Readings in

Classical Political Thought

Readings in

Classical Political Thought

Edited by
Peter J. Steinberger

Hackett Publishing Company, Inc.
Indianapolis/Cambridge

Copyright © 2000 by Hackett Publishing Company, Inc.

09 08 07 06 05 04 03 02 01 00   1 2 3 4 5 6 7 8 9 10

For further information, please address

Hackett Publishing Company, Inc.
P.O. Box 44937
Indianapolis, Indiana 46244-0937

www.hackettpublishing.com

Cover design by Brian Rak and John Pershing
Text design by Meera Dash

Library of Congress Cataloging-in-Publication Data

Readings in classical political thought / edited by Peter J. Steinberger.
        p.   cm.
Includes bibliographical references (p.).
ISBN 0-87220-513-4 (cloth)—ISBN 0-87220-512-6 (pbk.)
1. Political science—History.   I. Steinberger, Peter, J., 1948–
                JC51 .R43   2000
                320′.01—dc21
                99-059676

BRIEF CONTENTS

Preface   xi

I   Early Poets   1

        Homer, *Iliad*   4
        Hesiod, *Theogony*   10
                Works and Days   10
        Tyrtaeus of Sparta   13
        Solon of Athens   14
        Theognis of Megara   16

II   Presocratics and Sophists   17

        Heraclitus of Ephesus   20
        Protagoras   20
        Plato's *Protagoras*   21
        Gorgias, *In Praise of Helen*   25
        Antiphon   26
        The *Anonymus Iamblichi*   26

III   Historians   29

        Herodotus, *Histories*   32
        Thucydides, *History of the Peloponnesian War*   35

IV   Tragedians and Comedians   59

        Aeschylus, *The Furies*   62
        Aristophanes, *Clouds*   78
        Sophocles, *Antigone*   117

V   Socrates and Plato   **136**

    Euthyphro   139
    Apology   147
    Crito   159
    Republic   166
    Laws   317

VI   Aristotle   **358**

    Nicomachean Ethics   361
    Politics   377

VII   Cicero   **443**

    The Republic   446

VIII   Augustine   **461**

    City of God   463

IX   Thomas Aquinas   **505**

    Summa Theologica   508
    Statesmanship   542

X   Machiavelli   **547**

    Letter to Francesco Vettori   549
    The Prince   551
    Discourses   591

Works Cited   **623**

DETAILED CONTENTS

Preface   xi

I   Early Poets   1

         HOMER (Probably eighth century B.C.)   4
Iliad   4
  2.55–439
  12.297–342
  18.499–549
         HESIOD (c. 700 B.C.)   10
Theogony   10
  77–104
Works and Days   10
  204–428
         TYRTAEUS OF SPARTA (Seventh century B.C.)   13
Fragment 2
Fragment 4
         SOLON OF ATHENS (c. 640–560 B.C.)   14
Fragment 4
Fragments 5, 6, 7
Fragment 15
Fragment 32
Fragment 34
Fragment 36
Fragment 37
         THEOGNIS OF MEGARA (Sixth century B.C.)   16
  39–52

II   Presocratics and Sophists   17

         HERACLITUS OF EPHESUS (c. 540–480 B.C.)   20
  10.116–125

PROTAGORAS (c. 490–420 B.C.)   20
18.7, 20, 21

PLATO's *Protagoras*   21
320d–328d

GORGIAS (c. 483–385 B.C.)   25
In Praise of Helen   25
18.19

ANTIPHON (c. 480–411 B.C.)   26
19.2

THE *Anonymus Iamblichi*   26
19.13–15

III   **Historians**   29

HERODOTUS (c. 490–425 B.C.)   32
Histories   32
3.38, 80–82
5.78, 92

THUCYDIDES (c. 460–c. 399 B.C.)   35
History of the Peloponnesian War   35
1.20.2–22, 140–145
2.8, 35–54, 59–65
3.37–51, 81.2, 82–85
5.84–116

IV   **Tragedians and Comedians**   59

AESCHYLUS (525–456 B.C.)   62
The Furies   62
ARISTOPHANES (c. 445–385 B.C.)   78
Clouds   78
SOPHOCLES (c. 496–406/405 B.C.)   117
Antigone   117

V   **Socrates and Plato**   **136**

PLATO (427–347 B.C.)   139
Euthyphro   139
Apology   147
Crito   159
Republic   166

    Laws   317
      1–6 (abridged)
      7.793e–794d, 797a–798d, 800a–801e, 802e–803a
      8.835d–864c
      9.860d–864c
      10.885b–890e
      12.960e–969d

VI   **Aristotle**   **358**

                    ARISTOTLE (384–322 B.C.)   361
    Nicomachean Ethics   361
      1.1–5, 7–8
      2.1–6
      10.6–9
    Politics   377
      1.1–8, 13
      2.1–6, 9, 12
      3.1, 4, 6–9, 11, 12
      4.1, 3, 11
      5.1, 8–12
      6.1–5
      7.1–4, 8–11, 13–17
      8

VII   **Cicero**   **443**

              MARCUS TULLIUS CICERO (106–43 B.C.)   446
    The Republic   446
    (selections)

VIII **Augustine**   **461**

                 AUGUSTINE (354–430)   463
    City of God   463
      Preface
      1.1–2
      2.4, 15, 19–21
      3.21, 30
      4.4, 33
      5.9, 11, 15–17, 19, 24–26

8.3, 5, 6, 8, 10, 19
12.23–24, 27, 28
13.2, 10
14.4–6, 10–13, 15–16, 18, 22, 24, 25, 28
18.37, 39, 41
19.1–2, 4, 12, 13, 15–17, 19, 21, 23
22.27, 29, 30

IX   **Thomas Aquinas**   **505**

                    Thomas Aquinas (1225–1274)   508
            Summa Theologica   508
                I–II, qq 90–97
            Statesmanship   542
                1.1
                6

X   **Machiavelli**   **547**

                    Niccolò Machiavelli (1469–1527)   549
            Letter to Francesco Vettori   549
            The Prince   551
            Discourses   591
                Preface
                1–5, 9, 12, 13, 17, 18, 21, 27, 42, 46, 55, 58
                2.1, 29
                3.1–3, 29, 31

Works Cited   **623**

PREFACE

The ancient and classical tradition of Western political thought is bound up with—indeed, is part and parcel of—the ancient and classical tradition of Western literature. From Homer and the other early Greek poets to Plato and the other philosophers of Athens' Golden Age, fundamental questions of political life were a central and abiding preoccupation of intellectual and artistic endeavor, broadly conceived. Classical political thought thus manifests itself in a rather wide variety of literary genres: epic and lyric poetry, tragedy and comedy, history, philosophy.

In assembling this anthology, I have attempted to include all or nearly all of the major works that might plausibly be taught in an introductory undergraduate course on ancient political theory, political philosophy, or the history of political thought. The writings of Plato and Aristotle naturally take pride of place. But a proper understanding of those writings requires some attention to their contexts. The concerns of a Hesiod or a Herodotus, a Thucydides or a Sophocles, are reflected in and provide a focus for the more systematic discussions that we find in Plato's *Republic* or Aristotle's *Politics*. Similarly, the subsequent writings of Roman thinkers such as Cicero, Christian philosophers such as Augustine and Thomas Aquinas, and Renaissance authors such as Machiavelli help to demonstrate not only the influence and resonance but also the thematic significance of ancient Greek materials.

In recent years, some commentators have denied that the Western tradition of political thought is really a tradition at all. They have argued that political theory always arises in response to a particular set of controversies connected to a particular place and time, and that in treating such controversies political authors invariably invoke considerations of a narrowly partisan or ideological nature. No one can deny that writing about politics usually reflects, in one way or another, the immediate circumstances in which it is produced. But from this it hardly follows that the tradition is a myth. It is clear, for example, that Plato read and was influenced by Homer and the lyric poets, and that he had thought a great deal about the events described by Herodotus and Thucydides; that Aristotle was a student of Plato; that Cicero's *Republic* was profoundly influenced by Platonic and Aristotelian philosophy; that Augustine's *City of God* is, in large part, a commentary on Cicero; that the thought of Aquinas represents a massive engagement with Aristotle; that Machiavelli's writings are preoccupied with the political history and philosophy of the ancient world. The fundamental issues and ideas of political thinkers have been passed on from generation to generation and from era to era. They have been reformulated, reinterpreted, and revised, but their essential identity and force remains, to some significant degree, unchanged.

One such issue concerns the problem of nature (*physis*) and convention (*nomos*). Are moral truths—including political moral truths—true in virtue of the fundamental nature of the world itself? Do they, in other words, reflect unchanging and transcendent aspects of the way things really are? Or are they, to the contrary, merely products of the human imagination—rules or principles that we have constructed as circumstances allow, that seem to us useful and important, but that have moral force only insofar as we decide actually to observe them? This controversy, which was at the heart of the great discussions that took place between Socrates and the so-called Sophists, continues to preoccupy anyone today who would be interested in trying to distinguish political right from wrong.

A second issue concerns the relationship between our political commitments and our commitments in other, nonpolitical areas of organized human life. The state imposes on us certain obligations that may come into conflict with obligations demanded of us by our families, religious organizations, economic institutions, and the like. What is the nature of such conflicts and how are they to be resolved? When we encounter an Antigone who is forced to choose between her civic duties and her responsibilities to the gods, or a Socrates who must decide between a life of philosophy and a life of strict obedience to the government of his city, we are brought face-to-face with a kind of dilemma that recurs throughout history and that seems to be inherent in the very nature of political society.

A third issue centers around the problem of who should rule. In distinguishing monarchy, aristocracy, democracy, and other forms of government, Plato and Aristotle were exploring an already well-established set of questions—we find them in Herodotus, for example—and doing so in ways that would play a central role in virtually all subsequent political discourse. In this sense, the apparent hegemony of "democratic" ideals in contemporary political thought reflects an extremely rich, complex, and challenging set of questions and controversies that are far less well-settled than one might suppose.

Yet another issue—perhaps the most central of all—concerns the very idea of the state. What is the fundamental purpose of political society? What is the connection between the state itself and the particular institutions of government through which the state acts? What makes a state legitimate, and how do we distinguish authentic states from unauthorized, illegitimate pretenders? Questions such as these are asked by Machiavelli as much as by Aristotle, by Aquinas as much as by Herodotus. They are questions that we are still seeking to answer; and in approaching them, we can hardly do better than begin by studying in detail at least some of the more influential works of ancient political thought.

*

I wish to express my thanks, above all, to David Reeve. His help with this project—practical, personal, and intellectual—can hardly be overestimated. Indeed, without his advice and support, this volume would almost certainly not exist. I am also grateful to my colleague Walter Englert for his excellent suggestions and comments and to my editor Brian Rak for his wisdom and hard work. Finally, and as always, I am grateful to the intellectual community that is Reed College—colleagues, students, and staff—which is unusual, perhaps even unique, in the degree to which it honors and encourages serious intellectual endeavor.

I

EARLY POETS

Sometime around 1200 B.C., the part of the world that we now call Greece was plunged quite suddenly into a Dark Age, an age of nearly complete disintegration and decay that would last for at least two and possibly three centuries. The causes of this collapse have been much in dispute. It may have been that marauding peoples from the north, possibly Dorian tribes of Greek speakers who lived in northern Greece, overran and destroyed what had been a thriving culture. Perhaps a series of cataclysmic natural disasters were to blame—massive earthquakes or fires, epidemics or drought. Widespread economic failure may have led to violent unrest, or even revolution or civil war. But whatever the cause, historians now agree that an extraordinarily brilliant and powerful civilization, the Mycenaean, was rapidly and almost entirely obliterated, leaving in its wake a culture that could hardly be called brilliant or powerful in any respect.

The Mycenaean age is the period that Homer was thinking of when he composed his two great epic poems, the *Iliad* and the *Odyssey*. He viewed it as an age of heroes, and present-day historical and anthropological opinion suggests that it was a grand age indeed—a time of great kings and warrior leaders, of elaborate, fortified citadels, of prosperous towns and villages, of commerce and culture. Mycenaean traders traveled to Egypt and to Mesopotamia. Craftspeople produced statuary and pottery that was prized throughout the Mediterranean. Rulers established elaborate systems for keeping track of production and property ownership, as well as for levying taxes. Mycenaean armies may have been particularly formidable. If Homer is to be believed, Agamemnon's legions were composed of 60,000 soldiers who crossed the Aegean Sea in 1,186 ships and destroyed the great Asian city of Troy.

The ensuing Dark Age, in contrast, was dark in the extreme. From the twelfth to the tenth century B.C., or even to the ninth century, Greece experienced severe depopulation. The physical infrastructure—cities and roads—essentially fell apart. Systematic and centrally controlled arable farming quickly became a thing of the past, replaced by small-scale farming and stock-raising. There appears to have been little in the way of social organization beyond the localized tribe. The arts declined dramatically, and literacy probably disappeared altogether. In the words of historian Oswyn Murray, this was "the darkness of a primitive society with little material culture. . . ." The brilliant light of the Mycenaean world was utterly extinguished, and in its place came a world evidently poor in spirit as well as in resources.

Organized society in Greece gradually began to reemerge during the ninth and eighth centuries, and the epic poems of Homer may be best understood as a part of that reconstruction. The historical significance of this background needs to be kept clearly in mind. In composing poems about the Heroic Age of Agamemnon, Achilles, and Odysseus, Homer was attempting to describe a world that preceded him by about four hundred years, and he was seeking to do so without direct evidence of any kind. He had to rely solely on stories or myths handed down over the centuries. The inevitable result is that what Homer depicts in the *Iliad* and *Odyssey* undoubtedly tells us at least as much about eighth-century Greece—what is now called Archaic Greece—as it does about the Mycenaean world.

I have thus far spoken of "Homer" as the author of great epic poems. But the fact is that we know almost nothing of Homer himself, and there has long been deep disagreement about whether or not the *Iliad* and *Odyssey* were composed by a single individual. Indeed, most scholars now agree that these were originally oral compositions. In the 1920s, the great classicist Milman Parry argued that the structural character of the Homeric epics, especially their constantly repeated formulas and patterns, could be explained only if one assumed that the poems were actually composed in the process of being sung, hence that ancient epic poetry was in large part an improvisatory art form. In the 1930s, Parry confirmed his theory by discovering in Serbia—not far from Greece itself—illiterate bards who could recite poems the length of the *Odyssey*, making things up as they went along while remaining faithful to formal and metrical rules and composing tales of considerable complexity. Parry's astonishing research has led scholars to conclude that Homer's epics were essentially the product of an oral tradition that undoubtedly preceded by a great many years—even centuries—the actual production of written Homeric texts. The society portrayed in those texts would thus likely be an admixture of old and new, echoing the long-defunct Mycenaean age while at the same time reflecting important elements of the then-contemporary Archaic world.

Political life, as depicted in the *Iliad*, encompasses a variety of institutions and relationships that may or may not reveal the complexity of the poem's history. On the one hand, society is plainly monarchical. Cities are ruled by kings (*basileis*), and the power of the king seems to have been absolute. When Achilles decides to withdraw from the battle, so do his troops, without question or debate. On the other hand, the *Iliad* also speaks of many kings existing at the same time and in the same society. Not all of these kings seem to have been equal. Although Agamemnon, like Achilles, is a king, he is also more than that, a kind of king of Greek kings; and sometimes Homer uses a different word (*wanax*) to describe such a supreme ruler. But the supremacy of even this king is itself highly doubtful. Agamemnon cannot simply tell the other leaders, like Achilles, what to do. He must persuade them or negotiate with them, and it is far from certain that he will get his way. If the *Iliad* is to be believed, political society in Greece may have involved a kind of loose and fluid federation of aristocratic warriors, some of whom are more equal than others but all of whom retain an important degree of independence.

The *Iliad* also describes frequent assemblies in which leaders feel constrained to share their ideas with the rank and file. Homer never so much as implies that the masses of soldiers or citizens had any right to make, or even to influence, decisions. But the fact that such assemblies take place in the *Iliad* and seem to have been serious occasions strongly suggests that the political elite felt a genuine need to understand, and perhaps even to act in accordance with, prevailing sentiment. Again, whether or not Homeric politics reflects the realities of twelfth-century Mycenaean Greece or eighth-century Archaic Greece is a matter of historical dispute. But as the first great document of Western literature, the *Iliad* already speaks clearly to the fundamental theme of all political thought, namely, the proper relationship between leaders and followers, between the rulers and the ruled.

Such a theme is also to be found in the two important poems traditionally attributed to Hesiod, the *Theogony* and *Works and Days*. Composed perhaps around the year 700 B.C., these works are clearly the products of a reviving Greek civilization. The *Theogony*, which is a "history" of the gods, is our most important single source on ancient Greek religion. It describes the rise of the Olympian family, with Zeus at its head, and outlines the pantheon of traditional Greek divinities with their various roles and personalities. The work also functions as a kind of cosmogony—a story of the origin of the world itself. As such, it provides crucial information about the mind and mentality of Archaic Greece. Included here are brief but revealing views about political kingship, especially as regards the proper duties of the king and the sources of kingly authority.

In form, substance, and tone, *Works and Days* could hardly be more different from the *Theogony*. It presents itself as a kind of poetic letter from Hesiod to his ne'er-do-well brother Perses. As such, it is perhaps the first truly personal and autobiographical text of Western culture, a work that deals less with gods, heroes, and kings than with plain folk, and that provides a wealth of information regarding ordinary life in the Archaic Greek world. This text tells us much about agricultural practices and economic relations, about domestic life and moral attitudes, about interpersonal relations and the quality of daily life. *Works and Days* also functions as a species of "wisdom literature," a kind of ancient counterpart to Benjamin Franklin's *Farmer's Almanac*. Hesiod tells his brother how to farm, how to sail ships, when and whom to marry, and how to live a productive life. He offers a wide range of specific recommendations: "don't be tiresome at a potluck dinner . . . don't throw a man's poverty in his face . . . don't piss standing up while facing the sun . . . don't wash in a woman's bath-water . . . don't leave the wood rough on a house you're building. . . ." From these and numerous other injunctions and suggestions, we may surmise that Greeks in the eighth century had potluck dinners, recognized the psychology of poverty, took baths, built houses out of wood, thought about their bodily functions, and the like. It's also clear that they thought a great deal about political virtue. *Works and Days* is the first Greek text to speculate explicitly about the nature of justice (*dike*), and it does so in ways that we today can find intelligible and plausible. In this sense, we might say that the Western tradition of political thought really begins with Hesiod.

The continued development of Archaic Greek civilization in the seventh and sixth centuries saw the invention of a new literary genre, a kind of poetry called "lyric" because it was meant to be sung to the accompaniment of a lyre. A great deal of lyric poetry was produced during this period, and the range of poetic topics tells us much about life in Greece. Poems were written about love and war, about athletic contests and heroism, about drinking and old age and mortality and friendship. The subject of politics was not excluded. Tyrtaeus of Sparta (seventh century) is said to have written a poem about the Constitution of Sparta. That work is lost, but certain of his surviving poetic fragments speak to the importance of *eunomia*, or good laws, thereby establishing a significant contrast to the work of Homer and Hesiod, in which the emphasis seems to have been on the importance of good rulers. Solon of Athens (c. 640–c. 560) was one of the most influential political figures of ancient Greece. During a time of unrest and near civil war in Athens, he was called on to rewrite the city's laws and to establish peace between the wealthy aristocracy, on the one hand, and an increasingly oppressed class of commoners, on the other. His poems, which talk about the nature of class conflict in Archaic Greece, help clarify the sense in which justice and law had already become central political concepts. Theognis of Megara (sixth century), a prolific author of elegies, treats political themes at several points in his poetry. He worries about the dangers of hubristic tyrants and talks of the need for noble leaders who can help preserve the common good.

Further Reading: For a concise, highly readable, and extremely well-informed introduction to Bronze Age Greece, see M. I. Finley, *The World of Odysseus* (1954). Also highly recommended is Chapter 7 of John Chadwick's superb book, *The Decipherment of Linear B* (1958). An excellent general source on life in the emergent Iron Age is Oswyn Murray, *Early Greece* (1980). Also very important and informative is Anthony Snodgrass, *Archaic Greece* (1981). For a discussion of Milman Parry's immense contributions to the study of Homeric epic, see Albert Bates Lord, *The Singer of Tales* (1960). The literary and critical literature on Homer is immense, but a very good place to start would be Seth L. Schein, *The Mortal Hero: An Introduction to Homer's Iliad* (1984). See also the important book by J. M. Redfield, *Nature and Culture in the Iliad: The Tragedy of Hector* (1975).

Homer
(Probably eighth century B.C.)

Iliad

[For ten years, the army of Achaeans under the leadership of Agamemnon have laid siege to the Asian city of Troy, ostensibly because Paris, son of the Trojan king Priam, had seduced and abducted Helen, the wife of Agamemnon's brother, Menelaus. In Book 2 of the Iliad, Agamemnon has a disturbing dream that makes him wonder if the Archaeans shouldn't end their siege and return home in peace. He shares his concerns with the assembly of warriors, and a debate ensues.]

Agamemnon ordered the heralds
To call the Greeks to assembly.
The call went out, and the people gathered.
Agamemnon seated the elders first
By Nestor's ship and unfolded his plan:

"Listen, my friends. A dream from Zeus
Came to me last night in my sleep. It looked
Just like Nestor, same face, same build,
And it stood above my head and spoke:
'Asleep, son of Atreus, horsebreaker,
Wise man? You can't sleep all night.
All those decisions to make, so many people
Depending on you. I'll be brief.
I am a messenger from Zeus, who is
Far away, but loves you and pities you.
He orders you to arm your long-haired Greeks.
Now is your time to capture Troy.
The Olympian gods are no longer divided;
Hera has bent them all to her will
And targeted Troy for sorrow from Zeus.
Think it over.' The dream said all this
And off it flew, and I awoke from a sweet sleep.
We'd better move if we're going to get the men in
    armor.
But I'm going to test them first with a little speech,
The usual drill—order them to beat a retreat in their
    ships.
It's up to each one of you to persuade them to stay."

He had his say and sat down. Then up rose
Nestor, king of sandswept Pylos.
He was full of good will in the speech he made:

"Friends, Argive councillors and commanders:
If any other Greek told us this dream
We would call it a lie and turn our backs on him.
But this is a man with a claim to be
The best of the Greeks. We'd better move
If we're going to get them in armor."

And he headed out. The other commanders stood up,
Convinced he was right.

                                   The troops were moving now,

Swarming like insects over the beach, like bees
That hum from a hollow rock in an endless line
And fly in clusters over flowers in spring,
Grouping themselves in aerial throngs.

The Greeks made like that as they swarmed
Out of the ships and the huts clutched beneath them,
Filing through the deep sand into assembly,
Swept along by Zeus' emissary,
Wildfire Rumor. They milled about
In the assembly ground, and the earth
Groaned as the unruly crowd eased itself down,
And nine bawling heralds tried to stop their shouting
And get them to listen to their Zeus-spawned kings.
They settled down finally and kept their seats
And stopped all the noise.

                                   Up stood Lord Agamemnon,
Holding a staff.
                                   Hephaestus had crafted this staff
And Hephaestus had given it to Cronion Zeus.
Zeus in turn gave it to quicksilver Hermes
And Hermes to Pelops, the charioteer.
Pelops handed it on to Atreus,

Reprinted from Homer, *Iliad*, translated by Stanley Lombardo (Indianapolis: Hackett Publishing Company, 1997) by permission of the publisher.

And when Atreus died he left it to Thyestes.
Thyestes left it for Agamemnon to bear
And rule over the islands and all of Argos.
Leaning on it now he addressed the Greeks:

"Danaan heroes and soldiers,
                              Zeus
Is a hard god, friends. He's kept me in the dark
After all his promises and nods my way
That I'd raze Ilion's walls before sailing home.
It was all a lie, and I see now that his orders
Are for me to return to Argos in disgrace,
And this after all the armies I've destroyed.
I have no doubt that this is the high will
Of the god who has toppled so many cities
And will in the future, all glory to his power.
But it will be shame for generations to come,
That such a large and powerful army of Greeks
Has fought this futile war against a few puny men.
There is no end in sight, nor has there ever been.
Look, if the Greeks and the Trojans
Agreed to a truce, and both sides counted off—
All of the Trojans who live in the city
And all of the Greeks—and if we Greeks formed up
In platoons of ten, and each platoon picked a Trojan
To pour our wine, there would be many platoons
With no one to pour. That's how much our Greek
    forces
Outnumber the Trojans who live in the city.
It's their allies, reinforcements from other cities,
Who keep hitting me hard and won't let me capture
Ilion's serried fortress no matter how hard I try.
Nine years of great Zeus have passed.
Our ships' timbers are rotten and their tackle loose.
Our wives and little children are no doubt
Sitting at home waiting for us. And here we are,
The job that we came to do unfinished.
Now this is what I say, and I want us all to obey:
Let's clear out with our ships and head for home.
There's no more hope we will take Troy's tall town."

This speech roused the spirits of the rank and file,
The masses who had not been in on the council.

The army started to move on the shore.

                              Long waves form
On the Icarian Sea when winds East and South
Explode from the clouds of patriarch Zeus;
Or the West Wind rapes a field of deep wheat,
Rippling and tassling the ears as it blows.

So too these troop lines.
                              Then the shouting began,
And the mad rush to the ships, dust rising
In plumes from their feet as confused yells—
To fasten boathooks, clear out launchways
And drag the ships down to the shining sea—
Rose to the sky. They were going home.

They had already begun to remove the chocks
From under the hulls, and there might have been
An unordained homecoming then for the Greeks
If Hera had not had a word with Athena:

"This is awful. Child of Zeus, Mystic Daughter
Of the Aegis-Holder, are we going to allow
The Greeks to go home just like that, run away
To their own country over the sea's broad back?
They're just going to hand Priam and the Trojans
The glory, not to mention Helen of Argos,
For whose sake many a Greek has perished in Troy,
Far from his homeland. Go down there now
Along the ranks of the bronze-shirted Greeks,
And with your mild words restrain each man.
Don't let them haul their curved prows to the sea."

And Athena streaked down from Olympus' crags,
Her eyes like owls', grey in the blue air,
And came quickly to the ships in the beachhead
    camp.
She found Odysseus there, his mind like Zeus' own,
Standing in thought. He had not laid a hand
On his benched, black ship, and his heart was heavy.

The owl-eyed goddess stood close to him and said:

"Son of Laertes in the line of Zeus, wily Odysseus,
Are you Greeks going to run away just like that,
Home to your fatherland over the sea's broad back?
Are you just going to hand Priam and the Trojans
The glory, not to mention Helen of Argos,
For whose sake many a Greek has perished in Troy,
Far from his homeland? Now go down along
All the ships of the bronze-shirted Greeks,
And with your mild words restrain each man.
Don't them haul their curved prows to the sea."

Odysseus knew that voice, and he set off at a run,
Throwing his cloak behind him—Eurybates
The herald, his man from Ithaca, gathered it up—
And he went up to Agamemnon and got from him
His ancestral staff, that splinter of eternity,

And with it went along the ships of the Greeks.
Whenever he encountered a chieftain or the like,
He tried to restrain him with gentle words:

"What's gotten into you? I don't mean to frighten you
As if you were a coward, but sit down here yourself
And make your men sit down. You don't really know
Agamemnon's mind. He's just testing us now,
But before long he's going to come down on us hard.
Didn't we all hear what he said in council?
If he gets angry the whole army had better watch out.
Kings are bred by Zeus and have tempers to match."

But if he caught any of the ordinary soldiers yelling,
He would belt him with the staff and bawl him out:

"You there, who do you think you are? Sit still
And listen to your betters. You're a weakling,
Unfit for combat, a nothing in battle and in council.
Do you think every Greek here can be a king?
It's no good having a carload of commanders. We
    need
One commander, one king, the one to whom Zeus,
Son of Cronus the crooked, has given the staff
And the right to make decisions for his people."

And so Odysseus mastered the army. The men all
Streamed back from their ships and huts and
    assembled
With a roar.

> A wave from the restless, churning sea
> Crashes on a beach, and the water seethes and
>   thunders.

They had all dropped to the sand and were sitting
    there,
Except for one man, Thersites, a blathering fool
And a rabble rouser. This man had a repertory
Of choice insults he used at random to revile the
    nobles,
Saying anything he thought the soldiers would laugh
    at.
He was also the ugliest soldier at the siege of Troy,
Bowlegged, walked with a limp, his shoulders
Slumped over his caved-in chest, and up top
Scraggly fuzz sprouted on his pointy head.
Achilles especially hated him, as did Odysseus,
Because he was always provoking them. Now
He was screaming abuse at Agamemnon.

The Achaeans were angry with him and indignant,
But that didn't stop him from razzing the warlord:

"What's wrong, son of Atreus, something you need?
Your huts are filled with bronze, and with women
We Achaeans pick out and give to you first of all
Whenever we take some town. Are you short of gold?
Maybe some Trojan horse breeder will bring you
    some
Out of Ilion as ransom for his son
Whom I or some other Achaean has captured.
Maybe it's a young girl for you to make love to
And keep off somewhere for yourself. It's not right
For a leader to march our troops into trouble.
You Achaeans are a disgrace, Achaean women, not
    men!
Let's sail home in our ships and leave him here
To stew over his prizes so he'll have a chance to see
Whether he needs our help or not. Furthermore,
He dishonored Achilles, who's a much better man.
Achilles doesn't have an angry bone in his body,
Or this latest atrocity would be your last, son of
    Atreus!"

That was the abuse Agamemnon took
From the mouth of Thersites. Odysseus
Was on him in a flash, staring him down
With a scowl, and laid into him:

"Mind your tongue, Thersites. Better think twice
About being the only man here to quarrel with his
    betters.
I don't care how bell-toned an orator you are,
You're nothing but trash. There's no one lower
In all the army that followed Agamemnon to Troy.
You have no right even to mention kings in public,
Much less badmouth them so you can get to go
    home.
We have no idea how things are going to turn out,
What kind of homecoming we Achaeans will have.
Yet you have the nerve to revile Agamemnon,
Son of Atreus, the shepherd of his people,
Because the Danaan heroes are generous to him?
You think you can stand up in public and insult him?
Well, let me tell you something. I guarantee
That if I ever catch you running on at the mouth
    again
As you were just now, my name isn't Odysseus
And may I never again be called Telemachus' father
If I don't lay hold of you, strip your ass naked,

And run you out of the assembly and through the
    ships,
Crying at all the ugly licks I land on you."

And with that he whaled the staff down
On Thersites' back. The man crumpled in pain
And tears flooded his eyes. A huge bloody welt
Rose on his back under the gold stave's force,
And he sat there astounded, drooling with pain
And wiping away his tears. The troops, forgetting
Their disappointment, had a good laugh
At his expense, looking at each other and saying:

"Oh man! You can't count how many good things
Odysseus has done for the Greeks, a real leader
In council and in battle, but this tops them all,
The way he took that loudmouth out of commission.
I don't think he'll ever be man enough again
To rile the commanders with all his insults."

That's what they were saying in the ranks.

Then Odysseus, destroyer of cities, stood up
Holding the staff. Owl-eyed Athena transformed
    herself
Into a herald and silenced the troops
So that every last man in the Greek army
Would listen closely to what he had to say:

"Son of Atreus, the Greeks are out to make you,
My lord, the most despised man on earth,
And they have no intention of keeping the promise
They made to you when they set out from Argos—
Not to return until you pulled down Ilion's walls.
They are like little children or widow women,
The way they whine to each other about going home.
God knows it's hard enough to make a man give up
And go back. A man gets discouraged when he spends
Even one month away from his wife on his ship,
Battling winter winds and the surging sea.
For us, it's nine years we've been here now.
I can't blame our men for getting discouraged
As they wait beside their beaked ships. But still,
It would be a disgrace to go home empty-handed
After all this time. So bear up, friends,
And let's stay long enough to find out whether
Calchas has prophesied truly or not.
Everyone here—and I'm talking about all of us
Not carried off by the wings of death—remembers it.
It seems like just yesterday when the ships

Were mustered at Aulis with their cargo of sorrows
For Priam and the Trojans. We were gathered
Around a spring, offering sacrifice on sacred altars,
Perfect hecatombs, beneath a beautiful plane tree
From under which the shining water flowed.
Then we saw it: a serpent, its back blood-red,
Horrible—the Olympian himself
Must have brought it into the daylight.
It slithered out from the altar and up the plane tree.
A sparrow's fledglings were nested
On the topmost branch, eight little birds
Trembling under the leaves, or nine, counting
The mother who hatched them, and the serpent
Devoured them all as they cheeped pitifully.
The mother fluttered around, mourning her nestlings,
But he coiled and got her by the wing as she
    shrieked.
After he had eaten the sparrow and her young,
The very god who revealed him turned him to stone,
An unmistakable portent from Zeus, son of Cronus.
We stood there in awe of what had happened,
This prodigy that crept into our sacrifice.
Calchas was quick to pronounce its prophetic
    meaning:
'Why are you silent, all you long-haired Greeks?
This great portent is a message from Zeus,
Whose glory shall never die—a portent late in
    coming,
And late to be fulfilled. As this serpent devoured
The sparrow's children and the bird herself,
Eight hatchlings, nine, counting the mother,
So will we for as many years wage this war,
But in the tenth year we will capture the city.'
That was his prophecy, and it has all come true.
So let's have every Greek who ever strapped on armor
Stay put, until we capture Priam's great city!"

He finished. And the Greeks cheered, so loud
That the wooden hulls of the ships boomed
With their approval of godlike Odysseus' speech.

Then Nestor, the Gerenian rider, addressed them:

"Bah, you're carrying on like silly boys
Who have no business at all fighting a war.
What will become of our compacts and oaths?
Into the fire with our resolutions and plans,
The pure wine we poured out, the handclasps
We trusted in! We are wrangling with words now
And will not find thereby the ways or means

To stay the course for long.
                              Son of Atreus,
Assert yourself, and resume your command
Of the Greek forces in all their grueling battles.
To hell with those one or two Achaeans
With private plans—which will come to nothing—
To return to Argos before we know for sure
Whether Zeus' promise was a lie or not.
I say that the Aegis-Holder nodded his assent
On that day when the Argives came in their ships
With their cargo of carnage and death for the
   Trojans.
Lightning on the right, favorable signs revealed.
No man here should be in a hurry to go home
Until he has spent the night with some Trojan's wife
As revenge for Helen's struggles and groans.
But if anyone is so almighty eager
To go back home, let him touch his black ship—
So he can seal his fate before the whole army.
But now, my lord, be prudent and take the advice,
Hardly negligible, that I am about to give.
Divide the men by tribes and clans, Agamemnon,
So that clans and tribes can support each other.
If you do this and the army complies,
You will know which of your captains is a coward
And which is brave, and so too with the soldiers,
For they will fight as units. You will know too
Whether it is heaven's will that you not take the city
Or that your men are cowards and witless in war."

He spoke, and Lord Agamemnon answered:

"Once again, Nestor, the best speech of all.
Father Zeus, Athena, and Apollo, give me
Ten such counsellors, and Priam's city
Would lay her head in our lap, taken and ravaged.
But Zeus, son of Cronus, has given me grief,
Embroiling me in pointless quarrels.
Yes, Achilles and I argued over a girl,
And it was I who grew angry first.
If we two could agree, there would not be
The slightest postponement of evil for Troy.
But go eat now, so we can get this battle together.
Sharpen your spears and dress your shields,
Lay out fodder for your horses,
And inspect your chariots. We're going to war.
We're going to fight all day and hate every minute
Without any breaks until it's too dark to see.
It's going to be chests sweating under shield straps,
Hands sore from gripping spears, horses sweaty
From pulling us around in our polished cars.
And if I catch anyone even thinking about

Staying out of the fight back here with the ships,
The dogs and birds will have him by nightfall."

The cheer that followed this speech came on like a
wave

That pounds a high cliff, a wave swollen by wind
Against a jutting crag that is constantly worried
By wind-driven waves from every direction.

The men stood up and scattered to their ships,
Made fires in their huts and took their meal.
And each made sacrifice to his favorite god,
Praying to escape from battle alive.
The warlord Agamemnon sacrificed a fat bull,
Five years old, to Cronus' almighty son,
And he summoned the elders, the best of the
   Achaeans,
Nestor first of all, and the warlord Idomeneus,
Then the two Ajaxes, and Tydeus' son, Diomedes,
And as the sixth, Odysseus, Zeus' match in wisdom.
Menelaus, the rallier, came on his own,
Knowing what his brother was up against.
They stood 'round the ox and took up the barley
   grains,
And the warlord Agamemnon led them in prayer.

• • •

[*In Book 12, two warriors, Sarpedon and Glaucus,*
discuss the duties of aristocrats.]

The stones flew thick upon the Trojans
And upon the Greeks, and the wooden wall
Was beaten like a drum along its whole length.

For all this, though, Hector and his Trojans
Would never have broken the barred gate
Had not Zeus roused his own son, Sarpedon,
Against the Greeks, as a lion against cattle.
Sarpedon held before him a perfect shield,
Its bronze skin hammered smooth by the smith,
Who had stitched the leather beneath with gold
All around the rim. Holding this shield
And brandishing two spears, Sarpedon advanced.

The mountain lion has not fed for days
And is hungry and brave enough to enter
The stone sheep pen and attack the flocks.
Even if he finds herdsmen on the spot
With dogs and spears to protect the fold,

He will not be driven back without a try,
And either he leaps in and seizes a sheep
Or is killed by a spear, as human heroes are.

Godlike Sarpedon felt impelled
To rush the wall and tear it down.

He turned to Glaucus and said:

"Glaucus, you know how you and I
Have the best of everything in Lycia—
Seats, cuts of meat, full cups, everybody
Looking at us as if we were gods?
Not to mention our estates on the Xanthus,
Fine orchards and riverside wheat fields.
Well, now we have to take our stand at the front,
Where all the best fight, and face the heat of battle,
So that many an armored Lycian will say,
'So they're not inglorious after all,
Our Lycian lords who eat fat sheep
And drink the sweetest wine. No,
They're strong, and fight with our best.'
Ah, my friend, if you and I could only
Get out of this war alive and then
Be immortal and ageless all of our days.
I would never again fight among the foremost
Or send you into battle where men win glory.
But as it is, death is everywhere
In more shapes than we can count,
And since no mortal is immune or can escape,
Let's go forward, either to give glory
To another man or get glory from him."

Thus Sarpedon. Glaucus nodded, and the two of
   them
Moved out at the head of a great nation of Lycians.

• • •

[In Book 18, having learned that his close friend Patroclus has been killed by the Trojans, Achilles decides
to return to the battle. Hephaestus, god of the forge,
makes a shield for him and decorates it with scenes of
civic life.]

"Take heart, Thetis, and do not be distressed.
I only regret I do not have the power
To hide your son from death when it comes.

But armor he will have, forged to a wonder,
And its terrible beauty will be a marvel to men."

Hephaestus left her there and went to his bellows,
Turned them toward the fire and ordered them to
   work.
And the bellows, all twenty, blew on the crucibles,
Blasting out waves of heat in whatever direction
Hephaestus wanted as he hustled here and there
Around his forge and the work progressed.
He cast durable bronze onto the fire, and tin,
Precious gold and silver. Then he positioned
His enormous anvil up on its block
And grasped his mighty hammer
In one hand, and in the other his tongs.

He made a shield first, heavy and huge,
Every inch of it intricately designed.
He threw a triple rim around it, glittering
Like lightning, and he made the strap silver.
The shield itself was five layers thick, and he
Crafted its surface with all of his genius.

On it he made the earth, the sky, the sea,
The unwearied sun, and the moon near full,
And all the signs that garland the sky,
Pleiades, Hyades, mighty Orion,
And the Bear they also call the Wagon,
Which pivots in place and looks back at Orion
And alone is aloof from the wash of Ocean.

On it he made two cities, peopled
And beautiful. Weddings in one, festivals,
Brides led from their rooms by torchlight
Up through the town, bridal song rising,
Young men reeling in dance to the tune
Of lyres and flutes, and the women
Standing in their doorways admiring them.
There was a crowd in the market-place
And a quarrel arising between two men
Over blood money for a murder,
One claiming the right to make restitution,
The other refusing to accept any terms.
They were heading for an arbitrator
And the people were shouting, taking sides,
But heralds restrained them. The elders sat
On polished stone seats in the sacred circle
And held in their hands the staves of heralds.
The pair rushed up and pleaded their cases,
And between them lay two ingots of gold
For whoever spoke straightest in judgment.

Hesiod
(c. 700 B.C.)

Theogony

The nine daughters born of great Zeus,

Klio, Euterpe, Thalia, Melpomene,
Terpsichore, Erato, Polyhymnia, Ourania,

And Kalliope, the most important of all,

For she keeps the company of reverend kings.
When the daughters of great Zeus will honor a lord
Whose lineage is divine, and look upon his birth,
They distill a sweet dew upon his tongue,
And from his mouth words flow like honey. The
    people
All look to him as he arbitrates settlements
With judgments straight. He speaks out in sure tones
And soon puts an end even to bitter disputes.
A sound-minded ruler, when someone is wronged,
Sets things to rights in the public assembly,

Conciliating both sides with ease.
He comes to the meeting place propitiated as a
    god,
Treated with respect, preeminent in the crowd.
Such is the Muses' sacred gift to men.
For though it is singers and lyre players
That come from the Muses and far-shooting Apollo
And kings come from Zeus, happy is the man
Whom the Muses love. Sweet flows the voice from
    his mouth.
For if anyone is grieved, if his heart is sore
With fresh sorrow, if he is troubled, and a singer
Who serves the Muses chants the deeds of past men
Or the blessed gods who have their homes on
    Olympos,
He soon forgets his heartache, and of all his cares
He remembers none: the goddesses' gifts turn them
    aside.

Works and Days

This is the **Iron Age.**
                    Not a day goes by
A man doesn't have some kind of trouble.
Night too, just wearing him down. I mean
The gods send us terrible pain and vexation.
Still, there'll be some good mixed in with the evil,
And then Zeus will destroy this generation too,
Soon as they start being born grey around the
    temples.
Then fathers won't get along with their kids anymore,
Nor guests with hosts, nor partner with partner,
And brothers won't be friends, the way they used to be.
Nobody'll honor their parents when they get old
But they'll curse them and give them a hard time,
Godless rascals, and never think about paying them
    back
For all the trouble it was to raise them.
They'll start taking justice into their own hands,

Sacking each other's cities, no respect at all
For the man who keeps his oaths, the good man,
The just man. No, they'll keep all their praise
For the wrongdoer, the man who is violence
    incarnate,
And shame and justice will lie in their hands.
Some good-for-nothing will hurt a decent man
Slander him, and swear an oath on top of it.
Envy will be everybody's constant companion,
With her foul mouth and hateful face, relishing evil.
And then
                up to Olympos from the wide-pathed Earth,
                lovely apparitions wrapped in white veils,
                off to join the Immortals, abandoning
                    humans
There go **Shame** and **Nemesis.** And horrible suffering
Will be left for mortal men, and no defense against
    evil.

Reprinted from Hesiod, *Works and Days* and *Theogony*, translated by Stanley Lombardo (Indianapolis: Hackett Publishing Company,
1993) by permission of the publisher.

And here's a fable for kings, who'll not need it
    explained:

It's what the hawk said high in the clouds
As he carried off a speckle-throated nightingale
Skewered on his talons. She complained something
    pitiful,
And he made this high and mighty speech to her:
"No sense in your crying. You're in the grip of real
    strength now,
And you'll go where I take you, songbird or not.
I'll make a meal of you if I want, or I might let you
    go.
Only a fool struggles against his superiors.
He not only gets beat, but humiliated as well."

Thus spoke the hawk, the windlord, his long wings
    beating.

But you, Perses, you listed to Justice
And don't cultivate Violence.
                                    Violent behavior is bad
For a poor man. Even a rich man can't afford it
But it's going to bog him down in Ruin some day.
There's a better road around the other way
Leading to what's right. When it comes down to it
Justice beats out Violence. A fool learns this the hard
    way.
Also, Oath, who's a god, keeps up with crooked
    verdicts,
And there's a ruckus when the Lady Justice
Gets dragged through the streets by corrupt judges
Who swallow bribes and pervert their verdicts.
Later, she finds her way back into town, weeping,
Wrapped in mist, and she gives grief to the men
Who drove her out and didn't do right by her.

But when judges judge straight, for neighbors
As well as for strangers, and never turn their backs
On Justice, their city blossoms, their people bloom.
You'll find peace all up and down the land
And youngsters growing tall, because broad-browed
    Zeus
Hasn't marked them out for war. Nor do famine or
    blight
Ever afflict folk who deal squarely with each other.
They feast on the fruits of their tended fields,
And the earth bears them a good living too.
Mountain oaks yield them acorns at the crown,
Bees and honey from the trunk. Their sheep
Are hefty with fleece, and women bear children
Who look like their parents. In short, they thrive

On all the good things life has to offer, and they
Never travel on ships. The soil's their whole life.

But for those who live for violence and vice,
Zeus, Son of Kronos, broad-browed god, decrees
A just penalty, and often a whole city suffers
For one bad man and his damn fool schemes.
The Son of Kronos sends them disaster from heaven,
Famine and plague, and the folk wither away,
Women stop bearing children, whole families
Die off, by Zeus' Olympian will. Or another time
He might lay low their army, or tumble down
Their city's walls, or sink all their ships at sea.

Rulers and Lords! It's up to you
To observe this justice. There are, you know,
Immortal beings abroad in this world
Who do observe with what corruption and fraud
Men grind down their neighbors and destroy the state,
As if they'd never *heard* of angry gods.
Thirty thousand spirits there are on this earth
In the service of Zeus, watching the human race,
Overseeing trials for criminal acts. Invisible,
They roam all through the land, cloaked in mist.
And there's the Virgin Justice, Zeus' own daughter,
Honored and revered among the Olympian gods.
Whenever anyone hurts her by besmirching her
    name,
She sits down by the Son of Kronos, her father,
And speaks to him about men's unjust hearts
Until the people pay for their foolhardy rulers'
Unjust verdicts and biased decisions.
Guard against this, you bribe-eating lords.
Judge rightly. Forget your crooked deals.

Plan harm for another and harm yourself most,
The evil we hatch always comes home to roost.

The eye of Zeus sees all and knows all,
And, if he wants, he's looking here right now,
And the kind of justice this city harbors
Doesn't fool him one bit. As for me, I'd as soon
Not be a just man, not myself or my son.
It's no good at all for a man to be just
When the unjust man gets more than what's just.
But I don't look for Zeus in his wisdom
To bring things to that pass for a long time yet.

Perses, you take all this to heart. Listen
To what's right, and forget about violence.

The Son of Kronos has laid down the law for
   humans.
Fish and beasts and birds of prey feed on
Each other, since there's no justice among them.

But to men he gave justice, and that works out
All to the good. If you know in your heart what's right
And come out and say so, broad-bowed Zeus will
Give you prosperity. But if you bear false witness
Or lie under oath, and by damaging Justice
Ruin yourself beyond hope of cure, your bloodline
Will weaken and your descendants fade out. But a
   man
Who stands by his word leaves a strong line of
   kinfolk.

Now I'm speaking sense to you, Perses you fool.
It's easy to get all of Wickedness you want.
She lives just down the road a piece, and it's a
   smooth road too.
But the gods put Goodness where we have to sweat
To get at her. It's a long, uphill pull
And rough going at first. But once you reach the top
She's as easy to have as she was hard at first.

Best of all is the man who sees everything for himself,
Who looks ahead and sees what will be better in the
   end.
It's a good man too who knows how to take good
   advice.
But the man who can't see for himself nor take advice,
Now that kind of man is a real good-for-nothing.
So at least *listen*, Perses—you come from good
   stock—
And remember always to work. Work so Hunger'll
Hate you, and Demeter, the venerable crowned
   goddess,
Will smile on you and fill your barn with food.

Hunger is the lazy man's constant companion.
Gods hate him, and men do too, the loafer
Who lives like the stingless drones, wasting
The hive's honey without working themselves,
Eating free.
           You've got to *schedule* your work
So your sheds will stay full of each season's harvest.
It's work that makes men rich in flocks and goods.
When you work you're a lot dearer to the gods
And to people too. Everybody hates a lay-about.
Work's no disgrace; it's idleness that's a disgrace.

If you work, the lay-abouts will soon be envying you
Getting rich.
           With wealth comes honor and glory.
No matter your situation, it's better to work,
Better for you too, Perses, if you'd only
Get your mind off of other folks' property
And work at earning a living, as I keep telling you.

Shame is sometimes a blessing, sometimes a curse.
Shame, the bad kind, is the poor man's companion.
Shame for the poor, assurance for the rich.

Wealth's better not grabbed but given by the gods.
If a man lays hold of wealth by main force
Or if he pirates it with his tongue, as happens
All too often when greed hoodwinks a man's sense
And decency gets crowded out by its opposite,
The gods whittle him down just like that, shrink
His household, and he doesn't stay rich for long.
It's the same thing when somebody wrongs a
   suppliant
Or a guest, or gets into his brother's bed
And does with his sister-in-law what just isn't right,
Or like a damn fool wrongs an orphan
Or raises his voice to his old pappy, using
Harsh language with him when he's at death's door.
Zeus himself gets angry with a man like that
And in the end makes him pay for his wrongful acts.

But you keep your foolish heart away from such
   behavior,
And, according to your means, sacrifice to the gods,
Observing ritual purity when you burn the fat
   thighbones,
And on occasion appease them with libations and
   incense
Both before you sleep and when the holy light returns,
So may they bless you from propitious hearts, and you
Buy up other folks' farms instead of them buying
   yours.

Invite your friend to a feast, leave your enemy alone,
And be sure to invite the fellow who lives close by.
If you've got some kind of emergency on your hands,
Neighbors come lickety-split, kinfolk take a while.
A bad neighbor's as much a curse as a good one's a
   blessing.
You've got a real prize if you've got a good neighbor.
Nary an ox would be lost if it weren't for bad
   neighbors.
Get good measure from a neighbor and give back as
   good,

Measure for measure, or better if you're able,
So when you need something later you can count on
  him then.

Don't make dirty money; dirty money spells
  doomsday.
Return a friend's friendship and a visitor's visit.
Give gifts to the giver, give none to the non-giver.
The giver gets gifts, the non-giver gets naught.
And Give's a good girl, but Gimmee's a goblin.
The man who gives willingly, even if it costs him,
Takes joy in his giving and is glad in his heart.

But let a man turn greedy and grab for himself
Even something small, it'll freeze his heart stiff.

It's the saver staves off feverish starvation.
If you put away a little each day
Even that little will soon be a lot.

What's laid up at home doesn't worry a man.

Home's best for a body. It's a dangerous world.

It's great to help yourself from stores on hand
And a pain in the neck to need what's not there.

When a jar's full or nearly empty enjoy all you want.
Go easy in between. It's cheap to nurse the dregs.

Let the wages for a friend be settled on and fixed,
Even if he's your brother. You can shake hands and
  smile,
But get a witness. Trust and mistrust both ruin men.

Don't let a sashaying female pull the wool over your
  eyes
With her flirtatious lies. She's fishing for your barn.
Trust a woman and you'd as well trust a thief.

There should be only one son to support
The father's house. That's the way a family's wealth
  grows.
Die old if you leave a second son in the house.
Still, Zeus can easily supply plenty all around,
And more hands mean more help, and a bigger yield.

And if the spirit within you moves you to get rich,
Do as follows:

  Work, work, and then *work* some more.

Tyrtaeus of Sparta
(Seventh century B.C.)

FRAGMENT 2

For Zeus himself, the son of Kronos and husband of
  fair-garlanded
Hera, has granted this city to the descendants of
  Herakles,
together with whom, abandoning windy Erineos,
we came to the broad island of Pelops.

FRAGMENT 4

Having heard the voice of Phoibos, they brought
  home from Pytho

oracles of the god and words sure of fulfillment:
that deliberation should originate with the god-
  honored kings,
to whose care the lovely city of Sparta is entrusted,
and with the elders who take precedence by birth;
  and that thereafter the people,
answering back in accordance with straightforward
  ordinances,
should say things that are honorable and do all things
  that are right,
and offer this city no crooked counsel;
and that victory and power should attend on the mass
  of the people.
Such, in these matters, was Phoibos' revelation to the
  city.

Reprinted from *Greek Lyric: An Anthology in Translation,* translated by Andrew Miller (Indianapolis: Hackett Publishing Company, 1996) by permission of the publisher.

Solon of Athens
(c. 640–560 B.C.)

FRAGMENT 4

Our city will never be destroyed by Zeus's
ordinance and the purposes of the blessed immortal
    gods:
such is the great-hearted guardian who holds her
    hands over it,
Pallas Athena, she whose father is mighty.
No, it is the citizens themselves who in their
    witlessness
are bent on ruining their great city, putting trust in
    money;
and the leaders of the people are unjust in mind. In
    their case it is certain
that out of great arrogance many griefs must be
    endured;
for they do not know how to keep excess under
    restraint, nor how
to order the present joys of their feasting in
    tranquillity. . . .

. . . .

. . . they grow wealthy, putting trust in unjust
    deeds. . . .

. . . .

Neither sacred nor public property
do they spare, each stealing and plundering from a
    different source,
nor do they guard the holy foundations of Justice,
who is aware in silence of what is happening and
    what was before,
and who in time assuredly comes to exact payment.
This is already coming upon the entire city as an
    inescapable wound,
and it has quickly entered into base servitude,
which rouses civil discord and war from sleep—
war that destroys the lovely youth of many.
For by its enemies the surpassingly lovely town is
    quickly
worn away, amid conspiracies dear to those who do
    injustice.
These are the evils that range at large in the
    community; but of the poor,
many make their way to foreign lands,
having been sold off in bondage, fettered by shameful
    chains. . . .

. . . .

In this way public calamity comes to each man's home,
and the doors of the courtyard no longer can hold it
    back;
over the high wall it leaps, and assuredly it finds
even one who flees to the innermost corner of the
    room.
This is the lesson that my spirit urges me to teach the
    Athenians,
how many evils Unlawfulness brings about for the city,
while Lawfulness puts all things into good order and
    makes them sound,
and often places shackles about those who are unjust.
She smooths what is rough, puts an end to excess,
    enfeebles arrogance;
she withers the flowers of ruin as they spring up;
she straightens crooked judgments, and overbearing
    acts
she turns to gentleness; she puts an end to acts of
    dissension,
puts an end to the bitterness of painful strife: beneath
    her hand
all things among mankind are sound and prudent.

FRAGMENTS 5, 6, 7

For to the people I gave as much privilege as sufficed
    them,
neither taking away honor nor holding out still more.
As for those who had power and were admired for
    wealth,
I took care that they too should have no unseemly
    share.
I stood holding my strong shield about both parties,
allowing neither to gain victory unjustly.

. . . .

The people are likely to follow their leaders best
    under these conditions,
that they be neither given too much rein nor held too
    much in constraint.
For excess gives birth to arrogance, whenever great
    prosperity attends
on those among human beings whose minds are not
    sound.

. . . .

In actions of great importance it is difficult to please
    everyone.

Fragment 15

Many bad men are wealthy, and many good men are
    poor;
but we shall not exchange with them
our goodness for their wealth, because the one is sure
    forever,
while money belongs to different men at different
    times.

Fragment 32

. . . But if I spared my native
country, and did not lay my hands on tyranny
and implacable violence, staining and disgracing my
    reputation,
I feel no shame at this; for I believe that in this way I
    shall far outdo
all of mankind.

Fragment 34

But those who came for plunder were rich in hopes,
and each of them thought that he would find great
    prosperity
and that despite my smooth coaxing I would reveal a
    harsh intention.
Their thoughts and plans at the time were empty, and
    now in anger
they all look askance at me as if I were their enemy.
This is not right; for with the gods' aid I
    accomplished what I said I would,
and did not do other things without good reason; nor
    did it please me
to act in any way with tyrannical force, or to allow the
    base to hold
an equal share of their country's fertile soil with the
    noble.

Fragment 36

But as for me, which of the things for which I called
the people together did I not attain before I stopped?
In support of this before the court of Time

the supreme mother of the Olympian powers,
black Earth, can best bear witness. From her I once
took up the boundary stones that were fixed in many
    places,
so that she who was once in servitude is now free.
And to Athens, their god-founded homeland,
I brought back many men who had been sold off,
    some unjustly,
others justly, still others sent into exile by
the compulsive power of need, none of whom still
    spoke
the speech of Attika, wandering as they were in many
    places.
And as for those who here at home endured the
    shame
of servitude, in terror of their masters' ways,
I made them free. These things through power,
by fitting together force and justice,
I brought to pass, and so came through as I promised.
Laws too, however, alike for the base man and the
    noble,
fitting straightforward justice to each one's case,
I set down in writing. Another man who took up the
    goad as I did,
one who was ill-intentioned and greedy for
    possessions,
could not have restrained the people. For if I had
    been willing
to do what pleased their opponents at that time,
and then again what the other party had in mind for
    them,
this city would have been widowed of many men. .
For these reasons, mounting a defense in every
    quarter,
I turned and twisted like a wolf among many hounds.

Fragment 37

As for the people, if it is right to censure them openly,
the things that they now possess they never could
have seen in dreams . . .
And those of the greater sort, superior in force,
may praise me and regard me as their friend.
For if some other man had gained this honor,
he would not have restrained the people, nor would
    he have stopped
his churning until he had extracted the rich fat from
    the milk.
As for me, in the middle ground between the two
    parties
I stood like a boundary stone.

Theognis of Megara
(Sixth century B.C.)

Kyrnos, this city is pregnant, and I fear that it may
   give birth to a man
who will chastise and correct our wicked arrogance.
For though the citizens here are still of sound mind,
   their leaders
are on a fixed course to fall into great wickedness.
No city yet, Kyrnos, has ever been destroyed by noble
   men,
But when it pleases the base to grow arrogant,
and they corrupt the people and grant judgments to
   the unjust

for the sake of their own private gain and power,
do not expect that city to enjoy unshaken calm for
   long,
not even if it lies now in great quietness,
once base men set their hearts on things like these,
gains that come with hurt to the people.
For from these things come factions, the internecine
   slaughter of men,
and tyrants—may they never be pleasing to *this* city.

II
PRESOCRATICS AND SOPHISTS

The so-called Archaic period in Greece, dating roughly from 800 B.C. to 479 B.C., saw the emergence of a new kind of social order, what came to be called the "city state," or *polis*. The development of the *polis* was gradual and occurred differently in different parts of the Greek world. But by the time of the Persian Wars, in the early fifth century B.C., Greece was essentially composed of a myriad of independent, self-standing civic entities, each having its own constitution, social institutions, army, and government. These independent entities were not merely administrative in nature. They commanded the deep loyalty of their citizens. To have lived in Archaic Greece was to have been not solely, perhaps not even primarily, a Greek, but also a Spartan, a Corinthian, an Athenian, and so on.

Historians agree that the social and political structure of the *polis* was very different from that of Mycenaean (or Bronze Age) Greece, that is, the period before the Dark Age. Mycenaean society had been palace-centered. Social power was held largely by the king, or *wanax*, who exercised his power in conjunction with a complex array of courtiers and warriors and a professional class of palace scribes. The decision-making process—military, religious, and economic—was strongly centralized in the monarchy, even to the point that private commerce may have hardly existed at all. In such a society, fundamental questions about who should rule or what the appropriate form of government should be could not have been very salient. The authority of the king and of his advisers was taken for granted, and there was, as a result, little need for what we today think of as systematic political thought.

The collapse of Mycenaean civilization saw the end of Mycenaean kingship, and as the Greek world reemerged from the Dark Age, the issue of government and rulership became central indeed. Historian Jean-Pierre Vernant suggests that "with the disappearance of the *wanax*, who by superhuman power had unified a given order to the diverse groups that made up the kingdom, new problems emerged. How was order to arise out of discord between rival groups and the class of conflicting prerogatives and functions? How could a common life be founded on disparate elements? . . . How, on the social level, could one emerge from many and many from one?" Whereas all military, religious, and economic power in Mycenaean Greece had been centralized within the palace, Archaic Greek society saw a substantial division of social labor. This circumstance gave rise to fundamental political conflicts, and these, in turn, prompted people to begin thinking about a new set of questions. Who should rule—the military, the religious hierarchy, or the economic elite? What was the proper basis of political authority? What was the proper role of the citizen?

As a historical matter, the emergence of such issues was connected to two extraordinary and related cultural developments: the invention of philosophy and the discovery of politics. Disagreements about social authority and competition over social power provided a context for systematic thinking about the nature not only of the *polis* but also of the world itself. Mycenaean kings may have felt no need to justify their rule, but justifications were necessary in the Archaic city, where different kinds of individuals and institutions made contradictory claims to authority and where each group had to show how its own claims might be persuasive. The relative dispersion of political power, in other words, provided a natural context for the development of theory; and the development of theory, in turn, helped focus attention on questions of evidence and proof, hence on a kind of systematic, rational thinking that may be called philosophical or scientific. In such a circumstance, moreover, the characteristic features of what we now call politics—debate about policy and principles, disagreement and accommodation, the establishment of law—could flourish in a way that would have been difficult or impossible in the Bronze Age. It is no accident that the word *politics*, which is derived from the Greek word *polis*, describes a kind of activity that was, at least in the beginning, peculiar to and characteristic of the city-state.

In Aristotle's view, philosophy proper began in the sixth century B.C., with the so-called Milesian school of thinkers, of whom Thales was presumably the first, and among whom Anaximander and Anaximenes are also counted as major figures. Evidence about their thought is meager at best. Thales wrote nothing. Anaximander and Anaximenes wrote substantial treatises, but only fragments survive. From these fragments, however, and from later commentaries, we get a fairly clear sense of Milesian thought as signifying nothing less than a major intellectual revolution in Greek culture. A useful contrast can be set up with Homer and Hesiod. The epic poets sought to depict reality, to say how things in the world really are, and to help their listeners understand the world by using evocative language to tell revealing tales. In determining what was true, however, these poets relied on traditional and/or religious belief; and they sought not to evaluate and assess such belief but to express it as effectively as possible. In contrast, the Milesian thinkers wanted not merely to describe reality but to account for it, to explain how things were and why they were that way. In doing so, they presented not just *assertions* but also *arguments*, with which they tried to prove that their assertions about reality were true. They accepted nothing on mere faith. Claims had to be assessed and evaluated critically, that is, they had to be tested in terms of what was logically possible and what actually had been observed.

The Milesian thinkers thus engaged in a new kind of intellectual activity—systematic and rational argument and analysis—and were followed in this by a series of philosophical schools and individuals. Many of these latter came to be called "nature" philosophers. Such philosophers sought to describe and to account for the underlying nature of things, to identify that which was essential and that which was merely secondary, and to say what was the ultimate cause of reality. Some of them identified four fundamental elements in the world—earth, water, air, and fire—and disagreed about which was the more fundamental. Others, including the so-called Pythagoreans, speculated about the nature of *human* being and thereby helped to begin a long line of inquiry about the difficult and problematic connection between body and soul. Working in the late sixth and early fifth centuries B.C., Heraclitus placed a certain emphasis on the role of change in the world. He also wrote about moral and social issues—presumably in defense of an aristocratic politics—and some of his fragments on these subjects survive. In the fifth century, Parmenides of Elea claimed to have proven that the world is a single, seamless entity that is without beginning, without end, undivided, one.

Collectively, these thinkers are called Presocratics—they practiced philosophy before Socrates. A second group of thinkers, contemporaries of Socrates, were the so-called Sophists. They were itinerant, professional teachers and thinkers who studied, among other things, the rhetorical arts, and who for a fee provided a kind of practical training for the children of the elite. As such, they may well have been the first practitioners of what we today call higher education. They purported to possess a scientific understanding of language and of argument, and they claimed to be able to impart such an understanding to talented youth. Training of this kind would be immensely useful. Armed with a solid, technical background in rhetoric—in making effective speeches and in formulating persuasive arguments—students of the Sophists would be unusually well equipped to compete successfully in the world of affairs, for example, in the law courts and in the political arena.

The Sophistic movement marked a substantial departure from earlier Presocratic thinkers. The Sophists were not "nature" philosophers; their main concern was not primarily with the physical universe but rather with human affairs, including questions of ethics and politics. Moreover, they thought of argument not primarily as a means for getting at the truth of things but as a tool for leading a successful life. Indeed, their position was, in principle, highly critical of their Milesian and Eleatic predecessors, and their criticisms involved a sharp distinction between nature (*physis*) and convention (*nomos*).

Today we believe that the physical world operates according to, and can accurately be formulated in terms of, scientific laws. Such laws describe the universal, necessary, and immutable structure of things, the nature of reality; and to the degree that government and politics is lawlike, it too does—or should—reflect such an underlying nature. For many Presocratics, the truth of the world could be described in precisely this way—in terms of natural laws—and the task of the philosopher was none other than to discover and explain those laws. The Sophists generally disagreed. They argued that laws—certainly civic laws and possibly scientific laws—were based not in nature but in mere convention; therefore, these laws reflected not an eternal, underlying reality, but arbitrary, humanly constructed accommodations invented by people simply for reasons of convenience, tradition, or self-interest. Thus, the Sophists were relativists or pragmatists. They thought that truth depended in part on who was looking for it and in part on what interests would be served by believing in one theory versus another. Such a view came under sharp attack, first and most famously by Socrates, and then by Plato and Aristotle. Indeed, it is largely from these latter thinkers that words like *sophist* and *sophistry* received the negative connotations that they carry to this day.

Protagoras of Abdera was perhaps the most famous of the Sophists, an influential teacher who argued forcefully for relativism. Gorgias of Leontini, who held similar views, was particularly well-known for his admirable prose style. Both Protagoras and Gorgias were central characters in eponymous dialogues written by Plato. An important fragment from Antiphon argues for acting according to *physis* rather than *nomos*, whereas a passage from the so-called Anonymus Iamblichi takes roughly the opposite position.

Further Reading: An excellent place to start would be Richard D. McKirahan, Jr., *Philosophy before Socrates: An Introduction with Texts and Commentary* (1994). Another readable and reliable introduction is Edward Hussey, *The Presocratics* (1972). On Heraclitus, see the special issue of the journal *Monist* (1991), which is devoted to his thought. See also the commentary to be found in Charles H. Kahn, *The Art and Thought of Heraclitus* (1979). On the Sophists, see Jacqueline de Romilly, *The Great Sophists in Periclean Athens* (1992).

Heraclitus of Ephesus
(c. 540–480 B.C.)

Every grown man of the Ephesians should hang himself and leave the city to the boys; for they banished Hermodorus, the best man among them, saying "let no one of us excel, or if he does, be it elsewhere and among others."

May wealth never leave you, Ephesians, lest your wickedness be revealed.

One person is ten thousand to me if he is best.

A lifetime [or, eternity] is a child playing, playing checkers; the kingdom belongs to a child.

The people must fight for the law as for the city wall.

• • •

Willful violence (*hubris*) must be quenched more than a fire.

A person's character [or, individuality] is his divinity [or, guardian spirit].

It is not better for humans to get all they want.

It is better to conceal ignorance.

It is difficult to fight against anger, for whatever it wants it buys at the price of soul.

• • •

Protagoras
(c. 490–420 B.C.)

Concerning the gods I am unable to know either that they are or that they are not, or what their appearance is like. For many are the things that hinder knowledge: the obscurity of the matter and the shortness of human life.

• • •

A human being is the measure of all things—of things that are, that they are, and of things that are not, that they are not.

• • •

I do say that the truth is as I've written: each of us is the measure of the things which are and the things which are not. Nevertheless, there's an immense difference between one man and another in just this respect: the things which are and appear to one man are different from those which are and appear to another. As for wisdom or a wise man, I'm nowhere near saying there's no such thing; on the contrary, I do apply the word "wise" to precisely this sort of person: anyone who can effect a change in one of us, to whom bad things appear and are, and make good things both appear and be for him. . . . Remember the sort of thing you were saying

before: to a sick man what he eats appears, and is, bitter, whereas to a healthy man it is, and appears, the opposite. Now what must be done isn't to make either of them wiser, because that isn't even possible; nor is it to accuse the sick one of being ignorant because he makes the sort of judgments he does, and call the healthy one wise because he makes judgments of a different sort. What must be done is to effect a change in one direction; because one of the two conditions is better. In education too, in the same way, a change must be effected from one of two conditions to the better one; but whereas a doctor makes the change with drugs, a Sophist does it with things he says.

It's not that anyone ever makes someone whose judgments are false come, later on, to judge what's true: after all, it isn't possible to have in one's judgments the things which are not, or anything other than what one's experiencing, which is always true. What does happen, I think, is this: when, because of a harmful condition in his mind, someone has in his judgments things which are akin to that condition, then by means of a beneficial condition one makes

Reprinted from *Philosophy Before Socrates: An Introduction with Texts and Commentary*, by Richard D. McKirahan, Jr. (Indianapolis: Hackett Publishing Company, 1994) by permission of the publisher.

him have in his judgments things of that same sort—appearances which some people, because of ignorance, call true; but I call them better than the first sort, but not at all truer.

And as for the wise . . . where bodies are concerned, I say it's doctors who are the wise, and where plants are concerned, gardeners—because I claim that they, too, whenever any of their plants are sick, instill perceptions that are beneficial and healthy, and true, too, into them, instead of harmful ones. My claim is, too, that wise and good politicians make beneficial things, instead of harmful ones, seem to their states to be just. If any sort of thing seems just and admirable to any state, then it actually is just and admirable for it, as long as that state accepts it; but a wise man makes the beneficial things be and seem just and admirable to them, instead of any harmful things which used to be so for them. And according to the same principle the Sophist is wise, too, in that he can educate his pupils in that way.

Plato's *Protagoras*

[The most systematic account of Protagoras' political views is to be found in Plato's dialogue, the Protagoras. *Socrates asks Protagoras whether or not it is possible to teach someone what virtue is and how to be virtuous. Protagoras responds, first by telling a story, then by elaborating the story's implications.]*

320
d
"There once was a time when the gods existed but mortal races did not. When the time came for their appointed genesis, the gods molded them inside the earth, blending together earth and fire and various compounds of earth and fire. When they were ready to bring them to light the gods put Prometheus and Epimetheus in charge of decking them out and assigning to each its appropriate powers and abilities.

e
"Epimetheus begged Prometheus for the privilege of assigning the abilities himself. 'When I've completed the distribution,' he said, 'you can inspect it.' Prometheus agreed, and Epimetheus started distributing abilities.

321
"To some he assigned strength without quickness; the weaker ones he made quick. Some he armed; others he left unarmed but devised for them some other means for preserving themselves. He compensated for small size by issuing wings for flight or an underground habitat. Size was itself a safeguard for those he made large. And so on down the line, balancing his distribution, making adjustments, and taking precautions against the possible extinction of any of the races.

"After supplying them with defenses against mutual destruction, he devised for them protection against the weather. He clothed them with thick pelts and b tough hides capable of warding off winter storms, effective against heat, and serving also as built-in, natural bedding when they went to sleep. He also shod them, some with hooves, others with thick pads of bloodless skin. Then he provided them with various forms of nourishment, plants for some, fruit from trees for others, roots for still others. And there were some to whom he gave the consumption of other animals as their sustenance. To some he gave the capacity for few births; to others, ravaged by the former, he gave the capacity for multiple births, and so ensured the survival of their kind.

"But Epimetheus was not very wise, and he absent- c mindedly used up all the powers and abilities on the nonreasoning animals; he was left with the human race, completely unequipped. While he was floundering about at a loss, Prometheus arrived to inspect the distribution and saw that while the other animals were well provided with everything, the human race was naked, unshod, unbedded, and unarmed, and it was already the day on which all of them, human beings included, were destined to emerge from the earth into the light. It was then that Prometheus, d desperate to find some means of survival for the human race, stole from Hephaestus and Athena wisdom in the practical arts together with fire (without which this kind of wisdom is effectively useless) and gave them outright to the human race. The wisdom it

Reprinted from Plato, *Protagoras*, translated by Stanley Lombardo and Karen Bell (Indianapolis: Hackett Publishing Company, 1992) by permission of the publisher.

acquired was for staying alive; wisdom for living together in society, political wisdom, it did not acquire, because that was in the keeping of Zeus. Prometheus no longer had free access to the high citadel that is the house of Zeus, and besides this, the guards there

e were terrifying. But he did sneak into the building that Athena and Hephaestus shared to practice their arts, and he stole from Hephaestus the art of fire and

322 from Athena her arts, and he gave them to the human race. And it is from this origin that the resources human beings needed to stay alive came into being. Later, the story goes, Prometheus was charged with theft, all on account of Epimetheus.

"It is because humans had a share of the divine dispensation that they alone among animals worshipped the gods, with whom they had a kind of kinship, and erected altars and sacred images. It wasn't long before they were articulating speech and words and had invented houses, clothes, shoes, and blankets,

b and were nourished by food from the earth. Thus equipped, human beings at first lived in scattered isolation; there were no cities. They were being destroyed by wild beasts because they were weaker in every way, and although their technology was adequate to obtain food, it was deficient when it came to fighting wild animals. This was because they did not yet possess the art of politics, of which the art of war is a part. They did indeed try to band together and survive by founding cities. The outcome when they did so was that they wronged each other, because they did not possess the art of politics, and so they

c would scatter and again be destroyed. Zeus was afraid that our whole race might be wiped out, so he sent Hermes to bring justice and a sense of shame to humans, so that there would be order within cities and bonds of friendship to unite them. Hermes asked Zeus how he should distribute shame and justice to humans. 'Should I distribute them as the other arts were? This is how the others were distributed: one person practicing the art of medicine suffices for many ordinary people; and so forth with the other practitioners. Should I establish

d justice and shame among humans in this way, or distribute it to all?' 'To all,' said Zeus, 'and let all have a share. For cities would never come to be if only a few possessed these, as is the case with the other arts. And establish this law as coming

from me: Death to him who cannot partake of shame and justice, for he is a pestilence to the city.'

"And so it is, Socrates, that when the Athenians (and others as well) are debating architectural excellence, or the virtue proper to any other professional specialty, they think that only a few individuals have the right to advise them, and they do not accept advice e from anyone outside these select few. You've made this point yourself, and with good reason, I might add. But when the debate involves political excellence, which must proceed entirely from justice and 323 temperance, they accept advice from anyone, and with good reason, for they think that this particular virtue, political or civic virtue, is shared by all, or there wouldn't be any cities. This must be the explanation for it, Socrates.

"And so you won't think you've been deceived, consider this as further evidence for the universal belief that all humans have a share of justice and the rest of civic virtue. In the other arts, as you have said, if someone claims to be a good flute-player or whatever, but is not, people laugh at him or get angry with him, and his family comes round and remon- b strates with him as if he were mad. But when it comes to justice or any other social virtue, even if they know someone is unjust, if that person publicly confesses the truth about himself, they will call this truthfulness madness, whereas in the previous case they would have called it a sense of decency. They will say that everyone ought to claim to be just, whether they are c or not, and that it is madness not to pretend to justice, since one must have some trace of it or not be human.

"This, then, is my first point: It is reasonable to admit everyone as an adviser on this virtue, on the grounds that everyone has some share of it. Next I will attempt to show that people do *not* regard this virtue as natural or self-generated, but as something taught and carefully developed in those in whom it is developed.

"In the case of evils that men universally regard as d afflictions due to nature or bad luck, no one ever gets angry with anyone so afflicted or reproves, admonishes, punishes, or tries to correct them. We simply pity them. No one in his right mind would try to do anything like this to someone who is ugly, for example, or scrawny or weak. The reason is, I assume, that they know that these things happen to people as a

natural process or by chance, both these ills and their opposites. But in the case of the good things that
e accrue to men through practice and training and teaching, if someone does not possess these goods but rather their corresponding evils, he finds himself the object of anger, punishment, and reproof. Among
324 these evils are injustice, impiety, and in general everything that is opposed to civic virtue. Offenses in this area are always met with anger and reproof, and the reason is clearly that this virtue is regarded as something acquired through practice and teaching. The key, Socrates, to the true significance of punishment lies in the fact that human beings consider virtue to
b be something acquired through training. For no one punishes a wrong-doer in consideration of the simple fact that he has done wrong, unless one is exercising the mindless vindictiveness of a beast. Reasonable punishment is not vengeance for a past wrong—for one cannot undo what has been done—but is undertaken with a view to the future, to deter both the
c wrong-doer and whoever sees him being punished from repeating the crime. This attitude towards punishment as deterrence implies that virtue is learned, and this is the attitude of all those who seek requital in public or in private. All human beings seek requital from and punish those who they think have wronged them, and the Athenians, your fellow citizens, especially do so. Therefore, by my argument, the Athenians are among those who think that virtue is acquired and taught. So it is with good reason that your fellow citizens accept a blacksmith's or a cobbler's advice
d in political affairs. And they do think that virtue is acquired and taught. It appears to me that both these propositions have been sufficiently proved, Socrates.

"Now, on to your remaining difficulty, the problem you raise about good men teaching their sons everything that can be taught and making them wise in these subjects, but not making them better than anyone else in the particular virtue in which they themselves excel. On this subject, Socrates, I will abandon
e story for argument. Consider this: Does there or does there not exist one thing which all citizens must have for there to be a city? Here and nowhere else lies the solution to your problem. For if such a thing exists, and this one thing is not the art of the carpenter, the blacksmith, or the potter, but justice, and temperance,
325 and piety—what I may comprehensively term the

virtue of a man, and if this is the thing which everyone should share in and with which every man should act whenever he wants to learn anything or do anything, but should not act without it, and if we should instruct and punish those who do not share in it, b man, woman, and child, until their punishment makes them better, and should exile from our cities or execute whoever doesn't respond to punishment and instruction; if this is the case, if such is the nature of this thing, and good men give their sons an education in everything but this, then we have to be amazed at how strangely our good men behave. For we have shown that they regard this thing as teachable both in private and public life. Since it is something that can be taught and nurtured, is it possible that they have their sons taught everything in which there is no death penalty for not understanding it, but when their children are faced with the death penalty or exile if they fail to learn virtue and be nurtured in c it—and not only death but confiscation of property and, practically speaking, complete familial catastrophe—do you think they do not have them taught this or give them all the attention possible? We must think that they do, Socrates.

"Starting when they are little children and continuing as long as they live, they teach them and correct them. As soon as a child understands what is said to d him, the nurse, mother, tutor, and the father himself fight for him to be as good as he possibly can, seizing on every action and word to teach him and show him that this is just, that is unjust, this is noble, that is ugly, this is pious, that is impious, he should do this, he should not do that. If he obeys willingly, fine; if not, they straighten him out with threats and blows as if he were a twisted, bent piece of wood. After this they send him to school and tell his teachers to pay more atten- e tion to his good conduct than to his grammar or music lessons. The teachers pay attention to these things, and when the children have learned their letters and are getting to understand writing as well as the spoken language, they are given the works of good poets to read at their desks and have to learn them by heart, works 326 that contain numerous exhortations, many passages describing in glowing terms good men of old, so that the child is inspired to imitate them and become like them. In a similar vein, the music teachers too foster in their young pupils a sense of moral decency and

restraint, and when they learn to play the lyre they are
b taught the works of still more good poets, the lyric and
choral poets. The teachers arrange the scores and drill
the rhythms and scales into the children's souls, so that
they become gentler, and their speech and movements
become more rhythmical and harmonious. For all of
human life requires a high degree of rhythm and harmony. On top of all this, they send their children to an
athletic trainer so that they may have sound bodies in
c the service of their now fit minds and will not be forced
to cowardice in war or other activities through physical deficiencies.

"This is what the most able, i.e., the richest, do.
Their sons start going to school at the earliest age
d and quit at the latest age. And when they quit school,
the city in turn compels them to learn the laws and
to model their lives on them. They are not to act as
they please. An analogy might be drawn from the
practice of writing-teachers, who sketch the letters
faintly with a pen in workbooks for their beginning
students and have them write the letters over the
patterns they have drawn. In the same way the city
has drawn up laws invented by the great lawgivers in
the past and compels them to govern and be governed
by them. She punishes anyone who goes beyond these
laws, and the term for this punishment in your city
e and others is, because it is a corrective legal action,
'correction.'

"When so much care and attention is paid to virtue,
Socrates, both in public and private, are you still
puzzled about virtue being teachable? The wonder
would be if it were not teachable.

"Why, then, do many sons of good fathers never
amount to anything? I want you to understand this
too, and in fact it's no great wonder, if what I've just
327 been saying is true about virtue being something in
which no one can be a layman if there is to be a city.
For if what I am saying is true—and nothing could
be more true: Pick any other pursuit or study and
reflect upon it. Suppose, for instance, there could be
no city unless we were all flute-players, each to the
best of his ability, and everybody were teaching everybody else this art in public and private and reprimand-
ing the poor players and doing all this unstintingly,
b just as now no one begrudges or conceals his expertise
in what is just and lawful as he does his other professional expertise. For it is to our collective advantage
that we each possess justice and virtue, and so we all

gladly tell and teach each other what is just and
lawful. Well, if we all had the same eagerness and
generosity in teaching each other flute-playing, do
you think, Socrates, that the sons of good flute-players
would be more likely to be good flute-players than
the sons of poor flute-players? I don't think so at all.
When a son happened to be naturally disposed toward c
flute-playing, he would progress and become famous;
otherwise, he would remain obscure. In many cases
the son of a good player would turn out to be a poor
one, and the son of a poor player would turn out to
be good. But as flute-players, they would all turn out
to be capable when compared with ordinary people
who had never studied the flute. Likewise you must
regard the most unjust person ever reared in a human
society under law as a paragon of justice compared d
with people lacking education and lawcourts and the
pervasive pressure to cultivate virtue, savages such as
the playwright Pherecrates brought on stage at last
year's Lenaean festival. There's no doubt that if you
found yourself among such people, as did the misan-
thropes in that play's chorus, you would be delighted
to meet up with the likes of Eurybatus and e
Phrynondas and would sorely miss the immorality of
the people here. As it is, Socrates, you affect delicate
sensibilities, because everyone here is a teacher of
virtue, to the best of his ability, and you can't see a
single one. You might as well look for a teacher of 328
Greek; you wouldn't find a single one of those either.
Nor would you be any more successful if you asked
who could teach the sons of our craftsmen the very
arts which they of course learned from their fathers,
to the extent that their fathers were competent, and
their friends in the trade. It would be difficult to
produce someone who could continue their education, whereas it would be easy to find a teacher for
the totally unskilled. It is the same with virtue and
everything else. If there is someone who is the least
bit more advanced in virtue than ourselves, he is to
be cherished.

"I consider myself to be such a person, uniquely b
qualified to assist others in becoming noble and good,
and worth the fee that I charge and even more, so
much so that even my students agree. This is why I
charge according to the following system: a student c
pays the full price only if he wishes to; otherwise, he
goes into a temple, states under oath how much he
thinks my lessons are worth, and pays that amount.

"There you have it, Socrates, my mythic story and my argument that virtue is teachable and that the Athenians consider it to be so, and that it is no wonder that worthless sons are born of good fathers and good sons of worthless fathers, since even the sons of Po-lyclitus, of the same age as Paralus and Xanthippus here, are nothing compared to their father, and the *d* same is true for the sons of other artisans. But it is not fair to accuse these two yet; there is still hope for them, for they are young."

Gorgias
(c. 483–385 B.C.)

In Praise of Helen

I will set forth the reasons for which it was likely that Helen's voyage to Troy took place. (6) She did what she did through the will of Fate and the designs of the gods and decrees of Necessity or because she was taken by force, persuaded by words (*logoi*), or conquered by Love. . . . (8) Not even if speech (*logos*) persuaded and deceived her soul, is it hard to make a defense against this charge and free her from blame, as follows. *logos* is a powerful master, which by means of the smallest and most invisible body accomplishes most divine deeds. For it can put an end to fear, remove grief, instill joy, and increase pity. I will prove how this is so. (9) But it is to the opinion of my audience that I must prove it. I both consider and define all poetry to be speech (*logos*) with meter. Those who hear it are overcome with fearful shudder-ing, tearful pity, and mournful yearning, and over the good fortunes and ill-farings of other people and their affairs the soul experiences a feeling of its own, through the words (*logoi*). Come now, let me shift from one argument (*logos*) to another. (10) Inspired incantations bring on pleasure and bring away grief through words (*logoi*). For conversing with the soul's opinion the power of incantation charms, persuades, and changes it by witchcraft. Two arts of witchcraft and magic have been discovered—errors of the soul and deceptions of opinion. (11) All who have per-suaded or who persuade anyone of anything do so by fashioning false *logos*. For if on all subjects everyone had memory of the past, (a conception) of the present and foreknowledge of the future, *logos* would not be similarly similar as it is for people who, as things are, cannot easily remember the past, consider the present, or divine the future. Thus, on most matters, most people make opinion an adviser to their soul. But opinion is fallible and uncertain, and involves those who make use of it in fallible and uncertain successes. (12) What, then, keeps us from supposing that Helen too, against her will, came under the influence of *logoi* just as if she had been taken by the force of mighty men? For it was possible to see how persuasion prevails, which lacks the appearance of necessity but has the same power. For *logos*, which persuaded, compelled the soul, which it persuaded, both to believe what was said and to approve what was done. Therefore, the one who persuaded, since he compelled, is unjust, and the one who was persuaded, since she was compelled by *logos*, is wrongly blamed. (13) As to the fact that persuasion added to *logos* makes whatever impression it likes on the soul, one should attend first to the accounts (*logoi*) of the astron-omers, who replace one opinion with another and so make things incredible and unclear seem apparent to the eyes of opinion; second, to compulsory compe-titions which use speeches (*logoi*), in which a single *logos* written with art (*techne*) but not spoken with truth delights and persuades a large crowd; and third, to contests of philosophers' accounts (*logos*), in which is revealed how easily the swiftness of thought makes our confidence in our opinion change. (14) The power of *logos* has the same relation (*logos*) to the order of the soul as the order of drugs has to the nature of bodies. For as different drugs expel differ-ent humors from the body, and some put an end to

Reprinted from *Philosophy Before Socrates: An Introduction with Texts and Commentary,* by Richard D. McKirahan, Jr. (Indianapolis: Hackett Publishing Company, 1994) by permission of the publisher.

sickness and others to life, so some *logoi* cause grief, others joy, some fear, others render their hearers bold, and still others drug and bewitch the soul through an evil persuasion. (15) It has been stated that if she was persuaded by *logos* she did not do wrong but was unfortunate. . . . (21) By my account (*logos*) I have removed ill fame from a woman. I have stayed faithful to the rule (*nomos*) I stipulated at the beginning of my *logos*. I have attempted to put an end to the injustice of blame and ignorance of opinion. I wanted to write the *logos* as a praise of Helen and an entertainment for myself.

Antiphon
(c. 480–411 B.C.)

. . . Justice is a matter of not transgressing what the *nomoi* prescribe in whatever city you are a citizen of. A person would make most advantage of justice for himself if he treated the *nomoi* as important in the presence of witnesses, and treated the decrees of *physis* as important when alone and with no witnesses present. For the decrees of *nomoi* are extra additions, those of *physis* are necessary; those of the *nomoi* are the products of agreement, not of natural growth, whereas those of *physis* are the products of natural growth, not of agreement. If those who made the agreement do not notice a person transgressing the prescription of *nomoi*, he is free from both disgrace and penalty, but not so if they do notice him. But if, contrary to possibility, anyone violates any of the things which are innate by *physis*, the evil is no less if no one notices him and no greater if all observe. For he does not suffer harm as a result of opinion, but as a result of truth.

This is the entire purpose of considering these matters — that most of the things that are just according to *nomos* are established in a way which is hostile to *physis*. For *nomoi* have been established for the eyes, as to what they must see and what they must not, and for the ears, as to what they must hear and what they must not, and for the tongue, as to what it must say and what it must not, and for the hands, as to what they must do and what they must not, and for the feet, as to where they must go and where they must not, and for the mind, as to what it must desire and what it must not. Now the things from which the *nomoi* deter humans are no more in accord with or suited to *physis* than the things which they promote.

Living and dying are matters of *physis*, and living results for them from what is advantageous, dying from what is not advantageous. But the advantages which are established by the *nomoi* are bonds on *physis*, and those established by *physis* are free.

And so, things that cause distress, at least when thought of correctly, do not help *physis* more than things that give joy. Therefore, it will not be painful things rather than pleasant things which are advantageous. For things that are truly advantageous must not cause harm but benefit. Now the things that are advantageous by *physis* are among these. . . .

But according to *nomos*, those are correct who defend themselves after suffering and are not first to do wrong, and those who do good to parents who are bad to them, and who permit others to accuse them on oath but do not themselves accuse on oath. You will find most of these cases hostile to *physis*. They permit people to suffer more pain when less is possible and to have less pleasure when more is possible, and to receive injury when it is not necessary.

The *Anonymus Iamblichi*

No one should set out to maximize his own advantage or suppose that power used for one's advantage is *arete* and obedience to *nomoi* is cowardice. This is the most wicked thought and it results in everything diametrically opposed to what is good: evil and harm. For if humans were by *physis* unable to live singly but yielding to necessity came together to live with one another; and discovered all their life and their contrivances for living, but it is impossible for them to live with one another and to conduct their lives in the absence of *nomoi* (since that way they would suffer more damage than they would by living alone)—on account of these necessities *nomos* and justice are kings among humans and in no way can they depart. For they are firmly bound into our *physis*.

＊ ＊ ＊

If, then, someone were born who had from the beginning the following sort of *physis*: invulnerable in his flesh, not subject to disease, without feelings, superhuman, and hard as steel in body and soul—perhaps one might have thought that power used for personal advantage would be sufficient for such a person, since such a person could be scot-free even if he did not subject himself to the law (*nomos*). But this person does not think correctly. Even if there were such a person, though there could not be, he would survive by being an ally of the laws (*nomoi*) and of justice, strengthening them and using his might for them and for what assists them, but otherwise he could not last. For it would seem that all people would become enemies of a person with such a nature (*phunti*, related to *physis*), and through their own observance of *nomos* and their numbers they would overcome him by craft or force and would prevail. So it is obvious that power itself—real power—is preserved through *nomos* and justice.

＊ ＊ ＊

It is worthwhile to learn these facts about *eunomia* and *anomia*—how big the difference is between them, and that *eunomia* is the best thing both for the community and for the individual, and *anomia* is the worst, for the greatest harm arises immediately from *anomia*. Let us begin by indicating first what results from *eunomia*.

In the first place, trust arises from *eunomia*, and this benefits all people greatly and is one of the great goods. For as a result of it, money becomes available and so, even if there is little it is sufficient since it is in circulation, but without it not even a great deal of money would be enough. Fortunes and misfortunes in money and life are managed most suitably for people as a result of *eunomia*. For those enjoying good fortune can use it in safety and without danger of plots, while those suffering ill fortune are aided by the fortunate through their mutual dealings and trust, which result from *eunomia*. Through *eunomia*, moreover, the time people devote to *pragmata* [a word which can mean "government," "public business," or "troubles"] is idle, but that devoted to the activities of life is productive. In *eunomia* people are free from

the most unpleasant concern and engage in the most pleasant, since concern about *pragmata* is most unpleasant and concern about one's activities is most pleasant. Also, when they go to sleep, which is a rest from troubles for people, they go to it without fear and unworried about painful matters, and when they rise from it they have other similar experiences and do not suddenly become fearful. Nor after this very pleasant change [i.e., sleep] do they expect the day to bring poverty, but they look forward to it without fear directing their concern without grief towards the activities of life, lightening their labors with trust and confident hopes that they will get good things as a result. For all these things *eunomia* is responsible. And *war*, which is the source of the greatest evils for people, leading as it does to destruction and slavery—this too comes more to those who practice *anomia*, less to those practicing *eunomia*. There are many other goods found in *eunomia* which assist life, and also from it comes consolation for our difficulties.

These are the evils that come from *anomia*. In the first place, people do not have time for their activities and are engaged in the most unpleasant thing, *pragmata*, not activities, and because of mistrust and lack of mutual dealings they hoard money and do not make it available, so it becomes rare even if there is much. Ill fortune and good fortune minister to the opposite results [from what occurs under *eunomia*]: good fortune is not safe in *anomia*, but is plotted against, and bad fortune is not driven off but is strengthened through mistrust and the absence of mutual dealings. War from outside is more frequently brought against a land, and domestic faction comes from the same cause, and if it did not occur earlier it happens then. Also it happens that people are always involved in *pragmata* because of plots which come from one another, which force them to live constantly on guard and to make counterplots against each other. When they are awake their thoughts are not pleasant, and when they go to sleep their receptacle [i.e., sleep] is not pleasant but full of fear, and their awakening is fearful and frightening and leads a person to sudden memories of his troubles. These and all the previously mentioned evils result from *anomia*.

Also tyranny, so great and so foul an evil, arises from nothing else but *anomia*. Some people suppose—all who do not understand correctly—that a tyrant comes from some other source and that people are deprived of their freedom without being themselves responsible, but compelled by the tyrant when he has been established. But they do not consider this correctly. For whoever thinks that a king or a tyrant arises from anything else than *anomia* and personal advantage is an idiot. For when everyone turns to evil, this is what happens then. For it is impossible for humans to live without *nomoi* and justice. So when these two things—*nomos* and justice—are missing from the mass of the people, that is exactly when the guardianship and protection of them passes to a single person. How else could solitary rule be transferred to a single person unless the *nomos* had been driven out which benefited the mass of the people? For this man who is going to destroy justice and abolish *nomos* that is common and advantageous to all, must be made of steel if he intends to strip these things from the mass of the people, he being one and they many. But if he is made of flesh and is like the rest, he will not be able to accomplish this, but on the contrary if he reestablishes what is missing, he might be solitary ruler. This is why some people fail to notice this occurring when it does.

III

HISTORIANS

In 490 B.C., Persian troops acting on orders from the emperor Darius, invaded the Greek mainland. Their goal was to shore up the northwestern frontier of the burgeoning Persian empire. For several years, colonies in or near the Aegean Sea had rebelled against Persian rule, and they had done so with the aid of certain Greek city-states, most notably Athens. Persia had succeeded in suppressing the rebellions, but Darius was determined to punish the Greeks for their role in the uprisings and, in the process, to extend the already considerable reach of his empire.

By this time, Persia was the dominant power in the Mediterranean world. Under the leadership of Cyrus the Great, it had conquered the Babylonian empire, the Lydian kingdom in Asia Minor, and much of what we today call the Middle East, along with the Greek city-states of Ionia and the eastern Aegean. Cyrus himself was one of the most renowned leaders of antiquity (this is the same Cyrus who is praised in the Hebrew Bible for having freed the Israelites from the so-called Babylonian captivity). His successor, Cambyses, significantly enlarged the empire by conquering Egypt, thereby putting Persia in control of virtually the entire eastern rim of the Mediterranean, from the Hellespont to Libya. Darius succeeded Cambyses and sought to bring Persian power directly into Europe.

But the campaign proved to be a disaster for the Persians. In the famous and pivotal battle of Marathon, Greek forces under Athenian leadership, though badly outnumbered, routed the invaders. If Herodotus is to be believed—and this is a big if—Persia lost more than 6,000 men at Marathon, the Greeks but 192. The Persian army retreated in humiliation. Darius himself vowed retaliation, but he died before this was possible. His son and successor, Xerxes, was determined to avenge his father's defeat. In 480 B.C., an immense Persian army, estimated by modern historians to have had as many as 200,000 troops, once again invaded Greece.

The second Persian War was conducted on a far greater scale than the first. Whereas in the earlier conflict Athens had been nearly alone in defending the Greek mainland, the second war saw Sparta and other city-states join with Athens to create a more or less united front. A crucial battle occurred at Thermopylae, where a large Persian battalion was held in check for two crucial days by a tiny force of Spartan soldiers, all of whom ultimately died and were ever after honored as paragons of the Greek spirit. The Persians were eventually able to capture Athens itself; the city was abandoned by its residents, and the invaders plundered it, burning to the ground many of its most important structures. But in a crucial sea battle at Salamis, Greek forces dealt the Persians a crushing defeat; and in the ensuing land battle at Plataea, Greek armies routed the opposition, thereby ending, for all practical purposes, the Persian threat. The second Persian War established the power and independence of Greek city-states, and placed Athens squarely at the forefront. With this great victory in hand, Greece in general and Athens in particular could begin to enjoy what historians have come to call the Classical Age.

Our knowledge of the Persian Wars derives largely from Herodotus, whose *Histories* is the first great surviving prose work of Western literature. Indeed, it is no exaggeration to say that the very idea of writing history—of thinking historically—begins with this book. Herodotus pursues one overriding historical theme, the conflict between East and West, between Asia and Europe. He traces this conflict back to the Trojan War and sees in the Persian Wars the ultimate triumph of

Western values. In pursuing this theme, he places great emphasis on what we today would call culture. He contrasts the freedom and independence of Greek city-states with the slavishness of Persian culture, the open and deliberative nature of Greek politics with Persia's despotic form of rule, and the Greek emphasis on individuality and personal distinction with the Persian emphasis on the anonymity and insignificance of the average person. In these respects, Herodotus may be thought of not only as the first historian but also as the first anthropologist. Indeed, the second of the *Histories*'s eight books is devoted entirely to a detailed, historically grounded description of Egypt, apparently based at least in part on firsthand observation. It is important to note, moreover, that although Herodotus seems clearly concerned to sing the praises of Greek civilization, he is remarkably evenhanded with respect to other cultures. He finds much to admire in the Egyptians, for example, and believes many of their practices to be worth emulating.

In writing his account, Herodotus was clearly driven by the kind of interest in objectivity and truth that had been fostered by the Presocratic philosophers. In many cases, he provides alternative accounts of what happened in a particular place at a particular time, indicates his preference for one account over the others, and explains his preference by invoking basic criteria of reason and evidence. In discussing the Trojan War, for example, he doubts that Helen was actually in Troy during the conflict itself and provides what he believes to be clear and compelling reasons for his conclusion. In this and many other respects, he pointedly distinguishes his own enterprise from what he regards as the falsely historical, nonobjective work of Homer and the other epic poets.

If Herodotus was the so-called "father of history," then Thucydides was his immediate and arguably most illustrious heir. His topic, too, was war. But this was a different kind of war, and he wrote a different kind of history.

Victory over the Persians established a foundation for Athenian dominance in and around the Aegean; and this situation in turn was at least partly responsible for the development of deep conflicts among the various Greek city-states. Ultimately, those conflicts focused on the great rivalry between Athens and Sparta. In 433 B.C., a Corinthian colony called Corcyra—present-day Corfu—rebelled against Corinth and did so with the aid of Athenian forces. Other conflicts between Athens and Corinth eventually drew Corinth's ally Sparta into the controversy, and in 431 B.C., Sparta invaded Athens itself. Greek city-states essentially divided into two camps, and the war was fought at many locations throughout the Greek world. In part, the Peloponnesian War was a struggle between a land power and a sea power. Sparta's infantry was the strongest in Greece, while Athens had by far the best navy. But it was also a struggle between two different ways of life. Sparta was a conservative, inward-looking, landlocked, agrarian society, which was governed by an oligarchy and was famous for its disciplined, militaristic culture; its reputation was embodied in the heroes of Thermopylae. Athens, on the other hand, was a democratically governed commercial powerhouse, actively involved with trading partners throughout the Mediterranean; it was thought of as restless, innovative, and ambitious, and it was, of course, famous for its cultivation of the arts. These generalizations need to be pursued with care. Most present-day historians agree, for example, that despite its conservatism Spartan culture afforded women a much more central role in society than did Athenian culture. Nonetheless, the sharp contrast between the two dominant city-states is a fundamental motif of Thucydides' *History of the Peloponnesian War*.

Thucydides himself was an Athenian general during the early part of the war. In 424 B.C., he suffered an important defeat at Amphipolis, and as a result was removed from his command, condemned by Athens, and exiled for twenty years. These facts may help explain what some commentators believe to be a certain tendency in the *History* to look more favorably on Sparta than on Athens. Thucydides insists on his own objectivity, however. More generally, he pointedly contrasts his approach to history with that of Herodotus. Herodotus' goal was to recount the events of the Persian Wars as accurately as possible, to place those events in a larger historical context, and to explain what happened by pointing to the particular and unique differences between various cultures—Greek, Persian, Egyptian, and the like. Thucydides, on the other hand, claimed to be writing "for the ages" and suggested that his history would describe certain eternal truths about society and human nature, "covering laws" that are valid not just for the late fifth century B.C., but for all time.

The methodological differences between Herodotus and Thucydides are reflected in certain textual or literary differences. The most characteristic set pieces of Herodotus' *Histories* are sociological or anthropological accounts of particular societies, from which the author attempts to show how the activities of those societies followed naturally from their cultural predispositions. In Thucydides' *History*, on the other hand, the most famous set pieces are speeches or debates in which orators or discussants explain or justify actions on the basis of general, abstract principles that are not peculiar to any particular place or time. Included here are Pericles' Funeral Oration, the Mytilenian debate, and the Melian dialogue, all of which are literary masterpieces that present with uncommon power and clarity theoretical or ideological arguments that have been, and continue to be, extremely influential.

Further Reading: A very good introduction to Herodotus is John Gould, *Herodotus* (1989). Also highly recommended is the more recent book by James Romm, *Herodotus* (1998). An important and challenging historiographical study is Donald Lateiner, *The Historical Method of Herodotus* (1989). I am also much taken with the three essays contained in J. A. S. Evans, *Herodotus, Explorer of the Past* (1991). To my knowledge, the first attempt to compare and contrast the historical methods of Herodotus and Thucydides is Virginia Hunter, *Past and Process in Herodotus and Thucydides* (1982), which is highly recommended. Perhaps the best introduction to Thucydides himself is W. R. Connor, *Thucydides* (1984), which emphasizes, among other things, the literary dimensions of the *History*. Crucial for historical questions are the several books by Donald Kagan, including *The Outbreak of the Peloponnesian War* (1969) and *The Fall of the Athenian Empire* (1987). For an excellent treatment of a fundamental theme in Thucydides, see C. D. C. Reeve, "Thucydides on Human Nature," in *Political Theory* (1999).

Herodotus
(c. 490–c. 425 B.C.)

Histories

[In discussing the excesses of the Persian emperor Cambyses, Herodotus offers his view of the importance of nomos, *or custom.]*

[Book 3, Chapter 38] Thus it appears certain to me, by a great variety of proofs, that Cambyses was raving mad. Otherwise he would not have set out to mock holy rites and long-established customs. For if one were to offer men to select, out of all the customs in the world, those that seemed to them the best, they would examine all of them and end up preferring their own, so convinced are they that their own customs far surpass those of all others. Unless therefore, a man was mad, it is not likely that he would make sport of such matters. That people have this feeling about their customs may be seen by very many proofs, such as the following. Darius, after he became ruler, gathered certain Greeks who were at hand and asked how much money it would take to get them to eat the bodies of their fathers when they died. To which they answered that there was no sum of money that would tempt them to do such a thing. He then sent for certain Indians, of the race called Coalitions, men who eat their fathers, and asked them—while the Greeks stood by (and knew what he was saying with the help of an interpreter)—how much money it would take to get them to burn the bodies of their fathers when they died. The Indians exclaimed out loud and begged him not to say such things. Such is the usual way of men; and Pindar was right, in my judgment, when he said "Custom is the king over all."

[Having successfully overthrown the existing Persian rulers, Otanes, Megabyzus, and Darius debate the forms of government.]

[Book 3, Chapters 80–82] When five days were gone, and the hubbub had settled down, the conspirators met together to discuss the situation of affairs. At this meeting speeches were made, to which many of the Greeks give no credence, but they were made nevertheless. Otanes recommended that the management of public affairs should be entrusted to the majority. "To me," he said, "it seems advisable that we should no longer have a single man to rule us. The rule of one man is neither good nor pleasant. You cannot have forgotten to what lengths Cambyses went in his haughty tyranny, and the haughtiness of the Magi you yourselves have experienced. How indeed is it possible that monarchy should be a well-adjusted thing when it allows a man to do as he likes without being answerable? Such license is enough to stir strange and inappropriate thoughts in the heart of the worthiest of men. Give a person this power and immediately his virtues puff him up with pride while envy is so natural to humankind that it cannot but arise in him. But pride and envy together include all wickedness—both of them leading on to acts of savage violence. It is true that kings, possessing as they do all that anyone could desire, ought to be free of envy; but the contrary is seen in their conduct toward the citizens. They are jealous of the most virtuous among their subjects and wish them dead, while they take delight in the meanest and basest of citizens, being always ready to listen to the tales of slanderers. Besides, a king, more than anyone else, is unpredictable. Pay him respect in moderation, and he is angry because you do not show him more profound respect. Show him profound respect, and he is offended again because had claims that you are merely flattering him. But worst of all, he ignores the laws of the land, puts men to death without trial, and subjects women to violence. The rule of the many, on the other hand, has, in the first place, the fairest of names—*isonomy* or equality under the law. In addition, it is free from all those outrages that kings are apt to commit. Gov-

Adapted from *The History of Herodotus*, Volume 1 and 2, translated by George Rawlinson (London: J. M. Dent, 1910).

ernment positions are given out by lottery, the magistrate is answerable for what he does, and legislation rests with the people. I vote, therefore, that we do away with monarchy and raise the people to power. For the people are the embodiment of everything."

Such were the views of Otanes. Megabyzus spoke next and advised setting up an oligarchy. "In all that Otanes had said to persuade you to eliminate monarchy," he observed, "I fully concur; but his recommendation that we should call the people to power seems to me not the best advice. For there is nothing so void of understanding, nothing so capricious, as the uncontrollable rabble. It would be folly for men seeking to avoid the capriciousness of a tyrant to embrace the capriciousness of the unbridled mob. The tyrant, in all of his actions, at least knows what he is doing, but a mob is altogether devoid of knowledge; for how should there be any knowledge in a rabble—uneducated and with no natural sense of what is right and fit? It rushes wildly into political affairs with all the fury of a stream swollen in the winter, and confuses everything. Let the enemies of the Persians be ruled by democracies, but let us select from the citizenry a certain number of the worthiest individuals and put the government in their hands. In this way, we ourselves shall be among the governors; and since power will be entrusted to the best men, it is likely that the best counsels will prevail."

This was the advice that Megabyzus gave. After him came Darius, who spoke as follows: "All that Megabyzus said against democracy was well said, I think. But about oligarchy he did not speak wisely. For if we take these three forms of government—democracy, oligarchy, and monarchy—at their best, I maintain that monarchy far surpasses the other two. What government can possibly be better than that of the very best man in the whole state? The counsels of such a man are apt to be like himself, and so he governs the mass of the people so that they will be content. At the same time, his measure against evildoers are kept more secret than in other states. In oligarchies, where men vie with each other in the service of the commonwealth, fierce enmities are apt to arise between man and man, each wishing to be leader and to carry out his own measures. From this arises violent quarrels, which lead to open strife often ending in bloodshed. Monarchy is sure to follow, and this, too, shows how monarchy far surpasses all other forms of government. Again, in a democracy

there is certain to be mistakes or outrages. Such mistakes, however, do not lead to enmities but to close friendships, which are formed among the evildoers and who must stick together in order to carry on their villainy. And so things go on until a man stands forth as champion of the common good and puts down the evildoers. Immediately, the author of so great a service is admired by all, and thus comes to be appointed king. So that here, too, it is plain that monarchy is the best government. Lastly, to sum it all up, I ask: where was it that we obtained the freedom that we enjoy? Did democracy give to us, or oligarchy, or a monarch? As a single man reestablished our freedom for us, I vote to keep to the rule of one. Even apart from this, we ought not to change the laws of our forefathers when they work well, for to do so is not a good idea."

[Herodotus seeks to account for the success of Athens in dominating the Greek world.]

[Book 5, Chapter 78] The Athenians increased in strength. And it is plain enough, not from this instance alone but from many others, that freedom is an excellent thing. Even the Athenians, who when they were ruled by tyrants were no more courageous than any of their neighbors, became most courageous of all when freed from tyranny. Such things show that when they were being oppressed at home they let themselves be beaten in battle since they were working for a master. But as soon as they got their freedom, each man was eager to do the best he could for himself.

• • •

[Athenian dominance leads to tension among the Greek city-states, and this in turn prompts the following thoughts from Sosicles of Corinth on the evils of despotism.]

[Book 5, Chapter 92] "Surely heaven will soon be below, and the earth above, and men will henceforth live in the sea, and fish will take their place upon the dry land, since you, Lacedaemonians, propose to eliminate free governments in the cities of Greece and to set up tyrannies in their place. There is nothing in the whole world so unjust, nothing so bloody, as tyranny. If, however, it seems to you a desirable thing to have the cities under despotic rule, begin by putting a tyrant over yourselves before you establish despots in the other states. While you yourselves have always been unacquainted with tyranny, and are very careful to make sure that Sparta does not suffer from it, to act as you are now is to treat your allies unfairly. If you knew what tyranny was as well as we do, you would be better advised you now are in regard to it.

"The government at Corinth was once an oligarchy—a single race, called Bacchiadae, who intermarried only among themselves, controlled the government. Now it happened that Amphion, one of these, had daughter named Labda who was lame and whom therefore none of the Bacchiadae were willing to marry; so she was taken to wife by Aëtion, son of Echecrates, a man of the township of Petra who was, however, descended from the race of the Lapithae and of the house of Caeneus. Since he had no children either by this wife or any other, Aëtion went to Delphi to consult the oracle. Scarcely had he entered the temple when Pythia saluted him in these words:

No one honors thee now, Aëtion, worthy of honor—
Labda shall soon be a mother—her offspring a rock
*   that will one day*
Fall on the kingly race and right the city of Corinth.

By some chance this address of the oracle to Aëtion came to the ears of the Bacchiadae, who until then had been unable to perceive the meaning of another, earlier prophecy, which was also about Corinth and pointed to the same event. It said:

When amid the rocks an eagle shall bear a
*   carnivorous lion*
Might and fierce, he shall loosen the limbs of
*   many beneath them—*
Brood ye well upon this, all ye Corinthian people,
Ye who dwell by fair Pirene, and beetling Corinth.

The Bacchiadae had possessed this oracle for some time, but they were quite at a loss to know what it meant until they heard the response given to Aëtion. Then, however, they at once perceived its meaning, since the two agreed so well together. Nevertheless, though the significance of the first prophecy was now clear to them, they remained quiet, deciding to put to death the child that Aëtion was expecting. Thus,

as soon as this wife was delivered, they sent ten of their number to the township where Aëtion lived, with orders to kill the baby. So the men came to Petra and went into Aëtion's house and asked if they might see the child. And Labda, who knew nothing of their purpose but thought their questions arose from a kindly feeling toward her husband, brought the child and laid him in the arms of one of them. Now they had agreed that whoever first got hold of the child should dash it against the ground. But through providential luck, it happened that just as Labda put the baby into the man's arms, the baby smiled in his face. The man saw the smile and was touched with pity so that he could not kill it. He therefore passed it on to his neighbor, who gave it to a third; and so it went through all the ten without any one choosing to be the murderer. The mother received her child back, and the men went out of the house and stood near the door, and there blamed and reproached one another, chiefly accusing, however, the man who had first held the child because he had not done what had been agreed to. At last, after much time had been spent in this way, they decided to go into the house again and all take part in the murder.

"But it was fated that evil should come upon Corinth from the progeny of Aëtion. And so it happened that Labda, as she stood near the door, heard all that the men said to one another, and fearful of their changing their mind and returning to destroy her baby, she carried him off and hid him in what seemed to her the most unlikely place to be suspect, a corn bin. She knew that if they came back to look for the child, they would search all her house. And so they did, but not finding the child after looking everywhere, they thought it best to go away and declare to their superiors that they had indeed completed their task successfully. They reported as much on their return.

"Aëtion's son grew up and, in memory of the danger from which had escaped, was called Cypselus, after the corn bin. When he came to manhood, he went to Delphi and, after consulting the oracle, received a response that was two-sided:

See there comes to my dwelling a man much favor'd
*   of fortune, Cypselus, son of Aëtion, and king of*
*   the glorious Corinth,*
He and his children too, but not his children's
*   children,*

Such was the oracle; and Cypselus put so much faith in it that he immediately made his attempt and thereby became master of Corinth. Having thus become tyrant, he showed himself a harsh ruler—he drove many of the Corinthians into exile, deprived others of their fortunes and still more of their lives.

"His reign lasted thirty years and was prosperous to the end. He left his government to his son Periander. At the beginning of his reign, Periander was of a milder temper than his father. But later, after he corresponded by means of messengers with Thrasybulus, tyrant of Miletus, he became even bloodier than his father had been. On one occasion he sent a herald to ask Thrasybulus what form of government was the safest to establish in order to rule with honor. Thrasybulus led the messenger out of the city, and took him into a field of corn. While walking through the field, he asked him again and again about his coming from Corinth, breaking off and throwing away all of the ears of corn that had grown taller than the rest. He went through the whole field doing this, and destroyed thereby the best and richest part of the crop. Then, without a word, he sent the messenger back to Corinth. Periander was eager to know what Thrasybulus had advised, but the messenger reported that he had said nothing; and the messenger wondered why Periander had sent him to so strange a man, who seemed to have lost his senses since he did nothing but destroy his own property. And so he told Periander how Thrasybulus had behaved during the interview.

"Periander, understanding what that behavior meant and knowing that Thrasybulus was advising the destruction of all the leading citizens, began to treat his subjects with the very greatest cruelty. Where Cypselus had spared some, and had neither put them to death nor banished them, Periander completed what his father had left unfinished. One day he stripped all the women of Corinth stark naked, for the sake of his own wife Melissa. He had sent messengers into Thesprotia to consult the oracle of the dead upon the Acheron concerning something valuable that had been given to his safekeeping by a stranger. Melissa had appeared to the messengers but refused to speak or tell where the valuables were because, she said, she was cold for she had no clothes to keep her warm since the clothes that Periander had buried her in had not been burned. And this should indicate to Periander that what she said was true: 'the oven that was cold when he baked his loaves in it.'

"When this message was brought to him, Periander immediately made a proclamation that all wives of the Corinthians should go forth to the temple of Juno. So the women dressed themselves in their finest clothes and went to the temple, as if to a festival. Then, with the help of his guards, he stripped each one of them, free women and slaves alike. He put all of their clothes in a pit and, calling on the name of Melissa, burned them. Having done this, he again sent messengers to the oracle, and this time Melissa's ghost told them where to find the stranger's treasure.

"Such, Lacedaemonians, is tyranny."

Thucydides
(c. 460–c. 399 B.C.)

History of the Peloponnesian War

[*Thucydides discusses his historical method.*]

People take in reports about the past from each other all alike, without testing them—even reports about their own country. Most of the Athenians, for example, think that Hipparchus was tyrant when he was killed by Harmodius and Aristogeiton, and don't know that it was Hippias who was in power, since he was the eldest son of Pisistratus, and Hipparchus and Thessalus were his brothers. In fact, on the very day,

Reprinted from *Thucydides on Justice, Power, and Human Nature,* translated, with introduction and notes, by Paul Woodruff (Indianapolis: Hackett Publishing Company, 1993) by permission of the publisher.

and at the very moment of the deed, Harmodius and Aristogeiton suspected that some of their accomplices had told Hippias about the plot. So they avoided him as having been forewarned, but they still wanted to do something daring before they were captured. When they met Hipparchus by chance at the Leocorium, where he was organizing the Panathenaic Procession, they killed him.

Other Greeks have wrong opinions about many subjects that are current and not forgotten in the passage of time, for example, that the Lacedaemonian kings have two votes each, instead of one, and that they have a military unit there called "Pitanate," which never existed. That shows how much the search for truth strains the patience of most people, who would rather believe the first things that come to hand. [21] But if the evidence cited leads a reader to think that things were mostly as I have described them, he would not go wrong, as he would if he believed what the poets have sung about them, which they have much embellished, or what the prose-writers have strung together, which aims more to delight the ear than to be true. Their accounts cannot be tested, you see, and many are not credible, as they have achieved the status of myth over time. But the reader should believe that I have investigated these matters adequately, considering their antiquity, using the best evidence available. People always think the greatest war is the one they are fighting at the moment, and when that is over they are more impressed with wars of antiquity; but, even so, this war will prove, to all who look at the facts, that it was greater than the others.

[22] What particular people said in their speeches, either just before or during the war, was hard to recall exactly, whether they were speeches I heard myself or those that were reported to me at second hand. I have made each speaker say what I thought the situation demanded, keeping as near as possible to the general sense of what was actually said.

And as for the real action of the war, I did not think it right to set down either what I heard from people I happened to meet or what I merely believed to be true. Even for events at which I was present myself, I tracked down detailed information from other sources as far as I could. It was hard work to find out what happened, because those who were present at each event gave different reports, depending on which side they favored and how well they remembered.

This history may not be the most delightful to hear, since there is no mythology in it. But those who want to look into the truth of what was done in the past—which, given the human condition, will recur in the future, either in the same fashion or nearly so—those readers will find this *History* valuable enough, as this was composed to be a lasting possession and not to be heard for a prize at the moment of a contest.

[On the origins of the Peloponnesian War.]

The greatest action before this was the one against the Persians, and even that was decided quickly by two battles at sea and two on land. But the Peloponnesian war went on for a very long time and brought more suffering to Greece than had ever been seen before: never had so many cities been captured and depopulated (some by foreigners, others by Greeks themselves at war with one another—some of which were resettled with new inhabitants); never had so many people been driven from their countries or killed, either in the war itself or as a result of civil strife.

Tales told about earlier times, but scantily confirmed in actuality, suddenly ceased to be incredible: tales of earthquakes, which occurred over most of the earth at this time, quite violent ones—eclipses of the sun, which were more frequent than is recorded in earlier times—great droughts in some places followed by famine—and, what caused enormous harm and loss of life, the plague.

All these hardships came upon them during the war, which began when the Athenians and Peloponnesians broke the Thirty Years' Peace that had been agreed between them after the conquest of Euboea. I will first write down an account of the disputes that explain their breaking the Peace, so that no one will ever wonder from what ground so great a war could arise among the Greeks. I believe that the truest reason for the quarrel, though least evident in what was said at the time, was the growth of Athenian power, which put fear into the Lacedaemonians and so compelled them into war, while the explanations both sides gave in public for breaking the Peace and starting the war are as follows.

• • •

[*Sparta threatens war with Athens unless Athens gives up its claims on Potidaea, Aegina, and Megara. Pericles speaks to the assembly, arguing against giving in to Sparta's demands.*]

The Athenians called an assembly to consider their options, and decided to make up their minds and answer once and for all. Many people came forward to speak on each side; some thought they should go to war, others that they should rescind the Megarian Decree so that it would not stand in the way of peace. Then Pericles—who was at that time the foremost Athenian and the most able in speech or action—gave the following advice:

[140] My opinion has always been the same, Athenians: don't give in to the Peloponnesians. Of course I know the passion that leads people into war does not last when they're actually engaged in it; people change their minds with the circumstances. But I see I must still give nearly the same advice now as I gave before; and I insist that if you agree to this as common policy you support it even if things go badly for us—otherwise you've no right to boast of your intelligence if all goes well, since events can turn out as stupidly as people's intentions, and that is why we usually blame chance when things don't turn out as expected.

It is obvious that the Lacedaemonians have been plotting against us, now more than ever. We agreed in the Thirty Years' Peace to refer our differences to mutual arbitration, while each party kept what it had in the meanwhile. But they have not yet asked for arbitration, and they have not accepted our offers either; they prefer war to speeches as a means of clearing away the charges against them, and they're already giving orders when they come, instead of complaining as they did before. They are commanding us to leave Potidaea, restore autonomy to Aegina, and rescind our decree against Megara; now these latest arrivals are warning us to let the Greeks have their autonomy. No one should think that the war will be over a trifle if we do not rescind the Megarian decree (which is what they emphasize the most—that if we rescind the decree there won't be a war). There mustn't be any suspicion remaining among you that the war was over a small matter: this "little matter" holds all the firmness of your resolve, and the proof of our judgment. If you give way on these points you will immediately be ordered to give up something greater, since they will expect you to be afraid and give way over that as well. A stiff refusal from you, however, will teach them clearly to treat you more as equals.

[141] Make up your minds right now either to give in before we get hurt, or, if we do go to war—as *I* think best—not to yield to any demand whatever, great or small, and to hold on to our possessions without fear. The effect is the same—subjugation—whether the claim is large or small, so long as it comes as a command from equals to their neighbors, before arbitration.

Now as for the war and the resources on both sides, once you hear a detailed account you must see that we'll be just as strong as they will. First, the Peloponnesians work their own land and have no wealth either in private or public hands. Second, they have no experience of extended or overseas warfare, since their attacks on each other are kept brief by their poverty. Such people are unable to man ships or send out armies of foot soldiers with any frequency, for they'd be far from their own property while still depending on their own food supplies. Besides, they would be blockaded by sea. Wars must be supported by wealth that is available, not by forced contributions. And those who work their own land are more willing to risk their lives in war than their money, since they have some confidence of surviving but are not sure their money won't be spent, especially if their war should be prolonged (as is likely) beyond what they expected. The Peloponnesians and their allies are able to hold out against all the other Greeks in a single battle, but they are unable to make war against those whose preparations are different from their own. Their League does not have a common council to take quick decisive action as needed; instead, they all have equal votes, and because they are not akin each group pursues its own interest, which means that nothing gets decided. Some, you see, want more than anything to exact revenge, while others want to keep damage to their own property at a minimum. They take a long time before a meeting, and then devote only a fraction of it to any common business, while spending the greater part on their individual concerns. Meanwhile, no one thinks that his neglect of common interests will do any harm—let someone else look after his share of the common interest. The result is that no one notices how everyone's individual judgments are ruining the common good for them all.

[142] The main point however is that they will be hindered by lack of money, since they will have to delay action while they wait to raise funds. But in war, the critical moment will not wait. And we should not have a moment's fear of their fort-building or their navy. As for a fort in Attica, it would be hard enough in peace-time to build a citadel that would be our match, let alone in war, when we are fortified against it. If they build only an observation post, on the other hand, they may damage some of our land by raiding it, and they may take in runaway slaves; but this would not be enough to keep us from sailing to their land and building forts there or retaliating with our navy, which is our great strength.

Our naval experience has actually done us more good on land than their infantry experience has done for their navy. And they won't easily learn to be experts at sea. You yourselves have not yet mastered it completely, though you've been studying it since right after the Persians came; how then could men who are farmers rather than sailors do anything worthwhile? Besides, they'll have no chance to practice, because we will blockade them constantly with a large fleet. They might take courage from superior numbers, set their ignorance aside, and venture out against a light blockade; but if they are shut in by a large navy then they will not stir that way at all, their lack of practice will make them even less skillful than before, and they will be even more cautious because of that. Naval warfare requires professional knowledge as much as anything else does: it is not possible to learn by practicing it occasionally on the side; on the contrary, if you're studying naval warfare you can't do anything else on the side.

[143] What if they would carry off the money at Olympia or Delphi and try to hire away our foreign sailors at a larger salary? That would be dangerous to us only if we could not match them by manning a fleet with our own citizens and resident aliens. As it is, however, we *can* do this. Besides—and this is really decisive—we have more captains and junior officers among our citizens than all the rest of Greece, and they are better qualified, too. Furthermore, to say nothing of the risks involved, no sailor would agree to be outlawed by his own country, accept a weaker

chance of winning, and join forces with the other side for only a few days of bonus payments.

That is more or less how I think things stand for the Peloponnesians. As for us, our position is free of all the faults I found in theirs, and we have great advantages in other areas as well. If they invade our territory on foot, we shall go to theirs by sea. And the advantage will be ours even if we waste only part of the Peloponnesus while they waste all of Attica. They cannot replace their land without a battle, while we have plenty of land in the islands and on the mainland. That's how great a thing it is to have control of the sea!

Consider this: would we be any safer from attack if we were islanders? Now we should really think like islanders and give up our land and our farmhouses, but keep watch over the sea and our city. We must not get so angry over losing our farms that we engage the Peloponnesians in battle when they outnumber us. If we won, we would have to fight against just as many men again; and if we were defeated we would lose our allies, which are the source of our strength, as they'll not keep quiet unless we're strong enough to fight them. We mustn't cry over our land and farms, but save our mourning for the lives of men: farmland won't give us men, but men can win farmland. If I thought I could persuade you, I'd tell you to go out and destroy the farms yourselves, and prove to the Peloponnesians that you will never surrender in order to save your land.

[144] Many other things give me hope that we shall win through, unless you intend to enlarge your empire while still engaged in the war, or choose to take on new risks. I am more afraid of our own mistakes, you see, than I am of our opponents' schemes. But all this should come clear in another speech, at the time of action.

For the present, let us send the ambassadors back with this answer: (1) We will give the Megarians the use of our market and ports if the Lacedaemonians will cancel their policy of expelling us and our allies as aliens (since nothing in the treaty blocks either our current policy or theirs). Also, (2) we will give the Greek cities their autonomy (if they were autonomous when we signed the treaty), as soon as the Lacedaemonians grant autonomy to their own cities to enjoy as they see fit, and not merely to serve Lacedaemonian interests. And (3) we would like to go to arbitration in accordance with the treaty. We will not begin a war, but we will punish those who do.

This is an answer that follows justice and suits the dignity of our city as well. Nevertheless, you must realize that although we are being forced into this war, if we embrace it willingly we will have less pressure from the enemy. Remember too that the greatest danger gives rise to the greatest honor for a city or a private man. Our ancestors, after all, stood up to the Persians; they started with less than we have now, and even gave up what they had. It was more good planning than good luck, and more daring than power, that enabled them to repel the Persian king and raise our city to its present heights. We must measure up to our ancestors: resist our enemies in every possible way and try to deliver the city undiminished to those who come after.

[145] That was Pericles' speech. The Athenians thought his advice was best, and voted to do as he had told them. They answered the Lacedaemonians as he had proposed, in every particular and on the main point too: "They would do nothing on command, but were ready to resolve the accusations on a fair and equal basis by arbitration as specified in the treaty." Then the Lacedaemonians went home, and after that there came no more ambassadors.

• • •

[Thucydides describes why most Greeks supported Sparta.]

Neither side made small plans, and both put their whole strength into the war. This was only to be expected, for in the beginning of an enterprise everyone is most eager. Besides, there were many young men in the Peloponnesus at that time, and many in Athens, who for want of experience undertook the war quite willingly. And the rest of Greece watched in suspense as its two principal cities came into conflict. Many prophecies were told, and many sung by the priests of the oracles, both in the cities about to make war and in others. There was also an earthquake in Delos a little before this, where the earth had never been shaken before in the memory of the Greeks.

This was said to be a sign of what was going to happen afterwards, and people believed that. And if anything else of this sort happened by chance, people started looking for an explanation.

Men's sympathies for the most part went with the Lacedaemonians, especially because they gave out that they would recover the Greeks' liberty. Everyone, private citizens and cities alike, endeavored in word and deed to assist them as much as they could; and everyone thought that the affair would be held back if they were not part of it. That is how angry most people were against the Athenians, some out of the desire to be set free from their empire, and others for fear of falling under it.

[Pericles' Funeral Oration, one of the most famous speeches of Western history.]

[35] Most of those who have spoken before me on this occasion have praised the man who added this oration to our customs because it gives honor to those who have died in the wars; yet I would have thought it sufficient that those who have shown their mettle in action should also receive their honor in an action, as now you see they have, in this burial performed for them at public expense, so that the virtue of many does not depend on whether one person is believed to have spoken well or poorly.

It is a hard matter to speak in due measure when there is no firm consensus about the truth. A hearer who is favorable and knows what was done will perhaps think that a eulogy falls short of what he wants to hear and knows to be true; while an ignorant one will find some of the praise to be exaggerated, especially if he hears of anything beyond his own talent—because that would make him envious. Hearing another man praised is bearable only so long as the hearer thinks he could himself have done what he hears. But if a speaker goes beyond that, the hearer soon becomes envious and ceases to believe. Since our ancestors have thought it good, however, I too should follow the custom and endeavor to answer to the desires and opinions of every one of you, as far as I can.

[36] I will begin with our ancestors, since it is both just and fitting that they be given the honor of remembrance at such a time. Because they have

always lived in this land, they have so far always handed it down in liberty through their valor to successive generations up to now. They deserve praise; but our fathers deserve even more, for with great toil they acquired our present empire in addition to what they had received, and they delivered it in turn to the present generation. We ourselves who are here now in the prime of life have expanded most parts of the empire; and we have furnished the city with everything it needs to be self-sufficient both in peace and in war. The acts of war by which all this was attained, the valiant deeds of arms that we and our fathers performed against foreign or Greek invaders—these I will pass over, to avoid making a long speech on a subject with which you are well acquainted. But the customs that brought us to this point, the form of government and the way of life that have made our city great—these I shall disclose before I turn to praise the dead. I think these subjects are quite suitable for the occasion, and the whole gathering of citizens and guests will profit by hearing them discussed.

[37] We have a form of government that does not try to imitate the laws of our neighboring states. We are more an example to others, than they to us. In name, it is called a democracy, because it is managed not for a few people, but for the majority. Still, although we have equality at law for everyone here in private disputes, we do not let our system of rotating public offices undermine our judgment of a candidate's virtue; and no one is held back by poverty or because his reputation is not well-known, as long as he can do good service to the city. We are free and generous not only in our public activities as citizens, but also in our daily lives: there is no suspicion in our dealings with one another, and we are not offended by our neighbor for following his own pleasure. We do not cast on anyone the censorious looks that—though they are no punishment—are nevertheless painful. We live together without taking offense on private matters; and as for public affairs, we respect the law greatly and fear to violate it, since we are obedient to those in office at any time, and also to the laws—especially to those laws that were made to help people who have suffered an injustice, and to the unwritten laws that bring shame on their transgressors by the agreement of all.

[38] Moreover, we have provided many ways to give our minds recreation from labor: we have instituted regular contests and sacrifices throughout the year, while the attractive furnishings of our private homes give us daily delight and expel sadness. The greatness of our city has caused all things from all parts of the earth to be imported here, so that we enjoy the products of other nations with no less familiarity than we do our own.

[39] Then, too, we differ from our enemies in preparing for war: we leave our city open to all; and we have never expelled strangers in order to prevent them from learning or seeing things that, if they were not hidden, might give an advantage to the enemy. We do not rely on secret preparation and deceit so much as on our own courage in action. And as for education, our enemies train to be men from early youth by rigorous exercise, while we live a more relaxed life and still take on dangers as great as they do.

The evidence for this is that the Lacedaemonians do not invade our country by themselves, but with the aid of all their allies; when we invade our neighbors, however, we usually overcome them by ourselves without difficulty, even though we are fighting on hostile ground against people who are defending their own homes. Besides, no enemy has yet faced our whole force at once, because at the same time we are busy with our navy and sending men by land to many different places. But when our enemies run into part of our forces and get the better of them, they boast that they have beaten our whole force; and when they are defeated, they claim they were beaten by all of us. We are willing to go into danger with easy minds and natural courage rather than through rigorous training and laws, and that gives us an advantage: we'll never weaken ourselves in advance by preparing for future troubles, but we'll turn out to be no less daring in action than those who are always training hard. In this, as in other things, our city is worthy of admiration.

[40] We are lovers of nobility with restraint, and lovers of wisdom without any softening of character. We use wealth as an opportunity for action, rather than for boastful speeches. And as for poverty, we think there is no shame in confessing it; what is shameful is doing nothing to escape it. Moreover, the very men who take care of public affairs look after their own at the same time; and even those who are devoted to their own businesses know enough about the city's affairs. For we alone think that a man who

does not take part in public affairs is good for nothing, while others only say he is "minding his own business." We are the ones who develop policy, or at least decide what is to be done; for we believe that what spoils action is not speeches, but going into action without first being instructed through speeches. In this too we excel over others: ours is the bravery of people who think through what they will take in hand, and discuss it thoroughly; with other men, ignorance makes them brave and thinking makes them cowards. But the people who most deserve to be judged tough-minded are those who know exactly what terrors or pleasures lie ahead, and are not turned away from danger by that knowledge. Again we are opposite to most men in matters of virtue: we win our friends by doing them favors, rather than by accepting favors from them. A person who does a good turn is a more faithful friend: his goodwill towards the recipient preserves his feeling that he should do more; but the friendship of a person who has to return a good deed is dull and flat, because he knows he will be merely paying a debt—rather than doing a favor—when he shows his virtue in return. So that we alone do good to others not after calculating the profit, but fearlessly and in the confidence of our freedom.

[41] In sum, I say that our city as a whole is a lesson for Greece, and that each of us presents himself as a self-sufficient individual, disposed to the widest possible diversity of actions, with every grace and great versatility. This is not merely a boast in words for the occasion, but the truth in fact, as the power of this city, which we have obtained by having this character, makes evident.

For Athens is the only power now that is greater than her fame when it comes to the test. Only in the case of Athens can enemies never be upset over the quality of those who defeat them when they invade; only in our empire can subject states never complain that their rulers are unworthy. We are proving our power with strong evidence, and we are not without witnesses: we shall be the admiration of people now and in the future. We do not need Homer, or anyone else, to praise our power with words that bring delight for a moment, when the truth will refute his assumptions about what was done. For we have compelled all seas and all lands to be open to us by our daring; and we have set up eternal monuments on all sides, of our setbacks as well as of our accomplishments.

Such is the city for which these men fought valiantly and died, in the firm belief that it should never be destroyed, and for which every man of you who is left should be willing to endure distress.

[42] That is why I have spoken at such length concerning the city in general, to show you that the stakes are not the same, between us and the enemy—for their city is not like ours in any way—and, at the same time, to bring evidence to back up the eulogy of these men for whom I speak. The greatest part of their praise has already been delivered, for it was their virtues, and the virtues of men like them, that made what I praised in the city so beautiful. Not many Greeks have done deeds that are obviously equal to their own reputations, but these men have. The present end these men have met is, I think, either the first indication, or the final confirmation, of a life of virtue. And even those who were inferior in other ways deserve to have their faults overshadowed by their courageous deaths in war for the sake of their country. Their good actions have wiped out the memory of any wrong they have done, and they have produced more public good than private harm. None of them became a coward because he set a higher value on enjoying the wealth that he had; none of them put off the terrible day of his death in hopes that he might overcome his poverty and attain riches. Their longing to punish their enemies was stronger than this; and because they believed this to be the most honorable sort of danger, they chose to punish their enemies at this risk, and to let everything else go. The uncertainty of success they entrusted to hope; but for that which was before their eyes they decided to rely on themselves in action. They believed that this choice entailed resistance and suffering, rather than surrender and safety; they ran away from the word of shame, and stood up in action at risk of their lives. And so, in the one brief moment allotted them, at the peak of their fame and not in fear, they departed.

[43] Such were these men, worthy of their country. And you who remain may pray for a safer fortune, but you must resolve to be no less daring in your intentions against the enemy. Do not weigh the good they have done on the basis of one speech. Any long-winded orator could tell you how much good lies in resisting our enemies; but you already know this. Look instead at the power our city shows in action every day, and so become lovers of Athens. When the power

of the city seems great to you, consider then that this was purchased by valiant men who knew their duty and kept their honor in battle, by men who were resolved to contribute the most noble gift to their city: even if they should fail in their attempt, at least they would leave their fine character [*aretē*] to the city. For in giving their lives for the common good, each man won praise for himself that will never grow old; and the monument that awaits them is the most splendid—not where they are buried, but where their glory is laid up to be remembered forever, whenever the time comes for speech or action. For to famous men, all the earth is a monument, and their virtues are attested not only by inscriptions on stone at home; but an unwritten record of the mind lives on for each of them, even in foreign lands, better than any gravestone.

Try to be like these men, therefore: realize that happiness lies in liberty, and liberty in valor, and do not hold back from the dangers of war. Miserable men, who have no hope of prosperity, do not have a just reason to be generous with their lives; no, it is rather those who face the danger of a complete reversal of fortune for whom defeat would make the biggest difference: they are the ones who should risk their lives. Any man of intelligence will hold that death, when it comes unperceived to a man at full strength and with hope for his country, is not so bitter as miserable defeat for a man grown soft.

[44] That is why I offer you, who are here as parents of these men, consolation rather than a lament. You know your lives teem with all sorts of calamities, and that it is good fortune for anyone to draw a glorious end for his lot, as these men have done. While your lot was grief, theirs was a life that was happy as long as it lasted. I know it is a hard matter to dissuade you from sorrow, when you will often be reminded by the good fortune of others of the joys you once had; for sorrow is not for the want of a good never tasted, but for the loss of a good we have been used to having. Yet those of you who are of an age to have children may bear this loss in the hope of having more. On a personal level new children will help some of you forget those who are no more; while the city will gain doubly by this, in population and in security. It is not possible for people to give fair and just advice to the state, if they are not exposing their own children to the same danger when they advance a risky policy.

As for you who are past having children, you are to think of the greater part of your life as pure profit, while the part that remains is short and its burden lightened by the glory of these men. For the love of honor is the one thing that never grows old, and useless old age takes delight not in gathering wealth (as some say), but in being honored.

[45] As for you who are the children or the brothers of these men, I see that you will have considerable competition. Everyone is used to praising the dead, so that even extreme virtue will scarcely win you a reputation equal to theirs, but it will fall a little short. That is because people envy the living as competing with them, but they honor those who are not in their way, and their good will towards the dead is free of rivalry.

And now, since I must say something about feminine virtue, I shall express it in this brief admonition to you who are now widows: your glory is great if you do not fall beneath the natural condition of your sex, and if you have as little fame among men as is possible, whether for virtue or by way of reproach.

[46] Thus I have delivered, according to custom, what was appropriate in a speech, while those men who are buried here have already been honored by their own actions. It remains to maintain their children at the expense of the city until they grow up. This benefit is the city's victory garland for them and for those they leave behind after such contests as these, because the city that gives the greatest rewards for virtue has the finest citizens.

So now, when everyone has mourned for his own, you may go.

[Athens is afflicted by a plague, and this event seems to change, in many ways, the character of the city that Pericles had described in the Funeral Oration.]

In the very beginning of summer the Peloponnesians and their allies, with two-thirds of their forces as before, invaded Attica under the command of Archidamus, King of Lacedaemon. After they had settled in, they started wasting the country around them.

They had not been in Attica for many days when the plague first began among the Athenians. Although it was said to have broken out in many other places, particularly in Lemnos, no one could remember a disease that was so great or so destructive of human life breaking out anywhere before. Doctors, not knowing what to do, were unable to cope with it at first, and no other human knowledge was any use either. The doctors themselves died fastest, as they came to the sick most often. Prayers in temples, questions to oracles—all practices of that kind turned out to be useless also, and in the end people gave them up, defeated by the evil of the disease.

[48] They say it first began in the part of Ethiopia that is above Egypt, and from there moved down to Egypt and Libya and into most of the Persian Empire. It hit Athens suddenly, first infecting people in Piraeus [the port of Athens], with the result that they said the Peloponnesians must have poisoned the water tanks (they had no wells there at the time). Afterwards the plague moved inland to the city, where people died of it a good deal faster. Now anyone, doctor or layman, may say as much as he knows about where this probably came from, or what causes he thinks are powerful enough to bring about so great a change. For my part, I will only say what it was like: I will show what to look for, so that if the plague breaks out again, people may know in advance and not be ignorant. I will do this because I had the plague myself, and I myself saw others who suffered from it.

[49] This year of all years was the most free of other diseases, as everyone agrees. If anyone was sick before, his disease turned into this one. If not, they were taken suddenly, without any apparent cause, and while they were in perfect health. First they had a high fever in the head, along with redness and inflammation of the eyes; inside, the throat and tongue were bleeding from the start, and the breath was weird and unsavory. After this came sneezing and hoarseness, and soon after came a pain in the chest, along with violent coughing. And once it was settled in the stomach, it caused vomiting, and brought up, with great torment, all the kinds of bile that the doctors have named. Most of the sick then had dry heaves, which brought on violent spasms which were over quickly for some people, but not till long after for others. Outwardly their bodies were not very hot to the touch, and they were not pale but reddish, livid, and flowered with little pimples and ulcers; inwardly they were burning so much with fever that they could not bear to have the lighest clothes or linen garments on them—nothing but mere nakedness, and they

would have loved to throw themselves into cold water. Many of them who were not looked after did throw themselves into water tanks, driven mad by a thirst that was insatiable, although it was all the same whether they drank much or little. Sleeplessness and total inability to rest persisted through everything.

As long as the disease was at its height, the body did not waste away, but resisted the torment beyond all expectation, so that they either died after six or eight days from the burning inside them, or else, if they escaped that, then the disease dropped down into the belly, bringing severe ulceration and uncontrollable diarrhea; and many died later from the weakness this caused, since the disease passed through the whole body, starting with the head and moving down. And if anyone survived the worst of it, then the disease seized his extremities instead and left its mark there: it attacked the private parts, fingers, and toes. Many people escaped with the loss of these, while some lost their eyes as well. Some were struck by total amnesia as soon as they recovered, and did not know themselves or their friends.

[50] This was a kind of disease that defied explanation, and the cruelty with which it attacked everyone was too severe for human nature. What showed more clearly than anything else that it was different from the diseases that are bred among us was this: all the birds and beasts that feed on human flesh either avoided the many bodies that lay unburied, or tasted them and perished. Evidence for this was the obvious absence of such birds: they were not to be seen anywhere, and certainly not doing that. But this effect was more clearly observed in the case of dogs, because they are more familiar with human beings.

[51] Now this disease was generally as I have described it, if I may set aside the many variations that occurred as particular people had different experiences. During that time no one was troubled by any of the usual sicknesses, but whatever sickness came ended in this. People died, some unattended, and some who had every sort of care. There was no medical treatment that could be prescribed as beneficial, for what helped one patient did harm to another. Physical strength turned out to be of no avail, for the plague carried the strong away with the weak, no matter what regimen they had followed.

But the greatest misery of all was the dejection of mind in those who found themselves beginning to be sick, for as soon as they made up their minds it was hopeless, they gave up and made much less resistance to the disease. Another misery was their dying like sheep, as they became infected by caring for one another; and this brought about the greatest mortality. For if people held back from visiting each other through fear, then they died in neglect, and many houses were emptied because there was no one to provide care. If they did visit each other, they died, and these were mainly the ones who made some pretense to virtue. For these people would have been ashamed to spare themselves, and so they went into their friends' houses, especially in the end, when even family members, worn out by the lamentations of the dying, were overwhelmed by the greatness of the calamity. But those who had recovered had still more compassion, both on those who were dying and on those who were sick, because they knew the disease first-hand and were now out of danger, for this disease never attacked anyone a second time with fatal effect. And these people were thought to be blessedly happy, and through an excess of present joy they conceived a kind of light hope never to die of any other disease afterwards.

[52] The present affliction was aggravated by the crowding of country folk into the city, which was especially unpleasant for those who came in. They had no houses, and because they were living in shelters that were stifling in the summer, their mortality was out of control. Dead and dying lay tumbling on top of one another in the streets, and at every water fountain lay men half-dead with thirst. The temples also, where they pitched their tents, were all full of the bodies of those who died in them, for people grew careless of holy and profane things alike, since they were oppressed by the violence of the calamity, and did not know what to do. And the laws they had followed before concerning funerals were all disrupted now, everyone burying their dead wherever they could. Many were forced, by a shortage of necessary materials after so many deaths, to take disgraceful measures for the funerals of their relatives: when one person had made a funeral pyre, another would get before him, throw on his dead, and give it fire; others would come to a pyre that was already burning, throw on the bodies they carried, and go their way again.

[53] The great lawlessness that grew everywhere in the city began with this disease, for, as the rich sud-

denly died and men previously worth nothing took over their estates, people saw before their eyes such quick reversals that they dared to do freely things they would have hidden before—things they never would have admitted they did for pleasure. And so, because they thought their lives and their property were equally ephemeral, they justified seeking quick satisfaction in easy pleasures. As for doing what had been considered noble, no one was eager to take any further pains for this, because they thought it uncertain whether they should die or not before they achieved it. But the pleasure of the moment, and whatever contributed to that, were set up as standards of nobility and usefulness. No one was held back in awe, either by fear of the gods or by the laws of men: not by the gods, because men concluded it was all the same whether they worshipped or not, seeing that they all perished alike; and not by the laws, because no one expected to live till he was tried and punished for his crimes. But they thought that a far greater sentence hung over their heads now, and that before this fell they had a reason to get some pleasure in life.

[54] Such was the misery that weighed on the Athenians. It was very oppressive, with men dying inside the city and the land outside being wasted. At such a terrible time it was natural for them to recall this verse, which the older people said had been sung long ago:

> A Dorian war will come,
> and with it a plague.

People had disagreed about the wording of the verse: some said it was not *plague* (*loimos*) but *famine* (*limos*) that was foretold by the ancients; but on this occasion, naturally, the victory went to those who said "plague," for people made their memory suit their current experience. Surely, I think if there is another Dorian war after this one, and if a famine comes with it, it will be natural for them to recite the verse in that version.

Those who knew of it also recalled an oracle that was given to the Lacedaemonians when they asked the god [Apollo] whether they should start this war or not. The oracle had said: *they would win if they fought with all their might, and that he himself would take their part* [i.118]. Then they thought that their present misery was a fulfillment of the prophecy; the plague did begin immediately when the Peloponnesians invaded, and it had no appreciable effect in the Peloponnesus, but preyed mostly on Athens and after that in densely populated areas. So much for the plague.

• • •

[Pericles' last speech before he dies of the plague.]

[59] After their second invasion by the Peloponnesians, now that their land had been wasted a second time, and the plague was lying over them along with the war, the Athenians changed their minds and blamed Pericles for persuading them to make war—as if the troubles that had come their way were due to him—and were in a hurry to come to terms with the Lacedaemonians. They sent ambassadors to them, without effect. They were altogether at their wit's end, and so they attacked Pericles.

When he saw that they were angry over their present circumstances, and were doing exactly what he had expected, he called an assembly—he was still general at the time—intending to put heart into them, to turn aside their anger, and so to make their minds calmer and more confident.

He stood before them and spoke as follows:

[60] I expected you to get angry with me, and I can see why it has happened. I have called this assembly to remind you of certain points and to rebuke you for your misplaced anger at me and for your giving in too easily to misfortune.

I believe that if the city is sound as a whole, it does more good to its private citizens than if it benefits them as individuals while faltering as a collective unit. It does not matter whether a man prospers as an individual: if his country is destroyed, he is lost along with it; but if he meets with misfortune, he is far safer in a fortunate city than he would be otherwise. Since, therefore, a city is able to sustain its private citizens in whatever befalls them, while no one individual is strong enough to carry his city, are we not all obliged to defend it and not, as you are doing now, sacrifice our common safety? In your dismay at our misfortunes at home you are condemning yourselves along with me—me for advising you to go to war and yourselves for agreeing to it. And it is I at whom you are angry, a man who is second to

none (in my opinion) for recognizing and explaining what must be done—I, a patriot, beyond corruption. A man who knows something but cannot make it clear might as well have had nothing in mind at all; while a man who can do both will not give such loyal advice if he has no love for his city; and a man who has all this and loyalty too, but can be overcome by money, will sell anything for this alone. It follows that if you were persuaded to go to war because you thought I had all those qualities, even in a moderately higher degree than other people, there is no reason for me to bear a charge of injustice now.

[61] Of course, for people who have the choice and are doing well in other ways, it is very foolish to go to war. But if (as is the case with us) they are compelled either to submit directly to the rule of their neighbors, of else to take on great dangers in order to survive, a man who runs away from danger is more to be blamed than one who stands up to it.

For my part, I am the man I was. I have not shifted ground. It is you who are changing: you were persuaded to fight when you were still unharmed, but now that times are bad, you are changing your minds; and to your weak judgment my position does not seem sound. That is because you already feel the pain that afflicts you as individuals, while the benefit to us all has not yet become obvious; and now that this great reversal has come upon you in so short a time you are too low in your minds to stand by your decisions, for it makes your thoughts slavish when something unexpected happens suddenly and defies your best-laid plans. That is what has happened to you on top of everything else, mainly because of the plague.

Still, you live in a great city and have been brought up with a way of life that matches its greatness; so you should be willing to stand up to the greatest disasters rather than eclipse your reputation. (People think it equally right, you see, to blame someone who is so weak that he loses the glorious reputation that was really his, as it is to despise someone who has the audacity to reach for a reputation he should not have.)

So set aside the grief you feel for your individual losses, and take up instead the cause of our common safety.

[62] As for your fear that we will have a great deal of trouble in this war, and still be no closer to success, I have already said something that should be enough

for you: I proved many times that you were wrong to be suspicious of the outcome. I will tell you this, however, about your greatness in empire—something you never seem to think about, which I have not mentioned in my speeches. It is a rather boastful claim, and I would not bring it up now if I had not seen that you are more discouraged that you have reason to be. You think your empire extends only to your allies, but I am telling you that you are entirely the masters of one of the two usable parts of the world—the land and the sea. Of the sea, you rule as much as you use now, and more if you want. When you sail with your fleet as it is now equipped, there is no one who can stop you—not the King of Persia or any nation in existence. This power cannot be measured against the use of your land and homes, though you think it a great loss to be deprived of them. It makes no sense to take these so seriously; you should think of your land as a little kitchen garden, and your house as a rich man's trinket, of little value compared to this power. Keep in mind too that if we hold fast to our liberty and preserve it we will easily recover our land and houses; but people who submit to foreign domination will start to lose what they already had. Don't show yourselves to be doubly inferior to your ancestors, who took the empire—they did not inherit it from others—and, in addition, kept it safe and passed it on to you. No, what you should do is remember that it is more shameful to lose what you have than to fail in an attempt to get more. You should take on the enemy at close quarters, and go not only with pride, but with contempt. Even a coward can swell with pride, if he is lucky and ignorant; but you cannot have contempt for the enemy unless your confidence is based on a strategy to overcome them—which is your situation exactly. Even if you have only an even chance of winning, if you are conscious of your superiority it is safer for you to be daring, for in that case you do not depend on hope (which is bulwark only to those who have no resources at all), but on a strategy based on reality, which affords a more accurate prediction of the result.

[63] You have reason besides to support the dignity our city derives from her empire, in which you all take pride; you should not decline the trouble, unless you cease to pursue the honor, of empire. And do not think that the only thing we are fighting for is

our freedom from being subjugated: you are in danger of losing the empire, and if you do, the anger of the people you have ruled will raise other dangers. You are in no position to walk away from your empire, though some people might propose to do so from fear of the current situation, and act the part of virtue because they do not want to be involved in public affairs. You see, your empire is really like a tyranny— though it may have been thought unjust to seize, it is now unsafe to surrender. People who would persuade the city to do such a thing would quickly destroy it, and if they set up their own government they would destroy that too. For those who stay out of public affairs survive only with the help of other people who take action; and they are no use to a city that rules an empire, though in a subject state they may serve safely enough.

[64] Don't be seduced by this sort of men. After all, it was you who decided in favor of this war along with me; so don't be angry at me. What the enemy did when they invaded was just what was to be expected when we refused to submit to them; and this plague has struck contrary to all expectations—it is the only thing, of all that has happened, that has defied our hopes. I know that I have become hated largely because of this; but that is an injustice, unless you will also give me credit whenever you do better than you'd planned to do. What heaven sends we must bear with a sense of necessity, what the enemy does to us we must bear with courage—for that is the custom in our city; that is how it used to be, and that custom should not end with you.

Keep this in mind: our city is famous everywhere for its greatness in not yielding to adversity and in accepting so many casualties and so much trouble in war; besides, she has possessed great power till now, which will be remembered forever by those who come after us, even if we do give way a little now (for everything naturally goes into decline): Greeks that we are, we have ruled most of the Greeks, and held out in great wars against them, all together or one city at a time, and our city has the most wealth of every sort, and is the greatest. And yet a man of inaction would complain about this! No matter, anyone who is active will want to be like us, and those who do not succeed will envy us. To be hated and to cause pain is, at present, the reality for anyone who takes on the rule of others, and anyone who makes himself hated for matters of great consequence has made the right decision; for hatred does not last long, but the momentary brilliance of great actions lives on as a glory that will be remembered forever after.

As for you, keep your minds on the fine future you know will be yours, and on the shame you must avoid at this moment. Be full of zeal on both counts. Send no more heralds to the Lacedaemonians, and do not let them know how heavy your troubles are at present. The most powerful cities and individuals are the ones that are the least sensitive in their minds to calamity and the firmest in their actions to resist it.

[65] With this speech Pericles tried to appease the anger of the Athenians and to divert their attention from their present afflictions. They were persuaded on the public matter, and no longer sent embassies to the Lacedaemonians, but applied themselves more to the war. As individuals, however, they were upset by what had happened to them—the people were upset because they had been deprived of the little they had, and the powerful because they had lost their fine possessions in the country, along with their houses and costly furnishings. Most of all, however, it was because they had war instead of peace. As a group, they did not give up their anger against him until they had punished him with a fine. Not long after, however, as is common with a mob, they made him general again and turned all public affairs over to him, for their pain over their private domestic losses was dulled now, and they thought he was the best man to serve the needs of the city as a whole.

As long as he was at the head of the city in time of peace, he governed it with moderation and guarded it securely; and it was greatest under him. After the war was afoot, it was obvious that he also foresaw what the city could do in this. He lived two years and six months after the war began. And after his death his foresight about the war was even better recognized, for he told them that if they would be quiet and take care of their navy, and not seek to expand the empire during this war or endanger the city itself, they should then have the upper hand. But they did the opposite on all points, and in other things that seemed not to concern the war they managed the state for their private ambition and private gain, to the detriment of them-

selves and their allies. Whatever succeeded brought honor and profit mostly to private individuals, while whatever went wrong damaged the city in the war.

The reason for Pericles' success was this: he was powerful because of his prestige and his intelligence, and also because he was known to be highly incorruptible. He therefore controlled the people without inhibition, and was not so much led by them, as he led them. He would not humor the people in his speeches so as to get power by improper means, but because of their esteem for him he could risk their anger by opposing them. Therefore, whenever he saw them insolently bold out of season, he would put them into fear with his speeches; and again, when they were afraid without reason, he would raise up their spirits and give them courage. Athens was in name a democracy, but in fact was a government by its first man. But because those who came after were more equal among themselves, with everyone aiming to be the chief, they gave up taking care of the commonwealth in order to please the people.

Since Athens was a great imperial city, these mistakes led to many others, such as the voyage against Sicily, which was due not so much to mistaking the power of those they attacked, as it was to bad decisions on the part of the senders, which were no use to the people they sent. They weakened the strength of the army through private quarrels about popular leadership, and they troubled the state at home with discord for the first time. After their debacle in Sicily, when they lost most of their navy along with the rest of the expedition, and the city was divided by civil strife, they still held out eight years against their original enemies, who were now allied with the Sicilians, against most of their own rebellious allies besides, and also eventually against Cyrus, the son of the King of Persia, who took part with, and sent money to, the Peloponnesians to maintain their fleet. And they never gave in until they had brought about their own downfall through private quarrels.

So Pericles had more than enough reasons to predict that the city might easily outlast the Peloponnesians in this war.

[*The city of Mytilene has rebelled against Athens, and the Athenians assemble to decide how to respond. The debate between Cleon and Diodotus reflects the most fundamental arguments of political morality.]*

[37] For my part, I have often seen that a democracy is not capable of ruling an empire, and I see it most clearly now, in your change of heart concerning the Mytileneans. Because you are not afraid of conspiracies among yourselves in your daily life, you imagine you can be the same with your allies, and so it does not occur to you that when you let them persuade you to make a mistake, or you relent out of compassion, your softness puts you in danger and does not win you the affection of your allies; and you do not see that your empire is a tyranny, and that you have unwilling subjects who are continually plotting against you. They obey you not because of any good turns you might do them to your own detriment, and not because of any good will they might have, but only because you exceed them in strength. But it will be the worst mischief of all if none of our decisions stand firm, and if we never realize that a city with inferior laws is better if they are never relaxed than a city with good laws that have no force, that people are more use if they are sensible without education than if they are clever without self-control, and that the more common sort of people generally govern a city better than those who are more intelligent. For those intellectuals love to appear wiser than the laws and to win a victory in every public debate—as if there were no more important ways for them to show their wisdom! And that sort of thing usually leads to disaster for their city. But the other sort of people, who mistrust their own wits, are content to admit they know less than the laws and that they cannot criticize a speech as powerfully as a fine orator can; and so, as impartial judges rather than contestants, they govern a city for the most part very well. We should do the same, therefore, and not be carried away by cleverness and contests of wit, or give to you, the people, advice that runs against our own judgment.

[38] As for me, I have the same opinion I had before, and I am amazed at these men who have brought this matter of the Mytileneans into question again, thus causing a delay that works more to the advantage of those who have committed injustice. After a delay, you see, the victim comes at the wrongdoer with his anger dulled; but the punishment he gives right after an injury is the biggest and most appropriate. I am also amazed that there is anyone to oppose me, anyone who will try to prove that the injustice the Mytileneans have committed is good for us and that what goes wrong for us is really damaging to our allies. Clearly, he must have great trust in his eloquence if he is trying to make you believe that you did not decree what you decreed. Either that, or he has been bribed to try to lead you astray with a fine-sounding and elaborate speech.

Now the city gives prizes to others in contests of eloquence like this one, but the risks she must carry herself. You are to blame for staging these rhetorical contests so badly. The habits you've formed: why you merely look on at discussions, and real action is only a story to you! You consider proposals for the future on the basis of fine speeches, as if what they proposed were actually possible; and as for action in the past, you think that what has been done in front of your own eyes is less certain than what you have heard in the speeches of clever fault-finders. You are excellent men—at least for being deceived by novelties of rhetoric and for never wanting to follow advice that is tried and proved. You bow down like slaves to anything unusual, but look with suspicion on anything ordinary. Each of you wishes chiefly to be an effective speaker, but, if not, then you enter into competition with those who are. You don't want to be thought slow in following their meaning, so you applaud a sharp point before it is even made; and you are as eager to anticipate what will be said, as you are slow to foresee its consequences. You seek to hear about almost anything outside the experience of our daily lives, and yet you do not adequately understand what is right before your eyes. To speak plainly, you are so overcome with the delight of the ear that you are more like an audience for the sophists than an assembly deliberating for the good of the city.

[39] To put you out of these habits, I tell you that the Mytileneans have done us a far greater injustice than any other single city. For my part, I can forgive those cities that rebelled because they could not bear being ruled by us, or because they were compelled to do so by the enemy. But *these* people were islanders, their city was walled, and they had no fear of our enemies except by sea, where they were adequately protected by their fleet of triremes. Besides, they were governed by their own laws, and were held by us in

the highest honor. That they should have done this! What is it but a conspiracy or a betrayal? It is not a rebellion, for a rebellion can only come from people who have been violently oppressed, whereas these people have joined our bitterest enemies to destroy us! This is far worse than if they had made war on us to increase their own power.

They'd learned nothing from the example of their neighbors' calamities—everyone who has rebelled against us so far has been put down—and their prosperity did not make them at all cautious before rushing into danger. They were bold in the face of the future and they had hopes above their power to achieve, though below what they desired. And so they started this war, resolved to put strength before justice, for as soon as they thought they could win, they attacked us, who had done them no injustice.

It is usual for cities to turn insolent when they have suddenly come to great and unexpected prosperity. In general, good fortune is more secure in human hands when it comes in reasonable measure, than when it arrives unexpectedly; and, generally, it is easier to keep misfortune away than to preserve great happiness. Long ago we should have given the Mytileneans no more privileges than our other allies, and then they would not have come to this degree of insolence, for generally it is human nature to look with contempt on those who serve your interests, and to admire those who never give in to you.

They should be punished right now, therefore, as they deserve for their injustice. And do not put all the blame on the oligarchs and absolve the common people, for they all alike took up arms against you. The democrats could have come over to our side and would long since have recovered their city, but they thought it safer to join in the oligarchs' rebellion.

Now consider your allies. If you inflict the same punishment on those who rebel under compulsion by the enemy, as on those who rebel of their own accord, don't you think anyone would seize the slightest pretext to rebel, when if they succeed they will win their liberty, but if they fail they will suffer nothing that can't be mended? And then we would have to risk our lives and our money against one city after another. If we succeed we recover only a ruined city, and so lose its future revenue, on which our strength is based. But if we fail, we add these as new enemies to those we had before, and the time we need to spend fighting our old enemies we must use up fighting our own allies.

[40] We must not, therefore, give our allies any hope that pardon may be secured by bribery or by persuading us that "it is only human to err." For these people conspired against us in full knowledge and did us an injury of their own will, while only involuntary wrongs may be pardoned. Therefore I contend then and now that you ought not to alter your former decision, and you ought not to make the mistake of giving in to the three things that are most damaging to an empire: pity, delight in speeches, and a sense of fairness. It may be right to show pity to those who are like-minded, but not to those who will never have pity on us and who must necessarily be our enemies for ever after. As for the rhetoricians who delight you with their speeches—let them play for their prizes on matters of less weight, and not on a subject that will make the city pay a heavy price for a light pleasure, while the speakers themselves will be well rewarded for speaking well. And as for fairness, we should show that only towards people who will be our friends in the future, and not towards those who will still be as they are now if we let them live: our enemies.

In sum I say only this: if you follow my advice, you will do justice to the Mytileneans and promote your own interests at the same time. But if you see the matter differently, you will not win their favor; instead, you will be condemning yourselves: if they were right to rebel, you ought not to have been their rulers. But then suppose your empire is not justified: if you resolve to hold it anyway, then you must give these people an unreasonable punishment for the benefit of the empire, or else stop having an empire so that you can give charity without taking any risks.

If you keep in mind what it would have been reasonable for them to do to you if they had prevailed, then you—the intended victims—cannot turn out to be less responsive to perceived wrong than those who hatched the plot, and you *must* think they deserve the same punishment they'd have given you—especially since they were the first to commit an injustice. Those who wrong someone without any excuse are the ones who press him the hardest, even to the death, when they see how dangerous an enemy he will be if he survives; for (they will think) if one side is wronged without cause, and escapes, he will be more harsh than if the two sides had hated each other equally in the beginning.

Therefore, do not be traitors to yourselves. Recall as vividly as you can what they did to you, and how it was more important than anything else for you to defeat them then. Pay them back now, and do not be softened at the sight of their present condition, or forget how terrible a danger hung over us at that time. Give these people the punishment they deserve, and set up a clear example for our other allies, to show that the penalty for rebellion is death. Once they know this, you will less often have occasion to neglect your enemies and fight against your own allies.

[41] So spoke Cleon. After him, Diodotus, the son of Eucrates, who in the earlier assembly had strongly opposed putting the Mytileneans to death, came forward this time also, and spoke as follows:

[42] I find no fault with those who have brought the Mytilenean business forward for another debate, and I have no praise for those who object to our having frequent discussions on matters of great importance. In my opinion, nothing is more contrary to good judgment than these two—haste and anger. Of these, the one is usually thoughtless, while the other is ill-informed and narrow-minded. And anyone who contends that discussion is not instructive for action is either stupid or defending some private interest of his own. He is stupid if he thinks there is anything other than words that we can use to consider what lies hidden from sight in the future. And he has a private interest if he wants to persuade you to do something awful, but knows that a good speech will not carry a bad cause, and so tries to browbeat his opponents and audience with some good slander instead: the most difficult opponents are those who also accuse one of putting on a rhetorical show for a bribe. If the accusation were merely of ignorance, a speaker could lose his case and still go home with a reputation more for stupidity than injustice; but once corruption is imputed to him, then he will be under suspicion even if he wins, and if he loses he will be thought both stupid and unjust. Such accusations do not do the city any good, since it loses good advisers from fear of them. The city would do best if this kind of citizen had the least ability as speakers, for they would then persuade the city to fewer errors. A good citizen should not go about terrifying those who speak against him, but should try to look better in a fair debate. A sensible city should neither add to, nor reduce, the honor in which it holds its best advisers, nor should it punish or even dishonor those whose advice it does not take. This would make it less attractive for a successful speaker to seek greater popularity by speaking against his better judgment, or for an unsuccessful one to strive in this way to gratify the people and gain a majority.

[43] But we do the opposite of that here; and besides, if anyone is suspected of corruption, but gives the best advice anyway, we are so resentful of the profit we think he is making (though this is uncertain), that we give up benefits the city would certainly have received. It has become the rule also to treat good advice honestly given as being no less under suspicion than bad, so that a man who has something rather good to say must tell lies in order to be believed, just as a man who gives terrible advice must win over the people by deception. Because of these suspicions, ours is the only city that no one can possibly benefit openly, without deception, since if anyone does good openly to the city, his reward will be the suspicion that he had something secretly to gain from this.

But on the most important matters, such as these, we orators must decide to show more foresight than is found in your short-sighted citizens, especially since we stand accountable for the advice we give, but you listeners are not accountable to anyone, because if you were subject to the same penalties as the advisers you follow, you would make more sensible decisions. As it is, whenever you fail, you give in to your momentary anger and punish the man who persuaded you for his one error of judgment, instead of yourselves for the many mistakes in which you had a part.

[44] For my part, I did not come forward to speak about Mytilene with any purpose to contradict or to accuse. Our dispute, if we are sensible, will concern not their injustice to us, but our judgment as to what is best for us. Even if I proved them guilty of terrible injustice, I still would not advise the death penalty for this, unless that was to our advantage. Even if they deserved to be pardoned, I would not have you pardon them if it did not turn out to be good for the city. In my opinion, what we are discussing concerns the future more than the present. And as for this point that Cleon insists on—that the death penalty will be

to our advantage in the future, by keeping the others from rebelling—I maintain exactly the opposite view, and I too am looking at our future well-being. I urge you not to reject the usefulness of my advice in favor of the apparent attractions of his. In view of your present anger against the Mytileneans, you may agree that his argument is more in accord with justice. But we are not at law with them, and so have no need to speak of justice. We are in council instead, and must decide how the Mytileneans can be put to the best use for us.

[45] The death penalty has been ordained for many offenses in various cities, and these are minor offenses compared to this one; yet people still risk their lives when they are buoyed up by hope, and no one has ever gone into a dangerous conspiracy convinced that he would not succeed. What city would ever attempt a rebellion on the supposition that her resources, whether from home or from her alliance with other states, are too weak for this? They all have it by nature to do wrong, both men and cities, and there is no law that will prevent it. People have gone through all possible penalties, adding to them in the hope that fewer crimes will then be done to them by evildoers. It stands to reason that there were milder punishments in the old days, even for the most heinous crimes; but as the laws continued to be violated, in time most cities arrived at the death penalty. And still the laws are violated.

Either some greater terror than death must be found, therefore, or else punishment will not deter crime. Poverty compels the poor to be daring, while the powerful are led by pride and arrogance into taking more than their share. Each human condition is dominated by some great and incurable passion that impels people to danger. Hope and passionate desire, however, dominate every situation: with desire as the leader and hope as the companion, desire thinking out a plan, and hope promising a wealth of good fortune, these two cause the greatest mischief, and because they are invisible they are more dangerous than the evils we see. Besides these, fortune [*tuchē*] plays no less a part in leading men on, since she can present herself unexpectedly and excite you to take a risk, even with inadequate resources. This happens especially to cities, because of the serious issues at stake—their own freedom and their empire over others—and because an individual who is acting

with everyone else has an unreasonably high estimate of his own ability. In a word, it is an impossible thing—you would have to be simple-minded to believe that people can be deterred, by force of law or by anything else that is frightening, from doing what human nature is earnestly bent on doing.

[46] We should not, therefore, make a bad decision, relying on capital punishment to protect us, or set such hopeless conditions that our rebels have no opportunity to repent and atone for their crime as quickly as possible. Consider this: if a city in rebellion knew it could not hold out, as things are it would come to terms while it could still pay our expenses and make its remaining contributions; but if we take Cleon's way, wouldn't any city prepare better for a rebellion than they do now, and hold out in a siege to the very last, since it would mean the same whether they gave in late or early? And what is this if not harmful to us—to have the expense of a siege because they will not come to terms, and then, when we have taken a city, to find it ruined and to lose its revenue for the future? You see, our strength against our enemies depends on that revenue.

We should not, then, be strict judges in punishing offenders, and so harm ourselves; instead, we should look for a way to impose moderate penalties to ensure that we will in the future be able to make use of cities that can make us substantial payments. We should not plan to keep them in check by the rigor of laws, but by watching their actions closely. We are doing the opposite now, if we think we should punish cruelly a city that used to be free, was held in our empire by force, rebelled from us for a good reason—to restore its autonomy—and now has been defeated. What we ought to do in the case of a city of free men is not to impose extreme penalties after they rebel, but to be extremely watchful before they rebel, and to take care that the idea of rebellion never crosses their minds. And once we have overcome them, we should lay the fault upon as few of them as we can.

[47] Consider also how great a mistake you will be making on this score if you follow Cleon's advice: as things are, the democrats in all the cities are your friends, and either they do not join the oligarchs in rebellion or, if they are forced to, they remain hostile to the rebels, so that when you go to war with them, you have their common people on your side; but if you destroy the democrats of Mytilene, who had no

part in the rebellion, and who delivered the city into your hands of their own will as soon as they were armed, then you will, first, commit an injustice by killing those who have done you good service, and, second, accomplish exactly what oligarchs everywhere want the most: when they have made a city rebel, they will immediately have the democrats on their side, because you will have shown them in advance that those who are not guilty of injustice suffer the same penalty as those who are. And even if they were guilty, however, we should pretend that they were not, so that the only party still allied with us will not become our enemy. And in order to keep our empire intact, I think it much more advantageous for us to put up with an injustice willingly, than for us justly to destroy people we ought not to destroy. And as for Cleon's idea that justice and our own advantage come to the same in the case of punishment—these two cannot be found to coincide in the present case.

[48] Now I want you to accept my proposal because you see that it is the best course, and not because you are swayed more by pity or a sense of fairness. I would not have you influenced by those factors any more than Cleon would. But take my advice and judge the leaders of the rebellion at your leisure, while you let the rest enjoy their city. That will be good for the future, and it will strike fear into your enemies today. Those who plan well against their enemies, you see, are more formidable than those who attack with active force and foolishness combined.

[49] So spoke Diodotus. After these two quite opposite opinions were delivered, the Athenians were at odds with each other, and the show of hands was almost equal on both sides. But the opinion of Diodotus prevailed.

On this they immediately sent out another ship in haste, so they would not find the city already destroyed by coming in after the first ship (which had left a day and a night earlier). The Mytilenean ambassadors provided wine and barley cakes for the second ship and promised them great rewards if they overtook the first. And so they rowed in such haste that they ate their barley cakes steeped in wine and oil while they rowed, and took turns rowing while others slept. They were lucky in that there was no wind against them.

And since the first ship was not sailing in any haste on its perverse mission, while the second one hurried on in the manner described, the first ship did arrive first, but only by the time it took Paches to read the decree. He was about to execute the sentence when the second ship came in and prevented the destruction of the city. That was how close Mytilene came to destruction.

[50] As for the other men Paches had sent away as being most to blame for the rebellion, the Athenians did kill them as Cleon had advised, just over a thousand of them. They also razed the walls of Mytilene and confiscated their ships. Afterwards, they stopped collecting payments directly from Lesbos. Instead, they divided the land (all but that of Methymna) into three thousand allotments, of which they consecrated three hundred to the gods, the rest going to Athenians who were chosen by lot and sent out as allotment holders. The people of Lesbos were required to pay them two silver *minas* annually for each lot, and worked the land themselves. The Athenians also took over the communities that Mytilene had controlled on the mainland and made them subject to Athens. So ended the business on Lesbos.

[51] The same summer, after the recovery of Lesbos, the Athenians made war against the island of Minoa (which lies near Megara), under the command of Nicias. The Megarians had built a tower there for use as a garrison, and Nicias wanted it as an Athenian look-out post that would be nearer to Megara than Budorum or Salamis, so he could use it to prevent the Peloponnesians from sailing their triremes out of Megara unobserved (as had happened before with raiding expeditions) as well as from sending anything into Megara by sea. First he captured two towers on the side of the island facing Nisaea [the port of Megara], thus securing a passage for his ships between the mainland and the island; then he walled off the section that faced the mainland, (for it might have received aid by a bridge over the shallows where the island was near the mainland). He finished this in a few days and, after establishing a garrison in a fort there, went home with his army.

[Thucydides' harrowing description of civil war in Corcyra.]

[81.2] When the people of Corcyra heard that the Athenian ships were approaching, and that the Peloponnesians were leaving, they brought in the Messenian soldiers who had been outside into the city, and ordered the ships they had manned to come around into the Hyllaic port. While they were going around, the Corcyrean democrats killed all the opposing faction they could lay hands on; and as for the ones they had persuaded to man the ships, they killed them all as they disembarked. And they came to the temple of Hera and persuaded fifty of the oligarchic sympathizers who had taken sanctuary there to submit themselves to a trial; then they condemned them all to death. When they saw what was being done, most of the suppliants—all those who were not induced to stand trial by law—killed one another right there in the temple; some hanged themselves on trees, and everyone made away with himself by what means he could. For the seven days that the Athenian admiral Eurymedon stayed there with his sixty ships, the Corcyreans went on killing as many of their own people as they took to be their enemies. They accused them of subverting the democracy, but some of the victims were killed on account of private hatred, and some by their debtors for the money they had lent them. Every form of death was seen at this time; and (as tends to happen in such cases) there was nothing people would not do, and more: fathers killed their sons; men were dragged out of the temples and then killed hard by; and some who were walled up in the temple of Dionysus died inside it.

[82] So cruel was the course of this civil war [*stasis*], and it seemed all the more so because it was among the first of these. Afterwards, virtually all Greece was in upheaval, and quarrels arose everywhere between the democratic leaders, who sought to bring in the Athenians, and the oligarchs, who wanted to bring in the Lacedaemonians. Now in time of peace they could have had no pretext and would not have been so eager to call them in, but because it was war, and allies were to be had for either party to hurt their enemies and strengthen themselves at the same time, invitations to intervene came readily from those who wanted a new government. Civil war brought many hardships to the cities, such as happen and will always happen as long as human nature is the same, although they may be more or less violent or take different forms, depending on the circumstances in each case. In peace and prosperity, cities and private individuals alike are better minded because they are not plunged into the necessity of doing anything against their will; but war is a violent teacher: it gives most people impulses that are as bad as their situation when it takes away the easy supply of what they need for daily life.

Civil war ran through the cities; those it struck later heard what the first cities had done and far exceeded them in inventing artful means for attack and bizarre forms of revenge. And they reversed the usual way of using words to evaluate activities. Ill-considered boldness was counted as loyal manliness; prudent hesitation was held to be cowardice in disguise, and moderation merely the cloak of an unmanly nature. A mind that could grasp the good of the whole was considered wholly lazy. Sudden fury was accepted as part of manly valor, while plotting for one's own security was thought a reasonable excuse for delaying action. A man who started a quarrel was always to be trusted, while one who opposed him was under suspicion. A man who made a plot was intelligent if it happened to succeed, while one who could smell out a plot was deemed even more clever. Anyone who took precautions, however, so as not to need to do either one, had been frightened by the other side (they would say) into subverting his own political party. In brief, a man was praised if he could commit some evil action before anyone else did, or if he could cheer on another person who had never meant to do such a thing.

Family ties were not so close as those of the political parties, because their members would readily dare to do anything on the slightest pretext. These parties, you see, were not formed under existing laws for the good, but for avarice in violation of established law. And the oaths they swore to each other had their authority not so much by divine law, as by their being partners in breaking the law. And if their opponents gave a good speech, if they were the stronger party, they did not receive it in a generous spirit, but with an eye to prevent its taking effect.

To take revenge was of higher value than never to have received injury. And as for oaths of reconciliation (when there were any!), these were offered for the moment when both sides were at an impasse, and were in force only while neither side had help from abroad; but on the first opportunity, when one person saw the other unguarded and dared to act, he found his revenge sweeter because he had broken trust than if he had acted openly: he had taken the safer course, and he gave himself the prize for intelligence if he had triumphed by fraud. Evildoers are called skillful sooner than simpletons are called good, and people are ashamed to be called simpletons but take pride in being thought skillful.

The cause of all this was the desire to rule out of avarice and ambition, and the zeal for winning that proceeds from those two. Those who led their parties in the cities promoted their policies under decent-sounding names: "equality for ordinary citizens" [plēthous isonomia politikē] on one side, and "moderate aristocracy" [aristokratia sōphrōn] on the other. And though they pretended to serve the public in their speeches, they actually treated it as the prize for their competition; and striving by whatever means to win, both sides ventured on most horrible outrages and exacted even greater revenge, without any regard for justice or the public good. Each party was limited only by its own appetite at the time, and stood ready to satisfy its ambition of the moment either by voting for an unjust verdict or seizing control by force.

So neither side thought much of piety, but they praised those who could pass a horrible measure under the cover of a fine speech. The citizens who remained in the middle were destroyed by both parties, partly because they would not side with them, and partly for envy that they might escape in this way.

[83] Thus was every kind of wickedness afoot throughout all Greece by the occasion of civil wars. Simplicity, which is the chief cause of a generous spirit, was laughed down and disappeared. Citizens were sharply divided into opposing camps, and, without trust, their thoughts were in battle array. No speech was so powerful, no oath so terrible, as to overcome this mutual hostility. The more they reckoned up their chances, the less hope they had for a firm peace, and so they were all looking to avoid harm from each other, and were unable to rely on trust. For the most part, those with the weakest minds had the greatest success, since a sense of their own inferiority and the subtlety of their opponents put them into great fear that they would be overcome in debate or by schemes due to their enemies' intelli-

gence. They therefore went immediately to work against them in action, while their more intelligent opponents, scornful and confident that they could foresee any attack, thought they had no need to take by force what might be gotten by wit. They were therefore unprotected, and so more easily killed.

• • •

[85] Such was the anger that the Corcyreans expressed in their city—the first against fellow citizens.

Eurymedon and the Athenians sailed away with their ships. Later, refugees from Corcyra—about five hundred of them had escaped—seized forts on the mainland and took control of the Corcyrean territory opposite the island, which they used as a base for plundering Corcyra, causing considerable damage and a severe famine that broke out in the city. Meanwhile, they sent ambassadors to Lacedaemon and Corinth about going home. After a time, when nothing came of that, they got boats and hired mercenary soldiers, then crossed over to the island, about six hundred in all. There they burned their boats so that their only hope would be to take control of the land. They went up to Mt. Istone and built a fort there; then they preyed on those in the city and took control of the land.

• • •

[The famous Melian dialogue, focusing on the question of might and right.]

[84] (In 416) the Athenians made war against the island of Melos, with thirty ships of their own, six from Chios, and two from Lesbos. The Athenian contingent was twelve hundred hoplites, three hundred archers, and twenty mounted archers, while the allies, including islanders, contributed about fifteen hundred hoplites. The Melians are a colony of the Lacedaemonians, and so did not want to be subject to Athens as the other islands were. At the beginning, they had stayed at peace with both sides. Later on, however, when the Athenians drove them to it by wasting their land, they were openly at war.

Now the Athenian generals, Cleomedes and Tisias, set up camp in Melian territory with these forces. Before doing any harm to the Melian land, they first sent ambassadors to negotiate. The Melians refused to bring these ambassadors before the common people, but ordered them to deliver their message to a few officials and leading citizens. The Athenians spoke as follows:

[85] *Athenians:* Since we may not speak before the common people, for fear that they would be led astray if they heard our persuasive and unanswerable arguments all at once in a continuous speech—we know that is what you had in mind in bringing us to the few leading citizens—you who are sitting here should make your situation still more secure: answer every particular point, not in a single speech, but interrupting us immediately whenever we say anything that seems wrong to you. And first, tell us whether you like this proposal.

[86] *To this the Melian Council replied:* We would not find fault with the fairness of a leisurely debate, but these acts of war—happening right now, not in the future—do not seem to be consistent with that. We see that you have come to be judges of this proceeding, so we expect the result to be this: if we make the better case for justice and do not surrender because of that, we will have war; but if you win the argument, we will have servitude.

[87] *Athenians:* Well, then, if you came to this meeting to reason on the basis of suspicions about the future, or for any other purpose than to work out how to save your city on the basis of what you see here today—we should stop now. But if that is your purpose, let's speak to it.

[88] *Melians:* People in our situation can be expected to turn their words and thoughts to many things, and should be pardoned for that. Since, however, this meeting is to consider only the point of our survival, let's have our discussion on the terms you have proposed, if that is your decision.

[89] *Athenians:* For our part, we will not make a long speech no one would believe, full of fine moral arguments—that our empire is justified because we defeated the Persians, or that we are coming against you for an injustice you have done to us. And we don't want you to think you can persuade us by saying that you did not fight on the side of the Lacedaemonians in the war, though you were their colony, or that

you have done us no injustice. Instead, let's work out what we can do on the basis of what both sides truly accept: we both know that decisions about justice are made in human discussions only when both sides are under equal compulsion; but when one side is stronger, it gets as much as it can, and the weak must accept that.

[90] *Melians:* Well, then, since you put your interest in place of justice, our view must be that it is in your interest not to subvert this rule that is good for all: that a plea of justice and fairness should do some good for a man who has fallen into danger, if he can win over his judges, even if he is not perfectly persuasive. And this rule concerns you no less than us: if you ever stumble, you might receive a terrible punishment and be an example to others.

[91] *Athenians:* We are not downhearted at the prospect of our empire's coming to an end, though it may happen. Those who rule over others (such as the Lacedaemonians, who are not our present concern) are not as cruel to those they conquer as are a subject people who attack their rulers and overcome them. But let us be the ones to worry about that danger. We will merely declare that we are here for the benefit of our empire, and we will speak for the survival of your city: we would like to rule over you without trouble, and preserve you for our mutual advantage.

[92] *Melians:* But how could it be as much to our advantage to serve, as it is yours to rule?

[93] *Athenians:* Because if you obey, you will save yourselves from a very cruel fate; and we will reap a profit from you if we don't destroy you.

[94] *Melians:* So you would not accept a peaceful solution? We could be friends rather than enemies, and fight with neither side.

[95] *Athenians:* No. Your enmity does not hurt us as much as your friendship would. That would be a sign of our weakness to those who are ruled by us; but your hatred would prove our power.

[96] *Melians:* Why? Do your subjects reason so unfairly that they put us, who never had anything to do with you, in the same category as themselves, when most of them were your colonies, or else rebels whom you defeated?

[97] *Athenians:* Why not? They think we have as good a justification for controlling you as we do for them; they say the independent cities survive because they are powerful, and that we do not attack them because we are afraid. So when you have been trampled down by us, you will add not only to our empire, but to our security, by not staying independent. And this is especially true because you are islanders who are weaker than the others, and we are masters of the sea.

[98] *Melians:* But don't you think there is safety in our proposal of neutrality? Here again, since you have driven us away from a plea for justice, and are telling us to surrender to whatever is in your interest, we must show you what would be good for us, and try to persuade you that your interests coincide with ours. Won't this turn the people who are now neutral into your enemies? Once they've seen this, they will expect you to attack them eventually also. And what would this accomplish, but to make the enemies you already have still greater, and to make others your enemies against their will, when they would not have been so?

[99] *Athenians:* We do not think the free mainlanders will be terrible enemies to us; it will be long before they so much as keep guard against us. But islanders worry us—those outside the empire like you, and those under the empire who resent the force that keeps them that way—these may indeed act recklessly and bring themselves and us into foreseeable danger.

[100] *Melians:* Yes, but if you would face such extreme danger to retain your empire, and if your subjects would do so to get free of you, then wouldn't it be great weakness and cowardice on our part, since we are still free, not to go to every extreme rather than be your subjects?

[101] *Athenians:* No, not if you think sensibly. Your contest with us is not an equal match of courage against courage; no honor is lost if you submit. This is a conference about your survival and about not resisting those who are far stronger than you.

[102] *Melians:* But we know that in war the odds sometimes are more even than the difference in numbers between the two sides, and that if we yield, all our hope is lost immediately; but if we hold out, we can still hope to stand tall.

[103] *Athenians:* Hope! It *is* a comfort in danger, and though it may be harmful to people who have many other advantages, it will not destroy them. But people who put everything they have at risk will learn what hope is when it fails them, for hope is prodigal by nature; and once they have learned this, it is too late to take precautions for the future. Do not let this happen to you, since you are weak and have only this one throw of the dice. And do not be like the ordinary people who could use human means to save themselves but turn to blind hopes when they are forced to give up their sensible ones—to divination, oracles, and other such things that destroy men by giving them hope.

[104] *Melians:* You can be sure we think it hard to contend against your power and good fortune, unless we might do so on equal terms. Nevertheless, we trust that our good fortune will be no less than yours. The gods are on our side, because we stand innocent against men who are unjust. And as for power, what we lack will be supplied by the alliance we will make with the Lacedaemonians, who must defend us as a matter of honor, if only because we are related to them. So our confidence is not as totally unreasonable as you might think.

[105] *Athenians:* Well, the favor of the gods should be as much on our side as yours. Neither our principles nor our actions are contrary to what men believe about the gods, or would want for themselves. Nature always compels gods (we believe) and men (we are certain) to rule over anyone they can control. We did not make this law, and we were not the first to follow it; but we will take it as we found it and leave it to posterity forever, because we know that you would do the same if you had our power, and so would anyone else. So as far as the favor of the gods is

concerned, we have no reason to fear that we will do worse than you.

As for your opinion about the Lacedaemonians, your trust that they will help you in order to preserve their own honor—we admire your blessed innocence, but we don't envy you your foolishness. Granted, the Lacedaemonians do show a high degree of virtue towards each other according to their local customs; but one could say many things about their treatment of other people. We'll make this as brief and as clear as possible: of all the people we know, they are the ones who make it most obvious that they hold whatever pleases them to be honorable, and whatever profits them to be just. So your plan will not support your hope for survival, and it now seems reckless.

[106] *Melians*: But on that point we most firmly trust the Lacedaemonians to pursue their own advantage—*not* to betray their colonists, the Melians, for in doing so they would benefit their enemies by losing the confidence of their friends among the Greeks.

[107] *Athenians*: Don't you realize that advantage lies with safety, and that the pursuit of justice and honor brings danger? Which the Lacedaemonians are usually least willing to face?

[108] *Melians*: But we believe they will take a dangerous mission in hand for our sake. They will think it safer to do so for us than for anyone else, since we are close enough to the Peloponnesus for action, and we will be more faithful to them than others because our kinship gives us common views.

[109] *Athenians*: But the good will of those who call for help does not offer any security to those who might fight for them. They will be safe only if they have superior power in action. The Lacedaemonians are more aware of this than anyone else; at least they have no confidence in their own forces, and therefore take many allies along with them when they attack a neighbor. So while we are masters of the sea, you cannot reasonably expect them to cross over to an island.

[110] *Melians*: Yes, but they may have others to send. The Sea of Crete is wide; it is harder for its masters to seize ships there, than it is for people who

want to escape to slip through. And if the Lacedaemonians failed in this, they would turn their arms against your own land or the lands of your allies that have still not been invaded by Brasidas. And then you will be troubled about your own land, and that of your allies, and no longer about a country that does not concern you.

[111] *Athenians*: With your experience of what might happen, you are surely not unaware that Athens has never given up a single siege through fear of anyone else. We are struck by the fact that though you said you would confer about your survival, in all this discussion you have never mentioned a single thing that people could rely on and expect to survive. Your strongest points are mere hopes for the future, and your actual resources are too small for your survival in view of the forces arrayed against you. Your planning will be utterly irrational, unless (after letting us withdraw from the meeting) you decide on a more sensible policy. Do not be distracted by a sense of honor; this destroys people all too often, when dishonor and death stand before their eyes. Many have been so overcome by the power of this seductive word, "honor," that even when they foresee the dangers to which it carries them, they are drawn by a mere word into an action that is an irreparable disaster; and so, intentionally, they fall into a dishonor that is more shameful than mere misfortune, since it is due to their own foolishness.

You must guard against this if you are to deliberate wisely, and you must not think it unseemly for you to submit to a city of such great power, which offers such reasonable conditions—to be our allies, and to enjoy your own property under tribute to us. You are being given a choice between war and survival: do not make the wrong decision out of a passion for victory. Remember what is usually the best course: do not give way to equals, but have the right attitude towards your superiors and use moderation towards your inferiors. So think about this when we withdraw from the meeting, and keep this often in your mind: you are considering what to do for your country—your only country—and this one discussion will determine whether it meets success or failure.

[112] So the Athenians withdrew from the conference, and the Melians, left to themselves, decided

on much the same position as they had taken in the debate. Then the Melians answered as follows:

Melians: Athenians, our resolution is no different from what it was before: we will not, in a short time, give up the liberty in which our city has remained for the seven hundred years since its foundation. We will trust in the fortune of the gods, which has preserved it up to now, and in the help of men—the Lacedaemonians—and we will do our best to maintain our liberty. We offer this, however: we will be your friends; we will be enemies to neither side; and you will depart from our land, after making whatever treaty we both think fit.

[113] That was the answer of the Melians. As they broke off the conference, the Athenians said:

Athenians: It seems to us, on the basis of this discussion, that you are the only men who think you know the future more clearly than what is before your eyes, and who, through wishful thinking, see doubtful events as if they had already come to pass. You have staked everything on your trust in hope, good fortune, and the Lacedaemonians; and you will be ruined in everything.

[114] Then the Athenian ambassadors went back to their camp. When the generals saw that the Melians would not submit, they turned immediately to war and surrounded the Melian city with a wall, after dividing up the work with their allies. After that, the Athenians left a contingent of Athenian and allied troops there to guard the city by land and sea, and went home with the greater part of their army. The rest stayed behind to besiege the place.

[115] (About the same time, the Argives invaded the country around Phlious, where they were am-

bushed by Phlians and exiles from Argos, losing about eighty men. Meanwhile, the Athenians at Pylos brought in a great deal of plunder from the Lacedaemonians. The Lacedaemonians did not go to war over this, because that would have broken the treaty. Instead they proclaimed that any of their people could plunder the Athenians in return. The Corinthians were at war with the Athenians, but this was over certain disputes of their own, and the rest of the Peloponnesus kept quiet.)

The Melians, in a night attack, captured part of the Athenian wall opposite the market place, killed the men there, and brought in grain and as many supplies as they could. Then they went back and kept quiet. After that the Athenians maintained a better watch.

And so the summer ended.

[116] (The following winter, the Lacedaemonians were about to march into the land of Argos, but they returned when they found that the sacrifices for the border crossing were not favorable. The Argives suspected some of their own people of being involved in the Lacedaemonian plan; they captured some of them, and the rest escaped.)

About the same time, the Melians took another part of the Athenian wall, because there were not many men to guard it. After that another army came from Athens under the command of Philocrates. Now that the city was besieged in force, there was some treachery, and the Melians on their own initiative surrendered to the Athenians, to be dealt with as the Athenians decided: they killed all the men of military age and made slaves of the women and children. Later, they settled the place themselves, sending five hundred colonists.

IV
TRAGEDIANS AND
COMEDIANS

Among the many playwrights of Classical Greece who wrote tragedies, the works of only three Athenians—Aeschylus, Sophocles, and Euripides—survive. Aeschylus wrote eighty or ninety plays, seven of which have come down to us. We have seven of Sophocles' more than one hundred thirty plays. Nineteen of the ninety-two plays that Euripides is said to have written are extant.

Tragedy was undeniably a Greek invention. The very first tragedies were probably written and produced no earlier than the mid sixth century B.C., and evolved out of an earlier tradition of dithyrambic poetry. A dithyramb was a choral lyric poem that was sung in honor of Dionysus, the god of wine and ecstasy. It generally had narrative, as opposed to merely descriptive, content. Important lyric poets such as Simonides, Pindar, and Bacchylides wrote dithyrambs, and the genre was clearly an important part of Archaic Greek, and particularly Athenian, culture. Indeed, the performance of dithyrambs was a public event of some significance. Choirs composed of men and boys competed with one another for prizes at civic festivals, including the Great Dionysia at Athens, and such festivals were themselves major occurrences in the life of the city.

The development of tragedy out of dithyramb can be traced initially to an innovation of the late sixth century B.C., conventionally attributed to Thespis, from whose name the word *thespian* is derived. Thespis added to the unified chorus of the dithyramb a single, detached actor. This seemingly small change produced, in fact, an immense literary and cultural revolution. It completely altered the structure and the dynamic of choral performance. At the outset, the role of this new actor was simply to engage in question-and-answer dialogue with the chorus. But for the first time, the existence of such a role established at least the possibility of a kind of dual structure internal to the work, and the development of this structure—involving a certain tension between the chorus's and the actor's questions and answers—probably formed the basis for the very idea of drama. The political significance of such a development has been a matter of considerable speculation, but it almost certainly reflected the newfound preoccupation among Greeks with questions concerning the proper relationship between an individual citizen and his or her city. In tragedy, the chorus could function as a kind of fictionalized civic community—the body of citizens—upholding law and custom over against the more or less discrete individual—played by the actor—who finds himself or herself forced to deal with a range of conflicting moral claims.

Thespis' great innovation led to another, namely, the addition of a second actor by Aeschylus. Sophocles, in turn, added a third, and in doing so, he expanded exponentially the possibilities for dramatic narrative. Conflict could now occur not only between character and chorus but also among the characters themselves in shifting configurations, and this arrangement produced the specific genre that we call tragedy.

Critics since Aristotle have argued about the defining characteristics of tragedy as opposed to other dramatic forms, and it is not easy to find any kind of formal or substantive feature that would connect, say, the tragedies of Aeschylus with those of Shakespeare. Limiting ourselves to the Greek case, however, we may suggest that tragic plays essentially concern themselves with tragic situations, and that a tragic situation can be specifically defined as one in which a protagonist is forced to choose between two equally disastrous alternatives. In Sophocles' *Oedipus Tyrannus*, Oedipus himself must decide whether or not to pursue the underlying cause of his city's ills. Failure to do so means unacceptable suffering for the city and its citizens, and this is something that no king could countenance. Successful pursuit of the truth, however, means catastrophe of a different kind, both for Oedipus himself and for his family. Either way he loses, but the world offers him no third option. Similarly, the title character in the *Agamemnon* of Aeschylus must decide whether or not to sacrifice his daughter Iphigenia to the goddess Artemis. Again, failure to do so would ensure a kind of kingly failure, since without divine help, Agamemnon and his army would be unable to right the wrong committed by the Trojans when Paris seduced and ran off with Helen. But if Agamemnon propitiates the goddess by sacrificing his daughter, then he faces disaster of a different kind. Again, he is forced to choose one of two paths, each of which leads inevitably to calamity. For the Greek tragedians, human existence is filled with tragic situations of this kind. The artistic goal of the tragic playwright was to put us in touch with, and to help us feel as palpably as possible, this inescapable fact about ourselves and our condition.

Aeschylus' *The Furies* is the third part of a trilogy, itself referred to as the *Oresteia*. The trilogy in its entirety tells the story of Agamemnon's return from the Trojan War. In the *Agamemnon*, the first play in the trilogy, we learn that Agamemnon's wife, Clytemnestra, has taken up with someone else during her husband's long absence, in part because of Agamemnon's decision to sacrifice their daughter to Artemis. She plots to murder Agamemnon and succeeds in doing so, to the horror not only of their two surviving children, Electra and Orestes, but also of the citizens of Argos. Clytemnestra and her lover declare themselves rulers of the city, and the audience is led to believe that theirs will indeed be a despotic regime. In *The Libation Bearers*, the second play in the trilogy, the focus switches to Orestes. He has returned from exile and faces an archetypically tragic choice: he must either avenge his father by murdering his own mother or else do nothing at all, thereby profaning justice by leaving his father's murderer unpunished. In collaboration with Electra, he chooses the former course, killing both his mother and her lover. At the end of the play, he seeks to justify his deed, while knowing that he has gravely offended those powerful spirits—the Furies—whose job it is to punish anyone who commits murder within the family. In *The Furies*, Orestes is brought to trial for his deed. It is at this point that Aeschylus describes an extraordinary and monumental transition, from the justice of blood revenge and the vendetta to the rational, civic justice of law and legal procedure. Orestes' fate will be decided not by the angry Furies but by a judicial process. The trial is presided over by the goddess Athena—the personification of wisdom—and is decided by a tribunal of citizens. In the end, Orestes is acquitted, the Furies are conciliated, and the idea of law and impartial justice is hailed as a fundamental principle of civic life.

The *Antigone* of Sophocles pursues a rather different set of themes. It describes the fate of the title character, Oedipus' daughter. Her two brothers, Eteocles and Polyneices, have both been killed in battle. One brother fought on the side of the Theban regime, the other against it. The king of Thebes, Creon, decrees that the loyal brother, Eteocles, should be accorded an honorable burial but that the traitorous brother should not be buried at all. Antigone—who is betrothed to the king's son—believes both of her brothers to have been equally honorable, and so she defies the decree by burying Polyneices. She understands that she has violated the law of the city but declares that her act is sanctioned by the higher laws of the gods. Like Agamemnon and Orestes, Creon faces a tragic choice: to leave Antigone unpunished, thereby failing in his public trust by ignoring the distinction between loyalty and treason, or to punish his prospective daughter-in-law, thereby bringing disaster to his family.

Greek dramatists produced not just tragedies but comedies as well. The only complete comic works that we have from the fifth century B.C., are the eleven surviving plays of Aristophanes. Of these, *Clouds* is highly representative. In part it is a bawdy entertainment, in part a satire on "modern" Athenian life, and in part a serious commentary on law and moral values. The description of Strepsiades himself, the corrupt but bedeviled farmer, along with the account of his relationships with his spendthrift wife and his irresponsible son, tells us a great deal about life in classical Athens—about moneylenders, gambling, consumerism, and the like. In lampooning the emergent urban and intellectual culture of his day, Aristophanes may be thought of as a defender of older, simpler values, of a time when right actions were rewarded and crimes were punished, of an era when true logic could defeat false, sophistic logic. *Clouds* is also notable for its amusing but viciously satirical portrayal of Socrates. As such, it is absolutely crucial in understanding something of the historical context in which the trial of Socrates took place.

Further Reading: The articles contained in *Greek Tragedy and Political Theory* (1986), edited by J. Peter Euben, would provide a good introduction to the subject. A very interesting study of the political relevance of Aeschylus is Euben's "Justice in the *Oresteia*," in *American Political Science Review* (1982). For an excellent and quite comprehensive introductory treatment of Sophocles' *Antigone*, see Chapter 4 of Mary Whitlock Blundell, *Helping Friends and Harming Enemies: A Study in Sophocles and Greek Ethics* (1989). *Recapturing Sophocles' Antigone* (1998), by William Blake Tyrrell and Larry J. Bennett, provides a commentary that focuses on the original historical contexts in which the play would have been produced and performed. Chapter 5 of Charles Segal's *Sophocles' Tragic World: Divinity, Nature, Society* (1995) looks at *Antigone* from the perspective of contemporary literary theory. Also important and influential is George Steiner, *Antigones* (1984).

Aeschylus
(525–456 B.C.)

The Furies

Cast of Characters

THE PYTHIA	priestess of Apollo
APOLLO	son of Zeus
ORESTES	son of Agamemnon and Clytemnestra
THE GHOST OF CLYTEMNESTRA	slain queen of Argos
CHORUS	of Furies
ATHENA	patron goddess of Athens
ATHENIAN CITIZENS	
GROUP OF ATHENIAN WOMEN	

SCENE 1:   *The sanctuary of Apollo at Delphi.*

(Enter the Pythia from the stage right wing.)

PYTHIA:
First of the gods, foremost in my prayer,
I honor Gaia, the Earth Mother, the first seer,
then Themis, for it is said that she was the second
to take her mother's place of prophecy.
5 The third was Phoebe, a Titan, a daughter of the earth,
her place bestowed in peace by Themis.
Phoebe bequeathed it to Apollo at his birth,
hence Phoebus, the name that honored the gift.
He left the lake and ridge-backed land of Delos
10 and landed on Athena's ship-laden shores.
On he came to this land of Mt. Parnassus
with an Athenian escort paying him homage.
They were the road builders, the sons of Hephaestus;
they cleared the way, they tamed the frontier.
15 On came Apollo, and the people revered him,

and King Delphus, hand on helm, received him
with honors.
Zeus inspired, Apollo's mind swelled with the divine arts,
and he became the fourth to sit on this mantic throne,
the prophet of his father, the spokesman of Zeus.

These gods come first in my prayers, but Athena   20
who stands before the temple is foremost in my
speech,
and I revere the nymphs of the Corycian rock,
the cave beloved by birds, where the spirits dwell.
I remember that Dionysus inhabits in this land,
ever since he marshaled the Bacchae, weaving   25
the Destiny of Pentheus, the death of a hunted hare.
By the river of Pleistos and the power of Poseidon,
I call on Zeus the Fulfiller, the highest god,
as I go inside to take my seat as prophet.
Let this entrance surpass all times past   30
to be the best by far. If any Greeks are here
have them enter by lot, according to our custom.
Know that my prophecies are given by the god.

(The Pythia exits through the doors then immediately reenters, terrified and scurrying on all fours.)

Horrors! Horrors to tell! Horrors before my eyes,
they have repelled me from Apollo's house!   35
I am terrified, my legs have frozen in fear! I cannot stand,
I have to crawl out on my hands and knees.
A scared old woman is nothing, no more than a
helpless child.

I was entering the chamber where the wool wreaths   40
hang, and I saw a man by the center-stone,
stained in the sight of the gods and crouching
in supplication. His hands and drawn sword

Reprinted from Aeschylus, *Oresteia*, translated, with notes, by Peter Meineck (Indianapolis: Hackett Publishing Company, 1998) by permission of the publisher.

are dripping with blood, and he is clutching
a tall olive branch, rightly wreathed
45 with a full woolen shank of silvery fleece.
In front of this man was an astonishing throng
of women propped against the benches asleep.
No, not women, they were a hideous sight,
more like Gorgons, but worse, much worse.
50 I have seen paintings of the beasts that plagued
Phineus and stole his food, but the creatures in there
have no wings, they are dark, dank and disgusting.
Their foul stench and hideous breath forced me back,
and their eyes seep a repulsive, putrid pus.
55 They are wrapped in black dismal rags not fit for
    human sight.
A place of holy idols should not suffer such an evil ap-
    parition.
I have never known a race that spawned such crea-
    tures,
nor have I seen a land that could boast to have
    bred them
without suffering some terrible blight—terrible pain!
60 Apollo must decide what to do with them,
he is the master of this house,
he is the healer, the prophet,
he has the power to purify a house.

(Exit Pythia through the stage right wing.)

(Enter Orestes and Apollo from the door. The sleeping Furies are barely visible in the doorway.)

APOLLO:
I will not forsake you, I will protect you until the end,
65 I will stand by your side even when I am far, far away,
your enemies will never receive comfort from me.
You see those foul, frenzied creatures, they are
    trapped,
I have lulled the disgusting virgins to sleep.
They are the wizened ancient children, repugnant
70 to gods and untouched by man or beast.
The progeny of evil wallowing in misery
spewed from their infernal abyss, the bowels of hell.
Abhorred by men on earth and despised by the Olym-
    pian gods.
So run, run, flee these creatures, never weaken,
75 for they will drive you across continents,
to the ends of the earth, their feet pounding, on
    and on,
across the ocean, beyond the far seawashed lands.
But never stop, never weaken, you must endure

and reach the city of Athena, be her suppliant,
fall at her feet, hold her, clasp her wooden idol.   80
There you will find the judges of your cause,
and we will charm them with words, we will find a way
to finally free you from this ordeal. I will help you,
for it was I who persuaded you to kill your mother.

ORESTES:
Lord Apollo, you know how not to be unjust,   85
so learn how not to be neglectful.
You have the power for good, you can save me.

APOLLO:
Remember this, never let your mind be overcome
    by fear.
Hermes, paternal brother, be true to your title,
protect him, be his escort and his guide.   90
Be sure to guard my suppliant well,
Zeus respects the sacredness of the outcast.
Go quickly now and bring him back to the world
    of men.

(Exit Orestes through the stage left wing; exit Apollo
through doors.)

(Enter the ghost of Clytemnestra.)

CLYTEMNESTRA:
You sleep? What use are you asleep?
It is because of you that I am dishonored by the dead, 95
they charge me with the killings, accuse me,
and the dead are relentless in resentment.
I have no place, I am shunned in shame,
they indict me with the harshest blame,
I who suffered the cruelest pain from my closest kin. 100
There is no angry god to avenge me,
slaughtered by those mother-killing hands.
See my wounds—let them tear your hearts!

All those honeyed liquids and sweet libations   105
I poured for you, you lapped them up,
the dark nocturnal feasts I burned at the hearth,
in the dead of night, at the ungodly hour.
Now I see it all trampled underfoot.   110
He has gone, just skipped away like some fawn,
sprung from the midst of your hunting net,
turning back only to grin and mock you.
Hear me, I am pleading for my soul!
Mind me, underworld goddesses,   115
a dream of Clytemnestra is calling you.

(The Furies stir and groan.)

You whine while your man has fled and gone.
Even suppliants have allies, I have none.

120   *(They stir again.)*

Too much sleep, not enough pity for my pain.
Orestes, the mother-killer, has escaped!

(The Furies moan.)

You groan, yet sleep. Awake! Awake!
125 Why else do you exist if not to inflict evil?

(They moan again.)

So fatigue and sleep have conspired
to suck the strength of the furious serpent.

CHORUS:
Hunt!
       Hunt!
              Hunt!
                     Hunt!
130   *Hunt him!*

CLYTEMNESTRA:
You're preying on a dream, howling dogs,
hounding, hunting, chasing blood.
What are you doing? Wake up! Weariness will not
     win!
Sleep shall not rob your memories of my pain.
135 My scorn will stab your hearts,
a spur to prick the conscience of the just.
Let him feel the blast of your reeking, bloody breath,
bleed him dry and burn him in your stomach's fire.
On again! Hunt him down! Waste him away!

CHORUS:
Awake!
       Awake!
140   *All awake!*
Shake off sleep.
                  Up, up on your feet.
Seek out the truth of the dream.

(Exit Clytemnestra through the doors.)

*(Enter chorus one by one from the doors into the or-
chestra.)*

[Strophe 1]

No! No! Sisters we have been wronged!

All my work—all our work, for nothing! Nothing!

No! No! I can't bear the pain, it hurts! It hurts!   145

Unbearable pain!

Our prey has slipped the net, our victim has fled.

Sleep has beaten me, the hunt is lost.

[Antistrophe 1]

Son of Zeus, you are a thief!
The youth galloped past the ancient spirits,   150
but your sacred suppliant is a godless man,
a curse to those that raised him.
You have stolen the mother-killer, you, a god!
How can this be justice?

[Strophe 2]

The charge was leveled in my dream,   155
it lashed me like a chariot whip
held hard and strong,
it stung my mind, it thrashed my heart.

I felt the harsh crack and the searing smart   160
of the floggers punishing scourge.

[Antistrophe 2]

These new gods, this is how they behave,
their power exceeds the bounds of justice.
Their thrones are drenched in blood,
soaked from head to foot.   165

I see the center-stone stained,
defiled, accursed, grim with gore.

[Strophe 3]

The prophet has fouled his hearth and home,
sullied his own sanctuary, he invited it,
he encouraged it.   170

He flouts the law, puts men before gods,
he destroys the ancient lot of Destiny.

[Antistrophe 3]

He has wounded us, but the man will not escape,
175 *he can run to the ends of the earth, he'll never be free.*

He'll take the mark of murder to his grave,
more blood will come, on his own head be it.

(*Enter Apollo from the doors.*)

APOLLO:
Out I say! Get away from my house!
180 leave the prophetic chamber,
or feel the fangs of my winged serpents
flashing from my gold-stringed bow.
I'll pierce your guts, and you'll spew the black blood
and scum sucked from men, and choke on the putrid clots.
185 There is no place for you in this house, you have no
right here.
You belong where justice slaughters men for their
crimes,
where heads are cut off and eyes gouged out,
where a man's seed is killed by castration
and young boys are mutilated, their bull-spirits
crushed.
190 Go, follow the stonings, hear the tortured cries of men,
hover by the carcasses, staked out, driven through, impaled.
You crave your ghastly feast and the gods despise you.
Look at you! You are betrayed by your hideous shape,
you should cower in a cave, the carrion of a lion
195 gorged with blood. Never smear your filth on my
shrine.
Get out! Out, you headless herd, there's not a god
in heaven who would deign to be your shepherd.

CHORUS:
Lord Apollo, listen, it is our turn to speak.
200 You are not merely an accessory to this crime,
it was all your doing, you bear the blame.

APOLLO:
How? Tell me that, nothing more.

CHORUS:
Your oracle told the outcast to kill his mother.

APOLLO:
My oracle told him to exact revenge for his father,
what of it?

CHORUS:
You offered to shelter him, the blood still on his
hands.

APOLLO:
I told him to come to my house as a suppliant. 205

CHORUS:
But we brought him here and now you malign us.

APOLLO:
You should not come anywhere near my house.

CHORUS:
But it is our responsibility, it is our place.

APOLLO:
By what authority? Please proclaim your ancient prerogative.

CHORUS:
We drive mother-killers from their homes. 210

APOLLO:
And what do you do when a wife kills her husband?

CHORUS:
Then the killer would not be spilling kindred blood.

APOLLO:
Then you demean and dishonor
the marriage vows of Hera Fulfiller and Zeus.
Your statement discards Aphrodite to disgrace, 215
she, who seals the most cherished of mortal bonds.
The marriage of a man and woman is set by Destiny,
it is mightier than the oath and defended by Justice.
If you are prepared to allow murder in marriage,
and take no vengeance nor inflict your wrath, 220
then this manhunt of Orestes cannot be just.
I see that the one issue inflames your hearts,
but clearly for the other, you are unwilling to act.
I say the goddess Athena should preside over this case.

CHORUS:
We will never let that man be free, never! 225

APOLLO:
Well, chase him then, and suffer the consequences.

CHORUS:
I will not allow you to argue away our authority.

APOLLO:
Authority? If it was offered to me I would refuse it.

CHORUS:
Of course, for you are a mighty god enthroned by
   Zeus,
230 but we are forced on by the shedding of mother blood,
and Justice is best served by hunting the killer down.

(Exit Furies through the stage left wing.)

APOLLO:
He is in my sacred trust and I will protect him.
Gods and men fear nothing more than the rage
of a scorned suppliant denied his mercy.

(Exit Apollo through the doors.)

SCENE 2:   *Athens, at the foot of Athena's statue be-*
                  fore her temple.

(Enter Orestes from the stage left wing into the orchestra;
he falls at the altar.)

ORESTES:
235 Lady Athena, I have come at the command of Apollo,
greet this outcast with kind good grace.
I am not an untouchable, my hands are clean,
I am like a dulled blade, blunted in faraway homes,
beaten and battered on the roads of men.
240 I traveled the earth and spanned the seas,
following the oracle, the word of Apollo,
heading for your house, goddess, for your idol.
Now I'm here, I'll watch and wait for the final
   judgment.

(Enter the Furies from the stage left wing.)

CHORUS:
We have him! Look, the man-tracks, a fresh trail,
245 follow the silent evidence, it points the way.
Hound him, hunt him like a wounded fawn,
track the trace of a blood-splattered scent.
This deadly work, no man could bear it, gasping,
lung-splitting labor, sweeping across the earth,
250 skimming the seas in wingless flight,
swifter than a ship, bearing down on our prey.
He is here, skulking somewhere near,
I smell the welcome stench of human blood.

Look! Look!
255 *Look everywhere!*
The mother-killer must not escape, he must be pun-
   ished.

(The Furies see Orestes.)

There he is! He's taken sanctuary!
He's clinging to the idol of the goddess!
He wants to wipe his hands clean with a trial!   260
No! He has spilled his mother's blood!
It is done, drained away, it can't come back!
Swallowed by the earth, gone forever!
Blood must pay for blood!

(To Orestes)

                                    We will drink
the thick, red liquid libation of your limbs   265
and quench our thirst with a sickening toast.
We will bleed you dry then banish you below.
We'll see you in hell, one more for the wicked,
with the men who sinned against gods, guests,
and their own dear parents.   270
You'll suffer the pain that Justice ordains.
Mighty Hades balances the human ledger,
his final reckoning holds mortals to account,
deep in the depths of the earth everything
is remembered and etched on his mind.   275

ORESTES:
Evil has educated me. I have come to understand
many things, I know when to speak
and when to stay silent, and in this case
a wise teacher has told me to voice my case.
The blood on my hands has been worn to sleep,   280
the mark of mother-killing has been washed out.
The fresh stain was purged before Apollo's hearth,
cleansed by the blood of slaughtered swine.
It would take too long to tell you of all the homes
that sheltered me and yet were never tainted.   285
All things age and time can cleanse everything.
Now my pure and pious lips call on Athena,
queen of this country, to come to my aid.
Win without the spear, me, my country,
and all my Argive people, forevermore   290
trusted allies and confederates true.
She will come from the shores of Africa,
by the waters of Triton that bore her,
to lead the charge or to stand in defense,
she will enter the fight to rescue an ally.   295
She'll come striding the monstrous battleground,
surveying the field like a bold man of war.
I know she can hear me, I know she can save me.

CHORUS:
There is no salvation, not from Apollo, nor
    Athena.
300 You will be cast out, adrift, abandoned,
your tortured mind will never know happiness,
you'll be food for fiends, a blood-sucked shadow.
You refuse to answer? You spit on our words?
You are our sacrifice fatted for the feast,
305 you'll not be slashed at the altar, we'll eat you
    alive!
Now hear our song, our spellbinding song.

[Prelude]

Join our binding dance
the malignant music
unfolding the terror.
310 *Hear our share*
in the life of man,
for we are just and true.
Hold up clean hands
and clear wrath's trail,
315 *pass life free from harm.*
Should you, like him, stray to sin
and hide your murderous hands,
then we bear witness for the dead.
For bloodshed must be revenged,
320 *and we pursue it to the very end.*

[Strophe 1]

Mother who made me,
Mother Night hear me,
bred to avenge the sighted,
the blind, bred to avenge the dead.
Leto's child has stolen the hare,
Apollo tries to rob my rights,
we demand this sacrifice
325 *payment for mother-blood shed.*

[Refrain 1]

We sing for the victim
insanity's song,
330 *delirious, demented,*
the Furies' hymn,
spellbinding minds,
unstrung strains burning the brain.

[Antistrophe 1]

Our share of the thread
spun by the spirits of Destiny,   335
woven in permanent place.
We hunt down the mortal
compelled to kill kin,
hound him to hell,
down, down, deep in the earth,
he'll never be free, even in death.   340

[Refrain 1]

We sing for the victim
insanity's song:
delirious, demented,
the Furies' hymn:
spellbinding minds,   345
unstrung strains burning the brain.

[Strophe 2]

Our birthright, our share, ordained of old,
untouched by the deathless gods.   350
They never deign to sit at our feasts,
not for us the pure white robes,
they have no share in our dark rites.

[Refrain 2]

I reduce to ruin the House
that rears the brood of Ares   355
breeding kin killing kin.
Born of the blood, we hunt down
the killer, scorning his power,
casting bleak shadows of death.

[Antistrophe 2]

We eagerly fulfill this obligation,   360
absolving the gods from this care;
they need never hear these charges.
Zeus detests our gruesome kind,   365
and shuns us from his side.

[Strophe 3]

A man's esteem, the light of his life
can decay to disgrace once deep in the earth.
The black-clad chorus closes around,   370
feet pounding the furious dance.

[Refrain 3]

Leaping from the heights,
the hard, heavy downfall.
My foot stamps and cripples,
375 *the straining runner is brought down,*
crashing to ground, reduced by Ruin.

[Antistrophe 3]

He cannot see his downfall,
depravity drives him mad,
polluted mists cloud all reason.
Darkness hovers over his House,
380 *a sigh of grief breathes the doom.*

[Strophe 4]

And so it stands, this our craft,
fulfillment of the evil,
for remembrance is respect,
however much a man may beg.
385 *The gods hate our gory share,*
shunned in sunless grime.
Our rugged path is the only way
for both the living and the dead.

[Antistrophe 4]

What mortal man is not terrified,
390 *gripped in fear and horror*
to hear our sacred law
determined by Destiny's decree?
The gods yield this right,
it is our age-old prerogative,
395 *and though we dwell in sunless depths*
our underworld power stands respected.

(Enter Athena from the doors.)

ATHENA:
I heard a far cry for help from Scamander's
shores, where I claimed the land bestowed
by the warriors and chiefs of Greece.
400 The greatest share of the spear-won spoils,
branch and root, are mine for all time,
the choicest prize for Theseus' sons.
I have come stepping swiftly, stridently
my flailing Aegis whirling me wingless.
405 [yoking young steeds to my chariot.]

I see new visitors have come to my land,
an astounding sight, but I am not afraid.
Who or what are you? I speak to you all,
both the stranger crouched at my statue,
and you, inhuman grotesque creatures
fatherless by birth, and reared   410
by no goddesses known to the gods.
But prejudice is slander to the innocent,
and Justice should always be impartial.

CHORUS:
Daughter of Zeus, I will explain,   415
we are the eternal children of Night,
the curses that dwell deep in the earth.

ATHENA:
I know of your kind, I have heard your name.

CHORUS:
And you will soon hear of our authority.

ATHENA:
If you state your case clearly, I will learn it.   420

CHORUS:
We drive murderers from their homes.

ATHENA:
And where does this murder-hunt end?

CHORUS:
In a place that has never known joy.

ATHENA:
Is this your fugitive, are you hunting him?

CHORUS:
Yes, he saw fit to murder his mother.   425

ATHENA:
Was he forced? Did he fear the anger of another?

CHORUS:
What could goad a man to kill his own mother?

ATHENA:
There are two sides to this, it is only half-heard.

CHORUS:
But he will not swear the oath of innocence, nor
   accept our oath of his guilt.

ATHENA:
So you would rather be called just than act justly?   430

CHORUS:
What do you mean? You are wise, teach us.

ATHENA:
An oath must never triumph over Justice.

CHORUS:
Then question him, you judge the justice.

ATHENA:
Will you give the final say in this case to me?

CHORUS:
435 Yes, respect from you makes our respect due.

ATHENA:
Stranger, it is your turn to speak, to answer these
      charges.
Tell me where you are from, your family and your
      troubles,
then make your defense against these claims.
If it is your belief in Justice that has you huddling at
      my hearth,
440 clutching my statue, then your rights will be respected
and held sacred as a suppliant like Ixion before you.
Now address these issues and answer them clearly.

ORESTES:
Lady Athena, first of all please allow me to dispel
a misgiving I have over what you have just said to me.
445 I am not a suppliant, and it is not because my hands
are stained that I sit here at the foot of your image.
I have powerful proof that I am speaking the truth.
Divine law holds that a murderer must not speak
until a man who can perform the cleansing rite
450 sprinkles him with the blood of a suckling beast.
Also, I have long since been purged by the sacrifices
and lustral waters of all the homes that took me in.
So you see, the pollution must not be considered.
You will soon recognize my lineage.
455 I am an Argive, and you know my father well,
Agamemnon, the man who marshaled the fleet
and with your help, crushed the city of Troy.
Returning home he died a miserable death,
hacked down by my foul-minded mother,
460 shrouded in the intricate covert net,
the witness of the murder in the bath.
I was in exile then, but when I returned
I killed the woman who bore me. I do not deny it.
It was revenge for the murder of my beloved father.
465 Apollo was my accomplice, he shares the charge,

he lashed me with threats of heartwrenching pains
if I did not take action against the guilty ones.
You judge if I was just or not. I have made my case.
Whatever you decide, I will accept your verdict.

ATHENA:
This matter is too great to be decided by a mortal.   470
It is not even appropriate that I preside over
a murder trial that inflames such furious rage.
You have been tamed by the rites, fully cleansed
and have sought rightful sanctuary at my house.

(Indicating the Furies)

But Destiny has allotted their place, and it cannot   475
simply be dismissed, for if they were defeated
the wound of their resentment would seep malig-
      nant poison,
cursing the earth with an insufferable, perpetual
      plague.
So stands the case. Do I let you stay, or send you
      away?
An arduous decision, as either way will provoke di-   480
      vine wrath.
Because this case has become my responsibility
I will appoint the exemplary men of my city
as magistrates over murder, bound by a solemn oath,
for now and for ever, to serve this sacred court.
Summon your witnesses and gather your evidence,   485
prepare your sworn testimonies to support your cases.
I will select the finest of my citizens
who will strive to return an honest verdict,
uphold their pledge, and deliberate with judicial
      minds.

(Exit Athena through the doors.)

[Strophe 1]

CHORUS:
Catastrophe! Ancient   490
mandates will be usurped
should the corrupt plea
of the mother-killer prevail.
His crime will unite all mankind
in anarchy and lawlessness,   495
down through the generations,
children will be free to harm parents,
the fatal lesions tearing true.

[Antistrophe 1]

We are the Furies, sentinels,
500 but no longer will we keep watch
and rage against the depraved.
We will abandon all mankind.
Let slip the impending doom.
505 Let man appeal to man for heaven's help
and prophesy his neighbor's troubles.
Let him tell when the pain will ease and cease,
and offer the poor fool his ineffective cure.

[Strophe 2]

Now no one may call on us
when disaster rains down.
510 Yet they will clamor to cry,
"Justice, where are you!
Sovereign Furies!"
The tormented father,
the mother just wronged,
515 they will bemoan and wail
the collapse of the house of Justice.

[Antistrophe 2]

Fear has its place, it can be good,
it stands sentinel,
the watchman of the mind.
520 It can be beneficial
to suffer into sanity.
How can the man
or city that has no fear
to nourish the heart
525 ever have respect for Justice?

[Strophe 3]

Not a life of anarchy
nor the rule of tyranny.
Take the middle way endowed by gods
530 whatever course they sway.
In accord we sing measured words:
Outrage is Impiety's true child,
535 only a healthy mind provides
the good fortune so cherished,
the passion of all men's prayers.

[Antistrophe 3]

Know this now, know it all.
Respect Justice, never kick away
her altar for the glimpse of wealth.   540
The disgrace will be avenged,
for the end remains ordained.
Hold parents in the high esteem,   545
grace the sacred guest,
keep your house hospitable,
honor strangers with your good fortune.

[Strophe 4]

Freely embrace Justice   550
and you will surely prosper,
you will never know destruction.
The insolent violator heaping high
his unjust haul, hoarding his vicious
payload, will soon enough strike his sails   555
as his yardarm cracks and shatters,
against the blasts of suffering's storm.

[Antistrophe 4]

His cries for help fall on deaf ears
as he founders in the whirling currents.
The spirits see and mock the brazen man   560
who once boasted this could never be.
Helplessly drowning in a sea of sorrows,
his fortune submerged in a surge of woes,
wrecked upon the reef of Justice.
He is lost, unwept, unseen.   565

SCENE 3:   The hill of Ares (Areopagus) in Athens.

(Enter Athena from the doors.)

ATHENA:
Herald, summon the people to their places,
raise the Tyrrhenian war trumpet,
fill its bronze with mortal breath,
sound the piercing cry to call the people.

(Enter ten Athenian elders from the stage right wing into
the orchestra. They set two large voting urns.)

Be silent as the court convenes,   570
the city will learn my eternal laws,
the litigants will receive a fair trial
and hear a prudent judgment.

(Enter Apollo on the roof.)

Lord Apollo, you have your own jurisdiction;
575 tell me, how you are involved in this case?

APOLLO:
I have come to testify under the law.
This man is my suppliant and sought sanctuary
at my hearth, I purged him of his blood-guilt.
I stand as his advocate and share the blame
580 for the murder of his mother. I ask you
to decide this case. I seek your judgment.

ATHENA:
Begin the proceedings.

(To the Furies)

                                    Make your case.
The prosecution will present its arguments first.
Explain your accusations and set out your charges.

CHORUS:
585 Although we are many, we will be brief,

(To Orestes)

Answer our questions point for point.
Tell us first, did you kill your mother?

ORESTES:
I killed her, I do not deny it.

CHORUS:
There! The first of three falls.

ORESTES:
590 You boast before the bout is over. I am not yet down
for the count.

CHORUS:
Will you tell us how you killed her?

ORESTES:
I held my sword at her neck and slit her throat.

CHORUS:
Who persuaded you to do this, who advised it?

ORESTES:
It was the god's word, he will testify to that.

CHORUS:
595 The prophet guided you to kill your own mother?

ORESTES:
Yes, and as yet I have no regrets.

CHORUS:
You will, when the verdict places you in our grasp.

ORESTES:
I have faith in my father, help from beyond the grave.

CHORUS:
You trust the dead? You? The mother-killer!

ORESTES:
Yes, I killed her, because she was tainted with two 600
crimes.

CHORUS:
How? Explain that to the jury.

ORESTES:
She murdered her husband and she murdered my
father.

CHORUS:
But she was absolved by her death, while you still live.

ORESTES:
Then why did you not drive her out when she was
alive?

CHORUS:
She was not of the same blood as the man she mur- 605
dered.

ORESTES:
So do I share my mother's blood?

CHORUS:
You butcher! You grew in her womb, how can you
disown
the bond of blood between mother and child?

ORESTES:
Apollo guide me now, stand as my witness,
was Justice with me when I struck her down?   610
The deed was done, I did it, I do not deny it.
Consider the bloodshed and give your decision,
they must hear my side of this case, was I just?

APOLLO:
I say to you, and to this great court of Athena,
that he was just. I am the seer and I speak the truth. 615
No man, woman, or city has ever heard a word
from my seat of prophecy that was not
ordained by Zeus, the Olympian father.
Understand the force behind this just plea

620 and be sure you heed the will of my father,
for no oath can surpass the power of Zeus.

CHORUS:
Zeus? Are you saying Zeus gave you this oracle?
That he told Orestes to seek revenge for his father
by disregarding the honor he owed his mother?

APOLLO:
625 Clearly there is no comparison. He was avenging
the death
of a nobleman sceptered with Zeus-given honor.
The man was struck down by a woman, but not
in battle
by the furious flight of an Amazon's arrow.
No, you will hear how he died, Athena,
630 as will the jury who will decide the verdict.
He returned from the long war and in the balance
he had done well, and she welcomed him with kindness.
As he stepped from the bath, at the very edge,
she threw that shroud around him, tangling him
635 in the endless, intricate fabric—and then she
struck.
I have told you how this awe-inspiring man,
the First Sea Lord of the fleet, met his end.
It enrages the people to hear what she did,
as it should enrage you judges deciding this case.

CHORUS:
640 You say that Zeus has higher regard for a father's
destiny,
and yet he placed his own father, old Cronus, in
chains.
This seems to contradict your argument,
I call on the jurors to witness this.

APOLLO:
You repulsive hags! The gods detest you!
645 Chains can be broken, there is a remedy
and countless ways to be set free.
But once the dust has soaked up a man's blood
he is gone forever, nothing can bring him back.
Zeus has provided no magic charm for that,
650 though he has the power to change the course
of everything, breathlessly, at his whim.

CHORUS:
Look at how you justify his defense!
He spilled his own mother's blood on the ground,

and you would have him home in Argos at his fa-
ther's house?
Tell me, what communal altars could he worship at?   655
What clan could ever anoint and admit him?

APOLLO:
Then learn the truth, the one named mother
is not the child's true parent but the nurturer
of the newly sown seed. Man mounts to create life,
whereas woman is a stranger fostering a stranger,   660
nourishing the young, unless a god blights the birth.
I have proof that there can be a father without a
mother,
proof that what I say is true,
there stands your witness:

(Indicating Athena)

                          The child of Zeus.
She never grew in the darkness of a womb,   665
and no goddess could have borne such a child.

Athena, in all things I will do my utmost
to help your city and its people achieve greatness.
I sent this man to your house and hearth
that you may be bound in trust for all time   670
and that you would inherit a new ally, goddess.
Both he and his descendants true to you for ever,
the generations bonded in a covenant of faith.

ATHENA:
Have we heard enough? May I call on the jury
to deliberate and deliver their truthful verdict?   675

APOLLO:
We have shot all our defensive bolts.
I stay only to hear the decision in this dispute.

ATHENA:
Very well,

(To the Furies)

                    and how can I best appease you?

CHORUS:
You have heard what you have heard, may the jury
search
their hearts and respect their oath as they cast their 680
votes.

ATHENA:
Now hear my decree, people of Athens.
You are the first to judge a case of bloodshed.
And from this time on, the race of Aegeus
will forever uphold this judicial assembly.
685 When the Amazon warrior women invaded,
they pitched their camp on this rock of Ares.
Those foes of Theseus forced into your city and
   raised
their towering battlements that dwarfed your walls.
They dedicated this place for the war god,
690 and on this hill of Ares I will found my court.
From this rock shall come the respect to inspire
my citizens and the fear to restrain injustice,
constant through every long night and each bright
   day.
But the citizens must uphold the law
695 and there can be no deviation, for pure water
can never be drawn once the well has been
   fouled.
There will be no anarchy, nor the rule of tyranny.
Citizens, embrace the middle way, but never banish fear,
for the mortal who has no fear can never know
   Justice.
700 You must respect this court and you must fear it,
it is your best defense, for the stronger the bulwark,
the safer the city, and men will never know a city
   stronger,
whether it lies in the land of Pelops or in Scythian
   hills.
This tribunal will be untouchable, and not corrupt,
705 distinguished, but swift to act, the watchtower
of our country, the sentinel of safe, sound sleep.
I dedicate this address to my people, both now
and in the time to come. Let each man stand
and cast his ballot so we may decide this case,
710 and remember always to respect your oath.

(One by one, the ten jurors cast their votes.)

CHORUS:
I warn you, together we could curse your earth.
It would be wise not to dishonor us.

APOLLO:
And I remind you to heed my oracles, the word of
   Zeus;
do not deprive them of bearing their fruit.

CHORUS:
You are meddling in matters of blood, and it is not 715
   your place.
Your house will be unclean and your oracles tainted.

APOLLO:
So was Zeus mistaken when he offered sanctuary
to Ixion, the very first man to commit a murder?

CHORUS:
So you say, but if we do not receive some justice,
we will curse this land for the rest of time. 720

APOLLO:
You are a disgrace to the gods, young and old alike.
I will win, I will defeat you.

CHORUS:
Just like the time you interfered in the House of
   Pheres
and persuaded the spirits of Destiny to free a mortal
   from death.

APOLLO:
How can it not be just to aid the faithful man 725
especially in his time of greatest trouble?

CHORUS:
You obliterated age-old precedents,
you beguiled the ancient goddesses with wine.

APOLLO:
Soon enough you will lose this trial.
Spit your poison at your enemies. It will do them 730
   no harm.

CHORUS:
This youth rides roughshod over his elders,
but we will wait to hear the verdict
and then decide if this city will incur our wrath.

ATHENA:
Now my task is to make the last judgment,
and I cast my vote for Orestes. 735
I was born of no mother, and I defer to the male
in all things with all my heart, except for marriage,
as I will always be the child of my father.
Thus, I cannot give precedence to the woman's death:
she murdered her husband, the guardian of the 740
   House;
if the vote is split Orestes will be the winner.

Now the jury foremen will proceed with the count,
quickly, turn out the urns and tally the votes.

(The urns are emptied and the votes counted.)

ORESTES:
Apollo, lord of the light, what will be decided?

CHORUS:
745 Dark Mother Night, are you watching?

ORESTES:
Is it death at the end of a rope, or will I see the light
    of life?

CHORUS:
Is it the end for us or a new sanction of our authority?

APOLLO:
The ballots are out, make a careful count, be fair,
have respect for Justice as you divide the votes.
750 An ill-judged verdict could cause great harm,
and a single vote can restore a mighty House.

ATHENA:
Each side has received the same number of votes.
This man is acquitted of the charge of murder.

ORESTES:
Athena, you have saved my House!
755 I was denied the land of my fathers,
but you have restored me to my home.
The Greeks will say, "The man is Argive again.
He holds his father's House by the grace of Athena
and Apollo, ordained by the Savior, Zeus the Third."
760 Zeus marked the death of my father and saved
me from the litigants sent by my mother.
And as I leave for home I will make a great oath.
I swear to you, your land and your people,
that for the rest of time, no helmsman guiding
765 my country will ever raise a spear against you,
or march in force to do battle against this land.
I will protect this promise from beyond my grave
and will rise up and punish the oathbreaker.
I will slow their march to a disastrous crawl,
770 crush their spirits with the birds of ill omen,
force them down the path of penance and regret.
Yet if they respect this oath and forever honor
this city of Athena with their confederate spears,
I will bless them with good will and eternal kindness.
775 So farewell to you and the people of your city,

may your bouts be won, and your holds be strong,
may the safety of our spears bring victorious
    years.

*(Exit Orestes through the stage left wing. Exit Apollo from
the roof.)*

[Strophe 1]

CHORUS:
*You young gods have ridden roughshod over
the ancient ways, wrenched them from our grasp.
We are dishonored and dejected,*   780
*and our anger rises to ravage the land.
Venom boiled from grief,
seeping from seething hearts,
poison oozing on the earth,
sterile, stagnant pestilence
polluting the ground. Oh Justice! Justice!*   785
*Mortal infection will disease this place.
Ai, I lament, what will I do?
Scorned by the people,
unbearable mockery!
Ill-fated daughters of Night*   790
*you are cast out,
you are disgraced!*

ATHENA:
Be persuaded not to bear this burden of grief.
You were not defeated, the votes were even,   795
it was an honest verdict, there is no disgrace.
We heard the clear testimony of Zeus,
and it said that Orestes should not suffer,
it was evidenced by the prophet-god himself.
Now you threaten this land with your terrible wrath, 800
but curb your anger, do not poison the soil
by smearing your demonic venom, and ploughing
this fecund earth into a barren wasteland.
I swear by Justice that you will receive your due re-
    spect.
I will give you a shrine of the earth in this righ-   805
    teous land
and seat you on gleaming thrones beside an altar,
where my citizens will worship you with honor.

[Antistrophe 1]

CHORUS:
*You young gods have ridden roughshod over
the ancient ways, wrenched them from our grasp.*

810 *We are dishonored, and dejected,*
and our anger rises to ravage the land.
Venom boiled from grief,
seeping from the seething hearts,
poison oozing on the earth,
sterile, stagnant pestilence
815 *polluting the ground. Oh Justice! Justice!*
Mortal infection will disease this place.
Ai, I lament, what will I do?
Scorned by the people,
unbearable mockery!
820 *Ill-fated daughters of Night*
you are cast out,
you are disgraced!

ATHENA:
You are not disgraced, control your rage,
825 you are gods, do not devastate mortal land.
I put my trust in Zeus, it goes without saying,
and I am the only other god who holds the key
to the treasury where he stores the thunderbolts.
But they are not needed, let me persuade you instead:
830 don't let your malicious tongues lash this land
and curse the bounteous earth with blight.
Soothe to sleep your dark tide of bitter fury,
for you will be revered in honor and live here with me.
This magnificent city will sacrifice the first rites
835 of birth and marriage to you forevermore.
I know you will come to bless these words.

[Strophe 2]

CHORUS:
I must suffer this? Ancient wisdom
buried deep down under this land,
dishonored and despised!
840 *All is rage, breathe the fury!*
Oh the fury!
Oh!
Ah, the pain! stabbing, side-splitting pain!
Ai, Mother Night!
845 *Honors gone, stripped away,*
the cheating gods have left us nothing!

ATHENA:
I will indulge your anger because you are my elders
and in this respect you possess greater wisdom.
850 But Zeus has made my mind for good,
and I know that if you leave for foreign lands

I promise your hearts will long for Athens.
Here the passage of time will lead to honor,
my people will enshrine you on stately thrones
next to the house of Erechtheus, and a sacred   855
procession of men and women will grace you
with gifts unsurpassed in the mortal realm.
Leave your gory grindstones that whet the appetite
for blood, and sicken the stomachs of the young
with intoxicating ferocity and bloodthirsty rage.   860
The gamecock's violent heart will never beat
in their breasts, and throb to the pulse of Ares,
that internal hemorrhage that bleeds civil war.
Let our battles be abroad and let them come,
they will quench our thirst for fame and glory.   865
I damn the bird that fights its own and fouls the nest.
This is the choice I offer, you must decide.
Do good, gain goodness, receive goodly honors,
and take your share of this land beloved by gods.

[Antistrophe 2]

CHORUS:
I must suffer this? Ancient wisdom   870
buried deep down under this land,
dishonored and despised!
All is rage, breathe the fury!
Oh the fury!
Oh!   875
Ah, the pain! stabbing, side-splitting pain!
Ai, Mother Night!
Honors gone, stripped away,
the cheating gods leave us nothing!   880

ATHENA:
I will not tire of telling you the benefits I offer,
I will not let you ancient goddesses claim
that a younger god and her city's people
banished you, branded as outcasts.
If you have any respect for the power of Persuasion   885
let my words soothe and enchant you
to decide to stay. But if you do choose to leave,
it would be unjust to bring down your anger,
rage, and destruction upon these people,
for I have offered you a share in this land,   890
bestowed by Justice with eternal honor.

CHORUS:
Lady Athena, where is the place that will be mine?

ATHENA:
It is a place free from pain and suffering. Will you
    accept it?

CHORUS:
And if I do, what honors await me?

ATHENA:
895 No house will prosper without your help.

CHORUS:
And you would really give me that power?

ATHENA:
I will flourish the fortune of all your worshipers.

CHORUS:
And will you promise this for all eternity?

ATHENA:
Yes, I do not promise what I cannot fulfill.

CHORUS:
900 Your charms are working, the rage is subsiding.

ATHENA:
Then live beneath this earth befriended by my people.

CHORUS:
What song would you have me sing for this land?

ATHENA:
Nothing discordant with our mutual victory,
a blessing reaped from the earth, swept by the sea,
905 breathed on the wind down from the sky, brushing
the land with balmy breezes touched by the sun.
Then the fruits of the earth and plentiful herds
will flourish for my people, an everlasting harvest,
conserving the human seed, sowing new life,
910 cultivating the pious to make the righteous thrive.
I grow good men like the caring gardener
protecting this noble strain from the blight of sorrow.
You could give such blessings as I tend to the arts
    of war
the glorious challenge, for my quest is this city's
915 victorious pride of place, admired by all mankind.

[Strophe 1]

CHORUS:
We accept a home in this land of Pallas.
We will not dishonor a city ruled by Ares,

defender of gods and Zeus Almighty.
This sentinel of the sacred sites of Greece   920
is beloved by all the immortals.
Now for Athens we too will pray,
and we foresee a future bright,
the flourish of abundant life
flowing out from a fecund land,   925
sparkling in the sun's kind light

ATHENA:
With a mind for my people I do this,
I root to our earth the mighty, the resolute,
I settle these spirits here in our land,
appointed to share the rule   930
of the affairs of mortal man.
Ignore their heavy hand and the blows
rain down through life. Why?
From where? Sins unredeemed,
crimes of old will come before them,   935
and for the loud boasts a silent ruin
as hateful anger grinds to dust.

[Antistrophe 1]

CHORUS:
We sing of the gifts we will give:
no storm-winds will strike at your trees,
no searing heat will ever burn   940
scorching the earth, blistering your buds.
We will banish the baneful blights
that once condemned the crops to death.
Let Pan bless all your flocks with twins,
at lambing time, born fit and strong.
May the earth herself give birth   945
to Hermes' horde of buried wealth,
Fortune's bounty given by gods.

ATHENA:
Guardians of the city, do you hear
what they will bring to pass?
The gods above and those below   950
know the power of a Fury,
how they work their ways
and bring fulfillment to all mankind.
A celebration, a cause to rejoice,
or a life blinded by a flood of tears.   955

[Strophe 2]

CHORUS:
The murderous man-killing stroke
we forbid from taking young life,
so that now the lovely young girls
may come to know the marriage rites.
960 *Grant this, you mighty gods,*
grant this, sister Destiny,
daughters of Mother Night,
spirits of Justice and Right.
You have a share in every house,
965 *you bear down on every season.*
Justice is your communion,
you are honored by every god.

ATHENA:
Your minds are for my people,
the promise of your powers pleases me.
970 *When I faced your harsh rejections*
dear Persuasion watched over me,
leading my lips, training my tongue.
Zeus of Good Council prevailed,
bringing a victory for both,
975 *for common good, forevermore.*

[Antistrophe 2]

CHORUS:
I pray that the clash of civil war,
that unrelenting devastation,
never rages across this land.
980 *Let dust not drink the citizen's blood,*
may slaughter not breed slaughter.
No more blood-crazed retribution,
for this city will never feed Ruin.
Now let joy pay debts of joy,
985 *a commonwealth for friend and foe,*
one joint spirit shared by all,
a cure for the sufferings of all mankind.

ATHENA:
You see? They speak their minds,
they have found the path of good.
990 *In these fearsome faces*
I see great gain for this city,
kind minds for kind minds.
Honor them forevermore
and steer this land, our city,
995 *down the path of righteousness.*

[Strophe 3]

CHORUS:
Rejoice, rejoice for the fortune of Destiny.
Rejoice people of this city,
placed so close to Zeus himself,
cherished by Athena's great love.
As time goes, discretion comes, 1000
for you sit beneath Athena's wings
and you will be admired by Zeus.

(Enter a group of women from the stage right wing, carrying torches and folded crimson cloaks.)

ATHENA:
Rejoice with me, as I lead the way,
lit by holy light, raised by loyal escorts.
Down to the sacred chamber, down beneath 1005
the earth blessed by solemn sacrifice.
Here to stem the rise of destruction,
here to grow great gain for the land,
and here to sow the seeds of victory!
Citizens of Athens, sons of Cranaus, 1010
lead these sacred guests, lead the way.
May the people bless them kindly
for the great good blessings that they bring.

[Antistrophe 3]

CHORUS:
Rejoice, rejoice again for the city!
Rejoice, let it ring out aloud! 1015
All those who inhabit here,
both the divine and the mortal,
twin powers of Athena's land,
hold us guests in high esteem
and let good fortune bless your lives. 1020

ATHENA:
I thank you for your prayers and the vows you make
as I escort you by the gleaming light of brilliant torches
to your new home deep beneath this earth.
Go with my women, the sentinels of my shrine,
come to the core of the city, the heart of Athens, 1025
as this glorious procession ascends the rock of Theseus.
Come children, women and venerable ladies,
clothe them in robes of honor steeped in crimson,
lead on the light, burn high the torches.
This communion of kindness shining on our land 1030
will reap an eternal harvest of great, good men.

(The Furies are covered in crimson cloaks and escorted in procession out of the orchestra through the stage right wing as the women sing, leading the way.)

[Strophe 1]

WOMEN:
On, on to your home, mighty glorious,
childless children of Night, our kind escort.
1035 *Sing the blessing song, people of this land.*

[Antistrophe 1]

Deep, deep down in the earth's ancient cavern
we sacrifice, we honor and worship.
Sing the blessing song, people gathered here.

[Strophe 2]

Your gentle minds will be kind to our land.   1040
Come now you solemn goddesses, follow
in delight the way of the torchlight's flame.
Raise the hallowed cry, join our blessing our song!

[Antistrophe 2]

The peace for both citizen and settler
will last forevermore. All-seeing Zeus   1045
and Destiny, unite to seal our truce.
Raise the hallowed cry, join our blessing song!

(Exit all as the procession is led offstage. Athena stands in the doorway as the doors are finally closed.)

END

Aristophanes
(c. 445–385 B.C.)

Clouds

Cast of Characters

STREPSIADES	a rural Athenian
PHEIDIPPIDES	son of Strepsiades
HOUSEBOY	of Strepsiades
STUDENTS	of Socrates
SOCRATES	a philosopher
CHORUS	of Clouds
SUPERIOR ARGUMENT	
INFERIOR ARGUMENT	
FIRST CREDITOR	
SECOND CREDITOR	
CHAEREPHON	a philosopher
XANTHIAS	servant to Strepsiades

SCENE: *A house in Athens.*

(An old man named Strepsiades and his son Pheidippides are asleep. Strepsiades is tossing and turning and muttering to himself until he finally wakes up with a start.)

STREPSIADES:
Oh! Oh!
Oh, Zeus almighty! What a night!
It's never-ending! It must be morning soon.
I thought I heard the cock crow hours ago.
Just listen to those blasted servants, snoring away,   5
back in my day they'd have never dared to sleep in.
Damn this stupid war! It'll ruin us. I can't even beat
     my own slaves anymore
in case they sneak off and hide out in enemy territory!

(Pointing to Pheidippides)

Just look at him, the "refined young gentleman," he'll
     never see the sunrise,

Reprinted from Aristophanes, *Clouds, Wasps, Birds,* translated, with notes, by Peter Meineck (Indianapolis: Hackett Publishing Company, 1998) by permission of the publisher.

10 he'll just carry on, blissfully farting away under his
   five fluffy blankets.
It's all right for some! Oh, I'll just try and bury my
   head and ignore the snoring.

*(Strepsiades tries to go back to sleep, he tosses and turns
and then angrily throws off the covers in frustration.)*

It's no good, I just can't sleep!
I'm being bitten by debts and eaten away by stable
   bills.
Why? Because of this long-haired son of mine,
15 and all his riding events and chariot races.
He lives, breathes, and dreams horses!
It's already the 20th day of the month,
and the interest is due on the 30th. I'm finished!

(He calls out to a slave.)

Boy! Light a lamp and fetch my ledger!
20 I need to count up my debts and calculate the interest.

*(A slave hurries from the stage right door with some tablets
and a lamp. He hands the tablets to Strepsiades and holds
the lamp so he can read the accounts.)*

Now then, let's have a look at these debts:
"Twelve hundred drachmas owed to Pasias." Twelve
   hundred drachmas!
What on earth was that for? Oh, gods, I remember
   now, a horse for Pheidippides!
Twelve hundred drachmas? Ouch! I think I was the
   one taken for a ride.

*(Pheidippides, dreaming of chariot races, mutters in his
sleep.)*

PHEIDIPPIDES:
25 Philon, you cheat, keep to your own lane!

STREPSIADES:
You hear that! That's the problem right there.
He's constantly at the races, even in his sleep!

PHEIDIPPIDES:
How many turns must the war chariots make?

STREPSIADES:
Enough to turn your father into a pauper!
30 "What terrible debt shall strike after Pasias' bills?
Three hundred drachmas owed to Amynias
for a running board and a new set of wheels!"

PHEIDIPPIDES:
Make sure my horse has a roll before he goes home!

STREPSIADES:
It's my money those damned horses are rolling in!
While I am saddled with lawsuits and debts
and my creditors can't wait to seize my property.   35

(Pheidippides wakes up.)

PHEIDIPPIDES:
What is it, father? Is it really necessary to spend
the entire night twisting and writhing about?

STREPSIADES:
I'm being bitten to death . . . by bed bailiffs!

PHEIDIPPIDES:
Please, father. I am trying to get some sleep!

(Pheidippides settles down back to sleep.)

STREPSIADES:
Go on then, sleep away, soon enough all this will   40
   be yours.
My debts will be on your head one day! Sleep away,
   my boy.
Oh, I wish I had never met your mother, and I hope
   whoever it was
who introduced us dies a horribly cruel death!
Ah yes, those were the days, a lovely country life,
full of simple rustic pleasures. An unwashed, un-
   shaven heaven,
abounding with honey bees, shaggy sheep, lashings   45
   of olive oil . . .
then I married the niece of Megacles, son of Megacles.
I was just a plain country boy, but she was from the city
and had all these refined and delicate ways. A proper
   little lady.
And when we were joined together as man and wife,
   I went to bed
smelling fresh and fruity, like ripe figs and new wool. 50
She smelled of fine perfume, golden saffron, sexy
   kisses,
extravagance and luxury. Aphrodite all over and everywhere Eros.
Mind you, I can't say that she's lazy, not at all, she
   knew how to weave,
If you know what I mean. In-out, in-out, she loved
   to poke the thread!
It got to the point that I had to hold up my gown,
   show the evidence,

55 and tell her that it would wear out if she kept on
    whacking it like that!

(Strepsiades lifts his gown to reveal a limp phallus.)

HOUSEBOY:
There's no oil left in the lamp.

STREPSIADES:
Why did you use the thirstiest lamp in the house?
You've earned a beating. Come here.

HOUSEBOY:
                    Why should I?

STREPSIADES:
Because you inserted a thick wick, that's why!

(The houseboy exits through the stage right door.)

60 Where was I? Oh yes. Well, soon enough we had
    a son,
and then my troubles really began. The wife and I
    could not agree
on a name for the boy. She wanted something upper-
    class and horsy,
a name with *hippus* in it, like "Xanthippus," "Chaerip-
    pus," or "Callippides."
But I wanted to name him Pheidonides after his
    grandfather,
a good old-fashioned thrifty name.
65 We argued for ages, then eventually we reached a
    compromise
and gave him the name Pheidippides.
When he was little she used to take him in her arms
    and say,
"When you grow up, you'll be a rich man like un-
    cle Megacles
70 and drive a chariot through the city wearing a beauti-
    ful golden robe."
But I would tell him, "When you're big you'll be just
    like your father
and drive goats down from the mountains, wearing
    a lovely leather jerkin."
But he never listened to a single word I said,
it was like flogging a dead horse, and now the house-
    hold accounts
75 have a severe case of "galloping consumption."
I've been up all night trying to concoct a plan to get
    me out of this mess,

and I have found one drastic course, an extraordinary,
    supernatural trail.
If I can only persuade the lad to take it, I'll be saved!
Now then, let me think what would be the gentlest
    way to wake him up . . . ?

(Strepsiades leans over and whispers in Pheidippides' ear.)

Pheidipoo, little Pheidipoo . . .   80

*(There is no response from Pheidippides, Strepsiades be-
comes frustrated and shouts.)*

PHEIDIPPIDES!

(Pheidippides wakes with a start.)

PHEIDIPPIDES:
What! What do you want, father?

STREPSIADES:
Give me a kiss and take my hand.

(He does so.)

PHEIDIPPIDES:
All right. What is it?

STREPSIADES:
Tell me, son, do you love me?

PHEIDIPPIDES:
By Poseidon, god of horses, of course I do!

STREPSIADES:
I don't want to hear about the god of horses!
He's the very reason that I'm in this mess.   85
Listen, son, if you really love me, will you do what
    I ask?

PHEIDIPPIDES:
What would you like me to do?

STREPSIADES:
Turn your life around, right now,
do what I say, and go and learn.

PHEIDIPPIDES:
Learn what?   90

STREPSIADES:
Will you do it?

PHEIDIPPIDES:
(Exasperated) I'll do it, by Dionysus!

STREPSIADES:

Great! Now look over there *(he points to the stage left door)*.

Can you see that tiny doorway and that funny little house?

PHEIDIPPIDES:

I see it, what are you showing me, father?

STREPSIADES:

95 That, my boy, is the house of clever souls, the Pondertorium.

The men who live there are able to talk us into believing

that the universe is a casserole dish that covers us all

and we are the hot coals, nestling inside.

What's more, for a small fee, these gentleman they will teach you

how to successfully argue any case, right or wrong.

PHEIDIPPIDES:

100 Who are these people?

STREPSIADES:

I'm not sure I know their names, but they are all gentlemen,

good and true, and fine philosophers of the finite.

PHEIDIPPIDES:

Ughh! I know who you mean, that godforsaken bunch

of pasty looking frauds, going around barefoot!

You're talking about Socrates and Chaerephon!

STREPSIADES:

105 Shut up! Stop talking like a baby.

Consider your father's daily bread, there'll be none left,

unless you give up horse racing and sign up for classes.

PHEIDIPPIDES:

No, by Dionysus, no! Not even if you gave me

a pair of Leogoras' finest pheasants!

STREPSIADES:

110 Please! My darling little boy, I beg you. Go and be taught.

PHEIDIPPIDES:

But what do I need to learn?

STREPSIADES:

I have heard it said, that in this house reside two different

kinds of argument, one is called the Superior Argument,

whatever that is, and the other is known as the Inferior Argument.

Some men say that the Inferior Argument can debate 115 an unjust case

and win. All you have to do is learn this Inferior Argument for me,

then you can talk your way out of all the debts I've incurred

on your behalf, and I won't have to repay a single obol!

PHEIDIPPIDES:

No, I won't do it! How could I bear to show my pallid face

to all my friends in the cavalry? Wild horses couldn't 120 drag me in there!

STREPSIADES:

Then get out of my house, by Demeter! You'll not get another crumb

out of me. And that goes for your chariot stallion and your branded

thoroughbred. I've had enough of your horsing around!

PHEIDIPPIDES:

I'll just go to uncle Megacles. He'll make sure

that I'm not without horse and home! 125

(Exit Pheidippides through the stage right door.)

STREPSIADES:

I'm not down and out yet! With the help of the gods,

I'll enroll at the Pondertorium and learn it all myself!

(Strepsiades strides off toward the stage left door, then slows down and stops.)

Oh, I'm just a stupid old fool. How on earth can I be expected

to learn all those hair-splitting arguments at my age?

I'm far too old, and my mind's certainly not what it 130 used to be.

(He turns around and sets off for the stage right door, then suddenly stops.)

No! I have to do it! It's my one and only chance.

No more delaying, I'm going to walk right up and knock on the door!

(He marches purposefully up to the stage left door, knocks hard, and shouts out.)

Boy! Boy! Where are you? Boy!

(The stage left door-hatch opens suddenly.)

STUDENT:
Go to Hell!

(The student slams the hatch shut. Strepsiades knocks on the door again, and the hatch reopens.)

Who's there?

STREPSIADES:
Strepsiades, son of Pheidon, from Cicynna.

STUDENT:
135 Obviously an uneducated idiot! Don't you realize that you thoughtlessly
banged away at the door with such force that you may well have caused
the miscarriage of a brilliant new idea on the verge of discovery!

STREPSIADES:
I'm very sorry, I'm from far away, in the country.
What was it that may have "miscarried"?

(The student furtively looks around, then leans in to whisper.)

STUDENT:
140 Only students may be told such things. It is the sacred law.

(Strepsiades mimics the student's movements and also whispers.)

STREPSIADES:
It's quite all right, you can tell me,
I've come to sign up as a student in the Pondertorium.

(The stage left door opens, and the student breaks into normal speech.)

STUDENT:
Very well, but remember these things are holy mysteries and must
be kept secret. Just now, Socrates asked Chaerephon how many
145 feet a flea could jump, calculating the equation of one flea foot for a foot.
This question came to Chaerephon's mind, as the flea in question
had just bitten his eyebrow and leapt onto Socrates' head.

STREPSIADES:
How did he measure the distance?

STUDENT:
Expertly. He dipped the flea's feet in some melted wax,
and when it had dried, he carefully removed the 150 molds,
producing a pair of Persian booties in miniature.
He was halfway through measuring the distance when you . . .

STREPSIADES:
Zeus almighty! What a delicate, subtle intellect!

STUDENT:
You should have heard the new concept that Socrates recently announced.

STREPSIADES:
What concept? Tell me, I beg you!   155

STUDENT:
Chaerephon of Sphettus asked Socrates to pronounce his opinion on an important scientific matter.

STREPSIADES:
What was that?

STUDENT:
Whether the hum of a gnat is generated via its mouth or its anus.

STREPSIADES:
Really? And what did he find out about the gnat?

STUDENT:
He said that the intestine of a gnat is extremely constricted 160
and that air is pressed through this narrow conduit to the anus,
then the sphincter, acting as an oscillating cavity in close proximity
to a compressed channel, is forced to issue a vibrating sound
as a direct result of the wind acting upon it.

STREPSIADES:
So a gnat's arse is a trumpet! Who'd have thought it? 165
What an amazing display of rectumology; really gutsy stuff!

I'm sure Socrates could easily fend off hostile legal actions
with such a deep understanding of arseholes.

STUDENT:
Yesterday he was robbed of a stupendous new idea
  by a speckled gecko.

STREPSIADES:
170 What? Tell me more.

STUDENT:
He was preoccupied studying the lunar revolutions,
and as he stood there gaping at the night sky,
a speckled gecko on the roof shat right on his head.

STREPSIADES:
(Laughing) A speckled gecko shitting on Socrates, I
  like that.

STUDENT:
175 Then, last evening there was nothing for supper.

STREPSIADES:
Really? So how did he think he was going to get
  some oats?

STUDENT:
First, he laid the table by sprinkling a thin layer of
  ash over it,
then he bowed a skewer to form a pair of compasses,
  picked up
the bent legs . . . from the wrestling school and stole
  his cloak!

STREPSIADES:
180 Amazing! And to think, some people still think highly
  of Thales!
Come on, open, open the Pondertorium!
Quickly, I want to see *him*. I want to meet Socrates!
I can't wait any longer, I'm dying to learn. Open
  the door!

(The central doors open and the ekkyklema is rolled out on-stage. A group of four pallid, barefooted and shabbily dressed students are revealed busy with various activities.)

By Heracles! What on earth are these creatures!

STUDENT:
185 You seem surprised. What do you think they are?

STREPSIADES:
They look like a bunch of half-starved walking
  wounded to me.

(Pointing to a group of the students)

Why are they staring at the ground?

STUDENT:
They are seeking to know what lies beneath the earth.

STREPSIADES:
I see, they're looking for onions to eat. They don't
  need to waste time
pondering about that, I know just where they can
  find some lovely big ones.
(Pointing to another group) Why are they bending over 190
  like that?

STUDENT:
They are probing the nether regions of Erebus deep
  beneath Tartarus.

STREPSIADES:
Really? So why are their arses pointing at the sky?

STUDENT:
They are simultaneously studying "arse-stronomy"!
(To the students) Back inside! He must not find you 195
  out here.

STREPSIADES:
Hold on! Not so fast. Let them stay awhile,
I'd like to probe them with a penetrating point.

(Exit the students on the ekkyklema, which moves back behind the doors.)

STUDENT:
Sorry. It's against all the rules. It's not good for them
to spend too much time outside, exposed to the
  fresh air.

(Strepsiades notices a strange array of ludicrous scientific instruments.)

STREPSIADES:
What, in the name of the gods, might these be?   200

STUDENT:
This is for astronomy.

STREPSIADES:
What's this for?

STUDENT:
Geometry.

STREPSIADES:
Geometry? What's that?

STUDENT:
It is the science of measuring the land.

STREPSIADES:
I see, to measure out plots for the landlords?

STUDENT:
No, to measure land generally.

STREPSIADES:
205 Lovely! What a very democratic mechanism.

(The student shows Strepsiades a large map.)

STUDENT:
This is a map of the entire world. Look, here is Athens.

STREPSIADES:
Don't be stupid, that can't be Athens!
Where are all the jurors and the law courts?

STUDENT:
I'm telling you, this area is clearly the region of Attica.

STREPSIADES:
210 So where's my deme then? Where's Cicynna?

STUDENT:
I don't know! Over there somewhere. You see here,
    that is Euboea,
the long island lying off the coast.

STREPSIADES:
Yeah, me and Pericles really laid those revolting bas-
    tards out!
Where's Sparta then?

STUDENT:
Right here.

STREPSIADES:
215 That's far too close! You need to move it immediately!
You had better reponder that one, mate!

STUDENT:
But it's simply not possible just to . . .

STREPSIADES:
Then you'll get a beating, by Zeus . . .

*(Enter Socrates suspended over the stage on a rack by the
stage crane.)*

Who on earth is that man hanging about up there?

STUDENT:
Himself.

STREPSIADES:
Who's "Himself"?

STUDENT:
Socrates.

STREPSIADES:
Socrates! Call him over for me, will you?   220

STUDENT:
You call him! I'm, eh . . . very busy.

(Exit the student scurrying off through the stage left door.)

STREPSIADES:
Socrates! Oh Socrates!

SOCRATES:
Why do you call me, ephemeral creature?

STREPSIADES:
Socrates! What are you doing up there?

SOCRATES:
I walk the air in order to look down on the sun.   225

STREPSIADES:
But why do you need to float on a rack to scorn
    the gods?
If you have to do it, why not do it on the ground?

SOCRATES:
In order that I may make exact discoveries of the
    highest nature!
Thus, my mind is suspended to create only ele-
    vated notions.
The grains of these thoughts then merge with the   230
    similar
atmosphere of thin air! If I had remained earthbound
and attempted to scrutinize the heights, I would
    have found
nothing; for the earth forces the creative juices to
    be drawn
to its core, depriving one of the all important "water
    on the brain"!

STREPSIADES:

235 Eh?

You mean, you need a good brainwashing to think such thoughts?

Oh my dear Socrates, you must come down at once.

You must teach me all the things that I have come to learn.

(Socrates is lowered to the ground.)

SOCRATES:

And just why have you come?

STREPSIADES:

I want to learn to debate.

240 I'm being besieged by creditors, all my worldly goods are under threat of seizure, the bailiffs are banging on my door!

SOCRATES:

Did you fail to realize you were amassing such enormous debts?

STREPSIADES:

Oh, I tried to keep things on a tight rein, but it was like closing

the stable door after the horse had bolted. I want you to teach me

that other Argument of yours, the one that never pays its dues.

245 Name your price, whatever it takes, I swear by the gods to pay you!

SOCRATES:

(Laughing) "Swear by the gods"? We don't give credit to the gods here.

STREPSIADES:

Then how do you make oaths? This all sounds very Byzantine to me.

SOCRATES:

250 Do you really want to know the truth regarding matters of religion?

STREPSIADES:

I do, by Zeus! Is that possible?

SOCRATES:

And do you wish communion with the Clouds, to actually speak to our divinities?

STREPSIADES:

Oh, yes please!

SOCRATES:

Then lie down on this sacred couch.

STREPSIADES:

(He does so.) I'm lying down. 255

SOCRATES:

Here, take this ritual wreath.

(Socrates hands him a shabby-looking wreath.)

STREPSIADES:

A wreath? Gods no! Socrates, I don't want to be sacrificed!

You're not going to make a meal out of me!

SOCRATES:

Don't worry, it's just a part of the initiation rites, everyone has to do it.

STREPSIADES:

What do I get out of it?

SOCRATES:

Why, you will become a polished public speaker, a 260 rattling castanet,

the "flour" of finest orators. Now hold still . . .

(Socrates sprinkles flour over Strepsiades.)

STREPSIADES:

By Zeus, I'm no powder puff! I know when I'm getting a good dusting!

SOCRATES:

Silence! Speak no ill words, old man, and heed my invocation.

O master, our lord, infinite Air, upholder of the buoyant earth.

O radiant Ether, O reverend thunder-cracking 265 Clouds, ascend!

Reveal yourselves, sacred ladies, emerge for those with higher thoughts!

STREPSIADES:

Wait, wait! I need to wrap myself up first so I don't get soaked.

Dammit! I knew I shouldn't have left home without a hat.

SOCRATES:
Come, you illustrious Clouds, come and reveal yourselves to this mortal.

270 From the sacred snow-capped crests of Olympus, from
the festive spiraling

dances of the Sea-Nymphs in the lush gardens of the
Ocean father;

from the shimmering waters of the Nile where you
dip your golden goblets;

from lake Maeotis or the icy heights of Mount Mimas.
Hear my prayer!

Receive our sacrifice and bless our sacred rites.

(The Clouds are heard offstage.)

CHORUS:
Arise, appear, ever-soaring Clouds,
275 *The shape of shimmering drops assume.*
From mountain slopes, where forests crowd,
280 *From ocean depths where breakers boom.*

Look down upon the vales and hills,
See sacred earth where showers splash.
The holy rivers where rainfall spills,
285 *The roaring sea's rush and dash.*

Shake off the rain and misty haze,
A shining radiance warms the sky.
Upon this earth the Clouds will gaze
290 *Under the tireless gleam of heaven's eye.*

SOCRATES:
Oh, magnificent, revered Clouds, you heard my summons. You came!

Did you hear that sound? Those bellowing godlike
thunderclaps?

STREPSIADES:
I revere you too, oh illustrious Clouds! Let me answer
your rumbling part

with a rumbling fart! You've put the wind up me all
right, I'm all a jitter!

295 I don't know if it's right or wrong, but I need to take
a thundering crap!

SOCRATES:
Will you stop messing about and behaving like one
of those wretched comic playwrights!

Speak no ill words, a mighty flurry of goddesses is on
the move, singing as they go.

*(The chorus begins to enter the orchestra from left and
right. Strepsiades still cannot see them.)*

CHORUS:
On to Athens, maidens bearing rain,
The hallowed land of Cecrops' race,   300
Where the initiates seek to attain
Acceptance to a sacred place.

The house of Mysteries for holy rites   305
And massive temples with statues grand.
The godly processions to sacred sites,
The splendid sacrifices that crown the land.

Celebrations held throughout the year   310
Then sweet Dionysus comes in spring.
And the resonant tone of the pipes we hear
As the joyous chorus dance and sing.

STREPSIADES:
Zeus! Socrates, you must tell me, who are these ladies singing

this amazing song? Are they some new breed of fe-   315
male idols?

SOCRATES:
No, no, no. They are the heavenly Clouds, magnificent goddesses for men

of leisure. They grace us with our intellect, argumen-
tative skills, perception,

hyperbolization, circumlocution, pulverization, and
predomination!

STREPSIADES:
That's why my spirit has soared at the sound of
their voices!

I'm raring to split hairs, quibble over windy intricac-   320
ies, set notion

against notion, and strike down arguments within
counterarguments!

Oh, Socrates, I can't wait any longer, I've just got to
see them!

SOCRATES:
Then look over here, up at Mount Parnes. Here they
come, delicately wafting down.

STREPSIADES:
Where? Where? I can't see! Show me.

SOCRATES:
There, there. Can you see them all? Floating down
over hill and dale,

Look, there wafting toward us, to the left and right.   325

STREPSIADES:
What on earth are you talking about! I can't see anything!

SOCRATES:
Look there, in the wings!

STREPSIADES:
Yes, I think I . . . I can just about make something out.

SOCRATES:
Are you completely blind! Surely you can see them
   now?

   (The chorus is now assembled in the orchestra.)

STREPSIADES:
By Zeus! The Illustrious ones themselves, they're everywhere, all around us!

SOCRATES:
And to think that you never knew they were goddesses,
   you had no faith.

STREPSIADES:
330 I thought they were just a load of old vapor, all drizzle
   and fog!

SOCRATES:
Exactly, because you were unaware that they cultivate
   a slew of sophisticated scholars;
Prophets from the colonies, atmospheric therapists,
   long-haired loungers with jangling jewelry,
creators of complex, convoluted compositions, ethereal, immaterial, vacuous visionaries!
Intangible, insubstantial idleness sustained by waxing
   lyrical about the Clouds!

STREPSIADES:
335 Oh, I see! That's why they utter things like "the men-
   acing storm clouds advance, edged
with silver linings" and then call them "the billowing
   locks of hundred-headed Typhon,"
"furious gusts," "sky-borne cisterns," "jagged clawed
   birds soaring through the air,"
and sing about "torrents pouring down from rain filled
   clouds," and for that load
of hot air they get rewarded with beautiful fillets of
   fish and lovely little roasted thrushes!

SOCRATES:
340 Just think, it's all due to the Clouds.

STREPSIADES:
But if they are supposed to be Clouds, why do they
   look like women?
What happened? The Clouds up in the sky don't
   look like that.

SOCRATES:
Well, what do they look like?

STREPSIADES:
I don't really know just how to describe them exactly.
   Like a flock of woolly sheepskin rugs,
certainly not like women. I've never seen a Cloud
   with a nose before.

SOCRATES:
Really? Then answer this one question.   345

STREPSIADES:
Ask away.

SOCRATES:
Have you ever looked up at the Clouds and thought
   that they seemed
to assume the shape of, say a centaur, perhaps a
   leopard, or even a bull?

STREPSIADES:
I have, but so what?

SOCRATES:
The Clouds can assume any form they please. If they
   should happen to look down and spy
some long-haired, unkempt uncivilized type, say the
   son of Xenophantus, for example,
then they assume the form of a centaur in recognition 350
   of his true heart's desire.

STREPSIADES:
Ha! Then what if they see that fraudster, Simon, who
   robbed the public funds?

SOCRATES:
Then they assume his true likeness and turn into
   wolves.

STREPSIADES:
Oh! Now I know why they looked like a herd of deer
   the other day.
They must have recognized Cleonymus, the shield-
   shedder, for the cowardly bastard that he is.

SOCRATES:

355   Precisely, and now they have obviously just seen
      Cleisthenes, hence they become women!

STREPSIADES:

Oh, hail divine ladies! Please do for me what you do
   for others,
sing a song to reach the very heights of heaven.

CHORUS:

(To Strepsiades) Hail, O geriatric one, you who quest
   for artful words.
(To Socrates) Hail priest of pedantic prattle, what would
   you bid us do?
360   There are only two ethereal experts we hearken to:
Prodicus for his sheer wisdom and knowledge,
and you, for the way you strut around like a grand
   gander,
roll your eyes, go barefoot, endure all, and hold such
   high opinions.

STREPSIADES:

Good Earth! What vocals! Wondrous, sacred, marvelous!

SOCRATES:

365   You see, these are the only true gods, everything else
      is utter nonsense.

STREPSIADES:

What about Zeus? How can Olympian Zeus not be
   a god?

SOCRATES:

Zeus? Don't be absurd! Zeus doesn't exist.

STREPSIADES:

What are you saying? Who is it that makes rain, then?

SOCRATES:

Why, the Clouds of course! I'll prove it to you. Does
   it ever rain
370   without Clouds? No, and you would have thought
      that Zeus could
have made rain on his own if he so desired, without
   the help of the Clouds.

STREPSIADES:

And I always thought it was Zeus pissing through
   a sieve!
You certainly have a way with words, that makes
   complete sense.

But hold on, who makes the thunder that makes me
   shake in teror?

SOCRATES:

It is just the Clouds rocking in the sky.   375

STREPSIADES:

Is nothing sacred! How do they do that?

SOCRATES:

Simple. When they become completely saturated
   with moisture, they are forced
by Necessity to begin to oscillate to and fro. Every
   now and again they ram each other
and of course, being packed with precipitation,
   CRASH! A cloudburst!

STREPSIADES:

But surely someone must force them to move in the
   first place. That must be Zeus.

SOCRATES:

Not at all, it is the whirling of the Celestial Basin!   380

STREPSIADES:

Basin? So Zeus is no more and Basin is king now,
   is he?
But you haven't explained who it is that makes the
   thunder.

SOCRATES:

Listen! The Clouds become full of water and crash
   into each other,
thus they emit a thundering sound because of their
   sheer density.

STREPSIADES:

Do you seriously expect me to believe that?   385

SOCRATES:

Then allow me to demonstrate, using you as my
   example. Have you ever been
at the Panathenaea Festival, and eaten too much
   soup? What happened?
Your stomach suddenly became upset and started to
   rumble, yes?

STREPSIADES:

Yes, by Apollo. It grumbles and groans with all that
   soup sloshing around,
and then it makes a noise that sounds just like thunder. First of all

390 it's just a little splutter . . . Phuurrrt! Then it gets a
    bit louder . . . PHHUuuuurrtt!
And when I finally get to take a shit, it really thunders
    just like those clouds . . .
      . . . PHHHAAAARRRRAAARRRAAATTT!

SOCRATES:
My dear old fellow, if a tiny stomach such as yours
    can emit such a fart,
just think what a colossal thunder the vast atmosphere
    can produce.

STREPSIADES:
Yes, thunder and farter, they even sound the same.
395 But what about those flashing, fiery shafts of lightning
    that can burn
us to a crisp or at the least give us a good grilling
    every now and then?
Surely that is Zeus' instrument against oath-breakers.

SOCRATES:
You blithering, prehistoric, pre-cronian old fool!
If Zeus smites oath-breakers, why has he not inciner-
    ated Simon,
Cleonymus, or Theorus? They couldn't break more
    oaths if they tried!
Instead he strikes the temple at Cape Sunium and
400   turns his own oak trees to charcoal.
Everyone knows that an oath as solid as oak can't be
    broken. What was he thinking?

STREPSIADES:
I don't know, but it all sounds very convincing. So
    what's a thunderbolt then?

SOCRATES:
When an arid gust is blown up above and becomes
    trapped inside the clouds,
405 it tends to inflate them rather like a bladder; the sheer
    volume of air causes
the clouds to explode, and the compressed hot wind
    is forced out with such
terrific energy that in the process it bursts into sponta-
    neous flame.

STREPSIADES:
The exact same thing happened to me once at the
    Diasia feast.
I was cooking a nice big sausage for the family, and
    I completely

forgot to prick it. Well, it swelled right up and sud- 410
    denly BANG!
It blew up right in my face, and showered me with
    hot blood and fat!

CHORUS:
You come craving knowledge of the highest kind
So the Greeks will call you Athens' mastermind.
If you possess a brain fit for cogitation
And can suffer cold, stress, and deprivation.   415
If you can pace about and stand for hours
Not drink nor train by sheer willpower,
If you hold the clever soul in high regard,
Battling by the tongue will not be hard.

STREPSIADES:
My mind never rests, I'm as tough as old boots.   420
I've a mean, lean stomach, and I can live on roots.
Fear not, there's nothing that this body can't
    handle;
I'm ready to temper my spirit upon your anvil!

SOCRATES:
And do you repudiate all other gods, except those
    we venerate,
the holy trinity of Chaos, Clouds, and a confident
    tongue?

STREPSIADES:
I wouldn't even speak to a god if I met one, and you 425
    won't catch me
sacrificing, pouring libations, or burning incense on
    any of their altars.

CHORUS:
Then tell us, what is it you would like us to do for
    you? We will not fail you,
not if you pay us due honor and respect and come
    in search of knowledge.

STREPSIADES:
Reverend ladies! It's just a tiny little thing that I ask
    of you;
I wish to be the finest speaker in all of Greece, a 430
    hundred times over!

CHORUS:
So be it. From this day henceforth no man shall
    ever pass
more motions in the public assembly than you . . .

STREPSIADES:
No, no, no! I'm not interested in politics and carrying
    on in the assembly!
I want to twist Justice around and escape the clutches
    of my creditors.

CHORUS:
435 Then you will have your heart's desire, it is but a
    small thing you require.
Just place yourself into the hands of our leading dev-
    otees.

STREPSIADES:
I'll do it! I have to! I've got no choice, you see!
The horses and my marriage will be the death of me!

So here I am, take me now, I'm yours!
440 *Beat me, bruise me, it's in a very good cause.*
I'll starve, not bathe, shiver, shake, and freeze,
Feel free to tan my hide as often as you please!

I'll do anything to avoid the paying of my debts,
And men will come to realize my newly won assets.
445 *I'll be dangerous, mad, and devil-may-care,*
A low-down dirty liar, driven to despair!

A courthouse junkie blessed with the gift of gab,
A barrack-room lawyer and a filthy, oily rag!
450 *A chiseler, a shyster, a bullshitter and cheat,*
A miscreant, a twister, and a master of deceit!

Feed me on chop logic, I'll feast on your split hairs,
And all those who meet me should take extra care.
455 *So now I've told you what it is I yearn to be,*
Serve me to your students and make mincemeat out
    of me!

CHORUS:
I can't help but admire
his sheer strength of character.
Let me tell you this,
460 If you learn your lessons well,
Your very name will reach up
to resound in the heights of heaven!

STREPSIADES:
Then what lies in store for me?

CHORUS:
For the rest of your days you will be
the most blessed and envied of all men.   465

STREPSIADES:
Really?

CHORUS:
Of course!
Crowds will gather at your door
clamoring for any opportunity
to actually get to talk to you.   470
They'll all come in supplication,
seeking your sage advice.
You'll help them to decide vitally important
and extravagantly expensive issues,
issues suited to such an intellect as yours.   475
Now to enroll this old man in our educational
    program;
it is time to stimulate his mind and test his knowledge.

SOCRATES:
So, tell me a little about yourself.
I need to understand your particular personality traits.
Then I can correctly determine the best tactics to   480
    deploy.

STREPSIADES:
Tactics? Are you planning to lay siege to me?

SOCRATES:
No, no, I just want to analyze you a little.
Now then, are you in possession of a powerful
    memory?

STREPSIADES:
Well, that all depends. If someone owes me money,
it is quite superb, but if, on the other hand, I owe   485
    money,
then I'm afraid it has a tendency to let me down.

SOCRATES:
Then perhaps you have a particular penchant for
    oral recitation?

STREPSIADES:
(Laughing) Me? I'm certainly reticent to pay my
    debts!

SOCRATES:
Look, how on earth do you expect to learn anything?

STREPSIADES:
Oh, don't be such a worrier, I'll get the hang of it.

SOCRATES:
All right then, make sure that whenever I throw out some juicy bits
490   of heavenly wisdom that you snatch them up right away.

STREPSIADES:
(Laughing) What do you take me for, a dog?

SOCRATES:
You utter, uneducated barbarian oaf!
We may well have to beat some sense into this old fool.
Tell me, what would you do if someone were to hit you?

STREPSIADES:
495   I'd fall over! And I'd stay down too, at least until a witness
came along. Then I'd go and file assault charges
and get a hefty out-of-court settlement or some nice damages!

SOCRATES:
Remove your outer garment.

STREPSIADES:
What for, am I in trouble already?

SOCRATES:
No, all new initiates must disrobe.

STREPSIADES:
But, I promise I won't steal anything inside.

SOCRATES:
500   Just take the damn thing off, will you!

(Strepsiades takes off his tunic and gives it to Socrates, leaving him naked except for a loincloth.)

STREPSIADES:
If I work really hard and attend to my studies,
which of your followers can I ever hope to be like?

SOCRATES:
You should try to be like Chaerephon.

STREPSIADES:
Good gods no, I'll be as good as dead!

SOCRATES:
Will you please stop jabbering away.   505
Get a move on and follow me!

STREPSIADES:
All right, all right, but at least put a honey cake in my hand,
I'm scared, it's like descending into Trophonius' grotto.

SOCRATES:
Stop dilly-dallying at the door and come on!

(Enter Socrates and Strepsiades into the Pondertorium through the stage left door.)

CHORUS:
Good luck to this brave soul   510
Embarking on his quest,
Though he's old and gray
I know he'll do his best.
A dyed-in-the-wool spirit
Dipping into new ideas,   515
Such a radical education
For a man of advanced years.

[Parabasis]

(The chorus leader addresses the audience, speaking for Aristophanes.)

CHORUS:
Dear audience, allow me to speak candidly for a moment.
It is time to hear the truth, sworn by Dionysus, the very deity
that nurtured my rare talent and raised me to win 520
   great dramatic victories.
I thought that you were an intelligent audience, I thought that you would
truly enjoy this, the most intellectual of all my comedies.
I sweated night and day over a hot script to serve up to you
the very first taste of the fruits of my labor. But look what happened.
I was utterly defeated, thwarted by those other vile, 525
   despicable hacks!
And it is you people who must bear the blame for this disgrace,

for you should have known better. I did it all for you,
  and just look how you chose

to repay me! But never fear, I will always be here for
  those with the good taste

to fully appreciate the quality of my work. It was here,
  in this very theatre,

that my tale of the righteous boy and the little bugger
530   was so very well received.

It is true that I was not yet of an age to mother properly
  such a child, and so I exposed

my prodigy to be adopted by another in my stead.
  Then you, dear audience, you all

became its foster parents, it was you who nurtured it,
  you raised it.

Ever since then I have held you all in the highest
  esteem, and I always

swore by your sound judgment and prudent wisdom.
535   And now like Electra,

this comedy comes searching, hoping, seeking an
  audience equal in wit and intelligence,

and like the hair on Orestes' head, she'll know them
  when she sees them!

Contemplate for a moment, if you will, the value of
  her discreet sensibilities.

She does not dangle one of those huge, red-tipped ap-
  pendages

540   between her legs to get cheap laughs from the children among you.

She doesn't make rude jibes at the expense of bald
  men, and she categorically refuses

to perform any kind of suggestive dances. You will
  never see her leading actor

dressed up as an old man, running around, hitting
  all and sundry with a stick

to divert your attention from the poor quality of the
  rotten old jokes! What's more

you will certainly not encounter anybody charging
  onstage with flaming torches,

545   shouting Oh! Oh! No, this play comes here today
  trusting only in itself and its poetry,

and I, the playwright, am cast from the same mold.
  I have always been bold

(bold, not bald—I know I'm bald!), and I have never
  ever attempted to bamboozle you

by rehashing the same tired old material time and
  time again. No, I devote

every strain of my poetic fiber to the invention of
  brand new, cutting-edge comedy.

Every play has something different, something innovative, vivacious, and skillful.

When Cleon was at the peak of his powers, I slugged   550
  him in the stomach,

but I never hit the man when he was down. But just
  look at my rivals and how they

treated Hyperbolus, they walked all over him, not to
  mention the punishment they

dealt out to his poor old mother! It all started with
  Eupolis and that dreadful farce

of his, *Maricas*, blatant plagiarism! A disgusting imitation of my *Knights* with the totally

unnecessary addition of an inebriated old hag crudely
  gyrating in the dances.   555

The very same character, might I add, that we saw
  Phrynichus present

in his comedy about the women being fed to the
  sea creature!

Then came Hermippus, and his vicious attacks on
  Hyperbolus.

Soon everyone jumped on the Hyperbolus band
  wagon and were happily

dishing out the dirt, and worst of all stealing all my   560
  best eel gags!

If you find that kind of drivel amusing, you will never
  fully appreciate my work,

but those who enjoy my comedic innovations will be
  considered wise in years to come.

Zeus the highest god of all,
Greatest ruler, hear our call.

Come, Poseidon, with trident flashing,   565
From salty depths with breakers crashing.

The sky-father that witnessed our birth
Most sacred nurturer of life on earth.   570

The charioteer who fills our days,
With the light, heat, and brilliant rays.

To god and mortal, great power advance,
We call you all to join our dance!

  (The Clouds address the audience.)

Attention please, audience! It is time to prick your   575
  collective conscience.

You have performed us a great disservice, and we are
  here to chastise you for it!

No deity gives more to this city than we, and yet you
    fail to pay us the slightest respect!
We are the ones who are ever-present, and we con-
    stantly have your best interests
at heart, but you never pour us any libations or even
    offer a single sacrifice!
580 When you are about to embark on some futile armed
    campaign, we bellow noisily
and send sheets of rain. When you were holding
    elections for general and chose
that damned Paphlagonian tanner, we frowned down
    and thundered our dissent.
"Such sheets of fire, such bursts of horrid thunder."
    Even the moon reversed
585 her course, and the very sun in the sky snuffed his
    great wick and announced
that he would not rekindle his heavenly light if you
    nominated Cleon as General!
But in spite of everything, you still went ahead and
    voted for the man!
It has been said that bad decisions run rife in this
    city, and yet somehow the gods
always conspire to make everything turn out for the
    best. It is the same in this instance,
590 for there is a simple solution to turn this terrible error
    of judgment to your advantage.
Just go ahead and indict that gannet Cleon on charges
    of fraud and embezzlement,
clap him in the stocks, and lock him up. Lo and
    behold, out of your previous folly
shall come your salvation, everything will be as before,
back the way things were, to the very great benefit of
    your city.

595 *Come, Phoebus Apollo, lord of Delos,*
Leave Cynthus' rocks and come to us.

Come, Artemis, leave your house of gold,
Worshipped by Lydian daughters age-old.

600 *Goddess of the Aegis, protector of our city,*
Lady Athena, held in highest sanctity.

From Parnassus' towering heights,
Setting ablaze his pine torch light,

605 *The Bacchants of Delphi, wild and joyous,*
Come, festive god, come, Dionysus.

LEADER:
When we were on our way here, we happened to
    meet the Moon,
who told us to relay her benedictions to the Athenians
    and their allies.
However, she also informed us that she is very cross 610
    with you
and that you have treated her with disrespect, de-
    spite all
the wonderful things she has done for you all. Just
    think, she saves
you at least a drachma a month for all the torches
    you have no need of.
She's heard you telling your houseboys, "Don't bother
    with the lamp
tonight, my lad, the moonlight's nice and bright."   615
She does that for you and a lot more besides! She
    also informed us
that she is most displeased with all this fiddling about
    with the lunar cycle,
she says it is playing absolute havoc with the calendar,
    and she has received numerous
complaints from angry gods who have been cheated
    out of their due festival days!
To top it all, on sacred sacrificial days you are going 620
    around, torturing people
and sitting in court passing judgment when you
    should be worshipping.
There have even been times when the gods were
    partaking in a solemn memorial
service to Memnon or Sarpedon while you lot were
    pouring libations, drinking
and cavorting about all over the city—disgraceful!
    That is why Hyperbolus,
your elected religious remembrancer, had his wreath 625
    removed by the gods.
Now he knows that you should arrange your dates in
    concordance with the moon!

(Enter Socrates from the stage left door.)

SOCRATES:
By Breath, by Chaos, by Air!
I have never before encountered such a feeble-
    minded,
imbecilic, slow-witted country bumpkin in all my life!
He forgets the tiniest scraps of knowledge   630
before he's even had a chance to learn them!

(Calling into the Pondertorium)

Strepsiades! Come on out here, into the light,
Hurry up, and bring the couch with you.

*(Enter Strepsiades, still seminaked, from the stage left
door carrying a small couch. Like Socrates, he is now
barefoot.)*

STREPSIADES:
No need, the flea-infested thing can get up and walk
out on its own!

SOCRATES:
635 Put it down over there and listen carefully.

STREPSIADES:
All right.

SOCRATES:
Good, let's get started. Which facet of your intellect
do you wish to develop?
Perhaps you would like to use this opportunity to
master a subject you never had
the opportunity to learn before? Meter? Rhythm?
Scales?

STREPSIADES:
Scales! Only the other day that bastard grain merchant
640 fiddled me out of a full two measures!

SOCRATES:
Not those kind of scales, you idiot! I'm attempting to
engage you in a discussion
on music and poetry. Now, consider which measure
is more aesthetically pleasing,
the three-quarter beat or the four-quarter beat?

STREPSIADES:
Personally, I think the pint takes some beating!

SOCRATES:
Will you stop babbling such utter nonsense!

STREPSIADES:
645 It's not nonsense, everyone knows four quarts makes
a pint!

SOCRATES:
Oh damn you! You illiterate uneducated peasant!
Let's at least see if you can learn something about
rhythm.

STREPSIADES:
Rhythm? How is learning about rhythm going to buy
me barley?

SOCRATES:
A detailed knowledge of rhythm enables you to socialize effectively in polite
company and seem refined and cultured. You'll know   650
all about martial modes
and dactylic meter . . .

(Strepsiades looks confused.)

Beating the rhythm with your fingers!

STREPSIADES:
I know how to beat with my fingers, by Zeus!

SOCRATES:
You do? Tell me about it.

STREPSIADES:
Well when I was a young lad it was this . . .

(Strepsiades grabs and shuffles his phallus.)

SOCRATES:
Gods! You are nothing but a village idiot!   655

STREPSIADES:
You're the idiot, I don't want to learn any of this stuff.

SOCRATES:
Well, what DO you want to learn?

STREPSIADES:
The other thing, you know *(whispering)*: the Wrong
Argument.

SOCRATES:
That's an advanced class, you can't just start there,
you have to master the basics first,
such as the correct gender affiliation of certain types
of quadrapedic livestock.

STREPSIADES:
Livestock! I'm an expert. Let's see, masculine: 660
ram, billy-goat, bull, dog, chicken . . .

SOCRATES:
And the feminine?

STREPSIADES:
Ewe, nanny-goat, cow, bitch, chicken . . .

SOCRATES:
Aha! You called both the male and the female chicken.
You can't do that!

STREPSIADES:
What do you mean?

SOCRATES:
You said "chicken" and "chicken."

STREPSIADES:
665 By Poseidon, you're right! Well, what should I have said?

SOCRATES:
Chicken . . . and chickeness!

STREPSIADES:
Chickeness? That's a good one, by Air!
For just that single piece of learning
I should fill your meal-kneader with barley oats.

SOCRATES:
670 You've done it again, said another one. You used the masculine form
for meal-kneader, but it really should be feminine.

STREPSIADES:
What? I made a meal-kneader masculine?

SOCRATES:
Yes, just like Cleonymus.

STREPSIADES:
What do you mean?

SOCRATES:
Meal-kneader and Cleonymus are treated in the same manner.

STREPSIADES:
675 But Socrates, Cleonymus doesn't even own a meal kneader.
His "needs" are met by having his oats delivered by the back door,
if you, eh, know what I mean! What should I call it from now on?

SOCRATES:
The feminine form, that is "fe-meal kneader."

STREPSIADES:
So a meal-kneader needs a female to be a fe-meal kneader?

SOCRATES:
Exactly.

STREPSIADES:
I see, so I should have said, Cleonymus never needed   680
a female?

SOCRATES:
Yes. Well then, we must still educate you on proper names.
You need to know which are masculine and which are feminine.

STREPSIADES:
I know which are feminine all right.

SOCRATES:
Go on then.

(Strepsides lustfully imagines a group of well-known Athenian beauties.)

STREPSIADES:
Lysilla (*Wow wee!*), Philinna (*Oh yeah!*), Cleitagora (*Hubba, hubba*), and Demetria (*Ow!*).

SOCRATES:
And the masculine names?   685

(He imagines a collection of effeminate young men.)

STREPSIADES:
There's plenty: Philoxenus (*Luvvie!*), Melesias (*Big Boy!*), Amynias (*Hello sailor!*) . . .

SOCRATES:
Those are hardly masculine!

STREPSIADES:
You don't think they're masculine?

SOCRATES:
Absolutely not. If you saw Amynias, just how would you call out to him?

STREPSIADES:
Like this. "Coo-ee! Coo-ee! Amynia luvvie! Amynia   690
darling!"

SOCRATES:
I rest my case. You are clearly calling out to him like
   a woman,
and what's more, "Amynia" is feminine.

STREPSIADES:
That's what the old poof gets for dodging the draft.
But everyone knows Amynias is an old woman, I don't
   need to be taught that.

SOCRATES:
Be quiet by Zeus! Now lie down on the couch there.

STREPSIADES:
What for?

SOCRATES:
695   You need to concentrate on personal matters.

STREPSIADES:
No, I'm begging you! Don't make me lie down there.
   I can just as easily
do my personal concentrating on the bare earth!

SOCRATES:
I'm sorry, you simply have no choice.

STREPSIADES:
Oh no! Those fleas are going to have a field day
   feasting on me!

(Exit Socrates through the stage left door.)

CHORUS:
700   *So philosophize and cogitate,*
Intellectualize and ruminate.
Twist your thoughts, your mind must bend,
Through mental blocks and each dead end.
Let ideas jump and concepts fly,
705   *Don't let sweet sleep close your eyes.*

STREPSIADES:
Oh! Woe! Oh! Woe!

CHORUS:
What pains thee, art thou smitten?

STREPSIADES:
Misery! Agony! I'm being bitten!
They're leaping off this bed and biting
710   *Like Corinthians fleeing from the fighting!*
They've been gnawing on my bones all day,
They're sucking all my blood away!
They've champed my bollocks all red raw,

My poor old arse has never felt this sore!
These bugs will chew me half to death . . .   715

CHORUS:
I suggest you give that moaning a rest!

STREPSIADES:
Some hope you are, what bad advice!
I've lost money and health for a load of lice!
My very soul is bruised and beaten,
My clothes and shoes are all moth eaten.   720
So I sing to keep my spirits high,
But it's all over now, the end is nigh!

(Enter Socrates through the stage left door.)

SOCRATES:
What are you doing? You are supposed to be contemplating.

STREPSIADES:
I am, by Poseidon.

SOCRATES:
And just what, pray, have you been contemplating?

STREPSIADES:
I've been contemplating my future, once these bugs   725
   have finished me off!

SOCRATES:
Go to hell!

STREPSIADES:
Hell's right, chum! That's exactly what this is.

CHORUS:
Don't be so fainthearted, cover yourself up
and devise some fraudulent and illicit affair.

STREPSIADES:
Oh, if only instead of these lambskin covers,
I could get into an illicit affair!   730

*(Strepsiades covers himself up and lies on the couch. He
wriggles about, and then the covers rise, propped up by his
phallus. Socrates reenters.)*

SOCRATES:
All right, let's see how he's doing.
You there! Are you sleeping?

(Strepsiades pops his head out from under the fleece.)

STREPSIADES:
No, by Apollo, not me, no.

SOCRATES:
Have you been able to get a good grasp on anything?

STREPSIADES:
Eh . . . well, no, not really.

SOCRATES:
Nothing whatsoever?

STREPSIADES:
Well, my right hand has a good grasp on my prick
at the moment.

(Strepsiades removes the covers to reveal his erect phallus.)

SOCRATES:
735 Oh, by all the gods! Cover yourself up at once and
think about something else!

STREPSIADES:
But what? Tell me, Socrates, please.

SOCRATES:
No, you must discover that for yourself, then tell me
what it is you want.

STREPSIADES:
But you know very well what I want, I've told you a
thousand times:
It's my debts, I want to get out of paying them off!

SOCRATES:
740 All right then, cover yourself up and dissect your sup-
positions
into microscopic elements. Then consider the matter
in minute detail
thus arriving at a correct analysis derived from an
orthodox methodology.

*(Strepsiades pulls the fleece over his head and fidgets for a
while before lying down.)*

STREPSIADES:
Ohh! Ahh!

SOCRATES:
Stop fidgeting! Now, should your concept place you
in a quandary
move on, free your mind, then the idea can be set
in motion
745 once the innermost recesses of your intellect have
been unlocked.

(Strepsiades uncovers himself.)

STREPSIADES:
My beloved Socrates!

SOCRATES:
What is it?

(Strepsiades gets up on his feet and runs toward Socrates.)

STREPSIADES:
I've thought of an illicit idea for avoiding my debts!

SOCRATES:
Do divulge.

STREPSIADES:
Tell me this . . .

SOCRATES:
What, what?

STREPSIADES:
What if I got hold of a witch from Thessaly
and made her magic the moon out of the sky.   750
I could put it away in a dressing case like a mirror,
and hide it where no one would ever find it.

SOCRATES:
But how would that help you?

STREPSIADES:
How? If I stopped the moon from rising, then I
would never
have to pay the interest on any of my debts.   755

SOCRATES:
Why ever not?

STREPSIADES:
Because interest is always due at the end of the month,
when the new moon appears!

SOCRATES:
I see, here's another situation to consider. What would
you do
if a lawsuit was written up against you for five talents
in damages?
How would you go about having the case removed
from the record?

STREPSIADES:
Er, I've no idea, let me have a think about it.   760

(Strepsiades goes back under the fleece.)

SOCRATES:
Be sure not to constrict your imagination by keeping
    your thoughts wrapped up.
Let your mind fly through the air, but not too much.
    Think of your creativity
as a beetle on a string, airborne, but connected, flying,
    but not too high.

(He pops up from under the cover.)

STREPSIADES:
I've got it! A brilliant way of removing the lawsuit!
You're going to love this one.

SOCRATES:
765 Tell me more.

STREPSIADES:
Have you seen those pretty, see-through stones that
    the healers sell?
You know, the ones they use to start fires.

SOCRATES:
You mean glass.

STREPSIADES:
That's the stuff! If I had some glass, I could secretly
    position myself behind
770 the bailiff as he writes up the case on his wax tablet.
    Then I could aim the sun rays
at his docket and melt away the writing so there would
    be no record of my case!

SOCRATES:
Sweet charity! How "ingenious."

STREPSIADES:
Great! I've managed to erase a five-talent lawsuit.

SOCRATES:
Come on, then, chew this one over.

STREPSIADES:
775 I'm ready.

SOCRATES:
You're in court, defending a suit, and it looks like
    you will surely lose.
It's your turn to present your defense, and you have
    absolutely no witnesses.
How would you effectively contest the case and, more-
    over, win the suit itself?

STREPSIADES:
Easy!

SOCRATES:
Let's hear it then.

STREPSIADES:
During the case for the prosecution,   780
I would run off home and hang myself!

SOCRATES:
What are you talking about?

STREPSIADES:
By all the gods, it's foolproof! How can anybody sue
    me when I'm dead?

SOCRATES:
This is preposterous! I've had just about enough of
    this!
You'll get no more instruction from me.

STREPSIADES:
But Socrates, in the name of heaven, why not?

SOCRATES:
Because if I do manage to get something through to   785
    you, it is instantly
forgotten. Here, I'll prove it. What was the first thing
    I taught you?

STREPSIADES:
Mmmm, the first lesson, hang on, let me think, what
    was that, eh,
something female where we scatter our oats, oh I
    don't know!

SOCRATES:
You fossilized, forgetful old fool! Just piss off!   790

(Exit Socrates in disgust through the stage left door.)

STREPSIADES:
Oh no! I'm finished. This is terrible!
If I don't learn tongue-twisting, then I'm lost without
    a hope!
Clouds! You have to help me out. What can I do?

CHORUS:
You have a grownup son, don't you?
If you take our advice,   795
you will send him to take your place.

STREPSIADES:
Yes, I've a son, a refined, lovely lad, but he's not interested
in higher education. What else can I do?

CHORUS:
He's your son, is he not? Who is master of your house?

STREPSIADES:
800 Well, he's a passionate, spirited boy from a fine family,
the house of Coesyra, no less. But you're right, it's high time
I set him straight, and if he says no, then he's out on his ear
once and for all. Wait for me, I won't be long.

(Exit Strepsiades through the stage right door as the chorus serenades Socrates.)

CHORUS:
Now it is clear, once and for all
805 *The great benefits we bring to you,*
For this man is at your beck and call
To us alone, your prayers are due.

You've created one hysterical man,
810 *His excitement cannot be contained.*
Now quickly take him for all you can
For luck can change and drain away.

(Enter Pheidippides from the stage right door, chased by Strepsiades.)

STREPSIADES:
Get out! By Vapor, out of my house, once and for all.
815 Go and eat your uncle Megacles out of house and home!

PHEIDIPPIDES:
Father, whatever is the matter?
You are clearly insane, by Zeus!

STREPSIADES:
Listen to you, "By Zeus!" How childish!
Fancy believing in Olympian Zeus at your age.

PHEIDIPPIDES:
820 What on earth is so funny?

STREPSIADES:
You are, a young child like you with such old-fashioned ideas,

it's really quite ridiculous. But listen, come here, I want to reveal
something to you. When you understand, then, and only then, my son
will you truly be a man. But you must ensure that no one else knows this.

PHEIDIPPIDES:
Well, I'm here. Now what is it?   825

STREPSIADES:
Did you or did you not just swear to Zeus?

PHEIDIPPIDES:
I did.

STREPSIADES:
Now you'll see the benefits of education.
Pheidippides, there is no Zeus!

PHEIDIPPIDES:
What!

STREPSIADES:
Zeus is overthrown! Basin is king now!

PHEIDIPPIDES:
Ha! What rot!

STREPSIADES:
It's the truth.

PHEIDIPPIDES:
I don't believe you, who told you this nonsense?

STREPSIADES:
Socrates the Melian and Chaerephon,   830
and he's an expert in the true path of . . . fleas.

PHEIDIPPIDES:
Oh dear, your insanity is at a really advanced stage
if you have begun to follow the views of those maniacs.

STREPSIADES:
How dare you say such things! These are brilliant men
with superb minds. They live a simple frugal life 835
and refuse
to cut their hair, use soap, or set foot in a bathhouse.
But you, you've been taking yourself and my money
to the cleaners
for years, scrubbing away as if I was dead and buried!
Come on, hurry up, you have to go and learn in my place.

PHEIDIPPIDES:

840 What for? There's nothing even vaguely useful they
     could teach me.

STREPSIADES:

Nothing useful? What about all worldly knowledge,
     eh?
You could start off by learning what an imbecile
     you are.
Hang on, I've just had a thought. Wait here!

(Exit Strepsiades through the stage right door.)

PHEIDIPPIDES:

Dear me! Father is clearly completely deranged, what
     should I do?
845 I could have him tried in court and found legally in-
     competent,
or perhaps I had better book the undertaker right
     away.

*(Enter Strepsiades through the stage right door holding two
identical chickens.)*

STREPSIADES:

Now then, tell me what you would call this?

(Strepsiades holds up one of the chickens.)

PHEIDIPPIDES:

A chicken.

STREPSIADES:

Very good. And what would you call this?

(Strepsiades holds up the other chicken.)

PHEIDIPPIDES:

A chicken.

STREPSIADES:

Really? You would call them both by the same
     name, eh?
Now you really are being stupid. Here let me show
     you
850 so you will know next time you are asked; this one here
     is indeed called a "chicken" . . . but this is a "chick-
     eness."

PHEIDIPPIDES: *(Laughing)*

"Chickeness!" Is that an example of the "worldly
     knowledge"
that you learned in that house of stupid old clods?

*(Strepsiades throws the chickens off and starts to lead Phei-
dippides to the stage left door.)*

STREPSIADES:

It is, but son, I couldn't remember most of the stuff
     they taught,
every time I learned something I would forget it, I'm   855
     just too old and . . .

PHEIDIPPIDES:

That's why you've lost the clothes off your back, is it?

STREPSIADES:

They're not lost, just donated to my educational en-
     dowment.

PHEIDIPPIDES:

And just where are your shoes, you gullible old idiot?

STREPSIADES:

To quote Pericles, "They were spent on necessary ex-
     penses."
Come on, let's go. Do this one thing for your father,   860
     even if you
don't agree with it. I remember when you were a
     little six year old,
your little lisping voice begged me for a new toy cart
     as your festival
present, and I spent my first hard-earned obol of jury
     pay on you.

PHEIDIPPIDES:

Oh, all right then, but you'll regret this.   865

STREPSIADES:

Good lad, I knew you'd be persuaded. Socrates! Come
     out, come here!

(Enter Socrates from the stage left door.)

Here is my son, as promised. I persuaded him to
     come along
though he was dead set against it at first.

SOCRATES:

No, no, no, he simply will not do, he's a mere child.
     He would never
get the hang of the way we tackle things here. He
     just wouldn't grasp it.

PHEIDIPPIDES:

Grasp your own tackle and then go and hang yourself!   870

STREPSIADES:

Pheidippides! Watch your language in front of the
     teacher!

SOCRATES:
"Graaasp?" Just listen to his infantile diction!
What ever do you expect me to do with such flac-
cid lips?
How could he learn prevarication, incrimination, and
875 misrepresentation? Then again for the right course
fees
it may be possible, just look what a talent bought
for Hyperbolus!

STREPSIADES:
You can do it! He'll learn, he's a natural, you'll
find out!
You should have seen him when he was a little
lad, gifted!
A boy genius! He'd build the most beautiful mud
pies, carve
880 little boats, and make toy chariots out of old shoes,
and you can't
even begin to imagine the inventive little frogs he
made from
pomegranates. I want you to teach him those two Arguments,
the Superior, whatever that is, and the Inferior, you
know, the one
that can argue a wrongful case and defeat the Superior Argument.
885 If you can't manage both, then at least make him
learn the wrong one.

SOCRATES:
He can learn it from the Arguments themselves. I
must be off.

(Exit Socrates through the stage left door.)

STREPSIADES:
Remember, he needs to argue his way out of all types
of legitimate lawsuits!

(Enter the Superior Argument from the stage left door.)

SUPERIOR:
Come out, let the audience have a look at you!
890 You know how much you like to show off.

(Enter the Inferior Argument from the stage left door.)

INFERIOR:
Oh, "get you hence" dear *(he sees the audience)*. Ohhh!
What a crowd,

the more to witness your thrashing, the better. I just
love it!

SUPERIOR:
And who are you to think you can thrash me?

INFERIOR:
Just an argument.

SUPERIOR:
An Inferior Argument.

INFERIOR:
Oh, aren't you the high and mighty one! That may
be so darling,
but I'll still thrash you, all the same.   895

SUPERIOR:
Really? And just how do you plan to do that?

INFERIOR:
With innovative new ideas.

SUPERIOR:
Oh very chic, you're very fashionable aren't you,
thanks to these idiots *(indicating the audience)*.

INFERIOR:
On the contrary, they are of the highest intelligence.

SUPERIOR:
I'm going to annihilate you.

INFERIOR:
I see, how?

SUPERIOR:
Simply by stating my just argument.   900

INFERIOR:
Then let me start by defeating it with a counter-
argument,
because it is quite clear that Justice doesn't exist.

SUPERIOR:
Don't be ridiculous!

INFERIOR:
Well, where is she then?

SUPERIOR:
She resides with the gods on Olympus, as well you
know.

INFERIOR:
Well then, if Justice lives on Olympus,
905 why hasn't Zeus been punished for locking up his
    father, mmm?

SUPERIOR:
You're just spewing venom. Urghh! Get me a
    bucket, someone!

INFERIOR:
You're a doddering old relic.

SUPERIOR:
And you're a filthy queer!

INFERIOR:
Your words are strewn with roses!

SUPERIOR:
910 Freeloader!

INFERIOR:
You crown me with lilies!

SUPERIOR:
Father-beater!

INFERIOR:
You're completely unaware that you're showering me
    with gold.

SUPERIOR:
In my day, you'd be showered with lead!

INFERIOR:
Yes, I know but, my dear fellow, in these modern
    times we live in
all your worse name calling just pays me greater
    honor!

SUPERIOR:
You are completely contemptuous!

INFERIOR:
915 And you are absolutely archaic!

SUPERIOR:
It's your fault that the youth of today refuses
to attend school. You'll get your comeuppance,
you'll see, the Athenians will realize what fools
they've been to learn their lessons from the likes
    of you!

INFERIOR:
920 Pooh! You need to freshen up a bit.

SUPERIOR:
Oh, you've been busy all right, you worthless beggar.
You used to be the king of the scroungers,
gnawing on old sycophantic sayings from a tatty old
    swag bag.

INFERIOR:
How shrewd . . .

SUPERIOR:
How insane . . .   925

INFERIOR:
                                    . . . all that you've said I've done.

SUPERIOR:
                              . . . the city is to support you,
as you corrupt its young.

INFERIOR:
Don't even think about trying to teach this boy,
you crusty old Cronus!

SUPERIOR:
It is my duty, he needs to be saved from   930
the threat of spouting senseless gibberish.

INFERIOR:
(To Pheidippides) Come over here and ignore this reac-
    tionary old maniac.

SUPERIOR:
Keep away from him or you'll be sorry!

CHORUS:
Oh, stop all this fighting and arguing!

    (Addressing the Superior Argument)

Why don't you give an account of the schooling   935
you used to give in the old days,

    (Addressing the Inferior Argument)

                                                and then you
can tell us about your new educational methods.
Then this boy can hear your conflicting arguments,
make his own mind up, and enroll in the school of
    his choice.

SUPERIOR:
I see no reason why not.

INFERIOR:
I'm happy to do it.

CHORUS:
940 Good, who would like to speak first?

INFERIOR:
Oh, let him go first.
I want to hear what he has to say,
then I'm going to let my innovative phraseology fly
and shoot down his arguments once and for all.
945 My penetrating insights are like hornets,
and they'll prick him blind.
And if I hear so much as a peep out of him,
he'll wish he was dead and buried!

CHORUS:
Now our two antagonists
950 *Will decide which one is cleverest.*
The cut and thrust of confrontation,
A war of words and machination.
This ideological contest
Will decide which one is best.
955 *The end result of this demonstration*
Is the very future of education!

You crowned the older generation with your mo-
    rality,
960 now is your chance to proudly tell us exactly what
    you stand for.

SUPERIOR:
Then let me begin by explaining how education
    was run in the good old days
when my just cause was predominant and discre-
    tion was the aspiration of every man.
First, it was a given that boys should be seen and
    not heard and that students
should attend their district schools marching
    through the streets in orderly pairs
965 behind the lyre-master. Moreover, they were never
    allowed to wear cloaks,
even if the snow was falling as thick as porridge.
    These boys were then taught fine,
patriotic songs, and not to rub their thighs together
    while seated in the classroom!
Ah, yes what stirring hymns they would sing: "City-
    destroying Pallas" and "Hark I hear
a far-off tune," and they sung strong and proud like
    the manly fathers that raised them.
970 And if any boy engaged in classroom buffoonery or
    attempted to torture the music

by singing in the cacophonic, newfangled style of
    that awful lyre-plucker, Phrynis,
he was given a damned good thrashing for deliber-
    ately perverting the Muses!
Also, while sitting in the gymnasium the boys had
    to keep their legs closed in order
that they not expose the spectators to any inappro-
    priate and offensive sights.
When they stood up, they had to smooth the sand   975
    down where they were sitting
so that they would not leave behind any untoward
    impressions of their manhood.
No boy was permitted to oil himself below the
    waist, and consequently each
had a lovely soft down on his balls like a pair of
    fresh, ripe apricots . . .
They were not permitted to entice older lovers
    with effeminate voices,
or seductive looks, nor mince around pimping   980
    themselves out to all and sundry!
No taking the radish head during dinner, not grab-
    bing an elder's celery stick,
or pulling his parsley, no nibbling on tit-bits, no
    giggling at the table,
no sitting with legs crossed, no . . .

INFERIOR:
What a load of archaic claptrap! Your speech, sir,
    reeks of rotten old sacrificial beef,
it is crawling with grasshoppers and hums to the an- 985
    tiquated strains of Cedeides!

SUPERIOR:
Clearly you are missing the point. It was my system
    of student tutoring that raised
the men who fought so bravely at Marathon. All
    you do is train our young to be ashamed
of themselves and hide behind their cloaks. It
    grieves me to watch the war dance
at the Panathenaea and to have to see these wimpy
    lads who can barely lift a shield,
embarrassed at the sight of their own manly meat!   990
    It's a disgrace to Athena herself!
So come on young fellow, the choice is clear:
    choose me, the Superior Argument.
I'll teach you to detest hanging about in the mar-
    ketplace, and to keep out of public baths.
You'll learn to be ashamed of the shameful and to
    burn with indignation when you are ridiculed.

You'll gracefully let your elders and betters have
   your seat, and you will always treat your
parents with the utmost respect, you will do noth-
995   ing to harm your personal virtue.
No more chasing in and out of party girls' bed-
   rooms and running the risk of ruining your
reputation because of some harlot's love tokens. No
   more arguing with your father,
nor insulting his status by calling him a "crusty old
   fart" or "Cronus' older brother."
No, you'll come to respect all those years he spent
   raising you from a tiny little chick.

INFERIOR:
1000 Oh dear me, "young fellow," if you take his advice
   by Dionysus you'll turn out
like those dullard sons of Hippocrates, and be forever known as a little milksop.

SUPERIOR:
Don't listen to him, you'll be forever in the wrestling school, your bronzed body
glistening and hard. No wasting precious time twit-
   tering away on absurd topics
in the marketplace, nor bickering in the courts,
   splitting hairs, arguing the toss
1005 and wrangling over some insignificant little suit.
   We'll see you at the Academy,
bravely racing a friend under the boughs of holy
   olive-trees, your hair festooned
with fresh cut reeds, surrounded by sweet-scented
   wildflowers as the catkins
gently fall from the willows. There, you'll not have
   a care in the world, as the trees
rustle gently in the balmy breeze, and you partake
   of the joys of spring.
1010 This is the right way for you, my lad, and if you do
   what I say
you'll be eternally blessed
with a strapping body, a gleaming complexion,
   huge shoulders, a tiny little tongue,
big buttocks, and a small cock.
1015 Should you choose to follow the fashion currently
   in vogue amongst the young men of this city,
then it'll be pasty skin, round shoulders,
   concave chest, an enormous tongue,
no arse, a great hunk of meat, and a very long . . .
   turn of phrase!

He will have you believe that what should be   1020
   shameful
is beautiful, and what should be beautiful is made
   shameful.
Worst of all, in no time at all he'll turn you into
   an arse bandit
like that lecherous old queen, Antimachus.

CHORUS:

(Addressing the Superior Argument)

Such elevated sentiments   1025
Extolling high accomplishments,
Presenting such a fine defense
In praise of pride and sound good sense.
What blessed men you once did raise
Before our time, in olden days.   1030

(Addressing the Inferior Argument)

So be creative with your modern art.
This man has made a very good start.

If you want to avoid looking completely foolish and
   win this argument,
then I think you had better use some of your crafty   1035
   techniques.

INFERIOR:
In point of fact, I've been standing here for quite
   some time
literally busting a gut to confound his ridiculous statements
with my "counterintelligence." Why else do you think
   the philosophers
named me the Inferior Argument? Because it was I
   who created
the concept of disputing entrenched ideals and ethics.   1040
My dear boy, don't you see? To be able to take up
   the Inferior Argument and win
is worth far, far more than any number of silver coins
   you could care to count.
Let's examine these educational methods that he regards with such great confidence.
First of all, I clearly heard him say that he would
   abolish all bathing in warm water
Tell me, sir, if you will, the basis for your belief that   1045
   hot baths are bad?

SUPERIOR:
That they are most reprehensible and make the men who take them effeminate!

INFERIOR:
I've got you! You're quite pinned down and there's no escape!
Now tell me this, which son of Zeus do you believe has the finest
spirit and had successfully undertaken the most labors?

SUPERIOR:
1050 As far as I am concerned, there is no better man than Heracles.

INFERIOR:
Precisely! And have you ever seen a cold Heraclean bath?
And who could possibly be more manly than Heracles?

SUPERIOR:
That's exactly why the gymnasiums are empty, because the youth
of today are all at the bath houses spouting this kind of claptrap!

INFERIOR:
1055 Next, you take exception to our youngsters frequenting the public marketplace,
whereas I wholeheartedly recommend it. After all, if meeting in public is so appalling,
why does Homer describe Nestor and other men of wisdom as "public speakers"?
Let me now take up the issue of the tongue, which he states is not seemly for
the young to exercise. I have to disagree, and am of the opposite opinion.
1060 In addition, he pronounces that one must be discreet, a pair of fatal assumptions.
I would dearly love for you to tell me anyone who gained the slightest benefit
from behaving discreetly, just name them and prove me wrong.

SUPERIOR:
There's plenty. What about Peleus, he won a knife for his discretion.

INFERIOR:
A knife! What a delightful little thing to earn, by Zeus.
Even Hyperbolus, who's made a heap of cash swin- 1065 dling us all
at the lamp market, can't boast that he ever earned a knife!

SUPERIOR:
Thanks to his discretion, Peleus won the right to marry Thetis.

INFERIOR:
Yes, a little too discreet between the sheets, I heard, that's why
she ran out on him, because he simply wasn't outrageous enough in bed.
You know some women like it that way, you horny 1070 old Cronus stud!
Just consider, dear boy, what a life of discretion consists of,
and all the hedonistic delights you would miss out on—boys, girls,
drinking games, fancy food, fine wine, a good laugh.
How on earth could you endure life without these necessities?
Now, let us move on and discuss the needs of hu- 1075 man nature.
Suppose that you've been indulging in an illicit love affair. You are discovered!
A scandal! What will you do? You are finished, because you don't have the means
to argue your way out of trouble. But if you choose to make my acquaintance,
your nature can run free, with a spring in your step and a smile on your face,
and shameful thoughts will never even cross your 1080 mind. If the husband accuses you
of adultery, plead innocence and blame Zeus. Say that clearly he can't resist his lust
for women, so how can you, a mere mortal, be expected to have more strength than a god?

SUPERIOR:
Yes, but what if he takes your advice and gets punished by pubic plucking, scrotal singeing,
and a jolly good rectal radish ramming. No argument of yours is going to help him after that!

INFERIOR:
You mean people might think that he was gay? 1085

SUPERIOR:
Yes, what could possibly be worse than that?

INFERIOR:
Will you concede to me if I can prove this point
    to you?

SUPERIOR:
If you can, you'll not hear another peep out of me.

INFERIOR:
How would you describe most of our lawyers?

SUPERIOR:
1090 They're gay.

INFERIOR:
Quite right, and what about our tragic dramatists?

SUPERIOR:
All gay.

INFERIOR:
Yes, indeed. And our politicians?

SUPERIOR:
Definitely gay.

INFERIOR:
Then surely you must see that you are defending a
    lost cause.
1095 I mean, take a good look at the audience,
what would you call most of them?

SUPERIOR:
I'm looking.

INFERIOR:
And what do you see?

SUPERIOR:
By all the gods, most of them are . . . gay!

(He starts pointing at individual members of the audience.)

Well I know he is, and he definitely is,
1100 and that long-haired chap over there and . . . oh my!

INFERIOR:
Well then, what have you got to say for yourself now?

SUPERIOR:
I have to admit that you fuckers
have beaten me.
Here, take my cloak,
I think I might give it a try myself!

(Exit Superior Argument through the stage left door.)

INFERIOR:
(To Strepsiades) Well then, what do you think? Are you 1105
    and your son going to run off home,
or are you going to leave the boy with me to learn
    my oratorical arts?

STREPSIADES:
He's all yours to teach, and you have my permission
    to beat him too.
Remember, I want him to have a razor-sharp tongue,
    and fully
adjustable too, with one edge honed for petty lawsuits
    and the other
sharpened for cutting to the chase on more serious 1110
    matters.

INFERIOR:
Have no fear, he will return an expert in sophistry.

PHEIDIPPIDES:
I'll return a pasty-faced fiend, you mean!

CHORUS:
Go on, off you go.

*(Exit Inferior Argument and Pheidippides through the stage
left door into the Pondertorium.)*

I think that one day you may well
rue the day you did this.

*(Exit Strepsiades through the stage right door into his
house.)*

It's time to tell the judges why we should have first 1115
    prize,
And why honoring this Cloud chorus will prove ex-
    tremely wise.
When you're ploughing all your fields and you reach
    the sowing date,
We'll rain on your land first and make the others wait.
What's more, we'll watch your vines and carefully
    guard your crops.
We'll stop them getting parched and swamped by 1120
    huge raindrops.
But if on the other hand you mortals treat us with dis-
    respect
We goddesses will shower you with our malicious ef-
    fects.
Your lands will yield you nothing, your wine cel-
    lars deplete,

For your olives and your grapes will be pelted by
our sleet.
1125 When we see you baking bricks and laying tiles of clay,
We'll crack them with our hail, then wash them
all away.
Should a friend or family member happen to be wed,
We'll blow a gale all night and keep him from his bed.
You'd rather be in Egypt sizzling in the desert sun,
1130 Than make an unfair judgment and not vote us number one!

(Enter Strepsiades from the stage right door.)

STREPSIADES:
Let's see now; five, four, three, two . . . oh no, only
two more days
until the old-and-new day at the end of the month,
the day I fear
the most, the day that makes me tremble, the day
that gives me the jitters,
the day that debts are due! Every last one of my
creditors will have
1135 paid their court fees and are planning to destroy me,
once and for all!
They won't listen: I've pleaded with them to give me
more time, begged
to have my credit extended, implored them to write
off my debts.
But nothing works, they all want paying, they just
call me a criminal,
hurl abuse, and threaten me with the law! The unfeel-
ing bastards!

(He walks toward the stage left door.)

1140 Well, let them try it, that's what I say, they can take
me to court
for all I care, they'll be sorry, if my Pheidippides has
learned how
to talk the talk. Well there's only one way to find out,
I'll give the
Pondertorium a knock and see if he's ready.

(Strepsiades knocks on the door.)

Boy! Boy! Open up! Boy!

(Enter Socrates.)

SOCRATES:
1145 Ah, Strepsiades, good day to you.

STREPSIADES:
Likewise mate! I've brought you a little gift, here.

(Strepsiades hands Socrates a small bag of barley.)

It's right and proper to bring a present for the teacher.
Has my lad learned the argument, you know, the one
that did that little turn for us a while ago?

SOCRATES:
Indeed he has.

STREPSIADES:
Oh, Mistress of Misrepresentation, how marvelous!   1150

SOCRATES:
Now you will be able to contest all the litigation
you please.

STREPSIADES:
What? Even if a witness swore that they saw me
borrow the cash?

SOCRATES:
Even if there were a thousand witnesses!

(Strepsiades breaks into a joyous song.)

STREPSIADES:
Then be it known, let my shouts attest
That all the moneylenders have cause to mourn,   1155
For I banish your debts and compound interest.
I've no more need to endure your scorn.

For today my prodigy has sprung
From within these very walls
Armed with a glinting two-edged tongue   1160
To save my house and foes forestall.

So run and fetch him with a shout,
He will relieve his father's woes.
Call my child, have him come out,   1165
Come forth my son, it is time to go.

(Enter Pheidippides from the stage left door.)

SOCRATES:
I believe this is the man you are looking for.

STREPSIADES:
My dear boy! My dear, dear boy!

SOCRATES:
Take him and be on your way.

(Exit Socrates through the stage left door.)

STREPSIADES:
1170 My son! My child!
Hooray! Hooray!
Just let me look at you! What a lovely skin tone!
I can see the contention and the negation written all
over your face.
You look like a true Athenian now, with our characteristic "I've no idea
what you're talking about" look blooming in your
cheeks. Why, you've even
1175 picked up the look-of-righteous-indignation-even-when-
you're-in-the-wrong expression.
Now you can save me, since it was you who got me
into this mess in the first place.

PHEIDIPPIDES:
What are you are so afraid of?

STREPSIADES:
Why, the old-and-new day, of course!

PHEIDIPPIDES:
Are you trying to tell me that there's a day that's both
old and new?

STREPSIADES:
1180 Of course there is! It's the day when my creditors will
file their court deposits.

PHEIDIPPIDES:
Then, they'll lose their money, won't they? There's
no way that one day
can suddenly become two days, is there?

STREPSIADES:
Isn't there?

PHEIDIPPIDES:
Of course not. I mean that's like saying that a single
woman could be both
a young girl and an old woman at exactly the same
time.

STREPSIADES:
1185 But it's the law.

PHEIDIPPIDES:
No, no, no. They've obviously completely miscon-
strued the law.

STREPSIADES:
What does the law really mean, then?

PHEIDIPPIDES:
Solon, the elder statesman, was essentially a benefactor of the people, correct?

STREPSIADES:
What's that got to do with the old-and-new day?

PHEIDIPPIDES:
He was the one who decreed that there should be
two days
set aside for the issuing of court summonses, and that 1190
all deposits
must be lodged on the new day.

STREPSIADES:
Then why did he add the old day too?

PHEIDIPPIDES:
My dear fellow, to give the accused the opportunity
to settle out of court
one day prior to their scheduled trials. Then they
would avoid harassment
by their creditors until the actual morning of the 1195
new day.

STREPSIADES:
If that's the case, why do the court officials receive deposits
on the old *and* new day instead of just on the new day?

PHEIDIPPIDES:
Isn't it obvious, they're double-dipping.
They're just like the festival taste-testers
filching a foretaste of the fees as fast as is feasible! 1200

STREPSIADES:
Ha ha! You poor fools! You don't stand a chance!
Look at you simpletons sitting
out there, just begging to be ripped off by us members
of the intelligentsia!
You're dunderheads, clods, and empty vessels, nothing but a herd of sheep!
It is time I serenaded this splendid good fortune
with a nice hymn in honor of me and my son. 1205

(Strepsiades breaks into song.)

"O, Strepsiades, you are the lucky one
So fortunate and so wise,

You've raised a fine, upstanding son."
Thus my friends will eulogize.

1210 *When they find out I have a winner,*
You'll see the jealousy on their faces,
So let's celebrate with a great big dinner
Before you argue all my cases.

(Exit Strepsiades and Pheidippides through the stage right door. Enter First Creditor and a witness.)

FIRST CREDITOR:
So what's a man supposed to do, throw his own money
down the drain?
1215 Not likely, I shouldn't have felt so embarrassed, I
should have just said no
right when he asked me for the loan, then I wouldn't
be in this mess.

(Addressing the witness)

And I wouldn't have to waste your time dragging you
all the way down here
to witness a summons for money that was rightfully
mine in the first place.
Both ways I lose, either my money or the good will
of a neighbor.
1220 It's no good worrying about it, I have my duty as a
true Athenian,
I must go to court. I hereby summon Strepsiades to
appear in . . .

(Enter Strepsiades from the stage right door.)

STREPSIADES:
Who is it?

FIRST CREDITOR:
. . . in court on the old-and-new day.

STREPSIADES:
Did you hear that? He's summoned me on two differ-
ent days.
Why, pray, are you summoning me?

FIRST CREDITOR:
1225 You owe me twelve hundred drachmas. You borrowed
the money to purchase that dapple-gray horse.

STREPSIADES:
A horse! Did you hear that? Everyone knows that I
can't stand horses.

FIRST CREDITOR:
You made a sacred oath before the gods that you
would repay me.

STREPSIADES:
Indeed I did, but you see, that was before my lad Pheidippides
had gone and learned the unbeatable Argument.

FIRST CREDITOR:
I see, and I suppose now you think you can simply 1230
forgo your debts?

STREPSIADES:
Don't you think it's reasonable that I receive some
benefit from his education?

FIRST CREDITOR:
Well then, if that's the way you want it. Are you
willing to refute
your oath before the gods while standing on sacred
ground?

STREPSIADES:
Which particular gods?

FIRST CREDITOR:
Zeus, Hermes, and Poseidon.

STREPSIADES:
Of course! I'd even pay three obols for the privilege. 1235

*(The First Creditor is shocked and angry, becoming agi-
tated and animated.)*

FIRST CREDITOR:
By all the gods! May you be damned for your blasphemy!

*(Strepsiades grabs hold of the First Creditor and pats him
on the belly.)*

STREPSIADES:
You know if we were to split you open and rub
you down
with salt, your belly would make a lovely wineskin.

FIRST CREDITOR:
How dare you!

STREPSIADES:
It'd hold at least four jugs' worth.

FIRST CREDITOR:

1240 By Zeus almighty, by all the gods, you'll never get
away with this!

STREPSIADES:

Ha, ha! That's a good one that is, "by all the gods!"
Don't make me laugh!
Those of us "in the know" realize that Zeus is just
a joke.

FIRST CREDITOR:

I'm telling you, soon enough, you'll pay for this. Just
tell me one thing,
do you have any intention of paying what you owe me?

STREPSIADES:

1245 Hang on, I'll let you know . . .

(Strepsiades runs inside the stage right door.)

FIRST CREDITOR:

(To the witness) What's he up to now? Do you reckon
he's going to pay me?

(Strepsiades comes out again holding a kneading board.)

STREPSIADES:

Where's that man demanding money? Right then,
tell me what this is?

FIRST CREDITOR:

That? It's a meal-kneader, of course.

STREPSIADES:

And you have the gall to ask me for money! How
could you be so stupid?
1250 You won't catch me parting with a single obol to
such a moron.
You're the one who "needs the fee," it's obviously a
"fe-meal kneader."

(Strepsiades tries to dismiss the First Creditor.)

FIRST CREDITOR:

I take it that you have no intention of paying your debt.

STREPSIADES:

Not likely, now turn around, get off my doorstep, go
on, piss off!

FIRST CREDITOR:

I will go, straight to the court to lodge my deposit.
1255 I'll see you prosecuted if it's the last thing I do!

(Exit First Creditor and Witness.)

STREPSIADES:

You'll just be adding that to those twelve hundred
drachmas and increasing
your losses. Will you people never learn?
I feel sorry for him really, I mean, imagine not knowing your gender!

(Enter Second Creditor.)

SECOND CREDITOR:

Oh, no! No!

STREPSIADES:

Ah!
What now! Who the blazes is this chap, warbling   1260
dirges?
Looks like he's wandered away from a scene in a
tragedy.

SECOND CREDITOR:

Why do you care to know my name? I am
doomed, doomed!

STREPSIADES:

Well go and be doomed somewhere else, will you!

SECOND CREDITOR:

Oh, heartless demons, oh calamity that destroyed
my chariot!
Oh, Pallas Athena, you have brought me rack and   1265
ruin!

STREPSIADES:

The true tragedy is how you're mutilating those lines.

SECOND CREDITOR:

You may mock me, sir, but all I want is for your son
to repay
the money that he borrowed from me, particularly
in light
of my recent hapless misadventure.

STREPSIADES:

What money?   1270

SECOND CREDITOR:

The money that I lent him.

STREPSIADES:

Oh dear, I can see that you're in a bit of a mess.

SECOND CREDITOR:

I was rounding a bend and fell out of my chariot.

STREPSIADES:
Out of your mind, more like! I think you're the one who's
"round the bend," coming here spouting gibberish.

SECOND CREDITOR:
It is not gibberish, I just want to be repaid!

STREPSIADES:
1275 You're clearly quite insane, a lost cause, I'm afraid.

SECOND CREDITOR:
What do you mean?

STREPSIADES:
I believe that you have been knocked senseless, your
brain's addled.

SECOND CREDITOR:
And I believe that I'll be seeing you in court, by
Hermes,
if you don't pay me back the money that I'm owed!

STREPSIADES:
Tell me something, when Zeus makes it rain, do you
believe that he sends
1280 fresh water each time, or that the sun absorbs the
moisture from the earth,
reclaims it, and sends it back down again in the form
of a rain shower?

SECOND CREDITOR:
I have absolutely no idea, and I don't see what it has
to do with . . .

STREPSIADES:
Well how can you justify reclaiming your money
if you
don't understand the rudiments of meteorology?

SECOND CREDITOR:
1285 Listen, if you can't handle the whole payment this
month,
then how about just paying me the interest?

STREPSIADES:
What do you mean, "interest"? I'm not in the least
bit interested in your problems.

SECOND CREDITOR:
I mean the charge on the loan that increases in size
from day to day and month to month as time flows
on by.

STREPSIADES:
That's all very well, but do you think the sea   1290
has increased in size at all since olden times?

SECOND CREDITOR:
By Zeus, of course not, it would be against
the law of nature for the sea to change in size.

STREPSIADES:
Well then, you pitiful wretch, if the sea doesn't increase in size
with all the rivers flowing into it, who the blazes do
you think
you are to try and increase the size of your loan! Now   1295
bugger off
away from my house, or you'll get a damn good
prodding!

(*Strepsiades calls inside his house.*)

Boy! Bring me my cattle prod!

(*A slave rushes out of the stage right door with a cattle
prod.*)

SECOND CREDITOR:
Help! Somebody witness this!

(*Strepsiades starts prodding the Second Creditor.*)

STREPSIADES:
Giddy up! Get up there! Get going before I brand
your horse's arse!

SECOND CREDITOR:
This is outrageous! I protest!

(*Strepsiades continues his assault.*)

STREPSIADES:
Giddy up! Move it! Or I'll make a gelding out of you!   1300

(*The Second Creditor flees offstage, and Strepsiades calls
out after him.*)

Oh, you can move quickly enough when you want
to! You can take your
horses and your chariot wheels and stick them where
the sun don't shine!

(*Exit Strepsiades through the stage right door.*)

CHORUS:
Depravity often proves a fatal attraction
That can drive an old man to distraction.
This one thinks he can evade his debts,   1305

So he'll push his luck and hedge his bets.
But we all know that one day soon,
There will come an end to this honeymoon,
That will force our sophist roughly back
1310 *From his latest wicked track.*

For he will discover presently
The consequences of his desperate plea.
For his son has learned the wily art
1315 *Of successfully arguing the unjust part.*
He defeats all opponents however strong
Even when his case is plainly wrong.
But I have a feeling that these disputes
1320 *Will make him wish that his son was mute!*

(Enter a disheveled Strepsiades running out of the stage
right door.)

STREPSIADES:
Oh! Oh!
Help me! Friends, relatives, citizens, help!
Come quickly! I'm in terrible danger! Please!
I'm under attack, he's pummeling my head,
gashing my cheeks! Help me! Help me!

(Enter Pheidippides from the stage right door, looking very
smug.)

1325 You monster! You would dare to strike your own
father?

PHEIDIPPIDES:
That's right, old man.

STREPSIADES:
You hear that? He even admits to it!

PHEIDIPPIDES:
Freely.

STREPSIADES:
You're despicable, a father beater and a criminal!

PHEIDIPPIDES:
Oh, say those things again, more, more.
You know how I just love to be insulted.

STREPSIADES:
1330 You filthy arsehole!

PHEIDIPPIDES:
Please, keep showering me with roses.

STREPSIADES:
You would dare to raise a hand against your own
father?

PHEIDIPPIDES:
Of course I would by Zeus, and moreover I was perfectly
justified in giving you a beating, as well.

STREPSIADES:
You little bugger! How can striking your own father
ever be right?

PHEIDIPPIDES:
I'll prove it to you, by arguing my view, and I'll
win too.

STREPSIADES:
You'll never win on this point. It's impossible!   1335

PHEIDIPPIDES:
On the contrary, it'll be a walkover. So, decide
which of the two Arguments you want to present.

STREPSIADES:
Which two Arguments?

PHEIDIPPIDES:
The Superior or Inferior.

STREPSIADES:
It's unbelievable, and to think it was I who had you
educated to argue successfully against Justice.
But there's absolutely no way that you're going to   1340
be able
to convince me that it is right for a son to beat his
own father.

PHEIDIPPIDES:
Oh, but I shall convince you. In fact, you'll be so
convinced once you've heard
me out, that you'll have nothing at all worthwhile to
say on the matter.

STREPSIADES:
Go on then, let's hear what you have to say for yourself, I can't wait.

CHORUS:
Old man, it's time you started thinking   1345
About what you need to say to win,
He would not be quite so arrogant
If he did not have an argument.

So be aware of his self-assurance,
1350 *It is the reason for his insolence.*

CHORUS:
Please tell the chorus how you came to be involved
   in this dispute.
Tell us in your own words what actually happened.

STREPSIADES:
Oh, I'll tell you all right, you'll hear every sordid
   detail of this horrible squabble.
We were inside enjoying a nice dinner when I asked
   him to fetch his lyre
1355 and sing us an after dinner song. I suggested he do
   a bit of "Hark the Hallowed Ram
Was Shorn" by Simonides, but he would have none
   of it. No, he told me that strumming
a lyre and singing at dinner parties was "terribly passé"
   and said that only old women
grinding barley at the stone sing those kinds of
   songs anymore!

PHEIDIPPIDES:
Yes, and that explains why you received a thrashing.
   Who do you think you are,
1360 ordering me to croon some monotonous old song like
   a chirping grasshopper?

STREPSIADES:
That's exactly the kind of talk he was spouting inside,
   and what's more,
he even had the gall to announce that Simonides
   was a terrible poet!
I just couldn't believe my ears. Well, I swallowed my
   anger, for the moment,
and asked him ever so nicely to pick up the myrtle
   bough and recite a little
1365 Aeschylus for me, and do you know what he said!
   "Oh yes, Aeschylus, surely
the foremost of all poets at being loud, pompous,
   bombastic, and inaccessible."
Well, I nearly had a heart attack I was so angry at
   him, but yet again, I curbed
my fury and said calmly, "Why don't you come up
   with some of that clever
modern stuff, something from one of those fashionable poets you're always
1370 going on about." And with that he blurted out some
   disgusting lines from Euripides,

about a brother and sister going at it together! Well,
   that was it, the last straw,
I could contain myself no longer, and I let him have
   it, I told him
just what I thought and it wasn't pretty either, what's
   more he answered
me back with some of the foulest language I have
   ever heard. At that moment
he leapt to his feet and weighed into me, first pushing   1375
   and shoving, then he grabbed
my throat and started shaking me and punching and
   kicking. It was terrible!

PHEIDIPPIDES:
I was well within my rights to punish you, after you
   dared to insult a gifted man like Euripides.

STREPSIADES:
Gifted! He's just a . . . No, you'll only lay into me all
   over again.

PHEIDIPPIDES:
And I'd be justified too, by Zeus!

STREPSIADES:
How would you be justified? You insolent ruffian,   1380
   have you forgotten who raised you?
I was the one who had to listen to your lisping baby
   talk, when you went "wu-wu!"
I knew what you wanted and would fetch you something to drink. Then you would go
"foo-foo!" and daddy here would get you some bread.
   And when you cried "poo-poo!"
it was me who would pick you up, take you outside,   1385
   and let you do your little doo-doos!
But you, on the other hand, couldn't care less about
   my needs. Why just then, when you
were strangling me, I was completely ignored, even
   though I was screaming that I was
about to shit my pants, you just kept right on throttling
   away. You literally squeezed
the crap out of me, and I did my poo-poo right there
   and then!
It's a disgraceful way to treat your dear old dad.   1390

CHORUS:
The hearts of the young are all a flutter
To hear what words this lad might utter
To justify such disrespect
Could ever be deemed correct

1395 *For such an outcome would surely mean*
      That an old man's hide's not worth a bean!

CHORUS:
Now, you mover and shaker, you maestro of moder-
      nity, it is your turn.
You must persuade him to accept your point of view.

PHEIDIPPIDES:
Let me first say how pleasurable it is to be acquainted
      with modern ways and intelligent
1400 notions, for it enables one to disdain conventional
      practices from a superior vantage point.
When I filled my brain with only the mindless
      thoughts of horse riding I could hardly even blurt
out three words without making some stupid mistake.
      But thanks to my adversary here,
who saw to my education, I now possess a keen intel-
      lect and am proficient in finite conception,
subtle argument, and detailed contemplation. In ef-
      fect, I believe that I have the necessary skills
1405 to fully demonstrate that it is perfectly justified to
      discipline one's own father.

STREPSIADES:
I wish you'd go back to your horses, by Zeus! I would
      much rather have to pay
for a four-horse chariot team than run the risk of
      sustaining bodily harm every day!

PHEIDIPPIDES:
If I may be allowed to return to the point in my
      argument from where I was so rudely
interrupted. Tell me this, did you ever have occasion
      to beat me when I was a child?

STREPSIADES:
1410 Yes, but it was always for your own good. I had your
      best interests at heart.

PHEIDIPPIDES:
Then surely it is justified for me to beat you for your
      own good, if, by your definition,
"having someone else's best interests at heart" means
      to beat them? How is it justified
that your body should be protected against beatings
      but mine not? Is it not true that we
are both free men? "Suffer the little children, do you
      think the father should not?"
1415 No doubt you will attempt to defend yourself by stat-
      ing that it is quite legitimate for

this kind of punishment to be meted out to children,
      and yet, I would say that the
elderly are living a "second childhood." This being
      the case, surely it is only right
that the elderly should be chastised more severely
      than the young, as they should
have certainly learned right and wrong after a lifetime
      of experience.

STREPSIADES:
There's not a place in the world where it is legitimate 1420
      for a son to beat his father!

PHEIDIPPIDES:
But it is men who make legislation, men just like
      you and me. In past times,
one man simply persuaded another that this was the
      way things should be.
Therefore what is preventing me from similarly stat-
      ing a new "law" for times to come
specifying that sons should be permitted to beat their
      fathers in return?
"This will not be retroactive legislation, and all claims 1425
      for compensation for blows
previously sustained will not be considered and shall
      hereby be stricken from the record."
Examine chickens and other such farmyard animals,
      you will see that they freely
attack their fathers, and how are they so very different
      from us?
Except, of course, that they refrain from drafting
      statutes.

STREPSIADES:
If you're so keen to take after farmyard fowl, why 1430
      don't you start
eating chicken shit and roosting on a perch in the
      hen house?

PHEIDIPPIDES:
Sir, your analogy is hardly relevant, and I am sure
      Socrates would agree with me.

STREPSIADES:
Then stop hitting me, otherwise you'll come to re-
      gret it.

PHEIDIPPIDES:
And why would that be?

STREPSIADES:

1435 Well, when you have a son of your own,
you'll not have the right to beat him, as I did you!

PHEIDIPPIDES:

But what if I don't have a son, then I would have suffered
for nothing, and you'll be laughing at me from beyond the grave.

(Strepsiades addresses the audience.)

STREPSIADES:

You know what, friends, he does have a point, and it seems
only proper that we give the young the benefit of the doubt now and again.
I suppose it's only reasonable that we should suffer a little if we step out of line.

PHEIDIPPIDES:

1440 And another thing . . .

STREPSIADES:

No! I can't take it any more!

PHEIDIPPIDES:

Just listen, perhaps it will make your suffering seem not so bad.

STREPSIADES:

What are you talking about? Nothing could comfort my pain.

PHEIDIPPIDES:

I shall beat Mother just as I beat you.

STREPSIADES:

WHAT! What are you saying? This is going from bad to worse!

PHEIDIPPIDES:

1445 But I can use the inferior argument to defeat you on this very subject.
I can prove that it is right to beat one's mother.

STREPSIADES:

And what then?
What then? I ask you!
You're all doomed!
1450 You're going to throw yourself into the abyss.
You, Socrates, and that damned Inferior Argument!

(Strepsiades looks up and calls out.)

Clouds! This is all your fault, you're responsible!
I trusted you, I believed in you!

CHORUS:

You brought this trouble on yourself when you took
the twisting path of wickedness and deceit.   1455

STREPSIADES:

But why didn't you tell me that in the first place?
I'm just a simple old yokel. You lured me into this mess!

CHORUS:

But we always do this.
When we discover a mortal who becomes
enamored by vice, we drive them to despair.   1460
That is how we teach man to have proper respect for the gods.

STREPSIADES:

Oh, Clouds, you've treated me harshly, but you're right,
I should never have tried to get of out paying my debts.

(To Pheidippides)

Come on, my lad, let's get even with Socrates and Chaerephon,
those villains, it's high time they met their makers!   1465
Let's pay them back for the vile way they deceived us.

PHEIDIPPIDES:

But I must not offend my teachers.

STREPSIADES:

Yes, yes, and "we venerate Zeus protector of fathers."

PHEIDIPPIDES:

Just listen to you, "father Zeus." You're so old fashioned!
Zeus doesn't exist.   1470

STREPSIADES:

Yes he does.

PHEIDIPPIDES:

No he doesn't. "Zeus has been overthrown, Basin is king now."

STREPSIADES:

He hasn't been overthrown, I was misled by this basin.

(Indicating the wine basin set on a stand outside the Pondertorium)

Oh, what a stupid wretch I am, to believe that a piece
of clay pottery could ever be a god!

PHEIDIPPIDES:

1475   I've had enough of you. You can rant and rave to
yourself. I'm not listening!

*(Exit Pheidippides into the house, through the stage right
door.)*

STREPSIADES:

Oh, I must have been completely out of my mind,
to think I rejected the gods because Socrates told
me to.
Unbelievable! What was I thinking? Dear, dear
Hermes,
take pity on me, please be kind, don't destroy me now.
1480   I know I behaved like a raving maniac, but it was all
because of them
and their philosophical drivel. I need you now, help
me, tell me what
can I do to redeem myself? Should I file a lawsuit
against them?
What? What can I do?

(Strepsiades suddenly realizes what he must do.)

Yes, that's it, that's exactly right,
I'm not going to fiddle around with lawsuits, no,
I'll burn
1485   those babbling bastards out, that's what I'll do! Xan-
thias! Xanthias!
Come here at once and bring the ladder and an axe!

*(A slave comes running out of the stage right door with a
ladder and an axe. He lays the ladder on the scene
building.)*

I want you to climb up onto the roof of the Pondertorium
and do a hatchet job on their roof, and if you care anything
for your poor old master, you'll really bring the
house down
1490   on those charlatans. Light up a torch and hand it
to me!

(Xanthias hands him a flaming torch.)

Now it's my turn to call in the debts, those colossal
cheats
are going to pay dearly for what they put me through!

*(Strepsiades and Xanthias climb up onto the roof of the
scene building.)*

STUDENT:
Oh! Oh!

STREPSIADES:
"Come torch, send on your mighty blaze!"

*(Enter a student from the stage left door hatch, who sees
Strepsiades on the roof.)*

STUDENT 1:
You there! What are you up to?   1495

STREPSIADES:
I'm demonstrating to your rafters the finer points of
my axe!

(Enter another student from the window.)

STUDENT 2:
Ahhh! Who set our house on fire?

STREPSIADES:
You should know, you thieves, you lot stole his cloak!

STUDENT 1:
You'll kill us all! Kill us all!

STREPSIADES:
Well at least you're right about that, as long as I don't   1500
get carried away with my axe and come a cropper!

(Enter Socrates from the window.)

SOCRATES:
You up there, whatever do you think you are doing?

STREPSIADES:
I am "walking the air to look down on the sun!"

(Enter Chaerephon from the stage left door.)

CHAEREPHON:
Ahhh! Help! I'm suffocating!

SOCRATES
What about me? I'm going up in smoke!   1505

STREPSIADES:
It serves you right for daring to think that you could
snub the gods
and spy on the moon when she's all exposed. Outrageous!

Chase them down, smash bash and crash them! We'll
    teach them
a hundred lessons, but most of all never to offend
    the gods above!

(Exit Strepsiades and Xanthias into the Pondertorium.)

CHORUS:
And now it's time we closed this play   *1510*
We've performed enough for you today!

    (Exit the chorus rapidly offstage.)

END

Sophocles
(c. 496–406/405 B.C.)

Antigone

Characters

ANTIGONE

ISMENE

CHORUS OF THEBAN ELDERS

CREON

A GUARD

HAEMON

TEIRESIAS

A MESSENGER

EURYDICE

SCENE: *Thebes, before the royal palace. Antigone
and Ismene emerge from its great central
door.*

ANTIGONE:
My sister, my Ismene, do you know
of any suffering from our father sprung
that Zeus does not achieve for us survivors?
There's nothing grievous, nothing free from doom,
not shameful, not dishonored, I've not seen.
Your sufferings and mine.
And now, what of this edict which they say
the commander has proclaimed to the whole people?

Have you heard anything? Or don't you know
that the foes' trouble comes upon our friends?   *10*

ISMENE:
I've heard no word, Antigone, of our friends.
Not sweet nor bitter, since that single moment
when we two lost two brothers
who died on one day by a double blow.
And since the Argive army went away
this very night, I have no further news
of fortune or disaster for myself.

ANTIGONE:
I knew it well, and brought you from the house
for just this reason, that you alone may hear.

ISMENE:
What is it? Clearly some news has clouded you.   *20*

ANTIGONE:
It has indeed. Creon will give the one
of our two brothers honor in the tomb;
the other none.
Eteocles, with just entreatment treated,
as law provides he has hidden under earth
to have full honor with the dead below.
But Polyneices' corpse who died in pain,
they say he has proclaimed to the whole town
that none may bury him and none bewail,
but leave him unwept, untombed, a rich sweet sight
for the hungry birds' beholding.   *30*
Such orders they say the worthy Creon gives

Reprinted from Sophocles, *Antigone*, translated by Elizabeth Wyckoff, in *The Complete Greek Tragedies*, pp. 158–204, edited by
David Grene and Richmond Lattimore (Chicago: University of Chicago Press, 1954) by permission of the publisher.

to you and me—yes, yes, I say to *me*—
and that he's coming to proclaim it clear
to those who know it not.
Further: he has the matter so at heart
that anyone who dares attempt the act
will die by public stoning in the town.
So there you have it and you soon will show
if you are noble, or fallen from your descent.

ISMENE:
If things have reached this stage, what can I do,
40 poor sister, that will help to make or mend?

ANTIGONE:
Think will you share my labor and my act.

ISMENE:
What will you risk? And where is your intent?

ANTIGONE:
Will you take up that corpse along with me?

ISMENE:
To bury him you mean, when it's forbidden?

ANTIGONE:
My brother, and yours, though you may wish he
     were not.
I never shall be found to be his traitor.

ISMENE:
O hard of mind! When Creon spoke against it!

ANTIGONE:
It's not for him to keep me from my own.

ISMENE:
Alas. Remember, sister, how our father
50 perished abhorred, ill-famed.
Himself with his own hand, through his own curse
destroyed both eyes.
Remember next his mother and his wife
finishing life in the shame of the twisted strings.
And third two brothers on a single day,
Poor creatures, murdering, a common doom
each with his arm accomplished on the other.
And now look at the two of us alone.
We'll perish terribly if we force law
60 and try to cross the royal vote and power.
We must remember that we two are women
so not to fight with men.
And that since we are subject to strong power

we must hear these orders, or any that may be worse.
So I shall ask of them beneath the earth
forgiveness, for in these things I am forced,
and shall obey the men in power. I know
that wild and futile action makes no sense.

ANTIGONE:
I wouldn't urge it. And if now you wished
to act, you wouldn't please me as a partner.   70
Be what you want to; but that man shall I
bury. For me, the doer, death is best.
Friend shall I lie with him, yes friend with friend,
when I have dared the crime of piety.
Longer the time in which to please the dead
than that for those up here.
There shall I lie forever. You may see fit
to keep from honor what the gods have honored.

ISMENE:
I shall do no dishonor. But to act
against the citizens. I cannot.

ANTIGONE:
That's your protection. Now I go, to pile   80
the burial-mound for him, my dearest brother.

ISMENE:
Oh my poor sister. How I fear for you!

ANTIGONE:
For me, don't borrow trouble. Clear your fate.

ISMENE:
At least give no one warning of this act;
you keep it hidden, and I'll do the same.

ANTIGONE:
Dear God! Denounce me. I shall hate you more
if silent, not proclaiming this to all.

ISMENE:
You have a hot mind over chilly things.

ANTIGONE:
I know I please those whom I most should please.

ISMENE:
If but you can. You crave what can't be done.   90

ANTIGONE:
And so, when strength runs out, I shall give over.

ISMENE:
Wrong from the start, to chase what cannot be.

ANTIGONE:

If that's your saying, I shall hate you first,
and next the dead will hate you in all justice.
But let me and my own ill-counselling
suffer this terror. I shall suffer nothing
as great as dying with a lack of grace.

ISMENE:

Go, since you want to. But know this: you go
senseless indeed, but loved by those who love you.

*(Ismene returns to the palace; Antigone leaves by one of
the side entrances. The Chorus now enters from the other
side.)*

CHORUS:

Sun's own radiance, fairest light ever shone on the
100   gates of Thebes,
then did you shine, O golden day's
eye, coming over Dirce's stream,
on the Man who had come from Argos with all his
    armor
running now in headlong fear as you shook his bri-
    dle free.

110 He was stirred by the dubious quarrel of Polyneices.
    So, screaming shrill,
like an eagle over the land he flew,
covered with white-snow wing,
with many weapons,
with horse-hair crested helms.

He who had stood above our halls, gaping about our
    seven gates,
with that circle of thirsting spears.
120 Gone, without our blood in his jaws,
before the torch took hold on our tower-crown.
Rattle of war at his back; hard the fight for the drag-
    on's foe.

The boats of a proud tongue are for Zeus to hate.
So seeing them streaming on
130 in insolent clangor of gold,
he struck with hurling fire him who rushed
for the high wall's top,
to cry conquest abroad.

Swinging, striking the earth he fell
fire in hand, who in mad attack,
had raged against us with blasts of hate.
He failed. He failed of his aim.

For the rest great Ares dealt his blows about,
first in the war-team.   140

The captains stationed at seven gates
fought with seven and left behind
their brazen arms as an offering
to Zeus who is turner of battle.
All but those wretches, sons of one
    man,
one mother's sons, who sent their spears
each against each and found the share
of a common death together.

Great-named Victory comes to us
answering Thebe's warrior-joy.
Let us forget the wars just done   150
and visit the shrines of the gods.
All, with night-long dance which Bacchus will lead,
Who shakes Thebe's acres.

(Creon enters from the palace.)

Now here he comes, the king of the
    land,
Creon, Menoeceus' son,
Newly named by the gods' new fate.
What plan that beats about his mind
has made him call this council-session,   160
sending his summons to all?

CREON:

My friends, the very gods who shook the state
with mighty surge have set it straight again.
So now I sent for you, chosen from all,
first that I knew you constant in respect
to Laius' royal power; and again
when Oedipus had set the state to rights,
and when he perished, you were faithful still
in mind to the descendants of the dead.
When they two perished by a double fate,   170
on one day struck and striking and defiled
each by his own hand, now it comes that I
hold all the power and the royal throne
through close connection with the perished men.
You cannot learn of any man the soul,
the mind, and the intent until he shows
his practise of the government and law.
For I believe that who controls the state
and does not hold to the best plans of all,
but locks his tongue up through some kind of fear,   180
that he is worst of all who are or were.

And he who counts another greater friend
than his own fatherland, I put him nowhere.
So I—may Zeus all-seeing always know it—
could not keep silent as disaster crept
upon the town, destroying hope of safety.
Nor could I count the enemy of the land
friend to myself, not I who know so well
that she it is who saves us, sailing straight,
190 and only so can we have friends at all.
With such good rules shall I enlarge our state.
And now I have proclaimed their brother-edict.
In the matter of the sons of Oedipus,
citizens, know: Eteocles who died,
defending this our town with champion spear,
is to be covered in the grave and granted
all holy rites we give the noble dead.
But his brother Polyneices whom I name
200 the exile who came back and sought to burn
his fatherland, the gods who were his kin,
who tried to gorge on blood he shared, and lead
the rest of us as slaves—
it is announced that no one in this town
may give him burial or mourn for him.
Leave him unburied, leave his corpse disgraced,
a dinner for the birds and for the dogs.
Such is my mind. Never shall I, myself,
Honor the wicked and reject the just.
The man who is well-minded to the state
210 from me in death and life shall have his honor.

CHORUS:
This resolution, Creon, is your own,
in the matter of the traitor and the true.
For you can make such rulings as you will
about the living and about the dead.

CREON:
Now you be sentinels of the decree.

CHORUS:
Order some younger man to take this on.

CREON:
Already there are watchers of the corpse.

CHORUS:
What other order would you give us, then?

CREON:
Not to take sides with any who disobey.

CHORUS:
No fool is fool as far as loving death.   220

CREON:
Death is the price. But often we have known
men to be ruined by the hope of profit.

(Enter, from the side, a guard.)

GUARD:
Lord, I can't claim that I am out of breath
from rushing here with light and hasty step,
for I had many haltings in my thought
making me double back upon my road.
My mind kept saying many things to me:
"Why go where you will surely pay the price?"
"Fool, are you halting? And if Creon learns
from someone else, how shall you not be hurt?"   230
Turning this over, on I dilly-dallied.
And so a short trip turns itself to long.
Finally, though, my coming here won out.
If what I say is nothing, still I'll say it.
For I come clutching to one single hope
that I can't suffer what is not my fate.

CREON:
What is it that brings on this gloom of yours?

GUARD:
I want to tell you first about myself.
I didn't do it, didn't see who did it.
It isn't right for me to get in trouble.   240

CREON:
Your aim is good. You fence the fact around.
It's clear you have some shocking news to tell.

GUARD:
Terrible tidings make for long delays.

CREON:
Speak out the story, and then get away.

GUARD:
I'll tell you. Someone left the corpse just now,
burial all accomplished, thirsty dust
strewn on the flesh, the ritual complete.

CREON:
What are you saying? What man has dared to do it?

GUARD:
I wouldn't know. There were no marks of picks,
no grubbed-out earth. The ground was dry and
250   hard,
no trace of wheels. The doer left no sign.
When the first fellow on the day-shift showed us,
we all were sick with wonder.
For he was hidden, not inside a tomb,
light dust upon him, enough to turn the curse,
no wild beast's track, nor track of any hound
having been near, nor was the body torn.
260 We roared bad words about, guard against guard,
and came to blows. No one was there to stop us.
Each man had done it, nobody had done it
so as to prove it on him—we couldn't tell.
We were prepared to hold to red-hot iron,
to walk through fire, to swear before the gods
we hadn't done it, hadn't shared the plan,
when it was plotted or when it was done.
And last, when all our sleuthing came out nowhere,
one fellow spoke, who made our heads to droop
270 low toward the ground. We couldn't disagree.
We couldn't see a chance of getting off.
He said we had to tell you all about it.
We couldn't hide the fact.
So he won out. The lot chose poor old me
to win the prize. So here I am unwilling,
quite sure you people hardly want to see me.
Nobody likes the bringer of bad news.

CHORUS:
Lord, while he spoke, my mind kept on debating.
Isn't this action possibly a god's?

CREON:
280 Stop now, before you fill me up with rage,
or you'll prove yourself insane as well as old.
Unbearable, your saying that the gods
take any kindly forethought for this corpse.
Would it be they had hidden him away,
honoring his good service, his who came
to burn their pillared temples and their wealth,
even their land, and break apart their laws?
Or have you seen them honor wicked men?
It isn't so.
290 No, from the first there were some men in town
who took the edict hard, and growled against me,
who hid the fact that they were rearing back,
not rightly in the yoke, no way my friends.

These are the people—oh it's clear to me—
who have bribed these men and brought about the
    deed.
No current custom among men as bad
as silver currency. This destroys the state;
this drives men from their homes; this wicked teacher
drives solid citizens to acts of shame.
It shows men how to practise infamy   300
and know the deeds of all unholiness.
Every least hireling who helped in this
brought about then the sentence he shall have.
But further, as I still revere great Zeus,
understand this, I tell you under oath,
if you don't find the very man whose hands
buried the corpse, bring him for me to see,
not death alone shall be enough for you
till living, hanging, you make clear the crime.
For any future grabbings you'll have learned   310
where to get pay, and that it doesn't pay
to squeeze a profit out of every source.
For you'll have felt that more men come to doom
through dirty profits than are kept by them.

GUARD:
May I say something? Or just turn and go?

CREON:
Aren't you aware your speech is most unwel-
    come?

GUARD:
Does it annoy your hearing or your mind?

CREON:
Why are you out to allocate my pain?

GUARD:
The doer hurts your mind. I hurt your ears.

CREON:
You are a quibbling rascal through and through.   320

GUARD:
But anyhow I never did the deed.

CREON:
And you the man who sold your mind for money!

GUARD:
Oh!
How terrible to guess, and guess at lies!

CREON:
Go pretty up your guesswork. If you don't
show me the doers you will have to say
that wicked payments work their own revenge.

GUARD:
Indeed, I pray he's found, but yes or no,
taken or not as luck may settle it,
you won't see me returning to this place.
330 Saved when I neither hoped nor thought to be,
I owe the gods a mighty debt of thanks.

(Creon enters the palace. The Guard leaves by the way he came.)

CHORUS:
Many the wonders but nothing walks stranger than
   man.
The thing crosses the sea in the winter's storm,
making his path through the roaring waves.
And she, the greatest of gods, the earth—
ageless she is, and unwearied—he wears her away
340 as the ploughs go up and down from year to year
and his mules turn up the soil.

Gay nations of birds he snares and leads,
wild beast tribes and the salty brood of the sea,
with the twisted mesh of his nets, this clever man.
He controls with craft the beasts of the open air,
350 walkers on hills. The horse with his shaggy mane
he holds and harnesses, yoked about the neck,
and the strong bull of the mountain.

Language, and thought like the wind
and the feelings that make the town,
he has taught himself, and shelter against the cold,
refuge from rain. He can always help himself.
He faces no future helpless. There's only death
360 that he cannot find an escape from. He has contrived
refuge from illnesses once beyond all cure.

Clever beyond all dreams
the inventive craft that he has
which may drive him one time or another to well
   or ill.
When he honors the laws of the land and the gods'
   sworn right
370 high indeed in his city; but stateless the man

who dares to dwell with dishonor. Not by my
   fire,
never to share my thoughts, who does these things.

(The Guard enters with Antigone.)

My mind is split at this awful sight.
I know her. I cannot deny
Antigone is here.
Alas, the unhappy girl,
her unhappy father's child.   380
Oh what is the meaning of this?
It cannot be you that they bring
for breaking the royal law,
caught in open shame.

GUARD:
This is the woman who has done the deed.
We caught her at the burying. Where's the king?

(Creon enters.)

CHORUS:
Back from the house again just when he's needed.

CREON:
What must I measure up to? What has happened?

GUARD:
Lord, one should never swear off anything.
Afterthought makes the first resolve a liar.
I could have vowed I wouldn't come back here   390
after your threats, after the storm I faced.
But joy that comes beyond the wildest hope
is bigger than all other pleasure known.
I'm here, though I swore not to be, and bring
this girl. We caught her burying the dead.
This time we didn't need to shake the lots;
mine was the luck, all mine.
So now, lord, take her, you, and question her
and prove her as you will. But I am free.
And I deserve full clearance on this charge.   400

CREON:
Explain the circumstance of the arrest.

GUARD:
She was burying the man. You have it all.

CREON:
Is this the truth? And do you grasp its meaning?

GUARD:
I saw her burying the very corpse
you had forbidden. Is this adequate?

CREON:
How was she caught and taken in the act?

GUARD:
It was like this: when we got back again
struck with those dreadful threatenings of yours,
410 we swept away the dust that hid the corpse.
We stripped it back to slimy nakedness.
And then we sat to windward on the hill
so as to dodge the smell.
We poked each other up with growling threats
if anyone was careless of his work.
For some time this went on, till it was noon.
The sun was high and hot. Then from the
      earth
up rose a dusty whirlwind to the sky,
filling the plain, smearing the forest-leaves,
420 clogging the upper air. We shut our eyes,
sat and endured the plague the gods had sent.
So the storm left us after a long time.
We saw the girl. She cried the sharp and shrill
cry of a bitter bird which sees the nest
bare where the young birds lay.
So this same girl, seeing the body stripped,
cried with great groanings, cried a dreadful curse
upon the people who had done the deed.
Soon in her hands she brought the thirsty dust,
430 and holding high a pitcher of wrought bronze
she poured the three libations for the dead.
We saw this and surged down. We trapped her
      fast;
and she was calm. We taxed her with the deeds
both past and present. Nothing was denied.
And I was glad, and yet I took it hard.
One's own escape from trouble makes one glad;
but bringing friends to trouble is hard grief.
Still, I care less for all these second thoughts
440 than for the fact that I myself am safe.

CREON:
You there, whose head is drooping to the ground,
do you admit this, or deny you did it?

ANTIGONE:
I say I did it and I don't deny it.

CREON (to the guard):
Take yourself off wherever you wish to go
free of a heavy charge.

CREON (to Antigone):
You—tell me not at length but in a word.
You knew the order not to do this thing?

ANTIGONE:
I knew, of course I knew. The word was plain.

CREON:
And still you dared to overstep these laws?

ANTIGONE:
For me it was not Zeus who made that order.   450
Nor did that Justice who lives with the gods
      below
mark out such laws to hold among mankind.
Nor did I think your orders were so strong
that you, a mortal man, could over-run
the gods' unwritten and unfailing laws.
Not now, nor yesterday's, they always live,
and no one knows their origin in time.
So not through fear of any man's proud spirit
would I be likely to neglect these laws,
draw on myself the gods' sure punishment.
I knew that I must die; how could I not?   460
even without your warning. If I die
before my time, I say it is a gain.
Who lives in sorrows many as are mine
how shall he not be glad to gain his death?
And so, for me to meet this fate, no grief.
But if I left that corpse, my mother's son,
dead and unburied I'd have cause to grieve
as now I grieve not.
And if you think my acts are foolishness
the foolishness may be in a fool's eye.   470

CHORUS:
The girl is bitter. She's her father's child.
She cannot yield to trouble; nor could he.

CREON:
These rigid spirits are the first to fall.
The strongest iron, hardened in the fire,
most often ends in scraps and shatterings.
Small curbs bring raging horses back to terms.
Slave to his neighbor, who can think of pride?
This girl was expert in her insolence   480
when she broke bounds beyond established law.

Once she had done it, insolence the second,
to boast her doing, and to laugh in it.
I am no man and she the man instead
if she can have this conquest without pain.
She is my sister's child, but were she child
of closer kin than any at my hearth,
she and her sister should not so escape
their death and doom. I charge Ismene too.
490 She shared the planning of this burial.
Call her outside. I saw her in the house,
maddened, no longer mistress of herself.
The sly intent betrays itself sometimes
before the secret plotters work their wrong.
I hate it too when someone caught in crime
then wants to make it seem a lovely thing.

ANTIGONE:
Do you want more than my arrest and death?

CREON:
No more than that. For that is all I need.

ANTIGONE:
Why are you waiting? Nothing that you say
500 fits with my thought. I pray it never will.
Nor will you ever like to hear my words.
And yet what greater glory could I find
than giving my own brother funeral?
All these would say that they approved my act
did fear not mute them.
(A king is fortunate in many ways,
and most, that he can act and speak at will.)

CREON:
None of these others see the case this way.

ANTIGONE:
They see, and do not say. You have them cowed.

CREON:
510 And you are not ashamed to think alone?

ANTIGONE:
No, I am not ashamed. When was it shame
to serve the children of my mother's womb?

CREON:
It was not your brother who died against him, then?

ANTIGONE:
Full brother, on both sides, my parents' child.

CREON:
Your act of grace, in his regard, is crime.

ANTIGONE:
The corpse below would never say it was.

CREON:
When you honor him and the criminal just alike?

ANTIGONE:
It was a brother, not a slave, who died.

CREON:
Died to destroy this land the other guarded.

ANTIGONE:
Death yearns for equal law for all the dead.

CREON:
Not that the good and bad draw equal shares. 520

ANTIGONE:
Who knows that this is holiness below?

CREON:
Never the enemy, even in death, a friend.

ANTIGONE:
I cannot share in hatred, but in love.

CREON:
Then go down there, if you must love, and love
the dead. No woman rules me while I live.

(Ismene is brought from the palace under guard.)

CHORUS:
Look there! Ismene is coming out.
She loves her sister and mourns,
with clouded brow and bloodied cheeks,
tears on her lovely face. 530

CREON:
You, lurking like a viper in the house,
who sucked me dry. I looked the other way
while twin destruction planned against the throne.
Now tell me, do you say you shared this deed?
Or will you swear you didn't even know?

ISMENE:
I did the deed, if she agrees I did.
I am accessory and share the blame.

ANTIGONE:
Justice will not allow this. You did not
wish for a part, nor did I give you one.

ISMENE:
540 You are in trouble, and I'm not ashamed
to sail beside you into suffering.

ANTIGONE:
Death and the dead, they know whose act it was.
I cannot love a friend whose love is words.

ISMENE:
Sister, I pray, don't fence me out from honor,
from death with you, and honor done the dead.

ANTIGONE:
Don't die along with me, nor make your own
that which you did not do. My death's enough.

ISMENE:
When you are gone what life can be my friend?

ANTIGONE:
Love Creon. He's your kinsman and your care.

ISMENE:
550 Why hurt me, when it does yourself no good?

ANTIGONE:
I also suffer, when I laugh at you.

ISMENE:
What further service can I do you now?

ANTIGONE:
To save yourself. I shall not envy you.

ISMENE:
Alas for me. Am I ouside your fate?

ANTIGONE:
Yes. For you chose to live when I chose death.

ISMENE:
At least I was not silent. You were warned.

ANTIGONE:
Some will have thought you wiser. Some will not.

ISMENE:
And yet the blame is equal for us both.

ANTIGONE:
Take heart. You live. My life died long ago.
560 And that has made me fit to help the dead.

CREON:
One of these girls has shown her lack of sense
just now. The other had it from her birth.

ISMENE:
Yes, lord. When people fall in deep distress
their native sense departs, and will not stay.

CREON:
You chose your mind's distraction when you chose
to work out wickedness with this wicked girl.

ISMENE:
What life is there for me to live without her?

CREON:
Don't speak of her. For she is here no more.

ISMENE:
But will you kill your own son's promised bride?

CREON:
Oh, there are other furrows for his plough.

ISMENE:
But where the closeness that has bound these two? 570

CREON:
Not for my sons will I choose wicked wives.

ISMENE:
Dear Haemon, your father robs you of your rights.

CREON:
You and your marriage trouble me too much.

ISMENE:
You will take away his bride from your own son?

CREON:
Yes. Death will help me break this marriage off.

CHORUS:
It seems determined that the girl must die.

CREON:
You helped determine it. Now, no delay!
Slaves, take them in. They must be women now.
No more free running.
Even the bold will fly when they see Death   580
drawing in close enough to end their life.

(Antigone and Ismene are taken inside.)

CHORUS:
Fortunate they whose lives have no taste of pain.
For those whose house is shaken by the gods
escape no kind of doom. It extends to all the kin
like the wave that comes when the winds of Thrace
run over the dark of the sea.
590 The black sand of the bottom is brought from the
       depth;
the beaten capes sound back with a hollow cry.

Ancient the sorrow of Labdacus' house, I know.
Dead men's grief comes back, and falls on grief.
No generation can free the next.
One of the gods will strike. There is no escape.
So now the light goes out
600 for the house of Oedipus, while the bloody knife
cuts the remaining root. Folly and Fury have done
       this.

What madness of man, O Zeus, can bind your power?
Not sleep can destroy it who ages all,
nor the weariless months the gods have set. Unaged
       in time
610 monarch you rule of Olympus' gleaming light.
Near time, far future, and the past,
one law controls them all:
any greatness in human life brings doom.

Wandering hope brings help to many men.
But others she tricks from their giddy loves,
and her quarry knows nothing until he has walked
       into flame.
620 Word of wisdom it was when someone said,
"The bad becomes the good
to him a god would doom."
Only briefly is that one from under doom.

(Haemon enters from the side.)

Here is your one surviving son.
Does he come in grief at the fate of his bride,
630 in pain that he's tricked of his wedding?

CREON:
Soon we shall know more than a seer could tell us.
Son, have you heard the vote condemned your bride?
And are you here, maddened against your father,
or are we friends, whatever I may do?

HAEMON:
My father, I am yours. You keep me straight
with your good judgment, which I shall ever follow.
Nor shall a marriage count for more with me
than your kind leading.

CREON:
There's my good boy. So should you hold at heart
and stand behind your father all the way.   640
It is for this men pray they may beget
households of dutiful obedient sons,
who share alike in punishing enemies,
and give due honor to their father's friends.
Whoever breeds a child that will not help
what has he sown but trouble for himself,
and for his enemies laughter full and free?
Son, do not let your lust mislead your mind,
all for a woman's sake, for well you know
how cold the thing he takes into his arms   650
who has a wicked woman for his wife.
What deeper wounding than a friend no friend?
Oh spit her forth forever, as your foe.
Let the girl marry somebody in Hades.
Since I have caught her in the open act,
the only one in town who disobeyed,
I shall not now proclaim myself a liar,
but kill her. Let her sing her song of Zeus
who guards the kindred.
If I allow disorder in my house
I'd surely have to licence it abroad.   660
A man who deals in fairness with his own,
he can make manifest justice in the state.
But he who crosses law, or forces it,
or hopes to bring the rulers under him,
shall never have a word of praise from me.
The man the state has put in place must have
obedient hearing to his least command
when it is right, and even when it's not.
He who accepts this teaching I can trust,
ruler, or ruled, to function in his place,
to stand his ground even in the storm of spears,   670
a mate to trust in battle at one's side.
There is no greater wrong than disobedience.
This ruins cities, this tears down our homes,
this breaks the battle-front in panic-rout.
If men live decently it is because
discipline saves their very lives for them.
So I must guard the men who yield to order,

not let myself be beaten by a woman.
Better, if it must happen, that a man
should overset me.
680 I won't be called weaker than womankind.

CHORUS:
We think—unless our age is cheating us—
that what you say is sensible and right.

HAEMON:
Father, the gods have given men good sense,
the only sure possession that we have.
I couldn't find the words in which to claim
that there was error in your late remarks.
Yet someone else might bring some further light.
Because I am your son I must keep watch
on all men's doing where it touches you,
their speech, and most of all, their discontents.
690 Your presence frightens any common man
from saying things you would not care to hear.
But in dark corners I have heard them say
how the whole town is grieving for this girl,
unjustly doomed, if ever woman was,
to die in shame for glorious action done.
She would not leave her fallen, slaughtered brother
there, as he lay, unburied, for the birds
and hungry dogs to make an end of him.
Isn't her real desert a golden prize?
700 This is the undercover speech in town.
Father, your welfare is my greatest good.
What loveliness in life for any child
outweighs a father's fortune and good fame?
And so a father feels his children's faring.
Then, do not have one mind, and one alone
that only your opinion can be right.
Whoever thinks that he alone is wise,
his eloquence, his mind, above the rest,
come the unfolding, shows his emptiness.
710 A man, though wise, should never be ashamed
of learning more, and must unbend his mind.
Have you not seen the trees beside the torrent,
the ones that bend them saving every leaf,
while the resistant perish root and branch?
And so the ship that will not slacken sail,
the sheet drawn tight, unyielding, overturns.
She ends the voyage with her keel on top.
No, yield your wrath, allow a change of stand.
Young as I am, if I may give advice,
720 I'd say it would be best if men were born

perfect in wisdom, but that failing this
(which often fails) it can be no dishonor
to learn from others when they speak good sense.

CHORUS:
Lord, if your son has spoken to the point
you should take his lesson. He should do the same.
Both sides have spoken well.

CREON:
At my age I'm to school my mind by his?
This boy instructor is my master, then?

HAEMON:
I urge no wrong. I'm young, but you should watch
my actions, not my years, to judge of me.

CREON:
A loyal action, to respect disorder?   730

HAEMON:
I wouldn't urge respect for wickedness.

CREON:
You don't think she is sick with that disease?

HAEMON:
Your fellow-citizens maintain she's not.

CREON:
Is the town to tell me how I ought to rule?

HAEMON:
Now there you speak just like a boy yourself.

CREON:
Am I to rule by other mind than mine?

HAEMON:
No city is property of a single man.

CREON:
But custom gives possession to the ruler.

HAEMON:
You'd rule a desert beautifully alone.

CREON (to the Chorus):
It seems he's firmly on the woman's side.   740

HAEMON:
If you're a woman. It is you I care for.

CREON:
Wicked, to try conclusions with your father.

HAEMON:
When you conclude unjustly, so I must.

CREON:
Am I unjust, when I respect my office?

HAEMON:
You tread down the gods' due. Respect is gone.

CREON:
Your mind is poisoned. Weaker than a woman!

HAEMON:
At least you'll never see me yield to shame.

CREON:
Your whole long argument is but for her.

HAEMON:
And you, and me, and for the gods below.

CREON:
750 You shall not marry her while she's alive.

HAEMON:
Then she shall die. Her death will bring another.

CREON:
Your boldness has made progress. Threats, indeed!

HAEMON:
No threat, to speak against your empty plan.

CREON:
Past due, sharp lessons for your empty brain.

HAEMON:
If you weren't father, I should call you mad.

CREON:
Don't flatter me with "father," you woman's slave.

HAEMON:
You wish to speak but never wish to hear.

CREON:
You think so? By Olympus, you shall not
revile me with these tauntings and go free.
Bring out the hateful creature; she shall die
760 full in his sight, close at her bridegroom's side.

HAEMON:
Not at my side her death, and you will not
ever lay eyes upon my face again.
Find other friends to rave with after this.

(Haemon leaves, by one of the side entrances.)

CHORUS:
Lord, he has gone with all the speed of rage.
When such a man is grieved his mind is hard.

CREON:
Oh, let him go, plan superhuman action.
In any case the girls shall not escape.

CHORUS:
You plan for both the punishment of death?   770

CREON:
Not her who did not do it. You are right.

CHORUS:
And what death have you chosen for the other?

CREON:
To take her where the foot of man comes not.
There shall I hide her in a hollowed cave
living, and leave her just so much to eat
as clears the city from the guilt of death.
There, if she prays to Death, the only god
of her respect, she may manage not to die.
Or she may learn at last and even then
how much too much her labor for the dead.   780

(Creon returns to the palace.)

CHORUS:
Love unconquered in fight, love who falls on our
      havings.
You rest in the bloom of a girl's unwithered face.
You cross the sea, you are known in the wildest lairs.
Not the immortal gods can fly,
nor men of a day. Who has you within him is mad. 790

You twist the minds of the just. Wrong they pursue
      and are ruined.
You made this quarrel of kindred before us now.
Desire looks clear from the eyes of a lovely bride:
power as strong as the founded world.
For there is the goddess at play with whom no man 800
      can fight.

(Antigone is brought from the palace under guard.)

            Now I am carried beyond all bounds.
            My tears will not be checked.
            I see Antigone depart
            to the chamber where all men sleep.

ANTIGONE:

Men of my fathers' land, you see me go
my last journey. My last sight of the sun,
810 that never again. Death who brings all to sleep
takes me alive to the shore
of the river underground.
Not for me was the marriage-hymn, nor will anyone
    start the song
at a wedding of mine. Acheron is my mate.

CHORUS:

With praise as your portion you go
in fame to the vault of the dead.
Untouched by wasting disease,
820 not paying the price of the sword,
of your own motion you go.
Alone among mortals will you descend
in life to the house of Death.

ANTIGONE:

Pitiful was the death that stranger died,
our queen once, Tantalus' daughter. The rock
it covered her over, like stubborn ivy it grew.
Still, as she wastes, the rain
and snow companion her.
830 Pouring down from her mourning eyes comes the
    water that soaks the stone.
My own putting to sleep a god has planned like hers.

CHORUS:

God's child and god she was.
We are born to death.
Yet even in death you will have your fame,
to have gone like a god to your fate,
in living and dying alike.

ANTIGONE:

Laughter against me now. In the name of our fa-
    thers' gods,
840 could you not wait till I went? Must affront be thrown
    in my face?
O city of wealthy men.
I call upon Dirce's spring,
I call upon Thebe's grove in the armored plain,
to be my witnesses, how with no friend's mourning,
by what decree I go to the fresh-made prison-tomb.
850 Alive to the place of corpses, an alien still,
never at home with the living nor with the dead.

CHORUS:

You went to the furthest verge
of daring, but there you found
the high foundation of justice, and fell.
Perhaps you are paying your father's pain.

ANTIGONE:

You speak of my darkest thought, my pitiful fa-
    ther's fame,
spread through all the world, and the doom that 860
    haunts our house,
the royal house of Thebes.
My mother's marriage-bed.
Destruction where she lay with her husband-son,
my father. There are my parents and I their child.
I go to stay with them. My curse is to die unwed.
My brother, you found your fate when you found 870
    your bride,
found it for me as well. Dead, you destroy my life.

CHORUS:

You showed respect for the dead.
So we for you: but power
is not to be thwarted so.
Your self-sufficiency has brought you down.

ANTIGONE:

Unwept, no wedding-song, unfriended, now I go
the road laid down for me.
No longer shall I see this holy light of the sun.   880
No friend to bewail my fate.

(Creon enters from the palace.)

CREON:

When people sing the dirge for their own deaths
ahead of time, nothing will break them off
if they can hope that this will buy delay.
Take her away at once, and open up
the tomb I spoke of. Leave her there alone.
There let her choose: death, or a buried life.
No stain of guilt upon us in this case,
but she is exiled from our life on earth.   890

ANTIGONE:

O tomb, O marriage-chamber, hollowed out
house that will watch forever, where I go.
To my own people, who are mostly there;
Persephone has taken them to her.
Last of them all, ill-fated past the rest,
shall I descend, before my course is run.

Still when I get there I may hope to find
I come as a dear friend to my dear father,
to you, my mother, and my brother too.
900 All three of you have known my hand in death.
I washed your bodies, dressed them for the grave,
poured out the last libation at the tomb.
Last, Polyneices knows the price I pay
for doing final service to his corpse.
And yet the wise will know my choice was right.
Had I had children or their father dead,
I'd let them moulder. I should not have chosen
in such a case to cross the state's decree.
What is the law that lies behind these words?
One husband gone, I might have found another,
910 or a child from a new man in first child's place,
but with my parents hid away in death,
no brother, ever, could spring up for me.
Such was the law by which I honored you.
But Creon thought the doing was a crime,
a dreadful daring, brother of my heart.
So now he takes and leads me out by force.
No marriage-bed, no marriage-song for me,
and since no wedding, so no child to rear.
I go, without a friend, struck down by fate,
920 live to the hollow chambers of the dead.
What divine justice have I disobeyed?
Why, in my misery, look to the gods for help?
Can I call any of them my ally?
I stand convicted of impiety,
the evidence my pious duty done.
Should the gods think that this is righteousness,
in suffering I'll see my error clear.
But if it is the others who are wrong
I wish them no greater punishment than mine.

CHORUS:

                    The same tempest of mind
930   as ever, controls the girl.

CREON:

                    Therefore her guards shall regret
                    the slowness with which they move.

ANTIGONE:

                    That word comes close to death.

CREON:

                    You are perfectly right in that.

ANTIGONE:

                    O town of my fathers in Thebe's land,
                    O gods of our house.
                    I am led away at last.
                    Look, leaders of Thebes,   940
                    I am last of your royal line.
                    Look what I suffer, at whose command,
                    because I respected the right.

*(Antigone is led away. The slow procession should begin
during the preceding passage.)*

CHORUS:
Danaë suffered too.
She went from the light to the brass-built room,
chamber and tomb together. Like you, poor child,
she was of great descent, and more, she held and kept
the seed of the golden rain which was Zeus.   950
Fate has terrible power.
You cannot escape it by wealth or war.
No fort will keep it out, no ships outrun it.

Remember the angry king,
son of Dryas, who raged at the god and paid,
pent in a rock-walled prison. His bursting wrath
slowly went down. As the terror of madness went,
he learned of his frenzied attack on the god.   960
Fool, he had tried to stop
the dancing women possessed of god,
the fire of Dionysus, the songs and flutes.

Where the dark rocks divide
sea from sea in Thrace
is Salmydessus whose savage god   970
beheld the terrible blinding wounds
dealt to Phineus' sons by their father's wife.
Dark the eyes that looked to avenge their mother.
Sharp with her shuttle she struck, and blooded her
    hands.

Wasting they wept their fate,
settled when they were born   980
to Cleopatra, unhappy queen.
She was a princess too, of an ancient house,

reared in the cave of the wild north wind, her father.
Half a goddess but, child, she suffered like you.

*(Enter, from the side Teiresias, the blind prophet, led by a
boy attendant.)*

TEIRESIAS:
Elders of Thebes, we two have come one road,
two of us looking through one pair of eyes.
990 This is the way of walking for the blind.

CREON:
Teiresias, what news has brought you here?

TEIRESIAS:
I'll tell you. You in turn must trust the prophet.

CREON:
I've always been attentive to your counsel.

TEIRESIAS:
And therefore you have steered this city straight.

CREON:
So I can say how helpful you have been.

TEIRESIAS:
But now you are balanced on a razor's edge.

CREON:
What is it? How I shudder at your words!

TEIRESIAS:
You'll know, when you hear the signs that I have
    marked
1000 I sat where every bird of heaven comes
in my old place of augury, and heard
bird-cries I'd never known. They screeched about
goaded by madness, inarticulate.
I marked that they were tearing one another
with claws of murder. I could hear the wing-beats.
I was afraid, so straight away I tried
burnt sacrifice upon the flaming altar.
No fire caught my offerings. Slimy ooze
dripped on the ashes, smoked and sputtered there.
1010 Gall burst its bladder, vanished into vapor;
the fat dripped from the bones and would not burn.
These are the omens of the rites that failed,
as my boy here has told me. He's my guide
as I am guide to others.
Why has this sickness struck against the state?
Through your decision.
All of the altars of the town are choked

with leavings of the dogs and birds; their feast
was on that fated, fallen Polyneices.
So the gods will have no offering from us,
not prayer, nor flame of sacrifice. The birds   1020
will not cry out a sound I can distinguish,
gorged with the greasy blood of that dead man.
Think of these things, my son. All men may err
but error once committed, he's no fool
nor yet unfortunate, who gives up his stiffness
and cures the trouble he has fallen in.
Stubbornness and stupidity are twins.
Yield to the dead. Why goad him where he lies?
What use to kill the dead a second time?   1030
I speak for your own good. And I am right.
Learning from a wise counsellor is not pain
if what he speaks are profitable words.

CREON:
Old man, you all, like bowmen at a mark,
have bent your bows at me. I've had my share
of seers. I've been an item in your accounts.
Make profit, trade in Lydian silver-gold,
pure gold of India; that's your chief desire.
But you will never cover up that corpse.
Not if the very eagles tear their food   1040
from him, and leave it at the throne of Zeus.
I wouldn't give him up for burial
in fear of that pollution. For I know
no mortal being can pollute the gods.
O old Teiresias, human beings fall;
the clever ones the furthest, when they plead
a shameful case so well in hope of profit.

TEIRESIAS:
Alas!
What man can tell me, has he thought at all . . .

CREON:
What hackneyed saw is coming from your lips?

TEIRESIAS:
How better than all wealth is sound good counsel.   1050

CREON:
And so is folly worse than anything.

TEIRESIAS
And you're infected with that same disease.

CREON:
I'm reluctant to be uncivil to a seer . . .

TEIRESIAS:
You're that already. You have said I lie.

CREON:
Well, the whole crew of seers are money-mad.

TEIRESIAS:
And the whole tribe of tyrants grab at gain.

CREON:
Do you realize you are talking to a king?

TEIRESIAS:
I know. Who helped you save this town you hold?

CREON:
You're a wise seer, but you love wickedness.

TEIRESIAS:
1060 You'll bring me to speak the unspeakable, very soon.

CREON:
Well, speak it out. But do not speak for profit.

TEIRESIAS:
No, there's no profit in my words for you.

CREON:
You'd better realize that you can't deliver
my mind, if you should sell it, to the buyer.

TEIRESIAS:
Know well, the sun will not have rolled its course
many more days, before you come to give
corpse for these corpses, child of your own loins.
For you've confused the upper and lower worlds.
You sent a life to settle in a tomb;
1070 you keep up here that which belongs below
the corpse unburied, robbed of its release.
Not you, nor any god that rules on high
can claim him now.
You rob the nether gods of what is theirs.
So the pursuing horrors lie in wait
to track you down. The Furies sent by Hades
and by all gods will even you with your victims.
Now say that I am bribed! At no far time
shall men and women wail within your house.
1080 And all the cities that you fought in war
whose sons had burial from wild beasts, or dogs,
or birds that brought the stench of your great wrong
back to each hearth, they move against you now.
A bowman, as you said, I send my shafts,

now you have moved me, straight. You'll feel the
    wound.
Boy, take me home now. Let him spend his rage
on younger men, and learn to calm his tongue,
and keep a better mind than now he does.   1090

    (Exit.)

CHORUS:
Lord, he has gone. Terrible prophecies!
And since the time when I first grew grey hair
his sayings to the city have been true.

CREON:
I also know this. And my mind is torn.
To yield is dreadful. But to stand against him.
Dreadful to strike my spirit to destruction.

CHORUS:
Now you must come to counsel, and take advice.

CREON:
What must I do? Speak, and I shall obey.

CHORUS:
Go free the maiden from that rocky house.   1100
Bury the dead who lies in readiness.

CREON:
This is your counsel? You would have me yield?

CHORUS:
Quick as you can. The gods move very fast
when they bring ruin on misguided men.

CREON:
How hard, abandonment of my desire.
But I can fight necessity no more.

CHORUS:
Do it yourself. Leave it to no one else.

CREON:
I'll go at once. Come, followers, to your work.
You that are here round up the other fellows.
Take axes with you, hurry to that place
that overlooks us.   1110
Now my decision has been overturned
shall I, who bound her, set her free myself.
I've come to fear it's best to hold the laws
of old tradition to the end of life.

    (Exit.)

CHORUS:
God of the many names, Semele's golden child,
child of Olympian thunder, Italy's lord.
1120 Lord of Eleusis, where all men come
to mother Demeter's plain.
Bacchus, who dwell in Thebes,
by Ismenus' running water,
where wild Bacchic women are at home,
on the soil of the dragon seed.

Seen in the glaring flame, high on the double mount,
with the nymphs of Parnassus at play on the hill,
1130 seen by Kastalia's flowing stream.
You come from the ivied heights,
from green Euboea's shore.
In immortal words we cry
your name, lord, who watch the ways,
the many ways of Thebes.

This is your city, honored beyond the rest,
the town of your mother's miracle-death.
1140 Now, as we wrestle our grim disease,
come with healing step from Parnassus' slope
or over the moaning sea.

Leader in dance of the fire-pulsing stars,
overseer of the voices of night,
child of Zeus, be manifest,
1150 with due companionship of Maenad maids
whose cry is but your name

   (Enter one of those who left with Creon, as messenger.)

MESSENGER:
Neighbors of Cadmus, and Amphion's house,
there is no kind of state in human life
which I now dare to envy or to blame.
Luck sets it straight, and luck she overturns
the happy or unhappy day by day.
1160 No prophecy can deal with men's affairs.
Creon was envied once, as I believe,
for having saved this city from its foes
and having got full power in this land.
He steered it well. And he had noble sons.
Now everything is gone.
Yes, when a man has lost all happiness,
he's not alive. Call him a breathing corpse.
Be very rich at home. Live as a king.

But once your joy has gone, though these are left
they are smoke's shadow to lost happiness.   1170

CHORUS:
What is the grief of princes that you bring?

MESSENGER:
They're dead. The living are responsible.

CHORUS:
Who died? Who did the murder? Tell us now.

MESSENGER:
Haemon is gone. One of his kin drew blood.

CHORUS:
But whose arm struck? His father's or his own?

MESSENGER:
He killed himself. His blood is on his father.

CHORUS:
Seer, all too true the prophecy you told!

MESSENGER:
This is the state of things. Now make your plans.

   (Enter, from the palace, Eurydice.)

CHORUS:
Eurydice is with us now, I see.   1180
Creon's poor wife. She may have come by chance.
She may have heard something about her son.

EURYDICE:
I heard your talk as I was coming out
to greet the goddess Pallas with my prayer.
And as I moved the bolts that held the door
I heard of my own sorrow.
I fell back fainting in my women's arms.
But say again just what the news you bring.   1190
I, whom you speak to, have known grief before.

MESSENGER:
Dear lady, I was there, and I shall tell,
leaving out nothing of the true account.
Why should I make it soft for you with tales
to prove myself a liar? Truth is right.
I followed your husband to the plain's far edge,
where Polyneices' corpse was lying still
unpitied. The dogs had torn him all apart.   1200
We prayed the goddess of all journeyings,
and Pluto, that they turn their wrath to kindness,
we gave the final purifying bath,

then burned the poor remains on new-cut boughs,
and heaped a high mound of his native earth.
Then turned we to the maiden's rocky bed,
death's hollow marriage-chamber.
But, still far off, one of us heard a voice
in keen lament by that unblest abode.
He ran and told the master. As Creon came
1210 he heard confusion crying. He groaned and spoke:
"Am I a prophet now, and do I tread
the saddest of all roads I ever trod?
My son's voice crying! Servants, run up close,
stand by the tomb and look, push through the crevice
where we built the pile of rock, right to the entry.
Find out if that is Haemon's voice I hear
or if the gods are tricking me indeed."
We obeyed the order of our mournful master.
1220 In the far corner of the tomb we saw
her, hanging by the neck, caught in a noose
of her own linen veiling.
Haemon embraced her as she hung, and mourned
his bride's destruction, dead and gone below,
his father's actions, the unfated marriage.
When Creon saw him, he groaned terribly,
and went toward him, and called him with lament:
"What have you done, what plan have you caught up,
what sort of suffering is killing you?
1230 Come out, my child, I do beseech you, come!"
The boy looked at him with his angry eyes,
spat in his face and spoke no further word,
He drew his sword, but as his father ran,
he missed his aim. Then the unhappy boy,
in anger at himself, leant on the blade.
It entered, half its length, into his side.
While he was conscious he embraced the maiden,
holding her gently. Last, he gasped out blood,
red blood on her white cheek.
1240 Corpse on a corpse he lies. He found his marriage.
Its celebration in the halls of Hades.
So he has made it very clear to men
that to reject good counsel is a crime.

(Eurydice returns to the house.)

CHORUS:
What do you make of this? The queen has gone
in silence. We know nothing of her mind.

MESSENGER:
I wonder at her, too. But we can hope

that she has gone to mourn her son within
with her own women, not before the town.
She knows discretion. She will do no wrong.   1250

CHORUS:
I am not sure. This muteness may portend
as great disaster as a loud lament.

MESSENGER:
I will go in and see if some deep plan
hides in her heart's wild pain. You may be right.
There can be heavy danger in mute grief.

*(The messenger goes into the house. Creon enters with his
followers. They are carrying Haemon's body on a bier.)*

CHORUS:
But look, the king draws near.
His own hand brings
the witness of his crime,
the doom he brought on himself.   1260

CREON:
O crimes of my wicked heart,
harshness bringing death.
You see the killer, you see the kin he killed.
My planning was all unblest.
Son, you have died too soon.
Oh, you have gone away
through my fault, not your own.

CHORUS:
You have learned justice, though it comes too late. 1270

CREON:
Yes, I have learned in sorrow. It was a god who struck,
who has weighted my head with disaster; he drove
    me to wild strange ways,
his heavy heel on my joy.
Oh sorrows, sorrows of men.

(Re-enter the messenger, from a side door of the palace.)

MESSENGER:
Master, you hold one sorrow in your hands
but you have more, stored up inside the house.   1280

CREON:
What further suffering can come on me?

MESSENGER:
Your wife has died. The dead man's mother in deed,
poor soul, her wounds are fresh.

CREON:
Hades, harbor of all,
you have destroyed me now.
1290 Terrible news to hear, horror the tale you tell.
I was dead, and you kill me again.
Boy, did I hear you right?
Did you say the queen was dead,
slaughter on slaughter heaped?

(The central doors of the palace begin to open.)

CHORUS:
Now you can see. Concealment is all over.

(The doors are open, and the corpse of Eurydice is revealed.)

CREON:
My second sorrow is here. Surely no fate remains
which can strike me again. Just now, I held my son
   in my arms.
And now I see her dead.
1300 Woe for the mother and son.

MESSENGER:
There, by the altar, dying on the sword,
her eyes fell shut. She wept her older son
who died before, and this one. Last of all
she cursed you as the killer of her children.

CREON:
I am mad with fear. Will no one strike
and kill me with cutting sword?
1310 Sorrowful, soaked in sorrow to the bone!

MESSENGER:
Yes, for she held you guilty in the death
of him before you, and the elder dead.

CREON:
How did she die?

MESSENGER:
         Struck home at her own heart
when she had heard of Haemon's suffering.

CREON:
This is my guilt, all mine. I killed you, I say it clear.
Servants, take me away, out of the sight of men.   1320
I who am nothing more than nothing now.

CHORUS:
Your plan is good—if any good is left.
Beset to cut short our sorrow.

CREON:
Let me go, let me go. May death come quick,
bringing my final day.   1330
O let me never see tomorrow's dawn.

CHORUS:
That is the future's. We must look to now.
What will be is in other hands than ours.

CREON:
All my desire was in that prayer of mine.

CHORUS:
Pray not again. No mortal can escape
the doom prepared for him.

CREON:
Take me away at once, the frantic man who killed   1340
my son, against my meaning. I cannot rest.
My life is warped past cure. My fate has struck me
   down.

(Creon and his attendants enter the house.)

CHORUS:

    Our happiness depends
    on wisdom all the way.
    The gods must have their due.
    Great words by men of pride   1350
    bring greater blows upon them.
    So wisdom comes to the old.

V

SOCRATES AND PLATO

Our knowledge of Socrates comes almost entirely from Plato. Socrates himself wrote nothing, while Plato was a prolific author of philosophical dialogues. Thirty-seven of those dialogues have survived, and most of them—though not all—have Socrates as their main character. Socrates is known from two other contemporary sources, Aristophanes and Xenophon. But Aristophanes' portrayal of him in *Clouds*, though sufficient to show that Socrates was a well-known figure in Athens, is plainly motivated, at least in part, by the dramatic goals of a comic and satiric writer, while Xenophon's account, though highly sympathetic, does not reflect the depth and subtlety of Socratic thought.

Socrates was a teacher and a public philosopher, and his influence on all subsequent philosophy cannot be overestimated. Above all, he sought to address fundamental questions of an ethical nature, doing so by asking about the most basic moral concepts: virtue, courage, temperance, love, justice, and the like. Perhaps most important, his goal was to discover not simply what people thought about such things but what was actually true about them. This is to say that he believed our actions should be governed not by mere convention (*nomos*) but rather by a serious and systematic knowledge of the nature (*physis*) of things. A great many of his interlocutors were Sophists who denied either that there was an essential truth about right and wrong or that we could ever have knowledge of such a truth; and in this sense, Socrates was—contrary to Aristophanes' portrayal—the arch anti-Sophist.

In seeking the truth of things, Socrates famously pursued the method of *elenchus* or refutation, what is today rather loosely called the Socratic method. Socrates would ask someone about the nature of a particular moral concept, and his interlocutor would provide an opinion. Socrates would then ask about other opinions that the interlocutor might hold to very strongly and might not want to give up under any circumstance. If, then, it could be shown that the original opinion was inconsistent with the others—and this is typically what did happen—the original opinion would be refuted as incoherent. In the *Euthyphro*, for example, Socrates asks about the nature of piety. Euthyphro claims to know what piety is and offers an account of it. But Socrates then asks Euthyphro a series of questions concerning the gods and basic principles of logic. He shows that Euthyphro cannot consistently hold to his beliefs about those things and still keep his original account of piety. That account must therefore be replaced by a better account, one that comports with his more basic beliefs.

The *Euthyphro* also reflects another feature that is typical of Plato's Socratic dialogues, namely, that they are *aporetic*, that is, they often do not come to a clear, positive conclusion about the issue in question. At the end of the *Euthyphro*, we have a pretty good idea of why certain accounts of piety are untenable, but we still don't know what piety is. The *aporetic* nature of Socrates' conversations is consistent with his extraordinary, paradoxical, and inflammatory claim, made in the *Apology*, that he himself knows nothing, except that he alone knows that he knows nothing. Socrates' insistence on his own ignorance is a much disputed claim in the history of philosophy and is widely thought to reflect the fact that, as a literary matter, Plato's Socratic dialogues are rife with irony.

The trial and death of Socrates is one of the major events of the Western political tradition. Some have found in it a parallel to the crucifixion of Jesus. With Socrates, we have the first important instance of a sharp clash between philosophy and politics, between the single-minded pursuit of truth and the public's interest in the common good. It is important to note that Socrates was essentially accused of subversion. He was indicted on charges of believing in gods other than the orthodox gods of Athens, of teaching others to believe in those gods, and in general of making strong arguments seem weak, and weak ones strong—all of which was thought to undermine the authority of the state itself. These accusations are, in fact, not unrelated to what we find in Aristophanes' *Clouds*. But it also important to note that Socrates was accused, tried, and condemned by a democratic government. His death was the act not of a despot or jealous tyrant but of a legitimate, lawful, and apparently popular regime seeking to pursue the public interest. The trial of Socrates thus raises the most fundamental questions about the relationship between philosophical truth on the one hand and practical politics on the other.

These questions are treated systematically in Plato's *Republic*, arguably the most famous and possibly the greatest work of Western philosophy. Plato himself was born into a distinguished and venerable Athenian family. His father, Ariston, was evidently an illustrious figure and his stepfather, Pyrilampes, was known to be an intimate political ally of Pericles. His second cousin Critias was an important and influential leader of the oligarchic party in Athens, as was his uncle, Charmides. A young man with such a background would be presumed to seek and attain a position of leadership in the political affairs of the city. His family would have contemplated for him a future in politics, expecting him to follow in the footsteps of his father and stepfather and to assume, thereby, the prerogatives and responsibilities of his station.

But Plato chose otherwise. He fell deeply under the influence of Socrates, became Socrates' primary chronicler and greatest student, and gave up politics for a life of abstract, philosophical speculation. His dialogues are literary and philosophical masterpieces. Each of them presents a systematic conversation on a central topic in philosophy but does so by bringing together characters whose personalities and interactions both complicate and enrich the actual presentation of ideas.

Disentangling Plato's views from those of Socrates is a difficult business, which has long been a topic of scholarly debate. It seems clear, though, that the *Republic*, Plato's greatest work, is a "middle" or "late" dialogue and that it presents views that Socrates probably never articulated and might even have repudiated. It includes, early on, a fierce exchange about the concept of justice between Socrates and Thrasymachus, who presents a rather extreme view of Sophistic, conventionalist doctrine. Then, at the urging of two other interlocutors—Glaucon and Adeimantus, who happened to have been Plato's brothers—Socrates proceeds to construct an idea of the city-state, a *kallipolis* or beautiful city, that constitutes, according to Socrates, a kind of conceptual standard against which actual city-states are to be judged. In constructing the *kallipolis*, Plato has Socrates utilize a powerful, influential, and controversial analogy between the soul of the individual human being and the internal constitution of a just city. Just as the soul has three parts—an appetitive, a spirited, and a rational part—and just as a soul is healthy when the rational part rules the other two, so is a city composed of three classes—a business class, a warrior class, and a class of rational guardians—which are properly ordered when political power is entrusted to the guardians. In this sense, Platonic doctrine is sharply antidemocratic. It claims that those most capable of ruling should rule, and it holds that the rulers should do whatever is required—including, for example, implementing strict policies of censorship—in order to maintain the health and stability of the state.

Having outlined the idea of the state in Books 1 through 5, Plato then has Socrates answer a different kind of question: how can existing cities such as Athens, all of which are more or less corrupt, be reformed so that they can approximate as closely as possible the idea? Plato's famous reply is that kings should be philosophers, and philosophers kings. The deep tension between the political and the philosophical that seems evident in the trial and death of Socrates is now turned on its head. Philosophy is, in fact, the salvation of the political.

Such views are underwritten by an astonishing metaphysical doctrine, the so-called theory of forms. According to Plato, the only things that are really real—eternal, imperishable, unchangeable—are ideas. Empirical things, the things that we can observe with our physical senses, are essentially shadows of, merely temporary illustrations of, ideas. The chair that I am sitting on is a chair indeed. But it wouldn't be a chair—it couldn't be a chair—unless there were, independent of and prior to its existence, an idea of chair that makes this particular chair what it is in the first place; and when this particular chair ceases to exist, when it burns in a fire or is thrown away or broken to pieces, the idea of chair will continue to exist and will continue to make it possible for us to construct other particular chairs, each of which will similarly be a temporary embodiment of the idea. So too for cities. The *kallipolis* is the idea of the city. Particular cities are shadows—mere instantiations—of the idea. As craftsmen of cities, political leaders need to be able to understand the idea so that, in implementing policies, they can approximate it as closely as possible; and who could understand the idea of the city as clearly and comprehensively as the philosophers? Here, then, we have at least a part of the argument for the political rule of philosophy.

The *Laws* may be thought of as Plato's effort to think in detail about how best to implement the idea of the city. Socrates is entirely absent from the scene. An Athenian stranger leads a discussion aimed at developing a workable political constitution for a new Cretan colony. He and his friends propose numerous details of legislation, and their deliberations may well provide our best evidence about the practical political implications of Plato's abstract, philosophical doctrine.

Further Reading: Perhaps the most influential recent introduction to Socrates is Gregory Vlastos, *Socrates: Ironist and Moral Philosopher* (1991). It is highly recommended. Also important are two books by Thomas C. Brickhouse and Nicholas D. Smith, *Socrates on Trial* (1989) and *Plato's Socrates* (1994). A powerful defense of Socrates' argument in front of the jury is to be found in C. D. C. Reeve, *Socrates in the Apology* (1989). For the editor's view of the *Apology*, see Peter J. Steinberger, "Was Socrates Guilty as Charged? Apology 24c–28a," in *Ancient Philosophy* (Spring 1997).

The now-standard work on Plato's ethics is Terence Irwin, *Plato's Moral Theory* (1977). This is an extremely impressive piece of scholarship that traces in unusual detail the development of Plato's thought. A nice entryway into Plato's *Republic* is Julia Annas, *An Introduction to Plato's Republic*. Among recent commentaries, the most original, penetrating, and persuasive is surely C. D. C. Reeve's *Philosopher-Kings: The Argument of Plato's Republic* (1988). A very different kind of account is to be found in Leo Strauss, *The City and Man* (1978); a related view is presented in Arlene Saxonhouse, "Comedy in the Callipolis: Animal Imagery in the Republic," in *American Political Science Review* (1978). For the editor's view of some key issues in the *Republic*, see Peter J. Steinberger, "Who Is Cephalus," in *Political Theory* (May 1996), and Peter J. Steinberger, "Ruling: Guardians and Philosopher/Kings," in *American Political Science Review* (December 1989).

Plato

(427–347 B.C.)

Euthyphro

2 EUTHYPHRO: What's new, Socrates, to make you leave your usual haunts in the Lyceum and spend your time here by the king-archon's court? Surely you are not prosecuting anyone before the king-archon as I am?

SOCRATES: The Athenians do not call this a prosecution but an indictment, Euthyphro.

b EUTHYPHRO: What is this you say? Someone must have indicted you, for you are not going to tell me that you have indicted someone else.

SOCRATES: No indeed.

EUTHYPHRO: But someone else has indicted you?

SOCRATES: Quite so.

EUTHYPHRO: Who is he?

SOCRATES: I do not really know him myself, Euthyphro. He is apparently young and unknown. They call him Meletus, I believe. He belongs to the Pitthean deme, if you know anyone from that deme called Meletus, with long hair, not much of a beard, and a rather aquiline nose.

EUTHYPHRO: I don't know him, Socrates. What charge does he bring against you?

c SOCRATES: What charge? A not ignoble one I think, for it is no small thing for a young man to have knowledge of such an important subject. He says he knows how our young men are corrupted and who corrupts them. He is likely to be wise, and when he sees my ignorance corrupting his contemporaries, he d proceeds to accuse me to the city as to their mother. I think he is the only one of our public men to start out the right way, for it is right to care first that the young should be as good as possible, just as a good farmer is likely to take care of the young plants first, and of the others later. So, too, Meletus first gets rid 3 of us who corrupt the young shoots, as he says, and then afterwards he will obviously take care of the older ones and become a source of great blessings for the city, as seems likely to happen to one who started out this way.

EUTHYPHRO: I could wish this were true, Socrates, but I fear the opposite may happen. He seems to me to start out by harming the very heart of the city by attempting to wrong you. Tell me, what does he say you do to corrupt the young?

SOCRATES: Strange things, to hear him tell it, for b he says that I am a maker of gods, and on the ground that I create new gods while not believing in the old gods, he has indicted me for their sake, as he puts it.

EUTHYPHRO: I understand, Socrates. This is because you say that the divine sign keeps coming to you. So he has written this indictment against you as one who makes innovations in religious matters, and he comes to court to slander you, knowing that such things are easily misrepresented to the crowd. The same is true in my case. Whenever I speak of divine c matters in the assembly and foretell the future, they laugh me down as if I were crazy; and yet I have foretold nothing that did not happen. Nevertheless, they envy all of us who do this. One need not worry about them, but meet them head-on.

SOCRATES: My dear Euthyphro, to be laughed at does not matter perhaps, for the Athenians do not mind anyone they think clever, as long as he does not teach his own wisdom, but if they think that he makes others to be like himself they get angry, whether through envy, as you say, or for some d other reason.

EUTHYPHRO: I have certainly no desire to test their feelings towards me in this matter.

SOCRATES: Perhaps you seem to make yourself but rarely available, and not be willing to teach your own wisdom, but I'm afraid that my liking for people makes them think that I pour out to anybody anything I have to say, not only without charging a fee but even

Reprinted from Plato, *Five Dialogues*, translated by G. M. A. Grube (Indianapolis: Hackett Publishing Company, 1981) by permission of the publisher.

glad to reward anyone who is willing to listen. If then
e they were intending to laugh at me, as you say they
laugh at you, there would be nothing unpleasant in
their spending their time in court laughing and jesting, but if they are going to be serious, the outcome
is not clear except to you prophets.

EUTHYPHRO: Perhaps it will come to nothing, Socrates, and you will fight your case as you think best,
as I think I will mine.

SOCRATES: What is your case, Euthyphro? Are you
the defendant or the prosecutor?

EUTHYPHRO: The prosecutor.

SOCRATES: Whom do you prosecute?

EUTHYPHRO: One whom I am thought crazy to pros-
4 ecute.

SOCRATES: Are you pursuing someone who will
easily escape you?

EUTHYPHRO: Far from it, for he is quite old.

SOCRATES: Who is it?

EUTHYPHRO: My father.

SOCRATES: My dear sir! Your own father?

EUTHYPHRO: Certainly.

SOCRATES: What is the charge? What is the case
about?

EUTHYPHRO: Murder, Socrates.

SOCRATES: Good heavens! Certainly, Euthyphro,
b most men would not know how they could do this
and be right. It is not the part of anyone to do this,
but of one who is far advanced in wisdom.

EUTHYPHRO: Yes, by Zeus, Socrates, that is so.

SOCRATES: Is then the man your father killed one
of your relatives? Or is that obvious, for you would
not prosecute your father for the murder of a stranger.

EUTHYPHRO: It is ridiculous, Socrates, for you to
think that it makes any difference whether the victim
is a stranger or a relative. One should only watch
whether the killer acted justly or not; if he acted
justly, let him go, but if not, one should prosecute,
c if, that is to say, the killer shares your hearth and
table. The pollution is the same if you knowingly
keep company with such a man and do not cleanse
yourself and him by bringing him to justice. The
victim was a dependent of mine, and when we were
farming in Naxos he was a servant of ours. He killed
one of our household slaves in drunken anger, so my
father bound him hand and foot and threw him in
a ditch, then sent a man here to inquire from the
d priest what should be done. During that time he gave

no thought or care to the bound man, as being a
killer, and it was no matter if he died, which he did.
Hunger and cold and his bonds caused his death
before the messenger came back from the seer. Both
my father and my other relatives are angry that I
am prosecuting my father for murder on behalf of a
murderer when he hadn't even killed him, they say,
and even if he had, the dead man does not deserve
a thought, since he was a killer. For, they say, it is
e impious for a son to prosecute his father for murder.
But their ideas of the divine attitude to piety and
impiety are wrong, Socrates.

SOCRATES: Whereas, by Zeus, Euthyphro, you
think that your knowledge of the divine, and of piety
and impiety, is so accurate that, when those things
happened as you say, you have no fear of having acted
impiously in bringing your father to trial?

EUTHYPHRO: I should be of no use, Socrates, and
Euthyphro would not be superior to the majority of 5
men, if I did not have accurate knowledge of all
such things.

SOCRATES: It is indeed most important, my admirable Euthyphro, that I should become your pupil, and
as regards this indictment challenge Meletus about
these very things and say to him: that in the past too
I considered knowledge about the divine to be most
important, and that now that he says that I am guilty
of improvising and innovating about the gods I b
have become your pupil. I would say to him: "If,
Meletus, you agree that Euthyphro is wise in these
matters, consider me, too, to have the right beliefs
and do not bring me to trial. If you do not think so,
then prosecute that teacher of mine, not me, for
corrupting the older men, me and his own father, by
teaching me and by exhorting and punishing him."
If he is not convinced, and does not discharge me or
indict you instead of me, I shall repeat the same
challenge in court.

EUTHYPHRO: Yes, by Zeus, Socrates, and, if he
should try to indict me, I think I would find his weak c
spots and the talk in court would be about him rather
than about me.

SOCRATES: It is because I realize this that I am
eager to become your pupil, my dear friend. I know
that other people as well as this Meletus do not even
seem to notice you, whereas he sees me so sharply
and clearly that he indicts me for ungodliness. So
tell me now, by Zeus, what you just now maintained

you clearly knew: what kind of thing do you say that godliness and ungodliness are, both as regards murder and other things; or is the pious not the same and alike in every action, and the impious the opposite of all that is pious and like itself, and everything that is to be impious presents us with one form or appearance in so far as it is impious?

EUTHYPHRO: Most certainly, Socrates.

SOCRATES: Tell me then, what is the pious, and what the impious, do you say?

EUTHYPHRO: I say that the pious is to do what I am doing now, to prosecute the wrongdoer, be it about murder or temple robbery or anything else, whether the wrongdoer is your father or your mother or anyone else; not to prosecute is impious. And observe, Socrates, that I can cite powerful evidence that the law is so. I have already said to others that such actions are right, not to favor the ungodly, whoever they are. These people themselves believe that Zeus is the best and most just of the gods, yet they agree that he bound his father because he unjustly swallowed his sons, and that he in turn castrated his father for similar reasons. But they are angry with me because I am prosecuting my father for his wrongdoing. They contradict themselves in what they say about the gods and about me.

SOCRATES: Indeed, Euthyphro, this is the reason why I am a defendant in the case, because I find it hard to accept things like that being said about the gods, and it is likely to be the reason why I shall be told I do wrong. Now, however, if you, who have full knowledge of such things, share their opinions, then we must agree with them, too, it would seem. For what are we to say, we who agree that we ourselves have no knowledge of them? Tell me, by the god of friendship, do you really believe these things are true?

EUTHYPHRO: Yes, Socrates, and so are even more surprising things, of which the majority has no knowledge.

SOCRATES: And do you believe that there really is war among the gods, and terrible enmities and battles, and other such things as are told by the poets, and other sacred stories such as are embroidered by good writers and by representations of which the robe of the goddess is adorned when it is carried up to the Acropolis? Are we to say these things are true, Euthyphro?

EUTHYPHRO: Not only these, Socrates, but, as I was saying just now, I will, if you wish, relate many other things about the gods which I know will amaze you.

SOCRATES: I should not be surprised, but you will tell me these at leisure some other time. For now, try to tell me more clearly what I was asking just now, for, my friend, you did not teach me adequately when I asked you what the pious was, but you told me that what you are doing now, in prosecuting your father for murder, is pious.

EUTHYPHRO: And I told the truth, Socrates.

SOCRATES: Perhaps. You agree, however, that there are many other pious actions.

EUTHYPHRO: There are.

SOCRATES: Bear in mind then that I did not bid you tell me one or two of the many pious actions but that form itself that makes all pious actions pious, for you agreed that all impious actions are impious and all pious actions pious through one form, or don't you remember?

EUTHYPHRO: I do.

SOCRATES: Tell me then what this form itself is, so that I may look upon it, and using it as a model, say that any action of yours or another's that is of that kind is pious, and if it is not that it is not.

EUTHYPHRO: If that is how you want it, Socrates, that is how I will tell you.

SOCRATES: That is what I want.

EUTHYPHRO: Well then, what is dear to the gods is pious, what is not is impious.

SOCRATES: Splendid, Euthyphro! You have now answered in the way I wanted. Whether your answer is true I do not know yet, but you will obviously show me that what you say is true.

EUTHYPHRO: Certainly.

SOCRATES: Come then, let us examine what we mean. An action or a man dear to the gods is pious, but an action or a man hated by the gods is impious. They are not the same, but quite opposite, the pious and the impious. Is that not so?

EUTHYPHRO: It is indeed.

SOCRATES: And that seems to be a good statement?

EUTHYPHRO: I think so, Socrates.

SOCRATES: We have also stated that the gods are in a state of discord, that they are at odds with each other, Euthyphro, and that they are at enmity with each other. Has that, too, been said?

EUTHYPHRO: It has.

SOCRATES: What are the subjects of difference that cause hatred and anger? Let us look at it this way. If you and I were to differ about numbers as to which is the greater, would this difference make us enemies and angry with each other, or would we c proceed to count and soon resolve our difference about this?

EUTHYPHRO: We would certainly do so.

SOCRATES: Again, if we differed about the larger and the smaller, we would turn to measurement and soon cease to differ.

EUTHYPHRO: That is so.

SOCRATES: And about the heavier and the lighter, we would resort to weighing and be reconciled.

EUTHYPHRO: Of course.

SOCRATES: What subject of difference would make us angry and hostile to each other if we were unable to come to a decision? Perhaps you do not have an d answer ready, but examine as I tell you whether these subjects are the just and the unjust, the beautiful and the ugly, the good and the bad. Are these not the subjects of difference about which, when we are unable to come to a satisfactory decision, you and I and other men become hostile to each other whenever we do?

EUTHYPHRO: That is the difference, Socrates, about those subjects.

SOCRATES: What about the gods, Euthyphro? If indeed they have differences, will it not be about these same subjects?

EUTHYPHRO: It certainly must be so.

e SOCRATES: Then according to your argument, my good Euthyphro, different gods consider different things to be just, beautiful, ugly, good, and bad, for they would not be at odds with one another unless they differed about these subjects, would they?

EUTHYPHRO: You are right.

SOCRATES: And they like what each of them considers beautiful, good, and just, and hate the opposites of these?

EUTHYPHRO: Certainly.

SOCRATES: But you say that the same things are considered just by some gods and unjust by others, 8 and as they dispute about these things they are at odds and at war with each other. Is that not so?

EUTHYPHRO: It is.

SOCRATES: The same things then are loved by the gods and hated by the gods, and would be both god-loved and god-hated.

EUTHYPHRO: It seems likely.

SOCRATES: And the same things would be both pious and impious, according to this argument?

EUTHYPHRO: I'm afraid so.

SOCRATES: So you did not answer my question, you surprising man. I did not ask you what same thing is both pious and impious, and it appears that what is loved by the gods is also hated by them. So it is b in no way surprising if your present action, namely punishing your father, may be pleasing to Zeus but displeasing to Cronus and Uranus, pleasing to Hephaestus but displeasing to Hera, and so with any other gods who differ from each other on this subject.

EUTHYPHRO: I think, Socrates, that on this subject no gods would differ from one another, that whoever has killed anyone unjustly should pay the penalty.

SOCRATES: Well now, Euthyphro, have you ever c heard any man maintaining that one who has killed or done anything else unjustly should not pay the penalty?

EUTHYPHRO: They never cease to dispute on this subject, both elsewhere and in the courts, for when they have committed many wrongs they do and say anything to avoid the penalty.

SOCRATES: Do they agree they have done wrong, Euthyphro, and in spite of so agreeing do they nevertheless say they should not be punished?

EUTHYPHRO: No, they do not agree on that point.

SOCRATES: So they do not say or do just anything. For they do not venture to say this, or dispute that they must not pay the penalty if they have done wrong, d but I think they deny doing wrong. Is that not so?

EUTHYPHRO: That is true.

SOCRATES: Then they do not dispute that the wrongdoer must be punished, but they may disagree as to who the wrongdoer is, what he did and when.

EUTHYPHRO: You are right.

SOCRATES: Do not the gods have the same experience, if indeed they are at odds with each other about the just and the unjust, as your argument maintains? Some assert that they wrong one another, while others deny it, but no one among gods or men ventures to say that the wrongdoer must not be punished. e

EUTHYPHRO: Yes, that is true, Socrates, as to the main point.

SOCRATES: And those who disagree, whether men or gods, dispute about each action, if indeed the gods disagree. Some say it is done justly, others unjustly. Is that not so?

EUTHYPHRO: Yes, indeed.

9   SOCRATES: Come now, my dear Euthyphro, tell me, too, that I may become wiser, what proof you have that all the gods consider that man to have been killed unjustly who became a murderer while in your service, was bound by the master of his victim, and died in his bonds before the one who bound him found out from the seers what was to be done with him, and that it is right for a son to denounce and to prosecute his father on behalf of such a man.

b   Come, try to show me a clear sign that all the gods definitely believe this action to be right. If you can give me adequate proof of this, I shall never cease to extol your wisdom.

EUTHYPHRO: This is perhaps no light task, Socrates, though I could show you very clearly.

SOCRATES: I understand that you think me more dull-witted than the jury, as you will obviously show them that these actions were unjust and that all the gods hate such actions.

EUTHYPHRO: I will show it to them clearly, Socrates, if only they will listen to me.

c   SOCRATES: They will listen if they think you show them well. But this thought came to me as you were speaking, and I am examining it, saying to myself: "If Euthyphro shows me conclusively that all the gods consider such a death unjust, to what greater extent have I learned from him the nature of piety and impiety? This action would then, it seems, be hated by the gods, but the pious and the impious were not thereby now defined, for what is hated by the gods has also been shown to be loved by them." So I will not insist on this point; let us assume, if you wish, that all the gods con-

d   sider this unjust and that they all hate it. However, is this the correction we are making in our discussion, that what all the gods hate is impious, and what they all love is pious, and that what some gods love and others hate is neither or both? Is that how you now wish us to define piety and impiety?

EUTHYPHRO: What prevents us from doing so, Socrates?

SOCRATES: For my part nothing, Euthyphro, but you look whether on your part this proposal will enable you to teach me most easily what you promised.

EUTHYPHRO: I would certainly say that the pious   e   is what all the gods love, and the opposite, what all the gods hate, is the impious.

SOCRATES: Then let us again examine whether that is a sound statement, or do we let it pass, and if one of us, or someone else, merely says that something is so, do we accept that it is so? Or should we examine what the speaker means?

EUTHYPHRO: We must examine it, but I certainly think that this is now a fine statement.

SOCRATES: We shall soon know better whether it   10   is. Consider this: Is the pious being loved by the gods because it is pious, or is it pious because it is being loved by the gods?

EUTHYPHRO: I don't know what you mean, Socrates.

SOCRATES: I shall try to explain more clearly: we speak of something carried and something carrying, of something led and something leading, of something seen and something seeing, and you understand that these things are all different from one another and how they differ?

EUTHYPHRO: I think I do.

SOCRATES: So there is also something loved and—a different thing—something loving.

EUTHYPHRO: Of course.

SOCRATES: Tell me then whether the thing carried   b   is a carried thing because it is being carried, or for some other reason?

EUTHYPHRO: No, that is the reason.

SOCRATES: And the thing led is so because it is being led, and the thing seen because it is being seen?

EUTHYPHRO: Certainly.

SOCRATES: It is not being seen because it is a thing seen but on the contrary it is a thing seen because it is being seen; nor is it because it is something led that it is being led but because it is being led that it is something led; nor is something being carried because it is something carried, but it is something carried because it is being carried. Is what I want to   c   say clear, Euthyphro? I want to say this, namely, that if anything is being changed or is being affected in any way, it is not being changed because it is something changed, but rather it is something changed because it is being changed; nor is it being affected because it is something affected, but it is something affected because it is being affected. Or do you not agree?

EUTHYPHRO: I do.

SOCRATES: Is something loved either something changed or something affected by something?

EUTHYPHRO: Certainly.

SOCRATES: So it is in the same case as the things just mentioned; it is not being loved by those who love it because it is something loved, but it is something loved because it is being loved by them?

EUTHYPHRO: Necessarily.

d   SOCRATES: What then do we say about the pious, Euthyphro? Surely that it is being loved by all the gods, according to what you say?

EUTHYPHRO: Yes.

SOCRATES: Is it being loved because it is pious, or for some other reason?

EUTHYPHRO: For no other reason.

SOCRATES: It is being loved then because it is pious, but it is not pious because it is being loved?

EUTHYPHRO: Apparently.

SOCRATES: And yet it is something loved and god-loved because it is being loved by the gods?

EUTHYPHRO: Of course.

SOCRATES: Then the god-loved is not the same as the pious, Euthyphro, nor the pious the same as the god-loved, as you say it is, but one differs from the other.

e   EUTHYPHRO: How so, Socrates?

SOCRATES: Because we agree that the pious is being loved for this reason, that it is pious, but it is not pious because it is being loved. Is that not so?

EUTHYPHRO: Yes.

SOCRATES: And that the god-loved, on the other hand, is so because it is being loved by the gods, by the very fact of being loved, but it is not being loved because it is god-loved.

EUTHYPHRO: True.

SOCRATES: But if the god-loved and the pious were the same, my dear Euthyphro, then if the pious was being loved because it was pious, the god-loved would 11   also be being loved because it was god-loved; and if the god-loved was god-loved because it was being loved by the gods, then the pious would also be pious because it was being loved by the gods. But now you see that they are in opposite cases as being altogether different from each other: the one is such as to be loved because it is being loved, the other is being loved because it is such as to be loved. I'm afraid, Euthyphro, that when you were asked what piety is, you did not wish to make its nature clear to me, but you told me an affect or quality of it, that the pious has the quality of being loved by all the gods, but you have not yet told me what the pious is. Now, if b you will, do not hide things from me but tell me again from the beginning what piety is, whether being loved by the gods or having some other quality—we shall not quarrel about that—but be keen to tell me what the pious and the impious are.

EUTHYPHRO: But Socrates, I have no way of telling you what I have in mind, for whatever proposition we put forward goes around and refuses to stay put where we establish it.

SOCRATES: Your statements, Euthyphro, seem to belong to my ancestor, Daedalus. If I were stating them c and putting them forward, you would perhaps be making fun of me and say that because of my kinship with him my conclusions in discussion run away and will not stay where one puts them. As these propositions are yours, however, we need some other jest, for they will not stay put for you, as you say yourself.

EUTHYPHRO: I think the same jest will do for our discussion, Socrates, for I am not the one who makes them go round and not remain in the same place; it is you who are the Daedalus; for as far as I am con- d cerned they would remain as they were.

SOCRATES: It looks as if I was cleverer than Daedalus in using my skill, my friend, in so far as he could only cause to move the things he made himself, but I can make other people's move as well as my own. And the smartest part of my skill is that I am clever without wanting to be, for I would rather have your statements to me remain unmoved than possess the e wealth of Tantalus as well as the cleverness of Daedalus. But enough of this. Since I think you are making unnecessary difficulties, I am as eager as you are to find a way to teach me about piety, and do not give up before you do. See whether you think all that is pious is of necessity just.

EUTHYPHRO: I think so.

SOCRATES: And is then all that is just pious? Or is all that is pious just, but not all that is just pious, but 12 some of it is and some is not?

EUTHYPHRO: I do not follow what you are saying, Socrates.

SOCRATES: Yet you are younger than I by as much as you are wiser. As I say, you are making difficulties because of your wealth of wisdom. Pull yourself together, my dear sir, what I am saying is not difficult to grasp. I am saying the opposite of what the poet said who wrote:

You do not wish to name Zeus, who had done it, and who made
all things grow, for where there is fear there is also shame.

I disagree with the poet. Shall I tell you why?

EUTHYPHRO: Please do.

SOCRATES: I do not think that "where there is fear there is also shame," for I think that many people who fear disease and poverty and many other such things feel fear, but are not ashamed of the things they fear. Do you not think so?

EUTHYPHRO: I do indeed.

SOCRATES: But where there is shame there is also c fear. For is there anyone who, in feeling shame and embarrassment at anything, does not also at the same time fear and dread a reputation for wickedness?

EUTHYPHRO: He is certainly afraid.

SOCRATES: It is then not right to say "where there is fear there is also shame," but that where there is shame there is also fear, for fear covers a larger area than shame. Shame is a part of fear just as odd is a part of number, with the result that it is not true that where there is number there is also oddness, but that where there is oddness there is also number. Do you follow me now?

EUTHYPHRO: Surely.

SOCRATES: This is the kind of thing I was asking before, whether where there is piety there is also d justice, but where there is justice there is not always piety, for the pious is a part of justice. Shall we say that, or do you think otherwise?

EUTHYPHRO: No, but like that, for what you say appears to be right.

SOCRATES: See what comes next: if the pious is a part of the just, we must, it seems, find out what part of the just it is. Now if you asked me something of what we mentioned just now, such as what part of number is the even, and what number that is, I would say it is the number that is divisible into two equal, not unequal, parts. Or do you not think so?

EUTHYPHRO: I do.

SOCRATES: Try in this way to tell me what part of e the just the pious is, in order to tell Meletus not to wrong us any more and not to indict me for ungodliness, since I have learned from you sufficiently what is godly and pious and what is not.

EUTHYPHRO: I think, Socrates, that the godly and pious is the part of the just that is concerned with the care of the gods, while that concerned with the care of men is the remaining part of justice.

SOCRATES: You seem to me to put that very well, but I still need a bit of information. I do not know 13 yet what you mean by care, for you do not mean the care of the gods in the same sense as the care of other things, as, for example, we say, don't we, that not everyone knows how to care for horses, but the horse breeder does.

EUTHYPHRO: Yes, I do mean it that way.

SOCRATES: So horse breeding is the care of horses.

EUTHYPHRO: Yes.

SOCRATES: Nor does everyone know how to care for dogs, but the hunter does.

EUTHYPHRO: That is so.

SOCRATES: So hunting is the care of dogs.

EUTHYPHRO: Yes. b

SOCRATES: And cattle raising is the care of cattle.

EUTHYPHRO: Quite so.

SOCRATES: While piety and godliness is the care of the gods, Euthyphro. Is that what you mean?

EUTHYPHRO: It is.

SOCRATES: Now care in each case has the same effect; it aims at the good and the benefit of the object cared for, as you can see that horses cared for by horse breeders are benefited and become better. Or do you not think so?

EUTHYPHRO: I do.

SOCRATES: So dogs are benefited by dog breeding, cattle by cattle raising, and so with all the others. Or c do you think that care aims to harm the object of its care?

EUTHYPHRO: By Zeus, no.

SOCRATES: It aims to benefit the object of its care?

EUTHYPHRO: Of course.

SOCRATES: Is piety then, which is the care of the gods, also to benefit the gods and make them better? Would you agree that when you do something pious you make some one of the gods better?

EUTHYPHRO: By Zeus, no.

SOCRATES: Nor do I think that this is what you mean—far from it—but that is why I asked you what d you meant by the care of gods, because I did not believe you meant this kind of care.

EUTHYPHRO: Quite right, Socrates, that is not the kind of care I mean.

SOCRATES: Very well, but what kind of care of the gods would piety be?

EUTHYPHRO: The kind of care, Socrates, that slaves take of their masters.

SOCRATES: I understand. It is likely to be a kind of service of the gods.

EUTHYPHRO: Quite so.

SOCRATES: Could you tell me to the achievement of what goal service to doctors tends? Is it not, do you think, to achieving health?

EUTHYPHRO: I think so.

e SOCRATES: What about service to shipbuilders? To what achievement is it directed?

EUTHYPHRO: Clearly, Socrates, to the building of a ship.

SOCRATES: And service to housebuilders to the building of a house?

EUTHYPHRO: Yes.

SOCRATES: Tell me then, my good sir, to the achievement of what aim does service to the gods tend? You obviously know since you say that you, of all men, have the best knowledge of the divine.

EUTHYPHRO: And I am telling the truth, Socrates.

SOCRATES: Tell me then, by Zeus, what is that excellent aim that the gods achieve, using us as their servants?

EUTHYPHRO: Many fine things, Socrates.

14 SOCRATES: So do generals, my friend. Nevertheless you could easily tell me their main concern, which is to achieve victory in war, is it not?

EUTHYPHRO: Of course.

SOCRATES: The farmers too, I think, achieve many fine things, but the main point of their efforts is to produce food from the earth.

EUTHYPHRO: Quite so.

SOCRATES: Well then, how would you sum up the many fine things that the gods achieve?

EUTHYPHRO: I told you a short while ago, Socrates, that it is a considerable task to acquire any precise b knowledge of these things, but, to put it simply, I say that if a man knows how to say and do what is pleasing to the gods at prayer and sacrifice, those are pious actions such as preserve both private houses and public affairs of state. The opposite of these pleasing actions are impious and overturn and destroy everything.

SOCRATES: You could tell me in far fewer words, if you were willing, the sum of what I asked, Euthy- c phro, but you are not keen to teach me, that is clear. You were on the point of doing so, but you turned away. If you had given that answer, I should now have acquired from you sufficient knowledge of the nature of piety. As it is, the lover of inquiry must follow his beloved wherever it may lead him. Once more then, what do you say that piety and the pious are? Are they a knowledge of how to sacrifice and pray?

EUTHYPHRO: They are.

SOCRATES: To sacrifice is to make a gift to the gods, whereas to pray is to beg from the gods?

EUTHYPHRO: Definitely, Socrates.

SOCRATES: It would follow from this statement that d piety would be a knowledge of how to give to, and beg from, the gods.

EUTHYPHRO: You understood what I said very well, Socrates.

SOCRATES: That is because I am so desirous of your wisdom, and I concentrate my mind on it, so that no word of yours may fall to the ground. But tell me, what is this service to the gods? You say it is to beg from them and to give to them?

EUTHYPHRO: I do.

SOCRATES: And to beg correctly would be to ask from them things that we need?

EUTHYPHRO: What else?

SOCRATES: And to give correctly is to give them e what they need from us, for it would not be skillful to bring gifts to anyone that are in no way needed.

EUTHYPHRO: True, Socrates.

SOCRATES: Piety would then be a sort of trading skill between gods and men?

EUTHYPHRO: Trading yes, if you prefer to call it that.

SOCRATES: I prefer nothing, unless it is true. But tell me, what benefit do the gods derive from the gifts they receive from us? What they give us is obvious to all. There is for us no good that we do not receive from them, but how are they benefited by what they 15 receive from us? Or do we have such an advantage over them in the trade that we receive all our blessings from them and they receive nothing from us?

EUTHYPHRO: Do you suppose, Socrates, that the gods are benefited by what they receive from us?

SOCRATES: What could those gifts from us to the gods be, Euthyphro?

EUTHYPHRO: What else, do you think, than honor, reverence, and what I mentioned just now, gratitude?

b SOCRATES: The pious is then, Euthyphro, pleasing to the gods, but not beneficial or dear to them?

EUTHYPHRO: I think it is of all things most dear to them.

SOCRATES: So the pious is once again what is dear to the gods.

EUTHYPHRO: Most certainly.

SOCRATES: When you say this, will you be surprised if your arguments seem to move about instead of staying put? And will you accuse me of being Daedalus who makes them move, though you are yourself much more skillful than Daedalus and make them go round in a circle? Or do you not realize that our c argument has moved around and come again to the same place? You surely remember that earlier the pious and the god-loved were shown not to be the same but different from each other. Or do you not remember?

EUTHYPHRO: I do.

SOCRATES: Do you then not realize now that you are saying that what is dear to the gods is the pious? Is this not the same as the god-loved? Or is it not?

EUTHYPHRO: It certainly is.

SOCRATES: Either we were wrong when we agreed before, or, if we were right then, we are wrong now.

EUTHYPHRO: That seems to be so.

SOCRATES: So we must investigate again from the beginning what piety is, as I shall not willingly give up before I learn this. Do not think me unworthy, but concentrate your attention and tell the truth. For d you know it, if any man does, and I must not let you go, like Proteus, before you tell me. If you had no clear knowledge of piety and impiety you would never have ventured to prosecute your old father for murder on behalf of a servant. For fear of the gods you would have been afraid to take the risk lest you should not be acting rightly, and would have been ashamed before men, but now I know well that you believe you have e clear knowledge of piety and impiety. So tell me, my good Euthyphro, and do not hide what you think it is.

EUTHYPHRO: Some other time, Socrates, for I am in a hurry now, and it is time for me to go.

SOCRATES: What a thing to do, my friend! By going you have cast me down from a great hope I had, that I would learn from you the nature of the pious and 16 the impious and so escape Meletus' indictment by showing him that I had acquired wisdom in divine matters from Euthyphro, and my ignorance would no longer cause me to be careless and inventive about such things, and that I would be better for the rest of my life.

Apology

17 I do not know, men of Athens, how my accusers affected you; as for me, I was almost carried away in spite of myself, so persuasively did they speak. And yet, hardly anything of what they said is true. Of the many lies they told, one in particular surprised me, namely that you should be careful not to be deceived b by an accomplished speaker like me. That they were not ashamed to be immediately proved wrong by the facts, when I show myself not to be an accomplished speaker at all, that I thought was most shameless on their part—unless indeed they call an accomplished speaker the man who speaks the truth. If they mean that, I would agree that I am an orator, but not after their manner, for indeed, as I say, practically nothing they said was true. From me you will hear the whole c truth, though not, by Zeus, gentlemen, expressed in embroidered and stylized phrases like theirs, but things spoken at random and expressed in the first

Reprinted from Plato, *Five Dialogues*, translated by G. M. A. Grube (Indianapolis: Hackett Publishing Company, 1981) by permission of the publisher.

words that come to mind, for I put my trust in the justice of what I say, and let none of you expect anything else. It would not be fitting at my age, as it might be for a young man, to toy with words when I appear before you.

One thing I do ask and beg of you, gentlemen: if you hear me making my defense in the same kind of language as I am accustomed to use in the market-place by the bankers' tables, where many of you have heard me, and elsewhere, do not be surprised or
d create a disturbance on that account. The position is this: this is my first appearance in a lawcourt, at the age of seventy; I am therefore simply a stranger to the manner of speaking here. Just as if I were really a stranger, you would certainly excuse me if I spoke
18 in that dialect and manner in which I had been brought up, so too my present request seems a just one, for you to pay no attention to my manner of speech—be it better or worse—but to concentrate your attention on whether what I say is just or not, for the excellence of a judge lies in this, as that of a speaker lies in telling the truth.

It is right for me, gentlemen, to defend myself first against the first lying accusations made against me and my first accusers, and then against the later accu-
b sations and the later accusers. There have been many who have accused me to you for many years now, and none of their accusations are true. These I fear much more than I fear Anytus and his friends, though they too are formidable. These earlier ones, however, are more so, gentlemen; they got hold of most of you from childhood, persuaded you and accused me quite falsely, saying that there is a man called Socrates, a
c wise man, a student of all things in the sky and below the earth, who makes the worse argument the stronger. Those who spread that rumor, gentlemen, are my dangerous accusers, for their hearers believe that those who study these things do not even believe in the gods. Moreover, these accusers are numerous, and have been at it a long time; also, they spoke to you at an age when you would most readily believe them, some of you being children and adolescents, and they won their case by default, as there was no de-fense.

What is most absurd in all this is that one cannot even know or mention their names unless one of
d them is a writer of comedies. Those who maliciously and slanderously persuaded you—who also, when

persuaded themselves then persuaded others—all those are most difficult to deal with: one cannot bring one of them into court or refute him; one must simply fight with shadows, as it were, in making one's de-fense, and cross-examine when no one answers. I want you to realize too that my accusers are of two kinds: those who have accused me recently, and the old ones I mention; and to think that I must first defend myself against the latter, for you have also heard their accusations first, and to a much greater e extent than the more recent.

Very well then. I must surely defend myself and attempt to uproot from your minds in so short a time 19 the slander that has resided there so long. I wish this may happen, if it is in any way better for you and me, and that my defense may be successful, but I think this is very difficult and I am fully aware of how difficult it is. Even so, let the matter proceed as the god may wish, but I must obey the law and make my defense.

Let us then take up the case from its beginning. What is the accusation from which arose the slander b in which Meletus trusted when he wrote out the charge against me? What did they say when they slandered me? I must, as if they were my actual prose-cutors, read the affidavit they would have sworn. It goes something like this: Socrates is guilty of wrongdo-ing in that he busies himself studying things in the sky and below the earth; he makes the worse into the stronger argument, and he teaches these same things to others. You have seen this yourself in the comedy c of Aristophanes, a Socrates swinging about there, say-ing he was walking on air and talking a lot of other nonsense about things of which I know nothing at all. I do not speak in contempt of such knowledge, if someone is wise in these things—lest Meletus bring more cases against me—but, gentlemen, I have no part in it, and on this point I call upon the majority of you as witnesses. I think it right that all those of you who have heard me conversing, and many of you d have, should tell each other if anyone of you has ever heard me discussing such subjects to any extent at all. From this you will learn that the other things said about me by the majority are of the same kind.

Not one of them is true. And if you have heard from anyone that I undertake to teach people and charge a fee for it, that is not true either. Yet I think e it a fine thing to be able to teach people as Gorgias of Leontini does, and Prodicus of Ceos, and Hippias of Elis. Each of these men can go to any city and persuade the young, who can keep company with anyone of their own fellow citizens they want without paying, to leave the company of these, to join with themselves, pay them a fee, and be grateful to them besides. Indeed, I learned that there is another wise man from Paros who is visiting us, for I met a man who has spent more money on Sophists than everybody else put together, Callias, the son of Hipponicus. So I asked him—he has two sons—"Callias," I said, "if your sons were colts or calves, we could find and engage a supervisor for them who would make them excel in their proper qualities, some horse breeder or farmer. Now since they are men, whom do you have in mind to supervise them? Who is an expert in this kind of excellence, the human and social kind? I think you must have given thought to this since you have sons. Is there such a person," I asked, "or is there not?" "Certainly there is," he said. "Who is he?" I asked, "What is his name, where is he from? and what is his fee?" "His name, Socrates, is Evenus, he comes from Paros, and his fee is five minas." I thought Evenus a happy man, if he really possesses this art, and teaches for so moderate a fee. Certainly I would pride and preen myself if I had this knowledge, but I do not have it, gentlemen.

One of you might perhaps interrupt me and say: "But Socrates, what is your occupation? From where have these slanders come? For surely if you did not busy yourself with something out of the common, all these rumors and talk would not have arisen unless you did something other than most people. Tell us what it is, that we may not speak inadvisedly about you." Anyone who says that seems to be right, and I will try to show you what has caused this reputation and slander. Listen then. Perhaps some of you will think I am jesting, but be sure that all that I shall say is true. What has caused my reputation is none other than a certain kind of wisdom. What kind of wisdom? Human wisdom, perhaps. It may be that I really possess this, while those whom I mentioned just now are wise with a wisdom more than human; else I cannot explain it, for I certainly do not possess it, and whoever says I do is lying and speaks to slander me. Do not create a disturbance, gentlemen, even if you think I am boasting, for the story I shall tell does not originate with me, but I will refer you to a trustworthy source.

I shall call upon the god at Delphi as witness to the existence and nature of my wisdom, if it be such. You know Chaerephon. He was my friend from youth, and the friend of most of you, as he shared your exile and your return. You surely know the kind of man he was, how impulsive in any course of action. He went to Delphi at one time and ventured to ask the oracle—as I say, gentlemen, do not create a disturbance—he asked if any man was wiser than I, and the Pythian replied that no one was wiser. Chaerephon is dead, but his brother will testify to you about this.

Consider that I tell you this because I would inform you about the origin of the slander. When I heard of this reply I asked myself: "Whatever does the god mean? What is his riddle? I am very conscious that I am not wise at all; what then does he mean by saying that I am the wisest? For surely he does not lie; it is not legitimate for him to do so." For a long time I was at a loss as to his meaning; then I very reluctantly turned to some such investigation as this; I went to one of those reputed wise, thinking that there, if anywhere, I could refute the oracle and say to it: "This man is wiser than I, but you said I was." Then, when I examined this man—there is no need for me to tell you his name, he was one of our public men—my experience was something like this: I thought that he appeared wise to many people and especially to himself, but he was not. I then tried to show him that he thought himself wise, but that he was not. As a result he came to dislike me, and so did many of the bystanders. So I withdrew and thought to myself: "I am wiser than this man; it is likely that neither of us knows anything worthwhile, but he thinks he knows something when he does not, whereas when I do not know, neither do I think I know; so I am likely to be wiser than he to this small extent, that I do not think I know what I do not know." After this I approached another man, one of those thought to be wiser than he, and I thought the same thing, and so I came to be disliked both by him and by many others.

After that I proceeded systematically. I realized, to my sorrow and alarm, that I was getting unpopular, but I thought that I must attach the greatest importance to the god's oracle, so I must go to all those who had any reputation for knowledge to examine its meaning. And by the dog, gentlemen of the jury—for I must tell you the truth—I experienced something like this: in my investigation in the service of the god I found that those who had the highest reputation were nearly the most deficient, while those who were thought to be inferior were more knowledgeable. I must give you an account of my journeyings as if they were labors I had undertaken to prove the oracle irrefutable. After the politicians, I went to the poets, b the writers of tragedies and dithyrambs and the others, intending in their case to catch myself being more ignorant than they. So I took up those poems with which they seemed to have taken most trouble and asked them what they meant, in order that I might at the same time learn something from them. I am ashamed to tell you the truth, gentlemen, but I must. Almost all the bystanders might have explained the c poems better than their authors could. I soon realized that poets do not compose their poems with knowledge, but by some inborn talent and by inspiration, like seers and prophets who also say many fine things without any understanding of what they say. The poets seemed to me to have had a similar experience. At the same time I saw that, because of their poetry, they thought themselves very wise men in other respects, which they were not. So there again I withdrew, thinking that I had the same advantage over them as I had over the politicians.

Finally I went to the craftsmen, for I was conscious d of knowing practically nothing, and I knew that I would find that they had knowledge of many fine things. In this I was not mistaken; they knew things I did not know, and to that extent they were wiser than I. But, gentlemen of the jury, the good craftsmen seemed to me to have the same fault as the poets: each of them, because of his success at his craft, thought himself very wise in other most important e pursuits, and this error of theirs overshadowed the wisdom they had, so that I asked myself, on behalf of the oracle, whether I should prefer to be as I am, with neither their wisdom nor their ignorance, or to have both. The answer I gave myself and the oracle was that it was to my advantage to be as I am.

As a result of this investigation, gentlemen of the jury, I acquired much unpopularity, of a kind that is 23 hard to deal with and is a heavy burden; many slanders came from these people and a reputation for wisdom, for in each case the bystanders thought that I myself possessed the wisdom that I proved that my interlocu-

tor did not have. What is probable, gentlemen, is that in fact the god is wise and that his oracular response meant that human wisdom is worth little or nothing, and that when he says this man, Socrates, he is using b my name as an example, as if he said: "This man among you, mortals, is wisest who, like Socrates, understands that his wisdom is worthless." So even now I continue this investigation as the god bade me— and I go around seeking out anyone, citizen or stranger, whom I think wise. Then if I do not think he is, I come to the assistance of the god and show him that he is not wise. Because of this occupation, I do not have the leisure to engage in public affairs to any extent, nor indeed to look after my own, but I live in great poverty because of my service to the god.

Furthermore, the young men who follow me c around of their own free will, those who have most leisure, the sons of the very rich, take pleasure in hearing people questioned; they themselves often imitate me and try to question others. I think they find an abundance of men who believe they have some knowledge but know little or nothing. The result is that those whom they question are angry, not with themselves but with me. They say: "That man Socra- d tes is a pestilential fellow who corrupts the young." If one asks them what he does and what he teaches to corrupt them, they are silent, as they do not know, but, so as not to appear at a loss, they mention those accusations that are available against all philosophers, about "things in the sky and things below the earth," about "not believing in the gods" and "making the worse the stronger argument"; they would not want to tell the truth, I'm sure, that they have been proved to lay claim to knowledge when they know nothing. These people are ambitious, violent and numerous; they are continually and convincingly talking about e me; they have been filling your ears for a long time with vehement slanders against me. From them Meletus attacked me, and Anytus and Lycon, Meletus being vexed on behalf of the poets, Anytus on behalf of the craftsmen and the politicians, Lycon on behalf of the orators, so that, as I started out by saying, I 24 should be surprised if I could rid you of so much slander in so short a time. That, gentlemen of the jury, is the truth for you. I have hidden or disguised nothing. I know well enough that this very conduct makes me unpopular, and this is proof that what I b say is true, that such is the slander against me, and that such are its causes. If you look into this either now or later, this is what you will find.

Let this suffice as a defense against the charges of my earlier accusers. After this I shall try to defend myself against Meletus, that good and patriotic man, as he says he is, and my later accusers. As these are a different lot of accusers, let us again take up their sworn deposition. It goes something like this: Socrates is guilty of corrupting the young and of not believing in the gods in whom the city believes, but in other c new spiritual things? Such is their charge. Let us examine it point by point.

He says that I am guilty of corrupting the young, but I say that Meletus is guilty of dealing frivolously with serious matters, of irresponsibly bringing people into court, and of professing to be seriously concerned with things about none of which he has ever cared, and I shall try to prove that this is so. Come here and d tell me, Meletus. Surely you consider it of the greatest importance that our young men be as good as possible?—Indeed I do.

Come then, tell the jury who improves them. You obviously know, in view of your concern. You say you have discovered the one who corrupts them, namely me, and you bring me here and accuse me to the jury. Come, inform the jury and tell them who it is. You see, Meletus, that you are silent and know not what to say. Does this not seem shameful to you and a sufficient proof of what I say, that you have not been concerned with any of this? Tell me, my good e sir, who improves our young men?—The laws.

That is not what I am asking, but what person who has knowledge of the laws to begin with?—These jurymen, Socrates.

How do you mean, Meletus? Are these able to educate the young and improve them?—Certainly.

All of them, or some but not others?—All of them.

Very good, by Hera. You mention a great abun-25 dance of benefactors. But what about the audience? Do they improve the young or not?

—They do, too.

What about the members of Council?—The Councillors, also.

But, Meletus, what about the assembly? Do members of the assembly corrupt the young, or do they all improve them?—They improve them.

All the Athenians, it seems, make the young into fine good men, except me, and I alone corrupt them. Is that what you mean?—That is most definitely what I mean.

You condemn me to a great misfortune. Tell me: b does this also apply to horses do you think? That all men improve them and one individual corrupts them? Or is quite the contrary true, one individual is able to improve them, or very few, namely, the horse breeders, whereas the majority, if they have horses and use them, corrupt them? Is that not the case, Meletus, both with horses and all other animals? Of course it is, whether you and Anytus say so or not. It would be a very happy state of affairs if only one person corrupted our youth, while the others improved them.

You have made it sufficiently obvious, Meletus, c that you have never had any concern for our youth; you show your indifference clearly; that you have given no thought to the subjects about which you bring me to trial.

And by Zeus, Meletus, tell us also whether it is better for a man to live among good or wicked fellow citizens. Answer, my good man, for I am not asking a difficult question. Do not the wicked do some harm to those who are ever closest to them, whereas good people benefit them?

—Certainly.

And does the man exist who would rather be d harmed than benefited by his associates? Answer, my good sir, for the law orders you to answer. Is there any man who wants to be harmed?—Of course not.

Come now, do you accuse me here of corrupting the young and making them worse deliberately or unwillingly?—Deliberately.

What fellows, Meletus? Are you so much wiser at your age than I am at mine that you understand that wicked people always do some harm to their closest e neighbors while good people do them good, but I have reached such a pitch of ignorance that I do not realize this, namely that if I make one of my associates wicked I run the risk of being harmed by him so that I do such a great evil deliberately, as you say? I do not believe you, Meletus, and I do not think anyone else will. Either I do not corrupt the young or, if I 26 do, it is unwillingly, and you are lying in either case. Now if I corrupt them unwillingly, the law does not require you to bring people to court for such unwilling wrongdoings, but to get hold of them privately, to instruct them and exhort them; for clearly, if I learn better, I shall cease to do what I am doing unwillingly. You, however, have avoided my company and were unwilling to instruct me, but you bring me here, where the law requires one to bring those who are in need of punishment, not of instruction.

b
And so, gentlemen of the jury, what I said is clearly true: Meletus has never been at all concerned with these matters. Nonetheless tell us, Meletus, how you say that I corrupt the young; or is it obvious from your deposition that it is by teaching them not to believe in the gods in whom the city believes but in other new spiritual things? Is this not what you say I teach and so corrupt them?—That is most certainly what I do say.

c
Then by those very gods about whom we are talking, Meletus, make this clearer to me and to the jury: I cannot be sure whether you mean that I teach the belief that there are some gods—and therefore I myself believe that there are gods and am not altogether an atheist, nor am I guilty of that—not, however, the gods in whom the city believes, but others, and that this is the charge against me, that they are others. Or whether you mean that I do not believe in gods at all, and that this is what I teach to others.—This is what I mean, that you do not believe in gods at all.

d
You are a strange fellow, Meletus. Why do you say this? Do I not believe, as other men do, that the sun and the moon are gods?—No, by Zeus, jurymen, for he says that the sun is stone, and the moon earth.

My dear Meletus, do you think you are prosecuting Anaxagoras? Are you so contemptuous of the jury and think them so ignorant of letters as not to know that the books of Anaxagoras of Clazomenae are full of those theories, and further, that the young men learn
e
from me what they can buy from time to time for a drachma, at most, in the bookshops, and ridicule Socrates if he pretends that these theories are his own, especially as they are so absurd? Is that, by Zeus, what you think of me, Meletus, that I do not believe that there are any gods?—That is what I say, that you do not believe in the gods at all.

You cannot be believed, Meletus, even, I think, by yourself. The man appears to me, gentlemen of the jury, highly insolent and uncontrolled. He seems to have made this deposition out of insolence, violence 27 and youthful zeal. He is like one who composed a riddle and is trying it out: "Will the wise Socrates realize that I am jesting and contradicting myself, or shall I deceive him and others?" I think he contradicts himself in the affidavit, as if he said: "Socrates is guilty of not believing in gods but believing in gods," and surely that is the part of a jester!

Examine with me, gentlemen, how he appears to contradict himself, and you, Meletus, answer us. Re-
b
member, gentlemen, what I asked you when I began, not to create a disturbance if I proceed in my usual manner.

Does any man, Meletus, believe in human activities who does not believe in humans? Make him answer, and not again and again create a disturbance. Does any man who does not believe in horses believe in horsemen's activities? Or in flute-playing activities but not in flute-players? No, my good sir, no man could. If you are not willing to answer, I will tell you
c
and the jury. Answer the next question, however. Does any man believe in spiritual activities who does not believe in spirits?—No one.

Thank you for answering, if reluctantly, when the jury made you. Now you say that I believe in spiritual things and teach about them, whether new or old, but at any rate spiritual things according to what you say, and to this you have sworn in your deposition. But if I believe in spiritual things I must quite inevitably believe in spirits. Is that not so? It is indeed. I shall assume that you agree, as you do not answer. Do we
d
not believe spirits to be either gods or the children of gods? Yes or no?—Of course.

Then since I do believe in spirits, as you admit, if spirits are gods, this is what I mean when I say you speak in riddles and in jest, as you state that I do not believe in gods and then again that I do, since I do believe in spirits. If on the other hand the spirits are children of the gods, bastard children of the gods by nymphs or some other mothers, as they are said to be, what man would believe children of the gods to exist, but not gods? That would be just as absurd as to believe the young of horses and asses, namely
e
mules, to exist, but not to believe in the existence of horses and asses. You must have made this deposition, Meletus, either to test us or because you were at a loss to find any true wrongdoing of which to accuse me. There is no way in which you could persuade

anyone of even small intelligence that it is possible for one and the same man to believe in spiritual but
28 not also in divine things, and then again for that same man to believe neither in spirits nor in gods nor in heroes.

I do not think, gentlemen of the jury, that it requires a prolonged defense to prove that I am not guilty of the charges in Meletus' deposition, but this is sufficient. On the other hand, you know that what I said earlier is true, that I am very unpopular with many people. This will be my undoing, if I am undone, not Meletus or Anytus but the slanders and envy of
b many people. This has destroyed many other good men and will, I think, continue to do so. There is no danger that it will stop at me.

Someone might say: "Are you not ashamed, Socrates, to have followed the kind of occupation that has led to your being now in danger of death?" However, I should be right to reply to him: "You are wrong, sir, if you think that a man who is any good at all should take into account the risk of life or death; he should look to this only in his actions, whether what he does is right or wrong, whether he is acting like
c a good or a bad man." According to your view, all the heroes who died at Troy were inferior people, especially the son of Thetis who was so contemptuous of danger compared with disgrace. When he was eager to kill Hector, his goddess mother warned him, as I believe, in some such words as these: "My child, if you avenge the death of your comrade, Patroclus, and you kill Hector, you will die yourself, for your death is to follow immediately after Hector's." Hearing this, he despised death and danger and was much
d more afraid to live a coward who did not avenge his friends. "Let me die at once," he said, "when once I have given the wrongdoer his deserts, rather than remain here, a laughingstock by the curved ships, a burden upon the earth." Do you think he gave thought to death and danger?

This is the truth of the matter, gentlemen of the jury: wherever a man has taken a position that he believes to be best, or has been placed by his commander, there he must I think remain and face danger, without a thought for death or anything else,
e rather than disgrace. It would have been a dreadful way to behave, gentlemen of the jury, if, at Potidaea, Amphipolis and Delium, I had, at the risk of death, like anyone else, remained at my post where those

you had elected to command had ordered me, and then, when the god ordered me, as I thought and believed, to live the life of a philosopher, to examine myself and others, I had abandoned my post for fear 29 of death or anything else. That would have been a dreadful thing, and then I might truly have justly been brought here for not believing that there are gods, disobeying the oracle, fearing death, and thinking I was wise when I was not. To fear death, gentlemen, is no other than to think oneself wise when one is not, to think one knows what one does not know. No one knows whether death may not be the greatest of all blessings for a man, yet men fear it as if they knew that it is the greatest of evils. And surely it is the most blameworthy ignorance to believe that one b knows what one does not know. It is perhaps on this point and in this respect, gentlemen, that I differ from the majority of men, and if I were to claim that I am wiser than anyone in anything, it would be in this, that, as I have no adequate knowledge of things in the underworld, so I do not think I have. I do know, however, that it is wicked and shameful to do wrong, to disobey one's superior, be he god or man. I shall never fear or avoid things of which I do not know, whether they may not be good rather than things that c I know to be bad. Even if you acquitted me now and did not believe Anytus, who said to you that either I should not have been brought here in the first place, or that now I am here, you cannot avoid executing me, for if I should be acquitted, your sons would practice the teachings of Socrates and all be thoroughly corrupted; if you said to me in this regard: "Socrates, we do not believe Anytus now; we acquit you, but only on condition that you spend no more time on this investigation and do not practice philosophy, and if you are caught doing so you will die;" if, d as I say, you were to acquit me on those terms, I would say to you: "Gentlemen of the jury, I am grateful and I am your friend, but I will obey the god rather than you, and as long as I draw breath and am able, I shall not cease to practice philosophy, to exhort you and in my usual way to point out to any one of you whom I happen to meet: Good Sir, you are an Athenian, a citizen of the greatest city with the greatest reputation for both wisdom and power; are you not ashamed of e your eagerness to possess as much wealth, reputation and honors as possible, while you do not care for nor give thought to wisdom or truth, or the best possible state of your soul?" Then, if one of you disputes this and says he does care, I shall not let him go at once or leave him, but I shall question him, examine him and test him, and if I do not think he has attained the goodness that he says he has, I shall reproach 30 him because he attaches little importance to the most important things and greater importance to inferior things. I shall treat in this way anyone I happen to meet, young and old, citizen and stranger, and more so the citizens because you are more kindred to me. Be sure that this is what the god orders me to do, and I think there is no greater blessing for the city than my service to the god. For I go around doing nothing but persuading both young and old among you not to care for your body or your wealth in prefer- b ence to or as strongly as for the best possible state of your soul, as I say to you: "Wealth does not bring about excellence, but excellence makes wealth and everything else good for men, both individually and collectively."

Now if by saying this I corrupt the young, this advice must be harmful, but if anyone says that I give different advice, he is talking nonsense. On this point I would say to you, gentlemen of the jury: "Whether you believe Anytus or not, whether you acquit me or c not, do so on the understanding that this is my course of action, even if I am to face death many times." Do not create a disturbance, gentlemen, but abide by my request not to cry out at what I say but to listen, for I think it will be to your advantage to listen, and I am about to say other things at which you will perhaps cry out. By no means do this. Be sure that if you kill the sort of man I say I am, you will not harm me more than yourselves. Neither Meletus nor d Anytus can harm me in any way; he could not harm me, for I do not think it is permitted that a better man be harmed by a worse; certainly he might kill me, or perhaps banish or disfranchise me, which he and maybe others think to be great harm, but I do not think so. I think he is doing himself much greater harm doing what he is doing now, attempting to have a man executed unjustly. Indeed, gentlemen of the jury, I am far from making a defense now on my own behalf, as might be thought, but on yours, to prevent e you from wrongdoing by mistreating the god's gift to you by condemning me; for if you kill me you will not easily find another like me. I was attached to this

city by the god—though it seems a ridiculous thing to say—as upon a great and noble horse which was somewhat sluggish because of its size and needed to be stirred up by a kind of gadfly. It is to fulfill some such function that I believe the god has placed me in the city. I never cease to rouse each and every one of you, to persuade and reproach you all day long 31 and everywhere I find myself in your company.

Another such man will not easily come to be among you, gentlemen, and if you believe me you will spare me. You might easily be annoyed with me as people are when they are aroused from a doze, and strike out at me; if convinced by Anytus you could easily kill me, and then you could sleep on for the rest of your days, unless the god, in his care for you, sent you someone else. That I am the kind of person to be a gift of the god to the city you might realize from the fact that it does not seem like human nature for b me to have neglected all my own affairs and to have tolerated this neglect now for so many years while I was always concerned with you, approaching each one of you like a father or an elder brother to persuade you to care for virtue. Now if I profited from this by charging a fee for my advice, there would be some sense to it, but you can see for yourselves that, for all their shameless accusations, my accusers have not been able in their impudence to bring forward a c witness to say that I have ever received a fee or ever asked for one. I, on the other hand, have a convincing witness that I speak the truth, my poverty.

It may seem strange that while I go around and give this advice privately and interfere in private affairs, I do not venture to go to the assembly and there advise the city. You have heard me give the reason for this in many places. I have a divine or spiritual sign which Meletus has ridiculed in his deposition. This began d when I was a child. It is a voice, and whenever it speaks it turns me away from something I am about to do, but it never encourages me to do anything. This is what has prevented me from taking part in public affairs, and I think it was quite right to prevent me. Be sure, gentlemen of the jury, that if I had long ago attempted to take part in politics, I should have died long ago, and benefited neither you nor myself. e Do not be angry with me for speaking the truth; no man will survive who genuinely opposes you or any other crowd and prevents the occurrence of many

32 unjust and illegal happenings in the city. A man who really fights for justice must lead a private, not a public, life if he is to survive for even a short time.

I shall give you great proofs of this, not words but what you esteem, deeds. Listen to what happened to me, that you may know that I will not yield to any man contrary to what is right, for fear of death, even if I should die at once for not yielding. The things I shall tell you are commonplace and smack of the b lawcourts, but they are true. I have never held any other office in the city, but I served as a member of the Council, and our tribe Antiochis was presiding at the time when you wanted to try as a body the ten generals who had failed to pick up the survivors of the naval battle. This was illegal, as you all recognized later. I was the only member of the presiding committee to oppose your doing something contrary to the laws, and I voted against it. The orators were ready to prosecute me and take me away, and your shouts were egging them on, but I thought I should run any c risk on the side of law and justice rather than join you, for fear of prison or death, when you were engaged in an unjust course.

This happened when the city was still a democracy. When the oligarchy was established, the Thirty summoned me to the Hall, along with four others, and ordered us to bring Leon from Salamis, that he might be executed. They gave many such orders to many d people, in order to implicate as many as possible in their guilt. Then I showed again, not in words but in action, that, if it were not rather vulgar to say so, death is something I couldn't care less about, but that my whole concern is not to do anything unjust or impious. That government, powerful as it was, did not frighten me into any wrongdoing. When we left the Hall, the other four went to Salamis and brought in Leon, but I went home. I might have been put to e death for this, had not the government fallen shortly afterwards. There are many who will witness to these events.

Do you think I would have survived all these years if I were engaged in public affairs and, acting as a good man must, came to the help of justice and considered this the most important thing? Far from it, gentlemen of the jury, nor would any other man. 33 Throughout my life, in any public activity I may have engaged in, I am the same man as I am in private life. I have never come to an agreement with anyone to act unjustly, neither with anyone else nor with any one of those who they slanderously say are my pupils. I have never been anyone's teacher. If anyone, young or old, desires to listen to me when I am talking and dealing with my own concerns, I have never begrudged this to anyone, but I do not converse when I receive a fee and not when I do not. I am equally b ready to question the rich and the poor if anyone is willing to answer my questions and listen to what I say. And I cannot justly be held responsible for the good or bad conduct of these people, as I never promised to teach them anything and have not done so. If anyone says that he has learned anything from me, or that he heard anything privately that the others did not hear, be assured that he is not telling the truth.

Why then do some people enjoy spending consid- c erable time in my company? You have heard why, gentlemen of the jury, I have told you the whole truth. They enjoy hearing those being questioned who think they are wise, but are not. And this is not unpleasant. To do this has, as I say, been enjoined upon me by the god, by means of oracles and dreams, and in every other way that a divine manifestation has ever ordered a man to do anything. This is true, gentlemen, and can easily be established.

If I corrupt some young men and have corrupted d others, then surely some of them who have grown older and realized that I gave them bad advice when they were young should now themselves come up here to accuse me and avenge themselves. If they were unwilling to do so themselves, then some of their kindred, their fathers or brothers or other relations should recall it now if their family had been harmed by me. I see many of these present here, first Crito, my contemporary and fellow demesman, the e father of Critobulus here; next Lysanias of Sphettus, the father of Aeschines here; also Antiphon the Cephisian, the father of Epigenes; and others whose brothers spent their time in this way; Nicostratus, the son of Theozotides, brother of Theodotus, and Theodotus has died so he could not influence him; Paralius here, son of Demodocus, whose brother was Theages; 34 there is Adeimantus, son of Ariston, brother of Plato here; Acantidorus, brother of Apollodorus here.

I could mention many others, some one of whom surely Meletus should have brought in as witness in his own speech. If he forgot to do so, then let him do it now; I will yield time if he has anything of the kind to say. You will find quite the contrary, gentlemen. These men are all ready to come to the *b* help of the corruptor, the man who has harmed their kindred, as Meletus and Anytus say. Now those who were corrupted might well have reason to help me, but the uncorrupted, their kindred who are older men, have no reason to help me except the right and proper one, that they know that Meletus is lying and that I am telling the truth.

Very well, gentlemen of the jury. This, and maybe other similar things, is what I have to say in my *c* defense. Perhaps one of you might be angry as he recalls that when he himself stood trial on a less dangerous charge, he begged and implored the jury with many tears, that he brought his children and many of his friends and family into court to arouse as much pity as he could, but that I do none of these things, even though I may seem to be running the *d* ultimate risk. Thinking of this, he might feel resentful toward me and, angry about this, cast his vote in anger. If there is such a one among you—I do not deem there is, but if there is—I think it would be right to say in reply: My good sir, I too have a household and, in Homer's phrase, I am not born "from oak or rock" but from men, so that I have a family, indeed three sons, gentlemen of the jury, of whom one is an adolescent while two are children. Nevertheless, I will not beg you to acquit me by bringing them here. Why do I do none of these things? Not through *e* arrogance, gentlemen, nor through lack of respect for you. Whether I am brave in the face of death is another matter, but with regard to my reputation and yours and that of the whole city, it does not seem right to me to do these things, especially at my age and with my reputation. For it is generally believed, whether it be true or false, that in certain respects 35 Socrates is superior to the majority of men. Now if those of you who are considered superior, be it in wisdom or courage or whatever other virtue makes them so, are seen behaving like that, it would be a disgrace. Yet I have often seen them do this sort of thing when standing trial, men who are thought to be somebody, doing amazing things as if they thought it a terrible thing to die, and as if they were to be immortal if you did not execute them. I think these *b* men bring shame upon the city so that a stranger,

too, would assume that those who are outstanding in virtue among the Athenians, whom they themselves select from themselves to fill offices of state and receive other honors, are in no way better than women. You should not act like that, gentlemen of the jury, those of you who have any reputation at all, and if we do, you should not allow it. You should make it very clear that you will more readily convict a man who performs these pitiful dramatics in court and so makes the city a laughingstock, than a man who keeps quiet.

Quite apart from the question of reputation, gentle- men, I do not think it right to supplicate the jury and *c* to be acquitted because of this, but to teach and persuade them. It is not the purpose of a juryman's office to give justice as a favor to whoever seems good to him, but to judge according to law, and this he has sworn to do. We should not accustom you to perjure yourselves, nor should you make a habit of it. This is irreverent conduct for either of us.

Do not deem it right for me, gentlemen of the jury, that I should act towards you in a way that I do *d* not consider to be good or just or pious, especially, by Zeus, as I am being prosecuted by Meletus here for impiety; clearly, if I convinced you by my supplica- tion to do violence to your oath of office, I would be teaching you not to believe that there are gods, and my defense would convict me of not believing in them. This is far from being the case, gentlemen, for I do believe in them as none of my accusers do. I leave it to you and the god to judge me in the way that will be best for me and for you.

[The jury now gives its verdict of guilty, and Mele- tus asks for the penalty of death.]

There are many other reasons for my not being *e* angry with you for convicting me, gentlemen of the jury, and what happened was not unexpected. I am 36 much more surprised at the number of votes cast on each side for I did not think the decision would be by so few votes but by a great many. As it is, a switch of only thirty votes would have acquitted me. I think myself that I have been cleared on Meletus' charges, *b* and not only this, but it is clear to all that, if Anytus and Lycon had not joined him in accusing me, he would have been fined a thousand drachmas for not receiving a fifth of the votes.

He assesses the penalty at death. So be it. What counter-assessment should I propose to you, gentlemen of the jury? Clearly it should be a penalty I deserve, and what do I deserve to suffer or to pay because I have deliberately not led a quiet life but have neglected what occupies most people: wealth, household affairs, the position of general or public orator or the other offices, the political clubs and factions that exist in the city? I thought myself too *c* honest to survive if I occupied myself with those things. I did not follow that path that would have made me of no use either to you or to myself, but I went to each of you privately and conferred upon him what I say is the greatest benefit, by trying to persuade him not to care for any of his belongings before caring that he himself should be as good and as wise as possible, not to care for the city's possessions more than for the city itself, and to care for other *d* things in the same way. What do I deserve for being such a man? Some good, gentlemen of the jury, if I must truly make an assessment according to my deserts, and something suitable. What is suitable for a poor benefactor who needs leisure to exhort you? Nothing is more suitable, gentlemen, than for such a man to be fed in the Prytaneum much more suitable for him than for any one of you who has won a victory at Olympia with a pair or a team of horses. The *e* Olympian victor makes you think yourself happy; I make you be happy. Besides, he does not need food, but I do. So if I must make a just assessment of what I *37* deserve, I assess it as this: free meals in the Prytaneum.

When I say this you may think, as when I spoke of appeals to pity and entreaties, that I speak arrogantly, but that is not the case, gentlemen of the jury; rather it is like this: I am convinced that I never willingly wrong anyone, but I am not convincing you of this, for we have talked together but a short time. *b* If it were the law with us, as it is elsewhere, that a trial for life should not last one but many days, you would be convinced, but now it is not easy to dispel great slanders in a short time. Since I am convinced that I wrong no one, I am not likely to wrong myself, to say that I deserve some evil and to make some such assessment against myself. What should I fear? That I should suffer the penalty Meletus has assessed against me, of which I say I do not know whether it is good or bad? Am I then to choose in preference to this something that I know very well to be an evil

and assess the penalty at that? Imprisonment? Why *c* should I live in prison, always subjected to the ruling magistrates, the Eleven? A fine, and imprisonment until I pay it? That would be the same thing for me, as I have no money. Exile? for perhaps you might accept that assessment.

I should have to be inordinately fond of life, gentlemen of the jury, to be so unreasonable as to suppose that other men will easily tolerate my company and conversation when you, my fellow citizens, have been *d* unable to endure them, but found them a burden and resented them so that you are now seeking to get rid of them. Far from it, gentlemen. It would be a fine life at my age to be driven out of one city after another, for I know very well that wherever I go the young men will listen to my talk as they do here. If *e* I drive them away, they will themselves persuade their elders to drive me out; if I do not drive them away, their fathers and relations will drive me out on their behalf.

Perhaps someone might say: But Socrates, if you leave us will you not be able to live quietly, without talking? Now this is the most difficult point on which to convince some of you. If I say that it is impossible *38* for me to keep quiet because that means disobeying the god, you will not believe me and will think I am being ironical. On the other hand, if I say that it is the greatest good for a man to discuss virtue every day and those other things about which you hear me conversing and testing myself and others, for the unexamined life is not worth living for men, you will believe me even less.

What I say is true, gentlemen, but it is not easy to convince you. At the same time, I am not accustomed *b* to think that I deserve any penalty. If I had money, I would assess the penalty at the amount I could pay, for that would not hurt me, but I have none, unless you are willing to set the penalty at the amount I can pay, and perhaps I could pay you one mina of silver. So that is my assessment.

Plato here, gentlemen of the jury, and Crito and Critobulus and Apollodorus bid me put the penalty at thirty minae, and they will stand surety for the money. Well then, that is my assessment, and they will be sufficient guarantee of payment.

[The jury now votes again and sentences Socrates to death.]

c   It is for the sake of a short time, gentlemen of the jury, that you will acquire the reputation and the guilt, in the eyes of those who want to denigrate the city, of having killed Socrates, a wise man, for they who want to revile you will say that I am wise even if I am not. If you had waited but a little while, this would have happened of its own accord. You see my age, that I am already advanced in years and close

d   to death. I am saying this not to all of you but to those who condemned me to death, and to these same jurors I say: Perhaps you think that I was convicted for lack of such words as might have convinced you, if I thought I should say or do all I could to avoid my sentence. Far from it. I was convicted because I lacked not words but boldness and shamelessness and the willingness to say to you what you would most gladly have heard from me, lamentations and tears and my

e   saying and doing many things that I say are unworthy of me but that you are accustomed to hear from others. I did not think then that the danger I ran should make me do anything mean, nor do I now regret the nature of my defense. I would much rather die after this kind of defense than live after making the other kind. Neither I nor any other man should,

39 on trial or in war, contrive to avoid death at any cost. Indeed it is often obvious in battle that one could escape death by throwing away one's weapons and by turning to supplicate one's pursuers, and there are many ways to avoid death in every kind of danger if one will venture to do or say anything to avoid it. It is not difficult to avoid death, gentlemen of the jury,

b   it is much more difficult to avoid wickedness, for it runs faster than death. Slow and elderly as I am, I have been caught by the slower pursuer, whereas my accusers, being clever and sharp, have been caught by the quicker, wickedness. I leave you now, condemned to death by you, but they are condemned by truth to wickedness and injustice. So I maintain my assessment, and they maintain theirs. This perhaps had to happen, and I think it is as it should be.

c   Now I want to prophesy to those who convicted me, for I am at the point when men prophesy most, when they are about to die. I say gentlemen, to those who voted to kill me, that vengeance will come upon you immediately after my death, a vengeance much harder to bear than that which you took in killing me. You did this in the belief that you would avoid giving an account of your life, but I maintain that

quite the opposite will happen to you. There will be more people to test you, whom I now held back, but   d
you did not notice it. They will be more difficult to deal with as they will be younger and you will resent them more. You are wrong if you believe that by killing people you will prevent anyone from reproaching you for not living in the right way. To escape such tests is neither possible nor good, but it is best and easiest not to discredit others but to prepare oneself to be as good as possible. With this prophecy to you who convicted me, I part from you.

I should be glad to discuss what has happened with   e
those who voted for my acquittal during the time that the officers of the court are busy and I do not yet have to depart to my death. So, gentlemen, stay with me awhile, for nothing prevents us from talking to each other while it is allowed. To you, as being my   40
friends, I want to show the meaning of what has occurred. A surprising thing has happened to me, judges—you I would rightly call judges. At all previous times my familiar prophetic power, my spiritual manifestation, frequently opposed me, even in small matters, when I was about to do something wrong, but now that, as you can see for yourselves, I was faced with what one might think, and what is generally thought to be, the worst of evils, my divine sign has not opposed me, either when I left home at dawn,   b
or when I came into court, or at any time that I was about to say something during my speech. Yet in other talks it often held me back in the middle of my speaking, but now it has opposed no word or deed of mine. What do I think is the reason for this? I will tell you. What has happened to me may well be a good thing, and those of us who believe death to be an evil are certainly mistaken. I have convincing proof   c
of this, for it is impossible that my familiar sign did not oppose me if I was not about to do what was right.

Let us reflect in this way, too, that there is good hope that death is a blessing, for it is one of two things: either the dead are nothing and have no perception of anything, or it is, as we are told, a change and a relocating for the soul from here to another place. If   d
it is complete lack of perception, like a dreamless sleep, then death would be a great advantage. For I think that if one had to pick out that night during which a man slept soundly and did not dream, put beside it the other nights and days of his life, and then see how many days and nights had been better

and more pleasant than that night, not only a private person but the great king would find them easy to count compared with the other days and nights. If death is like this I say it is an advantage, for all eternity would then seem to be no more than a single night. If, on the other hand, death is a change from here to another place, and what we are told is true and all who have died are there, what greater blessing could there be, gentlemen of the jury? If anyone arriving in Hades will have escaped from those who call themselves judges here, and will find those true judges who are said to sit in judgment there, Minos and Rhadamanthus and Aeacus and Triptolemus and the other demi-gods who have been upright in their own life, would that be a poor kind of change? Again, what would one of you give to keep company with Orpheus and Musaeus, Hesiod and Homer? I am willing to die many times if that is true. It would be a wonderful way for me to spend my time whenever I met Palamedes and Ajax, the son of Telamon, and any other of the men of old who died through an unjust conviction, to compare my experience with theirs. I think it would be pleasant. Most important, I could spend my time testing and examining people there, as I do here, as to who among them is wise, and who thinks he is, but is not.

What would one not give, gentlemen of the jury, for the opportunity to examine the man who led the great expedition against Troy, or Odysseus, or Sisyphus, and innumerable other men and women one could mention. It would be an extraordinary happiness to talk with them, to keep company with them and examine them. In any case, they would certainly not put one to death for doing so. They are happier there than we are here in other respects, and for the rest of time they are deathless, if indeed what we are told is true.

You too must be of good hope as regards death, gentlemen of the jury, and keep this one truth in mind, that a good man cannot be harmed either in life or in death, and that his affairs are not neglected by the gods. What has happened to me now has not happened of itself, but it is clear to me that it was better for me to die now and to escape from trouble. That is why my divine sign did not oppose me at any point. So I am certainly not angry with those who convicted me, or with my accusers. Of course that was not their purpose when they accused and convicted me, but they thought they were hurting me, and for this they deserve blame. This much I ask from them: when my sons grow up, avenge yourselves by causing them the same kind of grief that I caused you, if you think they care for money or anything else more than they care for virtue, or if they think they are somebody when they are nobody. Reproach them as I reproach you, that they do not care for the right things and think they are worthy when they are not worthy of anything. If you do this, I shall have been justly treated by you, and my sons also.

Now the hour to part has come. I go to die, you go to live. Which of us goes to the better lot is known to no one, except the god.

Crito

SOCRATES: Why have you come so early, Crito? Or is it not still early?

CRITO: It certainly is.

SOCRATES: How early?

CRITO: Early dawn.

SOCRATES: I am surprised that the warder was willing to listen to you.

CRITO: He is quite friendly to me by now, Socrates. I have been here often and I have given him something.

SOCRATES: Have you just come, or have you been here for some time?

CRITO: A fair time.

SOCRATES: Then why did you not wake me right away but sit there in silence?

CRITO: By Zeus no, Socrates. I would not myself want to be in distress and awake so long. I have been surprised to see you so peacefully asleep. It was on purpose that I did not wake you, so that you should spend your time most agreeably. Often in the past

Reprinted from Plato, *Five Dialogues*, translated by G. M. A. Grube (Indianapolis: Hackett Publishing Company, 1981) by permission of the publisher.

throughout my life, I have considered the way you live happy, and especially so now that you bear your present misfortune so easily and lightly.

SOCRATES: It would not be fitting at my age to resent the fact that I must die now.

c   CRITO: Other men of your age are caught in such misfortunes, but their age does not prevent them resenting their fate.

SOCRATES: That is so. Why have you come so early?

CRITO: I bring bad news, Socrates, not for you, apparently, but for me and all your friends the news is bad and hard to bear. Indeed, I would count it among the hardest.

d   SOCRATES: What is it? Or has the ship arrived from Delos, at the arrival of which I must die?

CRITO: It has not arrived yet, but it will, I believe, arrive today, according to a message some men brought from Sunium, where they left it. This makes it obvious that it will come today, and that your life must end tomorrow.

SOCRATES: May it be for the best. If it so please the gods, so be it. However, I do not think it will arrive today.

44   CRITO: What indication have you of this?

SOCRATES: I will tell you. I must die the day after the ship arrives.

CRITO: That is what those in authority say.

SOCRATES: Then I do not think it will arrive on this coming day, but on the next. I take to witness of this a dream I had a little earlier during this night. It looks as if it was the right time for you not to wake me.

CRITO: What was your dream?

SOCRATES: I thought that a beautiful and comely woman dressed in white approached me. She called

b   me and said: "Socrates, may you arrive at fertile Phthia on the third day."

CRITO: A strange dream, Socrates.

SOCRATES: But it seems clear enough to me, Crito.

CRITO: Too clear it seems, my dear Socrates, but listen to me even now and be saved. If you die, it will not be a single misfortune for me. Not only will I be deprived of a friend, the like of whom I shall never find again, but many people who do not know

c   you or me very well will think that I could have saved you if I were willing to spend money, but that I did not care to do so. Surely there can be no worse reputation than to be thought to value money more

highly than one's friends, for the majority will not believe that you yourself were not willing to leave prison while we were eager for you to do so.

SOCRATES: My good Crito, why should we care so much for what the majority think? The most reasonable people, to whom one should pay more attention, will believe that things were done as they were done.

CRITO: You see, Socrates, that one must also pay   d attention to the opinion of the majority. Your present situation makes clear that the majority can inflict not the least but pretty well the greatest evils if one is slandered among them.

SOCRATES: Would that the majority could inflict the greatest evils, for they would then be capable of the greatest good, and that would be fine, but now they cannot do either. They cannot make a man either wise or foolish, but they inflict things haphazardly.

CRITO: That may be so. But tell me this, Socrates,   e are you anticipating that I and your other friends would have trouble with the informers if you escape from here, as having stolen you away, and that we should be compelled to lose all our property or pay heavy fines and suffer other punishment besides? If   45 you have any such fear, forget it. We would be justified in running this risk to save you, and worse, if necessary. Do follow my advice, and do not act differently.

SOCRATES: I do have these things in mind, Crito, and also many others.

CRITO: Have no such fear. It is not much money that some people require to save you and get you out of here. Further, do you not see that those informers are cheap, and that not much money would be needed to deal with them? My money is available and is, I think, sufficient. If, because of your affection   b for me, you feel you should not spend any of mine, there are those strangers here ready to spend money. One of them, Simmias the Theban, has brought enough for this very purpose. Cebes, too, and a good many others. So, as I say, do not let this fear make you hesitate to save yourself, nor let what you said in court trouble you, that you would not know what to do with yourself if you left Athens, for you would be   c welcomed in many places to which you might go. If you want to go to Thessaly, I have friends there who will greatly appreciate you and keep you safe, so that no one in Thessaly will harm you.

Besides, Socrates, I do not think that what you are doing is just, to give up your life when you can save it, and to hasten your fate as your enemies would hasten it, and indeed have hastened it in their wish to destroy you. Moreover, I think you are betraying *d* your sons by going away and leaving them, when you could bring them up and educate them. You thus show no concern for what their fate may be. They will probably have the usual fate of orphans. Either one should not have children, or one should share with them to the end the toil of upbringing and education. You seem to me to choose the easiest path, whereas one should choose the path a good and courageous man would choose, particularly when one claims throughout one's life to care for virtue.

e I feel ashamed on your behalf and on behalf of us, your friends, lest all that has happened to you be thought due to cowardice on our part: the fact that your trial came to court when it need not have done so, the handling of the trial itself, and now this absurd ending which will be thought to have got beyond our *46* control through some cowardice and unmanliness on our part, since we did not save you, or you save yourself, when it was possible and could be done if we had been of the slightest use. Consider, Socrates, whether this is not only evil, but shameful, both for you and for us. Take counsel with yourself, or rather the time for counsel is past and the decision should have been taken, and there is no further opportunity, for this whole business must be ended tonight. If we delay now, then it will no longer be possible, it will be too late. Let me persuade you on every count, Socrates, and do not act otherwise.

b SOCRATES: My dear Crito, your eagerness is worth much if it should have some right aim; if not, then the greater your keenness the more difficult it is to deal with. We must therefore examine whether we should act in this way or not, as not only now but at all times I am the kind of man who listens only to the argument that on reflection seems best to me. I cannot, now that this fate has come upon me, discard *c* the arguments I used; they seem to me much the same. I value and respect the same principles as before, and if we have no better arguments to bring up at this moment, be sure that I shall not agree with you, not even if the power of the majority were to frighten us with more bogeys, as if we were children, with threats of incarcerations and executions and con-

fiscation of property. How should we examine this matter most reasonably? Would it be by taking up first your argument about the opinions of men, whether it *d* is sound in every case that one should pay attention to some opinions, but not to others? Or was that well-spoken before the necessity to die came upon me, but now it is clear that this was said in vain for the sake of argument, that it was in truth play and nonsense? I am eager to examine together with you, Crito, whether this argument will appear in any way different to me in my present circumstances, or whether it remains the same, whether we are to abandon it or believe it. It was said on every occasion by those who thought they were speaking sensibly, as I have *e* just now been speaking, that one should greatly value some people's opinions, but not others. Does that seem to you a sound statement?

You, as far as a human being can tell, are exempt from the likelihood of dying tomorrow, so the present misfortune is not likely to lead you astray. Consider *47* then, do you not think it a sound statement that one must not value all the opinions of men, but some and not others, nor the opinions of all men, but those of some and not of others? What do you say? Is this not well said?

CRITO: It is.

SOCRATES: One should value the good opinions, and not the bad ones?

CRITO: Yes.

SOCRATES: The good opinions are those of wise men, the bad ones those of foolish men?

CRITO: Of course.

SOCRATES: Come then, what of statements such as this: Should a man professionally engaged in physical *b* training pay attention to the praise and blame and opinion of any man, or to those of one man only, namely a doctor or trainer?

CRITO: To those of one only.

SOCRATES: He should therefore fear the blame and welcome the praise of that one man, and not those of the many?

CRITO: Obviously.

SOCRATES: He must then act and exercise, eat and drink in the way the one, the trainer and the one who knows, thinks right, not all the others?

CRITO: That is so.

SOCRATES: Very well. And if he disobeys the one, *c* disregards his opinion and his praises while valuing those of the many who have no knowledge, will he not suffer harm?

CRITO: Of course.

SOCRATES: What is that harm, where does it tend, and what part of the man who disobeys does it affect?

CRITO: Obviously the harm is to his body, which it ruins.

SOCRATES: Well said. So with other matters, not to enumerate them all, and certainly with actions just and unjust, shameful and beautiful, good and bad, about which we are now deliberating, should we fol-
d low the opinion of the many and fear it, or that of the one, if there is one who has knowledge of these things and before whom we feel fear and shame more than before all the others. If we do not follow his directions, we shall harm and corrupt that part of ourselves that is improved by just actions and destroyed by unjust actions. Or is there nothing in this?

CRITO: I think there certainly is, Socrates.

SOCRATES: Come now, if we ruin that which is improved by health and corrupted by disease by not
e following the opinions of those who know, is life worth living for us when that is ruined? And that is the body, is it not?

CRITO: Yes.

SOCRATES: And is life worth living with a body that is corrupted and in bad condition?

CRITO: In no way.

SOCRATES: And is life worth living for us with that part of us corrupted that unjust action harms and just action benefits? Or do we think that part of us, whatever it is, that is concerned with justice and
48 injustice, is inferior to the body?

CRITO: Not at all.

SOCRATES: It is more valuable?

CRITO: Much more.

SOCRATES: We should not then think so much of what the majority will say about us, but what he will say who understands justice and injustice, the one, that is, and the truth itself. So that, in the first place, you were wrong to believe that we should care for the opinion of the many about what is just, beautiful, good, and their opposites. "But," someone might say "the many are able to put us to death."

b CRITO: That too is obvious, Socrates, and someone might well say so.

SOCRATES: And, my admirable friend, that argument that we have gone through remains, I think, as

before. Examine the following statement in turn as to whether it stays the same or not, that the most important thing is not life, but the good life.

CRITO: It stays the same.

SOCRATES: And that the good life, the beautiful life, and the just life are the same; does that still hold, or not?

CRITO: It does hold.

SOCRATES: As we have agreed so far, we must examine next whether it is just for me to try to get out of
c here when the Athenians have not acquitted me. If it is seen to be just, we will try to do so; if it is not, we will abandon the idea. As for those questions you raise about money, reputation, the upbringing of children, Crito, those considerations in truth belong to those people who easily put men to death and would bring them to life again if they could, without thinking; I mean the majority of men. For us, however, since our argument leads to this, the only valid consideration, as we were saying just now, is whether we should be acting rightly in giving money and gratitude to those who will lead me out of here, and ourselves
d helping with the escape, or whether in truth we shall do wrong in doing all this. If it appears that we shall be acting unjustly, then we have no need at all to take into account whether we shall have to die if we stay here and keep quiet, or suffer in another way, rather than do wrong.

CRITO: I think you put that beautifully, Socrates, but see what we should do.

SOCRATES: Let us examine the question together,
e my dear friend, and if you can make any objection while I am speaking, make it and I will listen to you, but if you have no objection to make, my dear Crito, then stop now from saying the same thing so often, that I must leave here against the will of the Athenians. I think it important to persuade you before I act, and not to act against your wishes. See whether the start of our inquiry is adequately stated, and try to answer
49 what I ask you in the way you think best.

CRITO: I shall try.

SOCRATES: Do we say that one must never in any way do wrong willingly, or must one do wrong in one way and not in another? Is to do wrong never good or admirable, as we have agreed in the past, or have all these former agreements been washed out during the last few days? Have we at our age failed to notice
b for some time that in our serious discussions we were

no different from children? Above all, is the truth such as we used to say it was, whether the majority agree or not, and whether we must still suffer worse things than we do now, or will be treated more gently, that nonetheless, wrongdoing or injustice is in every way harmful and shameful to the wrongdoer? Do we say so or not?

CRITO: We do.

SOCRATES: So one must never do wrong.

CRITO: Certainly not.

SOCRATES: Nor must one, when wronged, inflict wrong in return, as the majority believe, since one must never do wrong.

c   CRITO: That seems to be the case.

SOCRATES: Come now, should one mistreat anyone or not, Crito?

CRITO: One must never do so.

SOCRATES: Well then, if one is oneself mistreated, is it right, as the majority say, to mistreat in return, or is it not?

CRITO: It is never right.

SOCRATES: Mistreating people is no different from wrongdoing.

CRITO: That is true.

SOCRATES: One should never do wrong in return, nor mistreat any man, no matter how one has been
d   mistreated by him. And Crito, see that you do not agree to this, contrary to your belief. For I know that only a few people hold this view or will hold it, and there is no common ground between those who hold this view and those who do not, but they inevitably despise each other's views. So then consider very carefully whether we have this view in common, and whether you agree, and let this be the basis of our deliberation, that neither to do wrong nor to return a wrong is ever right, nor is bad treatment in return for bad treatment. Or do you disagree and do not share this view as a basis for discus-
e   sion? I have held it for a long time and still hold it now, but if you think otherwise, tell me now. If, however, you stick to our former opinion, then listen to the next point.

CRITO: I stick to it and agree with you. So say on.

SOCRATES: Then I state the next point, or rather I ask you: when one has come to an agreement that is just with someone, should one fulfill it or cheat on it?

CRITO: One should fulfill it.

SOCRATES: See what follows from this: if we leave
50 here without the city's permission, are we mistreating people whom we should least mistreat? And are we sticking to a just agreement, or not?

CRITO: I cannot answer your question, Socrates. I do not know.

SOCRATES: Look at it this way. If, as we were planning to run away from here, or whatever one should call it, the laws and the state came and confronted us and asked: "Tell me, Socrates, what are you intending to do? Do you not by this action you are attempting intend to destroy us, the laws, and indeed the whole   b city, as far as you are concerned? Or do you think it possible for a city not to be destroyed if the verdicts of its courts have no force but are nullified and set at naught by private individuals?" What shall we answer to this and other such arguments? For many things could be said, especially by an orator on behalf of this law we are destroying, which orders that the judgments of the courts shall be carried out. Shall   c we say in answer, "The city wronged me, and its decision was not right." Shall we say that, or what?

CRITO: Yes, by Zeus, Socrates, that is our answer.

SOCRATES: Then what if the laws said: "Was that the agreement between us, Socrates, or was it to respect the judgments that the city came to?" And if we wondered at their words, they would perhaps add: "Socrates, do not wonder at what we say but answer, since you are accustomed to proceed by question and   d answer. Come now, what accusation do you bring against us and the city, that you should try to destroy us? Did we not, first, bring you to birth, and was it not through us that your father married your mother and begat you? Tell you, do you find anything to criticize in those of us who are concerned with marriage?" And I would say that I do not criticize them. "Or in those of us concerned with the nurture of babies and the education that you too received? Were those assigned to that subject not right to instruct your father to educate you in the arts and in physical   e culture?" And I would say that they were right. "Very well," they would continue, "and after you were born and nurtured and educated, could you, in the first place, deny that you are our offspring and servant, both you and your forefathers? If that is so, do you think that we are on an equal footing as regards the right, and that whatever we do to you it is right for you to do to us? You were not on an equal footing with your father as regards the right, nor with your master if you had one, so as to retaliate for anything   51 they did to you, to revile them if they reviled you, to beat them if they beat you, and so with many other things. Do you think you have this right to retaliation against your country and its laws? That if we undertake to destroy you and think it right to do so, you can undertake to destroy us, as far as you can, in return? And will you say that you are right to do so, you who truly care for virtue? Is your wisdom such as not to realize that your country is to be honored more than your mother, your father and all your ancestors, that

b it is more to be revered and more sacred, and that it counts for more among the gods and sensible men, that you must worship it, yield to it and placate its anger more than your father's? You must either persuade it or obey its orders, and endure in silence whatever it instructs you to endure, whether blows or bonds, and if it leads you into war to be wounded or killed, you must obey. To do so is right, and one must not give way or retreat or leave one's post, but both in war and in courts and everywhere else, one

c must obey the commands of one's city and country, or persuade it as to the nature of justice. It is impious to bring violence to bear against your mother or father, it is much more so to use it against your country." What shall we say in reply, Crito, that the laws speak the truth, or not?

CRITO: I think they do.

SOCRATES: "Reflect now, Socrates," the laws might say "that if what we say is true, you are not treating us rightly by planning to do what you are planning. We have given you birth, nurtured you, educated

d you, we have given you and all other citizens a share of all the good things we could. Even so, by giving every Athenian the opportunity, once arrived at voting age and having observed the affairs of the city and us the laws, we proclaim that if we do not please him, he can take his possessions and go wherever he pleases. Not one of our laws raises any obstacle or forbids him, if he is not satisfied with us or the city, if one of you wants to go and live in a colony or wants

e to go anywhere else, and keep his property. We say, however, that whoever of you remains, when he sees how we conduct our trials and manage the city in other ways, has in fact come to an agreement with us to obey our instructions. We say that the one who disobeys does wrong in three ways, first because in us he disobeys his parents, also those who brought

him up, and because, in spite of his agreement, he neither obeys us nor, if we do something wrong, does 52 he try to persuade us to do better. Yet we only propose things, we do not issue savage commands to do whatever we order; we give two alternatives, either to persuade us or to do what we say. He does neither. We do say that you too, Socrates, are open to those charges if you do what you have in mind; you would be among, not the least, but the most guilty of the Athenians." And if I should say "Why so?" they might well be right to upbraid me and say that I am among the Athenians who most definitely came to that agreement with them. They might well say: "Socrates, we b have convincing proofs that we and the city were congenial to you. You would not have dwelt here most consistently of all the Athenians if the city had not been exceedingly pleasing to you. You have never left the city, even to see a festival, nor for any other reason except military service; you have never gone to stay in any other city, as people do; you have had no desire to know another city or other laws; we and c our city satisfied you.

"So decisively did you choose us and agree to be a citizen under us. Also, you have had children in this city, thus showing that it was congenial to you. Then at your trial you could have assessed your penalty at exile if you wished, and you are now attempting to do against the city's wishes what you could then have done with her consent. Then you prided yourself that you did not resent death, but you chose, as you said, death in preference to exile. Now, however, those words do not make you ashamed, and you pay no heed to us, the laws, as you plan to destroy us, d and you act like the meanest type of slave by trying to run away, contrary to your commitments and your agreement to live as a citizen under us. First then, answer us on this very point, whether we speak the truth when we say that you agreed, not only in words but by your deeds, to live in accordance with us." What are we to say to that, Crito? Must we not agree?

CRITO: We must, Socrates.

SOCRATES: "Surely," they might say, "you are breaking the commitments and agreements that you made with us without compulsion or deceit, and under no e pressure of time for deliberation. You have had seventy years during which you could have gone away if you did not like us, and if you thought our agreements unjust. You did not choose to go to Sparta or to Crete, which you are always saying are well governed, nor to any other city, Greek or foreign. You have been away from Athens less than the lame or the blind or other handicapped people. It is clear that the city has been outstandingly more congenial to you than to other Athenians, and so have we, the laws, for what city can please without laws? Will you then not now stick to our agreements? You will, Socrates, if we can persuade you, and not make yourself a laughingstock by leaving the city.

"For consider what good you will do yourself or your friends by breaking our agreements and committing such a wrong? It is pretty obvious that your friends will themselves be in danger of exile, disfranchisement and loss of property. As for yourself, if you go to one of the nearby cities—Thebes or Megara, both are well governed—you will arrive as an enemy to their government; all who care for their city will look on you with suspicion, as a destroyer of the laws. You will also strengthen the conviction of the jury that they passed the right sentence on you, for anyone who destroys the laws could easily be thought to corrupt the young and the ignorant. Or will you avoid cities that are well governed and men who are civilized? If you do this, will your life be worth living? Will you have social intercourse with them and not be ashamed to talk to them? And what will you say? The same as you did here, that virtue and justice are man's most precious possession, along with lawful behavior and the laws? Do you not think that Socrates would appear to be an unseemly kind of person? One must think so. Or will you leave those places and go to Crito's friends in Thessaly? There you will find the greatest license and disorder, and they may enjoy hearing from you how absurdly you escaped from prison in some disguise, in a leather jerkin or some other things in which escapees wrap themselves, thus altering your appearance. Will there be no one to say that you, likely to live but a short time more, were so greedy for life that you transgressed the most important laws? Possibly, Socrates, if you do not annoy anyone, but if you do, many disgraceful things will be said about you.

"You will spend your time ingratiating yourself with all men, and be at their beck and call. What will you do in Thessaly but feast, as if you had gone to a banquet in Thessaly? As for those conversations of yours about justice and the rest of virtue, where will they be? You say you want to live for the sake of your children, that you may bring them up and educate them. How so? Will you bring them up and educate them by taking them to Thessaly and making strangers of them, that they may enjoy that too? Or not so, but they will be better brought up and educated here, while you are alive, though absent? Yes, your friends will look after them. Will they look after them if you go and live in Thessaly, but not if you go away to the underworld? If those who profess themselves your friends are any good at all, one must assume that they will.

"Be persuaded by us who have brought you up, Socrates. Do not value either your children or your life or anything else more than goodness, in order that when you arrive in Hades you may have all this as your defense before the rulers there. If you do this deed, you will not think it better or more just or more pious here, nor will any one of your friends, nor will it be better for you when you arrive yonder. As it is, you depart, if you depart, after being wronged not by us, the laws, but by men; but if you depart after shamefully returning wrong for wrong and mistreatment for mistreatment, after breaking your agreements and commitments with us, after mistreating those you should mistreat least—yourself, your friends, your country and us—we shall be angry with you while you are still alive, and our brothers, the laws of the underworld, will not receive you kindly, knowing that you tried to destroy us as far as you could. Do not let Crito persuade you, rather than us, to do what he says."

Crito, my dear friend, be assured that these are the words I seem to hear, as the Corybants seem to hear the music of their flutes, and the echo of these words resounds in me, and makes it impossible for me to hear anything else. As far as my present beliefs go, if you speak in opposition to them, you will speak in vain. However, if you think you can accomplish anything, speak.

CRITO: I have nothing to say, Socrates.

SOCRATES: Let it be then, Crito, and let us act in this way, since this is the way the god is leading us.

Republic

Book I

327 I went down to the Piraeus yesterday with Glaucon, the son of Ariston. I wanted to say a prayer to the goddess, and I was also curious to see how they would manage the festival, since they were holding it for the first time. I thought the procession of the local residents was a fine one and that the one conducted by the Thracians was no less outstanding. After we had said our prayer and seen the procession, we started
b back towards Athens. Polemarchus saw us from a distance as we were setting off for home and told his slave to run and ask us to wait for him. The slave caught hold of my cloak from behind: Polemarchus wants you to wait, he said. I turned around and asked where Polemarchus was. He's coming up behind you, he said, please wait for him. And Glaucon replied: All right, we will.

c   Just then Polemarchus caught up with us. Adeimantus, Glaucon's brother, was with him and so were Niceratus, the son of Nicias, and some others, all of whom were apparently on their way from the procession.

Polemarchus said: It looks to me, Socrates, as if you two are starting off for Athens.

It looks the way it is, then, I said.

Do you see how many we are? he said.

I do.

Well, you must either prove stronger than we are, or you will have to stay here.

Isn't there another alternative, namely, that we persuade you to let us go?

But could you persuade us, if we won't listen?

Certainly not, Glaucon said.

Well, we won't listen; you'd better make up your mind to that.

Don't you know, Adeimantus said, that there is to
328 be a torch race on horseback for the goddess tonight?

On horseback? I said. That's something new. Are they going to race on horseback and hand the torches on in relays, or what?

In relays, Polemarchus said, and there will be an all-night festival that will be well worth seeing. After

dinner, we'll go out to look at it. We'll be joined there by many of the young men, and we'll talk. So don't go; stay.

It seems, Glaucon said, that we'll have to stay. b

If you think so, I said, then we must.

So we went to Polemarchus' house, and there we found Lysias and Euthydemus, the brothers of Polemarchus, Thrasymachus of Chalcedon, Charmantides of Paeania, and Clitophon the son of Aristonymus. Polemarchus' father, Cephalus, was also there, and I thought he looked quite old, as I hadn't seen him for some time. He was sitting on a sort of cushioned c chair with a wreath on his head, as he had been offering a sacrifice in the courtyard. There was a circle of chairs, and we sat down by him.

As soon as he saw me, Cephalus welcomed me and said: Socrates, you don't come down to the Piraeus to see us as often as you should. If it were still easy for me to walk to town, you wouldn't have to come here; we'd come to you. But, as it is, you ought to come here more often, for you should know that as the d physical pleasures wither away, my desire for conversation and its pleasures grows. So do as I say: Stay with these young men now, but come regularly to see us, just as you would to friends or relatives.

Indeed, Cephalus, I replied, I enjoy talking with the very old, for we should ask them, as we might ask those who have travelled a road that we too will probably have to follow, what kind of road it is, e whether rough and difficult or smooth and easy. And I'd gladly find out from you what you think about this, as you have reached the point in life the poets call "the threshold of old age." Is it a difficult time? What is your report about it?

By god, Socrates, I'll tell you exactly what I think. A number of us, who are more or less the same age, 329 often get together in accordance with the old saying. When we meet, the majority complain about the lost pleasures they remember from their youth, those of sex, drinking parties, feasts, and the other things that go along with them, and they get angry as if they had been deprived of important things and had lived well

Reprinted from Plato, *Five Dialogues*, translated by G. M. A. Grube (Indianapolis: Hackett Publishing Company, 1981) by permission of the publisher.

then but are now hardly living at all. Some others moan about the abuse heaped on old people by their relatives, and because of this they repeat over and over that old age is the cause of many evils. But I don't think they blame the real cause, Socrates, for if old age were really the cause, I should have suffered in the same way and so should everyone else of my age. But as it is, I've met some who don't feel like that in the least. Indeed, I was once present when someone asked the poet Sophocles: "How are you as far as sex goes, Sophocles? Can you still make love with a woman?" "Quiet, man," the poet replied, "I am very glad to have escaped from all that, like a slave who has escaped from a savage and tyrannical master." I thought at the time that he was right, and I still do, for old age brings peace and freedom from all such things. When the appetites relax and cease to importune us, everything Sophocles said comes to pass, and we escape from many mad masters. In these matters and in those concerning relatives, the real cause isn't old age, Socrates, but the way people live. If they are moderate and contented, old age, too, is only moderately onerous; if they aren't, both old age and youth are hard to bear.

I admired him for saying that and I wanted him to tell me more, so I urged him on: When you say things like that, Cephalus, I suppose that the majority of people don't agree, they think that you bear old age more easily not because of the way you live but because you're wealthy, for the wealthy, they say, have many consolations.

That's true; they don't agree. And there is something in what they say, though not as much as they think. Themistocles' retort is relevant here. When someone from Seriphus insulted him by saying that his high reputation was due to his city and not to himself, he replied that, had he been a Seriphian, he wouldn't be famous, but neither would the other even if he had been an Athenian. The same applies to those who aren't rich and find old age hard to bear: A good person wouldn't easily bear old age if he were poor, but a bad one wouldn't be at peace with himself even if he were wealthy.

Did you inherit most of your wealth, Cephalus, I asked, or did you make it for yourself?

What did I make for myself, Socrates, you ask. As a money-maker I'm in a sort of mean between my grandfather and my father. My grandfather and name-sake inherited about the same amount of wealth as I possess but multiplied it many times. My father, Lysanias, however, diminished that amount to even less than I have now. As for me, I'm satisfied to leave my sons here not less but a little more than I inherited.

The reason I asked is that you don't seem to love money too much. And those who haven't made their own money are usually like you. But those who have made it for themselves are twice as fond of it as those who haven't. Just as poets love their poems and fathers love their children, so those who have made their own money don't just care about it because it's useful, as other people do, but because it's something they've made themselves. This makes them poor company, for they haven't a good word to say about anything except money.

That's true.

It certainly is. But tell me something else. What's the greatest good you've received from being very wealthy?

What I have to say probably wouldn't persuade most people. But you know, Socrates, that when someone thinks his end is near, he becomes frightened and concerned about things he didn't fear before. It's then that the stories we're told about Hades, about how people who've been unjust here must pay the penalty there—stories he used to make fun of—twist his soul this way and that for fear they're true. And whether because of the weakness of old age or because he is now closer to what happens in Hades and has a clearer view of it, or whatever it is, he is filled with foreboding and fear, and he examines himself to see whether he has been unjust to anyone. If he finds many injustices in his life, he awakes from sleep in terror, as children do, and lives in anticipation of bad things to come. But someone who knows that he hasn't been unjust has sweet good hope as his constant companion—a nurse to his old age, as Pindar says, for he puts it charmingly, Socrates, when he says that when someone lives a just and pious life

> Sweet hope is in his heart,
> Nurse and companion to his age.
> Hope, captain of the ever-twisting
> Minds of mortal men.

How wonderfully well he puts that. It's in this connection that wealth is most valuable, I'd say, not for every

man but for a decent and orderly one. Wealth can
b do a lot to save us from having to cheat or deceive
someone against our will and from having to depart
for that other place in fear because we owe sacrifice
to a god or money to a person. It has many other
uses, but, benefit for benefit, I'd say that this is how
it is most useful to a man of any understanding.

A fine sentiment, Cephalus, but, speaking of this
c very thing itself, namely, justice, are we to say unconditionally that it is speaking the truth and paying
whatever debts one has incurred? Or is doing these
things sometimes just, sometimes unjust? I mean this
sort of thing, for example: Everyone would surely
agree that if a sane man lends weapons to a friend
and then asks for them back when he is out of his
mind, the friend shouldn't return them, and wouldn't
be acting justly if he did. Nor should anyone be
willing to tell the whole truth to someone who is out
of his mind.

d   That's true.

Then the definition of justice isn't speaking the
truth and repaying what one has borrowed.

It certainly is, Socrates, said Polemarchus, interrupting, if indeed we're to trust Simonides at all.

Well, then, Cephalus said, I'll hand over the argument to you, as I have to look after the sacrifice.

So, Polemarchus said, am I then to be your heir
in everything?

You certainly are, Cephalus said, laughing, and off
he went to the sacrifice.

Then tell us, heir to the argument, I said, just what
e Simonides stated about justice that you consider
correct.

He stated that it is just to give to each what is owed
to him. And it's a fine saying, in my view.

Well, now, it isn't easy to doubt Simonides, for
he's a wise and godlike man. But what exactly does
he mean? Perhaps you know, Polemarchus, but I
don't understand him. Clearly, he doesn't mean what
we said a moment ago, that it is just to give back
whatever a person has lent to you, even if he's out of
his mind when he asks for it. And yet what he has
lent to you is surely something that's owed to him,
332 isn't it?

Yes.

But it is absolutely not to be given to him when
he's out of his mind?

That's true.

Then it seems that Simonides must have meant
something different when he says that to return what
is owed is just.

Something different indeed, by god. He means that
friends owe it to their friends to do good for them,
never harm.

I follow you. Someone doesn't give a lender back
what he's owed by giving him gold, if doing so would
be harmful, and both he and the lender are friends. b
Isn't that what you think Simonides meant?

It is.

But what about this? Should one also give one's
enemies whatever is owed to them?

By all means, one should give them what is owed
to them. And in my view what enemies owe to each
other is appropriately and precisely—something
bad.

It seems then that Simonides was speaking in riddles—just like a poet!—when he said what justice is,
for he thought it just to give to each what is appropriate c
to him, and this is what he called giving him what
is owed to him.

What else did you think he meant?

Then what do you think he'd answer if someone
asked him: "Simonides, which of the things that are
owed or that are appropriate for someone or something to have does the craft we call medicine give,
and to whom or what does it give them?"

It's clear that it gives medicines, food, and drink
to bodies.

And what owed or appropriate things does the craft
we call cooking give, and to whom or what does it
give them?

It gives seasonings to food.   d

Good. Now, what does the craft we call justice
give, and to whom or what does it give it?

If we are to follow the previous answers, Socrates,
it gives benefits to friends and does harm to enemies.

Simonides means, then, that to treat friends well
and enemies badly is justice?

I believe so.

And who is most capable of treating friends well
and enemies badly in matters of disease and health?

A doctor.

And who can do so best in a storm at sea?   e

A ship's captain.

What about the just person? In what actions and what work is he most capable of benefiting friends and harming enemies?

In wars and alliances, I suppose.

All right. Now, when people aren't sick, Polemarchus, a doctor is useless to them?

True.

And so is a ship's captain to those who aren't sailing?

Yes.

And to people who aren't at war, a just man is useless?

No, I don't think that at all.

Justice is also useful in peacetime, then?

333   It is.

And so is farming, isn't it?

Yes.

For getting produce?

Yes.

And shoemaking as well?

Yes.

For getting shoes, I think you'd say?

Certainly.

Well, then, what is justice useful for getting and using in peacetime?

Contracts, Socrates.

And by contracts do you mean partnerships, or what?

I mean partnerships.

Is someone a good and useful partner in a game of checkers because he's just or because he's a check-
b ers player?

Because he's a checkers player.

And in laying bricks and stones, is a just person a better and more useful partner than a builder?

Not at all.

In what kind of partnership, then, is a just person a better partner than a builder or a lyre-player, in the way that a lyre-player is better than a just person at hitting the right notes?

In money matters, I think.

Except perhaps, Polemarchus, in using money, for whenever one needs to buy a horse jointly, I think a
c horse breeder is a more useful partner, isn't he?

Apparently.

And when one needs to buy a boat, it's a boatbuilder or a ship's captain?

Probably.

In what joint use of silver or gold, then, is a just person a more useful partner than the others?

When it must be deposited for safekeeping, Socrates.

You mean whenever there is no need to use them but only to keep them?

That's right.

Then it is when money isn't being used that justice is useful for it?

I'm afraid so.   d

And whenever one needs to keep a pruning knife safe, but not to use it, justice is useful both in partnerships and for the individual. When you need to use it, however, it is skill at vine pruning that's useful?

Apparently.

You'll agree, then, that when one needs to keep a shield or a lyre safe and not to use them, justice is a useful thing, but when you need to use them, it is soldiery or musicianship that's useful?

Necessarily.

And so, too, with everything else, justice is useless when they are in use but useful when they aren't?

It looks that way.

In that case, justice isn't worth much, since it is only useful for useless things. But let's look into the   e following point. Isn't the person most able to land a blow, whether in boxing or any other kind of fight, also most able to guard against it?

Certainly.

And the one who is most able to guard against disease is also most able to produce it unnoticed?

So it seems to me, anyway.

And the one who is the best guardian of an army is the very one who can steal the enemy's plans and dispositions?   334

Certainly.

Whenever someone is a clever guardian, then, he is also a clever thief.

Probably so.

If a just person is clever at guarding money, therefore, he must also be clever at stealing it.

According to our argument, at any rate.

A just person has turned out then, it seems, to be a kind of thief. Maybe you learned this from Homer, for he's fond of Autolycus, the maternal grandfather of Odysseus, whom he describes as better than every-   b one at lying and stealing. According to you, Homer, and Simonides, then, justice seems to be some sort of craft of stealing, one that benefits friends and harms enemies. Isn't that what you meant?

No, by god, it isn't. I don't know any more what I did mean, but I still believe that to benefit one's friends and harm one's enemies is justice.

Speaking of friends, do you mean those a person *c* believes to be good and useful to him or those who actually are good and useful, even if he doesn't think they are, and similarly with enemies?

Probably, one loves those one considers good and useful and hates those one considers bad and harmful.

But surely people often make mistakes about this, believing many people to be good and useful when they aren't, and making the opposite mistake about enemies?

They do indeed.

And then good people are their enemies and bad ones their friends?

That's right.

And so it's just to benefit bad people and harm *d* good ones?

Apparently.

But good people are just and able to do no wrong?

True.

Then, according to your account, it's just to do bad things to those who do no injustice.

No, that's not just at all, Socrates; my account must be a bad one.

It's just, then, is it, to harm unjust people and benefit just ones?

That's obviously a more attractive view than the other one, anyway.

Then, it follows, Polemarchus, that it is just for the many, who are mistaken in their judgment, to harm their friends, who are bad, and benefit their enemies, *e* who are good. And so we arrive at a conclusion opposite to what we said Simonides meant.

That certainly follows. But let's change our definition, for it seems that we didn't define friends and enemies correctly.

How did we define them, Polemarchus?

We said that a friend is someone who is believed to be useful.

And how are we to change that now?

Someone who is both believed to be useful and is useful is a friend; someone who is believed to be

useful but isn't, is believed to be a friend but isn't. And the same for the enemy.

According to this account, then, a good person will be a friend and a bad one an enemy.

Yes.

So you want us to add something to what we said before about justice, when we said that it is just to treat friends well and enemies badly. You want us to add to this that it is just to treat well a friend who is good and to harm an enemy who is bad?

Right. That seems fine to me.

Is it, then, the role of a just man to harm anyone?

Certainly, he must harm those who are both bad and enemies.

Do horses become better or worse when they are harmed?

Worse.

With respect to the virtue that makes dogs good or the one that makes horses good?

The one that makes horses good.

And when dogs are harmed, they become worse in the virtue that makes dogs good, not horses?

Necessarily.

Then won't we say the same about human beings, too, that when they are harmed they become worse *c* in human virtue?

Indeed.

But isn't justice human virtue?

Yes, certainly.

Then people who are harmed must become more unjust?

So it seems.

Can musicians make people unmusical through music?

They cannot.

Or horsemen make people unhorsemanlike through horsemanship?

No.

Well, then, can those who are just make people unjust through justice? In a word, can those who are good make people bad through virtue? *d*

They cannot.

It isn't the function of heat to cool things but of its opposite?

Yes.

Nor the function of dryness to make things wet but of its opposite?

Indeed.

Nor the function of goodness to harm but of its opposite?

Apparently.

And a just person is good?

Indeed.

Then, Polemarchus, it isn't the function of a just person to harm a friend or anyone else, rather it is the function of his opposite, an unjust person?

In my view that's completely true, Socrates.

If anyone tells us, then, that it is just to give to
e each what he's owed and understands by this that a just man should harm his enemies and benefit his friends, he isn't wise to say it, since what he says isn't true, for it has become clear to us that it is never just to harm anyone?

I agree.

You and I shall fight as partners, then, against anyone who tells us that Simonides, Bias, Pittacus, or any of our other wise and blessedly happy men said this.

I, at any rate, am willing to be your partner in the battle.

Do you know to whom I think the saying belongs
336 that it is just to benefit friends and harm enemies?

Who?

I think it belongs to Periander, or Perdiccas, or Xerxes, or Ismenias of Corinth, or some other wealthy man who believed himself to have great power.

That's absolutely true.

All right, since it has become apparent that justice and the just aren't what such people say they are, what else could they be?

While we were speaking, Thrasymachus had tried
b many times to take over the discussion but was restrained by those sitting near him, who wanted to hear our argument to the end. When we paused after what I'd just said, however, he couldn't keep quiet any longer. He coiled himself up like a wild beast about to spring, and he hurled himself at us as if to tear us to pieces.

Polemarchus and I were frightened and flustered as he roared into our midst: What nonsense have you two been talking, Socrates? Why do you act like idiots
c by giving way to one another? If you truly want to know what justice is, don't just ask questions and then refute the answers simply to satisfy your competitiveness or love of honor. You know very well that it is

easier to ask questions than answer them. Give an answer yourself, and tell us what you say the just is. And don't tell me that it's the right, the beneficial, d the profitable, the gainful, or the advantageous, but tell me clearly and exactly what you mean; for I won't accept such nonsense from you.

His words startled me, and, looking at him, I was afraid. And I think that if I hadn't seen him before he stared at me, I'd have been dumbstruck. But as it was, I happened to look at him just as our discussion began to exasperate him, so I was able to answer, e and, trembling a little, I said: Don't be too hard on us, Thrasymachus, for if Polemarchus and I made an error in our investigation, you should know that we did so unwillingly. If we were searching for gold, we'd never willingly give way to each other, if by doing so we'd destroy our chance of finding it. So don't think that in searching for justice, a thing more valuable than even a large quantity of gold, we'd mindlessly give way to one another or be less than completely serious about finding it. You surely mustn't think that, but rather—as I do—that we're incapable of finding it. Hence it's surely far more appropriate for us to be pitied by you clever people than to be given rough treatment. 337

When he heard that, he gave a loud, sarcastic laugh. By Heracles, he said, that's just Socrates' usual irony. I knew, and I said so to these people earlier, that you'd be unwilling to answer and that, if someone questioned *you*, you'd be ironical and do anything rather than give an answer.

That's because you're a clever fellow, Thrasymachus. You knew very well that if you ask someone how much twelve is, and, as you ask, you warn him by saying "Don't tell me, man, that twelve is twice six, or three b times four, or six times two, or four times three, for I won't accept such nonsense," then you'll see clearly, I think, that no one could answer a question framed like that. And if he said to you: "What are you saying, Thrasymachus, am I not to give any of the answers you mention, not even if twelve happens to be one of those things? I'm amazed. Do you want me to say something other than the truth? Or do you mean something else?" What answer would you give him? c

Well, so you think the two cases are alike?

Why shouldn't they be alike? But even if they aren't alike, yet seem so to the person you asked, do you think him any less likely to give the answer that seems right to him, whether we forbid him to or not?

Is that what you're going to do, give one of the forbidden answers?

I wouldn't be surprised—provided that it's the one that seems right to me after I've investigated the matter.

What if I show you a different answer about justice d than all these—and a better one? What would you deserve then?

What else than the appropriate penalty for one who doesn't know, namely, to learn from the one who does know? Therefore, that's what I deserve.

You amuse me, but in addition to learning, you must pay a fine.

I will as soon as I have some money.

He has some already, said Glaucon. If it's a matter of money, speak, Thrasymachus, for we'll all contribute for Socrates.

I know, he said, so that Socrates can carry on as e usual. He gives no answer himself, and then, when someone else does give one, he takes up the argument and refutes it.

How can someone give an answer, I said, when he doesn't know it and doesn't claim to know it, and when an eminent man forbids him to express the opinion he has? It's much more appropriate for you 338 to answer, since you say you know and can tell us. So do it as a favor to me, and don't begrudge your teaching to Glaucon and the others.

While I was saying this, Glaucon and the others begged him to speak. It was obvious that Thrasymachus thought he had a fine answer and that he wanted to earn their admiration by giving it, but he pretended that he wanted to indulge his love of victory by forcing me to answer. However, he agreed in the end, and b then said: There you have Socrates' wisdom; he himself isn't willing to teach, but he goes around learning from others and isn't even grateful to them.

When you say that I learn from others you are right, Thrasymachus, but when you say that I'm not grateful, that isn't true. I show what gratitude I can, but since I have no money, I can give only praise. But just how enthusiastically I give it when someone seems to me to speak well, you'll know as soon as you've answered, for I think that you will speak well.

Listen, then. I say that justice is nothing other than c the advantage of the stronger. Well, why don't you praise me? But then you'd do anything to avoid having to do that.

I must first understand you, for I don't yet know what you mean. The advantage of the stronger, you say, is just. What do you mean, Thrasymachus? Surely you don't mean something like this: Polydamus, the pancratist, is stronger than we are; it is to his advantage to eat beef to build up his physical strength; therefore, this food is also advantageous and just for us who are weaker than he is?   d

You disgust me, Socrates. Your trick is to take hold of the argument at the point where you can do it the most harm.

Not at all, but tell us more clearly what you mean.

Don't you know that some cities are ruled by a tyranny, some by a democracy, and some by an aristocracy?

Of course.

And in each city this element is stronger, namely, the ruler?

Certainly.

And each makes laws to its own advantage. Democracy makes democratic laws, tyranny makes tyrannical e laws, and so on with the others. And they declare what they have made—what is to their own advantage—to be just for their subjects, and they punish anyone who goes against this as lawless and unjust. This, then, is what I say justice is, the same in all cities, the advantage of the established rule. Since the established rule is surely stronger, anyone who reasons 339 correctly will conclude that the just is the same everywhere, namely, the advantage of the stronger.

Now I see what you mean. Whether it's true or not, I'll try to find out. But you yourself have answered that the just is the advantageous, Thrasymachus, whereas you forbade that answer to me. True, you've added "of the stronger" to it.

And I suppose you think that's an insignificant addition.   b

It isn't clear yet whether it's significant. But it is clear that we must investigate to see whether or not it's true. I agree that the just is some kind of advantage. But you add that it's *of the stronger*. I don't know about that. We'll have to look into it.

Go ahead and look.

We will. Tell me, don't you also say that it is just to obey the rulers?

I do.

And are the rulers in all cities infallible, or are they
c liable to error?

No doubt they are liable to error.

When they undertake to make laws, therefore, they
make some correctly, others incorrectly?

I suppose so.

And a law is correct if it prescribes what is to the
rulers' own advantage and incorrect if it prescribes
what is to their disadvantage? Is that what you mean?
It is.

And whatever laws they make must be obeyed by
their subjects, and this is justice?

Of course.

Then, according to your account, it is just to do
d not only what is to the advantage of the stronger, but
also the opposite, what is not to their advantage.

What are you saying?

The same as you. But let's examine it more fully.
Haven't we agreed that, in giving orders to their subjects, the rulers are sometimes in error as to what is
best for themselves, and yet that it is just for their
subjects to do whatever their rulers order? Haven't
we agreed to that much?

I think so.

Then you must also think that you have agreed
e that it is just to do what is disadvantageous to the
rulers and those who are stronger, whenever they
unintentionally order what is bad for themselves. But
you also say that it is just for the others to obey the
orders they give. You're terribly clever, Thrasymachus, but doesn't it necessarily follow that it is just
to do the opposite of what you said, since the weaker
are then ordered to do what is disadvantageous to
the stronger?

By god, Socrates, said Polemarchus, that's quite
340 clear.

If you are to be his witness anyway, said Clitophon, interrupting.

Who needs a witness? Polemarchus replied. Thrasymachus himself agrees that the rulers sometimes
order what is bad for themselves and that it is just for
the others to do it.

That, Polemarchus, is because Thrasymachus
maintained that it is just to obey the orders of the
rulers.

He also maintained, Clitophon, that the advantage
b of the stronger is just. And having maintained both
principles he went on to agree that the stronger some-

times gives orders to those who are weaker than he
is — in other words, to his subjects — that are disadvantageous to the stronger himself. From these agreements it follows that what is to the advantage of the
stronger is no more just than what is not to his advantage.

But, Clitophon responded, he said that the advantage of the stronger is what the stronger believes to
be his advantage. This is what the weaker must do,
and this is what he maintained the just to be.

That isn't what he said, Polemarchus replied.

It makes no difference, Polemarchus, I said. If
Thrasymachus wants to put it that way now, let's c
accept it. Tell me, Thrasymachus, is this what you
wanted to say the just is, namely, what the stronger
believes to be to his advantage, whether it is in fact
to his advantage or not? Is that what we are to say
you mean?

Not at all. Do you think I'd call someone who is
in error stronger at the very moment he errs?

I did think that was what you meant when you
agreed that the rulers aren't infallible but are liable
to error.

That's because you are a false witness in arguments,
Socrates. When someone makes an error in the treat- d
ment of patients, do you call him a doctor in regard
to that very error? Or when someone makes an error
in accounting, do you call him an accountant in
regard to that very error in calculation? I think that
we express ourselves in words that, taken literally, do
say that a doctor is in error, or an accountant, or a
grammarian. But each of these, insofar as he is what
we call him, never errs, so that, according to the e
precise account (and you are a stickler for precise
accounts), no craftsman ever errs. It's when his knowledge fails him that he makes an error, and in regard
to that error he is no craftsman. No craftsman, expert,
or ruler makes an error at the moment when he is
ruling, even though everyone will say that a physician
or a ruler makes errors. It's in this loose way that you
must also take the answer I gave earlier. But the most
precise answer is this. A ruler, insofar as he is a ruler, 341
never makes errors and unerringly decrees what is
best for himself, and this his subject must do. Thus,
as I said from the first, it is just to do what is to the
advantage of the stronger.

All right, Thrasymachus, so you think I'm a false
witness?

You certainly are.

And you think that I asked the questions I did in order to harm you in the argument?

I know it very well, but it won't do you any good.
b You'll never be able to trick me, so you can't harm me that way, and without trickery you'll never be able to overpower me in argument.

I wouldn't so much as try, Thrasymachus. But in order to prevent this sort of thing from happening again, define clearly whether it is the ruler and stronger in the ordinary sense or in the precise sense whose advantage you said it is just for the weaker to promote as the advantage of the stronger.

I mean the ruler in the most precise sense. Now practice your harm-doing and false witnessing on that if you can—I ask no concessions from you—but you certainly won't be able to.

Do you think that I'm crazy enough to try to shave
c a lion or to bear false witness against Thrasymachus?

You certainly tried just now, though you were a loser at that too.

Enough of this. Tell me: Is a doctor in the precise sense, whom you mentioned before, a money-maker or someone who treats the sick? Tell me about the one who is really a doctor.

He's the one who treats the sick.

What about a ship's captain? Is a captain in the precise sense a ruler of sailors or a sailor?

A ruler of sailors.

We shouldn't, I think, take into account the fact
d that he sails in a ship, and he shouldn't be called a sailor for that reason, for it isn't because of his sailing that he is called a ship's captain, but because of his craft and his rule over sailors?

That's true.

And is there something advantageous to each of these, that is, to bodies and to sailors?

Certainly.

And aren't the respective crafts by nature set over them to seek and provide what is to their advantage?

They are.

And is there any advantage for each of the crafts themselves except to be as complete or perfect as possible?

e What are you asking?

This: If you asked me whether our bodies are sufficient in themselves, or whether they need something else, I'd answer: "They certainly have needs. And

because of this, because our bodies are deficient rather than self-sufficient, the craft of medicine has now been discovered. The craft of medicine was developed to provide what is advantageous for a body." Do you think that I'm right in saying this or not?

You are right.

Now, is medicine deficient? Does a craft need some 342 further virtue, as the eyes are in need of sight, and the ears of hearing, so that another craft is needed to seek and provide what is advantageous to them? Does a craft itself have some similar deficiency, so that each craft needs another, to seek out what is to its advantage? And does the craft that does the seeking need still another, and so on without end? Or does each seek out what is to its own advantage by itself? Or does it need neither itself nor another craft to seek b out what is advantageous to it, because of its own deficiencies? Or is it that there is no deficiency or error in any craft? That it isn't appropriate for any craft to seek what is to the advantage of anything except that of which it is the craft? And that, since it is itself correct, it is without either fault or impurity, as long as it is wholly and precisely the craft that it is? Consider this with the preciseness of language you mentioned. Is it so or not?

It appears to be so.

Medicine doesn't seek its own advantage, then, but that of the body?
c

Yes.

And horse-breeding doesn't seek its own advantage, but that of horses? Indeed, no other craft seeks its own advantage—for it has no further needs—but the advantage of that of which it is the craft?

Apparently so.

Now, surely, Thrasymachus, the crafts rule over and are stronger than the things of which they are the crafts?

Very reluctantly, he conceded this as well.

No kind of knowledge seeks or orders what is advantageous to itself, then, but what is advantageous to the weaker, which is subject to it.
d

He tried to fight this conclusion, but he conceded it in the end. And after he had, I said: Surely, then, no doctor, insofar as he is a doctor, seeks or orders what is advantageous to himself, but what is advantageous to his patient? We agreed that a doctor in the precise sense is a ruler of bodies, not a money-maker. Wasn't that agreed?

Yes.

So a ship's captain in the precise sense is a ruler of sailors, not a sailor?

e   That's what we agreed.

Doesn't it follow that a ship's captain or ruler won't seek and order what is advantageous to himself, but what is advantageous to a sailor?

He reluctantly agreed.

So, then, Thrasymachus, no one in any position of rule, insofar as he is a ruler, seeks or orders what is advantageous to himself, but what is advantageous to his subjects; the ones of whom he is himself the craftsman. It is to his subjects and what is advantageous and proper to them that he looks, and everything he says and does he says and does for them.

When we reached this point in the argument, and
343 it was clear to all that his account of justice had turned into its opposite, instead of answering, Thrasymachus said: Tell me, Socrates, do you still have a wet nurse?

What's this? Hadn't you better answer *my* questions rather than asking *me* such things?

Because she's letting you run around with a snotty nose, and doesn't wipe it when she needs to! Why, for all she cares, you don't even know about sheep and shepherds.

Just what is it I don't know?

You think that shepherds and cowherds seek the
b   good of their sheep and cattle, and fatten them and take care of them, looking to something other than their master's good and their own. Moreover, you believe that rulers in cities—true rulers, that is— think about their subjects differently than one does about sheep, and that night and day they think of something besides their own advantage. You are so
c   far from understanding about justice and what's just, about injustice and what's unjust, that you don't realize that justice is really the good of another, the advantage of the stronger and the ruler, and harmful to the one who obeys and serves. Injustice is the opposite, it rules the truly simple and just, and those it rules do what is to the advantage of the other and stronger, and they make the one they serve happy, but themselves not at all. You must look at it as
d   follows, my most simple Socrates: A just man always gets less than an unjust one. First, in their contracts with one another, you'll never find, when the partnership ends, that a just partner has got more than an unjust one, but less. Second, in matters relating to

the city, when taxes are to be paid, a just man pays more on the same property, an unjust one less, but when the city is giving out refunds, a just man gets nothing, while an unjust one makes a large profit. e Finally, when each of them holds a ruling position in some public office, a just person, even if he isn't penalized in other ways, finds that his private affairs deteriorate because he has to neglect them, that he gains no advantage from the public purse because of his justice, and that he's hated by his relatives and acquaintances when he's unwilling to do them an unjust favor. The opposite is true of an unjust man in every respect. Therefore, I repeat what I said before: A person of great power outdoes everyone else. Consider him if you want to figure out how much more 344 advantageous it is for the individual to be just rather than unjust. You'll understand this most easily if you turn your thoughts to the most complete injustice, the one that makes the doer of injustice happiest and the sufferers of it, who are unwilling to do injustice, most wretched. This is tyranny, which through stealth or force appropriates the property of others, whether sacred or profane, public or private, not little by little, but all at once. If someone commits only one part of injustice and is caught, he's punished and greatly b reproached—such partly unjust people are called temple-robbers, kidnappers, housebreakers, robbers, and thieves when they commit these crimes. But when someone, in addition to appropriating their possessions, kidnaps and enslaves the citizens as well, instead of these shameful names he is called happy and blessed, not only by the citizens themselves, but c by all who learn that he has done the whole of injustice. Those who reproach injustice do so because they are afraid not of doing it but of suffering it. So, Socrates, injustice, if it is on a large enough scale, is stronger, freer, and more masterly than justice. And, as I said from the first, justice is what is advantageous to the stronger, while injustice is to one's own profit and advantage.

Having emptied this great flood of words into our ears all at once like a bath attendant, Thrasymachus d intended to leave. But those present didn't let him and made him stay to give an account of what he had said. I too begged him to stay, and I said to him: After hurling such a speech at us, Thrasymachus, do you intend to leave before adequately instructing us or finding out whether you are right or not? Or do *e* you think it a small matter to determine which whole way of life would make living most worthwhile for each of us?

Is *that* what I seem to you to think? Thrasymachus said.

Either that, or else you care nothing for us and aren't worried about whether we'll live better or worse lives because of our ignorance of what you say you know. So show some willingness to teach it to us. It wouldn't be a bad investment for you to be the benefactor of a group as large as ours. For my own *345* part, I'll tell you that I am not persuaded. I don't believe that injustice is more profitable than justice, not even if you give it full scope and put no obstacles in its way. Suppose that there *is* an unjust person, and suppose he *does* have the power to do injustice, whether by trickery or open warfare; nonetheless, he doesn't persuade me that injustice is more profitable *b* than justice. Perhaps someone here, besides myself, feels the same as I do. So come now, and persuade us that we are wrong to esteem justice more highly than injustice in planning our lives.

And how am I to persuade you, if you aren't persuaded by what I said just now? What more can I do? Am I to take my argument and pour it into your very soul?

God forbid! Don't do that! But, first, stick to what you've said, and then, if you change your position, do it openly and don't deceive us. You see, Thrasymachus, that having defined the true doctor—to continue ex- *c* amining the things you said before—you didn't consider it necessary later to keep a precise guard on the true shepherd. You think that, insofar as he's a shepherd, he fattens sheep, not looking to what is best for the sheep but to a banquet, like a guest about to be entertained at a feast, or to a future sale, like a money-maker rather than a shepherd. Shepherding is con- *d* cerned only to provide what is best for the things it is set over, and it is itself adequately provided with all it needs to be at its best when it doesn't fall short in any way of being the craft of shepherding. That's why I thought it necessary for us to agree before that every kind of rule, insofar as it rules, doesn't seek anything other than what is best for the things it rules and cares for, and this is true both of public and private kinds of *e* rule. But do you think that those who rule cities, the true rulers, rule willingly?

I don't think it, by god, I know it.

But, Thrasymachus, don't you realize that in other kinds of rule no one wants to rule for its own sake, but they ask for pay, thinking that their ruling will benefit not themselves but their subjects? Tell me, doesn't every craft differ from every other in having *346* a different function? Please don't answer contrary to what you believe, so that we can come to some definite conclusion.

Yes, that's what differentiates them.

And each craft benefits us in its own peculiar way, different from the others. For example, medicine gives us health, navigation gives us safety while sailing, and so on with the others?

Certainly.

And wage-earning gives us wages, for this is its function? Or would you call medicine the same as *b* navigation? Indeed, if you want to define matters precisely, as you proposed, even if someone who is a ship's captain becomes healthy because sailing is advantageous to his health, you wouldn't for that reason call his craft medicine?

Certainly not.

Nor would you call wage-earning medicine, even if someone becomes healthy while earning wages?

Certainly not.

Nor would you call medicine wage-earning, even if someone earns pay while healing?

No.   *c*

We are agreed, then, that each craft brings its own peculiar benefit?

It does.

Then whatever benefit all craftsmen receive in common must clearly result from their joint practice of some additional craft that benefits each of them?

So it seems.

And we say that the additional craft in question, which benefits the craftsmen by earning them wages, is the craft of wage-earning?

He reluctantly agreed.

Then this benefit, receiving wages, doesn't result from their own craft, but rather, if we're to examine *d* this precisely, medicine provides health, and wage-earning provides wages; house-building provides a house, and wage-earning, which accompanies it, provides a wage; and so on with the other crafts. Each of them does its own work and benefits the things it is set over. So, if wages aren't added, is there any benefit that the craftsman gets from his craft?

Apparently none.

But he still provides a benefit when he works for *e* nothing?

Yes, I think he does.

Then, it is clear now, Thrasymachus, that no craft or rule provides for its own advantage, but, as we've been saying for some time, it provides and orders for its subject and aims at its advantage, that of the weaker, not of the stronger. That's why I said just now, Thrasymachus, that no one willingly chooses to rule and to take other people's troubles in hand and straighten them out, but each asks for wages; for *347* anyone who intends to practice his craft well never does or orders what is best for himself—at least not when he orders as his craft prescribes—but what is best for his subject. It is because of this, it seems, that wages must be provided to a person if he's to be willing to rule, whether in the form of money or honor or a penalty if he refuses.

What do you mean, Socrates? said Glaucon. I know the first two kinds of wages, but I don't understand what penalty you mean or how you can call it a wage.

Then you don't understand the best people's kind of wages, the kind that moves the most decent to rule, when they are willing to rule at all. Don't you know *b* that the love of honor and the love of money are despised, and rightly so?

I do.

Therefore good people won't be willing to rule for the sake of either money or honor. They don't want to be paid wages openly for ruling and get called hired hands, nor to take them in secret from their rule and be called thieves. And they won't rule for the sake of honor, because they aren't ambitious honor-*c* lovers. So, if they're to be willing to rule, some compulsion or punishment must be brought to bear on them—perhaps that's why it is thought shameful to seek to rule before one is compelled to. Now, the greatest punishment, if one isn't willing to rule, is to be ruled by someone worse than oneself. And I think that it's fear of this that makes decent people rule when they do. They approach ruling not as something good or something to be enjoyed, but as something *d* necessary, since it can't be entrusted to anyone better than—or even as good as—themselves. In a city of good men, if it came into being, the citizens would fight in order *not to rule*, just as they do now in order to rule. There it would be quite clear that anyone who is really a true ruler doesn't by nature seek his own advantage but that of his subjects. And everyone, knowing this, would rather be benefited by others than take the trouble to benefit them. So I can't at all agree with Thrasymachus that justice is the advantage of the stronger—but we'll look further into that another time. What Thrasymachus is now say-*e* ing—that the life of an unjust person is better than that of a just one—seems to be of far greater importance. Which life would you choose, Glaucon? And which of our views do you consider truer?

I certainly think that the life of a just person is more profitable.

Did you hear all of the good things Thrasymachus listed a moment ago for the unjust life? *348*

I heard, but I wasn't persuaded.

Then, do you want us to persuade him, if we're able to find a way, that what he says isn't true?

Of course I do.

If we oppose him with a parallel speech about the blessings of the just life, and then he replies, and then we do, we'd have to count and measure the good things mentioned on each side, and we'd need a jury to decide the case. But if, on the other hand, *b* we investigate the question, as we've been doing, by seeking agreement with each other, we ourselves can be both jury and advocates at once.

Certainly.

Which approach do you prefer? I asked.

The second.

Come, then, Thrasymachus, I said, answer us from the beginning. You say that complete injustice is more profitable than complete justice?

I certainly do say that, and I've told you why. *c*

Well, then, what do you say about this? Do you call one of the two a virtue and the other a vice?

Of course.

That is to say, you call justice a virtue and injustice a vice?

That's hardly likely, since I say that injustice is profitable and justice isn't.

Then, what exactly do you say?

The opposite.

That justice is a vice?

No, just very high-minded simplicity.

Then do you call being unjust being low-minded?

No, I call it good judgment.

You consider unjust people, then, Thrasymachus, to be clever and good?

Yes, those who are completely unjust, who can bring cities and whole communities under their power. Perhaps, you think I meant pickpockets? Not that such crimes aren't also profitable, if they're not found out, but they aren't worth mentioning by comparison to what I'm talking about.

I'm not unaware of what you want to say. But I wonder about this: Do you really include injustice with virtue and wisdom, and justice with their opposites?

I certainly do.

That's harder, and it isn't easy now to know what to say. If you had declared that injustice is more profitable, but agreed that it is a vice or shameful, as some others do, we could have discussed the matter on the basis of conventional beliefs. But now, obviously, you'll say that injustice is fine and strong and apply to it all the attributes we used to apply to justice, since you dare to include it with virtue and wisdom.

You've divined my views exactly.

Nonetheless, we mustn't shrink from pursuing the argument and looking into this, just as long as I take you to be saying what you really think. And I believe that you aren't joking now, Thrasymachus, but are saying what you believe to be the truth.

What difference does it make to you, whether I believe it or not? It's *my account* you're supposed to be refuting.

It makes no difference. But try to answer this further question: Do you think that a just person wants to outdo someone else who's just?

Not at all, for he wouldn't then be as polite and innocent as he is.

Or to outdo someone who does a just action?

No, he doesn't even want to do that.

And does he claim that he deserves to outdo an unjust person and believe that it is just for him to do so, or doesn't he believe that?

He'd want to outdo him, and he'd claim to deserve to do so, but he wouldn't be able.

That's not what I asked, but whether a just person wants to outdo an unjust person but not a just one, thinking that this is what he deserves?

He does.

What about an unjust person? Does he claim that he deserves to outdo a just person or someone who does a just action?

Of course he does; he thinks he deserves to outdo everyone.

Then will an unjust person also outdo an *unjust* person or someone who does an *unjust* action, and will he strive to get the most he can for himself from everyone?

He will.

Then, let's put it this way: A just person doesn't outdo someone like himself but someone unlike himself, whereas an unjust person outdoes both like and unlike.

Very well put.

An unjust person is clever and good, and a just one is neither?

That's well put, too.

It follows, then, that an unjust person is like clever and good people, while the other isn't?

Of course that's so. How could he fail to be like them when he has their qualities, while the other isn't like them?

Fine. Then each of them has the qualities of the people he's like?

Of course.

All right, Thrasymachus. Do you call one person musical and another nonmusical?

I do.

Which of them is clever in music, and which isn't?

The musical one is clever, of course, and the other isn't.

And the things he's clever in, he's good in, and the things he isn't clever in, he's bad in?

Yes.

Isn't the same true of a doctor?

It is.

Do you think that a musician, in tuning his lyre and in tightening and loosening the strings, wants to outdo another musician, claiming that this is what he deserves?

I do not.

But he does want to outdo a nonmusician?

Necessarily.

What about a doctor? Does he, when prescribing food and drink, want to outdo another doctor or someone who does the action that medicine prescribes?

Certainly not.

But he does want to outdo a nondoctor?

Yes.

In any branch of knowledge or ignorance, do you think that a knowledgeable person would intentionally try to outdo other knowledgeable people or say something better or different than they do, rather than doing or saying the very same thing as those like him?

Well, perhaps it must be as you say.

And what about an ignorant person? Doesn't he want to outdo both a knowledgeable person and an b ignorant one?

Probably.

A knowledgeable person is clever?

I agree.

And a clever one is good?

I agree.

Therefore, a good and clever person doesn't want to outdo those like himself but those who are unlike him and his opposite.

So it seems.

But a bad and ignorant person wants to outdo both his like and his opposite.

Apparently.

Now, Thrasymachus, we found that an unjust person tries to outdo those like him and those unlike him? Didn't you say that?

I did.

And that a just person won't outdo his like but c his unlike?

Yes.

Then, a just person is like a clever and good one, and an unjust is like an ignorant and bad one.

It looks that way.

Moreover, we agreed that each has the qualities of the one he resembles.

Yes, we did.

Then, a just person has turned out to be good and clever, and an unjust one ignorant and bad.

Thrasymachus agreed to all this, not easily as I'm d telling it, but reluctantly, with toil, trouble, and— since it was summer—a quantity of sweat that was a wonder to behold. And then I saw something I'd never seen before—Thrasymachus blushing. But, in any case, after we'd agreed that justice is virtue and wisdom and that injustice is vice and ignorance, I said: All right, let's take that as established. But we also said that injustice is powerful, or don't you remember that, Thrasymachus?

I remember, but I'm not satisfied with what you're now saying. I could make a speech about it, but, if I did, I know that you'd accuse me of engaging in oratory. So either allow me to speak, or, if you want e to ask questions, go ahead, and I'll say, "All right," and nod yes and no, as one does to old wives' tales.

Don't do that, contrary to your own opinion.

I'll answer so as to please you, since you won't let me make a speech. What else do you want?

Nothing, by god. But if that's what you're going to do, go ahead and do it. I'll ask my questions.

Ask ahead.

I'll ask what I asked before, so that we may proceed with our argument about justice and injustice in an 351 orderly fashion, for surely it was claimed that injustice is stronger and more powerful than justice. But, now, if justice is indeed wisdom and virtue, it will easily be shown to be stronger than injustice, since injustice is ignorance (no one could now be ignorant of that). However, I don't want to state the matter so unconditionally, Thrasymachus, but to look into it in some such way as this. Would you say that it is unjust for b a city to try to enslave other cities unjustly and to hold them in subjection when it has enslaved many of them?

Of course, that's what the best city will especially do, the one that is most completely unjust.

I understand that's your position, but the point I want to examine is this: Will the city that becomes stronger than another achieve this power without justice, or will it need the help of justice?

If what you said a moment ago stands, and justice is cleverness or wisdom, it will need the help of justice, c but if things are as I stated, it will need the help of injustice.

I'm impressed, Thrasymachus, that you don't merely nod yes or no but give very fine answers.

That's because I'm trying to please you.

You're doing well at it, too. So please me some more by answering this question: Do you think that a city, an army, a band of robbers or thieves, or any other tribe with a common unjust purpose would be able to achieve it if they were unjust to each other?

No, indeed. d

What if they weren't unjust to one another? Would they achieve more?

Certainly.

Injustice, Thrasymachus, causes civil war, hatred, and fighting among themselves, while justice brings friendship and a sense of common purpose. Isn't that so?

Let it be so, in order not to disagree with you.

You're still doing well on that front. So tell me this: If the effect of injustice is to produce hatred wherever it occurs, then, whenever it arises, whether among free men or slaves, won't it cause them to hate one another, engage in civil war, and prevent
e them from achieving any common purpose?

Certainly.

What if it arises between two people? Won't they be at odds, hate each other, and be enemies to one another and to just people?

They will.

Does injustice lose its power to cause dissension when it arises within a single individual, or will it preserve it intact?

Let it preserve it intact.

Apparently, then, injustice has the power, first, to make whatever it arises in—whether it is a city, a family, an army, or anything else—incapable of
352 achieving anything as a unit, because of the civil wars and differences it creates, and, second, it makes that unit an enemy to itself and to what is in every way its opposite, namely, justice. Isn't that so?

Certainly.

And even in a single individual, it has by its nature the very same effect. First, it makes him incapable of achieving anything, because he is in a state of civil war and not of one mind; second, it makes him his own enemy, as well as the enemy of just people. Hasn't it that effect?

Yes.

And the gods too are just?

Let it be so.

So an unjust person is also an enemy of the gods,
b Thrasymachus, while a just person is their friend?

Enjoy your banquet of words! Have no fear, I won't oppose you. That would make these people hate me.

Come, then, complete the banquet for me by continuing to answer as you've been doing. We have shown that just people are cleverer and more capable of doing things, while unjust ones aren't even able to act together, for when we speak of a powerful
c achievement by unjust men acting together, what we

say isn't altogether true. They would never have been able to keep their hands off each other if they were completely unjust. But clearly there must have been some sort of justice in them that at least prevented them from doing injustice among themselves at the same time as they were doing it to others. And it was this that enabled them to achieve what they did. When they started doing unjust things, they were only halfway corrupted by their injustice (for those who are all bad and completely unjust are completely incapable of accomplishing anything). These are the things I understand to hold, not the ones you first maintained. We must now examine, as we proposed d before, whether just people also live better and are happier than unjust ones. I think it's clear already that this is so, but we must look into it further, since the argument concerns no ordinary topic but the way we ought to live.

Go ahead and look.

I will. Tell me, do you think there is such a thing as the function of a horse?

I do.   e

And would you define the function of a horse or of anything else as that which one can do only with it or best with it?

I don't understand.

Let me put it this way: Is it possible to see with anything other than eyes?

Certainly not.

Or to hear with anything other than ears?

No.

Then, we are right to say that seeing and hearing are the functions of eyes and ears?

Of course.

What about this? Could you use a dagger or a carving knife or lots of other things in pruning a vine? 353

Of course.

But wouldn't you do a finer job with a pruning knife designed for the purpose than with anything else?

You would.

Then shall we take pruning to be its function?

Yes.

Now, I think you'll understand what I was asking earlier when I asked whether the function of each thing is what it alone can do or what it does better than anything else.

I understand, and I think that this is the function of each.   b

All right. Does each thing to which a particular function is assigned also have a virtue? Let's go over the same ground again. We say that eyes have some function?

They do.

So there is also a virtue of eyes?

There is.

And ears have a function?

Yes.

So there is also a virtue of ears?

There is.

And all other things are the same, aren't they?

They are.

c And could eyes perform their function well if they lacked their peculiar virtue and had the vice instead?

How could they, for don't you mean if they had blindness instead of sight?

Whatever their virtue is, for I'm not now asking about that but about whether anything that has a function performs it well by means of its own peculiar virtue and badly by means of its vice?

That's true, it does.

So ears, too, deprived of their own virtue, perform their function badly?

That's right.

d And the same could be said about everything else?

So it seems.

Come, then, and let's consider this: Is there some function of a soul that you couldn't perform with anything else, for example, taking care of things, ruling, deliberating, and the like? Is there anything other than a soul to which you could rightly assign these, and say that they are its peculiar function?

No, none of them.

What of living? Isn't that a function of a soul?

It certainly is.

And don't we also say that there is a virtue of a soul?

We do.

Then, will a soul ever perform its function well,

e Thrasymachus, if it is deprived of its own peculiar virtue, or is that impossible?

It's impossible.

Doesn't it follow, then, that a bad soul rules and takes care of things badly and that a good soul does all these things well?

It does.

Now, we agreed that justice is a soul's virtue, and injustice its vice?

We did.

Then, it follows that a just soul and a just man will live well, and an unjust one badly.

Apparently so, according to your argument.

And surely anyone who lives well is blessed and happy, and anyone who doesn't is the opposite.   354

Of course.

Therefore, a just person is happy, and an unjust one wretched.

So be it.

It profits no one to be wretched but to be happy.

Of course.

And so, Thrasymachus, injustice is never more profitable than justice.

Let that be your banquet, Socrates, at the feast of Bendis.

Given by you, Thrasymachus, after you became gentle and ceased to give me rough treatment. Yet I haven't had a fine banquet. But that's my fault not yours. I seem to have behaved like a glutton, snatching   b at every dish that passes and tasting it before properly savoring its predecessor. Before finding the answer to our first inquiry about what justice is, I let that go and turned to investigate whether it is a kind of vice and ignorance or a kind of wisdom and virtue. Then an argument came up about injustice being more profitable than justice, and I couldn't refrain from abandoning the previous one and following up on that. Hence the result of the discussion, as far as I'm concerned, is that I know nothing, for when I don't   c know what justice is, I'll hardly know whether it is a kind of virtue or not, or whether a person who has it is happy or unhappy.

BOOK II

When I said this, I thought I had done with the   357 discussion, but it turned out to have been only a prelude. Glaucon showed his characteristic courage on this occasion too and refused to accept Thrasymachus' abandonment of the argument. Socrates, he said, do you want to seem to have persuaded us that it is better in every way to be just than unjust, or do you want truly to convince us of this?   b

I want truly to convince you, I said, if I can.

Well, then, you certainly aren't doing what you want. Tell me, do you think there is a kind of good we welcome, not because we desire what comes from it, but because we welcome it for its own sake—joy, for example, and all the harmless pleasures that have no results beyond the joy of having them?

Certainly, I think there are such things.

And is there a kind of good we like for its own sake c and also for the sake of what comes from it—knowing, for example, and seeing and being healthy? We welcome such things, I suppose, on both counts.

Yes.

And do you also see a third kind of good, such as physical training, medical treatment when sick, medicine itself, and the other ways of making money? We'd say that these are onerous but beneficial to us, and we wouldn't choose them for their own sakes, but for the sake of the rewards and other things that d come from them.

There is also this third kind. But what of it?

Where do you put justice?

I myself put it among the finest goods, as something 358 to be valued by anyone who is going to be blessed with happiness, both because of itself and because of what comes from it.

That isn't most people's opinion. They'd say that justice belongs to the onerous kind, and is to be practiced for the sake of the rewards and popularity that come from a reputation for justice, but is to be avoided because of itself as something burdensome.

I know that's the general opinion. Thrasymachus faulted justice on these grounds a moment ago and praised injustice, but it seems that I'm a slow learner.

Come, then, and listen to me as well, and see b whether you still have that problem, for I think that Thrasymachus gave up before he had to, charmed by you as if he were a snake. But I'm not yet satisfied by the argument on either side. I want to know what justice and injustice are and what power each itself has when it's by itself in the soul. I want to leave out of account their rewards and what comes from each of them. So, if you agree, I'll renew the argument of Thrasymachus. First, I'll state what kind of thing peo-c ple consider justice to be and what its origins are. Second, I'll argue that all who practice it do so unwillingly, as something necessary, not as something good. Third, I'll argue that they have good reason to act as they do, for the life of an unjust person is, they say, much better than that of a just one.

It isn't, Socrates, that I believe any of that myself. I'm perplexed, indeed, and my ears are deafened listening to Thrasymachus and countless others. But I've yet to hear anyone defend justice in the way I want, proving that it is better than injustice. I want d to hear it praised *by itself*, and I think that I'm most likely to hear this from you. Therefore, I'm going to speak at length in praise of the unjust life, and in doing so I'll show you the way I want to hear you praising justice and denouncing injustice. But see whether you want me to do that or not.

I want that most of all. Indeed, what subject could someone with any understanding enjoy discussing more often?

Excellent. Then let's discuss the first subject I mentioned—what justice is and what its origins are. e

They say that to do injustice is naturally good and to suffer injustice bad, but that the badness of suffering it so far exceeds the goodness of doing it that those who have done and suffered injustice and tasted both, but who lack the power to do it and avoid suffering it, decide that it is profitable to come to an agreement with each other neither to do injustice nor to suffer 359 it. As a result, they begin to make laws and covenants, and what the law commands they call lawful and just. This, they say, is the origin and essence of justice. It is intermediate between the best and the worst. The best is to do injustice without paying the penalty; the worst is to suffer it without being able to take revenge. Justice is a mean between these two extremes. People value it not as a good but because they are too weak to do injustice with impunity. Some-b one who has the power to do this, however, and is a true man wouldn't make an agreement with anyone not to do injustice in order not to suffer it. For him that would be madness. This is the nature of justice, according to the argument, Socrates, and these are its natural origins.

We can see most clearly that those who practice justice do it unwillingly and because they lack the power to do injustice, if in our thoughts we grant to c a just and an unjust person the freedom to do whatever they like. We can then follow both of them and see where their desires would lead. And we'll catch the just person red-handed travelling the same road as the unjust. The reason for this is the desire to outdo others and get more and more. This is what anyone's nature naturally pursues as good, but nature is forced by law into the perversion of treating fairness with respect.

The freedom I mentioned would be most easily realized if both people had the power they say the ancestor of Gyges of Lydia possessed. The story goes that he was a shepherd in the service of the ruler of Lydia. There was a violent thunderstorm, and an earthquake broke open the ground and created a chasm at the place where he was tending his sheep. Seeing this, he was filled with amazement and went down into it. And there, in addition to many other wonders of which we're told, he saw a hollow bronze horse. There were windowlike openings in it, and, peeping in, he saw a corpse, which seemed to be of more than human size, wearing nothing but a gold ring on its finger. He took the ring and came out of the chasm. He wore the ring at the usual monthly meeting that reported to the king on the state of the flocks. And as he was sitting among the others, he happened to turn the setting of the ring towards himself to the inside of his hand. When he did this, he became invisible to those sitting near him, and they went on talking as if he had gone. He wondered at this, and, fingering the ring, he turned the setting outwards again and became visible. So he experimented with the ring to test whether it indeed had this power—and it did. If he turned the setting inward, he became invisible; if he turned it outward, he became visible again. When he realized this, he at once arranged to become one of the messengers sent to report to the king. And when he arrived there, he seduced the king's wife, attacked the king with her help, killed him, and took over the kingdom.

Let's suppose, then, that there were two such rings, one worn by a just and the other by an unjust person. Now, no one, it seems, would be so incorruptible that he would stay on the path of justice or stay away from other people's property, when he could take whatever he wanted from the marketplace with impunity, go into people's houses and have sex with anyone he wished, kill or release from prison anyone he wished, and do all the other things that would make him like a god among humans. Rather his actions would be in no way different from those of an unjust person, and both would follow the same path. This, some would say, is a great proof that one is never just

willingly but only when compelled to be. No one believes justice to be a good when it is kept private, since, wherever either person thinks he can do injustice with impunity, he does it. Indeed, every man believes that injustice is far more profitable to himself than justice. And any exponent of this argument will say he's right, for someone who didn't want to do injustice, given this sort of opportunity, and who didn't touch other people's property would be thought wretched and stupid by everyone aware of the situation, though, of course, they'd praise him in public, deceiving each other for fear of suffering injustice. So much for my second topic.

As for the choice between the lives we're discussing, we'll be able to make a correct judgment about that only if we separate the most just and the most unjust. Otherwise we won't be able to do it. Here's the separation I have in mind. We'll subtract nothing from the injustice of an unjust person and nothing from the justice of a just one, but we'll take each to be complete in his own way of life. First, therefore, we must suppose that an unjust person will act as clever craftsmen do: A first-rate captain or doctor, for example, knows the difference between what his craft can and can't do. He attempts the first but lets the second go by, and if he happens to slip, he can put things right. In the same way, an unjust person's successful attempts at injustice must remain undetected, if he is to be fully unjust. Anyone who is caught should be thought inept, for the extreme of injustice is to be believed to be just without being just. And our completely unjust person must be given complete injustice; nothing may be subtracted from it. We must allow that, while doing the greatest injustice, he has nonetheless provided himself with the greatest reputation for justice. If he happens to make a slip, he must be able to put it right. If any of his unjust activities should be discovered, he must be able to speak persuasively or to use force. And if force is needed, he must have the help of courage and strength and of the substantial wealth and friends with which he has provided himself.

Having hypothesized such a person, let's now in our argument put beside him a just man, who is simple and noble and who, as Aeschylus says, doesn't want to be believed to be good but to be so. We must take away his reputation, for a reputation for justice would bring him honor and rewards, so that it wouldn't be clear whether he is just for the sake of justice itself or for the sake of those honors and rewards. We must strip him of everything except justice and make his situation the opposite of an unjust person's. Though he does no injustice, he must have the greatest reputation for it, so that his justice may be tested full-strength and not diluted by wrongdoing and what comes from it. Let him stay like that unchanged until he dies—just, but all his life believed to be unjust. In this way, both will reach the extremes, the one of justice and the other of injustice, and we'll be able to judge which of them is happier.

Whew! Glaucon, I said, how vigorously you've scoured each of the men for our competition, just as you would a pair of statues for an art competition.

I do the best I can, he replied. Since the two are as I've described, in any case, it shouldn't be difficult to complete the account of the kind of life that awaits each of them, but it must be done. And if what I say sounds crude, Socrates, remember that it isn't I who speak but those who praise injustice at the expense of justice. They'll say that a just person in such circumstances will be whipped, stretched on a rack, chained, blinded with fire, and, at the end, when he has suffered every kind of evil, he'll be impaled, and will realize then that one shouldn't want to be just but to be believed to be just. Indeed, Aeschylus' words are far more correctly applied to unjust people than to just ones, for the supporters of injustice will say that a really unjust person, having a way of life based on the truth about things and not living in accordance with opinion, doesn't want simply to be believed to be unjust but actually to be so—

> Harvesting a deep furrow in his mind,
> Where wise counsels propagate.

He rules his city because of his reputation for justice; he marries into any family he wishes; he gives his children in marriage to anyone he wishes; he has contracts and partnerships with anyone he wants; and besides benefiting himself in all these ways, he profits because he has no scruples about doing injustice. In any contest, public or private, he's the winner and outdoes his enemies. And by outdoing them, he becomes wealthy, benefiting his friends and harming his enemies. He makes adequate sacrifices to the gods and sets up magnificent offerings to them. He takes better care of the gods, therefore, (and, indeed, of the human beings he's fond of) than a just person does. Hence it's likely that the gods, in turn, will take better care of him than of a just person. That's what they say, Socrates, that gods and humans provide a better life for unjust people than for just ones.

When Glaucon had said this, I had it in mind to respond, but his brother Adeimantus intervened: You surely don't think that the position has been adequately stated?

Why not? I said.

The most important thing to say hasn't been said yet.

Well, then, I replied, a man's brother must stand by him, as the saying goes. If Glaucon has omitted something, you must help him. Yet what he has said is enough to throw me to the canvas and make me unable to come to the aid of justice.

Nonsense, he said. Hear what more I have to say, for we should also fully explore the arguments that are opposed to the ones Glaucon gave, the ones that praise justice and find fault with injustice, so that what I take to be his intention may be clearer.

When fathers speak to their sons, they say that one must be just, as do all the others who have charge of anyone. But they don't praise justice itself, only the high reputations it leads to and the consequences of being thought to be just, such as the public offices, marriages, and other things Glaucon listed. But they elaborate even further on the consequences of reputation. By bringing in the esteem of the gods, they are able to talk about the abundant good things that they themselves and the noble Hesiod and Homer say that the gods give to the pious, for Hesiod says that the gods make the oak trees

> Bear acorns at the top and bees in the
>   middle
> And make fleecy sheep heavy laden with wool

for the just, and tells of many other good things akin to these. And Homer is similar:

> When a good king, in his piety,
> Upholds justice, the black earth bears
> Wheat and barley for him, and his
>   trees are heavy with fruit.

> *His sheep bear lambs unfailingly,*
> *and the sea yields up its fish.*

Musaeus and his son make the gods give the just more headstrong goods than these. In their stories, they lead the just to Hades, seat them on couches, provide them with a symposium of pious people, crown them with wreaths, and make them spend all their time drinking—as if they thought drunkenness *d* was the finest wage of virtue. Others stretch even further the wages that virtue receives from the gods, for they say that someone who is pious and keeps his promises leaves his children's children and a whole race behind him. In these and other similar ways, they praise justice. They bury the impious and unjust in mud in Hades; force them to carry water in a sieve; bring them into bad repute while they're still alive, and all those penalties that Glaucon gave to the just *e* person they give to the unjust. But they have nothing else to say. This, then, is the way people praise justice and find fault with injustice.

Besides this, Socrates, consider another form of argument about justice and injustice employed both by private individuals and by poets. All go on repeating with one voice that justice and moderation are fine *364* things, but hard and onerous, while licentiousness and injustice are sweet and easy to acquire and are shameful only in opinion and law. They add that unjust deeds are for the most part more profitable than just ones, and, whether in public or private, they willingly honor vicious people who have wealth and other types of power and declare them to be happy. But they dishonor and disregard the weak and the poor, even though they agree that they are better than *b* the others.

But the most wonderful of all these arguments concerns what they have to say about the gods and virtue. They say that the gods, too, assign misfortune and a bad life to many good people, and the opposite fate to their opposites. Begging priests and prophets frequent the doors of the rich and persuade them that they possess a god-given power founded on sacrifices and incantations. If the rich person or any of *c* his ancestors has committed an injustice, they can fix it with pleasant rituals. Moreover, if he wishes to injure some enemy, then, at little expense, he'll be able to harm just and unjust alike, for by means of spells and enchantments they can persuade the gods

to serve them. And the poets are brought forward as witnesses to all these accounts. Some harp on the ease of vice, as follows:

> *Vice in abundance is easy to get;*
> *The road is smooth and begins beside you,* *d*
> *But the gods have put sweat between us*
> *and virtue,*

and a road that is long, rough, and steep. Others quote Homer to bear witness that the gods can be influenced by humans, since he said:

> *The gods themselves can be swayed by prayer,*
> *And with sacrifices and soothing promises,*
> *Incense and libations, human beings turn*
> *them from their purpose* *e*
> *When someone has transgressed and sinned.*

And they present a noisy throng of books by Musaeus and Orpheus, offspring as they say of Selene and the Muses, in accordance with which they perform their rituals. And they persuade not only individuals but whole cities that the unjust deeds of the living or the dead can be absolved or purified through ritual sacrifices and pleasant games. These initiations, as *365* they call them, free people from punishment hereafter, while a terrible fate awaits those who have not performed the rituals.

When all such sayings about the attitudes of gods and humans to virtue and vice are so often repeated, Socrates, what effect do you suppose they have on the souls of young people? I mean those who are clever and are able to flit from one of these sayings to another, so to speak, and gather from them an impression of what sort of person he should be and of how best to travel the road of life. He would surely ask himself Pindar's question, "Should I by justice or *b* by crooked deceit scale this high wall and live my life guarded and secure?" And he'll answer: "The various sayings suggest that there is no advantage in my being just if I'm not also thought just, while the troubles and penalties of being just are apparent. But they tell me that an unjust person, who has secured for himself a reputation for justice, lives the life of a god. Since, then, 'opinion forcibly overcomes truth' and 'controls happiness,' as the wise men say, I must *c* surely turn entirely to it. I should create a façade of illusory virtue around me to deceive those who come near, but keep behind it the greedy and crafty fox of the wise Archilochus."

"But surely," someone will object, "it isn't easy for vice to remain always hidden." We'll reply that nothing great is easy. And, in any case, if we're to be d happy, we must follow the path indicated in these accounts. To remain undiscovered we'll form secret societies and political clubs. And there are teachers of persuasion to make us clever in dealing with assemblies and law courts. Therefore, using persuasion in one place and force in another, we'll outdo others without paying a penalty.

"What about the gods? Surely, we can't hide from them or use violent force against them!" Well, if the gods don't exist or don't concern themselves with human affairs, why should we worry at all about hiding from them? If they do exist and do concern them-e selves with us, we've learned all we know about them from the laws and the poets who give their genealogies—nowhere else. But these are the very people who tell us that the gods can be persuaded and influenced by sacrifices, gentle prayers, and offerings. Hence, we should believe them on both matters or neither. If we believe them, we should be unjust and offer sacrifices from the fruits of our injustice. If we 366 are just, our only gain is not to be punished by the gods, since we lose the profits of injustice. But if we are unjust, we get the profits of our crimes and transgressions and afterwards persuade the gods by prayer and escape without punishment.

"But in Hades won't we pay the penalty for crimes committed here, either ourselves or our children's children?" "My friend," the young man will say as he does his calculation, "mystery rites have great power and the gods have great power of absolution. The greatest cities tell us this, as do those children b of the gods who have become poets and prophets."

Why, then, should we still choose justice over the greatest injustice? Many eminent authorities agree that, if we practice such injustice with a false façade, we'll do well at the hands of gods and humans, living and dying as we've a mind to. So, given all that has been said, Socrates, how is it possible for anyone of c any power—whether of mind, wealth, body, or birth—to be willing to honor justice and not laugh aloud when he hears it praised? Indeed, if anyone

can show that what we've said is false and has adequate knowledge that justice is best, he'll surely be full not of anger but of forgiveness for the unjust. He knows that, apart from someone of godlike character who is disgusted by injustice or one who has gained knowledge and avoids injustice for that reason, no one is d just willingly. Through cowardice or old age or some other weakness, people do indeed object to injustice. But it's obvious that they do so only because they lack the power to do injustice, for the first of them to acquire it is the first to do as much injustice as he can.

And all of this has no other cause than the one that led Glaucon and me to say to you: "Socrates, of all of you who claim to praise justice, from the original heroes of old whose words survive, to the men of the present day, not one has ever blamed injustice or e praised justice except by mentioning the reputations, honors, and rewards that are their consequences. No one has ever adequately described what each itself does of its own power by its presence in the soul of the person who possesses it, even if it remains hidden from gods and humans. No one, whether in poetry or in private conversations, has adequately argued that injustice is the worst thing a soul can have in it and that justice is the greatest good. If you had treated the subject in this way and persuaded us from youth, we wouldn't now be guarding against one another's 367 injustices, but each would be his own best guardian, afraid that by doing injustice he'd be living with the worst thing possible."

Thrasymachus or anyone else might say what we've said, Socrates, or maybe even more, in discussing justice and injustice—crudely inverting their powers, in my opinion. And, frankly, it's because I want to hear the opposite from you that I speak with all the b force I can muster. So don't merely give us a theoretical argument that justice is stronger than injustice, but tell us what each itself does, because of its own powers, to someone who possesses it, that makes injustice bad and justice good. Follow Glaucon's advice, and don't take reputations into account, for if you don't deprive justice and injustice of their true reputations and attach false ones to them, we'll say that you are not praising them but their reputations and that you're encouraging us to be unjust in secret. In that c case, we'll say that you agree with Thrasymachus that justice is the good of another, the advantage of the stronger, while injustice is one's own advantage and profit, though not the advantage of the weaker.

You agree that justice is one of the greatest goods, the ones that are worth getting for the sake of what comes from them, but much more so for their own d sake, such as seeing, hearing, knowing, being healthy, and all other goods that are fruitful by their own nature and not simply because of reputation. Therefore, praise justice as a good of that kind, explaining how — because of its very self — it benefits its possessors and how injustice harms them. Leave wages and reputations for others to praise.

Others would satisfy me if they praised justice and blamed injustice in that way, extolling the wages of one and denigrating those of the other. But you, unless you order me to be satisfied, wouldn't, for e you've spent your whole life investigating this and nothing else. Don't, then, give us only a theoretical argument that justice is stronger than injustice, but show what effect each has because of itself on the person who has it — the one for good and the other for bad — whether it remains hidden from gods and human beings or not.

While I'd always admired the natures of Glaucon 368 and Adeimantus, I was especially pleased on this occasion, and I said: You are the sons of a great man, and Glaucon's lover began his elegy well when he wrote, celebrating your achievements at the battle of Megara,

Sons of Ariston, godlike offspring of a famous man.

That's well said in my opinion, for you must indeed be affected by the divine if you're not convinced that injustice is better than justice and yet can speak on its behalf as you have done. And I believe that you b really are unconvinced by your own words. I infer this from the way you live, for if I had only your words to go on, I wouldn't trust you. The more I trust you, however, the more I'm at a loss as to what to do. I don't see how I can be of help. Indeed, I believe I'm incapable of it. And here's my evidence. I thought what I said to Thrasymachus showed that justice is better than injustice, but you won't accept it from me. On the other hand, I don't see how I can refuse my help, for I fear that it may even be impious to

have breath in one's body and the ability to speak and yet to stand idly by and not defend justice when it is being prosecuted. So the best course is to give c justice any assistance I can.

Glaucon and the others begged me not to abandon the argument but to help in every way to track down what justice and injustice are and what the truth about their benefits is. So I told them what I had in mind: The investigation we're undertaking is not an easy one but requires keen eyesight. Therefore, since we aren't clever people, we should adopt the method d of investigation that we'd use if, lacking keen eyesight, we were told to read small letters from a distance and then noticed that the same letters existed elsewhere in a larger size and on a larger surface. We'd consider it a godsend, I think, to be allowed to read the larger ones first and then to examine the smaller ones, to see whether they really are the same.

That's certainly true, said Adeimantus, but how is this case similar to our investigation of justice? e

I'll tell you. We say, don't we, that there is the justice of a single man and also the justice of a whole city?

Certainly.

And a city is larger than a single man?

It is larger.

Perhaps, then, there is more justice in the larger thing, and it will be easier to learn what it is. So, if you're willing, let's first find out what sort of thing justice is in a city and afterwards look for it in the 369 individual, observing the ways in which the smaller is similar to the larger.

That seems fine to me.

If we could watch a city coming to be in theory, wouldn't we also see its justice coming to be, and its injustice as well?

Probably so.

And when that process is completed, we can hope to find what we are looking for more easily?

Of course. b

Do you think we should try to carry it out, then? It's no small task, in my view. So think it over.

We have already, said Adeimantus. Don't even consider doing anything else.

I think a city comes to be because none of us is self-sufficient, but we all need many things. Do you think that a city is founded on any other principle?

No.

And because people need many things, and be-
c cause one person calls on a second out of one need
and on a third out of a different need, many people
gather in a single place to live together as partners
and helpers. And such a settlement is called a city.
Isn't that so?

It is.

And if they share things with one another, giving
and taking, they do so because each believes that this
is better for himself?

That's right.

Come, then, let's create a city in theory from its
beginnings. And it's our needs, it seems, that will
create it.

It is, indeed.

Surely our first and greatest need is to provide food
d to sustain life.

Certainly.

Our second is for shelter, and our third for clothes
and such.

That's right.

How, then, will a city be able to provide all this?
Won't one person have to be a farmer, another a
builder, and another a weaver? And shouldn't we add
a cobbler and someone else to provide medical care?

All right.

So the essential minimum for a city is four or
five men?

e Apparently.

And what about this? Must each of them contribute
his own work for the common use of all? For example,
will a farmer provide food for everyone, spending
quadruple the time and labor to provide food to be
shared by them all? Or will he not bother about that,
producing one quarter the food in one quarter the
370 time, and spending the other three quarters, one in
building a house, one in the production of clothes,
and one in making shoes, not troubling to associate
with the others, but minding his own business on
his own?

Perhaps, Socrates, Adeimantus replied, the way you
suggested first would be easier than the other.

That certainly wouldn't be surprising, for, even
as you were speaking it occurred to me that, in the
first place, we aren't all born alike, but each of us
differs somewhat in nature from the others, one being

suited to one task, another to another. Or don't you *b*
think so?

I do.

Second, does one person do a better job if he
practices many crafts or—since he's one person himself—if he practices one?

If he practices one.

It's clear, at any rate, I think, that if one misses the
right moment in anything, the work is spoiled.

It is.

That's because the thing to be done won't wait on
the leisure of the doer, but the doer must of necessity
pay close attention to his work rather than treating it
as a secondary occupation.   *c*

Yes, he must.

The result, then, is that more plentiful and better-
quality goods are more easily produced if each person
does one thing for which he is naturally suited, does
it at the right time, and is released from having to
do any of the others.

Absolutely.

Then, Adeimantus, we're going to need more than
four citizens to provide the things we've mentioned,
for a farmer won't make his own plough, not if it's
to be a good one, nor his hoe, nor any of his other
farming tools. Neither will a builder—and he, too, *d*
needs lots of things. And the same is true of a weaver
and a cobbler, isn't it?

It is.

Hence, carpenters, metal workers, and many other
craftsmen of that sort will share our little city and
make it bigger.

That's right.

Yet it won't be a huge settlement even if we add
cowherds, shepherds, and other herdsmen in order
that the farmers have cows to do their ploughing, the *e*
builders have oxen to share with the farmers in haul-
ing their materials, and the weavers and cobblers have
hides and fleeces to use.

It won't be a small one either, if it has to hold
all those.

Moreover, it's almost impossible to establish a city
in a place where nothing has to be imported.

Indeed it is.

So we'll need yet further people to import from
other cities whatever is needed.

Yes.

And if an importer goes empty-handed to another city, without a cargo of the things needed by the city from which he's to bring back what his own city
371 needs, he'll come away empty-handed, won't he?

So it seems.

Therefore our citizens must not only produce enough for themselves at home but also goods of the right quality and quantity to satisfy the requirements of others.

They must.

So we'll need more farmers and other craftsmen in our city.

Yes.

And others to take care of imports and exports. And they're called merchants, aren't they?

Yes.

So we'll need merchants, too.

Certainly.

And if the trade is by sea, we'll need a good many
b others who know how to sail.

A good many, indeed.

And how will those in the city itself share the things that each produces? It was for the sake of this that we made their partnership and founded their city.

Clearly, they must do it by buying and selling.

Then we'll need a marketplace and a currency for such exchange.

Certainly.

If a farmer or any other craftsman brings some of
c his products to market, and he doesn't arrive at the same time as those who want to exchange things with him, is he to sit idly in the marketplace, away from his own work?

Not at all. There'll be people who'll notice this and provide the requisite service—in well-organized cities they'll usually be those whose bodies are weakest and who aren't fit to do any other work. They'll stay
d around the market exchanging money for the goods of those who have something to sell and then exchanging those goods for the money of those who want them.

Then, to fill this need there will have to be retailers in our city, for aren't those who establish themselves in the marketplace to provide this service of buying and selling called retailers, while those who travel between cities are called merchants?

That's right.

There are other servants, I think, whose minds alone wouldn't qualify them for membership in our e society but whose bodies are strong enough for labor. These sell the use of their strength for a price called a wage and hence are themselves called wage-earners. Isn't that so?

Certainly.

So wage-earners complete our city?

I think so.

Well, Adeimantus, has our city grown to completeness, then?

Perhaps it has.

Then where are justice and injustice to be found in it? With which of the things we examined did they come in?

I've no idea, Socrates, unless it was somewhere in some need that these people have of one another. 372

You may be right, but we must look into it and not grow weary. First, then, let's see what sort of life our citizens will lead when they've been provided for in the way we have been describing. They'll produce bread, wine, clothes, and shoes, won't they? They'll build houses, work naked and barefoot in the summer, and wear adequate clothing and shoes in the winter. For b food, they'll knead and cook the flour and meal they've made from wheat and barley. They'll put their honest cakes and loaves on reeds or clean leaves, and, reclining on beds strewn with yew and myrtle, they'll feast with their children, drink their wine, and, crowned with wreaths, hymn the gods. They'll enjoy sex with one another but bear no more children than their resources allow, lest they fall into either poverty or war. c

It seems that you make your people feast without any delicacies, Glaucon interrupted.

True enough, I said, I was forgetting that they'll obviously need salt, olives, cheese, boiled roots, and vegetables of the sort they cook in the country. We'll give them desserts, too, of course, consisting of figs, chickpeas, and beans, and they'll roast myrtle and acorns before the fire, drinking moderately. And so they'll live in peace and good health, and when they d die at a ripe old age, they'll bequeath a similar life to their children.

If you were founding a city for pigs, Socrates, he replied, wouldn't you fatten *them* on the same diet?

Then how should I feed these people, Glaucon? I asked.

In the conventional way. If they aren't to suffer hardship, they should recline on proper couches, dine at a table, and have the delicacies and desserts that *e* people have nowadays.

All right, I understand. It isn't merely the origin of a city that we're considering, it seems, but the origin of a *luxurious* city. And that may not be a bad idea, for by examining it, we might very well see how justice and injustice grow up in cities. Yet the true city, in my opinion, is the one we've described, the healthy one, as it were. But let's study a city with a fever, if that's what you want. There's nothing to stop us. *373* The things I mentioned earlier and the way of life I described won't satisfy some people, it seems, but couches, tables, and other furniture will have to be added, and, of course, all sorts of delicacies, perfumed oils, incense, prostitutes, and pastries. We mustn't provide them only with the necessities we mentioned at first, such as houses, clothes, and shoes, but painting and embroidery must be begun, and gold, ivory, and the like acquired. Isn't that so?

b Yes.

Then we must enlarge our city, for the healthy one is no longer adequate. We must increase it in size and fill it with a multitude of things that go beyond what is necessary for a city—hunters, for example, and artists or imitators, many of whom work with shapes and colors, many with music. And there'll be poets and their assistants, actors, choral dancers, contractors, and makers of all kinds of devices, including, among other things, those needed for the adornment of women. And so we'll need more servants, *c* too. Or don't you think that we'll need tutors, wet nurses, nannies, beauticians, barbers, chefs, cooks, and swineherds? We didn't need any of these in our earlier city, but we'll need them in this one. And we'll also need many more cattle, won't we, if the people are going to eat meat?

Of course.

And if we live like that, we'll have a far greater *d* need for doctors than we did before?

Much greater.

And the land, I suppose, that used to be adequate to feed the population we had then, will cease to be adequate and become too small. What do you think?

The same.

Then we'll have to seize some of our neighbors' land if we're to have enough pasture and ploughland.

And won't our neighbors want to seize part of ours as well, if they too have surrendered themselves to the endless acquisition of money and have overstepped the limit of their necessities?

That's completely inevitable, Socrates.   *e*

Then our next step will be war, Glaucon, won't it?

It will.

We won't say yet whether the effects of war are good or bad but only that we've now found the origins of war. It comes from those same desires that are most of all responsible for the bad things that happen to cities and the individuals in them.

That's right.

Then the city must be further enlarged, and not just by a small number, either, but by a whole army, which will do battle with the invaders in defense of the city's substantial wealth and all the other things *374* we mentioned.

Why aren't the citizens themselves adequate for that purpose?

They won't be, if the agreement you and the rest of us made when we were founding the city was a good one, for surely we agreed, if you remember, that it's impossible for a single person to practice many crafts or professions well.

That's true.

Well, then, don't you think that warfare is a profession?   *b*

Of course.

Then should we be more concerned about cobbling than about warfare?

Not at all.

But we prevented a cobbler from trying to be a farmer, weaver, or builder at the same time and said that he must remain a cobbler in order to produce fine work. And each of the others, too, was to work all his life at a single trade for which he had a natural aptitude and keep away from all the others, so as not to miss the right moment to practice his own work *c* well. Now, isn't it of the greatest importance that warfare be practiced well? And is fighting a war so easy that a farmer or a cobbler or any other craftsman can be a soldier at the same time? Though no one can become so much as a good player of checkers or dice if he considers it only as a sideline and doesn't practice it from childhood. Or can someone pick up a shield or any other weapon or tool of war and immediately perform adequately in an infantry battle d or any other kind? No other tool makes anyone who picks it up a craftsman or champion unless he has acquired the requisite knowledge and has had sufficient practice.

If tools could make anyone who picked them up an expert, they'd be valuable indeed.

Then to the degree that the work of the guardians
e is most important, it requires most freedom from other things and the greatest skill and devotion.

I should think so.

And doesn't it also require a person whose nature is suited to that way of life?

Certainly.

Then our job, it seems, is to select, if we can, the kind of nature suited to guard the city.

It is.

By god, it's no trivial task that we've taken on. But insofar as we are able, we mustn't shrink from it.
375 No, we mustn't.

Do you think that, when it comes to guarding, there is any difference between the nature of a pedigree young dog and that of a well-born youth?

What do you mean?

Well, each needs keen senses, speed to catch what it sees, and strength in case it has to fight it out with what it captures.

They both need all these things.

And each must be courageous if indeed he's to fight well.

Of course.

And will a horse, a dog, or any other animal be courageous, if he isn't spirited? Or haven't you noticed just how invincible and unbeatable spirit is, so that
b its presence makes the whole soul fearless and unconquerable?

I have noticed that.

The physical qualities of the guardians are clear, then.

Yes.

And as far as their souls are concerned, they must be spirited.

That too.

But if they have natures like that, Glaucon, won't they be savage to each other and to the rest of the citizens?

By god, it will be hard for them to be anything else.

Yet surely they must be gentle to their own people
c and harsh to the enemy. If they aren't, they won't

wait around for others to destroy the city but will do it themselves first.

That's true.

What are we to do, then? Where are we to find a character that is both gentle and high-spirited at the same time? After all, a gentle nature is the opposite of a spirited one.

Apparently.

If someone lacks either gentleness or spirit, he can't be a good guardian. Yet it seems impossible to combine them. It follows that a good guardian cannot exist.   d

It looks like it.

I couldn't see a way out, but on reexamining what had gone before, I said: We deserve to be stuck, for we've lost sight of the analogy we put forward.

How do you mean?

We overlooked the fact that there *are* natures of the sort we thought impossible, natures in which these opposites are indeed combined.

Where?

You can see them in other animals, too, but especially in the one to which we compared the guardian, for you know, of course, that a pedigree dog naturally has a character of this sort—he is gentle as can be e to those he's used to and knows, but the opposite to those he doesn't know.

I do know that.

So the combination we want is possible after all, and our search for the good guardian is not contrary to nature.

Apparently not.

Then do you think that our future guardian, besides being spirited, must also be by nature philosophical?

How do you mean? I don't understand.   376

It's something else you see in dogs, and it makes you wonder at the animal.

What?

When a dog sees someone it doesn't know, it gets angry before anything bad happens to it. But when it knows someone, it welcomes him, even if it has never received anything good from him. Haven't you ever wondered at that?

I've never paid any attention to it, but obviously that is the way a dog behaves.

Surely this is a refined quality in its nature and one that is truly philosophical.   b

In what way philosophical?

Because it judges anything it sees to be either a friend or an enemy, on no other basis than that it knows the one and doesn't know the other. And how could it be anything besides a lover of learning, if it defines what is its own and what is alien to it in terms of knowledge and ignorance?

It couldn't.

But surely the love of learning is the same thing as philosophy or the love of wisdom?

It is.

Then, may we confidently assume in the case of a human being, too, that if he is to be gentle toward his own and those he knows, he must be a lover of learning and wisdom?

We may.

Philosophy, spirit, speed, and strength must all, then, be combined in the nature of anyone who is to be a fine and good guardian of our city.

Absolutely.

Then those are the traits a potential guardian would need at the outset. But how are we to bring him up and educate him? Will inquiry into that topic bring us any closer to the goal of our inquiry, which is to discover the origins of justice and injustice in a city? We want our account to be adequate, but we don't want it to be any longer than necessary.

I certainly expect, Glaucon's brother said, that such inquiry will further our goal.

Then, by god, Adeimantus, I said, we mustn't leave it out, even if it turns out to be a somewhat lengthy affair.

No, we mustn't.

Come, then, and just as if we had the leisure to make up stories, let's describe in theory how to educate our men.

All right.

What will their education be? Or is it hard to find anything better than that which has developed over a long period — physical training for bodies and music and poetry for the soul?

Yes, it would be hard.

Now, we start education in music and poetry before physical training, don't we?

Of course.

Do you include stories under music and poetry?

I do.

Aren't there two kinds of story, one true and the other false?

Yes.

And mustn't our men be educated in both, but first in false ones?

I don't understand what you mean.

Don't you understand that we first tell stories to children? These are false, on the whole, though they have some truth in them. And we tell them to small children before physical training begins.

That's true.

And that's what I meant by saying that we must deal with music and poetry before physical training.

All right.

You know, don't you, that the beginning of any process is most important, especially for anything young and tender? It's at that time that it is most malleable and takes on any pattern one wishes to impress on it.

Exactly.

Then shall we carelessly allow the children to hear any old stories, told by just anyone, and to take beliefs into their souls that are for the most part opposite to the ones we think they should hold when they are grown up?

We certainly won't.

Then we must first of all, it seems, supervise the storytellers. We'll select their stories whenever they are fine or beautiful and reject them when they aren't. And we'll persuade nurses and mothers to tell their children the ones we have selected, since they will shape their children's souls with stories much more than they shape their bodies by handling them. Many of the stories they tell now, however, must be thrown out.

Which ones do you mean?

We'll first look at the major stories, and by seeing how to deal with them, we'll see how to deal with the minor ones as well, for they exhibit the same pattern and have the same effects whether they're famous or not. Don't you think so?

I do, but I don't know which ones you're calling major.

Those that Homer, Hesiod, and other poets tell us, for surely they composed false stories, told them to people, and are still telling them.

Which stories do you mean, and what fault do you find in them?

The fault one ought to find first and foremost, especially if the falsehood isn't well told.

For example?

When a story gives a bad image of what the gods
e and heroes are like, the way a painter does whose
picture is not at all like the things he's trying to paint.

You're right to object to that. But what sort of thing
in particular do you have in mind?

First, telling the greatest falsehood about the most
important things doesn't make a fine story—I mean
Hesiod telling us about how Uranus behaved, how
Cronus punished him for it, and how he was in turn
378 punished by his own son. But even if it were true, it
should be passed over in silence, not told to foolish
young people. And if, for some reason, it has to be
told, only a very few people—pledged to secrecy and
after sacrificing not just a pig but something great
and scarce—should hear it, so that their number is
kept as small as possible.

Yes, such stories are hard to deal with.

And they shouldn't be told in our city, Adeimantus.
b Nor should a young person hear it said that in committing the worst crimes he's doing nothing out of the
ordinary, or that if he inflicts every kind of punishment on an unjust father, he's only doing the same
as the first and greatest of the gods.

No, by god, I don't think myself that these stories
are fit to be told.

Indeed, if we want the guardians of our city to
think that it's shameful to be easily provoked into
hating one another, we mustn't allow *any* stories about
c gods warring, fighting, or plotting against one another,
for they aren't true. The battles of gods and giants,
and all the various stories of the gods hating their
families or friends, should neither be told nor even
woven in embroideries. If we're to persuade our people that no citizen has ever hated another and that
it's impious to do so, then *that's* what should be
told to children from the beginning by old men and
women; and as these children grow older, poets
should be compelled to tell them the same sort of
d thing. We won't admit stories into our city—whether
allegorical or not—about Hera being chained by her
son, nor about Hephaestus being hurled from heaven
by his father when he tried to help his mother, who
was being beaten, nor about the battle of the gods in
Homer. The young can't distinguish what is allegorical from what isn't, and the opinions they absorb at
that age are hard to erase and apt to become unalter-
able. For these reasons, then, we should probably

take the utmost care to insure that the first stories
they hear about virtue are the best ones for them *e*
to hear.

That's reasonable. But if someone asked us what
stories these are, what should we say?

You and I, Adeimantus, aren't poets, but we *are*
founding a city. And it's appropriate for the founders *379*
to know the patterns on which poets must base their
stories and from which they mustn't deviate. But we
aren't actually going to compose their poems for
them.

All right. But what precisely are the patterns for
theology or stories about the gods?

Something like this: Whether in epic, lyric, or
tragedy, a god must always be represented as he is.

Indeed, he must.

Now, a god is really good, isn't he, and must be
described as such? *b*

What else?

And surely nothing good is harmful, is it?

I suppose not.

And can what isn't harmful do harm?

Never.

Or can what does no harm do anything bad?

No.

And can what does nothing bad be the cause of
anything bad?

How could it?

Moreover, the good is beneficial?

Yes.

It is the cause of doing well?

Yes.

The good isn't the cause of all things, then, but
only of good ones; it isn't the cause of bad ones.

I agree entirely. *c*

Therefore, since a god is good, he is not—as most
people claim—the cause of everything that happens
to human beings but of only a few things, for good
things are fewer than bad ones in our lives. He alone
is responsible for the good things, but we must find
some other cause for the bad ones, not a god.

That's very true, and I believe it.

Then we won't accept from anyone the foolish
mistake Homer makes about the gods when he says: *d*

There are two urns at the threshold of Zeus,
One filled with good fates, the other with
  bad ones....

and the person to whom he gives a mixture of these

> Sometimes meets with a bad fate, sometimes
>   with good,

but the one who receives his fate entirely from the second urn,

> Evil famine drives him over the divine earth.

e We won't grant either that Zeus is for us

> The distributor of both good and bad.

And as to the breaking of the promised truce by Pandarus, if anyone tells us that it was brought about by Athena and Zeus or that Themis and Zeus were responsible for strife and contention among the gods, we will not praise him. Nor will we allow the young 380 to hear the words of Aeschylus:

> A god makes mortals guilty
> When he wants utterly to destroy a house.

And if anyone composes a poem about the sufferings of Niobe, such as the one in which these lines occur, or about the house of Pelops, or the tale of Troy, or anything else of that kind, we must require him to say that these things are not the work of a god. Or, if they are, then poets must look for the kind of account of them that we are now seeking, and say that the actions of the gods are good and just, and b that those they punish are benefited thereby. We won't allow poets to say that the punished are made wretched and that it was a god who made them so. But we will allow them to say that bad people are wretched because they are in need of punishment and that, in paying the penalty, they are benefited by the gods. And, as for saying that a god, who is himself good, is the cause of bad things, we'll fight that in every way, and we won't allow anyone to say it in his own city, if it's to be well governed, or anyone to hear c it either—whether young or old, whether in verse or prose. These stories are not pious, not advantageous to us, and not consistent with one another.

I like your law, and I'll vote for it.

This, then, is one of the laws or patterns concerning the gods to which speakers and poets must conform, namely, that a god isn't the cause of all things but only of good ones.

And it's a fully satisfactory law.

What about this second law? Do you think that a god is a sorcerer, able to appear in different forms at d different times, sometimes changing himself from his own form into many shapes, sometimes deceiving us by making us think that he has done it? Or do you think he's simple and least of all likely to step out of his own form?

I can't say offhand.

Well, what about this? If he steps out of his own form, mustn't he either change himself or be changed by something else?   e

He must.

But the best things are least liable to alteration or change, aren't they? For example, isn't the healthiest and strongest body least changed by food, drink, and labor, or the healthiest and strongest plant by sun, wind, and the like?

Of course.   381

And the most courageous and most rational soul is least disturbed or altered by any outside affection?

Yes.

And the same account is true of all artifacts, furniture, houses, and clothes. The ones that are good and well made are least altered by time or anything else that happens to them.

That's right.

Whatever is in good condition, then, whether by nature or craft or both, admits least of being changed b by anything else.

So it seems.

Now, surely a god and what belongs to him are in every way in the best condition.

How could they fail to be?

Then a god would be least likely to have many shapes.

Indeed.

Then does he change or alter himself?

Clearly he does, if indeed he is altered at all.

Would he change himself into something better and more beautiful than himself or something worse and uglier?

It would have to be into something worse, if he's
c changed at all, for surely we won't say that a god is
deficient in either beauty or virtue.

Absolutely right. And do you think, Adeimantus,
that anyone, whether god or human, would deliberately make himself worse in any way?

No, that's impossible.

Is it impossible, then, for gods to want to alter
themselves? Since they are the most beautiful and
best possible, it seems that each always and unconditionally retains his own shape.

That seems entirely necessary to me.

Then let no poet tell us about Proteus or Thetis,
d or say that

> The gods, in the likeness of strangers from
>   foreign lands,
> Adopt every sort of shape and visit our cities.

Nor must they present Hera, in their tragedies or
other poems, as a priestess collecting alms for

> the life-giving sons of the Argive river Inachus,

or tell us other stories of that sort. Nor must mothers,
e believing bad stories about the gods wandering at
night in the shapes of strangers from foreign lands,
terrify their children with them. Such stories blaspheme the gods and, at the same time, make children
more cowardly.

They mustn't be told.

But though the gods are unable to change, do they
nonetheless make us believe that they appear in all
sorts of ways, deceiving us through sorcery?

Perhaps.

What? Would a god be willing to be false, either
382 in word or deed, by presenting an illusion?

I don't know.

Don't you know that a *true* falsehood, if one may
call it that, is hated by all gods and humans?

What do you mean?

I mean that no one is willing to tell falsehoods to
the most important part of himself about the most
important things, but of all places he is most afraid
to have falsehood there.

I still don't understand.

That's because you think I'm saying something
deep. I simply mean that to be false to one's soul b
about the things that are, to be ignorant and to have
and hold falsehood there, is what everyone would
least of all accept, for everyone hates a falsehood in
that place most of all.

That's right.

Surely, as I said just now, this would be most correctly called true falsehood—ignorance in the soul
of someone who has been told a falsehood. Falsehood
in words is a kind of imitation of this affection in the
soul, an image of it that comes into being after it and
is not a pure falsehood. Isn't that so?   c

Certainly.

And the thing that is really a falsehood is hated
not only by the gods but by human beings as well.

It seems so to me.

What about falsehood in words? When and to
whom is it useful and so not deserving of hatred?
Isn't it useful against one's enemies? And when any
of our so-called friends are attempting, through madness or ignorance, to do something bad, isn't it a
useful drug for preventing them? It is also useful in
the case of those stories we were just talking about,
the ones we tell because we don't know the truth
about those ancient events involving the gods. By d
making a falsehood as much like the truth as we can,
don't we also make it useful?

We certainly do.

Then in which of these ways could a falsehood be
useful to a god? Would he make false likenesses of
ancient events because of his ignorance of them?

It would be ridiculous to think that.

Then there is nothing of the false poet in a god?

Not in my view.

Would he be false, then, through fear of his enemies?

Far from it.   e

Because of the ignorance or madness of his family
or friends, then?

No one who is ignorant or mad is a friend of
the gods.

Then there's no reason for a god to speak falsely?

None.

Therefore the daemonic and the divine are in every
way free from falsehood.

Completely.

A god, then, is simple and true in word and deed. He doesn't change himself or deceive others by images, words, or signs, whether in visions or in dreams.

383   That's what I thought as soon as I heard you say it.

You agree, then, that this is our second pattern for speaking or composing poems about the gods: They are not sorcerers who change themselves, nor do they mislead us by falsehoods in words or deeds.

I agree.

So, even though we praise many things in Homer, we won't approve of the dream Zeus sent to Agamemnon, nor of Aeschylus when he makes Thetis say that

b Apollo sang in prophecy at her wedding:

> About the good fortune my children would
>   have,
> Free of disease throughout their long lives,
> And of all the blessings that the friendship of
>   the gods would bring me,
> I hoped that Phoebus' divine mouth would be
>   free of falsehood,
> Endowed as it is with the craft of prophecy.
> But the very god who sang, the one at the feast,
> The one who said all this, he himself it is
> Who killed my son.

Whenever anyone says such things about a god, we'll
c be angry with him, refuse him a chorus, and not allow his poetry to be used in the education of the young, so that our guardians will be as god-fearing and godlike as human beings can be.

I completely endorse these patterns, he said, and I would enact them as laws.

Book III

386   Such, then, I said, are the kinds of stories that I think future guardians should and should not hear about the gods from childhood on, if they are to honor the gods and their parents and not take their friendship with one another lightly.

I'm sure we're right about that, at any rate.

What if they are to be courageous as well? Shouldn't they be told stories that will make them least afraid of death? Or do you think that anyone
b ever becomes courageous if he's possessed by this fear?

No, I certainly don't.

And can someone be unafraid of death, preferring it to defeat in battle or slavery, if he believes in a Hades full of terrors?

Not at all.

Then we must supervise such stories and those who tell them, and ask them not to disparage the life in Hades in this unconditional way, but rather to praise it, since what they now say is neither true nor beneficial to future warriors.   c

We must.

Then we'll expunge all that sort of disparagement, beginning with the following lines:

> I would rather labor on earth in service to another,
> To a man who is landless, with little to live on,
> Than be king over all the dead.

and also these:

> He feared that his home should appear to
>   gods and men   d
> Dreadful, dank, and hated even by the gods.

and

> Alas, there survives in the Halls of Hades
> A soul, a mere phantasm, with its wits
>   completely gone.

and this:

> And he alone could think; the
>   others are flitting shadows.

and

> The soul, leaving his limbs, made its way to Hades,
> Lamenting its fate, leaving manhood and youth
>   behind.

and these: 387

> His soul went below the earth like smoke,
> Screeching as it went . . .

and

> As when bats in an awful cave
> Fly around screeching if one of them falls

From the cluster on the ceiling, all
clinging to one another,
So their souls went screeching . . .

We'll ask Homer and the other poets not to be angry
b if we delete these passages and all similar ones. It isn't
that they aren't poetic and pleasing to the majority of
hearers but that, the more poetic they are, the less
they should be heard by children or by men who are
supposed to be free and to fear slavery more than
death.

Most certainly.

And the frightening and dreadful names for the
underworld must be struck out, for example, "Cocy-
tus" and "Styx," and also the names for the dead, for
c example, "those below" and "the sapless ones," and
all those names of things in the underworld that make
everyone who hears them shudder. They may be all
well and good for other purposes, but we are afraid
that our guardians will be made softer and more
malleable by such shudders.

And our fear is justified.

Then such passages are to be struck out?

Yes.

And poets must follow the opposite pattern in
speaking and writing?

Clearly.

Must we also delete the lamentations and pitiful
d speeches of famous men?

We must, if indeed what we said before is compelling.

Consider though whether we are right to delete
them or not. We surely say that a decent man doesn't
think that death is a terrible thing for someone decent
to suffer—even for someone who happens to be his
friend.

We do say that.

Then he won't mourn for him as for someone who
has suffered a terrible fate.

Certainly not.

We also say that a decent person is most self-sufficient in living well and, above all others, has the least
e need of anyone else.

That's true.

Then it's less dreadful for him than for anyone else
to be deprived of his son, brother, possessions, or any
other such things.

Much less.

Then he'll least give way to lamentations and bear
misfortune most quietly when it strikes.

Certainly.

We'd be right, then, to delete the lamentations of
famous men, leaving them to women (and not even
to good women, either) and to cowardly men, so that
those we say we are training to guard our city will 388
disdain to act like that.

That's right.

Again, then, we'll ask Homer and the other poets
not to represent Achilles, the son of a goddess, as

Lying now on his side, now on his back, now again
On his belly; then standing up to wander distracted
This way and that on the shore of the unharvested sea.

Nor to make him pick up ashes in both hands and
pour them over his head, weeping and lamenting in b
the ways he does in Homer. Nor to represent Priam,
a close descendant of the gods, as entreating his
men and

Rolling around in dung,
Calling upon each man by name.

And we'll ask them even more earnestly not to make
the gods lament and say:

Alas, unfortunate that I am,
wretched mother of a great son. c

But, if they do make the gods do such things, at least
they mustn't dare to represent the greatest of the gods
as behaving in so unlikely a fashion as to say:

Alas, with my own eyes I see a man who is
most dear to me
Chased around the city, and my heart laments

or

Woe is me, that Sarpedon, who is most dear
to me, should be
Fated to be killed by Patroclus, the son of
Menoetius . . . d

If our young people, Adeimantus, listen to these stories without ridiculing them as not worth hearing, it's
hardly likely that they'll consider the things described

in them to be unworthy of mere human beings like themselves or that they'll rebuke themselves for doing or saying similar things when misfortune strikes. Instead, they'll feel neither shame nor restraint but groan and lament at even insignificant misfortunes.

e   What you say is completely true.

Then, as the argument has demonstrated—and we must remain persuaded by it until someone shows us a better one—they mustn't behave like that.

No, they mustn't.

Moreover, they mustn't be lovers of laughter either, for whenever anyone indulges in violent laughter, a violent change of mood is likely to follow.

So I believe.

Then, if someone represents worthwhile people as overcome by laughter, we won't approve, and we'll

389   approve even less if they represent gods that way.

Much less.

Then we won't approve of Homer saying things like this about the gods:

> And unquenchable laughter arose among the
>   blessed gods
> As they saw Hephaestus limping through the hall.

According to your argument, such things must be rejected.

If you want to call it mine, but they must be rejected

b   in any case.

Moreover, we have to be concerned about truth as well, for if what we said just now is correct, and falsehood, though of no use to the gods, is useful to people as a form of drug, clearly we must allow only doctors to use it, not private citizens.

Clearly.

Then if it is appropriate for anyone to use falsehoods for the good of the city, because of the actions of either enemies or citizens, it is the rulers. But everyone else must keep away from them, because for a private citizen to lie to a ruler is just as bad a

c   mistake as for a sick person or athlete not to tell the truth to his doctor or trainer about his physical condition or for a sailor not to tell the captain the facts about his own condition or that of the ship and the rest of its crew—indeed it is a worse mistake than either of these.

That's completely true.

And if the ruler catches someone else telling falsehoods in the city—   *d*

> Any one of the craftsmen,
> Whether a prophet, a doctor who heals the sick,
>   or a maker of spears

—he'll punish him for introducing something as subversive and destructive to a city as it would be to a ship.

He will, if practice is to follow theory.

What about moderation? Won't our young people also need that?

Of course.

And aren't these the most important aspects of moderation for the majority of people, namely, to obey the rulers and to rule the pleasures of drink, sex, and food for themselves?   *e*

That's my opinion at any rate.

Then we'll say that the words of Homer's Diomedes are well put:

> Sit down in silence, my friend, and be
>   persuaded by me.

and so is what follows:

> The Achaeans, breathing eagerness for battle,
> Marched in silence, fearing their commanders.

and all other such things.

Those *are* well put.

But what about this?

> Wine-bibber, with the eyes of a dog and
>   the heart of a deer

and the rest, is it—or any other headstrong words spoken in prose or poetry by private citizens against   390 their rulers—well put?

No, they aren't.

I don't think they are suitable for young people to hear—not, in any case, with a view to making them moderate. Though it isn't surprising that they are pleasing enough in other ways. What do you think?

The same as you.

What about making the cleverest man say that the finest thing of all is when

b
> The tables are well laden
> With bread and meat, and the winebearer
> Draws wine from the mixing bowl and
>   pours it in the cups.

or

> Death by starvation is the most pitiful fate.

Do you think that such things make for self-control in young people? Or what about having Zeus, when all the other gods are asleep and he alone is awake, c easily forget all his plans because of sexual desire and be so overcome by the sight of Hera that he doesn't even want to go inside but wants to possess her there on the ground, saying that his desire for her is even greater than it was when—without their parents' knowledge—they were first lovers? Or what about the chaining together of Ares and Aphrodite by Hephaestus—also the result of sexual passion?

No, by god, none of that seems suitable to me.

But if, on the other hand, there are words or deeds of famous men, who are exhibiting endurance in the d face of everything, surely they must be seen or heard. For example,

> He struck his chest and spoke to his heart:
> "Endure, my heart, you've suffered more
>   shameful things than this."

They certainly must.

Now, we mustn't allow our men to be money-lovers or to be bribable with gifts.

e Certainly not.

Then the poets mustn't sing to them:

> Gifts persuade gods, and gifts persuade revered kings.

Nor must Phoenix, the tutor of Achilles, be praised as speaking with moderation when he advises him to take the gifts and defend the Achaeans, but not to give up his anger without gifts. Nor should we think such things to be worthy of Achilles himself. Nor should we agree that he was such a money-lover that he would accept the gifts of Agamemnon or release 391 the corpse of Hector for a ransom but not otherwise.

It certainly isn't right to praise such things.

It is only out of respect for Homer, indeed, that I hesitate to say that it is positively impious to accuse Achilles of such things or to believe others who say them. Or to make him address Apollo in these words:

> You've injured me, Farshooter, most deadly of the gods;
> And I'd punish you, if I had the power.

Or to say that he disobeyed the river—a god—and was ready to fight it, or that he consecrated hair to b the dead Patroclus, which was already consecrated to a different river, Spercheius. It isn't to be believed that he did any of these. Nor is it true that he dragged the dead Hector around the tomb of Patroclus or massacred the captives on his pyre. So we'll deny that. Nor will we allow our people to believe that Achilles, who was the son of a goddess and of Peleus c (the most moderate of men and the grandson of Zeus) and who was brought up by the most wise Chiron, was so full of inner turmoil as to have two diseases in his soul—slavishness accompanied by the love of money, on the one hand, and arrogance towards gods and humans, on the other.

That's right.

We certainly won't believe such things, nor will we allow it to be said that Theseus, the son of Posidon, and Pirithous, the son of Zeus, engaged in terrible d kidnappings, or that any other hero and son of a god dared to do any of the terrible and impious deeds that they are now falsely said to have done. We'll compel the poets either to deny that the heroes did such things or else to deny that they were children of the gods. They mustn't say both or attempt to persuade our young people that the gods bring about evil or that heroes are no better than humans. As we said earlier, these things are both impious and untrue, e for we demonstrated that it is impossible for the gods to produce bad things.

Of course.

Moreover, these stories are harmful to people who hear them, for everyone will be ready to excuse himself when he's bad, if he is persuaded that similar things both are being done now and have been done in the past by

> Close descendants of the gods,
> Those near to Zeus, to whom belongs

The ancestral altar high up on Mount Ida,
In whom the blood of daemons has not weakened.

For that reason, we must put a stop to such stories,
lest they produce in the youth a strong inclination to
392 do bad things.

Absolutely.

Now, isn't there a kind of story whose content we
haven't yet discussed? So far we've said how one
should speak about gods, heroes, daemons, and things
in Hades.

We have.

Then what's left is how to deal with stories about
human beings, isn't it?

Obviously.

But we can't settle that matter at present.

Why not?

Because I think we'll say that what poets and prose-
writers tell us about the most important matters con-
b cerning human beings is bad. They say that many
unjust people are happy and many just ones wretched,
that injustice is profitable if it escapes detection, and
that justice is another's good but one's own loss. I
think we'll prohibit these stories and order the poets
to compose the opposite kind of poetry and tell the
opposite kind of tales. Don't you think so?

I know so.

But if you agree that what I said is correct, couldn't
I reply that you've agreed to the very point that is in
question in our whole discussion?

And you'd be right to make that reply.

Then we'll agree about what stories should be
c told about human beings only when we've discovered what sort of thing justice is and how by nature
it profits the one who has it, whether he is believed
to be just or not.

That's very true.

This concludes our discussion of the content of
stories. We should now, I think, investigate their style,
for we'll then have fully investigated both what should
be said and how it should be said.

I don't understand what you mean, Adeimantus responded.

But you must, I said. Maybe you'll understand it
d better if I put it this way. Isn't everything said by poets
and storytellers a narrative about past, present, or
future events?

What else could it be?

And aren't these narratives either narrative alone,
or narrative through imitation, or both?

I need a clearer understanding of that as well.

I seem to be a ridiculously unclear teacher. So,
like those who are incompetent at speaking, I won't
try to deal with the matter as a whole, but I'll take
up a part and use it as an example to make plain what
I want to say. Tell me, do you know the beginning of e
the *Iliad*, where the poet tells us that Chryses begs
Agamemnon to release his daughter, that Agamemnon harshly rejects him, and that, having failed,
Chryses prays to the god against the Achaeans?   393

I do.

You know, then, that up to the lines:

And he begged all the Achaeans
But especially the two sons of Atreus,
*   the commanders of the army,*

the poet himself is speaking and doesn't attempt to
get us to think that the speaker is someone other than
himself. After this, however, he speaks as if he were
Chryses and tries as far as possible to make us think
that the speaker isn't Homer but the priest himself—
an old man. And he composes pretty well all the rest b
of his narrative about events in Troy, Ithaca, and the
whole *Odyssey* in this way.

That's right.

Now, the speeches he makes and the parts between
them are both narrative?

Of course.

But when he makes a speech as if he were someone
else, won't we say that he makes his own style as c
much like that of the indicated speaker as possible?

We certainly will.

Now, to make oneself like someone else in voice
or appearance is to imitate the person one makes
oneself like.

Certainly.

In these passages, then, it seems that he and the
other poets effect their narrative through imitation.

That's right.

If the poet never hid himself, the whole of his
poem would be narrative without imitation. In order d
to prevent you from saying again that you don't understand, I'll show you what this would be like. If Homer

said that Chryses came with a ransom for his daughter to supplicate the Achaeans, especially the kings, and after that didn't speak as if he had become Chryses, but still as Homer, there would be no imitation but rather simple narrative. It would have gone something like this—I'll speak without meter since I'm no poet: "And the priest came and prayed that the gods would

e allow them to capture Troy and be safe afterwards, that they'd accept the ransom and free his daughter, and thus show reverence for the god. When he'd said this, the others showed their respect for the priest and consented. But Agamemnon was angry and ordered him to leave and never to return, lest his priestly wand and the wreaths of the god should fail to protect him. He said that, before freeing the daughter, he'd grow old in Argos by her side. He told Chryses to go away and not to make him angry, if he wanted to get

394 home safely. When the old man heard this, he was frightened and went off in silence. But when he'd left the camp he prayed at length to Apollo, calling him by his various titles and reminding him of his own services to him. If any of those services had been found pleasing, whether it was the building of temples or the sacrifice of victims, he asked in return that the arrows of the god should make the Achaeans pay for his tears." That is the way we get simple narrative

b without imitation.

I understand.

Then also understand that the opposite occurs when one omits the words between the speeches and leaves the speeches by themselves.

I understand that too. Tragedies are like that.

That's absolutely right. And now I think that I can

c make clear to you what I couldn't before. One kind of poetry and story-telling employs only imitation— tragedy and comedy, as you say. Another kind employs only narration by the poet himself—you find this most of all in dithyrambs. A third kind uses both— as in epic poetry and many other places, if you follow me.

Now I understand what you were trying to say.

Remember, too, that before all that we said that we had dealt with *what* must be said in stories, but that we had yet to investigate *how* it must be said.

Yes, I remember.

Well, this, more precisely, is what I meant: We

d need to come to an agreement about whether we'll allow poets to narrate through imitation, and, if so, whether they are to imitate some things but not others—and what things these are, or whether they are not to imitate at all.

I divine that you're looking into the question of whether or not we'll allow tragedy and comedy into our city.

Perhaps, and perhaps even more than that, for I myself really don't know yet, but whatever direction the argument blows us, that's where we must go.

Fine.

Then, consider, Adeimantus, whether our guardians should be imitators or not. Or does this also e follow from our earlier statement that each individual would do a fine job of one occupation, not of many, and that if he tried the latter and dabbled in many things, he'd surely fail to achieve distinction in any of them?

He would indeed.

Then, doesn't the same argument also hold for imitation—a single individual can't imitate many things as well as he can imitate one?

No, he can't.

Then, he'll hardly be able to pursue any worthwhile way of life while at the same time imitating many 395 things and being an imitator. Even in the case of two kinds of imitation that are thought to be closely akin, such as tragedy and comedy, the same people aren't able to do both of them well. Did you not just say that these were both imitations?

I did, and you're quite right that the same people can't do both.

Nor can they be both rhapsodes and actors.

True.

Indeed, not even the same actors are used for tragedy and comedy. Yet all these are imitations, aren't they? b

They are.

And human nature, Adeimantus, seems to me to be minted in even smaller coins than these, so that it can neither imitate many things well nor do the actions themselves, of which those imitations are likenesses.

That's absolutely true.

Then, if we're to preserve our first argument, that our guardians must be kept away from all other crafts so as to be the craftsmen of the city's freedom, and c be exclusively that, and do nothing at all except what contributes to it, they must neither do nor imitate anything else. If they do imitate, they must imitate from childhood what is appropriate for them, namely, people who are courageous, self-controlled, pious, and free, and their actions. They mustn't be clever at doing or imitating slavish or shameful actions, lest from enjoying the imitation, they come to enjoy the reality. Or haven't you noticed that imitations prac-

d ticed from youth become part of nature and settle into habits of gesture, voice, and thought?

I have indeed.

Then we won't allow those for whom we profess to care, and who must grow into good men, to imitate either a young woman or an older one, or one abusing her husband, quarreling with the gods, or bragging because she thinks herself happy, or one suffering misfortune and possessed by sorrows and lamenta-

e tions, and even less one who is ill, in love, or in labor.

That's absolutely right.

Nor must they imitate either male or female slaves doing slavish things.

No, they mustn't.

Nor bad men, it seems, who are cowards and are doing the opposite of what we described earlier, namely, libelling and ridiculing each other, using shameful language while drunk or sober, or wronging themselves and others, whether in word or deed, in the various other ways that are typical of such people.

396 They mustn't become accustomed to making themselves like madmen in either word or deed, for, though they must know about mad and vicious men and women, they must neither do nor imitate anything they do.

That's absolutely true.

Should they imitate metal workers or other craftsmen, or those who row in triremes, or their time-

b keepers, or anything else connected with ships?

How could they, since they aren't to concern themselves with any of those occupations?

And what about this? Will they imitate neighing horses, bellowing bulls, roaring rivers, the crashing sea, thunder, or anything of that sort?

They are forbidden to be mad or to imitate mad people.

If I understand what you mean, there is one kind of style and narrative that someone who is really a gentleman would use whenever he wanted to narrate something, and another kind, unlike this one, which his opposite by nature and education would favor, c and in which he would narrate.

Which styles are those?

Well, I think that when a moderate man comes upon the words or actions of a good man in his narrative, he'll be willing to report them as if he were that man himself, and he won't be ashamed of that kind of imitation. He'll imitate this good man most when he's acting in a faultless and intelligent manner, but he'll do so less, and with more reluctance, when d the good man is upset by disease, sexual passion, drunkenness, or some other misfortune. When he comes upon a character unworthy of himself, however, he'll be unwilling to make himself seriously resemble that inferior character—except perhaps for a brief period in which he's doing something good. Rather he'll be ashamed to do something like that, both because he's unpracticed in the imitation of such people and because he can't stand to shape and mold himself according to a worse pattern. He despises this in his mind, unless it's just done in play. e

That seems likely.

He'll therefore use the kind of narrative we described in dealing with the Homeric epics a moment ago. His style will participate both in imitation and in the other kind of narrative, but there'll be only a little bit of imitation in a long story? Or is there nothing in what I say?

That's precisely how the pattern for such a speaker must be.

As for someone who is not of this sort, the more inferior he is, the more willing he'll be to narrate 397 anything and to consider nothing unworthy of himself. As a result, he'll undertake to imitate seriously and before a large audience all the things we just mentioned—thunder, the sounds of wind, hail, axles, pulleys, trumpets, flutes, pipes, and all the other instruments, even the cries of dogs, sheep, and birds. And this man's style will consist entirely of imitation in voice and gesture, or else include only a small bit b of plain narrative.

That too is certain.

These, then, are the two kinds of style I was talking about.

There are these two.

The first of these styles involves little variation, so that if someone provides a musical mode and rhythm appropriate to it, won't the one who speaks correctly remain—with a few minor changes—pretty well *c* within that mode and rhythm throughout?

That's precisely what he'll do.

What about the other kind of style? Doesn't it require the opposite if it is to speak appropriately, namely, all kinds of musical modes and all kinds of rhythms, because it contains every type of variation?

That's exactly right.

Do all poets and speakers adopt one or other of these patterns of style or a mixture of both?

Necessarily.

What are we to do, then? Shall we admit all these *d* into our city, only one of the pure kinds, or the mixed one?

If my opinion is to prevail, we'll admit only the pure imitator of a decent person.

And yet, Adeimantus, the mixed style is pleasant. Indeed, it is by far the most pleasing to children, their tutors, and the vast majority of people.

Yes, it is the most pleasing.

But perhaps you don't think that it harmonizes with our constitution, because no one in our city is *e* two or more people simultaneously, since each does only one job.

Indeed, it doesn't harmonize.

And isn't it because of this that it's only in our city that we'll find a cobbler who is a cobbler and not also a captain along with his cobbling, and a farmer who is a farmer and not also a juror along with his farming, and a soldier who is a soldier and not a money-maker in addition to his soldiering, and so with them all?

That's true.

It seems, then, that if a man, who through clever 398 training can become anything and imitate anything, should arrive in our city, wanting to give a performance of his poems, we should bow down before him as someone holy, wonderful, and pleasing, but we should tell him that there is no one like him in our city and that it isn't lawful for there to be. We should pour myrrh on his head, crown him with wreaths, and send him away to another city. But, for our own good, we ourselves should employ a more austere and less pleasure-giving *b* poet and storyteller, one who would imitate the speech

of a decent person and who would tell his stories in accordance with the patterns we laid down when we first undertook the education of our soldiers.

That is certainly what we'd do if it were up to us.

It's likely, then, that we have now completed our discussion of the part of music and poetry that concerns speech and stories, for we've spoken both of what is to be said and of how it is to be said.

I agree.

Doesn't it remain, then, to discuss lyric odes and songs? *c*

Clearly.

And couldn't anyone discover what we would say about them, given that it has to be in tune with what we've already said?

Glaucon laughed and said: I'm afraid, Socrates, that I'm not to be included under "anyone," for I don't have a good enough idea at the moment of what we're to say. Of course, I have my suspicions.

Nonetheless, I said, you know that, in the first place, a song consists of three elements—words, harmonic mode, and rhythm. *d*

Yes, I do know that.

As far as words are concerned, they are no different in songs than they are when not set to music, so mustn't they conform in the same way to the patterns we established just now?

They must.

Further, the mode and rhythm must fit the words.

Of course.

And we said that we no longer needed dirges and lamentations among our words.

We did, indeed.

What are the lamenting modes, then? You tell me, since you're musical. *e*

The mixo-Lydian, the syntono-Lydian, and some others of that sort.

Aren't they to be excluded, then? They're useless even to decent women, let alone to men.

Certainly.

Drunkenness, softness, and idleness are also most inappropriate for our guardians.

How could they not be?

What, then, are the soft modes suitable for drinking-parties?

The Ionian and those Lydian modes that are said to be relaxed.

399   Could you ever use these to make people warriors?

Never. And now all you have left is the Dorian and Phrygian modes.

I don't know all the musical modes. Just leave me the mode that would suitably imitate the tone and rhythm of a courageous person who is active in battle or doing other violent deeds, or who is failing and
b facing wounds, death, or some other misfortune, and who, in all these circumstances, is fighting off his fate steadily and with self-control. Leave me also another mode, that of someone engaged in a peaceful, un-forced, voluntary action, persuading someone or ask-ing a favor of a god in prayer or of a human being through teaching and exhortation, or, on the other hand, of someone submitting to the supplications of another who is teaching him and trying to get him to change his mind, and who, in all these circum-stances, is acting with moderation and self-control, not with arrogance but with understanding, and is
c content with the outcome. Leave me, then, these two modes, which will best imitate the violent or voluntary tones of voice of those who are moderate and coura-geous, whether in good fortune or in bad.

The modes you're asking for are the very ones I mentioned.

Well, then, we'll have no need for polyharmonic or multistringed instruments to accompany our odes and songs.

It doesn't seem so to me at least.

Then we won't need the craftsmen who make trian-gular lutes, harps, and all other such multistringed
d and polyharmonic instruments.

Apparently not.

What about flute-makers and flute-players? Will you allow them into the city? Or isn't the flute the most "many-stringed" of all? And aren't the panhar-monic instruments all imitations of it?

Clearly.

The lyre and the cithara are left, then, as useful in the city, while in the country, there'd be some sort of pipe for the shepherds to play.

That is what our argument shows, at least.

Well, we certainly aren't doing anything new in
e preferring Apollo and his instruments to Marsyas and his.

By god, it doesn't seem as though we are.

And, by the dog, without being aware of it, we've been purifying the city we recently said was luxurious.

That's because we're being moderate.

Then let's purify the rest. The next topic after musi-cal modes is the regulation of meter. We shouldn't strive to have either subtlety or great variety in meter. Rather, we should try to discover what are the rhythms of someone who leads an ordered and courageous life and then adapt the meter and the tune to his words, not his words to them. What these rhythms 400 actually are is for you to say, just as in the case of the modes.

I really don't know what to say. I can tell you from observation that there are three basic kinds of metrical feet out of which the others are constructed, just as there are four in the case of modes. But I can't tell you which sort imitates which sort of life.

Then we'll consult with Damon as to which metri-cal feet are suited to slavishness, insolence, madness, b and the other vices and which are suited to their opposites. I think I've heard him talking about an enoplion, which is a composite metrical phrase (al-though I'm not clear on this), and also about dactylic or heroic meter, which he arranged, I don't know how, to be equal up and down in the interchange of long and short. I think he called one foot an iambus, another a trochee, assigning a long and a short to c both of them. In the case of some of these, I think he approved or disapproved of the tempo of the foot as much as of the rhythm itself, or of some combina-tion of the two—I can't tell you which. But, as I said, we'll leave these things to Damon, since to mark off the different kinds would require a long argument. Or do you think we should try it?

No, I certainly don't.

But you can discern, can't you, that grace and gracelessness follow good and bad rhythm respec-tively?

Of course.

Further, if, as we said just now, rhythm and mode must conform to the words and not vice versa, then d good rhythm follows fine words and is similar to them, while bad rhythm follows the opposite kind of words, and the same for harmony and disharmony.

To be sure, these things must conform to the words.

What about the style and content of the words themselves? Don't they conform to the character of the speaker's soul?

Of course.

And the rest conform to the words?

Yes.

Then fine words, harmony, grace, and rhythm follow simplicity of character—and I do not mean this
e in the sense in which we use "simplicity" as a euphemism for "simple-mindedness"—but I mean the sort of fine and good character that has developed in accordance with an intelligent plan.

That's absolutely certain.

And must not our young people everywhere aim at these, if they are to do their own work?

They must, indeed.

Now, surely painting is full of these qualities, as
401 are all the crafts similar to it; weaving is full of them, and so are embroidery, architecture, and the crafts that produce all the other furnishings. Our bodily nature is full of them, as are the natures of all growing things, for in all of these there is grace and gracelessness. And gracelessness, bad rhythm, and disharmony are akin to bad words and bad character, while their opposites are akin to and are imitations of the opposite, a moderate and good character.

Absolutely.

Is it, then, only poets we have to supervise, compel-
b ling them to make an image of a good character in their poems or else not to compose them among us? Or are we also to give orders to other craftsmen, forbidding them to represent—whether in pictures, buildings, or any other works—a character that is vicious, unrestrained, slavish, and graceless? Are we to allow someone who cannot follow these instructions to work among us, so that our guardians will
c be brought up on images of evil, as if in a meadow of bad grass, where they crop and graze in many different places every day until, little by little, they unwittingly accumulate a large evil in their souls? Or must we rather seek out craftsmen who are by nature able to pursue what is fine and graceful in their work, so that our young people will live in a healthy place and be benefited on all sides, and so that something of those fine works will strike their eyes and ears like a breeze that brings health from a good place, leading
d them unwittingly, from childhood on, to resemblance, friendship, and harmony with the beauty of reason?

The latter would be by far the best education for them.

Aren't these the reasons, Glaucon, that education in music and poetry is most important? First, because rhythm and harmony permeate the inner part of the soul more than anything else, affecting it most strongly and bringing it grace, so that if someone is properly educated in music and poetry, it makes him graceful, but if not, then the opposite. Second, because anyone who has been properly educated in *e* music and poetry will sense it acutely when something has been omitted from a thing and when it hasn't been finely crafted or finely made by nature. And since he has the right distastes, he'll praise fine things, be pleased by them, receive them into his soul, and, being nurtured by them, become fine and good. He'll rightly object to what is shameful, hating it while he's 402 still young and unable to grasp the reason, but, having been educated in this way, he will welcome the reason when it comes and recognize it easily because of its kinship with himself.

Yes, I agree that those are the reasons to provide education in music and poetry.

It's just the way it was with learning how to read. Our ability wasn't adequate until we realized that there are only a few letters that occur in all sorts of different combinations, and that—whether written *b* large or small—they were worthy of our attention, so that we picked them out eagerly wherever they occurred, knowing that we wouldn't be competent readers until we knew our letters.

True.

And isn't it also true that if there are images of letters reflected in mirrors or water, we won't know them until we know the letters themselves, for both abilities are parts of the same craft and discipline?

Absolutely.

Then, by the gods, am I not right in saying that neither we, nor the guardians we are raising, will be *c* educated in music and poetry until we know the different forms of moderation, courage, frankness, high-mindedness, and all their kindred, and their opposites too, which are moving around everywhere, and see them in the things in which they are, both themselves and their images, and do not disregard them, whether they are written on small things or large, but accept that the knowledge of both large and small letters is part of the same craft and discipline?

That's absolutely essential.

Therefore, if someone's soul has a fine and beautiful character and his body matches it in beauty and is thus in harmony with it, so that both share in the *d* same pattern, wouldn't that be the most beautiful sight for anyone who has eyes to see?

It certainly would.

And isn't what is most beautiful also most loveable?

Of course.

And a musical person would love such people most of all, but he wouldn't love anyone who lacked harmony?

No, he wouldn't, at least not if the defect was in the soul, but if it was only in the body, he'd put up *e* with it and be willing to embrace the boy who had it.

I gather that you love or have loved such a boy yourself, and I agree with you. Tell me this, however: Is excessive pleasure compatible with moderation?

How can it be, since it drives one mad just as much as pain does?

What about with the rest of virtue?

403   No.

Well, then, is it compatible with violence and licentiousness?

Very much so.

Can you think of a greater or keener pleasure than sexual pleasure?

I can't—or a madder one either.

But the right kind of love is by nature the love of order and beauty that has been moderated by education in music and poetry?

That's right.

Therefore, the right kind of love has nothing mad or licentious about it?

No, it hasn't.

Then sexual pleasure mustn't come into it, and *b* the lover and the boy he loves must have no share in it, if they are to love and be loved in the right way?

By god, no, Socrates, it mustn't come into it.

It seems, then, that you'll lay it down as a law in the city we're establishing that if a lover can persuade a boy to let him, then he may kiss him, be with him, and touch him, as a father would a son, for the sake of what is fine and beautiful, but—turning to the other things—his association with the one he cares *c* about must never seem to go any further than this, otherwise he will be reproached as untrained in music and poetry and lacking in appreciation for what is fine and beautiful.

That's right.

Does it seem to you that we've now completed our account of education in music and poetry? Anyway,

it has ended where it ought to end, for it ought to end in the love of the fine and beautiful.

I agree.

After music and poetry, our young people must be given physical training.

Of course.

In this, too, they must have careful education from childhood throughout life. The matter stands, I be- *d* lieve, something like this—but you, too, should look into it. It seems to me that a fit body doesn't by its own virtue make the soul good, but instead that the opposite is true—a good soul by its own virtue makes the body as good as possible. How does it seem to you?

The same.

Then, if we have devoted sufficient care to the mind, wouldn't we be right, in order to avoid having to do too much talking, to entrust it with the detailed supervision of the body, while we indicate only the general patterns to be followed?   *e*

Certainly.

We said that our prospective guardians must avoid drunkenness, for it is less appropriate for a guardian to be drunk and not to know where on earth he is than it is for anyone else.

It would be absurd for a guardian to need a guardian.

What about food? Aren't these men athletes in the greatest contest?

They are.

Then would the regimen currently prescribed for athletes in training be suitable for them?   *404*

Perhaps it would.

Yet it seems to result in sluggishness and to be of doubtful value for health. Or haven't you noticed that these athletes sleep their lives away and that, if they deviate even a little from their orderly regimen, they become seriously and violently ill?

I have noticed that.

Then our warrior athletes need a more sophisticated kind of training. They must be like sleepless hounds, able to see and hear as keenly as possible and to endure frequent changes of water and food, as well as summer and winter weather on their campaigns, without faltering in health.   *b*

That's how it seems to me, too.

Now, isn't the best physical training akin to the simple music and poetry we were describing a moment ago?

How do you mean?

I mean a simple and decent physical training, particularly the kind involved in training for war.

What would it be like?

You might learn about such things from Homer. You know that, when his heroes are campaigning, he doesn't give them fish to banquet on, even though they are by the sea in the Hellespont, nor boiled meat either. Instead, he gives them only roasted meat, which is the kind most easily available to soldiers, for it's easier nearly everywhere to use fire alone than to carry pots and pans.

That's right.

Nor, I believe, does Homer mention sweet desserts anywhere. Indeed, aren't even the other athletes aware that, if one's body is to be sound, one must keep away from all such things?

They're right to be aware of it, at any rate, and to avoid such things.

If you think that, then it seems that you don't approve of Syracusan cuisine or of Sicilian-style dishes.

I do not.

Then you also object to Corinthian girlfriends for men who are to be in good physical condition.

Absolutely.

What about the reputed delights of Attic pastries?

I certainly object to them, too.

I believe that we'd be right to compare this diet and this entire life-style to the kinds of lyric odes and songs that are composed in all sorts of modes and rhythms.

Certainly.

Just as embellishment in the one gives rise to licentiousness, doesn't it give rise to illness in the other? But simplicity in music and poetry makes for moderation in the soul, and in physical training it makes for bodily health?

That's absolutely true.

And as licentiousness and disease breed in the city, aren't many law courts and hospitals opened? And don't medicine and law give themselves solemn airs when even large numbers of free men take them very seriously?

How could it be otherwise?

Yet could you find a greater sign of bad and shameful education in a city than that the need for skilled doctors and lawyers is felt not only by inferior people and craftsmen but by those who claim to have been brought up in the manner of free men? Don't you think it's shameful and a great sign of vulgarity to be forced to make use of a justice imposed by others, as masters and judges, because you are unable to deal with the situation yourself?

I think that's the most shameful thing of all.

Yet isn't it even more shameful when someone not only spends a good part of his life in court defending himself or prosecuting someone else but, through inexperience of what is fine, is persuaded to take pride in being clever at doing injustice and then exploiting every loophole and trick to escape conviction—and all for the sake of little worthless things and because he's ignorant of how much better and finer it is to arrange one's own life so as to have no need of finding a sleepy or inattentive judge?

This case is even more shameful than the other.

And doesn't it seem shameful to you to need medical help, not for wounds or because of some seasonal illness, but because, through idleness and the life-style we've described, one is full of gas and phlegm like a stagnant swamp, so that sophisticated Asclepiad doctors are forced to come up with names like "flatulence" and "catarrh" to describe one's diseases?

It does. And those certainly are strange new names for diseases.

Indeed, I don't suppose that they even existed in the time of Asclepius himself. I take it as a proof of this that his sons at Troy didn't criticize either the woman who treated Eurypylus when he was wounded, or Patroclus who prescribed the treatment, which consisted of Pramnian wine with barley meal and grated cheese sprinkled on it, though such treatment is now thought to cause inflammation.

Yet it's a strange drink to give someone in that condition.

Not if you recall that they say that the kind of modern medicine that plays nursemaid to the disease wasn't used by the Asclepiads before Herodicus. He was a physical trainer who became ill, so he mixed physical training with medicine and wore out first himself and then many others as well.

How did he do that?

By making his dying a lengthy process. Always tending his mortal illness, he was nonetheless, it seems, unable to cure it, so he lived out his life under medical treatment, with no leisure for anything else whatever.

If he departed even a little from his accustomed regimen, he became completely worn out, but because his skill made dying difficult, he lived into old age.

That's a fine prize for his skill.

One that's appropriate for someone who didn't
c know that it wasn't because he was ignorant or inexperienced that Asclepius failed to teach this type of medicine to his sons, but because he knew that everyone in a well-regulated city has his own work to do and that no one has the leisure to be ill and under treatment all his life. It's absurd that we recognize this to be true of craftsmen while failing to recognize that it's equally true of those who are wealthy and supposedly happy.

How is that?

When a carpenter is ill, he expects to receive an
d emetic or a purge from his doctor or to get rid of his disease through surgery or cautery. If anyone prescribed a lengthy regimen to him, telling him that he should rest with his head bandaged and so on, he'd soon reply that he had no leisure to be ill and that life is no use to him if he has to neglect his work and always be concerned with his illness. After that
e he'd bid good-bye to his doctor, resume his usual way of life, and either recover his health or, if his body couldn't withstand the illness, he'd die and escape his troubles.

It is believed to be appropriate for someone like that to use medicine in this way.

Is that because his life is of no profit to him if he
407 doesn't do his work?

Obviously.

But the rich person, we say, has no work that would make his life unlivable if he couldn't do it.

That's what people say, at least.

That's because you haven't heard the saying of Phocylides that, once you have the means of life, you must practice virtue.

I think he must also practice virtue before that.

We won't quarrel with Phocylides about this. But let's try to find out whether the rich person must indeed practice virtue and whether his life is not worth living if he doesn't or whether tending an illness, while it is an obstacle to applying oneself to
b carpentry and the other crafts, is no obstacle whatever to taking Phocylides' advice.

But excessive care of the body, over and above physical training, is pretty well the biggest obstacle of all. It's troublesome in managing a household, in military service, and even in a sedentary public office.

Yet the most important of all, surely, is that it makes any kind of learning, thought, or private meditation c difficult, for it's always imagining some headaches or dizziness and accusing philosophy of causing them. Hence, wherever this kind of virtue is practiced and examined, excessive care of the body hinders it, for it makes a person think he's ill and be all the time concerned about his body.

It probably does.

Therefore, won't we say that Asclepius knew this, and that he taught medicine for those whose bodies are healthy in their natures and habits but have some specific disease? His medicine is for these people with d these habits. He cured them of their disease with drugs or surgery and then ordered them to live their usual life so as not to harm their city's affairs. But for those whose bodies were riddled with disease, he didn't attempt to prescribe a regimen, drawing off a little here and pouring in a little there, in order to make their life a prolonged misery and enable them to produce offspring in all probability like themselves. He didn't think that he should treat someone who couldn't live a normal life, since such a person would e be of no profit either to himself or to the city.

The Asclepius you're talking about was quite a statesman.

Clearly. And don't you see that because he was a statesman his sons turned out to be good men at Troy, practicing medicine as I say they did? Don't you 408 remember that they "sucked out the blood and applied gentle potions" to the wound Pandarus inflicted on Menelaus, but without prescribing what he should eat or drink after that, any more than they did for Eurypylus? They considered their drugs to be sufficient to cure men who were healthy and living an orderly life before being wounded, even if they happened to drink wine mixed with barley and cheese right after receiving their wounds. But they didn't b consider the lives of those who were by nature sick and licentious to be profitable either to themselves or to anyone else. Medicine isn't intended for such people and they shouldn't be treated, not even if they're richer than Midas.

The sons of Asclepius you're talking about were indeed very sophisticated.

Appropriately so. But Pindar and the tragedians don't agree with us. They say that Asclepius was the son of Apollo, that he was bribed with gold to heal a rich man, who was already dying, and that he was killed by lightning for doing so. But, in view of what we said before, we won't believe this. We'll say that c if Asclepius was the son of a god, he was not a money-grubber, and that if he was a money-grubber, he was not the son of a god.

That's right. But what do you say about the following, Socrates? Don't we need to have good doctors in our city? And the best will surely be those who have handled the greatest number of sick and of d healthy people. In the same way, the best judges will be those who have associated with people whose natures are of every kind.

I agree that the doctors and judges must be good. But do you know the kind I consider to be so?

If you'll tell me.

I'll try. But you ask about things that aren't alike in the same question.

In what way?

The cleverest doctors are those who, in addition to learning their craft, have had contact with the greatest number of very sick bodies from childhood on, have themselves experienced every illness, and e aren't very healthy by nature, for they don't treat bodies with their bodies, I suppose—if they did, we wouldn't allow their bodies to be or become bad. Rather they treat the body with their souls, and it isn't possible for the soul to treat anything well, if it is or has been bad itself.

That's right.

As for the judge, he *does* rule other souls with his 409 own soul. And it isn't possible for a soul to be nurtured among vicious souls from childhood, to associate with them, to indulge in every kind of injustice, and come through it able to judge other people's injustices from its own case, as it can diseases of the body. Rather, if it's to be fine and good, and a sound judge of just things, it must itself remain pure and have no experience of bad character while it's young. That's the reason, indeed, that decent people appear simple and easily deceived by unjust ones when they are b young. It's because they have no models in themselves

of the evil experiences of the vicious to guide their judgments.

That's certainly so.

Therefore, a good judge must not be a young person but an old one, who has learned late in life what injustice is like and who has become aware of it not as something at home in his own soul, but as something alien and present in others, someone who, after a long time, has recognized that injustice is bad by nature, not from his own experience of it, but through knowledge. c

Such a judge would be the most noble one of all.

And he'd be good, too, which was what you asked, for someone who has a good soul is good. The clever and suspicious person, on the other hand, who has committed many injustices himself and thinks himself a wise villain, appears clever in the company of those like himself, because he's on his guard and is guided by the models within himself. But when he meets with good older people, he's seen to be stupid, distrustful at the wrong time, and ignorant of what a sound character is, since he has no model of this d within himself. But since he meets vicious people more often than good ones, he seems to be clever rather than unlearned, both to himself and to others.

That's completely true.

Then we mustn't look for the good judge among people like that but among the sort we described earlier. A vicious person would never know either himself or a virtuous one, whereas a naturally virtuous person, when educated, will in time acquire knowledge of both virtue and vice. And it is someone like that who becomes wise, in my view, and not the bad person. e

I agree with you.

Then won't you legislate in our city for the kind of medicine we mentioned and for this kind of judging, so that together they'll look after those who are naturally well endowed in body and soul? But as for 410 the ones whose bodies are naturally unhealthy or whose souls are incurably evil, won't they let the former die of their own accord and put the latter to death?

That seems to be best both for the ones who suffer such treatment and for the city.

However, *our* young people, since they practice that simple sort of music and poetry that we said produces moderation, will plainly be wary of coming to need a judge.

That's right.

And won't a person who's educated in music and
b poetry pursue physical training in the same way, and choose to make no use of medicine except when unavoidable?

I believe so.

He'll work at physical exercises in order to arouse the spirited part of his nature, rather than to acquire the physical strength for which other athletes diet and labor.

That's absolutely right.

Then, Glaucon, did those who established education in music and poetry and in physical training do
c so with the aim that people attribute to them, which is to take care of the body with the latter and the soul with the former, or with some other aim?

What other aim do you mean?

It looks as though they established both chiefly for the sake of the soul.

How so?

Haven't you noticed the effect that lifelong physical training, unaccompanied by any training in music and poetry, has on the mind, or the effect of the opposite, music and poetry without physical training?

What effects are you talking about?

Savagery and toughness in the one case and softness
d and overcultivation in the other.

I get the point. You mean that those who devote themselves exclusively to physical training turn out to be more savage than they should, while those who devote themselves to music and poetry turn out to be softer than is good for them?

Moreover, the source of the savageness is the spirited part of one's nature. Rightly nurtured, it becomes courageous, but if it's overstrained, it's likely to become hard and harsh.

So it seems.

And isn't it the philosophic part of one's nature
e that provides the cultivation? If it is relaxed too far, it becomes softer than it should, but if properly nurtured, it is cultivated and orderly.

So it is.

Now, we say that our guardians must have both these natures.

They must indeed.

And mustn't the two be harmonized with each other?

Of course.

And if this harmony is achieved, the soul is both moderate and courageous?   411

Certainly.

But if it is inharmonious, it is cowardly and savage?

Yes, indeed.

Therefore, when someone gives music an opportunity to charm his soul with the flute and to pour those sweet, soft, and plaintive tunes we mentioned through his ear, as through a funnel, when he spends his whole life humming them and delighting in them, then, at first, whatever spirit he has is softened, just as iron is tempered, and from being hard and useless, it is made useful. But if he keeps at it unrelentingly and is beguiled by the music, after a time his spirit b
is melted and dissolved until it vanishes, and the very sinews of his soul are cut out and he becomes "a feeble warrior."

That's right.

And if he had a spiritless nature from the first, this process is soon completed. But if he had a spirited nature, his spirit becomes weak and unstable, flaring up at trifles and extinguished as easily. The result is that such people become quick-tempered, prone to anger, and filled with discontent, rather than spirited. c

That's certainly true.

What about someone who works hard at physical training and eats well but never touches music or philosophy? Isn't he in good physical condition at first, full of resolution and spirit? And doesn't he become more courageous than he was before?

Certainly.

But what happens if he does nothing else and never associates with the Muse? Doesn't whatever love of d
learning he might have had in his soul soon become enfeebled, deaf, and blind, because he never tastes any learning or investigation or partakes of any discussion or any of the rest of music and poetry, to nurture or arouse it?

It does seem to be that way.

I believe that someone like that becomes a hater of reason and of music. He no longer makes any use of persuasion but bulls his way through every situation by force and savagery like a wild animal, living in ignorance and stupidity without either rhythm or grace. e

That's most certainly how he'll live.

It seems, then, that a god has given music and physical training to human beings not, except incidentally, for the body and the soul but for the spirited and wisdom-loving parts of the soul itself, in order that these might be in harmony with one another, each being stretched and relaxed to the appropriate
412   degree.

It seems so.

Then the person who achieves the finest blend of music and physical training and impresses it on his soul in the most measured way is the one we'd most correctly call completely harmonious and trained in music, much more so than the one who merely harmonizes the strings of his instrument.

That's certainly so, Socrates.

Then, won't we always need this sort of person as an overseer in our city, Glaucon, if indeed its constitution is to be preserved?

It seems that we'll need someone like that most
b   of all.

These, then, are the patterns for education and upbringing. Should we enumerate the dances of these people, or their hunts, chases with hounds, athletic contests, and horse races? Surely, they're no longer hard to discover, since it's pretty clear that they must follow the patterns we've already established.

Perhaps so.

All right, then what's the next thing we have to determine? Isn't it which of these same people will rule and which be ruled?

c   Of course.

Now, isn't it obvious that the rulers must be older and the ruled younger?

Yes, it is.

And mustn't the rulers also be the best of them?

That, too.

And aren't the best farmers the ones who are best at farming?

Yes.

Then, as the rulers must be the best of the guardians, mustn't they be the ones who are best at guarding the city?

Yes.

Then, in the first place, mustn't they be knowledgeable and capable, and mustn't they care for the city?
d   That's right.

Now, one cares most for what one loves.

Necessarily.

And someone loves something most of all when he believes that the same things are advantageous to it as to himself and supposes that if it does well, he'll do well, and that if it does badly, then he'll do badly too.

That's right.

Then we must choose from among our guardians those men who, upon examination, seem most of all to believe throughout their lives that they must eagerly   e
pursue what is advantageous to the city and be wholly unwilling to do the opposite.

Such people would be suitable for the job at any rate.

I think we must observe them at all ages to see whether they are guardians of this conviction and make sure that neither compulsion nor magic spells will get them to discard or forget their belief that they must do what is best for the city.

What do you mean by discarding?

I'll tell you. I think the discarding of a belief is either voluntary or involuntary—voluntary when one learns that the belief is false, involuntary in the case of all true beliefs.   413

I understand voluntary discarding but not involuntary.

What's that? Don't you know that people are voluntarily deprived of bad things, but involuntarily deprived of good ones? And isn't being deceived about the truth a bad thing, while possessing the truth is good? Or don't you think that to believe the things that are is to possess the truth?

That's right, and I do think that people are involuntarily deprived of true opinions.

But can't they also be so deprived by theft, magic spells, and compulsion?   b

Now, I don't understand again.

I'm afraid I must be talking like a tragic poet! By "the victims of theft" I mean those who are persuaded to change their minds or those who forget, because time, in the latter case, and argument, in the former, takes away their opinions without their realizing it. Do you understand now?

Yes.

By "the compelled" I mean those whom pain or suffering causes to change their mind.

I understand that, and you're right.

The "victims of magic," I think you'd agree, are
c those who change their mind because they are under
the spell of pleasure or fear.

It seems to me that everything that deceives does
so by casting a spell.

Then, as I said just now, we must find out who
are the best guardians of their conviction that they
must always do what they believe to be best for the
city. We must keep them under observation from
childhood and set them tasks that are most likely to
make them forget such a conviction or be deceived
d out of it, and we must select whoever keeps on remembering it and isn't easily deceived, and reject the
others. Do you agree?

Yes.

And we must subject them to labors, pains, and
contests in which we can watch for these traits.

That's right.

Then we must also set up a competition for the
third way in which people are deprived of their convictions, namely, magic. Like those who lead colts
into noise and tumult to see if they're afraid, we must
expose our young people to fears and pleasures, testing
e them more thoroughly than gold is tested by fire. If
someone is hard to put under a spell, is apparently
gracious in everything, is a good guardian of himself
and the music and poetry he has learned, and if he
always shows himself to be rhythmical and harmonious, then he is the best person both for himself and
for the city. Anyone who is tested in this way as a
414 child, youth, and adult, and always comes out of it
untainted, is to be made a ruler as well as a guardian;
he is to be honored in life and to receive after his
death the most prized tombs and memorials. But
anyone who fails to prove himself in this way is to
be rejected. It seems to me, Glaucon, that rulers and
guardians must be selected and appointed in some
such way as this, though we've provided only a general
pattern and not the exact details.

It also seems to me that they must be selected in
this sort of way.

Then, isn't it truly most correct to call these people
b complete guardians, since they will guard against external enemies and internal friends, so that the one
will lack the power and the other the desire to harm
the city? The young people we've hitherto called

guardians we'll now call *auxiliaries* and supporters of
the guardians' convictions.

I agree.

How, then, could we devise one of those useful
falsehoods we were talking about a while ago, one
noble falsehood that would, in the best case, persuade c
even the rulers, but if that's not possible, then the
others in the city?

What sort of falsehood?

Nothing new, but a Phoenician story which describes something that has happened in many places.
At least, that's what the poets say, and they've persuaded many people to believe it too. It hasn't happened among us, and I don't even know if it could.
It would certainly take a lot of persuasion to get people
to believe it.

You seem hesitant to tell the story.

When you hear it, you'll realize that I have every
reason to hesitate.

Speak, and don't be afraid.

I'll tell it, then, though I don't know where I'll get
the audacity or even what words I'll use. I'll first try d
to persuade the rulers and the soldiers and then the
rest of the city that the upbringing and the education
we gave them, and the experiences that went with
them, were a sort of dream, that in fact they themselves, their weapons, and the other craftsmen's tools
were at that time really being fashioned and nurtured
inside the earth, and that when the work was com- e
pleted, the earth, who is their mother, delivered all
of them up into the world. Therefore, if anyone attacks
the land in which they live, they must plan on its
behalf and defend it as their mother and nurse and
think of the other citizens as their earthborn brothers.

It isn't for nothing that you were so shy about telling
your falsehood.

Appropriately so. Nevertheless, listen to the rest of
the story. "All of you in the city are brothers," we'll 415
say to them in telling our story, "but the god who made
you mixed some gold into those who are adequately
equipped to rule, because they are most valuable. He
put silver in those who are auxiliaries and iron and
bronze in the farmers and other craftsmen. For the
most part you will produce children like yourselves,
but, because you are all related, a silver child will
occasionally be born from a golden parent, and vice b
versa, and all the others from each other. So the first

and most important command from the god to the rulers is that there is nothing that they must guard better or watch more carefully than the mixture of metals in the souls of the next generation. If an offspring of theirs should be found to have a mixture of iron or bronze, they must not pity him in any way, but give him the rank appropriate to his nature and drive him out to join the craftsmen and farmers. But if an offspring of these people is found to have a mixture of gold or silver, they will honor him and take him up to join the guardians or the auxiliaries, for there is an oracle which says that the city will be ruined if it ever has an iron or a bronze guardian." So, do you have any device that will make our citizens believe this story?

I can't see any way to make them believe it themselves, but perhaps there is one in the case of their sons and later generations and all the other people who come after them.

I understand pretty much what you mean, but even that would help to make them care more for the city and each other. However, let's leave this matter wherever tradition takes it. And let's now arm our earthborn and lead them forth with their rulers in charge. And as they march, let them look for the best place in the city to have their camp, a site from which they can most easily control those within, if anyone is unwilling to obey the laws, or repel any outside enemy who comes like a wolf upon the flock. And when they have established their camp and made the requisite sacrifices, they must see to their sleeping quarters. What do you say?

I agree.

And won't these quarters protect them adequately both in winter and summer?

Of course, for it seems to me that you mean their housing.

Yes, but housing for soldiers, not for money-makers.

How do you mean to distinguish these from one another?

I'll try to tell you. The most terrible and most shameful thing of all is for a shepherd to rear dogs as auxiliaries to help him with his flocks in such a way that, through licentiousness, hunger, or some other bad trait of character, they do evil to the sheep and become like wolves instead of dogs.

That's certainly a terrible thing.

Isn't it necessary, therefore, to guard in every way against our auxiliaries doing anything like that to the citizens because they are stronger, thereby becoming savage masters instead of kindly allies?

It is necessary.

And wouldn't a really good education endow them with the greatest caution in this regard?

But surely they have had an education like that.

Perhaps we shouldn't assert this dogmatically, Glaucon. What we can assert is what we were saying just now, that they must have the right education, whatever it is, if they are to have what will most make them gentle to each other and to those they are guarding.

That's right.

Now, someone with some understanding might say that, besides this education, they must also have the kind of housing and other property that will neither prevent them from being the best guardians nor encourage them to do evil to the other citizens.

That's true.

Consider, then, whether or not they should live in some such way as this, if they're to be the kind of men we described. First, none of them should possess any private property beyond what is wholly necessary. Second, none of them should have a house or storeroom that isn't open for all to enter at will. Third, whatever sustenance moderate and courageous warrior-athletes require in order to have neither shortfall nor surplus in a given year they'll receive by taxation on the other citizens as a salary for their guardianship. Fourth, they'll have common messes and live together like soldiers in a camp. We'll tell them that they always have gold and silver of a divine sort in their souls as a gift from the gods and so have no further need of human gold. Indeed, we'll tell them that it's impious for them to defile this divine possession by any admixture of such gold, because many impious deeds have been done that involve the currency used by ordinary people, while their own is pure. Hence, for them alone among the city's population, it is unlawful to touch or handle gold or silver. They mustn't be under the same roof as it, wear it as jewelry, or drink from gold or silver goblets. In this way they'd save both themselves and the city. But if they acquire private land, houses, and currency themselves, they'll be household managers and farmers instead of guard-

b ians—hostile masters of the other citizens instead of their allies. They'll spend their whole lives hating and being hated, plotting and being plotted against, more afraid of internal than of external enemies, and they'll hasten both themselves and the whole city to almost immediate ruin. For all these reasons, let's say that the guardians must be provided with housing and the rest in this way, and establish this as a law. Or don't you agree?

I certainly do, Glaucon said.

Book IV

419 And Adeimantus interrupted: How would you defend yourself, Socrates, he said, if someone told you that you aren't making these men very happy and that it's their own fault? The city really belongs to them, yet they derive no good from it. Others own land, build fine big houses, acquire furnishings to go along with them, make their own private sacrifices to the gods, entertain guests, and also, of course, possess what you were talking about just now, gold and silver and all the things that are thought to belong to people who are blessedly happy. But one might well say that your guardians are simply settled in the city like mercenar-
420 ies and that all they do is watch over it.

Yes, I said, and what's more, they work simply for their keep and get no extra wages as the others do. Hence, if they want to take a private trip away from the city, they won't be able to; they'll have nothing to give to their mistresses, nothing to spend in whatever other ways they wish, as people do who are considered happy. You've omitted these and a host of other, similar facts from your charge.

Well, let them be added to the charge as well.

Then, are you asking how we should defend our-
b selves?

Yes.

I think we'll discover what to say if we follow the same path as before. We'll say that it wouldn't be surprising if these people were happiest just as they are, but that, in establishing our city, we aren't aiming to make any one group outstandingly happy but to make the whole city so, as far as possible. We thought that we'd find justice most easily in such a city and injustice, by contrast, in the one that is governed

worst and that, by observing both cities, we'd be able to judge the question we've been inquiring into for so long. We take ourselves, then, to be fashioning the *c* happy city, not picking out a few happy people and putting them in it, but making the whole city happy. (We'll look at the opposite city soon.)

Suppose, then, that someone came up to us while we were painting a statue and objected that, because we had painted the eyes (which are the most beautiful part) black rather than purple, we had not applied the most beautiful colors to the most beautiful parts of the statue. We'd think it reasonable to offer the following defense: "You mustn't expect us to paint the eyes so beautifully that they no longer appear to be eyes at all, and the same with the other parts. *d* Rather you must look to see whether by dealing with each part appropriately, we are making the whole statue beautiful." Similarly, you mustn't force us to give our guardians the kind of happiness that would make them something other than guardians. We know how to clothe the farmers in purple robes, *e* festoon them with gold jewelry, and tell them to work the land whenever they please. We know how to settle our potters on couches by the fire, feasting and passing the wine around, with their wheel beside them for whenever they want to make pots. And we can make all the others happy in the same way, so that the whole city is happy. Don't urge us to do this, however, for if we do, a farmer wouldn't be a farmer, nor a potter a potter, and none of the others would keep *421* to the patterns of work that give rise to a city. Now, if cobblers become inferior and corrupt and claim to be what they are not, that won't do much harm to the city. Hence, as far as they and the others like them are concerned, our argument carries less weight. But if the guardians of our laws and city are merely believed to be guardians but are not, you surely see that they'll destroy the city utterly, just as they alone have the opportunity to govern it well and make it happy.

If we are making true guardians, then, who are least likely to do evil to the city, and if the one who brought the charge is talking about farmers and ban-queters who are happy as they would be at a festival *b* rather than in a city, then he isn't talking about a city at all, but about something else. With this in mind, we should consider whether in setting up our guard-ians we are aiming to give them the greatest happi-

ness, or whether—since our aim is to see that the city as a whole has the greatest happiness—we must compel and persuade the auxiliaries and guardians to follow our other policy and be the best possible
c craftsmen at their own work, and the same with all the others. In this way, with the whole city developing and being governed well, we must leave it to nature to provide each group with its share of happiness.

I think you put that very well, he said.

Will you also think that I'm putting things well when I make the next point, which is closely akin to this one?

Which one exactly?

Consider whether or not the following things cor-
d rupt the other workers, so that they become bad.

What things?

Wealth and poverty.

How do they corrupt the other workers?

Like this. Do you think that a potter who has become wealthy will still be willing to pay attention to his craft?

Not at all.

Won't he become more idle and careless than he was?

Much more.

Then won't he become a worse potter?

Far worse.

And surely if poverty prevents him from having tools or any of the other things he needs for his craft, he'll produce poorer work and will teach his sons, or
e anyone else he teaches, to be worse craftsmen.

Of course.

So poverty and wealth make a craftsman and his products worse.

Apparently.

It seems, then, that we've found other things that our guardians must guard against in every way, to prevent them from slipping into the city unnoticed.

What are they?

Both wealth and poverty. The former makes for
422 luxury, idleness, and revolution; the latter for slavishness, bad work, and revolution as well.

That's certainly true. But consider this, Socrates: If our city hasn't got any money, how will it be able to fight a war, especially if it has to fight against a great and wealthy city?

Obviously, it will be harder to fight one such city
b and easier to fight two.

How do you mean?

First of all, if our city has to fight a city of the sort you mention, won't it be a case of warrior-athletes fighting against rich men?

Yes, as far as that goes.

Well, then, Adeimantus, don't you think that one boxer who has had the best possible training could easily fight two rich and fat nonboxers?

Maybe not at the same time.

Not even by escaping from them and then turning and hitting the one who caught up with him first, and doing this repeatedly in stifling heat and sun? c Wouldn't he, in his condition, be able to handle even more than two such people?

That certainly wouldn't be surprising.

And don't you think that the rich have more knowledge and experience of boxing than of how to fight a war?

I do.

Then in all likelihood our athletes will easily be able to fight twice or three times their own numbers in a war.

I agree, for I think what you say is right.

What if they sent envoys to another city and told them the following truth: "We have no use for gold d or silver, and it isn't lawful for us to possess them, so join us in this war, and you can take the property of those who oppose us for yourselves." Do you think that anyone hearing this would choose to fight hard, lean dogs, rather than to join them in fighting fat and tender sheep?

No, I don't. But if the wealth of all the cities came to be gathered in a single one, watch out that it doesn't endanger your nonwealthy city. e

You're happily innocent if you think that anything other than the kind of city we are founding deserves to be called *a city*.

What do you mean?

We'll have to find a greater title for the others because each of them is a great many cities, not *a* city, as they say in the game. At any rate, each of them consists of two cities at war with one another, that of the poor and that of the rich, and each of 423 these contains a great many. If you approach them as one city, you'll be making a big mistake. But if you approach them as many and offer to give to the one city the money, power, and indeed the very inhabitants of the other, you'll always find many allies and few enemies. And as long as your own city is moderately governed in the way that we've just arranged, it will, even if it has only a thousand men to fight for it, be the greatest. Not in reputation; I don't mean that, but the greatest in fact. Indeed, you won't find a city as great as this one among either Greeks or barbarians, although many that are many times its *b* size may seem to be as great. Do you disagree?

No, I certainly don't.

Then this would also be the best limit for our guardians to put on the size of the city. And they should mark off enough land for a city that size and let the rest go.

What limit is that?

I suppose the following one. As long as it is willing to remain *one* city, it may continue to grow, but it cannot grow beyond that point.

c That is a good limit.

Then, we'll give our guardians this further order, namely, to guard in every way against the city's being either small or great in reputation instead of being sufficient in size and one in number.

At any rate, that order will be fairly easy for them to follow.

And the one we mentioned earlier is even easier, when we said that, if an offspring of the guardians is inferior, he must be sent off to join the other citizens and that, if the others have an able offspring, he must *d* join the guardians. This was meant to make clear that each of the other citizens is to be directed to what he is naturally suited for, so that, doing the one work that is his own, he will become not many but one, and the whole city will itself be naturally one not many.

That *is* easier than the other.

These orders we give them, Adeimantus, are neither as numerous nor as important as one might think. Indeed, they are all insignificant, provided, as the saying goes, that they guard the one great thing, *e* though I'd rather call it sufficient than great.

What's that?

Their education and upbringing, for if by being well educated they become reasonable men, they will easily see these things for themselves, as well as all the other things we are omitting, for example, that marriage, the having of wives, and the procreation of children must be governed as far as possible by the old proverb: Friends possess everything in common.

That would be best.

And surely, once our city gets a good start, it will go on growing in a cycle. Good education and upbringing, when they are preserved, produce good natures, and useful natures, who are in turn well educated, grow up even better than their predecessors, both in their offspring and in other respects, just like other animals. *b*

That's likely.

To put it briefly, those in charge must cling to education and see that it isn't corrupted without their noticing it, guarding it against everything. Above all, they must guard as carefully as they can against any innovation in music and poetry or in physical training that is counter to the established order. And they should dread to hear anyone say:

> People care most for the song
> That is newest from the singer's lips.

Someone might praise such a saying, thinking that the poet meant not new songs but new ways of singing. *c* Such a thing shouldn't be praised, and the poet shouldn't be taken to have meant it, for the guardians must beware of changing to a new form of music, since it threatens the whole system. As Damon says, and I am convinced, the musical modes are never changed without change in the most important of a city's laws.

You can count me among the convinced as well, Adeimantus said.

Then it seems, I said, that it is in music and poetry that our guardians must build their bulwark. *d*

At any rate, lawlessness easily creeps in there unnoticed.

Yes, as if music and poetry were only play and did no harm at all.

It is harmless—except, of course, that when lawlessness has established itself there, it flows over little by little into characters and ways of life. Then, greatly increased, it steps out into private contracts, and from private contracts, Socrates, it makes its insolent way into the laws and government, until in the end it overthrows everything, public and private. *e*

Well, is that the way it goes?

I think so.

Then, as we said at first, our children's games must from the very beginning be more law-abiding, for if their games become lawless, and the children follow suit, isn't it impossible for them to grow up into good 425 and law-abiding men?

It certainly is.

But when children play the right games from the beginning and absorb lawfulness from music and poetry, it follows them in everything and fosters their growth, correcting anything in the city that may have gone wrong before—in other words, the very opposite of what happens where the games are lawless.

That's true.

These people will also discover the seemingly insignificant conventions their predecessors have destroyed.

Which ones?

Things like this: When it is proper for the young b to be silent in front of their elders, when they should make way for them or stand up in their presence, the care of parents, hair styles, the clothes and shoes to wear, deportment, and everything else of that sort. Don't you agree?

I do.

I think it's foolish to legislate about such things. Verbal or written decrees will never make them come about or last.

How could they?

At any rate, Adeimantus, it looks as though the start of someone's education determines what follows. c Doesn't like always encourage like?

It does.

And the final outcome of education, I suppose we'd say, is a single newly finished person, who is either good or the opposite.

Of course.

That's why I wouldn't go on to try to legislate about such things.

And with good reason.

Then, by the gods, what about market business, such as the private contracts people make with one another in the marketplace, for example, or contracts d with manual laborers, cases of insult or injury, the bringing of lawsuits, the establishing of juries, the payment and assessment of whatever dues are neces-

sary in markets and harbors, the regulation of market, city, harbor, and the rest—should we bring ourselves to legislate about any of these?

It isn't appropriate to dictate to men who are fine and good. They'll easily find out for themselves whatever needs to be legislated about such things. e

Yes, provided that a god grants that the laws we have already described are preserved.

If not, they'll spend their lives enacting a lot of other laws and then amending them, believing that in this way they'll attain the best.

You mean they'll live like those sick people who, through licentiousness, aren't willing to abandon their harmful way of life?

That's right.

And such people carry on in an altogether amusing fashion, don't they? Their medical treatment achieves 426 nothing, except that their illness becomes worse and more complicated, and they're always hoping that someone will recommend some new medicine to cure them.

That's exactly what happens to people like that.

And isn't it also amusing that they consider their worst enemy to be the person who tells them the truth, namely, that until they give up drunkenness, overeating, lechery, and idleness, no medicine, cautery, or surgery, no charms, amulets, or anything else b of that kind will do them any good?

It isn't amusing at all, for it isn't amusing to treat someone harshly when he's telling the truth.

You don't seem to approve of such men.

I certainly don't, by god.

Then, you won't approve either if a whole city behaves in that way, as we said. Don't you think that cities that are badly governed behave exactly like this when they warn their citizens not to disturb the city's whole political establishment on pain of death? The c person who is honored and considered clever and wise in important matters by such badly governed cities is the one who serves them most pleasantly, indulges them, flatters them, anticipates their wishes, and is clever at fulfillling them.

Cities certainly do seem to behave in that way, and I don't approve of it at all.

What about those who are willing and eager to serve such cities? Don't you admire their courage d and readiness?

I do, except for those who are deceived by majority approval into believing that they are true statesmen.

What do you mean? Have you no sympathy for such men? Or do you think it's possible for someone who is ignorant of measurement not to believe it himself when many others who are similarly ignorant *e* tell him that he is six feet tall?

No, I don't think that.

Then don't be too hard on them, for such people are surely the most amusing of all. They pass laws on the subjects we've just been enumerating and then amend them, and they always think they'll find a way to put a stop to cheating on contracts and the other things I mentioned, not realizing that they're really just cutting off a Hydra's head.

427   Yet that's all they're doing.

I'd have thought, then, that the true lawgiver oughtn't to bother with that form of law or constitution, either in a badly governed city or in a well-governed one—in the former, because it's useless and accomplishes nothing; in the latter, because anyone could discover some of these things, while the others follow automatically from the ways of life we established.

What is now left for us to deal with under the *b* heading of legislation?

For us nothing, but for the Delphic Apollo it remains to enact the greatest, finest, and first of laws.

What laws are those?

Those having to do with the establishing of temples, sacrifices, and other forms of service to gods, daemons, and heroes, the burial of the dead, and the services that ensure their favor. We have no knowledge of these things, and in establishing our city, if we have any understanding, we won't be persuaded to trust *c* them to anyone other than the ancestral guide. And this god, sitting upon the rock at the center of the earth, is without a doubt the ancestral guide on these matters for all people.

Nicely put. And that's what we must do.

Well, son of Ariston, your city might now be said *d* to be established. The next step is to get an adequate light somewhere and to call upon your brother as well as Polemarchus and the others, so as to look inside it and see where the justice and the injustice might be in it, what the difference between them is, and which of the two the person who is to be happy

should possess, whether its possession is unnoticed by all the gods and human beings or not.

You're talking nonsense, Glaucon said. You promised to look for them yourself because you said it was impious for you not to come to the rescue of justice in every way you could.   *e*

That's true, and I must do what I promised, but you'll have to help.

We will.

I hope to find it in this way. I think our city, if indeed it has been correctly founded, is completely good.

Necessarily so.

Clearly, then, it is wise, courageous, moderate, and just.

Clearly.

Then, if we find any of these in it, what's left over will be the ones we haven't found?

Of course.   428

Therefore, as with any other four things, if we were looking for any one of them in something and recognized it first, that would be enough for us, but if we recognized the other three first, this itself would be sufficient to enable us to recognize what we are looking for. Clearly it couldn't be anything other than what's left over.

That's right.

Therefore, since there are four virtues, mustn't we look for them in the same way?

Clearly.

Now, the first thing I think I can see clearly in the city is wisdom, and there seems to be something odd about it.   *b*

What's that?

I think that the city we described is really wise. And that's because it has good judgment, isn't it?

Yes.

Now, this very thing, good judgment, is clearly some kind of knowledge, for it's through knowledge, not ignorance, that people judge well.

Clearly.

But there are many kinds of knowledge in the city.

Of course.

Is it because of the knowledge possessed by its carpenters, then, that the city is to be called wise and sound in judgment?

Not at all. It's called skilled in carpentry because of that.   *c*

Then it isn't to be called wise because of the knowledge by which it arranges to have the best wooden implements.

No, indeed.

What about the knowledge of bronze items or the like?

It isn't because of any knowledge of that sort.

Nor because of the knowledge of how to raise a harvest from the earth, for it's called skilled in farming because of that.

I should think so.

Then, is there some knowledge possessed by some of the citizens in the city we just founded that doesn't judge about any particular matter but about the city as a whole and the maintenance of good relations, both internally and with other cities?

d

There is indeed.

What is this knowledge, and who has it?

It is guardianship, and it is possessed by those rulers we just now called complete guardians.

Then, what does this knowledge entitle you to say about the city?

That it has good judgment and is really wise.

Who do you think that there will be more of in our city, metal-workers or these true guardians?

e

There will be far more metal-workers.

Indeed, of all those who are called by a certain name because they have some kind of knowledge, aren't the guardians the least numerous?

By far.

Then, a whole city established according to nature would be wise because of the smallest class and part in it, namely, the governing or ruling one. And to this class, which seems to be by nature the smallest, belongs a share of the knowledge that alone among all the other kinds of knowledge is to be called wisdom.

429

That's completely true.

Then we've found one of the four virtues, as well as its place in the city, though I don't know how we found it.

Our way of finding it seems good enough to me.

And surely courage and the part of the city it's in, the part on account of which the city is called courageous, aren't difficult to see.

How is that?

Who, in calling the city cowardly or courageous, would look anywhere other than to the part of it that fights and does battle on its behalf?

b

No one would look anywhere else.

At any rate, I don't think that the courage or cowardice of its other citizens would cause the city itself to be called either courageous or cowardly.

No, it wouldn't.

The city is courageous, then, because of a part of itself that has the power to preserve through everything its belief about what things are to be feared, namely, that they are the things and kinds of things that the lawgiver declared to be such in the course of educating it. Or don't you call that courage?

c

I don't completely understand what you mean. Please, say it again.

I mean that courage is a kind of preservation.

What sort of preservation?

That preservation of the belief that has been inculcated by the law through education about what things and sorts of things are to be feared. And by preserving this belief "through everything," I mean preserving it and not abandoning it because of pains, pleasures, desires, or fears. If you like, I'll compare it to something I think it resembles.

d

I'd like that.

You know that dyers, who want to dye wool purple, first pick out from the many colors of wool the one that is naturally white, then they carefully prepare this in various ways, so that it will absorb the color as well as possible, and only at that point do they apply the purple dye. When something is dyed in this way, the color is fast—no amount of washing, whether with soap or without it, can remove it. But you also know what happens to material if it hasn't been dyed in this way, but instead is dyed purple or some other color without careful preparation.

e

I know that it looks washed out and ridiculous.

Then, you should understand that, as far as we could, we were doing something similar when we selected our soldiers and educated them in music and physical training. What we were contriving was nothing other than this: That because they had the proper nature and upbringing, they would absorb the laws in the finest possible way, just like a dye, so that their belief about what they should fear and all the rest would become so fast that even such extremely effective detergents as pleasure, pain, fear, and desire wouldn't wash it out—and pleasure is much more potent than any powder, washing soda, or soap. This power to preserve through everything the correct and

430

b

law-inculcated belief about what is to be feared and what isn't is what I call courage, unless, of course, you say otherwise.

I have nothing different to say, for I assume that you don't consider the correct belief about these same things, which you find in animals and slaves, and which is not the result of education, to be inculcated by law, and that you don't call it courage but something else.

c   That's absolutely true.

Then I accept your account of courage.

Accept it instead as my account of *civic* courage, and you will be right. We'll discuss courage more fully some other time, if you like. At present, our inquiry concerns not it but justice. And what we've said is sufficient for that purpose.

You're quite right.

There are now two things left for us to find in the city, namely, moderation and—the goal of our entire d   inquiry—justice.

That's right.

Is there a way we could find justice so as not to have to bother with moderation any further?

I don't know any, and I wouldn't want justice to appear first if that means that we won't investigate moderation. So if you want to please me, look for the latter first.

e   I'm certainly willing. It would be wrong not to be.

Look, then.

We will. Seen from here, it is more like a kind of consonance and harmony than the previous ones.

In what way?

Moderation is surely a kind of order, the mastery of certain kinds of pleasures and desires. People indicate as much when they use the phrase "self-control" and other similar phrases. I don't know just what they mean by them, but they are, so to speak, like tracks or clues that moderation has left behind in language. Isn't that so?

Absolutely.

Yet isn't the expression "self-control" ridiculous? The stronger self that does the controlling is the same as the weaker self that gets controlled, so that only 431   one person is referred to in all such expressions.

Of course.

Nonetheless, the expression is apparently trying to indicate that, in the soul of that very person, there is a better part and a worse one and that, whenever the naturally better part is in control of the worse, this is expressed by saying that the person is self-controlled or master of himself. At any rate, one praises someone by calling him self-controlled. But when, on the other hand, the smaller and better part is overpowered by the larger, because of bad upbringing or bad company, this is called being self-defeated or licentious   b and is a reproach.

Appropriately so.

Take a look at our new city, and you'll find one of these in it. You'll say that it is rightly called self-controlled, if indeed something in which the better rules the worse is properly called moderate and self-controlled.

I am looking, and what you say is true.

Now, one finds all kinds of diverse desires, pleasures, and pains, mostly in children, women, house-   c hold slaves, and in those of the inferior majority who are called free.

That's right.

But you meet with the desires that are simple, measured, and directed by calculation in accordance with understanding and correct belief only in the few people who are born with the best natures and receive the best education.

That's true.

Then, don't you see that in your city, too, the desires of the inferior many are controlled by the wisdom and desires of the superior few?   d

I do.

Therefore, if any city is said to be in control of itself and of its pleasures and desires, it is this one.

Absolutely.

And isn't it, therefore, also moderate because of all this?

It is.

And, further, if indeed the ruler and the ruled in any city share the same belief about who should rule,   e it is in this one. Or don't you agree?

I agree entirely.

And when the citizens agree in this way, in which of them do you say moderation is located? In the ruler or the ruled?

I suppose in both.

Then, you see how right we were to divine that moderation resembles a kind of harmony?

How so?

Because, unlike courage and wisdom, each of which resides in one part, making the city brave and wise respectively, moderation spreads throughout the whole. It makes the weakest, the strongest, and those in between—whether in regard to reason, physical strength, numbers, wealth, or anything else—all sing the same song together. And this unanimity, this agreement between the naturally worse and the naturally better as to which of the two is to rule both in the city and in each one, is rightly called moderation.

I agree completely.

All right. We've now found, at least from the point of view of our present beliefs, three out of the four virtues in our city. So what kind of virtue is left, then, that makes the city share even further in virtue? Surely, it's clear that it is justice.

That is clear.

Then, Glaucon, we must station ourselves like hunters surrounding a wood and focus our understanding, so that justice doesn't escape us and vanish into obscurity, for obviously it's around here somewhere. So look and try eagerly to catch sight of it, and if you happen to see it before I do, you can tell me about it.

I wish I could, but you'll make better use of me if you take me to be a follower who can see things when you point them out to him.

Follow, then, and join me in a prayer.

I'll do that, just so long as you lead.

I certainly will, though the place seems to be impenetrable and full of shadows. It is certainly dark and hard to search though. But all the same, we must go on.

Indeed we must.

And then I caught sight of something. Ah ha! Glaucon, it looks as though there's a track here, so it seems that our quarry won't altogether escape us.

That's good news.

Either that, or we've just been stupid.

In what way?

Because what we are looking for seems to have been rolling around at our feet from the very beginning, and we didn't see it, which was ridiculous of us. Just as people sometimes search for the very thing they are holding in their hands, so we didn't look in the right direction but gazed off into the distance, and that's probably why we didn't notice it.

What do you mean?

I mean that, though we've been talking and hearing about it for a long time, I think we didn't understand what we were saying or that, in a way, we were talking about justice.

That's a long prelude for someone who wants to hear the answer.

Then listen and see whether there's anything in what I say. Justice, I think, is exactly what we said must be established throughout the city when we were founding it—either that or some form of it. We stated, and often repeated, if you remember, that everyone must practice one of the occupations in the city for which he is naturally best suited.

Yes, we did keep saying that.

Moreover, we've heard many people say and have often said ourselves that justice is doing one's own work and not meddling with what isn't one's own.

Yes, we have.

Then, it turns out that this doing one's own work—provided that it comes to be in a certain way—is justice. And do you know what I take as evidence of this?

No, tell me.

I think that this is what was left over in the city when moderation, courage, and wisdom have been found. It is the power that makes it possible for them to grow in the city and that preserves them when they've grown for as long as it remains there itself. And of course we said that justice would be what was left over when we had found the other three.

Yes, that must be so.

And surely, if we had to decide which of the four will make the city good by its presence, it would be a hard decision. Is it the agreement in belief between the rulers and the ruled? Or the preservation among the soldiers of the law-inspired belief about what is to be feared and what isn't? Or the wisdom and guardianship of the rulers? Or is it, above all, the fact that every child, woman, slave, freeman, craftsman, ruler, and ruled each does his own work and doesn't meddle with what is other people's?

How could this fail to be a hard decision?

It seems, then, that the power that consists in everyone's doing his own work rivals wisdom, moderation,

and courage in its contribution to the virtue of the
e city.

It certainly does.

And wouldn't you call this rival to the others in its
contribution to the city's virtue justice?

Absolutely.

Look at it this way if you want to be convinced.
Won't you order your rulers to act as judges in the
city's courts?

Of course.

And won't their sole aim in delivering judgments
be that no citizen should have what belongs to another
or be deprived of what is his own?

They'll have no aim but that.

Because that is just?

Yes.

Therefore, from this point of view also, the having and doing of one's own would be accepted as
434 justice.

That's right.

Consider, then, and see whether you agree with
me about this. If a carpenter attempts to do the work
of a cobbler, or a cobbler that of a carpenter, or they
exchange their tools or honors with one another, or
if the same person tries to do both jobs, and all other
such exchanges are made, do you think that does any
great harm to the city?

Not much.

But I suppose that when someone, who is by nature
a craftsman or some other kind of money-maker, is
puffed up by wealth, or by having a majority of votes,
b or by his own strength, or by some other such thing,
and attempts to enter the class of soldiers, or one of
the unworthy soldiers tries to enter that of the judges
and guardians, and these exchange their tools and
honors, or when the same person tries to do all these
things at once, then I think you'll agree that these
exchanges and this sort of meddling bring the city
to ruin.

Absolutely.

Meddling and exchange between these three
classes, then, is the greatest harm that can happen to
the city and would rightly be called the worst thing
c someone could do to it.

Exactly.

And wouldn't you say that the worst thing that
someone could do to his city is injustice?

Of course.

Then, that exchange and meddling is injustice. Or
to put it the other way around: For the money-making,
auxiliary, and guardian classes each to do its own
work in the city, is the opposite. That's justice, isn't
it, and makes the city just?

I agree. Justice is that and nothing else.   d

Let's not take that as secure just yet, but if we find
that the same form, when it comes to be in each
individual person, is accepted as justice there as well,
we can assent to it. What else can we say? But if that
isn't what we find, we must look for something else
to be justice. For the moment, however, let's complete the present inquiry. We thought that, if we
first tried to observe justice in some larger thing that
possessed it, this would make it easier to observe in
a single individual. We agreed that this larger thing
is a city, and so we established the best city we could,
knowing well that justice would be in one that was e
good. So, let's apply what has come to light in the
city to an individual, and if it is accepted there, all
will be well. But if something different is found in
the individual, then we must go back and test that
on the city. And if we do this, and compare them
side by side, we might well make justice light up as 435
if we were rubbing fire-sticks together. And, when it
has come to light, we can get a secure grip on it
for ourselves.

You're following the road we set, and we must do
as you say.

Well, then, are things called by the same name,
whether they are bigger or smaller than one another,
like or unlike with respect to that to which that
name applies?

Alike.

Then a just man won't differ at all from a just city
in respect to the form of justice; rather he'll be like b
the city.

He will.

But a city was thought to be just when each of the
three natural classes within it did its own work, and
it was thought to be moderate, courageous, and wise
because of certain other conditions and states of
theirs.

That's true.

Then, if an individual has these same three parts
in his soul, we will expect him to be correctly called
by the same names as the city if he has the same c
conditions in them.

Necessarily so.

Then once again we've come upon an easy question, namely, does the soul have these three parts in it or not?

It doesn't look easy to me. Perhaps, Socrates, there's some truth in the old saying that everything fine is difficult.

Apparently so. But you should know, Glaucon, that, in my opinion, we will never get a precise answer d using our present methods of argument—although there is another longer and fuller road that does lead to such an answer. But perhaps we can get an answer that's up to the standard of our previous statements and inquiries.

Isn't that satisfactory? It would be enough for me at present.

In that case, it will be fully enough for me too.

Then don't weary, but go on with the inquiry.

Well, then, we are surely compelled to agree that e each of us has within himself the same parts and characteristics as the city? Where else would they come from? It would be ridiculous for anyone to think that spiritedness didn't come to be in cities from such individuals as the Thracians, Scythians, and others who live to the north of us who are held to possess spirit, or that the same isn't true of the love of learning, which 436 is mostly associated with our part of the world, or of the love of money, which one might say is conspicuously displayed by the Phoenicians and Egyptians.

It would.

That's the way it is, anyway, and it isn't hard to understand.

Certainly not.

But this *is* hard. Do we do these things with the same part of ourselves, or do we do them with three different parts? Do we learn with one part, get angry with another, and with some third part desire the pleasures of food, drink, sex, and the others that are closely akin to them? Or, when we set out after something, do we act with the whole of our soul, in each b case? This is what's hard to determine in a way that's up to the standards of our argument.

I think so too.

Well, then, let's try to determine in that way whether these parts are the same or different.

How?

It is obvious that the same thing will not be willing to do or undergo opposites in the same part of itself, in relation to the same thing, at the same time. So, if we ever find this happening in the soul, we'll know that we aren't dealing with one thing but many. c

All right.

Then consider what I'm about to say.

Say on.

Is it possible for the same thing to stand still and move at the same time in the same part of itself?

Not at all.

Let's make our agreement more precise in order to avoid disputes later on. If someone said that a person who is standing still but moving his hands and head is moving and standing still at the same time, we wouldn't consider, I think, that he ought to put it like that. What he ought to say is that one part of the person is standing still and another part is moving. Isn't that so? d

It is.

And if our interlocutor became even more amusing and was sophisticated enough to say that whole spinning tops stand still and move at the same time when the peg is fixed in the same place and they revolve, and that the same is true of anything else moving in a circular motion on the same spot, we wouldn't agree, because it isn't with respect to the same parts of themselves that such things both stand still and move. We'd say that they have an axis and a circumfer- e ence and that with respect to the axis they stand still, since they don't wobble to either side, while with respect to the circumference they move in a circle. But if they do wobble to the left or right, front or back, while they are spinning, we'd say that they aren't standing still in any way.

And we'd be right.

No such statement will disturb us, then, or make us believe that the same thing can be, do, or undergo opposites, at the same time, in the same respect, and in relation to the same thing. 437

They won't make me believe it, at least.

Nevertheless, in order to avoid going through all these objections one by one and taking a long time to prove them all untrue, let's hypothesize that this is corrrect and carry on. But we agree that if it should ever be shown to be incorrect, all the consequences we've drawn from it will also be lost.

We should agree to that.

Then wouldn't you consider all the following, whether they are doings or undergoings, as pairs of b opposites: Assent and dissent, wanting to have something and rejecting it, taking something and pushing it away?

Yes, they are opposites.

What about these? Wouldn't you include thirst, hunger, the appetites as a whole, and wishing and willing somewhere in the class we mentioned? Wouldn't you say that the soul of someone who has an appetite for a thing wants what he has an appetite for and takes to himself what it is his will to have, and that insofar as he wishes something to be given to him, his soul, since it desires this to come about, nods assent to it as if in answer to a question?

I would.

What about not willing, not wishing, and not having an appetite? Aren't these among the very opposites—cases in which the soul pushes and drives things away?

Of course.

Then won't we say that there is a class of things called appetites and that the clearest examples are hunger and thirst?

We will.

One of these is for food and the other for drink?

Yes.

Now, insofar as it is thirst, is it an appetite in the soul for more than that for which we say that it is the appetite? For example, is thirst thirst for hot drink or cold, or much drink or little, or, in a word, for drink of a certain sort? Or isn't it rather that, where heat is present as well as thirst, it causes the appetite to be for something cold as well, and where cold for something hot, and where there is much thirst because of the presence of muchness, it will cause the desire to be for much, and where little for little? But thirst itself will never be for anything other than what it is in its nature to be for, namely, drink itself, and hunger for food.

That's the way it is, each appetite itself is only for its natural object, while the appetite for something of a certain sort depends on additions.

Therefore, let no one catch us unprepared or disturb us by claiming that no one has an appetite for drink but rather good drink, nor food but good food, on the grounds that everyone after all has appetite for good things, so that if thirst is an appetite, it will be an appetite for good drink or whatever, and similarly with the others.

All the same, the person who says that has a point.

But it seems to me that, in the case of all things that are related to something, those that are of a particular sort are related to a particular sort of thing, while those that are merely themselves are related to a thing that is merely itself.

I don't understand.

Don't you understand that the greater is such as to be greater than something?

Of course.

Than the less?

Yes.

And the much greater than the much less, isn't that so?

Yes.

And the once greater to the once less? And the going-to-be greater than the going-to-be less?

Certainly.

And isn't the same true of the more and the fewer, the double and the half, heavier and lighter, faster and slower, the hot and the cold, and all other such things?

Of course.

And what about the various kinds of knowledge? Doesn't the same apply? Knowledge itself is knowledge of what can be learned itself (or whatever it is that knowledge is of), while a particular sort of knowledge is of a particular sort of thing. For example, when knowledge of building houses came to be, didn't it differ from the other kinds of knowledge, and so was called knowledge of building?

Of course.

And wasn't that because it was a different sort of knowledge from all the others?

Yes.

And wasn't it because it was of a particular sort of thing that it itself became a particular sort of knowledge? And isn't this true of all crafts and kinds of knowledge?

It is.

Well, then, this is what I was trying to say—if you understand it now—when I said that of all things that are related to something, those that are merely themselves are related to things that are merely themselves, while those that are of a particular sort are related to things of a particular sort. However, I don't mean that the sorts in question have to be the same for them both. For example, knowledge of health or disease isn't healthy or diseased, and knowledge of good and bad doesn't itself become good or bad. I mean that, when knowledge became, not knowledge of the thing itself that knowledge is of, but knowledge of something of a particular sort, the result was that it itself became a particular sort of knowledge, and this caused it to be no longer called knowledge without qualification, but—with the addition of the relevant sort—medical knowledge or whatever.

I understand, and I think that that's the way it is.

Then as for thirst, wouldn't you include it among things that are related to something? Surely thirst is related to . . .

I know it's related to drink.

Therefore a particular sort of thirst is for a particular sort of drink. But thirst itself isn't for much or little, good or bad, or, in a word, for drink of a particular sort. Rather, thirst itself is in its nature only for drink itself.

Absolutely.

Hence the soul of the thirsty person, insofar as he's thirsty, doesn't wish anything else but to drink, and it wants this and is impelled towards it.

Clearly.

Therefore, if something draws it back when it is thirsting, wouldn't that be something different in it from whatever thirsts and drives it like a beast to drink? It can't be, we say, that the same thing, with the same part of itself, in relation to the same, at the same time, does opposite things.

No, it can't.

In the same way, I suppose, it's wrong to say of the archer that his hands at the same time push the bow away and draw it towards him. We ought to say that one hand pushes it away and the other draws it towards him.

Absolutely.

Now, would we assert that sometimes there are thirsty people who don't wish to drink?

Certainly, it happens often to many different people.

What, then, should one say about them? Isn't it that there is something in their soul, bidding them to drink, and something different, forbidding them to do so, that overrules the thing that bids?

I think so.

Doesn't that which forbids in such cases come into play—if it comes into play at all—as a result of rational calculation, while what drives and drags them to drink is a result of feelings and diseases?

Apparently.

Hence it isn't unreasonable for us to claim that they are two, and different from one another. We'll call the part of the soul with which it calculates the rational part and the part with which it lusts, hungers, thirsts, and gets excited by other appetites the irrational appetitive part, companion of certain indulgences and pleasures.

Yes. Indeed, that's a reasonable thing to think.

Then, let these two parts be distinguished in the soul. Now, is the spirited part by which we get angry a third part or is it of the same nature as either of the other two?

Perhaps it's like the appetitive part.

But I've heard something relevant to this, and I believe it. Leontius, the son of Aglaion, was going up from the Piraeus along the outside of the North Wall when he saw some corpses lying at the executioner's feet. He had an appetite to look at them but at the same time he was disgusted and turned away. For a time he struggled with himself and covered his face, but, finally, overpowered by the appetite, he pushed his eyes wide open and rushed towards the corpses, saying, "Look for yourselves, you evil wretches, take your fill of the beautiful sight!"

I've heard that story myself.

It certainly proves that anger sometimes makes war against the appetites, as one thing against another.

Besides, don't we often notice in other cases that when appetite forces someone contrary to rational calculation, he reproaches himself and gets angry with that in him that's doing the forcing, so that of the two factions that are fighting a civil war, so to speak, spirit allies itself with reason? But I don't think you can say that you've ever seen spirit, either in yourself or anyone else, ally itself with an appetite to do what reason has decided must not be done.

No, by god, I haven't.

What happens when a person thinks that he has done something unjust? Isn't it true that the nobler he is, the less he resents it if he suffers hunger, cold, or the like at the hands of someone whom he believes to be inflicting this on him justly, and won't his spirit, as I say, refuse to be aroused?

That's true.

But what happens if, instead, he believes that someone has been unjust to him? Isn't the spirit within him boiling and angry, fighting for what he believes to be just? Won't it endure hunger, cold, and the like and keep on till it is victorious, not ceasing from noble actions until it either wins, dies, or calms down, *d* called to heel by the reason within him, like a dog by a shepherd?

Spirit is certainly like that. And, of course, we made the auxiliaries in our city like dogs obedient to the rulers, who are themselves like shepherds of a city.

You well understand what I'm trying to say. But also reflect on this further point.

e What?

The position of the spirited part seems to be the opposite of what we thought before. Then we thought of it as something appetitive, but now we say that it is far from being that, for in the civil war in the soul it aligns itself far more with the rational part.

Absolutely.

Then is it also different from the rational part, or is it some form of it, so that there are two parts in the soul—the rational and the appetitive—instead of three? Or rather, just as there were three classes in *441* the city that held it together, the money-making, the auxiliary, and the deliberative, is the spirited part a third thing in the soul that is by nature the helper of the rational part, provided that it hasn't been corrupted by a bad upbringing?

It must be a third.

Yes, provided that we can show it is different from the rational part, as we saw earlier it was from the appetitive one.

It isn't difficult to show that it is different. Even in small children, one can see that they are full of spirit right from birth, while as far as rational calculation is concerned, some never seem to get a share of it, *b* while the majority do so quite late.

That's really well put. And in animals too one can see that what you say is true. Besides, our earlier quotation from Homer bears it out, where he says,

He struck his chest and spoke to his heart.

For here Homer clearly represents the part that has *c* calculated about better and worse as different from the part that is angry without calculation.

That's exactly right.

Well, then, we've now made our difficult way through a sea of argument. We are pretty much agreed that the same number and the same kinds of classes as are in the city are also in the soul of each individual.

That's true.

Therefore, it necessarily follows that the individual is wise in the same way and in the same part of himself as the city.

That's right.

And isn't the individual courageous in the same way and in the same part of himself as the city? And *d* isn't everything else that has to do with virtue the same in both?

Necessarily.

Moreover, Glaucon, I suppose we'll say that a man is just in the same way as a city.

That too is entirely necessary.

And we surely haven't forgotten that the city was just because each of the three classes in it was doing its own work.

I don't think we could forget that.

Then we must also remember that each one of us in whom each part is doing its own work will himself be just and do his own. *e*

Of course, we must.

Therefore, isn't it appropriate for the rational part to rule, since it is really wise and exercises foresight on behalf of the whole soul, and for the spirited part to obey it and be its ally?

It certainly is.

And isn't it, as we were saying, a mixture of music and poetry, on the one hand, and physical training, on the other, that makes the two parts harmonious, stretching and nurturing the rational part with fine words and learning, relaxing the other part through soothing stories, and making it gentle by means of *442* harmony and rhythm?

That's precisely it.

And these two, having been nurtured in this way, and having truly learned their own roles and been educated in them, will govern the appetitive part, which is the largest part in each person's soul and is by nature most insatiable for money. They'll watch over it to see that it isn't filled with the so-called pleasures of the body and that it doesn't become so big and strong that it no longer does its own work but attempts to enslave and rule over the classes it isn't fitted to rule, thereby over- *b* turning everyone's whole life.

That's right.

Then, wouldn't these two parts also do the finest job of guarding the whole soul and body against external enemies—reason by planning, spirit by fighting, following its leader, and carrying out the leader's decisions through its courage?

Yes, that's true.

c And it is because of the spirited part, I suppose, that we call a single individual courageous, namely, when it preserves through pains and pleasures the declarations of reason about what is to be feared and what isn't.

That's right.

And we'll call him wise because of that small part of himself that rules in him and makes those declarations and has within it the knowledge of what is advantageous for each part and for the whole soul, which is the community of all three parts.

Absolutely.

And isn't he moderate because of the friendly and harmonious relations between these same parts, namely, when the ruler and the ruled believe in common that the rational part should rule and don't d engage in civil war against it?

Moderation is surely nothing other than that, both in the city and in the individual.

And, of course, a person will be just because of what we've so often mentioned, and in that way.

Necessarily.

Well, then, is the justice in us at all indistinct? Does it seem to be something different from what we found in the city?

It doesn't seem so to me.

If there are still any doubts in our soul about this, we could dispel them altogether by appealing to ordi-e nary cases.

Which ones?

For example, if we had to come to an agreement about whether someone similar in nature and training to our city had embezzled a deposit of gold or silver that he had accepted, who do you think would consider him to have done it rather than someone who 443 isn't like him?

No one.

And would he have anything to do with temple robberies, thefts, betrayals of friends in private life or of cities in public life?

No, nothing.

And he'd be in no way untrustworthy in keeping an oath or other agreement.

How could he be?

And adultery, disrespect for parents, and neglect of the gods would be more in keeping with every other kind of character than his.

With every one.

And isn't the cause of all this that every part within him does its own work, whether it's ruling or being b ruled?

Yes, that and nothing else.

Then, are you still looking for justice to be something other than this power, the one that produces men and cities of the sort we've described?

No, I certainly am not.

Then the dream we had has been completely fulfilled—our suspicion that, with the help of some god, we had hit upon the origin and pattern of justice right at the beginning in founding our city.   c

Absolutely.

Indeed, Glaucon, the principle that it is right for someone who is by nature a cobbler to practice cobblery and nothing else, for the carpenter to practice carpentry, and the same for the others is a sort of image of justice—that's why it's beneficial.

Apparently.

And in truth justice is, it seems, something of this sort. However, it isn't concerned with someone's doing his own externally, but with what is inside him, with what is truly himself and his own. One who is d just does not allow any part of himself to do the work of another part or allow the various classes within him to meddle with each other. He regulates well what is really his own and rules himself. He puts himself in order, is his own friend, and harmonizes the three parts of himself like three limiting notes in a musical scale—high, low, and middle. He binds together those parts and any others there may be in between, and from having been many things he becomes entirely one, moderate and harmonious. e Only then does he act. And when he does anything, whether acquiring wealth, taking care of his body, engaging in politics, or in private contracts—in all of these, he believes that the action is just and fine that preserves this inner harmony and helps achieve it, and calls it so, and regards as wisdom the knowledge that oversees such actions. And he believes that the

action that destroys this harmony is unjust, and calls it
444 so, and regards the belief that oversees it as ignorance.

That's absolutely true, Socrates.

Well, then, if we claim to have found the just man,
the just city, and what the justice is that is in them,
I don't suppose that we'll seem to be telling a complete falsehood.

No, we certainly won't.

Shall we claim it, then?

We shall.

So be it. Now, I suppose we must look for injustice.

Clearly.

Surely, it must be a kind of civil war between the
b three parts, a meddling and doing of another's work,
a rebellion by some part against the whole soul in
order to rule it inappropriately. The rebellious part
is by nature suited to be a slave, while the other part
is not a slave but belongs to the ruling class. We'll
say something like that, I suppose, and that the turmoil and straying of these parts are injustice, licentiousness, cowardice, ignorance, and, in a word, the
whole of vice.

That's what they are.

So, if justice and injustice are really clear enough
c to us, then acting justly, acting unjustly, and doing
injustice are also clear.

How so?

Because just and unjust actions are no different
for the soul than healthy and unhealthy things are
for the body.

In what way?

Healthy things produce health, unhealthy ones
disease.

Yes.

And don't just actions produce justice in the soul
d and unjust ones injustice?

Necessarily.

To produce health is to establish the components
of the body in a natural relation of control and being
controlled, one by another, while to produce disease
is to establish a relation of ruling and being ruled
contrary to nature.

That's right.

Then, isn't to produce justice to establish the parts
of the soul in a natural relation of control, one by
another, while to produce injustice is to establish a
relation of ruling and being ruled contrary to nature?

Precisely.

Virtue seems, then, to be a kind of health, fine
condition, and well-being of the soul, while vice is
disease, shameful condition, and weakness.   e

That's true.

And don't fine ways of living lead one to the possession of virtue, shameful ones to vice?

Necessarily.

So it now remains, it seems, to inquire whether it
is more profitable to act justly, live in a fine way, and 445
be just, whether one is known to be so or not, or to
act unjustly and be unjust, provided that one doesn't
pay the penalty and become better as a result of punishment.

But, Socrates, this inquiry looks ridiculous to me
now that justice and injustice have been shown to
be as we have described. Even if one has every kind
of food and drink, lots of money, and every sort of
power to rule, life is thought to be not worth living
when the body's nature is ruined. So even if someone
can do whatever he wishes, except what will free him b
from vice and injustice and make him acquire justice
and virtue, how can it be worth living when his soul—
the very thing by which he lives—is ruined and in
turmoil?

Yes, it is ridiculous. Nevertheless, now that we've
come far enough to be able to see most clearly that
this is so, we mustn't give up.

That's absolutely the last thing we must do.

Then come here, so that you can see how many
forms of vice there are, anyhow that I consider worthy c
of examination.

I'm following you, just tell me.

Well, from the vantage point we've reached in our
argument, it seems to me that there is one form of
virtue and an unlimited number of forms of vice,
four of which are worth mentioning.

How do you mean?

It seems likely that there are as many types of
soul as there are specific types of political constitution.

How many is that?

Five forms of constitution and five of souls.   d

What are they?

One is the constitution we've been describing. And
it has two names. If one outstanding man emerges
among the rulers, it's called a kingship; if more than
one, it's called an aristocracy.

That's true.

Therefore, I say that this is one form of constitution. Whether one man emerges or many, none of the significant laws of the city would be changed, if they *e* followed the upbringing and education we described.

Probably not.

BOOK V

449 This is the kind of city and constitution, then, that I call good and correct, and so too is this kind of man. And if indeed this is the correct kind, all the others—whether as city governments or as organizations of the individual soul—are bad and mistaken. Their badness is of four kinds.

What are they? he said.

I was going to enumerate them and explain how I thought they developed out of one another, but Polemarchus, who was sitting a little further away *b* than Adeimantus, extended his hand and took hold of the latter's cloak by the shoulder from above. He drew Adeimantus towards him, while he himself leaned forward and said something to him. We overheard nothing of what he said except the words "Shall we let it go, or what?"

We certainly won't let it go, Adeimantus said, now speaking aloud.

And I asked: What is it that you won't let go?

You, he said.

c For what reason in particular?

We think that you're slacking off and that you've cheated us out of a whole important section of the discussion in order to avoid having to deal with it. You thought we wouldn't notice when you said—as though it were something trivial—that, as regards wives and children, anyone could see that the possessions of friends should be held in common.

But isn't that right, Adeimantus?

Yes it is. But this "right," like the other things we've discussed, requires an explanation—in this case, an explanation of the manner in which they are to be held in common, for there may be many ways of doing *d* this. So don't omit telling us about the particular one you mean. We've been waiting for some time, indeed, for you to tell us about the production of children—how they'll be produced and, once born, how they'll be brought up—and about the whole subject of hav-

ing wives and children in common. We think that this makes a considerable difference—indeed all the difference—to whether a constitution is correct or not. So now, since you are beginning to describe another constitution before having adequately discussed these things, we are resolved, as you overheard, not to let you off until you explain all this as fully as the rest. *450*

Include me, Glaucon said, as a partner in this resolution.

In fact, Socrates, Thrasymachus added, you can take this as the resolution of all of us.

What a thing you've done, I said, in stopping me! What an argument you've started up again from the very beginning, as it were, about the constitution! I was delighted to think that it had already been described and was content to have these things accepted as they were stated before. You don't realize what a swarm of arguments you've stirred up by calling me to account now. I saw the swarm and passed the topic by in order to save us a lot of trouble. *b*

Well, said Thrasymachus, are we here to search for gold or to listen to an argument?

The latter, I said, but within reason.

It's within reason, Socrates, Glaucon said, for people with any understanding to listen to an argument of this kind their whole life long. So don't mind about us, and don't get tired yourself. Rather, tell us at length what your thoughts are on the topic we inquired about, namely, what the common possession of wives and children will amount to for the guardians and how the *c* children will be brought up while they're still small, for the time between birth and the beginning of education seems to be the most difficult period of all. So try to tell us what the manner of this upbringing must be.

It isn't an easy subject to explain, for it raises even more incredulity than the topics we've discussed so far. People may not believe that what we say is possible or that, even if it could be brought about, it would be for the best. It's for this reason that I hesitated to bring it up, namely, that our argument might seem to be no more than wishful thinking. *d*

Then don't hesitate, for your audience isn't inconsiderate, incredulous, or hostile.

Are you trying to encourage me by saying that?

I am.

Well, you're doing the opposite. Your encouragement would be fine, if I could be sure I was speaking with knowledge, for one can feel both secure and confident when one knows the truth about the dearest and most important things and speaks about them among those who are themselves wise and dear

e friends. But to speak, as I'm doing, at a time when one is unsure of oneself and searching for the truth,

451 is a frightening and insecure thing to do. I'm not afraid of being laughed at—that would be childish indeed. But I am afraid that, if I slip from the truth, just where it's most important not to, I'll not only fall myself but drag my friends down as well. So I bow to Adrastea for what I'm going to say, for I suspect that it's a lesser crime to kill someone involuntarily than to mislead people about fine, good, and just institutions. Since it's better to run this risk among enemies than among friends, you've well and truly

b encouraged me!

Glaucon laughed and said: Well, Socrates, if we suffer from any false note you strike in the argument, we'll release you and absolve you of any guilt as in a homicide case: your hands are clean, and you have not deceived us. So take courage and speak.

I will, for the law says that someone who kills involuntarily is free of guilt when he's absolved by the injured party. So it's surely reasonable to think the same is true in my case as well.

With that as your defense, speak.

Then I'll have to go back to what should perhaps

c have been said in sequence, although it may be that this way of doing things is in fact right and that after the completion of the male drama, so to speak, we should then go through the female one—especially as you insist on it so urgently.

For men born and educated as we've described there is, in my opinion, no right way to acquire and use women and children other than by following the road on which we started them. We attempted, in the argument, to set up the men as guardians of the herd.

Yes.

Then let's give them a birth and rearing consistent

d with that and see whether it suits us or not.

How?

As follows: Do we think that the wives of our guardian watchdogs should guard what the males guard, hunt with them, and do everything else in common with them? Or should we keep the women at home, as incapable of doing this, since they must bear and

rear the puppies, while the males work and have the entire care of the flock?

Everything should be in common, except that the females are weaker and the males stronger.   e

And is it possible to use any animals for the same things if you don't give them the same upbringing and education?

No, it isn't.

Therefore, if we use the women for the same things as the men, they must also be taught the same things.

Yes.   452

Now, we gave the men music and poetry and physical training.

Yes.

Then we must give these two crafts, as well as those having to do with warfare, to the women also to use in the same way as the men use them.

That seems to follow from what you say.

But perhaps much of what we are saying, since it is contrary to custom, would incite ridicule if it were carried out in practice as we've described.

It certainly would.

What is the most ridiculous thing that you see in it? Isn't it obviously the women exercising naked in the palestras with the men? And not just the young women, but the older ones too—like old men in gymnasiums who, even though their bodies are wrin-   b kled and not pleasant to look at, still love to do physical training.

Yes, that would look really ridiculous as things stand at present.

But surely, now that we've started to speak about this, we mustn't fear the various jokes that wits will make about this kind of change in music and poetry, physical training, and—last but not least—in bearing arms and riding horses.   c

You're right.

And now that we've begun to speak about this, we must move on to the tougher part of the law, begging these people not to be silly (though that is their own work!) but to take the matter seriously. They should remember that it wasn't very long ago that the Greeks themselves thought it shameful and ridiculous (as the majority of the barbarians still do) for even men to be seen naked and that when the Cretans and then the Lacedaemonians began the gymnasiums, the wits of those times could also have ridiculed it all. Or don't you think so?   d

I do.

But I think that, after it was found in practice to be better to strip than to cover up all those parts, then what was ridiculous to the eyes faded away in the face of what argument showed to be the best. This makes it clear that it's foolish to think that anything besides the bad is ridiculous or to try to raise a laugh at the sight of anything besides what's stupid or bad or (putting it the other way around) it's foolish to take
e seriously any standard of what is fine and beautiful other than the good.

That's absolutely certain.

However, mustn't we first agree about whether our proposals are possible or not? And mustn't we give to anyone who wishes the opportunity to question us—whether in jest or in earnest—about whether female human nature *can* share all the tasks of that
453 of the male, or none of them, or some but not others, and to ask in which class the waging of war belongs? Wouldn't this, as the best beginning, also be likely to result in the best conclusion?

Of course.

Shall we give the argument against ourselves, then, on behalf of those who share these reservations, so that their side of the question doesn't fall by default?
b There's no reason not to.

Then let's say this on their behalf: "Socrates and Glaucon, there's no need for others to argue with you, for you yourselves, when you began to found your city, agreed that each must do his own work in accordance with his nature."

And I think we certainly did agree to that.

"Can you deny that a woman is by nature very different from a man?"

Of course not.

"And isn't it appropriate to assign different work to each in accordance with its nature?"
c Certainly.

"How is it, then, that you aren't mistaken and contradicting yourselves when you say that men and women must do the same things, when their natures are so completely separate and distinct?"

Do you have any defense against that attack?

It isn't easy to think of one on the spur of the moment, so I'll ask you to explain the argument on our side as well, whatever it is.

This and many other such things, Glaucon, which I foresaw earlier, were what I was afraid of, so that I hesitated to tackle the law concerning the possession d and upbringing of women and children.

By god, it doesn't seem to be an easy topic.

It isn't. But the fact is that whether someone falls into a small diving pool or into the middle of the biggest ocean, he must swim all the same.

He certainly must.

Then we must swim too, and try to save ourselves from the sea of argument, hoping that a dolphin will pick us up or that we'll be rescued by some other desperate means.

It seems so.   e

Come, then. Let's see if we can find a way out. We've agreed that different natures must follow different ways of life and that the natures of men and women are different. But now we say that those different natures must follow the same way of life. Isn't that the accusation brought against us?

That's it exactly.

Ah! Glaucon, great is the power of the craft of disputation.   454

Why is that?

Because many fall into it against their wills. They think they are having not a quarrel but a conversation, because they are unable to examine what has been said by dividing it up according to forms. Hence, they pursue mere verbal contradictions of what has been said and have a quarrel rather than a conversation.

That does happen to lots of people, but it isn't happening to us at the moment, is it?

It most certainly is, for it looks to me, at any rate, as though we are falling into disputation against our will. b

How?

We're bravely, but in a quarrelsome and merely verbal fashion, pursuing the principle that natures that aren't the same must follow different ways of life. But when we assigned different ways of life to different natures and the same ones to the same, we didn't at all examine the form of natural difference and sameness we had in mind or in what regard we were distinguishing them.

No, we didn't look into that.

Therefore, we might just as well, it seems, ask ourselves whether the natures of bald and long-haired c men are the same or opposite. And, when we agree that they are opposite, then, if the bald ones are cobblers, we ought to forbid the long-haired ones to be cobblers, and if the long-haired ones are cobblers, we ought to forbid this to the bald ones.

That would indeed be ridiculous.

And aren't we in this ridiculous position because at that time we did not introduce every form of difference and sameness in nature, but focused on the one form of sameness and difference that was relevant to the particular ways of life themselves? We meant, for example, that a male and female doctor have souls of the same nature. Or don't you think so?

I do.

But a doctor and a carpenter have different ones?

Completely different, surely.

Therefore, if the male sex is seen to be different from the female with regard to a particular craft or way of life, we'll say that the relevant one must be assigned to it. But if it's apparent that they differ only in this respect, that the females bear children while the males beget them, we'll say that there has been no kind of proof that women are different from men with respect to what we're talking about, and we'll continue to believe that our guardians and their wives must have the same way of life.

And rightly so.

Next, we'll tell anyone who holds the opposite view to instruct us in this: With regard to what craft or way of life involved in the constitution of the city are the natures of men and women not the same but different?

That's a fair question, at any rate.

And perhaps he'd say, just as you did a moment ago, that it isn't easy to give an immediate answer, but with enough consideration it should not be difficult.

Yes, he might say that.

Shall we ask the one who raises this objection to follow us and see whether we can show him that no way of life concerned with the management of the city is peculiar to women?

Of course.

"Come, now," we'll say to him, "give us an answer: Is this what you meant by one person being naturally well suited for something and another being naturally unsuited? That the one learned it easily, the other with difficulty; that the one, after only a brief period of instruction, was able to find out things for himself, while the other, after much instruction, couldn't even remember what he'd learned; that the body of the one adequately served his thought, while the body of the other opposed his. Are there any other things besides these by which you distinguished those who are naturally well suited for anything from those who are not?"

No one will claim that there are any others.

Do you know of anything practiced by human beings in which the male sex isn't superior to the female in all these ways? Or must we make a long story of it by mentioning weaving, baking cakes, and cooking vegetables, in which the female sex is believed to excel and in which it is most ridiculous of all for it to be inferior?

It's true that one sex is much superior to the other in pretty well everything, although many women are better than many men in many things. But on the whole it is as you say.

Then there is no way of life concerned with the management of the city that belongs to a woman because she's a woman or to a man because he's a man, but the various natures are distributed in the same way in both creatures. Women share by nature in every way of life just as men do, but in all of them women are weaker than men.

Certainly.

Then shall we assign all of them to men and none to women?

How can we?

We'll say, I suppose, that one woman is a doctor, another not, and that one is musical by nature, another not.

Of course.

And, therefore, won't one be athletic or warlike, while another is unwarlike and no lover of physical training?

I suppose so.

Further, isn't one woman philosophical or a lover of wisdom, while another hates wisdom? And isn't one spirited and another spiritless?

That too.

So one woman may have a guardian nature and another not, for wasn't it qualities of this sort that we looked for in the natures of the men we selected as guardians?

Certainly.

Therefore, men and women are by nature the same with respect to guarding the city, except to the extent that one is weaker and the other stronger.

Apparently.

Then women of this sort must be chosen along
b with men of the same sort to live with them and share
their guardianship, seeing that they are adequate for
the task and akin to the men in nature.

Certainly.

And mustn't we assign the same way of life to the
same natures?

We must.

We've come round, then, to what we said before
and have agreed that it isn't against nature to assign
an education in music, poetry, and physical training
to the wives of the guardians.

Absolutely.

Then we're not legislating impossibilities or indulg-
c ing in mere wishful thinking, since the law we established is in accord with nature. It's rather the way
things are at present that seems to be against nature.

So it seems.

Now, weren't we trying to determine whether our
proposals were both possible and optimal?

Yes, we were.

And haven't we now agreed that they're possible?

Yes.

Then mustn't we next reach agreement about
whether or not they're optimal?

Clearly.

Should we have one kind of education to produce
women guardians, then, and another to produce men,
d especially as they have the same natures to begin with?

No.

Then, what do you think about this?

What?

About one man being better and another worse.
Or do you think they're all alike?

Certainly not.

In the city we're establishing, who do you think will
prove to be better men, the guardians, who receive the
education we've described, or the cobblers, who are
educated in cobblery?

Your question is ridiculous.

I understand. Indeed, aren't the guardians the best
e of the citizens?

By far.

And what about the female guardians? Aren't they
the best of the women?

They're by far the best.

Is there anything better for a city than having the
best possible men and women as its citizens?

There isn't.

And isn't it music and poetry and physical training,
lending their support in the way we described, that
bring this about? 457

Of course.

Then the law we've established isn't only possible;
it is also optimal for a city?

Yes.

Then the guardian women must strip for physical
training, since they'll wear virtue or excellence instead
of clothes. They must share in war and the other
guardians' duties in the city and do nothing else. But
the lighter parts must be assigned to them because
of the weakness of their sex. And the man who laughs
at naked women doing physical training for the sake
of what is best is "plucking the unripe fruit" of laugh- b
ter and doesn't know, it seems, what he's laughing at
or what he's doing, for it is and always will be the
finest saying that the beneficial is beautiful, while the
harmful is ugly.

Absolutely.

Can we say, then, that we've escaped one wave of
criticism in our discussion of the law about women,
that we haven't been altogether swept away by laying
it down that male and female guardians must share
their entire way of life, and that our argument is c
consistent when it states that this is both possible
and beneficial?

And it's certainly no small wave that you've escaped.

You won't think that it's so big when you get a
look at the next one.

Tell me about it, and I'll decide.

I suppose that the following law goes along with
the last one and the others that preceded it.

Which one?

That all these women are to belong in common
to all the men, that none are to live privately with any
man, and that the children, too, are to be possessed in
common, so that no parent will know his own off- d
spring or any child his parent.

This wave is far bigger than the other, for there's
doubt both about its possibility and about whether or
not it's beneficial.

I don't think that its being beneficial would be
disputed or that it would be denied that the common
possession of women and children would be the greatest good, if indeed it is possible. But I think that there

would be a lot of disagreement about whether or not it is possible.

e There could very well be dispute about both.

You mean that I'll have to face a coalition of arguments. I thought I'd escape one of them, if you believed that the proposal was beneficial, and that I'd have only the one about whether or not it's possible left to deal with.

But you didn't escape unobserved, so you have to give an argument for both.

Well, then, I'll have to accept my punishment. But do me this favor. Let me, as if on a holiday, do what lazy people do who feast on their own thoughts when

458 out for a solitary walk. Instead of finding out how something they desire might actually come about, these people pass that over, so as to avoid tiring deliberations about what's possible and what isn't. They assume that what they desire is available and proceed to arrange the rest, taking pleasure in thinking through everything they'll do when they have what they want, thereby making their lazy souls even lazier.

b I'm getting soft myself at the moment, so I want to delay consideration of the feasibility of our proposal until later. With your permission, I'll assume that it's feasible and examine how the rulers will arrange these matters when they come to pass. And I'll try to show that nothing could be more beneficial to the city and its guardians than those arrangements. These are the things I'll examine with you first, and I'll deal with the other question later, but only if you'll permit me to do it this way.

You have my permission, so carry on with your examination.

I suppose that our rulers and auxiliaries—if indeed they're worthy of the names—will be willing to com-

c mand and to obey respectively. In some cases, the rulers will themselves be obeying our laws, and in others, namely, the ones we leave to their discretion, they'll give directions that are in the spirit of our laws.

Probably so.

Then you, as their lawgiver, will select women just as you did men, with natures as similar to theirs as possible, and hand them over to the men. And since they have common dwellings and meals, rather than

d private ones, and live together and mix together both in physical training and in the rest of their upbringing, they will, I suppose, be driven by innate necessity to

have sex with one another. Or don't you think we're talking about necessities here?

The necessities aren't geometrical but erotic, and they're probably better than the others at persuading and compelling the majority of people.

That's right. But the next point, Glaucon, is that promiscuity is impious in a city of happy people, and the rulers won't allow it.

e

No, for it isn't right.

Then it's clear that our next task must be to make marriage as sacred as possible. And the sacred marriages will be those that are most beneficial.

Absolutely.

How, then, will they be most beneficial? Tell me this, Glaucon: I see that you have hunting dogs and 459 quite a flock of noble fighting birds at home. Have you noticed anything about their mating and breeding?

Like what?

In the first place, although they're all noble, aren't there some that are the best and prove themselves to be so?

There are.

Do you breed them all alike, or do you try to breed from the best as much as possible?

I try to breed from the best.

And do you breed from the youngest or the oldest or from those in their prime?

b

From those in their prime.

And do you think that if they weren't bred in this way, your stock of birds and dogs would get much worse?

I do.

What about horses and other animals? Are things any different with them?

It would be strange if they were.

Dear me! If this also holds true of human beings, our need for excellent rulers is indeed extreme.

It does hold of them. But what of it?

c

Because our rulers will then have to use a lot of drugs. And while an inferior doctor is adequate for people who are willing to follow a regimen and don't need drugs, when drugs are needed, we know that a bolder doctor is required.

That's true. But what exactly do you have in mind?

I mean that it looks as though our rulers will have to make considerable use of falsehood and deception

for the benefit of those they rule. And we said that
d all such falsehoods are useful as a form of drug.

And we were right.

Well, it seems we were right, especially where marriages and the producing of children are concerned.

How so?

It follows from our previous agreements, first, that the best men must have sex with the best women as frequently as possible, while the opposite is true of the most inferior men and women, and, second, that if our herd is to be of the highest possible quality, the former's offspring must be reared but not the
e latter's. And this must all be brought about without being noticed by anyone except the rulers, so that our herd of guardians remains as free from dissension as possible.

That's absolutely right.

Therefore certain festivals and sacrifices will be established by law at which we'll bring the brides and grooms together, and we'll direct our poets to compose appropriate hymns for the marriages that take place. We'll leave the number of marriages for
460 the rulers to decide, but their aim will be to keep the number of males as stable as they can, taking into account war, disease, and similar factors, so that the city will, as far as possible, become neither too big nor too small.

That's right.

Then there'll have to be some sophisticated lotteries introduced, so that at each marriage the inferior people we mentioned will blame luck rather than the rulers when they aren't chosen.

There will.

And among other prizes and rewards the young men who are good in war or other things must be
b given permission to have sex with the women more often, since this will also be a good pretext for having them father as many of the children as possible.

That's right.

And then, as the children are born, they'll be taken over by the officials appointed for the purpose, who may be either men or women or both, since our offices are open to both sexes.

Yes.

I think they'll take the children of good parents to
c the nurses in charge of the rearing pen situated in a separate part of the city, but the children of inferior parents, or any child of the others that is born defective, they'll hide in a secret and unknown place, as is appropriate.

It is, if indeed the guardian breed is to remain pure.

And won't the nurses also see to it that the mothers are brought to the rearing pen when their breasts have milk, taking every precaution to insure that no mother knows her own child and providing wet nurses if the mother's milk is insufficient? And won't they d take care that the mothers suckle the children for only a reasonable amount of time and that the care of sleepless children and all other such troublesome duties are taken over by the wet nurses and other attendants?

You're making it very easy for the wives of the guardians to have children.

And that's only proper. So let's take up the next thing we proposed. We said that the children's parents should be in their prime.

True.

Do you share the view that a woman's prime lasts about twenty years and a man's about thirty? e

Which years are those?

A woman is to bear children for the city from the age of twenty to the age of forty, a man from the time that he passes his peak as a runner until he reaches fifty-five.

At any rate, that's the physical and mental prime for both. 461

Then, if a man who is younger or older than that engages in reproduction for the community, we'll say that his offense is neither pious nor just, for the child he begets for the city, if it remains hidden, will be born in darkness, through a dangerous weakness of will, and without the benefit of the sacrifices and prayers offered at every marriage festival, in which the priests and priestesses, together with the entire city, ask that the children of good and beneficial parents may always prove themselves still better and more beneficial. b

That's right.

The same law will apply if a man still of begetting years has a child with a woman of child-bearing age without the sanction of the rulers. We'll say that he brings to the city an illegitimate, unauthorized, and unhallowed child.

That's absolutely right.

However, I think that when women and men have passed the age of having children, we'll leave them free to have sex with whomever they wish, with these exceptions: For a man—his daughter, his mother, his

c daughter's children, and his mother's ancestors; for a woman—her son and his descendants, her father and his ancestors. Having received these instructions, they should be very careful not to let a single fetus see the light of day, but if one is conceived and forces its way to the light, they must deal with it in the knowledge that no nurture is available for it.

That's certainly sensible. But how will they recognize their fathers and daughters and the others you

d mentioned?

They have no way of knowing. But a man will call all the children born in the tenth or seventh month after he became a bridegroom his sons, if they're male, and his daughters, if they're female, and they'll call him father. He'll call their children his grandchildren, and they'll call the group to which he belongs grandfathers and grandmothers. And those who were born at the same time as their mothers and fathers were having children they'll call their brothers and

e sisters. Thus, as we were saying, the relevant groups will avoid sexual relations with each other. But the law will allow brothers and sisters to have sex with one another if the lottery works out that way and the Pythia approves.

That's absolutely right.

This, then, Glaucon, is how the guardians of your city have their wives and children in common. We must now confirm that this arrangement is both consistent with the rest of the constitution and by far the best. Or how else are we to proceed?

462 In just that way.

Then isn't the first step towards agreement to ask ourselves what we say is the greatest good in designing the city—the good at which the legislator aims in making the laws—and what is the greatest evil? And isn't the next step to examine whether the system we've just described fits into the tracks of the good and not into those of the bad?

Absolutely.

Is there any greater evil we can mention for a city than that which tears it apart and makes it many instead of one? Or any greater good than that which

b binds it together and makes it one?

There isn't.

And when, as far as possible, all the citizens rejoice and are pained by the same successes and failures, doesn't this sharing of pleasures and pains bind the city together?

It most certainly does.

But when some suffer greatly, while others rejoice greatly, at the same things happening to the city or its people, doesn't this privatization of pleasures and pains dissolve the city?   c

Of course.

And isn't that what happens whenever such words as "mine" and "not mine" aren't used in unison? And similarly with "someone else's"?

Precisely.

Then, is the best-governed city the one in which most people say "mine" and "not mine" about the same things in the same way?

It is indeed.

What about the city that is most like a single person? For example, when one of us hurts his finger, the entire organism that binds body and soul together into a single system under the ruling part within it is aware of this, and the whole feels the pain together with the part that suffers. That's why we say that the man has a pain in his finger. And the same can be said about any part of   d a man, with regard either to the pain it suffers or to the pleasure it experiences when it finds relief.

Certainly. And, as for your question, the city with the best government *is* most like such a person.

Then, whenever anything good or bad happens to a single one of its citizens, such a city above all others will say that the affected part is its own and will share in the pleasure or pain as a whole.   e

If it has good laws, that must be so.

It's time now to return to our own city, to look there for the features we've agreed on, and to determine whether it or some other city possesses them to the greatest degree.

Then that's what we must do.

What about those other cities? Aren't there rulers and people in them, as well as in ours?   463

There are.

Besides fellow citizens, what do the people call the rulers in those other cities?

In many they call them despots, but in democracies they are called just this—rulers.

What about the people in our city? Besides fellow citizens, what do they call their rulers?

Preservers and auxiliaries.

And what do they in turn call the people?

Providers of upkeep and wages.

What do the rulers call the people in other cities?

Slaves.

And what do the rulers call each other?

Co-rulers.

And ours?

Co-guardians.

Can you tell me whether a ruler in those other cities could address some of his co-rulers as his kinsmen and others as outsiders?

Yes, many could.

And doesn't he consider his kinsman to be his own, and doesn't he address him as such, while he considers the outsider not to be his own?

He does.

What about your guardians? Could any of them consider a co-guardian as an outsider or address him as such?

There's no way he could, for when he meets any one of them, he'll hold that he's meeting a brother or sister, a father or mother, a son or daughter, or some ancestor or descendant of theirs.

You put that very well. But tell me this: Will your laws require them simply to use these kinship names or also to do all the things that go along with the names? Must they show to their "fathers" the respect, solicitude, and obedience we show to our parents by law? Won't they fare worse at the hands of gods and humans, as people whose actions are neither pious nor just, if they do otherwise? Will these be the oracular sayings they hear from all the citizens from their childhood on, or will they hear something else about their fathers—or the ones they're told are their fathers—and other relatives?

The former. It would be absurd if they only mouthed kinship names without doing the things that go along with them.

Therefore, in our city more than in any other, they'll speak in unison the words we mentioned a moment ago. When any one of them is doing well or badly, they'll say that "mine" is doing well or that "mine" is doing badly.

That's absolutely true.

Now, didn't we say that the having and expressing of this conviction is closely followed by the having of pleasures and pains in common?

Yes, and we were right.

Then won't our citizens, more than any others, have the same thing in common, the one they call "mine"? And, having that in common, won't they, more than any others, have common pleasures and pains?

Of course.

And, in addition to the other institutions, the cause of this is the having of wives and children in common by the guardians?

That more than anything else is the cause.

But we agreed that the having of pains and pleasures in common is the greatest good for a city, and we characterized a well-governed city in terms of the body's reaction to pain or pleasure in any one of its parts.

And we were right to agree.

Then, the cause of the greatest good for our city has been shown to be the having of wives and children in common by the auxiliaries.

It has.

And, of course, this is consistent with what we said before, for we said somewhere that, if they're going to be guardians, they mustn't have private houses, property, or possessions, but must receive their upkeep from the other citizens as a wage for their guardianship and enjoy it in common.

That's right.

Then isn't it true, just as I claimed, that what we are saying now, taken together with what we said before, makes even better guardians out of them and prevents them from tearing the city apart by not calling the same thing "mine"? If different people apply the term to different things, one would drag into his own house whatever he could separate from the others, and another would drag things into a different house to a different wife and children, and this would make for private pleasures and pains at private things. But our people, on the other hand, will think of the same things as their own, aim at the same goal, and, as far as possible, feel pleasure and pain in unison.

Precisely.

And what about lawsuits and mutual accusations? Won't they pretty well disappear from among them, because they have everything in common except their own bodies? Hence they'll be spared all the dissension that arises between people because of the possession of money, children, and families.

They'll necessarily be spared it.

Nor could any lawsuits for insult or injury justly occur among them, for we'll declare that it's a fine and just thing for people to defend themselves against others of the same age, since this will compel them to stay in good physical shape.

That's right.

465 This law is also correct for another reason: If a spirited person vents his anger in this way, it will be less likely to lead him into more serious disputes.

Certainly.

But an older person will be authorized to rule and punish all the younger ones.

Clearly.

And surely it's also obvious that a younger person won't strike or do any sort of violence to an older one or fail to show him respect in other ways, unless the rulers command it, for there are two guardians sufficient to prevent him from doing such things — shame and fear. Shame will prevent him from laying a hand on his parents, and so will the fear that the others would come to the aid of the victim, some as

b his sons, some as his brothers, and some as his fathers.

That's the effect they'll have.

Then, in all cases, won't the laws induce men to live at peace with one another?

Very much so.

And if there's no discord among the guardians, there's no danger that the rest of the city will break into civil war, either with them or among themselves.

Certainly not.

I hesitate to mention, since they're so unseemly, the pettiest of the evils the guardians would therefore escape: The poor man's flattery of the rich, the per-

c plexities and sufferings involved in bringing up children and in making the money necessary to feed the household, getting into debt, paying it off, and in some way or other providing enough money to hand over to their wives and household slaves to manage. All of the various troubles men endure in these matters are obvious, ignoble, and not worth discussing.

d They're obvious even to the blind.

They'll be free of all these, and they'll live a life more blessedly happy than that of the victors in the Olympian games.

How?

The Olympian victors are considered happy on account of only a small part of what is available to our guardians, for the guardians' victory is even greater, and their upkeep from public funds more complete. The victory they gain is the preservation of the whole city, and the crown of victory that they and their children receive is their upkeep and all the necessities of life. They receive rewards from their own city while they live, and at their death they're given a worthy burial.   e

Those are very good things.

Do you remember that, earlier in our discussion, someone — I forget who — shocked us by saying that we hadn't made our guardians happy, that it was possible for them to have everything that belongs to the citizens, yet they had nothing? We said, I think,   466 that if this happened to come up at some point, we'd look into it then, but that our concern at the time was to make our guardians true guardians and the city the happiest we could, rather than looking to any one group within it and molding it for happiness.

I remember.

Well, then, if the life of our auxiliaries is apparently much finer and better than that of Olympian victors, is there any need to compare it to the lives of cobblers, farmers, or other craftsmen?   b

Not in my opinion.

Then it's surely right to repeat here what I said then: If a guardian seeks happiness in such a way that he's no longer a guardian and isn't satisfied with a life that's moderate, stable, and — as we say — best, but a silly, adolescent idea of happiness seizes him and incites him to use his power to take everything in the city for himself, he'll come to know the true wisdom c of Hesiod's saying that somehow "the half is worth more than the whole."

If he takes my advice, he'll keep to his own life-style.

You agree, then, that the women and men should associate with one another in education, in things having to do with children, and in guarding the other citizens in the way we've described; that both when they remain in the city and when they go to war, they must guard together and hunt together like dogs and share in everything as far as possible; and that by d doing so they'll be doing what's best and not something contrary either to woman's nature as compared with man's or to the natural association of men and women with one another.

I agree.

Then doesn't it remain for us to determine whether it's possible to bring about this association among human beings, as it is among animals, and to say just how it might be done?

You took the words right out of my mouth.

As far as war is concerned, I think it's clear how
e they will wage it.

How so?

Men and women will campaign together. They'll take the sturdy children with them, so that, like the children of other craftsmen, they can see what they'll have to do when they grow up. But in addition to observing, they can serve and assist in everything to do with the war and help their mothers and fathers.
467 Haven't you noticed in the other crafts how the children of potters, for example, assist and observe for a long time before actually making any pots?

I have indeed.

And should these craftsmen take more care in training their children by appropriate experience and observation than the guardians?

Of course not; that would be completely ridiculous.

Besides, every animal fights better in the presence
b of its young.

That's so. But, Socrates, there's a considerable danger that in a defeat—and such things are likely to happen in a war—they'll lose their children's lives as well as their own, making it impossible for the rest of the city to recover.

What you say is true. But do you think that the first thing we should provide for is the avoidance of all danger?

Not at all.

Well, then, if people will probably have to face some danger, shouldn't it be the sort that will make them better if they come through it successfully?

Obviously.

And do you think that whether or not men who are going to be warriors observe warfare when they're still boys makes such a small difference that it isn't
c worth the danger of having them do it?

No, it does make a difference to what you're talking about.

On the assumption, then, that the children are to be observers of war, if we can contrive some way to keep them secure, everything will be fine, won't it?

Yes.

Well, then, in the first place, their fathers won't be ignorant, will they, about which campaigns are dangerous and which are not, but rather as knowledgeable about this as any human beings can be?   d

Probably so.

Then they'll take the children to some campaigns and not to others?

Correct.

And they'll put officers in charge of them whose age and experience qualifies them to be leaders and tutors?

Appropriately so.

But, as we say, the unexpected often occurs.

Indeed.

With this in mind, we must provide the children with wings when they're small, so that they can fly away and escape.

What do you mean?   e

We must mount them on horses as early as possible—not on spirited or aggressive horses, but on very fast and manageable ones—and when they've learned to ride, they must be taken to observe a war. In this way, they'll get the best look at their own work and, if the need arises, make the securest possible escape to safety, following their older guides.

I think you're right.

What about warfare itself? What attitude should your soldiers have to each other and to the enemy?   468
Are my views about this right or not?

First, tell me what they are.

If one of them leaves his post or throws away his shield or does anything else of that sort through cowardice, shouldn't he be reduced to being a craftsman or farmer?

Certainly.

And shouldn't anyone who is captured alive be left to his captors as a gift to do with as they wish?

Absolutely.   b

But don't you think that anyone who distinguishes himself and earns high esteem should, while still on the campaign, first be crowned with wreaths by each of the adolescents and children who accompany the expedition?

I do.

And what about shaken by the right hand?

That too.

But I suppose that you wouldn't go this far?

Namely?

That he should kiss and be kissed by each of them.

That most of all. And I'd add this to the law: As long as the campaign lasts, no one he wants to kiss shall be allowed to refuse, for then, if one of them happens to be in love with another, whether male or female, he'll be all the more eager to win the rewards of valor.

Excellent. And we've already stated that, since he's a good person, more marriages will be available to him, and he'll be selected for such things more frequently than the others, so that he'll beget as many children as possible.

Yes, we did say that.

Indeed, according to Homer too, it is just to honor in such ways those young people who are good, for he says that Ajax, when he distinguished himself in battle, "was rewarded with the long cut off the backbone." And that's an appropriate honor for a courageous young man, since it will both honor him and increase his strength.

That's absolutely right.

Then we'll follow Homer in these matters at least. And insofar as good people have shown themselves to be good, we'll honor them at sacrifices and all such occasions with hymns, "seats of honor, meats, and well-filled cups of wine," and in all the other ways we mentioned, so that, in addition to honoring good men and women, we'll continue to train them.

That's excellent.

All right. And as for those who died on the campaign, won't we say, first of all, that, if their deaths were distinguished, they belong to the golden race?

That above all.

And won't we believe with Hesiod that, whenever any of that race die, they become

469   *Sacred daemons living upon the earth,*
      Noble spirits, protectors against evil, guardians of
        articulate mortals?

We'll certainly believe that.

Then we'll inquire from the god what kind of distinguished funeral we should give to daemonic and godlike people, and we'll follow his instructions.

Of course.

And for the remainder of time, we'll care for their graves and worship at them as we would at those of daemons. And we'll follow the same rites for anyone whom we judge to have lived an outstandingly good life, whether he died of old age or in some other way.

That is only just.

Now, what about enemies? How will our soldiers deal with them?

In what respect?

First, enslavement. Do you think it is just for Greeks to enslave Greek cities, or, as far as they can, should they not even allow other cities to do so, and make a habit of sparing the Greek race, as a precaution against being enslaved by the barbarians?

It's altogether and in every way best to spare the Greek race.

Then isn't it also best for the guardians not to acquire a Greek slave and to advise the other Greeks not to do so either?

Absolutely. In that way they'd be more likely to turn against the barbarians and keep their hands off one another.

What about despoiling the dead? Is it a good thing to strip the dead of anything besides their armor after a victory? Or don't cowards make this an excuse for not facing the enemy—as if they were doing something of vital importance in bending over a corpse? And haven't many armies been lost because of such plundering?

Indeed, they have.

Don't you think it's slavish and money-loving to strip a corpse? Isn't it small-minded and womanish to regard the body as your enemy, when the enemy himself has flitted away, leaving behind only the instrument with which he fought? Or do you think such behavior any different from that of dogs who get angry with the stone that hits them and leave the thrower alone?

It's no different at all.

Then may our soldiers strip corpses or refuse the enemy permission to pick up their dead?

No, by god, they certainly may not.

Moreover, we won't take enemy arms to the temples as offerings, and if we care about the goodwill of other Greeks, we especially won't do this with *their* arms. Rather we'd be afraid of polluting the temples if we brought them such things from our own people, unless, of course, the god tells us otherwise.

That's absolutely right.

What about ravaging the land of the Greeks and burning their houses? Will your soldiers do things of this sort to their enemies?

I'd like to hear *your* opinion about that.

Well, I think they should do neither of these things but destroy the year's harvest only. Do you want me b to tell you why?

Of course.

It seems to me that as we have two names, "war" and "civil war," so there are two things and the names apply to two kinds of disagreements arising in them. The two things I'm referring to are what is one's own and akin, on the one hand, and what's foreign and strange, on the other. The name "civil war" applies to hostilities with one's own, while "war" applies to hostilities with strangers.

That's certainly to the point.

Then see whether this is also to the point: I say c that the Greek race is its own and akin, but is strange and foreign to barbarians.

That's right.

Then when Greeks do battle with barbarians or barbarians with Greeks, we'll say that they're natural enemies and that such hostilities are to be called war. But when Greeks fight with Greeks, we'll say that they are natural friends and that in such circumstances Greece is sick and divided into factions and that such d hostilities are to be called civil war.

I, at any rate, agree to think of it that way.

Now, notice that, wherever something of the sort that's currently called civil war occurs and a city is divided, if either party ravages the land of the others and burns their houses, it's thought that this is abominable and that neither party loves their city, since otherwise they'd never have ravaged their very nurse and mother. However, it *is* thought appropriate for the victors to carry off the harvest of the vanquished. Nonetheless, their attitude of mind should be that of e people who'll one day be reconciled and who won't always be at war.

This way of thinking is far more civilized than the other.

What about the city you're founding? It is Greek, isn't it?

It has to be.

Then, won't your citizens be good and civilized?

Indeed they will.

Then, won't they love Greece? Won't they consider Greece as their own and share the religion of the other Greeks?

Yes, indeed.

Then won't they consider their differences with Greeks—people who are their own—not as war but 471 as civil war?

Of course.

And won't they quarrel like people who know that one day they'll be reconciled?

Certainly.

Then they'll moderate their foes in a friendly spirit, not punish them with enslavement and destruction, for they're moderators, not enemies.

That's right.

And being Greeks, they won't ravage Greece or burn her houses, nor will they agree that in any of her cities all the inhabitants—men, women, and children—are their enemies, but that whatever differences arise are caused by the few enemies that any city inevitably contains. Because of this, because the majority are friendly, they won't ravage the country or destroy the houses, and they'll continue their quarrel only to the point at which those who caused it b are forced to pay the penalty by those who were its innocent victims.

I agree that this is the way our citizens must treat their enemies, and they must treat barbarians the way Greeks currently treat each other.

Then shall we also impose this law on the guardians: Neither ravage the country nor burn the houses? c

Consider it imposed. And let's also assume that this law and its predecessors are all fine. But I think, Socrates, that if we let you go on speaking about this subject, you'll never remember the one you set aside in order to say all this, namely, whether it's possible for this constitution to come into being and in what way it could be brought about. I agree that, if it existed, all the things we've mentioned would be good for the city in which they occurred. And I'll add some that you've left out. The guardians would be excellent fighters against an enemy because they'd be least likely to desert each other, since they know each other as brothers, fathers, and sons, and call each other by those names. Moreover, if their women joined their d campaigns, either in the same ranks or positioned in the rear to frighten the enemy and in case their help should ever be needed, I know that this would make them quite unbeatable. And I also see all the good things that they'd have at home that you've omitted.

e Take it that I agree that all these things would happen, as well as innumerable others, if this kind of constitution came into being, and say no more on that subject. But rather let's now try to convince ourselves that it is possible and how it is possible, and let the rest go.

This is a sudden attack that you've made on my
472 argument, and you show no sympathy for my delay. Perhaps you don't realize that, just as I've barely escaped from the first two waves of objections, you're bringing the third—the biggest and most difficult one—down upon me. When you see and hear it, you'll surely be completely sympathetic, and recognize that it was, after all, appropriate for me to hesitate and be afraid to state and look into so paradoxical a view.

The more you speak like that, the less we'll let you off from telling us how it's possible for this constitution
b to come into being. So speak instead of wasting time.

Well, then, we must first remember that we got to this point while trying to discover what justice and injustice are like.

We must. But what of it?

Nothing. But if we discover what justice is like, will we also maintain that the just man is in no way different from the just itself, so that he is like justice in every respect? Or will we be satisfied if he comes
c as close to it as possible and participates in it far more than anyone else?

We'll be satisfied with that.

Then it was in order to have a model that we were trying to discover what justice itself is like and what the completely just man would be like, if he came into being, and what kind of man he'd be if he did, and likewise with regard to injustice and the most unjust man. We thought that, by looking at how their relationship to happiness and its opposite seemed to us, we'd also be compelled to agree about ourselves as well, that the one who was most like them would
d have a portion of happiness most like theirs. But we weren't trying to discover these things in order to prove that it's possible for them to come into being.

That's true.

Do you think that someone is a worse painter if, having painted a model of what the finest and most beautiful human being would be like and having

rendered every detail of his picture adequately, he could not prove that such a man could come into being?

No, by god, I don't.

Then what about our own case? Didn't we say that we were making a theoretical model of a good city? *e*

Certainly.

So do you think that our discussion will be any less reasonable if we can't prove that it's possible to found a city that's the same as the one in our theory?

Not at all.

Then that's the truth of the matter. But if, in order to please you, I must also be willing to show how and under what conditions it would most be possible to found such a city, then you should agree to make the same concessions to me, in turn, for the purposes of this demonstration.

Which ones?

Is it possible to do anything in practice the same as in theory? Or is it in the nature of practice to grasp truth less well than theory does, even if some people don't think so? Will you first agree to this or not?   473

I agree.

Then don't compel me to show that what we've described in theory can come into being exactly as we've described it. Rather, if we're able to discover how a city could come to be governed in a way that most closely approximates our description, let's say that we've shown what you ordered us to show, namely, that it's possible for our city to come to be. Or wouldn't you be satisfied with that? *I* would be satisfied with it.   *b*

So would I.

Then next, it seems, we should try to discover and point out what's now badly done in cities that keeps them from being governed in that way and what's the smallest change that would enable our city to reach our sort of constitution—one change, if possible, or if not one, two, and if not two, then the fewest in number and the least extensive.

That's absolutely right.   *c*

There is one change we could point to that, in my opinion, would accomplish this. It's certainly neither small nor easy, but it is possible.

What is it?

Well, I've now come to what we likened to the greatest wave. But I shall say what I have to say, even if the wave is a wave of laughter that will simply drown me in ridicule and contempt. So listen to what I'm going to say.

Say on.

Until philosophers rule as kings or those who are now called kings and leading men genuinely and adequately philosophize, that is, until political power and philosophy entirely coincide, while the many natures who at present pursue either one exclusively are forcibly prevented from doing so, cities will have no rest from evils, Glaucon, nor, I think, will the human race. And, until this happens, the constitution we've been describing in theory will never be born to the fullest extent possible or see the light of the sun. It's because I saw how very paradoxical this statement would be that I hesitated to make it for so long, for it's hard to face up to the fact that there can be no happiness, either public or private, in any other city.

Socrates, after hurling a speech and statement like that at us, you must expect that a great many people (and not undistinguished ones either) will cast off their cloaks and, stripped for action, snatch any available weapon, and make a determined rush at you, ready to do terrible things. So, unless you can hold them off by argument and escape, you really will pay the penalty of general derision.

Well, you are the one that brought this on me.

And I was right to do it. However, I won't betray you, but rather defend you in any way I can—by goodwill, by urging you on, and perhaps by being able to give you more appropriate answers than someone else. So, with the promise of this assistance, try to show the unbelievers that things are as you say they are.

I must try it, then, especially since you agree to be so great an ally. If we're to escape from the people you mention, I think we need to define for them who the philosophers are that we dare to say must rule. And once that's clear, we should be able to defend ourselves by showing that the people we mean are fitted by nature both to engage in philosophy and to rule in a city, while the rest are naturally fitted to leave philosophy alone and follow their leader.

This would be a good time to give that definition.

Come, then, follow me, and we'll see whether or not there's some way to set it out adequately.

Lead on.

Do you need to be reminded or do you remember that, if it's rightly said that someone loves something, then he mustn't love one part of it and not another, but he must love all of it?

I think you'll have to remind me, for I don't understand it at all.

That would be an appropriate response, Glaucon, for somebody else to make. But it isn't appropriate for an erotically inclined man to forget that all boys in the bloom of youth pique the interest of a lover of boys and arouse him and that all seem worthy of his care and pleasure. Or isn't that the way you people behave to fine and beautiful boys? You praise a snub-nosed one as cute, a hook-nosed one you say is regal, one in between is well proportioned, dark ones look manly, and pale ones are children of the gods. And as for a honey-colored boy, do you think that this very term is anything but the euphemistic coinage of a lover who found it easy to tolerate sallowness, provided it was accompanied by the bloom of youth? In a word, you find all kinds of terms and excuses so as not to reject anyone whose flower is in bloom.

If you insist on taking me as your example of what erotically inclined men do, then, for the sake of the argument, I agree.

Further, don't you see wine-lovers behave in the same way? Don't they love every kind of wine and find any excuse to enjoy it?

Certainly.

And I think you see honor-lovers, if they can't be generals, be captains, and, if they can't be honored by people of importance and dignity, they put up with being honored by insignificant and inferior ones, for they desire the whole of honor.

Exactly.

Then do you agree to this or not? When we say that someone desires something, do we mean that he desires everything of that kind or that he desires one part of it but not another?

We mean he desires everything.

Then won't we also say that the philosopher doesn't desire one part of wisdom rather than another, but desires the whole thing?

Yes, that's true.

And as for the one who's choosy about what he learns, especially if he's young and can't yet give an account of what is useful and what isn't, we won't say that he is a lover of learning or a philosopher, for we wouldn't say that someone who's choosy about his food is hungry or has an appetite for food or is a lover of food—instead, we'd say that he is a bad eater.

And we'd be right to say it.

But the one who readily and willingly tries all kinds of learning, who turns gladly to learning and is insatiable for it, is rightly called a philosopher, isn't he?

d Then many strange people will be philosophers, for the lovers of sights seem to be included, since they take pleasure in learning things. And the lovers of sounds are very strange people to include as philosophers, for they would never willingly attend a serious discussion or spend their time that way, yet they run around to all the Dionysiac festivals, omitting none, whether in cities or villages, as if their ears were under contract to listen to every chorus. Are we to say that these people—and those who learn similar things or e petty crafts—are philosophers?

No, but they are *like* philosophers.

And who are the true philosophers?

Those who love the sight of truth.

That's right, but what exactly do you mean by it?

It would not be easy to explain to someone else, but I think that you will agree to this.

To what?

Since the beautiful is the opposite of the ugly, they are two.

476 Of course.

And since they are two, each is one?

I grant that also.

And the same account is true of the just and the unjust, the good and the bad, and all the forms. Each of them is itself one, but because they manifest themselves everywhere in association with actions, bodies, and one another, each of them appears to be many.

That's right.

So, I draw this distinction: On one side are those you just now called lovers of sights, lovers of crafts, and practical people; on the other side are those we are arguing about and whom one would alone b call philosophers.

How do you mean?

The lovers of sights and sounds like beautiful sounds, colors, shapes, and everything fashioned out of them, but their thought is unable to see and embrace the nature of the beautiful itself.

That's for sure.

In fact, there are very few people who would be able to reach the beautiful itself and see it by itself. Isn't that so?

Certainly.   c

What about someone who believes in beautiful things, but doesn't believe in the beautiful itself and isn't able to follow anyone who could lead him to the knowledge of it? Don't you think he is living in a dream rather than a wakened state? Isn't this dreaming: whether asleep or awake, to think that a likeness is not a likeness but rather the thing itself that it is like?

I certainly think that someone who does that is dreaming.

But someone who, to take the opposite case, believes in the beautiful itself, can see both it and the things that participate in it and doesn't believe that the participants are it or that it itself is the participants—is d he living in a dream or is he awake?

He's very much awake.

So we'd be right to call his thought knowledge, since he knows, but we should call the other person's thought opinion, since he opines?

Right.

What if the person who has opinion but not knowledge is angry with us and disputes the truth of what we are saying? Is there some way to console him and e persuade him gently, while hiding from him that he isn't in his right mind?

There must be.

Consider, then, what we'll say to him. Won't we question him like this? First, we'll tell him that nobody begrudges him any knowledge he may have and that we'd be delighted to discover that he knows something. Then we'll say: "Tell us, does the person who knows know something or nothing?" You answer for him.

He knows something.

Something that is or something that is not?

Something that is, for how could something that is not be known?   477

Then we have an adequate grasp of this: No matter how many ways we examine it, what is completely is completely knowable and what is in no way is in every way unknowable?

A most adequate one.

Good. Now, if anything is such as to be and also not to be, won't it be intermediate between what purely is and what in no way is?

Yes, it's intermediate.

Then, as knowledge is set over what is, while ignorance is of necessity set over what is not, mustn't we find an intermediate between knowledge and ignorance to be set over what is intermediate between what is and what is not, if there is such a

b thing?

Certainly.

Do we say that opinion is something?

Of course.

A different power from knowledge or the same?

A different one.

Opinion, then, is set over one thing, and knowledge over another, according to the power of each.

Right.

Now, isn't knowledge by its nature set over what is, to know it as it is? But first maybe we'd better be a bit more explicit.

How so?

Powers are a class of the things that are that enable

c us—or anything else for that matter—to do whatever we are capable of doing. Sight, for example, and hearing are among the powers, if you understand the kind of thing I'm referring to.

I do.

Here's what I think about them. A power has neither color nor shape nor any feature of the sort that many other things have and that I use to distinguish those things from one another. In the case of a power,

d I use only what it is set over and what it does, and by reference to these I call each the power it is: What is set over the same things and does the same I call the same power; what is set over something different and does something different I call a different one. Do you agree?

I do.

Then let's back up. Is knowledge a power, or what class would you put it in?

It's a power, the strongest of them all.

And what about opinion, is it a power or some

e other kind of thing?

It's a power as well, for it is what enables us to opine.

A moment ago you agreed that knowledge and opinion aren't the same.

How could a person with any understanding think that a fallible power is the same as an infallible one?

Right. Then we agree that opinion is clearly differ-

478 ent from knowledge.

It is different.

Hence each of them is by nature set over something different and does something different?

Necessarily.

Knowledge is set over what is, to know it as it is?

Yes.

And opinion opines?

Yes.

Does it opine the very thing that knowledge knows, so that the knowable and the opinable are the same, or is this impossible?

It's impossible, given what we agreed, for if a different power is set over something different, and opinion and knowledge are different powers, then the know- b able and the opinable cannot be the same.

Then, if what is is knowable, the opinable must be something other than what is?

It must.

Do we, then, opine what is not? Or is it impossible to opine what is not? Think about this. Doesn't someone who opines set his opinion over something? Or is it possible to opine, yet to opine nothing?

It's impossible.

But someone who opines opines some one thing?

Yes.

Surely the most accurate word for that which is not isn't "one thing" but "nothing"? c

Certainly.

But we had to set ignorance over what is not and knowledge over what is?

That's right.

So someone opines neither what is nor what is not?

How could it be otherwise?

Then opinion is neither ignorance nor knowledge?

So it seems.

Then does it go beyond either of these? Is it clearer than knowledge or darker than ignorance?

No, neither.

Is opinion, then, darker than knowledge but clearer than ignorance?

It is.

Then it lies between them? d

Yes.

So opinion is intermediate between those two?

Absolutely.

Now, we said that, if something could be shown, as it were, to be and not to be at the same time, it would be intermediate between what purely is and what in every way is not, and that neither knowledge nor ignorance would be set over it, but something intermediate between ignorance and knowledge?

Correct.

And now the thing we call opinion has emerged as being intermediate between them?

It has.

Apparently, then, it only remains for us to find *e* what participates in both being and not being and cannot correctly be called purely one or the other, in order that, if there is such a thing, we can rightly call it the opinable, thereby setting the extremes over the extremes and the intermediate over the intermediate. Isn't that so?

It is.

Now that these points have been established, I want *479* to address a question to our friend who doesn't believe in the beautiful itself or any form of the beautiful itself that remains always the same in all respects but who does believe in the many beautiful things—the lover of sights who wouldn't allow anyone to say that the beautiful itself is one or that the just is one or any of the rest: "My dear fellow," we'll say, "of all the many beautiful things, is there one that will not also appear ugly? Or is there one of those just things that will not also appear unjust? Or one of those pious things that will not also appear impious?"

There isn't one, for it is necessary that they appear *b* to be beautiful in a way and also to be ugly in a way, and the same with the other things you asked about.

What about the many doubles? Do they appear any the less halves than doubles?

Not one.

So, with the many bigs and smalls and lights and heavies, is any one of them any more the thing someone says it is than its opposite?

No, each of them always participates in both opposites.

Is any one of the manys what someone says it is, then, any more than it is not what he says it is?

No, they are like the ambiguities one is entertained with at dinner parties or like the children's riddle about the eunuch who threw something at a bat— *c* the one about what he threw at it and what it was in, for they are ambiguous, and one cannot understand them as fixedly being or fixedly not being or as both or as neither.

Then do you know how to deal with them? Or can you find a more appropriate place to put them than intermediate between being and not being? Surely, they can't *be* more than what is or *not be* more than what is not, for apparently nothing is darker than what is not or clearer than what is.   *d*

Very true.

We've now discovered, it seems, that according to the many conventions of the majority of people about beauty and the others, they are rolling around as intermediates between what is not and what purely is.

We have.

And we agreed earlier that anything of that kind would have to be called the opinable, not the knowable—the wandering intermediate grasped by the intermediate power.

We did.

As for those who study the many beautiful things but do not see the beautiful itself and are incapable *e* of following another who leads them to it, who see many just things but not the just itself, and so with everything—these people, we shall say, opine everything but have no knowledge of anything they opine.

Necessarily.

What about the ones who in each case study the things themselves that are always the same in every respect? Won't we say that they know and don't opine?

That's necessary too.

Shall we say, then, that these people love and embrace the things that knowledge is set over, as the *480* others do the things that opinion is set over? Remember we said that the latter saw and loved beautiful sounds and colors and the like but wouldn't allow the beautiful itself to be anything?

We remember, all right.

We won't be in error, then, if we call such people lovers of opinion rather than philosophers or lovers of wisdom and knowledge? Will they be angry with us if we call them that?

Not if they take my advice, for it isn't right to be angry with those who speak the truth.

As for those who in each case embrace the thing itself, we must call them philosophers, not lovers of opinion?

Most definitely.

Book VI

484 And so, Glaucon, I said, after a somewhat lengthy and difficult discussion, both the philosophers and the nonphilosophers have revealed who they are.

It probably wouldn't have been easy, he said, to have them do it in a shorter one.

Apparently not. But for my part, I think that the matter would have been better illuminated if we had only it to discuss and not all the other things that remain to be treated in order to discover the difference b between the just life and the unjust one.

What's our next topic?

What else but the one that's next in order? Since those who are able to grasp what is always the same in all respects are philosophers, while those who are not able to do so and who wander among the many things that vary in every sort of way are not philosophers, which of the two should be the leaders in a city?

What would be a sensible answer to that?

We should establish as guardians those who are clearly capable of guarding the laws and the ways of c life of the city.

That's right.

And isn't it clear that the guardian who is to keep watch over everything should be keen-sighted rather than blind?

Of course it's clear.

Do you think, then, that there's any difference between the blind and those who are really deprived of the knowledge of each thing that is? The latter have no clear model in their souls, and so they cannot—in the manner of painters—look to what is most true, make constant reference to it, and study it as exactly d as possible. Hence they cannot establish here on earth conventions about what is fine or just or good, when they need to be established, or guard and preserve them, once they have been established.

No, by god, there isn't much difference between them.

Should we, then, make these blind people our guardians or rather those who know each thing that is and who are not inferior to the others, either in experience or in any other part of virtue?

It would be absurd to choose anyone but philosophers, if indeed they're not inferior in these ways, for the respect in which they are superior is pretty well the most important one.

Then shouldn't we explain how it is possible for someone to have both these sorts of qualities? 485

Certainly.

Then, as we said at the beginning of this discussion, it is necessary to understand the nature of philosophers first, for I think that, if we can reach adequate agreement about that, we'll also agree that the same people *can* have both qualities and that no one but they should be leaders in cities.

How so?

Let's agree that philosophic natures always love the sort of learning that makes clear to them some feature of the being that always is and does not wander around b between coming to be and decaying.

And further, let's agree that, like the honor-lovers and erotically inclined men we described before, they love all such learning and are not willing to give up any part of it, whether large or small, more valuable or less so.

That's right.

Consider next whether the people we're describing must also have this in their nature. c

What?

They must be without falsehood—they must refuse to accept what is false, hate it, and have a love for the truth.

That's a reasonable addition, at any rate.

It's not only reasonable, it's entirely necessary, for it's necessary for a man who is erotically inclined by nature to love everything akin to or belonging to the boy he loves.

That's right.

And could you find anything that belongs more to wisdom than truth does?

Of course not.

Then is it possible for the same nature to be a philosopher—a lover of wisdom—and a lover of falsehood? d

Not at all.

Then someone who loves learning must above all strive for every kind of truth from childhood on.

Absolutely.

Now, we surely know that, when someone's desires incline strongly for one thing, they are thereby weakened for others, just like a stream that has been partly diverted into another channel.

Of course.

Then, when someone's desires flow towards learning and everything of that sort, he'd be concerned, I suppose, with the pleasures of the soul itself by itself, and he'd abandon those pleasures that come through the body—if indeed he is a true philosopher and not merely a counterfeit one.

e   That's completely necessary.

Then surely such a person is moderate and not at all a money-lover. It's appropriate for others to take seriously the things for which money and large expenditures are needed, but not for him.

That's right.

And of course there's also this to consider when you
486 are judging whether a nature is philosophic or not.

What's that?

If it is at all slavish, you should not overlook that fact, for pettiness is altogether incompatible with a soul that is always reaching out to grasp everything both divine and human as a whole.

That's completely true.

And will a thinker high-minded enough to study all time and all being consider human life to be something important?

He couldn't possibly.

b   Then will he consider death to be a terrible thing?

He least of all.

Then it seems a cowardly and slavish nature will take no part in true philosophy.

Not in my opinion.

And is there any way that an orderly person, who isn't money-loving, slavish, a boaster, or a coward, could become unreliable or unjust?

There isn't.

Moreover, when you are looking to see whether a soul is philosophic or not, you'll look to see whether it is just and gentle, from youth on, or savage and hard to associate with.

Certainly.

c   And here's something I think you won't leave out.

What?

Whether he's a slow learner or a fast one. Or do you ever expect anyone to love something when it pains him to do it and when much effort brings only small return?

No, it couldn't happen.

And what if he could retain nothing of what he learned, because he was full of forgetfulness? Could he fail to be empty of knowledge?

How could he?

Then don't you think that, if he's laboring in vain, he'd inevitably come to hate both himself and that activity in the end?

Of course.

Then let's never include a forgetful soul among those who are sufficiently philosophical for our purposes, but look for one with a good memory.   d

Absolutely.

Now, we'd certainly say that the unmusical and graceless element in a person's nature draws him to lack of due measure.

Of course.

And do you think that truth is akin to what lacks due measure or to what is measured?

To what is measured.

Then, in addition to those other things, let's look for someone whose thought is by nature measured and graceful and is easily led to the form of each thing that is.

Of course.

Well, then, don't you think the properties we've enumerated are compatible with one another and that each is necessary to a soul that is to have an   e
adequate and complete grasp of that which is?

They're all completely necessary.   487

Is there any objection you can find, then, to a way of life that no one can adequately follow unless he's by nature good at remembering, quick to learn, high-minded, graceful, and a friend and relative of truth, justice, courage, and moderation?

Not even Momus could find one.

When such people have reached maturity in age and education, wouldn't you entrust the city to them and to them alone?

And Adeimantus replied: No one would be able to contradict the things you've said, Socrates, but on each occasion that you say them, your hearers are affected in some such way as this. They think that,   b
because they're inexperienced in asking and answering questions, they're led astray a little bit by the argument at every question and that, when these little bits are added together at the end of the discussion, great is their fall, as the opposite of what they said at the outset comes to light. Just as inexperienced checkers players are trapped by the experts in the end and can't make a move, so they too are trapped in   c
the end and have nothing to say in this different kind

of checkers, which is played not with disks but with words. Yet the truth isn't affected by this outcome. I say this with a view to the present case, for someone might well say now that he's unable to oppose you as you ask each of your questions, yet he sees that of all those who take up philosophy—not those who merely dabble in it while still young in order to complete their upbringing and then drop it, but those d who continue in it for a longer time—the greatest number become cranks, not to say completely vicious, while those who seem completely decent are rendered useless to the city because of the studies you recommend.

When I'd heard him out, I said: Do you think that what these people say is false?

I don't know, but I'd be glad to hear what you think.

You'd hear that they seem to me to speak the truth.

How, then, can it be true to say that there will be e no end to evils in our cities until philosophers—people we agree to be useless—rule in them?

The question you ask needs to be answered by means of an image or simile.

And you, of course, aren't used to speaking in similes!

So! Are you making fun of me now that you've landed me with a claim that's so hard to establish? In any case, listen to my simile, and you'll appreciate 488 all the more how greedy for images I am. What the most decent people experience in relation to their city is so hard to bear that there's no other single experience like it. Hence to find an image of it and a defense for them, I must construct it from many sources, just as painters paint goat-stags by combining the features of different things. Imagine, then, that something like the following happens on a ship or on many ships. The shipowner is bigger and stronger than everyone else on board, but he's hard of hearing, b a bit short-sighted, and his knowledge of seafaring is equally deficient. The sailors are quarreling with one another about steering the ship, each of them thinking that he should be the captain, even though he's never learned the art of navigation, cannot point to anyone who taught it to him, or to a time when he learned it. Indeed, they claim that it isn't teachable and are ready to cut to pieces anyone who says that it is. They're always crowding around the shipowner, begging him and doing everything possible to get him

to turn the rudder over to them. And sometimes, if c they don't succeed in persuading him, they execute the ones who do succeed or throw them overboard, and then, having stupefied their noble shipowner with drugs, wine, or in some other way, they rule the ship, using up what's in it and sailing in the way that people like that are prone to do. Moreover, they call the person who is clever at persuading or forcing the shipowner to let them rule a "navigator," a "captain," and "one who knows ships," and dismiss anyone else d as useless. They don't understand that a true captain must pay attention to the seasons of the year, the sky, the stars, the winds, and all that pertains to his craft, if he's really to be the ruler of a ship. And they don't believe there is any craft that would enable him to determine how he should steer the ship, whether the others want him to or not, or any possibility of e mastering this alleged craft or of practicing it at the same time as the craft of navigation. Don't you think that the true captain will be called a real stargazer, a babbler, and a good-for-nothing by those who sail in ships governed in that way, in which such things happen? 489

I certainly do.

I don't think that you need to examine the simile in detail to see that the ships resemble cities and their attitude to the true philosophers, but you already understand what I mean.

Indeed, I do.

Then first tell this simile to anyone who wonders why philosophers aren't honored in the cities, and try to persuade him that there would be far more cause for wonder if they were honored. b

I will tell him.

Next tell him that what he says is true, that the best among the philosophers are useless to the majority. Tell him not to blame those decent people for this but the ones who don't make use of them. It isn't natural for the captain to beg the sailors to be ruled by him nor for the wise to knock at the doors of the rich—the man who came up with that wisecrack made a mistake. The natural thing is for the sick person, rich or poor, to knock at the doctor's door, and for anyone who needs to be ruled to knock at c the door of the one who can rule him. It isn't for the ruler, if he's truly any use, to beg the others to accept his rule. Tell him that he'll make no mistake in

likening those who rule in our cities at present to the
sailors we mentioned just now, and those who are
called useless stargazers to the true captains.

That's absolutely right.

Therefore, it isn't easy for the best ways of life
to be highly esteemed by people who, as in these
circumstances, follow the opposite ways. By far the
greatest and most serious slander on philosophy, how-
d ever, results from those who profess to follow the
philosophic way of life. I mean those of whom the
prosecutor of philosophy declared that the greatest
number are completely vicious and the most decent
useless. And I admitted that what he said was true,
didn't I?

Yes.

And haven't we explained why the decent ones
are useless?

Yes, indeed.

Then, do you next want us to discuss why it's inevitable that the greater number are vicious and to try
to show, if we can, that philosophy isn't responsible
e for this either?

Certainly.

Then, let's begin our dialogue by reminding ourselves of the point at which we began to discuss the
nature that someone must have if he is to become a
fine and good person. First of all, if you remember,
490 he had to be guided by the truth and always pursue
it in every way, or else he'd really be a boaster, with
no share at all in true philosophy.

That's what was said.

And isn't this view completely contrary to the opinions currently held about him?

It certainly is.

Then, won't it be reasonable for us to plead in his
defense that it is the nature of the real lover of learning
to struggle toward what is, not to remain with any of
the many things that are believed to be, that, as he
b moves on, he neither loses nor lessens his erotic love
until he grasps the being of each nature itself with
the part of his soul that is fitted to grasp it, because
of its kinship with it, and that, once getting near what
really is and having intercourse with it and having
begotten understanding and truth, he knows, truly
lives, is nourished, and—at that point, but not before—is relieved from the pains of giving birth?

That is the most reasonable defense possible.

Well, then, will such a person have any part in the
love of falsehood, or will he entirely hate it?

He'll hate it.   c

And if truth led the way, we'd never say, I suppose,
that a chorus of evils could ever follow in its train.

How could it?

But rather a healthy and just character, with moderation following it.

That's right.

What need is there, then, to marshal all over again
from the beginning the members of the philosophic
nature's chorus in their inevitable array? Remember
that courage, high-mindedness, ease in learning, and
a good memory all belong to it. Then you objected,
saying that anyone would be compelled to agree with
what we said, but that, if he abandoned the argument d
and looked at the very people the argument is about,
he'd say that some of them were useless, while the
majority had every kind of vice. So we examined the
reason for this slander and have now arrived at the
point of explaining why the majority of them are bad.
And it's for this reason that we've again taken up the
nature of the true philosophers and defined what it
necessarily has to be.

That's true.   e

We must now look at the ways in which this nature
is corrupted, how it's destroyed in many people, while
a small number (the ones that are called useless rather
than bad) escape. After that, we must look in turn at
the natures of the souls that imitate the philosophic
nature and establish themselves in its way of life, so
as to see what the people are like who thereby arrive 491
at a way of life they are unworthy of and that is beyond
them and who, because they often strike false notes,
bring upon philosophy the reputation that you said
it has with everyone everywhere.

In what ways are they corrupted?

I'll try to enumerate them for you if I can. I suppose
that everyone would agree that only a few natures
possess all the qualities that we just now said were
essential to becoming a complete philosopher and
that seldom occur naturally among human beings.
Or don't you think so?   b

I certainly do.

Consider, then, the many important ways in which
these few can be corrupted.

What are they?

What will surprise you most, when you hear it, is that each of the things we praised in that nature tends to corrupt the soul that has it and to drag it away from philosophy. I mean courage, moderation, and the other things we mentioned.

That does sound strange.

c Furthermore, all the things that are said to be good also corrupt it and drag it away—beauty, wealth, physical strength, relatives who are powerful in the city, and all that goes with these. You understand what I have in mind?

I do, and I'd be glad to learn even more about it.

If you correctly grasp the general point I'm after, it will be clear to you, and what I've said before won't seem so strange.

What do you want me to do?

d We know that the more vigorous any seed, developing plant, or animal is, the more it is deficient in the things that are appropriate for it to have when it is deprived of suitable food, season, or location. For the bad is more opposed to the good than is the merely not good.

Of course.

Then it's reasonable to say that the best nature fares worse, when unsuitably nurtured, than an ordinary one.

It is.

e Then won't we say the same thing about souls too, Adeimantus, that those with the best natures become outstandingly bad when they receive a bad upbringing? Or do you think that great injustices and pure wickedness originate in an ordinary nature rather than in a vigorous one that has been corrupted by its upbringing? Or that a weak nature is ever the cause of either great good or great evil?

No, you're right.

492 Now, I think that the philosophic nature as we defined it will inevitably grow to possess every virtue if it happens to receive appropriate instruction, but if it is sown, planted, and grown in an inappropriate environment, it will develop in quite the opposite way, unless some god happens to come to its rescue. Or do you agree with the general opinion that certain young people are actually corrupted by sophists—that there are certain sophists with significant influence on the young who corrupt them through private teaching? Isn't it rather the very people who say this who

are the greatest sophists of all, since they educate most completely, turning young and old, men and women, into precisely the kind of people they want b them to be?

When do they do that?

When many of them are sitting together in assemblies, courts, theaters, army camps, or in some other public gathering of the crowd, they object very loudly and excessively to some of the things that are said or done and approve others in the same way, shouting and clapping, so that the very rocks and surroundings echo the din of their praise or blame and double it. c In circumstances like that, what is the effect, as they say, on a young person's heart? What private training can hold out and not be swept away by that kind of praise or blame and be carried by the flood wherever it goes, so that he'll say that the same things are beautiful or ugly as the crowd does, follow the same way of life as they do, and be the same sort of person as they are?

He will be under great compulsion to do so, Socrates.   d

And yet we haven't mentioned the greatest compulsion of all.

What's that?

It's what these educators and sophists impose by their actions if their words fail to persuade. Or don't you know that they punish anyone who isn't persuaded, with disenfranchisement, fines, or death?

They most certainly do.

What other sophist, then, or what private conversations do you think will prevail in opposition to these?

I don't suppose that any will.   e

No, indeed, it would be very foolish even to try to oppose them, for there isn't now, hasn't been in the past, nor ever will be in the future anyone with a character so unusual that he has been educated to virtue in spite of the contrary education he received from the mob—I mean, a human character; the divine, as the saying goes, is an exception to the rule. You should realize that if anyone is saved and becomes what he ought to be under our present constitutions, he has been saved—you might rightly say—by 493 a divine dispensation.

I agree.

Well, then, you should also agree to this.

What?

Not one of those paid private teachers, whom the people call sophists and consider to be their rivals in craft, teaches anything other than the convictions that the majority express when they are gathered together. Indeed, these are precisely what the sophists call wisdom. It's as if someone were learning the moods and appetites of a huge, strong beast that he's rearing—

b how to approach and handle it, when it is most difficult to deal with or most gentle and what makes it so, what sounds it utters in either condition, and what sounds soothe or anger it. Having learned all this through tending the beast over a period of time, he calls this knack wisdom, gathers his information together as if it were a craft, and starts to teach it. In truth, he knows nothing about which of these convictions is fine or shameful, good or bad, just or unjust, but he applies all these names in accordance

c with how the beast reacts—calling what it enjoys good and what angers it bad. He has no other account to give of these terms. And he calls what he is compelled to do just and fine, for he hasn't seen and cannot show anyone else how much compulsion and goodness really differ. Don't you think, by god, that someone like that is a strange educator?

I do indeed.

Then does this person seem any different from the one who believes that it is wisdom to understand the

d moods and pleasures of a majority gathered from all quarters, whether they concern painting, music, or, for that matter, politics? If anyone approaches the majority to exhibit his poetry or some other piece of craftsmanship or his service to the city and gives them mastery over him to any degree beyond what's unavoidable, he'll be under Diomedean compulsion, as it's called, to do the sort of thing of which they approve. But have you ever heard anyone presenting an argument that such things are truly good and beautiful that wasn't absolutely ridiculous?

e No, and I don't expect ever to hear one.

Keeping all this in mind, recall the following question: Can the majority in any way tolerate or accept the reality of the beautiful itself, as opposed to the many beautiful things, or the reality of each thing

494 itself, as opposed to the corresponding many?

Not in any way.

Then the majority cannot be philosophic.

They cannot.

Hence they inevitably disapprove of those who practice philosophy?

Inevitably.

And so do all those private individuals who associate with the majority and try to please them.

Clearly.

Then, because of all that, do you see any salvation for someone who is by nature a philosopher, to insure that he'll practice philosophy correctly to the end? Think about what we've said before. We agreed that ease in learning, a good memory, courage, and high- b mindedness belong to the philosophic nature.

Yes.

And won't someone with a nature like that be first among the children in everything, especially if his body has a nature that matches that of his soul?

How could he not be?

Then I suppose that, as he gets older, his family and fellow citizens will want to make use of him in connection with their own affairs.

Of course.

Therefore they'll pay court to him with their requests and honors, trying by their flattery to secure c for themselves ahead of time the power that is going to be his.

That's what usually happens, at any rate.

What do you think someone like that will do in such circumstances, especially if he happens to be from a great city, in which he's rich, well-born, good-looking, and tall? Won't he be filled with impractical expectations and think himself capable of managing the affairs, not only of the Greeks, but of the barbarians as well? And as a result, won't he exalt himself to great heights and be brimming with pretension and pride that is empty and lacks understanding? d

He certainly will.

And if someone approaches a young man in that condition and gently tells him the truth, namely, that that there's no understanding in him, that he needs it, and that it can't be acquired unless he works like a slave to attain it, do you think that it will be easy for him to listen when he's in the midst of so many evils?

Far from it.

And even if a young man of that sort somehow sees the point and is guided and drawn to philosophy because of his noble nature and his kinship with e reason, what do you think those people will do, if they believe that they're losing their use of him and his companionship? Is there anything they won't do or say to him to prevent him from being persuaded? Or anything they won't do or say about his persuader—whether plotting against him in private or publicly bringing him into court—to prevent him from such persuasion?

495   There certainly isn't.

Then, is there any chance that such a person will practice philosophy?

None at all.

Do you see, then, that we weren't wrong to say that, when someone with a philosophic nature is badly brought up, the very components of his nature—together with the other so-called goods, such as wealth and other similar advantages—are themselves in a way the cause of his falling away from the philosophic way of life?

I do, and what we said was right.

These, then, are the many ways in which the best nature—which is already rare enough, as we said—is destroyed and corrupted, so that it cannot follow *b* the best way of life. And it is among these men that we find the ones who do the greatest evils to cities and individuals and also—if they happen to be swept that way by the current—the greatest good, for a petty nature will never do anything great, either to an individual or a city.

That's very true.

When these men, for whom philosophy is most *c* appropriate, fall away from her, they leave her desolate and unwed, and they themselves lead lives that are inappropriate and untrue. Then others, who are unworthy of her, come to her as to an orphan deprived of the protection of kinsmen and disgrace her. These are the ones who are responsible for the reproaches that you say are cast upon philosophy by those who revile her, namely, that some of those who consort with her are useless, while the majority deserve to suffer many bad things.

Yes, that is indeed what is said.

And it's a reasonable thing to say, for other little men—the ones who are most sophisticated at their own little crafts—seeing that this position, which is full of fine names and adornments, is vacated, leap *d* gladly from those little crafts to philosophy, like prisoners escaping from jail who take refuge in a temple.

Despite her present poor state, philosophy is still more high-minded than these other crafts, so that many people with defective natures desire to possess her, even though their souls are cramped and spoiled by the mechanical nature of their work, in just the way that their bodies are mutilated by their crafts and labors. Isn't that inevitable?   *e*

It certainly is.

Don't you think that a man of this sort looks exactly like a little bald-headed tinker who has come into some money and, having been just released from jail, has taken a bath, put on a new cloak, got himself up as a bridegroom, and is about to marry the boss's daughter because she is poor and abandoned?

They're exactly the same.   496

And what kind of children will that marriage produce? Won't they be illegitimate and inferior?

They have to be.

What about when men who are unworthy of education approach philosophy and consort with her unworthily? What kinds of thoughts and opinions are we to say they beget? Won't they truly be what are properly called sophisms, things that have nothing genuine about them or worthy of being called true wisdom?

That's absolutely right.

Then there remains, Adeimantus, only a very small group who consort with philosophy in a way that's worthy of her: A noble and well brought-up character, for example, kept down by exile, who remains with philosophy according to his nature because there is *b* no one to corrupt him, or a great soul living in a small city, who disdains the city's affairs and looks beyond them. A very few might be drawn to philosophy from other crafts that they rightly despise because they have good natures. And some might be held back by the bridle that restrains our friend Theages—for he's in every way qualified to be tempted away from philosophy, but his physical illness restrains him by keeping him out of politics. Finally, my own case *c* is hardly worth mentioning—my daemonic sign—because it has happened to no one before me, or to only a very few. Now, the members of this small group have tasted how sweet and blessed a possession philosophy is, and at the same time they've also seen the madness of the majority and realized, in a word, that hardly anyone acts sanely in public affairs and that there is no ally with whom they might go to the aid of justice and survive, that instead they'd perish d before they could profit either their city or their friends and be useless both to themselves and to others, just like a man who has fallen among wild animals and is neither willing to join them in doing injustice nor sufficiently strong to oppose the general savagery alone. Taking all this into account, they lead a quiet life and do their own work. Thus, like someone who takes refuge under a little wall from a storm of dust or hail driven by the wind, the philosopher—seeing others filled with lawlessness—is satisfied if he can somehow lead his present life free from injustice and impious acts and depart from it with good hope, e blameless and content.

Well, that's no small thing for him to have accom-497 plished before departing.

But it isn't the greatest either, since he didn't chance upon a constitution that suits him. Under a suitable one, his own growth will be fuller, and he'll save the community as well as himself. It seems to me that we've now sensibly discussed the reasons why philosophy is slandered and why the slanderer is unjust—unless, of course, you have something to add.

I have nothing to add on that point. But which of our present constitutions do you think is suitable for philosophers?

None of them. That's exactly my complaint: None b of our present constitutions is worthy of the philosophic nature, and, as a result, this nature is perverted and altered, for, just as a foreign seed, sown in alien ground, is likely to be overcome by the native species and to fade away among them, so the philosophic nature fails to develop its full power and declines into c a different character. But if it were to find the best constitution, as it is itself the best, it would be clear that it is really divine and that other natures and ways of life are merely human. Obviously you're going to ask next what the best constitution is.

You're wrong there; I wasn't going to ask that, but whether it was the constitution we described when we were founding our city or some other one.

In the other respects, it is that one. But we said even then that there must always be some people in the city who have a theory of the constitution, the same one that guided you, the lawgiver, when you d made the laws.

We did say that.

Yes, but we didn't emphasize it sufficiently, for fear of what your objections have made plain, namely, that its proof would be long and difficult. And indeed what remains is by no means easy to go through.

What's that?

How a city can engage in philosophy without being destroyed, for all great things are prone to fall, and, as the saying goes, fine things are really hard to achieve.

Nevertheless, to complete our discussion, we'll have to get clear about this.   e

If anything prevents us from doing it, it won't be lack of willingness but lack of ability. At least you'll see how willing I am, for notice again how enthusiastically and recklessly I say that the manner in which a city ought to take up the philosophic way of life is the opposite of what it does at present.

How?

At present, those who study philosophy do so as young men who have just left childhood behind and have yet to take up household management and money-making. But just when they reach the hardest 498 part—I mean the part that has to do with giving a rational account—they abandon it and are regarded as fully trained in philosophy. In later life, they think they're doing well if they are willing to be in an invited audience when others are doing philosophy, for they think they should do this only as a sideline. And, with a few exceptions, by the time they reach old age, their eagerness for philosophy is quenched more thoroughly than the sun of Heraclitus, which is never rekindled.   b

What should they do?

Entirely the opposite. As youths and children, they should put their minds to youthful education and philosophy and take care of their bodies at a time when they are growing into manhood, so as to acquire a helper for philosophy. As they grow older and their souls begin to reach maturity, they should increase their mental exercises. Then, when their strength begins to fail and they have retired from politics and military service, they should graze freely in the pastures of philosophy and do nothing else—I mean the ones who are to live happily and, in death, add a fitting destiny c in that other place to the life they have lived.

You seem to be speaking with true enthusiasm, Socrates. But I'm sure that most of your hearers, beginning with Thrasymachus, will oppose you with even greater enthusiasm and not be at all convinced.

Don't slander Thrasymachus and me just as we've become friends—not that we were enemies before. *d* We won't relax our efforts until we either convince him and the others or, at any rate, do something that may benefit them in a later incarnation, when, reborn, they happen upon these arguments again.

That's a short time you're talking about!

It's nothing compared to the whole of time. All the same, it's no wonder that the majority of people aren't convinced by our arguments, for they've never seen a *man* that fits our *plan* (and the rhymes of this sort they have heard are usually intended and not, like this one, the product of mere chance). That is *e* to say, they've never seen a man or a number of men who themselves rhymed with virtue, were assimilated to it as far as possible, and ruled in a city of the same *499* type. Or do you think they have?

I don't think so at all.

Nor have they listened sufficiently to fine and free arguments that search out the truth in every way for the sake of knowledge but that keep away from the sophistications and eristic quibbles that, both in public trials and in private gatherings, aim at nothing except reputation and disputation.

No, they haven't.

It was because of this, because we foresaw these difficulties, that we were afraid. Nonetheless, we were *b* compelled by the truth to say that no city, constitution, or individual man will ever become perfect until either some chance event compels those few philosophers who aren't vicious (the ones who are now called useless) to take charge of a city, whether they want to or not, and compels the city to obey them, or until a god inspires the present rulers and kings or their offspring with a true erotic love for true philosophy. Now, it cannot be reasonably maintained, in my view, *c* that either of these things is impossible, but if it could, we'd be justly ridiculed for indulging in wishful thinking. Isn't that so?

It is.

Then, if in the limitless past, those who were foremost in philosophy were forced to take charge of a city or if this is happening now in some foreign place far beyond our ken or if it will happen in the future, *d* we are prepared to maintain our argument that, at whatever time the muse of philosophy controls a city, the constitution we've described will also exist at that time, whether it is past, present, or future. Since it

is not impossible for this to happen, we are not speaking of impossibilities. That it is *difficult* for it to happen, however, we agree ourselves.

That's my opinion, anyway.

But the majority don't share your opinion—is that what you are going to say?

They probably don't.

You should not make such wholesale charges against the majority, for they'll no doubt come to a different opinion, if instead of indulging your love of *e* victory at their expense, you soothe them and try to remove their slanderous prejudice against the love of learning, by pointing out what you mean by a philosopher and by defining the philosophic nature and way of life, as we did just now, so that they'll *500* realize that you don't mean the same people as they do. And if they once see it your way, even you will say that they'll have a different opinion from the one you just attributed to them and will answer differently. Or do you think that anyone who is gentle and without malice is harsh with someone who is neither irritable nor malicious? I'll anticipate your answer and say that a few people may have such a harsh character, but not the majority.

And, of course, I agree.

Then don't you also agree that the harshness the majority exhibit towards philosophy is caused by those *b* outsiders who don't belong and who've burst in like a band of revellers, always abusing one another, indulging their love of quarrels, and arguing about human beings in a way that is wholly inappropriate to philosophy?

I do indeed.

No one whose thoughts are truly directed towards the things that are, Adeimantus, has the leisure to look down at human affairs or to be filled with envy and hatred by competing with people. Instead, as he looks at and studies things that are organized and *c* always the same, that neither do injustice to one another nor suffer it, being all in a rational order, he imitates them and tries to become as like them as he can. Or do you think that someone can consort with things he admires without imitating them?

I do not. It's impossible.

Then the philosopher, by consorting with what is ordered and divine and despite all the slanders around that say otherwise, himself becomes as divine and ordered as a human being can. *d*

That's absolutely true.

And if he should come to be compelled to put what he sees there into people's characters, whether into a single person or into a populace, instead of shaping only his own, do you think that he will be a poor craftsman of moderation, justice, and the whole of popular virtue?

He least of all.

And when the majority realize that what we are saying about the philosopher is true, will they be harsh with him or mistrust us when we say that the e city will never find happiness until its outline is sketched by painters who use the divine model?

They won't be harsh, if indeed they realize this.

501 But what sort of sketch do you mean?

They'd take the city and the characters of human beings as their sketching slate, but first they'd wipe it clean—which isn't at all an easy thing to do. And you should know that this is the plain difference between them and others, namely, that they refuse to take either an individual or a city in hand or to write laws, unless they receive a clean slate or are allowed to clean it themselves.

And they'd be right to refuse.

Then don't you think they'd next sketch the outline of the constitution?

Of course.

And I suppose that, as they work, they'd look often b in each direction, towards the natures of justice, beauty, moderation, and the like, on the one hand, and towards those they're trying to put into human beings, on the other. And in this way they'd mix and blend the various ways of life in the city until they produced a human image based on what Homer too called "the divine form and image" when it occurred among human beings.

That's right.

They'd erase one thing, I suppose, and draw in another until they'd made characters for human be- c ings that the gods would love as much as possible.

At any rate, that would certainly result in the finest sketch.

Then is this at all persuasive to those you said were straining to attack us—that the person we were praising is really a painter of constitutions? They were angry because we entrusted the city to him: Are they any calmer, now that they've heard what we had to say?

They'll be much calmer, if they have any moderation.

Indeed, how could they possibly dispute it? Will they deny that philosophers are lovers of what is or d of the truth?

That would be absurd.

Or that their nature as we've described it is close to the best?

They can't deny that either.

Or that such a nature, if it follows its own way. of life, isn't as completely good and philosophic as any other? Or that the people we excluded are more so?

Certainly not.   e

Then will they still be angry when we say that, until philosophers take control of a city, there'll be no respite from evil for either city or citizens, and the constitution we've been describing in theory will never be completed in practice?

They'll probably be less angry.

Then if it's all right with you, let's not say that they'll simply be less angry but that they'll become altogether gentle and persuaded, so that they'll be shamed into agreeing with us, if nothing else.   502

It's all right with me.

Let's assume, therefore, that they've been convinced on this point. Will anyone dispute our view that the offspring of kings or rulers could be born with philosophic natures?

No one would do that.

Could anyone claim that, if such offspring are born, they'll inevitably be corrupted? We agree ourselves that it's hard for them to be saved from corruption, but could anyone claim that in the whole of time not one of them could be saved?   b

How could he?

But surely one such individual would be sufficient to bring to completion all the things that now seem so incredible, provided that his city obeys him.

One would be sufficient.

If a ruler established the laws and ways of life we've described, it is surely not impossible that the citizens would be willing to carry them out.

Not at all.

And would it be either astonishing or impossible that others should think as we do?

I don't suppose it would.   c

But I think our earlier discussion was sufficient to show that these arrangements are best, if only they are possible.

Indeed it was.

Then we can now conclude that this legislation is best, if only it is possible, and that, while it is hard for it to come about, it is not impossible.

We can.

Now that this difficulty has been disposed of, we must deal with what remains, namely, how the saviors of our constitution will come to be in the city, what subjects and ways of life will cause them to come into being, and at what ages they'll take each of them up.

Indeed we must.

It wasn't very clever of me to omit from our earlier discussion the troublesome topics of acquiring wives, begetting children, and appointing rulers, just because I knew that the whole truth would provoke resentment and would be hard to bring about in practice, for as it turned out, I had to go through these matters anyway. The subject of women and children has been adequately dealt with, but that of the rulers has to be taken up again from the beginning. We said, if you remember, that they must show themselves to be lovers of their city when tested by pleasure and pain and that they must hold on to their resolve through labors, fears, and all other adversities. Anyone who was incapable of doing so was to be rejected, while anyone who came through unchanged—like gold tested in a fire—was to be made ruler and receive prizes both while he lived and after his death. These were the sort of things we were saying while our argument, afraid of stirring up the very problems that now confront us, veiled its face and slipped by.

That's very true; I do remember it.

We hesitated to say the things we've now dared to say anyway. So let's now also dare to say that those who are to be made our guardians in the most exact sense of the term must be philosophers.

Let's do it.

Then you should understand that there will probably be only a few of them, for they have to have the nature we described, and its parts mostly grow in separation and are rarely found in the same person.

What do you mean?

You know that ease of learning, good memory, quick wits, smartness, youthful passion, high-minded-ness, and all the other things that go along with these are rarely willing to grow together in a mind that will choose an orderly life that is quiet and completely stable, for the people who possess the former traits are carried by their quick wits wherever chance leads them and have no stability at all.

That's true.

On the other hand, people with stable characters, who don't change easily, who aren't easily frightened in battle, and whom one would employ because of their greater reliability, exhibit similar traits when it comes to learning: They are as hard to move and teach as people whose brains have become numb, and they are filled with sleep and yawning whenever they have to learn anything.

That's so.

Yet we say that someone must have a fine and goodly share of both characters, or he won't receive the truest education, honors, or rule.

That's right.

Then, don't you think that such people will be rare?

Of course.

Therefore they must be tested in the labors, fears, and pleasures we mentioned previously. But they must also be exercised in many other subjects—which we didn't mention but are adding now—to see whether they can tolerate the most important subjects or will shrink from them like the cowards who shrink from other tests.

It's appropriate to examine them like that. But what do you mean by the most important subjects?

Do you remember when we distinguished three parts in the soul, in order to help bring out what justice, moderation, courage, and wisdom each is?

If I didn't remember that, it wouldn't be just for me to hear the rest.

What about what preceded it?

What was that?

We said, I believe, that, in order to get the finest possible view of these matters, we would need to take a longer road that would make them plain to anyone who took it but that it was possible to give demonstrations of what they are that would be up to the standard of the previous argument. And you said that that would be satisfactory. So it seems to me that our discussion at that time fell short of exactness, but whether or not it satisfied you is for you to say.

I thought you gave us good measure and so, apparently, did the others.

Any measure of such things that falls short in any
c way of that which is is not good measure, for nothing incomplete is the measure of anything, although people are sometimes of the opinion that an incomplete treatment is nonetheless adequate and makes further investigation unnecessary.

Indeed, laziness causes many people to think that.

It is a thought that a guardian of a city and its laws can well do without.

Probably so.

Well, then, he must take the longer road and put as much effort into learning as into physical training, for otherwise, as we were just saying, he will never
d reach the goal of the most important subject and the most appropriate one for him to learn.

Aren't these virtues, then, the most important things? he asked. Is there anything even more important than justice and the other virtues we discussed?

There is something more important. However, even for the virtues themselves, it isn't enough to look at a mere sketch, as we did before, while neglecting the most complete account. It's ridiculous, isn't it, to strain every nerve to attain the utmost exactness and clarity about other things of little value and not to consider the most important things worthy of the
e greatest exactness?

It certainly is. But do you think that anyone is going to let you off without asking you what this most important subject is and what it concerns?

No, indeed, and you can ask me too. You've certainly heard the answer often enough, but now either you aren't thinking or you intend to make trouble for me again by interrupting. And I suspect the latter,
505 for you've often heard it said that the form of the good is the most important thing to learn about and that it's by their relation to it that just things and the others become useful and beneficial. You know very well now that I am going to say this, and, besides, that we have no adequate knowledge of it. And you also know that, if we don't know it, even the fullest possible knowledge of other things is of no benefit to us, any more than if we acquire any possession without the good of it. Or do you think that it is any advantage to have every kind of possession without the good of
b it? Or to know everything except the good, thereby knowing nothing fine or good?

No, by god, I don't.

Furthermore, you certainly know that the majority believe that pleasure is the good, while the more sophisticated believe that it is knowledge.

Indeed I do.

And you know that those who believe this can't tell us what sort of knowledge it is, however, but in the end are forced to say that it is knowledge of the good.

And that's ridiculous.

Of course it is. They blame us for not knowing the good and then turn around and talk to us as if we c did know it. They say that it is knowledge of the good—as if we understood what they're speaking about when they utter the word "good."

That's completely true.

What about those who define the good as pleasure? Are they any less full of confusion than the others? Aren't even they forced to admit that there are bad pleasures?

Most definitely.

So, I think, they have to agree that the same things are both good and bad. Isn't that true?

Of course.   d

It's clear, then, isn't it, why there are many large controversies about this?

How could it be otherwise?

And isn't this also clear? In the case of just and beautiful things, many people are content with what are believed to be so, even if they aren't really so, and they act, acquire, and form their own beliefs on that basis. Nobody is satisfied to acquire things that are merely believed to be good, however, but everyone wants the things that really *are* good and disdains mere belief here.

That's right.

Every soul pursues the good and does whatever it does for its sake. It divines that the good is something e but it is perplexed and cannot adequately grasp what it is or acquire the sort of stable beliefs it has about other things, and so it misses the benefit, if any, that even those other things may give. Will we allow the best people in the city, to whom we entrust everything, to be so in the dark about something of this kind and 506 of this importance?

That's the last thing we'd do.

I don't suppose, at least, that just and fine things will have acquired much of a guardian in someone who doesn't even know in what way they are good. And I divine that no one will have adequate knowledge of them until he knows this.

You've divined well.

But won't our constitution be perfectly ordered, if b a guardian who knows these things is in charge of it?

Necessarily. But, Socrates, you must also tell us whether you consider the good to be knowledge or pleasure or something else altogether.

What a man! It's been clear for some time that other people's opinions about these matters wouldn't satisfy you.

Well, Socrates, it doesn't seem right to me for you to be willing to state other people's convictions but not your own, especially when you've spent so much c time occupied with these matters.

What? Do you think it's right to talk about things one doesn't know as if one does know them?

Not as if one knows them, he said, but one ought to be willing to state one's opinions as such.

What? Haven't you noticed that opinions without knowledge are shameful and ugly things? The best of them are blind—or do you think that those who express a true opinion without understanding are any different from blind people who happen to travel the right road?

They're no different.

Do you want to look at shameful, blind, and crooked things, then, when you might hear illuminat-d ing and fine ones from other people?

By god, Socrates, Glaucon said, don't desert us with the end almost in sight. We'll be satisfied if you discuss the good as you discussed justice, moderation, and the rest.

That, my friend, I said, would satisfy me too, but I'm afraid that I won't be up to it and that I'll disgrace myself and look ridiculous by trying. So let's abandon the quest for what the good itself is for the time being, e for even to arrive at my own view about it is too big a topic for the discussion we are now started on. But I am willing to tell you about what is apparently an offspring of the good and most like it. Is that agreeable to you, or would you rather we let the whole matter drop?

It is. The story about the father remains a debt you'll pay another time.

I wish that I could pay the debt in full, and you 507 receive it instead of just the interest. So here, then,

is this child and offspring of the good. But be careful that I don't somehow deceive you unintentionally by giving you an illegitimate account of the child.

We'll be as careful as possible, so speak on.

I will when we've come to an agreement and recalled some things that we've already said both here and many other times.

Which ones?   b

We say that there are many beautiful things and many good things, and so on for each kind, and in this way we distinguish them in words.

We do.

And beauty itself and good itself and all the things that we thereby set down as many, reversing ourselves, we set down according to a single form of each, believing that there is but one, and call it "the being" of each.

That's true.

And we say that the many beautiful things and the rest are visible but not intelligible, while the forms are intelligible but not visible.

That's completely true.

With what part of ourselves do we see visible things?   c

With our sight.

And so audible things are heard by hearing, and with our other senses we perceive all the other perceptible things.

That's right.

Have you considered how lavish the maker of our senses was in making the power to see and be seen?

I can't say I have.

Well, consider it this way. Do hearing and sound need another kind of thing in order for the former to hear and the latter to be heard, a third thing in whose absence the one won't hear or the other be heard?   d

No, they need nothing else.

And if there are any others that need such a thing, there can't be many of them. Can you think of one?

I can't.

You don't realize that sight and the visible have such a need?

How so?

Sight may be present in the eyes, and the one who has it may try to use it, and colors may be present in things, but unless a third kind of thing is present, which is naturally adapted for this very purpose, you know that sight will see nothing, and the colors will e remain unseen.

What kind of thing do you mean?

I mean what you call light.

You're right.

Then it isn't an insignificant kind of link that con-
508 nects the sense of sight and the power to be seen—
it is a more valuable link than any other linked things
have got, if indeed light is something valuable.

And, of course, it's very valuable.

Which of the gods in heaven would you name as
the cause and controller of this, the one whose light
causes our sight to see in the best way and the visible
things to be seen?

The same one you and others would name. Obviously, the answer to your question is the sun.

And isn't sight by nature related to that god in
this way?

Which way?

Sight isn't the sun, neither sight itself nor that in
b which it comes to be, namely, the eye.

No, it certainly isn't.

But I think that it is the most sunlike of the senses.

Very much so.

And it receives from the sun the power it has, just
like an influx from an overflowing treasury.

Certainly.

The sun is not sight, but isn't it the cause of sight
itself and seen by it?

That's right.

Let's say, then, that this is what I called the offspring
of the good, which the good begot as its analogue.
What the good itself is in the intelligible realm, in
relation to understanding and intelligible things, the
c sun is in the visible realm, in relation to sight and
visible things.

How? Explain a bit more.

You know that, when we turn our eyes to things
whose colors are no longer in the light of day but in
the gloom of night, the eyes are dimmed and seem
nearly blind, as if clear vision were no longer in them.

Of course.

Yet whenever one turns them on things illuminated
by the sun, they see clearly, and vision appears in
d those very same eyes?

Indeed.

Well, understand the soul in the same way: When
it focuses on something illuminated by truth and what
is, it understands, knows, and apparently possesses
understanding, but when it focuses on what is mixed
with obscurity, on what comes to be and passes away,
it opines and is dimmed, changes its opinions this
way and that, and seems bereft of understanding.

It does seem that way.

So that what gives truth to the things known and
the power to know to the knower is the form of the
good. And though it is the cause of knowledge and
truth, it is also an object of knowledge. Both knowledge and truth are beautiful things, but the good is
other and more beautiful than they. In the visible
realm, light and sight are rightly considered sunlike,
but it is wrong to think that they are the sun, so here
it is right to think of knowledge and truth as goodlike
but wrong to think that either of them is the good—
for the good is yet more prized.

This is an inconceivably beautiful thing you're talking about, if it provides both knowledge and truth
and is superior to them in beauty. You surely don't
think that a thing like that could be pleasure.

Hush! Let's examine its image in more detail as
follows.

How?

You'll be willing to say, I think, that the sun not
only provides visible things with the power to be seen
but also with coming to be, growth, and nourishment,
although it is not itself coming to be.

How could it be?

Therefore, you should also say that not only do the
objects of knowledge owe their being known to the
good, but their being is also due to it, although the
good is not being, but superior to it in rank and power.

And Glaucon comically said: By Apollo, what a
daemonic superiority!

It's your own fault; you forced me to tell you my
opinion about it.

And I don't want you to stop either. So continue
to explain its similarity to the sun, if you've omitted anything.

I'm certainly omitting a lot.

Well, don't, not even the smallest thing.

I think I'll have to omit a fair bit, but, as far as is
possible at the moment, I won't omit anything voluntarily.

Don't.

Understand, then, that, as we said, there are these
two things, one sovereign of the intelligible kind and
place, the other of the visible (I don't say "of heaven"
so as not to seem to you to be playing the sophist

with the name). In any case, you have two kinds of thing, visible and intelligible.

Right.

It is like a line divided into two unequal sections. Then divide each section—namely, that of the visible and that of the intelligible—in the same ratio as the line. In terms now of relative clarity and opacity, one subsection of the visible consists of images. And by images I mean, first, shadows, then reflections in *e* water and in all close-packed, smooth, and shiny materials, and everything of that sort, if you under-*510* stand.

I do.

In the other subsection of the visible, put the originals of these images, namely, the animals around us, all the plants, and the whole class of manufactured things.

Consider them put.

Would you be willing to say that, as regards truth and untruth, the division is in this proportion: As the opinable is to the knowable, so the likeness is to the thing that it is like?

b Certainly.

Consider now how the section of the intelligible is to be divided.

How?

As follows: In one subsection, the soul, using as images the things that were imitated before, is forced to investigate from hypotheses, proceeding not to a first principle but to a conclusion. In the other subsection, however, it makes its way to a first principle that is *not* a hypothesis, proceeding from a hypothesis but without the images used in the previous subsection, using forms themselves and making its investigation through them.

I don't yet fully understand what you mean.

Let's try again. You'll understand it more easily *c* after the following preamble. I think you know that students of geometry, calculation, and the like hypothesize the odd and the even, the various figures, the three kinds of angles, and other things akin to these in each of their investigations, as if they knew them. They make these their hypotheses and don't think it necessary to give any account of them, either to themselves or to others, as if they were clear to everyone. And going from these first principles through *d* the remaining steps, they arrive in full agreement.

I certainly know that much.

Then you also know that, although they use visible figures and make claims about them, their thought isn't directed to them but to those other things that they are like. They make their claims for the sake of square itself and the diagonal itself, not the diagonal they draw, and similarly with the others. These figures that they make and draw, of which shadows and re- *e* flections in water are images, they now in turn use as images, in seeking to see those others themselves that one cannot see except by means of thought. *511*

That's true.

This, then, is the kind of thing that, on the one hand, I said is intelligible, and, on the other, is such that the soul is forced to use hypotheses in the investigation of it, not travelling up to a first principle, since it cannot reach beyond its hypotheses, but using as images those very things of which images were made in the section below, and which, by comparison to their images, were thought to be clear and to be valued as such.

I understand that you mean what happens in geometry and related sciences. *b*

Then also understand that, by the other subsection of the intelligible, I mean that which reason itself grasps by the power of dialectic. It does not consider these hypotheses as first principles but truly as hypotheses—but as stepping stones to take off from, enabling it to reach the unhypothetical first principle of everything. Having grasped this principle, it reverses itself and, keeping hold of what follows from it, comes down to a conclusion without making use of anything visible at all, but only of forms themselves, moving on from forms to forms, and ending in forms. *c*

I understand, if not yet adequately (for in my opinion you're speaking of an enormous task), that you want to distinguish the intelligible part of that which is, the part studied by the science of dialectic, as clearer than the part studied by the so-called sciences, for which their hypotheses are first principles. And although those who study the objects of these sciences are forced to do so by means of thought rather than sense perception, still, because they do not go back to a genuine first principle, but proceed from hypothe- *d* ses, you don't think that they understand them, even though, given such a principle, they are intelligible. And you seem to me to call the state of the geometers thought but not understanding, thought being intermediate between opinion and understanding.

Your exposition is most adequate. Thus there are four such conditions in the soul, corresponding to the four subsections of our line: Understanding for the highest, thought for the second, belief for the third, and imaging for the last. Arrange them in a ratio, and consider that each shares in clarity to the degree that the subsection it is set over shares in truth.

I understand, agree, and arrange them as you say.

BOOK VII

514 Next, I said, compare the effect of education and of the lack of it on our nature to an experience like this: Imagine human beings living in an underground, cavelike dwelling, with an entrance a long way up, which is both open to the light and as wide as the cave itself. They've been there since childhood, fixed in the same place, with their necks and legs fettered, able to see only in front of them, because their bonds prevent them from turning their heads around. Light is provided by a fire burning far above and behind them. Also behind them, but on higher ground, there is a path stretching between them and the fire. Imagine that along this path a low wall has been built, like the screen in front of puppeteers above which they show their puppets.

I'm imagining it.

Then also imagine that there are people along the wall, carrying all kinds of artifacts that project above it—statues of people and other animals, made out of stone, wood, and every material. And, as you'd expect, 515 some of the carriers are talking, and some are silent.

It's a strange image you're describing, and strange prisoners.

They're like us. Do you suppose, first of all, that these prisoners see anything of themselves and one another besides the shadows that the fire casts on the wall in front of them?

How could they, if they have to keep their heads motionless throughout life?

What about the things being carried along the wall? Isn't the same true of them?

Of course.

And if they could talk to one another, don't you think they'd suppose that the names they used applied to the things they see passing before them?

They'd have to.

And what if their prison also had an echo from the wall facing them? Don't you think they'd believe that the shadows passing in front of them were talking whenever one of the carriers passing along the wall was doing so?

I certainly do.

Then the prisoners would in every way believe that the truth is nothing other than the shadows of c those artifacts.

They must surely believe that.

Consider, then, what being released from their bonds and cured of their ignorance would naturally be like, if something like this came to pass. When one of them was freed and suddenly compelled to stand up, turn his head, walk, and look up toward the light, he'd be pained and dazzled and unable to see the things whose shadows he'd seen before. What do you think he'd say, if we told him that what he'd d seen before was inconsequential, but that now—because he is a bit closer to the things that are and is turned towards things that are more—he sees more correctly? Or, to put it another way, if we pointed to each of the things passing by, asked him what each of them is, and compelled him to answer, don't you think he'd be at a loss and that he'd believe that the things he saw earlier were truer than the ones he was now being shown?

Much truer.

And if someone compelled him to look at the light itself, wouldn't his eyes hurt, and wouldn't he turn e around and flee towards the things he's able to see, believing that they're really clearer than the ones he's being shown?

He would.

And if someone dragged him away from there by force, up the rough, steep path, and didn't let him go until he had dragged him into the sunlight, wouldn't he be pained and irritated at being treated that way? And when he came into the light, with the 516 sun filling his eyes, wouldn't he be unable to see a single one of the things now said to be true?

He would be unable to see them, at least at first.

I suppose, then, that he'd need time to get adjusted before he could see things in the world above. At first, he'd see shadows most easily, then images of men and other things in water, then the things them-selves. Of these, he'd be able to study the things in

the sky and the sky itself more easily at night, looking at the light of the stars and the moon, than during
b the day, looking at the sun and the light of the sun.

Of course.

Finally, I suppose, he'd be able to see the sun, not images of it in water or some alien place, but the sun itself, in its own place, and be able to study it.

Necessarily so.

And at this point he would infer and conclude that the sun provides the seasons and the years, governs everything in the visible world, and is in some way
c the cause of all the things that he used to see.

It's clear that would be his next step.

What about when he reminds himself of his first dwelling place, his fellow prisoners, and what passed for wisdom there? Don't you think that he'd count himself happy for the change and pity the others?

Certainly.

And if there had been any honors, praises, or prizes among them for the one who was sharpest at identifying the shadows as they passed by and who best remembered which usually came earlier, which later,
d and which simultaneously, and who could thus best divine the future, do you think that our man would desire these rewards or envy those among the prisoners who were honored and held power? Instead, wouldn't he feel, with Homer, that he'd much prefer to "work the earth as a serf to another, one without possessions," and go through any sufferings, rather than share their opinions and live as they do?
e I suppose he would rather suffer anything than live like that.

Consider this too. If this man went down into the cave again and sat down in his same seat, wouldn't his eyes — coming suddenly out of the sun like that — be filled with darkness?

They certainly would.

And before his eyes had recovered — and the adjustment would not be quick — while his vision was still dim, if he had to compete again with the perpetual
517 prisoners in recognizing the shadows, wouldn't he invite ridicule? Wouldn't it be said of him that he'd returned from his upward journey with his eyesight ruined and that it isn't worthwhile even to try to travel upward? And, as for anyone who tried to free them and lead them upward, if they could somehow get their hands on him, wouldn't they kill him?

They certainly would.

This whole image, Glaucon, must be fitted together with what we said before. The visible realm should
b be likened to the prison dwelling, and the light of the fire inside it to the power of the sun. And if you interpret the upward journey and the study of things above as the upward journey of the soul to the intelligible realm, you'll grasp what I hope to convey, since that is what you wanted to hear about. Whether it's true or not, only the god knows. But this is how I see it: In the knowable realm, the form of the good is the last thing to be seen, and it is reached only with difficulty. Once one has seen it, however, one must conclude that it is the cause of all that is correct and beautiful in anything, that it produces both light and
c its source in the visible realm, and that in the intelligible realm it controls and provides truth and understanding, so that anyone who is to act sensibly in private or public must see it.

I have the same thought, at least as far as I'm able.

Come, then, share with me this thought also: It isn't surprising that the ones who get to this point are unwilling to occupy themselves with human affairs and that their souls are always pressing upwards, eager to spend their time above, for, after all, this is surely what we'd expect, if indeed things fit the image I described before.
d It is.

What about what happens when someone turns from divine study to the evils of human life? Do you think it's surprising, since his sight is still dim, and he hasn't yet become accustomed to the darkness around him, that he behaves awkwardly and appears completely ridiculous if he's compelled, either in the courts or elsewhere, to contend about the shadows of justice or the statues of which they are the shadows and to dispute about the way these things are understood by people who have never seen justice itself?
e That's not surprising at all.

No, it isn't. But anyone with any understanding would remember that the eyes may be confused in
518 two ways and from two causes, namely, when they've come from the light into the darkness *and* when they've come from the darkness into the light. Realizing that the same applies to the soul, when someone sees a soul disturbed and unable to see something, he won't laugh mindlessly, but he'll take into consideration whether it has come from a brighter life and is dimmed through not having yet become accus-

tomed to the dark or whether it has come from greater ignorance into greater light and is dazzled by the increased brilliance. Then he'll declare the first soul happy in its experience and life, and he'll pity the b latter—but even if he chose to make fun of it, at least he'd be less ridiculous than if he laughed at a soul that has come from the light above.

What you say is very reasonable.

If that's true, then here's what we must think about these matters: Education isn't what some people declare it to be, namely, putting knowledge into souls c that lack it, like putting sight into blind eyes.

They do say that.

But our present discussion, on the other hand, shows that the power to learn is present in everyone's soul and that the instrument with which each learns is like an eye that cannot be turned around from darkness to light without turning the whole body. This instrument cannot be turned around from that which is coming into being without turning the whole soul until it is able to study that which is and the brightest thing that is, namely, the one we call the d good. Isn't that right?

Yes.

Then education is the craft concerned with doing this very thing, this turning around, and with how the soul can most easily and effectively be made to do it. It isn't the craft of putting sight into the soul. Education takes for granted that sight is there but that it isn't turned the right way or looking where it ought to look, and it tries to redirect it appropriately.

So it seems.

Now, it looks as though the other so-called virtues of the soul are akin to those of the body, for they really aren't there beforehand but are added later by e habit and practice. However, the virtue of reason seems to belong above all to something more divine, which never loses its power but is either useful and beneficial or useless and harmful, depending on the way it is turned. Or have you never noticed this about 519 people who are said to be vicious but clever, how keen the vision of their little souls is and how sharply it distinguishes the things it is turned towards? This shows that its sight isn't inferior but rather is forced to serve evil ends, so that the sharper it sees, the more evil it accomplishes.

Absolutely.

However, if a nature of this sort had been hammered at from childhood and freed from the bonds of kinship with becoming, which have been fastened to it by feasting, greed, and other such pleasures and which, like leaden weights, pull its vision down- b wards—if, being rid of these, it turned to look at true things, then I say that the same soul of the same person would see these most sharply, just as it now does the things it is presently turned towards.

Probably so.

And what about the uneducated who have no experience of truth? Isn't it likely—indeed, doesn't it follow necessarily from what was said before—that they will never adequately govern a city? But neither would those who've been allowed to spend their whole lives being educated. The former would fail because they don't have a single goal at which all their actions, c public and private, inevitably aim; the latter would fail because they'd refuse to act, thinking that they had settled while still alive in the faraway Isles of the Blessed.

That's true.

It is our task as founders, then, to compel the best natures to reach the study we said before is the most important, namely, to make the ascent and see the good. But when they've made it and looked sufficiently, we mustn't allow them to do what they're d allowed to do today.

What's that?

To stay there and refuse to go down again to the prisoners in the cave and share their labors and honors, whether they are of less worth or of greater.

Then are we to do them an injustice by making them live a worse life when they could live a better one?

You are forgetting again that it isn't the law's concern to make any one class in the city outstandingly e happy but to contrive to spread happiness throughout the city by bringing the citizens into harmony with each other through persuasion or compulsion and by making them share with each other the benefits that each class can confer on the community. The law produces such people in the city, not in order to allow them to turn in whatever direction they want, 520 but to make use of them to bind the city together.

That's true, I had forgotten.

Observe, then, Glaucon, that we won't be doing an injustice to those who've become philosophers in our city and that what we'll say to them, when we compel them to guard and care for the others, will be just. We'll say: "When people like you come to be in other cities, they're justified in not sharing in their city's labors, for they've grown there spontaneously, against the will of the constitution. And what grows of its own accord and owes no debt for its upbringing has justice on its side when it isn't keen to pay anyone for that upbringing. But we've made you kings in our city and leaders of the swarm, as it were, both for yourselves and for the rest of the city. You're better and more completely educated than the others and are better able to share in both types of life. Therefore each of you in turn must go down to live in the common dwelling place of the others and grow accustomed to seeing in the dark. When you are used to it, you'll see vastly better than the people there. And because you've seen the truth about fine, just, and good things, you'll know each image for what it is and also that of which it is the image. Thus, for you and for us, the city will be governed, not like the majority of cities nowadays, by people who fight over shadows and struggle against one another in order to rule—as if that were a great good—but by people who are awake rather than dreaming, for the truth is surely this: A city whose prospective rulers are least eager to rule must of necessity be most free from civil war, whereas a city with the opposite kind of rulers is governed in the opposite way."

Absolutely.

Then do you think that those we've nurtured will disobey us and refuse to share the labors of the city, each in turn, while living the greater part of their time with one another in the pure realm?

It isn't possible, for we'll be giving just orders to just people. Each of them will certainly go to rule as to something compulsory, however, which is exactly the opposite of what's done by those who now rule in each city.

This is how it is. If you can find a way of life that's better than ruling for the prospective rulers, your well-governed city will become a possibility, for only in it will the truly rich rule—not those who are rich in gold but those who are rich in the wealth that the happy must have, namely, a good and rational life. But if beggars hungry for private goods go into public life, thinking that the good is there for the seizing, then the well-governed city is impossible, for then

ruling is something fought over, and this civil and domestic war destroys these people and the rest of the city as well.

That's very true.

Can you name any life that despises political rule besides that of the true philosopher?

No, by god, I can't.

But surely it is those who are not lovers of ruling who must rule, for if they don't, the lovers of it, who are rivals, will fight over it.

Of course.

Then who will you compel to become guardians of the city, if not those who have the best understanding of what matters for good government and who have other honors than political ones, and a better life as well?

No one.

Do you want us to consider now how such people will come to be in our city and how—just as some are said to have gone up from Hades to the gods—we'll lead them up to the light?

Of course I do.

This isn't, it seems, a matter of tossing a coin, but of turning a soul from a day that is a kind of night to the true day—the ascent to what is, which we say is true philosophy.

Indeed.

Then mustn't we try to discover the subjects that have the power to bring this about?

Of course.

So what subject is it, Glaucon, that draws the soul from the realm of becoming to the realm of what is? And it occurs to me as I'm speaking that we said, didn't we, that it is necessary for the prospective rulers to be athletes in war when they're young?

Yes, we did.

Then the subject we're looking for must also have this characteristic in addition to the former one.

Which one?

It mustn't be useless to warlike men.

If it's at all possible, it mustn't.

Now, prior to this, we educated them in music and poetry and physical training.

We did.

And physical training is concerned with what comes into being and dies, for it oversees the growth and decay of the body.

Apparently.

So it couldn't be the subject we're looking for.

522   No, it couldn't.

Then, could it be the music and poetry we described before?

But that, if you remember, is just the counterpart of physical training. It educated the guardians through habits. Its harmonies gave them a certain harmoniousness, not knowledge; its rhythms gave them a certain rhythmical quality; and its stories, whether fictional or nearer the truth, cultivated other habits akin to these. But as for the subject you're looking for now,
b there's nothing like that in music and poetry.

Your reminder is exactly to the point; there's really nothing like that in music and poetry. But, Glaucon, what is there that does have this? The crafts all seem to be base or mechanical.

How could they be otherwise? But apart from music and poetry, physical training, and the crafts, what subject is left?

Well, if we can't find anything apart from these, let's consider one of the subjects that touches all of them.

What sort of thing?

For example, that common thing that every craft,
c every type of thought, and every science uses and that is among the first compulsory subjects for everyone.

What's that?

That inconsequential matter of distinguishing the one, the two, and the three. In short, I mean number and calculation, for isn't it true that every craft and science must have a share in that?

They certainly must.

Then so must warfare.

Absolutely.

In the tragedies, at any rate, Palamedes is always showing up Agamemnon as a totally ridiculous gen-
d eral. Haven't you noticed? He says that, by inventing numbers, he established how many troops there were in the Trojan army and counted their ships and everything else—implying that they were uncounted before and that Agamemnon (if indeed he didn't know how to count) didn't even know how many feet he had? What kind of general do you think that made him?

A very strange one, if that's true.

Then won't we set down this subject as compulsory
e for a warrior, so that he is able to count and calculate?

More compulsory than anything. If, that is, he's to understand anything about setting his troops in order or if he's even to be properly human.

Then do you notice the same thing about this subject that I do?

What's that?

That this turns out to be one of the subjects we were looking for that naturally lead to understanding. But no one uses it correctly, namely, as something that is really fitted in every way to draw one towards being.   523

What do you mean?

I'll try to make my view clear as follows: I'll distinguish for myself the things that do or don't lead in the direction we mentioned, and you must study them along with me and either agree or disagree, and that way we may come to know more clearly whether things are indeed as I divine.

Point them out.

I'll point out, then, if you can grasp it, that some sense perceptions don't summon the understanding to look into them, because the judgment of sense   b perception is itself adequate, while others encourage it in every way to look into them, because sense perception seems to produce no sound result.

You're obviously referring to things appearing in the distance and to trompe l'oeil paintings.

You're not quite getting my meaning.

Then what do you mean?

The ones that don't summon the understanding are all those that don't go off into opposite perceptions at the same time. But the ones that do go off in that way I call summoners—whenever sense perception   c doesn't declare one thing any more than its opposite, no matter whether the object striking the senses is near at hand or far away. You'll understand my meaning better if I put it this way: These, we say, are three fingers—the smallest, the second, and the middle finger.

That's right.

Assume that I'm talking about them as being seen from close by. Now, this is my question about them.

What?

It's apparent that each of them is equally a finger, and it makes no difference in this regard whether the finger is seen to be in the middle or at either end, whether it is dark or pale, thick or thin, or anything   d else of that sort, for in all these cases, an ordinary soul isn't compelled to ask the understanding what a finger is, since sight doesn't suggest to it that a finger is at the same time the opposite of a finger.

No, it doesn't.

Therefore, it isn't likely that anything of that sort e would summon or awaken the understanding.

No, it isn't.

But what about the bigness and smallness of fingers? Does sight perceive them adequately? Does it make no difference to it whether the finger is in the middle or at the end? And is it the same with the sense of touch, as regards the thick and the thin, the hard and the soft? And do the other senses reveal such things clearly and adequately? Doesn't each of them rather do the following: The sense set over the 524 hard is, in the first place, of necessity also set over the soft, and it reports to the soul that the same thing is perceived by it to be both hard and soft?

That's right.

And isn't it necessary that in such cases the soul is puzzled as to what this sense means by the hard, if it indicates that the same thing is also soft, or what it means by the light and the heavy, if it indicates that the heavy is light, or the light, heavy?

Yes, indeed, these are strange reports for the soul b to receive, and they do demand to be looked into.

Then it's likely that in such cases the soul, summoning calculation and understanding, first tries to determine whether each of the things announced to it is one or two.

Of course.

If it's evidently two, won't each be evidently distinct and one?

Yes.

Then, if each is one, and both two, the soul will understand that the two are separate, for it wouldn't c understand the inseparable to be two, but rather one.

That's right.

Sight, however, saw the big and small, not as separate, but as mixed up together. Isn't that so?

Yes.

And in order to get clear about all this, understanding was compelled to see the big and the small, not as mixed up together, but as separate—the opposite way from sight.

True.

And isn't it from these cases that it first occurs to us to ask what the big is and what the small is?

Absolutely.

And, because of this, we called the one the intelligible and the other the visible.

That's right. d

This, then, is what I was trying to express before, when I said that some things summon thought, while others don't. Those that strike the relevant sense at the same time as their opposites I call summoners, those that don't do this do not awaken understanding.

Now I understand, and I think you're right.

Well, then, to which of them do number and the one belong?

I don't know.

Reason it out from what was said before. If the one is adequately seen itself by itself or is so perceived by any of the other senses, then, as we were saying in the case of fingers, it wouldn't draw the soul towards being. But if something opposite to it is always seen e at the same time, so that nothing is apparently any more one than the opposite of one, then something would be needed to judge the matter. The soul would then be puzzled, would look for an answer, would stir up its understanding, and would ask what the one itself is. And so this would be among the subjects that lead the soul and turn it around towards the study of that which is. 525

But surely the sight of the one does possess this characteristic to a remarkable degree, for we see the same thing to be both one and an unlimited number at the same time.

Then, if this is true of the one, won't it also be true of all numbers?

Of course.

Now, calculation and arithmetic are wholly concerned with numbers.

That's right.

Then evidently they lead us towards truth. b

Supernaturally so.

Then they belong, it seems, to the subjects we're seeking. They are compulsory for warriors because of their orderly ranks and for philosophers because they have to learn to rise up out of becoming and grasp being, if they are ever to become rational.

That's right.

And our guardian must be both a warrior and a philosopher.

Certainly.

Then it would be appropriate, Glaucon, to legislate this subject for those who are going to share in the highest offices in the city and to persuade them to turn to calculation and take it up, not as laymen do, c but staying with it until they reach the study of the natures of the numbers by means of understanding itself, nor like tradesmen and retailers, for the sake of buying and selling, but for the sake of war and for ease in turning the soul around, away from becoming and towards truth and being.

Well put.

Moreover, it strikes me, now that it has been mentioned, how sophisticated the subject of calculation d is and in how many ways it is useful for our purposes, provided that one practices it for the sake of knowing rather than trading.

How is it useful?

In the very way we were talking about. It leads the soul forcibly upward and compels it to discuss the numbers themselves, never permitting anyone to propose for discussion numbers attached to visible or tangible bodies. You know what those who are clever in these matters are like: If, in the course of the argument, someone tries to divide the one itself, they laugh and won't permit it. If you divide it, they multi-e ply it, taking care that one thing never be found to be many parts rather than one.

That's very true.

Then what do you think would happen, Glaucon, 526 if someone were to ask them: "What kind of numbers are you talking about, in which the one is as you assume it to be, each one equal to every other, without the least difference and containing no internal parts?"

I think they'd answer that they are talking about those numbers that can be grasped only in thought and can't be dealt with in any other way.

Then do you see that it's likely that this subject b really is compulsory for us, since it apparently compels the soul to use understanding itself on the truth itself?

Indeed, it most certainly does do that.

And what about those who are naturally good at calculation or reasoning? Have you already noticed that they're naturally sharp, so to speak, in all subjects, and that those who are slow at it, if they're educated and exercised in it, even if they're benefited in no other way, nonetheless improve and become generally sharper than they were?

That's true.

Moreover, I don't think you'll easily find subjects c that are harder to learn or practice than this.

No, indeed.

Then, for all these reasons, this subject isn't to be neglected, and the best natures must be educated in it.

I agree.

Let that, then, be one of our subjects. Second, let's consider whether the subject that comes next is also appropriate for our purposes.

What subject is that? Do you mean geometry?

That's the very one I had in mind.

Insofar as it pertains to war, it's obviously appropriate, for when it comes to setting up camp, occupy- d ing a region, concentrating troops, deploying them, or with regard to any of the other formations an army adopts in battle or on the march, it makes all the difference whether someone is a geometer or not.

But, for things like that, even a little geometry— or calculation for that matter—would suffice. What we need to consider is whether the greater and more advanced part of it tends to make it easier to see the form of the good. And we say that anything has that e tendency if it compels the soul to turn itself around towards the region in which lies the happiest of the things that are, the one the soul must see at any cost.

You're right.

Therefore, if geometry compels the soul to study being, it's appropriate, but if it compels it to study becoming, it's inappropriate.

So we've said, at any rate.

Now, no one with even a little experience of geometry will dispute that this science is entirely the opposite 527 of what is said about it in the accounts of its practitioners.

How do you mean?

They give ridiculous accounts of it, though they can't help it, for they speak like practical men, and all their accounts refer to doing things. They talk of "squaring," "applying," "adding," and the like, whereas the entire subject is pursued for the sake of knowledge.   b

Absolutely.

And mustn't we also agree on a further point?

What is that?

That their accounts are for the sake of knowing what always is, not what comes into being and passes away.

That's easy to agree to, for geometry *is* knowledge of what always is.

Then it draws the soul towards truth and produces philosophic thought by directing upwards what we now wrongly direct downwards.

As far as anything possibly can.

Then as far as *we* possibly can, we must require those in your fine city not to neglect geometry in any way, for even its by-products are not insignificant.

What are they?

The ones concerned with war that you mentioned. But we also surely know that, when it comes to better understanding any subject, there is a world of difference between someone who has grasped geometry and someone who hasn't.

Yes, by god, a world of difference.

Then shall we set this down as a second subject for the young?

Let's do so, he said.

And what about astronomy? Shall we make it the third? Or do you disagree?

That's fine with me, for a better awareness of the seasons, months, and years is no less appropriate for a general than for a farmer or navigator.

You amuse me: You're like someone who's afraid that the majority will think he is prescribing useless subjects. It's no easy task—indeed it's very difficult—to realize that in every soul there is an instrument that is purified and rekindled by such subjects when it has been blinded and destroyed by other ways of life, an instrument that it is more important to preserve than ten thousand eyes, since only with it can the truth be seen. Those who share your belief that this is so will think you're speaking incredibly well, while those who've never been aware of it will probably think you're talking nonsense, since they see no benefit worth mentioning in these subjects. So decide right now which group you're addressing. Or are your arguments for neither of them but mostly for your own sake—though you won't begrudge anyone else whatever benefit he's able to get from them?

The latter: I want to speak, question, and answer mostly for my own sake.

Then let's fall back to our earlier position, for we were wrong just now about the subject that comes after geometry.

What was our error?

After plane surfaces, we went on to revolving solids before dealing with solids by themselves. But the right thing to do is to take up the third dimension right after the second. And this, I suppose, consists of cubes and of whatever shares in depth.

You're right, Socrates, but this subject hasn't been developed yet.

There are two reasons for that: First, because no city values it, this difficult subject is little researched. Second, the researchers need a director, for, without one, they won't discover anything. To begin with, such a director is hard to find, and, then, even if he could be found, those who currently do research in this field would be too arrogant to follow him. If an entire city helped him to supervise it, however, and took the lead in valuing it, then he would be followed. And, if the subject was consistently and vigorously pursued, it would soon be developed. Even now, when it isn't valued and is held in contempt by the majority and is pursued by researchers who are unable to give an account of its usefulness, nevertheless, in spite of all these handicaps, the force of its charm has caused it to develop somewhat, so that it wouldn't be surprising if it were further developed even as things stand.

The subject *has* outstanding charm. But explain more clearly what you were saying just now. The subject that deals with plane surfaces you took to be geometry.

Yes.

And at first you put astronomy after it, but later you went back on that.

In my haste to go through them all, I've only progressed more slowly. The subject dealing with the dimension of depth was next. But because it is in a ridiculous state, I passed it by and spoke of astronomy (which deals with the motion of things having depth) after geometry.

That's right.

Let's then put astronomy as the fourth subject, on the assumption that solid geometry will be available if a city takes it up.

That seems reasonable. And since you reproached me before for praising astronomy in a vulgar manner, I'll now praise it your way, for I think it's clear to everyone that astronomy compels the soul to look upward and leads it from things here to things there.

It may be obvious to everyone except me, but that's not my view about it.

Then what *is* your view?

As it's practiced today by those who teach philosophy, it makes the soul look very much downward.

How do you mean?

In my opinion, your conception of "higher studies" is a good deal too generous, for if someone were to study something by leaning his head back and studying ornaments on a ceiling, it looks as though you'd b say he's studying not with his eyes but with his understanding. Perhaps you're right, and I'm foolish, but I can't conceive of any subject making the soul look upward except one concerned with that which is, and that which is is invisible. If anyone attempts to learn something about sensible things, whether by gaping upward or squinting downward, I'd claim—since there's no knowledge of such things—that he never learns anything and that, even if he studies lying on c his back on the ground or floating on it in the sea, his soul is looking not up but down.

You're right to reproach me, and I've been justly punished, but what did you mean when you said that astronomy must be learned in a different way from the way in which it is learned at present if it is to be a useful subject for our purposes?

It's like this: We should consider the decorations in the sky to be the most beautiful and most exact of visible things, seeing that they're embroidered on a visible surface. But we should consider their motions d to fall far short of the true ones—motions that are really fast or slow as measured in true numbers, that trace out true geometrical figures, that are all in relation to one another, and that are the true motions of the things carried along in them. And these, of course, must be grasped by reason and thought, not by sight. Or do you think otherwise?

Not at all.

Therefore, we should use the embroidery in the sky as a model in the study of these other things. If someone experienced in geometry were to come upon plans very carefully drawn and worked out by Daeda- e lus or some other craftsman or artist, he'd consider them to be very finely executed, but he'd think it ridiculous to examine them seriously in order to find the truth in them about the equal, the double, or any 530 other ratio.

How could it be anything other than ridiculous?

Then don't you think that a real astronomer will feel the same when he looks at the motions of the stars? He'll believe that the craftsman of the heavens arranged them and all that's in them in the finest way possible for such things. But as for the ratio of night to day, of days to a month, of a month to a year, or of the motions of the stars to any of them or to each other, don't you think he'll consider it strange to believe that they're always the same and never b deviate anywhere at all or to try in any sort of way to grasp the truth about them, since they're connected to body and visible?

That's my opinion anyway, now that I hear it from you.

Then if, by really taking part in astronomy, we're to make the naturally intelligent part of the soul useful instead of useless, let's study astronomy by means of problems, as we do geometry, and leave the things in the sky alone. c

The task you're prescribing is a lot harder than anything now attempted in astronomy.

And I suppose that, if we are to be of any benefit as lawgivers, our prescriptions for the other subjects will be of the same kind. But have you any other appropriate subject to suggest?

Not offhand.

Well, there isn't just one form of motion but several. Perhaps a wise person could list them all, but there are two that are evident even to us. d

What are they?

Besides the one we've discussed, there is also its counterpart.

What's that?

It's likely that, as the eyes fasten on astronomical motions, so the ears fasten on harmonic ones, and that the sciences of astronomy and harmonics are closely akin. This is what the Pythagoreans say, Glaucon, and we agree, don't we?

We do.

Therefore, since the subject is so huge, shouldn't we ask them what they have to say about harmonic e motions and whether there is anything else besides them, all the while keeping our own goal squarely in view?

What's that?

That those whom we are rearing should never try to learn anything incomplete, anything that doesn't reach the end that everything should reach—the end we mentioned just now in the case of astronomy. Or don't you know that people do something similar in harmonics? Measuring audible consonances and 531 sounds against one another, they labor in vain, just like present-day astronomers.

Yes, by the gods, and pretty ridiculous they are too. They talk about something they call a "dense interval" or quartertone—putting their ears to their instruments like someone trying to overhear what the neighbors are saying. And some say that they hear a tone in between and that *it* is the shortest interval by which they must measure, while others argue that this tone sounds the same as a quarter tone. Both put ears
b before understanding.

You mean those excellent fellows who torment their strings, torturing them, and stretching them on pegs. I won't draw out the analogy by speaking of blows with the plectrum or the accusations or denials and boastings on the part of the strings; instead I'll cut it short by saying that these aren't the people I'm talking about. The ones I mean are the ones we just said we were going to question about harmonics, for
c they do the same as the astronomers. They seek out the numbers that are to be found in these audible consonances, but they do not make the ascent to problems. They don't investigate, for example, which numbers are consonant and which aren't or what the explanation is of each.

But that would be a superhuman task.

Yet it's useful in the search for the beautiful and the good. But pursued for any other purpose, it's useless.

Probably so.

Moreover, I take it that, if inquiry into all the subjects we've mentioned brings out their association and relationship with one another and draws conclu-
d sions about their kinship, it does contribute something to our goal and isn't labor in vain, but that otherwise it is in vain.

I, too, divine that this is true. But you're still talking about a very big task, Socrates.

Do you mean the prelude, or what? Or don't you know that all these subjects are merely preludes to the song itself that must also be learned? Surely you don't think that people who are clever in these matters
e are dialecticians.

No, by god, I don't. Although I have met a few exceptions.

But did it ever seem to you that those who can neither give nor follow an account know anything at all of the things we say they must know?

My answer to that is also no.

Then isn't this at last, Glaucon, the song that dialec-
532 tic sings? It is intelligible, but it is imitated by the

power of sight. We said that sight tries at last to look at the animals themselves, the stars themselves, and, in the end, at the sun itself. In the same way, whenever someone tries through argument and apart from all sense perceptions to find the being itself of each thing and doesn't give up until he grasps the good itself with understanding itself, he reaches the end of the intelligible, just as the other reached the end of b the visible.

Absolutely.

And what about this journey? Don't you call it dialectic?

I do.

Then the release from bonds and the turning around from shadows to statues and the light of the fire and, then, the way up out of the cave to the sunlight and, there, the continuing inability to look at the animals, the plants, and the light of the sun, but the newly acquired ability to look at divine images in water and shadows of the things that are, rather c than, as before, merely at shadows of statues thrown by another source of light that is itself a shadow in relation to the sun—all this business of the crafts we've mentioned has the power to awaken the best part of the soul and lead it upward to the study of the best among the things that are, just as, before, the clearest thing in the body was led to the brightest thing in the bodily and visible realm. d

I accept that this is so, even though it seems very hard to accept in one way and hard not to accept in another. All the same, since we'll have to return to these things often in the future, rather than having to hear them just once now, let's assume that what you've said is so and turn to the song itself, discussing it in the same way as we did the prelude. So tell us: what is the sort of power dialectic has, what forms is it divided into, and what paths does it follow? For these lead at last, it seems, towards that place which e is a rest from the road, so to speak, and an end of journeying for the one who reaches it.

You won't be able to follow me any longer, Glaucon, even though there is no lack of eagerness on my 533 part to lead you, for you would no longer be seeing an image of what we're describing, but the truth itself. At any rate, that's how it seems to me. That it is really so is not worth insisting on any further. But that there is some such thing to be seen, *that* is something we must insist on. Isn't that so?

Of course.

And mustn't we also insist that the power of dialectic could reveal it only to someone experienced in the subjects we've described and that it cannot reveal it in any other way?

That too is worth insisting on.

b At any rate, no one will dispute it when we say that there is no other inquiry that systematically attempts to grasp with respect to each thing itself what the being of it is, for all the other crafts are concerned with human opinions and desires, with growing or construction, or with the care of growing or constructed things. And as for the rest, I mean geometry and the subjects that follow it, we described them as to some extent grasping what is, for we saw that, while they do dream about what is, they are unable to command a waking view of it as long as they make c use of hypotheses that they leave untouched and that they cannot give any account of. What mechanism could possibly turn any agreement into knowledge when it begins with something unknown and puts together the conclusion and the steps in between from what is unknown?

None.

Therefore, dialectic is the only inquiry that travels this road, doing away with hypotheses and proceeding d to the first principle itself, so as to be secure. And when the eye of the soul is really buried in a sort of barbaric bog, dialectic gently pulls it out and leads it upwards, using the crafts we described to help it and cooperate with it in turning the soul around. From force of habit, we've often called these crafts sciences or kinds of knowledge, but they need another name, clearer than opinion, darker than knowledge. We called them thought somewhere before. But I presume that we won't dispute about a name when we e have so many more important matters to investigate.

Of course not.

It will therefore be enough to call the first section knowledge, the second thought, the third belief, and 534 the fourth imaging, just as we did before. The last two together we call opinion, the other two, intellect. Opinion is concerned with becoming, intellect with being. And as being is to becoming, so intellect is to opinion, and as intellect is to opinion, so knowledge is to belief and thought to imaging. But as for the ratios between the things these are set over and the division of either the opinable or the intelligible sec-

tion into two, let's pass them by, Glaucon, lest they involve us in arguments many times longer than the ones we've already gone through.

I agree with you about the others in any case, insofar as I'm able to follow.   b

Then, do you call someone who is able to give an account of the being of each thing dialectical? But insofar as he's unable to give an account of something, either to himself or to another, do you deny that he has any understanding of it?

How could I do anything else?

Then the same applies to the good. Unless someone can distinguish in an account the form of the good from everything else, can survive all refutation, as if in a battle, striving to judge things not in accordance c with opinion but in accordance with being, and can come through all this with his account still intact, you'll say that he doesn't know the good itself or any other good. And if he gets hold of some image of it, you'll say that it's through opinion, not knowledge, for he is dreaming and asleep throughout his present life, and, before he wakes up here, he will arrive in Hades and go to sleep forever.   d

Yes, by god, I'll certainly say all of that.

Then, as for those children of yours whom you're rearing and educating in theory, if you ever reared them in fact, I don't think that you'd allow them to rule in your city or be responsible for the most important things while they are as irrational as incommensurable lines.

Certainly not.

Then you'll legislate that they are to give most attention to the education that will enable them to ask and answer questions most knowledgeably?

I'll legislate it along with you.   e

Then do you think that we've placed dialectic at the top of the other subjects like a coping stone and that no other subject can rightly be placed above it, but that our account of the subjects that a future ruler must learn has come to an end?   535

Probably so.

Then it remains for you to deal with the distribution of these subjects, with the question of to whom we'll assign them and in what way.

That's clearly next.

Do you remember what sort of people we chose in our earlier selection of rulers?

Of course I do.

In the other respects, the same natures have to be chosen: we have to select the most stable, the most courageous, and as far as possible the most graceful. In addition, we must look not only for people who
b have a noble and tough character but for those who have the natural qualities conducive to this education of ours.

Which ones exactly?

They must be keen on the subjects and learn them easily, for people's souls give up much more easily in hard study than in physical training, since the pain—being peculiar to them and not shared with their body—is more their own.

That's true.

c We must also look for someone who has got a good memory, is persistent, and is in every way a lover of hard work. How else do you think he'd be willing to carry out both the requisite bodily labors and also complete so much study and practice?

Nobody would, unless his nature was in every way a good one.

In any case, the present error, which as we said before explains why philosophy isn't valued, is that she's taken up by people who are unworthy of her, for illegitimate students shouldn't be allowed to take her up, but only legitimate ones.

How so?

In the first place, no student should be lame in his
d love of hard work, really loving one half of it, and hating the other half. This happens when someone is a lover of physical training, hunting, or any kind of bodily labor and isn't a lover of learning, listening, or inquiry, but hates the work involved in them. And someone whose love of hard work tends in the opposite direction is also lame.

That's very true.

Similarly with regard to truth, won't we say that a soul is maimed if it hates a voluntary falsehood, can-
e not endure to have one in itself, and is greatly angered when it exists in others, but is nonetheless content to accept an involuntary falsehood, isn't angry when it is caught being ignorant, and bears its lack of learning easily, wallowing in it like a pig?

536 Absolutely.

And with regard to moderation, courage, high-mindedness, and all the other parts of virtue, it is also important to distinguish the illegitimate from the legitimate, for when either a city or an individual

doesn't know how to do this, it unwittingly employs the lame and illegitimate as friends or rulers for whatever services it wants done.

That's just how it is.

So we must be careful in all these matters, for if we bring people who are sound of limb and mind to so great a subject and training, and educate them in it, even justice itself won't blame us, and we'll save b the city and its constitution. But if we bring people of a different sort, we'll do the opposite, and let loose an even greater flood of ridicule upon philosophy.

And it would be shameful to do that.

It certainly would. But I seem to have done something a bit ridiculous myself just now.

What's that?

I forgot that we were only playing, and so I spoke too vehemently. But I looked upon philosophy as I c spoke, and seeing her undeservedly besmirched, I seem to have lost my temper and said what I had to say too earnestly, as if I were angry with those responsible for it.

That certainly wasn't my impression as I listened to you.

But it was mine as I was speaking. In any case, let's not forget that in our earlier selection we chose older people but that that isn't permitted in this one, for we mustn't believe Solon when he says that as someone grows older he's able to learn a lot. He can do d that even less well than he can run races, for all great and numerous labors belong to the young.

Necessarily.

Therefore, calculation, geometry, and all the preliminary education required for dialectic must be offered to the future rulers in childhood, and not in the shape of compulsory learning either.

Why's that?

Because no free person should learn anything like e a slave. Forced bodily labor does no harm to the body, but nothing taught by force stays in the soul.

That's true.

Then don't use force to train the children in these subjects; use play instead. That way you'll also see better what each of them is naturally fitted for.   537

That seems reasonable.

Do you remember that we stated that the children were to be led into war on horseback as observers and that, wherever it is safe to do so, they should be brought close and taste blood, like puppies?

I remember.

In all these things — in labors, studies, and fears — the ones who always show the greatest aptitude are to be inscribed on a list.

b At what age?

When they're released from compulsory physical training, for during that period, whether it's two or three years, young people are incapable of doing anything else, since weariness and sleep are enemies of learning. At the same time, how they fare in this physical training is itself an important test.

Of course it is.

And after that, that is to say, from the age of twenty, those who are chosen will also receive more honors than the others. Moreover, the subjects they learned in no particular order as children they must now
c bring together to form a unified vision of their kinship both with one another and with the nature of that which is.

At any rate, only learning of that sort holds firm in those who receive it.

It is also the greatest test of who is naturally dialectical and who isn't, for anyone who can achieve a unified vision is dialectical, and anyone who can't isn't.

I agree.

Well, then, you'll have to look out for the ones who most of all have this ability in them and who also remain steadfast in their studies, in war, and in
d the other activities laid down by law. And after they have reached their thirtieth year, you'll select them in turn from among those chosen earlier and assign them yet greater honors. Then you'll have to test them by means of the power of dialectic, to discover which of them can relinquish his eyes and other senses, going on with the help of truth to that which by itself is. And this is a task that requires great care.

What's the main reason for that?

Don't you realize what a great evil comes from
e dialectic as it is currently practiced?

What evil is that?

Those who practice it are filled with lawlessness.

They certainly are.

Do you think it's surprising that this happens to them? Aren't you sympathetic?

Why isn't it surprising? And why should I be sympathetic?

Because it's like the case of a child brought up surrounded by much wealth and many flatterers in a great and numerous family, who finds out, when he has become a man, that he isn't the child of his   538 professed parents and that he can't discover his real ones. Can you divine what the attitude of someone like that would be to the flatterers, on the one hand, and to his supposed parents, on the other, before he knew about his parentage, and what it would be when he found out? Or would you rather hear what I divine about it?

I'd rather hear your views.

Well, then, I divine that during the time that he didn't know the truth, he'd honor his father, mother, and the rest of his supposed family more than he would the flatterers, that he'd pay greater attention   b to their needs, be less likely to treat them lawlessly in word or deed, and be more likely to obey them than the flatterers in any matters of importance.

Probably so.

When he became aware of the truth, however, his honor and enthusiasm would lessen for his family and increase for the flatterers, he'd obey the latter far more than before, begin to live in the way that they did, and keep company with them openly, and, unless   c he was very decent by nature, he'd eventually care nothing for that father of his or any of the rest of his supposed family.

All this would probably happen as you say, but in what way is it an image of those who take up arguments?

As follows. We hold from childhood certain convictions about just and fine things; we're brought up with them as with our parents, we obey and honor them.

Indeed, we do.

There are other ways of living, however, opposite   d to these and full of pleasures, that flatter the soul and attract it to themselves but which don't persuade sensible people, who continue to honor and obey the convictions of their fathers.

That's right.

And then a questioner comes along and asks someone of this sort, "What is the fine?" And, when he answers what he has heard from the traditional lawgiver, the argument refutes him, and by refuting him often and in many places shakes him from his convictions, and makes him believe that the fine is no more

fine than shameful, and the same with the just, the good, and the things he honored most. What do you
e think his attitude will be then to honoring and obeying his earlier convictions?

Of necessity he won't honor or obey them in the same way.

Then, when he no longer honors and obeys those convictions and can't discover the true ones, will he be likely to adopt any other way of life than that
539 which flatters him?

No, he won't.

And so, I suppose, from being law-abiding he becomes lawless.

Inevitably.

Then, as I asked before, isn't it only to be expected that this is what happens to those who take up arguments in this way, and don't they therefore deserve a lot of sympathy?

Yes, and they deserve pity too.

Then, if you don't want your thirty-year-olds to be objects of such pity, you'll have to be extremely careful about how you introduce them to arguments.

That's right.

And isn't it one lasting precaution not to let them taste arguments while they're young? I don't suppose that it has escaped your notice that, when young
b people get their first taste of arguments, they misuse it by treating it as a kind of game of contradiction. They imitate those who've refuted them by refuting others themselves, and, like puppies, they enjoy dragging and tearing those around them with their arguments.

They're excessively fond of it.

Then, when they've refuted many and been refuted by them in turn, they forcefully and quickly fall into disbelieving what they believed before. And, as a re-
c sult, they themselves and the whole of philosophy are discredited in the eyes of others.

That's very true.

But an older person won't want to take part in such madness. He'll imitate someone who is willing to engage in discussion in order to look for the truth, rather than someone who plays at contradiction for sport. He'll be more sensible himself and will bring honor rather than discredit to the philosophical way
d of life.

That's right.

And when we said before that those allowed to take part in arguments should be orderly and steady by nature, not as nowadays, when even the unfit are allowed to engage in them—wasn't all that also said as a precaution?

Of course.

Then if someone continuously, strenuously, and exclusively devotes himself to participation in arguments, exercising himself in them just as he did in the bodily physical training, which is their counterpart, would that be enough?

Do you mean six years or four?
e

It doesn't matter. Make it five. And after that, you must make them go down into the cave again, and compel them to take command in matters of war and occupy the other offices suitable for young people, so that they won't be inferior to the others in experience. But in these, too, they must be tested to see whether they'll remain steadfast when they're pulled this way and that or shift their ground.
540

How much time do you allow for that?

Fifteen years. Then, at the age of fifty, those who've survived the tests and been successful both in practical matters and in the sciences must be led to the goal and compelled to lift up the radiant light of their souls to what itself provides light for everything. And once they've seen the good itself, they must each in
b turn put the city, its citizens, and themselves in order, using it as their model. Each of them will spend most of his time with philosophy, but, when his turn comes, he must labor in politics and rule for the city's sake, not as if he were doing something fine, but rather something that has to be done. Then, having educated others like himself to take his place as guardians of the city, he will depart for the Isles of the Blessed and dwell there. And, if the Pythia agrees, the city will publicly establish memorials and sacrifices to
c him as a daemon, but if not, then as a happy and divine human being.

Like a sculptor, Socrates, you've produced ruling men that are completely fine.

And ruling women, too, Glaucon, for you mustn't think that what I've said applies any more to men than it does to women who are born with the appropriate natures.

That's right, if indeed they are to share everything equally with the men, as we said they should.

Then, do you agree that the things we've said about the city and its constitution aren't altogether wishful thinking, that it's hard for them to come about, but not impossible? And do you also agree that they can come about only in the way we indicated, namely, when one or more true philosophers come to power in a city, who despise present honors, thinking them slavish and worthless, and who prize what is right and the honors that come from it above everything, and regard justice as the most important and most essential thing, serving it and increasing it as they set their city in order?

How will they do that?

They'll send everyone in the city who is over ten years old into the country. Then they'll take possession of the children, who are now free from the ethos of their parents, and bring them up in their own customs and laws, which are the ones we've described. This is the quickest and easiest way for the city and constitution we've discussed to be established, become happy, and bring most benefit to the people among whom it's established.

That's by far the quickest and easiest way. And in my opinion, Socrates, you've described well how it would come into being, if it ever did.

Then, isn't that enough about this city and the man who is like it? Surely it is clear what sort of man we'll say he has to be.

It is clear, he said. And as for your question, I think that we have reached the end of this topic.

Book VIII

Well, then, Glaucon, we've agreed to the following: If a city is to achieve the height of good government, wives must be in common, children and all their education must be in common, their way of life, whether in peace or war, must be in common, and their kings must be those among them who have proved to be best, both in philosophy and in warfare.

We have agreed to that, he said.

Moreover, we also agreed that, as soon as the rulers are established, they will lead the soldiers and settle them in the kind of dwellings we described, which are in no way private but common to all. And we also agreed, if you remember, what kind of possessions they will have.

I remember that we thought that none of them should acquire any of the things that the other rulers now do but that, as athletes of war and guardians, they should receive their yearly upkeep from the other citizens as a wage for their guardianship and look after themselves and the rest of the city.

That's right. But since we have completed this discussion, let's recall the point at which we began the digression that brought us here, so that we can continue on the same path from where we left off.

That isn't difficult, for, much the same as now, you were talking as if you had completed the description of the city. You said that you would class both the city you described and the man who is like it as good, even though, as it seems, you had a still finer city and man to tell us about. But, in any case, you said that, if this city was the right one, the others were faulty. You said, if I remember, that there were four types of constitution remaining that are worth discussing, each with faults that we should observe, and we should do the same for the people who are like them. Our aim was to observe them all, agree which man is best and which worst, and then determine whether the best is happiest and the worst most wretched or whether it's otherwise. I was asking you which four constitutions you had in mind when Polemarchus and Adeimantus interrupted. And that's when you took up the discussion that led here.

That's absolutely right.

Well, then, like a wrestler, give me the same hold again, and when I ask the same question, try to give the answer you were about to give before.

If I can.

I'd at least like to hear what four constitutions you meant.

That won't be difficult since they're the ones for which we have names. First, there's the constitution praised by most people, namely, the Cretan or Laconian. The second, which is also second in the praise it receives, is called oligarchy and is filled with a host of evils. The next in order, and antagonistic to it, is democracy. And finally there is genuine tyranny, surpassing all of them, the fourth and last of the diseased cities. Or can you think of another type of constitution—I mean another whose form is distinct

from these? Dynasties and purchased kingships and
other constitutions of that sort, which one finds no
less among the barbarians than among the Greeks,
are somewhere intermediate between these four.

At any event, many strange ones are indeed
talked about.

And do you realize that of necessity there are as
many forms of human character as there are of constitutions? Or do you think that constitutions are born
"from oak or rock" and not from the characters of
the people who live in the cities governed by them,
which tip the scales, so to speak, and drag the rest
along with them?

No, I don't believe they come from anywhere else.

Then, if there are five forms of city, there must
also be five forms of the individual soul.

Of course.

Now, we've already described the one that's like
aristocracy, which is rightly said to be good and just.

We have.

Then mustn't we next go through the inferior ones,
namely, the victory-loving and honor-loving (which
corresponds to the Laconian form of constitution),
followed by the oligarchic, the democratic, and the
tyrannical, so that, having discovered the most unjust
of all, we can oppose him to the most just? In this
way, we can complete our investigation into how pure
justice and pure injustice stand, with regard to the
happiness or wretchedness of those who possess them,
and either be persuaded by Thrasymachus to practice
injustice or by the argument that is now coming to
light to practice justice.

That's absolutely what we have to do.

Then, just as we began by looking for the virtues
of character in a constitution, before looking for them
in the individual, thinking that they'd be clearer in
the former, shouldn't we first examine the honor-
loving constitution? I don't know what other name
there is for it, but it should be called either timocracy
or timarchy. Then shouldn't we examine an individual who is related to that constitution, and, after that,
oligarchy and an oligarchic person, and democracy
and a democratic person? And finally, having come
to a city under a tyrant and having examined it,
shouldn't we look into a tyrannical soul, trying in
this way to become adequate judges of the topic we
proposed to ourselves?

That would be a reasonable way for us to go about
observing and judging, at any rate.

Well, then, let's try to explain how timocracy
emerges from aristocracy. Or is it a simple principle
that the cause of change in any constitution is civil
war breaking out within the ruling group itself, but
that if this group—however small it is—remains of
one mind, the constitution cannot be changed?

Yes, that's right.

How, then, Glaucon, will our city be changed?
How will civil war arise, either between the auxiliaries
and the rulers or within either group? Or do you want
us to be like Homer and pray to the Muses to tell us
"how civil war first broke out?" And shall we say that
they speak to us in tragic tones, as if they were in
earnest, playing and jesting with us as if we were
children?

What will they say?

Something like this. "It is hard for a city composed
in this way to change, but everything that comes into
being must decay. Not even a constitution such as
this will last forever. It, too, must face dissolution.
And this is how it will be dissolved. All plants that
grow in the earth, and also all animals that grow upon
it, have periods of fruitfulness and barrenness of both
soul and body as often as the revolutions complete the
circumferences of their circles. These circumferences
are short for the short-lived, and the opposite for their
opposites. Now, the people you have educated to be
leaders in your city, even though they are wise, still
won't, through calculation together with sense perception, hit upon the fertility and barrenness of the
human species, but it will escape them, and so they
will at some time beget children when they ought
not to do so. For the birth of a divine creature, there
is a cycle comprehended by a perfect number. For
a human being, it is the first number in which are
found root and square increases, comprehending
three lengths and four terms, of elements that make
things like and unlike, that cause them to increase
and decrease, and that render all things mutually
agreeable and rational in their relations to one another. Of these elements, four and three, married
with five, give two harmonies when thrice increased.
One of them is a square, so many times a hundred.
The other is of equal length one way but oblong.
One of its sides is one hundred squares of the rational

diameter of five diminished by one each or one hundred squares of the irrational diameter diminished by two each. The other side is a hundred cubes of three. This whole geometrical number controls better and worse births. And when your rulers, through ignorance of these births, join brides and grooms at the
d wrong time, the children will be neither good natured nor fortunate. The older generation will choose the best of these children but they are unworthy nevertheless, and when they acquire their fathers' powers, they will begin, as guardians, to neglect us Muses. First, they will have less consideration for music and poetry than they ought, then they will neglect physical training, so that your young people will become less well educated in music and poetry. Hence, rulers chosen
e from among them won't be able to guard well the testing of the golden, silver, bronze, and iron races, which are Hesiod's and your own. The intermixing of iron with silver and bronze with gold that results
547 will engender lack of likeness and unharmonious inequality, and these always breed war and hostility wherever they arise. Civil war, we declare, is always and everywhere 'of this lineage'."

And we'll declare that what the Muses say is right.

It must be, since they're Muses.

b What do the Muses say after that?

Once civil war breaks out, both the iron and bronze types pull the constitution towards money-making and the acquisition of land, houses, gold, and silver, while both the gold and silver types—not being poor, but by nature rich or rich in their souls—lead the constitution towards virtue and the old order. And thus striving and struggling with one another, they compromise on a middle way: They distribute the land and houses as private property, enslave and hold as serfs and servants those whom they previously guarded as free friends and providers of upkeep, and
c occupy themselves with war and with guarding against those whom they've enslaved.

I think that is the way this transformation begins.

Then, isn't this constitution a sort of midpoint between aristocracy and oligarchy?

Absolutely.

Then, if that's its place in the transformation, how will it be managed after the change? Isn't it obvious that it will imitate the aristocratic constitution in some
d respects and oligarchy in others, since it's between

them, and that it will also have some features of its own?

That's right.

The rulers will be respected; the fighting class will be prevented from taking part in farming, manual labor, or other ways of making money; it will eat communally and devote itself to physical training and training for war; and in all such ways, won't the constitution be like the aristocratic one?

Yes.

On the other hand, it will be afraid to appoint wise people as rulers, on the grounds that they are no e longer simple and earnest but mixed, and will incline towards spirited and simpler people, who are more naturally suited for war than peace; it will value the tricks and stratagems of war and spend all its time making war. Aren't most of these qualities peculiar 548 to it?

Yes.

Such people will desire money just as those in oligarchies do, passionately adoring gold and silver in secret. They will possess private treasuries and storehouses, where they can keep it hidden, and have houses to enclose them, like private nests, where they can spend lavishly either on women or on anyone else they wish. b

That's absolutely true.

They'll be mean with their own money, since they value it and are not allowed to acquire it openly, but they'll love to spend other people's because of their appetites. They'll enjoy their pleasures in secret, running away from the law like boys from their father, for since they've neglected the true Muse—that of discussion and philosophy—and have valued physical training more than music and poetry, they haven't been educated by persuasion but by force. c

The constitution you're discussing is certainly a mixture of good and bad.

Yes, it is mixed, but because of the predominance of the spirited element, one thing alone is most manifest in it, namely, the love of victory and the love of honor.

Very much so.

This, then, is the way this constitution would come into being and what it would be like, for, after all, we're only sketching the shape of the constitution in theory, not giving an exact account of it, since even *d* from a sketch we'll be able to discern the most just and the most unjust person. And, besides, it would be an intolerably long task to describe every constitution and every character without omitting any detail.

That's right.

Then who is the man that corresponds to this constitution? How does he come to be, and what sort of man is he?

I think, said Adeimantus, that he'd be very like Glaucon here, as far as the love of victory is concerned.

In that respect, I said, he might be, but, in the following ones, I don't think his nature would be similar.

e Which ones?

He'd be more obstinate and less well trained in music and poetry, though he's a lover of it, and he'd love to listen to speeches and arguments, though he's by no means a rhetorician. He'd be harsh to his slaves rather than merely looking down on them as 549 an adequately educated person does. He'd be gentle to free people and very obedient to rulers, being himself a lover of ruling and a lover of honor. However, he doesn't base his claim to rule on his ability as a speaker or anything like that, but, as he's a lover of physical training and a lover of hunting, on his abilities and exploits in warfare and warlike activities.

Yes, that's the character that corresponds to this constitution.

Wouldn't such a person despise money when he's young but love it more and more as he grows older, because he shares in the money-loving nature and *b* isn't pure in his attitude to virtue? And isn't that because he lacks the best of guardians?

What guardian is that? Adeimantus said.

Reason, I said, mixed with music and poetry, for it alone dwells within the person who possesses it as the lifelong preserver of his virtue.

Well put.

That, then, is a timocratic youth; he resembles the corresponding city.

c Absolutely.

And he comes into being in some such way as this. He's the son of a good father who lives in a city that isn't well governed, who avoids honors, office, lawsuits, and all such meddling in other people's affairs, and who is even willing to be put at a disadvantage in order to avoid trouble.

Then how does he come to be timocratic?

When he listens, first, to his mother complaining that her husband isn't one of the rulers and that she's at a disadvantage among the other women as a result. Then she sees that he's not very concerned about money and that he doesn't fight back when he's insulted, whether in private or in public in the courts, *d* but is indifferent to everything of that sort. She also sees him concentrating his mind on his own thoughts, neither honoring nor dishonoring her overmuch. Angered by all this, she tells her son that his father is unmanly, too easy-going, and all the other things that women repeat over and over again in such cases. *e*

Yes, Adeimantus said, it's like them to have many such complaints.

You know, too, I said, that the servants of men like that—the ones who are thought to be well disposed to the family—also say similar things to the son in private. When they see the father failing to prosecute someone who owes him money or has wronged him in some other way, they urge the son to take revenge on all such people when he grows up and to be more of a man than his father. The boy hears and sees the 550 same kind of things when he goes out: Those in the city who do their own work are called fools and held to be of little account, while those who meddle in other people's affairs are honored and praised. The young man hears and sees all this, but he also listens to what his father says, observes what he does from close at hand, and compares his ways of living with those of the others. So he's pulled by both. His father nourishes the rational part of his soul and makes it *b* grow; the others nourish the spirited and appetitive parts. Because he isn't a bad man by nature but keeps bad company, when he's pulled in these two ways, he settles in the middle and surrenders the rule over himself to the middle part—the victory-loving and spirited part—and becomes a proud and honor-loving man.

I certainly think that you've given a full account of how this sort of man comes to be.

Then we now have the second constitution and the second man. *c*

We have.

Then shall we next talk, as Aeschylus says, of "another man ordered like another city," or shall we follow our plan and talk about the city first?

We must follow our plan.

And I suppose that the one that comes after the present constitution is oligarchy.

And what kind of constitution would you call oligarchy?

The constitution based on a property assessment, in which the rich rule, and the poor man has no d share in ruling.

I understand.

So mustn't we first explain how timarchy is transformed into oligarchy?

Yes.

And surely the manner of this transformation is clear even to the blind.

What is it like?

The treasure house filled with gold, which each possesses, destroys the constitution. First, they find ways of spending money for themselves, then they stretch the laws relating to this, then they and their wives disobey the laws altogether.

They would do that.

And as one person sees another doing this and emulates him, they make the majority of the others e like themselves.

They do.

From there they proceed further into money-making, and the more they value it, the less they value virtue. Or aren't virtue and wealth so opposed that if they were set on a scales, they'd always incline in opposite directions?

That's right.

So, when wealth and the wealthy are valued or 551 honored in a city, virtue and good people are valued less.

Clearly.

And what is valued is always practiced, and what isn't valued is neglected.

That's right.

Then, in the end, victory-loving and honor-loving men become lovers of making money, or money-lovers. And they praise and admire wealthy people and appoint them as rulers, while they dishonor poor ones.

Certainly.

Then, don't they pass a law that is characteristic of an oligarchic constitution, one that establishes a wealth qualification—higher where the constitution is more oligarchic, less where it's less so—and pro-claims that those whose property doesn't reach the b stated amount aren't qualified to rule? And they either put this through by force of arms, or else, before it comes to that, they terrorize the people and establish their constitution that way. Isn't that so?

Of course it is.

Generally speaking, then, that's the way this kind of constitution is established.

Yes, but what is its character? And what are the faults that we said it contained?   c

First of all, the very thing that defines it is one, for what would happen if someone were to choose the captains of ships by their wealth, refusing to entrust the ship to a poor person even if he was a better captain?

They would make a poor voyage of it.

And isn't the same true of the rule of anything else whatsoever?

I suppose so.

Except a city? Or does it also apply to a city?

To it most of all, since it's the most difficult and most important kind of rule.

That, then, is one major fault in oligarchy.   d

Apparently.

And what about this second fault? Is it any smaller than the other?

What fault?

That of necessity it isn't one city but two—one of the poor and one of the rich—living in the same place and always plotting against one another.

By god, that's just as big a fault as the first.

And the following is hardly a fine quality either, namely, that oligarchs probably aren't able to fight a war, for they'd be compelled either to arm and use the majority, and so have more to fear from them than the enemy, or not to use them and show up as true oligarchs—few in number—on the battlefield. e At the same time, they'd be unwilling to pay merce-naries, because of their love of money.

That certainly isn't a fine quality either.

And what about the meddling in other people's affairs that we condemned before? Under this consti-tution, won't the same people be farmers, money-makers, and soldiers simultaneously? And do you think it's right for things to be that way?   552

Not at all.

Now, let's see whether this constitution is the first to admit the greatest of all evils.

Which one is that?

Allowing someone to sell all his possessions and someone else to buy them and then allowing the one who has sold them to go on living in the city, while belonging to none of its parts, for he's neither a money-maker, a craftsman, a member of the cavalry, or a hoplite, but a poor person without means.

b   It is the first to allow that.

At any rate, this sort of thing is not forbidden in oligarchies. If it were, some of their citizens wouldn't be excessively rich, while others are totally impoverished.

That's right.

Now, think about this. When the person who sells all his possessions was rich and spending his money, was he of any greater use to the city in the ways we've just mentioned than when he'd spent it all? Or did he merely seem to be one of the rulers of the city, while in truth he was neither ruler nor subject there, but only a squanderer of his property?

That's right. He seemed to be part of the city, but
c   he was nothing but a squanderer.

Should we say, then, that, as a drone exists in a cell and is an affliction to the hive, so this person is a drone in the house and an affliction to the city?

That's certainly right, Socrates.

Hasn't the god made all the winged drones stingless, Adeimantus, as well as some wingless ones, while other wingless ones have dangerous stings? And don't the stingless ones continue as beggars into old age, while those with stings become what we call evil-
d   doers?

That's absolutely true.

Clearly, then, in any city where you see beggars, there are thieves, pickpockets, temple-robbers, and all such evildoers hidden.

That is clear.

What about oligarchic cities? Don't you see beggars in them?

Almost everyone except the rulers is a beggar there.

Then mustn't we suppose that they also include
e   many evildoers with stings, whom the rulers carefully keep in check by force?

We certainly must.

And shall we say that the presence of such people is the result of lack of education, bad rearing, and a bad constitutional arrangement?

We shall.

This, then, or something like it, is the oligarchic city. It contains all these evils and probably others in addition.

That's pretty well what it's like.

Then, let's take it that we've disposed of the constitution called oligarchy—I mean the one that gets its 553 rulers on the basis of a property assessment—and let's examine the man who is like it, both how he comes to be and what sort of man he is.

All right.

Doesn't the transformation from the timocrat we described to an oligarch occur mostly in this way?

Which way?

The timocrat's son at first emulates his father and follows in his footsteps. Then he suddenly sees him crashing against the city like a ship against a reef, spilling out all his possessions, even his life. He had b held a generalship or some other high office, was brought to court by false witnesses, and was either put to death or exiled or was disenfranchised and had all his property confiscated.

That's quite likely.

The son sees all this, suffers from it, loses his property, and, fearing for his life, immediately drives from the throne in his own soul the honor-loving and spirited part that ruled there. Humbled by poverty, he turns greedily to making money, and, little by little, c saving and working, he amasses property. Don't you think that this person would establish his appetitive and money-making part on the throne, setting it up as a great king within himself, adorning it with golden tiaras and collars and girding it with Persian swords?

I do.

He makes the rational and spirited parts sit on the ground beneath appetite, one on either side, reducing d them to slaves. He won't allow the first to reason about or examine anything except how a little money can be made into great wealth. And he won't allow the second to value or admire anything but wealth and wealthy people or to have any ambition other than the acquisition of wealth or whatever might contribute to getting it.

There is no other transformation of a young man who is an honor-lover into one who is a money-lover that's as swift and sure as this.

Then isn't this an oligarchic man?   e

Surely, he developed out of a man who resembled the constitution from which oligarchy came.

Then let's consider whether he resembles the oligarchic constitution?

554   All right.

Doesn't he resemble it, in the first place, by attaching the greatest importance to money?

Of course.

And, further, by being a thrifty worker, who satisfies only his necessary appetites, makes no other expenditures, and enslaves his other desires as vain.

That's right.

A somewhat squalid fellow, who makes a profit from everything and hoards it—the sort the majority *b* admires. Isn't this the man who resembles such a constitution?

That's my opinion, anyway. At any rate, money is valued above everything by both the city and the man.

I don't suppose that such a man pays any attention to education.

Not in my view, for, if he did, he wouldn't have chosen a blind leader for his chorus and honored him most.

Good. But consider this: Won't we say that, because of his lack of education, the dronish appetites—some beggarly and others evil—exist in him, but that they're *c* forcibly held in check by his carefulness?

Certainly.

Do you know where you should look to see the evildoings of such people?

Where?

To the guardianship of orphans or something like that, where they have ample opportunity to do injustice with impunity.

True.

And doesn't this make it clear that, in those other contractual obligations, where he has a good reputation and is thought to be just, he's forcibly holding his other evil appetites in check by means of some decent part of himself? He holds them in check, not *d* by persuading them that it's better not to act on them or taming them with arguments, but by compulsion and fear, trembling for his other possessions.

That's right.

And, by god, you'll find that most of them have appetites akin to those of the drone, once they have other people's money to spend.

You certainly will.

Then someone like that wouldn't be entirely free from internal civil war and wouldn't be one but in some way two, though generally his better desires are in control of his worse.   *e*

That's right.

For this reason, he'd be more respectable than many, but the true virtue of a single-minded and harmonious soul far escapes him.

I suppose so.

Further, this thrifty man is a poor individual contestant for victory in a city or for any other fine and much-honored thing, for he's not willing to spend money for the sake of a fine reputation or on contests for such *555* things. He's afraid to arouse his appetites for spending or to call on them as allies to obtain victory, so he fights like an oligarch, with only a few of his resources. Hence he's mostly defeated but remains rich.

That's right.

Then have we any further doubt that a thrifty money-maker is like an oligarchic city?   *b*

None at all.

It seems, then, that we must next consider democracy, how it comes into being, and what character it has when it does, so that, knowing in turn the character of a man who resembles it, we can present him for judgment.

That would be quite consistent with what we've been doing.

Well, isn't the city changed from an oligarchy to a democracy in some such way as this, because of its insatiable desire to attain what it has set before itself as the good, namely, the need to become as rich as possible?

In what way?

Since those who rule in the city do so because they own a lot, I suppose they're unwilling to enact *c* laws to prevent young people who've had no discipline from spending and wasting their wealth, so that by making loans to them, secured by the young people's property, and then calling those loans in, they themselves become even richer and more honored.

That's their favorite thing to do.

So isn't it clear by now that it is impossible for a city to honor wealth and at the same time for its citizens to acquire moderation, but one or the other is inevitably neglected?   *d*

That's pretty clear.

Because of this neglect and because they encourage bad discipline, oligarchies not infrequently reduce people of no common stamp to poverty.

That's right.

And these people sit idle in the city, I suppose, with their stings and weapons—some in debt, some disenfranchised, some both—hating those who've acquired their property, plotting against them and others, and longing for a revolution.

They do.

The money-makers, on the other hand, with their eyes on the ground, pretend not to see these people, and by lending money they disable any of the remainder who resist, exact as interest many times the principal sum, and so create a considerable number of drones and beggars in the city.

A considerable number indeed.

In any case, they are unwilling to quench this kind of evil as it flares up in the city, either in the way we mentioned, by preventing people from doing whatever they like with their own property or by another law which would also solve the problem.

What law?

The second-best one, which compels the citizens to care about virtue by prescribing that the majority of voluntary contracts be entered into at the lender's own risk, for lenders would be less shameless then in their pursuit of money in the city and fewer of those evils we were mentioning just now would develop.

Far fewer.

But as it is, for all these reasons, the rulers in the city treat their subjects in the way we described. But as for themselves and their children, don't they make their young fond of luxury, incapable of effort either mental or physical, too soft to stand up to pleasures or pains, and idle besides?

Of course.

And don't they themselves neglect everything except making money, caring no more for virtue than the poor do?

Yes.

But when rulers and subjects in this condition meet on a journey or some other common undertaking—it might be a festival, an embassy, or a campaign, or they might be shipmates or fellow soldiers—and see one another in danger, in these circumstances are the poor in any way despised by the rich? Or rather isn't it often the case that a poor man, lean and suntanned, stands in battle next to a rich man, reared in the shade and carrying a lot of excess flesh, and sees him panting and at a loss? And don't you think

that he'd consider that it's through the cowardice of the poor that such people are rich and that one poor man would say to another when they met in private: "These people are at our mercy; they're good for nothing"?

I know very well that's what they would do.

Then, as a sick body needs only a slight shock from outside to become ill and is sometimes at civil war with itself even without this, so a city in the same condition needs only a small pretext—such as one side bringing in allies from an oligarchy or the other from a democracy—to fall ill and to fight with itself and is sometimes in a state of civil war even without any external influence.

Absolutely.

And I suppose that democracy comes about when the poor are victorious, killing some of their opponents and expelling others, and giving the rest an equal share in ruling under the constitution, and for the most part assigning people to positions of rule by lot.

Yes, that's how democracy is established, whether by force of arms or because those on the opposing side are frightened into exile.

Then how do these people live? What sort of constitution do they have? It's clear that a man who is like it will be democratic.

That is clear.

First of all, then, aren't they free? And isn't the city full of freedom and freedom of speech? And doesn't everyone in it have the license to do what he wants?

That's what they say, at any rate.

And where people have this license, it's clear that each of them will arrange his own life in whatever manner pleases him.

It is.

Then I suppose that it's most of all under this constitution that one finds people of all varieties.

Of course.

Then it looks as though this is the finest or most beautiful of the constitutions, for, like a coat embroidered with every kind of ornament, this city, embroidered with every kind of character type, would seem to be the most beautiful. And many people would probably judge it to be so, as women and children do when they see something multicolored.

They certainly would.

It's also a convenient place to look for a constitution.

Why's that?

Because it contains all kinds of constitutions on account of the license it gives its citizens. So it looks as though anyone who wants to put a city in order, as we were doing, should probably go to a democracy, as to a supermarket of constitutions, pick out whatever pleases him, and establish that.

He probably wouldn't be at a loss for models, at any rate.

In this city, there is no requirement to rule, even if you're capable of it, or again to be ruled if you don't want to be, or to be at war when the others are, or at peace unless you happen to want it. And there is no requirement in the least that you not serve in public office as a juror, if you happen to want to serve, even if there is a law forbidding you to do so. Isn't that a divine and pleasant life, while it lasts?

It probably is—while it lasts.

And what about the calm of some of their condemned criminals? Isn't that a sign of sophistication? Or have you never seen people who've been condemned to death or exile under such a constitution stay on at the center of things, strolling around like the ghosts of dead heroes, without anyone staring at them or giving them a thought?

Yes, I've seen it a lot.

And what about the city's tolerance? Isn't it so completely lacking in small-mindedness that it utterly despises the things we took so seriously when we were founding our city, namely, that unless someone had transcendent natural gifts, he'd never become good unless he played the right games and followed a fine way of life from early childhood? Isn't it magnificent the way it tramples all this underfoot, by giving no thought to what someone was doing before he entered public life and by honoring him if only he tells them that he wishes the majority well?

Yes, it's altogether splendid!

Then these and others like them are the characteristics of democracy. And it would seem to be a pleasant constitution, which lacks rulers but not variety and which distributes a sort of equality to both equals and unequals alike.

We certainly know what you mean.

Consider, then, what private individual resembles it. Or should we first inquire, as we did with the city, how he comes to be?

Yes, we should.

Well, doesn't it happen like this? Wouldn't the son of that thrifty oligarch be brought up in his father's ways?

Of course.

Then he too rules his spendthrift pleasures by force—the ones that aren't money-making and are called unnecessary.

Clearly.

But, so as not to discuss this in the dark, do you want us first to define which desires are necessary and which aren't?

I do.

Aren't those we can't desist from and those whose satisfaction benefits us rightly called necessary, for we are by nature compelled to satisfy them both? Isn't that so?

Of course.

So we'd be right to apply the term "necessary" to them?

We would.

What about those that someone could get rid of if he practiced from youth on, those whose presence leads to no good or even to the opposite? If we said that all of them were unnecessary, would we be right?

We would.

Let's pick an example of each, so that we can grasp the patterns they exhibit.

We should do that.

Aren't the following desires necessary: the desire to eat to the point of health and well-being and the desire for bread and delicacies?

I suppose so.

The desire for bread is necessary on both counts; it's beneficial, and unless it's satisfied, we die.

Yes.

The desire for delicacies is also necessary to the extent that it's beneficial to well-being.

Absolutely.

What about the desire that goes beyond these and seeks other sorts of foods, that most people can get rid of, if it's restrained and educated while they're young, and that's harmful both to the body and to the reason and moderation of the soul? Would it be rightly called unnecessary?

It would indeed.

Then wouldn't we also say that such desires are spendthrift, while the earlier ones are money-making, because they profit our various projects?

Certainly.

And won't we say the same about the desire for sex and about other desires?

Yes.

And didn't we say that the person we just now called a drone is full of such pleasures and desires, since he is ruled by the unnecessary ones, while a *d* thrifty oligarch is ruled by his necessary desires?

We certainly did.

Let's go back, then, and explain how the democratic man develops out of the oligarchic one. It seems to me as though it mostly happens as follows.

How?

When a young man, who is reared in the miserly and uneducated manner we described, tastes the honey of the drones and associates with wild and dangerous creatures who can provide every variety of multicolored pleasure in every sort of way, this, as you might suppose, is the beginning of his transformation *e* from having an oligarchic constitution within him to having a democratic one.

It's inevitable that this is how it starts.

And just as the city changed when one party received help from like-minded people outside, doesn't the young man change when one party of his desires receives help from external desires that are akin to them and of the same form?

Absolutely.

And I suppose that, if any contrary help comes to the oligarchic party within him, whether from his father or from the rest of his household, who exhort and reproach him, then there's civil war and counter-*560* revolution within him, and he battles against himself.

That's right.

Sometimes the democratic party yields to the oligarchic, so that some of the young man's appetites are overcome, others are expelled, a kind of shame rises in his soul, and order is restored.

That does sometimes happen.

But I suppose that, as desires are expelled, others akin to them are being nurtured unawares, and because of his father's ignorance about how to bring *b* him up, they grow numerous and strong.

That's what tends to happen.

These desires draw him back into the same bad company and in secret intercourse breed a multitude of others.

Certainly.

And, seeing the citadel of the young man's soul empty of knowledge, fine ways of living, and words of truth (which are the best watchmen and guardians of the thoughts of those men whom the gods love), they finally occupy that citadel themselves.

They certainly do. *c*

And in the absence of these guardians, false and boastful words and beliefs rush up and occupy this part of him.

Indeed, they do.

Won't he then return to these lotus-eaters and live with them openly? And if some help comes to the thrifty part of his soul from his household, won't these boastful words close the gates of the royal wall within him to prevent these allies from entering and refuse even to receive the words of older private individuals as ambassadors? Doing battle and controlling things themselves, won't they call reverence foolishness and *d* moderation cowardice, abusing them and casting them out beyond the frontiers like disenfranchised exiles? And won't they persuade the young man that measured and orderly expenditure is boorish and mean, and, joining with many useless desires, won't they expel it across the border?

They certainly will.

Having thus emptied and purged these from the soul of the one they've possessed and initiated in splendid rites, they proceed to return insolence, anarchy, extravagance, and shamelessness from exile in a *e* blaze of torchlight, wreathing them in garlands and accompanying them with a vast chorus of followers. They praise the returning exiles and give them fine names, calling insolence good breeding, anarchy freedom, extravagance magnificence, and shamelessness courage. Isn't it in some such way as this that someone who is young changes, after being brought up with necessary desires, to the liberation and release of use-*561* less and unnecessary pleasures?

Yes, that's clearly the way it happens.

And I suppose that after that he spends as much money, effort, and time on unnecessary pleasures as on necessary ones. If he's lucky, and his frenzy doesn't go too far, when he grows older, and the great tumult within him has spent itself, he welcomes back some of the exiles, ceases to surrender himself completely to the newcomers, and puts his pleasures on an equal *b* footing. And so he lives, always surrendering rule over himself to whichever desire comes along, as if it were chosen by lot. And when that is satisfied, he surrenders the rule to another, not disdaining any but satisfying them all equally.

That's right.

And he doesn't admit any word of truth into the guardhouse, for if someone tells him that some pleasures belong to fine and good desires and others to c evil ones and that he must pursue and value the former and restrain and enslave the latter, he denies all this and declares that all pleasures are equal and must be valued equally.

That's just what someone in that condition would do.

And so he lives on, yielding day by day to the desire at hand. Sometimes he drinks heavily while listening to the flute; at other times, he drinks only water and is on a diet; sometimes he goes in for physical training; d at other times, he's idle and neglects everything; and sometimes he even occupies himself with what he takes to be philosophy. He often engages in politics, leaping up from his seat and saying and doing whatever comes into his mind. If he happens to admire soldiers, he's carried in that direction, if money-makers, in that one. There's neither order nor necessity in his life, but he calls it pleasant, free, and blessedly happy, and he follows it for as long as he lives.

You've perfectly described the life of a man who e believes in legal equality.

I also suppose that he's a complex man, full of all sorts of characters, fine and multicolored, just like the democratic city, and that many men and women might envy his life, since it contains the most models of constitutions and ways of living.

That's right.

Then shall we set this man beside democracy as 562 one who is rightly called democratic?

Let's do so.

The finest constitution and the finest man remain for us to discuss, namely, tyranny and a tyrannical man.

They certainly do.

Come, then, how does tyranny come into being? It's fairly clear that it evolves from democracy.

It is.

And doesn't it evolve from democracy in much the b same way that democracy does from oligarchy?

What way is that?

The good that oligarchy puts before itself and because of which it is established is wealth, isn't it?

Yes.

And its insatiable desire for wealth and its neglect of other things for the sake of money-making is what destroyed it, isn't it?

That's true.

And isn't democracy's insatiable desire for what it defines as the good also what destroys it?

What do you think it defines as the good?

Freedom: Surely you'd hear a democratic city say that this is the finest thing it has, so that as a result it is the only city worth living in for someone who is c by nature free.

Yes, you often hear that.

Then, as I was about to say, doesn't the insatiable desire for freedom and the neglect of other things change this constitution and put it in need of a dictatorship?

In what way?

I suppose that, when a democratic city, athirst for freedom, happens to get bad cupbearers for its leaders, so that it gets drunk by drinking more than it should of the unmixed wine of freedom, then, unless the d rulers are very pliable and provide plenty of that freedom, they are punished by the city and accused of being accursed oligarchs.

Yes, that is what it does.

It insults those who obey the rulers as willing slaves and good-for-nothings and praises and honors, both in public and in private, rulers who behave like subjects and subjects who behave like rulers. And isn't it inevitable that freedom should go to all lengths in such a city?   e

Of course.

It makes its way into private households and in the end breeds anarchy even among the animals.

What do you mean?

I mean that a father accustoms himself to behave like a child and fear his sons, while the son behaves like a father, feeling neither shame nor fear in front of his parents, in order to be free. A resident alien or a foreign visitor is made equal to a citizen, and he is their equal.   563

Yes, that is what happens.

It does. And so do other little things of the same sort. A teacher in such a community is afraid of his students and flatters them, while the students despise their teachers or tutors. And, in general, the young imitate their elders and compete with them in word and deed, while the old stoop to the level of the young and are full of play and pleasantry, imitating the young for fear of appearing disagreeable and au-

b thoritarian.

Absolutely.

The utmost freedom for the majority is reached in such a city when bought slaves, both male and female, are no less free than those who bought them. And I almost forgot to mention the extent of the legal equal-ity of men and women and of the freedom in the relations between them.

What about the animals? Are we, with Aeschylus, going to "say whatever it was that came to our lips

c just now" about them?

Certainly. I put it this way: No one who hasn't experienced it would believe how much freer domes-tic animals are in a democratic city than anywhere else. As the proverb says, dogs become like their mis-tresses; horses and donkeys are accustomed to roam freely and proudly along the streets, bumping into anyone who doesn't get out of their way; and all the

d rest are equally full of freedom.

You're telling me what I already know. I've often experienced that sort of thing while travelling in the country.

To sum up: Do you notice how all these things together make the citizens' souls so sensitive that, if anyone even puts upon *himself* the least degree of slavery, they become angry and cannot endure it. And in the end, as you know, they take no notice of the laws, whether written or unwritten, in order to avoid

e having any master at all.

I certainly do.

This, then, is the fine and impetuous origin from which tyranny seems to me to evolve.

It is certainly impetuous. But what comes next?

The same disease that developed in oligarchy and destroyed it also develops here, but it is more wide-spread and virulent because of the general permissive-ness, and it eventually enslaves democracy. In fact, excessive action in one direction usually sets up a reaction in the opposite direction. This happens in seasons, in plants, in bodies, and, last but not least,

564 in constitutions.

That's to be expected.

Extreme freedom can't be expected to lead to any-thing but a change to extreme slavery, whether for a private individual or for a city.

No, it can't.

Then I don't suppose that tyranny evolves from any constitution other than democracy—the most severe and cruel slavery from the utmost freedom.

Yes, that's reasonable.

But I don't think that was your question. You asked what was the disease that developed in oligarchy and also in democracy, enslaving it.   *b*

That's true.

And what I had in mind as an answer was that class of idle and extravagant men, whose bravest mem-bers are leaders and the more cowardly ones followers. We compared them to stinged and stingless drones, respectively.

That's right.

Now, these two groups cause problems in any con-stitution, just as phlegm and bile do in the body. And it's against them that the good doctor and lawgiver of a city must take advance precautions, first, to pre-   *c* vent their presence and, second, to cut them out of the hive as quickly as possible, cells and all, if they should happen to be present.

Yes, by god, he must cut them out altogether.

Then let's take up the question in the following way, so that we can see what we want more clearly.

In what way?

Let's divide a democratic city into three parts in the-ory, this being the way that it is in fact divided. One part is this class of idlers, that grows here no less than in an oligarchy, because of the general permissiveness.   *d*

So it does.

But it is far fiercer in democracy than in the other.

How so?

In an oligarchy it is fierce because it's disdained, but since it is prevented from having a share in ruling, it doesn't get any exercise and doesn't become vigor-ous. In a democracy, however, with a few exceptions, this class is the dominant one. Its fiercest members do all the talking and acting, while the rest settle near the speaker's platform and buzz and refuse to tolerate the opposition of another speaker, so that, under a democratic constitution, with the few exceptions I referred to before, this class manages everything.   *e*

That's right.

Then there's a second class that always distinguishes itself from the majority of people.

Which is that?

When everybody is trying to make money, those who are naturally most organized generally become the wealthiest.

Probably so.

Then they would provide the most honey for the drones and the honey that is most easily extractable by them.

Yes, for how could anyone extract it from those who have very little?

Then I suppose that these rich people are called drone-fodder.

Something like that.

565 The people—those who work with their own hands—are the third class. They take no part in politics and have few possessions, but, when they are assembled, they are the largest and most powerful class in a democracy.

They are. But they aren't willing to assemble often unless they get a share of the honey.

And they always do get a share, though the leaders, in taking the wealth of the rich and distributing it to the people, keep the greater part for themselves.

b Yes, that is the way the people get their share.

And I suppose that those whose wealth is taken away are compelled to defend themselves by speaking before the people and doing whatever else they can.

Of course.

And they're accused by the drones of plotting against the people and of being oligarchs, even if they have no desire for revolution at all.

That's right.

So in the end, when they see the people trying to harm them, they truly do become oligarchs and c embrace oligarchy's evils, whether they want to or not. But neither group does these things willingly. Rather the people act as they do because they are ignorant and are deceived by the drones, and the rich act as they do because they are driven to it by the stinging of those same drones.

Absolutely.

And then there are impeachments, judgments, and trials on both sides.

That's right.

Now, aren't the people always in the habit of setting up one man as their special champion, nurturing him and making him great?

They are.

And it's clear that, when a tyrant arises, this special leadership is the sole root from which he sprouts.   d

It is.

What is the beginning of the transformation from leader of the people to tyrant? Isn't it clear that it happens when the leader begins to behave like the man in the story told about the temple of the Lycean Zeus in Arcadia?

What story is that?

That anyone who tastes the one piece of human innards that's chopped up with those of other sacrificial victims must inevitably become a wolf. Haven't you heard that story?   e

I have.

Then doesn't the same happen with a leader of the people who dominates a docile mob and doesn't restrain himself from spilling kindred blood? He brings someone to trial on false charges and murders him (as tyrants so often do), and, by thus blotting out a human life, his impious tongue and lips taste kindred citizen blood. He banishes some, kills others, and drops hints to the people about the cancellation of debts and the redistribution of land. And because of 566 these things, isn't a man like that inevitably fated either to be killed by his enemies or to be transformed from a man into a wolf by becoming a tyrant?

It's completely inevitable.

He's the one who stirs up civil wars against the rich.

He is.

And if he's exiled but manages, despite his enemies, to return, doesn't he come back as a full-fledged tyrant?

Clearly.

And if these enemies are unable to expel him or to put him to death by accusing him before the city,   b they plot secretly to kill him.

That's usually what happens at least.

And all who've reached this stage soon discover the famous request of the tyrant, namely, that the people give him a bodyguard to keep their defender safe for them.

That's right.

And the people give it to him, I suppose, because they *are* afraid for his safety but aren't worried at all about their own.

c   That's right.

And when a wealthy man sees this and is charged with being an enemy of the people because of his wealth, then, as the oracle to Croesus put it, he

> Flees to the banks of the many-pebbled Hermus,
> Neither staying put nor being ashamed of his
> cowardice.

He wouldn't get a second chance of being ashamed.

That's true, for if he was caught, he'd be executed.

He most certainly would.

But, as for the leader, he doesn't lie on the ground "mighty in his might," but, having brought down

d   many others, he stands in the city's chariot, a complete tyrant rather than a leader.

What else?

Then let's describe the happiness of this man and of the city in which a mortal like him comes to be.

Certainly, let's do so.

During the first days of his reign and for some time after, won't he smile in welcome at anyone he meets, saying that he's no tyrant, making all sorts of promises both in public and in private, freeing the people

e   from debt, redistributing the land to them and to his followers, and pretending to be gracious and gentle to all?

He'd have to.

But I suppose that, when he has dealt with his exiled enemies by making peace with some and destroying others, so that all is quiet on that front, the first thing he does is to stir up a war, so that the people will continue to feel the need of a leader.

Probably so.

But also so that they'll become poor through having

567   to pay war taxes, for that way they'll have to concern themselves with their daily needs and be less likely to plot against him.

Clearly.

Besides, if he suspects some people of having thoughts of freedom and of not favoring his rule, can't he find a pretext for putting them at the mercy of the enemy in order to destroy them? And for all these

reasons, isn't it necessary for a tyrant to be always stirring up war?

It is.

And because of this, isn't he all the more readily hated by the citizens?

b

Of course.

Moreover, don't the bravest of those who helped to establish his tyranny and who hold positions of power within it speak freely to each other and to him, criticizing what's happening?

They probably do.

Then the tyrant will have to do away with all of them if he intends to rule, until he's left with neither friend nor enemy of any worth.

Clearly.

He must, therefore, keep a sharp lookout for anyone who is brave, large-minded, knowledgeable, or rich. And so happy is he that he must be the enemy of them all, whether he wants to be or not, and plot   c
against them until he has purged them from the city.

That's a fine sort of purge!

Yes, for it's the opposite of the one that doctors perform on the body. They draw off the worst and leave the best, but he does just the opposite.

Yet I expect he'll have to do this, if he's really going to rule.

It's a blessedly happy necessity he's bound by, since it requires him either to live with the inferior majority,   d
even though they hate him, or not to live at all.

Yet that's exactly his condition.

And won't he need a larger and more loyal bodyguard, the more his actions make the citizens hate him?

Of course.

And who will these trustworthy people be? And where will he get them from?

They'll come swarming of their own accord, if he pays them.

Drones, by the dog! All manner of foreign drones! That's what I think you're talking about.

e

You're right.

But what about in the city itself? Wouldn't he be willing . . .

Willing to what?

To deprive citizens of their slaves by freeing them and enlisting them in his bodyguard?

He certainly would, since they'd be likely to prove most loyal to him.

What a blessedly happy sort of fellow you make the tyrant out to be, if these are the sort of people he employs as friends and loyal followers after he's done away with the earlier ones.

568 Nonetheless, they're the sort he employs.

And these companions and new citizens admire and associate with him, while the decent people hate and avoid him.

Of course.

It isn't for nothing, then, that tragedy in general has the reputation of being wise and that Euripides is thought to be outstandingly so.

Why's that?

Because among other shrewd things he said that "tyrants are wise who associate with the wise." And by "the wise" he clearly means the sort of people that b we've seen to be the tyrant's associates.

Yes. And he and the other poets eulogize tyranny as godlike and say lots of other such things about it.

Then, surely, since the tragic poets are wise, they'll forgive us and those whose constitutions resemble ours, if we don't admit them into our city, since they praise tyranny.

I suppose that the more sophisticated among c them will.

And so I suppose that they go around to other cities, draw crowds, hire people with fine, big, persuasive voices, and lead their constitutions to tyranny and democracy.

They do indeed.

And besides this, they receive wages and honors, especially—as one might expect—from the tyrants and, in second place, from the democracies, but the higher they go on the ascending scale of constitutions, d the more their honor falls off, as if unable to keep up with them for lack of breath.

Absolutely.

But we digress. So let's return to that fine, numerous, diverse, and ever-changing bodyguard of the tyrant and explain how he'll pay for it.

Clearly, if there are sacred treasuries in the city, he'll use them for as long as they last, as well as the property of the people he has destroyed, thus requiring smaller taxes from the people.

e What about when these give out?

Clearly, both he and his fellow revellers—his companions, male or female—will have to feed off his father's estate.

I understand. You mean that the people, who fathered the tyrant, will have to feed him and his companions.

They'll be forced to do so.

And what would you have to say about this? What if the people get angry and say, first, that it isn't just for a grown-up son to be fed by his father but, on the contrary, for the father to be fed by his son; second, that they didn't father him and establish him in power so that, when he'd become strong, they'd be enslaved to their own slave and have to feed both him and his 569 slaves, along with other assorted rabble, but because they hoped that, with him as their leader, they'd be free from the rich and the so-called fine and good people in the city; third, that they therefore order him and his companions to leave the city, just as a father might drive a son and his troublesome fellow revellers from his house?

Then, by god, the people will come to know what kind of creature they have fathered, welcomed, and made strong and that they are the weaker trying to drive out the stronger. b

What do you mean? Will the tyrant dare to use violence against his father or to hit him if he doesn't obey?

Yes—once he's taken away his father's weapons.

You mean that the tyrant is a parricide and a harsh nurse of old age, that his rule has become an acknowledged tyranny at last, and that—as the saying goes— by trying to avoid the frying pan of enslavement to free men, the people have fallen into the fire of having slaves as their masters, and that in the place of the great but inappropriate freedom they enjoyed under c democracy, they have put upon themselves the harshest and most bitter slavery to slaves.

That's exactly what I mean.

Well, then, aren't we justified in saying that we have adequately described how tyranny evolves from democracy and what it's like when it has come into being?

We certainly are, he said.

Book IX

It remains, I said, to consider the tyrannical man 571 himself, how he evolves from a democrat, what he is like when he has come into being, and whether he is wretched or blessedly happy.

Yes, he said, he is the one who is still missing.

And do you know what else I think is still missing? What?

I don't think we have adequately distinguished the kinds and numbers of our desires, and, if that subject isn't adequately dealt with, our entire investigation *b* will be less clear.

Well, isn't now as fine a time as any to discuss the matter?

It certainly is. Consider, then, what I want to know about our desires. It's this: Some of our unnecessary pleasures and desires seem to me to be lawless. They are probably present in everyone, but they are held in check by the laws and by the better desires in alliance with reason. In a few people, they have been eliminated entirely or only a few weak ones remain, *c* while in others they are stronger and more numerous.

What desires do you mean?

Those that are awakened in sleep, when the rest of the soul—the rational, gentle, and ruling part— slumbers. Then the beastly and savage part, full of food and drink, casts off sleep and seeks to find a way to gratify itself. You know that there is nothing it won't dare to do at such a time, free of all control by shame or reason. It doesn't shrink from trying to have sex with a mother, as it supposes, or with anyone *d* else at all, whether man, god, or beast. It will commit any foul murder, and there is no food it refuses to eat. In a word, it omits no act of folly or shamelessness.

That's completely true.

On the other hand, I suppose that someone who is healthy and moderate with himself goes to sleep only after having done the following: First, he rouses his rational part and feasts it on fine arguments and *e* speculations; second, he neither starves nor feasts his appetites, so that they will slumber and not disturb his best part with either their pleasure or their pain, *572* but they'll leave it alone, pure and by itself, to get on with its investigations, to yearn after and perceive something, it knows not what, whether it is past, present, or future; third, he soothes his spirited part in the same way, for example, by not falling asleep with his spirit still aroused after an outburst of anger. And when he has quieted these two parts and aroused the third, in which reason resides, and so takes his rest, you know that it is then that he best grasps the truth and that the visions that appear in his dreams are *b* least lawless.

Entirely so.

However, we've been carried away from what we wanted to establish, which is this: Our dreams make it clear that there is a dangerous, wild, and lawless form of desire in everyone, even in those of us who seem to be entirely moderate or measured. See whether you think I'm talking sense and whether or not you agree with me.

I do agree.

Recall, then, what we said a democratic man is like. He was produced by being brought up from youth by a thrifty father who valued only those desires that make money and who despised the unnecessary *c* ones that aim at frivolity and display. Isn't that right?

Yes.

And by associating with more sophisticated men, who are full of the latter desires, he starts to indulge in every kind of insolence and to adopt their form of behavior, because of his hatred of his father's thrift. But, because he has a better nature than his corrupters, he is pulled in both directions and settles down in the middle between his father's way of life and theirs. And enjoying each in moderation, as he supposes, he leads a life that is neither slavish nor lawless *d* and from having been oligarchic he becomes democratic.

That was and is our opinion about this type of man.

Suppose now that this man has in turn become older and that *he* has a son who is brought up in *his* father's ethos.

All right.

And further suppose that the same things that happened to his father now happen to him. First, he is led to all the kinds of lawlessness that those who are leading him call freedom. Then his father and the *e* rest of the household come to the aid of the middle desires, while the others help the other ones. Then, when those clever enchanters and tyrant-makers have no hope of keeping hold of the young man in any other way, they contrive to plant in him a powerful erotic love, like a great winged drone, to be the leader of those idle desires that spend whatever is at hand. Or do you think that erotic love is anything other *573* than an enormous drone in such people?

I don't think that it could be anything else.

And when the other desires—filled with incense, myrrh, wreaths, wine, and the other pleasures found in their company—buzz around the drone, nurturing it and making it grow as large as possible, they plant the sting of longing in it. Then this leader of the soul adopts madness as its bodyguard and becomes

b frenzied. If it finds any beliefs or desires in the man that are thought to be good or that still have some shame, it destroys them and throws them out, until it's purged him of moderation and filled him with imported madness.

You've perfectly described the evolution of a tyrannical man.

Is this the reason that erotic love has long been called a tyrant?

It looks that way.

Then doesn't a drunken man have something of

c a tyrannical mind?

Yes, he has.

And a man who is mad and deranged attempts to rule not just human beings, but gods as well, and expects that he will be able to succeed.

He certainly does.

Then a man becomes tyrannical in the precise sense of the term when either his nature or his way of life or both of them together make him drunk, filled with erotic desire, and mad.

Absolutely.

This, then, it seems, is how a tyrannical man comes to be. But what way does he live?

No doubt *you're* going to tell *me*, just as posers of

d riddles usually do.

I am. I think that someone in whom the tyrant of erotic love dwells and in whom it directs everything next goes in for feasts, revelries, luxuries, girlfriends, and all that sort of thing.

Necessarily.

And don't many terrible desires grow up day and night beside the tyrannical one, needing many things to satisfy them?

Indeed they do.

Hence any income someone like that has is soon spent.

Of course.

Then borrowing follows, and expenditure of

e capital.

What else?

And when everything is gone, won't the violent crowd of desires that has nested within him inevitably shout in protest? And driven by the stings of the other desires and especially by erotic love itself (which leads

all of them as its bodyguard), won't he become frenzied and look to see who possesses anything that he could take, by either deceit or force?

He certainly will.

Consequently, he must acquire wealth from every source or live in great pain and suffering.

He must.

And just as the pleasures that are latecomers outdo the older ones and steal away their satisfactions, won't the man himself think that he deserves to outdo his father and mother, even though he is younger than they are—to take and spend his father's wealth when he's spent his own share?

Of course.

And if they won't give it to him, won't he first try to steal it from them by deceitful means?

Certainly.

And if that doesn't work, wouldn't he seize it by force?

I suppose so.

And if the old man and woman put up a fight, would he be careful to refrain from acting like a tyrant?

I'm not very optimistic about their fate, if they do.

But, good god, Adeimantus, do you think he'd sacrifice his long-loved and irreplaceable mother for a recently acquired girlfriend whom he can do without? Or that for the sake of a newfound and replaceable boyfriend in the bloom of youth, he'd strike his

c aged and irreplaceable father, his oldest friend? Or that he'd make his parents the slaves of these others, if he brought them under the same roof?

Yes, indeed he would.

It seems to be a very great blessing to produce a tyrannical son!

It certainly does!

What about when the possessions of his father and mother give out? With that great swarm of pleasures

d inside him, won't he first try to break into someone's house or snatch someone's coat late at night? Then won't he try to loot a temple? And in all this, the old traditional opinions that he had held from childhood about what is fine or shameful—opinions that are accounted just—are overcome by the opinions, newly released from slavery, that are now the bodyguard of erotic love and hold sway along with it. When he himself was subject to the laws and his father and had

e a democratic constitution within him, these opinions

574

b

used only to be freed in sleep. Now, however, under the tyranny of erotic love, he has permanently become while awake what he used to become occasionally while asleep, and he won't hold back from any terrible murder or from any kind of food or act. But, rather, erotic love lives like a tyrant within him, in complete 575 anarchy and lawlessness as his sole ruler, and drives him, as if he were a city, to dare anything that will provide sustenance for itself and the unruly mob around it (some of whose members have come in from the outside as a result of his keeping bad company, while others have come from within, freed and let loose by his own bad habits). Isn't this the life that a tyrannical man leads?

It is indeed.

Now, if there are only a few such men in a city, and the rest of the people are moderate, this mob will leave the city in order to act as a bodyguard to b some other tyrant or to serve as mercenaries if there happens to be a war going on somewhere. But if they chance to live in a time of peace and quiet, they'll remain in the city and bring about lots of little evils.

What sort of evils do you mean?

They steal, break into houses, snatch purses, steal clothes, rob temples, and sell people into slavery. Sometimes, if they are good speakers, they become sycophants and bear false witness and accept bribes.

These evils *are* small, provided that there happen c to be only a few such people.

Yes, for small things are small by comparison to big ones. And when it comes to producing wickedness and misery in a city, all these evils together don't, as the saying goes, come within a mile of the rule of a tyrant. But when such people become numerous and conscious of their numbers, it is they—aided by the foolishness of the people—who create a tyrant. And he, more than any of them, has in his soul the greatest d and strongest tyrant of all.

Naturally, for he'd be the most tyrannical.

That's if the city happens to yield willingly, but if it resists him, then, just as he once chastised his mother and father, he'll now chastise his fatherland, if he can, by bringing in new friends and making his fatherland and his dear old motherland (as the Cretans call it) their slaves and keeping them that way, for this is surely the end at which such a man's desires are directed.

e It most certainly is.

Now, in private life, before a tyrannical man attains power, isn't he this sort of person—one who associates primarily with flatterers who are ready to obey him in everything? Or if he himself happens to need anything from other people, isn't he willing to fawn on them and make every gesture of friendship, as if he were dealing with his own family? But once he gets what 576 he wants, don't they become strangers again?

Yes, they certainly do.

So someone with a tyrannical nature lives his whole life without being friends with anyone, always a master to one man or a slave to another and never getting a taste of either freedom or true friendship.

That's right.

Wouldn't we be right to call someone like that untrustworthy?

Of course.

And isn't he as unjust as anyone can be? If indeed what we earlier agreed about justice was right.   b

And it certainly was right.

Then, let's sum up the worst type of man: His waking life is like the nightmare we described earlier.

That's right.

And he evolves from someone by nature most tyrannical who achieves sole rule. And the longer he remains tyrant, the more like the nightmare he becomes.

That's inevitable, said Glaucon, taking over the argument.

Well, then, I said, isn't the man who is clearly most vicious also clearly most wretched? And isn't the one who for the longest time is most of all a tyrant, most c wretched for the longest time? If, that is to say, truth rather than majority opinion is to settle these questions.

That much is certain, at any rate.

And isn't a tyrannical man like a city ruled by a tyrant, a democratic man like a city ruled by a democracy, and similarly with the others?

Of course.

And won't the relations between the cities with respect to virtue and happiness be the same as those between the men?

Certainly.   d

Then how does the city ruled by a tyrant compare to the city ruled by kings that we described first?

They are total opposites: one is the best, and the other the worst.

I won't ask you which is which, since it's obvious. But is your judgment the same with regard to their happiness and wretchedness? And let's not be dazzled by looking at one man—a tyrant—or at the few who surround him, but since it is essential to go into the city and study the whole of it, let's not give our opinion, till we've gone down and looked into every e corner.

That's right, for it's clear to everyone that there is no city more wretched than one ruled by a tyrant and none more happy than one ruled by kings.

Would I be right, then, to make the same challenge about the individuals, assuming, first, that the person 577 who is fit to judge them is someone who in thought can go down into a person's character and examine it thoroughly, someone who doesn't judge from outside, the way a child does, who is dazzled by the façade that tyrants adopt for the outside world to see, but is able to see right through that sort of thing? And, second, that he's someone—since we'd all listen to him if he were—who is competent to judge, because he has lived in the same house with a tyrant and witnessed his behavior at home and his treatment of each member of his household when he is stripped of his theatrical façade, and has also seen how he b behaves when in danger from the people? Shouldn't we ask the person who has seen all that to tell us how the tyrant compares to the others in happiness and wretchedness?

That's also right.

Then do you want us to pretend that we are among those who can give such a judgment and that we have already met tyrannical people, so that we'll have someone to answer our questions?

I certainly do.

Come, then, and look at it this way for me: Bearing c in mind the resemblance between the city and the man, look at each in turn and describe its condition.

What kinds of things do you want me to describe?

First, speaking of the city, would you say that a tyrannical city is free or enslaved?

It is as enslaved as it is possible to be.

Yet you see in it people who are masters and free.

I do see a few like that, but the whole city, so to speak, and the most decent part of it are wretched, dishonored slaves.

Then, if man and city are alike, mustn't the same d structure be in him too? And mustn't his soul be full

of slavery and unfreedom, with the most decent parts enslaved and with a small part, the maddest and most vicious, as their master?

It must.

What will you say about such a soul then? Is it free or slave?

Slave, of course.

And isn't the enslaved and tyrannical city least likely to do what it wants?

Certainly.

Then a tyrannical soul—I'm talking about the whole soul—will also be least likely to do what it wants and, forcibly driven by the stings of a dronish gadfly, will be full of disorder and regret.   e

How could it be anything else?

Is a tyrannically ruled city rich or poor?

Poor.

Then a tyrannical soul, too, must always be poor and unsatisfiable.   578

That's right.

What about fear? Aren't a tyrannical city and man full of it?

Absolutely.

And do you think that you'll find more wailing, groaning, lamenting, and grieving in any other city?

Certainly not.

Then, are such things more common in anyone besides a tyrannical man, who is maddened by his desires and erotic loves?

How could they be?

It is in view of all these things, I suppose, and others like them, that you judged this to be the most b wretched of cities.

And wasn't I right?

Of course you were. But what do you say about a tyrannical man, when you look at these same things?

He's by far the most wretched of all of them.

There you're no longer right.

How is that?

I don't think that this man has yet reached the extreme of wretchedness.

Then who has?

Perhaps you'll agree that this next case is even more wretched.

Which one?

The one who is tyrannical but doesn't live a private life, because some misfortune provides him with the c opportunity to become an actual tyrant.

On the basis of what was said before, I assume that what you say is true.

Yes, but in matters of this sort, it isn't enough just to assume these things; one needs to investigate carefully the two men in question by means of argument, for the investigation concerns the most important thing, namely, the good life and the bad one.

That's absolutely right.

Then consider whether I'm talking sense or not, for I think our investigation will be helped by the following examples.

What are they?

We should look at all the wealthy private citizens in our cities who have many slaves, for, like a tyrant, they rule over many, although not over so many as he does.

That's right.

And you know that they're secure and do not fear their slaves.

What have they got to be afraid of?

Nothing. And do you know why?

Yes. It's because the whole city is ready to defend each of its individual citizens.

You're right. But what if some god were to lift one of these men, his fifty or more slaves, and his wife and children out of the city and deposit him with his slaves and other property in a deserted place, where no free person could come to his assistance? How frightened would he be that he himself and his wife and children would be killed by the slaves?

Very frightened indeed.

And wouldn't he be compelled to fawn on some of his own slaves, promise them lots of things, and free them, even though he didn't want to? And wouldn't he himself have become a panderer to slaves?

He'd have to or else be killed.

What if the god were to settle many other neighbors around him, who wouldn't tolerate anyone to claim that he was the master of another and who would inflict the worst punishments on anyone they caught doing it?

I suppose that he'd have even worse troubles, since he'd be surrounded by nothing but vigilant enemies.

And isn't this the kind of prison in which the tyrant is held—the one whose nature is such as we have described it, filled with fears and erotic loves of all kinds? Even though his soul is really greedy for it,

he's the only one in the whole city who can't travel abroad or see the sights that other free people want to see. Instead, he lives like a woman, mostly confined to his own house, and envying any other citizen who happens to travel abroad and see something worthwhile.

That's entirely so.

Then, isn't this harvest of evils a measure of the difference between a tyrannical man who is badly governed on the inside—whom you judged to be most wretched just now—and one who doesn't live a private life but is compelled by some chance to be a tyrant, who tries to rule others when he can't even control himself. He's just like an exhausted body without any self-control, which, instead of living privately, is compelled to compete and fight with other bodies all its life.

That's exactly what he's like, Socrates, and what you say is absolutely true.

And so, Glaucon, isn't this a completely wretched condition to be in, and doesn't the reigning tyrant have an even harder life than the one you judged to be hardest?

He certainly does.

In truth, then, and whatever some people may think, a real tyrant is really a slave, compelled to engage in the worst kind of fawning, slavery, and pandering to the worst kind of people. He's so far from satisfying his desires in any way that it is clear— if one happens to know that one must study his whole soul—that he's in the greatest need of most things and truly poor. And, if indeed his state is like that of the city he rules, then he's full of fear, convulsions, and pains throughout his life. And it is like it, isn't it?

Of course it is.

And we'll also attribute to the man what we mentioned before, namely, that he is inevitably envious, untrustworthy, unjust, friendless, impious, host and nurse to every kind of vice, and that his ruling makes him even more so. And because of all these, he is extremely unfortunate and goes on to make those near him like himself.

No one with any understanding could possibly contradict you.

Come, then, and like the judge who makes the final decision, tell me who among the five—the king, the timocrat, the oligarch, the democrat, and the b tyrant—is first in happiness, who second, and so on in order.

That's easy. I rank them in virtue and vice, in happiness and its opposite, in the order of their appearance, as I might judge choruses.

Shall we, then, hire a herald, or shall I myself announce that the son of Ariston has given as his verdict that the best, the most just, and the most c happy is the most kingly, who rules like a king over himself, and that the worst, the most unjust, and the most wretched is the most tyrannical, who most tyrannizes himself and the city he rules?

Let it be so announced.

And shall I add to the announcement that it holds, whether these things remain hidden from every god and human being or not?

Add it.

Good. Then that is one of our proofs. And there'd be a second, if you happen to think that there is d anything in this.

In what?

In the fact that the soul of each individual is divided into three parts, in just the way that a city is, for that's the reason I think that there is another proof.

What is it?

This: it seems to me that there are three pleasures corresponding to the three parts of the soul, one peculiar to each part, and similarly with desires and kinds of rule.

What do you mean?

The first, we say, is the part with which a person learns, and the second the part with which he gets angry. As for the third, we had no one special name for it, since it's multiform, so we named it after the e biggest and strongest thing in it. Hence we called it the appetitive part, because of the intensity of its appetites for food, drink, sex, and all the things associated with them, but we also called it the money-loving part, because such appetites are most easily 581 satisfied by means of money.

And rightly so.

Then, if we said that its pleasure and love are for profit, wouldn't that best determine its central feature for the purposes of our argument and insure that we are clear about what we mean when we speak of this part of the soul, and wouldn't we be right to call it money-loving and profit-loving?

That's how it seems to me, at least.

What about the spirited part? Don't we say that it is wholly dedicated to the pursuit of control, victory, and high repute?

Certainly.   b

Then wouldn't it be appropriate for us to call it victory-loving and honor-loving?

It would be most appropriate.

Now, it is clear to everyone that the part with which we learn is always wholly straining to know where the truth lies and that, of the three parts, it cares least for money and reputation.

By far the least.

Then wouldn't it be appropriate for us to call it learning-loving and philosophical?

Of course.

And doesn't this part rule in some people's souls, while one of the other parts—whichever it happens to be—rules in other people's?   c

That's right.

And isn't that the reason we say that there are three primary kinds of people: philosophic, victory-loving, and profit-loving?

That's it precisely.

And also three forms of pleasure, one assigned to each of them?

Certainly.

And do you realize that, if you chose to ask three such people in turn to tell you which of their lives is most pleasant, each would give the highest praise to his own? Won't a money-maker say that the pleasure of being honored and that of learning are worth- d less compared to that of making a profit, if he gets no money from them?

He will.

What about an honor-lover? Doesn't he think that the pleasure of making money is vulgar and that the pleasure of learning—except insofar as it brings him honor—is smoke and nonsense?

He does.

And as for a philosopher, what do you suppose he thinks the other pleasures are worth compared to that of knowing where the truth lies and always being in e some such pleasant condition while learning? Won't he think that they are far behind? And won't he call them really necessary, since he'd have no need for them if they weren't necessary for life?

He will: we can be sure of that.

Then, since there's a dispute between the different forms of pleasure and between the lives themselves, not about which way of living is finer or more shameful or better or worse, but about which is more pleasant and less painful, how are we to know which of them is speaking most truly?

582

Don't ask me.

Look at it this way: How are we to judge things if we want to judge them well? Isn't it by experience, reason, and argument? Or could anyone have better criteria than these?

How could he?

Consider, then: Which of the three men has most experience of the pleasures we mentioned? Does a profit-lover learn what the truth itself is like or acquire more experience of the pleasure of knowing it than a philosopher does of making a profit?

b

There's a big difference between them. A philosopher has of necessity tasted the other pleasures since childhood, but it isn't necessary for a profit-lover to taste or experience the pleasure of learning the nature of the things that are and how sweet it is. Indeed, even if he were eager to taste it, he couldn't easily do so.

Then a philosopher is far superior to a profit-lover in his experience of both their pleasures.

c

He certainly is.

What about an honor-lover? Has he more experience of the pleasure of knowing than a philosopher has of the pleasure of being honored?

No, for honor comes to each of them, provided that he accomplishes his aim. A rich man is honored by many people, so is a courageous one and a wise one, but the pleasure of studying the things that are cannot be tasted by anyone except a philosopher.

Then, as far as experience goes, he is the finest judge of the three.

d

By far.

And he alone has gained his experience in the company of reason.

Of course.

Moreover, the instrument one must use to judge isn't the instrument of a profit-lover or an honor-lover but a philosopher.

What instrument is that?

Arguments, for didn't we say that we must judge by means of them?

Yes.

And argument is a philosopher's instrument most of all.

Of course.

Now, if wealth and profit were the best means of judging things, the praise and blame of a profit-lover would necessarily be truest.

e

That's right.

And if honor, victory, and courage were the best means, wouldn't it be the praise and blame of an honor-lover?

Clearly.

But since the best means are experience, reason, and argument . . .

The praise of a wisdom-lover and argument-lover is necessarily truest.

Then, of the three pleasures, the most pleasant is that of the part of the soul with which we learn, and the one in whom that part rules has the most pleasant life.

583

How could it be otherwise? A person with knowledge at least speaks with authority when he praises his own life.

To what life and to what pleasure does the judge give second place?

Clearly, he gives it to those of a warrior and honor-lover, since they're closer to his own than those of a money-maker.

Then the life and pleasure of a profit-lover come last, it seems.

Of course they do.

These, then, are two proofs in a row, and the just person has defeated the unjust one in both. The third is dedicated in Olympic fashion to Olympian Zeus the Savior. Observe then that, apart from those of a knowledgeable person, the other pleasures are neither entirely true nor pure but are like a shadow-painting, as I think I've heard some wise person say. And yet, if this were true, it would be the greatest and most decisive of the overthrows.

b

It certainly would. But what exactly do you mean?

I'll find out, if I ask the questions, and you answer.

c

Ask, then.

Tell me, don't we say that pain is the opposite of pleasure?

Certainly.

And is there such a thing as feeling neither pleasure nor pain?

There is.

Isn't it intermediate between these two, a sort of calm of the soul by comparison to them? Or don't you think of it that way?

I do.

And do you recall what sick people say when they're ill?

Which saying of theirs do you have in mind?

That nothing gives more pleasure than being healthy, but that they hadn't realized that it was most _d_ pleasant until they fell ill.

I do recall that.

And haven't you also heard those who are in great pain say that nothing is more pleasant than the cessation of their suffering?

I have.

And there are many similar circumstances, I suppose, in which you find people in pain praising, not enjoyment, but the absence of pain and relief from it as most pleasant.

That may be because at such times a state of calm becomes pleasant enough to content them.

And when someone ceases to feel pleasure, this _e_ calm will be painful to him.

Probably so.

Then the calm we described as being intermediate between pleasure and pain will sometimes be both.

So it seems.

Now, is it possible for that which is neither to become both?

Not in my view.

Moreover, the coming to be of either the pleasant or the painful in the soul is a sort of motion, isn't it?

Yes.

And didn't what is neither painful nor pleasant _584_ come to light just now as a calm state, intermediate between them?

Yes, it did.

Then, how can it be right to think that the absence of pain is pleasure or that the absence of pleasure is pain?

There's no way it can be.

Then it isn't right. But when the calm is next to the painful it appears pleasant, and when it is next to the pleasant it appears painful. However, there is nothing sound in these appearances as far as the truth about pleasure is concerned, only some kind of magic.

That's what the argument suggests, at any rate.

Take a look at the pleasures that don't come out of pains, so that you won't suppose in their case also _b_ that it is the nature of pleasure to be the cessation of pain or of pain to be the cessation of pleasure.

Where am I to look? What pleasures do you mean?

The pleasures of smell are especially good examples to take note of, for they suddenly become very intense without being preceded by pain, and when they cease they leave no pain behind. But there are plenty of other examples as well.

That's absolutely true.

Then let no one persuade us that pure pleasure is relief from pain or that pure pain is relief from _c_ pleasure.

No, let's not.

However, most of the so-called pleasures that reach the soul through the body, as well as the most intense ones are of this form—they are some kind of relief from pain.

Yes, they are.

And aren't the pleasures and pains of anticipation, which arise from the expectation of future pleasures or pains, also of this form?

They are.

Do you know what kind of thing they are and what they most resemble? _d_

No, what is it?

Do you believe that there is an up, a down, and a middle in nature?

I do.

And do you think that someone who was brought from down below to the middle would have any other belief than that he was moving upward? And if he stood in the middle and saw where he had come from, would he believe that he was anywhere other than the upper region, since he hasn't seen the one that is truly upper?

By god, I don't see how he could think anything else.

And if he was brought back, wouldn't he suppose that he was being brought down? And wouldn't he be right? _e_

Of course.

Then wouldn't all this happen to him because he is inexperienced in what is really and truly up, down, and in the middle?

Clearly.

Is it any surprise, then, if those who are inexperienced in the truth have unsound opinions about lots of other things as well, or that they are so disposed to pleasure, pain, and the intermediate state that, when they descend to the painful, they believe truly and are really in pain, but that, when they ascend 585 from the painful to the intermediate state, they firmly believe that they have reached fulfilllment and pleasure? They are inexperienced in pleasure and so are deceived when they compare pain to painlessness, just as they would be if they compared black to gray without having experienced white.

No, by god, I wouldn't be surprised. In fact, I'd be very surprised if it were any other way.

Think of it this way: Aren't hunger, thirst, and the b like some sort of empty states of the body?

They are.

And aren't ignorance and lack of sense empty states of the soul?

Of course.

And wouldn't someone who partakes of nourishment or strengthens his understanding be filled?

Certainly.

Does the truer filling up fill you with that which is less or that which is more?

Clearly, it's with that which is more.

And which kinds partake more of pure being? Kinds of filling up such as filling up with bread or drink or delicacies or food in general? Or the kind of filling up that is with true belief, knowledge, understanding, and, in sum, with all of virtue? Judge it this way: That c which is related to what is always the same, immortal, and true, is itself of that kind, and comes to be in something of that kind—this is more, don't you think, than that which is related to what is never the same and mortal, is itself of that kind, and comes to be in something of that kind?

That which is related to what is always the same is far more.

And does the being of what is always the same participate more in being than in knowledge?

Not at all.

Or more than in truth?

Not that either.

And if less in truth, then less in being also?

Necessarily.

And isn't it generally true that the kinds of filling up that are concerned with the care of the body share d less in truth and being than those concerned with the care of the soul?

Yes, much less.

And don't you think that the same holds of the body in comparison to the soul?

Certainly.

And isn't that which is more, and is filled with things that are more, really more filled than that which is less, and is filled with things that are less?

Of course.

Therefore, if being filled with what is appropriate to our nature is pleasure, that which is more filled with things that are more enjoys more really and truly a more true pleasure, while that which partakes of e things that are less is less truly and surely filled and partakes of a less trustworthy and less true pleasure.

That's absolutely inevitable.

Therefore, those who have no experience of reason or virtue, but are always occupied with feasts and the 586 like, are brought down and then back up to the middle, as it seems, and wander in this way throughout their lives, never reaching beyond this to what is truly higher up, never looking up at it or being brought up to it, and so they aren't filled with that which really is and never taste any stable or pure pleasure. Instead, they always look down at the ground like cattle, and, with their heads bent over the dinner table, they feed, fatten, and fornicate. To outdo others in these things, they kick and butt them with iron b horns and hooves, killing each other, because their desires are insatiable. For the part that they're trying to fill is like a vessel full of holes, and neither it nor the things they are trying to fill it with are among the things that are.

Socrates, you've exactly described the life of the majority of people, just like an oracle.

Then isn't it necessary for these people to live with pleasures that are mixed with pains, mere images and shadow-paintings of true pleasures? And doesn't the juxtaposition of these pleasures and pains make them appear intense, so that they give rise to mad erotic c passions in the foolish, and are fought over in just the way that Stesichorus tells us the phantom of Helen was fought over at Troy by men ignorant of the truth?

Something like that must be what happens.

And what about the spirited part? Mustn't similar things happen to someone who satisfies it? Doesn't his love of honor make him envious and his love of victory make him violent, so that he pursues the satisfaction of his anger and of his desires for honors and victories without calculation or understanding?

Such things must happen to him as well.

Then can't we confidently assert that those desires of even the money-loving and honor-loving parts that follow knowledge and argument and pursue with their help those pleasures that reason approves will attain the truest pleasures possible for them, because they follow truth, and the ones that are most their own, if indeed what is best for each thing is most its own?

And indeed it is best.

Therefore, when the entire soul follows the philosophic part, and there is no civil war in it, each part of it does its own work exclusively and is just, and in particular it enjoys its own pleasures, the best and truest pleasures possible for it.

Absolutely.

But when one of the other parts gains control, it won't be able to secure its own pleasure and will compel the other parts to pursue an alien and untrue pleasure.

That's right.

And aren't the parts that are most distant from philosophy and reason the ones most likely to do this sort of compelling?

They're much more likely.

And isn't whatever is most distant from reason also most distant from law and order?

Clearly.

And didn't the erotic and tyrannical desires emerge as most distant from these things?

By far.

And weren't the kingly and orderly ones least distant?

Yes.

Then I suppose that a tyrant will be most distant from a pleasure that is both true and his own and that a king will be least distant.

Necessarily.

So a tyrant will live most unpleasantly, and a king most pleasantly.

Necessarily.

Do you know how much more unpleasant a tyrant's life is than a king's?

I will if you tell me.

There are, it seems, three pleasures, one genuine and two illegitimate, and a tyrant is at the extreme end of the illegitimate ones, since he flees both law and reason and lives with a bodyguard of certain slavish pleasures. But it isn't easy, all the same, to say just how inferior he is to a king, except perhaps as follows. A tyrant is somehow third from an oligarch, for a democrat was between them.

Yes.

Then, if what we said before is true, doesn't he live with an image of pleasure that is third from an oligarch's with respect to truth?

He does.

Now, an oligarch, in turn, is third from a king, if we identify a king and an aristocrat.

Yes, he's third.

So a tyrant is three times three times removed from true pleasure.

Apparently so.

It seems then, on the basis of the magnitude of its number, that the image of tyrannical pleasure is a plane figure.

Exactly.

But then it's clear that, by squaring and cubing it, we'll discover how far a tyrant's pleasure is from that of a king.

It is clear to a mathematician, at any rate.

Then, turning it the other way around, if someone wants to say how far a king's pleasure is from a tyrant's, he'll find, if he completes the calculation, that a king lives seven hundred and twenty-nine times more pleasantly than a tyrant and that a tyrant is the same number of times more wretched.

That's an amazing calculation of the difference between the pleasure and pain of the two men, the just and the unjust.

Yet it's a true one, and one appropriate to human lives, if indeed days, nights, months, and years are appropriate to them.

And of course they are appropriate.

Then, if a good and just person's life is that much more pleasant than the life of a bad and unjust person, won't its grace, fineness, and virtue be incalculably greater?

By god, it certainly will.

All right, then. Since we've reached this point in
b the argument, let's return to the first things we said,
since they are what led us here. I think someone said
at some point that injustice profits a completely unjust
person who is believed to be just. Isn't that so?

It certainly is.

Now, let's discuss this with him, since we've agreed
on the respective powers that injustice and justice have.

How?

By fashioning an image of the soul in words, so
that the person who says this sort of thing will know
what he is saying.
c   What sort of image?

One like those creatures that legends tell us used
to come into being in ancient times, such as the
Chimera, Scylla, Cerberus, or any of the multitude
of others in which many different kinds of things are
said to have grown together naturally into one.

Yes, the legends do tell us of such things.

Well, then, fashion a single kind of multicolored
beast with a ring of many heads that it can grow
and change at will—some from gentle, some from
savage animals.

That's work for a clever artist. However, since words
d are more malleable than wax and the like, consider
it done.

Then fashion one other kind, that of a lion, and
another of a human being. But make the first much
the largest and the other second to it in size.

That's easier—the sculpting is done.

Now join the three of them into one, so that that
they somehow grow together naturally.

They're joined.

Then, fashion around them the image of one of
them, that of a human being so that anyone who sees
only the outer covering and not what's inside will
e think it is a single creature, a human being.

It's done.

Then, if someone maintains that injustice profits
this human being and that doing just things brings
no advantage, let's tell him that he is simply saying
that it is beneficial for him, first, to feed the multiform
beast well and make it strong, and also the lion and
all that pertains to him; second, to starve and weaken
589 the human being within, so that he is dragged along
wherever either of the other two leads; and, third, to
leave the parts to bite and kill one another rather

than accustoming them to each other and making
them friendly.

Yes, that's absolutely what someone who praises
injustice is saying.

But, on the other hand, wouldn't someone who
maintains that just things are profitable be saying,
first, that all our words and deeds should insure that
the human being within this human being has the
most control; second, that he should take care of
the many-headed beast as a farmer does his animals, b
feeding and domesticating the gentle heads and preventing the savage ones from growing; and, third, that
he should make the lion's nature his ally, care for
the community of all his parts, and bring them up
in such a way that they will be friends with each
other and with himself?

Yes, that's exactly what someone who praises justice
is saying.

From every point of view, then, anyone who praises
justice speaks truly, and anyone who praises injustice
speaks falsely. Whether we look at the matter from
the point of view of pleasure, good reputation, or
advantage, a praiser of justice tells the truth, while c
one who condemns it has nothing sound to say and
condemns without knowing what he is condemning.

In my opinion, at least, he knows nothing about it.

Then let's persuade him gently—for he isn't wrong
of his own will—by asking him these questions.
Should we say that this is the original basis for the
conventions about what is fine and what is shameful?
Fine things are those that subordinate the beastlike
parts of our nature to the human—or better, perhaps,
to the divine; shameful ones are those that enslave d
the gentle to the savage? Will he agree or what?

He will, if he takes my advice.

In light of this argument, can it profit anyone to
acquire gold unjustly if, by doing so, he enslaves the
best part of himself to the most vicious? If he got the
gold by enslaving his son or daughter to savage and
evil men, it wouldn't profit him, no matter how much e
gold he got. How, then, could he fail to be wretched
if he pitilessly enslaves the most divine part of himself
to the most godless and polluted one and accepts
golden gifts in return for a more terrible destruction
than Eriphyle's when she took the necklace in return 590
for her husband's soul?

A much more terrible one, Glaucon said. I'll answer for him.

And don't you think that licentiousness has long been condemned for just these reasons, namely, that because of it, that terrible, large, and multiform beast is let loose more than it should be?

Clearly.

And aren't stubbornness and irritability condemned because they inharmoniously increase and
b stretch the lionlike and snakelike part?

Certainly.

And aren't luxury and softness condemned because the slackening and loosening of this same part produce cowardice in it?

Of course.

And aren't flattery and slavishness condemned because they subject the spirited part to the moblike beast, accustoming it from youth on to being insulted for the sake of the money needed to satisfy the beast's insatiable appetites, so that it becomes an ape instead of a lion?
c They certainly are.

Why do you think that the condition of a manual worker is despised? Or is it for any other reason than that, when the best part is naturally weak in someone, it can't rule the beasts within him but can only serve them and learn to flatter them?

Probably so.

Therefore, to insure that someone like that is ruled by something similar to what rules the best person, we say that he ought to be the slave of that best person who has a divine ruler within himself. It isn't to harm
d the slave that we say he must be ruled, which is what Thrasymachus thought to be true of all subjects, but because it is better for everyone to be ruled by divine reason, preferably within himself and his own, otherwise imposed from without, so that as far as possible all will be alike and friends, governed by the same thing.

Yes, that's right.

This is clearly the aim of the law, which is the ally of everyone. But it's also our aim in ruling our children, we don't allow them to be free until we establish a constitution in them, just as in a city, and—by fostering their best part with our own—equip them with a guardian and ruler similar to our
591 own to take our place. Then, and only then, we set them free.

Clearly so.

Then how can we maintain or argue, Glaucon, that injustice, licentiousness, and doing shameful things are profitable to anyone, since, even though he may acquire more money or other sort of power from them, they make him more vicious?

There's no way we can.

Or that to do injustice without being discovered and having to pay the penalty is profitable? Doesn't the one who remains undiscovered become even more vicious, while the bestial part of the one who b is discovered is calmed and tamed and his gentle part freed, so that his entire soul settles into its best nature, acquires moderation, justice, and reason, and attains a more valuable state than that of having a fine, strong, healthy body, since the soul itself is more valuable than the body?

That's absolutely certain.

Then won't a person of understanding direct all his efforts to attaining that state of his soul? First, c he'll value the studies that produce it and despise the others.

Clearly so.

Second, he won't entrust the condition and nurture of his body to the irrational pleasure of the beast within or turn his life in that direction, but neither will he make health his aim or assign first place to being strong, healthy, and beautiful, unless he happens to acquire moderation as a result. Rather, it's clear that he will always cultivate the harmony of his body for the sake of the consonance in his soul.   d

He certainly will, if indeed he's to be truly trained in music and poetry.

Will he also keep order and consonance in his acquisition of money, with that same end in view? Or, even though he isn't dazzled by the size of the majority into accepting their idea of blessed happiness, will he increase his wealth without limit and so have unlimited evils?

Not in my view.

Rather, he'll look to the constitution within him and guard against disturbing anything in it, either by e too much money or too little. And, in this way, he'll direct both the increase and expenditure of his wealth, as far as he can.

That's exactly what he'll do.

And he'll look to the same thing where honors are concerned. He'll willingly share in and taste those 592 that he believes will make him better, but he'll avoid any public or private honor that might overthrow the established condition of his soul.

If that's his chief concern, he won't be willing to take part in politics.

Yes, by the dog, he certainly will, at least in his own kind of city. But he may not be willing to do so in his fatherland, unless some divine good luck chances to be his.

I understand. You mean that he'll be willing to take part in the politics of the city we were founding and describing, the one that exists in theory, for I don't think it exists anywhere on earth.

But perhaps, I said, there is a model of it in heaven, for anyone who wants to look at it and to make himself its citizen on the strength of what he sees. It makes no difference whether it is or ever will be somewhere, for he would take part in the practical affairs of that city and no other.

Probably so, he said.

BOOK X

Indeed, I said, our city has many features that assure me that we were entirely right in founding it as we did, and, when I say this, I'm especially thinking of poetry.

What about it in particular? Glaucon said.

That we didn't admit any that is imitative. Now that we have distinguished the separate parts of the soul, it is even clearer, I think, that such poetry should be altogether excluded.

What do you mean?

Between ourselves—for *you* won't denounce me to the tragic poets or any of the other imitative ones— all such poetry is likely to distort the thought of anyone who hears it, unless he has the knowledge of what it is really like, as a drug to counteract it.

What exactly do you have in mind in saying this?

I'll tell you, even though the love and respect I've had for Homer since I was a child make me hesitate to speak, for he seems to have been the first teacher and leader of all these fine tragedians. All the same, no one is to be honored or valued more than the truth. So, as I say, it must be told.

That's right.

Listen then, or, rather, answer.

Ask and I will.

Could you tell me what imitation in general is? I don't entirely understand what sort of thing imitations are trying to be.

Is it likely, then, that *I'll* understand?

That wouldn't be so strange, for people with bad eyesight often see things before those whose eyesight is keener.

That's so, but even if something occurred to me, I wouldn't be eager to talk about it in front of you. So I'd rather that you did the looking.

Do you want us to begin our examination, then, by adopting our usual procedure? As you know, we customarily hypothesize a single form in connection with each of the many things to which we apply the same name. Or don't you understand?

I do.

Then let's now take any of the manys you like. For example, there are many beds and tables.

Of course.

But there are only two forms of such furniture, one of the bed and one of the table.

Yes.

And don't we also customarily say that their makers look towards the appropriate form in making the beds or tables we use, and similarly in the other cases? Surely no craftsman makes the form itself. How could he?

There's no way he could.

Well, then, see what you'd call *this* craftsman?

Which one?

The one who makes all the things that all the other kinds of craftsmen severally make.

That's a clever and wonderful fellow you're talking about.

Wait a minute, and you'll have even more reason to say that, for this same craftsman is able to make, not only all kinds of furniture, but all plants that grow from the earth, all animals (including himself), the earth itself, the heavens, the gods, all the things in the heavens and in Hades beneath the earth.

He'd be amazingly clever!

You don't believe me? Tell me, do you think that there's no way any craftsman could make all these things, or that in one way he could and in another he couldn't? Don't you see that there is a way in which you yourself could make all of them?

What way is that?

It isn't hard: You could do it quickly and in lots of places, especially if you were willing to carry a mirror with you, for that's the quickest way of all. With it you can quickly make the sun, the things in the heavens, the earth, yourself, the other animals, manufactured items, plants, and everything else mentioned just now.

Yes, I could make them appear, but I couldn't make the things themselves as they truly are.

Well put! You've extracted the point that's crucial to the argument. I suppose that the painter too belongs to this class of makers, doesn't he?

Of course.

But I suppose you'll say that he doesn't truly make the things he makes. Yet, in a certain way, the painter does make a bed, doesn't he?

Yes, he makes the appearance of one.

What about the carpenter? Didn't you just say that he doesn't make the form—which is our term for the being of a bed—but only *a* bed?

Yes, I did say that.

Now, if he doesn't make the being of a bed, he isn't making that which is, but something which is like that which is, but is not it. So, if someone were to say that the work of a carpenter or any other craftsman is completely that which is, wouldn't he risk saying what isn't true?

That, at least, would be the opinion of those who busy themselves with arguments of this sort.

Then let's not be surprised if the carpenter's bed, too, turns out to be a somewhat dark affair in comparison to the true one.

All right.

Then, do you want us to try to discover what an imitator is by reference to these same examples?

I do, if you do.

We get, then, these three kinds of beds. The first is in nature a bed, and I suppose we'd say that a god makes it, or does someone else make it?

No one else, I suppose.

The second is the work of a carpenter.

Yes.

And the third is the one the painter makes. Isn't that so?

It is.

Then the painter, carpenter, and god correspond to three kinds of bed?

Yes, three.

Now, the god, either because he didn't want to or because it was necessary for him not to do so, didn't make more than one bed in nature, but only one, the very one that is the being of a bed. Two or more of these have not been made by the god and never will be.

Why is that?

Because, if he made only two, then again one would come to light whose form they in turn would both possess, and *that* would be the one that is the being of a bed and not the other two.

That's right.

The god knew this, I think, and wishing to be the real maker of the truly real bed and not just *a* maker of *a* bed, he made it to be one in nature.

Probably so.

Do you want us to call him its natural maker or something like that?

It would be right to do so, at any rate, since he is by nature the maker of this and everything else.

What about a carpenter? Isn't he the maker of a bed?

Yes.

And is a painter also a craftsman and maker of such things?

Not at all.

Then what do you think he does do to a bed?

He imitates it. He is an imitator of what the others make. That, in my view, is the most reasonable thing to call him.

All right. Then wouldn't you call someone whose product is third from the natural one an imitator?

I most certainly would.

Then this will also be true of a tragedian, if indeed he is an imitator. He is by nature third from the king and the truth, as are all other imitators.

It looks that way.

We're agreed about imitators, then. Now, tell me this about a painter. Do you think he tries in each case to imitate the thing itself in nature or the works of craftsmen?

The works of craftsmen.

As they are or as they appear? You must be clear about that.

How do you mean?

Like this. If you look at a bed from the side or the front or from anywhere else is it a different bed each time? Or does it only appear different, without being at all different? And is that also the case with other things?

That's the way it is—it appears different without being so.

Then consider this very point: What does painting
b do in each case? Does it imitate that which is as it is, or does it imitate that which appears as it appears? Is it an imitation of appearances or of truth?

Of appearances.

Then imitation is far removed from the truth, for it touches only a small part of each thing and a part that is itself only an image. And that, it seems, is why it can produce everything. For example, we say that a painter can paint a cobbler, a carpenter, or any other craftsman, even though he knows nothing about
c these crafts. Nevertheless, if he is a good painter and displays his painting of a carpenter at a distance, he can deceive children and foolish people into thinking that it is truly a carpenter.

Of course.

Then this, I suppose, is what we must bear in mind in all these cases. Hence, whenever someone tells us that he has met a person who knows all the crafts as well as all the other things that anyone else knows and that his knowledge of any subject is more exact than any of theirs is, we must assume that we're
d talking to a simple-minded fellow who has apparently encountered some sort of magician or imitator and been deceived into thinking him omniscient and that the reason he has been deceived is that he himself can't distinguish between knowledge, ignorance, and imitation.

That's absolutely true.

Then, we must consider tragedy and its leader, Homer. The reason is this: We hear some people say that poets know all crafts, all human affairs concerned
e with virtue and vice, and all about the gods as well. They say that if a good poet produces fine poetry, he must have knowledge of the things he writes about, or else he wouldn't be able to produce it at all. Hence, we have to look to see whether those who tell us this have encountered these imitators and have been so deceived by them that they don't realize that their works are at the third remove from that which is and are easily produced without knowledge of the truth
599 (since they are only images, not things that are), or whether there is something in what these people say,

and good poets really do have knowledge of the things most people think they write so well about.

We certainly must look into it.

Do you think that someone who could make both the thing imitated and its image would allow himself to be serious about making images and put this at the forefront of his life as the best thing to do? b

No, I don't.

I suppose that, if he truly had knowledge of the things he imitates, he'd be much more serious about actions than about imitations of them, would try to leave behind many fine deeds as memorials to himself, and would be more eager to be the subject of a eulogy than the author of one.

I suppose so, for these things certainly aren't equally valuable or equally beneficial either.

Then let's not demand an account of any of these professions from Homer or the other poets. Let's not ask whether any of them is a doctor rather than an imitator of what doctors say, or whether any poet of c the old or new school has made anyone healthy as Asclepius did, or whether he has left any students of medicine behind as Asclepius did his sons. And let's not ask them about the other crafts either. Let's pass over all that. But about the most important and most beautiful things of which Homer undertakes to speak—warfare, generalship, city government, and people's education—about these it *is* fair to question him, asking him this: "Homer, if you're not third from the truth about virtue, the sort of craftsman of d images that we defined an imitator to be, but if you're even second and capable of knowing what ways of life make people better in private or in public, then tell us which cities are better governed because of you, as Sparta is because of Lycurgus, and as many others—big and small—are because of many other men? What city gives you credit for being a good lawgiver who benefited it, as Italy and Sicily do to e Charondas, and as we do to Solon? Who gives such credit to you?" Will he be able to name one?

I suppose not, for not even the Homeridae make that claim for him.

Well, then, is any war in Homer's time remembered that was won because of his generalship and advice? 600

None.

Or, as befits a wise man, are many inventions and useful devices in the crafts or sciences attributed to

Homer, as they are to Thales of Miletus and Anachar-sis the Scythian?

There's nothing of that kind at all.

Then, if there's nothing of a public nature, are we told that, when Homer was alive, he was a leader in the education of certain people who took pleasure in associating with him in private and that he passed on
b a Homeric way of life to those who came after him, just as Pythagoras did? Pythagoras is particularly loved for this, and even today his followers are conspicuous for what they call the Pythagorean way of life.

Again, we're told nothing of this kind about Homer. If the stories about him are true, Socrates, his compan-ion, Creophylus, seems to have been an even more ridiculous example of education than his name sug-gests, for they tell us that while Homer was alive,
c Creophylus completely neglected him.

They do tell us that. But, Glaucon, if Homer had really been able to educate people and make them better, if he'd known about these things and not merely about how to imitate them, wouldn't he have had many companions and been loved and honored by them? Protagoras of Abdera, Prodicus of Ceos, and a great many others are able to convince anyone who associates with them in private that he wouldn't be able to manage his household or city unless they
d themselves supervise his education, and they are so intensely loved because of this wisdom of theirs that their disciples do everything but carry them around on their shoulders. So do you suppose that, if Homer had been able to benefit people and make them more virtuous, his companions would have allowed either him or Hesiod to wander around as rhapsodes? In-stead, wouldn't they have clung tighter to them than to gold and compelled them to live with them in their homes, or, if they failed to persuade them to do so, wouldn't they have followed them wherever they
e went until they had received sufficient education?

It seems to me, Socrates, that what you say is en-tirely true.

Then shall we conclude that all poetic imitators, beginning with Homer, imitate images of virtue and all the other things they write about and have no grasp of the truth? As we were saying just now, a painter, though he knows nothing about cobblery, can make what seems to be a cobbler to those who
601 know as little about it as he does and who judge things by their colors and shapes.

That's right.

And in the same way, I suppose we'll say that a poetic imitator uses words and phrases to paint col-ored pictures of each of the crafts. He himself knows nothing about them, but he imitates them in such a way that others, as ignorant as he, who judge by words, will think he speaks extremely well about cobblery or generalship or anything else whatever, provided—so great is the natural charm of these things—that he speaks with meter, rhythm, and harmony, for if you strip a poet's works of their musical colorings and b take them by themselves, I think you know what they look like. You've surely seen them.

I certainly have.

Don't they resemble the faces of young boys who are neither fine nor beautiful after the bloom of youth has left them?

Absolutely.

Now, consider this. We say that a maker of an image—an imitator—knows nothing about that which is but only about its appearance. Isn't that so? c

Yes.

Then let's not leave the discussion of this point halfway, but examine it fully.

Go ahead.

Don't we say that a painter paints reins and a mouth-bit?

Yes.

And that a cobbler and a metal-worker makes them?

Of course.

Then, does a painter know how the reins and mouth-bit have to be? Or is it the case that even a cobbler and metal-worker who make them don't know this, but only someone who knows how to use them, namely, a horseman?

That's absolutely true.

And won't we say that the same holds for every-thing?

What?

That for each thing there are these three crafts, one that uses it, one that makes it, and one that d imitates it?

Yes.

Then aren't the virtue or excellence, the beauty and correctness of each manufactured item, living creature, and action related to nothing but the use for which each is made or naturally adapted?

They are.

It's wholly necessary, therefore, that a user of each thing has most experience of it and that he tell a maker which of his products performs well or badly in actual use. A flute-player, for example, tells a flute-maker about the flutes that respond well in actual playing and prescribes what kind of flutes he is to

e make, while the maker follows his instructions.

Of course.

Then doesn't the one who knows give instructions about good and bad flutes, and doesn't the other rely on him in making them?

Yes.

Therefore, a maker—through associating with and having to listen to the one who knows—has right opinion about whether something he makes is fine

602 or bad, but the one who knows is the user.

That's right.

Does an imitator have knowledge of whether the things he makes are fine or right through having made use of them, or does he have right opinion about them through having to consort with the one who knows and being told how he is to paint them?

Neither.

Therefore an imitator has neither knowledge nor right opinion about whether the things he makes are fine or bad.

Apparently not.

Then a poetic imitator is an accomplished fellow when it comes to wisdom about the subjects of his poetry!

Hardly.

Nonetheless, he'll go on imitating, even though he doesn't know the good or bad qualities of anything,

b but what he'll imitate, it seems, is what appears fine or beautiful to the majority of people who know nothing.

Of course.

It seems, then, that we're fairly well agreed that an imitator has no worthwhile knowledge of the things he imitates, that imitation is a kind of game and not something to be taken seriously, and that all the tragic poets, whether they write in iambics or hexameters, are as imitative as they could possibly be.

That's right.

Then is this kind of imitation concerned with some-

c thing that is third from the truth, or what?

Yes, it is.

And on which of a person's parts does it exert its power?

What do you mean?

This: Something looked at from close at hand doesn't seem to be the same size as it does when it is looked at from a distance.

No, it doesn't.

And something looks crooked when seen in water and straight when seen out of it, while something else looks both concave and convex because our eyes are deceived by its colors, and every other similar sort of confusion is clearly present in our soul. And it is because they exploit this weakness in our nature that *trompe l'oeil* painting, conjuring, and other forms of d trickery have powers that are little short of magical.

That's true.

And don't measuring, counting, and weighing give us most welcome assistance in these cases, so that we aren't ruled by something's looking bigger, smaller, more numerous, or heavier, but by calculation, measurement, or weighing?

Of course.

And calculating, measuring, and weighing are the work of the rational part of the soul. e

They are.

But when this part has measured and has indicated that some things are larger or smaller or the same size as others, the opposite appears to it at the same time.

Yes.

And didn't we say that it is impossible for the same thing to believe opposites about the same thing at the same time?

We did, and we were right to say it.

Then the part of the soul that forms a belief contrary to the measurements couldn't be the same as the part that believes in accord with them. 603

No, it couldn't.

Now, the part that puts its trust in measurement and calculation is the best part of the soul.

Of course.

Therefore, the part that opposes it is one of the inferior parts in us.

Necessarily.

This, then, is what I wanted to get agreement about when I said that painting and imitation as a whole produce work that is far from the truth, namely, that imitation really consorts with a part of us that is far from reason, and the result of their being friends and companions is neither sound nor true. b

That's absolutely right.

Then imitation is an inferior thing that consorts with another inferior thing to produce an inferior off-spring.

So it seems.

Does this apply only to the imitations we see, or does it also apply to the ones we hear—the ones we call poetry?

It probably applies to poetry as well.

However, we mustn't rely solely on a mere probability based on the analogy with painting; instead, we must go directly to the part of our thought with which poetic imitations consort and see whether it is inferior *c* or something to be taken seriously.

Yes, we must.

Then let's set about it as follows. We say that imitative poetry imitates human beings acting voluntarily or under compulsion, who believe that, as a result of these actions, they are doing either well or badly and who experience either pleasure or pain in all this. Does it imitate anything apart from this?

Nothing.

Then is a person of one mind in all these circumstances? Or, just as he was at war with himself in matters of sight and held opposite beliefs about the *d* same thing at the same time, does he also fight with himself and engage in civil war with himself in matters of action? But there is really no need for us to reach agreement on this question now, for I remember that we already came to an adequate conclusion about all these things in our earlier arguments, when we said that our soul is full of a myriad of such oppositions at the same time.

And rightly so.

It *was* right, but I think we omitted some things *e* then that we must now discuss.

What are they?

We also mentioned somewhere before that, if a decent man happens to lose his son or some other prized possession, he'll bear it more easily than the other sorts of people.

Certainly.

But now let's consider this. Will he not grieve at all, or, if that's impossible, will he be somehow measured in his response to pain?

The latter is closer to the truth.

Now, tell me this about him: Will he fight his pain *604* and put up more resistance to it when his equals can see him or when he's alone by himself in solitude?

He'll fight it far more when he's being seen.

But when he's alone I suppose he'll venture to say and do lots of things that he'd be ashamed to be heard saying or seen doing.

That's right.

And isn't it reason and law that tells him to resist his pain, while his experience of it tells him to give in? *b*

True.

And when there are two opposite inclinations in a person in relation to the same thing at the same time, we say that he must also have two parts.

Of course.

Isn't one part ready to obey the law wherever it leads him?

How so?

The law says, doesn't it, that it is best to keep as quiet as possible in misfortunes and not get excited about them? First, it isn't clear whether such things will turn out to be good or bad in the end; second, it doesn't make the future any better to take them hard; third, human affairs aren't worth taking very seriously; and, finally, grief prevents the very thing *c* we most need in such circumstances from coming into play as quickly as possible.

What are you referring to?

Deliberation. We must accept what has happened as we would the fall of the dice, and then arrange our affairs in whatever way reason determines to be best. We mustn't hug the hurt part and spend our time weeping and wailing like children when they trip. Instead, we should always accustom our souls to turn as quickly as possible to healing the disease and putting the disaster right, replacing lamentation with cure. *d*

That would be the best way to deal with misfortune, at any rate.

Accordingly, we say that it is the best part of us that is willing to follow this rational calculation.

Clearly.

Then won't we also say that the part that leads us to dwell on our misfortunes and to lamentation, and that can never get enough of these things, is irrational, idle, and a friend of cowardice?

We certainly will.

Now, this excitable character admits of many multi-colored imitations. But a rational and quiet character, *e* which always remains pretty well the same, is neither easy to imitate nor easy to understand when imitated, especially not by a crowd consisting of all sorts of people gathered together at a theater festival, for the experience being imitated is alien to them.

605 Absolutely.

Clearly, then, an imitative poet isn't by nature related to the part of the soul that rules in such a character, and, if he's to attain a good reputation with the majority of people, his cleverness isn't directed to pleasing it. Instead, he's related to the excitable and multicolored character, since it is easy to imitate.

Clearly.

Therefore, we'd be right to take him and put him beside a painter as his counterpart. Like a painter, he produces work that is inferior with respect to truth and that appeals to a part of the soul that is similarly b inferior rather than to the best part. So we were right not to admit him into a city that is to be well-governed, for he arouses, nourishes, and strengthens this part of the soul and so destroys the rational one, in just the way that someone destroys the better sort of citizens when he strengthens the vicious ones and surrenders the city to them. Similarly, we'll say that an imitative poet puts a bad constitution in the soul of each individual by making images that are far removed from the truth and by gratifying the irrational c part, which cannot distinguish the large and the small but believes that the same things are large at one time and small at another.

That's right.

However, we haven't yet brought the most serious charge against imitation, namely, that with a few rare exceptions it is able to corrupt even decent people, for that's surely an altogether terrible thing.

It certainly is, if indeed it can do that.

Listen, then, and consider whether it can or not. When even the best of us hear Homer or some other tragedian imitating one of the heroes sorrowing and making a long lamenting speech or singing and beat-d ing his breast, you know that we enjoy it, give ourselves up to following it, sympathize with the hero, take his sufferings seriously, and praise as a good poet the one who affects us most in this way.

Of course we do.

But when one of us suffers a private loss, you realize that the opposite happens. We pride ourselves if we are able to keep quiet and master our grief, for we think that this is the manly thing to do and that the e behavior we praised before is womanish.

I do realize that.

Then are we right to praise it? Is it right to look at someone behaving in a way that we would consider unworthy and shameful and to enjoy and praise it rather than being disgusted by it?

No, by god, that doesn't seem reasonable.

No, at least not if you look at it in the following way. 606 How?

If you reflect, first, that the part of the soul that is forcibly controlled in our private misfortunes and that hungers for the satisfaction of weeping and wailing, because it desires these things by nature, is the very part that receives satisfaction and enjoyment from poets, and, second, that the part of ourselves that is best by nature, since it hasn't been adequately educated either by reason or habit, relaxes its guard over the lamenting part when it is watching the sufferings of somebody else. The reason it does so is this: It b thinks that there is no shame involved for it in praising and pitying another man who, in spite of his claim to goodness, grieves excessively. Indeed, it thinks that there is a definite gain involved in doing so, namely, pleasure. And it wouldn't want to be deprived of that by despising the whole poem. I suppose that only a few are able to figure out that enjoyment of other people's sufferings is necessarily transferred to our own and that the pitying part, if it is nourished and strengthened on the sufferings of others, won't be easily held in check when we ourselves suffer.

That's very true. c

And doesn't the same argument apply to what provokes laughter? If there are any jokes that you yourself would be ashamed to tell but that you very much enjoy hearing and don't detest as something evil in comic plays or in private, aren't you doing the same thing as in the case of what provokes pity? The part of you that wanted to tell the jokes and that was held back by your reason, for fear of being thought a buffoon, you then release, not realizing that, by making it strong in this way, you will be led into becoming a figure of fun where your own affairs are concerned.

Yes, indeed.

And in the case of sex, anger, and all the desires, pleasures, and pains that we say accompany all our d actions, poetic imitation has the very same effect on us. It nurtures and waters them and establishes them as rulers in us when they ought to wither and be ruled, for that way we'll become better and happier rather than worse and more wretched.

I can't disagree with you.

And so, Glaucon, when you happen to meet those *e* who praise Homer and say that he's the poet who educated Greece, that it's worth taking up his works in order to learn how to manage and educate people, and that one should arrange one's whole life in accordance with his teachings, you should welcome these people and treat them as friends, since they're as good 607 as they're capable of being, and you should agree that Homer is the most poetic of the tragedians and the first among them. But you should also know that hymns to the gods and eulogies to good people are the only poetry we can admit into our city. If you admit the pleasure-giving Muse, whether in lyric or epic poetry, pleasure and pain will be kings in your city instead of law or the thing that everyone has always believed to be best, namely, reason.

That's absolutely true.

Then let this be our defense—now that we've re*b* turned to the topic of poetry—that, in view of its nature, we had reason to banish it from the city earlier, for our argument compelled us to do so. But in case we are charged with a certain harshness and lack of sophistication, let's also tell poetry that there is an ancient quarrel between it and philosophy, which is evidenced by such expressions as "the dog yelping and shrieking at its master," "great in the empty eloquence of fools," "the mob of wise men that has *c* mastered Zeus," and "the subtle thinkers, beggars all." Nonetheless, if the poetry that aims at pleasure and imitation has any argument to bring forward that proves it ought to have a place in a well-governed city, we at least would be glad to admit it, for we are well aware of the charm it exercises. But, be that as it may, to betray what one believes to be the truth is impious. What about you, Glaucon, don't you feel the charm of the pleasure-giving Muse, especially *d* when you study her through the eyes of Homer?

Very much so.

Therefore, isn't it just that such poetry should return from exile when it has successfully defended itself, whether in lyric or any other meter?

Certainly.

Then we'll allow its defenders, who aren't poets themselves but lovers of poetry, to speak in prose on its behalf and to show that it not only gives pleasure but is beneficial both to constitutions and to human life. Indeed, we'll listen to them graciously, for we'd certainly profit if poetry were shown to be not only pleasant but also beneficial. *e*

How could we fail to profit?

However, if such a defense isn't made, we'll behave like people who have fallen in love with someone but who force themselves to stay away from him, because they realize that their passion isn't beneficial. In the same way, because the love of this sort of poetry has been implanted in us by the upbringing we have received under our fine constitutions, we are well disposed to any proof that it is the best and truest thing. But if it isn't able to produce such a defense, 608 then, whenever we listen to it, we'll repeat the argument we have just now put forward like an incantation so as to preserve ourselves from slipping back into that childish passion for poetry which the majority of people have. And we'll go on chanting that such poetry is not to be taken seriously or treated as a serious undertaking with some kind of hold on the truth, but that anyone who is anxious about the constitution within him must be careful when he hears it and must continue to believe what we have said *b* about it.

I completely agree.

Yes, for the struggle to be good rather than bad is important, Glaucon, much more important than people think. Therefore, we mustn't be tempted by honor, money, rule, or even poetry into neglecting justice and the rest of virtue.

After what we've said, I agree with you, and so, I think, would anyone else.

And yet we haven't discussed the greatest rewards and prizes that have been proposed for virtue. *c*

They must be inconceivably great, if they're greater than those you've already mentioned.

Could anything really great come to pass in a short time? And isn't the time from childhood to old age short when compared to the whole of time?

It's a mere nothing.

Well, do you think that an immortal thing should be seriously concerned with that short period rather than with the whole of time? *d*

I suppose not, but what exactly do you mean by this?

Haven't you realized that our soul is immortal and never destroyed?

He looked at me with wonder and said: No, by god, I haven't. Are you really in a position to assert that?

I'd be wrong not to, I said, and so would you, for it isn't difficult.

It is for me, so I'd be glad to hear from you what's not difficult about it.

Listen, then.

Just speak, and I will.

Do you talk about good and bad?

I do.

And do you think about them the same way I do?

What way is that?

The bad is what destroys and corrupts, and the good is what preserves and benefits.

I do.

And do you say that there is a good and a bad for everything? For example, ophthalmia for the eyes, sickness for the whole body, blight for grain, rot for wood, rust for iron or bronze. In other words, is there, as I say, a natural badness and sickness for pretty well everything?

There is.

And when one of these attaches itself to something, doesn't it make the thing in question bad, and in the end, doesn't it disintegrate it and destroy it wholly?

Of course.

Therefore, the evil that is natural to each thing and the bad that is peculiar to it destroy it. However, if they don't destroy it, nothing else will, for the good would never destroy anything, nor would anything neither good nor bad.

How could they?

Then, if we discover something that has an evil that makes it bad but isn't able to disintegrate and destroy it, can't we infer that it is naturally incapable of being destroyed?

Probably so.

Well, what about the soul? Isn't there something that makes it bad?

Certainly, all the things we were mentioning: Injustice, licentiousness, cowardice, and lack of learning.

Does any of these disintegrate and destroy the soul? Keep your wits about you, and let's not be deceived into thinking that, when an unjust and foolish person is caught, he has been destroyed by injustice, which is evil in a soul. Let's think about it this way instead: Just as the body is worn out, destroyed, and brought to the point where it is a body no longer by disease, which is evil in a body, so all the things we mentioned just now reach the point at which they cease to be what they are through their own peculiar evil, which attaches itself to them and is present in them. Isn't that so?

Yes.

Then look at the soul in the same way. Do injustice and the other vices that exist in a soul—by their very presence in it and by attaching themselves to it—corrupt it and make it waste away until, having brought it to the point of death, they separate it from the body?

That's not at all what they do.

But surely it's unreasonable to suppose that a thing is destroyed by the badness proper to something else when it is not destroyed by its own?

That is unreasonable.

Keep in mind, Glaucon, that we don't think that a body is destroyed by the badness of food, whether it is staleness, rottenness, or anything else. But if the badness of the food happens to implant in the body an evil proper to a body, we'll say that the body was destroyed by its own evil, namely, disease. But, since the body is one thing and food another, we'll never judge that the body is destroyed by the badness of food, unless it implants in it the body's own natural and peculiar evil.

That's absolutely right.

By the same argument, if the body's evil doesn't cause an evil in the soul that is proper to the soul, we'll never judge that the soul, in the absence of its own peculiar evil, is destroyed by the evil of something else. We'd never accept that *anything* is destroyed by an evil proper to something else.

That's also reasonable.

Then let's either refute our argument and show that we were wrong, or, as long as it remains unrefuted, let's never say that the soul is destroyed by a fever or any other disease or by killing either, for that matter, not even if the body is cut up into tiny pieces. We mustn't say that the soul is even close to being destroyed by these things until someone shows us that these conditions of the body make the soul more unjust and more impious. When something has the evil proper to something else in it, but its own peculiar evil is absent, we won't allow anyone to say that it is destroyed, no matter whether it is a soul or anything else whatever.

And you may be sure that no one will ever prove that the souls of the dying are made more unjust by death.

But if anyone dares to come to grips with our argument, in order to avoid having to agree that our souls are immortal, and says that a dying man does become more vicious and unjust, we'll reply that, if what he says is true, then injustice must be as deadly to unjust people as a disease, and those who catch it *d* must die of it because of its own deadly nature, with the worst cases dying quickly and the less serious dying more slowly. As things now stand, however, it isn't like that at all. Unjust people do indeed die of injustice, but at the hands of others who inflict the death penalty on them.

By god, if injustice were actually fatal to those who contracted it, it wouldn't seem so terrible, for it would be an escape from their troubles. But I rather think that it's clearly the opposite, something that kills other *e* people if it can, while, on top of making the unjust themselves lively, it even brings them out at night. Hence it's very far from being deadly to its possessors.

You're right, for if the soul's own evil and badness isn't enough to kill and destroy it, an evil appointed for the destruction of something else will hardly kill it. Indeed, it won't kill anything at all except the very thing it is appointed to destroy.

"Hardly" is right, or so it seems.

Now, if the soul isn't destroyed by a single evil, whether its own or something else's, then clearly it *611* must always be. And if it always is, it is immortal.

Necessarily so.

So be it. And if it is so, then you realize that there would always be the same souls, for they couldn't be made fewer if none is destroyed, and they couldn't be made more numerous either. If anything immortal is increased, you know that the increase would have to come from the mortal, and then everything would end up being immortal.

That's true.

Then we mustn't think such a thing, for the argument doesn't allow it, nor must we think that the soul *b* in its truest nature is full of multicolored variety and unlikeness or that it differs with itself.

What do you mean?

It isn't easy for anything composed of many parts to be immortal if it isn't put together in the finest way, yet this is how the soul now appeared to us.

It probably isn't easy.

Yet our recent argument and others as well compel us to believe that the soul *is* immortal. But to see the soul as it is in truth, we must not study it as it is while it is maimed by its association with the body and other evils—which is what we were doing earlier— *c* but as it is in its pure state, that's how we should study the soul, thoroughly and by means of logical reasoning. We'll then find that it is a much finer thing than we thought and that we can see justice and injustice as well as all the other things we've discussed far more clearly. What we've said about the soul is true of it as it appears at present. But the condition in which we've studied it is like that of the sea god Glaucus, whose primary nature can't easily be made out by those who catch glimpses of him. Some of the original parts have been broken off, *d* others have been crushed, and his whole body has been maimed by the waves and by the shells, seaweeds, and stones that have attached themselves to him, so that he looks more like a wild animal than his natural self. The soul, too, is in a similar condition when we study it, beset by many evils. That, Glaucon, is why we have to look somewhere else in order to discover its true nature.

To where?

To its philosophy, or love of wisdom. We must realize what it grasps and longs to have intercourse *e* with, because it is akin to the divine and immortal and what always is, and we must realize what it would become if it followed this longing with its whole being, and if the resulting effort lifted it out of the sea in which it now dwells, and if the many stones *612* and shells (those which have grown all over it in a wild, earthy, and stony profusion because it feasts at those so-called happy feastings on earth) were hammered off it. Then we'd see what its true nature is and be able to determine whether it has many parts or just one and whether or in what manner it is put together. But we've already given a decent account, I think, of what its condition is and what parts it has when it is immersed in human life.

We certainly have.

And haven't we cleared away the various other objections to our argument without having to invoke the rewards and reputations of justice, as you said Homer and Hesiod did? And haven't we found that *b* justice itself is the best thing for the soul itself, and that the soul—whether it has the ring of Gyges or even it together with the cap of Hades—should do just things?

We have. That's absolutely true.

Then can there now be any objection, Glaucon, if in addition we return to justice and the rest of virtue both the kind and quantity of wages that they obtain for the soul from human beings and gods, whether in this life or the next?

None whatever.

Then will you give me back what you borrowed from me during the discussion?

What are you referring to in particular?

I granted your request that a just person should seem unjust and an unjust one just, for you said that, even if it would be impossible for these things to remain hidden from both gods and humans, still, this had to be granted for the sake of argument, so that justice itself could be judged in relation to injustice itself. Don't you remember that?

It would be wrong of me not to.

Well, then, since they've now been judged, I ask that the reputation justice in fact has among gods and humans be returned to it and that we agree that it does indeed have such a reputation and is entitled to carry off the prizes it gains for someone by making him seem just. It is already clear that it gives good things to anyone who is just and that it doesn't deceive those who really possess it.

That's a fair request.

Then won't you first grant that it doesn't escape the notice of the gods at least as to which of the two is just and which isn't?

We will.

Then if neither of them escapes the gods' notice, one would be loved by the gods and the other hated, as we agreed at the beginning.

That's right.

And won't we also agree that everything that comes to someone who is loved by gods, insofar as it comes from the gods themselves, is the best possible, unless it is the inevitable punishment for some mistake he made in a former life?

Certainly.

Then we must suppose that the same is true of a just person who falls into poverty or disease or some other apparent evil, namely, that this will end well for him, either during his lifetime or afterwards, for the gods never neglect anyone who eagerly wishes to become just and who makes himself as much like a god as a human can by adopting a virtuous way of life.

It makes sense that such a person not be neglected by anyone who is like him.

And mustn't we suppose that the opposite is true of an unjust person?

Definitely.

Then these are some of the prizes that a just person, but not an unjust one, receives from the gods.

That's certainly my opinion.

What about from human beings? What does a just person get from them? Or, if we're to tell the truth, isn't this what happens? Aren't clever but unjust people like runners who run well for the first part of the course but not for the second? They leap away sharply at first, but they become ridiculous by the end and go off uncrowned, with their ears drooping on their shoulders like those of exhausted dogs, while true runners, on the other hand, get to the end, collect the prizes, and are crowned. And isn't it also generally true of just people that, towards the end of each course of action, association, or life, they enjoy a good reputation and collect the prizes from other human beings?

Of course.

Then will you allow me to say all the things about them that you yourself said about unjust people? I'll say that it is just people who, when they're old enough, rule in their own cities (if they happen to want ruling office) and that it is they who marry whomever they want and give their children in marriage to whomever they want. Indeed, all the things that you said about unjust people I now say about just ones. As for unjust people, the majority of them, even if they escape detection when they're young, are caught by the end of the race and are ridiculed. And by the time they get old, they've become wretched, for they are insulted by foreigners and citizens, beaten with whips, and made to suffer those punishments, such as racking and burning, which you rightly described as crude. Imagine that I've said that they suffer all such things, and see whether you'll allow me to say it.

Of course I will. What you say is right.

Then these are the prizes, wages, and gifts that a just person receives from gods and humans while he is alive and that are added to the good things that justice itself provides.

Yes, and they're very fine and secure ones too.

Yet they're nothing in either number or size compared to those that await just and unjust people after death. And these things must also be heard, if both are to receive in full what they are owed by the argument.

Then tell us about them, for there aren't many
b things that would be more pleasant to hear.

It isn't, however, a tale of Alcinous that I'll tell you but that of a brave Pamphylian man called Er, the son of Armenias, who once died in a war. When the rest of the dead were picked up ten days later, they were already putrefying, but when he was picked up, his corpse was still quite fresh. He was taken home, and preparations were made for his funeral. But on the twelfth day, when he was already laid on the funeral pyre, he revived and, having done so, told what he had seen in the world beyond. He said that, after his soul had left him, it travelled together with
c many others until they came to a marvellous place, where there were two adjacent openings in the earth, and opposite and above them two others in the heavens, and between them judges sat. These, having rendered their judgment, ordered the just to go upwards into the heavens through the door on the right, with signs of the judgment attached to their chests, and the unjust to travel downward through the opening on the left, with signs of all their deeds on their
d backs. When Er himself came forward, they told him that he was to be a messenger to human beings about the things that were there, and that he was to listen to and look at everything in the place. He said that he saw souls departing after judgment through one of the openings in the heavens and one in the earth, while through the other two souls were arriving. From the door in the earth souls came up covered with dust and dirt and from the door in the heavens souls came down pure. And the souls who were arriving
e all the time seemed to have been on long journeys, so that they went gladly to the meadow, like a crowd going to a festival, and camped there. Those who knew each other exchanged greetings, and those who come up from the earth asked those who came down from the heavens about the things there and were in turn questioned by them about the things below. And so they told their stories to one another, the former
615 weeping as they recalled all they had suffered and seen on their journey below the earth, which lasted a thousand years, while the latter, who had come

from heaven, told about how well they had fared and about the inconceivably fine and beautiful sights they had seen. There was much to tell, Glaucon, and it took a long time, but the main point was this: For each in turn of the unjust things they had done and for each in turn of the people they had wronged, they paid the penalty ten times over, once in every century of their journey. Since a century is roughly the length of a human life, this means that they paid a tenfold b penalty for each injustice. If, for example, some of them had caused many deaths by betraying cities or armies and reducing them to slavery or by participating in other wrongdoing, they had to suffer ten times the pain they had caused to each individual. But if they had done good deeds and had become just and pious, they were rewarded according to the same scale. He said some other things about the stillborn and those who had lived for only a short time, but they're not worth recounting. And he also spoke of c even greater rewards or penalties for piety or impiety towards gods or parents and for murder with one's own hands.

For example, he said he was there when someone asked another where the great Ardiaeus was. (This Ardiaeus was said to have been tyrant in some city in Pamphylia a thousand years before and to have killed his aged father and older brother and committed many other impious deeds as well.) And he said that the one who was asked responded: "He hasn't d arrived here yet and never will, for this too was one of the terrible sights we saw. When we came near the opening on our way out, after all our sufferings were over, we suddenly saw him together with some others, pretty well all of whom were tyrants (although there were also some private individuals among them who had committed great crimes). They thought that they were ready to go up, but the opening wouldn't e let them through, for it roared whenever one of these incurably wicked people or anyone else who hadn't paid a sufficient penalty tried to go up. And there were savage men, all fiery to look at, who were standing by, and when they heard the roar, they grabbed some of these criminals and led them away, but they bound the feet, hands, and head of Ardiaeus and the others, threw them down, and flayed them. Then they dragged them out of the way, lacerating them on 616 thorn bushes, and telling every passer-by that they were to be thrown into Tartarus, and explaining why they were being treated in this way." And he said that of their many fears the greatest each one of them had was that the roar would be heard as he came up and that everyone was immensely relieved when silence greeted him. Such, then, were the penalties and punishments and the rewards corresponding to them.

Each group spent seven days in the meadow, and on the eighth they had to get up and go on a journey. On the fourth day of that journey, they came to a place where they could look down from above on a straight column of light that stretched over the whole of heaven and earth, more like a rainbow than anything else, but brighter and more pure. After another day, they came to the light itself, and there, in the middle of the light, they saw the extremities of its bonds stretching from the heavens, for the light binds the heavens like the cables girding a trireme and holds its entire revolution together. From the extremities hangs the spindle of Necessity, by means of which all the revolutions are turned. Its stem and hook are of adamant, whereas in its whorl adamant is mixed with other kinds of material. The nature of the whorl was this: Its shape was like that of an ordinary whorl, but, from what Er said, we must understand its structure as follows. It was as if one big whorl had been made hollow by being thoroughly scooped out, with another smaller whorl closely fitted into it, like nested boxes, and there was a third whorl inside the second, and so on, making eight whorls altogether, lying inside one another, with their rims appearing as circles from above, while from the back they formed one continuous whorl around the spindle, which was driven through the center of the eighth. The first or outside whorl had the widest circular rim; that of the sixth was second in width; the fourth was third; the eighth was fourth; the seventh was fifth; the fifth was sixth; the third was seventh; and the second was eighth. The rim of the largest was spangled; that of the seventh was brightest; that of the eighth took its color from the seventh's shining on it; the second and fifth were about equal in brightness, more yellow than the others; the third was the whitest in color; the fourth was rather red; and the sixth was second in whiteness. The whole spindle turned at the same speed, but, as it turned, the inner spheres gently revolved in a direction opposite to that of the whole. Of these inner spheres, the eighth was the fastest; second came the seventh, sixth, and fifth, all at the same speed; it seemed to them that the fourth was third in its speed of revolution; the fourth, third; and the second, fifth. The spindle itself turned on the lap of Necessity. And up above on each of the rims of the circles stood a Siren, who accompanied its revolution, uttering a single sound, one single note. And the concord of the eight notes produced a single harmony. And there were three other beings sitting at equal distances from one another, each on a throne. These were the Fates, the daughters of Necessity: Lachesis, Clotho, and Atropos. They were dressed in white, with garlands on their heads, and they sang to the music of the Sirens. Lachesis sang of the past, Clotho of the present, and Atropos of the future. With her right hand, Clotho touched the outer circumference of the spindle and helped it turn, but left off doing so from time to time; Atropos did the same to the inner ones; and Lachesis helped both motions in turn, one with one hand and one with the other.

When the souls arrived at the light, they had to go to Lachesis right away. There a Speaker arranged them in order, took from the lap of Lachesis a number of lots and a number of models of lives, mounted a high pulpit, and spoke to them: "Here is the message of Lachesis, the maiden daughter of Necessity: 'Ephemeral souls, this is the beginning of another cycle that will end in death. Your daemon or guardian spirit will not be assigned to you by lot; you will choose him. The one who has the first lot will be the first to choose a life to which he will then be bound by necessity. Virtue knows no master; each will possess it to a greater or less degree, depending on whether he values or disdains it. The responsibility lies with the one who makes the choice; the god has none.'" When he had said this, the Speaker threw the lots among all of them, and each—with the exception of Er, who wasn't allowed to choose—picked up the one that fell next to him. And the lot made it clear to the one who picked it up where in the order he would get to make his choice. After that, the models of lives were placed on the ground before them. There were far more of them than there were souls present, and they were of all kinds, for the lives of animals were there, as well as all kinds of human lives. There were tyrannies among them, some of which lasted throughout life, while others ended halfway through in poverty, exile, and beggary. There were lives of famous men, some of whom were famous for the beauty of their appearance, others for their strength or athletic prowess, others still for their high birth and the virtue or excellence of their ancestors. And there were also lives of men b who weren't famous for any of these things. And the same for lives of women. But the arrangement of the soul was not included in the model because the soul is inevitably altered by the different lives it chooses. But all the other things were there, mixed with each other and with wealth, poverty, sickness, health, and the states intermediate to them.

Now, it seems that it is here, Glaucon, that a human being faces the greatest danger of all. And because of this, each of us must neglect all other subjects and c be most concerned to seek out and learn those that will enable him to distinguish the good life from the bad and always to make the best choice possible in every situation. He should think over all the things we have mentioned and how they jointly and severally determine what the virtuous life is like. That way he will know what the good and bad effects of beauty are when it is mixed with wealth, poverty, and a d particular state of the soul. He will know the effects of high or low birth, private life or ruling office, physical strength or weakness, ease or difficulty in learning, and all the things that are either naturally part of the soul or are acquired, and he will know what they achieve when mixed with one another. And from all this he will be able, by considering the nature of the soul, to reason out which life is better and which worse and to choose accordingly, calling a life worse if it leads the soul to become more unjust, e better if it leads the soul to become more just, and ignoring everything else: We have seen that this is the best way to choose, whether in life or death. Hence, we must go down to Hades holding with adamantine determination to the belief that this is so, lest we be dazzled there by wealth and other such 619 evils, rush into a tyranny or some other similar course of action, do irreparable evils, and suffer even worse ones. And we must always know how to choose the mean in such lives and how to avoid either of the extremes, as far as possible, both in this life and in all those beyond it. This is the way that a human b being becomes happiest.

Then our messenger from the other world reported that the Speaker spoke as follows: "There is a satisfactory life rather than a bad one available even for the one who comes last, provided that he chooses it rationally and lives it seriously. Therefore, let not the first be careless in his choice nor the last discouraged."

He said that when the Speaker had told them this, the one who came up first chose the greatest tyranny. In his folly and greed he chose it without adequate examination and didn't notice that, among other evils, he was fated to eat his own children as a part of it. c When he examined at leisure, the life he had chosen, however, he beat his breast and bemoaned his choice. And, ignoring the warning of the Speaker, he blamed chance, daemons, or guardian spirits, and everything else for these evils but himself. He was one of those who had come down from heaven, having lived his previous life under an orderly constitution, where he had participated in virtue through habit and without philosophy. Broadly speaking, indeed, most of those who were caught out in this way were souls who had d come down from heaven and who were untrained in suffering as a result. The majority of those who had come up from the earth, on the other hand, having suffered themselves and seen others suffer, were in no rush to make their choices. Because of this and because of the chance of the lottery, there was an interchange of goods and evils for most of the souls. However, if someone pursues philosophy in a sound manner when he comes to live here on earth and if the lottery doesn't make him one of the last to choose, e then, given what Er has reported about the next world, it looks as though not only will he be happy here, but his journey from here to there and back again won't be along the rough underground path, but along the smooth heavenly one.

Er said that the way in which the souls chose their lives was a sight worth seeing, since it was pitiful, funny, and surprising to watch. For the most part, 620 their choice depended upon the character of their former life. For example, he said that he saw the soul that had once belonged to Orpheus choosing a swan's life, because he hated the female sex because of his death at their hands, and so was unwilling to have a woman conceive and give birth to him. Er saw the soul of Thamyris choosing the life of a nightingale, a swan choosing to change over to a human life, and other musical animals doing the same thing. The twentieth soul chose the life of a lion. This was the b soul of Ajax, son of Telamon. He avoided human life because he remembered the judgment about the armor. The next soul was that of Agamemnon, whose sufferings also had made him hate the human race, so he changed to the life of an eagle. Atalanta had been assigned a place near the middle, and when she saw great honors being given to a male athlete, she chose his life, unable to pass them by. After her, he saw the soul of Epeius, the son of Panopeus, taking

c on the nature of a craftswoman. And very close to last, he saw the soul of the ridiculous Thersites clothing itself as a monkey. Now, it chanced that the soul of Odysseus got to make its choice last of all, and since memory of its former sufferings had relieved its love of honor, it went around for a long time, looking for the life of a private individual who did his own work, and with difficulty it found one lying off somewhere neglected by the others. He chose it gladly and said that he'd have made the same choice even if

d he'd been first. Still other souls changed from animals into human beings, or from one kind of animal into another, with unjust people changing into wild animals, and just people into tame ones, and all sorts of mixtures occurred.

After all the souls had chosen their lives, they went forward to Lachesis in the same order in which they had made their choices, and she assigned to each the daemon it had chosen as guardian of its life and

e fulfiller of its choice. This daemon first led the soul under the hand of Clotho as it turned the revolving spindle to confirm the fate that the lottery and its own choice had given it. After receiving her touch, he led the soul to the spinning of Atropos, to make what had been spun irreversible. Then, without turn-

ing around, they went from there under the throne of Necessity and, when all of them had passed through, they travelled to the Plain of Forgetfulness in burning, choking, terrible heat, for it was empty 621 of trees and earthly vegetation. And there, beside the River of Unheeding, whose water no vessel can hold, they camped, for night was coming on. All of them had to drink a certain measure of this water, but those who weren't saved by reason drank more than that, and as each of them drank, he forgot everything and went to sleep. But around midnight there was a clap of thunder and an earthquake, and they were suddenly b carried away from there, this way and that, up to their births, like shooting stars. Er himself was forbidden to drink from the water. All the same, he didn't know how he had come back to his body, except that waking up suddenly he saw himself lying on the pyre at dawn.

And so, Glaucon, his story wasn't lost but preserved, and it would save us, if we were persuaded by it, for we would then make a good crossing of the River of c Forgetfulness, and our souls wouldn't be defiled. But if we are persuaded by me, we'll believe that the soul is immortal and able to endure every evil and every good, and we'll always hold to the upward path, practicing justice with reason in every way. That way we'll be friends both to ourselves and to the gods while we remain here on earth and afterwards—like victors in the games who go around collecting their prizes— d we'll receive our rewards. Hence, both in this life and on the thousand-year journey we've described, we'll do well and be happy.

Laws

CHARACTERS
An Athenian Stranger, Clinias of Crete, Megillus of Lacedaemon

Book I

ATH. To whom do you ascribe the authorship of your legal arrangements, Strangers? To a god or to some man?

CLIN. To a god, Stranger, most rightfully to a god. We Cretans call Zeus our lawgiver; while in Lacedaemon, where our friend here has his home, I believe they claim Apollo as theirs. Is not that so, Megillus?

MEG. Yes.

ATH. Do you then, like Homer, say that Minos used to go every ninth year to hold converse with his father Zeus, and that he was guided by his divine oracles in laying down the laws for your cities?

Reprinted by permission of the publishers and the Loeb Classical Library from Plato, *Laws*, Volumes 1 and 2, translated by R. G. Bury, Cambridge, Mass.: Harvard University Press, 1926.

CLIN. So our people say. And they say also that his brother Rhadamanthys—no doubt you have heard the name—was exceedingly just. And certainly we Cretans would maintain that he won this title owing to his righteous administration of justice in those days.

ATH. Yes, his renown is indeed glorious and well befitting a son of Zeus. And, since you and our friend Megillus were both brought up in legal institutions of so noble a kind, you would, I imagine, have no aversion to our occupying ourselves as we go along in discussion on the subject of government and laws. Certainly, as I am told, the road from Cnosus to the cave and temple of Zeus is a long one, and we are sure to find, in this sultry weather, shady resting-places among the high trees along the road: in them we can rest ofttimes, as befits our age, beguiling the time with discourse, and thus complete our journey in comfort.

CLIN. True, Stranger; and as one proceeds further one finds in the groves cypress-trees of wonderful height and beauty, and meadows too, where we may rest ourselves and talk.

ATH. You say well.

CLIN. Yes, indeed: and when we set eyes on them we shall say so still more emphatically. So let us be going, and good luck attend us!

ATH. Amen! And tell me now, for what reason did your law ordain the common meals you have, and your gymnastic schools and military equipment?

CLIN. Our Cretan customs, Stranger, are, as I think, such as anyone may grasp easily. As you may notice, Crete, as a whole, is not a level country, like Thessaly: consequently, whereas the Thessalians mostly go on horseback, we Cretans are runners, since this land of ours is rugged and more suitable for the practice of foot-running. Under these conditions we are obliged to have light armor for running and to avoid heavy equipment; so bows and arrows are adopted as suitable because of their lightness. Thus all these customs of ours are adapted for war, and, in my opinion, this was the object which the lawgiver had in view when he ordained them all. Probably this was his reason also for instituting common meals: he saw how soldiers, all the time they are on campaign, are obliged by force of circumstances to mess in common, for the sake of their own security. And herein, as I think, he condemned the stupidity of the mass of men in failing to perceive that all are involved ceaselessly in a life-

long war against all States. If, then, these practices are necessary in war—namely, messing in common for safety's sake, and the appointment of relays of officers and privates to act as guards—they must be carried out equally in time of peace. For (as he would say) "peace," as the term is commonly employed, is nothing more than a name, the truth being that every State is, by a law of nature, engaged perpetually in an informal war with every other State. And if you look at the matter from this point of view you will find it practically true that our Cretan lawgiver ordained all our legal usages, both public and private, with an eye to war, and that he therefore charged us with the task of guarding our laws safely, in the conviction that without victory in war nothing else, whether possession or institution, is of the least value, but all the goods of the vanquished fall into the hands of the victors.

ATH. Your training, Stranger, has certainly, as it seems to me, given you an excellent understanding of the legal practices of Crete. But tell me this more clearly still: by the definition you have given of the well-constituted State you appear to me to imply that it ought to be organized in such a way as to be victorious in war over all other States. Is that so?

CLIN. Certainly it is; and I think that our friend here shares my opinion.

MEG. No Lacedaemonian, my good sir, could possibly say otherwise.

ATH. If this, then, is the right attitude for a State to adopt toward a State, is the right attitude for village toward village different?

CLIN. By no means.

ATH. It is the same, you say?

CLIN. Yes.

ATH. Well then, is the same attitude right also for one house in the village toward another, and for each man toward every other?

CLIN. It is.

ATH. And must each individual man regard himself as his own enemy? Or what do we say when we come to this point?

CLIN. O Stranger of Athens—for I should be loth to call you a man of Attica, since methinks you deserve rather to be named after the goddess Athena, seeing that you have made the argument more clear by taking it back again to its starting-point; whereby you will the more easily discover the justice of our recent statement that, in the mass, all men are both publicly and privately the enemies of all, and individually also each man is his own enemy.

ATH. What is your meaning, my admirable sir?

CLIN. It is just in this war, my friend, that the victory over self is of all victories the first and best while self-defeat is of all defeats at once the worst and the most shameful. For these phrases signify that a war against self exists within each of us.

ATH. Now let us take the argument back in the reverse direction. Seeing that individually each of us is partly superior to himself and partly inferior, are we to affirm that the same condition of things exists in house and village and State, or are we to deny it?

CLIN. Do you mean the condition of being partly self-superior and partly self-inferior?

ATH. Yes.

CLIN. That, too, is a proper question; for such a condition does most certainly exist, and in States above all. Every State in which the better class is victorious over the populace and the lower classes would rightly be termed "self-superior," and would be praised most justly for a victory of this kind; and conversely, when the reverse is the case.

ATH. Well then, leaving aside the question as to whether the worse element is ever superior to the better (a question which would demand a more lengthy discussion), what you assert, as I now perceive, is this—that sometimes citizens of one stock and of one State who are unjust and numerous may combine together and try to enslave by force those who are just but fewer in number, and wherever they prevail such a State would rightly be termed "self-inferior" and bad, but "self-superior" and good wherever they are worsted.

CLIN. This statement is indeed most extraordinary, Stranger; none the less we cannot possibly reject it.

ATH. Stay a moment: here too is a case we must further consider. Suppose there were a number of brothers, all sons of the same parents, it would not be at all surprising if most of them were unjust and but few just.

CLIN. It would not.

ATH. And, moreover, it would ill beseem you and me to go a-chasing after this form of expression, that if the bad ones conquered the whole of this family

and house should be called "self-inferior," but "self-superior" if they were defeated; for our present reference to the usage of ordinary speech is not concerned with the propriety or impropriety of verbal phrases but with the essential rightness or wrongness of laws.

CLIN. Very true, Stranger.

MEG. And finely spoken, too, up to this point, as I agree.

ATH. Let us also look at this point: the brothers we have just described would have, I suppose, a judge?

CLIN. Certainly.

ATH. Which of the two would be the better—a judge who destroyed all the wicked among them and charged the good to govern themselves, or one who made the good members govern and, while allowing the bad to live, made them submit willingly to be governed? And there is a third judge we must mention (third and best in point of merit)—if indeed such a judge can be found—who in dealing with a single divided family will destroy none of them but reconcile them and succeed, by enacting laws for them, in securing amongst them thence-forward permanent friendliness.

CLIN. A judge and lawgiver of that kind would be by far the best.

ATH. But mark this: his aim, in the laws he enacted for them, would be the opposite of war.

CLIN. That is true.

ATH. And what of him who brings the State into harmony? In ordering its life would he have regard to external warfare rather than to the internal war, whenever it occurs, which goes by the name of "civil" strife? For this is a war as to which it would be the desire of every man that, if possible, it should never occur in his own State, and that, if it did occur, it should come to as speedy an end as possible.

CLIN. Evidently he would have regard to civil war.

ATH. And would anyone prefer that the citizens should be obliged to devote their attention to external enemies after internal concord had been secured by the destruction of one section and the victory of their opponents rather than after the establishment of friendship and peace by terms of conciliation?

CLIN. Everyone would prefer the latter alternative for his own State rather than the former.

ATH. And would not the lawgiver do the same?

CLIN. Of course.

ATH. Would not every lawgiver in all his legislation aim at the highest good?

CLIN. Assuredly.

ATH. The highest good, however, is neither war nor civil strife—which things we should pray rather to be saved from—but peace one with another and friendly feeling. Moreover, it would seem that the victory we mentioned of a State over itself is not one of the best things but one of those which are necessary. For imagine a man supposing that a human body was best off when it was sick and purged with physic, while never giving a thought to the case of the body that needs no physic at all! Similarly, with regard to the well-being of a State or an individual, that man will never make a genuine statesman who pays attention primarily and solely to the needs of foreign warfare, nor will he make a finished lawgiver unless he designs his war legislation for peace rather than his peace legislation for war.

CLIN. This statement, Stranger, is apparently true; yet, unless I am much mistaken, our legal usages in Crete, and in Lacedaemon too, are wholly directed toward war.

ATH. Very possibly; but we must not now attack them violently, but mildly interrogate them, since both we and your legislators are earnestly interested in these matters. Pray follow the argument closely. Let us take the opinion of Tyrtaeus (an Athenian by birth and afterward a citizen of Lacedaemon), who, above all men, was keenly interested in our subject. This is what he says: "Though a man were the richest of men, though a man possessed goods in plenty (and he specifies nearly every good there is), if he failed to prove himself at all times most valiant in war, no mention should I make of him, nor take account of him at all." No doubt you also have heard these poems; while our friend Megillus is, I imagine, surfeited with them.

MEG. I certainly am.

CLIN. And I can assure you they have reached Crete also, shipped over from Lacedaemon.

ATH. Come now, let us jointly interrogate this poet somehow on this wise: "O Tyrtaeus, most inspired of poets (for assuredly you seem to us both wise and good in that you have eulogized excellently those who excel in war), concerning this matter we three—Megillus, Clinias of Cnosus, and myself—are already in entire accord with you, as we suppose; but we wish

to be assured that both we and you are alluding to the same persons. Tell us then: do you clearly recognize, as we do, two distinct kinds of war?" In reply to this I suppose that even a much less able man than Tyrtaeus would state the truth, that there are two kinds, the one being that which we all call "civil," which is of all wars the most bitter, as we said just now, while the other kind, as I suppose we shall all agree, is that which we engage in when we quarrel with foreigners and aliens—a kind much milder than the former.

CLIN. Certainly.

ATH. "Come, then, which kind of warriors, fighting in which kind of war, did you praise so highly, while blaming others? Warriors, apparently, who fight in war abroad. At any rate, in your poems you have said that you cannot abide men who dare not

face the gory fray and smite the foe in close combat."

Then we should proceed to say, "It appears, O Tyrtaeus, that you are chiefly praising those who achieve distinction in foreign and external warfare." To this, I presume, he would agree, and say "Yes"?

CLIN. Of course.

ATH. Yet, brave though these men are, we still maintain that they are far surpassed in bravery by those who are conspicuously brave in the greatest of wars; and we also have a poet for witness—Theognis (a citizen of Sicilian Megara), who says:

In the day of grievous feud, O Cyrnus, the loyal warrior is worth his weight in silver and gold.

Such a man, in a war much more grievous, is, we say, ever so much better than the other—nearly as much better, in fact, as the union of justice, prudence and wisdom with courage is better than courage by itself alone. For a man would never prove himself loyal and sound in civil war if devoid of goodness in its entirety; whereas in the war of which Tyrtaeus speaks there are vast numbers of mercenaries ready to die fighting "with well-planted feet apart," of whom the majority, with but few exceptions, prove themselves reckless, unjust, violent, and pre-eminently foolish. What, then, is the conclusion to which our present discourse is tending, and what point is it trying to make clear by these statements? Plainly it is this:

both the Heaven-taught legislator of Crete and every legislator who is worth his salt will most assuredly legislate always with a single eye to the highest goodness and to that alone; and this (to quote Theognis) consists in "loyalty in danger," and one might term it "complete righteousness." But that goodness which Tyrtaeus specially praised, fair though it be and fitly glorified by the poet, deserves nevertheless to be placed no higher than fourth in order and estimation.

CLIN. We are degrading our own lawgiver, Stranger, to a very low level!

ATH. Nay, my good Sir, it is ourselves we are degrading, in so far as we imagine that it was with a special view to war that Lycurgus and Minos laid down all the legal usages here and in Lacedaemon.

CLIN. How, then, ought we to have stated the matter?

ATH. In the way that is, as I think, true and proper when talking of a divine hero. That is to say, we should state that he enacted laws with an eye not to some one fraction, and that the most paltry, of goodness, but to goodness as a whole, and that he devised the laws themselves according to classes, though not the classes which the present devisers propound. For everyone now brings forward and devises just the class which he needs: one man deals with inheritances and heiresses, another with cases of battery, and so on in endless variety. But what we assert is that the devising of laws, when rightly conducted, follows the procedure which we have now commenced. Indeed, I greatly admire the way you opened your exposition of the laws; for to make a start with goodness and say that that was the aim of the lawgiver is the right way. But in your further statement that he legislated wholly with reference to a fraction of goodness, and that the smallest fraction, you seemed to me to be in error, and all this latter part of my discourse was because of that. What then is the manner of exposition I should have liked to have heard from you? Shall I tell you?

CLIN. Yes, by all means.

ATH. "O Stranger" (thus you ought to have said), "it is not for nothing that the laws of the Cretans are held in superlatively high repute among all the Hellenes. For they are true laws inasmuch as they effect the well-being of those who use them by supplying all things that are good. Now goods are of two kinds, human and divine; and the human goods are dependent on the divine, and he who receives the greater acquires also the less, or else he is bereft of both. The lesser goods are those of which health ranks first, beauty second; the third is strength, in running and all other bodily exercises; and the fourth is wealth—no blind god Plutus, but keen of sight, provided that he has wisdom for companion. And wisdom, in turn, has first place among the goods that are divine, and rational temperance of soul comes second; from these two, when united with courage, there issues justice, as the third; and the fourth is courage. Now all these are by nature ranked before the human goods, and verily the lawgiver also must so rank them. Next, it must be proclaimed to the citizens that all the other instructions they receive have these in view; and that, of these goods themselves, the human look up to the divine, and the divine to reason as their chief. And in regard to their marriage connections, and to their subsequent breeding and rearing of children, male and female, both during youth and in later life up to old age, the lawgiver must supervise the citizens, duly apportioning honor and dishonor; and in regard to all their forms of intercourse he must observe and watch their pains and pleasures and desires and all intense passions, and distribute praise and blame correctly by the means of the laws themselves. Moreover, in the matter of anger and of fear, and of all the disturbances which befall souls owing to misfortune, and of all the avoidances thereof which occur in good-fortune, and of all the experiences which confront men through disease or war or penury or their opposites—in regard to all these definite instruction must be given as to what is the right and what the wrong disposition in each case. It is necessary, in the next place, for the lawgiver to keep a watch on the methods employed by the citizens in gaining and spending money, and to supervise the associations they form with one another, and the dissolutions thereof, whether they be voluntary or under compulsion; he must observe the manner in which they conduct each of these mutual transactions, and note where justice obtains and where it is lacking. To those that are obedient he must assign honors by law, but on the disobedient he must impose duly appointed penalties. Then finally, when he arrives at the completion of the whole constitution, he has to consider in what manner in each case the burial of the dead should be carried out, and what honors should be assigned to them. This being settled, the framer of the laws will hand over all his statutes to the charge of Wardens—guided some by wisdom, others by true opinion—to the end that Reason, having bound all into one single system, may declare them to be ancillary neither to wealth nor ambition, but to temperance and justice." In this manner, Stranger, I could have wished (and I wish it still) that you had fully explained how all these regulations are inherent in the reputed laws of Zeus and in those of the Pythian Apollo which were ordained by Minos and Lycurgus, and how their systematic arrangement is quite evident to him who, whether by art or practice, is an expert in law, although it is by no means obvious to the rest of us.

CLIN. What then, Stranger, should be the next step in our argument?

• • •

ATH. Evidently, then, you are both ready to play your part as listeners. But as for my part, though the will is there, to compass the task is hard: still, I must try. In the first place, then, our argument requires that we should define education and describe its effects: that is the path on which our present discourse must proceed until it finally arrives at the god of Wine.

CLIN. By all means let us do so, since it is your wish.

ATH. Then while I am stating how education ought to be defined, you must be considering whether you are satisfied with my statement.

CLIN. Proceed with your statement.

ATH. I will. What I assert is that every man who is going to be good at any pursuit must practice that special pursuit from infancy, by using all the implements of his pursuit both in his play and in his work. For example, the man who is to make a good builder must play at building toy houses, and to make a good farmer he must play at tilling land; and those who are rearing them must provide each child with toy tools modeled on real ones. Besides this, they ought to have elementary instruction in all the necessary subjects—the carpenter, for instance, being taught in play the use of rule and measure, the soldier taught riding or some similar accomplishment. So, by means of their games, we should endeavor to turn the tastes and desires of the children in the direction of that object which forms their ultimate goal. First and foremost, education, we say, consists in that right nurture which most strongly draws the soul of the child when at play to a love for that pursuit of which, when he becomes a man, he must possess a perfect mastery. Now consider, as I said before, whether, up to this point, you are satisfied with this statement of mine.

CLIN. Certainly we are.

ATH. But we must not allow our description of education to remain indefinite. For at present, when censuring or commending a man's upbringing, we describe one man as educated and another as uneducated, though the latter may often be uncommonly well educated in the trade of a peddler or a skipper, or some other similar occupation. But we, naturally, in our present discourse are not taking the view that such things as these make up education: the education we speak of is training from childhood in goodness, which makes a man eagerly desirous of becoming a perfect citizen, understanding how both to rule and be ruled righteously. This is the special form of nurture to which, as I suppose, our present argument would confine the term "education"; whereas an upbringing which aims only at money-making or physical strength, or even some mental accomplishment devoid of reason and justice, it would term vulgar and illiberal and utterly unworthy of the name "education." Let us not, however, quarrel over a name, but let us abide by the statement we agreed upon just now, that those who are rightly educated become, as a rule, good, and that one should in no case disparage education, since it stands first among the finest gifts that are given to the best men; and if ever it errs from the right path, but can be put straight again, to this task every man, so long as he lives, must address himself with all his might.

CLIN. You are right, and we agree with what you say.

ATH. Further, we agreed long ago that if men are capable of ruling themselves, they are good, but if incapable, bad.

CLIN. Quite true.

ATH. Let us, then, re-state more clearly what we meant by this. With your permission, I will make use of an illustration in the hope of explaining the matter.

CLIN. Go ahead.

ATH. May we assume that each of us by himself is a single unit?

CLIN. Yes.

ATH. And that each possesses within himself two antagonistic and foolish counselors, whom we call by the names of pleasure and pain?

CLIN. That is so.

ATH. And that, besides these two, each man possesses opinions about the future, which go by the general name of "expectations"; and of these, that which precedes pain bears the special name of "fear," and that which precedes pleasure the special name of "confidence"; and in addition to all these there is "calculation," pronouncing which of them is good, which bad; and "calculation," when it has become the public decree of the State, is named "law."

CLIN. I have some difficulty in keeping pace with you: assume, however, that I do so, and proceed.

MEG. I am in exactly the same predicament.

ATH. Let us conceive of the matter in this way. Let us suppose that each of us living creatures is an ingenious puppet of the gods, whether contrived by way of a toy of theirs or for some serious purpose — for as to that we know nothing; but this we do know, that these inward affections of ours, like sinews or cords, drag us along and, being opposed to each other, pull one against the other to opposite actions; and herein lies the dividing line between goodness and badness. For, as our argument declares, there is one of these pulling forces which every man should always follow and nohow leave hold of, counteracting thereby the pull of the other sinews: it is the leading-string, golden and holy, of "calculation," entitled the public law of the State; and whereas the other cords are hard and steely and of every possible shape and semblance, this one is flexible and uniform, since it is of gold. With that most excellent leading-string of the law we must needs co-operate always; for since calculation is excellent, but gentle rather than forceful, its leading-string needs helpers to ensure that the golden kind within us may vanquish the other kinds. In this way our story comparing ourselves to puppets will not fall flat, and the meaning of the terms "self-superior" and "self-inferior" will become somewhat more clear, and also how necessary it is for the individual man to grasp the true account of these inward pulling forces and to live in accordance therewith, and how necessary for the State (when it has received such an account either from a god or from a man who knows) to make this into a law for itself and be guided thereby in its intercourse both with itself and with all other States. Thus both badness and goodness would be differentiated for us more clearly; and these having become more evident, probably education also and the other institutions will appear less obscure; and about the institution of the wine-party in particular it may very likely be shown that it is by no means, as might be thought, a paltry matter which it is absurd to discuss at great length but rather a matter which fully merits prolonged discussion.

• • •

ATH. Are not these the conditions in which we are of the character described — anger, lust, insolence, ignorance, covetousness, and extravagance; and these also — wealth, beauty, strength, and everything which intoxicates a man with pleasure and turns his head? And for the purpose, first, of providing a cheap and comparatively harmless test of these conditions, and, secondly, of affording practice in them, what more suitable pleasure can we mention than wine, with its playful testing — provided that it is employed at all carefully? For consider: in the case of a man whose disposition is morose and savage (whence spring numberless iniquities), is it not more dangerous to test him by entering into money transactions with him, at one's own personal risk, than by associating with him with the help of Dionysus and his festive insight? And when a man is a slave to the pleasures of sex, is it not a more dangerous test to entrust to him one's own daughters and sons and wife, and thus imperil one's own nearest and dearest, in order to discover the disposition of his soul? In fact, one might quote innumerable instances in a vain endeavor to show the full superiority of this playful method of inspection which is without either serious consequence or costly damage. Indeed, so far as that is concerned, neither the Cretans, I imagine, nor any other people would dispute the fact that herein we have a fair test of man by man, and that for cheapness, security, and speed it is superior to all other tests.

CLIN. That certainly is true.

ATH. This then — the discovery of the natures and conditions of men's souls — will prove one of the things most useful to that art whose task it is to treat them; and that art is (as I presume we say) the art of politics: is it not so?

CLIN. Undoubtedly.

Book II

ATH. . . . In all education and music in your countries, is not this your teaching? You oblige the poets to teach that the good man, since he is temperate and just, is fortunate and happy, whether he be great or small, strong or weak, rich or poor; whereas, though he be richer even "than Cinyras or Midas," if he be unjust, he is a wretched man and lives a miserable life. Your poet says—if he speaks the truth—"I would spend no word on the man, and hold him in no esteem," who without justice performs or acquires all the things accounted good; and again he describes how the just man "drives his spear against the foe at close quarters," whereas the unjust man dares not "to look upon the face of bloody death," nor does he outpace in speed of foot "the north wind out of Thrace," nor acquire any other of the things called "good." For the things which most men call good are wrongly so described. Men say that the chief good is health, beauty the second, wealth the third; and they call countless other things "goods"—such as sharpness of sight and hearing, and quickness in perceiving all the objects of sense; being a king, too, and doing exactly as you please; and to possess the whole of these goods and become on the spot an immortal, that, as they say, is the crown and top of all felicity. But what you and I say is this—that all these things are very good as possessions for men who are just and holy, but for the unjust they are (one and all, from health downward) very bad; and we say too that sight and hearing and sensation and even life itself are very great evils for the man endowed with all the so-called goods, but lacking in justice and all virtue, if he is immortal for ever, but a lesser evil for such a man if he survives but a short time. This, I imagine, is what you (like myself) will persuade or compel your poets to teach, and compel them also to educate your youth by furnishing them with rhythms and harmonies in consonance with this teaching. Am I not right? Just consider: what I assert is that what are called "evils" are good for the unjust, but evil for the just, while the so-called "goods" are really good for the good, but bad for the bad. Are you in accord with me, then—that was my question—or how stands the matter?

CLIN. We are, apparently, partly in accord, but partly quite the reverse.

ATH. Take the case of a man who has health and wealth and absolute power in perpetuity—in addition to which I bestow on him, if you like, matchless strength and courage, together with immortality and freedom from all the other "evils" so-called—but a man who has within him nothing but injustice and insolence: probably I fail to convince you that the man who lives such a life is obviously not happy but wretched?

CLIN. Quite true.

ATH. Well, then, what ought I to say next? Do you not think that if a man who is courageous, strong, beautiful, and rich, and who does exactly as he likes all his life long, is really unjust and insolent, he must necessarily be living a base life? Probably you will agree at any rate to call it "base"?

CLIN. Certainly.

ATH. And also a bad life?

CLIN. We would not go so far as to admit that.

ATH. Well, would you admit the epithets "unpleasant" and "unprofitable to himself"?

CLIN. How could we agree to such further descriptions?

ATH. "How?" do you ask? Only (as it seems, my friend) if some god were to grant us concord, since at present we are fairly at discord one with another. In my opinion these facts are quite indisputable—even more plainly so, my dear Clinias, than the fact that Crete is an island; and were I a legislator, I should endeavour to compel the poets and all the citizens to speak in this sense; and I should impose all but the heaviest of penalties on anyone in the land who should declare that any wicked men lead pleasant lives, or that things profitable and lucrative are different from things just; and there are many other things contrary to what is now said, as it seems, by Cretans and Lacedaemonians—and of course by the rest of mankind—which I should persuade my citizens to proclaim. For, come now, my most excellent sirs, in the name of Zeus and Apollo, suppose we should interrogate those very gods themselves who legislated for you, and ask: "Is the most just life the most pleasant; or are there two lives, of which the one is most pleasant, the other most just?" If they replied that there were two, we might well ask them further, if we were to put the correct question: "Which of the two ought one to describe as the happier, those that live the most just or those that live the most pleasant life?" If they replied, "Those that live the most pleasant life," that would be a monstrous statement in their mouths. But I prefer not to ascribe such statements to gods, but rather to ancestors and lawgivers: imagine, then, that the questions I have put have been put to an ancestor and lawgiver, and that he has stated that the man who lives the most pleasant life is the happiest. In the next place I would say to him this: "O father, did you not desire me to live as happily as possible? Yet you never ceased bidding me constantly to live as justly as possible." And hereby, as I think, our lawgiver or ancestor would be shown up as illogical and incapable of speaking consistently with himself. But if, on the other hand, he were to declare the most just life to be the happiest, everyone who heard him would, I suppose, enquire what is the good and charm it contains which is superior to pleasure, for which the lawgiver praises it. For, apart from pleasure, what good could accrue to a just man? "Come, tell me, is fair fame and praise from the mouths of men and gods a noble and good thing, but unpleasant, while ill-fame is the opposite?" "By no means, my dear lawgiver," we shall say. And is it unpleasant, but noble and good, neither to injure anyone nor be injured by anyone, while the opposite is pleasant, but ignoble and bad?

CLIN. By no means.

ATH. So then the teaching which refuses to separate the pleasant from the just helps, if nothing else, to induce a man to live the holy and just life, so that any doctrine which denies this truth is, in the eyes of the lawgiver, most shameful and most hateful; for no one would voluntarily consent to be induced to commit an act, unless it involves as its consequence more pleasure than pain. Now distance has the effect of befogging the vision of nearly everybody, and of children especially; but our lawgiver will reverse the appearance by removing the fog, and by one means or another—habituation, commendation, or argument—will persuade people that their notions of justice and injustice are illusory pictures, unjust objects appearing pleasant and just objects most unpleasant to him who is opposed to justice, through being viewed from his own unjust and evil standpoint, but when seen from the standpoint of justice, both of them appear in all ways entirely the opposite.

CLIN. So it appears.

ATH. In point of truth, which of the two judgments shall we say is the more authoritative—that of the worse soul or that of the better?

CLIN. That of the better, undoubtedly.

ATH. Undoubtedly, then, the unjust life is not only more base and ignoble, but also in very truth more unpleasant, than the just and holy life.

CLIN. It would seem so, my friends, from our present argument.

ATH. And even if the state of the case were different from what it has now been proved to be by our argument, could a lawgiver who was worth his salt find any more useful fiction than this (if he dared to use any fiction at all in addressing the youths for their good), or one more effective in persuading all men to act justly in all things willingly and without constraint?

CLIN. Truth is a noble thing, Stranger, and an enduring; yet to persuade men of it seems no easy matter.

ATH. Be it so; yet it proved easy to persuade men of the Sidonian fairy-tale, incredible though it was, and of numberless others.

CLIN. What tales?

ATH. The tale of the teeth that were sown, and how armed men sprang out of them. Here, indeed, the lawgiver has a notable example of how one can, if he tries, persuade the souls of the young of anything, so that the only question he has to consider in his inventing is what would do most good to the State, if it were believed; and then he must devise all possible means to ensure that the whole of the community constantly, so long as they live, use exactly the same language, so far as possible, about these matters, alike in their songs, their tales, and their discourses. If you, however, think otherwise, I have no objection to your arguing in the opposite sense.

CLIN. Neither of us, I think, could possibly argue against your view.

• • •

BOOK III

ATH. Our States, I presume, must have rulers and subjects.

CLIN. Of course.

ATH. Very well then: what and how many are the agreed rights or claims in the matter of ruling and being ruled, alike in States, large or small, and in households? Is not the right of father and mother one of them? And in general would not the claim of parents to rule over offspring be a claim universally just?

CLIN. Certainly.

ATH. And next to this, the right of the noble to rule over the ignoble; and then, following on these as a third claim, the right of older people to rule and of younger to be ruled.

CLIN. To be sure.

ATH. The fourth right is that slaves ought to be ruled, and masters out to rule.

CLIN. Undoubtedly.

ATH. And the fifth is, I imagine, that the stronger should rule and the weaker be ruled.

CLIN. A truly compulsory form of rule!

ATH. Yes, and one that is very prevalent among all kinds of creatures, being "according to nature," as Pindar of Thebes once said. The most important right is, it would seem, the sixth, which ordains that the man without understanding should follow, and the wise man lead and rule. Nevertheless, my most sapient Pindar, this is a thing that I, for one, would hardly assert to be against nature, but rather according thereto—the natural rule of law, without force, over willing subjects.

CLIN. A very just observation.

ATH. Heaven's favor and good-luck mark the seventh form of rule, where we bring a man forward for a casting of lots, and declare that if he gains the lot he will most justly be ruler, but if he fails he shall take his place among the ruled.

CLIN. Very true.

ATH. "Seest thou, O lesislator"—it is thus we might playfully address one of those who lightly start on the task of legislation—"how many are the rights pertaining to rulers, and how they are essentially opposed to one another? Herein we have now discovered a source of factions, which thou must remedy. So do thou, in the first place, join with us in enquiring how it came to pass, and owing to what transgression of those rights, that the kings of Argos and Messene brought ruin alike on themselves and on the Hellenic power, splendid as it was at that epoch. Was it not through ignorance of that most true saying of Hesiod that 'oftimes the half is greater than the whole'?"

CLIN. Most true, indeed.

ATH. Is it our view, then, that this causes ruin when it is found in kings rather than when found in peoples?

CLIN. Probably this is, in the main, a disease of kings, in whom luxury breeds pride of life.

ATH. Is it not plain that what those kings strove for first was to get the better of the established laws, and that they were not in accord with one another about the pledge which they had approved both by word and by oath; and this discord—reputed to be wisdom, but really, as we affirm, the height of ignorance—owing to its grating dissonance and lack of harmony, brought the whole Greek world to ruin?

CLIN. It would seem so, certainly.

ATH. Very well then: what precaution ought the legislator to have taken at that time in his enactments, to guard against the growth of this disorder? Verily, to perceive that now requires no great sagacity, nor is it a hard thing to declare; but the man who foresaw it in those days—if it could possibly have been foreseen—would have been a wiser man than we.

MEG. To what are you alluding?

ATH. If one looks at what has happened, Megillus, among you Lacedaemonians, it is easy to perceive, and after perceiving to state, what ought to have been done at that time.

MEG. Speak still more clearly.

ATH. The clearest statement would be this—

MEG. What?

ATH. If one neglects the rule of due measure, and gives things too great in power to things too small—sails to ships, food to bodies, offices of rule to souls—then everything is upset, and they run, through excess of insolence, some to bodily disorders, others to that offspring of insolence, injustice. What, then, is our conclusion? Is it not this? There does not exist, my friends, a mortal soul whose nature, when young and irresponsible, will ever be able to stand being in the highest ruling position upon earth without getting surfeited in mind with that greatest of disorders, folly, and earning the detestation of its nearest friends; and when this occurs, it speedily ruins the soul itself and annihilates the whole of its power. To guard against this, by perceiving the due measure, is the task of the great lawgiver. So the most duly reasonable conjecture we can now frame as to what took place at that epoch appears to be this—

MEG. What?

ATH. To begin with, there was a god watching over you; and he, foreseeing the future, restricted within due bounds the royal power by making your kingly line no longer single but twofold. In the next place, some man, in whom human nature was blended with power divine, observing your government to be still swollen with fever, blended the self-willed force of the royal strain with the temperate potency of age, by making the power of the eight-and-twenty elders of equal weight with that of the kings in the greatest matters. Then your "third savior," seeing your government still fretting and fuming, curbed it, as one may say, by the power of the ephors, which was not far removed from government by lot. Thus, in your case, according to this account, owing to its being blended of the right elements and possessed of due measure, the kingship not only survived itself but ensured the survival of all else. For if the matter had lain with Temenus and Cresphontes and the lawgivers of their day—whosoever those lawgivers really were—even the portion of Aristodemus could never have survived, for they were not fully expert in the art of legislation; otherwise they could hardly have deemed it sufficient to moderate by means of sworn pledges a youthful soul endowed with power such as might develop into a tyranny; but now God has shown of what kind the government ought to have been then, and ought to be now, if it is to endure. That we should understand this, after the occurrence, is—as I said before—no great mark of sagacity, since it is by no means difficult to draw an inference from an example in the past; but if, at the time, there had been anyone who foresaw the result and was able to moderate the ruling powers and unify them—such a man would have preserved all the grand designs then formed, and no Persian or other armament would ever have set out against Greece, or held us in contempt as a people of small account.

CLIN. True.

ATH. The way they repulsed the Persians, Clinias, was disgraceful. But when I say "disgraceful," I do not imply that they did not win fine victories both by land and sea in those victorious campaigns: what I call "disgraceful" is this—that, in the first place, one only of those three States defended Greece, while the other two were so basely corrupt that one of them actually prevented Lacedaemon from assisting Greece by warring against her with all its might, and Argos, the other—which stood first of the three in the days of the Dorian settlement—when summoned to help against the barbarian, paid no heed and gave no help. Many are the discreditable charges one would have to bring against Greece in relating the events of that war; indeed, it would be wrong to say that Greece defended herself, for had not the bondage that threatened her been warded off by the concerted policy of the Athenians and Lacedaemonians, practically all the Greek races would have been confused together by now, and barbarians confused with Greeks and Greeks with barbarians—just as the races under the Persian empire today are either scattered abroad or jumbled together and live in a miserable plight. Such, O Megillus and Clinias, are the charges we have to make against the so-called statesmen and lawgivers, both of the past and of the present, in order that, by investigating their causes, we may discover what different course ought to have been pursued; just as, in the case before us, we called it a blunder to establish by law a government that is great or unblended, our idea being that a State ought to be free and wise and in friendship with itself, and that the lawgiver should legislate with a view to this. Nor let it surprise us that, while we have often already proposed ends which the legislator should, as we say, aim at in his legislation, the various ends thus proposed are apparently different. One needs to reflect that wisdom and friendship, when stated to be the aim in view, are not really different aims, but identical; and, if we meet with many other such terms, let not this fact disturb us.

CLIN. We shall endeavor to bear this in mind as we traverse the arguments again. But for the moment, as regards friendship, wisdom, and freedom—tell us, what was it you intended to say that the lawgiver ought to aim at?

ATH. Listen. There are two mother-forms of constitution, so to call them, from which one may truly say all the rest are derived. Of these the one is properly termed monarchy, the other democracy, the extreme case of the former being the Persian polity, and of the latter the Athenian; the rest are practically all, as I said, modifications of these two. Now it is essential for a polity to partake of both these two forms, if it is to have freedom and friendliness combined with wisdom. And that is what our argument intends to enjoin, when it declares that a State which does not partake of these can never be rightly constituted.

CLIN. It could not.

ATH. Since the one embraced monarchy and the other freedom, unmixed and in excess, neither of them has either in due measure: your Laconian and Cretan States are better in this respect, as were the Athenian and Persian in old times—in contrast to their present condition.

• • •

ATH. We said that the lawgiver must aim, in his legislation, at three objectives—to make the State he is legislating for free, and at unity with itself, and possessed of sense. That was so, was it not?

MEG. Certainly.

ATH. With these objects in view, we selected the most despotic of polities and the most absolutely free, and are now enquiring which of these is rightly constituted. When we took a moderate example of each— of despotic rule on the one hand, and liberty on the other—we observed that there they enjoyed prosperity in the highest degree; but when they advanced, the one to the extreme of slavery, the other to the extreme of liberty, then there was no gain to either the one or the other.

MEG. Most true.

ATH. With the same objects in view we surveyed, also, the settling of the Doric host and the homes of Dardanus at the foot of the hills and the colony by the sea and the first men who survived the Flood, together with our previous discourses concerning music and revelry, as well as all that preceded these. The object of all these discourses was to discover how best a State might be managed, and how best the individual citizen might pass his life. But as to the value of our conclusions, what test can we apply in conversing among ourselves, O Megillus and Clinias?

CLIN. I think, Stranger, that I can perceive one. It is a piece of good luck for me that we have dealt with all these matters in our discourse. For I myself have now come nearly to the point when I shall need them, and my meeting with you and Megillus here was quite opportune. I will make no secret to you of what has befallen me; nay, more, I count it to be a sign from Heaven. The most part of Crete is undertaking to found a colony, and it has given charge of the undertaking to the Cnosians, and the city of Cnosus

has entrusted it to me and nine others. We are bidden also to frame laws, choosing such as we please either from our own local laws or from those of other countries, taking no exception to their alien character, provided only that they seem superior. Let us, then, grant this favor to me, and yourselves also; let us select from the statements we have made, and build up by arguments the framework of a State, as though we were erecting it from the foundation. In this way we shall be at once investigating our theme, and possibly I may also make use of our framework for the State that is to be formed.

ATH. Your proclamation, Clinias, is certainly not a proclamation of war! So, if Megillus has no objection, you may count on me to do all I can to gratify your wish.

CLIN. It is good to hear that.

MEG. And you can count on me too.

CLIN. Splendid of you both! But, in the first place, let us try to found the State by word.

BOOK IV

ATH. . . . No man ever makes laws, but chances and accidents of all kinds, occurring in all sorts of ways, make all our laws for us. For either it is a war that violently upsets polities and changes laws, or it is the distress due to grievous poverty. Diseases, too, often force on revolutions, owing to the inroads of pestilences and recurring bad seasons prolonged over many years. Foreseeing all this, one might deem it proper to say—as I said just now—that no mortal man frames any law, but human affairs are nearly all matters of pure chance. But the fact is that, although one may appear to be quite right in saying this about sea-faring and the arts of the pilot, the physician, and the general, yet there really is something else that we may say with equal truth about these same things.

CLIN. What is that?

ATH. That God controls all that is, and that Chance and Occasion co-operate with God in the control of all human affairs. It is, however, less harsh to admit that these two must be accompanied by a third factor, which is Art. For that the pilots' art should co-operate with Occasion—verily I, for one, should esteem that a great advantage. Is it not so?

CLIN. It is.

ATH. Then we must grant that this is equally true in the other cases also, by parity of reasoning, including the case of legislation. When all the other conditions are present which a country needs to possess in the way of fortune if it is ever to be happily settled, then every such State needs to meet with a lawgiver who holds fast to truth.

CLIN. Very true.

ATH. Would not, then, the man who possessed art in regard to each of the crafts mentioned be able to pray aright for that condition which, if it were given by Chance, would need only the supplement of his own art?

CLIN. Certainly.

ATH. And if all the other craftsmen mentioned just now were bidden to state the object of their prayers, they could do so, could they not?

CLIN. Of course.

ATH. And the lawgiver, I suppose, could do likewise?

CLIN. I suppose so.

ATH. "Come now, O lawgiver," let us say to him, "what are we to give you, and what condition of State, to enable you, when you receive it, thenceforward to manage the State by yourself satisfactorily?"

CLIN. What is the next thing that can rightly be said?

ATH. You mean, do you not, on the side of the lawgiver?

CLIN. Yes.

ATH. This is what he will say: "Give me the State under a monarchy; and let the monarch be young, and possessed by nature of a good memory, quick intelligence, courage and nobility of manner; and let that quality, which we formerly mentioned as the necessary accompaniment of all the parts of virtue, attend now also on our monarch's soul, if the rest of his qualities are to be of any value."

CLIN. Temperance, as I think, Megillus, is what the Stranger indicates as the necessary accompaniment. Is it not?

ATH. Yes, Clinias; temperance, that is, of the ordinary kind; not the kind men mean when they use academic language and identify temperance with wisdom, but that kind which by natural instinct springs up at birth in children and animals, so that some are not incontinent, others continent, in respect of pleasures; and of this we said that, when isolated from the numerous so-called "goods," it was of no account. You understand, of course, what I mean.

CLIN. Certainly.

ATH. Let our monarch, then, possess this natural quality in addition to the other qualities mentioned, if the State is to acquire in the quickest and best way possible the constitution it needs for the happiest kind of life. For there does not exist, nor could there ever arise, a quicker and better form of constitution than this.

CLIN. How and by what argument, Stranger, could one convince oneself that to say this is to speak the truth?

ATH. It is quite easy to perceive at least this, Clinias, that the facts stand by nature's ordinance in the way described.

CLIN. In what way do you mean? On condition, do you say, that there should be a monarch who was young, temperate, quick at learning, with a good memory, brave and of a noble manner?

ATH. Add also "fortunate"—not in other respects, but only in this, that in his time there should arise a praiseworthy lawgiver, and that, by a piece of good fortune, the two of them should meet; for if this were so, then God would have done nearly everything that he does when he desires that a State should be eminently prosperous. The second best condition is that there should arise two such rulers; then comes the third best, with three rulers; and so on, the difficulty increasing in proportion as the number becomes greater, and *vice versa*.

CLIN. You mean, apparently, that the best State would arise from a monarchy, when it has a first-rate lawgiver and a virtuous monarch, and these are the conditions under which the change into such a State could be effected most easily and quickly; and, next to this, from an oligarchy—or what is it you mean?

ATH. Not at all: the easiest step is from a monarchy, the next easiest from a monarchic constitution, the third from some form of democracy. An oligarchy, which comes fourth in order, would admit of the growth of the best State only with the greatest difficulty, since it has the largest number of rulers. What I say is that the change takes place when nature supplies a true lawgiver, and when it happens that his policy is shared by the most powerful persons in the State; and wherever the State authorities are at once strongest and fewest in number, then and there the changes are usually carried out with speed and facility.

CLIN. How so? We do not understand.

ATH. Yet surely it has been stated not once, I imagine, but many times over. But you, very likely, have never so much as set eyes on a monarchical State.

CLIN. No, nor have I any craving for such a sight.

ATH. You would, however, see in it an illustration of what we spoke of just now.

CLIN. What was that?

ATH. The fact that a monarch, when he decides to change the moral habits of a State, needs no great efforts nor a vast length of time, but what he does need is to lead the way himself first along the desired path, whether it be to urge the citizens toward virtue's practices or the contrary; by his personal example he should first trace out the right lines, giving praise and honor to these things, blame to those, and degrading the disobedient according to their several deeds.

CLIN. Yes, we may perhaps suppose that the rest of the citizens will quickly follow the ruler who adopts such a combination of persuasion and force.

ATH. Let none, my friends, persuade us that a State could ever change its laws more quickly or more easily by any other way than by the personal guidance of the rulers: no such thing could ever occur, either now or hereafter. Indeed, that is not the result which we find it difficult or impossible to bring about; what is difficult to bring about is rather that result which has taken place but rarely throughout long ages, and which, whenever it does take place in a State, produces in that State countless blessings of every kind.

CLIN. What result do you mean?

ATH. Whenever a heaven-sent desire for temperate and just institutions arises in those who hold high positions—whether as monarchs, or because of conspicuous eminence of wealth or birth, or, haply, as displaying the character of Nestor, of whom it is said that, while he surpassed all men in the force of his eloquence, still more did he surpass them in temperance. That was, as they say, in the Trojan age, certainly not in our time; still, if any such man existed, or shall exist, or exists among us now, blessed is the life he leads, and blessed are they who join in listening to the words of temperance that proceed out of his mouth. So likewise of power in general, the same rule holds good: whenever the greatest power coincides in

man with wisdom and temperance, then the germ of the best polity is planted; but in no other way will it ever come about. Regard this as a myth oracularly uttered, and let us take it as proved that the rise of a well-governed State is in one way difficult, but in another way—given, that is, the condition we mention—it is easier by far and quicker than anything else.

CLIN. No doubt.

ATH. Let us apply the oracle to your State, and so try, like greybeard boys, to model its laws by our discourse.

CLIN. Yes, let us proceed, and delay no longer.

ATH. Let us invoke the presence of the God at the establishment of the State; and may he hearken, and hearkening may he come, propitious and kindly to us-ward, to help us in the fashioning of the State and its laws.

CLIN. Yes, may he come!

ATH. Well, what form of polity is it that we intend to impose upon the State?

CLIN. What, in particular, do you refer to? Explain still more clearly. I mean, is it a democracy, an oligarchy, an aristocracy, or a monarchy? For certainly you cannot mean a tyranny: that we can never suppose.

ATH. Come now, which of you two would like to answer me first and tell me to which of these kinds his own polity at home belongs?

MEG. Is it not proper that I, as the elder, should answer first?

CLIN. No doubt.

MEG. In truth, Stranger, when I reflect on the Lacedaemonian polity, I am at a loss to tell you by what name one should describe it. It seems to me to resemble a tyranny, since the board of ephors it contains is a marvelously tyrannical feature; yet sometimes it strikes me as, of all States, the nearest to a democracy. Still, it would be totally absurd to deny that it is an aristocracy; while it includes, moreover, a life monarchy, and that the most ancient of monarchies, as is affirmed, not only by ourselves, but by all the world. But now that I am questioned thus suddenly, I am really, as I said, at a loss to say definitely to which of these polities it belongs.

CLIN. And I, Megillus, find myself equally perplexed; for I find it very difficult to affirm that our Cnosian polity is any one of these.

ATH. Yes, my good Sirs; for you do, in fact, partake in a number of polities. But those we named just now are not polities, but arrangements of States which rule or serve parts of themselves, and each is named after the ruling power.

• • •

ATH. . . . We deny that laws are true laws unless they are enacted in the interest of the common weal of the whole State. But where the laws are enacted in the interest of a section, we call them "feudalities" rather than "polities"; and the "justice" they ascribe to such laws is, we say, an empty name. Our reason for saying this is that in your State we shall assign office to a man, not because he is wealthy, nor because he possesses any other quality of the kind—such as strength or size or birth; but the ministration of the laws must be assigned, as we assert, to that man who is most obedient to the laws and wins the victory for obedience in the State—the highest office to the first, the next to him that shows the second degree of mastery, and the rest must similarly be assigned, each in succession, to those that come next in order. And those who are termed "magistrates" I have now called "ministers" of the laws, not for the sake of coining a new phrase, but in the belief that salvation, or ruin, for a State hangs upon nothing so much as this. For wherever in a State the law is subservient and impotent, over that State I see ruin impending; but wherever the law is lord over the magistrates, and the magistrates are servants to the law, there I descry salvation and all the blessings that the gods bestow on States.

BOOK V

Of all the goods, for gods and men alike, truth stands first. Thereof let every man partake from his earliest days, if he purposes to become blessed and happy, that so he may live his life as a true man so long as possible. He is a trusty man; but untrustworthy is the man who loves the voluntary lie; and senseless is the man who loves the involuntary lie; and neither of these two is to be envied. For everyone that is either faithless or foolish is friendless; and since, as time goes on, he is found out, he is making for himself, in his woeful old-age, at life's close, a complete solitude, wherein his life becomes almost equally desolate whether his companions and children are living or dead. He that does no wrong is indeed a man

worthy of honor; but worthy of twice as much honor as he, and more, is the man who, in addition, consents not to wrongdoers when they do wrong; for while the former counts as one man, the latter counts as many, in that he informs the magistrates of the wrongdoing of the rest. And he that assists the magistrates in punishing, to the best of his power—let him be publicly proclaimed to be the Great Man of the State and perfect, the winner of the prize for excellence.

Upon temperance and upon wisdom one should bestow the same praise, and upon all the other goods which he who possesses them can not only keep himself, but can share also with others. He that thus shares these should be honored as highest in merit; and he that would fain share them but cannot, as second in merit; while if a man is jealous and unwilling to share any good things with anyone in a friendly spirit, then the man himself must be blamed, but his possession must not be disesteemed any the more because of its possessor—rather one should strive to gain it with all one's might. Let every one of us be ambitious to gain excellence, but without jealousy. For a man of this character enlarges a State, since he strives hard himself and does not thwart the others by calumny; but the jealous man, thinking that calumny of others is the best way to secure his own superiority, makes less effort himself to win true excellence, and disheartens his rivals by getting them unjustly blamed; whereby he causes the whole State to be ill-trained for competing in excellence, and renders it, for his part, less large in fair repute. Every man ought to be at once passionate and gentle in the highest degree. For, on the one hand, it is impossible to escape from other men's wrongdoings, when they are cruel and hard to remedy, or even wholly irremediable, otherwise than by victorious fighting and self-defence, and by punishing most rigorously; and this no soul can achieve without noble passion. But, on the other hand, when men commit wrongs which are remediable, one should, in the first place, recognize that every wrongdoer is a wrongdoer involuntarily; for no one anywhere would ever voluntarily acquire any of the greatest evils, least of all in his own most precious possessions. And most precious in very truth to every man is, as we have said, the soul. No one, therefore, will voluntarily admit into this most precious thing the greatest evil and live possessing it all his life long. Now while in general the wrongdoer and he that has these evils are to be pitied, it is permissible to show pity to the man that has evils that are remediable, and to abate one's passion and treat him gently, and not to keep on raging like a scolding wife; but in dealing with the man who is totally and obstinately perverse and wicked one must give free course to wrath. Wherefore we affirm that it behooves the good man to be always at once passionate and gentle.

There is an evil, great above all others, which most men have, implanted in their souls, and which each one of them excuses in himself and makes no effort to avoid. It is the evil indicated in the saying that every man is by nature a lover of self, and that it is right that he should be such. But the truth is that the cause of all sins in every case lies in the person's excessive love of self. For the lover is blind in his view of the object loved, so that he is a bad judge of things just and good and noble, in that he deems himself bound always to value what is his own more than what is true; for the man who is to attain the title of "Great" must be devoted neither to himself nor to his own belongings, but to things just, whether they happen to be actions of his own or rather those of another man. And it is from this same sin that every man has derived the further notion that his own folly is wisdom; whence it comes about that though we know practically nothing, we fancy that we know everything; and since we will not entrust to others the doing of things we do not understand, we necessarily go wrong in doing them ourselves. Wherefore every man must shun excessive self-love, and ever follow after him that is better than himself, allowing no shame to prevent him from so doing.

Precepts that are less important than these and oftentimes repeated—but no less profitable—a man should repeat to himself by way of reminder; for where there is a constant efflux, there must also be corresponding influx, and when wisdom flows away, the proper influx consists in recollection; wherefore men must be restrained from untimely laughter and tears, and every individual, as well as the whole State, must charge every man to try to conceal all show of extreme joy or sorrow, and to behave himself seemly, alike in good fortune and in evil, according as each man's Genius ranges itself—hoping always that God will diminish the troubles that fall upon them by the blessings which he bestows, and will change for the better the present evils; and as to their blessings, hoping that they, contrariwise, will, with the help of good fortune, be increased. In these hopes, and in the recollections of all these truths, it behoves every man to live, sparing no pains, but constantly recalling them clearly to the recollection both of himself and of his neighbor, alike when at work and when at play.

Thus, as regards the right character of institutions and the right character of individuals, we have now laid down practically all the rules that are of divine sanction. Those that are of human origin we have not stated as yet, but state them we must; for our converse is with men, not gods. Pleasures, pains and desires are by nature especially human; and from these, of necessity, every mortal creature is, so to say, suspended and dependent by the strongest cords of influence. Thus one should commend the noblest life, not merely because it is of superior fashion in respect of fair repute, but also because, if a man consents to taste it and not shun it in his youth, it is superior likewise in that which all men covet—an excess, namely, of joy and a deficiency of pain throughout the whole of life. That this will clearly be the result, if a man tastes of it rightly, will at once be fully evident. But wherein does this "rightness" consist? That is the question which we must now, under the instruction of our Argument, consider; comparing the more pleasant life with the more painful, we must in this wise consider whether this mode is natural to us, and that other mode unnatural. We desire that pleasure should be ours, but pain we neither choose nor desire; and the neutral state we do not desire in place of pleasure, but we do desire it in exchange for pain; and we desire less pain with more pleasure, but we do not desire less pleasure with more pain; and when the two are evenly balanced, we are unable to state any clear preference. Now all these states—in their number, quantity, intensity, equality, and in the opposites thereof—have, or have not, influence on desire, to govern its choice of each. So these things being thus ordered of necessity, we desire that mode of life in which the feelings are many, great, and intense, with those of pleasure predominating, but we do not desire the life in which the feelings of pain predominate; and contrariwise, we do not desire the life in which the feelings are few, small, and gentle, if the painful predominate, but if the pleasurable predominate, we do desire it. Further, we must regard the life in which there is an equal balance of pleasure and pain as we previously regarded the neutral state: we desire the balanced life in so far as it exceeds the painful life in point of what we like, but we do not desire it in so far as it exceeds the pleasant lives in point of the things we dislike. The lives of us men must all be regarded as naturally bound up in these feelings, and what kinds of lives we naturally desire is what we must distinguish; but if we assert that we desire anything else, we only say so through ignorance and inexperience of the lives as they really are.

What, then, and how many are the lives in which a man—when he has chosen the desirable and voluntary in preference to the undesirable and the involuntary, and has made it into a private law for himself, by choosing what is at once both congenial and pleasant and most good and noble—may live as happily as man can? Let us pronounce that one of them is the temperate life, one the wise, one the brave, and let us class the healthy life as one; and to these let us oppose four others—the foolish, the cowardly, the licentious, and the diseased. He that knows the temperate life will set it down as gentle in all respects, affording mild pleasures and mild pains, moderate appetites and desires void of frenzy; but the licentious life he will set down as violent in all directions, affording both pains and pleasures that are extreme, appetites that are intense and maddening, and desires the most frenzied possible; and whereas in the temperate life the pleasures outweigh the pains, in the licentious life the pains exceed the pleasures in extent, number, and frequency. Whence it necessarily results that the one life must be naturally more pleasant, the other more painful to us; and it is no longer possible for the man who desires a pleasant life voluntarily to live a licentious life, but it is clear by now (if our argument is right) that no man can possibly be licentious voluntarily: it is owing to ignorance incontinence, or both, that the great bulk of mankind live lives lacking in temperance. Similarly with regard to the diseased life and the healthy life, one must observe that while both have pleasures and pains, the pleasures exceed the pains in health, but the pains the pleasures in disease. Our desire in the choice of lives is not that pain should be in excess, but the life we have judged the more pleasant is that in which pain is exceeded by

pleasure. We will assert, then, that since the temperate life has its feelings smaller, fewer and lighter than the licentious life, and the wise life than the foolish, and the brave than the cowardly, and since the one life is superior to the other in pleasure, but inferior in pain, the brave life is victorious over the cowardly and the wise over the foolish; consequently the one set of lives ranks as more pleasant than the other: the temperate, brave, wise, and healthy lives are more pleasant than the cowardly, foolish, licentious, and diseased. To sum up, the life of bodily and spiritual virtue, as compared with that of vice, is not only more pleasant, but also exceeds greatly in nobility, rectitude, virtue, and good fame, so that it causes the man who lives it to live ever so much more happily than he who lives the opposite life.

Thus far we have stated the prelude of our laws, and here let that statement end: after the prelude must necessarily follow the tune—or rather, to be strictly accurate, a sketch of the State-organization. Now, just as in the case of a piece of webbing, or any other woven article, it is not possible to make both warp and woof of the same materials, but the stuff of the warp must be of better quality—for it is strong and is made firm by its twistings, whereas the woof is softer and shows a due degree of flexibility—from this we may see that in some such way we must mark out those who are to hold high offices in the State and those who are to hold low offices, after applying in each case an adequate educational test. For of State organization there are two divisions, of which the one is the appointment of individuals to office, the other the assignment of laws to the offices.

• • •

Book VI

ATH. . . . It is imperatively necessary for you to choose your Law-wardens first with the utmost care.

CLIN. What means can we find for this, or what rule?

ATH. This: I assert, O ye sons of Crete, that, since the Cnosians take precedence over most of the Cretan cities, they should combine with those who have come into this community to select thirty-seven persons in all from their own number and the community—nineteen from the latter body, and the rest from Cnosus itself; and those men the Cnosians should make over to your State, and they should make you in person a citizen of this colony and one of the eighteen—using persuasion or, possibly, a reasonable degree of compulsion.

CLIN. Why, pray, have not you also, Stranger, and Megillus lent us a hand in our constitution?

ATH. Athens is haughty, Clinias, and Sparta also is haughty, and both are far distant: but for you this course is in all respects proper, as it is likewise for the rest of the founders of the colony, to whom also our recent remarks about you apply. Let us, then, assume that this would be the most equitable arrangement under the conditions at present existing. Later on, if the constitution still remains, the selection of officials shall take place as follows:—In the selection of officials all men shall take part who carry arms, as horse-soldiers or foot-soldiers, or who have served in war so far as their age and ability allowed. They shall make the selection in that shrine which the State shall deem the most sacred; and each man shall bring to the altar of the god, written on a tablet, the name of his nominee, with his father's name and that of his tribe and of the deme he belongs to, and beside these he shall write also his own name in like manner. Any man who chooses shall be permitted to remove any tablet which seems to him to be improperly written, and to place it in the market-place for not less than thirty days. The officials shall publicly exhibit, for all the State to see, those of the tablets that are adjudged to come first, to the number of 300; and all the citizens shall vote again in like manner, each for whomsoever of these he wishes. Of these, the officials shall again exhibit publicly the names of those who are adjudged first, up to the number of 100. The third time, he that wishes shall vote for whomsoever he wishes out of the hundred, passing between slain victims as he does so: then they shall test the thirty-seven men who have secured most votes, and declare them to be magistrates.

Who, then, are the men, O Clinias and Megillus, who shall establish in our State all these regulations concerning magisterial offices and tests? We perceive (do we not?) that for States that are thus getting into harness for the first time some such persons there must necessarily be; but who they can be, before any officials exist, it is impossible to see. Yet somehow or other they must be there—and men, too, of no mean quality, but of the highest quality possible. For, as the saying goes, "well begun is half done," and every man always commends a good beginning; but it is truly, as I think, something more than the half, and no man has ever yet commended as it deserves a beginning that is well made.

CLIN. Very true.

ATH. Let us not then wittingly leave this first step unmentioned, nor fail to make it quite clear to ourselves how it is to be brought about. I, however, am by no means fertile in resource, save for one statement which, in view of the present situation, it is both necessary and useful to make.

CLIN. What statement is that?

ATH. I assert that the State for whose settlement we are planning has nobody in the way of parents except that State which is founding it, though I am quite aware that many of the colony-States often have been, and will be, at feud with those which founded them. But now, on the present occasion, just as a child in the present helplessness of childhood—in spite of the likelihood of his being at enmity with his parents at some future date—loves his parents and is loved by them, and always flies for help to his kindred and finds in them, and them alone, his allies—so now, as I assert, this relationship exists ready-made for the Cnosians toward the young State, owing to their care for it, and for the young State toward the Cnosians. I state once more, as I stated just now—for there is no harm in duplicating a good statement—that the Cnosians must take a share in caring for all these matters, choosing out not less than 100 men of those who have come into the colony, the oldest and best of them they are able to select; and of the Cnosians themselves let there be another hundred. This joint body must, I say, go to the new State and arrange in common that the magistrates be appointed according to the laws and be tested after appointment. When this has been done, then the Cnosians must dwell in Cnosus, and the young State must endeavor by its own efforts to secure for itself safety and success. As to the men who belong to the thirty and seven, let us select them for the following purposes: First, they shall act as Wardens of the laws, and secondly as Keepers of the registers in which every man writes out for the officials the amount of his property, omitting four minae if he be of the highest property-class, three if he be of the second class, two if he be of the third, and one if he be of the fourth class. And should anyone be proved to possess anything else beyond what is registered, all such surplus shall be confiscated; and in addition he shall be liable to be brought to trial by anyone who wishes to prosecute—a trial neither noble nor fair of name, if he be convicted of despising law because of lucre. So he that wishes shall charge him with profiteering, and prosecute him by law before the Law-wardens themselves; and if the defendant be convicted, he shall take no share of the public good, and whenever the State makes a distribution, he shall go portionless, save for his allotment, and he shall be registered as a convicted criminal, where anyone who chooses may read his sentence, as long as he lives. A Law-warden shall hold office for no more than twenty years, and he shall be voted into office when he is not under fifty years of age. If he is elected at the age of sixty, he shall hold office for ten years only; and by the same rule, the more he exceeds the minimum age, the shorter shall be his term of office; so that if he lives beyond the age of seventy, he must no longer fancy that he can remain among these officials holding an office of such high importance.

So, for the Law-wardens, let us state that these three duties are imposed on them, and as we proceed with the laws, each fresh law will impose upon these men whatever additional duties they ought to be charged with beyond those now stated.

* * *

The Boulé (or "Council") shall consist of thirty dozen—as the number 360 is well-adapted for the sub-divisions: they shall be divided into four groups; and 90 councillors shall be voted for from each of the property-classes. First, for councillors from the highest property-class all the citizens shall be compelled to vote, and whoever disobeys shall be fined with the fine decreed. When these have been voted for, their names shall be recorded. On the next day those from the second class shall be voted for, the procedure being similar to that on the first day. On the third day, for councillors from the third class anyone who chooses shall vote; and the voting shall be compulsory for members of the first three classes, but those of the fourth and lowest class shall be let off the fine, in case any of them do not wish to vote. On the fourth day, for those from the fourth and lowest class all shall vote; and if any member of the third or fourth class does not wish to vote, he shall be let off the fine; but any member of the first or second class who fails to vote shall be fined—three times the amount of the first fine in the case of a member of the second class, and four times in the case of one of the first class. On the fifth day the officials shall publish the names recorded for all the citizens to see; and for these every man shall vote, or else be fined with the first fine; and when they have selected 180 from each of the classes, they shall choose out by lot one-half of this number, and test them; and these shall be the Councillors for the year.

The selection of officials that is thus made will form a mean between a monarchic constitution and a democratic; and midway between these our constitution should always stand. For slaves will never be friends with masters, nor bad men with good, even when they occupy equal positions—for when equality is given to unequal things, the resultant will be unequal, unless due measure is applied; and it is because of these two conditions that political organizations are filled with feuds. There is an old and true saying that "equality produces amity," which is right well and fitly spoken; but what the equality is which is capable of doing this is a very troublesome question, since it is very far from being clear. For there are two kinds of equality which, though identical in name, are often almost opposites in their practical results. The one of these any State or lawgiver is competent to apply in the assignment of honors—namely, the equality determined by measure, weight, and number—by simply employing the lot to give even results in the distributions; but the truest and best form of equality is not an easy thing for everyone to discern. It is the judgment of Zeus, and men it never assists save in small measure, but in so far as it does assist either States or individuals, it produces all things good; for it dispenses more to the greater and less to the smaller, giving due measure to each according to nature; and with regard to honors also, by granting the greater to those that are greater in goodness, and the less to those of the opposite character in respect of goodness and education, it assigns in proportion what is fitting to each. Indeed, it is precisely this which constitutes for us "political justice," which is the object we must strive for, Clinias; this equality is what we must aim at, now that we are settling the

State that is being planted. And whoever founds a State elsewhere at any time must make this same object the aim of his legislation—not the advantage of a few tyrants, or of one, or of some form of democracy, but justice always; and this consists in what we have just stated, namely, the natural equality given on each occasion to things unequal. None the less, it is necessary for every State at times to employ even this equality in a modified degree, if it is to avoid involving itself in intestine discord, in one section or another—for the reasonable and considerate, wherever employed, is an infringement of the perfect and exact, as being contrary to strict justice; for the same reason it is necessary to make use also of the equality of the lot, on account of the discontent of the masses, and in doing so to pray, calling upon God and Good Luck to guide for them the lot aright toward the highest justice. Thus it is that necessity compels us to employ both forms of equality; but that form, which needs good luck, we should employ as seldom as possible.

The State which means to survive must necessarily act thus, my friends, for the reasons we have stated. For just as a ship when sailing on the sea requires continual watchfulness both by night and day, so likewise a State, when it lives amidst the surge of surrounding States and is in danger of being entrapped by all sorts of plots, requires to have officers linked up with officers from day to night and from night to day, and guardians succeeding guardians, and being succeeded in turn, without a break. But since a crowd of men is incapable of ever performing any of these duties smartly, the bulk of the Councillors must necessarily be left to stay most of their time at their private business, to attend to their domestic affairs; and we must assign a twelfth part of them to each of the twelve months, to furnish guards in rotation, so as promptly to meet any person coming either from somewhere abroad or from their own State, in case he desires to give information or to make enquiries about some matter of international importance; and so as to make replies, and, when the State has asked questions, to receive the replies; and above all, in view of the manifold innovations that are wont to occur constantly in States, to prevent if possible their occurrence, and in case they do occur, to ensure that the State may perceive and remedy the occurrence as quickly as possible. For these reasons, this presidential

section of the State must always have the control of the summoning and dissolving of assemblies, both the regular legal asssemblies and those of an emergency character. Thus a twelfth part of the Council will be the body that manages all these matters, and each such part shall rest in turn for eleven-twelfths of the year: in common with the rest of the officials, this twelfth section of the Council must keep its watch in the State over these matters continually.

• • •

Next, as regards possessions, what should a man possess to form a reasonable amount of substance? As to most chattels, it is easy enough both to see what they should be and to acquire them; but servants present all kinds of difficulties. The reason is that our language about them is partly right and partly wrong; for the language we use both contradicts and agrees with our practical experience of them.

MEG. What mean we by this? We are still in the dark, Stranger, as to what you refer to.

ATH. That is quite natural, Megillus. For probably the most vexed problem in all Hellas is the problem of the Helot-system of the Lacedaemonians, which some maintain to be good, others bad; a less violent dispute rages round the subjection of the Mariandyni to the slave-system of the Heracleotes, and that of the class of Penestae to the Thessalians. In view of these and similar instances, what ought we to do about this question of owning servants? The point I happened to mention in the course of my argument—and about which you naturally asked me what I referred to— was this. We know, of course, that we would all agree that one ought to own slaves that are as docile and good as possible; for in the past many slaves have proved themselves better in every form of excellence than brothers or sons, and have saved their masters and their goods and their whole houses. Surely we know that this language is used about slaves?

MEG. Certainly.

ATH. And is not the opposite kind of language also used—that the soul of a slave has no soundness in it, and that a sensible man should never trust that class at all? And our wisest poet, too, in speaking of Zeus, declared that—

Of half their wits far-thundering Zeus bereaves
Those men on whom the day of bondage falls.

Thus each party adopts a different attitude of mind: the one places no trust at all in the servant-class, but, treating them like brute beasts, with goads and whips they make the servants' souls not merely thrice but fifty times enslaved; whereas the other party act in precisely the opposite way.

MEG. Just so.

CLIN. Since this difference of opinion exists, Stranger, what ought we to do about our own country, in regard to the owning of slaves and their punishment?

ATH. Well now, Clinias, since man is an intractable creature, it is plain that he is not at all likely to be or become easy to deal with in respect of the necessary distinction between slave and free-born master in actual experience.

CLIN. That is evident.

ATH. The slave is no easy chattel. For actual experience shows how many evils result from slavery—as in the frequent revolts in Messenia, and in the States where there are many servants kept who speak the same tongue, not to speak of the crimes of all sorts committed by the "Corsairs," as they are called, who haunt the coasts of Italy, and the reprisals therefor. In view of all these facts, it is really a puzzle to know how to deal with all such matters. Two means only are left for us to try—the one is, not to allow the slaves, if they are to tolerate slavery quietly, to be all of the same nation, but, so far as possible, to have them of different races—and the other is to accord them proper treatment, and that not only for their sakes, but still more for the sake of ourselves. Proper treatment of servants consists in using no violence towards them, and in hurting them even less, if possible, than our own equals. For it is his way of dealing with men whom it is easy for him to wrong that shows most clearly whether a man is genuine or hypocritical in his reverence for justice and hatred of injustice. He, therefore, that in dealing with slaves proves himself, in his character and action, undefiled by what is unholy or unjust will best be able to sow a crop of goodness— and this we may say, and justly say, of every master, or king, and of everyone who possesses any kind of absolute power over a person weaker than himself. We ought to punish slaves justly, and not to make them conceited by merely admonishing them as we would free men. An address to a servant should be mostly a simple command: there should be no jesting with servants, either male or female, for by a course of excessively foolish indulgence in their treatment of their slaves, masters often make life harder both for themselves, as rulers, and for their slaves, as subject to rule.

CLIN. That is true.

• • •

BOOK VII

ATH. . . .To form the character of the child over three and up to six years old there will be need of games: by then punishment must be used to prevent their getting pampered—not, however, punishment of a degrading kind, but just as we said before, in the case of slaves, that one should avoid enraging the persons punished by using degrading punishments, or pampering them by leaving them unpunished, so in the case of the free-born the same rule holds good. Children of this age have games which come by natural instinct; and they generally invent them of themselves whenever they meet together. As soon as they have reached the age of three, all the children from three to six must meet together at the village temples, those belonging to each village assembling at the same place. Moreover, the nurses of these children must watch over their behavior, whether it be orderly or disorderly; and over the nurses themselves and the whole band of children one of the twelve women already elected must be appointed annually to take charge of each band, the appointment resting with the Law-wardens. These women shall be elected by the women who have charge of the supervision of marriage, one out of each tribe and all of a like age. The woman thus appointed shall pay an official visit to the temple every day, and she shall employ a State servant and deal summarily with male or female slaves and strangers; but in the case of citizens, if the person protests against the punishment, she shall bring him for trial before the city-stewards; but if no protest is made, she shall inflict summary justice equally on citizens. After the age of six, each sex shall be kept separate, boys spending their time with boys, and likewise girls with girls; and when it is necessary for them to begin lessons, the boys must go to teachers of riding, archery, javelin-throwing and slinging, and the girls also, if they agree to it, must share in the lessons, and especially such as relate to the use of arms. For, as regards the view now prevalent regarding these matters, it is based on almost universal ignorance.

• • •

ATH. I assert that there exists in every State a complete ignorance about children's games—how that they are of decisive importance for legislation, as determining whether the laws enacted are to be permanent or not. For when the program of games is prescribed and secures that the same children always play the same games and delight in the same toys in the same way and under the same conditions, it allows the real and serious laws also to remain undisturbed; but when these games vary and suffer innovations, among other constant alterations the children are always shifting their fancy from one game to another, so that neither in respect of their own bodily gestures nor in respect of their equipment have they any fixed and acknowledged standard of propriety and impropriety; but the man they hold in special honor is he who is always innovating or introducing some novel device in the matter of form or color or something of the sort; whereas it would be perfectly true to say that a State can have no worse pest than a man of that description, since he privily alters the characters of the young, and causes them to contemn what is old and esteem what is new. And I repeat again that there is no greater mischief a State can suffer than such a dictum and doctrine: just listen while I tell you how great an evil it is.

CLIN. Do you mean the way people rail at antiquity in States?

ATH. Precisely.

CLIN. That is a theme on which you will find us no grudging listeners, but the most sympathetic possible.

ATH. I should certainly expect it to be so.

CLIN. Only say on.

ATH. Come now, let us listen to one another and address one another on this subject with greater care than ever. Nothing, as we shall find, is more perilous than change in respect of everything, save only what is bad—in respect of seasons, winds, bodily diet, mental disposition, everything in short with the solitary exception, as I said just now, of the bad. Accordingly, if

one considers the human body, and sees how it grows used to all kinds of meats and drinks and exercises, even though at first upset by them, and how presently out of these very materials it grows flesh that is akin to them, and acquiring thus a familiar acquaintance with, and fondness for, all this diet, lives a most healthy and pleasant life; and further, should a man be forced again to change back to one of the highly-reputed diets, how he is upset and ill at first, and recovers with difficulty as he gets used again to the food—it is precisely the same, we must suppose, with the intellects of men and the nature of their souls. For if there exist laws under which men have been reared up and which (by the blessing of Heaven) have remained unaltered for many centuries, so that there exists no recollection or report of their ever having been different from what they now are—then the whole soul is forbidden by reverence and fear to alter any of the things established of old. By hook or by crook, then, the lawgiver must devise a means whereby this shall be true of his State. Now here is where I discover the means desired:—Alterations in children's games are regarded by all lawgivers (as we said above) as being mere matters of play, and not as the causes of serious mischief; hence, instead of forbidding them, they give in to them and adopt them. They fail to reflect that those children who innovate in their games grow up into men different from their fathers; and being thus different themselves, they seek a different mode of life, and having sought this, they come to desire other institutions and laws; and none of them dreads the consequent approach of that result which we described just now as the greatest of all banes to a State. The evil wrought by changes in outward forms would be of less importance; but frequent changes in matters involving moral approval and disapproval are, as I maintain, of extreme importance, and require the utmost caution.

CLIN. Most certainly.

ATH. Well, then, do we still put our trust in those former statements of ours, in which we said that matters of rhythm and music generally are imitations of the manners of good or bad men? Or how do we stand?

CLIN. Our view at least remains unaltered.

ATH. We assert, then, that every means must be employed, not only to prevent our children from desiring to copy different models in dancing or singing, but also to prevent anyone from tempting them by the inducement of pleasures of all sorts.

CLIN. Quite right.

ATH. To attain this end, can any one of us suggest a better device than that of the Egyptians?

CLIN. What device is that?

ATH. The device of consecrating all dancing and all music. First, they should ordain the sacred feasts, by drawing up an annual list of what feasts are to be held, and on what dates, and in honour of what special gods and children of gods and daemons; and they should ordain next what hymn is to be sung at each of the religious sacrifices, and with what dances each such sacrifice is to be graced; these ordinances should be first made by certain persons, and then the whole body of citizens, after making a public sacrifice to the Fates and all the other deities, should consecrate with a libation these ordinances—dedicating each of the hymns to their respective gods and divinities. And if any man proposes other hymns or dances besides these for any god, the priests and priestesses will be acting in accordance with both religion and law when, with the help of the Law-wardens, they expel him from the feast; and if the man resists expulsion, he shall be liable, so long as he lives, to be prosecuted for impiety by anyone who chooses.

CLIN. That is right.

ATH. Since we find ourselves now dealing with this theme, let us behave as befits ourselves.

CLIN. In what respect?

ATH. Every young man—not to speak of old men—on hearing or seeing anything unusual and strange, is likely to avoid jumping to a hasty and impulsive solution of his doubts about it, and to stand still; just as a man who has come to a crossroads and is not quite sure of his way, if he be traveling alone, will question himself, or if traveling with others, will question them too about the matter in doubt, and refuse to proceed until he has made sure by investigation of the direction of his path. We must now do likewise. In our discourse about laws, the point which has now occurred to us being strange, we are bound to investigate it closely; and in a matter so weighty we, at our age, must not lightly assume or assert that we can make any reliable statement about it on the spur of the moment.

CLIN. That is very true.

ATH. We shall, therefore, devote some time to this subject, and only when we have investigated it thoroughly shall we regard our conclusions as certain. But lest we be uselessly hindered from completing the ordinance which accompanies the laws with which we are now concerned, let us proceed to their conclusion. For very probably (if Heaven so will) this exposition, when completely brought to its conclusion, may also clear up the problem now before us.

CLIN. Well said, Stranger: let us do just as you say.

ATH. Let the strange fact be granted, we say, that our hymns are now made into "nomes" (laws), just as the men of old, it would seem, gave this name to harp-tunes,—so that they, too, perhaps, would not wholly disagree with our present suggestion, but one of them may have divined it vaguely, as in a dream by night or a waking vision: anyhow, let this be the decree on the matter:—In violation of public tunes and sacred songs and the whole choristry of the young, just as in violation of any other "nome" (law), no person shall utter a note or move a limb in the dance. He that obeys shall be free of all penalty; but he that disobeys shall (as we said just now) be punished by the Law-wardens, the priestesses and the priests. Shall we now lay down these enactments in our statements?

CLIN. Yes, lay them down.

ATH. How shall we enact these rules by law in such a way as to escape ridicule? Let us consider yet another point concerning them. The safest plan is to begin by framing in our discourse some typical cases, so to call them; one such case I may describe in this way. Suppose that, when a sacrifice is being performed and the offerings duly burned, some private worshipper—a son or a brother—when standing beside the altar and the offering, should blaspheme most blasphemously, would not his voice bring upon his father and the rest of the family a feeling of despair and evil forebodings?

CLIN. It would.

ATH. Well, in our part of the world this is what happens, one may almost say, in nearly every one of the States. Whenever a magistrate holds a public sacrifice, the next thing is for a crowd of choirs—not merely one—to advance and take their stand, not at a distance from the altars, but often quite close to them; and then they let out a flood of blasphemy over the sacred offerings, racking the souls of their audience with words, rhythms, and tunes most dolorous, and the man that succeeds at once in drawing most tears from the sacrificing city carries off the palm of victory. Must we not reject such a custom as this? For if it is ever really necessary that the citizens should listen to such doleful strains, it would be more fitting that the choirs that attend should be hired from abroad, and that not on holy days but only on fast-days—just as a corpse is escorted with Carian music by hired mourners. Such music would also form the fitting accompaniment for hymns of this kind; and the garb befitting these funeral hymns would not be any crowns nor gilded ornaments, but just the opposite—for I want to get done with this subject as soon as I can. Only I would have us ask ourselves again this single question—are we satisfied to lay this down as our first typical rule for hymns?

CLIN. What rule?

ATH. That of auspicious speech; and must we have a kind of hymn that is altogether in all respects auspicious? Or shall I ordain that it shall be so, without further questioning?

CLIN. By all means ordain it so; for that is a law carried by a unanimous vote.

ATH. What then, next to auspicious speech, should be the second law of music? Is it not that prayers should be made on each occasion to those gods to whom offering is made?

CLIN. Certainly.

ATH. The third law, I suppose, will be this—that the poets, knowing that prayers are requests addressed to gods, must take the utmost care lest unwittingly they request a bad thing as though it were a good thing; for if such a prayer were made, it would prove, I fancy, a ludicrous blunder.

CLIN. Of course.

ATH. Did not our argument convince us, a little while ago, that no Plutus either in gold or in silver should dwell enshrined within the State?

CLIN. It did.

ATH. What then shall we say that this statement serves to illustrate? Is it not this—that the tribe of poets is not wholly capable of discerning very well what is good and what not? For surely when a poet, suffering from this error, composes prayers either in speech or in song, he will be making our citizens contradict ourselves in their prayers for things of the greatest moment; yet this, as we have said, is an error than which few are greater. So shall we also lay down

this as one of our laws and typical cases regarding music?

CLIN. What law? Explain it to us more clearly.

ATH. The law that the poet shall compose nothing which goes beyond the limits of what the State holds to be legal and right, fair and good; nor shall he show his compositions to any private person until they have first been shown to the judges appointed to deal with these matters, and to the Law-wardens, and have been approved by them. And in fact we have judges appointed in those whom we selected to be the legislators of music and in the supervisor of education. Well then, I repeat my question—is this to be laid down as our third law, typical case, and example? What think you?

CLIN. Be it laid down by all means.

ATH. Next to these, it will be most proper to sing hymns and praise to the gods, coupled with prayers; and after the gods will come prayers combined with praise to daemons and heroes, as is befitting to each.

CLIN. To be sure.

ATH. This done, we may proceed at once without scruple to formulate this law:—all citizens who have attained the goal of life and have wrought with body or soul noble works and toilsome, and have been obedient to the laws, shall be regarded as fitting objects for praise.

CLIN. Certainly.

ATH. But truly it is not safe to honor with hymns and praises those still living, before they have traversed the whole of life and reached a noble end. All such honors shall be equally shared by women as well as men who have been conspicuous for their excellence.

● ● ●

ATH. . . . For females, too, my law will lay down the same regulations as for men, and training of an identical kind. I will unhesitatingly affirm that neither riding nor gymnastics, which are proper for men, are improper for women. I believe the old tales I have heard, and I know now of my own observation, that there are practically countless myriads of women called Sauromatides, in the district of Pontus, upon whom equally with men is imposed the duty of handling bows and other weapons, as well as horses, and who practice it equally. In addition to this I allege the following argument. Since this state of things can exist, I affirm that the practice which at present prevails in our districts is a most irrational one—

namely, that men and women should not all follow the same pursuits with one accord and with all their might. For thus from the same taxation and trouble there arises and exists half a State only instead of a whole one, in nearly every instance; yet surely this would be a surprising blunder for a lawgiver to commit.

CLIN. So it would seem; yet truly a vast number of the things now mentioned, Stranger, are in conflict with our ordinary polities.

ATH. Well, but I said that we should allow the argument to run its full course, and when this is done we should adopt the conclusion we approve.

CLIN. In this you spoke most reasonably; and you have made me now chide myself for what I said. So say on now what seems good to you.

ATH. What seems good to me, Clinias, as I said before, is this—that if the possibility of such a state of things taking place had not been sufficiently proved by facts, then it might have been possible to gainsay our statement; but as it is, the man who rejects our law must try some other method, nor shall we be hereby precluded from asserting in our doctrine that the female sex must share with the male, to the greatest extent possible, both in education and in all else. For in truth we ought to conceive of the matter in this light. Suppose that women do not share with men in the whole of their mode of life, must they not have a different system of their own?

CLIN. They must.

ATH. Then which of the systems now in vogue shall we prescribe in preference to that fellowship which we are now imposing upon them? Shall it be that of the Thracians, and many other tribes, who employ their women in tilling the ground and minding oxen and sheep and toiling just like slaves? Or that which obtains with us and all the people of our district? The way women are treated with us at present is this— we huddle all our goods together, as the saying goes, within four walls, and then hand over the dispensing of them to the women, together with the control of the shuttles and all kinds of wool-work. Or again, shall we prescribe for them, Megillus, that midway system, the Laconian? Must the girls share in gymnastics and music, and the women abstain from wool-work, but weave themselves instead a life that is not trivial at all nor useless, but arduous, advancing as it were halfway in the path of domestic tendance and

management and child-nurture, but taking no share in military service; so that, even if it should chance to be necessary for them to fight in defense of their city and their children, they will be unable to handle with skill either a bow (like the Amazons) or any other missile, nor could they take spear and shield, after the fashion of the Goddess, so as to be able nobly to resist the wasting of their native land, and to strike terror—if nothing more—into the enemy at the sight of them marshaled in battle-array? If they lived in this manner, they certainly would not dare to adopt the fashion of the Sauromatides, whose women would seem like men beside them. So in regard to this matter, let who will commend your Laconian lawgivers: as to my view, it must stand as it is. The lawgiver ought to be whole-hearted, not half-hearted—letting the female sex indulge in luxury and expense and disorderly ways of life, while supervising the male sex; for thus he is actually bequeathing to the State the half only, instead of the whole, of a life of complete prosperity.

MEG. What are we to do, Clinias? Shall we allow the Stranger to run down our Sparta in this fashion?

CLIN. Yes: now that we have granted him free speech we must let him be, until we have discussed the laws fully.

MEG. You are right.

• • •

ATH. ... The actions of ugly bodies and ugly ideas and of the men engaged in ludicrous comic-acting, in regard to both speech and dance, and the representations given by all these comedians—all this subject we must necessarily consider and estimate. For it is impossible to learn the serious without the comic, or any one of a pair of contraries without the other, if one is to be a wise man; but to put both into practice is equally impossible, if one is to share in even a small measure of virtue; in fact, it is precisely for this reason that one should learn them—in order to avoid ever doing or saying anything ludicrous, through ignorance, when one ought not; we will impose such mimicry on slaves and foreign hirelings, and no serious attention shall ever be paid to it, nor shall any free man or free woman be seen learning it, and there must always be some novel feature in their mimic shows. Let such, then, be the regulations for all those laughable amusements which we all call "comedy," as laid down both by law and by argument. Now as to what are called our "serious" poets, the tragedians — suppose that some of them were to approach us and put some such question as this — "O Strangers, are we, or are we not, to pay visits to your city and country, and traffic in poetry? Or what have you decided to do about this?" What would be the right answer to make to these inspired persons regarding the matter? In my judgment, this should be the answer — "Most excellent of Strangers, we ourselves, to the best of our ability, are the authors of a tragedy at once superlatively fair and good; at least, all our polity is framed as a representation of the fairest and best life, which is in reality, as we assert, the truest tragedy. Thus we are composers of the same things as yourselves, rivals of yours as artists and actors of the fairest drama, which, as our hope is, true law, and it alone, is by nature competent to complete. Do not imagine, then, that we will ever thus lightly allow you to set up your stage beside us in the marketplace, and give permission to those imported actors of yours, with their dulcet tones and their voices louder than ours, to harangue women and children and the whole populace, and to say not the same things as we say about the same institutions, but, on the contrary, things that are, for the most part, just the opposite. In truth, both we ourselves and the whole State would be absolutely mad, were it to allow you to do as I have said, before the magistrates had decided whether or not your compositions are deserving of utterance and suited for publication. So now, ye children and offspring of Muses mild, do ye first display your chants side by side with ours before the rulers; and if your utterances seem to be the same as ours or better, then we will grant you a chorus, but if not, my friends, we can never do so."

Let such, then, be the customs ordained to go with the laws regarding all choristry and the learning thereof — keeping distinct those for slaves and those for masters — if you agree.

CLIN. Of course we now agree to it.

• • •

BOOK VIII

ATH. . . . When in my discourse I came to the subject of education, I saw young men and maidens consorting with one another affectionately; and, naturally, a feeling of alarm came upon me, as I asked myself how one is to manage a State like this in which young men and maidens are well-nourished but exempt from those severe and menial labors which are the surest means of quenching wantonness, and where the chief occupation of everyone all through life consists in sacrifices, feasts, and dances. In a State such as this, how will the young abstain from those desires which frequently plunge many into ruin — all those desires from which reason, in its endeavor to be law, enjoins abstinence? That the laws previously ordained serve to repress the majority of desires is not surprising; thus, for example, the proscription of excessive wealth is of no small benefit for promoting temperance, and the whole of our education-system contains laws useful for the same purpose; in addition to this, there is the watchful eye of the magistrates, trained to fix its gaze always on this point and to keep constant watch on the young people. These means, then, are sufficient (so far as any human means suffice) to deal with the other desires. But when we come to the amorous passions of children of both sexes and of men for women and women for men — passions which have been the cause of countless woes both to individuals and to whole States — how is one to guard against these, or what remedy can one apply so as to find a way of escape in all such cases from a danger such as this? It is extremely difficult, Clinias. For whereas, in regard to other matters not a few, Crete generally and Lacedaemon furnish us (and rightly) with no little assistance in the framing of laws which differ from those in common use — in regard to the passions of sex (for we are alone by ourselves) they contradict us absolutely. If we were to follow in nature's steps and enact that law which held good before the days of Laïus, declaring that it is right to refrain from indulging in the same kind of intercourse with men and boys as with women, and adducing as evidence thereof the nature of wild beasts, and pointing out how male does not touch male for this purpose, since it is unnatural — in all this we would probably be using an argument neither convincing nor in any way consonant with your States. Moreover, that object which, as we affirm, the lawgiver ought always to have in view does not agree with these practices. For the enquiry we always make is this — which of the proposed laws tends toward virtue and which not. Come then, suppose we grant that this practice is now legalized, and that it is noble and in no way ignoble, how far would it promote virtue? Will it engender in the soul of him who is seduced a courageous character, or in the soul of the seducer the quality of temperance? Nobody would ever believe this; on the contrary, as all men will blame the cowardice of the man who always yields to pleasures and is never able to hold out against them, will they not likewise reproach that man who plays the woman's part with the resemblance he bears to his model? Is there any man, then, who will ordain by law a practice like that? Not one, I should say, if he has a notion of what true law is. What then do we declare to be the truth about this matter? It is necessary to discern the real nature of friendship and desire and love (so-called), if we are to determine them rightly; for what causes the utmost confusion and obscurity is the fact that this single term embraces these two things, and also a third kind compounded of them both.

CLIN. How so?

ATH. Friendship is the name we give to the affection of like for like, in point of goodness, and of equal for equal; and also to that of the needy for the rich, which is of the opposite kind; and when either of these feelings is intense we call it "love."

CLIN. True.

ATH. The friendship which occurs between opposites is terrible and fierce and seldom reciprocal among men, while that based on similarity is gentle and reciprocal throughout life. The kind which arises from a blend of these presents difficulties—first, to discover what the man affected by this third kind of love really desires to obtain, and, in the next place, because the man himself is at a loss, being dragged in opposite directions by the two tendencies—of which the one bids him to enjoy the bloom of his beloved, while the other forbids him. For he that is in love with the body and hungering after its bloom, as it were that of a ripening peach, urges himself on to take his fill of it, paying no respect to the disposition of the beloved; whereas he that counts bodily desire as but secondary, and puts longing looks in place of love, with soul lusting really for soul, regards the bodily satisfaction of the body as an outrage, and, reverently worshipping temperance, courage, nobility, and wisdom, will desire to live always chastely in company with the chaste object of his love. But the love which is blended of these two kinds is that which

we have described just now as third. Since, then, love has so many varieties, ought the law to prohibit them all and prevent them from existing in our midst, or shall we not plainly wish that the kind of love which belongs to virtue and desires the young to be as good as possible should exist within our State, while we shall prohibit, if possible, the other two kinds? Or what is our view, my dear Megillus?

MEG. Your description of the subject, Stranger, is perfectly correct.

ATH. It seems that, as I expected, I have gained your assent; so there is no need for me to investigate your law, and its attitude toward such matters, but simply to accept your agreement to my statement. Later on I will try to charm Clinias also into agreeing with me on this subject. So let your joint admission stand at that, and let us by all means proceed with our laws.

MEG. Quite right.

ATH. I know of a device at present for enacting this law, which is in one way easy, but in another quite the hardest possible.

MEG. Explain your meaning.

ATH. Even at present, as we are aware, most men, however lawless they are, are effectively and strictly precluded from sexual commerce with beautiful persons—and that not against their will, but with their own most willing consent.

MEG. On what occasions do you mean?

ATH. Whenever any man has a brother or sister who is beautiful. So too in the case of a son or daughter, the same unwritten law is most effective in guarding men from sleeping with them, either openly or secretly, or wishing to have any connection with them—nay, most men never so much as feel any desire for such connection.

MEG. That is true.

ATH. Is it not, then, by a brief sentence that all such pleasures are quenched?

MEG. What sentence do you mean?

ATH. The sentence that these acts are by no means holy, but hated of God and most shamefully shameful. And does not the reason lie in this, that nobody speaks of them otherwise, but every one of us, from the day of his birth, hears this opinion expressed always and everywhere, not only in comic speech, but often also in serious tragedy—as when there is brought on to the stage a Thyestes or an Oedipus, or a Macareus having secret intercourse with a sister, and all these are seen inflicting death upon themselves willingly as a punishment for their sins?

MEG. Thus much at least you are quite right in saying—that public opinion has a surprising influence, when there is no attempt by anybody ever to breathe a word that contradicts the law.

ATH. Then is it not true, as I said just now, that when a lawgiver wishes to subdue one of those lusts which especially subdue men, it is easy for him at least to learn the method of mastering them—that it is by consecrating this public opinion in the eyes of all alike—bond and free, women and children, and the whole State—that he will effect the firmest security for this law.

MEG. Certainly; but how it will ever be possible for him to bring it about that all are willing to say such a thing—

ATH. A very proper observation. That was precisely the reason why I stated that in reference to this law I know of a device for making a natural use of reproductive intercourse—on the one hand, by abstaining from the male and not slaying of set purpose the human stock, nor sowing seed on rocks and stones where it can never take root and have fruitful increase; and, on the other hand, by abstaining from every female field in which you would not desire the seed to spring up. This law, when it has become permanent and prevails—if it has rightly become dominant in other cases, just as it prevails now regarding intercourse with parents—is the cause of countless blessings. For, in the first place, it follows the dictates of nature, and it serves to keep men from sexual rage and frenzy and all kinds of fornication, and from excess in meats and drinks, and it ensures in husbands fondness for their own wives: other blessings also would ensue, in infinite number, if one could make sure of this law. Possibly, however, some young bystander, rash and of superabundant virility, on hearing of the passing of this law, would denounce us for making foolish and impossible rules, and fill all the place with his outcries; and it was in view of this that I made the statement that I knew of a device to secure the permanence of this law when passed which is at once the easiest of all devices and the hardest. For while it is very easy to perceive that this is possible, and how it is possible—since we affirm that this rule, when duly consecrated, will dominate all souls, and

cause them to dread the laws enacted and yield them entire obedience—yet it has now come to this, that men think that, even so, it is unlikely to come about—just in the same way as, in the case of the institution of public meals, people refuse to believe that it is possible for the whole State to be able to continue this practice constantly; and that, too, in spite of the evidence of facts and the existence of the practice in your countries; and even there, as applied to women, the practice is regarded as non-natural. Thus it was that, because of the strength of this unbelief, I said that it is most difficult to get both these matters permanently legalized.

MEG. And you were right in that.

ATH. Still, to show that it is not beyond the power of man, but possible, would you like me to try to state an argument which is not without some plausibility?

CLIN. Certainly.

ATH. Would a man be more ready to abstain from sex-indulgence, and to consent to carry out the law on this matter soberly, if he had his body not ill-trained, but in good condition, than if he had it in bad condition?

CLIN. He would be much more ready if it were not ill-trained.

ATH. Do we not know by report about Iccus of Tarentum, because of his contests at Olympia and elsewhere—how, spurred on by ambition and skill, and possessing courage combined with temperance in his soul, during all the period of his training (as the story goes) he never touched a woman, nor yet a boy? And the same story is told about Crison and Astylus and Diopompus and very many others. And yet, Clinias, these men were not only much worse educated in soul than your citizens and mine, but they also possessed much more sexual vigor of body.

CLIN. That this really happened in the case of these athletes is indeed, as you say, confidently affirmed by the ancients.

ATH. Well then, if those men had the fortitude to abstain from that which most men count bliss for the sake of victory in wrestling, running, and the like, shall our boys be unable to hold out in order to win a much nobler victory—that which is the noblest of all victories, as we shall tell them from their childhood's days, charming them into belief, we hope, by tales and sentences and songs.

CLIN. What victory?

ATH. Victory over pleasures—which if they win, they will live a life of bliss, but if they lose, the very opposite. Furthermore, will not the dread that this is a thing utterly unholy give them power to master those impulses which men inferior to themselves have mastered?

CLIN. It is certainly reasonable to suppose so.

ATH. Now that we have reached this point in regard to our regulation, but have fallen into a strait because of the cowardice of the many, I maintain that our regulation on this head must go forward and proclaim that our citizens must not be worse than fowls and many other animals which are produced in large broods, and which live chaste and celibate lives without sexual intercourse until they arrive at the age for breeding; and when they reach this age they pair off, as instinct moves them, male with female and female with male; and thereafter they live in a way that is holy and just, remaining constant to their first contracts of love: surely our citizens should at least be better than these animals. If, however, they become corrupted by most of the other Hellenes or barbarians, through seeing and hearing that among them the "lawless Love" (as it is called) is of very great power, and thus become unable to overcome it, then the Law-wardens, acting as lawgivers, must devise for them a second law.

CLIN. What law do you recommend them to make if that which is now proposed slips out of their grasp?

ATH. Evidently that law which comes next to it as second.

CLIN. What is that?

ATH. One ought to put the force of pleasures as far as possible out of gear, by diverting its increase and nutriment to another part of the body by means of exercise. This would come about if indulgence in sexual intercourse were devoid of shamelessness; for if, owing to shame, people indulged in it but seldom, in consequence of this rare indulgence they would find it a less tyrannical mistress. Let them, therefore, regard privacy in such actions as honorable—sanctioned both by custom and by unwritten law; and want of privacy—yet not the entire avoidance of such actions—as dishonorable. Thus we shall have a second standard of what is honorable and shameful established by law and possessing a second degree of rectitude; and those people of depraved character, whom we describe as "self-inferior," and who form a single

kind, shall be hemmed in by three kinds of force and compelled to refrain from law-breaking.

CLIN. What kinds?

ATH. That of godly fear, and that of love of honor, and that which is desirous of fair forms of soul, not fair bodies. The things I now mention are, perhaps, like the visionary ideals in a story; yet in very truth, if only they were realized, they would prove a great blessing in every State. Possibly, should God so grant, we might forcibly effect one of two things in this matter of sex-relations—either that no one should venture to touch any of the noble and freeborn save his own wedded wife, nor sow any unholy and bastard seed in fornication, nor any unnatural and barren seed in sodomy—or else we should entirely abolish love for males, and in regard to that for women, if we enact a law that any man who has intercourse with any women save those who have been brought to his house under the sanction of Heaven and holy marriage, whether purchased or otherwise acquired, if detected in such intercourse by any man or woman, shall be disqualified from any civic commendation, as being really an alien—probably such a law would be approved as right. So let this law—whether we ought to call it one law or two—be laid down concerning sexual commerce and love affairs in general, as regards right and wrong conduct in our mutual intercourse due to these desires.

MEG. For my own part, Stranger, I should warmly welcome this law; but Clinias must tell us himself what his view is on the matter.

CLIN. I shall do so, Megillus, when I deem the occasion suitable; but for the present let us allow the Stranger to proceed still further with his laws.

MEG. You are right.

• • •

BOOK IX

ATH. I believe that I expressly stated in our previous discourse—or, if I did not do it before, please assume that I now assert—

CLIN. What?

ATH. That all bad men are in all respects unwillingly bad; and, this being so, our next statement must agree therewith.

CLIN. What statement do you mean?

ATH. This—that the unjust man is, indeed, bad, but the bad man is unwillingly bad. But it is illogical to suppose that a willing deed is done unwillingly; therefore he that commits an unjust act does so unwillingly in the opinion of him who assumes that injustice is involuntary—a conclusion which I also must now allow; for I agree that all men do unjust acts unwillingly; so, since I hold this view—and do not share the opinion of those who, through contentiousness or arrogance, assert that, while there are some who are unjust against their will, yet there are also many who are unjust willingly—how am I to prove consistent with my own statements? Suppose you two, Megillus and Clinias, put this question to me—"If this is the state of the case, Stranger, what counsel do you give us in regard to legislating for the Magnesian State? Shall we legislate or shall we not?" "Legislate by all means," I shall reply. "Will you make a distinction, then, between voluntary and involuntary wrongdoings, and are we to enact heavier penalties for the crimes and wrongdoings that are voluntary, and lighter penalties for the others? Or shall we enact equal penalties for all, on the view that there is no such thing as a voluntary act of injustice?"

CLIN. What you say, Stranger, is quite right: so what use are we to make of our present arguments?

ATH. A very proper question! The use we shall make of them, to begin with, is this—

CLIN. What?

ATH. Let us recall how, a moment ago, we rightly stated that in regard to justice we are suffering from the greatest confusion and inconsistency. Grasping this fact, let us again question ourselves—"As to our perplexity about these matters, since we have neither got it clear nor defined the point of difference between those two kinds of wrongdoing, voluntary and involuntary, which are treated as legally distinct in every State by every legislator who has ever yet appeared— as to this, is the statement we recently made to stand, like a divine oracle, as a mere *ex cathedra* statement, unsupported by any proof, and to serve as a kind of master-enactment?" That is impossible; and before we legislate we are bound first to make it clear somehow that these wrongdoings are twofold, and wherein their difference consists, in order that when we impose the penalty on either kind, everyone may

follow our rules, and be able to form some judgment regarding the suitability or otherwise of our enactments.

CLIN. What you say, Stranger, appears to us to be excellent: we ought to do one of two things—either not assert that all unjust acts are involuntary, or else make our distinctions first, then prove the correctness of that assertion.

ATH. Of these alternatives the first is to me quite intolerable—namely, not to assert what I hold to be the truth—for that would be neither a lawful thing to do nor a pious. But as to the question how such acts are twofold—if the difference does not lie in that between the voluntary and the involuntary, then we must try to explain it by means of some other distinction.

CLIN. Well, certainly, Stranger, about this matter there is no other plan we can possibly adopt.

ATH. It shall be done. Come now, in dealings and intercourse between citizens, injuries committed by one against another are of frequent occurrence, and they involve plenty of the voluntary as well as of the involuntary.

CLIN. To be sure!

ATH. Let no one put down all injuries as acts of injustice and then regard the unjust acts involved as twofold in the way described, namely, that they are partly voluntary and partly involuntary (for, of the total, the involuntary injuries are not less than the voluntary either in number or in magnitude); but consider whether in saying what I am now going to say I am speaking sense or absolute nonsense. For what I assert, Megillus and Clinias, is not that, if one man harms another involuntarily and without wishing it, he acts unjustly though involuntarily, nor shall I legislate in this way, pronouncing this to be an involuntary act of injustice, but I will pronounce that such an injury is not an injustice at all, whether it be a greater injury or a less. And, if my view prevails, we shall often say that the author of a benefit wrongly done commits an injustice; for as a rule, my friends, neither when a man gives some material object to another, nor when he takes it away, ought one to term such an act absolutely just or unjust, but only when a man of just character and disposition does any benefit or injury to another—that is what the lawgiver must look at; he must consider these two things, injustice and injury, and the injury inflicted he must make good so far as possible by legal means; he must conserve what is lost, restore what has been broken down, make whole what is wounded or dead; and when the several injuries have been atoned for by compensation, he must endeavor always by means of the laws to convert the parties who have inflicted them and those who have suffered them from a state of discord to a state of amity.

CLIN. He will be right in doing that.

ATH. As regards unjust injuries and gains, in case one man causes another to gain by acting unjustly toward him, all such cases as are curable we must cure, regarding them as diseases of the soul. And we should affirm that our cure for injustice lies in this direction—

CLIN. What direction?

ATH. In this—that whenever any man commits any unjust act, great or small, the law shall instruct him and absolutely compel him for the future either never willingly to dare to do such a deed, or else to do it ever so much less often, in addition to paying for the injury. To effect this, whether by action or speech, by means of pleasures and pains, honors and dishonors, money-fines and money-gifts, and in general by whatsoever means one can employ to make men hate injustice and love (or at any rate not hate) justice—this is precisely the task of laws most noble. But for all those whom he perceives to be incurable in respect of these matters, what penalty shall the lawgiver enact, and what law? The lawgiver will realise that in all such cases not only is it better for the sinners themselves to live no longer, but also that they will prove of a double benefit to others by quitting life—since they will both serve as a warning to the rest not to act unjustly, and also rid the State of wicked men—and thus he will of necessity inflict death as the chastisement for their sins, in cases of this kind, and of this kind only.

CLIN. What you have said seems very reasonable; but we should be glad to hear a still clearer statement respecting the difference between injury and injustice, and how the distinction between the voluntary and the involuntary applies in these cases.

ATH. I must endeavor to do as you bid me, and explain the matter. No doubt in conversing with one another you say and hear said at least thus much about the soul, that one element in its nature (be it affection or part) is "passion," which is an inbred quality of a contentious and pugnacious kind, and one that overturns many things by its irrational force.

CLIN. Of course.

ATH. Moreover, we distinguish "pleasure" from passion, and we assert that its mastering power is of an opposite kind, since it effects all that its intention desires by a mixture of persuasion and deceit.

CLIN. Exactly.

ATH. Nor would it be untrue to say that the third cause of sins is ignorance. This cause, however, the lawgiver would do well to subdivide into two, counting ignorance in its simple form to be the cause of minor sins, and in its double form—where the folly is due to the man being gripped not by ignorance only, but also by a conceit of wisdom, as though he had full knowledge of things he knows nothing at all about—counting this to be the cause of great and brutal sins when it is joined with strength and might, but the cause of childish and senile sins when it is joined with weakness; and these last he will count as sins and he will ordain laws, as for sinners, but laws that will be, above all others, of the most mild and merciful kind.

CLIN. That is reasonable.

ATH. And pretty well everyone speaks of one man being "superior," another "inferior," to pleasure or to passion; and they are so.

CLIN. Most certainly.

ATH. But we have never heard it said that one man is "superior," another "inferior," to ignorance.

CLIN. Quite true.

ATH. And we assert that all these things urge each man often to go counter to the actual bent of his own inclination.

CLIN. Very frequently.

ATH. Now I will define for you, clearly and without complication, my notion of justice and injustice. The domination of passion and fear and pleasure and pain and envies and desires in the soul, whether they do any injury or not, I term generally "injustice"; but the belief in the highest good—in whatsoever way either States or individuals think they can attain to it—if this prevails in their souls and regulates every man, even if some damage be done, we must assert that everything thus done is just, and that in each man the part subject to this governance is also just, and best for the whole life of mankind, although most men suppose that such damage is an involuntary injustice. But we are not now concerned with a verbal dispute. Since, however, it has been shown that there are three kinds of sinning, we must first of all recall these still more clearly to mind. Of these, one kind, as we know, is painful; and that we term passion and fear.

CLIN. Quite so.

ATH. The second kind consists of pleasure and desires; the third, which is a distinct kind, consists of hopes and untrue belief regarding the attainment of the highest good. And when this last kind is subdivided into three, five classes are made, as we now assert; and for these five classes we must enact distinct laws, of two main types.

CLIN. What are they?

ATH. The one concerns acts done on each occasion by violent and open means, the other acts done privily under cover of darkness and deceit, or sometimes acts done in both these ways—and for acts of this last kind the laws will be most severe, if they are to prove adequate.

•   •   •

BOOK X

ATH. . . . We shall state for cases of violence one universally inclusive principle of law, to this effect:— No one shall carry or drive off anything which belongs to others, nor shall he use any of his neighbor's goods unless he has gained the consent of the owner; for from such action proceed all the evils above mentioned—past, present, and to come. Of the rest, the most grave are the licentious and outrageous acts of the young; and outrages offend most gravely when they are directed against sacred things, and they are especially grave when they are directed against objects which are public as well as holy, or partially public, as being shared in by the members of a tribe or other similar community. Second, and second in point of gravity, come offenses against sacred objects and tombs that are private; and third, offenses against parents, when a person commits the outrage otherwise

than in the cases already described. A fourth kind of outrage is when a man, in defiance of the magistrates, drives or carries off or uses any of their things without their own consent; and a fifth kind will be an outrage against the civil right of an individual private citizen which calls for judicial vindication. To all these severally one all-embracing law must be assigned. As to temple-robbing, whether done by open violence or secretly, it has been already stated summarily what the punishment should be; and in respect of all the outrages, whether of word or deed, which a man commits, either by tongue or hand, against the gods, we must state the punishment he should suffer, after we have first delivered the admonition. It shall be as follows:—No one who believes, as the laws prescribe, in the existence of the gods has ever yet done an impious deed voluntarily, or uttered a lawless word: he that acts so is in one or other of these three conditions of mind—either he does not believe in what I have said; or, secondly, he believes that the gods exist, but have no care for men; or, thirdly, he believes that they are easy to win over when bribed by offerings and prayers.

CLIN. What, then, shall we do or say to such people?

ATH. Let us listen first, my good sir, to what they, as I imagine, say mockingly, in their contempt for us.

CLIN. What is it?

ATH. In derision they would probably say this: "O Strangers of Athens, Lacedaemon, and Crete, what you say is true. Some of us do not believe in gods at all; others of us believe in gods of the kinds you mention. So we claim now, as you claimed in the matter of laws, that before threatening us harshly, you should first try to convince and teach us, by producing adequate proofs, that gods exist, and that they are too good to be wheedled by gifts and turned aside from justice. For as it is, this and such as this is the account of them we hear from those who are reputed the best of poets, orators, seers, priests, and thousands upon thousands of others; and consequently most of us, instead of seeking to avoid wrongdoing, do the wrong and then try to make it good. Now from lawgivers like you, who assert that you are gentle rather than severe, we claim that you should deal with us first by way of persuasion; and if what you say about the existence of the gods is superior to the arguments of others in point of truth, even though it be but little superior in eloquence, then probably you would succeed in convincing us. Try then, if you think this reasonable, to meet our challenge."

CLIN. Surely it seems easy, Stranger, to assert with truth that gods exist?

ATH. How so?

CLIN. First, there is the evidence of the earth, the sun, the stars, and all the universe, and the beautiful ordering of the seasons, marked out by years and months; and then there is the further fact that all Greeks and barbarians believe in the existence of gods.

ATH. My dear sir, these bad men cause me alarm—for I will never call it "awe"—lest haply they scoff at us. For the cause of the corruption in their case is one you are not aware of; since you imagine that it is solely by their incontinence in regard to pleasures and desires that their souls are impelled to that impious life of theirs.

CLIN. What other cause can there be, Stranger, besides this?

ATH. One which you, who live elsewhere, could hardly have any knowledge of or notice at all.

CLIN. What is this cause you are now speaking of?

ATH. A very grievous unwisdom which is reputed to be the height of wisdom.

CLIN. What do you mean?

ATH. We at Athens have accounts preserved in writing (though, I am told, such do not exist in your country, owing to the excellence of your polity), some of them being in a kind of metre, others without metre, telling about the gods: the oldest of these accounts relate how the first substance of Heaven and all else came into being, and shortly after the beginning they go on to give a detailed theogony, and to tell how, after they were born, the gods associated with one another. These accounts, whether good or bad for the hearers in other respects, it is hard for us to censure because of their antiquity; but as regards the tendance and respect due to parents, I certainly would never praise them or say that they are either helpful or wholly true accounts. Such ancient accounts, however, we may pass over and dismiss: let them be told in the way best pleasing to the gods. It is rather the novel views of our modern scientists that we must hold responsible as the cause of mischief. For the result of the arguments of such people is

this—that when you and I try to prove the existence of the gods by pointing to these very objects—sun, moon, stars, and earth—as instances of deity and divinity, people who have been converted by these scientists will assert that these things are simply earth and stone, incapable of paying any heed to human affairs, and that these beliefs of ours are speciously tricked out with arguments to make them plausible.

CLIN. The assertion you mention, Stranger, is indeed a dangerous one, even if it stood alone; but now that such assertions are legion, the danger is still greater.

ATH. What then? What shall we say? What must we do? Are we to make our defense as it were before a court of impious men, where someone had accused us of doing something dreadful by assuming in our legislation the existence of gods? Or shall we rather dismiss the whole subject and revert again to our laws, lest our prelude prove actually more lengthy than the laws? For indeed our discourse would be extended in no small degree if we were to furnish those men who desire to be impious with an adequate demonstration by means of argument concerning those subjects which ought, as they claimed, to be discussed, and so to convert them to fear of the gods, and then finally, when we had caused them to shrink from irreligion, to proceed to enact the appropriate laws.

CLIN. Still, Stranger, we have frequently (considering the shortness of the time) made this very statement—that we have no need on the present occasion to prefer brevity of speech to lengthiness (for, as the saying goes, "no one is chasing on our heels"); and to show ourselves choosing the briefest in preference to the best would be mean and ridiculous. And it is of the highest importance that our arguments, showing that the gods exist and that they are good and honor justice more than do men, should by all means possess some degree of persuasiveness; for such a prelude is the best we could have in defense, as one may say, of all our laws. So without any repugnance or undue haste, and with all the capacity we have for endowing such arguments with persuasiveness, let us expound them as fully as we can, and without any reservation.

ATH. This speech of yours seems to me to call for a prefatory prayer, seeing that you are so eager and ready; nor is it possible any longer to defer our statement. Come, then; how is one to argue on behalf of the existence of the gods without passion? For we needs must be vexed and indignant with the men who have been, and now are, responsible for laying on us this burden of argument, through their disbelief in those stories which they used to hear, while infants and sucklings, from the lips of their nurses and mothers—stories chanted to them, as it were, in lullabies, whether in jest or in earnest; and the same stories they heard repeated also in prayers at sacrifices, and they saw spectacles which illustrated them, of the kind which the young delight to see and hear when performed at sacrifices; and their own parents they saw showing the utmost zeal on behalf of themselves and their children in addressing the gods in prayers and supplications, as though they most certainly existed; and at the rising and setting of the sun and moon they heard and saw the prostrations and devotions of all the Greeks and barbarians, under all conditions of adversity and prosperity, directed to these luminaries, not as though they were not gods, but as though they most certainly were gods beyond the shadow of a doubt—all this evidence is contemned by these people, and that for no sufficient reason, as everyone endowed with a grain of sense would affirm; and so they are now forcing us to enter on our present argument. How, I ask, can one possibly use mild terms in admonishing such men, and at the same time teach them, to begin with, that the gods do exist? Yet one must bravely attempt the task; for it would never do for both parties to be enraged at once—the one owing to greed for pleasure, the other with indignation at men like them.

So let our prefatory address to the men thus corrupted in mind be dispassionate in tone, and, quenching our passion, let us speak mildly, as though we were conversing with one particular person of the kind described, in the following terms: "My child, you are still young, and time as it advances will cause you to reverse many of the opinions you now hold: so wait till then before pronouncing judgment on matters of most grave importance; and of these the gravest of all—though at present you regard it as naught—is the question of holding a right view about the gods and so living well, or the opposite. Now in the first place, I should be saying what is irrefutably true if I pointed out to you this signal fact, that neither you by yourself nor yet your friends are the first and foremost to adopt this opinion about the gods; rather is it true that people who suffer from this disease are always springing up, in greater or less numbers. But I, who have met with many of these people, would declare this to you, that not a single man who from his youth had adopted this opinion, that the gods have no existence, has ever yet continued till old age constant in the same view; but the other two false notions about the gods do remain—not, indeed, with many, but still with some—the notion, namely, that the gods exist, but pay no heed to human affairs, and the other notion that they do pay heed, but are easily won over by prayers and offerings. For a doctrine about them that is to prove the truest you can possibly form you will, if you take my advice, wait, considering the while whether the truth stands thus or otherwise, and making enquiries not only from all other men, but especially from the lawgiver; and in the meantime do not dare to be guilty of any impiety in respect of the gods. For it must be the endeavor of him who is legislating for you both now and hereafter to instruct you in the truth of these matters.

CLIN. Our statement thus far, Stranger, is most excellent.

ATH. Very true, O Megillus and Clinias; but we have plunged unawares into a wondrous argument.

CLIN. What is it you mean?

ATH. That which most people account to be the most scientific of all arguments.

CLIN. Explain more clearly.

ATH. It is stated by some that all things which are coming into existence, or have or will come into existence, do so partly by nature, partly by art, and partly owing to chance.

CLIN. Is it not a right statement?

ATH. It is likely, to be sure, that what men of science say is true. Anyhow, let us follow them up, and consider what it is that the people in their camp really intend.

CLIN. By all means let us do so.

ATH. It is evident, they assert, that the greatest and most beautiful things are the work of nature and of chance, and the lesser things that of art—for art receives from nature the great and primary products as existing, and itself molds and shapes all the smaller ones, which we commonly call "artificial."

CLIN. How do you mean?

ATH. I will explain it more clearly. Fire and water and earth and air, they say, all exist by nature and chance, and none of them by art; and by means of these, which are wholly inanimate, the bodies which come next—those, namely, of the earth, sun, moon and stars—have been brought into existence. It is by chance all these elements move, by the interplay of their respective forces, and according as they meet together and combine fittingly—hot with cold, dry with moist, soft with hard, and all such necessary mixtures as result from the chance combination of these opposites—in this way and by these means they have brought into being the whole Heaven and all that is in the Heaven, and all animals, too, and plants—after that all the seasons had arisen from these elements; and all this, as they assert, not owing to reason, nor to any god or art, but owing, as we have said, to nature and chance. As a later product of these, art comes later; and it, being mortal itself and of mortal birth, begets later playthings which share but little in truth, being images of a sort akin to the arts themselves—images such as painting begets, and music, and the arts which accompany these. Those arts which really produce something serious are such as share their effect with nature—like medicine, agriculture, and gymnastic. Politics too, as they say, shares to a small extent in nature, but mostly in art; and in like manner all legislation which is based on untrue assumptions is due, not to nature, but to art.

CLIN. What do you mean?

ATH. The first statement, my dear sir, which these people make about the gods is that they exist by art and not by nature—by certain legal conventions which differ from place to place, according as each tribe agreed when forming their laws. They assert, moreover, that there is one class of things beautiful by nature, and another class beautiful by convention; while as to things just, they do not exist at all by nature, but men are constantly in dispute about them and continually altering them, and whatever alteration they make at any time is at that time authoritative, though it owes its existence to art and the laws, and not in any way to nature. All these, my friends, are views which young people imbibe from men of science, both prose-writers and poets, who maintain that the height of justice is to succeed by force; whence it comes that the young people are afflicted with a plague of impiety, as though the gods were

not such as the law commands us to conceive them; and, because of this, factions also arise, when these teachers attract them toward the life that is right "according to nature," which consists in being master over the rest in reality, instead of being a slave to others according to legal convention.

CLIN. What a horrible statement you have described, Stranger! And what widespread corruption of the young in private families as well as publicly in the States!

ATH. That is indeed true, Clinias. What, then, do you think the lawgiver ought to do, seeing that these people have been armed in this way for a long time past? Should he merely stand up in the city and threaten all the people that unless they affirm that the gods exist and conceive them in their minds to be such as the law maintains; and so likewise with regard to the beautiful and the just and all the greatest things, as many as relate to virtue and vice, that they must regard and perform these in the way prescribed by the lawgiver in his writings; and that whosoever fails to show himself obedient to the laws must either be put to death or else be punished, in one case by stripes and imprisonment, in another by degradation, in others by poverty and exile? But as to persuasion, should the lawgiver, while enacting the people's laws, refuse to blend any persuasion with his statements, and thus tame them so far as possible?

CLIN. Certainly not, Stranger; on the contrary, if persuasion can be applied in such matters in even the smallest degree, no lawgiver who is of the slightest account must ever grow weary, but must (as they say) "leave no stone unturned" to reinforce the ancient saying that gods exist, and all else that you recounted just now; and law itself he must also defend and art, as things which exist by nature or by a cause not inferior to nature, since according to right reason they are the offspring of mind, even as you are now, as I think, asserting; and I agree with you.

ATH. What now, my most ardent Clinias? Are not statements thus made to the masses difficult for us to keep up with in argument, and do they not also involve us in arguments portentously long?

CLIN. Well now, Stranger, if we had patience with ourselves when we discoursed at such length on the subjects of drinking and music, shall we not exercise patience in dealing with the gods and similar subjects? Moreover, such a discourse is of the greatest help for intelligent legislation, since legal ordinances when put in writing remain wholly unchanged, as though ready to submit to examination for all time, so that one need have no fear even if they are hard to listen to at first, seeing that even the veriest dullard can come back frequently to examine them, nor yet if they are lengthy, provided that they are beneficial. Consequently, in my opinion, it could not possibly be either reasonable or pious for any man to refrain from lending his aid to such arguments to the best of his power.

MEG. What Clinias says, Stranger, is, I think, most excellent.

• • •

BOOK XII

ATH. Did we not say that we must have in our State a synod of the following kind:—The ten senior members, at the moment, of the body of Law-wardens shall form the synod, in company with all who have won the award of merit; and, moreover, those inspectors who have gone abroad to discover if they could hear of anything pertinent to the safe-keeping of laws, and who, in the belief that they have succeeded, have come safely home again, shall, after undergoing a searching test, be deemed worthy to take part in the synod? In addition to these, every member must bring with him one of the young men, not less than thirty years old, whom he has first selected as being both by nature and training a suitable person; after selecting him, he shall introduce him among the members, and if they also approve, he shall keep him as a colleague, but if they disapprove, the fact of his original selection must be concealed from all the rest, and especially from the person thus rejected. The synod must meet at an early hour, when everyone has his time most free from other business, private or public. Was it not some such organisation as this that we described in our previous discourse?

CLIN. It was.

ATH. Resuming, then, the subject of this synod, I will say this:—If one were to lay this down as an anchor for the whole State, possessing all the requisite

conditions—then, I affirm, it would secure the salvation of all that we desire.

CLIN. How so?

ATH. Now will be the time for us to display no lack of zeal in declaring truly what follows.

CLIN. Excellently spoken! Proceed as you propose.

ATH. One ought to observe, Clinias, in regard to every object, in each of its operations, what constitutes its appropriate savior—as, for example, in an animal, the soul and the head are eminently such by nature.

CLIN. How do you mean?

ATH. Surely it is the goodness of those parts that provides salvation to every animal.

CLIN. How?

ATH. By the existence of reason in the soul, in addition to all its other qualities, and by the existence of sight and hearing, in addition to all else, in the head; thus, to summarize the matter, it is the combination of reason with the finest senses, and their union in one, that would most justly be termed the salvation of each animal.

CLIN. That is certainly probable.

ATH. It is probable. But what kind of reason is it which, when combined with senses, will afford salvation to ships in stormy weather and calm? On shipboard is it not the pilot and the sailors who, by combining the senses with the pilot reason, secure salvation both for themselves and for all that belongs to the ship?

CLIN. Of course.

ATH. There is no need of many examples to illustrate this. Consider, for instance, what would be the right mark for a general to set up to shoot at in the case of an army, or the medical profession in the case of a human body, if they were aiming at salvation. Would not the former make victory his mark, and mastery over the enemy, while that of the doctors and their assistants would be the providing of health to the body?

CLIN. Certainly.

ATH. But if a doctor were ignorant of that bodily condition which we have now called "health," or a general ignorant of victory, or any of the other matters we have mentioned, could he possibly be thought to possess reason about any of these things?

CLIN. How could he?

ATH. What, now, shall we say about a State? If a man were to be plainly ignorant as regards the political mark to be aimed at, would he, first of all, deserve the title of magistrate, and, secondly, would he be able to secure the salvation of that object concerning the aim of which he knows nothing at all?

CLIN. How could he?

ATH. So now, in our present case, if our settlement of the country is to be finally completed, there must, it would seem, exist in it some element which knows, in the first place, what that political aim, of which we are speaking, really is, and, secondly, in what manner it may attain this aim, and which of the laws, in the first instance, and secondly of men, gives it good counsel or bad. But if any State is destitute of such an element, it will not be surprising if, being thus void of reason and void of sense, it acts at haphazard always in all its actions.

CLIN. Very true.

ATH. In which, then, of the parts or institutions of our State have we now got anything so framed as to prove an adequate safeguard of this kind? Can we answer that question?

CLIN. No, Stranger; at least, not clearly. But if I must make a guess, it seems to me that this discourse of yours is leading up to that synod which has to meet at night, as you said just now.

ATH. An excellent reply, Clinias! And, as our present discourse shows, this synod must possess every virtue; and the prime virtue is not to keep shifting its aim among a number of objects, but to concentrate its gaze always on one particular mark, and at that one mark to shoot, as it were, all its arrows continually.

CLIN. Most certainly.

ATH. So now we shall understand that it is by no means surprising if the legal customs in States keep shifting, seeing that different parts of the codes in each State look in different directions. And, in general, it is not surprising that, with some statesmen, the aim of justice is to enable a certain class of people to rule in the State (whether they be really superior, or inferior), while with others the aim is how to acquire health (whether or not they be somebody's slaves); and others again direct their efforts to winning a life of freedom. Still others make two objects at once the joint aim of their legislation—namely, the gaining of freedom for themselves, and mastery over other States; while those who are the wisest of all, in their own conceit, aim not at one only, but at the sum total of these and the like objects, since they are

unable to specify any one object of pre-eminent value toward which they would desire all else to be directed.

CLIN. Then, Stranger, was not the view we stated long ago the right one? We said that all our laws must always aim at one single object, which, as we agreed, is quite rightly named "virtue."

ATH. Yes.

CLIN. And we stated that virtue consists of four things.

ATH. Certainly.

CLIN. And that the chief of all the four is reason, at which the other three, as well as everything else, should aim.

ATH. You follow us admirably, Clinias; and now follow us in what comes next. In the case of the pilot, the doctor, and the general, reason is directed, as we said, towards the one object of aim which is proper in each case; and now we are at the point of examining reason in the case of a statesman, and, addressing it as a man, we shall question it thus:—"O admirable sir, what is your aim? Medical reason is able to state clearly the one single object at which it aims; so you will be unable to state your one object—you who are superior, as perhaps you will say, to all the wise?" Can you two, Megillus and Clinias, define that object on his behalf, and tell me what you say it is, just as I, on behalf of many others, defined their objects for you?

CLIN. We are totally unable to do so.

ATH. Well then, can you declare that we need zeal in discerning both the object itself as a whole and the forms it assumes?

CLIN. Illustrate what you mean by "the forms" you speak of.

ATH. For example, when we said that there are four forms of virtue, obviously, since there are four, we must assert that each is a separate one.

CLIN. Certainly.

ATH. And yet we call them all by one name: we assert that courage is virtue, and wisdom virtue, and the other two likewise, as though they were really not a plurality, but solely this one thing—virtue.

CLIN. Very true.

ATH. Now it is not hard to explain wherein these two (and the rest) differ from one another, and how they have got two names; but to explain why we have given the one name "virtue" to both of them (and to the rest) is no longer an easy matter.

CLIN. How do you mean?

ATH. It is not hard to make clear my meaning. Let one of us adopt the role of questioner, the other of answerer.

CLIN. In what way?

ATH. Do you ask me this question—why, when calling both the two by the single name of "virtue," did we again speak of them as two—courage and wisdom? Then I shall tell you the reason—which is, that the one of them has to do with fear, namely courage, in which beasts also share, and the characters of very young children; for a courageous soul comes into existence naturally and without reasoning, but without reasoning there never yet came into existence, and there does not nor ever will exist, a soul that is wise and rational, it being a distinct kind.

CLIN. That is true.

ATH. Wherein they differ and are two you have now learnt from my reply. So do you, in turn, inform me how it is that they are one and identical. Imagine you are also going to tell me how it is that, though four, they are yet one; and then, after you have shown me how they are one, do you again ask me how they are four. And after that, let us enquire regarding the person who has full knowledge of any objects which possess both a name and a definition, whether he ought to know the name only, and not know the definition, or whether it is not a shameful thing for a man worth anything to be ignorant of all these points in regard to matters of surpassing beauty and importance.

CLIN. It would certainly seem to be so.

ATH. For the lawgiver and the Law-warden, and for him who thinks he surpasses all men in virtue and who has won prizes for just such qualities, is there anything more important than these very qualities with which we are now dealing—courage, temperance, justice, and wisdom?

CLIN. Impossible.

ATH. In regard to these matters, is it not right that the interpreters, the teachers, the lawgivers, as the wardens of the rest, in dealing with him that requires knowledge and information, or with him that requires punishment and reproof for his sin, should excel all others in the art of instructing him in the quality of vice and virtue and exhibiting it fully? Or is some poet who comes into the State, or one who calls himself a trainer of youth, to be accounted evidently superior to him that has won prizes for all the virtues? In a State like that, where there are no wardens who are competent both in word and deed, and possessed of a competent knowledge of virtue—is it surprising, I ask, if such a State, all unwarded as it is, suffers the same fate as do many of the States which exist today?

CLIN. Not at all, I should say.

ATH. Well then, must we do what we now propose, or what? Must we contrive how our wardens shall have a more accurate grasp of virtue, both in word and deed, than the majority of men? For otherwise, how shall our State resemble a wise man's head and senses, on the ground that it possesses within itself a similar kind of wardenship?

CLIN. What is this resemblance we speak of, and wherein does it consist?

ATH. Evidently we are comparing the State itself to the skull; and, of the wardens, the younger ones, who are selected as the most intelligent and nimble in every part of their souls, are set, as it were, like the eyes, in the top of the head, and survey the State all round; and as they watch, they pass on their perceptions to the organs of memory—that is, they report to the elder wardens all that goes on in the State—while the old men, who are likened to the reason because of their eminent wisdom in many matters of importance, act as counselors, and make use of the young men as ministers and colleagues also in their counsels, so that both these classes by their co-operation really effect the salvation of the whole State. Is this the way, or ought we to contrive some other? Should the State, do you think, have all its members equal, instead of having some more highly trained and educated?

CLIN. Nay, my good sir, that were impossible.

ATH. We must proceed, then, to expound a type of education that is higher than the one previously described.

CLIN. I suppose so.

ATH. Will the type which we hinted at just now prove to be that which we require?

CLIN. Certainly.

ATH. Did we not say that he who is a first-class craftsman or warden, in any department, must not only be able to pay regard to the many, but must be able also to press toward the One so as to discern it and, on discerning it, to survey and organize all the rest with a single eye to it?

CLIN. Quite right.

ATH. Can any man get an accurate vision and view of any object better than by being able to look from the many and dissimilar to the one unifying form?

CLIN. Probably not.

ATH. It is certain, my friend, rather than probable, that no man can possibly have a clearer method than this.

CLIN. I believe you, Stranger, and I assent; so let us employ this method in our subsequent discourse.

ATH. Naturally we must compel the wardens also of our divine polity to observe accurately, in the first place, what that identical element is which pervades all the four virtues, and which—since it exists as a unity in courage, temperance, justice, and wisdom—may justly be called, as we assert, by the single name of "virtue." This element, my friends, we must now (if we please) hold very tight, and not let go until we have adequately explained the essential nature of the object to be aimed at—whether, that is, it exists by nature as a unity, or as a whole, or as both, or in some other way. Else, if this eludes us, can we possibly suppose that we shall adequately grasp the nature of virtue, when we are unable to state whether it is many or four or one? Accordingly, if we follow our own counsel, we shall contrive somehow, by hook or by crook, that this knowledge shall exist in our State. Should we decide, however, to pass it over entirely—pass it over we must.

CLIN. Nay, Stranger, in the name of the Stranger's God, we must by no means pass over a matter such as this, since what you say seems to us most true. But how is this to be contrived?

ATH. It is too early to explain how we are to contrive it: let us first make sure that we agree among ourselves as to whether or not we ought to do so.

CLIN. Well, surely we ought, if we can.

ATH. Very well then; do we hold the same view about the fair and the good? Ought our wardens to know only that each of these is a plurality, or ought they also to know how and wherein they are each a unity?

CLIN. It is fairly obvious that they must necessarily also discern how these are a unity.

ATH. Well then, ought they to discern it, but be unable to give a verbal demonstration of it?

CLIN. Impossible! The state of mind you describe is that of a slave.

ATH. Well then, do we hold the same view about all forms of goodness, that those who are to be real wardens of the laws must really know the true nature of them, and be capable both of expounding it in word and conforming to it in deed, passing judgment on fair actions and foul according to their real character?

CLIN. Certainly.

ATH. And is not one of the fairest things the doctrine about the gods, which we expounded earnestly—to know both that they exist, and what power they manifestly possess, so far as a man is capable of learning these matters; so that while one should pardon the mass of the citizens if they merely follow the letter of the law, one must exclude from office those who are eligible for wardenship, unless they labor to grasp all the proofs there are about the existence of gods? Such exclusion from office consists in refusing ever to choose as a Law-warden, or to number among those approved for excellence, a man who is not divine himself, nor has spent any labor over things divine.

CLIN. It is certainly just, as you say, that the man who is idle or incapable in respect of this subject should be strictly debarred from the ranks of the noble.

ATH. Are we assured, then, that there are two causes, amongst those we previously discussed, which lead to faith in the gods?

CLIN. What two?

ATH. One is our dogma about the soul—that it is the most ancient and divine of all the things whose motion, when developed into "becoming," provides an ever-flowing fount of "being"; and the other is our dogma concerning the ordering of the motion of the stars and all the other bodies under the control of reason, which has made a "cosmos" of the All. For no man that views these objects in no careless or amateurish way has ever proved so godless as not to be affected by them in a way just the opposite of that which most people expect. For they imagine that those who study these objects in astronomy and the other necessary allied arts become atheists through observing, as they suppose, that all things come into being by necessary forces and not by the mental energy of the will aiming at the fulfilment of good.

CLIN. What in fact is the real state of the case?

ATH. The position at present is, as I said, exactly the opposite of what it was when those who considered these objects considered them to be soulless. Yet even then they were objects of admiration, and the conviction which is now actually held was suspected by all who studied them accurately—namely, that if they were soulless, and consequently devoid of reason, they could never have employed with such precision calculations so marvelous; and even in those days there were some who dared to hazard the statement that reason is the orderer of all that is in the heavens. But the same thinkers, through mistaking the nature of the soul and conceiving her to be posterior, instead of prior, to body, upset again (so to say) the whole universe, and most of all themselves; for as regards the visible objects of sight, all that moves in the heavens appeared to them to be full of stones, earth and many other soulless bodies which dispense the causes of the whole cosmos. These were the views which, at that time, caused these thinkers to incur many charges of atheism and much odium, and which also incited the poets to abuse them by likening philosophers to "dogs howling at the moon," with other such senseless slanders. But today, as we have said, the position is quite the reverse.

CLIN. How so?

ATH. It is impossible for any mortal man to become permanently god-fearing if he does not grasp the two truths now stated—namely, how that the soul is oldest of all things that partake of generation, and is immortal, and rules over all bodies—and in addition to this, he must also grasp that reason which, as we have often affirmed, controls what exists among the stars, together with the necessary preliminary sciences; and he must observe also the connection therewith of musical theory, and apply it harmoniously to the institutions and rules of ethics; and he must be able to give a rational explanation of all that admits of rational explanation. He that is unable to master these sciences, in addition to the popular virtues, will never make a competent magistrate of the whole State, but only a minister to other magistrates. And now, O Megillus and Clinias, it is time at last to consider whether, in addition to all the previous laws which we have stated, we shall add this also—that the nocturnal synod of magistrates shall be legally established, and shall participate in all the education we have de-

scribed, to keep ward over the State, and to secure its salvation; or what are we to do?

CLIN. Of course we shall add this law, my excellent sir, if we can possibly do so, even to a small extent.

ATH. Then, verily, let us all strive to do so. And herein you will find me a most willing helper, owing to my very long experience and study of this subject; and perhaps I shall discover other helpers also besides myself.

CLIN. Well, Stranger, we most certainly must proceed on that path along which God too, it would seem, is conducting us. But what is the right method for us to employ—that is what we have now got to discover and state.

ATH. It is not possible at this stage, Megillus and Clinias, to enact laws for such a body, before it has been duly framed; when it is, its members must themselves ordain what authority they should possess; but it is already plain that what is required in order to form such a body, if it is to be rightly formed, is teaching by means of prolonged conferences.

CLIN. How so? What now are we to understand by this observation?

ATH. Surely we must first draw up a list of all those who are fitted by age, intellectual capacity, and moral character and habit for the office of warden; but as regards the next point, the subjects they should learn—these it is neither easy to discover for oneself nor is it easy to find another who has made the discovery and learn from him. Moreover, with respect to the limits of time, when and for how long they ought to receive instruction in each subject, it were idle to lay down written regulations; for even the learners themselves could not be sure that they were learning at the opportune time until each of them had acquired within his soul some knowledge of the subject in question. Accordingly, although it would be wrong to term all these matters "indescribable," they should be termed "imprescribable," seeing that the prescribing of them beforehand does nothing to elucidate the question under discussion.

CLIN. What then must we do, Stranger, under these circumstances?

ATH. Apparently, my friends, we must "take our chance with the crowd" (as the saying is), and if we are willing to put the whole polity to the hazard and throw (as men say) three sixes or three aces, so it must be done; and I will go shares with you in the hazard by declaring and explaining my views concerning education and nurture, the subject now started anew in our discourse; but truly the hazard will be no small one, nor comparable to any others. And you, Clinias, I specially exhort to take good heed to this matter. For as concerns the State of the Magnesians—or whoever else, by the god's direction, gives your State its name—if you frame it aright, you will achieve most high renown, or at any rate you will inevitably gain the reputation of being the boldest of all your successors. If so be that this divine synod actually comes into existence, my dear colleagues, we must hand over to it the State; and practically all our present lawgivers agree to this without dispute. Thus we shall have as an accomplished fact and waking reality that result which we treated but a short while ago in our discourse as a mere dream, when we constructed a kind of picture of the union of the reason and the head—if, that is to say, we have the members carefully selected and suitably trained, and after their training quartered in the acropolis of the country, and thus finally made into wardens, the like of whom we have never before seen in our lives for excellence in safeguarding.

MEG. My dear Clinias, from all that has now been said it follows that either we must forgo the idea of settling the State, or else we must detain this Stranger here, and by prayers and every possible means secure his co-operation in the task of settling the State.

CLIN. That is most true, Megillus; I will do as you say, and do you yourself assist me.

MEG. Assist you I will.

VI
ARISTOTLE

For twenty years, Aristotle was a pupil of Plato in the Academy. One can only speculate at the extraordinary interactions that must have taken place between two of the most profound geniuses that the world has known. On Plato's death in 347 B.C., Aristotle left Athens, and in 342 he was hired to be the tutor for Alexander, son of the king of Macedon, Philip II. It is likely that Aristotle taught his pupil primarily about literature, but it is also possible that the curriculum included an education in political matters and that this stimulated Aristotle's own interest in politics. In 335 B.C., Alexander succeeded his father on the throne, and in an astonishingly short period—twelve years in all—he conquered much of the known world, including virtually all of Greece and Asia Minor, Persia, and a good deal of northern Africa, and ultimately moved his armies deep into present-day India.

Aristotle himself played no role in these activities. He had returned to Athens on his pupil's accession to the throne and pursued there his career as a teacher, scientist, and philosopher. What Alexander the Great had accomplished in twelve years on the battlefield was almost certainly exceeded—indeed, far exceeded—by what his former teacher was able to accomplish during the same period in the intellectual field. Aristotle's school became known as the Lyceum, and his pupils were called Peripatetics, named for the covered courtyard (*peripatos*) at the school where students and faculty walked together while engaging in scholarly discussions. Although an enormous body of Aristotle's own writing has come down to us, this represents only a relatively small part of what he actually produced during his life. His early philosophical dialogues, probably similar in form to the dialogues of Plato, are now lost, as are most of the encyclopedic collections of historical and scientific facts that he compiled. What remains, however, are works of immense philosophical importance. Included are the following:

- *Works on logic.* To the best of our knowledge, Aristotle was the first person to explore the science of correct reasoning itself, i.e., what it means to think clearly and accurately. He provided accounts both of deductive logic—the formal analysis of analytic truth—and of inductive logic. Those accounts, which are stunning in their scope and accuracy, are to a great extent still valid today.
- *Works on metaphysics.* Aristotle follows Plato in searching for the underlying, unobservable form of observable things, but he differs from Plato in finding the form to be immanent in the thing itself and in believing that observable things are not mere shadows but have real substance. Central here is his claim that the essence of a particular thing is to be found, at least in part, in its "final cause," or its function. The function of a chair is to be sat on. This assertion means that the essence of any particular chair is the quality of its being useful for sitting. Such an account provides us not only with an understanding of chairs but also with a standard by which to evaluate particular chairs. If one chair is a better chair than another chair, this condition cannot be because that chair is prettier or more costly, but only because it is better for sitting.

- *Works in natural science*. Aristotle produced important treatises on physics, biology, astronomy, and weather, as well as on the nature of the soul. The scope of learning and depth of insight that is contained in these works is nothing less than staggering.
- *Works on poetry and rhetoric*. In addition to everything else, Aristotle is arguably the first systematic literary critic. His *Poetics* includes sustained analysis of the nature of tragedy and comedy, as well as important discussions of epic poetry in general and Homeric epic in particular. His *Rhetoric* presents a detailed and still-influential account of the art of persuasion.

Aristotle also wrote crucial works in the area of politics and morality. His *Politics* is, along with Plato's *Republic*, one of the two great political works of antiquity. Central to his discussion is an account of the essence of—the metaphysics of—the *polis*. We find here, among other things, his famous assertion that man is by nature a political animal, by which Aristotle means that the proper condition of humans is to live in a city-state. Forms of social organization that are smaller than the city-state, such as families, villages, and tribes, are functionally inadequate to provide people with what they need in order to live appropriately human lives; larger forms of social organization are, in these respects, bloated and superfluous. It is interesting to note that Aristotle defended the idea of the city-state at a time when the city-states of Greece were themselves being absorbed into an immense imperial state, which first was led by Aristotle's erstwhile employer, Philip II, and subsequently by his own former student, Alexander.

In Aristotle, then, we find the roots of an idea that would prove to have enormous and lasting impact: the idea that individual human beings can improve themselves as individuals, can become better human beings, simply by living and participating in a *polis*. This is an idea—perhaps our first systematic idea—of citizenship. It suggests that to live a good life is to live a life of political involvement, of engagement in the world of public affairs, hence a life of civic virtue. Aristotle agrees with Plato that not all human beings are equally suited to such involvement. He is no egalitarian and is, among other things, a sturdy defender of slavery (though only for people who are naturally suited to being slaves). But his account of plausible and virtuous political regimes is broader than Plato's, and he is particularly important for having sung the praises of a "mixed regime" composed, in various measure, of monarchical, aristocratic, and democratic elements. The idea of the mixed regime would become central to the ideology of republican Rome, as articulated by Cicero, among others, and would inform the deliberations of the American Founding Fathers, who in producing the United States Constitution were producing a form of government deeply rooted in Aristotelian principles.

The *Nicomachean Ethics*—one of two important ethical treatises that Aristotle wrote—deals with the most fundamental kinds of moral questions. It argues that the goal of human life is *eudaimonia*, a word that is typically and correctly translated as "happiness" but that means happiness only in the broadest sense to connote a kind of satisfaction or peace of mind associated with people who are flourishing. In order to flourish, humans must live in accordance with their distinctive natures; and what distinguishes humans in general from all other creatures is their capacity for reason. A natural and virtuous life, a life that is most likely to make us truly happy, is thus a life lived rationally. But what kinds of specific choices would a rational person make? Aristotle has a great deal to say about this, but most of his answers reflect a fundamental and famous principle of practical reason: in all things, choose the mean. In seeking to satisfy our appetites, for example, neither excess (i.e., gluttony) nor deficiency (i.e., extreme asceticism) are likely to make us happy. *Eudaimonia* is to be found in a middle ground, through due proportion. A virtuous person is one who habitually chooses the mean; and in politics, this choice again speaks strongly to the virtue of a mixed regime, one that is midway between the extremes of unrestrained autocracy on the one hand and excessive democracy on the other.

Further Reading: A very good starting place would be *Aristotle's Political Theory: An Introduction* (1977), by R. G. Mulgan. Even better, in my opinion, is Michael Davis, *The Politics of Philosophy: A Commentary on Aristotle's Politics* (1996). For two quite different but stimulating studies, see Stephen Salkever, *Finding the Mean: Theory and Practice in Aristotle's Political Philosophy* (1990), and Bernard Yack, *The Problems of a Political Animal: Community, Justice and Conflict in Aristotelian Political Thought* (1993).

On Aristotle's ethical theory, see especially C. D. C. Reeve, *Practices of Reason: Aristotle's Nicomachaean Ethics* (1992), a substantial and very challenging work. Also, see Richard Kraut, *Aristotle on the Human Good* (1989). Both of these books in part build on and react to two fine earlier studies, *Reason and the Human Good in Aristotle* (1975), by John M. Cooper, and *Aristotle's Theory of Moral Insight* (1983), by Troels Engberg-Pedersen. For a discussion of Aristotle's idea of practical wisdom, see Peter J. Steinberger, *The Concept of Political Judgment* (1993).

Aristotle
(384–322 B.C.)

Nicomachean Ethics

Book 1

1

1094a Every craft and every investigation, and likewise every action and decision, seems to aim at some good; hence the good has been well described as that at which everything aims.

However, there is an apparent difference among the ends aimed at. For the end is sometimes an activ-
5 ity, sometimes a product beyond the activity; and when there is an end beyond the action, the product is by nature better than the activity.

Since there are many actions, crafts and sciences, the ends turn out to be many as well; for health is the end of medicine, a boat of boatbuilding, victory of generalship, and wealth of household manage-
10 ment.

But whenever any of these sciences are subordinate to some one capacity—as e.g. bridlemaking and every other science producing equipment for horses are subordinate to horsemanship, while this and every action in warfare and in turn subordinate to general-ship, and in the same way other sciences are subordi-nate to further ones—in each of these the end of the
15 ruling science is more choiceworthy than all the ends subordinate to it, since it is the end for which those ends are also pursued. And here it does not matter whether the ends of the actions are the activities themselves, or some product beyond them, as in the sciences we have mentioned.

2

Suppose, then, that (a) there is some end of the things we pursue in our actions which we wish for because of itself, and because of which we wish for the other things; and (b) we do not choose everything because 20 of something else, since (c) if we do, it will go on without limit, making desire empty and futile; then clearly (d) this end will be the good, i.e. the best good.

Then surely knowledge of this good is also of great importance for the conduct of our lives, and if, like archers, we have a target to aim at, we are more likely to hit the right mark. If so, we should try to grasp, in 25 outline at any rate, what the good is, and which science or capacity is concerned with it.

It seems to concern the most controlling science, the one that, more than any other, is the ruling sci-ence. And political science apparently has this char-acter.

(1) For it is the one that prescribes which of the sciences ought to be studied in cities, and which ones 1094b each class in the city should learn, and how far.

(2) Again, we see that even the most honoured capacities, e.g. generalship, household management and rhetoric, are subordinate to it.

(3) Further, it uses the other sciences concerned with action, and moreover legislates what must be 5 done and what avoided.

Hence its end will include the ends of the other sciences, and so will be the human good.

[This is properly called political science;] for though admittedly the good is the same for a city as for an individual, still the good of the city is apparently a greater and more complete good to acquire and preserve. For while it is satisfactory to acquire and preserve the good even for an individual, it is finer and more divine to acquire and preserve it for a people 10 and for cities. And so, since our investigation aims at these [goods, for an individual and for a city], it is a sort of political science.

Reprinted from Aristotle, *Nicomachean Ethics*, translated, with introduction and notes, by Terence Irwin (Indianapolis: Hackett Publishing Company, 1985) by permission of the publisher.

3

Our discussion will be adequate if its degree of clarity fits the subject-matter; for we should not seek the same degree of exactness in all sorts of arguments alike, any more than in the products of different crafts.

15 Moreover, what is fine and what is just, the topics of inquiry in political science, differ and vary so much that they seem to rest on convention only, not on nature. Goods, however, also vary in the same sort of way, since they cause harm to many people; for it has happened that some people have been destroyed because of their wealth, others because of their bravery.

Since these, then, are the sorts of things we argue 20 from and about, it will be satisfactory if we can indicate the truth roughly and in outline; since [that is to say] we argue from and about what holds good usually [but not universally], it will be satisfactory if we can draw conclusions of the same sort.

Each of our claims, then, ought to be accepted in the same way [as claiming to hold good usually], since the educated person seeks exactness in each 25 area to the extent that the nature of the subject allows; for apparently it is just as mistaken to demand demonstrations from a rhetorician as to accept [merely] persuasive arguments from a mathematician.

Further, each person judges well what he knows, 1095a and is a good judge about that; hence the good judge in a particular area is the person educated in that area, and the unconditionally good judge is the person educated in every area.

This is why a youth is not a suitable student of political science; for he lacks experience of the actions in life which political science argues from and about.

Moreover, since he tends to be guided by his feel- 5 ings, his study will be futile and useless; for its end is action, not knowledge. And here it does not matter whether he is young in years or immature in character, since the deficiency does not depend on age, but results from being guided in his life and in each of his pursuits by his feelings; for an immature person, like an incontinent person, gets no benefit from his knowledge.

10 If, however, we are guided by reason in forming our desires and in acting, then this knowledge will be of great benefit.

These are the preliminary points about the student, about the way our claims are to be accepted, and about what we intend to do.

4

Let us, then, begin again. Since every sort of knowledge and decision pursues some good, what is that 15 good which we say is the aim of political science? What [in other words] is the highest of all the goods pursued in action?

As far as its name goes, most people virtually agree [about what the good is], since both the many and the cultivated call it happiness, and suppose that living well and doing well are the same as being happy. But they disagree about what happiness is, and the 20 many do not give the same answer as the wise.

For the many think it is something obvious and evident, e.g. pleasure, wealth, or honor, some thinking one thing, others another; and indeed the same person keeps changing his mind, since in sickness he thinks it is health, in poverty wealth. And when they are conscious of their own ignorance, they admire 25 anyone who speaks of something grand and beyond them.

[Among the wise,] however, some used to think that besides these many goods there is some other good that is something in itself, and also causes all these goods to be goods.

Presumably, then, it is rather futile to examine all these beliefs, and it is enough to examine those that are most current or seem to have some argument 30 for them.

We must notice, however, the difference between arguments from origins and arguments toward origins. For indeed Plato was right to be puzzled about this, when he used to ask if [the argument] set out from the origins or led toward them—just as on a race course the path may go from the starting-line to the 1095b far end, or back again.

For while we should certainly begin from origins that are known, things are known in two ways; for some are known to us, some known unconditionally [but not necessarily known to us]. Presumably, then, the origin we should begin from is what is known to us.

This is why we need to have been brought up in fine habits if we are to be adequate students of what 5

is fine and just, and of political questions generally. For the origin we begin from is the belief that something is true, and if this is apparent enough to us, we will not, at this stage, need the reason why it is true in addition; and if we have this good upbringing, we have the origins to begin from, or can easily acquire them. Someone who neither has them nor can ac-
10 quire them should listen to Hesiod: "He who understands everything himself is best of all; he is noble also who listens to one who has spoken well; but he who neither understands it himself nor takes to heart what he hears from another is a useless man."

5

But let us begin again from [the common beliefs]
15 from which we digressed. For, it would seem, people quite reasonably reach their conception of the good,
17, 18 i.e. of happiness, from the lives [they lead]; for there are roughly three most favored lives—the lives of
19 gratification, of political activity, and, third, of study.
16   The many, the most vulgar, would seem to conceive the good and happiness as pleasure, and hence
17 they also like the life of gratification. Here they appear
19 completely slavish, since the life they decide on is
20 a life for grazing animals; and yet they have some argument in their defense, since many in positions of power feel the same way as Sardanapallus [and also choose this life].

The cultivated people, those active [in politics], conceive the good as honor, since this is more or less the end [normally pursued] in the political life. This, however, appears to be too superficial to be what we are seeking, since it seems to depend more on those
25 who honor than on the one honored, whereas we intuitively believe that the good is something of our own and hard to take from us.

Further, it would seem, they pursue honor to convince themselves that they are good; at any rate, they seek to be honored by intelligent people, among people who know them, and for virtue. It is clear, then,
30 that in the view of active people at least, virtue is superior [to honor].

Perhaps, indeed, one might conceive virtue more than honor to be the end of the political life. However, this also is apparently too incomplete [to be the good]. For, it seems, someone might possess virtue but be

asleep or inactive throughout his life; or, further, he 1096a might suffer the worst evils and misfortunes; and if this is the sort of life he leads, no one would count him happy, except to defend a philosopher's paradox. Enough about this, since it has been adequately discussed in the popular works also.

The third life is the life of study, which we will 5 examine in what follows.

The money-maker's life is in a way forced on him [not chosen for itself]; and clearly wealth is not the good we are seeking, since it is [merely] useful, [choiceworthy only] for some other end. Hence one would be more inclined to suppose that [any of] the goods mentioned earlier is the end, since they are liked for themselves. But apparently they are not [the end] either; and many arguments have been pre- 10 sented against them. Let us, then, dismiss them.

7

But let us return once again to the good we are looking 1097a for, and consider just what it could be, since it is apparently one thing in one action or craft, and another thing in another; for it is one thing in medicine, another in generalship, and so on for the rest.

What, then, is the good in each of these cases? Surely it is that for the sake of which the other things are done; and in medicine this is health, in general- 20 ship victory, in housebuilding a house, in another case something else, but in every action and decision it is the end, since it is for the sake of the end that everyone does the other things.

And so, if there is some end of everything that is pursued in action, this will be the good pursued in action; and if there are more ends than one, these will be the goods pursued in action.

Our argument has progressed, then, to the same conclusion [as before, that the highest end is the 25 good]; but we must try to clarify this still more.

Though apparently there are many ends, we choose some of them, e.g. wealth, flutes and, in general, instruments, because of something else; hence it is clear that not all ends are complete. But the best good is apparently something complete. Hence, if only one end is complete, this will be what we are looking for; and if more than one are complete, the most complete of 30 these will be what we are looking for.

An end pursued in itself, we say, is more complete than an end pursued because of something else; and an end that is never choiceworthy because of something else is more complete than ends that are choiceworthy both in themselves and because of this end; and hence an end that is always [choiceworthy, and also] choiceworthy in itself, never because of something else, is unconditionally complete.

Now happiness more than anything else seems un-1097b conditionally complete, since we always [choose it, and also] choose it because of itself, never because of something else.

Honor, pleasure, understanding and every virtue we certainly choose because of themselves, since we would choose each of them even if it had no further result, but we also choose them for the sake of happi-5 ness, supposing that through them we shall be happy. Happiness, by contrast, no one ever chooses for their sake, or for the sake of anything else at all.

The same conclusion [that happiness is complete] also appears to follow from self-sufficiency, since the complete good seems to be self-sufficient.

Now what we count as self-sufficient is not what suffices for a solitary person by himself, living an 10 isolated life, but what suffices also for parents, children, wife and in general for friends and fellow-citizens, since a human being is a naturally political [animal]. Here, however, we must impose some limit; for if we extend the good to parents' parents and children's children and to friends of friends, we shall go on without limit; but we must examine this another time.

Anyhow, we regard something as self-sufficient 15 when all by itself it makes a life choiceworthy and lacking nothing; and that is what we think happiness does.

Moreover, we think happiness is most choiceworthy of all goods, since it is not counted as one good among many. If it were counted as one among many, then, clearly, we think that the addition of the smallest of goods would make it more choiceworthy; for [the smallest good] that is added becomes an extra quantity of goods [so creating a good larger than the original good], and the larger of two goods is always more choiceworthy. [But we do not think any addition 20 can make happiness more choiceworthy; hence it is most choiceworthy.]

Happiness, then, is apparently something complete and self-sufficient, since it is the end of the things pursued in action.

But presumably the remark that the best good is happiness is apparently something [generally] agreed, and what we miss is a clearer statement of what the best good is.

Well, perhaps we shall find the best good if we first find the function of a human being. For just as 25 the good, i.e. [doing] well, for a flautist, a sculptor, and every craftsman, and, in general, for whatever has a function and [characteristic] action, seems to depend on its function, the same seems to be true for a human being, if a human being has some function.

Then do the carpenter and the leatherworker have their functions and actions, while a human being has 30 none, and is by nature idle, without any function? Or, just as eye, hand, foot and, in general, every [bodily] part apparently has its functions, may we likewise ascribe to a human being some function besides all of theirs?

What, then, could this be? For living is apparently shared with plants, but what we are looking for is the special function of a human being; hence we should 1098a set aside the life of nutrition and growth. The life next in order is some sort of life of sense-perception; but this too is apparently shared, with horse, ox and every animal. The remaining possibility, then, is some sort of life of action of the [part of the soul] that has reason.

Now this [part has two parts, which have reason in different ways], one as obeying the reason [in the other part], the other as itself having reason and think-5 ing. [We intend both.] Moreover, life is also spoken of in two ways [as capacity and as activity], and we must take [a human being's special function to be] life as activity, since this seems to be called life to a fuller extent.

(a) We have found, then, that the human function is the soul's activity that expresses reason [as itself having reason] or requires reason [as obeying reason]. (b) Now the function of F, e.g. of a harpist, is the same in kind, so we say, as the function of an excellent F, e.g. an excellent harpist. (c) The same is true unconditionally in every case, when we add to the 10 function the superior achievement that expresses the virtue; for a harpist's function, e.g. is to play the harp,

and a good harpist's is to do it well. (d) Now we take the human function to be a certain kind of life, and take this life to be the soul's activity and actions that express reason. (e) [Hence by (c) and (d)] the excellent man's function is to do this finely and well. (f)
15 Each function is completed well when its completion expresses the proper virtue. (g) Therefore [by (d), (e) and (f)] the human good turns out to be the soul's activity that expresses virtue.

And if there are more virtues than one, the good will express the best and most complete virtue. Moreover, it will be in a complete life. For one swallow does not make a spring, nor does one day; nor, simi-
20 larly, does one day or a short time make us blessed and happy.

This, then, is a sketch of the good; for, presumably, the outline must come first, to be filled in later. If the sketch is good, then anyone, it seems, can advance and articulate it, and in such cases time is a good
25 discoverer or [at least] a good co-worker. That is also how the crafts have improved, since anyone can add what is lacking [in the outline].

However, we must also remember our previous remarks, so that we do not look for the same degree of exactness in all areas, but the degree that fits the subject-matter in each area and is proper to the investigation. For the carpenter's and the geometer's inquir-
30 ies about the right angle are different also; the carpenter's is confined to the right angle's usefulness for his work, whereas the geometer's concerns what, or what sort of thing, the right angle is, since he studies the truth. We must do the same, then, in other areas too, [seeking the proper degree of exactness], so that digressions do not overwhelm our main task.

1098b Nor should we make the same demand for an explanation in all cases. Rather, in some cases it is enough to prove that something is true without explaining why it is true. This is so, e.g. with origins, where the fact that something is true is the first principle, i.e. the origin.

Some origins are studied by means of induction, some by means of perception, some by means of some
5 sort of habituation, and others by other means. In each case we should try to find them out by means suited to their nature, and work hard to define them well. For they have a great influence on what follows; for the origin seems to be more than half the whole,

and makes evident the answer to many of our questions.

8

However, we should examine the origin not only from the conclusion and premises [of a deductive 10 argument], but also from what is said about it; for all the facts harmonize with a true account, whereas the truth soon clashes with a false one.

Goods are divided, then, into three types, some called external, some goods of the soul, others goods of the body; and the goods of the soul are said to be 15 goods to the fullest extent and most of all, and the soul's actions and activities are ascribed to the soul. Hence the account [of the good] is sound, to judge by this belief anyhow—and it is an ancient belief agreed on by philosophers.

Our account is also correct in saying that some sort of actions and activities are the end; for then the end turns out to be a good of the soul, not an external good. 20

The belief that the happy person lives well and does well in action also agrees with our account, since we have virtually said that the end is a sort of living well and doing well in action.

Further, all the features that people look for in happiness appear to be true of the end described in our account. For to some people it seems to be virtue; to others intelligence; to others some sort of wisdom; 25 to others again it seems to be these, or one of these, involving pleasure or requiring its addition; and others add in external prosperity as well.

Some of these views are traditional, held by many, while others are held by a few reputable men; and it is reasonable for each group to be not entirely in error, but correct on one point at least, or even on most points.

First, our account agrees with those who say happi- 30 ness is virtue [in general] or some [particular] virtue; for activity expressing virtue is proper to virtue. Presumably, though, it matters quite a bit whether we suppose that the best good consists in possessing or in using, i.e. in a state or in an activity [that actualizes the state]. For while someone may be in a state that achieves no good, if, e.g. he is asleep or inactive in 1099a some other way, this cannot be true of the activity; for it will necessarily do actions and do well in them. And just as Olympic prizes are not for the finest and strongest, but for contestants, since it is only these who win; so also in life [only] the fine and good people who act correctly win the prize.

Moreover, the life of these [active] people is also pleasant in itself. For being pleased is a condition of the soul, [hence included in the activity of the soul]. Further, each type of person finds pleasure in whatever he is called a lover of, so that a horse, e.g. pleases the horse-lover, a spectacle the lover of spectacles, and similarly what is just pleases the lover of justice, and in general what expresses virtue pleases the lover of virtue. Hence the things that please most people conflict, because they are not pleasant by nature, whereas the things that please lovers of what is fine are things pleasant by nature; and actions expressing virtue are pleasant in this way; and so they both please lovers of what is fine and are pleasant in themselves.

Hence their life does not need pleasure to be added [to virtuous activity] as some sort of ornament; rather, it has its pleasure within itself. For besides the reasons already given, someone who does not enjoy fine actions is not good; for no one would call him just, e.g., if he did not enjoy doing just actions, or generous if he did not enjoy generous actions, and similarly for the other virtues. If this is so, then actions expressing the virtues are pleasant in themselves.

Moreover, these actions are good and fine as well as pleasant; indeed, they are good, fine and pleasant more than anything else, since on this question the excellent person has good judgment, and his judgment agrees with our conclusions.

Happiness, then, is best, finest and most pleasant, and these three features are not distinguished in the way suggested by the Delian inscription: "What is most just is finest; being healthy is most beneficial; but it is most pleasant to win our heart's desire." For all three features are found in the best activities, and happiness we say is these activities, or [rather] one of them, the best one.

Nonetheless, happiness evidently also needs external goods to be added [to the activity], as we said, since we cannot, or cannot easily, do fine actions if we lack the resources.

1099b For, first of all, in many actions we use friends, wealth and political power just as we use instruments.

Further, deprivation of certain [externals]—e.g. good birth, good children, beauty—mars our blessedness; for we do not altogether have the character of happiness if we look utterly repulsive or are ill-born, solitary or childless, and have it even less, presumably, if our children or friends are totally bad, or were good but have died.

And so, as we have said, happiness would seem to need this sort of prosperity added also; that is why some people identify happiness with good fortune, while others [reacting from one extreme to the other] identify it with virtue.

BOOK 2

1

Virtue, then, is of two sorts, virtue of thought and virtue of character. Virtue of thought arises and grows mostly from teaching, and hence needs experience and time. Virtue of character [i.e. of *ēthos*] results from habit [*ethos*]; hence its name 'ethical', slightly varied from '*ethos*'.

Hence it is also clear that none of the virtues of character arises in us naturally.

For if something is by nature [in one condition], habituation cannot bring it into another condition. A stone, e.g., by nature moves downward, and habituation could not make it move upward, not even if you threw it up ten thousand times to habituate it; nor could habituation make fire move downward, or bring anything that is by nature in one condition into another condition.

Thus the virtues arise in us neither by nature nor against nature. Rather, we are by nature able to acquire them, and reach our complete perfection through habit.

Further, if something arises in us by nature, we first have the capacity for it, and later display the activity. This is clear in the case of the senses; for we did not acquire them by frequent seeing or hearing, but already had them when we exercised them, and did not get them by exercising them.

Virtues, by contrast, we acquire, just as we acquire crafts, by having previously activated them. First we learn a craft by producing the same product that we must produce when we have learned it, becoming builders, e.g., by building and harpists by playing the harp; so also, then, we become just by doing just 1103b actions, temperate by doing temperate actions, brave by doing brave actions.

What goes on in cities is evidence for this also. For the legislator makes the citizens good by habituating 5 them, and this is the wish of every legislator; if he fails to do it well he misses his goal. [The right] habituation is what makes the difference between a good political system and a bad one.

Further, just as in the case of a craft, the sources and means that develop each virtue also ruin it. For playing the harp makes both good and bad harpists, and it is analogous in the case of builders and all the 10 rest; for building well makes good builders, building badly, bad ones. If it were not so, no teacher would be needed, but everyone would be born a good or a bad craftsman.

It is the same, then, with the virtues. For actions 15 in dealings with [other] human beings make some people just, some unjust; actions in terrifying situations and the acquired habit of fear or confidence make some brave and others cowardly. The same is true of situations involving appetites and anger; for one or another sort of conduct in these situations 20 makes some people temperate and gentle, others intemperate and irascible.

To sum up, then, in a single account: A state [of character] arises from [the repetition of] similar activities. Hence we must display the right activities, since differences in these imply corresponding differences in the states. It is not unimportant, then, to acquire one sort of habit or another, right from our youth; 25 rather, it is very important, indeed all-important.

2

Our present inquiry does not aim, as our others do, at study; for the purpose of our examination is not to know what virtue is, but to become good, since 30 otherwise the inquiry would be of no benefit to us. Hence we must examine the right way to act, since, as we have said, the actions also control the character of the states we acquire.

First, then, actions should express correct reason. That is a common [belief], and let us assume it; later

we will say what correct reason is and how it is related to the other virtues.

But let us take it as agreed in advance that every 1104a account of the actions we must do has to be stated in outline, not exactly. As we also said at the start, the type of accounts we demand should reflect the subject-matter; and questions about actions and expediency, like questions about health, have no fixed [and invariable answers].

And when our general account is so inexact, the 5 account of particular cases is all the more inexact. For these fall under no craft or profession, and the agents themselves must consider in each case what the opportune action is, as doctors and navigators do.

The account we offer, then, in our present inquiry 10 is of this inexact sort; still, we must try to offer help.

First, then, we should observe that these sorts of states naturally tend to be ruined by excess and deficiency. We see this happen with strength and health, which we mention because we must use what is evident as a witness to what is not. For both excessive 15 and deficient exercises ruin strength; and likewise, too much or too little eating or drinking ruins health, while the proportionate amount produces, increases and preserves it.

The same is true, then, of temperance, bravery and the other virtues. For if, e.g., someone avoids and is 20 afraid of everything, standing firm against nothing, he becomes cowardly, but if he is afraid of nothing at all and goes to face everything, he becomes rash. Similarly, if he gratifies himself with every pleasure and refrains from none, he becomes intemperate, but if he avoids them all, as boors do, he becomes some sort of insensible person. Temperance and bravery, 25 then, are ruined by excess and deficiency but preserved by the mean.

The same actions, then, are the sources and causes both of the emergence and growth of virtues and of their ruin; but further, the activities of the virtues will be found in these same actions. For this is also true 30 of more evident cases, e.g. strength, which arises from eating a lot and from withstanding much hard labor, and it is the strong person who is most able to do these very things. It is the same with the virtues. Refraining from pleasures make us become temperate, and when we have become temperate we are 35 most able to refrain from pleasures. And it is similar 1104b with bravery; habituation in disdaining what is fearful and in standing firm against it makes us become brave, and when we have become brave we shall be most able to stand firm.

3

But [actions are not enough]; we must take as a sign of someone's state his pleasure or pain in consequence of his action. For if someone who abstains from bodily pleasures enjoys the abstinence itself, then he is temperate, but if he is grieved by it, he is intemperate. Again, if he stands firm against terrifying situations and enjoys it, or at least does not find it painful, then he is brave, and if he finds it painful, he is cowardly.

[Pleasures and pains are appropriately taken as signs] because virtue of character is concerned with pleasures and pains.

(1) For it is pleasure that causes us to do base actions, and pain that causes us to abstain from fine ones. Hence we need to have had the appropriate upbringing—right from early youth, as Plato says— to make us find enjoyment or pain in the right things; for this is the correct education.

(2) Further, virtues are concerned with actions and feelings; but every feeling and every action implies pleasure or pain; hence, for this reason too, virtue is concerned with pleasures and pains.

(3) Corrective treatment [for vicious actions] also indicates [the relevance of pleasure and pain], since it uses pleasures and pains; it uses them because such correction is a form of medical treatment, and medical treatment naturally operates through contraries.

(4) Further, as we said earlier, every state of soul is naturally related to and concerned with whatever naturally makes it better or worse; and pleasures and pains make people worse, from pursuing and avoiding the wrong ones, at the wrong time, in the wrong ways, or whatever other distinctions of that sort are needed in an account.

These [bad effects of pleasure and pain] are the reason why people actually define the virtues as ways of being unaffected and undisturbed [by pleasures and pains]. They are wrong, however, because they speak [of being unaffected] unconditionally, not of being unaffected in the right or wrong way, at the right or wrong time, and the added specifications.

We assume, then, that virtue is the sort of state [with the appropriate specifications] that does the best actions concerned with pleasures and pains, and that vice is the contrary. The following points will also make it evident that virtue and vice are concerned with the same things.

(5) There are three objects of choice—fine, expedient and pleasant—and three objects of avoidance— their contraries, shameful, harmful and painful. About all these, then, the good person is correct and the bad person is in error, and especially about pleasure. For pleasure is shared with animals, and implied by every object of choice, since what is fine and what is expedient appear pleasant as well.

(6) Further, since pleasure grows up with all of us from infancy on, it is hard to rub out this feeling that is dyed into our lives; and we estimate actions as well [as feelings], some of us more, some less, by pleasure and pain. Hence, our whole inquiry must be about these, since good or bad enjoyment or pain is very important for our actions.

(7) Moreover, it is harder to fight pleasure than to fight emotion, [though that is hard enough], as Heracleitus says. Now both craft and virtue are concerned in every case with what is harder, since a good result is even better when it is harder. Hence, for this reason also, the whole inquiry, for virtue and political science alike, must consider pleasures and pains; for if we use these well, we shall be good, and if badly, bad.

In short, virtue is concerned with pleasures and pains; the actions that are its sources also increase it or, if they are done differently, ruin it; and its activity is concerned with the same actions that are its sources.

4

However, someone might raise this puzzle: "What do you mean by saying that to become just we must first do just actions and to become temperate we must first do temperate actions? For if we do what is grammatical or musical, we must already be grammarians or musicians. In the same way, then, if we do what is just or temperate, we must already be just or temperate."

But surely this is not so even with the crafts, for it is possible to produce something grammatical by chance or by following someone else's instructions. To be a grammarian, then, we must both produce

something grammatical and produce it in the way in
25 which the grammarian produces it, i.e. expressing
grammatical knowledge that is in us.

Moreover, in any case what is true of crafts is not
true of virtues. For the products of a craft determine by
their own character whether they have been produced
well; and so it suffices that they are in the right state
when they have been produced. But for actions expressing virtue to be done temperately or justly [and
hence well] it does not suffice that they are themselves
30 in the right state. Rather, the agent must also be in
the right state when he does them. First, he must
know [that he is doing virtuous actions]; second, he
must decide on them, and decide on them for themselves; and, third, he must also do them from a firm
and unchanging state.

1105b As conditions for having a craft these three do not
count, except for the knowing itself. As a condition
for having a virtue, however, the knowing counts for
nothing, or [rather] for only a little, whereas the other
two conditions are very important, indeed all-important. And these other two conditions are achieved by
5 the frequent doing of just and temperate actions.

Hence actions are called just or temperate when
they are the sort that a just or temperate person would
do. But the just and temperate person is not the one
who [merely] does these actions, but the one who
also does them in the way in which just or temperate
people do them.

10 It is right, then, to say that a person comes to be
just from doing just actions and temperate from doing
temperate actions; for no one has even a prospect of
becoming good from failing to do them.

The many, however, do not do these actions but take
refuge in arguments, thinking that they are doing philosophy, and that this is the way to become excellent
15 people. In this they are like a sick person who listens
attentively to the doctor, but acts on none of his instructions. Such a course of treatment will not improve the
state of his body; any more than will the many's way of
doing philosophy improve the state of their souls.

5

Next we must examine what virtue is. Since there
20 are three conditions arising in the soul—feelings,
capacities and states—virtue must be one of these.

By feelings I mean appetite, anger, fear, confidence, envy, joy, love, hate, longing, jealousy, pity,
in general whatever implies pleasure or pain.

By capacities I mean what we have when we are
said to be capable of these feelings—capable of, e.g., 25
being angry or afraid or feeling pity.

By states I mean what we have when we are well
or badly off in relation to feelings. If, e.g., our feeling
is too intense or slack, we are badly off in relation to
anger, but if it is intermediate, we are well off; and
the same is true in the other cases.

First, then, neither virtues nor vices are feelings.
(a) For we are called excellent or base in so far as 30
we have virtues or vices, not in so far as we have
feelings. (b) We are neither praised nor blamed in
so far as we have feelings; for we do not praise the
angry or the frightened person, and do not blame the
person who is simply angry, but only the person who 1106a
is angry in a particular way. But we are praised or
blamed in so far as we have virtues or vices. (c) We
are angry and afraid without decision; but the virtues
are decisions of some kind, or [rather] require decision. (d) Besides, in so far as we have feelings, we
are said to be moved; but in so far as we have virtues 5
or vices, we are said to be in some condition rather
than moved.

For these reasons the virtues are not capacities
either; for we are neither called good nor called bad
in so far as we are simply capable of feelings. Further,
while we have capacities by nature, we do not become 10
good or bad by nature; we have discussed this before.

If, then, the virtues are neither feelings nor capacities, the remaining possibility is that they are states.
And so we have said what the genus of virtue is.

6

But we must say not only, as we already have, that it
is a state, but also what sort of state it is. 15

It should be said, then, that every virtue causes its
possessors to be in a good state and to perform their
functions well; the virtue of eyes, e.g., makes the eyes
and their functioning excellent, because it makes us
see well; and similarly, the virtue of a horse makes
the horse excellent, and thereby good at galloping, 20
at carrying its rider and at standing steady in the face
of the enemy. If this is true in every case, then the

virtue of a human being will likewise be the state that makes a human being good and makes him perform his function well.

25 We have already said how this will be true, and it will also be evident from our next remarks, if we consider the sort of nature that virtue has.

In everything continuous and divisible we can take more, less and equal, and each of them either in the object itself or relative to us; and the equal is some intermediate between excess and deficiency.

30 By the intermediate in the object I mean what is equidistant from each extremity; this is one and the same for everyone. But relative to us the intermediate is what is neither superfluous nor deficient; this is not one, and is not the same for everyone.

If, e.g., ten are many and two are few, we take six as intermediate in the object, since it exceeds [two] 35 and is exceeded [by ten] by an equal amount, [four]; this is what is intermediate by numerical proportion. 1106b But that is not how we must take the intermediate that is relative to us. For if, e.g., ten pounds [of food] are a lot for someone to eat, and two pounds a little, it does not follow that the trainer will prescribe six, since this might also be either a little or a lot for the person who is to take it—for Milo [the athlete] a little, but for the beginner in gymnastics a lot; and the same is true for running and wrestling. In this 5 way every scientific expert avoids excess and deficiency and seeks and chooses what is intermediate— but intermediate relative to us, not in the object.

This, then, is how each science produces its product well, by focusing on what is intermediate and making the product conform to that. This, indeed, 10 is why people regularly comment on well-made products that nothing could be added or subtracted, since they assume that excess or deficiency ruins a good [result] while the mean preserves it. Good craftsmen also, we say, focus on what is intermediate when they 15 produce their product. And since virtue, like nature, is better and more exact than any craft, it will also aim at what is intermediate.

By virtue I mean virtue of character; for this [pursues the mean because] it is concerned with feelings and actions, and these admit of excess, deficiency and an intermediate condition. We can be afraid, e.g., or be confident, or have appetites, or get angry, or feel pity, in general have pleasure or pain, both 20 too much and too little, and in both ways not well;

but [having these feelings] at the right times, about the right things, toward the right people, for the right end, and in the right way, is the intermediate and best condition, and this is proper to virtue. Similarly, actions also admit of excess, deficiency and the intermediate condition.

Now virtue is concerned with feelings and actions, 25 in which excess and deficiency are in error and incur blame, while the intermediate condition is correct and wins praise, which are both proper features of virtue. Virtue, then, is a mean, in so far as it aims at what is intermediate.

Moreover, there are many ways to be in error, since badness is proper to what is unlimited, as the 30 Pythagoreans pictured it, and good to what is limited; but there is only one way to be correct. That is why error is easy and correctness hard, since it is easy to miss the target and hard to hit it. And so for this reason also excess and deficiency are proper to vice, the mean to virtue; "for we are noble in only one 35 way, but bad in all sorts of ways."

Virtue, then, is (a) a state that decides, (b) [consisting] in a mean, (c) the mean relative to us, (d) which 1107a is defined by reference to reason, (e) i.e., to the reason by reference to which the intelligent person would define it. It is a mean between two vices, one of excess and one of deficiency.

It is a mean for this reason also: Some vices miss what is right because they are deficient, others because they are excessive, in feelings or in actions, 5 while virtue finds and chooses what is intermediate.

Hence, as far as its substance and the account stating its essence are concerned, virtue is a mean; but as far as the best [condition] and the good [result] are concerned, it is an extremity.

But not every action or feeling admits of the mean. For the names of some automatically include base- 10 ness, e.g. spite, shamelessness, envy [among feelings], and adultery, theft, murder, among actions. All of these and similar things are called by these names because they themselves, not their excesses or deficiencies, are base.

Hence in doing these things we can never be correct, but must invariably be in error. We cannot do 15 them well or not well—e.g. by committing adultery with the right woman at the right time in the right way; on the contrary, it is true unconditionally that to do any of them is to be in error.

[To think these admit of a mean], therefore, is like thinking that unjust or cowardly or intemperate action 20 also admits of a mean, an excess and a deficiency. For then there would be a mean of excess, a mean of deficiency, an excess of excess and a deficiency of deficiency.

Rather, just as there is no excess or deficiency of temperance or of bravery, since the intermediate is a sort of extreme [in achieving the good], so also there is no mean, and no excess or deficiency, of these [vicious actions] either, but whatever way anyone does 25 them, he is in error. For in general there is no mean of excess or of deficiency, and no excess or deficiency of a mean.

Book 10

6

1176a We have now finished our discussion of the types of virtue; of friendship; and of pleasure. It remains for us to discuss happiness in outline, since we take this to be the end of human [aims]. Our discussion will be shorter if we first take up again what we said before.

We said, then, that happiness is not a state. For if it were, someone might have it and yet be asleep for 35 his whole life, living the life of a plant, or suffer the 1176b greatest misfortunes. If we do not approve of this, we count happiness as an activity rather than a state, as we said before.

Some activities are necessary, i.e. choiceworthy for some other end, while others are choiceworthy in themselves. Clearly, then, we should count happiness as one of those activities that are choiceworthy in 5 themselves, not as one of those choiceworthy for some other end. For happiness lacks nothing, but is self-sufficient; and an activity is choiceworthy in itself when nothing further beyond it is sought from it.

This seems to be the character of actions expressing virtue; for doing fine and excellent actions is choiceworthy for itself.

But pleasant amusements also [seem to be choice-10 worthy in themselves]. For they are not chosen for other ends, since they actually cause more harm than benefit, by causing neglect of our bodies and possessions.

Moreover, most of those people congratulated for their happiness resort to these sorts of pastimes. Hence people who are witty participants in them have a good reputation with tyrants, since they offer themselves 15 as pleasant [partners] in the tyrant's aims, and these are the sort of people the tyrant requires. And so these amusements seem to have the character of happiness because people in supreme power spend their leisure in them.

However, these sorts of people are presumably no evidence. For virtue and understanding, the sources of excellent activities, do not depend on holding supreme power. Further, these powerful people have had no 20 taste of pure and civilized pleasure, and so they resort to bodily pleasures. But that is no reason to think these pleasures are most choiceworthy, since boys also think that what they honor is best. Hence, just as different things appear honorable to boys and to men, it is reasonable that in the same way different things appear honorable to base and to decent people.

As we have often said, then, what is honourable 25 and pleasant is what is so to the excellent person; and to each type of person the activity expressing his own proper state is most choiceworthy; hence the activity expressing virtue is most choiceworthy to the excellent person [and hence is most honorable and pleasant].

Happiness, then, is not found in amusement; for it would be absurd if the end were amusement, and our lifelong efforts and sufferings aimed at amusing 30 ourselves. For we choose practically everything for some other end—except for happiness, since it is [the] end; but serious work and toil aimed [only] at amusement appears stupid and excessively childish. Rather, it seems correct to amuse ourselves so that we can do something serious, as Anacharsis says; for amusement would seem to be relaxation, and it is because we cannot toil continuously that we require 35 relaxation. Relaxation, then, is not [the] end, since we pursue it [to prepare] for activity.   1177a

Further, the happy life seems to be a life expressing virtue, which is a life involving serious actions, and not consisting in amusement.

Besides, we say that things to be taken seriously are better than funny things that provide amusement, and that in each case the activity of the better part 5 and the better person is more serious and excellent; and the activity of what is better is superior, and thereby has more the character of happiness.

Moreover, anyone at all, even a slave, no less than the best person, might enjoy bodily pleasures; but no one would allow that a slave shares in happiness, if one does not [also allow that the slave shares in the sort of] life [needed for happiness]. Happiness, then, is found not in these pastimes, but in the activities
10 expressing virtue, as we also said previously.

7

If happiness, then, is activity expressing virtue, it is reasonable for it to express the supreme virtue, which will be the virtue of the best thing.

The best is understanding, or whatever else seems
15 to be the natural ruler and leader, and to understand what is fine and divine, by being itself either divine or the most divine element in us.

Hence complete happiness will be its activity expressing its proper virtue; and we have said that this activity is the activity of study. This seems to agree with what has been said before, and also with the truth.
20 For this activity is supreme, since understanding is the supreme element in us, and the objects of understanding are the supreme objects of knowledge.

Besides, it is the most continuous activity, since we are more capable of continuous study than of any continuous action.

We think pleasure must be mixed into happiness; and it is agreed that the activity expressing wisdom
25 is the pleasantest of the activities expressing virtue. At any rate, philosophy seems to have remarkably pure and firm pleasures; and it is reasonable for those who have knowledge to spend their lives more pleasantly than those who seek it.

Moreover, the self-sufficiency we spoke of will be found in study above all.

For admittedly the wise person, the just person and the other virtuous people all need the good things
30 necessary for life. Still, when these are adequately supplied, the just person needs other people as partners and recipients of his just actions; and the same is true of the temperate person and the brave person and each of the others.

But the wise person is able, and more able the wiser he is, to study even by himself; and though he
1177b presumably does it better with colleagues, even so he

is more self-sufficient than any other [virtuous person].

Besides, study seems to be liked because of itself alone, since it has no result beyond having studied. But from the virtues concerned with action we try to a greater or lesser extent to gain something beyond the action itself.

Happiness seems to be found in leisure, since we 5 accept trouble so that we can be at leisure, and fight wars so that we can be at peace. Now the virtues concerned with action have their activities in politics or war, and actions here seem to require trouble.

This seems completely true for actions in war, since no one chooses to fight a war, and no one continues it, for the sake of fighting a war; for someone would 10 have to be a complete murderer if he made his friends his enemies so that there could be battles and killings.

But the actions of the politician require trouble also. Beyond political activities themselves these actions seek positions of power and honors; or at least they seek happiness for the politician himself and for his fellow-citizens, which is something different from political science itself, and clearly is sought on the 15 assumption that it is different.

Hence among actions expressing the virtues those in politics and war are pre-eminently fine and great; but they require trouble, aim at some [further] end, and are choiceworthy for something other than themselves.

But the activity of understanding, it seems, is superior in excellence because it is the activity of study, 20 aims at no end beyond itself and has its own proper pleasure, which increases the activity. Further, selfsufficiency, leisure, unwearied activity (as far as is possible for a human being), and any other features ascribed to the blessed person, are evidently features of this activity.

Hence, a human being's complete happiness will 25 be this activity, if it receives a complete span of life, since nothing incomplete is proper to happiness.

Such a life would be superior to the human level. For someone will live it not in so far as he is a human being, but in so far as he has some divine element in him. And the activity of this divine element is as much superior to the activity expressing the rest of virtue as this element is superior to the compound. 30 Hence if understanding is something divine in comparison with a human being, so also will the life that expresses understanding be divine in comparison with human life.

We ought not to follow the proverb-writers, and "think human, since you are human," or "think mortal, since you are mortal." Rather, as far as we can, we ought to be pro-immortal, and go to all lengths to live a life that expresses our supreme element; for however much this element may lack in bulk, by much more it surpasses everything in power and value.

1178a

Moreover, each person seems to be his understanding, if he is his controlling and better element; it would be absurd, then, if he were to choose not his own life, but something else's.

5   And what we have said previously will also apply now. For what is proper to each thing's nature is supremely best and pleasantest for it; and hence for a human being the life expressing understanding will be supremely best and pleasantest, if understanding above all is the human being. This life, then, will also be happiest.

8

The life expressing the other kind of virtue [i.e., the kind concerned with action] is [happiest] in a second-ary way because the activities expressing this virtue are human.

10

For we do just and brave actions, and the others expressing the virtues, in relation to other people, by abiding by what fits each person in contracts, services, all types of actions, and also in feelings; and all these appear to be human conditions.

15   Indeed, some feelings actually seem to arise from the body; and in many ways virtue of character seems to be proper to feelings.

Besides, intelligence is yoked together with virtue of character, and so is this virtue with intelligence. For the origins of intelligence express the virtues of character; and correctness in virtues of character expresses intelligence. And since these virtues are also connected to feelings, they are concerned with the compound. Since the virtues of the compound are human virtues, the life and the happiness expressing these virtues is also human.

20

The virtue of understanding, however, is separated [from the compound]. Let us say no more about it, since an extract account would be too large a task for our present project.

Moreover, it seems to need external supplies very little, or [at any rate] less than virtue of character needs them. For grant that they both need necessary goods, and to the same extent, since there will be only a very small difference even though the politician labors more about the body and such-like. Still, there will be a large difference in [what is needed] for the [proper] activities [of each type of virtue].

25

For the generous person will need money for generous actions; and the just person will need it for paying debts, since wishes are not clear, and people who are not just pretend to wish to do justice. Similarly, the brave person will need enough power, and the temperate person will need freedom [to do intemperate actions], if they are to achieve anything that the virtue requires. For how else will they, or any other virtuous people, make their virtue clear?

30

Moreover, it is disputed whether it is decision or actions that is more in control of virtue, on the assumption that virtue depends on both. Well, certainly it is clear that what is complete depends on both; but for actions many external goods are needed, and the greater and finer the actions the more numerous are the external goods needed.

35

1178b

But someone who is studying needs none of these goods, for that activity at least; indeed, for study at least, we might say they are even hindrances.

In so far as he is a human being, however, and [hence] lives together with a number of other human beings, he chooses to do the actions expressing virtue. Hence he will need the sorts of external goods [that are needed for the virtues], for living a human life.

5

In another way also it appears that complete happiness is some activity of study. For we traditionally suppose that the gods more than anyone are blessed and happy; but what sorts of actions ought we to ascribe to them? Just actions? Surely they will appear ridiculous making contracts, returning deposits and so on. Brave actions? Do they endure what [they find] frightening and endure dangers because it is fine? Generous actions? Whom will they give to? And surely it would be absurd for them to have currency or anything like that. What would their temperate

10

15 actions be? Surely it is vulgar praise to say that they do not have base appetites. When we go through them all, anything that concerns actions appears trivial and unworthy of the gods.

20 However, we all traditionally suppose that they are alive and active, since surely they are not asleep like Endymion. Then if someone is alive, and action is excluded, and production even more, what is left but study? Hence the gods' activity that is superior in blessedness will be an activity of study. And so the human activity that is most akin to the gods' will, more than any others, have the character of happiness.

25 A sign of this is the fact that other animals have no share in happiness, being completely deprived of this activity of study. For the whole life of the gods is blessed, and human life is blessed to the extent that it has something resembling this sort of activity; but none of the other animals is happy, because none of them shares in study at all. Hence happiness extends just as far as study extends, and the more some-
30 one studies, the happier he is, not coincidentally but in so far as he studies, since study is valuable in itself. And so [on this argument] happiness will be some kind of study.

However, the happy person is a human being, and so will need external prosperity also; for his nature is
35 not self-sufficient for study, but he needs a healthy body, and needs to have food and the other services provided.

1179a Still, even though no one can be blessedly happy without external goods, we must not think that to be happy we will need many large goods. For self-sufficiency and action do not depend on excess, and we can do fine actions even if we do not rule earth and sea; for even from moderate resources we can
5 do the actions expressing virtue. This is evident to see, since many private citizens seem to do decent actions no less than people in power do—even more, in fact. It is enough if moderate resources are provided; for the life of someone whose activity expresses virtue will be happy.
10 Solon surely described happy people well, when he said they had been moderately supplied with external goods, had done what he regarded as the finest actions, and had lived their lives temperately. For it is possible to have moderate possessions and still to do the right actions.

And Anaxagoras would seem to have supposed that the happy person was neither rich nor powerful, since he said he would not be surprised if the happy person 15 appeared an absurd sort of person to the many. For the many judge by externals, since these are all they perceive.

Hence the beliefs of the wise would seem to accord with our arguments.

These considerations do indeed produce some confidence. The truth, however, in questions about action is judged from what we do and how we live, 20 since these are what control [the answers to such questions]. Hence we ought to examine what has been said by applying it to what we do and how we live; and if it harmonizes with what we do, we should accept it, but if it conflicts we should count it [mere] words.

The person whose activity expresses understanding and who takes care of understanding would seem to be in the best condition, and most loved by the gods. 25 For if the gods pay some attention to human beings, as they seem to, it would be reasonable for them to take pleasure in what is best and most akin to them, namely understanding; and reasonable for them to benefit in return those who most of all like and honour understanding, on the assumption that these people attend to what is beloved by the gods, and act correctly and finely.

Clearly, all this is true of the wise person more 30 than anyone else; hence he is most loved by the gods. And it is likely that this same person will be happiest; hence the wise person will be happier than anyone else on this argument too.

9

We have now said enough in outlines about happiness and the virtues, and about friendship and pleasure also. Should we then think that our decision [to study 35 these] has achieved its end? On the contrary, the aim of studies about action, as we say, is surely not to 1179b study and know about each thing, but rather to act on our knowledge. Hence knowing about virtue is not enough, but we must also try to possess and exercise virtue, or become good in any other way.

Now if arguments were sufficient by themselves to 5 make people decent, the rewards they would com-

mand would justifiably have been many and large, as Theognis says, and rightly bestowed. In fact, however, arguments seem to have enough influence to stimulate and encourage the civilized ones among the young people, and perhaps to make virtue take possession of a well-born character that truly loves what is
10 fine; but they seem unable to stimulate the many toward being fine and good.

For the many naturally obey fear, not shame; they avoid what is base because of the penalties, not because it is disgraceful. For since they live by their feelings, they pursue their proper pleasures and the sources of them, and avoid the opposed pains, and
15 have not even a notion of what is fine and [hence] truly pleasant, since they have had no taste of it.

What argument could reform people like these? For it is impossible, or not easy, to alter by argument what has long been absorbed by habit; but, presumably, we should be satisfied to achieve some share in virtue when we already have what we seem to need to become decent.
20 Some think it is nature that makes people good; some think it is habit; some think it is teaching.

The [contribution] of nature clearly is not up to us, but results from some divine cause in those who have it, who are the truly fortunate ones.

Arguments and teaching surely do not influence
25 everyone, but the soul of the student needs to have been prepared by habits for enjoying and hating finely, like ground that is to nourish seed. For someone whose life follows his feelings would not even listen to an argument turning him away, or comprehend it [if he did listen]; and in that state how could he be persuaded to change? And in general feelings seem to yield to force, not to argument.
30 Hence we must already in some way have a character suitable for virtue, fond of what is fine and objecting to what is shameful.

But it is hard for someone to be trained correctly for virtue from his youth if he has not been brought up under correct laws, since the many, especially the young, do not find it pleasant to live in a temperate and resistant way. Hence laws must prescribe their
35 upbringing and practices; for they will not find these things painful when they get used to them.
1180a Presumably, however, it is not enough to get the correct upbringing and attention when they are young; rather, they must continue the same practices

and be habituated to them when they become men. Hence we need laws concerned with these things also, and in general with all of life. For the many yield to compulsion more than to argument, and to 5 sanctions more than to what is fine.

This, some think, is why legislators should urge people towards virtue and exhort them to aim at what is fine, on the assumption that anyone whose good habits have prepared him decently will listen to them, but should impose corrective treatments and penalties on anyone who disobeys or lacks the right nature, and completely expel an incurable. For the decent 10 person, it is assumed, will attend to reason because his life aims at what is fine, while the base person, since he desires pleasure, has to receive corrective treatment by pain, like a beast of burden; that is why it is said that the pains imposed must be those most contrary to the pleasures he likes.

As we have said, then, someone who is to be good 15 must be finely brought up and habituated, and then must live in decent practices, doing nothing base either willingly or unwillingly. And this will be true if his life follows some sort of understanding and correct order that has influence over him.

A father's instructions, however, lack this influence and compelling power; and so in general do the in- 20 structions of an individual man, unless he is a king or someone like that. Law, however, has the power that compels; and law is reason that proceeds from a sort of intelligence and understanding. Besides, people become hostile to an individual human being who opposes their impulses even if he is correct in opposing them; whereas a law's prescription of what is decent is not burdensome.

And yet, only in Sparta, or in a few other cities as 25 well, does the legislator seem to have attended to upbringing and practices. In most other cities they are neglected, and each individual citizen lives as he wishes, "laying down the rules for his children and wife," like a Cyclops.

It is best, then, if the community attends to upbringing, and attends correctly. If, however, the community 30 neglects it, it seems fitting for each individual to promote the virtue of his children and his friends — to be able to do it, or at least to decide to do it.

From what we have said, however, it seems he will be better able to do it if he acquires legislative science. For, clearly, attention by the community works 35 through laws, and decent attention works through excellent laws; and whether the laws are written or unwritten, for the education of one or of many, seems unimportant, as it is in music, gymnastics and other practices. For just as in cities the provisions of law and the [prevailing] types of character have influence, similarly a father's words and habits have influence, and all the more because of kinship and because of the benefits he does; for his children are already fond of him and naturally ready to obey.

Moreover, education adapted to an individual is actually better than a common education for everyone, just as individualized medical treatment is better. For though generally a feverish patient benefits from rest and starvation, presumably some patient does not; nor does the boxing instructor impose the same way of fighting on everyone. Hence it seems that treatment in particular cases is more exactly right when each person gets special attention, since he then more often gets the suitable treatment.

Nonetheless a doctor, a gymnastics trainer and everyone else will give the best individual attention if they also know universally what is good for all, or for these sorts. For sciences are said to be, and are, of what is common [to many particular cases].

Admittedly someone without scientific knowledge may well attend properly to a single person, if his experience has allowed him to take exact note of what happens in each case, just as some people seem to be their own best doctors, though unable to help anyone else at all. None the less, presumably, it seems that someone who wants to be an expert in a craft and a branch of study should progress to the universal, and come to know that, as far as possible; for that, as we have said, is what the sciences are about.

Then perhaps also someone who wishes to make people better by his attention, many people or few, should try to acquire legislative science, if we will become good through laws. For not just anyone can improve the condition of just anyone, or the person presented to him; but if anyone can it is the person with knowledge, just as in medical science and the others that require attention and intelligence.

Next, then, should we examine whence and how someone might acquire legislative science? Just as in other cases [we go to the practitioner], should we go to the politicians? For, as we saw, legislative science seems to be a part of political science.

But is the case of political science perhaps apparently different from the other sciences and capacities? For evidently in others the same people, e.g. doctors or painters, who transmit the capacity to others actively practice it themselves. By contrast, it is the sophists who advertise that they teach politics but none of them practices it. Instead, those who practice it are the political activists, and they seem to act on some sort of capacity and experience rather than thought.

For evidently they neither write nor speak on such questions, though presumably it would be finer to do this than to compose speeches for the law courts or the Assembly; nor have they made politicians out of their own sons or any other friends of theirs. And yet it would be reasonable for them to do this if they were able; for there is nothing better than the political capacity that they could leave to their cities, and nothing better that they could decide to produce in themselves, or, therefore, in their closest friends.

Certainly experience would seem to contribute quite a lot; otherwise people would not have become better politicians by familiarity with politics. Hence those who aim to know about political science would seem to need experience as well.

By contrast, those of the sophists who advertise [that they teach political science] appear to be a long way from teaching; for they are altogether ignorant about the sort of thing political science is, and the sorts of things it is about. For if they had known what it is, they would not have taken it to be the same as rhetoric, or something inferior to it, or thought it an easy task to assemble the laws with good reputations and then legislate. For they think they can select the best laws, as though the selection itself did not require comprehension, and as though correct judgment were not the most important thing, as it is in music.

It is those with experience in each area who judge the products correctly and who comprehend the method or way of completing them, and what fits with what; for if we lack experience, we must be satisfied with noticing that the product is well or badly made, as with painting. Now laws would seem to be the products of political science; how, then, could someone acquire legislative science, or judge which laws are best, from laws alone? For neither do we appear to become experts in medicine by reading textbooks.

And yet doctors not only try to describe the [recognized] treatments, but also distinguish different [physical] states, and try to say how each type of patient might be cured and must be treated. And what they say seems to be useful to the experienced, though useless to the ignorant.

Similarly, then, collections of laws and political systems might also, presumably, be most useful if we are capable of studying them and of judging what is done finely or in the contrary way, and what sorts of [elements] fit with what. Those who lack the [proper] state [of experience] when they go through these collections will not manage to judge finely, unless they can do it all by themselves [without training], though they might come to comprehend them better by going through them.

Since, then, our predecessors have left the area of legislation uncharted, it is presumably better to examine it ourselves instead, and indeed to examine political systems in general, and so to complete the philosophy of human affairs, as far as we are able.

First, then, let us try to review any sound remarks our predecessors have made on particular topics. Then let us study the collected political systems, to see from them what sorts of things preserve and destroy cities, and political systems of different types; and what causes some cities to conduct politics well, and some badly.

For when we have studied these questions, we will perhaps grasp better what sort of political system is best; how each political system should be organized so as to be best; and what habits and laws it should follow.

Politics

Book I

Chapter 1

We see that every city-state is a community of some sort, and that every community is established for the sake of some good (for everyone performs every action for the sake of what he takes to be good). Clearly, then, while every community aims at some good, the community that has the most authority of all and encompasses all the others aims highest, that is to say, at the good that has the most authority of all. This community is the one called a city-state, the community that is political.

Those, then, who think that the positions of statesman, king, household manager, and master of slaves are the same, are not correct. For they hold that each of these differs not in kind, but only in whether the subjects ruled are few or many: that if, for example, someone rules few people, he is a master; if more, a household manager; if still more, he has the position of statesman or king — the assumption being that there is no difference between a large household and a small city-state. As for the positions of statesman and king, they say that someone who is in charge by

himself has the position of king, whereas someone who follows the principles of the appropriate science, ruling and being ruled in turn, has the position of statesman. But these claims are not true. What I am saying will be clear, if we examine the matter according to the method of investigation that has guided us elsewhere. For as in other cases, a composite has to be analyzed until we reach things that are incomposite, since these are the smallest parts of the whole, so if we also examine the parts that make up a city-state, we shall see better both how these differ from each other, and whether or not it is possible to gain some expertise in connection with each of the things we have mentioned.

Chapter 2

If one were to see how these things develop naturally from the beginning, one would, in this case as in others, get the best view of them. First, then, those who cannot exist without each other necessarily form a couple, as [1] female and male do for the sake of procreation (they do not do so from deliberate choice, but, like other animals and plants, because the urge

Reprinted from Aristotle, *Politics*, translated, with introduction and notes, by C. D. C. Reeve (Indianapolis: Hackett Publishing Company, 1998) by permission of the publisher.

to leave behind something of the same kind as themselves is natural), and [2] as a natural ruler and what is naturally ruled do for the sake of survival. For if something is capable of rational foresight, it is a natural ruler and master, whereas whatever can use its body to labor is ruled and is a natural slave. That is why the same thing is beneficial for both master and slave.

There is a natural distinction, of course, between what is female and what is servile. For, unlike the blacksmiths who make the Delphian knife, nature produces nothing skimpily, but instead makes a single thing for a single task, because every tool will be made best if it serves to perform one task rather than many. Among non-Greeks, however, a woman and a slave occupy the same position. The reason is that they do not have anything that naturally rules; rather their community consists of a male and a female slave. That is why our poets say "it is proper for Greeks to rule non-Greeks," implying that non-Greek and slave are in nature the same.

The first thing to emerge from these two communities is a household, so that Hesiod is right when he said in his poem, "First and foremost: a house, a wife, and an ox for the plow." For an ox is a poor man's servant. The community naturally constituted to satisfy everyday needs, then, is the household; its members are called "meal-sharers" by Charondas and "manger-sharers" by Epimenides the Cretan. But the first community constituted out of several households for the sake of satisfying needs other than everyday ones is a village.

As a colony or offshoot from a household, a village seems to be particularly natural, consisting of what some have called "sharers of the same milk," sons and the sons of sons. That is why city-states were originally ruled by kings, as nations still are. For they were constituted out of people who were under kingships; for in every household the eldest rules as a king. And so the same holds in the offshoots, because the villagers are blood relatives. This is what Homer is describing when he says: "Each one lays down the law for his own wives and children." For they were scattered about, and that is how people dwelt in the distant past. The reason all people say that the gods too are ruled by a king is that they themselves were ruled by kings in the distant past, and some still are. Human beings model the shapes of the gods on

their own, and do the same to their way of life as well.

A complete community constituted out of several villages, once it reaches the limit of total self-sufficiency, practically speaking, is a city-state. It comes to be for the sake of living, but it remains in existence for the sake of living well. That is why every city-state exists by nature, since the first communities do. For the city-state is their end, and nature is an end; for we say that each thing's nature—for example, that of a human being, a horse, or a household—is the character it has when its coming-into-being has been completed. Moreover, that for the sake of which something exists, that is to say, its end, is best, and self-sufficiency is both end and best.

It is evident from these considerations, then, that a city-state is among the things that exist by nature, that a human being is by nature a political animal, and that anyone who is without a city-state, not by luck but by nature, is either a poor specimen or else superhuman. Like the one Homer condemns, he too is "clanless, lawless, and homeless." For someone with such a nature is at the same time eager for war, like an isolated piece in a board game.

It is also clear why a human being is more of a political animal than a bee or any other gregarious animal. Nature makes nothing pointlessly, as we say, and no animal has speech except a human being. A voice is a signifier of what is pleasant or painful, which is why it is also possessed by the other animals (for their nature goes this far: they not only perceive what is pleasant or painful but signify it to each other). But speech is for making clear what is beneficial or harmful, and hence also what is just or unjust. For it is peculiar to human beings, in comparison to the other animals, that they alone have perception of what is good or bad, just or unjust, and the rest. And it is community in these that makes a household and a city-state.

The city-state is also prior in nature to the household and to each of us individually, since a whole is necessarily prior to its parts. For if the whole body is dead, there will no longer be a foot or a hand, except homonymously, as one might speak of a stone "hand" (for a dead hand will be like that); but everything is defined by its task and by its capacity; so that in such condition they should not be said to be the same things but homonymous ones. Hence that the city-

state is natural and prior in nature to the individual
25 is clear. For if an individual is not self-sufficient when
separated, he will be like all other parts in relation
to the whole. Anyone who cannot form a community
with others, or who does not need to because he is
self-sufficient, is no part of a city-state—he is either
30 a beast or a god. Hence, though an impulse toward
this sort of community exists by nature in everyone,
whoever first established one was responsible for the
greatest of goods. For as a human being is the best
of the animals when perfected, so when separated
from law and justice he is worst of all. For injustice
is harshest when it has weapons, and a human being
grows up with weapons for virtue and practical wisdom to use, which are particularly open to being
used for opposite purposes. Hence he is the most
35 unrestrained and most savage of animals when he
lacks virtue, as well as the worst where food and sex
are concerned. But justice is a political matter; for
justice is the organization of a political community,
and justice decides what is just.

Chapter 3

1253b Since it is evident from what parts a city-state is constituted, we must first discuss household management,
for every city-state is constituted from households.
The parts of household management correspond in
turn to the parts from which the household is constituted, and a complete household consists of slaves
and free. But we must first examine each thing in
5 terms of its smallest parts, and the primary and smallest parts of a household are master and slave, husband
and wife, father and children. So we shall have to
examine these three things to see what each of them
is and what features it should have. The three in
question are [1] mastership, [2] "marital" science (for
we have no word to describe the union of woman
10 and man), and [3] "procreative" science (this also
lacks a name of its own). But there is also a part
which some believe to be identical to household management, and others believe to be its largest part. We
shall have to study its nature too. I am speaking of
what is called wealth acquisition.
15   But let us first discuss master and slave, partly to
see how they stand in relation to our need for necessities, but at the same time with an eye to knowledge

about this topic, to see whether we can acquire some
better ideas than those currently entertained. For, as
we said at the beginning, some people believe that
mastership is a sort of science, and that mastership,
household management, statesmanship, and the science of kingship are all the same. But others believe
that it is contrary to nature to be a master (for it is
by law that one person is a slave and another free, 20
whereas by nature there is no difference between
them), which is why it is not just either; for it involves force.

Chapter 4

Since property is part of the household, the science
of property acquisition is also a part of household
management (for we can neither live nor live well
without the necessities). Hence, just as the specialized
crafts must have their proper tools if they are going 25
to perform their tasks, so too does the household
manager. Some tools are inanimate, however, and
some are animate. The ship captain's rudder, for example, is an inanimate tool, but his lookout is an
animate one; for where crafts are concerned every
assistant is classed as a tool. So a piece of property is 30
a tool for maintaining life; property in general is the
sum of such tools; a slave is a piece of animate property
of a sort; and all assistants are like tools for using tools.
For, if each tool could perform its task on command or
by anticipating instructions, and if like the statues of
Daedalus or the tripods of Hephaestus—which the 35
poet describes as having "entered the assembly of the
gods of their own accord"—shuttles wove cloth by
themselves, and picks played the lyre, a master craftsman would not need assistants, and masters would
not need slaves.

What are commonly called tools are tools for pro- 1254a
duction. A piece of property, on the other hand, is
for action. For something comes from a shuttle beyond the use of it, but from a piece of clothing or a
bed we get only the use. Besides, since action and
production differ in kind, and both need tools, their 5
tools must differ in the same way as they do. Life
consists in action, not production. Therefore, slaves
too are assistants in the class of things having to do
with action. Pieces of property are spoken of in the
same way as parts. A part is not just a part of another

10 thing, but is *entirely* that thing's. The same is also true of a piece of property. That is why a master is just his slave's *master*, not his simply, while a slave is not just his master's *slave*, he is entirely his.

It is clear from these considerations what the nature and capacity of a slave are. For anyone who, despite being human, is by nature not his own but someone 15 else's is a natural slave. And he is someone else's when, despite being human, he is a piece of property; and a piece of property is a tool for action that is separate from its owner.

Chapter 5

But whether anyone is really like that by nature or not, and whether it is better or just for anyone to be a slave or not (all slavery being against nature) — these are the things we must investigate next. And it is not difficult either to determine the answer by argument or to learn it from actual events. For ruling and being 20 ruled are not only necessary, they are also beneficial, and some things are distinguished right from birth, some suited to rule and others to being ruled. There are many kinds of rulers and ruled, and the better the ruled are, the better the rule over them always 25 is; for example, rule over humans is better than rule over beasts. For a task performed by something better is a better task, and where one thing rules and another is ruled, they have a certain task. For whenever a number of constituents, whether continuous with one another or discontinuous, are combined into one 30 common thing, a ruling element and a subject element appear. These are present in living things, because this is how nature as a whole works. (Some rule also exists in lifeless things: for example, that of a harmony. But an examination of that would perhaps take us too far afield.)

Soul and body are the basic constituents of an animal: the soul is the natural ruler; the body the 35 natural subject. But of course one should examine what is natural in things whose condition is natural, not corrupted. One should therefore study the human being too whose soul and body are in the best possible condition; one in whom this is clear. For in depraved people, and those in a depraved condition, the body will often seem to rule the soul, because their condition is bad and unnatural.

1254b

At any rate, it is, as I say, in an animal that we can first observe both rule of a master and rule of a statesman. For the soul rules the body with the rule of a master, whereas understanding rules desire with 5 the rule of a statesman or with the rule of a king. In these cases it is evident that it is natural and beneficial for the body to be ruled by the soul, and for the affective part to be ruled by understanding (the part that has reason), and that it would be harmful to everything if the reverse held, or if these elements were equal. The same applies in the case of human beings with respect to the other animals. For domestic animals are by nature better than wild ones, and it 10 is better for all of them to be ruled by human beings, since this will secure their safety. Moreover, the relation of male to female is that of natural superior to natural inferior, and that of ruler to ruled. But, in fact, the same holds true of all human beings. 15

Therefore those people who are as different from others as body is from soul or beast from human, and people whose task, that is to say, the best thing to come from them, is to use their bodies are in this condition — those people are natural slaves. And it is better for them to be subject to this rule, since it is also better for the other things we mentioned. For 20 he who can belong to someone else (and that is why he actually does belong to someone else), and he who shares in reason to the extent of understanding it, but does not have it himself (for the other animals obey not reason but feelings), is a natural slave. The difference in the use made of them is small, since both slaves and domestic animals help provide the necessities with their bodies. 25

Nature tends, then, to make the bodies of slaves and free people different too, the former strong enough to be used for necessities, the latter useless for that sort of work, but upright in posture and possessing all the other qualities needed for political life — qualities 30 divided into those needed for war and those for peace. But the opposite often happens as well: some have the bodies of free men; others, the souls. This, at any rate, is evident: if people were born whose bodies alone were as excellent as those found in the statues of the gods, everyone would say that those who were 35 substandard deserved to be their slaves. And if this is true of the body, it is even more justifiable to make such a distinction with regard to the soul; but the soul's beauty is not so easy to see as the body's.

1255a

It is evident, then, that there are some people, some of whom are naturally free, others naturally slaves, for whom slavery is both just and beneficial.

Chapter 6

But it is not difficult to see that those who make the opposite claim are also right, up to a point. For slaves and slavery are spoken of in two ways: for there are also slaves—that is to say, people who are in a state
5 of slavery—by *law*. The law is a sort of agreement by which what is conquered in war is said to belong to the victors. But many of those conversant with the law challenge the justice of this. They bring a writ of illegality against it, analogous to that brought against a speaker in the assembly. Their supposition is that it is monstrous if someone is going to be the subject and slave to whatever has superior power and is able
10 to subdue him by force. Some hold the latter view, others the former; and this is true even among the wise.

The reason for this dispute, and for the overlap in the arguments, is this: virtue, when it is equipped with resources, is in a way particularly adept in the use of force; and anything that conquers always does
15 so because it is outstanding in *some* good quality. This makes it seem that force is not without virtue, and that only the justice of the matter is in dispute. For one side believes that justice is benevolence, whereas the other believes that it is precisely the rule of the more powerful that is just. At any event, when these accounts are disentangled, the other arguments
20 have neither force nor anything else to persuade us that the one who is more virtuous should not rule or be master.

Then there are those who cleave exclusively, as they think, to justice of a sort (for law is justice of a sort), and maintain that enslavement in war is just. But at the same time they imply that it is not just. For it is possible for wars to be started unjustly, and no one would say that someone is a slave if he did
25 not deserve to be one; otherwise, those regarded as the best born would be slaves or the children of slaves, if any of them were taken captive and sold. That is why indeed they are not willing to describe *them*, but only non-Greeks, as slaves. Yet, in saying this, they
30 are seeking precisely the natural slave we talked about

in the beginning. For they have to say that some people are slaves everywhere, whereas others are slaves nowhere.

The same holds of noble birth. Nobles regard themselves as well born wherever they are, not only when they are among their own people, but they regard non-Greeks as well born only when they are at home. They imply a distinction between a good birth and freedom that is unqualified and one that is not un-qualified. As Theodectes' Helen says: "Sprung from 35 divine roots on both sides, who would think that I deserve to be called a slave?" But when people say this, they are in fact distinguishing slavery from free-dom, well born from low born, in terms of virtue and vice alone. For they think that good people come 40 from good people in just the way that human comes from human, and beast from beast. But often, though nature does have a tendency to bring this about, it is 1255b nevertheless unable to do so.

It is clear, then, that the objection with which we began has something to be said for it, and that the one lot are not always natural slaves, nor the other naturally free. But it is also clear that in some cases 5 there is such a distinction—cases where it is beneficial and just for the one to be master and the other to be slave, and where the one ought to be ruled and the other ought to exercise the rule that is natural for him (so that he is in fact a master), and where misrule harms them both. For the same thing is beneficial for both part and whole, body and soul; and a slave 10 is a sort of part of his master—a sort of living but separate part of his body. Hence, there is a certain mutual benefit and mutual friendship for such mas-ters and slaves as deserve to be by nature so related. When their relationship is not that way, however, but is based on law, and they have been subjected to force, the opposite holds. 15

Chapter 7

It is also evident from the foregoing that the rule of a master is not the same as rule of a statesman and that the other kinds of rule are not all the same as one another, though some people say they are. For rule of a statesman is rule over people who are natu-rally free, whereas that of a master is rule over slaves; rule by a household manager is a monarchy, since

every household has one ruler; rule of a statesman is
20 rule over people who are free and equal.

A master is so called not because he possesses a
science but because he is a certain sort of person.
The same is true of slave and free. None the less,
there could be such a thing as mastership or slave-
craft; for example, the sort that was taught by the man
in Syracuse who for a fee used to train slave boys in
25 their routine services. Lessons in such things might
well be extended to include cookery and other services of that type. For different slaves have different
tasks, some of which are more esteemed, others more
concerned with providing the necessities: "slave is
superior to slave, master to master," as the proverb
30 says. All such sciences, then, are the business of slaves.

Mastership, on the other hand, is the science of using
slaves; for it is not in acquiring slaves but in using them
that someone is a master. But there is nothing grand
or impressive about this science. The master needs to
know how to command the things that the slave needs
35 to know how to do. Hence for those who have the resources not to bother with such things, a steward takes
on this office, while they themselves engage in politics
or philosophy. As for the science of acquiring slaves
(the just variety of it), it is different from both of these,
and is a kind of warfare or hunting.

These, then, are the distinctions to be made regarding slave and master.

Chapter 8

Since a slave has turned out to be part of property,
1256a let us now study property and wealth acquisition generally, in accordance with our guiding method. The
first problem one might raise is this: Is wealth acquisition the same as household management, or a part
of it, or an assistant to it? If it is an assistant, is it in
5 the way that shuttle making is assistant to weaving,
or in the way that bronze smelting is assistant to statue
making? For these do not assist in the same way: the
first provides tools, whereas the second provides the
matter. (By the matter I mean the substrate, that out
of which the product is made—for example, wool for
10 the weaver and copper for the bronze smelter.)

It is clear that household management is not the
same as wealth acquisition, since the former uses resources, while the latter provides them; for what sci-

ence besides household management uses what is in
the household? But whether wealth acquisition is a part
of household management or a science of a different
kind is a matter of dispute. For if someone engaged in
wealth acquisition has to study the various sources of
wealth and property, and property and wealth have 15
many different parts, we shall first have to investigate
whether farming is a part of household management
or some different type of thing, and likewise the supervision and acquisition of food generally.

But there are many kinds of food too. Hence the
lives of both animals and human beings are also of 20
many kinds. For it is impossible to live without food,
so that differences in diet have produced different
ways of life among the animals. For some beasts live
in herds and others live scattered about, whichever
is of benefit for getting their food, because some of
them are carnivorous, some herbivorous, and some 25
omnivorous. So, in order to make it easier for them
to get hold of these foods, nature has made their ways
of life different. And since the same things are not
naturally pleasant to each, but rather different things
to different ones, among the carnivores and herbivores
themselves the ways of life are different.

Similarly, among human beings too; for their ways
of life differ a great deal. The idlest are nomads; for 30
they live a leisurely life, because they get their food
effortlessly from their domestic animals. But when
their herds have to change pasture, they too have to
move around with them, as if they were farming a
living farm. Others hunt for a living, differing from
one another in the sort of hunting they do. Some live 35
by raiding; some—those who live near lakes, marshes,
rivers, or a sea containing fish—live from fishing;
and some from birds or wild beasts. But the most
numerous type lives off the land and off cultivated 40
crops. Hence the ways of life, at any rate those whose
fruits are natural and do not provide food through
exchange or commerce, are roughly speaking these:
nomadic, raiding, fishing, hunting, farming. But 1256b
some people contrive a pleasant life by combining
several of these, supplementing their way of life where
it has proven less than self-sufficient; for example,
some live both a nomadic and a raiding life, others,
both a farming and a hunting one, and so on, each 5
spending their lives as their needs jointly compel.

It is evident that nature itself gives such property
to all living things, both right from the beginning,

when they are first conceived, and similarly when they have reached complete maturity. Animals that 10 produce larvae or eggs produce their offspring together with enough food to last them until they can provide for themselves. Animals that give birth to live offspring carry food for their offspring in their own bodies for a certain period, namely, the natural substance we call milk. Clearly, then, we must suppose 15 in the case of fully developed things too that plants are for the sake of animals, and that the other animals are for the sake of human beings, domestic ones both for using and eating, and most but not all wild ones for food and other kinds of support, so that clothes 20 and the other tools may be got from them. If then nature makes nothing incomplete or pointless, it must have made all of them for the sake of human beings. That is why even the science of warfare, since hunting is a part of it, will in a way be a natural part of property acquisition. For this science ought to be used not only against wild beasts but also against those human 25 beings who are unwilling to be ruled, but naturally suited for it, as this sort of warfare is naturally just.

One kind of property acquisition is a natural part of household management, then, in that a store of the goods that are necessary for life and useful to the community of city-state or household either must be available to start with, or household management 30 must arrange to make it available. At any rate, true wealth seems to consist in such goods. For the amount of this sort of property that one needs for the self-sufficiency that promotes the good life is not unlimited, though Solon in his poetry says it is: "No boundary to wealth has been established for human beings." But such a limit or boundary has been established, 35 just as in the other crafts. For none has any tool unlimited in size or number, and wealth is a collection of tools belonging to statesmen and household managers.

It is clear, then, that there is a natural kind of property acquisition for household managers and statesmen, and it is also clear why this is so.

Chapter 13

1259b It is evident, then, that household management is 20 more seriously concerned with human beings than with inanimate property, with their virtue more than

with its (which we call wealth), and with the virtue of free people more than with that of slaves.

The first problem to raise about slaves, then, is this: Has the slave some other virtue more estimable than those he has as a tool or servant, such as temperance, courage, justice, and other such states of character? Or has he none besides those having to do with the 25 physical assistance he provides? Whichever answer one gives, there are problems. If slaves have temperance and the rest, in what respect will they differ from the free? If they do not, absurdity seems to result, since slaves are human and have a share in reason. Roughly the same problem arises about women and children. Do they too have virtues? Should women 30 be temperate, courageous, and just, or a child be temperate or intemperate? Or not?

The problem of natural rulers and natural subjects, and whether their virtue is the same or different, needs to be investigated in general terms. If both of them should share in what is noble-and-good, why should one of them rule once and for all and the 35 other be ruled once and for all? (It cannot be that the difference between them is one of degree. Ruling and being ruled differ in kind, but things that differ in degree do not differ in that way.) On the other hand, if the one shares in what is noble-and-good, and not the other, that would be astonishing. For if the ruler is not going to be temperate and just, how will he rule well? And if the subject is not going to be, how will he be ruled well? For if he is intemperate 40 and cowardly, he will not perform any of his duties. 1260a It is evident, therefore, that both must share in virtue, but that there are differences in their virtue (as there are among those who are naturally ruled).

Consideration of the soul leads immediately to this view. The soul by nature contains a part that rules 5 and a part that is ruled, and we say that each of them has a different virtue, that is to say, one belongs to the part that has reason and one to the nonrational part. It is clear, then, that the same holds in the other cases as well, so that most instances of ruling and being ruled are natural. For free rules slaves, male rules female, and man rules child in different ways, 10 because, while the parts of the soul are present in all these people, they are present in different ways. The deliberative part of the soul is entirely missing from a slave; a woman has it but it lacks authority; a child has it but it is incompletely developed. We must

suppose, therefore, that the same necessarily holds of
15 the virtues of character too: all must share in them,
but not in the same way; rather, each must have a
share sufficient to enable him to perform his own
task. Hence a ruler must have virtue of character
complete, since his task is unqualifiedly that of a
master craftsman, and reason is a master craftsman,
but each of the others must have as much as pertains
to him. It is evident, then, that all those mentioned
have virtue of character, and that temperance, cour-
20 age, and justice of a man are not the same as those
of a woman, as Socrates supposed: the one courage
is that of a ruler, the other that of an assistant, and
similarly in the case of the other virtues too.

If we investigate this matter in greater detail, it will
become clear. For people who talk in generalities,
25 saying that virtue is a good condition of the soul, or
correct action, or something of that sort, are deceiving
themselves. It is far better to enumerate the virtues,
as Gorgias does, than to define them in this general
way. Consequently, we must take what the poet says
about a woman as our guide in every case: "To a
woman silence is a crowning glory"—whereas this
does not apply to a man. Since a child is incompletely
30 developed, it is clear that his virtue too does not
belong to him in relation to himself but in relation
to his end and his leader. The same holds of a slave
in relation to his master. But we said that a slave is
useful for providing the necessities, so he clearly needs
35 only a small amount of virtue—just so much as will
prevent him from inadequately performing his tasks
through intemperance or cowardice.

If what we have now said is true, one might raise the
problem of whether vulgar craftsmen too need to have
virtue; for they often fail to perform their tasks through
intemperance. Or are the two cases actually very different? For a slave shares his master's life, whereas a vulgar
40 craftsman is at a greater remove, and virtue pertains to
him to just the extent that slavery does; for a vulgar
1260b craftsman has a kind of delimited slavery. Moreover, a
slave is among the things that exist by nature, whereas
no shoemaker is, nor any other sort of craftsman. It is
evident, then, that the cause of such virtue in a slave
must be the master, not the one who possesses the science of teaching him his tasks. Hence those who deny
5 reason to slaves, but tell us to give them orders only,
are mistaken; for slaves should be admonished more
than children.

But we may take these matters to be determined
in this way. As for man and woman, father and children, the virtue relevant to each of them, what is
good in their relationship with one another and what 10
is not good, and how to achieve the good and avoid
the bad—it will be necessary to go through all these
in connection with the constitutions. For every household is part of a city-state, these are parts of a household, and the virtue of a part must be determined by
looking to the virtue of the whole. Hence both women
and children must be educated with an eye to the 15
constitution, if indeed it makes any difference to the
virtue of a city-state that its children be virtuous, and
its women too. And it must make a difference, since
half the free population are women, and from children come those who participate in the constitution.

So, since we have determined some matters, and 20
must discuss the rest elsewhere, let us regard the
present discussion as complete, and make a new beginning. And let us first investigate those who have
expressed views about the best constitution.

Book II

Chapter 1

Since we propose to study which political community
is best of all for people who are able to live as ideally
as possible, we must investigate other constitutions
too, both some of those used in city-states that are
said to be well governed, and any others described 30
by anyone that are held to be good, in order to see
what is correct or useful in them, but also to avoid
giving the impression that our search for something
different from them results from a desire to be clever.
Let it be held, instead, that we have undertaken this
inquiry because the currently available constitutions
are not in good condition. 35

We must begin, however, at the natural starting
point of this investigation. For all citizens must share
everything, or nothing, or some things but not others.
It is evidently impossible for them to share nothing.
For a constitution is a sort of community, and so they 40
must, in the first instance, share their location; for
one city-state occupies one location, and citizens
share that one city-state. But is it better for a city- 1261a

state that is to be well managed to share everything possible? Or is it better to share some things but not others? For the citizens could share children, women, and property with one another, as in Plato's *Republic*. For Socrates claims there that children, women, and property should be communal. So is what we have now better, or what accords with the law described in the *Republic*?

Chapter 2

That women should be common to all raises many difficulties. In particular, it is not evident from Socrates' arguments why he thinks this legislation is needed. Besides, the end he says his city-state should have is impossible, as in fact described, yet nothing has been settled about how one ought to delimit it. I am talking about the assumption that it is best for a city-state to be as far as possible all one unit; for that is the assumption Socrates adopts. And yet it is evident that the more of a unity a city-state becomes, the less of a city-state it will be. For a city-state naturally consists of a certain multitude; and as it becomes more of a unity, it will turn from a city-state into a household, and from a household into a human being. For we would surely say that a household is more of a unity than a city-state and an individual human being than a household. Hence, even if someone could achieve this, it should not be done, since it will destroy the city-state.

A city-state consists not only of a number of people, but of people of different kinds, since a city-state does not come from people who are alike. For a city-state is different from a military alliance. An alliance is useful because of the weight of numbers, even if they are all of the same kind, since the natural aim of a military alliance is the sort of mutual assistance that a heavier weight provides if placed on a scales. A nation will also differ from a city-state in this sort of way, provided the multitude is not separated into villages, but is like the Arcadians. But things from which a unity must come differ in kind. That is why reciprocal equality preserves city-states, as we said earlier in the *Ethics*, since this must exist even among people who are free and equal. For they cannot all rule at the same time, but each can rule for a year or some other period. As a result they all rule, just as all would be shoemakers and carpenters if they

changed places, instead of the same people always being shoemakers and the others always carpenters. But since it is better to have the latter also where a political community is concerned, it is clearly better, where possible, for the same people always to rule. But among those where it is not possible, because all are naturally equal, and where it is at the same time just for all to share the benefits or burdens of ruling, it is at least possible to approximate to this if those who are equal take turns and are similar when out of office. For they rule and are ruled in turn, just as if they had become other people. It is the same way among those who are ruling; some hold one office, some another.

It is evident from these considerations that a city-state is not a natural unity in the way some people say it is, and that what has been alleged to be the greatest good for city-states destroys them, whereas what is good for a thing preserves it. It is also evident on other grounds that to try to make a city-state too much a unity is not a better policy. For a household is more self-sufficient than a single person, and a city-state than a household; and a city-state tends to come about as soon as a community's population is large enough to be fully self-sufficient. So, since what is more self-sufficient is more choiceworthy, what is less a unity is more choiceworthy than what is more so.

Chapter 3

But even if it is best for a community to be as much a unity as possible, this does not seem to have been established by the argument that everyone says "mine" and "not mine" at the same time (for Socrates takes this as an indication that his city-state is completely one). For "all" is ambiguous. If it means each individually, perhaps more of what Socrates wants will come about, since each will then call the same woman his wife, the same person his son, the same things his property, and so on for each thing that befalls him. But this is not in fact how those who have women and children in common will speak. They will *all* speak, but not *each*. And the same goes for property: all, not each. It is evident, then, that there is an equivocation involved in "all say." (For "all," "both," "odd," and "even," are ambiguous, and give rise to contentious arguments even in discussion.) Hence in one sense it would be good if all said the same, but not possible, whereas in the other sense it is in no way conducive to concord.

But the phrase is also harmful in another way, since what is held in common by the largest number of people receives the least care. For people give most attention to their own property, less to what is communal, or only as much as falls to them to give. For apart from anything else, the thought that someone 35 else is attending to it makes them neglect it the more (just as a large number of household servants sometimes give worse service than a few). Each of the citizens acquires a thousand sons, but they do not belong to him as an individual: any of them is equally 40 the son of any citizen, and so will be equally neglected 1262a by them all. Besides, each says "mine" of whoever among the citizens is doing well or badly in this sense, that he is whatever fraction he happens to be of a certain number. What he really means is "mine or so-and-so's," referring in this way to each of the thousand or however many who constitute the city-state. And even then he is uncertain, since it is not clear 5 who has had a child born to him, or one who once born survived. Yet is this way of calling the same thing "mine" as practiced by each of two or ten thousand people really better than the way they in fact use "mine" in city-states? For the same person is called "my son" by one person, "my brother" by another, "my 10 cousin" by a third, or something else in virtue of some other connection of kinship or marriage, one's own marriage, in the first instance, or that of one's relatives. Still others call him "my fellow clansman" or "my fellow tribesman." For it is better to have a cousin of one's own than a son in the way Socrates describes.

Moreover, it is impossible to prevent people from having suspicions about who their own brothers, sons, 15 fathers, and mothers are. For the resemblances that occur between parents and children will inevitably be taken as evidence of this. And this is what actually happens, according to the reports of some of those who write accounts of their world travels. They say that some of the inhabitants of upper Libya have their 20 women in common, and yet distinguish the children on the basis of their resemblance to their fathers. And there are some women, as well as some females of other species such as mares and cows, that have a strong natural tendency to produce offspring resem-

bling their sires, like the mare in Pharsalus called "Just."

Chapter 4

Moreover, there are other difficulties that it is not easy for the establishers of this sort of community to 25 avoid, such as voluntary or involuntary homicides, assaults, or slanders. None of these is pious when committed against fathers, mothers, or not too distant relatives (just as none is even against outsiders). Yet they are bound to occur even more frequently among those who do not know their relatives than among 30 those who do. And when they do occur, the latter can perform the customary expiation, whereas the former cannot.

It is also strange that while making sons communal, he forbids sexual intercourse only between lovers, but does not prohibit sexual love itself or the other practices which, between father and son or a pair of brothers, are most indecent, since even the love alone 35 is. It is strange, too, that Socrates forbids such sexual intercourse solely because the pleasure that comes from it is so intense, but regards the fact that the lovers are father and son or brother and brother as making no difference. 40

It would seem more useful to have the farmers rather than the guardians share their women and children. For there will be less friendship where women and children are held in common. But it is 1262b the *ruled* who should be like that, in order to promote obedience and prevent rebellion.

In general, the results of such a law are necessarily the opposite of those of a good law, and the opposite 5 of those that Socrates aims to achieve by organizing the affairs of children and women in this way. For we regard friendship as the greatest of goods for city-states, since in this condition people are least likely to factionalize. And Socrates himself particularly praises unity in a city-state, something that is held to be, and that he himself says is, the result of friendship. 10 (Similarly, in the erotic dialogues, we know that Aristophanes says that lovers, because of their excessive friendship, want to grow together and become one instead of two. The result in such circumstances, however, is that one or both has necessarily perished.)

But in a city-state this sort of community inevitably makes friendship watery, in that father hardly ever says "mine" of son, or son of father. For just as adding a lot of water to a drop of sweet wine makes the mixture undetectable, so it is with the kinship connections expressed in these names, since in a constitution of this sort a father has least reason to cherish his sons as sons, or a son his father as a father, or brothers each other as brothers. For there are two things in particular that cause human beings to love and cherish something: their own and their favorite. And neither can exist among those governed in this way.

But there is also a lot of confusion about the way in which the children, once born, will be transferred from the farmers and craftsmen to the guardians, and vice versa. Those who do the transferring and receiving are sure to know who has been transferred to whom. Besides, in these cases the results we mentioned earlier must of necessity happen even more often — I mean assaults, love affairs, and murders. For those who have been transferred to the other citizens will no longer call the guardians "brothers," "children," "fathers," or "mothers," nor will those who have been transferred to the guardians use these terms of the other citizens, so as to avoid committing, through kinship, any such offenses.

So much for our conclusions about community of women and children.

Chapter 5

The next topic to investigate is property, and how those in the best constitution should arrange it. Should it be owned in common, or not? One could investigate these questions even in isolation from the legislation dealing with women and children. I mean even if women and children belong to separate individuals, which is in fact the practice everywhere, it still might be best for property either to be owned or used communally. For example, [1] the land might be owned separately, while the crops grown on it are communally stored and consumed (as happens in some nations). [2] Or it might be the other way around: the land might be owned and farmed communally, while the crops grown on it are divided up among individuals for their private use (some non-

Greeks are also said to share things in this way). [3] Or both the land and the crops might be communal.

If the land is worked by others, the constitution is different and easier. But if the citizens do the work for themselves, property arrangements will give rise to a lot of discontent. For if the citizens happen to be unequal rather than equal in the work they do and the profits they enjoy, accusations will inevitably be made against those who enjoy or take a lot but do little work by those who take less but do more. It is generally difficult to live together and to share in any human enterprise, particularly in enterprises such as these. Travelers away from home who share a journey together show this clearly. For most of them start quarreling because they annoy one another over humdrum matters and little things. Moreover, we get especially irritated with those servants we employ most regularly for everyday services.

These, then, and others are the difficulties involved in the common ownership of property. The present practice, provided it was enhanced by virtuous character and a system of correct laws, would be much superior. For it would have the good of both — by "of both" I mean of the common ownership of property and of private ownership. For while property should be in some way communal, in general it should be private. For when care for property is divided up, it leads not to those mutual accusations, but rather to greater care being given, as each will be attending to what is his own. But where use is concerned, virtue will ensure that it is governed by the proverb "friends share everything in common."

Such a practice is already present in outline form in some city-states, which implies that it is not impracticable. In well-managed city-states, in particular, some elements exist, whereas others could come to be. For although each citizen does own private property, he makes part of it available for his friends to use and keeps part for his own use. For example, in Sparta they pretty much have common use of each other's slaves, and dogs and horses also; and when on a journey in the countryside, they may take what provisions they need from the fields. Evidently, then, it is better for property to be private and its use communal. It is the legislator's special task to see that people are so disposed.

40   Besides, to regard a thing as one's own makes an enormous difference to one's pleasure. For the love each person feels for himself is no accident, but is
1263b something natural. Selfishness is rightly criticized. But it is not just loving oneself, it is loving oneself more than one should, just as in the case of the love of money (since practically everyone does love each
5   of these things). Moreover, it is very pleasant to help one's friends, guests, or companions, and do them favors, as one can if one has property of one's own. But those who make the city-state too much a unity by abolishing private property exclude these pleasures. They also openly take away the tasks of two of the virtues: of temperance in regard to women (for it is a fine thing to stay away from another man's woman
10   out of temperance), and generosity with one's property, since one cannot show oneself to be generous, nor perform any generous action (for it is in the use made of property that generosity's task lies).
15   Such legislation may seem attractive, and humane. For anyone who hears it accepts it gladly, thinking that all will have an amazing friendship for all, particularly when someone blames the evils now existing in constitutions on property's not being communal
20   (I mean lawsuits brought against one another over contracts, perjury trials, and flattery of the rich). Yet none of these evils is caused by property not being communal but by vice. For we see that those who own and share communal property have far more disagreements than those whose property is separate.
25   But we consider those disagreeing over what they own in common to be few, because we compare them with the many whose property is private. Furthermore, it would be fair to mention not only how many evils people will lose through sharing, but also how many good things. The life they would lead seems to be totally impossible.
      One has to think that the reason Socrates goes
30   astray is that his assumption is incorrect. For a household and a city-state must indeed be a unity up to a point, but not totally so. For there is a point at which it will, as it goes on, not be a city-state, and another at which, by being nearly not a city-state, it will be a worse one. It is as if one were to reduce a harmony
35   to a unison, or a rhythm to a single beat. But a city-state consists of a multitude, as we said before, and should be unified and made into a community by means of education. It is strange, at any rate, that

the one who aimed to bring in education, and who believed that through it the city-state would be excellent, should think to set it straight by measures of this sort, and not by habits, philosophy, and laws—as in Sparta and Crete, where the legislator aimed to make property communal by means of the messes.   40
      And we must not overlook this point, that we should 1264a consider the immense period of time and the many years during which it would not have gone unnoticed if these measures were any good. For practically speaking all things have been discovered, although some have not been collected, and others are known about but not used. The matter would become particularly evident, however, if one could see such a constitution 5 actually being instituted. For it is impossible to construct his city-state without separating the parts and dividing it up into common messes or into clans and tribes. Consequently, nothing else will be legislated except that the guardians should not do any farming, which is the very thing the Spartans are trying to 10 enforce even now.
      But the fact is that Socrates has not said, nor is it easy to say, what the arrangement of the constitution as a whole is for those who participate in it. The multitude of the other citizens constitute pretty well the entire multitude of his city-state, yet nothing has been determined about them, whether the farmers too should have communal property or each his own 15 private property, or whether their women and children should be private or communal. If all is to be common to all in the same way, how will they differ from the guardians? And how will they benefit from submitting to their rule? Or what on earth will prompt them to submit to it—unless the guardians adopt some clever stratagem like that of the Cretans? For the Cretans allow their slaves to have the same other 20 things as themselves, and forbid them only the gymnasia and the possession of weapons. On the other hand, if they too are to have such things, as they do in other city-states, what sort of community will it be? For it will inevitably be two city-states in one, and those 25 opposed to one another. For he makes the guardians into a sort of garrison, and the farmers, craftsmen, and the others into the citizens. Hence the indictments, lawsuits, and such other bad things as he says exist in other city-states will all exist among them. And yet Socrates claims that because of their education they will not need many regulations, such as town or mar- 30

ket ordinances and others of that sort. Yet he gives this education only to the guardians. Besides, he gives the farmers authority over their property, although he requires them to pay a tax. But this is likely to make them much more difficult and presumptuous than the helots, serfs, and slaves that some people have today.

35   But be that as it may, whether these matters are similarly essential or not, nothing at any rate has been determined about them; neither are the related questions of what constitution, education, and laws they will have. The character of these people is not easy to discover, and the difference it makes to the preservation of the community of the guardians is not small. But if Socrates is going to make their women communal and their

1264b property private, who will manage the household in the way the men manage things in the fields? Who will manage it, indeed, if the farmers' women and property are communal? It is futile to draw a comparison with wild beasts in order to show that women should have

5   the same way of life as men: wild beasts do not go in for household management.

The way Socrates selects his rulers is also risky. He makes the same people rule all the time, which becomes a cause of conflict even among people with no merit, and all the more so among spirited and

10   warlike men. But it is evident that he has to make the same people rulers, since the gold from the god has not been mixed into the souls of one lot of people at one time and another at another, but always into the same ones. He says that the god, immediately at their birth, mixed gold into the souls of some, silver into others, and bronze and iron into those who are

15   going to be craftsmen and farmers.

Moreover, even though Socrates deprives the guardians of their happiness, he says that the legislator should make the whole city-state happy. But it is impossible for the whole to be happy unless all, most, or some of its parts are happy. For happiness is not

20   made up of the same things as evenness, since the latter can be present in the whole without being present in either of the parts, whereas happiness cannot. But if the guardians are not happy, who is? Surely not the skilled craftsmen or the multitude of vulgar craftsmen.

These, then, are the problems raised by the constitution Socrates describes, and there are others that

25   are no less great.

Chapter 6

Pretty much the same thing holds in the case of the *Laws*, which was written later, so we had better also briefly examine the constitution there. In fact, Socrates has settled very few topics in the *Republic*: the way in which women and children should be shared in common; the system of property; and the organiza-

30   tion of the constitution. For he divides the multitude of the inhabitants into two parts: the farmers and the defensive soldiers. And from the latter he takes a third, which is the part of the city-state that deliberates and is in authority. But as to whether the farmers and skilled craftsmen will participate in ruling to some extent or not at all, and whether or not they are to own weapons and join in battle—Socrates has settled

35   nothing about these matters. He does think, though, that guardian women should join in battle and receive the same education as the other guardians. Otherwise, he has filled out his account with extraneous discussions, including those about the sort of education the

40   guardians should receive.

1265a Most of the *Laws* consist, in fact, of laws, and he has said little about the constitution. He wishes to make it more generally attainable by actual city-states, yet he gradually turns it back toward the other constitution. For, with the exception of the communal possession of women and property, the other things

5   he puts in both constitutions are the same: the same education, the life of freedom from necessary work, and, on the same principles, the same messes—except that in this constitution he says that there are to be messes for women too; and whereas the other one consisted of one thousand weapon owners, this one is to consist of five thousand. All the Socratic dialogues

10   have something extraordinary, sophisticated, innovative, and probing about them; but it is perhaps difficult to do everything well. Consider, for example, the multitude just mentioned. We must not forget that it would need a territory the size of Babylon or some other unlimitedly large territory to keep five thousand people in idleness, and a crowd of women and

15   servants along with them, many times as great. We should assume ideal conditions, to be sure, but nothing that is impossible.

It is stated that a legislator should look to just two things in establishing his laws: the territory and the people. But it would also be good to add the neighbor-

20

ing regions too, if first, the city-state is to live a political life, not a solitary one; for it must then have the weapons that are useful for waging war not only on its own territory but also against the regions outside

25 it. But if one rejects such a life, both for the individual and for the city-state in common, the need to be formidable to enemies is just as great, both when they are invading its territory and when they are staying away from it.

The amount of property should also be looked at, to see whether it would not be better to determine it differently and on a clearer basis. He says that a person should have as much as he needs in order to

30 live temperately, which is like saying "as much as he needs to live well." For the formulation is much too general. Besides, it is possible to live a temperate life but a wretched one. A better definition is "temperately and generously"; for when separated, the one will lead to poverty, the other to luxury. For these are the only choiceworthy states that bear on the use of

35 property. One cannot use property either mildly or courageously, for example, but one can use it temperately and generously. Hence, too, the states concerned with its use must be these.

It is also strange to equalize property and not to regu-

40 late the number of citizens, leaving the birth rate unrestricted in the belief that the existence of infertility will keep it sufficiently steady no matter how many births there are, because this seems to be what happens in actual city-states. But the same exactness on this mat-

1265b ter is not required in actual city-states as in this one. For in actual city-states no one is left destitute, because property can be divided among however great a number. But, in this city-state, property is indivisible, so that excess children will necessarily get nothing, no matter

5 whether they are few or many. One might well think instead that it is the birth rate that should be limited, rather than property, so that no more than a certain number are born. (One should fix this number by looking to the chances that some of those born will not survive, and that others will be childless.) To leave the

10 number unrestricted, as is done in most city-states, inevitably causes poverty among the citizens; and poverty produces faction and crime. In fact, Pheidon of Corinth, one of the most ancient legislators, thought that the number of citizens should be kept the same as the number of household estates, even if initially they all

15 had estates of unequal size. But in the *Laws*, it is just the

opposite. Our own view as to how these things might be better arranged, however, will have to be given later.

Another topic omitted from the *Laws* concerns the rulers: how they will differ from the ruled. He says that just as warp and woof come from different sorts of wool, so should ruler be related to ruled. Further- 20 more, since he permits a person's total property to increase up to five times its original value, why should this not also hold of land up to a certain point? The division of homesteads also needs to be examined, in case it is disadvantageous to household management. For he assigns two of the separate homesteads resulting from the division to each individual; but it is difficult to run two households. 25

The overall organization tends to be neither a democracy nor an oligarchy but midway between them; it is called a polity, since it is made up of those with hoplite weapons. If, of the various constitutions, he is establishing this as the one generally most acceptable to actual city-states, his proposal is perhaps good, but if as next best after the first constitution, it is 30 not good. For one might well commend the Spartan constitution, or some other more aristocratic one. Some people believe, indeed, that the best constitution is a mixture of all constitutions, which is why 35 they commend the Spartan constitution. For some say that it is made up of oligarchy, monarchy, and democracy; they say the kingship is a monarchy, the office of senators an oligarchy, and that it is governed democratically in virtue of the office of the overseers (because the overseers are selected from the people as a whole). Others of them say that the overseership is a tyranny, and that it is governed democratically 40 because of the messes and the rest of daily life. But in the *Laws* it is said that the best constitution should be composed of democracy and tyranny, constitutions 1266a one might well consider as not being constitutions at all, or as being the worst ones of all. Therefore, the proposal of those who mix together a larger number is better, because a constitution composed of a larger number is better. 5

Next, the constitution plainly has no monarchical features at all, but only oligarchic and democratic ones, with a tendency to lean more toward oligarchy. This is clear from the method of selecting officials. For to select by lot from a previously elected pool is common to both. But it is oligarchic to require richer people to attend the assembly, to vote for officials,

10 and to perform any other political duties, without requiring these things of the others. The same is true of the attempt to ensure that the majority of officials come from among the rich, with the most important ones coming from among those with the highest property assessment.

He also makes the election of the council oligarchic. First, everyone is required to elect candidates from the
15 first property-assessment class, then again in the same way from the second, then from members of the third—except that not everyone was required to elect candidates from members of it or of the fourth class, and only members of the first and second classes are required to elect candidates from members of the fourth. Then from these, he says, an equal number must be selected from each assessment class. As a re-
20 sult, those from the highest assessment classes will be more numerous and better, since some of the common people will not vote because they are not required to.

It is evident from this, and from what we shall say later when our investigation reaches this sort of constitution, that such a constitution should not be
25 constituted out of democracy and monarchy. As for the elections of officials, electing from the elected is dangerous. For, if even a relatively small number of people combine, the election will always turn out the way they want.

This, then, is how things stand concerning the
30 constitution of the *Laws*.

Chapter 9

1269a There are two things to investigate about the constitution of Sparta, of Crete, and, in effect, about the other
30 constitutions also. First, is there anything legislated in it that is good or bad as compared with the best organization? Second, is there anything legislated in it that is contrary to the fundamental principle or character of the intended constitution?

It is generally agreed that to be well-governed a constitution should have leisure from necessary tasks. But
35 the way to achieve this is not easy to discover. For the Thessalian serfs often attacked the Thessalians, just as the helots—always lying in wait, as it were, for their masters' misfortunes—attacked the Spartans. Nothing like this has so far happened in the case of the Cretans.
40 Perhaps the reason is that, though they war with one

another, the neighboring city-states never ally themselves with the rebels: it benefits them to do so, since 1269b they also possess subject peoples themselves. Sparta's neighbors, on the other hand, the Argives, Messenians, and Arcadians, were all hostile. The Thessalians, too, 5 first experienced revolts because they were still at war with their neighbors, the Achaeans, Perrhaebeans, and Magnesians. If nothing else, it certainly seems that the management of serfs, the proper way to live together with them, is a troublesome matter. For if they are given license, they become arrogant and claim to merit equality with those in authority, but if they live miserably, they hate and conspire. It is clear, then, that those 10 whose system of helotry leads to these results still have not found the best way.

Furthermore, the license where their women are concerned is also detrimental both to the deliberately chosen aims of the constitution and to the happiness of the city-state as well. For just as a household has a 15 man and a woman as parts, a city-state, too, is clearly to be regarded as being divided almost equally between men and women. So in all constitutions in which the position of women is bad, half the city-state should be regarded as having no laws. And this is exactly what has happened in Sparta. For the legislator, wishing the whole city-state to have endurance, makes his wish evident where the men are concerned, but has been negli- 20 gent in the case of the women. For being free of all constraint, they live in total intemperance and luxury. The inevitable result, in a constitution of this sort, is that wealth is esteemed. This is particularly so if the citizens are dominated by their women, like most military and warlike races (except for the Celts and some 25 others who openly esteemed male homosexuality). So it is understandable why the original author of the myth of Ares and Aphrodite paired the two; for all warlike men seem obsessed with sexual relations with either men or women. That is why the same happened to the 30 Spartans, and why in the days of their hegemony, many things were managed by women. And yet what difference is there between women rulers and rulers ruled by women? The result is the same. Audacity is not useful in everyday matters, but only, if at all, in war. Yet Spartan women were very harmful even here. They 35 showed this quite clearly during the Theban invasion; for they were of no use at all, like women in other city-states, but caused more confusion than the enemy.

So it seems that license with regard to women initially occurred in Sparta for explicable reasons. For Spartan men spent a great deal of time away from home
40 during their wars with the Argives, and again with the Arcadians and Messenians. So when leisure returned,
1270a they placed themselves in the hands of their legislator, already prepared thanks to military life, which includes
5 many parts of virtue. But we are told that when he attempted to bring the women under his laws, they resisted and he retreated. These, then, are the causes of what happened, and so, clearly, of the present error as well. But of course we are not investigating the question
10 of whom we should excuse and whom not, but what is correct and what is not.

The fact that the position of women is not well handled seems not only to create a certain unseemliness in the constitution, as we said before, but also to contribute something to the love of money. For what one might criticize next, after the foregoing, is the uneven distribution of property. For because some of the Spar-
15 tans came to own too much wealth and others very little, the land passed into the hands of a few. This is poorly organized by the laws as well. For the legislator
20 quite rightly made it improper to buy or sell an existing landholding, but he left owners free to give or bequeath their land if they wished, even though this inevitably leads to the same results as the other. Indeed, nearly two-fifths of all the land belongs to the women, both because many become heiresses and because large dowries are given. It would have been better if it had
25 been organized so that there was no dowry or only a small or moderate one. But, as it is, one may marry an heiress daughter to whomever one wishes, and if a man dies intestate, the person he leaves as his heir gives her to whom he likes. As a result, in a land capable of supporting fifteen hundred cavalry and thirty thousand
30 hoplites, there were fewer than a thousand. The very facts have clearly shown that the organization of these matters served them badly. For their city-state did not withstand one single blow, but was ruined because of its shortage of men.

It is said that at the time of their early kings, they used to give a share in the constitution to others, so that
35 there was no shortage of men, despite lengthy wars. Indeed, they say that there were once ten thousand Spartiates. Whether this is true or not, a better way to keep high the number of men in a city-state is by leveling property. But the law dealing with the procreation

of children militates against this reform. For the legislator, intending there to be as many Spartiates as possible, 1270b encourages people to have as many children as possible, since there is a law exempting a father of three sons from military service, and a father of four from all taxes. But it is evident that if many children are born, and the land is correspondingly divided, many people will 5 inevitably become poor.

Matters relating to the board of overseers are also badly organized. For this office has sole authority over the most important matters; but the overseers are drawn from among the entire people, so that often very poor men enter it who, because of their poverty, 10 are open to bribery. (This has been shown on many occasions in the past too, and recently among the Andrians; for some, corrupted by bribes, did everything in their power to destroy the entire city-state.) Moreover, because the office is too powerful—in fact, equal in power to a tyranny—even the kings were forced to curry favor with the overseers. And this too has harmed the constitution, for from an aristocracy 15 a democracy was emerging.

Admittedly, the board of overseers does hold the constitution together; for the people remain contented because they participate in the most important office. So, whether it came about because of the legislator or by luck, it benefits Spartan affairs. For 20 if a constitution is to survive, every part of the city-state must want it to exist and to remain as it is. And the kings want this because of the honor given to them; the noble-and-good, because of the senate (since this office is a reward of virtue); and the people, because of the board of overseers (since selections for 25 it are made from all). Still, though the overseers should be chosen from all, it should not be by the present method, which is exceedingly childish.

Furthermore, the overseers have authority over the most important judicial decisions, though they are ordinary people. Hence it would be better if they decided cases not according to their own opinion, but in accordance with what is written, that is to say, 30 laws. Again, the overseers' lifestyle is not in keeping with the aim of the constitution. For it involves too much license, whereas in other respects it is too austere, so that they cannot endure it, but secretly escape from the law and enjoy the pleasures of the body. 35

Matters relating to the senate also do not serve the Spartans well. If the senators were decent people,

with an adequate general education in manly virtue, one might well say that this office benefits the city-state. Although, one might dispute about whether they ought to have lifelong authority in important matters, since the mind has its old age as well as the
40 body. But when they are educated in such a way that even the legislator himself doubts that they are good
1271a men, it is not safe. And in fact in many matters of public concern, those who have participated in this office have been conspicuous in taking bribes and showing favoritism. This is precisely why it is better that the senators not be exempt from INSPECTION, as
5 they are at present. It might seem that the overseers should inspect every office, but this would give too much to the board of overseers, and is not the way we say inspections should be carried out.

The method of electing senators is also defective. Not only is the selection made in a childish way, but
10 it is wrong for someone worthy of the office to ask for it: a man worthy of the office should hold it whether he wants to or not. But the fact is that the legislator is evidently doing the same thing here as in the rest of the constitution. He makes the citizens love honor and then takes advantage of this fact in
15 the election of the senators; for no one would ask for office who did not love honor. Yet the love of honor and of money are *the* causes of most voluntary wrong-doings among human beings.

The question of whether or not it is better for city-states to have a kingship must be discussed later; but it is better to choose each new king, not as now, but
20 on the basis of his own life. (It is clear that even the Spartan legislator himself did not think it possible to make the kings noble-and-good. At any rate he dis-trusts them, on the grounds that they are not suffi-ciently good men. That is precisely why they used to send out a king's opponents as fellow ambassadors, and why they regard faction between the kings as a
25 safeguard for the city-state.)

Nor were matters relating to the messes (or so-called *phiditia*) well legislated by the person who first established them. For they ought to be publicly supported, as they are in Crete. But among the Spar-tans each individual has to contribute, even though some are extremely poor and unable to afford the
30 expense. The result is thus the opposite of the legisla-tor's deliberately chosen aim. He intended the institu-tion of messes to be democratic, but, legislated as

they are now, they are scarcely democratic at all, since the very poor cannot easily participate in them.
35 Yet their traditional way of delimiting the Spartan constitution is to exclude from it those who cannot pay this contribution.

The law dealing with the admirals has been criti-cized by others, and rightly so, since it becomes a cause of faction. For the office of admiral is estab-lished against the kings, who are permanent generals,
40 as pretty much another kingship.

One might also criticize the fundamental prin-ciple of the legislator as Plato criticized it in the
1271b *Laws*. For the entire system of their laws aims at a part of virtue, military virtue, since this is useful for conquest. So, as long as they were at war, they re-mained safe. But once they ruled supreme, they started to decline, because they did not know how to be at leisure, and had never undertaken any kind of
5 training with more authority than military training. Another error, no less serious, is that although they think (rightly) that the good things that people com-pete for are won by virtue rather than by vice, they also suppose (not rightly) that these goods are better than virtue itself.

Matters relating to public funds are also badly orga-
10 nized by the Spartiates. For they are compelled to fight major wars, yet the public treasury is empty, and taxes are not properly paid; for, as most of the land belongs to the Spartiates, they do not scrutinize one another's tax payments. Thus the result the legislator has produced is the opposite of beneficial: he has
15 made his city-state poor and the private individuals into lovers of money.

So much for the Spartan constitution. For these are the things one might particularly criticize in it.

Chapter 12

Some of those who have had something to say about
1273b a constitution took no part in political actions, but always lived privately. About them pretty much every-thing worth saying has been said. Others became
30 legislators, engaging in politics themselves, some in their own city-states, others in foreign ones as well. Some of these men crafted laws only, whereas others, such as Lycurgus and Solon, crafted a constitution too, for they established both laws and constitutions.

35   We have already discussed that of the Spartans. As for Solon, some think he was an excellent legislator because: he abolished an oligarchy which had become too unmixed; he put an end to the slavery of the common people; and he established the ancestral democracy, by mixing the constitution well. For they think the council of the Areopagus is oligarchic; the election
40   of officials aristocratic; and the courts democratic. But
1274a it seems that the first two, the council and the election of officials, existed already, and Solon did not abolish them. On the other hand, by making law courts open to all, he did set up the democracy. That, indeed, is why some people criticize him. They say that when he gave law courts selected by lot authority over all legal cases, he destroyed the other things. For when this ele-
5   ment became powerful, those who flattered the common people like a tyrant changed the constitution into the democracy we have now: Ephialtes and Pericles curtailed the power of the Areopagus, and Pericles introduced payment for jurors. In this way, each popular leader enhanced the power of the people and led them
10   on to the present democracy.

It seems that this did not come about through Solon's deliberate choice, however, but rather more by accident. For the common people were the cause of Athens's naval supremacy during the Persian wars. As a result, they became arrogant, and chose inferior people as their popular leaders when decent people opposed their policies. Solon, at any rate, seems to
15   have given the people only the minimum power necessary, that of electing and inspecting officials (since if they did not even have authority in these, the people would have been enslaved and hostile). But he drew all the officials from among the notable and rich: the
20   *pentakosiomedimnoi*, the *zeugitai*, and the third class, the so-called *hippeis*. But the fourth class, the *thetes*, did not participate in any office.

Book III

Chapter 1

1274b When investigating constitutions, and what each is and is like, pretty well the first subject of investigation concerns a city-state, to see what the city-state is. For as things stand now, there are disputes about this.

Some people say, for example, that a city-state performed a certain action, whereas others say that it was not the city-state that performed the action, but rather the oligarchy or the tyrant did. We see, too, 35 that the entire occupation of statesmen and legislators concerns city-states. Moreover, a constitution is itself a certain organization of the inhabitants of a city-state. But since a city-state is a composite, one that is a whole and, like any other whole, constituted out of many parts, it is clear that we must first inquire into citizens. For a city-state is some sort of multitude 40 of citizens. Hence we must investigate who should be called a citizen, and who the citizen is. For there is often dispute about the citizen as well, since not 1275a everyone agrees that the same person is a citizen. For the sort of person who is a citizen in a democracy is often not one in an oligarchy.

We should leave aside those who acquire the title of citizen in some exceptional way; for example, those who are made citizens. Nor is a citizen a citizen 5 through residing in a place, for resident aliens and slaves share the dwelling place with him. Again, those who participate in the justice system, to the extent of prosecuting others in the courts or being judged there themselves, are not citizens: parties to treaties can also do that (though in fact in many places the participation of resident aliens in the justice system 10 is not even complete, but they need a sponsor, so that their participation in this sort of communal relationship is in a way incomplete). Like minors who are too young to be enrolled in the citizen lists or old people who have been excused from their civic duties, they must be said to be citizens *of a sort*, but not unqualified citizens. Instead, a qualification must 15 be added, such as "incomplete" or "superannuated" or something else like that (it does not matter what, since what we are saying is clear). For we are looking for the unqualified citizen, the one whose claim to citizenship has no defect of this sort that needs to be rectified (for one can raise and solve similar problems 20 about those who have been disenfranchised or exiled).

The unqualified citizen is defined by nothing else so much as by his participation in judgment and office. But some offices are of limited tenure, so they cannot be held twice by the same person at all, or can be held again only after a definite period. Another 25 person, however, holds office indefinitely, such as the juror or assemblyman. Now someone might say that

the latter sort are not officials at all, and do not, because of this, participate in any office as such. Yet surely it would be absurd to deprive of office those who have the most authority. But let this make no difference, since the argument is only about a word. For what a juror and an assemblyman have in com-
30 mon lacks a name that one should call them both. For the sake of definition, let it be indefinite office. We take it, then, that those who participate in office in this way are citizens. And this is pretty much the definition that would best fit all those called citizens.

We must not forget, however, that in case of things
35 in which what underlies differs in kind (one coming first, another second, and so on), a common element either is not present at all, insofar as these things are such, or only in some attenuated way. But we see that constitutions differ in kind from one another, and that some are posterior and others prior; for mistaken or deviant constitutions are necessarily posterior
1275b to those that are not mistaken. (What we mean by "deviant" will be apparent later.) Consequently, the citizen in each constitution must also be different.

That is precisely why the citizen that we defined is above all a citizen in a democracy, and may possibly be one in other constitutions, but not necessarily. For
5 some constitutions have no "the people" or assemblies they legally recognize, but only specially summoned councils and judicial cases decided by different bodies. In Sparta, for example, some cases concerning contracts are tried by one overseer, others by another,
10 whereas cases of homicide are judged by the senate, and other cases by perhaps some other official. It is the same way in Carthage, since there certain officials decide all cases. None the less, our definition of a citizen admits of correction. For in the other constitutions, it is not the holder of indefinite office who is assemblyman and juror, but someone whose office is definite. For it is either to some or to all of the latter
15 that deliberation and judgment either about some or about all matters is assigned.

It is evident from this who the citizen is. For we can now say that someone who is eligible to participate in deliberative and judicial office is a citizen in this city-state, and that a city-state, simply speaking, is a
20 multitude of such people, adequate for life's self-sufficiency.

Chapter 4

The next thing to investigate after what we have just *1276b* discussed is whether the virtue of a good man and of a good citizen should be regarded as the same, or not the same. But surely if we should indeed investigate this, the virtue of a citizen must first be grasped in some sort of outline.

Just as a sailor is one of a number of members of a community, so, we say, is a citizen. And though 20 sailors differ in their capacities (for one is an oarsman, another a captain, another a lookout, and others have other sorts of titles), it is clear both that the most exact account of the virtue of each sort of sailor will be peculiar to him, and similarly that there will also be some common account that fits them all. For the 25 safety of the voyage is a task of all of them, since this is what each of the sailors strives for. In the same way, then, the citizens too, even though they are dissimilar, have the safety of the community as their task. But the community is the constitution. Hence the virtue of a citizen must be suited to his constitution. Consequently, if indeed there are several kinds 30 of constitution, it is clear that there cannot be a single virtue that is the virtue—the complete virtue—of a good citizen. But the good man, we say, does express a single virtue: the complete one. Evidently, then, it is possible for someone to be a good citizen without having acquired the virtue expressed by a good 35 man.

By going through problems in a different way, the same argument can be made about the best constitution. If it is impossible for a city-state to consist entirely of good people, and if each must at least perform his own task well, and this requires virtue, and if it is impossible for all the citizens to be similar, then the virtue of a citizen and that of a good man cannot be 40 a single virtue. For that of the good citizen must be *1277a* had by all (since this is necessary if the city-state is to be best), but the virtue of a good man cannot be had by all, unless all the citizens of a good city-state are necessarily good men. Again, since a city-state consists of dissimilar elements (I mean that just as an animal consists in the first instance of soul and 5 body, a soul of reason and desire, a household of man and woman, and property of master and slave, so a city-state, too, consists of all these, and of other dissimilar kinds in addition), then the citizens cannot all

10 have one virtue, any more than can the leader of a chorus and one of its ordinary members.

It is evident from these things, therefore, that the virtue of a man and of a citizen cannot be unqualifiedly the same.

But will there, then, be anyone whose virtue is the same both as a good citizen and as a good man? We say, indeed, that an excellent ruler is good and 15 possesses practical wisdom, but that a citizen need not possess practical wisdom. Some say, too, that the education of a ruler is different right from the beginning, as is evident, indeed, from the sons of kings being educated in horsemanship and warfare, and from Euripides saying "No subtleties for me . . . but what the city-state needs," (since this implies that rulers should get a special sort of education). But if 20 the virtue of a good ruler is the same as that of a good man, and if the man who is ruled is also a citizen, then the virtue of a citizen would not be unqualifiedly the same as the virtue of a man (though that of a certain sort of citizen would be), since the virtue of a ruler and that of a citizen would not be the same. Perhaps this is why Jason said that he went hungry except when he was a tyrant. He meant that he did not know how to be a private individual.

25 Yet the capacity to rule and be ruled is at any rate praised, and being able to do both well is held to be the virtue of a citizen. So if we take a good man's virtue to be that of a ruler, but a citizen's to consist in both, then the two virtues would not be equally praiseworthy.

Since, then, both these views are sometimes accepted, that ruler and ruled should learn different 30 things and not the same ones, and that a citizen should know and share in both, we may see what follows from that. For there is a rule by a master, by which we mean the kind concerned with the necessities. The ruler does not need to know how to produce these, but rather how to make use of those who do. 35 In fact, the former is servile. (By "the former" I mean actually knowing how to perform the actions of a servant.) But there are several kinds of slaves, we say, since their tasks vary. One part consists of those tasks performed by manual laborers. As their very name implies, these are people who work with their hands. 1277b Vulgar craftsmen are included among them. That is why among some peoples in the distant past craftsmen did not participate in office until extreme democracy

arose. Accordingly, the tasks performed by people ruled in this way should not be learned by a good person, nor by a statesman, nor by a good citizen, except perhaps to satisfy some personal need of his own (for then it is no longer a case of one person 5 becoming master and the other slave).

But there is also a kind of rule exercised over those who are similar in birth and free. This we call "political" rule. A ruler must learn it by being ruled, just as one learns to be a cavalry commander by serving under a cavalry commander, or to be a general by 10 serving under a general, or under a major or a company commander to learn to occupy the office. Hence this too is rightly said, that one cannot rule well without having been ruled. And whereas the virtues of these *are* different, a good citizen must have the knowledge and ability both to be ruled and to rule, and this is the virtue of a citizen, to know the rule 15 of free people from both sides.

In fact, a good man too possesses both, even if a ruler does have a different kind of justice and temperance. For if a good person is ruled, but is a free citizen, his virtue (justice, for example) will clearly not be of one kind, but includes one kind for ruling and another for being ruled, just as a man's and a woman's courage and temperance differ. For a man 20 would seem a coward if he had the courage of a woman, and a woman would seem garrulous if she had the temperance of a good man, since even household management differs for the two of them (for his task is to acquire property and hers to preserve it). Practical wisdom is the only virtue peculiar to a ruler; 25 for the others, it would seem, must be common to both rulers and ruled. At any rate, practical wisdom is not the virtue of one who is ruled, but true opinion is. For those ruled are like makers of flutes, whereas rulers are like the flute players who use them.

So then, whether the virtue of a good man is the 30 same as that of an excellent citizen or different, and how they are the same and how different, is evident from the preceding.

Chapter 6

Since these issues have been determined, the next 1278b thing to investigate is whether we should suppose that there is just one kind of constitution or several, and, if there are several, what they are, how many they are, and how they differ.

A constitution is an organization of a city-state's various offices but, particularly, of the one that has authority over everything. For the governing class has authority in every city-state, and the governing class is the constitution. I mean, for example, that in democratic city-states the people have authority, whereas in oligarchic ones, by contrast, the few have it, and we also say the constitutions of these are different. And we shall give the same account of the other constitutions as well.

First, then, we must set down what it is that a city-state is constituted for, and how many kinds of rule deal with human beings and communal life. In our first discussions, indeed, where conclusions were reached about household management and rule by a master, it was also said that a human being is by nature a political animal. That is why, even when they do not need one another's help, people no less desire to live together, although it is also true that the common benefit brings them together, to the extent that it contributes some part of living well to each. This above all is the end, then, whether of everyone in common or of each separately. But human beings also join together and maintain political communities for the sake of life by itself. For there is perhaps some share of what is noble in life alone, as long as it is not too overburdened with the hardships of life. In any case, it is clear that most human beings are willing to endure much hardship in order to cling to life, as if it had a sort of joy inherent in it and a natural sweetness.

But surely it is also easy to distinguish at least the kinds of rule people talk about, since we too often discuss them in our own external works. For rule by a master, although in truth the same thing is beneficial for both natural masters and natural slaves, is nevertheless rule exercised for the sake of the master's own benefit, and only coincidentally for that of the slave. For rule by a master cannot be preserved if the slave is destroyed. But rule over children, wife, and the household generally, which we call household management, is either for the sake of the ruled or for the sake of something common to both. Essentially, it is for the sake of the ruled, as we see medicine, physical training, and the other crafts to be, but coincidentally it might be for the sake of the rulers as

1279a

well. For nothing prevents the trainer from sometimes being one of the athletes he is training, just as the captain of a ship is always one of the sailors. Thus a trainer or a captain looks to the good of those he rules, but when he becomes one of them himself, he shares coincidentally in the benefit. For the captain is a sailor, and the trainer, though still a trainer, becomes one of the trained.

Hence, in the case of political office too, where it has been established on the basis of equality and similarity among the citizens, they think it right to take turns at ruling. In the past, as is natural, they thought it right to perform public service when their turn came, and then to have someone look to *their* good, just as they had earlier looked to his benefit when they were in office. Nowadays, however, because of the profits to be had from public funds and from office, people want to be in office continuously, as if they were sick and would be cured by being always in office. At any rate, perhaps the latter would pursue office in that way.

It is evident, then, that those constitutions that look to the common benefit turn out, according to what is unqualifiedly just, to be correct, whereas those which look only to the benefit of the rulers are mistaken and are deviations from the correct constitutions. For they are like rule by a master, whereas a city-state is a community of free people.

Chapter 7

Now that these matters have been determined, we must next investigate how many kinds of constitutions there are and what they are, starting first with the correct constitutions. For once they have been defined, the deviant ones will also be made evident.

Since "constitution" and "governing class" signify the same thing, and the governing class is the authoritative element in any city-state, and the authoritative element must be either one person, or few, or many, then whenever the one, the few, or the many rule for the common benefit, these constitutions must be correct. But if they aim at the private benefit, whether of the one or the few or the multitude, they are deviations (for either the participants should not be called citizens, or they should share in the benefits).

A monarchy that looks to the common benefit we customarily call a kingship; and rule by a few but more than one, an aristocracy (either because the 35 best people rule, or because they rule with a view to what is best for the city-state and those who share in it). But when the multitude governs for the common benefit, it is called by the name common to all constitutions, namely, *politeia*. Moreover, this happens reasonably. For while it is possible for one or a few to be outstandingly virtuous, it is difficult for a larger 40 number to be accomplished in every virtue, but it 1279b can be so in military virtue in particular. That is precisely why the class of defensive soldiers, the ones who possess the weapons, has the most authority in this constitution.

Deviations from these are tyranny from kingship, oligarchy from aristocracy, and democracy from pol- 5 ity. For tyranny is rule by one person for the benefit of the monarch, oligarchy is for the benefit of the rich, and democracy is for the benefit of the poor. But none is for their common profit.

Chapter 8

10 We should say a little more about what each of these constitutions is. For certain problems arise, and when one is carrying out any investigation in a philosophical manner, and not merely with a practical purpose in view, it is appropriate not to overlook or omit any- 15 thing, but to make the truth about each clear.

A tyranny, as we said, exists when a monarchy rules the political community like a master; in an oligarchy those in authority in the constitution are the ones who have property. A democracy is the opposite; those who do not possess much property, and are poor, are in authority. The first problem concerns this defini- 20 tion. Suppose that the majority were rich and had authority in the city-state; yet there is a democracy whenever the majority has authority. Similarly, to take the opposite case, suppose the poor were fewer in number than the rich, but were stronger and had authority in the constitution; yet when a small group has authority it is said to be an oligarchy. It would seem, then, that these constitutions have not been 25 well defined. But even if one combines being few with being rich in one case, and being a majority with being poor in the other, and describes the consti-

tutions accordingly (oligarchy as that in which the rich are few in number and hold the offices, and democracy as that in which the poor are many and hold them), another problem arises. For what are we 30 to call the constitutions we just described, those where the rich are a majority and the poor a minority, but each has authority in its own constitution—if indeed there is no other constitution besides those just mentioned?

What this argument seems to make clear is that it is a coincidence that the few have authority in oligarchies and the many in democracies, a result of 35 the fact that everywhere the rich are few and the poor many. That is why, indeed, the reasons just mentioned are not the reasons for the differences. What does distinguish democracy and oligarchy from one another is poverty and wealth: whenever some, 40 whether a minority or a majority, rule because of their wealth, the constitution is necessarily an oligar- 1280a chy, and whenever the poor rule, it is necessarily a democracy. But it turns out, as we said, that the former are in fact few and the latter many. For only a few people are rich, but all share in freedom; and these 5 are the reasons they both dispute over the constitution.

Chapter 9

The first thing one must grasp, however, is what people say the defining marks of oligarchy and democracy are, and what oligarchic and democratic justice are. For [1] they all grasp justice of a sort, but they go only to a certain point and do not discuss the whole of what is just in the most authoritative sense. For example, justice seems to be equality, and it is, but 10 not for everyone, only *for equals*. Justice also seems to be inequality, since indeed it is, but not for everyone, only *for unequals*. They disregard the "for whom," however, and judge badly. The reason is that the judgment concerns themselves, and most people are pretty poor judges about what is their own. 15

So since what is just is just *for certain people*, and consists in dividing things and people in the same way (as we said earlier in the *Ethics*), they agree about what constitutes equality in the thing but disagree about it in the people. This is largely because of what was just mentioned, that they judge badly about what 20 concerns themselves, but also because, since they are both speaking up to a point about justice of a sort, they think they are speaking about what is unqualifiedly just. For one lot thinks that if they are unequal in one respect (wealth, say) they are wholly unequal, whereas the other lot thinks that if they are equal in one respect (freedom, say) they are wholly equal. But about the most authoritative considerations they do not speak.

25 For suppose people constituted a community and came together for the sake of property; then their participation in a city-state would be proportional to their property, and the oligarchic argument would as a result seem to be a powerful one. (For it is not just that someone who has contributed only one mina to a sum of one hundred minas should have equal shares in that sum, whether of the principal or of the interest, 30 with the one who has contributed all the rest.) But suppose [2] they do not do so only for the sake of life, but rather for the sake of living well, since otherwise there could be a city-state of slaves or animals, whereas in fact there is not, because these share neither in happiness nor in a life guided by deliberative choice.

And suppose [3] they do not do so for the sake of an alliance to safeguard themselves from being wronged by anyone, nor [4] to facilitate exchange 35 and mutual assistance, since otherwise the Etruscans and the Carthaginians, and all those who have treaties with one another would virtually be citizens of one city-state. To be sure, they have import agreements, treaties about refraining from injustice, and formal 40 documents of alliance, but no offices common to all of them have been established to deal with these matters; instead each city-state has different ones. Nor 1280b are those in one city-state concerned with what sort of people the others should be, or that none of those covered by the agreements should be unjust or vicious in any way, but only that neither city-state acts unjustly toward the other. But those who are concerned with 5 good government give careful attention to political virtue and vice. Hence it is quite evident that the city-state (at any rate, the one truly so called and not just for the sake of argument) must be concerned with virtue. For otherwise the community becomes an alliance that differs only in location from other alliances in which the allies live far apart, and law 10 becomes an agreement, "a guarantor of just behav-

ior toward one another," as the sophist Lycophron said, but not such as to make the citizens good and just.

It is evident that this is right. For even if [5] one were to bring their territories together into one, so that the city-state of the Megarians was attached to that of the Corinthians by walls, it still would not be a single city-state. Nor would it be so if their citizens 15 intermarried, even though this is one of the forms of community characteristic of city-states. Similarly, if there were some who lived separately, yet not so separately as to share nothing in common, and had laws against wronging one another in their business transactions (for example, if one were a carpenter, another a farmer, another a cobbler, another something else 20 of that sort, and their number were ten thousand), yet they shared nothing else in common besides such things as exchange and alliance — not even in this case would there be a city-state.

What, then, is the reason for this? Surely, it is not because of the nonproximate nature of their community. For suppose they joined together while continuing to share in that way, but each nevertheless treated 25 his own household like a city-state, and the others like a defensive alliance formed to provide aid against wrongdoers only. Even then this still would not be thought a city-state by those who make a precise study of such things, if indeed they continued to associate with one another in the same manner when together as when separated.

Evidently, then, a city-state is not [5] a sharing of a common location, and does not exist for the purpose of [4] preventing mutual wrongdoing and [3] exchan- 30 ging goods. Rather, while these must be present if indeed there is to be a city-state, when all of them *are* present there is still not yet a city-state, but [2] only when households and families live well as a community whose end is a complete and self-sufficient life. But this will not be possible unless they do inhabit one and the same location and practice 35 intermarriage. That is why marriage connections arose in city-states, as well as brotherhoods, religious sacrifices, and the leisured pursuits of living together. For things of this sort are the result of friendship, since the deliberative choice of living together constitutes friendship. The end of the city-state is living well, then, but these other things are for the sake of the end. And a city-state is the community of families

40 and villages in a complete and self-sufficient life,
1281a which we say is living happily and nobly.

So political communities must be taken to exist for
the sake of noble actions, and not for the sake of living
together. Hence those who contribute the most to *this*
sort of community have a larger share in the city-state
5 than those who are equal or superior in freedom or
family but inferior in political virtue, and those who
surpass in wealth but are surpassed in virtue.

It is evident from what has been said, then, that
[1] those who dispute about constitutions all speak
10 about a *part* of justice.

Chapter 11

As for the other cases, we may let them be the topic of
a different discussion. But the view that the multitude
rather than the few best people should be in authority
40 would seem to be held, and while it involves a problem, it perhaps also involves some truth. For the
many, who are not as individuals excellent men, nevertheless can, when they have come together, be bet-
1281b ter than the few best people, not individually but
collectively, just as feasts to which many contribute
are better than feasts provided at one person's expense.
For being many, each of them can have some part
of virtue and practical wisdom, and when they come
5 together, the multitude is just like a single human
being, with many feet, hands, and senses, and so too
for their character traits and wisdom. That is why the
many are better judges of works of music and of
the poets. For one of them judges one part, another
another, and all of them the whole thing.
10 It is in this way that excellent men differ from each
of the many, just as beautiful people are said to differ
from those who are not beautiful, and as things painted by craft are superior to real things: they bring
together what is scattered and separate into one—
although, at least if taken separately, this person's eye
and some other feature of someone else will be more
beautiful than the painted ones.
15 Whether this superiority of the many to the few
excellent people can exist in the case of every people
and every multitude is not clear. Though presumably,
by Zeus, it is clear that in some of them it cannot
possibly do so, since the same argument would apply
to beasts. For what difference is there, practically

speaking, between some people and beasts? But nothing prevents what has been said from being true of 20
some multitude.

By means of these considerations, too, one might
solve the problem mentioned earlier and also the
related one of what the free should have authority
over, that is to say, the multitude of the citizens who
are not rich and have no claim whatsoever arising 25
from virtue. For it would not be safe to have them
participate in the most important offices, since, because of their lack of justice and practical wisdom,
they would inevitably act unjustly in some instances
and make mistakes in others. On the other hand, to
give them no share and not to allow them to participate at all would be cause for alarm. For a state in
which a large number of people are excluded from
office and are poor must of necessity be full of enemies. The remaining alternative, then, is to have them 30
participate in deliberation and judgment, which is
precisely why Solon and some other legislators arrange to have them elect and inspect officials, but
prevent them from holding office alone. For when
they all come together their perception is adequate,
and, when mixed with their betters, they benefit their 35
states, just as a mixture of roughage and pure food-
concentrate is more useful than a little of the latter
by itself. Taken individually, however, each of them
is an imperfect judge.

But this organization of the constitution raises problems itself. In the first place, it might be held that
the same person is able to judge whether or not
someone has treated a patient correctly, and to treat 40
patients and cure them of disease when it is present—
namely, the doctor. The same would also seem to
hold in other areas of experience and other crafts.
Therefore, just as a doctor should be inspected by 1282a
doctors, so others should also be inspected by their
peers. But "doctor" applies to the ordinary practitioner
of the craft, to a master craftsman, and thirdly, to
someone with a general education in the craft. For
there are people of this third sort in (practically speak- 5
ing) all the crafts. And we assign the task of judging
to generally educated people no less than to experts.

Moreover, it might be held that election is the
same way, since choosing correctly is also a task for
experts: choosing a geometer is a task for expert geometers, for example, and choosing a ship's captain is a
task for expert captains. For even if some laymen are 10

also involved in the choice of candidates in the case of some tasks and crafts, at least they do not play a larger role than the experts. According to this argument, then, the multitude should not be given authority over the election or inspection of officials.

But perhaps not all of these things are correctly stated, both because according to the earlier argument the multitude may not be too servile, since each may be a worse judge than those who know, but a better or no worse one when they all come together; and because there are some crafts in which the maker might not be either the only or the best judge — the ones where those who do not possess the craft nevertheless have knowledge of its products. For example, the maker of a house is not the only one who has some knowledge about it; the one who uses it is an even better judge (and the one who uses is the household manager). A captain, too, judges a rudder better than a carpenter, and a guest, rather than the cook, a feast.

This problem might be held to be adequately solved in such a way. But there is another connected with it. For it is held to be absurd for inferior people to have authority over more important matters than decent people do. But inspections and elections of officials are very important things. And in some constitutions, as we said, these are assigned to the people, since the assembly has authority over all such matters. And yet those with low property assessments and of whatever age participate in the assembly, and in deliberation and decision, whereas those with high property assessment are the treasurers and generals and hold the most important offices.

But one can, in fact, also solve this problem in the same way. For perhaps these things are also correctly organized. For it is neither the individual juror, nor the individual councilor, nor the individual assemblyman who is ruling, but the court, the council, and the people, whereas each of the individuals mentioned is only a part of these. (By "part" I mean the councilor, the assemblyman, and the juror.) Hence it is just for the multitude to have authority over the more important matters. For the people, the council, and the court consist of many individuals, and their collective property assessment is greater than the assessment of those who, whether individually or in small groups, hold the important offices. So much for how these matters should be determined.

As to the first problem we mentioned, it makes nothing else so evident as that the laws, when correctly established, should be in authority, and that the ruler, whether one or many, should have authority over only those matters on which the laws cannot pronounce with precision, because it is not easy to make universal declarations about everything.

It is not yet clear, however, what correctly established laws should be like, and the problem stated earlier remains to be solved. For the laws must necessarily be bad or good, and just or unjust, at the same time and in the same way as the constitutions. Still, at least it is evident that the laws must be established to suit the constitution. But if this is so, it is clear that laws that accord with the correct constitutions must be just, and those that accord with the deviant constitutions not just.

Chapter 12

Since in every science and craft the end is a good, the greatest and best good is the end of the science or craft that has the most authority of all of them, and this is the science of statesmanship. But the political good is justice, and justice is the common benefit. Now everyone holds that what is just is some sort of equality, and up to a point, at least, all agree with what has been determined in those philosophical works of ours dealing with ethical issues. For justice is something to someone, and they say it should be something equal to those who are equal. But equality in what and inequality in what, should not be overlooked. For this involves a problem and political philosophy.

Someone might say, perhaps, that offices should be unequally distributed on the basis of superiority in any good whatsoever, provided the people did not differ in their remaining qualities but were exactly similar, since where people differ, so does what is just and what accords with merit. But if this is true, then those who are superior in complexion, or height, or any other good whatsoever will get more of the things with which political justice is concerned. And isn't that plainly false? The matter is evident in the various sciences and capacities. For among flute players equally proficient in the craft, those who are of better birth do not get more or better flutes, since they will not play the flute any better if they do. It is the superior performers who should also

35 get the superior instruments. If what has been said is somehow not clear, it will become so if we take it still further. Suppose someone is superior in flute playing, but is very inferior in birth or beauty; then, even if each of these (I mean birth and beauty) is a greater good than flute playing, and is proportionately more superior to

40 flute playing than he is superior in flute playing, he should still get the outstanding flutes. For the superior-

1283a ity in wealth and birth would have to contribute to the performance, but in fact they contribute nothing to it.

Besides, according to this argument every good would have to be commensurable with every other. For if being a certain height counted more, height in gen-

5 eral would be in competition with both wealth and freedom. So if one person is more outstanding in height than another is in virtue, and if height in general is of more weight than virtue, then all goods would be commensurable. For if a certain amount of size is better than a certain amount of virtue, it is clear that some amount of the one is equal to some amount of the other. Since this is impossible, it is clear that in political mat-

10 ters, too, it is reasonable not to dispute over political office on the basis of just any sort of inequality. For if some are slow runners and others fast, this is no reason for the latter to have more and the former less: it is in athletic competitions that such a difference wins honor. The dispute must be based on the things from

15 which a city-state is constituted. Hence the well-born, the free, and the rich reasonably lay claim to office. For there must be both free people and those with assessed property, since a city-state cannot consist entirely of poor people, any more than of slaves. But if these things are needed in a city-state, so too, it is clear, are justice and political virtue, since a city-state cannot be man-

20 aged without these. Rather, without the former a city-state cannot exist, and without the latter it cannot be well managed.

Book IV

Chapter 1

1288b Among all the crafts and sciences that are concerned not only with a part but that deal completely with some one type of thing, it belongs to a single one to study what is appropriate for each type. For example: what sort of physical training is beneficial for what sort of body, that is to say, what sort is best (for the sort that is appropriate for the sort of body that is naturally best and best equipped is necessarily best), and what single sort of training is appropriate for most

15 bodies (since this too is a task for physical training). Further, if someone wants neither the condition nor the knowledge required of those involved in competition, it belongs no less to coaches and physical trainers to provide this capacity too. We see a similar thing in medicine, ship building, clothing manufacture,

20 and every other craft.

Consequently, it is clear that it belongs to the same science to study: [1] What the best constitution is, that is to say, what it must be like if it is to be most ideal, and if there were no external obstacles. Also [2] which constitution is appropriate for which city-states. For achieving the best constitution is perhaps

25 impossible for many; and so neither the unqualifiedly best constitution nor the one that is best in the circumstances should be neglected by the good legislator and true statesman. Further, [3] which constitution is best given certain assumptions. For a statesman must be able to study how any given constitution might initially come into existence, and how, once in existence, it might be preserved for the longest

30 time. I mean, for example, when some city-state happens to be governed neither by the best constitution (not even having the necessary resources) nor by the best one possible in the existing circumstances, but by a worse one. Besides all these things, a statesman should know [4] which constitution is most appropriate for all city-states. Consequently, those who have

35 expressed views about constitutions, even if what they say is good in other respects, certainly fail when it comes to what is useful. For one should not study only what is best, but also what is possible, and similarly what is easier and more attainable by all. As it is, however, some seek only the constitution that is highest and requires a lot of resources, while others,

40 though they discuss a more attainable sort, do away with the constitutions actually in place, and praise the Spartan or some other. But what should be done is to introduce the sort of organization that people will be easily persuaded to accept and be able to 1289a

participate in, given what they already have, as it is no less a task to reform a constitution than to establish one initially, just as it is no less a task to correct what we have learned than to learn it in the first place. That is why, in addition to what has just been mentioned, a statesman should also be able to help existing constitutions, as was also said earlier. But this is impossible if he does not know [5] how many kinds of constitutions there are. As things stand, however, some people think that there is just one kind of democracy and one of oligarchy. But this is not true. So one must not overlook the varieties of each of the constitutions, how many they are and how many ways they can be combined. And [6] it is with this same practical wisdom that one should try to see both which laws are best and which are appropriate for each of the constitutions. For laws should be established, and all do establish them, to suit the constitution and not the constitution to suit the laws. For a constitution is the organization of offices in city-states, the way they are distributed, what element is in authority in the constitution, and what the end is of each of the communities. Laws, apart from those that reveal what the constitution is, are those by which the officials must rule, and must guard against those who transgress them. Clearly, then, a knowledge of the varieties of each constitution and of their number is also necessary for establishing laws. For the same laws cannot be beneficial for all oligarchies or for all democracies — if indeed there are several kinds, and not one kind of democracy nor one kind of oligarchy only.

Chapter 3

1289b The reason why there are several constitutions is that every city-state has several parts. For in the first place, we see that all city-states are composed of households; and, next, that within this multitude there have to be some who are rich, some who are poor, and some who are in the middle; and that of the rich and of the poor, the one possessing weapons and the other without weapons. We also see that the people comprise a farming part, a trading part, and a vulgar craftsman part. And among the notables there are differences in wealth and in extent of their property — as, for example, in the breeding of horses, since this

is not easy for those without wealth to do. (That is 35 why, indeed, there were oligarchies among those city-states in ancient times whose power lay in their cavalry, and who used horses in wars with their neighbors — as, for example, the Eretrians did, and the Chalcidians, the Magnesians on the river Menander, and many of the others in Asia.) There are also differ- 40 ences based on birth, on virtue, and on everything else of the sort that we characterized as part of a city-state in our discussion of aristocracy, since there we 1290a distinguished the number of parts that are necessary to any city-state. For sometimes all of these parts participate in the constitution, sometimes fewer of them, sometimes more.

It is evident, therefore, that there must be several 5 constitutions that differ in kind from one another, since these parts themselves also differ in kind. For a constitution is the organization of offices, and all consitutions distribute these either on the basis of the power of the participants, or on the basis of some sort of equality common to them (I mean, for example, of the poor or of the rich, or some equality common 10 to both). Therefore, there must be as many constitutions as there are ways of organizing offices on the basis of the superiority and varieties of the parts.

But there are held to be mainly two constitutions: just as the winds are called north or south, and the others deviations from these, so there are also said to be two constitutions, democracy and oligarchy. For 15 aristocracy is regarded as a sort of oligarchy, on the grounds that it is a sort of rule by the few, whereas a so-called polity is regarded as a sort of democracy, just as the west wind is regarded as northerly, and the east as southerly. According to some people, the same thing also happens in the case of harmonies, which are regarded as being of two kinds, the Dorian 20 and the Phrygian, and the other arrangements are called either Phrygian types or Dorian types. People are generally accustomed, then, to think of constitutions in this way. But it is truer and better to distinguish them, as we have, and say that two constitutions (or one) are well formed, and that the others are 25 deviations from them, some from the well-mixed "harmony," and others from the best constitution, the more tightly controlled ones and those that are more like the rule of a master being more oligarchic, and the unrestrained and soft ones democratic.

Chapter 11

1295a What is the best constitution, and what is the best life for most city-states and most human beings, judging neither by a virtue that is beyond the reach of ordinary people, nor by a kind of education that requires natural gifts and resources that depend on luck, nor by the ideal constitution, but by a life that most people can share and a constitution in which most city-states 30 can participate? For the constitutions called aristocracies, which we discussed just now, either fall outside the reach of most city-states or border on so-called polities (that is why the two have to spoken about as one).

35 Decision about all these matters depends on the same elements. For if what is said in the *Ethics* is right, and a happy life is the one that expresses virtue and is without impediment, and virtue is a mean, then the middle life, the mean that each sort of person can actually achieve, must be best. These same defining principles must also hold of the virtue and vice 40 of a city-state or a constitution, since a constitution is a sort of life of city-state.

1295b In all city-states, there are three parts of the city-state: the very rich, the very poor; and, third, those in between these. So, since it is agreed that what is moderate and in a mean is best, it is evident that 5 possessing a middle amount of the goods of luck is also best. For it most readily obeys reason, whereas whatever is exceedingly beautiful, strong, well born, or wealthy, or conversely whatever is exceedingly poor, weak, or lacking in honor, has a hard time obeying reason. For the former sort tend more toward arrogance and major vice, whereas the latter tend too 10 much toward malice and petty vice; and wrongdoing is caused in the one case by arrogance and in the other by malice. Besides, the middle classes are least inclined either to avoid ruling or to pursue it, both of which are harmful to city-states.

Furthermore, those who are superior in the goods 15 of luck (strength, wealth, friends, and other such things) neither wish to be ruled nor know how to be ruled (and this is a characteristic they acquire right from the start at home while they are still children; for because of their luxurious lifestyle they are not accustomed to being ruled, even in school). Those, on the other hand, who are exceedingly deprived of such goods are too humble. Hence the latter do not know how to rule, but only how to be ruled in the way slaves are ruled, whereas the former do not know how to be ruled in any way, but only how to rule as 20 masters rule. The result is a city-state consisting not of free people but of slaves and masters, the one group full of envy and the other full of arrogance. Nothing is further removed from a friendship and a community that is political. For community involves friendship, since enemies do not wish to share even a journey in common. But a city-state, at least, tends to consist as much as possible of people who are equal and similar, and this condition belongs particularly to 25 those in the middle. Consequently, this city-state, the one constituted out of those from which we say the city-state is naturally constituted, must of necessity be best governed. Moreover, of all citizens, those in the middle survive best in city-states. For neither do they desire other people's property as the poor do, nor do 30 other people desire theirs, as the poor desire that of the rich. And because they are neither plotted against nor engage in plotting, they live out their lives free from danger. That is why Phocylides did well to pray: "Many things are best for those in the middle. I want to be in the middle in a city-state."

It is clear, therefore, that the political community that depends on those in the middle is best too, and that city-states can be well governed where those in 35 the middle are numerous and stronger, preferably than both of the others, or, failing that, than one of them. For it will tip the balance when added to either and prevent the opposing extremes from arising. That is precisely why it is the height of good luck if those who are governing own a middle or adequate amount 40 of property, because when some people own an excessive amount and the rest own nothing, either extreme 1296a democracy arises or unmixed oligarchy or, as a result of both excesses, tyranny. For tyranny arises from the most vigorous kind of democracy and oligarchy, but much less often from middle constitutions or those close to them. We will give the reason for this later 5 when we discuss changes in constitutions.

That the middle constitution is best is evident, since it alone is free from faction. For conflicts and dissensions seldom occur among the citizens where there are many in the middle. Large city-states are also freer from faction for the same reason, namely, that more are many in the middle. In small city-states, on the other hand, it is easy to divide all the citizens 10 into two, so that no middle is left and pretty well everyone is either poor or rich. Democracies are also more stable and longer lasting than oligarchies because of those in the middle (for they are more numer-

15 ous in democracies than in oligarchies and participate in office more), since when the poor predominate without these, failure sets in and they are quickly ruined. The fact that the best legislators have come from the middle citizens should be regarded as evidence of this. For Solon was one of these, as is clear from his poems, as were Lycurgus (for he was not a

20 king), Charondas, and pretty well most of the others.

It is also evident from these considerations why most constitutions are either democratic or oligarchic. For because the middle class in them is often small, whichever of the others preponderates (whether the

25 property owners or the people), those who overstep the middle way conduct the constitution to suit themselves, so that it becomes either a democracy or an oligarchy. In addition to this, because of the conflicts and fights that occur between the people and the rich, whenever one side or the other happens to gain more power than its opponents, they establish neither

30 a common constitution nor an equal one, but take their superiority in the constitution as a reward of their victory and make in the one case a democracy and in the other an oligarchy. Then too each of those who achieved leadership in Greece has looked to their own constitutions and established either democracies or oligarchies in city-states, aiming not at the

35 benefit of these city-states but at their own. As a consequence of all this, the middle constitution either never comes into existence or does so rarely and in few places. For among those who have previously held positions of leadership, only one man has ever been persuaded to introduce this kind of organization, and it has now become customary for those in city-

40 states not even to wish for equality, but either to seek
1296b rule or to put up with being dominated.

What the best constitution is, then, and why it is so is evident from these considerations. As for the other constitutions (for there are, as we say, several kinds of democracies and of oligarchies), which of them is to be put first, which second, and so on in

5 the same way, according to whether it is better or worse, is not hard to see now that the best has been determined. For the one nearest to this must of necessity always be better and one further from the middle

worse—provided one is not judging on the basis of certain assumptions. I say "on the basis of certain assumptions," because it often happens that, while one constitution is more choiceworthy, nothing pre- 10 vents a different one from being more beneficial for some.

Book V

Chapter 1

Pretty well all the other topics we intended to treat 1301a have been discussed. Next, after what has been said, we should investigate: [1] the sources of change in constitutions, how many they are and of what sort; [2] what things destroy each constitution; [3] from what sort into what sort they principally change; further, [4] the ways to preserve constitutions in general and each constitution in particular; and, finally, [5] the means by which each constitution is principally preserved.

We should take as our initial starting point that 25 many constitutions have come into existence because, though everyone agrees about justice (that is to say, proportional equality), they are mistaken about it, as we also mentioned earlier. For democracy arose from those who are equal in some respect thinking themselves to be unqualifiedly equal; for because they are equally free, they think they are unqualifiedly equal. 30 Oligarchy, on the other hand, arose from those who are unequal in some respect taking themselves to be wholly unequal; for being unequal in property, they take themselves to be unqualifiedly unequal. The result is that the former claim to merit an equal share of everything, on the grounds that they are all equal, whereas the latter, being unequal, seek to get more (for a bigger share is an unequal one). All these consti- 35 tutions possess justice of a sort, then, although unqualifiedly speaking they are mistaken. And this is why, when one or another of them does not participate in the constitution in accordance with their assumption, they start faction. However, those who would be most justified in starting faction, namely, those who are outstandingly virtuous, are the least likely to do so. 40 For they alone are the ones it is most reasonable to 1301b regard as unqualifiedly unequal. There are also certain people, those of good birth, who suppose that they do not merit a merely equal share because they are unequal in this way. For people are thought to be noble when they have ancestral wealth and virtue behind them.

5   These, practically speaking, are the origins and sources of factions, the factors that lead people to start it. Hence the changes that are due to faction are also of two kinds. [1] For sometimes people aim to change the established constitution to one of another kind—for example, from democracy to oligarchy, or from oligarchy to democracy, or from these to polity or aristocracy, or the latter into the former. [2] But

10   sometimes instead of trying to change the established constitution (for example, an oligarchy or a monarchy), they deliberately choose to keep it, but [2.1] want to have it in their own hands. Again, [2.2] it may be a question of degree: where there is an oligarchy, the aim may be to make the governing class

15   more oligarchic or less so; where there is a democracy, the aim may be to make it more democratic or less so; and similarly, in the case of the remaining constitutions, the aim may be to tighten or loosen them. Again, [2.3] the aim may be to change a certain part of the constitution, for example, to establish or abolish a certain office, as some say Lysander tried to abolish

20   the kingship in Sparta, and King Pausanias the overseership. In Epidamnus too the constitution was partially altered, since a council replaced the tribal rulers, though it is still the case that only those members of the governing class who actually hold office are obliged to attend the public assembly when election to office is taking place. (Having a single supreme official was also an oligarchic feature of this consti-

25   tution.)

      For faction is everywhere due to inequality, when unequals do not receive proportionately unequal things (for example, a permanent kingship is unequal if it exists among equals). For people generally engage in faction in pursuit of equality. But equality is of two sorts: numerical equality and equality according

30   to merit. By numerical equality I mean being the same and equal in number or magnitude. By equality according to merit I mean what is the same and equal in ratio. For example, three exceeds two and two exceeds one by a numerical amount. But four exceeds two and two exceeds one in ratio. For two and one

35   are equal parts of four and two, since both are halves.

But, though people agree that what is unqualifiedly just is what is according to merit, they still disagree, as we said earlier. For some consider themselves wholly equal if they are equal in a certain respect, whereas others claim to merit an unequal share of everything if they are unequal in a certain respect.

      That is also why two constitutions principally arise: democracy and oligarchy. For good birth and virtue 40 are found in few people, whereas wealth and freedom are more widespread. For no city-state has a hundred good and well-born men, but there are rich ones in 1302a many places. But it is a bad thing for a constitution to be organized unqualifiedly and entirely in accord with either sort of equality. This is evident from what actually happens, since no constitution of this kind is stable. The reason is that when one begins from an erroneous beginning, something bad inevitably 5 results in the end. Hence numerical equality should be used in some cases, and equality according to merit in others. Nevertheless, democracy is more stable and freer from faction than oligarchy. For in oligarchies, *two* sorts of faction arise, one among the oligarchs themselves and another against the people. In democ- 10 racies, on the other hand, the only faction is against the oligarchs, since there is none worth mentioning among the people themselves. Besides, a constitution based on the middle classes is closer to a democracy than to an oligarchy, and it is the most secure constitution of this kind.   15

Chapter 8

Our next topic is the preservation of constitutions 1307b generally and each kind of constitution separately. [1] It is clear, in the first place, that if we know what destroys a constitution, we also know what preserves it. For opposites are productive of opposite things, and destruction is opposite to preservation. In well-mixed constitutions, then, if care should be taken to 30 ensure that no one breaks the law in other ways, small violations should be particularly guarded against. For illegality creeps in unnoticed, in just the way that property gets used up by frequent small expenditures: the expense goes unnoticed because it does not occur all at once. For the mind is led to reason fallaciously 35 by them, as in the sophistical argument "if each is small, all are also." In one way this is true; in another false: the whole composed of all the parts is not small, but it is composed of small parts. One thing to guard against, then, is destruction that has a starting point of this sort.

[2] Secondly, we must not put our faith in the devices that are designed to deceive the multitude, since they are shown to be useless by the facts. (I mean the sort of devices used in constitutions that we discussed earlier.)

[3] Next, we should notice that not only some aristocracies but also some oligarchies survive, not because their constitutions are secure, but because those in office treat well both those outside the constitution and those in the governing class. They do this by not being unjust to the nonparticipants and by bringing their leading men into the constitution; by not being unjust to those who love honor by depriving them of honor, or to the many by depriving them of profit; and by treating each other, the ones who do participate, in a democratic manner. For what democrats seek to extend to the multitude, namely, equality, is not only just for those who are similar but also beneficial. That is why, if the governing class is large, many democratic legislative measures prove beneficial, for example, having offices be tenable for six months in order that all those who are similar can participate in them. For those who are similar are already a people of a sort, which is why popular leaders arise even among them, as we mentioned earlier. Furthermore, oligarchies and aristocracies of this sort are less likely to fall into the hands of dynasties. For officials who rule a short time cannot so easily do wrong as those who rule a long time. For this is what causes tyrannies to arise in oligarchies and democracies, since in both constitutions, the ones who attempt to establish a tyranny are either the most powerful (popular leaders in democracies, dynasts in oligarchies) or those who hold the most important offices, and hold them for a long time.

[4] Constitutions are preserved not only because of being far away from what destroys them, but sometimes too because they are nearby. For fear makes people keep a firmer grip on the constitution. Hence those who are concerned about their constitution should excite fears and make faraway dangers seem close at hand, so that the citizens will defend the constitution and, like sentries on night-duty, never relax their guard.

[5] Moreover, one should try to guard against the rivalries and factions of the notables, both by means of the laws and by preventing those who are not involved in the rivalry from getting caught up in it themselves. For it takes no ordinary person to recognize an evil right from the beginning but a man who is a statesman.

[6] As for change from an oligarchy or a polity because of property assessments—if it occurs while the assessments remain the same but money becomes more plentiful, it is beneficial to discover what the total communal assessment is compared with that of the past; with that of last year's in city-states with annual assessment, with that of three or five years ago in larger city-states. If the total is many times greater or many times less than it was when the rates qualifying someone to participate in the constitution were established, it is beneficial to have a law that tightens or relaxes the assessment; tightening it in proportion to the increase if the total has increased, relaxing it or making it less if the total has decreased. For when oligarchies and polities do not do this, the result is that if the total has decreased, an oligarchy arises from the latter and a dynasty from the former, and if it has increased, a democracy arises from a polity and either a polity or a democracy from an oligarchy.

[7] It is a rule common to democracy, oligarchy, monarchy, and every constitution not to allow anyone to grow too great or out of all due proportion, but to try to give small honors over a long period of time rather than large ones quickly. For people are corrupted by major honors, and not every man can handle good luck. Failing that, constitutions should at least try not to take away all at once honors that have been awarded all at once, but to do so gradually. They should try to regulate matters by means of the laws, indeed, so as to ensure that no one arises who is far superior in power because of his friends or wealth. Failing that, they should ensure that such men are removed from the city-state by being ostracized.

[8] But since people also attempt to stir up change because of their private lives, an office should be set up to keep an eye on those whose lifestyles are not beneficial to the constitution, whether to the democracy in a democracy, to the oligarchy in an oligarchy, or similarly for each of the other constitutions. For the same reasons, one must guard against the prospering of the city-state one part at a time. A remedy for

this is always to place the conduct of affairs and the offices in the hands of opposite parts. (I mean that the decent are opposite to the multitude, the poor to the rich.) Another remedy is to try to mix the multitude of the poor with that of the rich or to increase the middle class, since this dissolves faction caused by inequality.

[9] But the most important thing in every constitution is for it have the laws and the management of other matters organized in such a way that it is impossible to make a profit from holding office. One should pay particular heed to this in oligarchies. For the many are not as resentful at being excluded from office—they are even glad to be given the leisure to attend to their private affairs—as they are when they think that officials are stealing public funds. At any rate, they are then pained both at not sharing in office and at not sharing in its profits. Indeed, the only way it is possible for democracy and aristocracy to coexist is if someone instituted this, since it would then be possible for both the notables and the multitude to have what they want. For allowing everyone to hold office is democratic, but having the notables actually hold the offices is aristocratic. But this is what will happen if it is impossible to profit from office. For the poor will not want to hold office, because there is no profit in it, but will prefer to attend to their private affairs, whereas the rich will be able to hold it, because they need no support from public funds. The result will be that the poor will become rich through spending their time working, and the notables will not have to be ruled by anybody and everybody. But to prevent public funds from being stolen, the transfer of the money should take place in the presence of all citizens, and copies of the accounts should be deposited with each clan, company, and tribe. And to ensure that people will hold office without seeking profit, there should be a law that assigns honors to reputable officials.

[10] In democracies, the rich should be treated with restraint, not only by not having redistributions of their property but by not having redistributions of their incomes either (as happens unnoticed in some constitutions). It is also better to prevent the rich, even if they are willing to do so, from taking on expensive but useless public services, such as equipping choruses, officiating at torch races, and other

similar things. In an oligarchy, on the other hand, one should take good care of the poor, and distribute offices that yield some gain to them. If a rich person treats them arrogantly, his punishment should be greater than if he treated a member of his own class arrogantly. Inheritances should be passed on not by bequest but by kinship, and the same person should not receive more than one inheritance. In this way, property holdings would be more equitable, and more of the poor could join the ranks of the rich. It is beneficial, both in democracy and in oligarchy, to give either equality or preference in all other matters to those who participate least in the constitution, the rich in a democracy and the poor in an oligarchy. But the offices of the constitution that have supreme authority should be kept solely or largely in the hands of those who do participate in the constitution.

Chapter 9

Those who are to hold the offices with supreme authority should possess three qualities: first, friendship for the established constitution; next, the greatest possible capacity for the tasks of office; third, in each constitution the sort of virtue or justice that is suited to the constitution (for if what is just is not the same in all constitutions, there must be differences in the virtue of justice as well). But there is a problem. When all of these qualities are not found in the same person, how is the choice to be made? For example, if one man is an expert general but is vicious and no friend to the constitution, whereas another is just and friendly to it, how should the choice be made? It seems that one should consider two things: which quality does everyone have a larger share in, and which a smaller one? That is why, in the case of a generalship, one should consider experience more than virtue. For everyone shares in generalship less, but in decency more. In the case of guardianship or stewardship, on the other hand, the opposite holds. For these require more virtue than the many possess, but the knowledge they require is common to all. One might also raise the following problem. If someone has the capacity for the tasks of office as well as friendship for the constitution, why does he also need virtue, since even the first two will produce beneficial results? Or is it possible for someone who possesses these two qualities to be weak-willed, so that just as people can fail to serve their own interests well even though they have the knowledge and are friendly to themselves, so nothing prevents them from behaving in the same way where the common interest is concerned?

Simply speaking, everything in laws that we say is beneficial to constitutions also preserves those consti-
15 tutions, as does the most important fundamental principle, so often mentioned, of keeping watch to ensure that the multitude that wants the constitution is stronger than the multitude that does not.

In addition to all this, one thing must not be overlooked, which is in fact overlooked by deviant constitutions: the mean. For many of the things that are
20 held to be democratic destroy democracies, and many that are held to be oligarchic destroy oligarchies. But those who think that this is the only kind of virtue push the constitution to extremes. They do not know that constitutions are just like parts of the body. A straight nose is the most beautiful, but one that deviates from being straight and tends toward being hooked or snub can nevertheless still be beautiful to
25 look at. Yet if it is tightened still more toward the extreme, the part will first be thrown out of due proportion, and in the end it will cease to look like a nose at all, because it has too much of one and too little of the other of these opposites. The same holds of the other parts as well. This can also happen in
30 the case of the constitutions. For it is possible for an oligarchy or a democracy to be adequate even though it has diverged from the best organization. But if someone tightens either of them more, he will first make the constitution worse, and in the end it will
35 not be a constitution at all. That is why legislators and statesmen should not be ignorant about which democratic features preserve a democracy and which destroy it, or which oligarchic features have these effects on an oligarchy. For neither of these constitutions can exist and survive without rich people and the multitude, but when a leveling of property occurs, the resulting constitution is necessarily of a different
40 kind. Hence by destroying these classes through ex-
1310a treme legislation, they destroy their constitution.

A mistake is made in both democracies and oligarchies. In democracies popular leaders make it where the multitude have authority over the laws. For they divide the city-state in two by always fighting with the rich, yet they should do the opposite, and always 5 be regarded as spokesmen for the rich. In oligarchies, the oligarchs should be regarded as spokesmen for the people, and should take oaths that are the opposite of the ones they take nowadays. For in some oligarchies, they now swear "and I will be hostile to the people and will plan whatever wrongs I can against them." But they ought to hold and to seem to hold 10 the opposite view, and declare in their oaths that "I will not wrong the people."

But of all the ways that are mentioned to make a constitution last, the most important one, which everyone now despises, is for citizens to be educated in a way that suits their constitutions. For the most beneficial laws, even when ratified by all who are 15 engaged in politics, are of no use if people are not habituated and educated in accord with the constitution — democratically if the laws are democratic and oligarchically if they are oligarchic. For if weakness of will indeed exists in a single individual, it also exists in a city-state. But being educated in a way that suits the constitution does not mean doing whatever 20 pleases the oligarchs or those who want a democracy. Rather, it means doing the things that will enable the former to govern oligarchically and the latter to have a democratic constitution. In present-day oligarchies, however, the sons of the rulers live in luxury, whereas the sons of the poor are hardened by exercise and toil, so that the poor are more inclined to stir up change and are better able to do so. In those 25 democracies that are held to be particularly democratic, the very opposite of what is beneficial has become established. The reason for this is that they define freedom incorrectly. For there are two things by which democracy is held to be defined: by the majority being in supreme authority and by freedom. For justice is held to be equality; equality is for the opinion of the multitude to be in authority; and free- 30 dom is doing whatever one likes. So in democracies of this sort everyone lives as he likes, and "according to his fancy," as Euripides says. But this is bad. For living in a way that suits the constitution should be considered not slavery, but salvation. 35

Such, then, simply speaking, are the sources of change and destruction in constitutions, and the factors through which they are preserved and maintained.

Chapter 10

It remains to go through monarchy too, both the sources of its destruction and the means by which it 40 is naturally preserved. What happens in the case of kingships and tyrannies is pretty much similar to what 1310b we said happens in constitutions. For kingship is akin to aristocracy, and tyranny is a combination of ultimate oligarchy and ultimate democracy. That is why, indeed, tyranny is also the most harmful to those it 5 rules, seeing that it is composed of two bad constitutions and involves the deviations and errors of both.

Each of these kinds of monarchy comes to be from directly opposite circumstances. For kingship came into existence to help the decent against the people, 10 and a king is selected from among the decent men on the basis of a superiority in virtue, or in the actions that spring from virtue, or on the basis of a superiority of family of this sort. A tyrant, on the other hand, comes from the people (that is to say, the multitude) to oppose the notables, so that the people may suffer no injustice at their hands. This is evident from what has happened. For almost all tyrants began as popular 15 leaders who were trusted because they abused the notables. For some tyrannies were established in this way in city-states that had already grown large. Other earlier ones arose when kings departed from ancestral customs and sought to rule more in the manner of a master. Others were established by people elected to the offices that have supreme authority; for in 20 ancient times, the people appointed "doers of the people's business" and "sacred ambassadors" to serve for long periods of time. Still others arose in oligarchies that gave a single elected official authority over the most important offices. For in all these ways people could easily become tyrants if only they wished, 25 because of the power they already possessed through the kingship or through other high office. Thus Pheidon of Argos and others became tyrants having already ruled as kings; the Ionian tyrants and Phalaris as a result of their high office; and Panaetius in Leontini, Cypselus in Corinth, Pisistratus in Athens, Dionysius 30 in Syracuse, and likewise others, from having been popular leaders.

Kingship is, then, as we said, an organization like aristocracy, since it is based on merit, whether individual or familial virtue, or on benefactions, or on these together with the capacity to perform them. For all those who obtained this office either had benefited or were capable of benefiting their city-states or nations. 35 Some, like Codrus, saved their people from enslavement in war; others, like Cyrus, set them free; others acquired or settled territory, like the kings of the Spartans, Macedonians, and Molossians. A king tends 40 to be a guardian, seing to it that property owners suffer no injustice and the people no arrogance. But 1311a tyranny, as has often been said, never looks to the common benefit except for the sake of private profit. A tyrant aims at what is pleasant; a king at what is noble; and that is why it is characteristic of a tyrant to be most acquisitive of wealth and of a king to 5 be most acquisitive of what is noble. Also, a king's bodyguard consists of citizens, whereas a tyrant's consists of foreigners.

That tyranny has the vices of both democracy and oligarchy is evident. From oligarchy comes its taking 10 wealth to be its end (for, indeed, only in this way can the tyrant possibly maintain his bodyguard and his luxury), and its mistrust of the multitude (which is why, indeed, tyrants deprive them of weapons). It is common to both constitutions (oligarchy and tyranny) to ill-treat the multitude, drive them out of the town, and disperse them. From democracy, on the other hand, comes its 15 hostility to the notables, its destruction of them both by covert and overt means, and its exiling of them as rivals in the craft of ruling and impediments to its rule. For it is from the notables that conspiracies arise, since some of them wish to rule themselves, and others not to be enslaved. Hence too the advice that Periander 20 gave to Thrasybulus when he cut down the tallest ears of corn, namely, that it is always necessary to do away with the outstanding citizens.

As has pretty much been said, then, one should consider the sources of change both in constitutions and in monarchies to be the same. For it is because of injustice, fear, and contemptuous treatment that 25 many subjects attack monarchies. In the case of injustice, arrogance is the principal cause, but sometimes too the seizure of private property. The ends sought are also the same there as in tyrannies and kingships, since monarchs possess the great wealth and high 30 office that everyone desires.

In some cases, attack is directed against the person of the rulers; in others, against their office. Those caused by arrogance are directed against the person. Arrogance has many forms, but each of them is a

35 cause of anger; and most angry people act out of revenge, not ambition. For example, the attack on the Pisistratids took place because they abused Harmodius' sister and showed contempt for Harmodius himself (for Harmodius attacked because of his sister, and Aristogeiton because of Harmodius). People plotted against Periander, tyrant of Ambracia, because 40 once when he was drinking with his boyfriend, he 1311b asked whether he was pregnant by him yet. Philip was attacked by Pausanias because he allowed him to be treated arrogantly by Attalus and his coterie. Amyntas the Little was attacked by Derdas because he boasted of having deflowered him. The same is true of the attack on Evagoras of Cyprus by a eunuch; 5 he felt arrogantly treated because Evagoras' son had taken away his wife.

Many attacks have also occurred because of the shameful treatment of other people's bodies by certain monarchs. The attack on Archelaus by Crataeas is an example. For Crataeas always felt disgust at their sex- 10 ual relations, so that even a lesser excuse than the fact that Archelaus did not give him one of his daughters in marriage, though he had agreed to do so, would have been enough. (Instead, when hard pressed in the war against Sirras and Arrabaeus, Archelaus gave his elder daughter to the king of Elimeia and the younger one to his own son Amyntas, thinking that this would be likely to prevent Amyntas from quarreling with his son by Cleopatra.) In any case, the source 15 of Crataeas' estrangement was his disgust at his sexual activities with Archelaus. Hellanocrates of Larisa joined him in the attack for the same reason. For because Archelaus deflowered him and then persistently refused to return him to his home as promised, he thought that the king's sexual relations with him 20 were motivated by arrogance rather than sexual desire. Python and Heracleides of Aenus, on the other hand, killed Cotys to avenge their father. But Adamas revolted on the grounds of arrogant treatment, because he had been castrated by him when he was a boy.

Many people, outraged by blows to their bodies, have, on the grounds of arrogant treatment, killed or tried to kill those responsible, even those who held 25 office or were associated with kingly dynasties. For example, when the Penthilids of Mytilene went around beating up people with clubs, Megacles and his friends attacked and killed them. Later, Smerdis killed Penthilus because he had dragged him away from his wife and beaten him. Decamnichus became leader of the revolt against Archelaus and was the 30 first to incite his adversaries. The reason for his anger was that Archelaus had handed him over to the poet Euripides for flogging (Euripides had been enraged by a remark he had made about his bad breath). Many others have been killed or plotted against for 35 reasons such as these.

Similar attacks also occur out of fear, which is a cause of change in monarchies and constitutions, as we mentioned. For example, Artapanes killed Xerxes because he feared that he would be accused in connection with the murder of Darius. Artapanes had hanged him without being ordered to do so by Xerxes, thinking he would be pardoned, since Xerxes would not remember what orders he had given on account of his dining.

Other attacks on monarchs have been motivated 40 by contempt. Thus, if what the storytellers say is true, a man killed Sardanapalus out of contempt because he saw him carding wool with the women (though 1312a if this is not true of Sardanapalus, it might well be true of someone else). And Dion attacked Dionysius the Younger out of contempt, when he saw that the citizens had the same reactions to his always being 5 drunk. Even a monarch's friends sometimes attack him out of contempt. For the fact that they are trusted makes them contemptuous and confident they will not be discovered. And those who think they have the power to take over as ruler attack out of contempt in a way. For it is because of their power and the contempt for the danger their power gives them that 10 they are ready to try their luck. That is why generals attack their monarchs. For example, Cyrus attacked Astyages out of contempt both for his lifestyle and for his power, which had declined while he was living in luxury. And Seuthes the Thracian attacked Amadocus while he was his general.

Others attack monarchs from several of these mo- 15 tives, as Mithridates attacked Ariobarzanes out of contempt and out of a desire for profit. Attempts of this sort are made principally by those of a bold nature who are assigned to military office by their monarch. For boldness is courage combined with power, and it is because of both of these that people attack and think that they will easily prevail. 20

In cases where the attack is motivated by love of honor, however, the explanation is of a different sort from those previously discussed. For some attack tyrants because they see great profit and high office in store for themselves, but this is not why someone whose attack is motivated by love of honor deliberately chooses to take the risk. The former attack for the reasons mentioned, but the latter do so for the same reason that they would do any other extraordinary deed that made a name for themselves and made them notable in the eyes of others: because they want not monarchy but fame. Nevertheless, very few people are impelled by this sort of motive, since it presupposes a total disregard for their own safety in the event that the action is not successful. They must be guided by the same fundamental principle as Dion (something that is not easy for most people). For Dion accompanied by a small force marched against Dionysius, saying that whatever point he was able to reach, he would be satisfied to have completed that much of the enterprise, and that if, for example, he were killed after having just set foot on land, he would have a noble death.

Like each of the other constitutions, one way a tyranny is destroyed is from the outside, if there is a more powerful constitution opposed to it. For the wish to destroy a tyranny will clearly be present, because the deliberate choices of the two are opposed; and people always do what they wish when they have the power. The constitutions opposed to tyranny are democracy, kingship, and aristocracy. Democracy is opposed to it as "potter to potter" (as Hesiod puts it), since the extreme sort of democracy is also a tyranny. Kingship and aristocracy are opposed to it because of opposition of constitution. That is why the Spartans overthrew a large number of tyrannies, as did the Syracusans while they were well governed.

Another way a tyranny is destroyed is from within, when those participating in it start a faction. This happened in the tyranny of the family of Gelon and, in our own time, in that of the family of Dionysius. The tyranny of Gelon was destroyed when Thrasyboulus, the brother of Hiero, curried favor with Gelon's son and led him into a life of sensual pleasure, in order that he himself might rule. The family got together to destroy not the entire tyranny, but Thrasyboulus. But those who joined them seized the opportunity and expelled all of them. Dion, who was related by marriage to Dionysius, marched against him, won

over the people, and expelled him, but was himself killed afterwards.

The two principal motives people have for attacking tyrannies are hatred and contempt. Of them, hatred always attaches to tyrants, but many overthrows are due to contempt. Evidence of this is the fact that most of those who won the office of tyrant held onto it, whereas their successors almost all lost it right away. For living lives of indulgence, they easily became contemptible and gave others ample opportunity to attack them. Anger must also be considered a part of the hatred, since in a way it gives rise to the same sorts of actions. Often, in fact, it is more conducive to action than hatred. For angry people attack more vehemently because passion does not employ rational calculation. People are particularly apt to be led by their angry spirit on account of arrogant treatment. This was the cause of both the overthrow of the Pisistratid tyranny and that of many others. But hatred employs calculation more than anger does. For anger involves pain, and pain makes rational calculation difficult; but hatred does not involve pain.

To speak summarily, however, the causes that we said destroy unmixed or extreme oligarchies and extreme democracies should also be regarded as destroying tyranny. For these are in fact divided tyrannies.

Kingship is destroyed least by outside factors, which is also why it is long-lasting. The sources of its destruction generally come from within. It is destroyed in two ways: first, when those who participate in the kingship start faction, and, second, when the kings try to manage affairs in a more tyrannical fashion, claiming that they deserve to have authority over more areas than is customary, and to be beyond the law. Kingships no longer arise nowadays, but if any do happen to occur, they tend more to be tyrannical monarchies. This is because kingship is rule over willing subjects and has authority over more important matters. But nowadays there are numerous men of equal quality, although none so outstanding as to measure up to the magnitude and dignity of the office of king. Hence people are unwilling to put up with this sort of rule. And if someone comes to exercise it, whether through force or deceit, this is immediately held to be a tyranny.

In the case of kingships based on lineage, there is something besides the factors already mentioned that

should be considered a cause of their destruction, namely, the fact that many kings easily become objects of contempt and behave arrogantly, even though they exercise kingly office, not tyrannical power. For then overthrow is easy. For a king whose subjects are unwilling immediately ceases to be a king whereas a
15 tyrant can rule even unwilling subjects.

Monarchies are destroyed for these reasons, then, and for others of the same sort.

Chapter 11

It is clear, to put it simply, that monarchies are preserved by the opposite causes. But kingships in particular are preserved by being made more moderate.
20 For the fewer areas over which kings have authority, the longer must their office remain intact. For they themselves become less like masters, more equal in their characters, and less envied by those they rule. That is also why the kingships of the Molossians lasted a long time, and that of the Spartans as well. In the latter case it was because the office was divided into
25 two parts from the beginning, and again because Theopompus, besides moderating it in other ways, instituted the office of the overseers. By diminishing the power of the kingship he increased its duration, so that in a way he made it greater, not lesser. He is supposed to have given precisely this answer, indeed,
30 when his wife asked him whether he was not ashamed to hand over a lesser kingship to his sons than the one he had inherited from his father: "Certainly not," he said, "for I am handing over one that will be longer lasting."

Tyrannies are preserved in two quite opposite ways.
35 One of them is traditional and is the way most tyrants exercise their rule. Periander of Corinth is said to have instituted most of its devices, but many may also be seen in the Persian empire. These include the device we mentioned some time ago as tending to preserve a tyranny (to the extent that it can be pre-
40 served): [1] cutting down the outstanding men and eliminating the high-minded ones. Others are: [2] Prohibiting messes, clubs, education, and other things
1313b of that sort. [3] Keeping an eye on anything that typically engenders two things: high-mindedness and mutual trust. [4] Prohibiting schools and other gather-

ings connected with learning, and doing everything to ensure that people are as ignorant of one another as possible, since knowledge tends to give rise to 5 mutual trust. [5] Requiring the residents to be always in public view and to pass their time at the palace gates. For their activities will then be hard to keep secret and they will become humble-minded from always acting like slaves. [6] Imposing all the other restrictions of a similar nature that are found in Persian and non-Greek tyrannies (for they are all capable of producing the same effect). 10

[7] Another is trying to let nothing done or said by any of his subjects escape notice, but to retain spies, like the so-called women informers of Syracuse, or the eavesdroppers that Hiero sent to every meeting or gathering. For people speak less freely when they 15 fear the presence of such spies, and if they do speak freely, they are less likely to go unnoticed. [8] Another is to slander people to one another, setting friend against friend, the people against the notables, and the rich against themselves. [9] It is also tyrannical to impoverish the people, so that they cannot afford a militia and are so occupied with their daily work that they lack the leisure for plotting. The pyramids 20 of Egypt, the Cypselid monuments, the construction of the temple of Olympian Zeus by the Pisistratids, and the works on Samos commissioned by Polycrates are all examples of this. For all these things have the same result, lack of leisure and poverty for the ruled. [10] And there is taxation, as in Syracuse, when, 25 during the reign of Dionysius, taxation ate up a person's entire estate in five years. [11] A tyrant also engages in warmongering in order that his subjects will lack leisure and be perpetually in need of a leader. And while a kingship is preserved by its friends, it is the mark of a tyrant to distrust his friends, on the 30 grounds that while all his subjects wish to overthrow him, these are particularly capable of doing so.

All the practices found in the extreme kind of democracy are also characteristic of a tyranny: [12] the dominance of women in the household, in order that they may report on the men, and [13] the license of slaves for the same reason. For slaves and women 35 not only do not plot against tyrants but, because they prosper under them, are inevitably well disposed toward tyrannies and toward democracies as well (for the people too aspire to be a monarch). That is why a flatterer is honored in both constitutions—in democracies, the popular leader (for the popular leader

40 is a flatterer of the people), in tyrannies, those who are obsequious in their dealings with the tyrant, which is precisely a task for flattery. For that is also why

1314a tyranny loves vice. For tyrants delight in being flattered. But no free-minded person would flatter them. On the contrary, decent people act out of friendship, not flattery. The vicious are also useful for vicious

5 tasks—"nail to nail," as the saying goes. And it is characteristic of a tyrant not to delight in anyone who is dignified or free-minded. For a tyrant thinks that he alone deserves to be like that. But anyone who is a rival in dignity or free-mindedness robs tyranny of its superiority and its status as a master of slaves, and so tyrants hate him as a threat to their rule. And it is also characteristic of a tyrant to have foreigners rather than people from the city-state as dinner guests and

10 companions, on the grounds that the former are hostile to him, whereas the latter oppose him in nothing.

These devices are characteristic of tyrants and help preserve their rule, but there is no vice they leave out. They all fall into three categories, broadly speak-

15 ing. For tyranny aims at three things: first, that the ruled think small, for a pusillanimous person would plot against no one; second, that they distrust one another, for a tyranny will not be overthrown until some people trust each other. This is also why tyrants attack decent people. They view them as harmful to

20 their rule not only because they refuse to be ruled as by a master, but also because they command trust among both themselves and others, and do not inform on one another or on anyone else. Third, that the ruled be powerless to act. For no one tries to do what is impossible, and so no one tries to overthrow a

25 tyranny if he lacks the power. Thus the wishes of tyrants may be reduced in fact to these three defining principles, since all tyrannical aims might be reduced to these three tenets: that the ruled not trust one another; that they be powerless; that they think small.

This, then, is one way in which the preservation of tyrannies comes about. The other involves precau-

30 tions that are pretty much the opposite of those just discussed. One may grasp it by considering the destruction of kingships. For just as one way to destroy a kingship is to make its rule more tyrannical, so one way to preserve a tyranny is to make it more like a

35 kingship. One thing only must be safeguarded, the tyrant's power, so he can rule not just willing subjects but unwilling ones as well. For if this power is lost, the tyranny is also. But while this must remain a basic principle, a tyrant should perform or seem to perform everything else in a noble, kingly fashion.

First, then, [1] he should seem to take care of 40 public funds. He should not squander them on gifts that enrage the multitude, taking money from people 1314b who are laboring and toiling in penury, and lavishing it on prostitutes, foreigners, and craftsmen. He should also render an account of funds received and expended, as some tyrants in the past have done. For 5 in this way, he will give the impression of managing the city-state like the head of a household rather than a tyrant. He should not be afraid of running short of funds, since he has authority over the city-state. At any event, it is even more beneficial for tyrants who are often away on foreign campaigns to do this than to amass a great hoard of wealth and leave it behind. For those who guard the city-state will be less likely 10 to seize his things. A tyrant on a foreign campaign has more to fear from such guards, indeed, than from the citizens. For the citizens accompany him, while the guards stay behind. Next, it should appear that taxes and public services exist for the purposes of 15 administration, and to meet the needs of military emergencies. In a word: a tyrant should pose as a guardian and steward of the public funds, not of his own private estate.

[2] He should also appear not harsh but dignified, the kind of person who inspires awe rather than fear in those who meet him. But this is not easily achieved if he is contemptible. That is why even if a tyrant 20 neglects the other virtues, he must cultivate military virtue and get himself a reputation for it.

Furthermore, [3] not only should he himself avoid any appearance of behaving arrogantly toward any teenage boys and girls among his subjects, but neither should any of his followers. The women of his house- 25 hold should also be similarly respectful toward other women, as the arrogant behavior of women has caused the downfall of many tyrannies. Where bodily pleasures are concerned, the tyrant should do the opposite of what some in fact do. For they not only begin their debaucheries at dawn and continue them for days on 30 end, but they also wish to be seen doing so by others, in order that they may be admired as happy and blessed. But above all the tyrant should be moderate in such matters, or failing that, he should at least avoid exhibiting his indulgence to others. For it is not easy to attack or despise a sober or wakeful man, 35 but it is easy to attack or despise a drunk or drowsy one.

[4] A tyrant must do the opposite of pretty well all the things we mentioned a while back. For he must lay out and beautify the city-state as if he were a household steward rather than a tyrant.

Again, [5] a tyrant should always be seen to be very zealous about matters concerning the gods, but without appearing foolish in the process. For people are less afraid of suffering illegal treatment at the 40 hands of such people. And if they regard their ruler 1315a as a god-fearing man who pays heed to the gods, they plot against him less, since they think that he has the gods on his side.

[6] A tyrant should so honor those who prove to be good in any area that they do not expect that they 5 would be more honored by citizens living under their own laws. He should bestow such honors himself, but punishments should be administered by other officials and by the courts. But it is a precaution common to every sort of monarchy not to make any one man important, but where necessary to elevate several, so that they will keep an eye on one another. If it happens to be necessary to make one man important, however, at all events it should not be someone 10 of courageous character. For men of this sort are the most enterprising in any sphere of action. And if it is considered necessary to remove someone from power, his prerogatives should be taken away gradually, not all at once.

[7] A tyrant should refrain from all forms of arrogance, and from two in particular: corporal punish- 15 ment and arrogance toward adolescents. This is particularly true where those who love honor are concerned. For while lovers of money resent contemptuous acts affecting their property, honor lovers and decent human beings resent those involving dis- 20 honor. Hence either he should not treat people in these ways or else he should appear to punish like a father, not out of contempt; and to engage in sexual relations with young people out of sexual desire, and not as if it were a prerogative of his office. And as a general rule, he should compensate apparent dishonors with yet greater honors. Of those who make at- 25 tempts on his life, a tyrant should most fear and take

the greatest precautions against those who are ready to sacrifice their own lives to destroy him. Hence he should be particularly wary of people who think that he has behaved arrogantly toward them or those they happen to cherish. For people who attack out of anger are careless of themselves. As Heraclitus said, "Anger is a hard enemy to combat, because it pays for what 30 it wants with life."

[8] Since city-states consist of two parts, poor and rich, it is best if both believe that they owe their safety to the tyrant's rule, and that neither is unjustly treated by the other because of it. But whichever of them is the stronger should be particularly attached to his 35 rule, so that with his power thus increased he will not need to free slaves or confiscate weapons. For the latter of the two parts added to his force will be enough to make them stronger than attackers.

But it is superfluous to discuss all such measures 40 in detail. For their aim is evident. A tyrant should appear to his subjects not as a tyrant but as a head of household and a kingly man, not as an embezzler 1315b but as a steward. He should also pursue the moderate things in life, not excess, maintaining close relations with the notables, while playing the popular leader with the many. For as a result, not only will his rule necessarily be nobler and more enviable, but since he rules better people who have not been humiliated he will not end up being hated and feared. And his 5 rule will be longer lasting, and his character will either be nobly disposed to virtue or else half good, not vicious but half vicious. 10

Chapter 12

Yet, the shortest-lived of all constitutions are oligarchy and tyranny. For the longest lasting tyranny was that of Orthagoras and his sons in Sicyon. It lasted a hundred years. This was because they treated their subjects moderately and were subservient to the laws in many 15 areas; Cleisthenes, in particular, was also not easy to despise because of his ability in battle; and they acted as popular leaders by looking after the people's interests in various ways. At any rate, Cleisthenes is said to have given a crown to the judge who denied him victory in a competition. And some say that the seated figure in the marketplace is a statue of the man who gave the verdict. They also say that Pisistratus once 20 allowed himself to be summoned for trial before the Areopagus.

The second longest tyranny was that of the Cypselids in Corinth, which lasted seventy-three years and six months. For Cypselus was tyrant for thirty years, Periander for forty and a half, and Psammeticus, the son of Gorgus, for three. The reasons it lasted are also the same. Cypselus was a popular leader who went without a bodyguard throughout his rule; and Periander, though he became tyrannical, was able in battle.

The third was that of the Pisistratids in Athens. But it was not continuous. For Pisistratus went into exile twice, so that in a period of thirty-three years he was tyrant for seventeen. Since his sons ruled for eighteen years, the tyranny lasted for thirty-five years altogether.

The longest lasting of the remaining tyrannies was the one associated with Gelon and Hiero at Syracuse. Yet even this did not last long, just eighteen years total. For Gelon was tyrant for seven and died in the eighth; Hiero for ten; whereas Thrasyboulus was expelled after ten months. But the majority of tyrannies have all been quite short-lived.

The various causes that destroy constitutions and monarchies, and also those that preserve them, have now pretty well all been discussed.

In the *Republic* Socrates discusses change, but he does not discuss it well. For in the case of the first and best constitution he does not discuss the change peculiar to it. For he claims that its cause is that nothing is permanent, but that everything undergoes a sort of cyclical change, and that the origin of this lies in the elements four and three, which "married with five, give two harmonies," whenever the number of this figure becomes cubed. His idea is that nature sometimes produces people who are mediocre and stronger than education. Perhaps he is not wrong in saying this, since there may be some people who are ineducable and cannot become good men. But how could this sort of change be any more peculiar to the constitution he says is best than common to all the others and to everything that comes into existence? Yes, and is it during this period of time, due to which, as he says, everything changes, that even things that did not begin to exist at the same time change at the same time? If something comes into existence on the day before the completion of the cycle, for example, does it still change at the same time as everything

else? Furthermore, why does the best constitution change into a constitution of the Spartan sort? For all constitutions more often change into their opposites than into the neighboring one. The same remark also applies to the other changes. For he says that the Spartan constitution changes to an oligarchy, then to a democracy, then to a tyranny. Yet change may also occur in the opposite direction. For example, from democracy to oligarchy, and to it more than to monarchy.

Moreover, he does not tell us whether tyranny undergoes change, or what causes it to change, if it does. Nor does he tell us what sort of constitution it changes into. The reason for this is that he could not easily have told us, since the matter is undecidable, although according to him it should change into his first or best constitution, since that would make the cycle continuous. But in fact tyranny can also change into another tyranny, as the constitution at Sicyon changed from the tyranny of Myron to that of Cleisthenes; into oligarchy, like that of Antileon in Chalcis; into democracy, like that of Gelon and his family at Syracuse; and into aristocracy, like that of Charillus in Sparta [or the one in Carthage].

Change also occurs from oligarchy to tyranny, as happened in most of the ancient oligarchies in Sicily: in Leontini, it was to the tyranny of Panaetius; in Gela, to that of Cleander; in Rhegium, to that of Anaxilaus; and similarly in many other city-states. It is also absurd to hold that a constitution changes into an oligarchy because the office holders are money lovers and acquirers of wealth, and not because those who are far superior in property holdings think it unjust for those who do not own anything to participate equally in the city-state with those who do. And in many oligarchies office holders are not only not allowed to acquire wealth, but there are laws to prevent it. On the other hand, in Carthage, which is governed timocratically, the officials do engage in acquiring wealth, and it has not yet undergone change.

It is also absurd to claim that an oligarchic city-state is really two city-states, one of the rich and one of the poor. For why is this any more true of it than of the Spartan constitution, or any other constitution where the citizens do not all own an equal amount of property or are not all similarly good men? And even when no one becomes any poorer than he was, constitutions still undergo change from oligarchy to democracy, if the poor become a majority, or from democracy to oligarchy, if the rich happen to be more powerful than the multitude, and the latter are careless, while the former set their mind to change. Also, though there are many reasons why oligarchies change into democracies, Socrates mentions but one: poverty caused by riotous living and paying interest on loans—as if all or most of the citizens were rich at the start. But this is false. Rather, when some of the leading men lose their properties, they stir up change; but when some of the others do so, nothing terrible happens. And even when change does occur, it is no more likely to result in a democracy than in some other constitution. Besides, if people have no share in office or are treated unjustly or arrogantly, they start factions and change constitutions, even if they have not squandered all their property through being free to do whatever they like (the cause of which, Socrates says, is too much freedom).

Although there are many kinds of oligarchies and democracies, Socrates discusses their changes as if there were only one of each.

Book VI

Chapter 1

We have already discussed the number and varieties of the deliberative and authoritative elements of constitutions, the ways of organizing offices and courts, which is suited to which constitution, and also what the origins and causes are of the destruction and preservation of constitutions. But since it turned out that there are several kinds of democracies, and similarly of the other constitutions, we would do well to consider whatever remains to be said about these, and to determine which ways of organizing things are appropriate for and beneficial to each of them.

Moreover, we have to investigate the combinations of all the ways of organizing the things we mentioned. For these, when coupled, cause constitutions to overlap, resulting in oligarchic aristocracies and democratically inclined polities. I mean those couplings which should be investigated but at present have not been. For example, where the deliberative part and the part that deals with the choice of officials are organized oligarchically, but the part that deals with the courts is aristocratic; or where the part that deals with the courts and the deliberative part are oligarchic, and the part that deals with the choice of officials is aristocratic; or where, in some other way, not all the parts appropriate to the constitution are combined.

We have already discussed the question of which kind of democracy is suited to which kind of city-state; similarly, which kind of oligarchy is suited to which kind of people; and which of the remaining constitutions is beneficial for which. Still, since we should make clear not only which kind of constitution is best for a city-state, but also how it and the other kinds should be established, let us briefly go through this. We may begin with democracy, since that will at the same time throw some light on the opposite constitution, the one some call oligarchy.

To carry out this inquiry, we need to grasp all the features that are democratic and that are held to go along with democracy. For it is as a result of the way these are combined that the various kinds of democracy arise, and more than one variety of each kind of democracy. For there are *two* reasons why there are several kinds of democracy. The first is the one mentioned earlier, that there are different kinds of people. For there is the multitude of farmers, that of vulgar craftsmen, and that of laborers. And when the first of these is added to the second, and the third again to both of them, it not only affects the quality of the democracy for better or worse, it also changes its kind. But the second reason is the one we are discussing now. For the features that go along with democracy and are held to be appropriate to this kind of constitution, when they are differently combined, cause democracies to differ, since a few of these features will go with one kind of democracy, more with a second, and all of them with a third. It is useful to be familiar with each of them, whether for the purpose of establishing whichever kind of democracy one happens to want, or for that of reforming an existing kind. For those who are establishing a constitution try to combine all the features that are in keeping with its fundamental principle. But they err in doing so, as was pointed out earlier in our discussions of what causes the destruction and preservation of constitutions.

Let us now discuss the fundamental principles, character, and aims of the various kinds of democracy.

Chapter 2

40 The fundamental principle of the democratic constitution is freedom. For it is commonly asserted that freedom is shared only in this sort of constitution, 1317b since it is said that all democracies have it as their aim. One component of freedom is ruling and being ruled in turn. For democratic justice is based on numerical equality, not on merit. But if this is what 5 justice is, then of necessity the multitude must be in authority, and whatever seems right to the majority, this is what is final and this is what is just, since they say that each of the citizens should have an equal share. The result is that the poor have more authority than the rich in democracies. For they are the majority, and majority opinion is in authority. This, then, 10 is one mark of freedom which all democrats take as a goal of their constitution. Another is to live as one likes. This, they say, is the result of freedom, since that of slavery is not to live as one likes. This, then, is the second goal of democracy. From it arises the 15 demand not to be ruled by anyone, or failing that, to rule and be ruled in turn. In this way the second goal contributes to freedom based on equality.

From these presuppositions and this sort of principle arise the following democratic features: [1] Having all choose officials from all. [2] Having all rule each 20 and each in turn rule all. [3] Having all offices, or all that do not require experience or skill, filled by lot. [4] Having no property assessment for office, or one as low as possible. [5] Having no office, or few besides military ones, held twice or more than a few times by the same person. [6] Having all offices or as many as possible be short-term. [7] Having all, or 25 bodies selected from all, decide all cases, or most of them, and the ones that are most important and involve the most authority, such as those having to do with the inspection of officials, the constitution, or private contracts. [8] Having the assembly have authority over everything or over all the important things, but having no office with authority over any- 30 thing or over as little as possible. The council is the most democratic office in city-states that lack adequate resources to pay everyone, but where such resources exist even this office is stripped of its power. For when the people are well paid, they take all decisions into their own hands (as we said in the inquiry preceding this one). [9] Having pay provided,

preferably for everyone, for the assembly, courts, and 35 public offices, or failing that, for service in the offices, courts, council, and assemblies that are in authority, or for those offices that require their holders to share a mess. Besides, since oligarchy is defined by family, wealth, and education, their opposites (low birth, pov- 40 erty, and vulgarity) are held to be characteristically democratic. [10] Furthermore, it is democratic to have no office be permanent; and if such an office happens to survive an ancient change, to strip it of 1318a its power, at least, and have it filled by lot rather than by election.

These, then, are the features commonly found in democracies. And from the type of justice that is agreed to be democratic, which consists in everyone having numerical equality, comes what is held to be most of all a democracy and a rule by the people, 5 since equality consists in the poor neither ruling more than the rich nor being alone in authority, but in all ruling equally on the basis of numerical equality, since in that way they would consider equality and freedom to be present in the constitution. 10

Chapter 3

The next problem that arises is how they will achieve this equality. Should they divide assessed property so that the property of five hundred citizens equals that of a thousand others, and then give equal power to the thousand as to the five hundred? Or is this not the way to produce numerical equality? Should they instead divide as before, then take an equal number of citizens from the five hundred as from the thousand 15 and give them authority over the elections and the courts? Is this the constitution that is most just from the point of view of democratic justice? Or is it the one based on quantity? For democrats say that whatever seems just to the greater number constitutes justice, whereas oligarchs say that it is whatever seems just to those with the most property. For they say that quantity of property should be the deciding factor. 20 But both views are unequal and unjust. For if justice is whatever the few decide, we have tyranny, since if one person has more than the others who are rich, then, from the point of view of oligarchic justice, it is just for him alone to rule. On the other hand, if justice is what the numerical majority decide, they

25 will commit injustice by confiscating the property of the wealthy few (as we said earlier).

What sort of equality there might be, then, that both would agree on is something we must investigate in light of the definitions of justice they both give. For they both say that the opinion of the majority of the citizens should be in authority. So let this stand, though not fully. Instead, since there are in fact two

30 classes in a city-state, the rich and the poor, whatever is the opinion of both or of a majority of each should have authority. But if they are opposed, the opinion of the majority (that is to say, the group whose assessed property is greater) should prevail. Suppose, for example, that there are ten rich citizens and twenty poor ones, and that six of the rich have voted against fifteen of the poorer ones, whereas four of the rich have

35 sided with the poor, and five of the poor with the rich. When the assessed properties of both the rich and the poor on each side are added together, the side whose assessed property is greater should have authority. If the amounts happen to be equal, this should be considered a failure for both sides, as it is at present when the assembly or the court is split,

40 and the question must be decided by lot or something

1318b else of that sort.

Even if it is very difficult to discover the truth about what equality and justice demand, however, it is still easier than to persuade people of it when they have the power to be acquisitive. For equality and justice are always sought by the weaker party; the strong pay

5 no heed to them.

Chapter 4

Of the four kinds of democracy, the first in order is the best, as we said in the discussions before these. It is also the oldest of them all. But I call it first as one might distinguish people. For the first or best kind of people is the farming kind, and so it is also possible to create a democracy where the multitude

10 live by cultivating the land or herding flocks. For because they do not have much property, they lack leisure and cannot attend meetings of the assembly frequently. And because they do not have the necessities, they are busy at their tasks and do not desire other people's property. Indeed, they find working more pleasant than engaging in politics and holding

office, where no great profit is to be had from office, 15 since the many seek money more than honor. Evidence of this is that they even put up with the ancient tyrannies, and continue to put up with oligarchies, so long as no one prevents them from working or takes anything away from them. For in no time some of them become rich, while the others at least escape 20 poverty. Besides, having authority over the election and inspection of officials will give them what they need, if they do have any love of honor. In fact, in some democracies, the multitude do not participate in the election of officials; instead, electors are selected from all the citizens by turns, as in Mantinea; yet if they have authority over deliberation, they are 25 content. (This arrangement too should be regarded as a form of democracy, as it was at Mantinea.)

That is why, indeed, in the aforementioned kind of democracy, it is both beneficial and customary for all the citizens to elect and inspect officials and sit on juries, but for the holders of the most important offices to be elected from those with a certain amount 30 of assessed property (the higher the office, the higher the assessment), or alternatively for officials not to be elected on the basis of property assessments at all, but on the basis of ability. People governed in this way are necessarily governed well; the offices will always be in the hands of the best, while the people will consent and will not envy the decent; and this organization is necessarily satisfactory to the decent 35 and reputable people, since they will not be ruled by their inferiors, and will rule justly because the others have authority over the inspection of officials. For to be under constraint, and not to be able to do whatever seems good, is beneficial, since freedom to do whatever one likes leaves one defenseless against the bad 40 things that exist in every human being. So the neces- 1319a sary result, which is the very one most beneficial in constitutions, is that the decent people rule without falling into wrongdoing and the multitude are in no way short-changed.

It is evident, then, that this is the best of the democracies, and also the reason why: that it is because the 5 people are of a certain kind. And for the purpose of establishing a farming people, some of the laws that existed in many city-states in ancient times are extremely useful, for example, prohibiting the ownership of more than a certain amount of land under any circumstances, or else more than a certain amount situated between a given place and the city-state's town. And there used to be a law in many city-states (at any rate, in ancient times) forbidding even the sale of the original allotments of land, and also one, said to derive from Oxylus, with a similar sort of effect, forbidding lending against more than a certain portion of each person's land. Nowadays, however, one should also attempt reform by using the law of the Aphytaeans, as it too is useful for the purpose under discussion. For though the citizens of Aphytis are numerous and have little land, they all engage in farming, because property assessments are based not on whole estates but on such small subdivisions of them that even the poor can exceed the assessment.

After the multitude of farmers, the best sort of people consists of herdsmen, who get their living from livestock. For herding is in many respects similar to farming, and where military activities are concerned, they are particularly well prepared, because they are physically fit and able to live in the open. The other multitudes, of which the remaining kinds of democracies are composed, are almost all very inferior to these. For their way of life is bad, and there is no element of virtue involved in the task to which the multitude of vulgar craftsmen, tradesmen, and laborers put their hand. Furthermore, because they wander around the marketplace and town, practically speaking this entire class can easily attend the assembly. Farmers, on the other hand, because they are scattered throughout the countryside, neither attend so readily nor have the same need for this sort of meeting. But where the lay of the land is such that the countryside is widely separated from the city-state, it is even easier to create a democracy that is serviceable and a constitution. For the multitude are forced to make their settlements out in the country areas, so that, even if there is a whole crowd that frequents the marketplace, one should simply not hold assemblies in democracies without the multitude from the country.

How, then, the best or first kind of democracy should be established has been described. But how the others should be established is also evident. For they should deviate in order from the best kind, always excluding a worse multitude.

The ultimate democracy, because everyone participates in it, is not one that every city-state can afford; nor can it easily endure, if its laws and customs are not well put together. (The factors that cause the destruction of this and other constitutions have pretty well all been discussed earlier.) With a view to establishing this sort of democracy and making the people powerful, the leaders usually admit as many as possible to citizenship, including not only the legitimate children of citizens but even the illegitimate ones, and those descended from citizens on only one side (I mean their mother's or their father's). For this whole class are particularly at home in this sort of democracy. This, then, is how popular leaders usually establish such a constitution; yet they should add citizens only up to the point where the multitude outnumber the notables and middle classes, and not go beyond this. For when they do overshoot it, they make the constitution more disorderly and provoke the notables to such an extent that they find the democracy hard to endure (which was in fact the cause of the faction at Cyrene). For a small class of worthless people gets overlooked, but as it grows larger it gets more noticed.

Also useful to a democracy of this kind are the sorts of institutions that Cleisthenes used in Athens when he wanted to increase the power of the democracy, and that those setting up the democracy used at Cyrene. For different and more numerous tribes and clans should be created, private cults should be absorbed into a few public ones, and every device should be used to mix everyone together as much as possible and break up their previous associations. Furthermore, all tyrannical institutions are held to be democratic. I mean, for example, the lack of supervision of slaves (which may really be beneficial to a democracy up to a certain point), or of women or children, and allowing everyone to live as he likes. For many people will support a constitution of this sort, since for the many it is more pleasant to live in a disorderly fashion than in a temperate one.

Chapter 5

For a legislator, however, or for those seeking to establish a constitution of this kind, setting it up is not the most important task nor indeed the only one, but rather ensuring its preservation. For it is not difficult for those who govern themselves in any old way to continue for a day or even for two or three days. That is why legislators should make use of our earlier

studies of what causes the preservation and destruction of constitutions, and from them try to institute stability, carefully avoiding the causes of destruction, while establishing the sort of laws, both written and
40 unwritten, which best encompass the features that
1320a preserve constitutions. They should consider a measure to be democratic or oligarchic not if it will make the city-state be as democratically governed or as oligarchically governed as possible, but if it will make it be so for the longest time.

Popular leaders nowadays, however, in their efforts to curry favor with the people, confiscate a lot of
5 property by means of the courts. That is why those who care about the constitution should counteract this by passing a law that nothing confiscated from a condemned person should become common property, but sacred property instead. For wrongdoers will be no less deterred, since they will be fined in the same way as before, whereas the crowd will less fre-
10 quently condemn defendants, since they will gain nothing by doing so. Public lawsuits too should always be kept to an absolute minimum, and those who bring frivolous ones should be deterred by large fines. For they are usually brought against notables, not democrats; but all the citizens should be well disposed
15 toward the constitution, or, failing that, they should at least not regard those in authority as their enemies.

Since the ultimate democracies have large populations that cannot easily attend the assembly without wages, where they also happen to have a dearth of revenues, this is hostile to the notables. For the wages
20 have to be obtained from taxes, confiscations of property, and corrupt courts—things that have already brought down many democracies. Where revenues are lacking, then, few assemblies should be held, and courts with many jurors should be in session for only a few days. For this helps reduce the fears of the
25 notables about expense, provided the rich are not paid for jury service but only the poor. It also greatly improves the quality of decisions in lawsuits; for the rich are unwilling to be away from their private affairs for many days, but are willing to be so for brief periods.

Where there are revenues, however, one should not do what popular leaders do nowadays. For they
30 distribute any surplus, but people no sooner get it than they want the same again. Helping the poor in this way, indeed, is like pouring water into the proverbial leaking jug. But the truly democratic man

should see to it that the multitude are not too poor (since this is a cause of the democracy's being a corrupt one). Measures must, therefore, be devised to ensure long-term prosperity. And, since this is also beneficial to the rich, whatever is left over from the 35 revenues should be collected together and distributed in lump sums to the poor, particularly if enough can be accumulated for the acquisition of a plot of land, or failing that, for a start in trade or farming. And if this cannot be done for all, distribution should instead be by turns on the basis of tribe or some other part. 1320b In the meantime the rich should be taxed to provide pay for necessary meetings of the assembly, while being released from useless sorts of public service.

It is by governing in this sort of way that the Carthaginians have won the friendship of their people, since they are always sending some of them out to 5 their subject city-states to become rich. But it is also characteristic of notables who are cultivated and sensible to divide the poor amongst themselves and give them a start in some line of work. It is a good thing too to imitate the policy of the Tarentines, who retain the goodwill of the multitude by giving communal use of their property to the poor. They also divide all 10 their offices into two classes, those that are elected and those chosen by lot: those by lot, so the people participate; those elected, so they are governed better. But this can also be done by dividing the same office between those people chosen by lot and those elected. 15

We have said, then, how democracies should be established.

BOOK VII

Chapter 1

Anyone who intends to investigate the best constitution in the proper way must first determine which life is most choiceworthy, since if this remains un- 15 clear, what the best constitution is must also remain unclear. For it is appropriate for those to fare best who live in the best constitution their circumstances allow—provided nothing contrary to reasonable expectation occurs. That is why we should first come to some agreement about what the most choiceworthy life is for practically speaking everyone, and then determine whether it is the same for an individual as for a community, or different.

Since, then, I consider that I have already expressed much that is adequate about the best life in the "external" works, I propose to make use of them here as well. For since, in the case of one division at least, there are three groups—external goods, goods of the body, and goods of the soul—surely no one would raise a dispute and say that not all of them need be possessed by those who are blessedly happy. For no one would call a person blessedly happy who has no shred of courage, temperance, justice, or practical wisdom, but is afraid of the flies buzzing around him, stops at nothing to gratify his appetite for food or drink, betrays his dearest friends for a pittance, and has a mind as foolish and prone to error as a child's or a madman's. But while almost all accept these claims, they disagree about quantity and relative superiority. For they consider any amount of virtue, however small, to be sufficient, but seek an unlimitedly excessive amount of wealth, possessions, power, reputation, and the like.

We, however, will say to them that it is easy to reach a reliable conclusion on these matters even from the facts themselves. For we see that the virtues are not acquired and preserved by means of external goods, but the other way around, and we see that a happy life for human beings, whether it consists in pleasure or virtue or both, is possessed more often by those who have cultivated their characters and minds to an excessive degree, but have been moderate in their acquisition of external goods, than by those who have acquired more of the latter than they can possibly use, but are deficient in the former. Moreover, if we investigate the matter on the basis of argument, it is plain to see. For external goods have a limit, as does any tool, and all useful things are useful for something; so excessive amounts of them must harm or bring no benefit to their possessors. In the case of each of the goods of the soul, however, the more excessive it is, the more useful it is (if these goods too should be thought of as useful, and not simply as noble).

It is generally clear too, we shall say, that the relation of superiority holding between the best condition of each thing and that of others corresponds to that holding between the things whose conditions we say they are. So since the soul is unqualifiedly more valuable, and also more valuable to us, than possessions or the body, its best states must be proportionally better than theirs. Besides, it is for the sake of the soul that these things are naturally choiceworthy, and every sensible person should choose them for its sake, not the soul for theirs.

We may take it as agreed, then, that each person has just as much happiness as he has virtue, practical wisdom, and the action that expresses them. We may use god as evidence of this. For he is blessedly happy, not because of any external goods but because of himself and a certain quality in his nature. This is also the reason that good luck and happiness are necessarily different. For chance or luck produces goods external to the soul, but no one is just or temperate as a result of luck or because of luck.

The next point depends on the same arguments. The happy city-state is the one that is best and acts nobly. It is impossible for those who do not do noble deeds to act nobly; and no action, whether a man's or a city-state's, is noble when separate from virtue and practical wisdom. But the courage, justice, and practical wisdom of a city-state have the same capacity and are of the same kind as those possessed by each human being who is said to be just, practically wise, and temperate.

So much, then, for the preface to our discussion. For we cannot avoid talking about these issues altogether, but neither can we go through all the arguments pertaining to them, since that is a task for another type of study. But for now, let us assume this much, that the best life, both for individuals separately and for city-states collectively, is a life of virtue sufficiently equipped with the resources needed to take part in virtuous actions. With regard to those who dispute this, if any happen not to be persuaded by what has been said, we must ignore them in our present study, but investigate them later.

Chapter 2

It remains to say whether the happiness of each individual human being is the same as that of a city-state or not. But here too the answer is evident, since everyone would agree that they are the same. For those who suppose that living well for an individual consists in wealth will also call a whole city-state

blessedly happy if it happens to be wealthy. And those
10 who honor the tyrannical life above all would claim
that the city-state that rules the greatest number is
happiest. And if someone approves of an individual
because of his virtue, he will also say that the more
excellent city-state is happier.

Two questions need to be investigated, however.
First, which life is more choiceworthy, the one that
involves taking part in politics with other people and
15 participating in a city-state, or the life of an alien cut
off from the political community? Second, and regardless of whether participating in a city-state is more
choiceworthy for everyone or for most but not for all,
which constitution, which condition of the city-state,
20 is best? This second question, and not the one about
what is choiceworthy for the individual, is a task for
political thought or theory. And since that is the investigation we are now engaged in, whereas the former is a
further task, our task is the second question.

It is evident that the best constitution must be that
organization in which anyone might do best and live
25 a blessedly happy life. But the very people who agree
that the most choiceworthy life is the life of virtue
are the ones who dispute about whether it is the
political life of action that is worthy of choice or
rather the one released from external concerns—a
contemplative life, for example, which some say is
the only life for a philosopher. For it is evident that
almost all of those, past or present, with the greatest
love for the honor accorded to virtue have chosen
30 between these two lives (I mean the political life
and the philosophic one). And it makes no small
difference on which side the truth lies, since anyone
with sound practical wisdom at least must organize
his affairs by looking to the better target—and this
applies to human beings individually and to the constitution communally.

35 Some people think that ruling over one's neighbors
like a master involves one of the greatest injustices,
and that rule of a statesman, though it involves no
injustice, does involve an impediment to one's own
well-being. Others think almost the opposite, they say
that an active, political life is the only one for a man,
40 since the actions expressing each of the virtues are
no more available to private individuals than to those
engaged in communal affairs and politics. Some give
1324b this reply, then, but others claim that only a constitution that involves being a master or tyrant is happy.

For some people, indeed, the fundamental aim of
the constitution and the laws just is to rule their
neighbors like a master. That is why, even though
most customs have been established pretty much at 5
random in most cases, anywhere the laws have to
some extent a single aim, it is always domination. So
in Sparta and Crete the educational system and most
of the laws are set up for war. Besides, all the nations
that have the power to be acquisitive honor military 10
power—for example, the Scythians, Persians, Thracians, and Celts. Indeed, some of them even have
laws designed to foster military virtue. It is said that
in Carthage, for example, they receive armlets as
decorations for each campaign in which they take
part. There was once a law in Macedonia too that 15
any man who had not killed an enemy must wear a
halter for a belt. Among the Scythians, when the cup
passes around at a feast, those who have not killed
an enemy are not permitted to drink from it. And
among the Iberians, a warlike race, they place small
obelisks in the earth around a man's tomb to show
the number of enemies he has killed. And there are 20
many other similar practices among other peoples,
some prescribed by law, others by custom.

Yet to anyone willing to investigate the matter, it
would perhaps seem quite absurd if the task of a
statesman involved being able to study ways to rule
or master his neighbors, whether they are willing or 25
not. For how could this be a political or legislative
task, when it is not even lawful? But to rule not only
justly but also unjustly is unlawful, whereas it is quite
possible to dominate unjustly. Certainly, this is not
what we see in the other sciences; for it is not the
doctor's or captain's task to use force on his patients 30
or passengers if he cannot persuade them. Yet many
seem to think that statesmanship is the same as mastership, and what they all say is unjust or nonbeneficial
when it is done to them, they are not ashamed to do
to others. For they seek just rule for themselves, but 35
pay no attention to justice in their dealings with others. It is absurd to deny, however, that one thing is
fit to be a master and another not fit to be a master.
So, if indeed one is that way, one should not try to
rule as a master over everyone, but only over those
who are fit to be ruled by a master. Similarly, one
should not hunt human beings for a feast or sacrifice,
but only animals that are fit to be hunted for these 40
purposes: and that is any wild animal that is edible.

Furthermore, it is possible for even a single city-state to be happy all by itself, provided it is well 1325a governed, since it is possible for a city-state to be settled somewhere by itself and to employ excellent laws. And *its* constitution will not be organized for the purposes of war or of dominating its enemies (for we are assuming that it has none).

5 It is clear, therefore, that all military practices are to be regarded as noble, not when they are pursued as the highest end of all, but only when they are pursued for the sake of the highest end. The task of an excellent legislator, then, is to study how a city-state, a race of men, or any other community can come to have a share in a good life and in the happi-10 ness that is possible for them. There will be differences, of course, in some of the laws that are instituted, and if there are neighboring peoples, it belongs to legislative science to consider what sorts of military training are needed in relation to which sorts of people and which measures are to be used in relation to each.

But the question of which end the best constitution 15 should aim at will receive a proper investigation later.

Chapter 3

We must now reply to the two sides who agree that the virtuous life is most choiceworthy, but disagree about how to practice it. For some rule out the holding of political office and consider that the life of a free person is both different from that of a statesman and the most choiceworthy one of all. But others 20 consider that the political life is best, since it is impossible for someone inactive to do or act well, and that doing well and happiness are the same. We must reply that they are both partly right and partly wrong. On the one hand, it is true to say that the life of a free person is better than that of a master. For there is certainly nothing grand about using a slave as a 25 slave, since ordering people to do necessary tasks is in no way noble. None the less, it is wrong to consider that every kind of rule is rule by a master. For the difference between rule over free people and over slaves is no smaller than the difference between being naturally free and being a natural slave. We have 30 adequately distinguished them in our first discussions. On the other hand, to praise inaction more than

action is not correct either. For happiness is action, and many noble things reach their end in the actions of those who are just and temperate.

Perhaps someone will take these conclusions to imply, however, that having authority over everyone is what is best. For in that way one would have author-35 ity over the greatest number of the very noblest actions. It would follow that someone who has the power to rule should not surrender it to his neighbor but take it away from him, and that a father should disregard his children, a child his father, a friend his friend, and pay no attention to anything except ruling. For what is best is most choiceworthy, and doing well is best. 40

What they say is perhaps true, if indeed those who use force and commit robbery will come to possess 1325b the most choiceworthy thing there is. But perhaps they cannot come to possess it, and the underlying assumption here is false. For someone cannot do noble actions if he is not as superior to those he rules as a husband is to his wife, a father to his children, or a master to his slaves. Therefore, a transgressor 5 could never make up later for his deviation from virtue. For among those who are similar, ruling and being ruled in turn is just and noble, since this is equal or similar treatment. But unequal shares for equals or dissimilar ones for similars is contrary to nature; and nothing contrary to nature is noble. Hence when someone else has superior virtue and 10 his power to do the best things is also superior, it is noble to follow and just to obey him. But he should possess not virtue alone, but also the power he needs to do these things.

If these claims are correct, and we should assume that happiness is doing well, then the best life, whether for a whole city-state collectively or for an individual, would be a life of action. Yet it is not 15 necessary, as some suppose, for a life of action to involve relations with other people, nor are those thoughts alone active which we engage in for the sake of action's consequences; the study and thought that are their own ends and are engaged in for their own sake are much more so. For to do or act well is 20 the end, so that action of a sort is the end too. And even in the case of actions involving external objects, the one who does them most fully is, strictly speaking, the master craftsman who directs them by means of his thought.

Moreover, city-states situated by themselves, which have deliberately chosen to live that way, do not necessarily have to be inactive, since activity can take
25 place even among their parts. For the parts of a city-state have many sorts of communal relationships with one another. Similarly, this holds for any human being taken singly. For otherwise god and the entire universe could hardly be in a fine condition; for they have no external actions, only the internal ones proper to them.

30 It is evident, then, that the same life is necessarily best both for each human being and for city-states and human beings collectively.

Chapter 4

Since what has just been said about these matters was by way of a preface, and since we studied the various constitutions earlier, the starting point for the
35 remainder of our investigation is first to discuss the conditions that should be presupposed to exist by the ideal city-state we are about to construct. For the best constitution cannot come into existence without commensurate resources. Hence we should presuppose that many circumstances are as ideal as we could wish, although none should be impossible. I have in mind, for example, the number of citizens and the
40 size of the territory. For other craftsmen—for example, a weaver or a shipbuilder—should also be supplied with suitable material to work on, and the better
1326a the material that has been prepared, the finer the product of their craft must necessarily be. So too a statesman or legislator should be supplied with proper material in a suitable condition.

5 First among the political resources needed for a city-state is the multitude of people. How many should there be of them, and of what sort? Similarly for the territory, how large should it be, and of what nature? Most people suppose that a happy city-state must be a great one, but even if what they suppose is true, they are ignorant of the quality that makes a
10 city-state great or small. For they judge a city-state to be great if the number of its inhabitants is large, whereas they ought to look not to number but to ability. For a city-state too has a task to perform, so that the city-state that is best able to complete it is the one that should be considered greatest. Similarly,

one should say that Hippocrates is a greater doctor than someone who exceeds him in physical size, not 15 a greater human being.

Yet even if one had to judge the greatness of a city-state by looking to the multitude, this should not be any chance multitude (for city-states inevitably contain a large number of slaves, resident aliens, and foreigners), but rather to those who are *part* of it, that 20 is to say, those who form one of the parts from which a city-state is properly constituted. For possessing a superior number of these is the sign of a great city-state. A city-state that can send a large number of vulgar craftsmen out to war, on the other hand, but only a few hoplites, cannot possibly be great. For a great city-state is not the same as a densely populated one.

Furthermore it is evident from the facts at least 25 that it is difficult, perhaps impossible, for an overly populated city-state to be well governed. At any rate, among those that are held to be nobly governed, we see none that fails to restrict the size of its population. Argument also convinces us that this is clearly so. For law is a kind of organization, and good government must of necessity be good organization. But an 30 excessively large number of things cannot share in organization. For that would be a task for a divine power, the sort that holds the entire universe together. For beauty is usually found in number and magnitude. Hence a city-state whose size is fixed by the aforementioned limit must also be the most beautiful. But the size of city-state, like everything else, has a 35 certain scale: animals, plants, and tools. For when each of them is neither too small nor too excessively large, it will have its own proper capacity; otherwise, it will either be wholly deprived of its nature or be in poor condition. For example, a ship that is one span [seven and a half inches] long will not be a ship at all, nor will one of two stades [twelve hundred feet]; and 40 as it approaches a certain size, it will sail badly, because it either is still too small or still too large. Similarly for 1326b a city-state: one that consists of too few people is not self-sufficient (whereas a city-state is self-sufficient), but one that consists of too many, while it is self-sufficient in the necessities, the way a nation is, is still no city-state, since it is not easy for it to have a constitution. For who will be the general of its excessively large mul- 5 titude, and who, unless he has the voice of Stentor, will serve as its herald?

Hence the first city-state to arise is the one composed of the first multitude large enough to be self-sufficient with regard to living the good life as a political community. It is also possible for a city-state that exceeds this one in number to be a greater city-
10 state, but, as we said, this is not possible indefinitely. The limit to its expansion can easily be seen from the facts. For a city-state's actions are either those of the rulers or those of the ruled. And a ruler's task is to issue orders and decide. But in order to decide
15 lawsuits and distribute offices on the basis of merit, each citizen must know what sorts of people the other citizens are. For where they do not know this, the business of electing officials and deciding lawsuits must go badly, since to act haphazardly is unjust in both these proceedings. But this is plainly what occurs in an overly populated city-state. Besides, it is easy
20 for resident aliens and foreigners to participate in the constitution, since the excessive size of the population makes escaping detection easy. It is clear, then, that the best limit for a city-state is this: it is the greatest size of multitude that promotes life's self-sufficiency and that can be easily surveyed as a whole. The size of
25 the city-state, then, should be determined in this way.

Chapter 8

1328a Since, as in the case of every other naturally constituted whole, the things that it cannot exist without are not all parts of it, clearly the things that are neces-
25 sary for the existence of a city-state should not be assumed to be parts of it either, and likewise for any other community that constitutes a single type of thing. For communities should have one thing that is common and the same for all their members, whether they share in it equally or unequally: for example, food, a piece of territory, or something else of this sort. But whenever one thing is for the sake of another and the other is the end for whose sake it is, they have nothing in common except that one produces and the other gets produced. I mean, for example,
30 the relationship of every tool or craftsman to the work produced. For the house and the builder have nothing in common. Rather, the builder's craft is for the sake of the house. That is why, though city-states need property, property is not a part of a city-state. Among
35 the parts of property are many living things, but a

city-state is a community of similar people aiming at the best possible life.

Since happiness is the best thing, however, and it is some sort of activation or complete exercise of virtue, and since, as it happens, some people are able to share in happiness, whereas others are able to do so only to a small degree or not at all, it is clear that this is why there are several kinds and varieties of 40 city-state and a plurality of constitutions. For it is by seeking happiness in different ways and by different means that individual groups of people create differ- 1328b ent ways of life and different constitutions.

But we must also investigate the question of how many of these things there are that a city-state cannot exist without. For what we are calling the parts of a city-state would of necessity be included among them. So we must determine the number of tasks there are, since this will make the answer clear. First, there should be a food supply. Second, crafts (for life needs 5 many tools). Third, weapons; for the members of the community must also have weapons of their own, both in order to rule (since there are people who disobey) and in order to deal with outsiders who attempt to wrong them. Fourth, a ready supply of 10 wealth, both for internal needs and for wars. Fifth, but of primary importance, the supervision of religious matters, which is called a priesthood. Sixth, and most necessary of all, judgment about what is beneficial and what is just in their relations with one another. These, then, are the tasks that need to be done in practically speaking every city-state. For a city-state is 15 not just any chance multitude, but one that is self-sufficient with regard to life, as we say; and if any of these tasks is lacking, a community cannot be unqualifiedly self-sufficient. Hence a city-state must be organized around these tasks. So there should be 20 a multitude of farmers to provide the food, craftsmen, soldiers, rich people, priests, and people to decide matters of necessity and benefit.

Chapter 9

Having determined these matters, it remains to investigate whether everyone should share in all the tasks we mentioned (for it is possible for all the same people to be farmers, craftsmen, deliberators and judges), or 25 whether different people should be assigned to each of them, or whether some tasks are necessarily specialized, whereas others can be shared by everyone. But it is not the same in every constitution. For it is possible, as we said, for everyone to share every task, or for not everyone to share in every task, but certain people in certain ones. For these differences too make constitutions differ. In democracies everyone shares in everything, whereas in oligarchies it is the opposite.

Since we are investigating the best constitution, however, the one that would make a city-state most happy—and happiness cannot exist apart from virtue, as was said earlier—it evidently follows that in a city-state governed in the finest manner, possessing men who are unqualifiedly just (and not given certain assumptions), the citizens should not live the life of a vulgar craftsman or tradesman. For lives of these sorts are ignoble and inimical to virtue. Nor should those who are going to be citizens engage in farming, since leisure is needed both to develop virtue and to engage in political actions.

But since the best city-state contains both a military part and one that deliberates about what is beneficial and makes judgments about what is just, and since it is evident that these, more than anything else, are parts of the city-state, should these tasks also be assigned to different people, or are both to be assigned to the same people? This is also evident, because in one way the tasks should be assigned to the same people, and in another they should be assigned to different ones. For since the best time for each of the two tasks is different, in that one requires practical wisdom and the other physical strength, they should be assigned to different people. On the other hand, since those capable of using and resisting force cannot possibly tolerate being ruled continuously, for this reason the two tasks should be assigned to the same people. For those who control the weapons also control whether a constitution will survive or not. The only course remaining, then, is for the constitution to assign both tasks to the same people, but not at the same time. Instead, since it is natural for physical strength to be found among younger men and practical wisdom among older ones, it is beneficial and just to assign the tasks to each group on the basis of age, since this division is based on merit.

Moreover, the property should belong to them. For the citizens must be well supplied with resources, and these people are the citizens. For the class of vulgar craftsmen does not participate in the city-state, nor does any other class whose members are not "craftsmen of virtue." This is clear from our basic assumption. For happiness necessarily accompanies virtue, and a city-state must not be called happy by looking at just a part, but by looking at all the citizens. It is also evident that the property should be theirs, since the farmers must be either slaves or non-Greek subject peoples.

Of the things we listed earlier, then, only the class of priests remains. Its organization is also evident. No farmer or vulgar craftsman should be appointed a priest, since it is appropriate for the gods to be honored by citizens. But because the political or citizen class is divided into two parts, the military and the deliberative, and because it is appropriate for those who have retired because of age to render service to the gods and find rest, the priesthoods should be assigned to them.

We have now discussed the things without which a city-state cannot be constituted, and how many parts of a city-state there are. Farmers, craftsmen, and the laboring class generally are necessary for the existence of city-states, but the military and deliberative classes are a city-state's parts. Each of these classes is separate from the others, some permanently, others by turns.

Chapter 10

Those who philosophize about constitutions, whether nowadays or in recent times, seem not to be the only ones to recognize that a city-state should be divided into separate classes, and that the military class should be different from the class of farmers. For it is still this way even today in Egypt and Crete, Sesostris having made such a law for Egypt, so it is said, and Minos for Crete.

messes also seem to be an ancient organization; they arose in Crete during the reign of Minos, but those in Italy are much older. Local historians say that the Oenotrians changed their name to Italians when a certain Italus who settled there became their king. It was because of him that the promontory of Europe that lies between the Gulfs of Scylletium and Lametius (which are a half-day's journey apart) was given the name Italy. It was Italus, they say, who made the nomadic Oenotrians into farmers, enacted laws for them, and first introduced messes. That is why some of his descendants still use messes even today, as well as some of his other laws. Those living near Tyrrhenia were the Opicians, who were then (as now) called Ausonians; those living near Iapygia and the Ionian Gulf, in a region called Siritis, were the Chonians, who were related to the Oenotrians by race. So it was in this region that messes were first organized. The separation of the political multitude into classes, on the other hand, originated in Egypt, for the kingship of Sesostris is much earlier than that of Minos. We should take it, indeed, that pretty well everything else too has been discovered many times, or rather an infinite number of times, in the long course of history. For our needs are likely to teach the necessities, and once they are present, the things that add refinement and luxury to life quite naturally develop. Hence we should suppose that the same is true of matters pertaining to constitutions. That all such matters are ancient is indicated by the facts about Egypt. For the Egyptians are held to be the most ancient people, and they have always had laws and a political organization. Therefore, one should make adequate use of what has been discovered, but also try to investigate whatever has been overlooked.

We said earlier that the territory should belong to those who possess weapons and participate in the constitution; we explained why the class of farmers should be different from them; and we discussed how much territory there should be and of what sort. Our first task now is to discuss the distribution of land, who the farmers should be, and what sort of people they should be. We do not agree with those who claim that property should be communally owned, but it should be commonly used, as it is among friends, and no citizen should be in need of sustenance. As for messes, everyone agrees that it is useful for well-organized city-states to have them. (Our own reasons for agreeing with this will be stated later.) All the citizens should participate in these meals, even though it is not easy for the poor to contribute the required amount from their private resources and maintain the rest of their household as well. Furthermore, expenses relating to the gods should be shared in common by the entire city-state.

So the territory must be divided into two parts, one of which is communal and another that belongs to private individuals. And each of these must again be divided in two: one part of the communal land should be used to support public services to the gods, the other to defray the cost of messes; one part of the private land should be located near the frontiers, the other near the city-state, so that, with two allotments assigned to each citizen, all of them may share in both locations. This not only accords with justice and equality, but ensures greater unanimity in the face of wars with neighbors. For wherever things are not this way, some citizens make light of feuds with bordering city-states, while others are overly and ignobly concerned about them. That is why some city-states have a law that prohibits those who dwell close to the border from participating in deliberations about whether to go to war with neighboring peoples, because their private interests are thought to prevent them from deliberating well. For these reasons, then, the land must be divided in the way we described.

As for the farmers, ideally speaking, they should be racially heterogeneous and spiritless slaves, since they would then be useful workers, unlikely to stir up change. As a second best, they should be non-Greek subject peoples, similar in nature to the slaves just mentioned. Those who work on private land should be the private possessions of the owners; those who work on the communal land should be communal property. Later we shall discuss how slaves should be treated and why it is better to hold out freedom as a reward to all slaves.

Chapter 11

We said earlier that a city-state should have as much access to land and sea, and indeed to its entire territory, as circumstances allow. As regards its own situation, one should ideally determine its site by looking to four factors. The first is health, since it is a necessity. City-states that slope toward the east, that is, toward the winds that blow from the direction of the rising sun, are healthier. Those that slope away from the north wind are second healthiest, since they have milder winters. A further factor is that the city-state should be well sited for political and military activities. As regards military activities, the city-state should be easy for the citizens themselves to march out from but difficult for their enemies to approach and blockade. It should also possess a plentiful water supply of its own, especially springs. But if it does not, the construction of many large reservoirs for rain water has been found as a way to prevent the supply from running short when the citizens are kept away from their territory by war. Since we must of necessity consider the health of the inhabitants, and it depends on the city-state being well situated on healthy ground and facing in a healthy direction, and second, on 10 using healthy water supplies, this too should be matter of more than incidental concern. For the things our bodies use most frequently and in the greatest quantity contribute most to health, and water and air are by 15 nature of this sort. Hence if it happens that all the springs are not equally healthy or if the healthy ones are not abundant, well-planned city-states should keep apart those suitable for drinking from those used for other purposes.

The same type of fortification is not beneficial for all constitutions. For example, an acropolis [hill fort] is suitable for an oligarchy or a monarchy; one on level ground for a democracy. An aristocracy, on the 20 other hand, should have neither of these, but rather a number of strongholds.

Where private dwellings are concerned, the modern Hippodamean scheme of laying them out in straight rows is considered pleasanter and more useful for general purposes. But, when it comes to security in wartime, the opposite plan, which prevailed in ancient times, is thought to be better. For it makes 25 it difficult for foreign troops to enter and for attackers to find their way around. Hence the best city-state should share in the features of both plans. This is possible if the houses are laid out like vine "clumps" (as some farmers call them), that is, if certain parts and areas are laid out in straight rows, but not the city-state as a whole. In this way, both safety and 30 beauty will be well served.

Some people say that city-states that lay claim to virtue should not have walls. But this is a very old-fashioned notion. Especially when it is plain to see that city-states that pride themselves on not having walls are refuted by the facts. It may not be noble to seek safety behind fortified walls against an evenly 35 matched or only slightly more numerous foe, but it can and does happen that the superior numbers of the attackers are too much for human virtue or the virtue of a small number of people. Hence if the city-state is to survive without suffering harm or arrogant 40 treatment, it should be left to military expertise to

determine what the most secure kind of fortified walls are for it to have, particularly now that the invention of projectiles and siege engines has reached such a *1331a* high degree of precision. To claim that city-states should not have surrounding walls is like flattening the mountains and trying to make the territory easy to invade, or like not having walls for private houses, 5 on the grounds that they make the inhabitants cowardly. Furthermore, we should not forget that the inhabitants of a city-state with surrounding walls can treat it either as having walls or as not having them, whereas the inhabitants of a city-state without walls lack this option. Given that this is how things stand, a city-state not only should have surrounding walls, 10 it should take care to ensure that they both enhance the beauty of the city-state and satisfy military requirements, especially those brought to light by recent discoveries. For just as attackers are always busily concerned with new ways to get the better of city- 15 states, so too, though some defensive devices have already been discovered, defenders should keep searching for and thinking out new ones. For when people are well prepared in the first place, no one even thinks of attacking them.

Chapter 13

But we must now discuss the constitution itself, and *1331b* from which and what sorts of people a city-state should be constituted if it is to be blessedly happy and well governed. In all cases, well-being consists in two 25 things: setting up the aim and end of action correctly and discovering the actions that bear on it. These factors can be in harmony with one another or in disharmony. For people sometimes set up the end 30 well but fail to achieve it in action; and sometimes they achieve everything that promotes the end, but the end they set up is a bad one. Sometimes they make both mistakes. For example, in medicine it sometimes happens that doctors are neither correct in their judgment about what condition a healthy body should be in, nor successful in producing the 35 condition they have set up as their end. In the crafts and sciences both of these have to be under control, the end and the actions directed toward it. It is evident that everyone aims at living well and at happiness. But while some can achieve these ends, others, whether 40 because of luck or because of something in their nature, cannot. For we also need resources in order 1332a to live a good life, although we need fewer of them if we are in a better condition, more if we are in a worse one. Others, though they could achieve happiness, search for it in the wrong place from the outset. But since we are proposing to look at the best constitution, and this is the one under which a city-state will be best governed, and since a city-state is best 5 governed under a constitution that would above all make it possible for the city-state to be happy, it is clear that we should not overlook the question of what happiness actually is.

We say, and we have given this definition in our ethical works (if anything in those discussions is of service), that happiness is a complete activation or use of virtue, and not a qualified use but an unquali- 10 fied one. By "qualified uses" I mean those that are necessary; by "unqualified" I mean those that are noble. For example, in the case of just actions, just retributions and punishments spring from virtue, but are necessary uses of it, and are noble only in a necessary way, since it would be more choiceworthy if no individual or city-state needed such things. On 15 the other hand, just actions that aim at honors and prosperity are unqualifiedly noblest. The former involve choosing something that is somehow bad, whereas the latter are the opposite: they construct and generate goods. To be sure, an excellent man will deal with poverty, disease, and other sorts of bad 20 luck in a noble way. But blessed happiness requires their opposites. For according to the definition established in our ethical works, an excellent man is the sort whose virtue makes *unqualifiedly* good things good *for him*. Clearly, then, his use of them must also be unqualifiedly good and noble. That is why people think that external goods are the causes of 25 happiness. Yet we might as well hold that a lyre is the cause of fine and brilliant lyre playing, and not the performer's craft. It follows, then, from what has been said, that some goods must be there to start with, whereas others must be provided by the legislator. That is why we pray that our city-state will be ideally equipped with the goods that luck controls 30 (for we assume that luck does control them). When we come to making the city-state excellent, however, that is no longer a task for luck but one for scientific knowledge and deliberate choice. A city-state is excel-

lent, however, because the citizens who participate in the constitution are excellent; and in our city-state all the citizens participate in the constitution. The matter we have to investigate, therefore, is how a man becomes excellent. For even if it is possible for all 35 the citizens to be collectively excellent without being so individually, the latter is still more choiceworthy, since if each is excellent, all are.

But surely people become excellent because of three things. The three are nature, habit, and reason. For first [1] one must possess a certain nature from 40 birth, namely, that of a human, and not that of some other animal. Similarly, one's body and soul must be of a certain sort. But in the case of some of these qualities, there is no benefit in just being born with them, because they are altered by our habits. [2] 1332b For some qualities are naturally capable of being developed by habit either in a better direction or in a worse one. The other animals mostly live under the guidance of nature alone, although some are guided a little by habit. [3] But human beings live under the guidance of reason as well, since they alone have reason. Consequently, all three of these factors need 5 to be harmonized with one another. For people often act contrary to their habits and their nature because of reason, if they happen to be persuaded that some other course of action is better.

We have already determined the sorts of natures people should have if it is to be easy for the legislator to take them in hand. Everything thereafter is a task for education. For some things are learned by habituation, others by instruction. 10

Chapter 14

Since every political community is composed of rulers and ruled, we must investigate whether rulers and ruled should be the same or different throughout life. For clearly their education must correspond to this 15 division. Now if they differed from one another as much as gods and heroes are believed to differ from human beings, if the former were so greatly superior, first in body and then in soul, that their superiority was indisputable and manifest to those they ruled— 20 it would clearly be altogether better if the same people always ruled and the others were always ruled. But this is not easy to achieve, and there are not, as Scylax says there are in India, kings that are so superior to the ruled. Evidently, then, and for many different reasons, it is necessary for all to share alike in ruling and being ruled in turn. For equality consists in giving the same to those who are alike, and it is difficult for a constitution to last if its organization is contrary to justice. For the citizens being ruled will be joined by those in the surrounding territory who want to stir up change, and the governing class cannot possibly be numerous enough to be more powerful than all of them.

Surely it is indisputable, however, that the rulers should be different from the ruled. Hence the legislator should investigate the question of how this is to be achieved, and how they should share with one another. We discussed this earlier, for nature itself settled the choice by making part of the same species younger and part older, the former fit to be ruled and the latter to rule. For young people do not object to being ruled, or think themselves better than their rulers, particularly when they are going to be compensated for their contribution when they reach the proper age. We must conclude, therefore, that rulers and ruled are in one way the same and in another different. Consequently, their education too must be in one way the same and in another different. For if someone is going to rule well, as the saying goes, he should first have been ruled.

As we said in our first discussions, however, there is a kind of rule that is for the sake of the ruler and a kind that is for the sake of the ruled. The former, we say, is rule by a master, the latter rule over free people. Now some commands differ not with respect to the tasks they assign but with respect to that for the sake of which they are done. That is why it is noble even for free young men to perform many of the tasks that are held to be appropriate for slaves. For the difference between noble and shameful actions does not lie so much in the acts themselves as in their ends, on that for the sake of which they are performed. Since we say that the virtue of a citizen or ruler is the same as that of the best man, and that the same man should be ruled first and a ruler later, the legislator should make it his business to determine how and through what practices men become good, and what the end of the best life is.

The soul is divided into two parts, one of which has reason intrinsically, whereas the other does not,

but is capable of listening to it, and we say that the virtues of the latter entitle a man to be called, in a certain way, good. As to the question of which of these the end is more particularly found in, to those who make the distinction we mentioned it is not unclear what must be said. For the worse part is always for the sake of the better, and this is as evident in the products of the crafts as it is in those of nature. But the part that has reason is better; and it, in accordance with our usual way of dividing, is divided in two: for there is practical reason and theoretical reason. So it is clear that the rational part of the soul must also be divided in the same manner. Actions too, we will say, are divided analogously, and those that belong to the naturally better part must be more choiceworthy to anyone who can carry out all or only two of them. For what is most choiceworthy for each individual is always this: to attain what is highest. But the whole of life too is divided into work and leisure, war and peace, and of actions some are necessary or useful, others noble. And the same choice must be made among these as among the parts of the soul and their actions. War must be chosen for the sake of peace, work for the sake of leisure, necessary and useful things for the sake of noble ones.

A statesman must, therefore, look to all these things, particularly to those that are better and those that are ends, and legislate in a way that suits the parts of the soul and their actions. And he should legislate in the same way where life and the divisions of actions are concerned. For one should be able to work or go to war, but even better able to remain at peace and leisure; able to perform necessary or useful actions, but better able to perform noble ones. These then are the aims that should be kept in view when educating citizens, both when they are still children and whenever else they need education.

It is evident, however, that those Greeks who are currently held to be best governed, and the legislators who established their constitutions, did not organize the various aspects of their constitutions to promote the best end. Nor did they organize their laws and educational system to promote all the virtues, but instead were vulgarly inclined to promote the ones held to be more useful and more conducive to acquisition. Some later writers have expressed the same opinion in the same spirit. For they praise the Spartan constitution and express admiration for the aim of its legislator, because his entire legislation was intended to promote conquest and war. What they say is easy to refute by argument, and has now been refuted by

15 the facts too. For most human beings are eager to rule as masters over many because it provides a ready supply of the goods of luck. And Thibron and all these other writers are no different: they admire the

20 Spartan legislator because by training the Spartans to face danger he enabled them to rule over many. And yet it is clear, now that their empire is no longer in their hands at any rate, that the Spartans are not a happy people, and that their legislator is not a good one. Moreover, it is absurd if it was by keeping to his laws and putting them into practice without impedi-

25 ment that they lost their fine way of life. They are also incorrect in their conception of the sort of rule a legislator should be seen to honor. For rule over free people is nobler and more virtuous than rule by a master. Besides, one should not consider a city-state

30 happy or praise its legislator because he trained it to conquer and rule its neighbors, since such things involve great harm. For clearly any citizen who is able to should also try to acquire the power to rule his own city-state. Yet this is precisely what the Spartans accused their king, Pausanias, of doing, even though he held so high an office.

Arguments and laws of this sort are not worthy of a statesman, then, nor are they beneficial or true. For

35 the same things are best both for individuals and for communities, and it is these that a legislator should implant in the souls of human beings. Training in war should not be undertaken for the sake of reducing those who do not deserve it to slavery, but, first, to

40 avoid becoming enslaved to others; second, to pursue a position of leadership in order to benefit the ruled, not to be masters of all of them; and, third, to be

1334a masters of those who deserve to be slaves.

Both facts and arguments testify, then, that the legislator should give more serious attention to how to organize his legislation, both the part that deals with military affairs and the part that deals with other

5 matters, for the sake of peace and leisure. For most city-states of the sort described remain secure while they are at war, but come to ruin once they have acquired empire. Like an iron sword, they lose their edge when they remain at peace. But the one respon- sible is their legislator, who did not educate them to

10 be able to be at leisure.

Chapter 15

Since it is evident that human beings have the same end, both individually and collectively, and since the best man and the best constitution must of necessity have the same aim, it is evident that the virtues suit- able for leisure should be present in both. For, as has been said repeatedly, peace is the end of war, and 15 leisure of work. Some of the virtues useful for leisure and leisured pursuits accomplish their task while one is actually at leisure, but others do so while one is at work. For many necessities must be present in order for leisure to be possible. That is why it is appropriate for our city-state to have temperance, courage, and endurance. For as the proverb says, there is no leisure 20 for slaves, and people who are unable to face danger courageously are the slaves of their attackers. Courage and endurance are required for work, philosophy for leisure, and temperance and justice for both, but particularly for peace and leisure. For war compels people to be just and temperate, but the enjoyment 25 of good luck and the leisure that accompanies peace tend to make them arrogant. Much justice and tem- perance are needed, therefore, by those who are held to be doing best and who enjoy all the things regarded 30 as blessings; people like those, if there are any, who live in the isles of the blessed, as the poets call them. For they will be most in need of philosophy, temper- ance, and justice the more they live at leisure amidst an abundance of such goods. It is evident, then, why a city-state that is to be happy and good should share in these virtues. For it is shameful to be unable to 35 make use of good things, but it is even more shameful to be unable to make use of them in leisure time— to make it plain that we are good men when working or at war, but slaves when at peace and leisure. That is why one should not cultivate virtue as the city-state of the Spartans does. For the difference between the 40 Spartans and others is not that they consider different 1334b things to be the greatest goods, but that they believe that these goods are obtained by means of a particular virtue. And because they consider these goods and the enjoyment of them to be better than the enjoyment of the virtues, [they train themselves only in the virtue that is useful for acquiring them, and ignore the virtue that is exercised in leisure.] But it is evident from what we have said, that [the latter virtue should be cultivated] on its own account. We must now

study how and through what means this will come
about.

We distinguished earlier three requirements: nature, habit, and reason. We have already determined the natural qualities our citizens should have. It remains to study whether they are to be educated through reason first or through habits. For the harmony between those should be the best kind of harmony. For it is possible for someone's reason to have missed the best supposition and for him to be led similarly astray by his habits.

This much at least is evident. First, procreation, like the production of any other kind of thing, has a starting point, and some starting points have ends that are the starting points of further ends. But reason and understanding constitute our natural end. Hence they are the ends that procreation and the training of our habits should be organized to promote. Second, just as soul and body are two, so we see that the soul has two parts as well, one that is nonrational and one that has reason. Their states are also two in number, desire and understanding. And just as the development of the body is prior to that of the soul, so the nonrational part is prior to the rational. This too is evident. For spirit, wish, and also appetite are present in children right from birth, whereas reasoning and understanding naturally develop as they grow older. That is why supervision of the body comes first and precedes that of the soul; then comes supervision of appetite or desire. But supervision of desire should be for the sake of understanding, and that of the body for the sake of the soul.

Chapter 16

Since, then, the legislator should see to it from the start that the bodies of children being reared develop in the best possible way, he must first supervise the union of the sexes, and determine what sorts of people should have marital relations with one another, and when. In legislating for this community, he should have regard both to the people involved and to their life spans, so that they reach the same stage of life at the same time: that is to say, there should be no disharmony between their procreative powers, as happens when the man is still capable of procreating but the woman is not, or when the woman is capable

and the man not, since these things cause conflicts and disagreements among couples.

Next, he should have regard to the difference in age between parents and children. For children should not be too far removed in age from their fathers, since the gratitude of children is of no benefit to older fathers, and the assistance of such fathers is of no benefit to their children. But they should not be too close in age either, since this leads to many difficulties. For there is less respect for them, as for contemporaries, and the closeness in age leads to conflict over the management of the household.

Third, to return to the point at which we began this digression, the legislator should ensure that the bodies of those who are born are as he wishes.

These results can pretty well all be achieved by a single sort of supervision. For in the majority of cases, a man's fertility comes to an end at a maximum age of seventy, and a woman's at fifty. Hence the beginning of their sexual union should be so timed that they reach their decline simultaneously. The coupling of young people, however, is a bad thing from the point of view of childbearing. For in all animals the young are more likely to bear offspring that are imperfect, female, or undersized, and so the same must occur in human beings as well. The following is evidence of this. In all those city-states in which the coupling of young men and women is the local custom, people's bodies are imperfect and undersized. Second, young women have longer labors, and more of them die in childbirth. According to some accounts, indeed, the well-known oracle was given to the Troezenians not because of anything to do with the harvest but because their custom of marrying off younger women resulted in so many deaths. Third, with regard to temperance or chastity, it is beneficial for women to be given in marriage when they are older, since women who have had sex when they are young are held to be more licentious. Fourth, if males have sex while their bodies are still growing, this is held to impair their growth; for this growth too takes a definite period of time, after which it is no longer extensive. It is fitting, therefore, for the women to be married at around the age of eighteen; the men at thirty-seven or a little before. At those ages, sexual union will occur when their bodies are in their prime, and will end, conveniently for both, at the time when they cease to be fertile. As to difference in age between

parents and children, if the children are born soon after marriage occurs, as can reasonably be expected, they will be at the beginning of their prime when their father's period of vigor has come to an end, at
35 around the age of seventy.

We have said when sexual union should occur; as for the season, however, one should use the time many people use. For nowadays they correctly set aside the winter as the time to begin this sort of cohabitation. In addition, couples should study for themselves what is said by doctors and natural scien-
40 tists about procreation. For doctors have adequately discussed the times that are right as regards the body, and natural scientists have discussed the winds, favor-
1335b ing northerly over southerly ones.

As to the bodily characteristics in parents that are most beneficial to the offspring being produced, we must deal with that topic at greater length in our discussion of the supervision of children. It is suffi-
5 cient to speak of it in outline now. Neither the physical condition of athletes nor one that is overly reliant on medical treatment and poorly suited to exertion is useful from the point of view of health or procreation, or is the condition needed in a good citizen. But the condition that is a mean between these two *is* useful for these purposes. The proper physical condition, therefore, is one that is achieved by exertion, but not by violent exertion, and that promotes not just one thing, as the athletic condition does, but the
10 actions of free people. And these should be provided to women and men alike. Even pregnant women should take care of their bodies and not stop exercising or adopt a meager diet. The legislator can easily prevent them from doing these things by requiring them
15 to take a walk every day to worship the gods whose assigned prerogative is to watch over birth. But in contrast with their bodies, it is appropriate for their minds to remain somewhat inactive. For unborn children obviously draw resources from their mothers, just as plants do from the earth.

As to the question of whether to rear offspring or expose them, there should be a law against rearing
20 deformed ones, but where it is because of the number of children, if it happens that the way custom is organized prohibits the exposure of offspring once they are born, a limit should be imposed on procreation. And if some people have sex in violation of this regulation and conceive a child, it should be

aborted before the onset of sensation and life. For sensation and life distinguish what is pious from what 25 is impious here.

Since we have specified the earliest age at which men and women should begin their sexual union, we should also specify the appropriate length of time for them to perform public service by having children. For the offspring of parents who are too old, like those of parents who are too young, are imperfect in both 30 body and mind, and those of people who have actually reached old age are weak. Hence we should define the length of the time in question by reference to the time when the mind is in its prime. In most cases, this occurs around the fiftieth year, as some of the poets who measure age in periods of seven years have pointed out. Therefore, men who exceed this age by 35 four or five years should be released from procreating for the community. If they have sex after that, it should be evident that it is for the sake of health, or for some other such reason.

As to having sex with another man or another woman when one is a husband or referred to as such, it should be regarded as shameful to be openly involved in any form of it with anyone. If a man is 40 discovered doing something of this sort during his period of procreation, he should be punished with a loss of honor appropriate to his offense.   1336a

Chapter 17

It should be recognized that the sort of nourishment children are given once they are born makes a large difference to the strength of their bodies. It is evident to anyone who investigates the other animals or those 5 nations concerned to cultivate a military disposition that the nourishment particularly suited to children's bodies has a lot of milk in it but very little wine, because of the diseases it produces. Furthermore, it is also beneficial for them to make whatever movements are possible at that age. But to prevent curvature of the limbs, due to softness, there are certain mechan- 10 ical devices, which some nations already employ, to keep their bodies straight. It is beneficial, too, to habituate children to the cold right from the time they are small, since this is very useful both from the point of view of health and from that of military affairs. That is why many non-Greeks have the custom

15 of submerging newborn children in a cold river, whereas many others—for example, the Celts—dress them in light clothing. For whenever it is possible to create habits, it is better to create them right from the start, but to do so gradually. And because their bodily condition is hot, children are naturally suited
20 to being trained to bear the cold.

In the first stage of life, then, it is beneficial to adopt this sort of supervision as well as any other similar to it. During the next stage, which lasts until the age of five, it is not a good idea to have children engage in any kind of learning or any necessary tasks, lest it interfere with their growth. But they should
25 engage in enough exercise to avoid physical laziness, and this should be provided to them through play and other such activities. But the games they play should not be either unfit for free people or exerting or undisciplined. As for the kinds of stories and fables
30 children of this age should listen to, the officials called child supervisors should deal with that issue. For all such things should pave the way for their later pursuits. Hence many of the games they play should imitate the serious occupations of later life. Those in the *Laws* who prevent children from screaming and crying are wrong to prohibit such things, for they
35 contribute to growth, since they are a sort of exercise for the body. For holding the breath gives strength to those who are exerting themselves, and this is just what occurs in children when they are screaming their lungs out.

The child supervisors should pay attention to the
10 way the children pursue leisure. In particular, they should ensure that they pursue it as little as possible in the company of slaves. For, at this age, and until
1336b they are seven, children must be educated in the household. So it is reasonable to expect that they will pick up some taint of servility from what they see and hear even at that early age. The legislator should altogether outlaw shameful talk from the city-state, as he would any other shameful thing, since by speaking
5 lightly of a shameful activity one comes closer to doing it. He should particularly outlaw it among children, so that they neither say nor hear anything of the sort. If it happens, none the less, that any free man who is not yet old enough to have been given a seat at the messes is found saying or doing something
10 forbidden, he should be punished by being dishonored or beaten. But if he is older than this, he should be punished with those dishonors usually reserved for the unfree, because he has acted in a manner characteristic of slaves.

Since we are outlawing shameful talk, it is evident that we should also outlaw looking at unseemly pictures or stories. The officials should ensure, therefore, that there are no statues or pictures representing un- 15 seemly acts, except those kept in the temples of those gods at whose festivals custom permits even mockery to occur. Custom allows men of suitable age to pay this sort of honor to the gods on behalf of themselves and of their wives and children. But younger people should not be permitted to witness iambus or comedy until they have reached the age when it is appropriate 20 for them to recline at the communal table and drink wine, and their education has rendered them immune to the harm such things can do.

Our present discussion of this issue has been cursory. Later we must stop and determine it at greater 25 length, first raising the problem of whether the attendance of the young at such performances should or should not be prohibited, and if so how it should be handled. It was right to touch on it at this juncture, however, but only to the extent necessary for present purposes. Perhaps Theodorus, the tragic actor, put the point rather well. He said that he never allowed any other actor, not even an incompetent one, to play a part before he did, because audiences become accustomed to the voice they hear first. The same 30 is true of our relationships with people and things; whatever we encounter first we like better. That is why everything bad or vulgar should be alien to the young, particularly if it involves vice or malice.

When children reach the age of five, they should 35 spend the two years till they are seven as observers of the lessons they themselves will eventually have to learn. There are then two stages in their education that should be distinguished, from age seven to puberty and from puberty to age twenty-one. For those who divide the stages of life into seven-year periods 40 are for the most part correct. But one should be guided by a natural division, since every craft and 1337a every sort of education is intended to supplement nature. First, then, we should investigate whether some organization should be established to deal with the children; second, whether it is beneficial for their supervision to be established by the community or arranged on a private basis (as is the case in most city- 5 states nowadays); and third, what sort of supervision it should be.

Book VIII

Chapter 1

No one would dispute, therefore, that legislators should be particularly concerned with the education of the young, since in city-states where this does not occur, the constitutions are harmed. For education should suit the particular constitution. In fact, the character peculiar to each constitution usually safe-
15 guards it as well as establishes it initially (for example, the democratic character, a democracy; and the oli-garchic one, an oligarchy), and a better character is always the cause of a better constitution. Besides, prior education and habituation are required in order to perform certain elements of the task of any capacity or craft. Hence it is clear that this also holds for the
20 activities of virtue.

Since the whole city-state has one single end, how-ever, it is evident that education too must be one and the same for all, and that its supervision must be communal, not private as it is at present, when each
25 individual supervises his own children privately and gives them whatever private instruction he thinks best. Training for communal matters should also be communal.

At the same time, one should not consider any citizen as belonging to himself alone, but as all be-longing to the city-state, since each is a part of the city-state. And it is natural for the supervision of each part to look to the supervision of the whole. For this
30 reason one might praise the Spartans, since they pay the most serious attention to their children, and do so as a community.

Chapter 2

It is evident, then, that there should be legislation regarding education, and that education should be communal. But the questions of what kind of educa-tion there should be and how it should be carried
35 out should not be neglected. In fact, there is dispute at present about what its tasks are. For not all consider

that the young should learn the same things, whether to promote virtue or the best life; nor is it evident whether it is more appropriate for education to de-velop the mind or the soul's character.

Investigation of the education we see around us results in confusion, since it is not at all clear whether people should be trained in what is useful for life, in 40 what conduces to virtue, or in something out of the ordinary. For all of these proposals have acquired some advocates. Besides, there is no agreement about what promotes virtue. For, in the first place, people do not all esteem the same virtue, so they quite under- 1337b standably do not agree about the training needed for it.

That children should be taught those useful things that are really necessary, however, is not unclear. But it is evident that they should not be taught all of them, since there is a difference between the tasks of the free and those of the unfree, and that they 5 should share only in such useful things as will not turn them into vulgar craftsmen. (Any task, craft, or branch of learning should be considered vulgar if it 10 renders the body or mind of free people useless for the practices and activities of virtue. That is why the crafts that put the body into a worse condition and work done for wages are called vulgar; for they debase the mind and deprive it of leisure.)

Even in the case of some of the sciences that are suitable for a free person, while it is not unfree to participate in them up to a point, to study them too 15 assiduously or exactly is likely to result in the harms just mentioned. What one acts or learns *for* also makes a big difference. For what one does for one's own sake, for the sake of friends, or on account of virtue is not unfree, but someone who does the same thing for others would often be held to be acting like a hired laborer or a slave.   20

Chapter 3

The subjects that are now established tend in two directions, as was mentioned earlier. But generally speaking there are four that are customarily taught: reading and writing, gymnastics, music, and fourth (but only occasionally), drawing. Reading, writing, 25 and drawing are taught because they are useful for life and have many applications; gymnastics is taught

because it contributes to courage; but in the case of music a problem immediately arises. Nowadays, most people take part in music for the sake of pleasure. But those who originally included it as a part of educa-
30 tion did so, as has often been said, because nature itself aims not only at the correct use of work but also at the capacity for noble leisured activity. Since this is the starting point for everything else, I propose to discuss it once again.

If both are required, but leisured activity is more choiceworthy than work and is its end, we should try to discover what people should do for leisured activity.
35 For surely they should not be amusing themselves, otherwise amusement would have to be our end in life. But if that is impossible, and if amusements are more to be used while one is at work (for one who exerts himself needs relaxation, relaxation is the end of amusement, and work is accompanied by toil and strain), then we should, for this reason, permit amuse-
40 ment, but we should be careful to use it at the right time, dispensing it as a medicine for the ills of work. For this sort of motion of the soul is relaxing and restful because of the pleasure it involves.

1338a   Leisured activity is itself held to involve pleasure, happiness, and living blessedly. This is not available to those who are working, however, but only to those who are engaged in leisured activity. For one who is working is doing so for the sake of some end he does
5 not possess, whereas happiness *is* an end that everyone thinks is accompanied not by pain but by pleasure. This pleasure is not the same for everyone, however, but each takes it to be what suits himself and his condition, and the best person takes it to be the best pleasure, the one that comes from the noblest things. It is evident, then, that we should learn and be taught
10 certain things that promote leisured activity. And these subjects and studies are undertaken for their own sake, whereas those relating to work are necessary and for the sake of things other than themselves.

It is for this reason that our predecessors assigned music a place in education. They did not do so because they supposed: that it is necessary for life (for
15 it is nothing of the sort); or that, like reading and writing, it is useful for making money, managing a household, acquiring further learning, or for a large number of political activities; or that, like gymnastics, it promotes health and vigor, for we see that neither
20 of these results from music. What remains, then, is

that music is for pursuit in leisure, which is evidently the very reason our predecessors included it in education. For they give it a place among the leisured pursuits they considered appropriate for free people. Hence Homer's instruction to "call the bard alone to the rich banquet." And he goes on to mention certain 25 others who "call the bard that he may bring delight to all." Elsewhere, Odysseus says that the best leisured pursuit is when men are enjoying good cheer and "the banqueters seated in due order throughout the hall, give ear to the bard." It is evident, then, that there is a certain kind of education that children must be given not because it is useful or necessary but 30 because it is noble and suitable for a free person. But the number of subjects involved (whether one or many), what they are, and how they should be taught—these are questions that must be discussed later on. But as things stand, a certain amount of progress has been made, because we have some evidence from the ancients about the educational sub- 35 jects they established, music being an obvious case in point.

Furthermore, it is clear that children should be taught some useful subjects (such as reading and writing) not only because of their utility, but also because many other areas of study become possible through them. Similarly, they should be taught draw- 40 ing not in order to avoid making mistakes in their private purchases or being cheated when buying or selling products, but rather because it makes them 1338b contemplate the beauty of bodies. It is completely inappropriate for magnanimous and free people to be always asking what use something is.

Since it is evident that education through habituation must come before education through reason, and that education of the body must come before education of the mind, it clearly follows that children 5 must be put in the hands of physical trainers who will bring their bodies into a certain condition, and coaches who will teach them to do certain physical tasks.

Chapter 4

At present, the city-states that are thought to be most concerned with children turn them into athletes, and thus distort the shape and development of their bod- 10

ies; whereas the Spartans, though they do not make this mistake, none the less brutalize their children through rigorous exertion, thinking that this will greatly enhance their courage. Yet, as we have said many times, the supervision of children should not
15 aim to promote just one virtue, especially not this one. But even if this one were the aim, the Spartans do not succeed in producing it. For in other animals or in non-Greek nations, we do not find that courage goes along with the greatest savagery, but that it goes along with a tamer, lionlike character. Many of these
20 nations think nothing of killing and cannibalizing people—for example, the Achaeans and Heniochi, who live around the Black Sea. And there are similar peoples on the mainland, and others who are even worse. These nations are skilled in raiding, to be sure, but of courage they have no share.

Besides, we know that even the Spartans, who were
25 superior to others as long as they alone persisted in their devotion to rigorous exertion, are now inferior to others in both gymnastic and military contests. They were superior to others not because they trained their young people in that rigorous way, but only because they had training, while their adversaries had none.

So nobility, not brutality, should play the leading role here. For no wolf or other wild beast faces danger
30 when it is noble to do so, but a good man does. Those who throw the young into too much of this sort of rigorous exertion and leave them without training in what is necessary produce people who are truly vulgar. For they make them useful to statesmanship for one
35 task only, and one at which they are worse than other people, as our argument shows. One should judge the Spartans on the basis not of their earlier deeds, but of their present ones. For now there are people who rival them in education, whereas earlier there were none.

We have agreed, then, that we must make use of gymnastics, and how it is to be employed. Until children reach puberty they should be given lighter exer-
40 cises, but a strict diet and strenuous exertions should be forbidden, so that nothing impedes their growth. It is no small indication that such exertions can have
1339a this impeding effect that one finds only two or three people on the list of Olympic victors who were victorious both as men and as boys, because the training of the young, and the strenuous exercises involved,

robs them of their strength. But when they have spent the three years after puberty on other studies, it is 5 appropriate for them to spend the next period of their lives exerting themselves and maintaining a strict diet. For one should not exert the mind and the body at the same time, since these kinds of exertion naturally produce opposite effects: exerting the body impedes the mind and exerting the mind impedes the body. 10

Chapter 5

As for music, we have mentioned some of the problems in our earlier discussion. But it will be well to take them up again now and develop them further, in order to provide a sort of prelude to the arguments that might be made in an exposition of the subject. For it is not easy to determine what the power of music is, or why one should take part in it. Is it for 15 the sake of amusement and relaxation, like sleep and drink? Sleep and drink are not in themselves serious matters; they are pleasant, and at the same time they "put an end to care," as Euripides says. That is why people include music in the same class as sleep and drink, indeed, and treat them all in the same way. 20 They also include dancing in this class. Or should we believe instead that music contributes something to virtue, on the grounds that, just as gymnastics gives us a body of a certain quality, so music has the power to give us a character of a certain quality, by instilling the habits that enable us to enjoy ourselves in the right way? Or does music contribute something to 25 leisured pursuits and to practical wisdom (which must be set down as third among the possibilities that are mentioned)?

It is clear that the young should not be educated for the sake of amusement. For while they are learning they are not amusing themselves, since learning is a painful process. On the other hand, it is not appropriate to give children of that age leisured pursuits, 30 since the end (something complete) is not appropriate for someone who is incomplete. But perhaps it might be held that the serious activities of children are undertaken for the sake of their amusement when they have become men and are complete. If that were true, however, why should they have to learn music themselves? Why shouldn't they be like the kings of the Persians and the Medes, and take part in musical learning and its pleasure through listening to others performing? Aren't those who have made music their very task and craft bound to produce something better than those who devote only as much time to it as is needed to learn it? On the other hand, if they have to study music in depth, they would also have to take up the activity of cooking delicacies. But that is absurd.

The same problem arises, however, even if music is able to improve people's character. Why should they learn it themselves, rather than being like the Spartans, who enjoy the music of others in the right way and are able to judge it? For the Spartans do not learn it themselves, but are still able, so they say, to determine which melodies are good and which are not.

The same argument also applies if music is to be used to promote well-being and the leisured pursuits appropriate to someone who is free. Why should they learn it themselves rather than benefiting from the fact that others practice it? In this regard, we may consider the conception we have of the gods; for Zeus himself does not sing or accompany poets on the lyre. On the contrary, we even say that musicians are vulgar craftsmen, and that a true man would not perform music unless he were drunk or amusing himself.

Perhaps we should investigate these matters later on, however. The question we must first investigate is whether music is to be included in education or not, and in which of the three areas we mentioned earlier its power lies: amusement, education, or leisured pursuits. It seems reasonable to assign it to, and it seems to have a share in, all three. For amusement is for the sake of relaxation, and relaxation is of necessity pleasant, since it is a sort of cure for the pain caused by one's exertions. It is generally agreed, moreover, that one's leisured pursuits should be not only noble but also pleasant, since happiness is both. But everyone says that music is among the very greatest pleasures, whether it is unadorned or with voice accompaniment. At any rate, Museus says that "singing is the most pleasant thing for mortals." That is why, because of its power to delight, it is reasonably included in social gatherings and among leisured pursuits.

One might suppose, then, that young people should be educated in music for this reason too. For harmless pleasures are suitable not only because they promote the end of life, but because they promote relaxation too. But since people rarely achieve this end, whereas they do frequently relax and make use of amusements (not only because relaxation and amusements lead to other things, but also because of the pleasure they provide), it would be useful to allow the young to find rest from time to time in the pleasures of music.

What has happened, however, is that people make amusement their end. For the end perhaps involves a certain pleasure (though not just any chance one), and in their search for it they mistake amusement for it, because it has a certain similarity to the end of action. For the end is not choiceworthy for the sake of what will come later, and these sorts of amusements are not choiceworthy for what will come later, but because of things that have happened already (exertions and pains, for example). One might plausibly conclude, therefore, that this is the reason people try to achieve happiness by means of pleasant amusements. But people do not take part in music for that reason alone, it seems, but also because it is useful for promoting relaxation.

Yet we must investigate whether this effect of music is not simply coincidental, whereas its true nature is more estimable than the usefulness we mentioned suggests, and whether one should not take part only in the common pleasure that derives from music (a pleasure everyone perceives, since it is of a natural sort, and so is agreeable to people of all ages and characters), but see whether music influences one's character and soul in some way. This would be clear if one came to be of a certain quality in one's character because of music. But that we do indeed come to be of a certain quality is evident on many different grounds, and not least from the melodies of Olympus. For it is generally agreed that they cause souls to become inspired, and inspiration is an emotion that affects the character of one's soul.

Moreover, everyone who listens to representations comes to have the corresponding emotions, even when the rhythms and melodies these representations contain are taken in isolation. And since music happens to be one of the pleasures, and virtue is a matter of enjoying, loving, and hating in the right way, it is clear that nothing is more important than that one should learn to judge correctly and get into the habit of enjoying decent characters and noble actions. But rhythms and melodies contain the greatest likenesses of the true natures of anger, gentleness, courage, temperance, and their opposites, and of all the other components of character as well. The facts make this clear. For when we listen to such representations our souls are changed. But getting into the habit of being pained or pleased by likenesses is close to being in the same condition where the real things are concerned. For example, if 25 someone enjoys looking at an image of something for no other reason than because of its shape or form, he is bound to enjoy looking at the very thing whose image he is looking at.

It happens, however, that other perceptible objects, such as those of touch or taste, contain no likenesses of the components of character, although the objects of sight contain faint ones. For there are a few shapes 30 that do contain such likenesses, and everyone perceives them. Still, they are not really likenesses of the components of character; rather, the shapes and colors that are produced are signs of characters, and are derived from a body in the grip of the emotions. This is not to 35 deny, however, that insofar as it also makes a difference which of these objects we look at, the young should look at the works of Polygnotus or any other painter or sculptor who deals with character, not those of Pauson.

It is evident, however, that melodies themselves contain representations of the components of character. For, in the first place, harmonies have divergent na- 40 tures, so that listeners are affected differently and do not respond in the same way to each one. They respond to some (for example, the so-called Mixo-Lydian) in a 1340b more mournful and solemn way; to others (for example, the more relaxed modes), their response is more tender minded; their response to the Dorian (which is held to be the only mode that produces this effect) is particularly balanced and composed, whereas the Phrygian causes them to be inspired. These views have 5 been well discussed by those who have philosophized about this type of education, since they base their arguments on the facts themselves. The same also holds of the different rhythms. Some have a steadying character, others get us moving; and some of these movements are more slavish or boorish, whereas others are more 10 free.

It is evident from all these considerations that music has the power to produce a certain quality in the character of our souls. And if it has this power, children should clearly be introduced to music and educated in it. Besides, education in music is appropriate to their youthful nature. For on account of their age, the young 15 are unwilling to put up with anything that is unsweetened with pleasure, and music is something naturally

sweet. Also there seems to be a natural affinity for harmonic modes and rhythms. That is why many of the wise say the soul is a harmony, others that it has a harmony.

Chapter 6

We must now discuss the problem we mentioned earlier of whether or not the young ought to learn to sing and to play an instrument themselves. It is not 20 difficult to see, of course, that if someone takes part in performance himself, it makes a great difference in the development of certain qualities, since it is difficult if not impossible for people to become excellent judges of performance if they do not take part in it. At the same time, children should have some- 25 thing to keep them occupied, and the rattle of Archytas, which is given to young children to keep them from breaking things in the house, should be considered a good invention, since youngsters cannot keep still. A rattle is suitable for children in their infancy, then, and education is a rattle for older children. 30

These considerations make it evident that children should be educated in music so as to be able to take part in its performance. Moreover, it is not difficult to determine what is suitable or unsuitable for them at various ages, or to solve the problem raised by those who say that to care about performance is vulgar. For, first, since one should take part in performance in order to judge, for this reason they should engage in 35 performance while they are young and stop performing when they are older, but be able to judge which melodies are noble and enjoy them in the right way, because of what they learned while they were young. As for the objection raised by some people, that performing music makes one vulgar, it is not difficult to 40 refute, if we investigate the extent to which those being educated in political virtue should take part in performance, what sorts of melodies and rhythms they should take part in, and on which sorts of instruments 1341a they should learn (since this too probably makes a difference). The refutation depends on these issues. For it is quite possible that certain styles of music *do* have the effect we mentioned. It is evident, then, that learning music should not be an impediment to later 5 activities, or make children's bodies into those of vulgar craftsmen, useless for military or political training, current employment, or later studies.

This could be achieved where lessons in music are concerned if the students do not exert themselves to learn either what is needed for professional competi-
10 tion or the astonishing or out-of-the-ordinary works which have now made their way into competitions and from there into education, but rather learn the ones not of this sort and only up to the point at which they are able to enjoy noble melodies and rhythms,
15 instead of just the common sort of music, which appeals even to some of the other animals, and to the majority of slaves and children as well.

It is also evident from these considerations what sorts of instruments should be used. Flutes should not be introduced into their education, nor should the cithara, or any other professional instruments of that sort. They should learn only those instruments that will make them good listeners, whether to musical educa-
20 tion or to education of any other sort. Besides, the flute has more to do with religious frenzy than with character, and so the correct occasions for its use are those where observing has the power to purify rather than educate. The fact that playing the flute interferes with
25 speech also tells against its use in education.

For these reasons, our predecessors were right to reject the practice of having the young or the free play the flute, even when they had played it earlier. For when they came to have more leisure as a result of greater prosperity, and took greater pride in their virtue, and had in addition reflected on their accomplishments both before and after the Persian Wars,
30 they seized indiscriminately on every sort of learning and pursued them all. Hence they also included flute playing among their studies. In Sparta, there was even a patron of the theater who played the flute himself to accompany his own chorus. And in Athens flute playing became such a local custom that most free
35 people took part in it, as is clear from the tablet Thrasippus, the theater patron, set up for Ecphantides. Later, when they were better able to distinguish what does promote virtue from what does not, they rejected flute playing because of their experience with it. And the same thing happened to many other ancient instruments (for example, the pektis and the
40 barbitos), those that enhance the pleasure of people who listen for embellishments (the heptagon, the trigona, and the sambukai), and all those requiring professional knowledge. The story told by the ancients 1341b about flutes is also plausible. They say that Athena invented flutes, but discarded them. There is nothing wrong with saying that the goddess did this out of annoyance at how flute playing distorted her face, 5 but the more likely explanation is that the flute does nothing to develop the mind, whereas we attribute scientific knowledge and craft to Athena.

We reject professional education in instruments, then, (and by professional education I mean the kind that aims at competition). For the performer does not 10 take part in this kind of education for the sake of his own virtue but to give his audience pleasure, and a boorish pleasure at that. That is precisely why we judge this sort of activity to be more appropriate for hired laborers than for free men. For performers do indeed become vulgar, since the end they aim at is a base one. The listener, because he is boorish himself, 15 typically has an influence on the music, in that he imparts certain qualities to the professionals who perform for him, and to their bodies as well, because of the movements he requires them to make.

Chapter 7

As for harmonies and rhythms and their role in education, we should also investigate: whether all the harmonies and rhythms should be used, or whether we 20 should divide them; whether the same division should be established for those who are at work on their education, or a third class introduced. Since we can certainly see that music consists of melody making and rhythms, we should not neglect the power that each of these has to promote education but ask 25 whether we should prefer music that has a good melody or the kind that has a good rhythm. But since I consider that current experts on music as well as those in philosophy who happen to be experienced in issues pertaining to musical education say many good things on these topics, I shall refer anyone who wants a precise account of each particular to their works. 30 Here, however, the discussion concerns legislation, and we shall speak in outline only.

Since we accept the division made by some people in philosophy who divide melodies into those relating to character, action, and inspiration, claiming that the harmonies are by nature peculiarly suited to these

35 particular melodies, one being suited to one melody, and another to another; and since we claim that music should not be used for the sake of one benefit but several—for it is for the sake of education and purification (I shall not elaborate on what I mean by purification here, but I shall return to it in my work on poetics and discuss it in greater detail), and third, for

40 leisured pursuit, for rest, and for the relaxation of one's tensions—it is evident that all the harmonies

1342a are to be used, but that they are not all to be used in the same way. The ones that most pertain to character should be used in education, whereas those that pertain to action or inspiration should be used for listening to while others perform them. For any emotion

5 that strongly affects some people's souls (for example, pity, fear, or inspiration) is present in everyone, although to a greater or lesser degree. For there are some who are prone to become possessed by this motion. But under the influence of sacred melodies (when they make use of the ones that induce a frenzy in their souls), we see that they calm down, as if

10 they had received medical treatment and a purifying purgation. The same thing, then, must be experienced by those who are prone to pity or fear, by those who are generally emotional, and by others to the extent that they share in these emotions: they all undergo a kind of purification and get a pleasant feeling of relief. In a similar way, the purifying melo-

15 dies provide harmless enjoyment for people.

That is why competitors who perform music for the theater should be permitted to use such harmonies and melodies. But since theater audiences are of two kinds, one free and generally educated, the other boorish and composed of vulgar craftsmen, hired laborers, and other people of that sort, the latter too

20 must be provided with competitions and spectacles for the purposes of relaxation. Just as there are souls that are distorted from the natural state, so too there are deviant harmonies and melodies that are strained and over-ornamented, and what gives each person

25 pleasure is what is akin to his nature. Hence those who compete before a theater audience of the second sort should be permitted to use the second type of music.

But, as we said, the melodies and harmonies that pertain to character should be used for education. The Dorian is of this sort, as we said earlier, but we

30 should accept any other that passes the inspection

carried out for us by those who share in the practice of philosophy and musical education. The Socrates of the *Republic* was not right to retain only the Phrygian along with the Dorian, however, particularly since he includes the flute among the instruments he rejects. For the Phrygian has the same power among the harmonies that the flute has among the instruments, 1342b since both are frenzied and emotional. For all Bacchic frenzy and all motions of that sort are more closely associated with the flute than with any of the other instruments, whereas among the harmonies, 5 the Phrygian melodies are the ones that are suited to them. Poetry shows this clearly. For example, the dithyramb is generally held to be Phrygian. And experts on these matters cite many instances to prove this, notably the fact that when Philoxenus tried to compose a dithyramb—*The Mysians*—in Dorian, he 10 could not do it, but the very nature of his material forced him back into Phrygian, which is the harmony naturally appropriate to it. As for the Dorian, everyone agrees that it is the steadiest and has a more courageous character than any other. Besides, we praise what is in a mean between two extremes, and say that it is what we should pursue. So, since the Dorian 15 has this nature, when compared to the other harmonies, it is evident that Dorian melodies are more suitable for the education of younger people.

There are two things to aim at: what is possible and what is suitable. And each individual should undertake what is more possible and more suitable for him. But possibility and suitability are determined by one's stage of life. For example, it is not easy for 20 people exhausted by age to sing harmonies that are strained—nature recommends the relaxed harmonies at their stage of life. That is why some musical experts rightly criticize Socrates because he rejected the relaxed harmonies for the purposes of education, not because they have the power that drink has of produc- 25 ing Bacchic frenzy, but because like drink they make us weak. So, with an eye to that future stage of life— old age—children *should* take up harmonies and melodies of this relaxed sort. Moreover, if there is a certain sort of harmony that is suited to childhood, 30 because it has the power to provide both order and education at the same time (as seems particularly true of the Lydian harmony), then it is evident that these three things must be made the defining principles of education: the mean, the possible, and the suitable.

VII

CICERO

In 133 B.C., Tiberius Sempronius Gracchus, tribune of the people of Rome and the leading advocate of reforms favoring the plebeian classes, was assassinated—Plutarch indicates that he was clubbed to death—during a riot precipitated by his political enemies, the senatorial elite. Twelve years later, his brother Gaius, whose credentials and platform were strikingly similar, met a virtually identical fate. Thus began one hundred years of upheaval and civil war, involving great rivalries between Marius and Sulla, Caesar and Pompey, Octavian and Mark Antony, and culminating in the destruction of the Roman republic and the establishment of imperial government—a government that would last, in one form or another, for more than four centuries.

Marcus Tullius Cicero lived his entire life (106–43 B.C.) during these troubled times. A politician of great importance and influence who in the year 63 B.C., was elected consul, the highest office of Rome, Cicero was a staunch supporter of traditional republican values, an opponent of Julius Caesar and, even more strongly, of Caesar's successor Antony (who was responsible for Cicero's murder). Cicero was also without doubt the leading literary and intellectual figure of his day, the most famous orator of Roman history, and a prolific author who was more responsible than anyone else for introducing Greek philosophical ideas into the Roman world.

In the first century B.C., Greek philosophy was composed primarily of four distinct schools: the *Academy* (roughly, the intellectual heirs of Plato), the *Peripatetics* (Aristotelians), *Stoicism*, and *Epicureanism*. Cicero, who had formal training in three of these (Aristotelianism being the exception), was deeply influenced by all. He often regarded himself as an Academic, and this preference might lead one to suspect that he was simply a Platonist. But things were not quite so simple, since by the time of Cicero, the Academy had come to adopt a type of skeptical viewpoint that Plato himself would almost certainly have disavowed. More generally, on questions of ethics and politics, it seems that Cicero's thought owes much more to Stoic influence. Indeed, we can say with some confidence that his main works of political relevance—*De Officiis* (*On Duties*), *De Finibus* (*The Supreme Good*), *De Legibus* (*The Laws*), and *De Republica* (*The Republic*)—constitute the most complete statement of Stoic political thought ever produced.

As such, these works mark an extraordinary and dramatic change from the tradition of Plato and Aristotle, a change that amply reflects the new realities of the Roman world. It is true that much of Cicero seems quite similar to what we have already encountered in the Greek writers: the best life is the life lived in accordance with nature; nature itself prescribes to us a life of virtue, and this means that honorable behavior is far more important for us than the acquisition of superficial material rewards; nature, moreover, is a structure of rationality, something that we can come to understand through our own powers of reasoning, and this understanding implies that our lives should be guided not by our appetites but by the faculty of rational thought. In Cicero, however, such claims lead in rather new directions. Specifically, he believed that since nature was a single, unified force governing the entire world, and since reason was a single, objective faculty of thought more or less common to all humans, the kinds of local distinctions that were so important to earlier thinkers—Greek versus barbarian, Athenian versus Spartan, etc.—were in fact relatively unimportant. Humankind is of a piece. We are far more alike than we are different; and one implication of this similarity is that nature prescribes rules of conduct that apply not primarily to this or that particular city, or to this or that particular race of people, but to the entire species. Cicero used the phrase "natural law" to describe such rules. In doing so, he initiated a tradition of natural law speculation that would forever after play a fundamental role in Western political thought.

Cicero also believed that each of us, individually, is by nature more similar to one another than not, and that our various differences of achievement and temperament are due less to innate differences of ability than to accidents of habit and circumstance. Compared with Plato and Aristotle, he was an egalitarian. Natural law applies to all of us equally, and we are all more or less equally able to understand it and to behave accordingly.

In each of these respects, Cicero was producing a political philosophy well-suited to an age in which the multiplicity and variety of independent city-states, characteristic of Plato's time, had been replaced by a single world-state, the Roman Empire. Instead of the *polis*, there was a *cosmopolis*. One consequence of this change was that to be a human being was primarily to be a citizen of the empire, and that this was true whether or not one happened to live in the city of Rome itself, or in Transalpine Gaul (what now is called France), or in the Roman Province of Asia (part of present-day Turkey), and so on. But there was a further implication here: the idea of *cosmopolis*, along with the comparative devaluation of local or communal ties, had the effect of giving newfound importance to the individual qua individual. The identity and value of each person became less closely bound up with his or her particular social connections—with peculiarities of language, history, and local custom—than with the more abstract fact that each of us is, like every one else, a citizen of the world empire. Such ideas had a profound influence on early Christian thought, as exemplified most of all by Augustine, whose *City of God* quotes Cicero's *Republic* frequently and at great length.

To these broadly Stoic views, Cicero added a particular theory of government itself, specifically, a preference for the so-called mixed regime. Like Plato and Aristotle before him, he thought that the basic government types were three in number: monarchy, aristocracy, and democracy; and he agreed, further, that each had its strengths and weaknesses. But unlike Plato (although rather like Aristotle), he felt that the best regime was one that contained elements of all three in roughly equal measure. Moreover, he believed that he had found a concrete model for such a regime in the traditional Roman republic itself, a complex structure of offices dominated by a traditional senatorial elite but with—at least in theory—significant democratic and monarchical aspects. Such a model was described most systematically by the second-century B.C., Greek historian Polybius, with whose work Cicero was very familiar; and Cicero's own account of it exercised, in turn, a great influence on numerous subsequent thinkers, including James Madison and the other founders of the United States Constitution.

The imaginary dialogue of *The Republic* takes place in 129 B.C., four years after the death of Tiberius Gracchus. The central character, Scipio Africanus the Younger (c. 185–129 B.C.), was himself a major figure of Roman history. He was the adopted grandson of the Africanus who defeated Hannibal at Zama in 202 B.C., a battle that ended the second Punic War; and Scipio himself was a distinguished military and political leader during whose consulate (in 146 B.C.) Carthage was defeated for a third and final time, thereby establishing beyond all doubt Rome's total domination of the Mediterranean world. But Scipio's reputation and eminence was as much cultural and intellectual as it was political. As leader of the so-called Scipionic Circle, he patronized and surrounded himself with the leading authors and scholars of his time, including the comic poet Terence, the Stoic philosopher Panaetius, and the previously mentioned historian Polybius. In many respects, these individuals established the very foundations of the Roman literary tradition, of which Cicero was the next great practitioner, and Scipio's role in nurturing and supporting this group can hardly be overestimated. His reputation as a person of culture and learning who was, at the same time, deeply involved in public service must have made him, in Cicero's eyes, an ideal vehicle through which to express Stoic political ideals.

Each of the other individuals present in the dialogue was also a historical figure of consequence. Laelius, a soldier and literary patron, was well-known as Scipio's closest friend; Philus was consul in 136 B.C.; Manilius and Scaevola were both influential legal scholars.

Further Reading: A good general introduction is F. E. Adcock, *Roman Political Ideas and Practice* (1964). The most influential recent treatment of the historical background is Ronald Syme, *The Roman Revolution* (1960), a difficult but very important book that looks closely at the complexity and shifting alliances of Roman politics. On Cicero himself, see Elizabeth Rawson, *Cicero: A Portrait* (1983), and R. E. Smith, *Cicero the Statesman* (1966). For at least part of the philosophical background, see Brad Inwood, *Ethics and Human Action in Early Stoicism* (1985).

Marcus Tullius Cicero
(106–43 B.C.)

The Republic

XXXI. SCIPIO: Every state varies according to the character and inclination of its sovereign. Consequently, no state except one in which the people have supreme power provides a habitation for liberty, than which surely nothing can be sweeter. But if liberty is not equally enjoyed by all the citizens, it is not liberty at all. And yet, how can all citizens have an equal share in liberty—I pass over the citizens in a monarchy, for there, of course, the subjection of the people is neither concealed nor questionable—but even in those states in which all men are nominally free? They do, of course, cast their votes; they elect the civil and military officials; their suffrages are solicited for purposes of election and legislation. Nevertheless, the powers which they bestow they would have bestow, even against their will; and they do not possess the powers which others seek to obtain from them. For they have no share in military commands, or in advisory councils, or in special jury panels. These offices are in fact reserved to men of ancient family or to men of wealth. But in a free people, as at Rhodes or at Athens, there is no citizen who [is not eligible to all the offices of state]. . . .

• • •

XXXII. SCIPIO: [The advocates of democracy] affirm that, [when] one man or a few men become wealthier and more powerful than the other citizens, their pride and arrogance give rise [to special privileges], because the inactive and the weak give way and submit to the pretensions of the rich. So long, however, as the people actually retain their power, these thinkers hold that no form of government is better, more liberal, or more prosperous, since the people have control over legislation, the administration of justice, the making of war and peace, the concluding of treaties, and over the civil status and property of each individual citizen. This, according to their view, is the only form of government which can properly be called a commonwealth, that is, the people's affair; and therefore, while there are many instances where the people's affair is freed from the yoke of kings and patricians, there is none of a free people's demanding a king or an aristocratic form of government. They assert, moreover, that it is not right for democracy in general to be condemned because an uncontrolled populace has defects; that, so long as a people is harmonious and subordinates everything to its safety and freedom, there is no form of government less subject to revolution or more stable; and that the kind of state in which harmony is most easily attained is one in which the interests of all the citizens are the same. Dissension, as they hold, arises from diversity of interests, whenever the well-being of some is contrary to the well-being of others. Consequently, when the government was in the hands of aristocrats, the form of the state has never remained stable. Still less has this been the case with monarchies, for, in Ennius' words,

In a kingdom there is no sacred fellowship or trust.

Since, then, law is the bond that holds political society together, and since equality of rights is a part of law, by what principle of right can an association of citizens be held together, when the status of these citizens is not equal? For, if it is not thought desirable that property should be equally distributed, and if the natural capacities of all men cannot possibly be equal, yet certainly all who are citizens of the same commonwealth ought to enjoy equal rights in their mutual relations. What, indeed, is a state, if it is not an association of citizens united by law? . . .

XXXIII. In fact, [the advocates of democracy] do not think that the other forms of government deserve

Reprinted from *On the Commonwealth*, edited by George Holland Sabine and Stanley Barney Smith (Upper Saddle River, N.J.: Prentice-Hall, Inc., 1976) by permission of the publisher.

even the names by which they would be called. Why, indeed, should I apply the word king—a name which belongs properly to Jupiter the Most High—to a human being who is greedy for lordship and exclusive dominion and who is the slave-driver of an oppressed people? Should I not rather call him a tyrant? For mercy is as possible in a tyrant as cruelty in a king. Accordingly, the only concern of the people is whether they are the slaves of a kindly or of a harsh master, since under this form of government they are inevitably the slaves of someone. Moreover, how was it that, at the time when Spartan political institutions were supposedly at their best, this famous people contrived to have only good and just kings, although they had to take as king anyone who happened to be born of the royal family? And as for aristocrats, who can tolerate those who have assumed this title, not as the result of popular grant but as the result of their own election? What, I ask, is the criterion by which your aristocrat is judged? Is it learning, or culture, or scholarly tastes, as I hear?

• • •

XXXIV. SCIPIO: If a state [chooses its rulers] at haphazard, it will be overthrown as quickly as a ship will founder if its pilot is chosen by lot from among the passengers. But if a free people chooses those to whose guidance it will submit itself, and if it chooses for this purpose all its best citizens—provided, of course, that the people wish to be secure—surely, then, the safety of the state has been founded upon the wisdom of its ablest members. This is particularly true since nature has contrived to make the men who are superior in courage and ability rule over the weak, and the weak willing to submit themselves to the best. This perfect relationship between men has been overthrown, according to the partizans of aristocracy, by the false notions that prevail about human excellence. For, as few men possess excellence, so few are able to recognize and judge it. Thus, being ignorant of its nature, the masses suppose that men of wealth, influence, and important family connections are the best. When, as a result of this error on the part of the commons, the wealth rather than the excellence of a few men has come to control the state, these leaders cling stubbornly to the title of aristocrats, utterly lacking though they may be in the substance of excellence. For riches and reputation and power, if devoid of wisdom and of moderation in conduct and

in the exercise of authority, are characterized by shamelessness and insufferable arrogance. There is, indeed, no uglier kind of state than one in which the richest men are thought to be the best.

On the other hand, when excellence governs the commonwealth, what can be more glorious? For then he who rules over others is not himself the slave of any base desire; the requirements which he lays upon his fellow-citizens he has fulfilled himself; he does not impose upon the people laws which he does not himself obey; he holds up his own life before his fellow-citizens as the law by which they may guide their lives. If one such man were able to accomplish effectively all the business of the state, there would be no need for others; and if the body of citizens could always discover this perfect ruler and agree in regard to him, no one would demand specially chosen leaders. The difficulty of determining policy wisely has caused the transfer of authority from the king to several persons; and, conversely, the ignorance and recklessness of the commons have caused it to pass from the many to the few. Thus, between the weakness inherent in a single ruler and the recklnessness inherent in the many, aristocracy has come to hold a middle place. Nothing, in fact, can be more perfectly balanced; and as long as an aristocracy guards the state, the people are necessarily in the happiest condition, since they are free from all care and anxiety. Their ease has been put into the safe-keeping of others, who must protect it and take care that nothing arises to make the people believe that their interests are being neglected by their leaders.

Now the equal rights of which democracies are so fond cannot be maintained. Indeed, no matter how free and untrammeled popular governments may be, they are still exceptionally prone to confer many favors on many men, and show decided preferences in the matter of individuals and in the matter of high rank. And what is called equality is, in reality, extremely unequal. For when the same importance is attached to the high and the low—and in every community these two classes necessarily exist—that very equality is most unequal. Such a condition cannot arise in states that are governed by aristocracies.

Arguments of much this character, Laelius, and others of the same kind, are usually put forward by those who praise most highly the aristocratic form of government.

XXXV. LAELIUS: But of the three simple forms of state, Scipio, which do you especially approve?

SCIPIO: You frame your question well when you ask, "Which of the three" I especially approve, because I do not approve any one of them considered separately and by itself. I prefer rather the mixed form, which is a combination of all three, to any one taken by itself. Still, if I had to express preference for one of the unmixed forms, I should choose monarchy [and accord it first place. In this kind of state] we find that the king is described as if he were a father, planning for his subjects as if they were his children, and zealously protecting them [but never reducing them to subjection. Thus it is much better for the weak and ignorant] to be guarded by the care of one man, who is at once the strongest and the best man in the state. There are, to be sure, the aristocrats, who claim that they do this better than the king, and assert that there would be greater wisdom in a number of men than in one, and withal the same justice and good faith. Finally, the people themselves declare loudly that they do not wish to obey either one man or several. Nothing, they say, is sweeter than freedom, even to wild beasts; and no citizen possesses freedom when he is subject either to a king or to an aristocracy.

Thus I prefer monarchy for the love which the king bears to his subjects; aristocracy for its wisdom in counsel; and democracy for its freedom. When I compare them, I find it hard to decide which feature we desire the most.

LAELIUS: I suppose so, but the rest of the subject can hardly be developed if you leave this point unsettled.

XXXVI. SCIPIO: Then let us imitate Aratus, for when he addresses himself to treat an important subject, he thinks it necessary to begin with Jupiter.

LAELIUS: What has Jupiter to do with it, or what resemblance does this discussion bear to Aratus' poem?

SCIPIO: This resemblance: it is proper for us to begin our discourse with him who all men, learned and unlearned alike, agree is the sole king of all gods and men.

LAELIUS: But why?

SCIPIO: Why do you suppose, except for the reason that is before your very eyes? It may be that the rulers of states, with an eye to the practical side of life, created this belief in order that it might be thought that there was one king in heaven, who, as Homer says, moved all Olympus with his nod and was considered both king and father of all creatures. In this case the belief finds powerful support and a cloud of witnesses, if we may so describe all the witnesses in the world, in the circumstance that all peoples in decrees—passed of course by their rulers—have expressed their agreement that nothing is superior to monarchy, since they believe that all the gods are ruled by a single divinity. Or, on the other hand, it may be that the belief rests, as we have been taught, upon the errors of ignorant men and is like the myths. Nevertheless, let us hear the views of those whom I may call the common teachers of educated men, who see with their eyes, as it were, those things which we scarcely know by hearsay.

LAELIUS: And who are the men you refer to?

SCIPIO: Those who by their investigations into natural philosophy have come to the conclusion that the whole world [is governed] by [a single] soul.

• • •

XXXVII. SCIPIO: If you like, Laelius, I shall give you witnesses that are neither too ancient nor at all uncivilized.

LAELIUS: That is the kind of witness I want.

SCIPIO: Do you note that our own city has been less than four hundred years without kings?

LAELIUS: That is a fact. It is less than four hundred years.

SCIPIO: And is four hundred years a very long time in the life of a city or state?

LAELIUS: In fact, the state is hardly full grown in that time.

SCIPIO: Then within these four hundred years there was a king at Rome?

LAELIUS: Yes, and a proud one, too.

SCIPIO: How was it before his time?

LAELIUS: Before him there was a very just king, and so on back to Romulus, who was king six hundred years ago.

SCIPIO: Then it was not very long ago that even Romulus was king?

LAELIUS: Not at all. Greece was already growing old in his time.

SCIPIO: Tell me, now, surely Romulus was not a king of barbarians?

LAELIUS: If, as the Greeks say, every people is either Greek or barbarian, then I am afraid that he was a king of barbarians. But if we use the word to refer to manners rather than to language, then I deem the Romans to be no more barbarians than the Greeks.

SCIPIO: For the purpose in hand, we are interested not in their race but in their natural capacities. For if these men, who were both intelligent and comparatively modern, were willing to have kings, then the witnesses on whom I rely are neither too ancient nor uncivilized and barbarous.

XXXVIII. LAELIUS: I see, Scipio, that you are ready enough with your authorities; but for my part I, like any good judge, am more influenced by proofs than by witnesses.

SCIPIO: Very well, Laelius, take this proof drawn from your own feelings.

LAELIUS: What feelings?

SCIPIO: Those which you experienced if by any chance or at any time you felt yourself in a passion with someone.

LAELIUS: I have had that experience oftener than I should have liked.

SCIPIO: And when you are angry, do you let anger master your whole mind?

LAELIUS: No, I assure you. On the contrary, I imitate the famous Archytas of Tarentum, who, having gone to his country estate and having found that everything had been done contrary to his orders, said to his steward: "You good-for-nothing fellow! I should have beaten the life out of you, if I were not so angry."

SCIPIO: Excellent! Then Archytas rightly regarded anger—which is, of course, at odds with intelligence—as a sort of insurrection in the soul, and wished to quell it by reason. Now if to anger you add greed, the love of power and fame, and the lusts of the flesh, you see that, if there is a kind of royal power in the souls of men, it will be the dominion exercised by this one element, namely, reason. For reason is the best part of the soul; and so long as it is lord, there is no place for the lusts, for anger, or for any irrational impulse.

LAELIUS: That is true.

SCIPIO: Do you then approve of a soul so regulated?

LAELIUS: There is indeed nothing of which I approve more.

SCIPIO: Then you would not approve, if the lusts of the flesh, which are without number, or the angry passions, should drive out reason and possess the entire soul?

LAELIUS: On the contrary, I should think that nothing was more wretched than such a soul or a man who had such a soul.

SCIPIO: Then you approve, if all the parts of the soul are subject to kingly rule, and if reason is their king?

LAELIUS: Yes, such an arrangement I approve.

SCIPIO: Why, then, are you in doubt as to your conclusion about the state? If political power should be divided among several persons, you can immediately see that there will be no commanding authority, for an authority which is not a unit cannot exist.

XXXIX. LAELIUS: But what difference, pray, is there between a single ruler or several, if justice exists in the several?

SCIPIO: Since I have found that the witnesses whom I have called do not influence you greatly, Laelius, I shall continue to use you as a witness in order to prove my case.

LAELIUS: Me? How will you do that?

SCIPIO: Not long ago when we were on your estate at Formiae, I noticed that you strictly charged your slaves to take their orders from one person only.

LAELIUS: Of course, from the steward.

SCIPIO: Well, now, when you are at home, do several persons manage your affairs?

LAELIUS: No; only one person manages my affairs.

SCIPIO: Surely no one except yourself rules your household?

LAELIUS: Of course not.

SCIPIO: Then do you not agree that in the state also the rule of an individual, provided it be just, is the best?

LAELIUS: You almost force me to agree with you.

XL. SCIPIO: You will be more ready to agree, Laelius, if I leave out of account such analogies as, for example, the fact that it is better to put a ship in charge of one pilot, or a sick man under the care of one physician, supposing, of course, that these men are worthy of their callings, than to entrust such matters to several persons, and if I go on to more important considerations.

LAELIUS: What are the more important considerations that you refer to?

SCIPIO: Why, you see, do you not, that it was the insolence and arrogance of one man, namely Tarquinius, which brought the name of king into detestation among the Romans?

LAELIUS: I do indeed see it.

SCIPIO: Then you also see — and this is a topic which I think I shall elaborate in the course of the discussion — that, after the expulsion of Tarquinius, the people ran riot in an astonishing orgy of license. At that time innocent persons were driven into exile; the estates of many were confiscated; the consuls were established, holding office for only a year; the fasces were lowered before the people as a token of respect; appeals to the centuries were granted for all sorts of cases; the plebs seceded; and finally everything was so conducted that all power was in the hands of the people.

LAELIUS: It is exactly as you say.

SCIPIO: This condition, however, holds only in time of peace and quiet. For you may play the fool as long as you have nothing to fear, as on a ship [in calm weather] and often even in disease if it is not critical. But the passenger calls for a single skilled pilot when the seas begin suddenly to rise; and the invalid calls for a single doctor when his illness takes a turn for the worse. In the same way, our people in the peaceful course of civil affairs command and threaten the magistrates themselves, obstruct them, seek the aid of one against another, or carry an appeal from their decision to the centuries. But in war the people obey their magistrates as if they were kings, for then their safety is of more moment than their mere whim. In really serious wars, indeed, our people have decided that all military power should be in the hands of an officer who has no colleague and whose very name signifies the extent of his power. The word dictator is derived, indeed, from the fact that this magistrate is appointed, but in our records you see, Laelius, that he is called the master of the people.

LAELIUS: I see.

SCIPIO: Wisely, therefore, did our ancestors [provide for the appointment of such an officer]. . . .

• • •

XLI. SCIPIO: When a people has been deprived of a just king, "longing possesses their divine hearts," as Ennius says [when describing the people's feelings] after the death of an excellent king:

Among themselves
Thus men communed: O Romulus, O Romulus divine,
How excellently didst thou, whom gods begot, guard
   thy country!
O father, O ancestor, O scion sprung from the gods!

Lord and master are names which the people never applied to those rulers whom they had justly obeyed; nor did they call them even kings. They called them guardians of their country or fathers or gods. And not without reason, either, if we consider the next words of their apostrophe:

Thou didst guide us onwards into the shores of light.

Life, renown, and glory, according to the people, were procured for them by the justice of the king. The same affectionate regard for kings would have continued in the hearts of subsequent generations, if the kings had retained the truly royal character. But you see that one king's injustice caused the total ruin of that form of commonwealth.

LAELIUS: I see indeed; and I am eager to learn the cycles of political change, both as they affect our state and as they affect every state.

XLII. SCIPIO: After I have set forth my views about the form of state that I consider the best, I must certainly discuss with considerable care the revolutions that occur in governments, though I do not think that my favorite type of mixed government will readily be subject to them.

In a kingdom, however, the first and most certain change is that which occurred under Tarquinius: when the king ceases to rule justly, the royal form of government is straightway destroyed. The king becomes a tyrant; and tyranny, though closest to the best type, is the worst of all states. If, as is usually the case, the tyrant is crushed by the leading citizens, the commonwealth enjoys the second of the three forms of government I mentioned. For there is a certain regal or paternal element in the council of chief men who study to serve well the people's needs. If, on the other hand, the people themselves have slain or driven out the tyrant, they govern with considerable restraint so long as they are prudent and wise. Taking pride in their achievement, they are willing to guard the commonwealth which they have established. But let us suppose that the people have revolted against a just king or have deprived such a ruler of his royal power, or again let us suppose — what more frequently happens — that they have even tasted the blood of the foremost citizens and have made the whole state subserve their lust. If this happens — and, believe me, there is no sea so hard to calm and no fire so hard to check as the vengeance of the unrestrained mob—then that condition exists which Plato vividly describes. I wish that I could render it adequately into Latin. It is hard to do, but I shall try it.

XLIII. "Once the insatiable gullet of the people is parched with a thirst for freedom and once the thirsty populace has been led by its bad servants to drain draughts, not of decently blended, but of undiluted freedom, they are continually censuring and accusing and incriminating their magistrates and leaders; and unless the latter supinely yield and grant freedom in generous measure, the people call them masters, kings, and tyrants." I feel sure that you are familiar with this passage.

Laelius: Perfectly familiar.

Scipio: Then Plato continues: "Those who obey their leaders are harassed by such a democracy and reproached with being willing slaves. Magistrates who are willing to perform their public duties as if they were merely private citizens, and those private citizens who would do away with all distinctions which mark off the magistrates, are extolled to the skies and rewarded with honors. Thus, it inevitably comes about that under such a government everything is full of liberty. No authority is exercised in any private home, and the evil extends even to the dump animals, until finally the father fears his son, the son slights his father, and every feeling of respect is gone. Thus men are indeed free. There is no distinction between citizen and foreigner; teachers fear their pupils and flatter them; pupils scorn their teachers; the young affect the gravity of age; and old men revert to youthful pranks in order not to be tiresome and displeasing to the young. Even slaves conduct themselves with undue freedom; and wives enjoy the same rights as their husbands. And even the dogs and the horses and the asses live in such an atmosphere of freedom that they run on us and make us give them the right of way. From this boundless license," Plato continues, "the following result inevitably follows: so sensitive and effeminate do the feelings of the citizens become that, if the least restraint is applied to them, they are enraged and cannot endure it. Then they begin to ignore the laws also, and so are completely without any master."

XLIV. Laelius: You have exactly rendered Plato's words.

Scipio: This extreme of license, which is their only idea of freedom—to return now to Plato—is a sort of root from which the tyrant springs and, if I may say so, is born. Even as the extreme power of the aristocracy brings about the downfall of the aristocracy, so freedom itself punishes with slavery a people whose freedom has no bounds. Thus, every extreme—in climate, in fertility, or in health—which has been too pleasant, passes generally into the opposite extreme. This happens especially in the case of states, where the extreme of freedom becomes, both for peoples and for individuals, the extreme of slavery. Thus, from perfect freedom arises the tyrant, bringing with him arbitrary and oppressive subjection. Out of the untamed, or better still, the bestial populace, there is generally chosen a champion to guide them against their former leaders, who by this time have been overwhelmed and driven from their positions of authority. Overreaching and vicious, such a champion wantonly assails men who have often earned the gratitude of the state. He curries favor with the people by giving them the property of others as well as his own. Because he is still a private citizen, and because the insecurity of his position makes him afraid, great powers are granted him and are never resigned; and, as happened with Peisistratus at Athens, his person is protected even by armed guards. The final stage is reached when the tyrant tyranizes over the very citizens who have elevated him to his tyranny.

If the tyrant is overthrown by citizens with aristocratic leanings, as often happens, constitutional government is revived. If, on the other hand, political adventurers cause his downfall, there develops that turbulent oligarchy which is merely another form of tyranny. This kind of oligarchical state often arises also from the good form of aristocracy, when some lack of rectitude has corrupted the leaders themselves. The government is thus bandied about like a ball: tyrants receive it from kings; from tyrants it passes either to aristocrats or to the people; and from the people to oligarchs or tyrants. The same form of government is never long retained.

XLV. In view of these facts, monarchy is, in my judgment, far the best of the three simple types of states. But even monarchy will be excelled by the kind of state that is formed by an equal balancing and blending of the three unmixed types. For I hold it desirable, first, that there should be a dominant and royal, element in the commonwealth; second, that some powers should be granted and assigned to the influence of the aristocracy; and third, that certain matters should be reserved to the people for decision and judgment. Such a government insures at once an element of equality, without which the people can hardly be free, and an element of strength. For, whereas the three forms of simple state which we mentioned first readily lapse into the perverted forms opposed to their respective virtues—tyranny arising from monarchy, oligarchy from aristocracy, and turbulent ochlocracy from democracy—and whereas the types themselves are often discarded for new ones, this instability can hardly occur in the mixed and judiciously blended form of state, unless its leaders fall into exceptional degradation. There is, indeed, no cause for change when each individual is firmly set in his proper place, and when there is no inferior position into which he may rapidly decline.

XLVI. But I am afraid, Laelius and my other wise and gracious friends, that if I continue longer in this strain you will find my discourse more after the manner of a dogmatic pedagogue than in the spirit of a fellow-student of politics. I shall accordingly enter at once into a discussion of those topics which are familiar ground to all of you but about which questions were put to me some time ago. It is, indeed, my judgment, opinion, and conviction that of all forms of government there is none which for organization, distribution of power, and respect for authority is to be compared with that constitution which our fathers received from their ancestors and have bequeathed to us. If you approve this course, I shall comply with the wish, which you really expressed, to hear from me facts which you knew yourselves; and I shall show at once the character and supreme excellence of our state. The Roman commonwealth will be the model; and to it I shall apply, if I can, all that I must say about the perfect state. If I can persevere in this course to the end, I feel that I shall have more than completely performed the task which Laelius assigned me.

XLVII. LAELIUS: Your task it is, Scipio, and yours alone. Who, in fact, could speak better than you either about the customs of our ancestors—since your own ancestors were so distinguished—or about the best form of state—in which, if we ever get it, no one indeed could play a more distinguished role than you

play even now—or about policies aimed to meet the future—since you have banished the two terrors that threatened our city and have provided for its future welfare?

•   •   •

XXIII. SCIPIO: I hold that the best constituted state is one which is formed by the due combination of the three simple types, monarchy, aristocracy, and democracy, and which does not arouse a wild and untamed spirit [in its citizens] by punishing. . . .

SCIPIO: . . .[Carthage was] sixty-[five] years older [than Rome], for it was founded thirty-nine years before the first Olympiad. And Lycurgus was the earliest to come to nearly the same conclusion. Accordingly, the even balance of governmental elements in the composite form of state which we have been discussing appears to me to have been common to the Roman constitution and to these other governments. But the peculiar and incomparable excellence of our government in its present form I shall analyze, if I can, in greater detail. It will be found to consist in a quality the like of which can be discovered in no other state. The elements which I have been hitherto explaining were blended in the Roman monarchy, at Sparta, and at Carthage, but so blended that the balance between them was not maintained. For in a state in which one man holds perpetual power—and especially if his power be royal—his authority predominates; and such a commonwealth cannot fail to be a monarchy both in fact and name, even if there is also a senate, as was the case at Rome under the kings or at Sparta under the laws of Lycurgus, or if the people themselves possess a certain degree of authority, as was the case in the Roman monarchy. Moreover, the monarchical form of government is particularly unstable because failure on the part of a single individual easily sweeps it headlong to utter ruin. In itself monarchy is not only unobjectionable but, if I were to give my approval to any simple type of state, is probably far preferable to either of the other two simple types, as long as it preserves its own proper nature. Still, it is inherent in the nature of monarchy that the permanent authority, the sense of justice, and the wisdom of a single individual control the safety, the political equality, and the peace of the citizens. A people who live under a monarchy are wholly deprived of many blessings. The first of these is liberty, which consists not in being subject to a lawful master but in being subject to no master at all. . . .

* * *

XXIV. SCIPIO: For this arbitrary and cruel tyrant was long blessed by fortune in his public acts. He conquered all Latium in war and captured and sacked Suessa Pometia, a wealthy and populous city. Having thus enriched himself with a great treasure of gold and silver, he redeemed his father's vow by building the temple to Jupiter on the Capitoline. He also founded colonies, and in accordance with the custom of the people from whom he had sprung, he sent splendid gifts, the first-fruits of his spoils, to Apollo at Delphi.

XXV. In these circumstances there will occur a change in the political cycle, the natural course and revolution of which you must learn to recognize in their beginnings. The highest achievement of political wisdom, with which all our discussion deals, is to perceive the tortuous path followed by public affairs, in order that we may know the tendency of each change and thus be able to retard the movement or forestall it. Now the king of whom I speak, polluted first by the murder of an excellent ruler, was not sound of mind. Since he himself feared the extreme punishment merited by his crime, he desired to be feared by others. Moreover, relying upon his victories and his wealth, he took delight in lawless violence, and could not control either his own conduct or the lusts of his kindred. The result was that his elder son violated Lucretia, the daughter of Tricipitinus and the wife of Collatinus, and the modest and well-born woman slew herself because of this assault. Then Lucius Brutus, a man distinguished both for his ability and for his character, lifted from the shoulders of his fellow-citizens the unjust yoke of oppressive servitude. Though Brutus held no public office, he upheld the whole common weal. Thus he was the first man in our commonwealth to teach the lesson that, when it is a question of preserving the liberty of the citizens, there is no such thing as private station. He began and led a revolution, and as a consequence of the fresh charge brought by the father and kindred of Lucretia, added to the memory of the arrogance of Tarquinius and the many wrongs committed by him and his sons, the state decreed the exile of the king himself, his children, and the whole line of the Tarquinii.

XXVI. Do you see, then, how a king developed into a tyrant and how a defect on the part of one man turned the state from a good form into a thoroughly bad one? In Tarquinius we see a master of the people such as the Greeks call a tyrant. A king, on the other hand, they define as one who cherishes the interests of his people like a parent, and who preserves his subjects in the best possible mode of life. Monarchy is undoubtedly a good type of state, as I have said, but it nevertheless has a tendency or, as I might say, a leaning towards the worst type. For once the king has adopted a form of rule which is unjust and arbitrary, he becomes forthwith a tyrant, than whom no creature more foul, or loathsome, or detestable to gods or men can be imagined. Though he is formed in the image of man, the monstrous ferocity of his character surpasses that of the wildest of beasts. Who can justly give the title of human being to one who, in his dealings with his fellow citizens and indeed with the entire human race, does not desire the bond of a common law and the relationships involved in civilized life? But this topic will engage us at another and more suitable time, when the development of our subject prompts us to criticise those who have sought to set up tyrannical power even in a state already free.

XXVII. Such is the first origin of the tyrant, for this was the name which the Greeks applied to an arbitrary ruler. The Romans have used the word "king" to mean all who held absolute and perpetual authority over their people. Thus, it has been said that Spurius Cassius, Marcus Manlius, and Spurius Maelius desired to set up a "kingdom," and recently [the same charge was made against Tiberius Gracchus].

* * *

XXVIII. [The senators] at Sparta [Lycurgus] are called ["elders"]. In number they were far too few, being only twenty-eight. In their hands he desired the chief deliberative power to rest, whereas the king exercised the chief military and executive authority. Our statesmen adopted from him the same arrangement and, translating his terms, gave the name senate to the body of those whom he had called elders. Romulus, as we have already said, pursued the same course when the senators were chosen. Nevertheless, the power, authority, and title of king predominate. Suppose that you grant some authority to the people also, as both Lycurgus and Romulus did; you will not thereby satisfy their desire for liberty, but you will fire them with the love of liberty by giving them an opportunity merely to taste it. The fear will always hang over them that the king may become an arbitrary ruler, as generally happens. Precarious, therefore, is the lot of a people which is dependent, as I have previously said, on the caprice or character of a single man.

XXIX. Accordingly, let this be the first type, form, and origin of the tyrant. We have found it in the government which Romulus established after consulting the auspices, and not in that commonwealth which, according to the version written by Plato, Socrates himself sketched in the famous dialogue on the state. We have found how a man like Tarquinius completely subverted monarchy, not by usurping new authority but by using arbitrarily the authority which he had. Now let us imagine the antithesis of this tyrant, a ruler who is good and wise and versed in all that contributes to the advantage and prestige of the state; who is, as it were, the guardian and steward of the commonwealth, for so we should call anyone who directs and pilots the state. You should bend all your efforts to recognize such a man, since it is he who can protect the state by his wisdom and services. . . .

• • •

XXX. . . . [Plato] sought . . . and he created a state which must be regarded as an impractical ideal rather than one whose realization can be expected. It was drawn in the smallest dimensions possible; and while it could not exist, it was one in which the theory of political relations could be fully understood. On the other hand, if I can at all accomplish my purpose, I shall strive to follow the same principles which Plato perceived, and to illustrate them, not in an unreal and shadowy state, but in our own glorious commonwealth. I shall do this, in order to place my finger, as it were, upon the cause of every good and evil in the state.

The period of royal government, together with the interregna, occupied a little more than two hundred and forty years. After the expulsion of Tarquinius, the Roman people hated the name of king as intensely as they had loved it after the death or, as we should say, departure of Romulus. Thus, whereas at the earlier time they could not be without a king, after the expulsion of Tarquinius they could not abide the title of king.

• • •

XXXI. Thus, after that celebrated form of government set up by Romulus had stood firm for about two hundred and forty years that whole law was abrogated. As a result of this feeling our ancestors then exiled Collatinus, innocent though he was, because they were suspicious of his kinship with Tarquinius, and they banished the rest of the Tarquinii because of the hostility felt toward their name. Because of the same feeling Publius Valerius first ordered the fasces to be lowered after he had begun to speak in a formal gathering of the citizens. He also moved his house down to the foot of Mount Velia, after he noticed that the people's suspicions were aroused by his beginning to build at a higher point on the hill, just where King Tullus had lived. But the act by which Valerius especially showed himself a friend of the people was the proposal of a law — the first passed in the assembly of the centuries — prohibiting any magistrate from executing or flogging a Roman citizen without permitting an appeal to the centuries. Even in the time of the kings there had existed the right to appeal from their decisions, as our pontifical books assert and as the augural records also show. Moreover, it is clear from many provisions of the Twelve Tables that an appeal was permitted from every conviction on a criminal charge. And the tradition that there was no right of appeal from the decision of the Decemvirs, who reduced the law to writing, is itself sufficient evidence that an appeal would lie from decisions of the other magistrates. The law of the consuls Lucius Valerius Potitus and Marcus Horatius Barbatus, men who were wisely democratic in the interest of harmony, enacted that no magistrate should be constituted from whose decisions an appeal would not lie. Finally, the three Porcian Laws, which, as you know, are named for the three Porcii, really added nothing new except the clause setting the penalty for violation.

To resume then: After the passage of the law we have mentioned on the right of appeal, Publicola at once ordered the axes to be withdrawn from the fasces, and on the following day he secured the election of Spurius Lucretius as his colleague, and commanded his lictors to be transferred to Lucretius because he was the elder. He was the first also to establish the rule that the lictors should precede each consul in alternate months. The design of this plan was that there should not be more symbols of authority in a free people than there had been under the monarchy.

Publicola, I should certainly judge, was a man of no mean ability, since he made it easier to maintain the authority of the nobility by giving freedom in moderation to the people. It is not without reason that I now descant upon these events, which you find so ancient and out of date. On the contrary, I use notable personalities and periods to mark out such types of men and achievement as the remainder of my discussion will treat.

XXXII. Accordingly, at this period the senate maintained the commonwealth in the following condition: the people, though free, performed few functions by themselves; the senate carried on the greater share of public business by virtue of its prestige and customary authority; and the consuls possessed a power which, though annual in duration, was royal in its legal nature. The provision which was really the chief factor in preserving the ascendancy of the nobility was rigidly maintained, namely, that enactments by the people were not binding unless they had received the sanction of the senate. It was also at this same period, about ten years after the establishment of the consulate, that the first dictator, Titus Larcius, was appointed. This form of authority was a strange phenomenon and seemed a close approximation to kingship; nevertheless, all the chief powers of government were then wielded by the senate with full authority granted by the people. Great were the exploits in war performed in those ages by brave men invested with the supreme military command, either as dictators or consuls.

XXXIII. In the very nature of things, however, it was inevitable that the people, once they were freed from the kings, should demand for themselves a greater degree of authority. This enlargement of their power they attained, after a brief interval of about sixteen years, in the consulate of Postumus Cominius and Spurius Cassius. There was perhaps no element of design in this change, but there is a principle of growth inherent in public affairs which often overrides design. For you should master the principle which I laid down at the beginning: Unless there is in the state such an equal distribution of legal rights, functions, and duties that the magistrates possess an adequate power, the council of the chief men an adequate influence, and the people an adequate measure of liberty, the balance of the commonwealth cannot be preserved unchanged. Thus, when the question of debt had thrown the state into disorder,

the common people seized first the Sacred Mountain and later the Aventine. Not even Lycurgus, for all his discipline, reined back the Greeks from constitutional change. For even at Sparta, in the kingship of Theopompus, there were set up five magistrates called ephors, while in Crete there were ten officials named kosmoi, whose duty was to limit the power of the kings, just as at Rome the tribunes of the plebs were established to limit the authority of the consuls.

• • •

XXII. Laelius: There is in fact a true law—namely, right reason—which is in accordance with nature, applies to all men, and is unchangeable and eternal. By its commands this law summons men to the performance of their duties; by its prohibitions it restrains them from doing wrong. Its commands and prohibitions always influence good men, but are without effect upon the bad. To invalidate this law by human legislation is never morally right, nor is it permissible ever to restrict its operation, and to annul it wholly is impossible. Neither the senate nor the people can absolve us from our obligation to obey this law, and it requires no Sextus Aelius to expound and interpret it. It will not lay down one rule at Rome and another at Athens, nor will it be one rule today and another tomorrow. But there will be one law, eternal and unchangeable, binding at all times upon all peoples; and there will be, as it were, one common master and ruler of men, namely God, who is the author of this law, its interpreter, and its sponsor. The man who will not obey it will abandon his better self, and, in denying the true nature of a man, will thereby suffer the severest of penalties, though he has escaped all the other consequences which men call punishment.

• • •

XXXIII. Laelius: There is no form of state to which I should sooner deny the name of commonwealth than to one which is wholly in the hands of the masses. For if we decided that Syracuse was not a commonwealth, and that Agrigentum and Athens were not commonwealths when they were subject to tyrants, and that Rome was not a commonwealth when it was subject to the decemvirs, I do not see why the word commonwealth is any more appropriate for a city enslaved by a mob. For in the first place, as I see the matter, a people does not exist unless, as you have excellently defined it, Scipio, the group is held together by a common agreement about law and right. But the mob that you describe is as tyrannous as if it were a single usurper; in one respect it is even worse, for there is nothing more odious than this monster which apes the appearance and usurps the name of a people. . . .

• • •

XXXV. SCIPIO: I am aware, Spurius, of your rooted dislike of the popular form of government. And although it can be regarded more favorably than you are wont to regard it, still I agree that of the three [unmixed] forms of government none is less worthy of approval. However, I do not agree with you that aristocrats are better than a king. For if it is wisdom that governs the commonwealth, what difference does it make whether this wisdom is found in one man or in several? But we are deceived by a certain fallacy in this mode of argument. For when aristocracy is called a government by the best men, it seems as if no other government can be better. For how can anything be supposed to be better than the best? On the other hand, when we speak of a king, the idea of an unjust king, no less than that of a just one, presents itself to our minds. But the unjust king does not enter into the question when we are investigating royal government as such. If you will consider Romulus or Pompilius or Tullus as the typical king, you will perhaps not think so ill of monarchy.

• • •

THE DREAM OF SCIPIO

IX. After my arrival in Africa—where, as you know, I served under Manius Manilius as military tribune of the fourth legion—my first desire was to meet King Masinissa, who, for very good reasons, was a close friend of our family. When I met him, the aged prince embraced me and burst into tears. After a brief space he looked up into the sky and said: "To thee, O mighty Sun, and to you, ye other dwellers in heaven, I give thanks because, ere I depart this life, I behold in my kingdom and within this palace Publius Cornelius Scipio whose very name gives me new life. So constantly does my heart muse on the memory of his grandfather, that excellent man and invincible general." Then I questioned him about his kingdom, and he asked me about the condition of our common-

wealth; and we spent the day together in lengthy conversation.

X. I was then entertained with princely splendor, and we prolonged our discussion late into the night. For the venerable man spoke of nothing except Africanus, and recalled not only all that he had done but even all that he had said. I was exhausted both by my journey and by the lateness of the hour. Accordingly, when we separated to retire, a deeper sleep than usual took me in its embrace. What ensued had its origin, I suppose, in the matter of our conversation. For quite regularly the subjects of our thought and discourse suggest our dreams, as Ennius writes that he dreamt of Homer, who no doubt was frequently the theme of his waking thought and conversation. Thus it happened that Africanus appeared to me, in a form which was more familiar from his death mask than from the man himself. When I recognized him, I confess that I was stricken with fear. But he said, "Be calm, Scipio; banish your fears, and inscribe my words in your memory.

XI. "Do you see that city?" From a lofty station, bright and glittering and filled with stars, he pointed out Carthage. "Do you see that city which I forced to obey the Roman people, but which now begins anew those ancient wars and cannot be at peace? Although you who now come to besiege it are as yet hardly a soldier, in three years you will be consul and will overthrow it, and the cognomen which now you inherit from me you will then have won for yourself by your own achievements. After you have destroyed Carthage, celebrated your triumph, been censor, and traveled on an embassy through Egypt, Syria, Asia, and Greece, a second time you will be chosen consul, though absent from Rome, and by destroying Numantia you will bring to a close Rome's greatest war. But when you have been borne to the Capitol in your triumphal chariot, you will find the commonwealth thrown into utter confusion by the designs of my grandson.

XII. "Then, Africanus, you must show to your country the light of your courage, your character, and your wisdom. But I see, as it were, the course of your destiny then becoming uncertain. For when your life has passed through eight times seven yearly revolutions of the sun, and when these two numbers, seven and eight—each of which is considered perfect for a special reason—have by their natural cycle completed the span allotted you by destiny, then to you alone, because of your renown, the whole state will turn. On you the senate, all patriotic citizens, the allies, and the Latins will fix their eyes. On you alone the safety of the state will rest. In a word, you must be dictator and must set the state in order—if only you escape the godless hands of your kindred."

At any exclamation from Laelius and at the deeper groans of the others, Scipio gently smiled. "Hush," said he, "pray, do not break my slumber. Hear yet a little longer what remains for me to tell."

XIII. "Yet, Africanus, that you may be more zealous in guarding your country, be assured of this: All men who have saved or benefited their native land, or have enhanced its power, are assigned an especial place in heaven where they may enjoy a life of eternal bliss. For the supreme god who rules the entire universe finds nothing, at least among earthly objects, more pleasing than the societies and groups of men, united by law and right, which are called states. The rulers and saviors of states set forth from that place and to that place return."

XIV. At these words I was greatly frightened, less by fear of death than by the thought of treachery at the hands of my kindred. Nevertheless, I asked Africanus whether he and my father Paulus and the others whom we supposed dead were still living. "In truth," he replied, "only those are alive who have escaped the bondage of the flesh as from a prison, while that which you call life is in reality death. Do you not behold your father Paulus coming toward you?" When I saw him, I poured forth a flood of tears, but Paulus embraced me and bade me not to weep.

XV. As soon as I mastered my tears and regained the power of speech, I said, "O father most excellent and holy, since true life is here, as Africanus tells me, why, I ask you, do I linger upon earth? Why may I not hasten to come to you?" "That may not be," he replied, "for, until God, to whom belongs this whole world before your eyes, shall free you from the body's prison, you may not enter this place. For the human race was born subject to the condition that they should guard the sphere which you see in the center of the heavens and which is called the earth. To them souls were given, drawn from those eternal fires which you name constellations and stars. These heavenly bodies are round like spheres. They are quickened

by divine intelligences and complete their cycles and rotations with wonderful swiftness. For this reason, Publius, you and all loyal men must retain the soul in its fleshy prison, and unless he who has bestowed the soul upon you so commands, you must not abandon human life, lest you seem to have deserted the earthly tasks imposed by God.

XVI. "But even as your grandfather here before you, even as I who begot you, so do you, Scipio, cultivate justice and loyalty, which is a noble spirit when shown towards parents and kindred, but noblest when shown towards your country. Such a life is the way to heaven and to the company of those whose life on earth is done and who, released from the body, inhabit the region which you behold, and which, after the Greeks, you name the Milky Way."

The place was a glittering circle that shone with exceeding brilliance in the midst of fiery stars. As I gazed down from it all other objects seemed dazzling and wonderful. There were stars which we have never seen from this earth of ours, and all of them had magnitudes such as we have never supposed to exist. The smallest of them was situated most remote from the heaven [of the fixed stars] and nearest to the earth, and shone with borrowed light. Moreover, the stars greatly surpassed the earth in size, and now the earth itself appeared so small that I felt ashamed of our empire, by which we cover a point, as it were, upon its surface.

XVII. Since I was observing the earth more intently than aught else, Africanus said, "How long, I ask you, will your thoughts be fixed upon the earth? Do you not perceive the heavenly spaces into which you have come? The universe is formed of nine circles or spheres, as we should more properly call them. One of these is the heaven [of the fixed stars]; it is on the exterior of the universe, embracing all the other orbs, and is the supreme god himself who constrains and includes the remaining spheres. In it are placed the eternal courses of the rolling stars. Beneath this outer circle are the seven orbs which revolve in a direction opposite to that of the heavens. The outermost of these spheres belongs to the planet which men on earth call Saturn. The next is the luminary called Jupiter, benign and propitious to the human race, and next the ruddy star, feared by earth, which you call Mars. Below Mars comes the sun, which holds almost the midregion [between the earth and the heavens] and is the leader, chief, and director of the other stars, and the mind which keeps the universe in balance. Such is his greatness that he encompasses and fills the whole world with his light. In the sun's train, like comrades, follow the spheres of Venus and Mercury. The lowest globe carries the moon, which is kindled by the rays of the sun. All below the moon is mortal and transitory, except the souls which the gods have bestowed on man, while all above the moon is immortal. The earth, which occupies the ninth position, is the center of the universe. It does not move, it is the lowest of the spheres, and all heavy bodies are swept to it by gravity."

XVIII. When I recovered from the astonishment with which I was gazing upon this spectacle, I asked, "What is this mighty yet delightful sound which fills my ears?" "That," he replied, "is the melody produced by the swift movement of the spheres themselves. It is blended from notes of different pitch, and while the intervals between them are unequal, their differences are marked with exact proportion, and by a blending of high with low notes various concordant effects are harmoniously achieved. Motions so vast cannot sweep on in silence. It is natural, furthermore, for one extremity to have a low pitch while the opposite has a high pitch. Accordingly, the heaven's outermost sphere, which carries the stars and which revolves more rapidly, moves with a high and lively tone. On the other hand, the lowest pitch is the moon's, which is the innermost of the spheres. For the earth, which is the ninth planet, [does not produce any tone, since it] remains motionless and abides in one place, occupying the center of the universe. The eight [other] cycles, however—two of which [Mercury and Venus] move with the same velocity—produce seven notes of different pitch, and the number seven is, in a sense, the bond which holds the entire universe together. This method of creating harmony scholars have imitated in vocal and instrumental music, and have thus won for themselves a return to this place, even as other men have done who, blessed with pre-eminent ability, have devoted their lives on earth to studying the ways of heaven. The sound which we hear has filled and deafened man's ears, since no sense is more easily blunted than hearing. Thus, the people who live near what are called the cataracts of the Nile, where the river sweeps down from high mountains, have lost the power of hearing

because of the roar of waters, and similarly the sound caused by the swift revolution of the whole universe is so overwhelming that human ears are insensible to it. In the same way, you cannot gaze directly at the sun; its rays overcome your sight and vision."

XIX. Though I was filled with awe at the celestial harmonies, I kept turning my eyes constantly towards the earth. "I see," said Africanus, "that you still contemplate the abode and home of man. If the earth appears insignificant to you—as indeed it is—ever lift up your eyes to these heavenly realms and despise the concerns of men. For what fame can you win among men or what renown worthy of your striving? You perceive that the earth is peopled only in scattered and restricted regions, and that even within the patches where men live—if I may use the word patches—there are interspersed great tracts of desert. You see not only that the inhabitants are so dissevered that nothing can be interchanged, but also that some live in the same longitude with you but in the opposite latitude, some in the same latitude but in the opposite longitude, and some are even diametrically on the opposite side of the earth. From such as these assuredly you can hope for no renown.

XX. "You perceive, moreover, that the earth is also adorned and encircled with what we may call girdles. Two of these zones are exactly opposite to one another and, lying beneath the very poles of the heavens, are congealed with ice. On the other hand, the middle zone, which is the largest, is parched by the sun's heat. Two are habitable, and of these the southern zone, in which the inhabitants are your antipodes, touches you not at all. There remains, then, the northern zone in which you dwell. Consider how small a portion of it concerns you. For all the territory which you possess is narrow from north to south and, while broader from east to west, is in fact only a small island surrounded by the body of water which you on earth call either the Atlantic, or the Great Sea, or Oceanus. But though you call it great, you see how insignificant it is! Has your fame, or the fame of any of us, been able to spread beyond the lands which you know and possess, and to pass over the Caucasus, which you see here, or to cross the Ganges, there? Is there anyone in the other extremities of the earth, whether in the east, west, north, or south, who will hear your name? And when you leave out these regions, you see how little is the world in which your ambition strives to make a show. And how short-lived will be the speech even of those who speak our name!

XXI. "Even if the children of generations to come should desire to recount to their posterity the praise of our several achievements which they have heard from their fathers, the destruction of the earth by fire or flood—disasters bound to recur at fixed periods—preclude our winning lasting, to say nothing of immortal, fame. Indeed, what matters it if the men who come after you will have your name upon their lips when the men who lived before you never mentioned you?

XXII. "And yet the earlier generation was quite as numerous as the later and was certainly composed of better men. [What matters human fame], especially when [we consider that], even of the men who can hear our name, there is not one who can remember the events of a single year? For while men loosely define a year as the time necessary for a revolution of the sun—that is, of a single star—in reality a year can truly be said to have completed its course only when all the stars have returned to the original positions whence they set out, and when after a long interval they have brought back the same arrangement throughout the whole heavens. In this cosmic year I do not dare to say how many generations of men are included. Once, when the soul of Romulus entered these heavenly regions, men thought that the sun disappeared and was blotted out. Only when the sun has again passed into eclipse in the same region of the sky and at the same time, and when all the planets and stars have likewise returned to their original positions, are you to understand that a year has passed. Of this year be assured that the twentieth part has not yet revolved.

XXIII. "If, then, you give up the hope of returning to this place where all blessings await great and distinguished men, how puerile is the renown conferred by man, lasting as it does for only a small portion of a single year! But if you wish to look on high and to contemplate this abode and eternal home, you will not yield to the flattery of the rabble or set your hopes upon the rewards that men may give. Excellence itself, by its own inherent charm, must draw you towards true glory. What others say about you must be their concern; nothing will prevent their talking. All that they may say, however, is confined to the narrow limits you perceive; it is never lasting in the case of any man, but is obscured when men die and is blotted out when posterity forgets."

XXIV. After he had spoken thus, I answered: "Since, Africanus, there is, as it were, a path which leads to heaven and which lies open to men who have earned their country's gratitude, I shall strive for so glorious a reward even more earnestly than I have. And yet from boyhood I have followed in my father's footsteps and in yours and have not tarnished your glory." "Strive earnestly," he replied, "and be assured that only this body of yours, and not your real self, is mortal. For you are not the mere physical form that you appear to be; but the real man is the soul and not that physical body which men can point to. Know, then, that your true nature is divine, if indeed it is a divine principle which lives, feels, remembers, and foresees, and which rules, guides, and activates the body beneath its sway, even as the supreme god directs the universe. And as the world, which is in part mortal, is stirred to motion by God Himself, who lives forever, so the frail body is quickened by an immortal soul.

XXV. "For whatever possesses the power of ceaseless movement is eternal. On the other hand, whatever imparts movement to other things and is itself set in motion by external objects must end its life when its movement ends. Accordingly, only that which moves with self-originating motion never ceases to be moved, because it is never abandoned by itself; and it is, moreover, the source and beginning of motion for all other things that move. Beginning has no source, since all things arise from beginning, while beginning itself can spring only from itself. For that which took its beginning from something else could not be a beginning. If, then, beginning is never born, neither does it ever die. For beginning, if destroyed, will never itself receive new life from another source, nor will it create anything else from itself, since all things must arise from a beginning. Thus, it follows that the beginning of movement is derived from that which moves with self-originating motion and which can neither be born nor die. Otherwise, the whole heaven and the universe would collapse and stand still and would never receive any impulse by which they might again be stirred to motion.

XXVI. "Since, therefore, it is clear that whatever is self-moving is eternal, who will deny that this power has been given to soul? For everything that is stirred to movement by external forces is lifeless, but whatever possesses life is moved by an inner and inherent impulse. And this impulse is the very essence and power of soul. If, then, soul be the only thing which is self-moving, assuredly it is not created but is eternal. Train it in the noblest ways! Now the noblest concerns of the soul have to do with the security of your country, and the soul which is employed and disciplined in such pursuits will fly more speedily to this abode, its natural home. This journey it will make the swifter, if it looks abroad, while still imprisoned in the flesh, and if, by meditating upon that which lies beyond it, it divorces itself as far as may be from the body. For the souls of men who have surrendered themselves to carnal delights, who have made themselves as it were slaves of the passions, and who have been prompted by lust to violate the laws of gods and men, wander about near the earth itself, after their escape from the body, and do not return hither until they have been driven about for many ages."

He departed; I awoke from sleep.

VIII
AUGUSTINE

In 410 A.D., the city of Rome was overrun and sacked by an army of Goths led by their king, Alaric. This historical event, which would have worldwide impact, signaled what many centuries later came to be called the decline and fall of the Roman empire. In the eighteenth century, Edward Gibbon, who wrote a multivolume history of that title, argued that the collapse of Rome in the face of barbarian invasions from the north could in large part be attributed to Christianity. Classical culture — a culture of learning and the arts, of philosophy and public-spiritedness — had flourished for eight hundred years or more. From the defeat of the Persians in 479 B.C., to the conquest of much of the known world under the Scipios, Julius Caesar, and the emperor Augustus, the superiority — and, above all, the practical utility — of the values and principles of Greco-Roman civilization could hardly be denied. But when the emperor Constantine converted to Christianity in the early fourth century A.D., he began what developed rapidly into a process of decay and decline. By embracing Christian doctrine, the leaders of the Roman state abandoned the culture of Solon and Pericles, of Plato and Aristotle, of Cicero, Augustus, Trajan, Hadrian — a culture that had placed the highest value on civic involvement and that had brought to large parts of the globe the benefits of wise government.

Gibbons's claims were astonishing and compelling, but also not entirely new. Indeed, Christianity had been blamed for Rome's decline virtually from the beginning. Writers in late antiquity saw that Christian doctrine contemplated a new kind of relationship between the individual human being and his or her political state. They worried that this new relationship would weaken the state, leaving it vulnerable to the predations of the untutored north and thereby paving the way for a government of darkness and despotism.

Augustine's *City of God*, one of the great works of Christian theology, was written at least in part to defend Christianity against these kinds of criticisms. Augustine himself was the Bishop of Hippo, an ancient city in north Africa. His father had been a pagan, his mother a Christian, and he himself had been classically educated (though in Latin, not Greek). While still a young man, he became a professor of rhetoric in Milan. But there he came under the influence of Milan's great bishop, Ambrose, and thus began his gradual embrace of Christian doctrine. Augustine's *Confessions*, a major work of autobiography, describes his ultimate conversion to Christianity as well as his continuing and ongoing interest in classical philosophy. Indeed, there is a sense in which classical and Christian cultures come together for the first time in the thought, and in the person, of Augustine of Hippo, and his mature theology may be regarded as a kind of Christianized Platonism.

Defending Christianity against the charge that it had undermined the Roman empire — indeed, producing a coherent Christian doctrine of politics — was no easy matter, for Christianity seemed to be peculiarly unpolitical. Unlike the Hebrew Bible, the New Testament does not contemplate the creation of a discrete and independent political community, nor does it provide a detailed code of laws that might govern a community of the kind that we encounter, for example, in Leviticus. The Gospels themselves, and Paul's Epistles as well, seem to provide conflicting evidence about the relationship between spiritual and temporal life. And how can a state hope to defend itself against barbarian invaders if it follows Christ's admonition to turn the other cheek?

But indeed, the problem is even more serious than this. For in its very essence, Christian doctrine seems to teach that the value of life is to be found in a kind of salvation to be enjoyed only in the afterlife and that what happens to us on earth is therefore comparatively unimportant. Faith promises us eternal redemption, a kind of oneness with God that will exist forever or, indeed, outside time itself. Compared with this—compared with eternal salvation—how much importance could we possibly attach to our relatively brief moment of earthly existence, the mere sixty or eighty or even hundred years of biological life? With heaven looming in the background, the business of living out our physical lives—and of managing and organizing those lives through government and politics—seems trivial at best, distracting at worst. After all, a life seriously devoted to public affairs— the kind of life that Cicero recommended—would seem to be a life insufficiently dedicated to that in the world which is truly important, namely, Jesus Christ.

In dealing with this issue, Augustine treats a wide range of topics. His starting point and his constant touchstone is Cicero. Indeed, one might say that the *City of God* is an effort to show how Ciceronian political theory can be rendered both intelligible in and useful for a Christian world. The text quotes Cicero's *Republic* often and at length, and in doing so it considers a wide variety of fundamental themes. We find here, for example, an account of moral life in Rome, in which Augustine uses Cicero himself to show that the problem of moral decay and political weakness preceded by a great many years the advent of Christianity. He discusses the question of reason and faith, the role of the Roman empire in God's unfolding plan, and the notion of an ideal Christian ruler. He presents his extremely influential views on the idea of original sin and on the nature of the good life. Of most importance, he describes the differences and relationships between the two great cities, the city of man and the city of God. He believes that to live in the city of man is to live a life of the flesh, a carnal existence, and that this is vastly inferior to the spiritual existence that one can enjoy in the city of God. But he also believes that true religion demands of us that we obey our temporal rulers and that this effort actually strengthens, rather than weakens, good government. Obedience to the state is not something chosen merely for the sake of convenience; it is, rather, a religious duty, something sanctioned and required by the law of God. In this way, the Ciceronian insistence on civic virtue and the Pauline emphasis on faith and spirituality are shown to be not contradictory but entirely compatible; and on that basis, a follower of Augustine might well conclude that the decline and fall of the Roman empire could be attributed to a deficiency, rather than to an excess, of Christian influence.

Further Reading: Augustine's own *Confessions*, an autobiographical work, is a literary and philosophical masterpiece that can serve as a splendid introduction to his life and thought. For the historical background, see the excellent book by Peter Brown, *The World of Late Antiquity* (1989). On Augustine's political thought, see William Connolly, *The Augustinian Imperative: A Reflection on the Politics of Morality* (1993). Also see *Moral Foundations of Constitutional Thought: Current Problems, Augustinian Prospects* (1990), by Graham Walker.

Augustine
(354–430)

City of God

BOOK I

Preface

I have undertaken to defend the most glorious city of God against those who prefer their own gods to the founder of that city. This defense, which I promised you, my dearest son Marcellinus, considers the city of God both in the fleeting course of time when, living by faith, it travels among the impious and also in the stability of its eternal abode. It now awaits that stability through patience, "until justice is turned into judgment" (Ps 93:15); but then it will obtain, through its excellence, final victory and perfect peace. The task which I undertake is great and arduous, but God is our help (Ps 61:9).

I am aware of the powers required to persuade the proud of how great the virtue of humility is. It brings about a loftiness that human arrogance cannot seize but which divine grace gives, a loftiness that transcends all earthly triumphs wavering in unstable mutability. The king and founder of this city of which we will be speaking has made clear the meaning of the divine law in the Scriptures of his people, in which it is said, "God resists the proud, but gives grace to the humble" (Prv 3:34; Jas 4:6; 1 Pt 5:5). However, this privilege, which belongs to God, the swollen spirit of the proud soul also grasps at, for it loves to be praised in these words: "to spare the defeated and to conquer the proud." Thus, I must not pass over in silence the subject of the earthly city which, even as, in its quest to dominate, it enslaves peoples, is itself dominated by the very lust to dominate. If the ability is given to me, I will speak of this earthly city insofar as the plan of this work requires.

Chapter 1

The reason for this is that the enemies against which the city of God must be defended come out of the earthly city. Many of them, once the error of impiety is corrected, become quite suitable citizens of the city of God. However, many of them are so ablaze with the fire of hatred and are so ungrateful for the obvious benefits of the redeemer of the city of God that they still speak against that city even though they could not today utter a single word against it if, while fleeing the hostile sword, they had not found the life of which they are so proud in its sacred places. Are not even those Romans whom the barbarians spared on account of Christ now hostile to the name of Christ? The shrines of the martyrs and basilicas of the apostles testify to this, for they took in both their own and strangers who were fleeing the sack of the city.

All the way up to those places the bloodthirsty enemy raged. There the raving of the butcher recognized its limit. There even the ones who were spared outside of those places were led by merciful foes, so that they would not be attacked by other foes who did not have such mercy. Moreover, even those who elsewhere were raging cruelly in wild fury held back all savage slaying and curbed all greed for getting captives after they came to those places where what the law of war allows was forbidden. In this way many escaped who now disparage these Christian times.

The evil things which the earthly city endured they impute to Christ. The good things which occurred on account of Christ, resulting in their being alive due to the respect given to Christ, they do not impute to our Christ but to their own fate. If they were to discern correctly the rough and harsh suffering they

Reprinted from Augustine, *Political Writings*, translated by Michael W. Tkacz and Douglas Kries (Indianapolis: Hackett Publishing Company, 1994) by permission of the publisher.

endured at the hands of their foes, they ought to ascribe it to that divine providence which customarily uses wars to improve or obliterate the corrupt ways of men. That providence also makes the lives of the just and praiseworthy strong through such afflictions, and having found them acceptable, it either conveys them to a better place or detains them in this world for other purposes.

Contrary to the customs of war, the cruel barbarians spared them. Some they spared wherever they found them on account of the name of Christ; others they spared in the largest places most consecrated to the name of Christ. These places were selected on account of their capacity to hold a great multitude, so that the mercy would be more abundant. This they ought to attribute to these Christian times; hence, they ought to give thanks to God; hence, in order to escape the punishment of eternal fire they ought to run truthfully to his name—the name which many of them mendaciously usurped in order to escape the punishment of temporal destruction. Among those whom you see insolently and shamelessly insulting the servants of Christ are many who would not have escaped destruction and annihilation unless they had pretended to be servants of Christ. And now his name, to which they fled with deceitful mouths in order to enjoy temporal light, they resist through ungrateful pride, a most impious insanity, and a perverse heart, only to be punished in everlasting darkness.

Chapter 2

Many wars have been recorded which were waged either before the founding of Rome or since its birth and hegemony. Let the enemies of the city of God read these accounts, and let them show us a single city seized by foreigners where the troops who took it spared those they found taking refuge in the temples of their gods; or let them show us when a barbarian leader, upon storming a town, ordered that none of those found in this or that temple were to be harmed.

Did not Aeneas see Priam before the altars "defiling by his blood the fires he himself had consecrated"? Did not Diomedes and Ulysses "cut down the guards of the supreme citadel, seize the sacred statue, and with bloody hands boldly grasp the sacred ribbons of

the virgin goddess"? The next passage in the *Aeneid*, "from that point the hopes of the Greeks ebbed and slipping backwards retreated," is not true, for indeed what happened next was that the Greeks conquered; next they destroyed Troy with sword and fire; next they hacked Priam to pieces as he fled to the altars.

Certainly Troy did not perish because it lost Minerva, for what had Minerva herself lost first so that she might perish? Perhaps her guards? This is quite true, for once they were killed, she could be carried away. It was not the men who were being protected by the image, but the image by the men. How then could she be worshipped in order that she might guard the fatherland and the citizens, when she was unable to guard her own guards?

Book II

Chapter 4

Why were the gods of the Romans unwilling to take care that they did not have the worst sort of morals? To be sure, the true God justifiably neglected those who did not worship him. But why did those gods, whose worship ungrateful men complain is prohibited to them, establish no laws to guide their worshippers in living well? Certainly, it was right that, just as these worshippers were concerned with the worship of their gods, so the gods should have been concerned with their worshippers' conduct.

Our adversaries respond that anyone who is evil is so by his own will. Who would deny this? Even so, it was the obligation of the gods men consulted not to keep hidden the precepts of the good life from the peoples who worshipped them, but to promulgate them clearly. Through soothsayers they should have called upon and convinced sinners, openly warned those doing evil of punishment, and promised reward to those living rightly. When, though, did such a message ever shake the temples of those gods with a prompt and clear voice?

As adolescents, we too used to attend their absurd and sacrilegious spectacles. We would watch the entranced dervishes and listen to the musicians. We would take pleasure in the shameful games that were put on for the gods and goddesses, especially for the virgin Caelestis and Berecynthia, the mother of all the gods. On the solemn day of her purification, the vilest actors publicly chanted before her couch things so indecent that they were unfit, I do not need to say for the mother of the gods, but even for the mothers of senators or any decent men. Indeed, such shameful things were not even fit for the mothers of those disgusting actors. There is, in the human respect for parents, something that even depravity cannot destroy. Those actors themselves would have been ashamed to say or do at home in the presence of their mothers the filthy things in which they publicly engaged in the presence of the mother of the gods and a teeming crowd of watchers and listeners of both sexes. If this crowd was present because drawn by curiosity, it should have departed in confusion because of the offense to its modesty.

If these rites are sacred, what is sacrilege? If these rites are purification, what is pollution? These rites were called "trays," as if a banquet were being celebrated at which impure demons fed on delicacies. Who does not realize what sort of spirits delight in such obscenities except those who are either unaware of the existence of impure spirits who, under the name of "gods," deceive human beings, or those who live in such a way as to seek the favor and fear the anger of these gods rather than of the true God?

Chapter 15

Is it not flattery rather than reason that led them to choose their false gods? They did not consider Plato, whom they regard as a demigod and who labored with so many arguments to keep human morals from being corrupted by the evils of the mind (the ones most to be avoided), worthy of even a small shrine. Rather, they preferred their own Romulus to many other gods, even though their more or less secret doctrine ranks him as a demigod rather than a god. Indeed, they even appointed a *flamen* for him. This was a kind of priest so distinguished in Roman religion — the distinction was symbolized by their conical hats — that only three divinities had *flamens* appointed for them: Dialis for Jupiter, Martialis for Mars, and Quirinalis for Romulus. . . .

Chapter 19

Look at the Roman republic which, "having changed little by little from the most beautiful and best, has become the worst and most disgraceful." I am not the first to say this. Their own authors, from whom we learned it for a fee, said it long before the coming of Christ. Look at how, before the coming of Christ and after the destruction of Carthage, "the morals of the ancestors were not changed little by little as previously, but swept away by a torrent to such an extent that the youth were corrupted by luxury and greed."

Let them read to us the precepts against luxury and greed given to the Roman people by their gods. If only these gods had kept silent about chastity and modesty and not demanded from the people shameful and disgraceful things, giving them a pernicious authority through their false divinity. Let them read our many precepts against luxury and greed given through the prophets, the Holy Gospel, the Acts of the Apostles, and the epistles. Such precepts are everywhere read to the people gathered to hear them. How excellent and divine they sound, not like the clatter of philosophical disputation, but like the oracle of God sounding from the clouds.

Nevertheless, they do not blame their own gods for the luxury, the greed, and the wild and dissolute morals which, prior to the coming of Christ, changed the republic into "the worst and most disgraceful." Instead they reproach the Christian religion for any sort of distress which their pride and voluptuousness has suffered in recent times.

If "the kings of the earth and all peoples, leaders and all judges of the earth, youths and maidens, the youthful and the elderly" (Ps 148:11–12), those of every age capable of understanding, both sexes, even those very tax collectors and soldiers that John the baptist addressed (Lk 3:12–14) — if they would hear and obey the precepts of the Christian religion concerning just and upright morals, then the republic would embellish the domain of the present life with its own happiness and would ascend to eternal life to reign in supreme happiness. However, because this person hears, that one scorns, and many are better friends with the evil allurements of the vices than with the advantageous austerity of the virtues, the servants of Christ—whether kings or leaders or judges, whether soldiers or inhabitants of the provinces, whether rich or poor, whether free or slave, whether male or female—are commanded to endure even "the worst and most disgraceful" republic, if it is necessary, and through that endurance to prepare an illustrious place for themselves in that most holy and majestic assembly of angels, in that heavenly republic where the will of God is law.

Chapter 20

. . . What sane man would not compare this republic, I do not say to the Roman empire, but to the palace of Sardanapalus, a king so given to sensual pleasures that he had it inscribed on his tomb that in death he possessed only those things which his passion had absorbed and consumed while he was alive? With this sort of king, who, indulgent himself, would not oppose their indulgence with any severity, the people would more freely consecrate a temple and *flamen* to him than the ancient Romans did to Romulus.

Chapter 21

If our enemies scorn the author who said that the Roman republic was the "worst and the most disgraceful," and if they do not care about the great shame and degradation of the "worst and most disgraceful" morals that fill it, but care only that it stand firm and survive, then let them hear no more about how it became the worst and most disgraceful, as Sallust narrates. Instead, let them hear that, as Cicero argues, the republic had already at that time utterly perished and no longer existed at all.

Cicero brings forth Scipio, the destroyer of Carthage himself, discussing the republic at a time when there was already foreboding that it was about to perish through the corruption described by Sallust. . . . At the end of the second book, Scipio says,

> Among lyres and flutes or singing voices, a certain harmony must be maintained out of the different sounds. Trained ears cannot bear false or discordant notes. This harmony, full of concord and agreement, is produced from the regulation of the most dissimilar voices. In the same way, the city, having

been regulated by reason, harmonizes through a consensus of dissimilar elements from the upper, lower, and middle classes, just like musical notes. What the musicians call "harmony" in music, is "concord" in a city, a bond of preservation that is the tightest and the best of all in a republic, and in no way can it exist without justice.

After Scipio discusses somewhat more broadly and fully how great an advantage justice is to a city and how great a disadvantage is its absence, Philus, one of those present at the discussion, wades in and demands that this question be treated more thoroughly and that more be said about justice on account of what was then commonly supposed, namely, that a republic cannot be ruled without injustice. Scipio accordingly agrees that this question must be discussed and explicated. He replies that he thinks there is nothing that has already been said about a republic that could serve as a basis for proceeding further, unless it can be firmly established not only that it is false that a republic cannot be ruled without injustice, but also that it is most true that a republic cannot be ruled without supreme justice.

The explication of this question is put off until the following day, when it is argued out with great conflict in the third book. Philus himself takes up the cause of those who think that without injustice a republic cannot be governed. Above all else, he apologizes for doing so, in order that it would not be believed that he himself actually held this position. He zealously pleads the cause of injustice against justice. Using arguments and examples resembling the truth, he undertakes to show that injustice is useful for a republic and justice useless. Then Laelius, at the request of all the others, sets forth to defend justice and protects, to the extent that he is able, the position that nothing is so inimical to a city as injustice and that a republic cannot be governed or stand firm at all without a great deal of justice.

After this question is treated to an extent that is viewed as sufficient, Scipio returns to the point where the discussion was interrupted. He repeats and recommends his brief definition of a republic, stating that a republic is "the affair of a people." However, he defines a "people" to be not every fellowship of a multitude, but a "fellowship united through a consensus concerning right and a sharing of advantage."

Next, he shows the great advantage of definition in argumentation, and from his own definitions he then concludes that a republic, i.e. the affair of a people, exists when a people is governed well and justly, whether it is by a single king, a few aristocrats, or the whole people. However, when a king is unjust, he calls him, according to the Greek usage, a tyrant; when the aristocrats are unjust, he says their fellowship is a faction; when the people itself is unjust, he finds no customary name for it, unless it would also be called tyranny. In these latter three cases, he does not show that such a republic is then corrupt, as he had argued on the previous day. Rather, reasoning from his definitions, he teaches that a republic does not exist at all, because there is no "affair of the people" when a tyrant or a faction seize it. Nor is the people then a people if it is unjust, because there is no multitude united through a consensus concerning right and a sharing of advantage, as "people" was defined.

Therefore, when the Roman republic was of the quality described by Sallust, it was not then "the worst and most disgraceful," as he had said, but it did not exist at all according to this line of reasoning, which this dialogue on the republic conducted among the great leaders of that age makes clear. Also, Cicero himself, speaking in his own name and not in the person of Scipio or anyone else, quotes a verse from the poet Ennius at the beginning of Book 5: "The Roman republic stands firm on the morals and men of yesteryear." Cicero goes on to say,

> This verse, through both its brevity and truth, seems to me to be just like a statement from some oracle. If the city had not had such morals, then men could not have founded or preserved for so long a republic ruling so far and wide; nor could the morals have done so, if these men had not been leaders. Thus, before our time, the morality of the forefathers brought forth outstanding men, and superior men maintained the old morality and the ways of our ancestors. Our age, however, has received the republic like a remarkable painting which is fading with age, and not only has it neglected to restore its original colors, but it has not even bothered to preserve, so to speak, its shape and basic outlines. What remains from the ancient morals upon which Ennius and the Roman republic stands firm? We see that they have fallen into such oblivion that not

only are they not practiced, but they are not even known. What shall I say of the men of our time? The morals themselves perished because of a lack of men. Not only must we answer for such a crime, but we must, as it were, plead our case against a capital charge. We preserve the republic in word, but the thing itself we lost long ago, and this is due not to some accident, but to our own vices.

Indeed, Cicero was confessing these things long after the death of Africanus, whom he portrays in the argument in his books *On the Republic*; nevertheless, this was still before the coming of Christ. If these views had been thought and stated while the Christian religion was growing strong, who among our enemies would not have been of the opinion that the Christians should be blamed for them? Why, then, did their gods not bother to prevent the ruin and loss of the republic that Cicero, long before Christ came in the flesh, so mournfully laments as lost? Those who praise that republic even for those "men and morals of yesteryear" must consider whether true justice flourished in it or whether perhaps even then it was something that did not live through morals but was depicted through colors. Cicero himself unwittingly expresses this when he commends the painting.

However, we will examine this elsewhere, if God is willing. In the appropriate place, I will attempt to show that according to the definitions of Cicero concerning what a "republic" is and what a "people" is, which were succinctly set forth in the speeches of Scipio (and also confirmed by many statements either of Cicero's own or of other speakers who are portrayed in the same dialogue), the republic never existed because true justice was never present in it. According to more accepted definitions, however, a certain sort of republic did exist, and it was directed better by the earlier Romans than by the later ones. Nevertheless, true justice does not exist except in that republic whose founder and ruler is Christ—if it is admitted that it, too, may be called a "republic," since we cannot deny that it is "the affair of the people." Yet even if such a use of this name "republic," which is commonly used for other things and in other ways, is perhaps too far removed from normal usage, certainly there is true justice in that city of which the Sacred Scripture says, "Glorious things are said about you, O city of God" (Ps 87:3).

Book III

Chapter 21

. . . In the last Punic War, during a single campaign led by the younger Scipio (who on account of it also won for himself the title of "Africanus"), the rival of Roman dominion was utterly destroyed. From that time on, however, the Roman republic was oppressed by burdens of evils. Indeed, the very prosperity and security of Rome's affairs led, on account of the Romans' exceedingly corrupt morals, to those burdensome evils. Thus, Carthage harmed Rome more by being so swiftly overthrown than it had previously harmed her by being for so long her adversary.

Caesar Augustus seems in every way to have wrested from the Romans their liberty, which, even in their own eyes, was no longer glorious but full of contention and destruction as it lost vigor and languished. He subjected all affairs to monarchic rule and, as it were, restored and revived the republic that was crumbling from the morbidity of old age. . . .

Chapter 30

With what effrontery, with what boldness, with what impudence with what foolishness—or rather insanity—do they not attribute those disasters of the past to their own gods while they attribute the disasters of today to our Christ? The cruel civil wars were more bitter than all of the foreign wars, as is admitted by their own historians. These civil wars not only afflicted the republic, but are judged to have completely destroyed it. They began long before the coming of Christ, and, by a long series of criminal causes, led from the wars of Marius and Sulla to the wars of Sertorius and Catiline (of whom one was proscribed and the other supported by Sulla); and from this war to the war of Lepidus and Catulus (of whom one wanted to repeal the acts of Sulla and the other to defend them); and from this war to the war of Pompey and Caesar (of whom Pompey was a follower of Sulla, whose power he equalled or even surpassed, while Caesar could not bear Pompey's power because he did not have it himself; yet he exceeded it when Pompey was defeated and killed). This led to the other

Caesar, afterwards called Augustus, during whose rule Christ was born.

Augustus himself waged many civil wars and in these many illustrious men died. Among them was Cicero, that eloquent master of the art of ruling a republic. Consider the conquerer of Pompey, Gaius Caesar, who acted with clemency in civil victory and granted his adversaries life and dignity: a conspiracy of noble senators, asserting that he desired to be king and claiming to act for the sake of the liberty of the republic, assassinated him, cutting him down in the Curia itself. Then Antony, a man of quite different morals, corrupted and polluted with every vice, seemed to covet his power, but was vehemently opposed by Cicero for the sake of that same liberty of the fatherland. There then emerged that young man of remarkable character, the other Caesar, adopted by Gaius Caesar as his son, who, as I said, was afterwards called Augustus. This young Caesar was favored by Cicero so that his power might be used against Antony. Cicero hoped that he would depose Antony, put an end to his depotism, and establish a free republic. However, Cicero was so blind and improvident that the same young man, whose prestige and power he supported, permitted Cicero himself to be killed as a token of his reconciliation with Antony. As for the liberty of the republic, which Cicero had many times proclaimed, young Caesar brought it under his own control.

Book IV

Chapter 4

Without justice, what are kingdoms but great robber bands. What are robber bands but small kingdoms? The band is itself made up of men, is ruled by the command of a leader, and is held together by a social pact. Plunder is divided in accordance with an agreed-upon law. If this evil increases by the inclusion of dissolute men to the extent that it takes over territory, establishes headquarters, occupies cities, and subdues peoples, it publically assumes the title of kingdom! This title is manifestly conferred on it, not because greed has been removed, but because impunity has been added. A fitting and true response was once given to Alexander the Great by an apprehended pirate. When asked by the king what he thought he was doing by infesting the sea, he replied with noble insolence, "What do you think you are doing by infesting the whole world? Because I do it with one puny boat, I am called a pirate; because you do it with a great fleet, you are called an emperor."

Chapter 33

God, the author and giver of happiness, because he alone is the true God, is the one who gives earthly kingdoms to both the good and the evil. He does not do this blindly or, as it were, fortuitously—because he is God, not fortune—but according to the order of things and times that is hidden from us but well-known to him. God, however, is not subject to this order of times but rules it as Lord and orders it as governor. Happiness he gives only to the good. Servants can have or lack it and kings can have or lack it, but it shall be complete in that life where no one is a servant. Therefore, he gives earthly kingdoms to the good or the evil so that his worshippers, who are still children as regard moral progress, may not desire these gifts from him as something great. It is the sacrament of the Old Testament, in which the New Testament is hidden, that there even earthly gifts are promised, for even then spiritual people understood, though they did not yet openly declare, the eternity symbolized by these temporal things and the gifts of God in which true happiness may be found.

Book V

Chapter 9

The way in which Cicero takes on the task of refuting the Stoics indicates that he thought that his argument would have no effect unless he had first destroyed fortune-telling. He does this by denying that there is any knowledge of the future. He contends with all his powers that neither God nor man has such knowledge and that future events cannot be predicted. He therefore denies the foreknowledge of God and attempts to refute all prophecies, even those clearer than the light, by using empty arguments and by

opposing certain oracles that are easily refuted—though even these oracles are not really refuted by him.

In refuting the conjectures of the astrologers, however, his argument succeeds because their views are of the sort which self-destruct and refute themselves. Even so, those who assert that the stars determine fate are far more tolerable than those who deny the foreknowledge of the future, for to assert that God exists and at the same time to deny that he has foreknowledge of future events is clearly madness. . . .

No matter how vexed and tortuous the philosophers' debates and disputes may be, just as we confess the supreme and true God, so we also confess his will and his supreme power and foreknowledge. We are not afraid that what we do voluntarily might actually be done involuntarily because he, whose foreknowledge is infallible, foreknew that we would do it. It was this fear which concerned Cicero and caused him to oppose foreknowledge. It also caused the Stoics to hold that things do not always happen from necessity, even though they maintained that everything happens according to fate.

What was it, then, that concerned Cicero about the foreknowledge of the future, so that he tried to undermine it through detestable argumentation? It was undoubtedly this: if the future is foreknown, then things will happen in the order in which they are foreknown to happen, and if they happen in this order, then the order of things is, with respect to God who foreknows it, certain; and if the order of things is certain, then the order of causes is certain, because nothing happens without some efficient cause; but if there is such a certain order of causes according to which everything that happens does in fact happen, then, according to Cicero, everything which happens happens by fate. If, however, this is so, then nothing is in our own power and there is no free choice of the will. If we concede this, he says, then all of human life is subverted. The giving of laws is frustrated, as are blame, praise, criticism, and exhortation. There is no justice at all in establishing rewards for the good and punishments for the wicked.

In order that such consequences, which are so disgraceful and absurd and harmful to human affairs, might not follow, Cicero rejects foreknowledge of the future and binds the religious mind in a dilemma, so that it must choose one of these two: either there is something subject to our will or there is foreknowledge of the future. He thinks that both cannot be true: if one is affirmed, the other is destroyed. If we would choose foreknowledge of the future, free choice of the will is destroyed; if we would choose free choice of the will, foreknowledge of the future is destroyed. . . .

We, against such bold sacrilege and impiety, say both that God knows everything before it happens and that we do by our will whatever we know and feel does not happen unless it is willed by us. We do not claim that everything happens by fate; in fact, we say that nothing happens by fate. We point out that the term "fate" is meaningless in its customary usage of referring to the position of the stars when someone was conceived or born, for it asserts something that is not real. We do not deny the order of causes in which the will of God has the greatest power, nor do we designate it by means of the word "fate," unless we take "fate" to mean "what is spoken," deriving it from *fari*, which means "to speak." After all, we cannot deny that it is written in the Sacred Scriptures that "God spoke once; I have heard these two things: that power belongs to God, and to you, Lord, belongs mercy, and you give back to each according to his works" (Ps 62:12). . . .

Even if the order of all causes is certain to God, it does not follow that nothing depends on the free choice of our own wills. Our wills are themselves included in that order of causes which is known with certainty by God and which is contained in his foreknowledge, for human wills are the causes of human actions. He who foreknew all the causes of things could not be ignorant of our wills, which he foreknew as causes of our actions.

Even the concession which Cicero grants, that nothing happens unless preceded by an efficient cause, is sufficient to refute him on this question. How does it help him to say that nothing happens without a cause, but that not all causes are causes of fate, since there are also fortuitous, natural, and voluntary causes? That he admits that everything which happens would not happen unless it were preceded by a cause is enough to refute him. We say that those causes termed "fortuitous"—from which the word "fortune" is taken—are not non-existent, but that they are hidden. We attribute them either

to the will of God or to the will of spirits of some kind. Concerning natural causes, we in no way separate them from the will of him who is the author and founder of all nature. Voluntary causes belong to God or angels or men or animals of various sorts—if the movements by which animals devoid of reason seek or avoid various things according to their own natures should really be called "voluntary." When I speak of the wills of the angels, I mean both the wills of the good angels, called the angels of God, and of the wicked angels, called the angels of the devil, or demons. So, too, by the wills of men I mean both the wills of the good and of the wicked.

From all this we conclude that the only efficient causes of all the things which occur are voluntary causes; that is, they are causes which come from that nature which is the spirit of life. To be sure, the air itself and the wind are also called "spirit," but because they are material, they are not the spirit of life. The spirit of life, however, which gives life to all things and is the creator of every body and every created spirit, is God himself, who is indeed uncreated spirit. In his will is the supreme power which assists the good wills of created spirits and judges the evil ones. He orders all of them, granting powers to some and not granting them to others. Just as he is the creator of all natures, so he is the giver of all powers, but not of all wills. Evil wills do not come from him, as they are contrary to the nature which does come from him. Bodies are mostly subject to wills—some to ours (that is, to the wills of all living mortal creatures, and more to the wills of human beings than to the wills of animals) and others to the wills of angels. Yet all bodies are subordinate to the will of God, to whom all wills are also subject, for wills have no power except that which he has given them.

The cause of things, therefore, which makes but is not made, is God. All other causes both make and are made; such are all created spirits, especially rational spirits. Material causes, therefore, which are made rather than make, are not to be considered among the efficient causes because they can only do what the wills of spirits do with them. In what way, therefore, does the order of causes which is certain in the foreknowledge of God necessitate that there should be nothing dependent on our wills when our wills have a large place in that very order of causes? . . .

Our wills, then, also have just so much power as God willed and foreknew that they would have. Therefore, whatever power they have, they possess with the utmost certainty, and what they are about to do, they are most surely about to do, for he whose foreknowledge is infallible foreknew that they would have the power to do it and would in fact do it. Thus, if I should choose to apply the name of "fate" to anything at all, I would say that the fate of the weaker is the will of the stronger, who has the weaker in his power, rather than say that the order of causes which the Stoics call "fate"—not by ordinary usage, but by their own custom—takes away the free choice of our will.

Chapter 11

The supreme and true God, with his Word and Holy Spirit who are three in one, the one all-powerful God, creator and maker of every soul and body, the God who bestows not vain but true happiness by allowing people to participate in himself, who made man a rational animal with soul and body, who, when man sinned, neither allowed man to go unpunished nor abandoned him without mercy; who gave, to both the good and the evil, being, which they share with stones, the vegetable life shared with trees, the sensitive life shared with the beasts, and the intellectual life shared with the angels alone; from whom is every kind, every species, every order; from whom are measure, number, weight; from whom is everything having existence in nature, of whatever kind and value; from whom are the seeds of forms and the forms of seeds, and the movements of seeds and of forms; who gave also to flesh its origin, beauty, health, fertility, disposition of parts, healthy balance; who also gave to the nonintellective soul memory, sense, appetite, and to the rational soul in addition to these mind, intelligence, and will; who has not neglected to give, not only to the heavens and the earth, not only to angels and men, but even to the entrails of the lowest, feeblest creature, to the bird's pinfeather, to the plant's tiny flower, and to the tree's leaf, a harmony of its parts and a certain peace—never should this God be thought to have wanted the kingdoms of human beings and their dominations and servitudes to be alien from the laws of his providence.

Chapter 15

God would not grant men such as these Roman heroes eternal life with his holy angels in his heavenly city. True piety leads to that society, but true piety does not offer that religious worship that the Greeks call *latreia* to any but the one true God. If he were not to grant the earthly glory of the most supreme empire to them, the reward for their good qualities, that is, the virtues with which they strained themselves to attain such great glory, would not be paid. Indeed, it is for that reason, so that they might receive glory from human beings, that such men are seen doing anything good. It was about them that the Lord said, "Amen, I say to you, you have received your reward" (Mt 6:2).

They scorned their own private goods for the sake of the common good, that is, for the republic, and for its treasury. They resisted avarice. They concerned themselves with their country's affairs through their generous advice. Crimes and vices were punished according to their laws. Through these qualities they sought, as if by a true path, honor, power, and glory. They were honored among nearly all peoples; they imposed the laws of their own empire on many peoples; and today they are glorified by the literature and history of almost all peoples. They have no reason to complain about the justice of the supreme and true God. "They have received their reward."

Chapter 16

Very different, however, is the reward of the saints. They have here endured reproaches for the sake of God's truth, which is hateful to those who desire this world. That city is everlasting. There none are born because none die. There exists true and complete felicity—not a goddess, but a gift from God. We have received from there the pledge of faith; while on our journey, we sigh for that city's beauty. There the sun does not rise on the good and the evil (Mt 5:45), but the Sun of Justice (Mal 4:2) protects the good alone. There no great industry will be needed to fill the public treasury by constricting private property, because there the common treasury is truth.

Therefore, it was not only for the sake of rewarding the citizens of Rome that the empire and glory had been so uniquely extended. It was also for the sake of the citizens of that eternal city, so that during their journeys here they might diligently and soberly contemplate these examples and learn what love they owe to the heavenly country on account of eternal life if the earthly country was loved so much by its citizens on account of human glory.

Chapter 17

Concerning this life of mortals, which is lived and ended in a few days, what difference does it make whose governance a man who is about to die lives under, so long as those who rule do not compel him to impiety and sin? Did the Romans harm those peoples on whom they imposed their laws when they conquered them, except insofar as there was a great slaughter in the wars? If it had been done with their consent, it would have been accomplished with greater success, but there would have been no glory of conquest. The Romans themselves lived under the laws they imposed on others. If this had been done without Mars and Bellona so that there would have been no place for Victory (there is no conquering where there is no fighting), would not the condition of the Romans and the other peoples have been the same? Would this not have especially been the case if what was later done most humanely and acceptably had been done earlier; namely, that all who belonged to the Roman Empire were granted access to the society of the city and became Roman citizens? In this way, what was once the privilege of a few became the privilege of all, except that the lower classes, which had no lands of their own, lived at public expense. Under good public administration, their support might have been offered more willingly through agreement rather than, as was the case, through extorting it from conquered peoples. . . .

Consider what great things they scorned, what things they endured, the desires they conquered for the sake of human glory. Consider that they earned glory as a sort of reward for each virtue. Let this consideration be useful to us for suppressing our pride. That city in which it has been promised to us to rule surpasses this one as far as heaven is distant from the earth, eternal life from temporal joy, solid

glory from empty praise, the company of angels from the company of mortals, the glory of he who made the sun and the moon from the light of the sun and the moon. The citizens of so great a country may not think themselves to have accomplished anything very great if, in order to attain it, they have done some good or suffered some evil, while these Romans did such great things and suffered such great harms for this earthly land which they already inhabited. Especially consider that the forgiveness of sins which gathers citizens into the eternal land has a shadowy resemblance in that asylum of Romulus, to which impunity for all sorts of crimes drew together the multitude from which that city was founded.

Chapter 19

There is a great difference between the desire for human glory and the desire for domination. To be sure, one who takes excessive delight in human glory can readily become one who ardently aspires to dominate; nevertheless those who desire true glory, even of human praise, will avoid displeasing those who think well of them. After all, many people are competent judges of many good moral qualities, even though they do not possess them. By means of these good moral qualities those men strive for glory, honor, and domination, and Sallust says of them, "They strive in the true way." . . .

He who scorns glory and is avid for domination is worse than the beasts in the vices of cruelty and extravagance. Certain Romans were like this, for although they did not care about esteem, they were not without the desire to dominate. History testifies that many were like this. Nero Caesar was the first to reach the summit and, as it were, the citadel, of this vice. So great was his extravagance that one would have thought that there was no manliness to be feared in him. So great was his cruelty that, had the contrary not been known, one would have thought there was nothing effeminate in his character.

Nonetheless, the power to dominate is not given even to these men except by the providence of the most high God, when he judges that the condition of human affairs is worthy of such masters. The divine voice speaks openly concerning this when the wisdom of God says, "Through me kings rule, and tyrants hold the earth through me" (Prv 8:15). To prevent our interpreting the word "tyrants" here not as "the worst and wicked kings" but in the old sense of "strong men" (as Virgil used it when he says, "There will be peace for me when tyrants join right hands"), Scripture speaks most openly of God in another place: "He makes a hypocritical man to reign on account of the perversity of the people" (Jb 34:30).

Although I have demonstrated, to the extent of my ability, why the one true and just God assisted the Romans, who were good according to a certain earthly standard, to obtain the glory of so great an empire, there may be even another, more hidden cause, resulting from the diverse merits of the human race known better to God than to us. Let it be agreed, though, among all who are truly pious, that no one lacking true piety, which is the true worship of the true God, can have true virtue. Let it also be agreed that virtue is not true when it serves human glory. Nevertheless, those who are not citizens of the eternal city, which is called "the city of God" in the Sacred Scriptures, are more useful to the earthly city when they at least have that virtue which serves human glory than if they had none at all. Nothing, however, could be more felicitous for human affairs than that those living well and endowed with true piety, if they have the knowledge of ruling peoples, might also, by God's mercy, have the power. . . .

Chapter 24

We do not claim that certain Christian emperors were happy because they ruled a long time, or, in dying a peaceful death, left their sons to succeed them as emperor, or conquered the enemies of the republic, or were able to both guard against and suppress the attempts of hostile citizens rising against them. These gifts or other comforts of this sorrowful life were even earned by demon-worshippers who do not belong to the kingdom of God to which these emperors belong. All this happened through the mercy of God, so that those who believe in him would not desire these things as though they were the highest good. We do claim that the Christian emperors are happy if they rule justly and if, instead of being exalted by the

praises of those who pay them the highest honors and by the groveling of those who salute them with excessive humility, they remember instead that they are human beings. We claim that they are happy if they make their power the servant of God's majesty by using it for the greatest possible extension of his worship; if they fear and love and worship God; if they love that kingdom in which they are not afraid to share power more than their earthly kingdom; if they are slow to punish and ready to pardon; if they apply that punishment as necessary to govern and defend the republic and not in order to indulge their own hatred; if they grant pardon, not so that crime should be unpunished, but in the hope of correction; if they compensate with the gentleness of mercy and the liberality of benevolence for whatever severe measure they may be compelled to decree; if their extravagance is as much restrained as it might have been unrestrained; if they prefer to rule evil desires rather than any people one might name; and if they do all these things from love of eternal happiness rather than ardor for empty glory, and if they do not fail to offer to the true God who is their God the sacrifices of humility, contrition, and prayer for their sins. Such Christian emperors, we claim, are happy in the present through hope, and are happy afterwards, in the future, in the enjoyment of happiness itself, when what we wait for will have come.

Chapter 25

The good God did not want men who believe that he is to be worshipped for the sake of eternal life to think that, since the evil spirits have great power over these high positions and earthly kingdoms, nobody could attain such things unless he called upon demons. Consequently, God gave the emperor Constantine, who was not a worshipper of demons but of the true God himself, such earthly gifts as nobody would dare to wish for. God also granted to him the honor of founding a city, a partner in Roman rule, the daughter of Rome itself, but without any temple or likeness of demons. He reigned for a long time as sole augustus and held and defended the whole Roman world. In administering and waging wars he was most victorious, and in oppressing tyrants he was prosperous in every way. After a long life, he died of illness and old age, leaving sons to succeed him as emperor.

Yet, on the other hand, so that no emperor should become a Christian in order to earn the happiness of Constantine rather than for the sake of eternal life, God carried away Jovian far sooner than Julian. He also permitted Gratian to be killed by the sword of a tyrant, though in a far less severe manner than Pompey the Great, who worshiped the so-called gods of the Romans. Pompey could not be avenged by Cato, to whom he had left the civil wars as, in a way, an inheritance; Gratian, however—even though pious souls do not require such solace—was avenged by Theodosius. Gratian had made Theodosius his associate in ruling the empire, even though Gratian had a younger brother of his own, because he was more eager for a faithful alliance than excessive power.

Chapter 26

Theodosius not only preserved during the lifetime of Gratian that faithfulness which was owed to him, but also after his death. Gratian's murderer Maximus expelled Gratian's younger brother Valentinian, but Theodosius, like a good Christian, took Valentinian, still a child, under his protection as a ward in his part of the empire and looked after him with fatherly affection. . . .

Later, when Maximus's success was making him dangerous, Theodosius, in the middle of difficult anxieties, was not drawn away to unlawful and sacrilegious curiosities, but contacted John, who lived as a hermit in Egypt. Theodosius had learned that this servant of God whose reputation was spreading was granted the gift of prophecy. John assured him of victory. At once Theodosius destroyed the tyrant Maximus and, with the greatest kindness and reverence, restored the boy Valentinian to his share of the empire from which he had had to flee. . . .

Theodosius was unlike Cinna, Marius, Sulla, and other such men, who did not wish civil wars to end even when they were finished. Instead of wanting to harm anyone when the wars were finished, he grieved that they had begun at all. Through all of these events from the beginning of his rule, he did not cease to help the church, laboring against the impious, by means of the most just and merciful laws. The heretical Valens, favoring the Arians, vehemently afflicted the church; Theodosius, however, took more joy in belonging to the church than he did in being a king on earth. The idols of the pagans he ordered everywhere thrown down, understanding well enough that not even earthly gifts are in the power of demons, but in that of the true God.

Further, what could be more admirable than his religious humility? He was driven by the uproar of certain people who were close to him to avenge the most grievous crime of the Thessalonians, which, at the intercession of the bishops, he had previously promised to pardon. He was then corrected by the discipline of the church and did penance in such a way that the people, praying, wept more at the sight of the imperial highness prostrated on account of them than they feared his anger at their sin. These and similar good works, which would take long to commemorate, he carried with him from this life, which, no matter what human summits and pinnacles are attained, is only a temporal mist (Jas 4:14). . . .

BOOK VIII

Chapter 3

Socrates is remembered as the first to turn the whole of philosophy to the reforming and arranging of morals, for all philosophers before him instead expended their greatest efforts on investigating physical—that is, natural—things. However, it does not seem to me to be possible to conclude for certain just why Socrates did this. Was he turning his mind away from the weariness of obscure and uncertain things and toward the discovery of something clear and certain that was necessary for the happy life, since this is the single goal for the sake of which the industry of all philosophers is seen to have stayed up late and toiled? Or, as certain more benevolent people suspect of him, was he unwilling that minds made impure by earthly desire should strive to attain divine things? Indeed, he would see such minds inquiring about the causes of things, but, as he believed the first and highest of the causes to be only in the will of the one and highest god, he did not think they could be grasped except by a purified mind. Therefore, he recommended that one eagerly pursue the required cleansing of life through good morals. In this way the mind, unencumbered by the weight of lusts, might raise itself to eternal things by its natural vigor, and so contemplate with a purified intelligence the nature of immaterial and unchangeable light, where the causes of all created natures have their stable dwelling.

Nevertheless, it is known that he would agitate and manipulate the foolishness of ignorant men who believed that they knew something. He did this by means of a marvelous and pleasant style of discussion and a most cutting wit, either confessing his ignorance or dissimulating his knowledge even about questions concerning morals, to which it seemed that he had directed the whole of his attention. Because of this, he was condemned on a false charge by his enraged adversaries and punished by death. After that, however, the city of Athens itself, which had publicly condemned him, publicly mourned him. The indignation of the people turned against his two accusors to such an extent that one of them perished due to the violence of the multitude and the other evaded a similar punishment by a voluntary and permanent exile.

So glowing were the reports of the life and death of Socrates that he left behind many followers of his philosophy. These eagerly engaged in debate about the moral questions which treat the highest good, the good by which man is able to become happy. Because all arguments are set in motion, defended, and destroyed in the disputations of Socrates, the position of Socrates himself on the highest good was not very clear. Each follower took what appealed to him and picked what seemed to him to be the ultimate good. The "ultimate good" is the name given to that which makes one happy when one attains it. In this way, the Socratics came to hold different opinions concerning this end among themselves, so that (what is scarcely believable about the followers of a single teacher) some, such as Aristippus, said that the good was pleasure; others, such as Antisthenes, virtue. Others have still other views, and it would be tedious to recount them all.

Chapter 5

If Plato said that the wise man imitates, knows, and loves this god, and is happy through participating in him, what need is there to examine the rest of the philosophers? No one comes closer to us than the Platonists. Consequently, let not only the mythical theology, entertaining impious minds with the crimes of the gods, give precedence to them, but also the civil theology, in which impure demons, leading peoples given to earthly delights astray in the name of the gods, wanted to have human errors as their own divine honors. Such demons excite their worshippers through the filthiest cravings to treat the sport of watching their crimes as though it was their worship. The spectators themselves thus provide an even more delightful sport for the demons. Even if some honorable things are done in the temples, they are defiled by their being joined to the obscenities of the theatres, and whatever disgraceful things are done in the theatres are praised in comparison to the foulness of the temples.

The views of Varro, according to which the sacred rites are interpreted as if they refer to the sky, the earth, and the origin and progress of mortal things, must also give precedence to the Platonists. The reason for this is that the rites do not have the meanings that he attempts to suggest, and thus his attempt does not yield truth. Even if the rites did have these meanings, the rational soul still ought not worship as god those things which are placed beneath it by the order of nature, nor ought it place above itself as gods those things over which it has been placed by the true God. Also, those books that Numa Pompilius took care to hide by having them buried with himself, which were then turned up by a plough and ordered to be burned by the senate, in fact pertained to the same sacred rites and must likewise give precedence to the Platonists. . . .

Therefore, let these two theologies, the mythical and the civil, give way to the Platonic philosophers who said that the true God is the author of all things, the illuminator of truth, and the lavish bestower of happiness. Let also the other philosophers, who fancied the principles of nature to be material because their minds were surrendered to their bodies, give way to these great men who recognized such a great god. . . .

Some of them, such as the Epicureans, believed that living things could come into being from non-living things. Others believed that both living and non-living things come into being from a living thing, but that material things still proceed from a material thing. The Stoics thought fire—one of the four material elements of which this visible world is composed—to be both living and wise, the maker of the world itself and everything in it: in short, they thought fire to be god.

These and other similar philosophers were able to consider only what their hearts, entangled in the senses of the flesh, said to them. Certainly, they had within themselves something they did not see, and they pictured in their own minds what they had seen externally, even when they did not see it but only thought about it. Yet, what is viewed in such thinking is no longer a body, but the likeness of a body. Moreover, that whereby this likeness of a body is seen in the mind is itself neither a body nor a likeness of a body, and that whereby the likeness of a body is seen and judged to be beautiful or deformed, is surely better than what is judged. This thing by which the likeness of a body is seen and judged is the understanding of man and the nature of the rational soul. Certainly it is not a body, since that likeness of a body that is seen and judged by the thinking mind is itself not a body. Therefore, the mind is neither earth, nor sky, nor air, nor fire, which are the four material bodies called "elements," of which we see the material world to be constructed. Moreover, if our mind is not material, in what way is God, the creator of mind, material?

Therefore, as was said above, let these philosophers also give precedence to the Platonists. Those, too, who were embarrassed to say that God is material but still thought that our minds are of the same nature as God, must likewise give way. They did not take into account the great changeability of the soul, for it is an abomination to attribute such changeability to the divine nature. Yet, they respond that the nature of the soul is changed by the body, since in itself the soul is unchangeable. They could just as well say that flesh is wounded by some body, since in itself the flesh is not capable of being wounded! In a word, what cannot be changed can be changed by nothing, while what can be changed by a body is able to be changed by something and therefore cannot rightly be said to be unchangeable.

Chapter 6

Thus, those philosophers, whom we see deservedly surpassing the rest in fame and glory, realized that no material body is God. In seeking God, then, they transcended all material bodies. They realized that whatever is changeable is not the highest God. Therefore, in seeking the highest God, they transcended every soul and every changeable spirit.

Next, they realized that, in any changeable thing, the form by which the thing is—no matter what it is, in what way it is, or what sort of nature it is—cannot exist except through him who truly exists, since he is unchangeable. Hence, the matter of the whole world—its shapes, qualities, and ordered movements; its elements arranged from heaven to earth and whatever bodies that are in them—cannot exist except through him who exists simply. Neither can any life exist except through him—whether it is the life of nutrition and preservation, such as the life which is present in trees; or the life which in addition also senses, such as is present in animals; or the life which does these things and also understands, such as is present in man; or the life which has no need of being sustained by nutrition but only preserves, senses, and understands, such as is present in angels.

The reason for this is that being and living are not distinct in him, as if he could exist without being alive. Neither are living and understanding distinct in him, as if he could live without understanding. Neither are understanding and being happy distinct in him, as if he could understand without being happy. Instead, his living, understanding, and being happy are his very being.

From this unchangeability and simplicity of God, the Platonists understood that he made all things and that he himself could not have been made by anyone. They considered that whatever exists is either body or life, and that life is something superior to body, and that the form of body is sensible but that of life intelligible. Consequently, they placed the intelligible form higher than the sensible. By "sensible," we mean those things which can be sensed through the vision and touch of the body. By "intelligible," we mean those things which can be understood through the pondering of the mind, for there is no bodily excellence—whether in the condition of a body, such as in shape, or in the motion of a body, such as in song—that is not judged by the mind. Indeed, that would not be possible unless a superior form of these things existed in the mind without the bulging of mass, the clamor of voice, and the extension of space or time.

Yet, unless the mind was also changeable, one person would not be a better judge of sensible forms than another. In fact, though, a clever person is a better judge than a dullard, a skilled person than an unskilled, a well-trained person than one in training. Indeed, the very same person, when he improves, is certainly a better judge afterward than before. Whatever admits of more or less, however, is without doubt changeable.

From this argument, the Platonists, who were clever, learned, and trained in these matters, easily concluded that the primary form is not in those things which have been convincingly proven to be changeable. In their view, both body and soul admit of greater or lesser degrees of form, and thus, if they could lack all form, they would not exist at all. They saw that something exists in which exists the primary form, which is unchangeable and therefore not admitting of degrees of comparison. They quite correctly believed that the beginning of things is there, that it was not made, and that from it everything was made. Thus, "what is known of God, he himself made clear to them when they perceived and understood his invisible and everlasting power and divinity through created things" (Rom 1:19–20), for all visible and temporal things were created by him.

Let these remarks suffice for a discussion of that part of philosophy that the Platonists call "physics" or "natural philosophy."

Chapter 8

The remaining part of the Platonists' philosophy is morals, which is called "ethics" in Greek. Here the supreme good is sought, the good to which we refer everything that we do, desiring it not for the sake of something else, but for its very own sake. Obtaining it, we require nothing further in order to be happy. It is truly called the "end," because we want everything else for the sake of this, but this we want only for itself.

Some have said that this good which makes one happy comes from the body, others that it comes from the mind, and others that it comes from both. They saw that man himself consists of mind and body and they therefore believed that well-being for themselves could come from one or the other of these two or from both together—from a sort of final good, through which they would be happy and to which they would refer everything they did, without seeking further for that to which everything must be referred. Thus, those who are said to have added a third class of goods called "extrinsic"—goods such as honor, glory, wealth, and things of that sort—did not add these things as though they were the final good. That is to say, they did not add these things as though they ought to be desired for their own sake, but for the sake of something else. This class of goods is good for good people but bad for bad people.

Thus, whether they sought the good of man from the mind, the body, or both, they thought that nothing other than what derives from man was to be sought. Those who sought the good of man in the body sought it in the inferior part of man; those who sought it in the soul in the better part; and those who sought it in both, in the whole of man. Yet, whether they sought it in either part or in the whole, they sought it nowhere except in man. Those three different views, however, have produced not only three, but many dissenting schools of philosophers, because different philosophers have held different opinions about the good of the body, the good of the mind, and the good of both together.

So then, let all these philosophers give precedence to those who have said that man is happy not by enjoying the body or the mind, but by enjoying God, not as the mind enjoys the body or itself, nor as one friend enjoys another, but as the eye enjoys light, if an analogy can be made between those two things. If God will be my help, this analogy will be clarified, insofar as it is possible, in another place. For now, let it suffice to remember that Plato determined that the final good is to live according to virtue and that this is possible only to one who knows and imitates God, and that there is no other cause of happiness. He did not doubt that to study philosophy is to love God, whose nature is immaterial. From this it certainly follows that the one who loves wisdom (for that is what "philosopher" means), will be happy when he begins to attain God. Although one who attains what he loves is not necessarily happy (for many, by loving the things that are unworthy of love, are miserable, and they are more miserable when they attain them), no one is happy who loves what he does not attain. Even those who love things unworthy of love think that they are happy not by loving but by attaining them. Who, therefore, except the most miserable, denies that anyone who attains what he loves, and loves the true and highest good, is happy? Plato says that God himself is the true and highest good. Thus, because philosophy reaches for a happy life, Plato wants a philosopher to be a lover of God, so that by loving God he might be happy in attaining him.

Chapter 10

A Christian educated only in ecclesiastical writings might perhaps be ignorant of the name of the Platonists and might not know of the existence of the two kinds of Greek-speaking philosophers, the Ionian and the Italian. Nevertheless, such a person is not so deaf to human affairs that he does not know that philosophers profess either the enthusiasm for wisdom or else the actual possession of it. A Christian, however, is wary of those who philosophize according to the elements of this world and not according to God, who made the world. He is warned by the precept of the apostle and faithfully hears what has been said: "Be on your guard that no one deceives you through philosophy and the empty seduction of the elements of the world" (Col 2:8).

Next, in order that he does not judge all philosophers to be like those, a Christian hears the same apostle say about some of them, "Because what is known of God has been made clear to them, for God made it clear to them; from the creation of the world his invisible and everlasting power and divinity are perceived, having been understood through created things" (Rom 1:19–20). Furthermore, speaking to the Athenians, after he had said a great thing about God which few can understand—namely, that "in him we live and move and are"—the apostle added, "as even some of your own have said" (Acts 17:28).

The Christian knows very well to be on guard even against these philosophers when they err on certain matters, for where it was said that God has made clear

his invisible perfections through the perception and understanding of created things, it was also said that they have not correctly worshipped God himself because they offered the divine honors due only to him to other, unworthy things: "Knowing God, they did not glorify and give thanks to him as God, but they lapsed into empty speculation and their foolish hearts were darkened. Saying that they were wise, they became fools, and they exchanged the glory of the incorruptible God for an image bearing the likeness of corruptible man, or birds, or four-footed animals, or serpents" (Rom 1:21–23). In this passage, the apostle is referring to the Romans, Greeks, and Egyptians, who prided themselves on their famous wisdom.

We shall argue with them about that later on. Still, we prefer them to the rest of the philosophers, for they agree with us concerning the one God, the author of the universe, who is not only immaterial and above all material things, but also incorruptible and above all souls, our beginning, our light, and our good.

Perhaps a Christian, ignorant of their writings, does not use in argumentation words that he has not learned. Perhaps he does not use the Latin word "natural" or the Greek word "physics" to name that part of philosophy in which the investigation of nature is treated, nor the term "rational" or "logic" to name that part in which it is asked in what way one is able to comprehend truth, nor the terms "moral" or "ethics" to name that part which treats morals and the final good to be sought and the ultimate evil to be avoided. Yet he is not therefore ignorant that it is from the one, true, and supreme God that we have the nature by which we have been made according to his image, the teaching by which we know both him and ourselves, and the grace by which we are made happy by clinging to him.

This, then, is the reason why we prefer the Platonists to the rest. The other philosophers wore away their abilities and enthusiasm in inquiring after the causes of things and the manner of learning and living. These Platonists, having recognized God's existence, discovered there the cause of the ordered universe, the light of truth which we long to understand, and the fountain of happiness, made for drinking. Therefore, if either these Platonists or any other philosophers among the peoples think these things about God, they think as we do. It is better, however, to plead this cause with the Platonists, for their writings are better known. The Greeks, whose language is preeminent among the peoples, resoundingly praise their writings, and the Latins, persuaded either by their excellence or their glory, have studied them most enthusiastically and made them more well-known and illustrious by translating them into our language.

Chapter 19

Shall I not summon the public itself as a clear witness against the arts of magic, on which some who are excessively wretched and impious even pride themselves? Why are those arts so harshly punished by the severity of law if they are the works of deities who should be worshipped? Is it perhaps because Christians instituted those laws which punish the magical arts? . . . Did not Cicero relate that in the Twelve Tables, which are the oldest laws of the Romans, the magical arts were listed and a punishment established for those who practiced them?

Finally, when Apuleius himself was accused of practicing the magical arts, surely no one will claim his judges were Christians! If he knew that the practices with which he was charged were divine and pious and in accord with the works of divine power, not only should he have confessed them but professed them, accusing instead the laws which prohibited and condemned things which ought to have been considered admirable and venerable. Had he done so, either he would have persuaded the judges to his own opinion or, if they had ruled in accord with the unjust laws and had punished him with death for proclaiming and praising such things, the demons would have repaid him with gifts worthy of a soul which did not fear the loss of human life in order to proclaim their divine works. He would have been like our martyrs, who, when the Christian religion was charged against them as a crime, knew that salvation and the greatest eternal glory would be theirs through the Christian faith. They chose not to evade temporal punishment by denying their faith, but instead, by confessing, professing, and proclaiming it, by enduring all things faithfully and courageously for it and by dying with the composure of piety, they compelled the laws to blush with shame and caused them to be changed.

There still exists, however, a most complete and eloquent oration by this Platonic philosopher in which he defends himself against the crime of practicing the arts of magic by claiming to be a stranger to them. He does not want to be judged innocent except by repudiating what an innocent person cannot commit. Moreover, he also says that all the miracles of the magicians, whom he rightly thinks ought to be condemned, result from the teachings and works of demons. . . .

Book XII

Chapter 23

God was not ignorant of the fact that man would sin and, having sinned, would then be subject to death and would therefore give birth to human beings who would die. He also knew that mortals would commit such great sins that even the beasts, who lack rational will and were created from earth and water in great numbers, would live more peacefully among their own kind than men, who had originally been generated from one man as a means of commending concord. Even lions or dragons have never waged such wars among their own kind as men have waged against one another. God, however, foresaw that, by his grace, a holy people would be called into adoption (Gal 4:5) with their sins forgiven. He foresaw that they would be justified by the Holy Spirit and united in community with the holy angels in eternal peace, when the final enemy, death, was destroyed (1 Cor 15:26). God also knew that this people would benefit from the consideration that he built up the human race from one man in order to show them how pleasing unity even in the midst of plurality is to him.

Chapter 24

God, therefore, made man in his own image. He created man with a soul gifted with reason and intellect, by which he might excel all the animals that move on land or fly or swim, and which do not have minds of this kind. Having formed man out of the dust of the earth he gave him a soul of the kind I have described. Either he had already made it and gave it to man by breathing it into him, or else he made it by breathing into him, so that God willed that the breath which he breathed into man would be his soul. . . . After his own manner, he also made a wife for man to aid him in the work of generating his kind, and he formed her from a bone taken out of the man's side.

We should not think of this work in a carnal way, as if God worked in the way we usually see craftsmen work, using their hands and earthly matter of some sort, applying their skill to the production of some material object. God's hand is his power, and he, working invisibly, makes visible things. This, however, is judged mythical rather than true by those who use common and everyday works to measure the power and wisdom whereby God understands and is able to produce without seeds the very seeds themselves. Because they do not know about the things that were first established, they find them unbelievable—as though what they do know about human conception and birth would not seem even less believable if they were told to someone who knew nothing about them. Yet, most people attribute the causes of these things as well to natural bodies rather than to the work of the divine mind.

Chapter 27

Plato attributed the creation of certain living things to minor gods who were made by the highest God, and he wished us to understand by this that their immortal part was taken from the highest God himself and the mortal part from the lower gods. He did not want us to think of our souls as coming from these lower gods, but our bodies. Porphyry holds that in order to be purified the soul must escape from the body. Plato and the Platonists agree with this and think that those who have lived an immoderate and dishonorable life must return to the mortal body to pay the penalty for such living. Plato thinks they must return even to the bodies of beasts, but Porphyry thinks they must return only to human bodies. It follows that the gods they speak of, and which they wish us to worship as our parents and makers, are really nothing other than the makers of our shackles and chains. They are not our creators, but our incarcerators and jailers, who lock us up in a very

bitter and burdensome prison. Therefore, let the Platonists either stop threatening us with our bodies as a punishment for our souls or stop urging us to worship those gods whose work in us the Platonists themselves exhort us to avoid and escape by all the means in our power! Indeed, both views are as false as can be!

Our souls do not return to this life to be punished, nor is there any other creator of anything in heaven or on earth than he who made heaven and earth. If there is no other cause for living in the body than to undergo punishment, how can it be that, as Plato himself says elsewhere, the world, in order to be most beautiful and most perfect, is filled with every kind of living being, both mortal and immortal. Further, if our creation as mortal beings with bodies is a divine gift, how can it be a punishment to return to this body, that is, to a divine blessing? Even more, if God, as Plato constantly asserts, contains in his eternal intelligence all the forms of the whole world and of all living beings, how can it be that he did not create them himself? Is it possible that he was unwilling to create those things, the plan of which was contained in his ineffable and ineffably praiseworthy mind?

Chapter 28

True religion, then, properly acknowledges and proclaims that the creator of the whole universe is also the creator of all living beings, that is, the creator of both souls and bodies. For the reason that I have stated, and perhaps for another greater albeit hidden reason, one single human being was made by him in his image, preeminent among earthly things. However, that human being was not left alone, for nothing is so social by nature and yet so full of discord by vice as is this race. Nothing more appropriate could be spoken by human nature about guarding against the rise of the vice of discord or about healing it once it has arisen, than the remembrance that God willed to create as a single being the parent from whom the whole multitude was to be propagated, in order that through this reminder the concord of unity might be maintained even in multiplicity. Indeed, that the woman was made for the man and from his side also clearly signifies how affectionate the union of husband and wife ought to be.

Because they were first, these works of God are for that reason unusual. However, anyone who does not believe that they are marvels should not believe that any deeds are marvels; nor would these works be called "marvels" if they had been produced in the usual course of nature. Yet does anything arise without purpose under the great governance of divine providence, even though its reason may be hidden? A certain holy psalm says, "Come and see the works of the Lord, what marvels he has placed upon the earth" (Ps 46:8). . . .

Because this book must now be concluded, let us consider that in this man who was made first there had arisen—not yet openly but already in the foreknowledge of God—two societies or cities among human beings. From him there were to be all human beings, some to be punished in the society of the wicked angels, others to be rewarded in the society of the good ones. Although the judgment of God is hidden, it is nevertheless just. Since it is written in Scripture, "All the ways of the Lord are mercy and truth" (Ps 25:10), his grace cannot be unjust, nor his justice cruel.

Book XIII

Chapter 2

I see that it is necessary to speak a little more diligently about death. Although the human soul is correctly said to be immortal, it also has a certain death of its own. It is called immortal because it does not stop living and feeling in some way, however small. The body, though, is called mortal because it can lose all life and cannot live on its own. The death of the soul occurs when God leaves it, just as the death of the body occurs when the soul leaves it. Therefore, the death of both, which is the death of the whole man, occurs when the soul, abandoned by God, abandons the body. In this case, God is not the life of the soul nor is the soul the life of the body.

This death of the whole man is followed by what the authority of the divine pronouncements call "the second death" (Rev 2:11; 20:6 and 14; 21:8). The Saviour referred to this when he said, "Fear the one who is able to destroy both the soul and the body in hell" (Mt 10:28). Because this does not occur before the soul is joined to the body in such a way that the two cannot be separated, it may be wondered how the body can be said to be killed by a death in which it is not abandoned by the soul but rather remains alive and sensitive to pain. In that final and everlasting punishment, which we shall look at more closely in the proper place, the soul is rightly said to die because it does not live from God. How, though, can we say that the body is dead, since it lives from the soul? After all, if it were not alive it could not feel the torments that will follow the resurrection. Is it because any kind of life is good but pain is evil, so that we should not say that the body lives when its soul is a cause of pain rather than of life?

The soul lives from God when it lives well, for it cannot live well unless God brings about good in it. The body lives from the soul when the soul lives in the body, whether the soul lives from God or not. The life in the bodies of the impious is not the life of the soul but of the body. It is a life that even dead souls, that is, abandoned by God, are able to bestow on their bodies, since the little life they have on their own, which makes them immortal, does not go away. In the final damnation, even though man does not stop feeling, there is good reason to call this "death" rather than "life" because his feeling is neither sweet with pleasure nor healthy with rest but painful with punishment. It is called a second death because it follows the first, which separates two conjoined natures, whether they be God and the soul or the soul and the body. Concerning the first or bodily death, therefore, we can say that it is good for the good and evil for the evil. The second death, however, because it belongs to none of the good, is without doubt good for no one.

Chapter 10

As soon as we begin to live in this dying body, each one of our actions hastens the approach of death. At every moment of this life (if it is to be called life) our mutability tends toward death. There is certainly no one who is not nearer to death this year than last, tomorrow than today, today than yesterday, a short time from now than now, and now than a short time ago. The amount of time that we have lived is subtracted from our whole life span and what remains is daily being shortened. Our whole life is nothing but a race toward death in which no one is permitted to stand still for a time or to go more slowly, for all men are driven forward with equal momentum and equal speed. One whose life was short lived through a day no more quickly than one whose life was longer. While equal moments were snatched from both equally, one was nearer and the other more remote from the goal to which both were racing at equal speed. It is one thing to make a longer journey and another thing to walk at a slower pace. Accordingly, the one who lives longer on his way to death does not proceed at a slower pace but completes a longer journey.

Further, if each person begins to die—that is, to be in death—as soon as death has begun to act in him by taking away life (for when all life has been taken away a man will not then be "in" death but "after" death), then all begin to be in death as soon as they begin to live. What else is happening in all one's days, hours, and individual moments until death is completed? After this comes the time after death, rather than the time during which life was being withdrawn, which was the time in death. Man, therefore, is never in life from the moment he comes to be in this dying rather than living body—that is, if he cannot be in life and death at once. Or should we say that he is in both? Is he in life, which he lives until all is consumed, but in death too, which he dies as his life is consumed? If he is not in life, what is it which is consumed until all is gone? If he is not in death, what is this consumption itself? When the whole of life has been consumed from the body, the term "after death" would be meaningless unless that consumption were death. When life has been entirely consumed, if a man is not in death but after death, then when is he in death, except when life is being consumed?

Book XIV

Chapter 4

. . . I have said that two different and contrary cities have sprung up, because some live according to the flesh and others according to the spirit. To put this

another way, some live according to man and some according to God. Thus, Paul says very clearly to the Corinthians, "When there is envy and conflict among you, are you not being carnal and walking according to man?" (1 Cor 3:3). To walk according to man, then, is to be carnal, because "flesh," which is part of a human being, stands for the whole human being.

The very same people that he calls "carnal," he had earlier called "animal," saying,

Among men, who knows what belongs to a man except the spirit of man which is in him? In the same way, nobody knows what belongs to God except the spirit of God. We have not, however, received the spirit of this world, but the spirit which is from God, so that we might know those things which are given to us by God. We speak of these things, not in the words taught by human wisdom, but in words taught by the spirit, likening spiritual things with spiritual. The animal man does not perceive what belongs to the spirit of God, for such things are foolishness to him" (1 Cor 2:11–14)

It is to such people—that is, the animal—that Paul later says, "I was not able to speak to you, brothers, as spiritual people, but only as carnal people" (1 Cor 3:1). With both "animal" and "carnal," Paul's manner of speaking is the same: the part represents the whole. Both the soul and the flesh, which are parts of a human being, can signify the whole human being. Therefore, animal man and carnal man are not different, but the same—that is, man living according to man. . . .

Chapter 5

There is no need to blame the nature of the flesh for our sins and defects and in so doing wrong the creator, because within its own kind and order the flesh is good. It is not good, however, to live according to a created good by turning our backs on the goodness of the creator. This is true whether we choose to live according to the flesh or according to the soul or according to the whole human being which is composed of flesh and soul (and which can be designated by either the word "flesh" alone or the word "soul" alone). Thus, he who praises the nature of the soul as the highest good and condemns the nature of the flesh as evil loves the soul in a carnal way and flees the flesh in a carnal way, for this view is based on human vanity not divine truth. Indeed, unlike the Manichaeans, the Platonists do not despise the nature of the earthly body as evil, because they attribute to God the creator all the elements of which this visible and tangible world is composed, and their qualities. . . .

Chapter 6

The condition of the human will is of great importance, for if the will is twisted, its acts will be twisted. If, on the other hand, it is upright, not only will its acts be blameless but even praiseworthy. The will is in all the soul's acts. Indeed, these acts are nothing other than acts of the will. After all, what are desire and joy except the will consenting to the things that we will? What are fear and sadness except the will dissenting from the things that we do not will? When we consent to seeking the things that we will, this is called "desire." When we consent to enjoying the things we will, it is called "joy." In the same way, when we dissent from the things that we do not will to happen, such an act of will is called "fear." When we will to avoid the things that happen even though we did not will them to happen, this is called "sadness." In general, as the human will is attracted or repelled in accordance with the variety of things that are sought or shunned, so it is changed and turned into this or that attraction or repulsion.

Therefore, the human being who lives according to God and not according to man should be a lover of good and, consequently, a hater of evil. Because no one is evil by nature but only by defect, he who lives according to God ought to have a perfect hatred for evil. Thus, he will never hate the man on account of the defect nor love the defect on account of the man, but hate the defect and love the man. Once the defect is healed, what will remain is everything that ought to be loved and nothing that ought to be hated.

Chapter 10

It is not unreasonable to ask whether before the fall the first human being, or rather the first human beings (indeed, there was a marriage of two people), had in their animal bodies such sentiments as we will lack in our spiritual bodies when sin is at last purged and ended. If they did, how were they happy in that memorable place of bliss we call "paradise"? After all, who can be called absolutely happy if he is troubled by fear or suffering?

What could men fear or suffer in the midst of such an abundance of goods, where neither death nor sickness of the body was feared, where nothing was missing which a good will might want, and where nothing was present which might prevent a human being from living a happy life, both physically and mentally? Their love of God was undisturbed, as was their love for each other in marriage, living in a faithful and sincere partnership. From this love came great joy, because what they loved was always present. The avoidance of sin was tranquil, and as long as this lasted no evil from any source capable of causing sadness could invade their lives.

Or could it have been that those first human beings did strongly desire to touch and eat the forbidden fruit but were afraid to die? Did desire and fear, then, already plague them, even in that place? By no means! We cannot consider this to have been true where there was no sin. Indeed, it is a sin to desire those things which God's law prohibits and to abstain from them out of fear of punishment rather than love of justice. By no means, I say, should we think that before the fall there was already the same sort of sin committed with respect to that forbidden fruit as the one of which the Lord speaks when he says: "If someone should look at a woman with lust, he has already committed adultery with her in his heart" (Mt 5:28).

Therefore, just as the first human beings were happy and free from mental distress and bodily discomfort, so the whole human society would have been happy if these first human beings had not transmitted this evil to their posterity and if each of their descendants had not committed in iniquity what they would receive in condemnation.

This happiness would have continued until, by that blessing which says, "Increase and multiply" (Gn 1:28), the number of predestined saints had been completed. They would have then been given that higher happiness which the most blessed angels have been given, where it would be certain that no one would sin and no one would die. Such would have been the life of the saints without the experience of labor, sorrow, and death. It is just this sort of life that the saints will enjoy when, after having experienced these evils, their bodies are resurrected from the dead and restored to incorruptibility.

Chapter 11

Yet, because God foresees everything, he knew that human beings would sin. We ought, then, to make our declarations about the holy city according to what God foresaw and planned, and not according to what cannot attain the status of knowledge for us since it was not in God's plan. Man could not alter the divine plan by his sin, as if God could be forced to change what he has established. God's foreknowledge antici- pated how evil man, whom he created good, would become, as well as what good God himself would still draw forth from him. Even though God is said to change what he establishes (so that in a metaphori- cal way the Scriptures even say that God repented), this is said with respect to what human beings had expected or with respect to the order of natural causes, and not with respect to what the Almighty foreknew he would do.

Therefore, God, as it is written, "made man up- right" (Eccl 7:29) and hence possessing a good will. If man had not had a good will, he would not have been upright. A good will, therefore, is the work of God and he created man with it. The first evil will, which preceded all evil human works, was less a single deed than a falling away from the work of God to its own works. Thus, works are evil because they are done according to the will itself rather than according to God. The will, or the human being himself insofar as his will is evil, is like the bad tree producing bad fruit (Mt 7:17).

Further, although an evil will is not according to nature, but contrary to nature, since it is a defect, it nevertheless belongs to the nature of which it is a defect, for it cannot exist except in a nature. Moreover, it can only exist in a nature created from nothing and not in another the creator generates from himself, as he generated the Word through which all things were made. Even if God formed human beings from the dust of the earth, that same earth and all earthly materials come completely from nothing, as does the soul, which God made from nothing and gave to the body when he created man.

Even though evils are allowed to exist in order to demonstrate how the most provident justice of the creator can use them for good, they are nevertheless so overpowered by goods that goods can exist without them. This is the case with the true and highest God himself, as well as with every invisible and visible creature above the misty air of the heavens. Evils, on the other hand, cannot exist without goods, because the natures in which evils exist are good insofar as they are natures. Moreover, evil is removed not by removing any nature or part of a nature that evil brings to a thing, but by healing and correcting what evil has damaged and deformed.

The choice of the will, then, is truly free when it is not the slave of vices and sins. Such freedom was given by God. Lost through its own fault, it cannot be returned except by God, who is the only one who had the ability to give it in the first place. Thus, the Truth proclaims: "If the Son frees us, then we are truly free" (Jn 8:36). This is the same as saying: If the Son saves you, you are truly saved. Indeed, he is our liberator insofar as he is our savior.

Man once lived according to God in a corporeal and spiritual paradise. This was not simply a corporeal paradise for the good of the body and not a spiritual paradise for the good of the mind. Nor was it simply a spiritual paradise offering human beings enjoyment through the internal senses and not also a corporeal paradise offering them enjoyment through the exter- nal senses. . . .

Chapter 12

One might be disturbed by the question, Why is human nature not changed by other sins as it was by the sinful collusion of those first two human beings? The first sin subjected human nature to a corruption we see and feel, and thus to death also. Human nature was perturbed and tossed about by many and contrary emotions to which it was not subject in paradise before the fall, even though it existed in an animal body. If, as I said, anyone is troubled by this, he ought not suppose that the first sin was trivial and unimportant simply because it was about food—a food that was not evil and injurious except insofar as it was forbidden. Nor should one think that God would have created and planted anything evil in such a happy place.

Rather, obedience was commanded by God's precept. This virtue is, as it were, the mother and guardian of all the virtues in a rational creature. For such a creature, submission is advantageous, whereas exercising its own will against the one who created it is ruinous. The prohibition against eating this one kind of food where there was such an abundance of other kinds was such an easy precept to observe and such a brief one to remember, especially since the will was not yet opposed by desire, which only followed afterwards as the punishment for the sin! Hence, the injustice in violating the precept was all the greater given the extreme ease by which it might have been kept.

Chapter 13

The first human beings, having become evil in secret, openly fell into disobedience. After all, the evil work would not have been done unless an evil will preceded it. Further, how can the will begin to be evil except through pride? Thus, "The beginning of all sin is pride" (Sir 10:13). What, though, is pride, but the longing for wrongful exaltation? This exalting is wrong when the mind deserts the principle to which it ought to cling and becomes, as it were, its own principle. This happens when it takes too much pleasure in itself and falls away from that unchangeable good which ought to please it much more than it is able to please itself. This falling away comes from the will itself because, if the will had remained established in the love of the higher unchangeable good — through which it is illuminated so that it might understand and is inflamed so that it might love — then it would not have turned away to find satisfaction in itself, thereby making itself cold and dark. The woman would not have believed that the serpent spoke the truth; nor would the man have placed the will of his wife over the precept of God, thinking the transgression against this precept a venial matter and not abandoning the partner of his life, even though the partnership was one of sin.

It follows that the evil act — that is, the transgression involved in eating the prohibited food — was perpetrated by those who were already evil. That evil fruit could only come from an evil tree (Mt 7:18). That the tree should become evil was contrary to nature, because it could only come about through a defect of the will, which is contrary to nature. A nature, though, could not be deformed through a defect unless it were made from nothing. Thus, its existence as a nature results from its being created by God, but its falling away from God results from its being made from nothing. When human beings turned away from God in this way, they did not fall into pure nothingness. Rather, as a result of their being inclined to themselves they became less than they were when they clung to him who exists most perfectly. . . .

Therefore, humility is especially recommended in the city of God as it journeys in this world. The humility of the king of this city, who is Christ, is especially proclaimed. The opposite of this virtue, the defect of pride, especially dominates his adversary, who is the devil, as is said in Holy Scripture. Surely, this is the great difference that can be discerned between the two cities of which we are speaking. The one is a society of the pious and the other of the impious, each having its own angels associated with it. In the one prevailed the love of God; in the other, the love of oneself. . . .

Chapter 15

. . . Whoever thinks that this sort of condemnation is either excessive or unjust does not know how to judge the gravity of a sin that was so easy to avoid. Just as Abraham's obedience is rightly proclaimed to be great because what he was commanded to do — kill his son — was most difficult, so in paradise the disobedience was even greater because what was commanded was not at all difficult. Just as the obedience of the second man was more praiseworthy because he "became obedient even to death" (Phil 2:8), so the disobedience of the first man was more detestable because he became disobedient even to death. Indeed, where the penalty laid down for disobedience is great and the matter commanded by the Creator is easy, who can sufficiently explain how evil it is not to obey in an easy matter the command of so great a power threatening so great a punishment?

To put it briefly, in the punishment of that sin, what was the retribution for disobedience if not disobedience itself? What else is man's misery if not his disobedience to himself? Because he was unwilling to do what he could, now he wants to do what he cannot. Even though he could not do everything in paradise before the fall, he did not want to do what he could not do and so was able to do everything he wanted. . . .

Bodily pain is nothing but an aversion of the soul arising from the flesh and a sort of dissenting from what happens to the flesh, just as the mental pain called "sadness" is a dissenting from those things which happen to us against our will. Sadness, however, is most often preceded by fear, which is in the soul, not in the flesh. Bodily pain is not preceded by any sort of fear that would be experienced in the flesh before the pain.

Pleasure, on the other hand, is preceded by a certain craving that is felt in the flesh as its own desire, as in hunger thirst, and what with respect to the genital organs is usually called "lust" — although this is also the general term for all desire. The ancients, for example, defined anger as nothing other than the lust for revenge, even though a man is sometimes angry even at inanimate things, which do not feel his vengeance, as when he smashes a style or breaks a pen which writes badly. Although irrational, this is still a sort of lust for revenge and, so to speak, a strange shadow of the notion of retribution, according to which those who do evil should suffer it.

Therefore, there is a lust for revenge that is called "anger." There is a lust to possess money called "greed." There is a lust to overcome in any way whatsoever called "stubbornness." There is a lust for glory called "bragging." There are many and various lusts, some having names of their own and some not. Who, indeed, can easily say what we should call that lust to dominate, which is often so strong in the souls of tyrants, as civil wars testify?

Chapter 16

Therefore, there are lusts for many things, but when "lust" is used without specifying the object, then what usually occurs to the mind is almost always the lust

involving the arousal of the private parts of the body. This lust overcomes not only the whole body, nor only outwardly, but also inwardly; it carries away the whole human being with a conjunction and mixture of mental emotion and bodily craving, so that the resulting pleasure is the greatest of all bodily pleasures. Indeed, at the moment when it reaches its high point, almost all sharpness and, one could say, alertness of thought are overwhelmed.

What friend of wisdom and holy joy, living the married life but, as the apostle warns, "knowing that he possesses his vessel in holiness and honor, not in the affliction of desire, as do the peoples who do not know God" (1 Thes 4:4–5), would not prefer, if he could, to procreate children without this lust? If this could be done, then in performing the duty to procreate the bodily parts created for this purpose would not be excited by the agitation of lust, but would function at the command of the will, as do other parts of the body in the exercise of their functions.

In fact, not even lovers of this pleasure, whether they seek it in marital intercourse or in shameful impurity, are moved to it whenever they might wish. Rather, sometimes the impulse troubles them when they do not want it and sometimes it deserts them when they do, the mind seething with the desire while the body is cold. Thus, astonishingly, lust not only fails to serve the will to bring forth children, but also the lust for lascivious gratification. Although it is often completely opposed to the resisting mind, it is sometimes opposed to itself, moving the mind, but leaving the body unmoved.

Chapter 18

The act itself to which one is impelled by such lust is always done in secret, not only in the case of rape, which requires a hiding place to escape human law courts, but also in the use of prostitutes, which the earthly city disgracefully allows. Although the law of that city does not punish this act, even lust that is permitted and unpunished avoids public scrutiny. On account of a natural sense of shame, secrecy is provided even in brothels, and it was easier for lewdness to do without the restrictions of legal prohibitions than for shamelessness to remove the hiding places of that foulness. Indeed, even the disgraceful call this prostitution disgraceful; though they love it, they dare not indulge it openly.

What about marital intercourse, which, according to the matrimonial code of law, is done for the procreation of children? Although it is right and honorable, is not even it performed in a private room away from witnesses? Before the bridegroom even begins to caress the bride, does he not send out all the servants and even the groomsmen and anyone else who had been permitted to enter the bridal chamber on account of kinship? Since, as "the greatest Roman authority on eloquence" said, all right acts wish to be placed in the light—or in other words, wish to be known—this right act wishes to be known yet blushes to be seen. Who does not know what a married couple do in order to bear children? Is this not why wives are married with such celebration? Nonetheless, when this act which brings about children is performed, not even those children who have already been born are allowed to witness it. Thus, this right act seeks to be known by the light of the mind but hides from the light of the eyes. Why is this so if not because that act, which by nature is fitting and decent, is done with shame, which is the penalty for sin?

Chapter 22

I have no doubt that, according to the blessing of God, to increase, multiply, and fill the earth is the gift of marriage as God established it from the beginning, before the fall. He created a male and a female, a sexual difference quite evident in the flesh. It was to this work of God that the blessing was attached, for when the scripture says, "Male and female he created them," it continues, 'God blessed them saying, "increase and multiply and fill the earth and dominate it"' (Gn 1:27–28), and so on.

Although all of this can be appropriately understood in a spiritual way, male and female cannot be understood as a metaphor for two things existing in a single human being simply because there is plainly in him one thing which rules and another which is ruled. Rather, it is a great absurdity to deny that, as is most evident, human beings were created male and female with bodies of different sexes in order that they might increase, multiply, and fill the earth by generating offspring. When the Lord was asked whether it was permitted for someone to divorce his wife for any reason, since Moses permitted a decree of divorce to be given on account of the hardness of the hearts of the Israelites, his answer was not about the spirit which commands, nor about the flesh which obeys, nor about the rational soul which rules, nor about irrational desire which is ruled, nor about contemplative virtue which is higher, nor about active virtue which is subordinate, nor about the understanding of the mind, nor about the senses of the body, but clearly about the union of marriage by which both sexes are mutually bound to each other. He said, "Have you not read that he who created them in the beginning, created them male and female and said to them: 'for this reason a man will leave his father and mother and cling to his wife and the two will become one flesh?' So they are not now two, but one flesh. Therefore, what God has joined, man must not separate" (Mt 19:4–5).

It is certain, then, that the first human beings were created male and female, as we see and know two human beings of different sexes to be now. They are called "one" either because of the marriage union or because of the origin of the woman who was created from the side of the man. Through this original example, a precedent which God established, the apostle admonishes everyone that men should love their wives (Eph 5:25; Col 3:19).

Chapter 24

When, and as often as, it was necessary to produce offspring, the man would have planted the seed and the woman would have received it, their genital organs being moved by the will, not by the excitement of lust. We not only move at will those parts of the body composed of rigid and jointed bones—such as hands, feet, and fingers—but also the nonrigid parts having pliant tendons. When we want, we can move them by shaking, extend them by stretching, bend them by twisting, and harden them by constricting, as we do with the mouth and face. The lungs, which are the softest of the internal organs except for the marrow—and because of this are protected in the cavity of the chest—serve the will by inhaling and exhaling and by emitting or modifying sounds, like the bellows of blacksmiths or organists. They do this in breathing, blowing, speaking, shouting, and singing. I omit here discussion of certain animals who are naturally able to move a particular place on the hide that covers their whole bodies if they feel something there that they want to drive away. This ability is so developed that by a quivering of the hide they can not only shake off flies that have settled on them but also spears that have pierced them.

Could it be true that, because human beings lack this ability, the creator was not able to give it to whatever living things he wished? Thus, human beings, too, might have been able to have the obedience of their lower parts had they not lost it through their own disobedience. Indeed, it was not difficult for God to form them in such a way that those parts of the body which are now moved only by lust should have been moved only by the will. . . .

Chapter 25

No one lives as he wishes save the happy, and no one is happy save the just. Even the just man himself does not live as he wishes until he has reached that place where he cannot in any way die, be deceived, or be hurt, and until he is certain that these things will never happen to him. Indeed, his nature requires this, and he will not be fully and perfectly happy until he attains what his nature requires.

What human being is now able to live as he wishes when life itself is not in his power? Though he wants to live, he is compelled to die. In what way, then, does he live as he wishes when he does not live as long as he wishes? If he wishes to die, in what way is he able to live as he wishes when he does not wish to live? Furthermore, if he wishes to die, not because he does not wish to live, but so that after death he might live a better life, he is still not yet living as he wishes, but will do so when, by dying, he has attained what he wishes.

Look at a man living as he wishes because he tortured and commanded himself not to wish what he cannot have and to wish only what he can. As Terence says, "Because you cannot do what you want, want what you can do." Is a person like this happy because he is patiently miserable? One does not possess the happy life if one does not love it. Further, if

the happy life is loved and possessed, it is necessary that it be loved more than anything else, because everything else that is loved must be loved for the sake of that happy life. Moreover, if the happy life is loved as much as it deserves to be (for he is not happy who does not love the happy life as it deserves to be loved), then he who loves it in this way cannot but wish it to be eternal. Therefore, life will be happy only when it is eternal.

Chapter 28

The two cities, therefore, were created by two loves: the earthly city by love of oneself, even to the point of contempt for God; the heavenly city by the love of God, even to the point of contempt for oneself. The first glories in itself, the second in the Lord. The first seeks glory from human beings; God, who is the witness of the conscience, is the greatest glory of the other. The first lifts its head in its own glory; the second says to its God, "You are my glory and the one who raises my head" (Ps 3:3). The first, its princes and the nations that it subjugates, is dominated by the lust to dominate; in the second, all mutually serve one another in charity, the leaders through their counsel and the subjects through their obedience. The first, in its princes, loves its own strength; the second says to its God, "I will love you, Lord, my strength" (Ps 18:1).

Therefore, the wise of the first city, living according to man, have sought the goods of the body or of the soul or of both. Those among them who were able to know God "did not honor him as God or give him thanks, but they disappeared into their own thoughts and their foolish hearts were darkened, and all the while they were telling themselves they were wise"— that is, dominated by pride, they exalted themselves in their own wisdom—"and became fools, changing the glory of the incorruptible God into the images of corruptible man, birds, four-footed animals, and serpents"—for in adoring images of this sort they were either leaders or followers of the people—"and they honored and served creatures more than the creator, who is blessed forever" (Rom 1:21–25). In the other city, there is nothing of human wisdom except the piety by which the true God is rightly worshipped, for it expects to find its reward in the company of the holy ones, not only of human beings, but also of angels, "so that God may be all in all" (1 Cor 15:28).

Book XVIII

Chapter 37

In the age of our prophets, those writings were already known to almost all peoples, and especially in the era following the prophets, lived the gentile philosophers who were first called by the name of "philosopher." The name begins with Pythagoras of Samos, who was distinguished and well-known at the time when the Jews were freed from their captivity. Much more so, then, are the rest of the philosophers found to have lived after the prophets. Socrates of Athens himself, the teacher of all who were most illustrious at that time, pre-eminent in that part of philosophy called "moral" or "practical," is found after Esra in the *Chronicles*. Not long after, Plato, who far surpassed the rest of the disciples of Socrates, was born.

Even if we count the earlier philosophers, who were not yet called such—namely, The Seven Wise Men, and then the physicists who succeeded Thales and imitated his zeal in scrutinizing the nature of things, such as Anaximander, Anaximenes, and Anaxagoras, and not a few others prior to Pythagoras, the first philosopher to profess the name—they did not, regarded as a group, precede our prophets in time. Indeed, Thales, after whom came the rest, is reported to have been prominent during the reign of Romulus, when the river of prophecy burst forth from the fountains of Israel in the writings which would flow across the whole world.

Therefore, only those theological poets Orpheus, Linus, Musaeus, and any others that there may have been among the Greeks, are found to have been prior to these Hebrew prophets, whose writings we hold as authoritative. None of those poets, however, temporally preceded Moses, our true theologian, who truly proclaimed the one true God, whose writings are now first in the authoritative canon. Thus, the Greeks, in whose language the literature of this world has most streamed forth, have no reason to brag about their own wisdom if it does not seem to be superior to or at least older than our religion, which is the true wisdom. . . .

Chapter 39

. . . Accordingly, let no people vainly pride itself about the antiquity of its own wisdom being superior to our patriarchs and prophets, in whom there is divine wisdom. Egypt is accustomed to glory falsely and inanely about the antiquity of its own teachings, yet its wisdom, such as it is, is found not to have preceded in time the wisdom of our patriarchs. Nor will anyone dare to say that the Egyptians were expert in their wonderful learning before they knew letters, that is, before Isis arrived and taught them such things.

Furthermore, what is that memorable teaching of the Egyptians, which is called "wisdom," except primarily astronomy and other such learning that is customarily used more to exercise wittiness than to illuminate minds with true wisdom? Insofar as this Egyptian learning pertains to philosophy, which professes to teach something whereby human beings might be made happy, studies of that sort became illustrious in Egypt around the time of Mercury, whom they have called Trismegistus. This was certainly long before the wise men or the philosophers of Greece, but nevertheless after Abraham, Isaac, Jacob, and Joseph, and long after Moses himself, for Atlas, the great astronomer, is found to have lived in the time in which Moses was born, and Atlas was the brother of Prometheus and the maternal grandfather of Mercury the elder, whose grandson was this Mercury Trismegistus.

Chapter 41

However, let us now set aside the study of history. The philosophers themselves, from whom we have digressed to consider that subject, do not seem to have labored in their own studies for any other reason than to discover in what manner one must live in order to be fit to embrace happiness. Why then did the students disagree with their teachers, and why did the fellow students disagree among themselves, if not because those human beings have sought happiness by means of human sensation and human reason? To be sure, it might have been a zeal for self-aggrandizement, by which everyone desires to be seen as wiser and smarter than others and in no way bound by the thoughts of others, but the inventor of his own teachings and opinions. Nevertheless, I concede that some or even most of them broke with their teachers or fellow students because of a love of truth, so that they might argue for that which they thought—either correctly or incorrectly—to be the truth.

What does human misery do, to what extent and in what manner does it reach out to attain happiness, if divine authority does not lead it? Far be it from our authors, to whom the canon of sacred writings is not without reason fixed and limited, to disagree among themselves in any way! Thus, it is not without merit that so many and such numerous peoples, both on farms and in cities, both learned and unlearned—and not merely a few babblers in contentious disputations in schools and gymnasia—have believed that God has spoken to or through our authors as they were writing those canonical books. There ought to have been only a few of these authors, in order that what ought to be dear to religion not become cheap by being abundant. Nevertheless, they ought not be so few that their agreement not be astonishing. Among the multitude of philosophers who have also left behind a monument of their teachings through their literary labors, it is not easy to discover any two who are in agreement with each other about everything. It would take too long, however, to prove that in this work. . . .

On the other hand, that race, that people, that city, that republic, those Israelites, to whom the eloquence of God was entrusted, in no way mixed together pseudo-prophets with true ones by tolerating them all as though they were the same. Those, however, who were in accord with each other and were without any dissent were recognized and known to be truthful authors of sacred writings. These authors were "philosophers"—that is, lovers of wisdom. They were their wise men, their theologians, their prophets, their teachers of righteousness and piety. Whoever thought and lived according to them thought and lived not according to man but according to God, who spoke through them. If a sacrilege is prohibited in their writings, God has prohibited it. If it is said, "Honor your father and your mother," God commands it. If

it is said, "You shall not commit adultery, you shall not kill a human being, you shall not steal," and so forth, such things are not uttered by a human mouth but by a divine oracle.

Among their false opinions, certain philosophers were able to discern some truth: the truth that God made this world and that he administers it through the greatest providence, the truth about the honorable character of the virtues, about the love of one's country, about the faithfulness of friends, about good deeds and everything pertaining to upright morals. Even though these philosophers did not know to what end and in what manner all these things needed to be directed, they struggled through laborious disputations to persuade people of them. These truths were commended to the people of Israel by prophetic—that is, by divine—voices, although through human beings; they were not inculcated through the strife of argumentation. This was so that those who would learn of these truths would be afraid to scorn not the wittiness of human beings but the eloquence of God.

Book XIX

Chapter 1

Because I see that I must next discuss the proper ends of the two cities—namely, the earthly and the heavenly—I must first explain, insofar as the limits imposed by the plan of this work allow, the arguments by which mortals have struggled to make themselves happy in the misery of this life. This is necessary in order to clarify the difference between their futilities and our hope, which God has given us, and its object, namely true happiness, which God will give us. This will be done not only through divine authority, but also, for the sake of unbelievers, through reason.

Concerning the ends of goods and evils, philosophers have engaged in many and varied disputes among themselves; but the question they have pursued with the greatest effort, turning it over in their minds, is, What makes man happy? Indeed, our final good is that for the sake of which other things are desired, but which is itself desired for its own sake; and the final evil is that on account of which other things are avoided, but which is avoided on its own account. Hence, we now call the "final good" not that through which good is destroyed, and so ceases to exist, but that through which it is perfected, and so exists fully; and we call the "final evil" not that through which evil ceases to be, but that through which it produces its greatest harm. Thus, these ends are the supreme good and the supreme evil.

As I said, many who have professed the study of wisdom in the futility of this age have worked hard to discover these ends, as well as to obtain the supreme good and to avoid the supreme evil in this life. Although they wandered off in different directions, nevertheless the limit of nature did not permit them to deviate from the path of truth so far that they failed to place the final good and final evil in the soul, in the body, or in both. To this tripartite division of schools Marcus Varro, in his book, *On Philosophy*, directed his attention, diligently and subtly scrutinizing a large number of different teachings. By applying certain distinctions he easily arrived at 288 possible — though not necessarily actual — schools. . . .

Chapter 2

Then there are those three kinds of life: the first is the leisurely — but not slothful — life, devoted to contemplating or seeking the truth; the second is the busy life devoted to conducting human affairs; and the third is the life which mixes both of these kinds. When it is asked which of these three ought to be chosen, the final good is not being disputed. What is considered by that question is which of these three brings difficulty or assistance for seeking or preserving the final good. When anyone attains the final good, he is forthwith made happy. However, the life devoted to learned leisure, to public business, or to performing both alternately does not necessarily make one happy. Certainly, many are able to live in one or another of these three ways, but err with respect to desiring the final good by which man is made happy.

Therefore, it is one thing to ask about the final good and the final evil, and the answer to that question distinguishes every single one of the philosophical schools. It is quite another thing to ask questions about the social life, the hesitation of the Academics, the dress and diet of the Cynics, and the three kinds of life — the leisurely, the active, and the combined.

The final good and evil are not disputed in any of these questions.

By using these four distinctions — that is, the distinctions derived from the social life, the new Academics, the Cynics, and the three kinds of life — Marcus Varro reaches 288 schools. If there are other distinctions, they could be added in the same way. By removing all of those four distinctions, because they do not bear upon the question of pursuing the supreme good and thus do not give rise to what can properly be called "schools," he returns to those twelve in which it is asked, What is the good of man, the pursuit of which makes man happy? From these twelve, he shows that one is true and the rest false. . . .

To Varro, it seemed proper that these three schools be treated carefully. He asked, Which ought to be chosen? True reason does not permit more than one to be true, whether it is among these three or — as we will see later on — somewhere else. In the meantime, we will examine, as briefly and clearly as we can, how Varro chooses one of these three. Certainly, these three schools arise as follows: either the primary goods of nature are chosen for the sake of virtue, or virtue is chosen for the sake of the primary goods of nature, or both — that is, both virtue and the primary goods of nature — are chosen for their own sakes.

Chapter 4

If, then, we are asked what the city of God would reply to each of these questions, and, most importantly, what it thinks about the final good and final evil, it will reply that eternal life is the supreme good and eternal death the supreme evil, and that in order to attain the one and avoid the other, we must live rightly. That is why it is written, "The just man lives by faith" (Gal 3:11), for we do not at present see our good and thus must seek it through believing, nor does our living rightly derive from ourselves, except insofar as he, who gave the very faith through which we believe ourselves to be in need of help from him, helps us in our believing and praying.

Those, however, who have held that the final good and evil are in this life, whether they place the supreme good in the body, in the soul, or in both — and indeed, to express it more explicitly, whether they place it in pleasure or in virtue or both; whether in rest or virtue or in both; whether in pleasure and rest simultaneously or in virtue or in all these; whether in the primary things of nature or in virtue or in all these—they wanted to be happy here and now and, through an astonishing vanity, they wanted to be made happy by their own actions. The Truth ridiculed them through the prophet, saying, "The Lord knows the thoughts of men" (Ps 94:11), or, as the apostle Paul puts this testimony, "The Lord knows the thoughts of the wise, that they are vain" (1 Cor 3:20).

Indeed, who is able, however great the flood of his eloquence, to expound the miseries of this life? Cicero lamented them, as well as he was able, in the *Consolation* on the death of his daughter, but how much was he able to do? In truth, when, where, and in what way can those things called the primary goods of nature be so well possessed in this life that they are not tossed about under the sway of unforeseen accidents? What pain contrary to pleasure, what restlessness contrary to rest, could not befall the body of a wise man? Certainly, the amputation or the debility of a man's limbs destroys his soundness, deformity his beauty, feebleness his health, exhaustion his strength, numbness or slowness his mobility. Which of these is it that cannot overcome the flesh of a wise person? The postures and movements of the body, when they are fitting and harmonious, are likewise numbered among the primary goods of nature. Yet what if some state of ill health causes the limbs to shake and tremble? What if the spine is so curved that the hands are forced to touch the ground, making the man a sort of quadruped? Is not every type of posture and movement of the body distorted?

What about the primary things of the mind itself, which are called goods? Sense and intellect are placed first since on account of them perception and comprehension of the truth are possible. Yet what sort of and how much sensation remains if, to say nothing of other things, a man becomes deaf and blind? Indeed, if reason and intelligence recede from someone rendered insane by some illness, where would those faculties slumber? The mad, when they speak or act, do many absurd things, for the most part unrelated—indeed, even opposed—to their own good intentions and inclinations. When we either reflect on or observe what they say and do, if we consider them properly, we are barely—if at all—able to contain our tears. What shall I say of those who suffer the assault of

demons? Where is their own intelligence hidden or buried when an evil spirit uses both their soul and their body according to its own will? Who is confident that this evil cannot befall a wise man in this life? Next, how well and to what extent do we perceive truth in this flesh, when, as we read in the true book of Wisdom, "The corruptible body weighs down the soul and the earthly dwelling oppresses the intelligence as it considers many things" (Wis 9:15)? An "impulse" or "appetite for action," if in this way Latin rightly names that which the Greeks call *hormé*, is counted as one of the primary goods of nature. Yet is it not precisely that which also produces those miserable motions and deeds of the insane which horrify us when sense is distorted and reason is put to sleep?

Further, virtue itself, which is not among the primary goods of nature because it is added afterward through education, claims to be the highest of human goods; and yet what does it do except conduct perpetual wars with vices, not external but internal ones, not those of others but our very own? Is this not the particular struggle of that virtue which in Greek is named *sóphrosyné*, in Latin "temperance," by which the carnal passions are curbed so that they do not drag the mind into consenting to every sort of shameful action? Vice is never absent when, in the words of the apostle, "The flesh desires in opposition to the spirit." To this vice there is a contrary virtue, when, as the same apostle says: "The spirit desires in opposition to the flesh. For these," he says, "are at war with each other, so that what you will is not what you do" (Gal 5:17). What, however, do we will to do when we will to be perfected by the supreme good? It can only be that the flesh not desire in opposition to the spirit and that this vice opposed to what the spirit desires not be in us. We are not strong enough to do this in this life, however much we will, but with the help of God, let us at least not surrender the spirit and so yield to the flesh warring against the spirit, and be dragged into sinning by our own consent. Therefore, let us not believe that, as long as we are in this internal war, we have already attained our happiness, which we will to attain by conquering the flesh. And who is so utterly wise as to have no conflict at all with his lusts?

What about the virtue called prudence? Does not its total vigilance consist in distinguishing goods from evils, so that in seeking the former and avoiding the latter no error sneaks in? Yet in this way does not prudence itself give evidence that we are among evils or that evils are within us? Prudence teaches that evil is consenting to the desire to sin and that good is withholding consent to that desire. Nevertheless, that evil, to which prudence teaches us not to consent, and to which temperance enables us not to consent, is not removed from this life by either prudence or temperance.

What about justice, whose function is to render to each his due, thereby establishing in man a certain just order of nature, so that the soul is subordinated to God, and the flesh to the soul, and consequently the flesh and the soul to God? Does it not demonstrate in performing this function that it is still laboring at its task instead of resting in the completion of its goal? Surely, the less the soul keeps God in its own thoughts, the less it is subordinated to him; and the more the flesh desires in opposition to the spirit, the less is it subordinated to the soul. Therefore, as long as there is in us this weakness, this plague, this weariness, how shall we dare to say that we are already made well? If we are not yet made well, how shall we dare to say that we are already happy in the attainment of final happiness?

As for the virtue called courage, no matter how wise one may be, it bears the clearest witness to human evils, which is forced to endure patiently. I am astonished to see with what boldness the Stoic philosophers contend that such evils are not evils, yet they allow that if evils become so great that a wise man cannot or ought not endure them, he may be driven to bring about his own death and leave this life. So great is the stupid pride of these men that, while holding that the final good is found in this life and that they are made happy by their own efforts, their wise man (that is, the man whom they describe with an amazing inanity) is one who—even if he is made blind, deaf, dumb, and lame, even if he is tormented by pain and assailed by any other such evils that could be spoken or thought, so that he is driven to bring about his own death—is still not ashamed to call this life so composed of evils "happy"!

O happy life, which seeks the help of death in order to be ended! If it is happy, he should remain in it. In what way are those things not evils? They conquer the good of courage and not only compel the same courage to yield to themselves, but also to rave, so that it both calls the same life happy and persuades one to flee it! Who is so blind that he does not see that if it is happy, one ought not flee it? In saying that such a life must be fled, they openly admit the weakness of their position. The neck of their pride having been broken, why they do not also admit that such a life is miserable? I ask, did Cato kill himself because of endurance or lack of endurance? He would not have done it, except that he could not bear to endure the victory of Caesar. Where is the courage here? Truly, it yielded; truly, it surrendered; truly, it was so completely overcome that it abandoned, deserted, and fled the happy life. Or was it not then happy? Clearly, it was miserable. In what sense, then, were there no evils which made life miserable and something necessary to flee? . . .

If virtues are true—and true virtues cannot exist except in those who possess true piety—they do not profess to be able to protect the men who have them from suffering miseries. True virtues are not such liars as to profess this. They do, however, profess that human life, which is compelled by the great number and magnitude of evils in this world to be miserable, is happy through hope in a future world, and in the same way made well. Indeed, how can it be happy until it is made well? And thus the apostle Paul, speaking not of imprudent, impatient, intemperate, and unjust men, but of men living according to true piety, and thereby having true virtues, says: "By hope we are made well. However, hope that is seen is not hope, for how can one hope for what one sees? However, if we hope for what we do not see, we look forward to it with patience" (Rom 8:24–25).

Therefore, as we are made well by hope, so we are made happy by hope; and as we do not presently possess well-being, but look forward to it in the future "with patience," so it is with happiness. This is because we are now among evils, which we must endure patiently, until we arrive at those goods in which we will find only indescribable delight and none of the things which we must now endure. Such well-being, which we will find in the future world, will itself be final happiness. Because they do not see this happiness, the philosophers refuse to believe in it, but struggle to fabricate for themselves in this life an utterly false happiness through a virtue as dishonest as it is proud.

Chapter 12

Anyone who pays any attention to human affairs and our common human nature, recognizes as I do that just as there is no one who does not wish to be joyful, so there is no one who does not wish to have peace. Indeed, even those who want war want nothing other than to achieve victory; by warring, therefore, they desire to attain a glorious peace. What else is victory, unless triumphing over the opposition? When this has happened, there will be peace. Therefore, even those who are eager to exercise the military virtues by commanding or fighting wage war with the intention of peace. Consequently, the desired end of war is peace, for everyone seeks peace, even by waging war, but no one seeks war by making peace.

Even those who want the peace they now have to be disturbed do not hate peace, but they desire to change the peace according to their own wishes. Thus, they are not unwilling that there be peace, but they want it on their own terms. Furthermore, even if they have separated themselves from others through sedition, when they conspire or plot amongst themselves they do not achieve what they intend unless they have some sort of peace. Likewise, robbers themselves want to have peace with their partners, so that they might more violently and safely attack the peace of others. Perhaps one person is so strong and so wary of conspiring with others that he does not ally himself to any partners. Waiting in ambush and prevailing alone, he gains plunder by crushing and annihilating whom he can. Still, with those whom he cannot kill and from whom he wants to hide what he does, he certainly has some sort of a shadow of peace.

In his home, with his wife and children and anyone else who might be there, he surely strives to be at peace. Their complying with his command is no doubt pleasing. If they do not do so, he is enraged; he rebukes and punishes them. He establishes peace in his own home, if it is necessary, even by brutality. He thinks that peace is not possible unless the rest of the household is subject to a ruler, and in his own home he himself is that ruler. That is why, if the service of a great multitude, or of cities, or peoples is offered to him, so that they would serve him in the same manner as he wanted to be served in his own household, then he would no longer conceal himself like a bandit in a hideout, but raise himself up like a visible king, although the same desire and malice would abide in him. Thus, all desire to have peace with their own associates, whom they want to live according to their own decree. Indeed, they want, if they are able, to make even those against whom they wage war into their own associates, and to impose on them, when conquered, the laws of their own peace.

Let us imagine someone of the sort sung about in poetry and myth, someone whom, perhaps because of his unsociability and savageness, they have preferred to call "semihuman" rather than "human." His kingdom was the solitude of his horrible cave. So extraordinary was his malice that a name was invented from it, for in the Greek language evil is called *kakos*, which is what he was named. He had no wife with whom to carry on endearing conversation, no little children to play with, no older children to give orders to, no friends with whom to enjoy speaking. He did not even enjoy the society of his father Vulcan, compared to whom he was happier simply because he had not generated such a monster as himself. He gave nothing to anyone, but took from whomever he could whatever and whenever he wanted.

Nevertheless, in the very solitude of his own cave, in which, as is said, "the ground was always reeking with fresh carnage," he wanted nothing other than peace—a peace in which no one would molest him, in which the quiet was not disturbed by the violence of anyone or the fear of it. Further, he desired to be at peace with his body, and to the extent that he was at peace with it, all was well with him. When he commanded, the limbs of his body submitted. Yet, his own morality rebelled against him out of need and stirred up sedition through hunger, aiming to dissociate and exclude the soul from the body. In order to make peace with that morality as quickly as possible, he plundered, he killed, and he devoured. Though monstrous and savage, he was nevertheless monstrously and savagely providing for the peace of his own life and well-being. Moreover, if he had been willing to make peace with others while he was striving to make peace in his cave and in himself, he would not have been called evil or a monster or semihuman. Also, if the appearance of his body and his breathing horrible fire frightened human society, possibly he was not so much savage because of a desire for harming but because of the necessity of his staying alive.

He might not, however, have even existed, or, what is more believable, he might not have been the same as the description given by the vanity of poetry, for if Cacus were not blamed too much, Hercules would be praised too little. Therefore, it is better, as I have said, to believe that a human or semihuman of that sort never existed, as is the case with many of the imaginings of the poets.

Even the most savage wild animals, from whom Cacus got part of his wildness (for he was even said to be half-wild), care for their own species by means of a certain peace. They do this by associating, begetting, bearing, cherishing, and nourishing the offspring, even though they are for the most part insociable and solitary. I do not mean those animals such as sheep, deer, doves, starlings, and bees, but those such as lions, wolves, foxes, eagles, and owls. Indeed, what tigress, pacifying her wildness, does not gently purr and caress her young? What kite, however much it circles its prey alone, does not unite with a mate, put together a nest, warm the eggs, nourish the young birds, and, as if with the mother of his family, keep peace in his domestic society as much as he can? How much more is man brought by the laws of his nature, as it were, to enter into society and keep peace with all men to the extent that he is able?

After all, even the evil wage war for the sake of the peace of their own associates, and they would want to make everyone their own, if they could, so that everyone and everything would be enslaved to one individual. How would that happen if they did not consent to his peace, either through love or fear? In this manner, pride imitates God in a distorted way. It hates equality with partners under God, but wants to impose its own domination upon its partners in place of God. Consequently, it hates the just peace of God and loves its own iniquitous peace. Nevertheless, it is not able not to love some sort of peace. Truly, there is no defect so contrary to nature that it wipes away even the last vestiges of nature. Accordingly, he who knows to prefer the upright to the deformed, and the ordered to the distorted, sees that the peace of the iniquitous, in comparison to the peace of the just, should not be called "peace" at all. However, it is necessary that even what is distorted

be at peace in some way with a part of the things in which it exists or from which it is established. Otherwise, it would not exist at all.

This is just like if someone were to hang with his head downward. The position of the body and the order of the limbs would certainly be distorted, because what nature demands to be above is below, and what it wants to be below is above. This distortion disturbs the peace of the flesh and for that reason is painful. It is nevertheless true that the soul is at peace with the body and is busy struggling for its well-being, and thus there is someone suffering. If the soul departs, having been driven out by the pain, as long as the structure of the limbs remains, so does a certain amount of peace, and thus there is still something hanging there. Because the earthly body tends toward the earth and is resisted by the chain by which it is suspended, it tends to the order of its own peace and requests in a weighty voice, as it were, a place where it might rest. Now lifeless and without any sense, nevertheless it does not depart from the peace of its own natural order, either when it has it or when it reaches toward it.

If embalming portions and treatments are applied, which do not allow the form of the cadaver to break up and dissolve, a sort of peace still unites certain parts to other parts and connects the whole mass in its suitable and therefore peaceful place in the earth. If no one applies the treatment for burying, however, then the cadaver disintegrates in the course of nature. It is in a state of disturbance due to dissenting vapors which are disagreeable to our senses (for this is what is smelled in putrefication), until it is assimilated to the elements of the world and gradually, little by little, separates into their peace. Nevertheless, in no way is anything withdrawn from the laws of the supreme creator and governor by whom the peace of the universe is administered, for even if tiny animals are born from the cadaver of a greater animal, by the same law of the creator each little body serves its own little soul in the well-being of peace. Even if the flesh of the dead is devoured by other animals, wherever it is carried, whatever the things to which it is joined, whatever the things into which it is changed and altered, it finds these same laws diffused throughout all things for the well-being of every mortal species, making peace by harmonizing suitable elements.

Chapter 13

Thus, the peace of the body is the ordered proportion of its parts. The peace of the irrational soul is the ordered repose of the appetites. The peace of the rational soul is the ordered agreement of knowledge and action. The peace of the body and the soul is the ordered life and well-being of a living thing. The peace between a mortal man and God is an ordered obedience, in faith, under the eternal law.

The peace among human beings is ordered concord. The peace of the household is an ordered concord concerning commanding and obeying among those who dwell together. The peace of the city is an ordered concord concerning commanding and obeying among the citizens. The peace of the heavenly city is a fellowship perfectly ordered and harmonious, enjoying God and each other in God. The peace of all things is the tranquility of order.

Order is the arrangement of things equal and unequal, alloting to each its own position. Hence, the miserable indeed lack the tranquility of order in which there is no disturbance, since insofar as they are miserable, they certainly are not at peace. Nevertheless, since they are deservedly and justly miserable, they are not, in their very own misery, able to be outside that order. They are surely not united to the happy, but, by the law of order, are separated from them. When they are free from disturbance, they are adjusted to the circumstances in which they find themselves by a harmony of some degree. Thus, some tranquility of order belongs to them, and so some peace. Therefore, the reason they are miserable is because, even if they have some freedom from concern and are not suffering, they are still not in a position where they ought to be exempt from concern and suffering. They are more miserable, however, if they are not at peace with the very law by which the order of nature is administered.

Moreover, when they suffer, they suffer in that part in which a disturbance of peace occurs, but there is still peace in that part not disturbed by suffering and in the structure itself, which is not dissolved. As, therefore, there is a kind of life without suffering, but suffering cannot exist without some life, so there is a kind of peace without any war, but war cannot exist without some peace. This does not follow because of what war itself is, but because it is waged by those or in those who are natural beings in some way. They would not exist at all, unless they remained in a peace of some sort.

Accordingly, there is a nature in which there is no evil, or even in which there can be no evil, but there cannot be a nature in which there is no good. Thus, not even the nature of the devil himself, insofar as it is a nature, is evil. Rather, it is the distortion of that nature that makes it evil. Hence, he did not stand firm in the truth, but he did not escape the judgment of the truth. He did not remain in the tranquility of order, but he nevertheless did not avoid the power of the one who orders. The goodness of God, which is in the devil's nature, does not remove him from the justice of God, which orders by punishing him. God did not then reproach the good that he created, but the evil that the devil has committed. Neither does God take away all that he gave to the devil's nature, but some he takes and some he leaves, so that there might be something to suffer the loss of what was taken away. That very suffering is a witness to the good taken away and the good left behind, for unless good were left behind, the devil could not suffer because of the good lost. . . .

Therefore, God, who founded all natures most wisely and ordered them most justly, who established the mortal human race as the greatest embellishment of the earth, gave to mankind certain goods suitable for this life. These goods include a temporal peace proportional to the short span of a mortal life, a peace involving health, preservation, and the society of one's own kind. They also include the things necessary for guarding or recovering this peace (such as what is appropriately and fittingly present to the senses: light, sound, breathable air, drinkable water, and whatever is suitable for feeding, covering, healing, and adorning the body). All this was given through the most equitable stipulation, that he who uses such mortal goods rightly, adapting them to the peace of mortals, would receive more and better goods; namely, the peace of immortality and the glory and honor suitable to it, in an eternal life which is for enjoying God and one's neighbor in God. He, however, who uses mortal goods wrongly, would lose them and would not receive eternal ones.

Chapter 15

God said, "Let him have dominion over the fish of the sea and the winged things of the heavens and all the crawling things which crawl upon the earth" (Gn 1:26). He did not will that the rational being, having been made according to his own image, dominate any except the irrational beings; he did not will that man dominate man, but that man dominate the beasts. Therefore, the first just men were established as shepherds of beasts rather than as kings of men, so that even in this way God might suggest what the order of creatures requires and what the reward of sinners drives away. Surely it is understood that the condition of slavery is rightly imposed on the sinner. Accordingly, nowhere in the scripture do we read the word "slave" before the just Noah punished the sin of his son with this word. Thus, he earned the name through fault, not through nature. . . .

The first cause of slavery, then, is sin, with the result that man is placed under man by the bondage of this condition. This does not happen except through the judgment of God, in whom there is no iniquity, and who knows how to distribute the various punishments according to the merits of the delinquent. Yet, as the Lord above says, "Anyone who sins is a slave of sin" (Jn 8:34), and thus indeed many religious people enslaved to iniquitous masters are nevertheless not enslaved to the free: "For by whatever one has been conquered, to that one has also been made a slave" (2 Pt 2:19). And it is certainly a happier condition to be enslaved to a man than to a lust, since the very lust for dominating—not to mention others—ravishes the hearts of mortals by a most savage mastery. In that order of peace by which some are subordinated to others, humility is as beneficial to the enslaved as pride is harmful to the dominating.

Nevertheless, by the nature in which God first established man, no one is a slave of man or of sin. It is also true that penal slavery is ordained by that law which commands the preservation and prohibits the disturbance of the natural order, because if nothing had been done contrary to that law, there would have been nothing requiring the restraint of penal slavery. That is why the apostle also warns slaves to be subject to their masters and to serve with good will and from the heart (Eph 6:5), so that if they are not able to be freed by their masters, they might make their slavery in a certain sense free, by serving not with the cunning of fear, but with the faithfulness of affection, until iniquity is transformed and all human rule and power are made void, and God is all in all (1 Cor 15:24, 28).

Chapter 16

. . . Those who are true "fathers of their families" are concerned that all in their family—the slaves as well as the children—should worship and be reconciled to God. Such fathers desire and long to come to the heavenly household, where the duty of ruling mortals is not necessary because the duty of being concerned for the welfare of those already happy in that immortality will no longer be necessary. Until that home is reached, fathers ought to endure more because they rule than slaves do because they serve.

If, however, anyone in the household opposes the domestic peace through disobedience, he is disciplined by word or by whip or by any other kind of just and legitimate punishment, to the extent that human society allows. Such discipline is for the profit of the one being disciplined, so that he is readjusted to the peace from which he had departed. After all, just as it is not kindness to help someone when it would cause him to lose a greater good, so it is not innocence to spare punishment and permit someone to fall more grievously into wickedness. Therefore, in order to be innocent, duty demands not only that one not bring evil to anyone, but also that one restrain another from sin or punish his sin, so that either the person who is punished might be set straight by the experience or others frightened by his example.

Hence, because the human household ought to be the beginning or the building block of the city, and because every beginning is directed to some end of its own kind and every part to the integrity of the whole whose part it is, the consequence is clearly that domestic peace is directed to civic peace. That is to say, the ordered concord concerning commanding and obeying of those dwelling together is directed to the ordered concord concerning commanding and obeying of the citizens. Accordingly, the father of the family should obtain the precepts by which he rules his household from the laws of the city, so that his household might be adapted to the peace of the city.

Chapter 17

The household of those who do not live by faith chases an earthly peace consisting of the affairs and advantages of this temporal life. The household of human beings living by faith, on the other hand, looks forward to the future, to those things which are promised as eternal, and makes use of temporal and earthly things like a traveller. Those things do not seize such a person and turn him away from the path to God. They do not increase the burdens of "the corruptible body which weighs down the soul" (Wis 9:15), but sustain him for more easily enduring them. Consequently, both sorts of men and both sorts of households use the things necessary for this mortal life, but the end of such use is unique to each and varies greatly. So also the earthly city, which does not live by faith, desires earthly peace and it secures the concord concerning commanding and obeying of the citizens, so that there might be a certain orderly arrangement of human wills concerning the things pertaining to mortal life. The heavenly city, however, or rather the part of it which journeys in this mortal life and lives by faith, necessarily uses this peace, too, until the very mortality which makes such a peace necessary might pass away.

Because of this, so long as it leads the life of a captive, as it were, journeying within the earthly city, already having received a promise of redemption and a spiritual gift as a pledge of it, the heavenly city has no doubts about conforming to the laws of the earthly city which administer the things required for the sustainance of the mortal life. Because mortality itself is common to both of the cities, concord between them is preserved with respect to those things pertaining to the mortal life. . . .

So long as this heavenly city journeys on the earth, it calls forth citizens from all peoples and gathers a society of foreigners speaking all languages. It is not troubled at all about differences in customs, laws, and institutions by which the earthly peace is either sought or maintained. So long as they do not impede the religion which teaches the worship of the one, supreme, and true God, the heavenly city abrogates or

destroys none of them, but indeed observes and follows them, for whatever the diversities of different nations, they nevertheless strive toward the one and the same end of earthly peace.

Hence, even the heavenly city uses the earthly peace on its journey, and it is concerned about and desires the orderly arrangement of human wills concerning the things pertaining to mortal human nature, insofar as it is agreeable to sound piety and religion. It directs the earthly peace to the heavenly peace, which is so truly peace that it must be held and said that the only peace, at least of rational creatures, is the most ordered and most harmonious society enjoying God and each other in God. When that peace comes, there will not be mortal life, but a whole and certain life; not the ensouled body weighing down the soul in its corruption (Wis 9:15), but a spiritual body with no wants and with every part subordinated to the will. While it journeys, the heavenly city possesses this peace in faith, and out of this faith it lives justly when it directs to the attainment of that peace whatever good actions it performs toward God, and also those performed toward the neighbor, since the life of this city is certainly social.

Chapter 19

The style of dress or manner of living in which anyone follows the faith that leads to God does not matter to the heavenly city, so long as these are not in contradiction with the divine precepts. Thus, even philosophers, when they become Christians, are not required to change their style of dress or eating customs, which do not impede religion, though they are required to change their false teachings. Accordingly, that city does not care at all about the distinction that Varro made concerning the Cynics, so long as nothing is done basely or intemperately.

With respect to those three kinds of life, the leisurely, the active, and the combination of the two, although every one, through sound faith, can lead his life according to any one of them and attain the everlasting reward, what one holds through the love of truth and what one expends through the duty of charity are nevertheless important. Thus, no one ought to be so leisurely that he does not, in his leisure, consider the advantage of his neighbor; neither should anyone be so active that he does not consider the contemplation of God to be necessary.

In leisure, one ought not delight in slothful idleness, but in either the investigation or discovery of truth, so that everyone advances in it and does not withhold his discoveries from others. In action, no one ought to love honor or power in this life, because all is vanity under the sun (Eccl 1:2–3). Rather, the work itself that is done through the same honor or power should be loved, if it is done rightly and profitably. That is to say, it should be loved if it advances the well-being of the subjects, which is according to God, as we have argued earlier.

Because of this the apostle said, "He who desires the episcopacy desires a good work" (1 Tm 3:1). He wanted to explain that the name "episcopacy" is the name of a work not of an honor. Indeed, the word is Greek, and it comes from the fact that he who is set over others "superintends" them; that is, he exercises care for them. Indeed, the Greek word *skopos* means intention; therefore, for *episkopein* we can say, if we want, "superintend." Consequently, he who desires to be over others rather than to benefit others should understand that he is not a bishop.

Thus, no one is prohibited from zealousness for knowledge of the truth, because the life of learned leisure pertains to what is praiseworthy. On the other hand, to desire high position, without which a people cannot be ruled, is indecent, even if the position is held and administered in a decent manner. Because of this, charity for truth seeks holy leisure, while the requirements of charity accept just activity. If this latter burden is not imposed, one is free to grasp for and to contemplate truth. If, however, the burden is imposed, accepting it is on account of the requirements of charity. Even in this instance, however, delight in the truth is not abandoned completely, otherwise that sweetness might be lost and these requirements crush us.

Chapter 21

It is at this place that I will explain, as briefly and clearly as I can, what in the second book of this work I promised that I would demonstrate; namely, that, according to the definition that Scipio uses in the *Republic* of Cicero, there never was a Roman repub-

lic. He succinctly defines a "republic" as "the affair of a people." If this definition is true, there never was a Roman republic, because Rome never was the affair of a people, which is Scipio's definition of a republic.

The reason for this is that he defined "a people" as "a fellowship of a multitude united through a consensus concerning right and a sharing of advantage." What he calls "a consensus concerning right" he explains in the dialogue by making it clear that it is not possible for a republic to be managed without justice. Therefore, where there is no true justice, there can be no right. What is done by right is indeed done justly; what is done unjustly, however, cannot be done by right. The iniquitous institutions of human beings must not be said or thought to exist by right, because even those institutions say that right flows from the fountain of justice, and that what is customarily said by those who do not understand right correctly—i.e. that right is the advantage of the strongest—is false.

Accordingly, where there is no true justice, there can be no fellowship of men united through a consensus concerning right, and therefore there can be no people according to the definition of Scipio or Cicero. Moreover, if there is no people, neither can there be an affair of a people, but only of some sort of a multitude which is not worthy of the name of "a people." Consequently, if a republic is "the affair of a people," and there is no people which is not "united by means of a consensus concerning right," and there is no right where there is no justice, without doubt it must be concluded that where there is no justice, there is no republic.

Furthermore, justice is that virtue which distributes to everyone his due. What sort of justice is it, then, that takes a man away from the true God and subjects him to unclean demons? Is *this* to distribute to each his due? Or, is he who takes the ground purchased by someone and gives it to another who has no right to it unjust, but he who takes himself away from the dominion of the God who made him and enslaves himself to malicious spirits just?

Certainly, the cause of justice against injustice is argued very energetically and forcefully in that very same book, *The Republic*. Earlier, the case of injustice against justice was considered and it was said that the republic could not stand firm or be managed except through injustice. It was set down as the most powerful part of the argument that it was unjust for men to serve other men as their masters, but that unless the imperial city to whom the great republic belongs follows such injustice it is not able to rule its provinces. The response from the side of justice was that this rule over the inhabitants of the provinces is just because servitude is advantageous for such men and is done for their benefit when it is done correctly—that is, when the license for wrongdoing is taken away from the wicked. Also, it was argued that they will be in a better condition as a result of having been subdued, because they were in a worse condition before being subdued.

In order to strengthen this reasoning, a famous example was stated as though it was borrowed from nature: "Why, then, does God rule man, the soul rule the body, the reason rule lust and the rest of the corrupt parts of the soul?" Plainly, this example teaches well that servitude is advantageous to some and that serving God is indeed advantageous to all. In serving God, the soul correctly rules the body, and the reason in the soul subordinated to the Lord God correctly rules lust and the rest of the corrupt parts of the soul. Thus, when a man does not serve God, what in him can be reckoned to belong to justice? Indeed, when not serving God, the soul can in no way justly rule the body, or human reason the vices. Furthermore, if there is not any justice in such a man, without doubt neither is there any in a fellowship of human beings which consists of such men. Therefore, this is not that "consensus concerning right" which makes a multitude of human beings a "people," whose affair is called a "republic."

What shall I say concerning that "advantage," the sharing of which also unites a fellowship of men so that it is named "a people," as stipulated by the definition? If you carefully direct your attention, you will see that there is no advantage to any who live impiously, as do all who do not serve God but serve the demons who, the more impious they are, the more they want to receive sacrifice as gods, even though they are the most unclean spirits of all. Yet, what we have said about the consensus concerning right I think is sufficient to make it apparent that, according to this definition, there is no people which might be said to be a republic in which there is no justice.

If our enemies say that the Romans have not served unclean spirits but good and holy gods in their republic, must what we have already said sufficiently, indeed more than sufficiently, be repeated yet again? Who, except the excessively stupid or the shamelessly contentious, having arrived at this point after reading the earlier books of this work, finds it possible to doubt but that the Romans have up to this point served evil and impure demons? Nevertheless, in order to say no more about the sort of gods they are worshiping with sacrifices, I instead cite what is written in the law of the true God: "Anyone sacrificing to the gods, except only to the Lord, will be eradicated" (Ex 22:20). Thus, he who admonishes with such a threat did not want either good gods or evil ones to receive sacrifice.

Chapter 23

... We ourselves—his city—are the best and most radiant sacrifice. We celebrate this mystery through our offerings, which are known to the faithful, as we have argued in the preceding books. Indeed, through the Hebrew prophets the divine oracles thundered that the offering of sacrificial victims by the Jews, a foreshadowing of the future, would cease, and that peoples from the rising of the sun to its setting would offer one sacrifice, as we see happening now. From these oracles we have taken as much as seemed sufficient and have already sprinkled them throughout this work.

Thus, justice exists when the one and supreme God rules his obedient city according to his grace, so that it does not sacrifice to any whatsoever except Him alone. As a result, in everyone belonging to that same city and obeying God, the soul faithfully commands the body, and reason the corrupt parts of the soul, in accord with the lawful order. Consequently, just like a single just man, a fellowship and a people of just men lives by faith, which works through love, by which man loves God as God ought to be loved, and his neighbor as himself. Where that justice does not exist, truly there is no "fellowship of men united through a consensus concerning right and a sharing of advantage." If this justice does not exist, then a people does not exist, if this is the true definition of a people. Therefore, neither does a republic exist, for there is no affair of a people where there is no people.

Book XXII

Chapter 27

Plato and Porphyry each said certain things, and if they had been able to communicate them to each other, they might perhaps have become Christians. Plato said that souls are not able to exist in eternity without bodies, for he said that after quite a long period of time the souls of even the wise return to bodies. Porphyry, however, said that a fully purified soul, when it has returned to the Father, will never return to the evils of the world. Accordingly, suppose that Plato had given to Porphyry the truth that he had seen—that even the fully purified souls of the just and the wise will return to human bodies—and that Porphyry had likewise given to Plato the truth which he had seen—that no holy souls will return to the miseries of corruptible bodies. Each would not then have had only a single truth, but both would have had both truths. I think that they would have seen that it follows both that souls return to their bodies and also that they receive the sort of bodies in which they might live happily and immortally. The reason is that, according to Plato, even holy souls will return to human bodies; and according to Porphyry, holy souls will not return to the evils of this world.

Hence, let Porphyry say with Plato, "Holy souls will return to bodies," and let Plato say with Porphyry, "Holy souls will not return to evils," and they will both agree that holy souls return to bodies in which no evils are suffered. Such bodies will be nothing other than the sort of bodies which God promises—happy souls living in eternity with their own eternal flesh. As far as I can tell, they would both readily concede to us that those who profess that the souls of the saints will return to immortal bodies would also allow that they return to their own bodies, the bodies in which they endured the evils of this world and in which they worshipped God in piety and fidelity so that they might be freed from those evils.

Chapter 29

Let us now consider, to the extent that the Lord deigns to assist us, what the saints will do in their immortal and spiritual bodies, with their flesh living not carnally but spiritually. In truth, though, I do not know what that activity—or rather that rest and leisure—will be, for I have not ever seen it through my bodily senses. If I say that I have seen it mentally, by means of my understanding, then what is our understanding compared to that excellence? As the apostle says, "There is the peace of God which surpasses all understanding" (Phil 4:7). What understanding does he mean, except ours, or perhaps even that of the holy angels? Indeed, he does not mean God's understanding. If, then, the saints will live in the peace of God, surely they will live in that peace which surpasses all understanding. That it surpasses our understanding, there is no doubt. If, however, it surpasses even that of the angels, so that it would seem that he who said "all understanding" did not leave out them, then we ought to take this passage to mean that neither we nor any angel are able to know the peace of God by which God himself is peaceful, as God knows it. Thus, this peace surpasses every understanding—with the exception, surely, of his own.

Yet, because we have been made partakers of his peace according to our own capacity, we know that highest peace within ourselves and among ourselves and with him, to the highest extent of which we are capable. In the same way, the holy angels know it according to their own capacity. The capacity of human beings, however, is now far below that of the angels, no matter what mental progress human beings might make. Indeed, one must consider how great that man was who said, "We know in part and we prophesy in part, until that which is perfect arrives" and "Now we see reflections obscurely, but then we will see face to face" (1 Cor 13:9,12). The holy angels, who are also called "our angels," see that way already.

They are called "our" angels because, torn away from the power of darkness, given the pledge of the Spirit, and carried over to the kingdom of Christ, we have already begun to belong to those angels with whom we will live together in the holy and supremely sweet city of God itself, about which I have already written so many books. In this way, then, the angels of God are our angels, just as the Christ of God is our Christ. They belong to God because they did not abandon him; they belong to us because they have begun to have us as fellow citizens. Moreover, the Lord Jesus said, "See to it that you do not despise one of these little ones, for I say to you, their angels in heaven always see the face of my father who is in heaven" (Mt 18:10). Therefore, as they see, so will we see; but we do not see in that way yet. It is on account of this that the apostle says what I cited just a moment ago: "Now we see reflections obscurely, but then we will see face to face." That vision is preserved for us as the reward of faith; the apostle John says of it, "When he appears, we will be like him, for we will see him as he is" (1 Jn 3:2). The "face" of God must be understood as his manifestation, not as the part of a body such as we have and call by that name.

Consequently, when I am asked what the saints will do in that spiritual body, I do not say that I already see, but I say what I believe, according to what I read in the psalm: "I believed, and hence I have spoken" (Ps 116:10). Thus I say that they will see God in the body itself, but whether they will see God through the body itself, as we now see the sun, the moon, the stars, the sea, and the earth and the things that are in it through the body, is no small question. It is difficult to assert that the saints will then have such bodies that they will not be able to close and open their eyes whenever they want; yet it is more difficult to assert that anyone there who closes his eyes will not see God. . . .

The question is whether the saints will see God through the eyes of the body when they have them open. If, in the spiritual body, the eyes—which are, of course, also spiritual—will be able to see only as much as these eyes which we have now, then without doubt they will not be able to see God. Consequently, such eyes will be of a very different power than the ones we have now if that immaterial nature which is not contained in space but is completely present everywhere will be seen through them. While we say that God is both in heaven and in earth—in fact, he himself says through the prophet, "I fill heaven and earth" (Jer 23:24)—we are not about to say that God has one part in heaven and another part on earth; rather, he is entirely in heaven and entirely on earth, not at alternating periods of time but both at the same time, as no material nature can be. Hence, the power of those eyes will be greatly enhanced, not so that they might see more keenly than certain snakes or eagles are thought to see (for however great their keenness of perceiving, animals also see nothing other than material things), but so that they might also see immaterial things. . . .

If we could be completely certain about the reasoning of the philosophers when they argue that intelligible things are seen by the gaze of the mind and sensible things—that is, bodily things—by the sense of the body in such a way that the mind is not able to look upon intelligible things through the body nor bodily things through itself, then indeed it would be certain that God could in no way be seen through the eyes of even a spiritual body. Both true reason and prophetic authority ridicule that line of reasoning, however. Indeed, who is so averse to the truth that he dares to say that God does not know material things? Does God therefore have a body with eyes, through which he is able to learn about material things? . . .

Therefore, as it is agreed that material things are seen by spirit, what if the power of the spiritual body will be such that spirit might also be seen by the body? After all, "God is spirit" (Jn 4:24). Moreover, everyone knows his own life—the life by which he now lives in the body and the life which makes his earthly limbs grow and makes them alive—not through material eyes but through an inner sense. Yet everyone sees the lives of others through the body, even though the lives of others are invisible. On what basis do we distinguish living bodies from non-living ones, unless we see bodies and, at the same time, the lives which we would not be able to see except through the body? With material eyes, however, we do not see lives without bodies.

Accordingly, it could happen, and it is quite believable, that we will then see the worldly bodies belonging to the new heaven and the new earth in such a way that, through the bodies which we will wear and which we will observe, we will see, with the most transparent clarity, wherever we turn our eyes, God—present everywhere, governing the whole universe, material things included. It will not be as it is now, when the invisible realities of God are observed through understanding the things which have been made, observed through an obscure reflection and in part (Rom 1:20; 1 Cor 13:12). Now the faith by which we believe is more important in us than the material things we perceive through the material eyes.

The human beings among whom we live are living and show the motions of life, so that when looking at them we do not believe but see that they are alive. Even though we are not able to see that they are alive without their bodies, we nevertheless observe the life in them through their bodies, without the slightest doubt. In the same way, wherever we will turn those spiritual eyes of our bodies, we will also behold through our bodies the immaterial God ruling over all things.

Therefore, either God will be seen through those eyes in such a way that they will have some capacity similar to the mind through which even immaterial nature will be perceived—though this is either difficult or impossible to demonstrate through any examples or testimonies of divine Scripture—or else, what is easier to understand, God will be so known and so visible to us that he will be seen in spirit by each of us in each of us, seen by everyone in everyone else, seen in himself, seen in the new heaven and the new earth and in every creature which will then exist, seen even in every body through bodies, wherever the eyes of the spiritual body will direct their penetrating view. Even our thoughts will be open to each other, for the words of the apostle will then be fulfilled. After he had said, "Do not judge before the time," he then added, "until the Lord comes, both bringing to light things hidden in darkness and making the thoughts of the heart manifest; then each person will have his praise from God" (1 Cor 4:5).

Chapter 30

How great will be that happiness where there will be no evil, where no good will be concealed, where there will be leisure for the praises of God, who will be all in all! I do not know what else would be done where there will be no inactivity due to any idleness nor any labor due to any need. I am also advised about this by the sacred song, when I read or hear, "Happy are those who dwell in your house; they will praise you forever" (Ps 84:4).

Because there will be no necessity then, but a full, certain, secure, and everlasting happiness, every limb and organ of the incorruptible body, which we now see assigned to the various tasks of necessity, will be proficient in the praising of God. All those numbers of the harmony of the body, concerning which I have spoken already, which are now hidden, will not be hidden then, but arranged through the whole body, both inside and out. With the other great and marvelous things that will be seen there, they will inflame rational minds through a delight in rational beauty into praising such a great artificer. I do not presume to define rashly what the movements of such bodies will be there, for I am not able to unravel that question. Nevertheless, both their movement and posture, like their appearance itself, will be fitting, whatever they will be, for only what is fitting will exist there. Certainly, wherever the spirit will want to be, the body will be there immediately, and the spirit will not want anything that could not be fitting for the spirit of the body.

True glory will be there; no one will be praised through error or flattery. True honor, which will be denied to no one worthy, will be offered to no one unworthy. No one unworthy, however, will even seek it, for only the worthy will be permitted to be there. True peace will be there, for no one will suffer opposition, either from himself or from another. The reward of virtue will be God himself, who gave the virtue and promised himself as its reward, for there could be nothing better or greater. Indeed, what else did he mean when he said through the prophet, "I will be their God, and they will be my people" (Lv 26:12) except "I will be what satisfies them; I will be everything that is properly desired by human beings— life and health and nourishment and abundance and glory and honor and peace and all good things"? The saying of the apostle, "so that God may be all in all" (1 Cor 15:28), is correctly understood in this way also. He himself, who will be seen without end, loved without surfeit, and praised without fatigue, will be the end of our desires. This gift, this affection, this activity, will surely be common to all just as eternal life itself is common to all.

Who is fit to ponder, much less to declare, what degrees of honor and glory according to merit there will be? That there will be such degrees is not to be doubted. That happy city will see this great good in itself also: no inferior will envy any superior, just as now the rest of the angels do not envy the archangels. No one will want what he has not received, although he will be tied by a supremely peaceful bond of concord to the one who has received it, just as in the body the finger does not want to be the eye, though the peaceful joining of the whole body contains both of these. In this way, therefore, anyone who has a lesser gift than another will also have this gift: he will not want more. . . .

The free will of that city will be one in all and indivisible in each. Freed from every evil and filled with every good, it will enjoy the delight of eternal gladness without ceasing. Having forgotten all sins and all punishments, it will not therefore forget its own liberation and so be ungrateful to its own liberator. Insofar, then, as they pertain to rational knowledge, that city remembers its own past evils completely; insofar as they pertain to sense experience, it forgets them completely.

The most expert physician knows almost all the diseases of the body as they are known by that art. Not having suffered the diseases himself, however, he does not generally know them as they are felt by the body. Thus, there are two ways of knowing evils: in one way, evils are not concealed from the power of the mind; in another, they cling to sensory experience. Indeed, in one way, every vice is known through the teaching of wisdom; in another way, they are known through the dissolute life of foolishness. Accordingly, there are also two ways of forgetting evils. One who has studied and learned them forgets them in one way; one who has experienced and suffered them forgets them in another. The first forgets if he neglects the study of evils; the second if he is rid of misery.

It is according to his second manner of forgetting that the saints will not remember past evils. They will be rid of all evils in such a way that every sensation of them will be thoroughly deleted. Nevertheless, not only their own past evils, but even the everlasting miseries of the condemned, will not be concealed from their power of knowing, which will be great in them. Otherwise, if they will not know that they themselves were wretched, how, as the psalm says, "will they sing of the mercies of the Lord forever" (Ps 89:2)? Surely there will be nothing more delightful for that city than this song to the glory of the grace of Christ, by whose blood we have been freed.

There will these words be accomplished: "Rest, and see that I am God" (Ps 46:11). . . . This Sabbath will be more apparent if the number of the ages is enumerated just like the number of the days of creation, as if the days of creation correspond to those periods of time which have been expressed by the Scriptures, for one discovers that there are seven such ages. The first age, corresponding to the first day, extends from Adam up until the flood; the second age, extending from there up until Abraham, is not equal in time to the first, but in the number of generations—indeed, they are each found to have had ten. From that point there follow, as the evangelist Matthew divides them, three ages until the coming of Christ. Each of those three extend fourteen generations: from Abraham until David is the first; from David until the exile in Babylon is the second; and from the exile until the birth of Christ in the flesh is the third. Thus, five ages have been completed.

The sixth is occurring now. It should not be estimated by any set number of generations, since the scripture says, "It is not for you to know the time, which the Father, in his own power, has established" (Acts 1:7). After this age God will rest, as on the seventh day, when he will cause the seventh day— and we will be that day—to rest in God himself. To discuss thoroughly each of these ages in turn at the present time would be tedious. Nevertheless, this seventh age will be our Sabbath. Its end will not be at sunset, but will be the Lord's day—an eternal eighth day sanctified by the resurrection of Christ, which prefigures the eternal rest, not only of the spirit but also of the body. There we will rest and see, see and love, love and praise. Behold what will be in the end without end! For what else will our end be, except to reach the kingdom in which there is no end?

I think that I have, with the help of the Lord, fulfilled my obligation of writing this enormous work. May those for whom it is too little or too much pardon me. May those for whom it is just sufficient give solemn thanks, not to me, but to God with me.

IX
THOMAS AQUINAS

Medieval political thought might plausibly be summarized as a struggle among four distinct and competing conceptions of political society. According to one such conception, the proper form of political society was the *nation-state* governed by a king. Political order would flourish most naturally in a single, circumscribed territory with a population having a more or less shared and undifferentiated historical, linguistic, ethnic, and cultural background. The regime would be a secular one, politics being no place for the clergy, and the regime would achieve stability by relying on the unity of the ruling power—the monarchy itself—along with the unified customs of the citizenry.

Posed against this model was the conception of a *papal state* in which temporal powers would be subservient to ecclesiastical ones. The argument for such a conception involved theological considerations. Truth and morality were ultimately to be found in the word of Christ and in divine grace; and as the ordained interpreters of the truth, it was the clergy—and the pope in particular—who ought to have authority with respect to all facets of human existence, the political included. How could a Christian commonwealth be truly Christian unless it was governed, in the last analysis, by the ministers of God?

A third approach conceived of political society as an *empire*. In the year 800, Charlemagne had been declared Holy Roman Emperor, and this event helped establish the idea of a secular state that would find unity not in particular territorial, linguistic, or cultural traditions, as would the nation-state, but in the larger commonalities of Christianity itself. Germans, Italians, Spaniards, and the rest might be different from one another in any number of ways; but insofar as they were all Christian, their similarities outweighed their differences. They formed a larger community, rooted in spiritual considerations, and ought therefore to be governed by a single government— one that reflected, however, Christ's injunction to render under Caesar the things that are properly Caesar's.

A fourth model involved a reformulated version of the ancient *city-state*. Such a model was especially important in medieval Italy, where autonomous and powerful city-states flourished and where a distinctive ideology of civic, republican independence had begun to emerge. Here, again, the ruling powers would be secular rather than clerical; but the underlying basis of unity would be found in the intimacy of the city itself, where the interconnectedness of citizens and their various interests could be experienced literally every day.

All such views were essentially partisan in nature, but each of them sought, to one degree or another, a larger theoretical or philosophical grounding. One possible foundation of this kind was provided by the most important philosopher and theologian of the Middle Ages, Thomas Aquinas. In seeking to provide a metaphysical account of the idea of the state, St. Thomas may be thought to have summarized and synthesized the premodern approach to politics and to have established thereby a systematic understanding of political society that would provide the crucial background against which the founders of modern politics—preeminently Machiavelli and Hobbes—would develop their bold new ideas.

In the thirteenth century, William of Moerbeke produced the first direct translation of Aristotle's *Politics* from the Greek to the Latin. In doing so, he made an important contribution to the astonishing explosion of interest in Aristotle that galvanized and revolutionized the intellectual life of the West. No one was more caught up in this occurrence than St. Thomas. His own texts refer to Aristotle simply as "the Philosopher," and it is not too much of an exaggeration to say that St. Thomas's life's work, and his great achievement, was to show how it might be possible to be an Aristotelian and a Christian at the same time.

It is important to remember that Aristotle was a pagan philosopher who lived three centuries before the birth of Christ. He was, moreover, committed to the authority of human reason. The truth of the world was something to be discovered through logic and science, and Aristotle himself pursued a philosophical method in which mystery and mysticism could play no role whatever. Like any rationalist, he thought that belief ought to be based solely on evidence and proof and that opinions grounded in other kinds of considerations could not possibly have any plausible claim to truth. Against this background, consider the immensely influential views of St. Paul, who argued that Christianity was fundamentally a matter of faith, hence irreducible to any kind of rational formula. Indeed, it sometimes seems that, for Paul, genuine faith is best demonstrated precisely in those circumstances that are least amenable to rational analysis. If we can believe in the word of God even where reason strongly urges us not to, then this is the most authentic evidence of our devotion to Jesus.

The immense edifice of Thomistic philosophy is largely designed to show that the truths of rational philosophy and those of Christian faith are, in fact, not incompatible but are merely two different sides of the same coin. Reason and revelation mutually reinforce one another. Crucial to St. Thomas's view is the connection between natural law and divine law. Divine law is the revealed law of God—something to be apprehended through faith and religious devotion—and is the highest law of all. But God chooses to communicate to us in a second way, through natural law. Natural law is, in effect, a version of divine law constructed in such a way so as to be accessible to those who would employ the distinctive and defining faculty of human beings, the faculty of reason. If we utilize that faculty—roughly as Aristotle prescribed—we will come to understand the teaching of natural law and hence will come to understand the truth of the world. Our understanding will not be as exalted or as penetrating as if we had directly apprehended divine law itself, through faith and revelation. Our purchase of the truth will be less secure and more superficial. But we will know the truth nonetheless, and this knowledge will allow us, among other things, to live our lives in an ethical and upstanding manner—a manner of which God would approve—and to construct our political institutions with similar rectitude. In this last respect, St. Thomas produced a political philosophy remarkably faithful to its Aristotelian roots, one that emphasized the essentially political nature of human beings and that focused on the need for kings to govern their communities with a view toward serving and enhancing the public interest.

In proposing such a reconciliation of classical and Christian thought, St. Thomas was proposing a doctrine deeply offensive to many of the ecclesiastical powers of his day, a doctrine for which he himself was severely condemned. The allure of Aristotelianism and the power of the Thomistic synthesis proved to be irresistible, however. Thomas Aquinas died in 1274. Scarcely fifty years later, he attained sainthood in the Catholic church, and he remains to this day the most influential of all Catholic theologians and political theorists.

Further Reading: The best place to start would be Chapter 2 of *The Medieval Contribution to Political Thought* (1939) by Alexander Passerin D'Entreves. Also relevant and helpful by Passerin D'Entreves is his *Natural Law* (1951). A classic study of medieval political thought is Otto von Gierke, *Political Theories of the Middle Age* (1900). For a more recent study, see Mark C. Murphy, "Consent, Custom and the Common Good in Aquinas's Account of Political Authority," in *Review of Politics* (1997).

Thomas Aquinas
(1225–1274)

Summa Theologica

QUESTION 90
OF THE ESSENCE OF LAW

[In Four Articles]

We have now to consider the extrinsic principles of acts. Now the extrinsic principle inclining to evil is the devil, of whose temptations we have spoken in the First Part. But the extrinsic principle moving to good is God, Who both instructs us by means of His law and assists us by His grace; wherefore, in the first place, we must speak of law; in the second place, of grace.

Concerning law, we must consider (1) law itself in general; (2) its parts. Concerning law in general, three points offer themselves for our consideration: (1) its essence; (2) the different kinds of law; (3) the effects of law.

Under the first head, there are four points of inquiry: (1) Whether law is something pertaining to reason? (2) concerning the end of law; (3) its cause; (4) the promulgation of law.

First Article
Is Law Something Pertaining to Reason?

We proceed thus to the First Article:

Objection 1. It would seem that law is not something pertaining to reason. For the Apostle says: "I see another law in my members," etc. But nothing pertaining to reason is in the members, since the reason does not make use of a bodily organ. Therefore, law is not something pertaining to reason.

Obj. 2. Further, in the reason there is nothing else but power, habit, and act. But law is not the power itself of reason. In like manner, neither is it a habit of reason, because the habits of reason are the intellectual virtues of which we have spoken above. Nor, again, is it an act of reason because then law would cease when the act of reason ceases, for instance, while we are asleep. Therefore, law is nothing pertaining to reason.

Obj. 3. Further, the law moves those who are subject to it to act aright. But it belongs properly to the will to move to act, as is evident from what has been said above. Therefore, law pertains not to the reason but to the will, according to the words of the Jurist: "Whatever pleases the ruler has the force of law."

On the contrary, It belongs to the law to command and to forbid. But it belongs to reason to command, as stated above. Therefore, law is something pertaining to reason.

I answer that Law is a certain rule and measure of acts whereby man is induced to act or is restrained from acting; for *lex* (law) is derived from *ligare* (to bind) because it binds one to act. Now the rule and measure of human acts is reason, which is the first principle of human acts, as is evident from what has been stated above, since it belongs to reason to direct to the end, which is the first principle in all matters of action, according to the Philosopher. Now, that which is the principle in any genus is the rule and measure of that genus, for instance, unity in the genus of numbers, and the first movement in the genus of movements. Consequently, it follows that law is something pertaining to reason.

Reply Obj. 1. Since law is a kind of rule and measure, it may be in something in two ways. First, as in that which measures and rules; and since this is proper to reason, it follows that, in this way, law is in reason alone. Second, as in that which is measured and ruled. In this way, law is in all those things that are inclined to something by reason of some law, so that any inclination arising from a law may be called a law, not essentially but by participation as it were.

Reprinted from Aquinas, *On Law, Morality, and Politics*, edited, with introduction, by William P. Baumgarth and Richard J. Regan, S.J. (Cambridge, Mass.: Avatar Books of Cambridge, 1988) by permission of the publisher.

And thus the inclination of the members to concupiscence is called "the law of the members."

Reply Obj. 2. Just as, in external action, we may consider the work and the work done—for instance, the work of building and the house built, so in the acts of reason we may consider the act itself of reason, i.e., to understand and to reason, and something produced by this act. With regard to the speculative reason, this is first of all the definition; secondly, the proposition; thirdly, the syllogism or argument. And since also the practical reason makes use of a kind of syllogism in respect to the work to be done, as stated above and as the Philosopher teaches, hence we find in the practical reason something that holds the same position in regard to operations as, in the speculative intellect, the proposition holds in regard to conclusions. Suchlike universal propositions of the practical intellect that are directed to actions have the nature of law. And these propositions are sometimes under our actual consideration, while sometimes they are retained in the reason by means of a habit.

Reply Obj. 3. Reason has its power of moving from the will, as stated above, for it is due to the fact that one wills the end that the reason issues its commands as regards things ordained to the end. But in order that the volition of what is commanded may have the nature of law, it needs to be in accord with some rule of reason. And in this sense is to be understood the saying that the will of the ruler has the force of law; otherwise, the ruler's will would savor of lawlessness rather than of law.

Second Article
Is the Law Always Directed to the Common Good?

We proceed thus to the Second Article:

Obj. 1. It would seem that the law is not always directed to the common good as to its end. For it belongs to law to command and to forbid. But commands are directed to certain individual goods. Therefore, the end of the law is not always the common good.

Obj. 2. Further, the law directs man in his actions. But human actions are concerned with particular matters. Therefore, the law is directed to some particular good.

Obj. 3. Further, Isidore says, "If the law is based on reason, whatever is based on reason will be a law." But reason is the foundation not only of what is ordained to the common good but also of that which is directed to private good. Therefore, the law is not only directed to the common good but also to the private good of an individual.

On the contrary, Isidore says that "Laws are enacted for no private profit but for the common benefit of the citizens."

I answer that, As stated above, the law belongs to that which is a principle of human acts because it is their rule and measure. Now, as reason is a principle of human acts, so in reason itself there is something which is the principle in respect of all the rest; wherefore to this principle chiefly and mainly law must needs be referred. Now the first principle in practical matters, which are the object of the practical reason, is the last end, and the last end of human life is bliss or happiness, as stated above. Consequently, the law must needs regard principally the relationship to happiness. Moreover, since every part is ordained to the whole as imperfect to perfect, and since a single man is a part of the perfect community, the law must needs regard properly the relationship to universal happiness. Wherefore the Philosopher, in the above definition of legal matters, mentions both happiness and the body politic, for he says that we call those legal matters just "which are adapted to produce and preserve happiness and its parts for the body politic" since the political community is a perfect community, as he says in *Politics* I, 1.

Now, in every genus, that which belongs to it most of all is the principle of the others, and the others belong to that genus in subordination to that thing; thus fire, which is chief among hot things, is the cause of heat in mixed bodies, and these are said to be hot insofar as they have a share of fire. Consequently, since the law is chiefly ordained to the common good, any other precept in regard to some individual work must needs be devoid of the nature of a law, save insofar as it is ordered to the common good. Therefore, every law is ordained to the common good.

Reply Obj. 1. A command denotes an application of a law to matters regulated by the law. Now the order to the common good, at which the law aims, is applicable to particular ends. And in this way, commands are given even concerning particular matters.

Reply Obj. 2. Actions are indeed concerned with particular matters, but those particular matters are referable to the common good, not as to a common genus or species, but as to a common final cause, according as the common good is said to be the common end.

Reply Obj. 3. Just as nothing stands firm with regard to the speculative reason except that which is traced back to the first indemonstrable principles, so nothing stands firm with regard to the practical reason unless it be directed to the last end which is the common good, and whatever stands to reason in this sense has the nature of a law.

Third Article
Is the Reason of Any Person Competent to Make Laws?

We proceed thus to the Third Article:

Obj. 1. It would seem that the reason of any person is competent to make laws. For the Apostle says that "when the Gentiles, who have not the law, do by nature those things that are of the law, . . . they are a law to themselves." Now he says this of all in general. Therefore, anyone can make a law for himself.

Obj. 2. Further, as the Philosopher says, "The intention of the lawgiver is to lead men to virtue." But every man can lead another to virtue. Therefore, the reason of any man is competent to make laws.

Obj. 3. Further, just as the ruler of a political community governs the political community, so every father of a family governs his household. But the ruler of a political community can make laws for the political community. Therefore, every father of a family can make laws for his household.

On the contrary, Isidore says, "A law is an ordinance of the people, whereby something is sanctioned by nobles together with commoners." Not everyone, therefore, is competent to make law.

I answer that Law, properly speaking, regards first and chiefly an ordering to the common good. Now to order anything to the common good belongs either to the whole people or to someone who is the vicegerent of the whole people. And, therefore, the making of law belongs either to the whole people or to a public personage who has care of the whole people, since, in all other matters, the directing of anything to the end concerns him to whom the end belongs.

Reply Obj. 1. As stated above, law is in a person not only as in one that rules but also by participation

as in one that is ruled. In the latter way, each one is a law to himself, insofar as he shares the direction that he receives from one who rules him. Hence the same text goes on, "who show the work of the law written in their hearts."

Reply Obj. 2. A private person cannot lead another to virtue efficaciously, for he can only advise, and if his advice be not taken, it has no coercive power, such as the law should have in order to prove an efficacious inducement to virtue, as the Philosopher says. But this coercive power is vested in the whole people or in some public personage to whom it belongs to inflict penalties, as we shall state further on. Wherefore, the framing of laws belongs to him alone.

Reply Obj. 3. As one man is a part of the household, so a household is a part of the political community, and the political community is a perfect community, according to *Politics* I, 1. And, therefore, as the good of one man is not the last end but is ordained to the common good, so too the good of one household is ordained to the good of a single political community, which is a perfect community. Consequently, he that governs a family can indeed make certain commands or ordinances but not such as to have properly the nature of law.

Fourth Article
Is Promulgation Essential to a Law?

We proceed thus to the Fourth Article:

Obj. 1. It would seem that promulgation is not essential to a law. For the natural law above all has the nature of law. But the natural law needs no promulgation. Therefore, it is not essential to a law that it be promulgated.

Obj. 2. Further, it belongs properly to a law to bind one to do or not to do something. But the obligation of fulfilling a law touches not only those in whose presence it is promulgated but also others. Therefore, promulgation is not essential to a law.

Obj. 3. Further, the obligation of a law extends even to the future since "laws are binding in matters of the future," as the jurists say. But promulgation is made to those who are present. Therefore, it is not essential to a law.

On the contrary, It is laid down in the *Decretum,* dist. 4, that "Laws are established when they are promulgated."

I answer that, As stated above, a law is imposed on others by way of a rule and measure. Now a rule or measure is imposed by being applied to those who are to be ruled and measured by it. Wherefore, in order that a law obtain the binding force which is proper to a law, it must needs be applied to the men who have to be ruled by it. Such application is made by its being notified to them by promulgation. Wherefore promulgation is necessary for the law to obtain its force.

Thus, from the four preceding articles, the definition of law may be gathered, and it is nothing else than a certain ordinance of reason for the common good, made by him who has care of the community, and promulgated.

Reply Obj. 1. The natural law is promulgated by the very fact that God instilled it into men's minds so as to be known by them naturally.

Reply Obj. 2. Those who are not present when a law is promulgated are bound to observe the law, insofar as it is notified or can be notified to them by others after it has been promulgated.

Reply Obj. 3. The promulgation that takes place now extends to future time by reason of the durability of written characters, by which means it is continually promulgated. Hence Isidore says that "*lex* (law) is derived from *legere* (to read) because it is written."

QUESTION 91
OF THE VARIOUS KINDS OF LAW

[In Six Articles]

We must now consider the various kinds of law, under which head there are six points of inquiry: (1) Whether there is an eternal law? (2) Whether there is a natural law? (3) Whether there is a human law? (4) Whether there is a divine law? (5) Whether there is one divine law or several? (6) Whether there is a law of sin?

First Article
Is There an Eternal Law?

We proceed thus to the First Article:

Obj. 1. It would seem that there is no eternal law because every law is imposed on someone. But there was not someone from eternity on whom a law could be imposed since God alone was from eternity. Therefore, no law is eternal.

Obj. 2. Further, promulgation is essential to law. But promulgation could not be from eternity because there was no one to whom it could be promulgated from eternity. Therefore, no law can be eternal.

Obj. 3. Further, a law implies order to an end. But nothing ordained to an end is eternal, for the last end alone is eternal. Therefore, no law is eternal.

On the contrary, Augustine says, "That law which is the supreme reason cannot be understood to be otherwise than unchangeable and eternal."

I answer that, As stated above, a law is nothing else but a dictate of practical reason in the ruler who governs a perfect community. Now it is evident, granted that the world is ruled by divine providence, as was stated in the First Part, that the whole community of the universe is governed by divine reason. Wherefore, the very idea of the government of things in God the Ruler of the universe has the nature of a law. And since the divine reason's conception of things is not subject to time but is eternal, according to Pr. 8:23, therefore it is that this kind of law must be called eternal.

Reply Obj. 1. Those things that are not in themselves exist with God inasmuch as they are foreknown and preordained by Him, according to Rom. 4:17, "Who calls those things that are not, as those that are." Accordingly, the eternal concept of the divine law bears the nature of an eternal law insofar as it is ordained by God to the government of things foreknown by Him.

Reply Obj. 2. Promulgation is made by word of mouth or in writing, and in both ways the eternal law is promulgated, because both the divine word and the writing of the Book of Life are eternal. But the promulgation cannot be from eternity on the part of the creature that hears or reads.

Reply Obj. 3. The law implies order to an end actively, insofar as it directs certain things to an end, but not passively—that is to say, the law itself is not ordained to an end—except accidentally, in a governor whose end is extrinsic to him, and to which end his law must needs be ordained. But the end of the divine government is God Himself, and His law is not distinct from Himself. Wherefore the eternal law is not ordained to another end.

Second Article
Is There a Natural Law in Us?

We proceed thus to the Second Article:

Obj. 1. It would seem that there is no natural law in us because man is governed sufficiently by the eternal law; for Augustine says that "the eternal law is that by which it is right that all things should be most orderly." But nature does not abound in superfluities, as neither does it fail in necessaries. Therefore, there is no natural law in man.

Obj. 2. Further, by the law man is directed in his acts to the end, as stated above. But the directing of human acts to their end is not by nature, as is the case in irrational creatures, which act for an end solely by their natural appetite, whereas man acts for an end by his reason and will. Therefore, there is no natural law for man.

Obj. 3. Further, the more a man is free, the less is he under the law. But man is freer than all other animals on account of his free will, with which he is endowed above all other animals. Since, therefore, other animals are not subject to a natural law, neither is man subject to a natural law.

On the contrary, A gloss on Rom. 2:14 ("When the Gentiles, who have not the law, do by nature those things that are of the law") comments as follows: "Although they have no written law, yet they have the natural law, whereby each one knows, and is conscious of, what is good and what is evil."

I answer that, As stated above, law, being a rule and measure, can be in a person in two ways: in one way, as in him that rules and measures; in another way, as in that which is ruled and measured, since a thing is ruled and measured insofar as it partakes of the rule or measure. Wherefore, since all things subject to divine providence are ruled and measured by the eternal law, as was stated above, it is evident that all things partake somewhat of the eternal law insofar as, namely, from its being imprinted on them, they derive their respective inclinations to their proper acts and ends. Now among all others, the rational creature is subject to divine providence in a more excellent way, insofar as it partakes of a share of providence, by being provident both for itself and for others. Wherefore it has a share of the eternal reason, whereby it has a natural inclination to its proper act and end, and this participation of the eternal law in

the rational creature is called the natural law. Hence the Psalmist, after saying "offer up the sacrifice of justice," as though someone asked what the works of justice are, adds: "Many say, 'Who shows us good things?',", in answer to which question he says: "The light of Your countenance, O lord, is signed upon us"; thus implying that the light of natural reason, whereby we discern what is good and what is evil, which pertains to the natural law, is nothing else than an imprint on us of the divine light. It is therefore evident that the natural law is nothing else than the rational creature's participation of the eternal law.

Reply Obj. 1. This argument would hold if the natural law were something different from the eternal law, whereas it is nothing but a participation thereof, as stated above.

Reply Obj. 2. Every act of reason and will in us is derived from that which is according to nature, as stated above; for every act of reasoning is based on principles that are known naturally, and every act of appetite in respect of the means is derived from the natural appetite in respect of the last end. Accordingly, the first direction of our acts to their end must needs be in virtue of the natural law.

Reply Obj. 3. Even irrational animals partake in their own way of the eternal reason, just as the rational creature does. But because the rational creature partakes thereof in an intellectual and rational manner, therefore the participation of the eternal law in the rational creature is properly called a law, since a law is something pertaining to reason, as stated above. Irrational creatures, however, do not partake thereof in a rational manner, wherefore, there is no participation of the eternal law in them, except by way of similitude.

Third Article
Is There a Human Law?

We proceed thus to the Third Article:

Obj. 1. It would seem that there is not a human law. For the natural law is a participation of the eternal law, as stated above. Now, through the eternal law, "all things are most orderly," as Augustine states. Therefore, the natural law suffices for the ordering of all human affairs. Consequently, there is no need for a human law.

Obj. 2. Further, a law has the nature of a measure, as stated above. But human reason is not a measure of things, but vice versa, as stated in *Metaphysics* IX, 1. Therefore, no law can emanate from human reason.

Obj. 3. Further, a measure should be most certain, as stated in *Metaphysics* 10. But the dictates of human reason in matters of conduct are uncertain, according to Wisdom 9:14: "The thoughts of mortal men are fearful, and our counsels uncertain." Therefore, no law can emanate from human reason.

On the contrary, Augustine distinguishes two kinds of law: the one eternal; the other temporal, which he calls human.

I answer that, As stated above, a law is a certain dictate of practical reason. Now it is to be observed that the same procedure takes place in the practical and in the speculative reason, for each proceeds from principles to conclusions, as stated above (ibid.). Accordingly, we conclude that just as, in the speculative reason, from naturally known indemonstrable principles we draw the conclusions of the various sciences, the knowledge of which is not imparted to us by nature but acquired by the efforts of reason, so too it is from the precepts of the natural law, as from general and indemonstrable principles, that the human reason needs to proceed to certain particular determinations of the laws. These particular determinations, devised by human reason, are called human laws, provided the other essential conditions of law be observed as stated above. Wherefore, Tully says in his *Rhetoric* that "justice has its source in nature; thence certain things came into custom by reason of their utility; afterward these things which emanated from nature and were approved by custom were sanctioned by fear and reverence for the law."

Reply Obj. 1. The human reason cannot have a full participation of the dictate of the divine reason but according to its own mode and imperfectly. Consequently, as on the part of the speculative reason, by a natural participation of divine wisdom, there is in us the knowledge of certain general principles but not proper knowledge of each single truth, such as that contained in the divine wisdom, so too on the part of the practical reason, man has a natural participation of the eternal law according to certain general principles but not as regards the particular determinations of individual cases, which are, however, contained in the eternal law. Hence the need for human reason to proceed further to particular legal sanctions.

Reply Obj. 2. Human reason is not of itself the rule of things, but the principles impressed on it by nature are general rules and measures of all things relating to human conduct, whereof the natural reason is the rule and measure, although it is not the measure of things that are from nature.

Reply Obj. 3. The practical reason is concerned with practical matters, which are singular and contingent, but not with necessary things, with which the speculative reason is concerned. Wherefore human laws cannot have that inerrancy that belongs to the demonstrated conclusions of sciences. Nor is it necessary for every measure to be altogether unerring and certain but according as it is possible in its own particular genus.

Fourth Article
Was There Any Need for a Divine Law?

We proceed thus to the Fourth Article:

Obj. 1. It would seem that there was no need for a divine law because, as stated above, the natural law is a participation in us of the eternal law. But the eternal law is a divine law, as stated above. Therefore, there is no need for a divine law in addition to the natural law and human laws derived therefrom.

Obj. 2. Further, it is written that "God left man in the hand of his own counsel." Now counsel is an act of reason, as stated above. Therefore, man was left to the direction of his reason. But a dictate of human reason is a human law, as stated above. Therefore, there is no need for man to be governed also by a divine law.

Obj. 3. Further, human nature is more self-sufficing than irrational creatures. But irrational creatures have no divine law besides the natural inclination impressed on them. Much less, therefore, should the rational creature have a divine law in addition to the natural law.

On the contrary, David prayed God to set His law before him, saying: "Set before me for a law the way of Your justifications, O Lord."

I answer that, Besides the natural and the human law, it was necessary for the directing of human life to have a divine law. And this for four reasons. First, because it is by law that man is directed how to perform his proper acts in view of his last end. And, indeed, if man were ordained to no other end than that which is proportionate to his natural faculty, there would be no need for man to have any further direction on the part of his reason beyond the natural law and human law which is derived from it. But since man is ordained to an end of eternal happiness which is inproportionate to man's natural faculty, as stated above, therefore it was necessary that, besides the natural and the human law, man should be directed to his end by a law given by God.

Secondly, because, on account of the uncertainty of human judgment, especially on contingent and particular matters, different people form different judgments on human acts, whence also different and contrary laws result. In order, therefore, that man may know without any doubt what he ought to do and what he ought to avoid, it was necessary for man to be directed in his proper acts by a law given by God, for it is certain that such a law cannot err.

Thirdly, because man can make laws in those matters of which he is competent to judge. But man is not competent to judge of interior movements that are hidden but only of exterior acts which appear, and yet, for the perfection of virtue, it is necessary for man to conduct himself aright in both kinds of acts. Consequently, human law could not sufficiently curb and direct interior acts, and it was necessary for this purpose that a divine law should supervene.

Fourthly, because, as Augustine says, human law cannot punish or forbid all evil deeds, since, while aiming at doing away with all evils, it would do away with many good things and would hinder the advance of the common good, which is necessary for human intercourse. In order, therefore, that no evil might remain unforbidden and unpunished, it was necessary for the divine law to supervene, whereby all sins are forbidden.

And these four causes are touched upon in Ps. 118:8, where it is said: "The law of the Lord is unspotted," i.e., allowing no foulness of sin, "converting souls" because it directs not only exterior but also interior acts, "the testimony of the Lord is faithful" because of the certainty of what is true and right, "giving wisdom to little ones" by directing man to an end supernatural and divine.

Reply Obj. 1. By natural law, the eternal law is participated in in proportion to the capacity of human nature. But to his supernatural end, man needs to be directed in a yet higher way. Hence the additional law given by God whereby man shares more perfectly in the eternal law.

Reply Obj. 2. Counsel is a kind of inquiry; hence it must proceed from some principles. Nor is it enough for it to proceed from principles imparted by nature, which are the precepts of the natural law, for the reasons given above, but there is need for certain additional principles, namely, the precepts of the divine law.

Reply Obj. 3. Irrational creatures are not ordained to an end higher than that which is proportionate to their natural powers; consequently, the comparison fails.

Fifth Article
Is There But One Divine Law?

We proceed thus to the Fifth Article:

Obj. 1. It would seem that there is but one divine law because, where there is one king in one kingdom, there is but one law. Now the whole of mankind is compared to God as to one king, according to Ps. 46:8: "God is the King of all the earth." Therefore, there is but one divine law.

Obj. 2. Further, every law is directed to the end which the lawgiver intends for those for whom he makes the law. But God intends one and the same thing for all men, since, according to 1 Tim. 2:4, "He will have all men to be saved and to come to the knowledge of the truth." Therefore, there is but one divine law.

Obj. 3. Further, the divine law seems to be closer to the eternal law, which is one, than the natural law, according as the revelation of grace is of a higher order than natural knowledge. Therefore, much more is the divine law only one.

On the contrary, The Apostle says, "The priesthood being translated, it is necessary that a translation also be made of the law." But the priesthood is twofold, as stated in the same passage, viz., the levitical priesthood and the priesthood of Christ. Therefore, the divine law is twofold, namely, the Old Law and the New Law.

I answer that, As stated in the First Part, distinction is the cause of number. Now, things may be distinguished in two ways. First, as those things that are altogether specifically different, e.g., a horse and an ox. Secondly, as perfect and imperfect in the same species, e.g., a boy and a man, and in this way the divine law is divided into Old and New. Hence the Apostle compares the state of man under the Old Law to that of a child "under a pedagogue" but the state under the New Law to that of a full-grown man who is "no longer under a pedagogue."

Now the perfection and imperfection of these two laws is to be taken in connection with the three conditions pertaining to law, as stated above. For, in the first place, it belongs to law to be directed to the common good as to its end, as stated above. This good may be twofold. It may be a sensible and earthly good, and to this, man was directly ordained by the Old Law; wherefore, at the very outset of the law, the people were invited to the earthly kingdom of the Canaanites. Again, it may be an intelligible and heavenly good, and to this man is ordained by the New Law. Wherefore, at the very beginning of His preaching, Christ invited men to the kingdom of heaven, saying: "Do penance, for the kingdom of heaven is at hand." Hence Augustine says that "promises of temporal goods are contained in the Old Testament, for which reason it is called old, but the promise of eternal life belongs to the New Testament."

Secondly, it belongs to the law to direct human acts according to the order of righteousness, wherein also the New Law surpasses the Old Law since it directs our internal acts, according to Mt. 5:20: "Unless your justice abound more than that of the Scribes and Pharisees, you shall not enter into the kingdom of heaven." Hence the saying that "the Old Law restrains the hand, but the New Law controls the mind."

Thirdly, it belongs to the law to induce men to observe its commandments. This the Old Law did by the fear of punishment, but the New Law by love, which is poured into our hearts by the grace of Christ bestowed in the New Law but foreshadowed in the Old. Hence Augustine says that "there is little difference between the Law and the Gospel—fear and love."

Reply Obj. 1. As the father of a family issues different commands to children and to adults, so also the one King, God, in His one kingdom, gave one law to men while they were yet imperfect and another more perfect law when, by the preceding law, they had been led to a greater capacity for divine things.

Reply Obj. 2. The salvation of man could not be achieved otherwise than through Christ, according to Acts 4:12: "There is no other name . . . given to men whereby we must be saved." Consequently, the law that brings all to salvation could not be given perfectly until after the coming of Christ. But, before His coming, it was necessary to give to the people of whom Christ was to be born a law containing certain rudiments of righteousness unto salvation in order to prepare them to receive Him.

Reply Obj. 3. The natural law directs man by way of certain general precepts common to both the perfect and the imperfect; wherefore it is one and the same for all. But the divine law directs man also in certain particular matters to which the perfect and imperfect do not stand in the same relation. Hence the necessity for the divine law to be twofold, as already explained.

Sixth Article
Is There a Law of Concupiscence *(Fomes)?*

We proceed thus to the Sixth Article:

Obj. 1. It would seem that there is no law of concupiscence. For Isidore says that the "law is based on reason." But concupiscence is not based on reason but deviates from it. Therefore, concupiscence has not the nature of a law.

Obj. 2. Further, every law is binding, so that those who do not obey it are called transgressors. But man is not called a transgressor from not following the instigations of concupiscence but rather from his following them. Therefore, concupiscence has not the nature of a law.

Obj. 3. Further, the law is ordained to the common good, as stated above. But concupiscence inclines us, not to the common good, but to our own private good. Therefore, concupiscence does not have the nature of a law.

On the contrary, The Apostle says, "I see another law in my members fighting against the law of my mind."

I answer that, As stated above, the law, as to its essence, resides in him that rules and measures, but, by way of participation, in that which is ruled and measured, so that every inclination or ordination which may be found in things subject to the law is called a law by participation, as stated above (ibid.). Now those who are subject to a law may receive a twofold inclination from the lawgiver. First, insofar as he directly inclines his subjects to something, sometimes indeed different subjects to different acts; in this way, we may say that there is a military law and a mercantile law. Secondly, indirectly; thus by the very fact that a lawgiver deprives a subject of some dignity, the latter passes into another order so as to be under another law, as it were; thus if a soldier is discharged from the army, he becomes a subject of rural or mercantile legislation.

Accordingly, under the divine lawgiver, various creatures have various natural inclinations, so that what is, as it were, a law for one is against the law for another; thus I might say that fierceness is, in a way, the law of a dog but against the law of a sheep or another meek animal. And so the law of man, which, by the divine ordinance, is allotted to him according to his proper condition, is that he should act in accordance with reason, and this law was so effective in the first state that nothing either beside or against reason could take man unawares. But when man turned his back on God, he fell under the influence of his sensual impulses—in fact, this happens to each one individually the more he deviates from the path of reason—so that, after a fashion, he is likened to the beasts that are led by the impulse of sensuality, according to Ps. 58:21: "Man, when he was in honor, did not understand; he has been compared to senseless beasts and made like to them."

So, then, this very inclination of sensuality, which is called concupiscence, in other animals has simply the nature of a law (yet only insofar as a law may be said to be in such things) by reason of a direct inclination. But in man, it has not the nature of law in this way; rather is it a deviation from the law of reason. But since, by divine justice, man is destitute of original justice, and his reason bereft of its vigor, this impulse of sensuality whereby he is led, insofar as it is a penalty following from the divine law depriving man of his proper dignity, has the nature of a law.

Reply Obj. 1. This argument considers concupiscence in itself as an incentive to evil. It is not thus that it has the nature of a law, as stated above, but according as it results from the justice of the divine law; it is as though we were to say that the law allows a nobleman to be condemned to servile tasks for some misdeed.

Reply Obj. 2. This argument considers law in the light of a rule or measure, for it is in this sense that those who deviate from the law become transgressors. But concupiscence is not a law in this respect but by a kind of participation, as stated above.

Reply Obj. 3. This argument considers concupiscence as to its proper inclination and not as to its origin. And yet, if the inclination of sensuality be considered as it is in other animals, thus it is ordained to the common good, namely, to the preservation of nature in the species or in the individual. And this is in man also, insofar as sensuality is subject to reason. But it is called concupiscence insofar as it strays from the order of reason.

Question 92
Of the Effects of Law

[In Two Articles]

We must now consider the effects of law, under which head there are two points of inquiry: (1) Whether an effect of law is to make men good? (2) Whether the effects of law are to command, to forbid, to permit, and to punish, as the Jurist states?

First Article
Is an Effect of Law to Make Men Good?

We proceed thus to the First Article:

Obj. 1. It seems that it is not an effect of law to make men good. For men are good through virtue, since virtue, as stated in *Ethics* II, 6, is "that which makes its subject good." But virtue is in man from God alone, because He it is Who "works it in us without us," as we stated above in giving the definition of virtue. Therefore, the law does not make men good.

Obj. 2. Further, law does not profit a man unless he obeys it. But the very fact that a man obeys a law is due to his being good. Therefore, in man, goodness is presupposed to the law. Therefore, the law does not make men good.

Obj. 3. Further, law is ordained to the common good, as stated above. But some behave well in things regarding the community who behave ill in things regarding themselves. Therefore, it is not the business of the law to make men good.

Obj. 4. Further, some laws are tyrannical, as the Philosopher says. But a tyrant does not intend the good of his subjects but considers only his own profit. Therefore, law does not make men good.

On the contrary, The Philosopher says that the "intention of every lawgiver is to make men good."

I answer that, As stated above, a law is nothing else than a dictate of reason in the ruler by which his subjects are governed. Now the virtue of any subordinate thing consists in its being well subordinated to that by which it is regulated; thus we see that the virtue of the irascible and concupisible faculties consists in their being obedient to reason, and accordingly, "the virtue of every subject consists in his being well subjected to his ruler," as the Philosopher says. But every law aims at being obeyed by those who are subject to it. Consequently, it is evident that the proper effect of law is to lead its subjects to their proper virtue, and since virtue is "that which makes its subjects good," it follows that the proper effect of law is to make those to whom it is given good, either simply or in some particular respect. For if the intention of the lawgiver is fixed on true good, which is the common good regulated according to divine justice, it follows that the effect of the law is to make men good simply. If, however, the intention of the lawgiver is fixed on that which is not simply good but useful or pleasurable to himself or in opposition to divine justice, then the law does not make men good simply but in respect to that particular government. In this way, good is found even in things that are bad of themselves; thus a man is called a good robber because he works in a way that is adapted to his end.

Reply Obj. 1. Virtue is twofold, as explained above, viz., acquired and infused. Now the fact of being accustomed to an action contributes to both, but in different ways; for it causes the acquired virtue, while it disposes to infused virtue and preserves and fosters it when it already exists. And since law is given for the purpose of directing human acts, as far as human acts conduce to virtue, so far does law make men good. Wherefore the Philosopher says in the second book of the *Politics* that "lawgivers make men good by habituating them to good works."

Reply Obj. 2. It is not always through perfect virtue that one obeys the law, but sometimes it is through fear of punishment, and sometimes from the mere dictate of reason, which is a beginning of virtue, as stated above.

Reply Obj. 3. The goodness of any part is considered in comparison with the whole; hence Augustine says that "unseemly is the part that harmonizes not with the whole." Since, then, every man is a part of the political community, it is impossible that a man be good unless he be well proportionate to the common good, nor can the whole be well consistent unless its parts be proportionate to it. Consequently, the common good of the political community cannot flourish unless the citizens be virtuous, at least those whose business it is to govern. But it is enough for the good of the community that the other citizens be so far virtuous that they obey the commands of their rulers. Hence the Philosopher says that "the virtue of a ruler is the same as that of a good man, but the virtue of any common citizen is not the same as that of a good man."

Reply Obj. 4. A tyrannical law, through not being according to reason, is not a law, absolutely speaking, but rather a perversion of law, and yet insofar as it is something in the nature of a law, it aims at the citizens being good. For all it has in the nature of a law consists in its being an ordinance made by a superior to his subjects and aims at being obeyed by them, which is to make them good, not simply but with respect to that particular government.

Second Article
Are the Acts of Law Suitably Assigned?

We proceed thus to the Second Article:

Obj. 1. It would seem that the acts of law are not suitably assigned as consisting in "command," "prohibition," "permission," and "punishment." For "every law is a general precept," as the Jurist states. But command and precept are the same. Therefore, the other three are superfluous.

Obj. 2. Further, the effect of a law is to induce its subjects to good, as stated above. But counsel aims at a higher good than a command does. Therefore, it belongs to law to counsel rather than to command.

Obj. 3. Further, just as punishment stirs a man to good deeds, so does reward. Therefore, if to punish is reckoned an effect of law, so also is to reward.

Obj. 4. Further, the intention of a lawgiver is to make men good, as stated above. But he that obeys the law merely through fear of being punished is not good, because "although a good deed may be done through servile fear, i.e., fear of punishment, it is not done well," as Augustine says. Therefore, punishment is not a proper effect of law.

On the contrary, Isidore says, "Every law either permits something, as: 'A brave man may demand his reward,' or forbids something, as: 'No man may ask a consecrated virgin in marriage,' or punishes, as: 'Let him that commits a murder be put to death.' "

I answer that, Just as an assertion is a dictate of reason asserting something, so is a law a dictate of reason commanding something. Now it is proper to reason to lead from one thing to another. Wherefore, just as, in demonstrative sciences, the reason leads us from certain principles to assent to the conclusion, so it induces us by some means to assent to the precept of the law.

Now the precepts of law are concerned with human acts, in which the law directs, as stated above.

Again, there are three kinds of human acts; for, as stated above, some acts are good generically, viz., acts of virtue, and in respect of these, the act of the law is a precept or command, for "the law commands all acts of virtue." Some acts are evil generically, viz., acts of vice, and in respect of these, the law forbids. Some acts are generically indifferent, and in respect of these, the law permits; and all acts that are either not distinctly good or not distinctly bad may be called indifferent. And it is the fear of punishment that law makes use of in order to ensure obedience, in which respect punishment is an effect of law.

Reply Obj. 1. Just as to cease from evil is a kind of good, so a prohibition is a kind of precept, and accordingly, taking precept in a wide sense, every law is a kind of precept.

Reply Obj. 2. To advise is not a proper act of law but may be within the competency even of a private person, who cannot make a law. Wherefore, too, the Apostle, after giving a certain counsel says: "I speak, not the Lord." Consequently, it is not reckoned as an effect of law.

Reply Obj. 3. To reward may also pertain to anyone, but to punish pertains to none but the framer of the law, by whose authority the pain is inflicted. Wherefore, to reward is not reckoned an effect of law, but only to punish.

Reply Obj. 4. From becoming accustomed to avoid evil and fulfill what is good, through fear of punishment, one is sometimes led on to do so likewise with delight and of one's own accord. Accordingly, law, even by punishing, leads men on to being good.

QUESTION 93
OF THE ETERNAL LAW

[In Six Articles]

We must now consider each law by itself, and (1) the eternal law, (2) the natural law, (3) the human law, (4) the Old Law, (5) the New Law, which is the law of the Gospel. Of the sixth law, which is the law of concupiscence, suffice what we have said when treating of original sin.

Concerning the first, there are six points of inquiry: (1) What is the eternal law? (2) Whether it is known to all? (3) Whether every law is derived from it? (4) Whether necessary things are subject to the eternal law? (5) Whether natural contingencies are subject to the eternal law? (6) Whether all human things are subject to it?

First Article
Is the Eternal Law a Sovereign
Type Existing in God?

We proceed thus to the First Article:

Obj. 1. It would seem that the eternal law is not a sovereign type existing in God. For there is only one eternal law. But there are many types of things in the divine mind, for Augustine says that God "made each thing according to its type." Therefore, the eternal law does not seem to be a type existing in the divine mind.

Obj. 2. Further, it is essential to a law that it be promulgated by word, as stated above. But Word is a personal name in God, as stated in the First Part, whereas type refers to the essence. Therefore, the eternal law is not the same as a divine type.

Obj. 3. Further, Augustine says, "We see a law above our minds, which is called truth." But the law which is above our minds is the eternal law. Therefore, truth is the eternal law. But the idea of truth is not the same as the idea of a type. Therefore, the eternal law is not the same as the sovereign type.

On the contrary, Augustine says that "the eternal law is the sovereign type, to which we must always conform."

I answer that, Just as in every artificer there pre-exists a type of the things that are made by his art, so too in every governor there must pre-exist the type of the order of those things that are to be done by those who are subject to his government. And just as the type of the things yet to be made by an art is called the art or exemplar of the products of that art, so too the type in him who governs the acts of his subjects has the nature of a law, provided the other conditions be present which we have mentioned above. Now God, by His wisdom, is the creator of all things, in relation to which He stands as the artificer to the products of His art, as stated in the First Part. Moreover, He governs all the acts and movements that are to be found in each single creature, as was also stated in the First Part. Wherefore, as the type of the divine wisdom, inasmuch as by it all things are created, has the nature of art, exemplar, or idea, so the type of divine wisdom, as moving all things to their due end, has the nature of law. Accordingly, the eternal law is nothing else than the type of divine wisdom, as directing all actions and movements.

Reply Obj. 1. Augustine is speaking in that passage of the ideal types which regard the proper nature of each single thing, and consequently, in them there is a certain distinction and plurality according to their different relations to things, as stated in the First Part. But law is said to direct acts by ordaining them to the common good, as stated above. And things which are in themselves different may be considered as one according as they are ordained to one common thing. Wherefore the eternal law is one since it is the type of this order.

Reply Obj. 2. With regard to any sort of word, two points may be considered: viz., the word itself and that which is expressed by the word. For the spoken word is something uttered by the mouth of man and expresses that which is signified by the human word. The same applies to the human mental word, which is nothing else than something conceived by the mind, by which man expresses his thoughts mentally. So, then, in God, the Word conceived by the intellect of the Father is the name of a person, but all things that are in the Father's knowledge, whether they refer to the essence or to the persons or to the works of God are expressed by this Word, as Augustine declares. And among other things expressed by this Word, the eternal law itself is expressed thereby. Nor does it follow that the eternal law is a personal name in God, yet it is appropriated to the Son on account of the kinship between type and word.

Reply Obj. 3. The types of the divine intellect do not stand in the same relation to things as the types of the human intellect. For the human intellect is measured by things, so that a human concept is not true by reason of itself but by reason of its being consonant with things, since an opinion is true or false depending on whether a thing is or is not. But the divine intellect is the measure of things since each thing has so far truth in it as it represents the divine intellect, as was stated in the First Part. Consequently, the divine intellect is true in itself, and its type is truth itself.

Second Article
Is the Eternal Law Known to All?

We proceed thus to the Second Article:

Obj. 1. It would seem that the eternal law is not known to all because, as the Apostle says, "the things that are of God no man knows, but the Spirit of God." But the eternal law is a type existing in the divine mind. Therefore, it is unknown to all save God alone.

Obj. 2. Further, as Augustine says, "the eternal law is that by which it is right that all things should be most orderly." But all do not know how all things are most orderly. Therefore, all do not know the eternal law.

Obj. 3. Further, Augustine says that "the eternal law is not subject to the judgment of man." But according to *Ethics* I, "Any man can judge well of what he knows." Therefore, the eternal law is not known to us.

On the contrary, Augustine says that "knowledge of the eternal law is imprinted on us.

In answer that A thing may be known in two ways: first, in itself; secondly, in its effect, wherein some likeness of that thing is found; thus someone not seeing the sun in its substance may know it by its rays. So, then, no one can know the eternal law as it is in itself except God and the blessed who see Him in His essence. But every rational creature knows it in its reflection, greater or less. For every knowledge of truth is a kind of reflection and participation of the eternal law, which is the unchangeable truth, as Augustine says. Now, all men know the truth to a certain extent, at least as to the common principles of the natural law, and as to the others, they partake of the knowledge of truth, some more, some less, and in this respect are more or less cognizant of the eternal law.

Reply Obj. 1. We cannot know the things that are of God as they are in themselves, but they are made known to us in their effects, according to Rom. 1:20: "The invisible things of God . . . are clearly seen, being understood by the things that are made."

Reply Obj. 2. Although each one knows the eternal law according to his own capacity, in the way explained above, yet no one can comprehend it, for it cannot be made perfectly known by its effects. Therefore, it does not follow that anyone who knows the eternal law in the way aforesaid knows also the whole order of things whereby they are most orderly.

Reply Obj. 3. To judge of a thing may be understood in two ways. First, as when a cognitive power judges of its proper object, according to Job 12:11: "Does not the ear discern words, and the palate of him that eats, the taste?" It is to this kind of judgment that the Philosopher alludes when he says that "anyone can judge well of what he knows," by judging, namely, whether what is put forward is true. In another way, we speak of a superior judging of a subordinate by a kind of practical judgment as to whether he should be such and such or not. And thus none can judge of the eternal law.

Third Article
Is Every Law Derived from the Eternal Law?

We proceed thus to the Third Article:

Obj. 1. It would seem that not every law is derived from the eternal law. For there is a law of concupis-

cence, as stated above, which is not derived from that divine law which is the eternal law, since thereunto pertains the "prudence of the flesh," of which the Apostle says that "it cannot be subject to the law of God." Therefore, not every law is derived from the eternal law.

Obj. 2. Further, nothing unjust can be derived from the eternal law, because, as stated above, "the eternal law is that according to which it is right that all things should be most orderly." But some laws are unjust, according to Is. 10:1: "Woe to them that make wicked laws." Therefore, not every law is derived from the eternal law.

Obj. 3. Further, Augustine says that "the law which is framed for ruling the people rightly permits many things which are punished by divine providence." But the type of divine providence is the eternal law, as stated above. Therefore, not even every good law is derived from the eternal law.

On the contrary, Divine wisdom says, "By Me kings reign, and lawgivers decree just things." But the type of divine wisdom is the eternal law, as stated above. Therefore, all laws proceed from the eternal law.

I answer that, As stated above, law denotes a kind of plan directing acts toward an end. Now wherever there are movers ordained to one another, the power of the second mover must needs be derived from the power of the first mover, since the second mover does not move except insofar as it is moved by the first. Wherefore we observe the same in all those who govern, so that the plan of government is derived by secondary governors from the governor-in-chief; thus the plan of what is to be done in a political community flows from the king's command to his inferior administrators, and again in things of art, the plan of whatever is to be done by art flows from the chief craftsman to the undercraftsmen who work with their hands. Since, then, the eternal law is the plan of government in the Chief Governor, all the plans of government in the inferior governors must be derived from the eternal law. But these plans of inferior governors are all other laws besides the eternal law. Therefore, all laws, insofar as they partake of right reason, are derived from the eternal law. Hence Augustine says that, "in temporal law, there is nothing just and lawful but what man has drawn from the eternal law."

Reply Obj. 1. Concupiscence has the nature of law in man insofar as it is a punishment resulting from divine justice, and in this respect, it is evident that it is derived from the eternal law. But insofar as it denotes a proneness to sin, it is contrary to the divine law and has not the nature of law, as stated above.

Reply Obj. 2. Human law has the nature of law insofar as it partakes of right reason, and it is clear that, in this respect, it is derived from the eternal law. But insofar as it deviates from reason, it is called an unjust law and has the nature, not of law, but of violence. Nevertheless, even an unjust law, insofar as it retains some appearance of law through being framed by one who is in power, is derived from the eternal law, since all power is from the Lord God, according to Romans.

Reply Obj. 3. Human law is said to permit certain things, not as approving of them, but as being unable to direct them. And many things are directed by the divine law, which human law is unable to direct, because more things are subject to a higher than to a lower cause. Hence the very fact that human law does not meddle with matters it cannot direct comes under the ordination of the eternal law. It would be different were human law to sanction what the eternal law condemns. Consequently, it does not follow that human law is not derived from the eternal law, but that it is not on a perfect equality with it.

Fourth Article
Are Necessary and Eternal Things Subject to the Eternal Law?

We proceed thus to the Fourth Article:

Obj. 1. It would seem that necessary and eternal things are subject to the eternal law, for whatever is reasonable is subject to reason. But the divine will is reasonable, for it is just. Therefore, it is subject to reason. But the eternal law is the divine reason. Therefore, God's will is subject to the eternal law. But God's will is eternal. Therefore, eternal and necessary things are subject to the eternal law.

Obj. 2. Further, whatever is subject to the King is subject to the King's law. Now the Son, according to 1 Cor. "shall be subject . . . to God the Father . . . when He shall have delivered up the Kingdom to Him." Therefore, the Son, Who is eternal, is subject to the eternal law.

Obj. 3. Further, the eternal law is divine providence as a type. But many necessary things are subject to

divine providence; for instance, the stability of incorporeal substances and of the heavenly bodies. Therefore, even necessary things are subject to the eternal law.

On the contrary, Things that are necessary cannot be otherwise and consequently need no restraining. But laws are imposed on men in order to restrain them from evil, as explained above. Therefore, necessary things are not subject to the law.

I answer that, As stated above, the eternal law is the type of the divine government. Consequently, whatever is subject to the divine government is subject to the eternal law, while if anything is not subject to the divine government, neither is it subject to the eternal law. The application of this distinction may be gathered by looking around us. For those things are subject to human government which can be done by man, but what pertains to the nature of man is not subject to human government, for instance, that he should have a soul, hands, or feet. Accordingly, all that is in things created by God, whether it be contingent or necessary, is subject to the eternal law, while things pertaining to the divine nature or essence are not subject to the eternal law but are the eternal law itself.

Reply Obj. 1. We may speak of God's will in two ways. First, as to the will itself, and thus, since God's will is His very essence, it is subject neither to the divine government nor to the eternal law but is the same thing as the eternal law. Secondly, we may speak of God's will as to the things themselves that God wills about creatures, which things are subject to the eternal law insofar as they are planned by divine wisdom. In reference to these things, God's will is said to be reasonable, though, regarded in itself, it should rather be called their type.

Reply Obj. 2. God the Son was not made by God but was naturally born of God. Consequently, He is not subject to divine providence or to the eternal law but rather is Himself the eternal law by a kind of appropriation, as Augustine explains. But He is said to be subject to the Father by reason of His human nature, in respect of which also the Father is said to be greater than He.

The Third Objection we grant, because it deals with those necessary things that are created.

Reply Obj. 4. As the Philosopher says, some necessary things have a cause of their necessity, and thus they derive from something else the fact that they cannot be otherwise. And this is in itself a most effective restraint, for whatever is restrained is said to be restrained insofar as it cannot do otherwise than it is allowed to.

Fifth Article
Are Natural Contingents Subject to the Eternal Law?

We proceed thus to the Fifth Article:

Obj. 1. It would seem that natural contingents are not subject to the eternal law because promulgation is essential to law, as stated above. But a law cannot be promulgated except to rational creatures to whom it is possible to make an announcement. Therefore, only rational creatures are subject to the eternal law, and consequently, natural contingents are not.

Obj. 2. Further, "Whatever obeys reason partakes somewhat of reason," as stated in *Ethics* I, 13. But the eternal law is the supreme type, as stated above. Since, then, natural contingents do not partake of reason in any way but are altogether void of reason, it seems that they are not subject to the eternal law.

Obj. 3. Further, the eternal law is most efficient. But, in natural contingents, defects occur. Therefore, they are not subject to the eternal law.

On the contrary, It is written: "When He compassed the sea with its bounds and set a law to the waters, that they should not pass their limits."

I answer that We must speak otherwise of the law of man than of the eternal law, which is the law of God. For the law of man extends only to rational creatures subject to man. The reason of this is because law directs the actions of those that are subject to the government of someone; wherefore, properly speaking, none imposes a law on his own actions. Now, whatever is done regarding the use of irrational things subject to man is done by the act of man himself moving those things, for these irrational creatures do not move themselves but are moved by others, as stated above. Consequently, man cannot impose laws on irrational beings, however much they may be subject to him. But he can impose laws on rational beings subject to him insofar as, by his command or pronouncement of any kind, he imprints on their minds a rule which is a principle of action.

Now, just as man, by such pronouncement, impresses a kind of inward principle of action on the man that is subject to him, so God imprints on the whole of nature the principles of its proper actions. And so, in this way, God is said to command the whole of nature, according to Ps. 148:6: "He has made a decree, and it shall not pass away." And thus all actions and movements of the whole of nature are subject to the eternal law. Consequently, irrational creatures are subject to the eternal law through being moved by divine providence, but not, as rational creatures are, through understanding the divine commandment.

Reply Obj. 1. The impression of an inward active principle is to natural things what the promulgation of law is to men because law, by being promulgated, imprints on man a directive principle of human actions, as stated above.

Reply Obj. 2. Irrational creatures neither partake of, nor are obedient to, human reason, whereas they do partake of the divine reason by obeying it, because the power of divine reason extends over more things than human reason does. And as the members of the human body are moved at the command of reason and yet do not partake of reason, since they have no apprehension subordinate to reason, so too irrational creatures are moved by God without on that account being rational.

Reply Obj. 3. Although the defects which occur in natural things are outside the order of particular causes, they are not outside the order of universal causes, especially of the First Cause, i.e., God, from Whose providence nothing can escape, as stated in the First Part. And since the eternal law is the type of divine providence, as stated above, hence the defects of natural things are subject to the eternal law.

Sixth Article
Are All Human Affairs Subject to the Eternal Law?

We proceed thus to the Sixth Article:

Obj. 1. It would seem that not all human affairs are subject to the eternal law, for the Apostle says, "If you are led by the spirit you are not under the law." But the righteous, who are the sons of God by adoption, are led by the spirit of God, according to

Romans: "Whosoever are led by the Spirit of God, they are the sons of God." Therefore, not all men are under the eternal law.

Obj. 2. Further, the Apostle says, "The prudence of the flesh is an enemy to God, for it is not subject to the law of God." But many are those in whom the prudence of the flesh dominates. Therefore, all men are not subject to the eternal law, which is the law of God.

Obj. 3. Further, Augustine says that "the eternal law is that by which the wicked deserve misery, the good a life of blessedness." But those who are already blessed, and those who are already lost, are not in the state of merit. Therefore, they are not under the eternal law.

On the contrary, Augustine says, "Nothing evades the laws of the most high Creator and Governor, for by Him the peace of the universe is administered."

I answer that There are two ways in which a thing is subject to the eternal law, as explained above, first, by partaking of the eternal law by way of knowledge; secondly, by way of action and passion, i.e., by partaking of the eternal law by way of an inward motive principle; and in the second way, irrational creatures are subject to the eternal law, as stated above (ibid.). But since the rational nature, together with that which it has in common with all creatures, has something proper to itself inasmuch as it is rational, consequently it is subject to the eternal law in both ways; because while each rational creature has some knowledge of the eternal law, as stated above, it also has a natural inclination to that which is in harmony with the eternal law, for "we are naturally adapted to be the recipients of virtue."

Both ways, however, are imperfect and to a certain extent corrupted in the wicked, because in them the natural inclination to virtue is corrupted by vicious habits, and, moreover, the natural knowledge of good is darkened by passions and habits of sin. But, in the good, both ways are found more perfect, because in them, besides the natural knowledge of good, there is the added knowledge of faith and wisdom, and again, besides the natural inclination to good, there is the added interior motive of grace and virtue.

Accordingly, the good are perfectly subject to the eternal law, as always acting according to it, whereas the wicked are subject to the eternal law imperfectly as to their actions, since both their knowledge of good and their inclination thereto are imperfect. But this imperfection on the part of action is supplied on the part of passion insofar as they suffer what the eternal law decrees concerning them, according as they fail to act in harmony with that law. Hence Augustine says, "I esteem the righteous act according to the eternal law," and: "Out of the just misery of the souls which deserted Him, God knew how to furnish the inferior parts of His creation with most suitable laws."

Reply Obj. 1. This saying of the Apostle may be understood in two ways. First, so that a man is said to be under the law through being pinned down thereby against his will, as by a load. Hence, on the same passage, a gloss says that "he is under the law who refrains from evil deeds through fear of the punishment threatened by the law and not from love of virtue." In this way, the spiritual man is not under the law because he fulfills the law willingly, through charity which is poured into his heart by the Holy Spirit. Secondly, it can be understood as meaning that the works of a man who is led by the Holy Spirit are works of the Holy Spirit rather than his own. Therefore, since the Holy Spirit is not under the law, as neither is the Son, as stated above, it follows that such works, insofar as they are of the Holy Spirit, are not under the law. The Apostle witnesses to this when he says, "Where the Spirit of the Lord is, there is liberty."

Reply Obj. 2. The prudence of the flesh cannot be subject to the law of God as regards action since it inclines to actions contrary to the divine law; yet it is subject to the law of God as regards passion since it deserves to suffer punishment according to the law of divine justice. Nevertheless, in no man does the prudence of the flesh dominate so far as to destroy the whole good of his nature, and consequently, there remains in man the inclination to act in accordance with the eternal law. For we have seen above that sin does not destroy entirely the good of nature.

Reply Obj. 3. A thing is maintained in the end and moved toward the end by one and the same cause; thus gravity which makes a heavy body rest in the lower place is also the cause of its being moved thither. We, therefore, reply that as it is according to the eternal law that some deserve happiness, others unhappiness, so it is by the eternal law that some are maintained in a happy state, others in an unhappy state. Accordingly, both the blessed and the damned are under the eternal law.

Question 94
Of the Natural Law

[In Six Articles]

We must now consider the natural law, concerning which there are six points of inquiry: (1) What is the natural law? (2) What are the precepts of the natural law? (3) Whether all acts of virtue are prescribed by the natural law? (4) Whether the natural law is the same in all? (5) Whether it is changeable? (6) Whether it can be abolished from the heart of man?

First Article
Is the Natural Law a Habit?

We proceed thus to the First Article:

Obj. 1. It would seem that the natural law is a habit because, as the Philosopher says, "there are three things in the soul: power, habit, and passion." But the natural law is not one of the soul's powers, nor is it one of the passions, as we may see by going through them one by one. Therefore, the natural law is a habit.

Obj. 2. Further, Basil says that the conscience or "*synderesis* is the law of our mind," which can only apply to the natural law. But *synderesis* is a habit, as was shown in the First Part. Therefore, the natural law is a habit.

Obj. 3. Further, the natural law abides in man always, as will be shown further on. But man's reason, to which the law pertains, does not always think about the natural law. Therefore, the natural law is not an act but a habit.

On the contrary, Augustine says that "a habit is that whereby something is done when necessary." But such is not the natural law since it is in infants and in the damned who cannot act by it. Therefore, the natural law is not a habit.

I answer that A thing may be called a habit in two ways. First, properly and essentially, and thus the natural law is not a habit. For it has been stated above that the natural law is something appointed by reason,

just as a proposition is a work of reason. Now, that which a man does is not the same as that whereby he does it, for he makes a becoming speech by the habit of grammar. Since, then, a habit is that by which we act, a law cannot be a habit properly and essentially.

Secondly, the term "habit" may be applied to that which we hold by a habit; thus faith may mean that which we hold by faith. And accordingly, since the precepts of the natural law are sometimes considered by reason actually, while sometimes they are in the reason only habitually, in this way the natural law may be called a habit. Thus, in speculative matters, the indemonstrable principles are not the habit itself whereby we hold those principles but are the principles the habit of which we possess.

Reply Obj. 1. The Philosopher proposes there to discover the genus of virtue, and since it is evident that virtue is a principle of action, he mentions only those things which are principles of human acts, viz., powers, habits, and passions. But there are other things in the soul besides these three: there are acts; thus to will is in the one that wills; again, things known are in the knower. Moreover, its own natural properties are in the soul, such as immortality and the like.

Reply Obj. 2. Synderesis is said to be the law of our mind because it is a habit containing the precepts of the natural law, which are the first principles of human actions.

Reply Obj. 3. This argument proves that the natural law is held habitually, and this is granted.

To the argument advanced in the contrary sense we reply that sometimes a man is unable to make use of that which is in him habitually on account of some impediment; thus, on account of sleep, a man is unable to use the habit of reasoning. In like manner, through the deficiency of his age, a child cannot use the habit of understanding principles, or the natural law, which is in him habitually.

Second Article
Does the Natural Law Contain Several Precepts or One Only?

We proceed thus to the Second Article:

Obj. 1. It would seem that the natural law contains, not several precepts, but one only. For law is a kind of precept, as stated above. If, therefore, there were many precepts of the natural law, it would follow that there are also many natural laws.

Obj. 2. Further, the natural law is consequent to human nature. But human nature as a whole is one, though, as to its parts, it is manifold. Therefore, either there is but one precept of the law of nature, on account of the unity of nature as a whole, or there are many by reason of the number of parts of human nature. The result would be that even things relating to the inclination of the concupiscible faculty belong to the natural law.

Obj. 3. Further, law is something pertaining to reason, as stated above. Now, reason is but one in man. Therefore, there is only one precept of the natural law.

On the contrary, The precepts of the natural law in man stand in relation to practical matters as the first principles to matters of demonstration. But there are several first indemonstrable principles. Therefore, there are also several precepts of the natural law.

I answer that, As stated above, the precepts of the natural law are to the practical reason what the first principles of demonstrations are to the speculative reason because both are self-evident principles. Now a thing is said to be self-evident in two ways: first, in itself; secondly, in relation to us. Any proposition is said to be self-evident in itself if its predicate is contained in the notion of the subject, although, to one who knows not the definition of the subject, it happens that such a proposition is not self-evident. For instance, this proposition, "Man is a rational being," is in its very nature self-evident, since who says "man" says "a rational being," and yet to one who knows not what a man is, this proposition is not self-evident. Hence it is that, as Boethius says, certain axioms or propositions are universally self-evident to all, and such are those propositions whose terms are known to all, as "Every whole is greater than its part," and, "Things equal to one and the same are equal to one another." But some propositions are self-evident only to the wise who understand the meaning of the terms of such propositions; thus to one who understands that an angel is not a body, it is self-evident that an angel is not circumspectively in a place, but this is not evident to the unlearned, for they cannot grasp it.

Now, a certain order is to be found in those things that are apprehended universally. For that which,

before aught else, falls under apprehension, is "being," the notion of which is included in all things whatsoever a man apprehends. Wherefore the first indemonstrable principle is that the same thing cannot be affirmed and denied at the same time, which is based on the nature of "being" and "not-being," and on this principle all others are based, as it is stated in *Metaphysics* IV. Now, as "being" is the first thing that falls under the apprehension simply, so "good" is the first thing that falls under the apprehension of the practical reason, which is directed to action, since every agent acts for an end under the aspect of good. Consequently, the first principle in the practical reason is one founded on the notion of good, viz., that good is that which all things seek after. Hence this is the first precept of law, that good is to be done and pursued, and evil is to be avoided. All other precepts of the natural law are based upon this, so that whatever the practical reason naturally apprehends as man's good (or evil) belongs to the precepts of the natural law as something to be done or avoided.

Since, however, good has the nature of an end, and evil the nature of a contrary, hence it is that all those things to which man has a natural inclination are naturally apprehended by reason as being good and, consequently, as objects of pursuit, and their contraries as evil and objects of avoidance. Wherefore the order of the precepts of the natural law is according to the order of natural inclinations. Because in man there is first of all an inclination to good in accordance with the nature which he has in common with all substances, inasmuch as every substance seeks the preservation of its own being according to its nature, and by reason of this inclination, whatever is a means of preserving human life and of warding off its obstacles to the natural law. Secondly, there is in man an inclination to things that pertain to him more specially according to that nature which he has in common with other animals, and in virtue of this inclination, those things are said to belong to the natural law "which nature has taught to all animals," such as sexual intercourse, education of offspring, and so forth. Thirdly, there is in man an inclination to good according to the nature of his reason, which nature is proper to him; thus man has a natural inclination to know the truth about God and to live in society, and in this respect, whatever pertains to this inclination belongs to the natural law, for instance, to shun ignorance, to avoid offending those among whom one has to live, and other such things regarding the above inclination.

Reply Obj. 1. All these precepts of the law of nature have the character of one natural law inasmuch as they flow from one first precept.

Reply Obj. 2. All the inclinations of any parts whatsoever of human nature, e.g., of the concupiscible and irascible parts, insofar as they are ruled by reason, belong to the natural law and are reduced to one first precept, as stated above, so that the precepts of the natural law are many in themselves but are based on one common foundation.

Reply Obj. 3. Although reason is one in itself, yet it directs all things regarding man, so that whatever can be ruled by reason is contained under the law of reason.

Third Article
Are All Acts of Virtue Prescribed by the Natural Law?

We proceed thus to the Third Article:

Obj. 1. It would seem that not all acts of virtue are prescribed by the natural law because, as stated above, it is essential to a law that it be ordained to the common good. But some acts of virtue are ordained to the private good of the individual, as is evident especially in regard to acts of temperance. Therefore, not all acts of virtue are the subject of natural law.

Obj. 2. Further, every sin is opposed to some virtuous act. If, therefore, all acts of virtue are prescribed by the natural law, it seems to follow that all sins are against nature, whereas this applies to certain special sins.

Obj. 3. Further, those things which are according to nature are common to all. But acts of virtue are not common to all, since a thing is virtuous in one and vicious in another. Therefore, not all acts of virtue are prescribed by the natural law.

On the contrary, Damascene says that "virtues are natural." Therefore, virtuous acts also are a subject of the natural law.

I answer that We may speak of virtuous acts in two ways: first, under the aspect of virtuous; secondly, as such and such acts considered in their proper species.

If, then, we speak of acts of virtue considered as virtuous, thus all virtuous acts belong to the natural law. For it has been stated that to the natural law belongs everything to which a man is inclined according to his nature. Now each thing is inclined naturally to an operation that is suitable to it according to its form; thus fire is inclined to give heat. Wherefore, since the rational soul is the proper form of man, there is in every man a natural inclination to act according to reason, and this is to act according to virtue. Consequently, considered thus, all acts of virtue are prescribed by the natural law, since each one's reason naturally dictates to him to act virtuously. But if we speak of virtuous acts considered in themselves, i.e., in their proper species, thus not all virtuous acts are prescribed by the natural law; the many things are done virtuously to which nature does not incline at first, but which, through the inquiry of reason, have been found by men to be conducive to well-living.

Reply Obj. 1. Temperance is about the natural concupiscences of food, drink, and sexual matters, which are indeed ordained to the natural common good, just as other matters of law are ordained to the moral common good.

Reply Obj. 2. By human nature we may mean either that which is proper to man—and in this sense all sins, as being against reason, are also against nature, as Damascene states—or we may mean that nature which is common to man and other animals, and in this sense certain special sins are said to be against nature; thus, contrary to heterosexual intercourse, which is natural to all animals, is male homosexual union, which has received the special name of the unnatural vice.

Reply Obj. 3. This argument considers acts in themselves. For it is owing to the various conditions of men that certain acts are virtuous for some as being proportionate and becoming to them, while they are vicious for others as being out of proportion to them.

Fourth Article
Is the Natural Law the Same in All Men?

We proceed thus to the Fourth Article:

Obj. 1. It would seem that the natural law is not the same in all. For it is stated in the *Decretum* that "the natural law is that which is contained in the Law and the Gospel." But this is not common to all men because, as it is written, "all do not obey the gospel." Therefore, the natural law is not the same in all men.

Obj. 2. Further, "Things which are according to the law are said to be just," as stated in *Ethics* V. But it is stated in the same book that nothing is so universally just as not to be subject to change in regard to some men. Therefore, even the natural law is not the same in all men.

Obj. 3. Further, as stated above, to the natural law belongs everything to which a man is inclined according to his nature. Now, different men are naturally inclined to different things, some to the desire of pleasures, others to the desire of honors, and other men to other things. Therefore, there is not one natural law for all.

On the contrary, Isidore says, "The natural law is common to all nations."

I answer that, As stated above, to the natural law belong those things to which a man is inclined naturally, and among these, it is proper to man to be inclined to act according to reason. Now the process of reason is from the common to the proper, as stated in *Phys.* I. The speculative reason, however, is differently situated in this matter from the practical reason. For, since the speculative reason is concerned chiefly with necessary things, which cannot be otherwise than they are, its proper conclusions, like the universal principles, contain the truth without fail. The practical reason, on the other hand, is concerned with contingent matters, about which human actions are concerned, and consequently, although there is necessity in the general principles, the more we descend to matters of detail, the more frequently we encounter deviations. Accordingly, then, in speculative matters, truth is the same for all men both as to principles and as to conclusions, although the truth is not known to all as regards the conclusions but only as regards the principles which are called common notions. But in matters of action, truth or practical rectitude is not the same for all as to matters of detail but only as to the general principles, and where there is the same rectitude in matters of detail, it is not equally known to all.

It is, therefore, evident that, as regards the general principles, whether of speculative or practical reason, truth or rectitude is the same for all and is equally known by all. As to the proper conclusions of the speculative reason, the truth is the same for all but is not equally known to all; thus it is true for all that the three angles of a triangle are together equal to two right angles, although it is not known to all. But as to the proper conclusions of the practical reason, neither is the truth or rectitude the same for all, nor, where it is the same, is it equally known by all. Thus it is right and true for all to act according to reason, and from this principle, it follows as a proper conclusion that goods entrusted to another should be restored to their owner. Now this is true for the majority of cases, but it may happen in a particular case that it would be injurious, and therefore unreasonable, to restore goods held in trust, for instance, if they are claimed for the purpose of fighting against one's country. And this principle will be found to fail the more according as we descend further into detail, e.g., if one were to say that goods held in trust should be restored with such and such a guarantee or in such and such a way, because the greater the number of conditions added, the greater the number of ways in which the principle may fail, so that it be not right to restore or not to restore.

Consequently, we must say that the natural law as to general principles is the same for all both as to rectitude and as to knowledge. But as to certain matters of detail, which are conclusions, as it were, of those general principles, it is the same for all in the majority of cases both as to rectitude and as to knowledge, and yet, in some few cases, it may fail both as to rectitude by reason of certain obstacles (just as natures subject to generation and corruption fail in some few cases on account of some obstacle) and as to knowledge, since, in some, the reason is perverted by passion or evil habit or an evil disposition of nature; thus, formerly, theft, although it is expressly contrary to the natural law, was not considered wrong among the Germans, as Julius Caesar relates.

Reply Obj. 1. The meaning of the sentence quoted is not that whatever is contained in the Law and the Gospel belongs to the natural law, since they contain many things that are above nature, but that whatever belongs to the natural law is fully contained in them. Wherefore Gratian, after saying that "the natural law is what is contained in the Law and the Gospel," adds at once, by way of example, "by which everyone is commanded to do to others as he would be done by."

Reply Obj. 2. The saying of the Philosopher is to be understood of things that are naturally just, not as general principles but as conclusions drawn from them, having rectitude in the majority of cases but failing in a few.

Reply Obj. 3. As, in man, reason rules and commands the other powers, so all the natural inclinations belonging to the other powers must needs be directed according to reason. Wherefore it is universally right for all men that all their inclinations should be directed according to reason.

Fifth Article
Can the Natural Law Be Changed?

We proceed thus to the Fifth Article:

Obj. 1. It would seem that the natural law can be changed because, on Sir. 17:9, "He gave them instructions, and the law of life," a gloss says: "He wished the law of the letter to be written in order to correct the law of nature." But that which is corrected is changed. Therefore, the natural law can be changed.

Obj. 2. Further, the slaying of the innocent, adultery, and theft are against the natural law. But we find these things changed by God, as when God commanded Abraham to slay his innocent son, and when He ordered the Jews to borrow and purloin the vessels of the Egyptians, and when He commanded Hosea to take to himself "a wife of fornications." Therefore, the natural law can be changed.

Obj. 3. Further, Isidore says that "the possession of all things in common and universal freedom are matters of natural law." But these things are seen to be changed by human laws. Therefore, it seems that the natural law is subject to change.

On the contrary, It is said in the *Decretum:* "The natural law dates from the creation of the rational creature. It does not vary according to time but remains unchangeable."

I answer that A change in the natural law may be understood in two ways. First, by way of addition. In this sense, nothing hinders the natural law from being changed, since many things, for the benefit of human life, have been added over and above the natural law both by the divine law and by human laws.

Secondly, a change in the natural law may be understood by way of subtraction, so that what previously was according to the natural law ceases to be so. In this sense, the natural law is altogether unchangeable in its first principles, but in its secondary principles, which, as we have said, are like certain proper conclusions closely related to the first principles, the natural law is not changed so that what it prescribes be not right in most cases. But it may be changed in some particular cases of rare occurrence through some special causes hindering the observance of such precepts, as stated above.

Reply Obj. 1. The written law is said to be given for the correction of the natural law, either because it supplies what was wanting to the natural law or because the natural law was perverted in the hearts of some men as to certain matters, so that they esteemed those things good which are naturally evil, which perversion stood in need of correction.

Reply Obj. 2. All men alike, both guilty and innocent, die the death of nature, which death of nature is inflicted by the power of God on account of original sin, according to 1 Kings: "The Lord kills and makes alive." Consequently, by the command of God, death can be inflicted on any man, guilty or innocent, without any injustice whatever. In like manner, adultery is intercourse with another's wife, who is allotted to him by the law handed down by God. Consequently, intercourse with any woman, by the command of God, is neither adultery nor fornication. The same applies to theft, which is the taking of another's property. For whatever is taken by the command of God, to Whom all things belong, is not taken against the will of its owner, whereas it is in this that theft consists. Nor is it only in human things that whatever is commanded by God is right but also in natural things— whatever is done by God is, in some way, natural, as stated in the First Part.

Reply Obj. 3. A thing is said to belong to the natural law in two ways. First, because nature inclines thereto, e.g., that one should not do harm to another. Secondly, because nature did not bring in the contrary; thus we might say that for man to be naked is of the natural law because nature did not give him clothes, but art invented them. In this sense, "the possession of all things in common and universal freedom" are said to be of the natural law because, to wit, the distinction of possessions and slavery were not brought in by nature but devised by human reason for the benefit of human life. Accordingly, the law of nature was not changed in this respect except by addition.

Sixth Article
Can the Law of Nature Be Abolished from the Heart of Man?

We proceed thus to the Sixth Article:

Obj. 1. It would seem that the natural law can be abolished from the heart of man because, on Rom. 2:14, "When the Gentiles who have not the law," etc., a gloss says that "the law of righteousness, which sin had blotted out, is graven on the heart of man when he is restored by grace." But the law of righteousness is the law of nature. Therefore, the law of nature can be blotted out.

Obj. 2. Further, the law of grace is more efficacious than the law of nature. But the law of grace is blotted out by sin. Much more, therefore, can the law of nature be blotted out.

Obj. 3. Further, that which is established by law is made just. But many things are legally established which are contrary to the law of nature. Therefore, the law of nature can be abolished from the heart of man.

On the contrary, Augustine says, "Thy law is written in the hearts of men, which iniquity itself effaces not." But the law which is written in men's hearts is the natural law. Therefore, the natural law cannot be blotted out.

I answer that, As stated above, there belong to the natural law, first, certain most general precepts that are known to all; and secondly, certain secondary and more detailed precepts which are, as it were, conclusions following closely from first principles. As to those general principles, the natural law, in the abstract, can nowise be blotted out from men's hearts. But it is blotted out in the case of particular action insofar as reason is hindered from applying the general principles to a particular point of practice on account of concupiscence or some other passion, as stated above. But as to the other, i.e., the secondary precepts, the natural law can be blotted out from the human heart either by evil persuasions, just as in speculative matters errors occur in respect of necessary conclusions, or by vicious customs and corrupt habits, as among some men theft and even unnatural

vices, as the Apostle states, were not esteemed sinful.

Reply Obj. 1. Sin blots out the law of nature in particular cases, not universally, except perchance in regard to the secondary precepts of the natural law, in the way stated above.

Reply Obj. 2. Although grace is more efficacious than nature, yet nature is more essential to man and therefore more enduring.

Reply Obj. 3. The argument is true of the secondary precepts of the natural law, against which some legislators have framed certain enactments which are unjust.

QUESTION 95
OF HUMAN LAW

[In Four Articles]

We must now consider human law, and (1) this law considered in itself; (2) its power; (3) its mutability. Under the first head, there are four points of inquiry: (1) its utility; (2) its origin; (3) its quality; (4) its divisions.

First Article
Was It Useful for Laws to Be Framed by Men?

We proceed thus to the First Article:

Obj. 1. It would seem that it was not useful for laws to be framed by men because the purpose of every law is that man be made good thereby, as stated above. But men are more to be induced to be good willingly by means of admonitions than against their will by means of laws. Therefore, there was no need to frame laws.

Obj. 2. Further, as the Philosopher says, "men have recourse to a judge as to justice in the flesh." But justice in the flesh is better than inanimate justice, which is contained in laws. Therefore, it would have been better for the execution of justice to be entrusted to the decision of judges than to frame laws in addition.

Obj. 3. Further, every law is framed for the direction of human actions, as is evident from what has been stated above. But since human actions are about singulars, which are infinite in number, matters pertaining to the direction of human actions cannot be taken into sufficient consideration except by a wise man who looks into each one of them. Therefore, it would have been better for human acts to be directed by the judgment of wise men than by the framing of laws. Therefore, there was no need of human laws.

On the contrary, Isidore says, "Laws were made that, in fear thereof, human audacity might be held in check, that innocence might be safeguarded in the midst of wickedness, and that the dread of punishment might prevent the wicked from doing harm." But these things are most necessary to mankind. Therefore, it was necessary that human laws should be made.

I answer that, As stated above, man has a natural aptitude for virtue, but the perfection of virtue must be acquired by man by means of some kind of training. Thus we observe that man is helped by industry in his necessities, for instance, in food and clothing. Certain beginnings of these he has from nature, viz., his reason and his hands, but he has not the full complement, as other animals have to whom nature has given sufficiency of clothing and food. Now, it is difficult to see how man could suffice for himself in the matter of this training, since the perfection of virtue consists chiefly in withdrawing man from undue pleasures, to which, above all, man is inclined, and especially the young, who are more capable of being trained. Consequently, a man needs to receive this training from another whereby to arrive at the perfection of virtue. And as to those young people who are inclined to acts of virtue by their good natural disposition or by custom, or rather by the gift of God, paternal training suffices, which is by admonitions. But since some are found to be depraved and prone to vice and not easily amenable to words, it was necessary for such to be restrained from evil by force and fear in order that they might at least desist from evildoing and leave others in peace, and that they themselves, by being habituated in this way, might be brought to do willingly what hitherto they did from fear and thus become virtuous. Now this kind of training which compels through fear of punishment is the discipline of laws. Therefore, in order that man might have peace and virtue, it was necessary for laws to be framed, for, as the Philosopher says, "a man is the most noble of animals if he be perfect in virtue, so is he the lowest of all if he be severed from law

and justice." Because man can use his reason to devise means of satisfying his lusts and evil passions, which other animals are unable to do.

Reply Obj. 1. Men who are well disposed are led willingly to virtue by being admonished better than by coercion, but men who are evilly disposed are not led to virtue unless they are compelled.

Reply Obj. 2. As the Philosopher says, "It is better that all things be regulated by law than left to be decided by judges," and this for three reasons. First, because it is easier to find a few wise men competent to frame right laws than to find the many who would be necessary to judge aright of each single case. Secondly, because those who make laws consider long beforehand what laws to make, whereas judgment on each single case has to be pronounced as soon as it arises, and it is easier for man to see what is right by taking many instances into consideration than by considering one solitary fact. Thirdly, because lawgivers judge in the abstract and of future events, whereas those who sit in judgment judge of things present, toward which they are affected by love, hatred, or some kind of cupidity; wherefore their judgment is perverted.

Since, then, the embodied justice of the judge is not found in every man, and since it can be deflected, therefore it was necessary, whenever possible, for the law to determine how to judge, and for very few matters to be left to the decision of men.

Reply Obj. 3. Certain individual facts which cannot be covered by the law "have necessarily to be committed to judges," as the Philosopher says in the same passage, for instance, "concerning something that has happened or not happened" and the like.

Second Article
Is Every Human Law Derived from the Natural Law?

We proceed thus to the Second Article:

Obj. 1. It would seem that not every human law is derived from the natural law. For the Philosopher says that "the legal just is that which originally was a matter of indifference." But those things which arise from the natural law are not matters of indifference. Therefore, the enactments of human laws are not all derived from the natural law.

Obj. 2. Further, positive law is contrasted with natural law, as stated by Isidore and the Philosopher.

But those things which flow as conclusions from the general principles of the natural law belong to the natural law, as stated above. Therefore, that which is established by human law does not belong to the natural law.

Obj. 3. Further, the law of nature is the same for all, since the Philosopher says that "the natural just is that which is equally valid everywhere." If, therefore, human laws were derived from the natural law, it would follow that they too are the same for all, which is clearly false.

Obj. 4. Further, it is possible to give a reason for things which are derived from the natural law. But "it is not possible to give the reason for all the legal enactments of the lawgivers," as the Jurist says. Therefore, not all human laws are derived from the natural law.

On the contrary, Tully says, "Things which emanated from nature and were approved by custom were sanctioned by fear and reverence for the laws."

I answer that, As Augustine says, "that which is not just seems to be no law at all"; wherefore the force of a law depends on the extent of its justice. Now, in human affairs a thing is said to be just from being right according to the rule of reason. But the first rule of reason is the law of nature, as is clear from what has been stated above. Consequently, every human law has just so much of the nature of law as it is derived from the law of nature. But if, in any point, it deflects from the law of nature, it is no longer a law but a perversion of law.

But it must be noted that something may be derived from the natural law in two ways: first, as a conclusion from premises; secondly, by way of determination of certain generalities. The first way is like to that by which, in the sciences, demonstrated conclusions are drawn from the principles, while the second mode is likened to that whereby, in the arts, general forms are particularized as to details; thus the craftsman needs to determine the general form of a house to some particular shape. Some things are, therefore, derived from the general principles of the natural law by way of conclusion, e.g., that "one must not kill" may be derived as a conclusion from the principle that "one should do harm to no man"; while some are derived therefrom by way of determination, e.g., the law of nature has it that the evildoer should be punished; but that he be punished in this or that

way is not directly by natural law but is a certain determination of it.

Accordingly, both modes of derivation are found in the human law. But those things which are derived in the first way are contained in human law, not as emanating therefrom exclusively but having some force from the natural law also. But those things which are derived in the second way have no other force than that of human law.

Reply Obj. 1. The Philosopher is speaking of those enactments which are by way of determination or specification of the precepts of the natural law.

Reply Obj. 2. This argument avails for those things that are derived from the natural law by way of conclusions.

Reply Obj. 3. The general principles of the natural law cannot be applied to all men in the same way on account of the great variety of human affairs, and hence arises the diversity of positive laws among various people.

Reply Obj. 4. These words of the Jurist are to be understood as referring to decisions of rulers in determining particular points of the natural law, on which determinations the judgment of expert and prudent men is based as on its principle, insofar, to wit, as they see at once what is the best thing to decide.

Hence the Philosopher says that, in such matters, "we ought to pay as much attention to the undemonstrated sayings and opinions of persons who surpass us in experience, age, and prudence as to their demonstrations."

Third Article
Is Isidore's Description of the Quality of Positive Law Appropriate?

We proceed thus to the Third Article:

Obj. 1. It would seem that Isidore's description of the quality of positive law is not appropriate when he says: "Law shall be virtuous, just, possible, according to nature, in agreement with the customs of the country, suitable to place and time, necessary, useful, clearly expressed lest by its obscurity it lead to misunderstanding, framed for no private benefit but for the common good." Because he had previously expressed the quality of law in three conditions, saying that "law is anything founded on reason provided that it foster religion, be helpful to discipline, and further the common weal." Therefore, it was needless to add any further conditions to these.

Obj. 2. Further, justice is included in virtue, as Tully says. Therefore, after saying "virtuous," it was superfluous to add "just."

Obj. 3. Further, written law is distinct from custom, according to Isidore. Therefore, it should not be stated in the definition of law that it is "in agreement with the customs of the country."

Obj. 4. Further, a thing may be necessary in two ways. It may be necessary simply because it cannot be otherwise, and that which is necessary in this way is not subject to human judgment. Wherefore human law is not concerned with necessity of this kind. Again, a thing may be necessary for an end, and this necessity is the same as usefulness. Therefore, it is superfluous to say both "necessary" and "useful."

On the contrary stands the authority of Isidore.

I answer that, Whenever a thing is for an end, its form must be determined proportionately to that end, as the form of a saw is such as to be suitable for cutting (*Physics* I, 9). Again, everything that is ruled and measured must have a form proportionate to its rule and measure. Now both these conditions are verified of a human law since it is both something ordained to an end and is a rule or measure ruled or measured by a higher measure. And this higher measure is twofold, viz., the divine law and the natural law, as explained above. Now, the end of human law is to be useful to man, as the Jurist states. Wherefore Isidore, in determining the nature of law, lays down, at first, three conditions: viz., that it "foster religion," inasmuch as it is proportionate to the divine law; that it be "helpful to discipline," inasmuch as it is proportionate to the natural law; and that it "further the common weal," inasmuch as it is proportionate to the utility of mankind.

All the other conditions mentioned by him are reduced to these three. For it is called "virtuous" because it fosters religion. And when he goes on to say that it should be "just, possible, according to nature, in agreement with the customs of the country, adapted to place and time," he implies that it should be helpful to discipline. For human discipline depends, first, on the order of reason, to which he refers by saying "just"; secondly, it depends on the ability of the agent because discipline should be adapted to each one

according to his ability, taking also into account the ability of nature (for the same burdens should be not laid on children as on adults), and should be accorded to human customs since man cannot live alone in society, paying no heed to others; thirdly, it depends on certain circumstances, in respect of which he says, "adapted to place and time." The remaining words, "necessary," "useful," etc., mean that law should further the common weal, so that "necessity" refers to the removal of evils, "usefulness" to the attainment of good, "clearness of expression" to the need of preventing any harm ensuing from the law itself. And since, as stated above, law is ordained to the common good this is expressed in the last part of the description.

This suffices for the *Replies* to the *Objections*.

Fourth Article
Is Isidore's Division of Human Laws Appropriate?

We proceed thus to the Fourth Article:

Obj. 1. It would seem that Isidore wrongly divided human statutes or human law. For, under this law, he includes the "law of nations," so called, because, as he says, "nearly all nations use it." But as he says, "natural law is that which is common to all nations." Therefore, the law of nations is not contained under positive human law but rather under natural law.

Obj. 2. Further, those laws which have the same force seem to differ not formally but only materially. But "statutes, decrees of the commonality, senatorial decrees," and the like which he mentions, all have the same force. Therefore, they do not differ except materially. But art takes no notice of such a distinction since it may go on to infinity. Therefore, this division of human laws is not appropriate.

Obj. 3. Further, just as, in the political community, there are princes, priests, and soldiers, so are there other human offices. Therefore, it seems that, as this division includes "military law," and "public law" referring to priests and magistrates, so also it should include other laws pertaining to other offices of the political community.

Obj. 4. Further, those things that are accidental should be passed over. But it is accidental to law that it be framed by this or that man. Therefore, it is unreasonable to divide laws according to the names of lawgivers, so that one be called the "Cornelian" law, another the "Falcidian" law, etc.

On the contrary, The authority of Isidore (*Obj. 1*) suffices.

I answer that A thing can of itself be divided in respect of something contained in the notion of that thing. Thus a soul, either rational or irrational, is contained in the notion of animal, and, therefore, animal is divided properly and of itself in respect of its being rational or irrational but not in the point of its being white or black, which are entirely beside the notion of animal. Now, in the notion of human law, many things are contained in respect of any of which human law can be divided properly and of itself. For in the first place, it belongs to the notion of human law to be derived from the law of nature, as explained above. In this respect, positive right is divided into the "right among nations" and civil right according to the two ways in which something may be derived from the law of nature, as stated above. Because to the right among nations belong those things which are derived from the law of nature as conclusions from premises, e.g., just buyings and sellings and the like, without which men cannot live together, which is a point of the law of nature since man is by nature a social animal, as is proved in *Politics* I, 1. But those things which are derived from the law of nature by way of particular determination belong to the civil right according as each political community decides on what is best for itself.

Secondly, it belongs to the notion of human law to be ordained to the common good of the political community. In this respect, human law may be divided according to the different kinds of men who work in a special way for the common good, e.g., priests by praying to God for the people, princes by governing the people, soldiers by fighting for the safety of the people. Wherefore certain special kinds of law are adapted to these men.

Thirdly, it belongs to the notion of human law to be framed by that one who governs the political community, as shown above. In this respect, there are various human laws according to the various forms of government. Of these, according to the Philosopher, one is monarchy, i.e., when the state is governed by one, and then we have "royal ordinances." Another form is aristocracy, i.e., government by the best men

or men of highest rank, and then we have the "authoritative legal opinions" ("*responsa prudentum*") and "decrees of the senate" ("*senatusconsulta*"). Another form is oligarchy, i.e., government by a few rich and powerful men, and then we have "praetorian," also called "honorary," law. Another form of government is that of the people, which is called democracy, and there we have "decrees of the commonality" ("*plebiscita*"). There is also tyrannical government, which is altogether corrupt, which, therefore, has no corresponding law. Finally, there is a form of government made up of all these, and which is the best; and in this respect, we have "law sanctioned by nobles together with commoners," as stated by Isidore.

Fourthly, it belongs to the notion of human law to direct human actions. In this respect, according to the various matters of which the law treats, there are various kinds of laws, which are sometimes named after their authors: thus we have the *Lex Julia* about adultery, the *Lex Cornelia* concerning assassins, and so on, differentiated in this way not on account of the authors but on account of the matters to which they refer.

Reply Obj. 1. The law of nations is indeed in some way natural to man insofar as he is a reasonable being, because it is derived from the natural law by way of a conclusion that is not very remote from its premises. Wherefore men easily agreed thereto. Nevertheless, it is distinct from the natural law, especially from that natural law which is common to all animals.

The *Replies* to the other *Objections* are evident from what has been said.

QUESTION 96
OF THE POWER OF HUMAN LAW

[In Six Articles]

We must now consider the power of human law. Under this head, there are six points of inquiry: (1) Whether human law should be framed for the community? (2) Whether human law should repress all vices? (3) Whether human law is competent to direct all acts of virtue? (4) Whether it binds man in conscience? (5) Whether all men are subject to human law? (6) Whether those who are under the law may act beside the letter of the law?

First Article
Should Human Law Be Framed for the Community Rather Than for the Individual?

We proceed thus to the First Article:

Obj. 1. It would seem that human law should be framed, not for the community, but rather for the individual. For the Philosopher says that "the legal just . . . includes all particular acts of legislation . . . and all those matters which are the subject of decrees," which are also individual matters, since decrees are framed about individual actions. Therefore, law is framed not only for the community but also for the individual.

Obj. 2. Further, law is the director of human acts, as stated above. But human acts are about individual matters. Therefore, human laws should be framed, not for the community, but rather for the individual.

Obj. 3. Further, law is a rule and measure of human acts, as stated above. But a measure should be most certain, as stated in *Metaphysics* X. Since, therefore, in human acts no general proposition can be so certain as not to fail in some individual cases, it seems that laws should be framed not in general but for individual cases.

On the contrary, The Jurist says that "laws should be made to suit the majority of instances, and they are not framed according to what may possibly happen in an individual case."

I answer that Whatever is for an end should be proportionate to that end. Now the end of law is the common good, because, as Isidore says, "Law should be framed, not for any private benefit, but for the common good of all the citizens." Hence human laws should be proportionate to the common good. Now the common good comprises many things. Wherefore law should take account of many things, as to persons, as to occupations, and as to times, because the political community is composed of many citizens and its good is procured by many actions; nor is it established to endure for only a short time but to last for all time, by the citizens succeeding one another, as Augustine says.

Reply Obj. 1. The Philosopher divides the "legal just," i.e., positive law, into three parts. For some things are laid down simply in a general way, and these are

the general laws. Of these, he says that "the legal is that which originally was a matter of indifference, but which, when enacted is so no longer," as the fixing of the ransom of a captive. Some things affect the community in one respect and individuals in another. These are called "privileges," i.e., "private laws," as it were, because they regard private persons, although their power extends to many matters, and in regard to these, he adds: "and further all prescriptions in particular cases." Other matters are legal, not through being laws but through being applications of general laws to particular cases; such are decrees which have the force of law, and in regard to these, he adds: "all matters subject to decrees."

Reply Obj. 2. A principle of direction should be applicable to many; wherefore the Philosopher says that all things belonging to one genus are measured by one which is the first in that genus. For if there were as many rules or measures as there are things measured or ruled, they would cease to be of use, since their use consists in being applicable to many things. Hence law would be of no use if it did not extend further than to one single act because the decrees of prudent men are made for the purpose of directing individual actions, whereas law is a general precept, as stated above.

Reply Obj. 3. "We must not seek the same degree of certainty in all things." Consequently, in contingent matters such as natural and human things, it is enough for a thing to be certain as being true in the greater number of instances, though at times and less frequently it fail.

Second Article
Does It Belong to Human Law to Repress All Vices?

We proceed thus to the Second Article:

Obj. 1. It would seem that it belongs to human law to repress all vices. For Isidore says that "laws were made in order that, in fear thereof, man's audacity might be held in check." But it would not be held in check sufficiently unless all evils were repressed by law. Therefore, human law should repress all evils.

Obj. 2. Further, the intention of the lawgiver is to make the citizens virtuous. But a man cannot be virtuous unless he forbear from all kinds of vice. Therefore, it belongs to human law to repress all vices.

Obj. 3. Further, human law is derived from the natural law, as stated above. But all vices are contrary to the law of nature. Therefore, human law should repress all vices.

On the contrary, We read in *De libero arbitrio:* "It seems to me that the law which is written for the governing of the people rightly permits these things, and that divine providence punishes them." But divine providence punishes nothing but vices. Therefore, human law rightly allows some vices by not repressing them.

I answer that, As stated above, law is imposed as a certain rule or measure of human actions. Now, a measure should be homogeneous with that which it measures, as stated in *Metaphysics* X, since different things are measured by different measures. Wherefore laws imposed on men should also be in keeping with their condition, for, as Isidore says, law should be "possible both according to nature and according to the customs of the country." Now, possibility or faculty of action is due to an interior habit or disposition, since the same thing is not possible to one who has not a virtuous habit as is possible to one who has. Thus, the same is not possible to a child as to a full-grown man, for which reason, the law for children is not the same as for adults, since many things are permitted to children which in an adult are punished by law or at any rate are open to blame. In like manner, many things are permissible to men not perfect in virtue which would be intolerable in a virtuous man.

Now, human law is framed for a number of human beings, the majority of whom are not perfect in virtue. Wherefore, human laws do not forbid all vices from which the virtuous abstain but only the more grievous vices from which it is possible for the majority to abstain and chiefly those that are to the hurt of others, without the prohibition of which human society could not be maintained; thus human law prohibits murder, theft, and suchlike.

Reply Obj. 1. Audacity seems to refer to the assailing of others. Consequently, it belongs to those sins chiefly whereby one's neighbor is injured, and these sins are forbidden by human law, as stated.

Reply Obj. 2. The purpose of human law is to lead men to virtue, not suddenly but gradually. Wherefore it does not lay upon the multitude of imperfect men the burdens of those who are already virtuous, viz.,

that they should abstain from all evil. Otherwise, these imperfect ones, being unable to bear such precepts, would break out into yet greater evils; thus it is written: "He that violently blows his nose, brings out blood," and that if "new wine," i.e., precepts of a perfect life, is "put into old bottles," i.e., into imperfect men, "the bottles break, and the wine runs out," i.e., the precepts are despised, and those men, from contempt, break out into evils worse still.

Reply Obj. 3. The natural law is a participation in us of the eternal law, while human law falls short of the eternal law. Now Augustine says: "The law which is framed for the government of political communities allows and leaves unpunished many things that are punished by divine providence. Nor, if this law does not attempt to do everything, is this a reason why it should be blamed for what it does." Wherefore, too, human law does not prohibit everything that is forbidden by the natural law.

Third Article
Does Human Law Prescribe Acts of All the Virtues?

We proceed thus to the Third Article:

Obj. 1. It would seem that human law does not prescribe acts of all the virtues. For vicious acts are contrary to acts of virtue. But human law does not prohibit all vices, as stated above. Therefore, neither does it prescribe all acts of virtue.

Obj. 2. Further, a virtuous act proceeds from a virtue. But virtue is the end of law, so that whatever is from a virtue cannot come under a precept of law. Therefore, human law does not prescribe all acts of virtue.

Obj. 3. Further, law is ordained to the common good, as stated above. But some acts of virtue are ordained not to the common good but to private good. Therefore, the law does not prescribe all acts of virtue.

On the contrary, The Philosopher says that the law "prescribes the performance of the acts of a brave man . . . and the acts of the temperate man . . . and the acts of the meek man and in like manner as regards the other virtues and vices prescribing the former, forbidding the latter."

I answer that The species of virtues are distinguished by their objects, as explained above. Now all the objects of virtues can be referred either to the private good of an individual or to the common good of the multitude; thus matters of fortitude may be achieved either for the safety of the political community or for upholding the rights of a friend, and in like manner with the other virtues. But law, as stated above, is ordained to the common good. Wherefore, there is no virtue whose acts cannot be prescribed by the law. Nevertheless, human law does not prescribe concerning all the acts of every virtue but only in regard to those that are ordained to the common good—either immediately, as when certain things are done directly for the common good, or mediately, as when a lawgiver prescribes certain things pertaining to good training whereby the citizens are disciplined in the upholding of the common good of justice and peace.

Reply Obj. 1. Human law does not forbid all vicious acts by the obligation of a precept, as neither does it prescribe all acts of virtue. But it forbids certain acts of each vice, just as it prescribes some acts of each virtue.

Reply Obj. 2. An act is said to be an act of virtue in two ways. First, from the fact that a man does something virtuous; thus the act of justice is to do what is right, and an act of fortitude is to do brave things—and in this way law prescribes certain acts of virtue. Secondly, an act of virtue is when a man does a virtuous thing in a way in which a virtuous man does it. Such an act always proceeds from virtue, and it does not come under a precept of law but is the end at which every lawgiver aims.

Reply Obj. 3. There is no virtue whose act is not ordainable to the common good, as stated above, either mediately or immediately.

Fourth Article
Does Human Law Bind a Man in Conscience?

We proceed thus to the Fourth Article:

Obj. 1. It would seem that human law does not bind a man in conscience. For an inferior power has no jurisdiction in a court of higher power. But the power of man which frames human law is beneath the divine power. Therefore, human law cannot impose its precept in a divine court, such as is the court of conscience.

Obj. 2. Further, the judgment of conscience depends chiefly on the commandments of God. But sometimes God's commandments are made void by human laws, according to Mt. 15:6: "You have made void the commandment of God for your tradition." Therefore, human law does not bind a man in conscience.

Obj. 3. Further, human laws often bring loss of character and injury on man, according to Is. 10:1: "Woe to them that make wicked laws, and when they write, write injustice; to oppress the poor in judgment and do violence to the cause of the humble of My people." But it is lawful for anyone to avoid oppression and violence. Therefore, human laws do not bind man in conscience.

On the contrary, It is written: "This is thanksworthy, if for conscience . . . a man endure sorrows, suffering wrongfully."

I answer that Laws framed by man are either just or unjust. If they be just, they have the power of binding in conscience from the eternal law whence they are derived, according to Pr. 8:15: "By Me kings reign, and lawgivers decree just things." Now laws are said to be just from the end, when, to wit, they are ordained to the common good, and from their author, that is to say, when the law that is made does not exceed the power of the lawgiver, and from their form, when, to wit, burdens are laid on the subjects according to an equality of proportion and with a view to the common good. For, since one man is a part of the community, each man, in all that he is and has, belongs to the community, just as a part, in all that it is, belongs to the whole; wherefore nature inflicts a loss on the part in order to save the whole, so that, on this account, such laws as these which impose proportionate burdens are just and binding in conscience and are legal laws.

On the other hand, laws may be unjust in two ways: first, by being contrary to human good, through being opposed to the things mentioned above—either in respect of the end, as when an authority imposes on his subjects burdensome laws conducive, not to the common good, but rather to his own cupidity or vainglory; or in respect of the author, as when a man makes a law that goes beyond the power committed to him; or in respect of the form, as when burdens are imposed unequally on the community, although with a view to the common good. The like are acts of violence rather than laws, because, as Augustine says, "A law that is not just, seems to be no law at all." Wherefore such laws do not bind in conscience, except perhaps in order to avoid scandal or disturbance, for which cause a man should even yield his right, according to Mt. 5:40, 41: "If a man . . . take away your coat, let go your cloak also unto him, and whosoever will force you one mile, go with him other two."

Secondly, laws may be unjust through being opposed to the divine good; such are the laws of tyrants inducing to idolatry or to anything else contrary to the divine law, and laws of this kind must nowise be observed because, as stated in Acts 5:29, "we ought to obey God rather than men."

Reply Obj. 1. As the Apostle says, all human power is from God . . .; "therefore, he that resists the power" in matters that are within its scope "resists the ordinance of God," so that he becomes guilty according to his conscience.

Reply Obj. 2. This argument is true of laws that are contrary to the commandments of God, which is beyond the scope of (human) power. Wherefore in such matters human law should not be obeyed.

Reply Obj. 3. This argument is true of a law that inflicts unjust hurt on its subjects. The power that man holds from God does not extend to this; wherefore neither in such matters is man bound to obey the law, provided he avoid giving scandal or inflicting a more grievous hurt.

Fifth Article
Are All Subject to the Law?

We proceed thus to the Fifth Article:

Obj. 1. It would seem that not all are subject to the law. For those alone are subject to a law for whom a law is made. But the Apostle says: "The law is not made for the just man." Therefore, the just are not subject to the law.

Obj. 2. Further, Pope Urban says: "He that is guided by a private law need not for any reason be bound by the public law." Now all spiritual men are led by the private law of the Holy Spirit, for they are the sons of God, of whom it is said: "Whosoever are led by the Spirit of God, they are the sons of God." Therefore, not all men are subject to human law.

Obj. 3. Further, the Jurist says that "the ruler is exempt from the laws." But he that is exempt from the law is not bound thereby. Therefore, not all are subject to the law.

On the contrary, The Apostle says, "Let every soul be subject to the higher powers." But subjection to a power seems to imply subjection to the laws framed by that power. Therefore, all men should be subject to human law.

I answer that, As stated above, the notion of law contains two things: first, that it is a rule of human acts; secondly, that it has coercive power. Wherefore a man may be subject to law in two ways. First, as the regulated is subject to the regulator, and, in this way, whoever is subject to a power is subject to the law framed by that power. But it may happen in two ways that one is not subject to a power. In one way, by being altogether free from its authority; hence the subjects of one city or kingdom are not bound by the laws of the sovereign of another city or kingdom, since they are not subject to his authority. In another way, by being under a yet higher law; thus the subject of a proconsul should be ruled by his command but not in those matters in which the subject receives his orders from the emperor, for in these matters he is not bound by the mandate of the lower authority since he is directed by that of a higher. In this way, one who is simply subject to a law may not be subject thereto in certain matters in respect of which he is ruled by a higher law.

Secondly, a man is said to be subject to a law as the coerced is subject to the coercer. In this way, the virtuous and righteous are not subject to the law but only the wicked. Because coercion and violence are contrary to the will, but the will of the good is in harmony with the law, whereas the will of the wicked is discordant from it. Wherefore, in this sense, the good are not subject to the law but only the wicked.

Reply Obj. 1. This argument is true of subjection by way of coercion, for, in this way, "the law is not made for the just men," because "they are a law to themselves" since they "show the work of the law written in their hearts," as the Apostle says. Consequently, the law does not enforce itself upon them as it does on the wicked.

Reply Obj. 2. The law of the Holy Spirit is above all law framed by man, and, therefore, spiritual men, insofar as they are led by the law of the Holy Spirit, are not subject to the law in those matters that are inconsistent with the guidance of the Holy Spirit. Nevertheless, the very fact that spiritual men are subject to law is due to the leading of the Holy Spirit, according to 1 Pet.: "Be you subject ... to every human creature for God's sake."

Reply Obj. 3. The ruler is said to be "exempt from the law" as to its coercive power, since, properly speaking, no man is coerced by himself, and law has no coercive power save from the power of the ruler. Thus, then, is the ruler said to be exempt from the law because none is competent to pass sentence on him if he acts against the law. Wherefore on Ps. 50:6: "To You only have I sinned," a gloss says that "there is no man who can judge the deeds of a king." But as to the directive force of law, the ruler is subject to the law by his own will, according to the statement that "whatever law a man makes for another, he should keep himself." And a wise authority says: "Obey the law that you make yourself." Moreover, the Lord reproaches those who "say and do not," and who "bind heavy burdens and lay them on men's shoulders, but with a finger of their own, they will not move them." Hence, in the judgment of God, the ruler is not exempt from the law as to its directive force, but he should fulfill it of his own free will and not of constraint. Again, the ruler is above the law insofar as, when it is expedient, he can change the law and dispense from it according to time and place.

Sixth Article
May He Who Is under a Law Act beside the Letter of the Law?

We proceed thus to the Sixth Article:

Obj. 1. It seems that he who is subject to a law may not act beside the letter of the law. For Augustine says: "Although men judge about temporal laws when they make them, yet, when once they are made and confirmed, they must pass judgment, not on them but according to them." But if anyone disregard the letter of the law, saying that he observes the intention of the lawgiver, he seems to pass judgment on the law. Therefore, it is not right for one who is under a law to disregard the letter of the law in order to observe the intention of the lawgiver.

Obj. 2. Further, he alone is competent to interpret the law who can make the law. But those who are subject to the law cannot make the law. Therefore, they have no right to interpret the intention of the lawgiver but should always act according to the letter of the law.

Obj. 3. Further, every wise man knows how to explain his intention by words. But those who framed the laws should be reckoned wise, for Wisdom says: "By Me kings reign, and lawgivers decree just things." Therefore, we should not judge of the intention of the lawgiver otherwise than by the words of the law.

On the contrary, Hilary says, "The meaning of what is said is according to the motive for saying it, because things are not subject to speech, but speech to things." Therefore, we should take more account of the motive of the lawgiver than to his very words.

I answer that, As stated above, every law is directed to the common weal of men and derives the force and nature of law accordingly, but it has no power to oblige morally if it fails to be so directed. Hence the Jurist says: "By no reason of law or favor of equity is it allowable for us to interpret harshly and render burdensome those useful measures which have been enacted for the welfare of man." Now, it happens often that the observance of some point of law conduces to the common weal in the majority of instances, and yet in some cases is very hurtful. Since, then, the lawgiver cannot have in view every single case, he shapes the law according to what happens most frequently, by directing his attention to the common good. Wherefore, if a case arise wherein the observance of that law would be hurtful to the general welfare, it should not be observed. For instance, suppose that, in a besieged city, it be an established law that the gates of the city are to be kept closed, this is good for public welfare as a general rule, but if it were to happen that the enemy are in pursuit of certain citizens who are defenders of the city, it would be a great loss to the city if the gates were not opened to them, and so, in that case, the gates ought to be opened, contrary to the letter of the law, in order to maintain the common weal, which the lawgiver had in view.

Nevertheless, it must be noted that if the observance of the law according to the letter does not involve any sudden risk needing instant remedy, it is not competent for everyone to expound what is useful and what is not useful to the political community; those alone can do this who are in authority, and who, on account of suchlike cases, have the power to dispense from the laws. If, however, the peril be so sudden as not to allow of the delay involved by referring the matter to authority, the mere necessity brings with it a dispensation, since necessity knows no law.

Reply Obj. 1. He who in a case of necessity acts beside the letter of the law does not judge of the law but of a particular case in which he sees that the letter of the law is not to be observed.

Reply Obj. 2. He who follows the intention of the lawgiver does not interpret the law indiscriminately but in a case in which it is evident, by reason of the manifest harm, that the lawgiver intended otherwise. For if it be a matter of doubt, he must either act according to the letter of the law or consult those in power.

Reply Obj. 3. No man is so wise as to be able to take account of every single case; wherefore he is not able sufficiently to express in words all those things that are suitable for the end he has in view. And even if a lawgiver were able to take all the cases into consideration, he ought not to mention them all, in order to avoid confusion, but should frame the law according to that which is of most common occurrence.

QUESTION 97
OF CHANGE IN LAWS

[In Four Articles]

We must now consider change in laws, under which head there are four points of inquiry: (1) Whether human law is changeable? (2) Whether it should always be changed whenever something better occurs? (3) Whether it is abolished by custom, and whether custom obtains the force of law? (4) Whether the application of human law should be changed by dispensation of those in authority?

First Article
Should Human Law Be Changed in Any Way?

We proceed thus to the First Article:

Obj. 1. It would seem that human law should not be changed in any way at all because human law is derived from the natural law, as stated above. But the natural law endures unchangeably. Therefore, human law should also remain without any change.

Obj. 2. Further, as the Philosopher says, a measure should be absolutely stable. But human law is the measure of human acts, as stated above. Therefore, it should remain without change.

Obj. 3. Further, it is of the essence of law to be just and right, as stated above. But that which is right once is right always. Therefore, that which is law once should be always law.

On the contrary, Augustine says, "A temporal law, however just, may be justly changed in course of time."

I answer that, As stated above, human law is a dictate of reason whereby human acts are directed. Thus there may be two causes for the just change of human law: one on the part of reason; the other on the part of man, whose acts are regulated by law. The cause on the part of reason is that it seems natural to human reason to advance gradually from the imperfect to the perfect. Hence, in speculative sciences, we see that the teaching of the early philosophers was imperfect, and that it was afterward perfected by those who succeeded them. So also in practical matters; for those who first endeavored to discover something useful for the human community, not being able by themselves to take everything into consideration, set up certain institutions which were deficient in many ways, and these were changed by subsequent lawgivers who made institutions that might prove less frequently deficient in respect of the common weal.

On the part of man, whose acts are regulated by law, the law can be rightly changed on account of the changed condition of man, to whom different things are expedient according to the difference of his condition. An example is proposed by Augustine:

If the people have a sense of moderation and responsibility and are most careful guardians of the common weal, it is right to enact a law allowing such a people to choose their own magistrates for the government of the commonwealth. But if, as time goes on, the same people become so corrupt as to sell their votes and entrust the government to scoundrels and criminals, then the right of appointing their public officials is rightly forfeit to such a people, and the choice devolves to a few good men.

Reply Obj. 1. The natural law is a participation of the eternal law, as stated above, and, therefore, endures without change, owing to the unchangeableness and perfection of the divine reason, the Author of nature. But the reason of man is changeable and imperfect; wherefore his law is subject to change. Moreover, the natural law contains certain universal precepts which are everlasting, whereas human law contains certain particular precepts according to various emergencies.

Reply Obj. 2. A measure should be as enduring as possible. But nothing can be absolutely unchangeable in things that are subject to change. And, therefore, human law cannot be altogether unchangeable.

Reply Obj. 3. Of corporeal objects, "right" ["straight"] is predicated absolutely and, therefore, as far as itself is concerned, always remains "right." But "right" is predicated of law with reference to the common weal, to which one and the same thing is not always adapted, as stated above; wherefore, rectitude of this kind is subject to change.

Second Article
Should Human Law Always Be Changed Whenever Something Better Occurs?

We proceed thus to the Second Article:

Obj. 1. It would seem that human law should be changed whenever something better occurs because human laws are devised by human reason, like other arts. But in the other arts, the tenets of former times give place to others if something better occurs. Therefore, the same should apply to human laws.

Obj. 2. Further, by taking note of the past, we can provide for the future. Now unless human laws had been changed when it was found possible to improve them, considerable inconvenience would have ensued because the laws of old were crude in many points. Therefore, it seems that laws should be changed whenever anything better occurs to be enacted.

Obj. 3. Further, human laws are enacted about single acts of man. But we cannot acquire perfect knowledge in singular matters except by experience, which "requires time," as stated in *Ethics* II, 1. Therefore, it seems that, as time goes on, it is possible for something better to occur for legislation.

On the contrary, It is stated in the *Decretum:* "It is absurd and a detestable shame that we should suffer

those traditions to be changed which we have received from the fathers of old."

I answer that, As stated above, human law is rightly changed insofar as such change is conducive to the common weal. But, to a certain extent, the mere change of law is of itself prejudicial to the common good because custom avails much for the observance of laws, seeing that what is done contrary to general custom, even in slight matters, is looked upon as grave. Consequently, when a law is changed, the binding power of the law is diminished insofar as custom is abolished. Wherefore, human law should never be changed unless, in some way or other, the common weal be compensated according to the extent of the harm done in this respect. Such compensation may arise either from some very great and very evident benefit conferred by the new enactment or from the extreme urgency of the case, due to the fact that either the existing law is clearly unjust or its observance extremely harmful. Wherefore the Jurist says that "in establishing new laws, there should be evidence of the benefit to be derived before departing from a law which has long been considered just."

Reply Obj. 1. Rules of art derive their force from reason alone, and, therefore, whenever something better occurs, the rule followed hitherto should be changed. But "laws derive very great force from custom," as the Philosopher states; consequently, they should not be quickly changed.

Reply Obj. 2. This argument proves that laws ought to be changed, not in view of any improvement but for the sake of a great benefit or in a case of great urgency, as stated above. This answer applies also to the *Third Objection.*

Third Article
Can Custom Obtain Force of Law?

We proceed thus to the Third Article:

Obj. 1. It would seem that custom cannot obtain force of law nor abolish a law because human law is derived from the natural law and from the divine law, as stated above. But human custom cannot change either the law of nature or the divine law. Therefore, neither can it change human law.

Obj. 2. Further, many evils cannot make one good. But he who first acted against the law did evil. Therefore, by multiplying such acts, nothing good is the result. Now a law is something good, since it is a rule of human acts. Therefore, law is not abolished by custom so that the mere custom should obtain force of law.

Obj. 3. Further, the framing of laws belongs to those public men whose business it is to govern the community; wherefore private individuals cannot make laws. But custom grows by the acts of private individuals. Therefore, custom cannot obtain force of law so as to abolish the law.

On the contrary, Augustine says, "The customs of God's people and the institutions of our ancestors are to be considered as laws. And those who throw contempt on the customs of the Church ought to be punished as those who disobey the law of God."

I answer that All law proceeds from the reason and will of the lawgiver: the divine and natural laws from the reasonable will of God, the human law from the will of man regulated by reason. Now just as human reason and will, in practical matters, may be made manifest by speech, so may they be made known by deeds, since, seemingly, a man chooses as good that which he carries into execution. But it is evident that, by human speech, law can be both changed and expounded insofar as it manifests the interior movement and thought of human reason. Wherefore, by actions also, especially if they be repeated so as to make a custom, law can be changed and expounded, and also something can be established which obtains force of law insofar as, by repeated external actions, the inward movement of the will and concepts of reason are most effectually declared; for when a thing is done again and again, it seems to proceed from a deliberate judgment of reason. Accordingly, custom has the force of labor, abolishes law, and is the interpreter of law.

Reply Obj. 1. The natural and divine laws proceed from the divine will, as stated above. Wherefore, they cannot be changed by a custom proceeding from the will of man but only by divine authority. Hence it is that no custom can prevail over the divine or natural laws, for Isidore says: "Let custom yield to authority; evil customs should be eradicated by law and reason."

Reply Obj. 2. As stated above, human laws fail in some cases; wherefore, it is possible sometimes to act beside the law, namely, in a case where the law fails, yet the act will not be evil. And when such cases are multiplied, by reason of some change in man, then custom shows that the law is no longer useful, just as it might be declared by the verbal promulgation of a law to the contrary. If, however, the same reason remains for which the law was useful hitherto, then it is not the custom that prevails against the law but the law that overcomes the custom, unless perhaps the sole reason for the law seeming useless be that it is not "possible according to the custom of the country," which has been stated to be one of the conditions of law. For it is not easy to set aside the custom of a whole people.

Reply Obj. 3. The people among whom a custom is introduced may be of two conditions. For if they are free and able to make their own laws, the consent of the whole people expressed by a custom counts far more in favor of a particular observance than does the authority of the ruler, who has not the power to frame laws except as representing the people. Wherefore, although single individuals cannot make laws, yet the whole people can. If, however, the people have not the free power to make their own laws or to abolish a law made by a higher authority, nevertheless, with such a people, a prevailing custom obtains force of law insofar as it is tolerated by those to whom it belongs to make laws for that people, because, by the very fact that they tolerate it, they seem to approve of that which is introduced by custom.

Fourth Article
Can the Rulers of the People Dispense from Human Laws?

We proceed thus to the Fourth Article:

Obj. 1. It would seem that the rulers of the people cannot dispense from human laws. For the law is established for the "common weal," as Isidore says. But the common good should not be set aside for the private convenience of an individual, because, as the Philosopher says, "the good of the nation is more godlike than the good of one man." Therefore, it seems that a man should not be dispensed from acting in compliance with the general rule.

Obj. 2. Further, those who are placed over others are commanded as follows: "You shall hear the little as well as the great; neither shall you respect any man's person, because it is the judgment of God." But to allow one man to do that which is equally forbidden to all seems to be respect of persons. Therefore, the rulers of a community cannot grant such dispensations, since this is against a precept of the divine law.

Obj. 3. Further, human law, in order to be just, should accord with the natural and divine laws, else it would not "foster religion nor be helpful to discipline," which is a requisite of law as laid down by Isidore. But no man can dispense from the divine and natural laws. Neither, therefore, can he dispense from the human law.

On the contrary, The Apostle says, "A dispensation is committed to me."

I answer that Dispensation, properly speaking, denotes a measuring out to individuals of some common goods; thus the head of a household is called a dispenser because, to each member of the household, he distributes work and necessaries of life in due weight and measure. Accordingly, in every community, a man is said to dispense from the very fact that he directs how some general precept is to be fulfilled by each individual. Now it happens at times that a precept which is conducive to the common weal as a general rule is not good for a particular individual or in some particular case, either because it would hinder some greater good or because it would be the occasion of some evil, as explained above. But it would be dangerous to leave this to the discretion of each individual, except perhaps by reason of an evident and sudden emergency, as stated above (ibid.). Consequently, he who is placed over a community is empowered to dispense in a human law that rests upon his authority, so that, when the law fails in its application to persons or circumstances, he may allow the precept of the law not to be observed. If, however, he grant this permission without any such reason and of his mere will, he will be an unfaithful or an imprudent dispenser: unfaithful if he has not the common good in view; imprudent if he ignores the reasons for granting dispensations. Hence our Lord says: "Who, think you, is the faithful and wise dispenser, whom his lord sets over his family?"

Reply Obj. 1. When a person is dispensed from observing the general law, this should not be done to the prejudice of, but with the intention of benefiting, the common good.

Reply Obj. 2. It is not "respect of persons" if unequal measures are served out to those who are themselves unequal. Wherefore, when the condition of any person requires that he should reasonably receive special treatment, it is not "respect of persons" if he be the object of a special favor.

Reply Obj. 3. Natural law, so far as it contains general precepts, which never fail, does not allow of dispensation. In the other precepts, however, which are as conclusions of the general precepts, man sometimes grants a dispensation: for instance, that a loan should not be paid back to the betrayer of his country, or something similar. But to the divine law, each man stands as a private person to the public law to which he is subject. Wherefore, just as none can dispense from public human law except the man from whom the law derives its authority or his delegate, so, in the precepts of the divine law, which are from God, none can dispense but God or the man to whom He may give special power for that purpose.

Statesmanship

ON KINGSHIP

To the King of Cyprus

Book One

Chapter One

It is necessary for men living together to be ruled diligently by a king.

Our primary intention requires that we explain what is to be understood by the name "king." In all things, however, which are ordered to some goal, by which we can proceed in more than one way, there is a need for some directing principle, by which the task may be brought rightly to completion. For even a ship, randomly moved to and fro by different winds, will not reach her destined goal unless she is directed by the effort of the helmsman to her port. There is a certain goal for man towards which his whole life and deeds are ordered, since he acts by his intelligence, which is clearly to act with some goal in mind. It happens that people proceed towards their intended goal in different ways, which the very diversity of human endeavors and actions makes clear.

Therefore, man needs some directing principle to attain that goal. However, every man is endowed by nature with the light of reason, by which he may be directed in his actions to his goal. So, if it were fitting for man to live alone, as in the case of many animals, no other direction would be needed regarding that goal, but each would be a king unto himself under God, the highest king, inasmuch as in his actions he would direct himself by the light of reason divinely given to him.

Man is by nature, however, a social and political animal, living amid a multitude of his kind; more so, indeed, than is the case with all other animals, which natural necessity itself makes clear. For nature prepares for other animals their food, their covering of fur, their means of defense (such as teeth, horns, claws, or at least swiftness of flight). For man, however, none of these were provided by nature, but instead of all of these, reason was given to him, by which, through the labor of his hands, he would be able to fashion for himself all these things, but for the fashioning of all of which one man alone would not suffice. For one man alone, by his own devices, could not sufficiently make his way through life. It is, therefore, natural for man that he live in the companionship of many of his kind.

Moreover, instinct is given to other animals by which they discover all those things which are useful or dangerous, as the sheep instinctively recognizes the wolf as its enemy. Certain animals know instinctively that some herbs are medicinal and know instinctively other things necessary for their life. Man has a natural knowledge of those things which are necessary for survival, but only in a general way, insofar as, so to speak, being gifted by reason, he can pass from natural principles to the recognition of those particulars which are necessary for human life. It is not possible, though, that a single person could achieve all this knowledge by his own power of reason. It is, therefore, necessary for man to live in society with his fellows, so that one may be aided by another and that different persons may be engaged in making different discoveries through their respective powers of reason; one, for example, in medicine, another in this field, another in that. This point is made most clearly evident by this—that it is man's distinctive

trait to speak, whereby one man can fully express his thought to others. Other animals can express to each other in a general way their feelings, as dogs express anger when they bark and other animals express their feelings in diverse ways. Man communicates with his fellows more than any other animal we see living in a group, such as cranes, ants, and bees. Reflecting upon this Solomon says, "It is better to be two than to be one. They have been enriched in one another's company." If it is natural that man live in society with his fellows, it is necessary that there be some power in men by which that group be ruled. If there be a group of people, with each one looking solely after his own interest, that group would break up into many parts unless, indeed, there were also someone taking care of those things pertaining to the good of the group, just as the body of a man or of any animal would fall apart unless there were some general ruling principle in the body which has as its interest the common good of all the members. Reflecting upon this Solomon says, "Where there is no governor, the people scatter." This happens reasonably enough. The particular and the common are not the same: the particular differentiates; the common unites. Different things, however, are the result of different causes. It is necessary, therefore, that, besides that which moves each towards his own private good, there be something else that moves towards the common good of the group. Therefore, in all things which are ordered to one goal, there is to be found some ruling principle. Thus, in the universe of bodies, divine Providence rules, by a certain order, other bodies by the first (that is, the heavenly) body and by that order all bodies are ruled by the rational creature. In every man, the soul rules the body, and, between the spirited and desiring parts of the soul, reason assigns an order. Again, among the members of the body, one is the chief, and it moves the others, whether it be the heart or the head. There has to be, therefore, some ruling principle in every group.

Even so, in those things which are directed to a goal, things can proceed rightly or not rightly. So, in ruling a group, it may be found that such is done rightly or not rightly. Each thing is directed rightly when it is brought to its fitting goal and not rightly when the goal is not fitting. The goal befitting a community of free men is different from that befitting a community of slaves. For the free man is the cause of his own actions; the slave, as such, belongs to another. If, therefore, a community of free men be ordered by a governor to the common good of that group, that will be a rule both right and just, as befits free men. If, in fact, his rule is directed, not to the common good of the group, but to the private advantage of the ruler, that will be a rule both unjust and perverse; wherefore the Lord warns such rulers through Ezechiel, saying, "Woe to the shepherds who feed themselves" (as if seeking their private advantage), "Should not the flocks be fed by the shepherds?" However, shepherds should seek the good of the flock, and, indeed, rulers the good of that group subject to them.

If, therefore, an unjust rule is exercised by one man alone, who seeks his own advantage from that rule, not the good of the group subject to him, such a ruler is called a tyrant, a name derived from strength, since, indeed, he oppresses by his power; he does not rule by justice. Therefore, among the ancients, powerful men were called tyrants. If, though, an unjust rule be exercised not by one alone but by several who are few, it is called oligarchy, that is, rule by the few, insofar as the few indeed oppress the common people for the sake of wealth, distinguishing themselves from the tyrant solely by being more than one. If wicked rule is exercised by many, it is termed democracy, that is, rule by the people, insofar as indeed the mass of common folk, by the force of numbers, oppresses the rich. Thus the whole of the people will be, as it were, one tyrant.

We must, in like manner, distinguish different just constitutions. If things are administered by some group, it is called by the common name "polity," as, for instance, when a group of soldiers rules a city or a province. If things are administered by few, this constitution is called aristocracy, that is, the best rule or rule by the best, who, therefore, are termed "the best men." If, indeed, a just constitution is exercised by one man alone, he is properly called king; therefore, the Lord through Ezechiel says, "My servant David will be a king over all, and he will be the one shepherd of all of them." Hence it is obvious that the very concept of a king entails that there be one who presides, and that he be the shepherd seeking the common good of the group and not his own advantage.

Since, then, it is necessary for man to live in society with his fellows, because by himself he could not secure those things necessary for life if he would remain in a solitary existence, it is a consequence that the companionship of many would be more complete to the extent that it will be more sufficient in itself for the necessities of life. There is, however, a certain sufficiency for life in the single family of one household (as much, that is, as suffices for the natural acts of nutrition and procreation and similar things); in one quarter of a city, there is as much sufficiency as is required for a single craft. In a city, however, (which is a complete community), there is as much as suffices for all the necessities of life, yet still much more in a province because of the need for defense and of the mutual aid of allies against the public enemy. Therefore, he who rules a complete community, that is, a city or a province, is justly termed king; he who rules a household is called father of the family, but not king. A father has a certain likeness to a king, because of which kings are sometimes called the fathers of peoples.

It is clear from our discussion that king is one who rules the multitude in a city or a province for the common good; therefore, Solomon says, "The king rules all lands which are subject to him."

Chapter Six

The rule of one man is unqualifiedly the best. The community ought to provide that certain circumstances should be prevented, so that a king will not become a tyrant; yet, even if he does become a tyrant, this should be tolerated so that greater evils can be avoided.

Since, then, the rule of one man ought to be what we above all choose, because such a rule is the best, and since it happens that such a rule might change into tyranny, which is the worst kind of rule, as is clear from our remarks above, every effort must be carefully made so that the community is provided with a king in such a way that it will not fall under a tyrant. First, it is necessary that whoever is elevated to the rank of king, by those responsible for doing so, have the kind of character that makes it unlikely that he would stoop to tyranny. Therefore Samuel, praising God's providence regarding the institution of a king, says, "The Lord sought out for Himself a man according to His heart, and the Lord commanded him to be a leader over his people." Next, the governance of a kingdom must be arranged so that there is no opportunity given for a king who has been instituted to act as a tyrant. At the same time his power should be moderated so that he cannot easily stoop to tyranny. We will consider how to do this below. Finally, we certainly have to be concerned about what must be done if, nevertheless, a king lapses into behaving as a tyrant.

If, indeed, there is not an excess of tyranny, it is more profitable to put up with a milder tyranny for the time being than, by opposing the tyrant, to run into many dangers more grievous than the tyranny itself. There is a possibility that if those who oppose the tyrant do not succeed, then the enraged tyrant would become even more savage. Even if the opponents of the tyrant are successful, from this very success most grave divisions often arise among the people: the community splinters on the question of the nature of the constitution, either during the insurrection against the tyrant or after his overthrow. It even happens that, while the community drives out the tyrant with somebody's help, that person, having received power, takes over the tyrant's role himself, and fearing to suffer from someone else what he did himself to another, oppresses his subjects with an even weightier enslavement. Thus, then, it regularly happens in the case of tyranny that a latter tyrant is more oppressive than his predecessor, for he does not give up the preceding oppression but rather thinks up new forms out of the malice of his heart. This is the reason that, when at the time that everyone in Syracuse desired the death of Dionysius, some old lady persistently prayed that he might be unharmed and might outlive her. When he found this out, he questioned her intention. She replied, "When I was a little girl we had an oppressive tyrant; I wanted him dead. He was killed, and a somewhat more harsh tyrant succeeded him. I thought the end of his domination would be great. We began to have a third ruler harsher still: yourself. So if you were taken away from us, a worse would follow you."

And if an excessive tyranny is intolerable, it has seemed to some that the virtue of the more powerful men entitles them to kill the tyrant and, for the sake of the liberation of the community, to place themselves in danger of death. There is an example of this in the Old Testament itself. For Ehud killed a certain Eglon, King of Moab, who oppressed the people of God with a weighty enslavement, by thrusting a dagger into Eglon's thigh, and he was made judge of the people. But this does not conform to apostolic teachings. Peter teaches us that we ought to be reverently submissive not only to good and gentle rulers but even to overbearing ones: "This is indeed a grace if, because of awareness of God, someone bears up with suffering unjustly inflicted troubles." Thus, when many Roman emperors persecuted the faith of Christ in a tyrannical way, a great crowd (no less of the nobility than of the common folk) were converted to the faith, making no resistance, but they are praised for enduring death for Christ patiently and with spirited courage. This is clearly the case with the holy legion of Thebes. It must be judged that Ehud killed somebody who was more the public enemy than a ruler of the people, though a tyrannical one. Thus also we read in the Old Testament that those who killed Joash, King of Juda, were killed themselves, although he had departed from the worship of God, but their children were spared according to the command of the law. It would be dangerous for the community and its rulers if anybody by private initiative were to attempt to kill its public officers, even if they were tyrants. It is more often the case that evil persons expose themselves to such great dangers than do the good. For evil persons, it is common that the rule of kings is no less burdensome than is that of tyrants, since according to the saying of Solomon, "A wise king scatters the impious." It is, therefore, more likely that from this sort of presumption danger to the community would occur from the loss of a king than any relief from the removal of a tyrant.

It seems, then, that actions should arise more from public authority against the brutality of tyrants than from anybody's private initiative. In the first place, if by right a certain community is entitled to provide itself with a king, it is not unjust that the installed king be deposed by that same community or that his power be curtailed, if the royal power is abused tyrannically. Nor must it be thought that such a community acts unfaithfully when it deposes a tyrant, even if it had subjected itself to him beforehand in perpetuity. For he himself deserved this: since he had not acted faithfully in discharging the royal office, so the covenant made by his subjects might likewise not be kept. Thus the Romans deposed Tarquin the Proud as king (whom they had accepted as such), because of his tyranny and that of his sons, and replaced the royal power by a lesser, that is, consular, power. Thus, also, Domitian, who succeeded the most moderate emperor, his father Vespasian, and his brother Titus, was killed by the Roman Senate when he exercised tyrannical power, and everything that he did wickedly to the Romans was justly and usefully revoked and rendered invalid by Senatorial edict. Thus it was that Blessed John the Evangelist, who was exiled by that same Domitian to the island of Patmos, was sent back to Ephesus by Senatorial edict.

If, however, by right some superior authority is entitled to provide a king for a community, the remedy for the iniquity of the tyrant must be awaited from that party. Thus the Jews deferred to Caesar Augustus in their complaint about Archelaus, who had already begun to rule in Judea in place of his father Herod, having imitated his father's malice. At first, therefore, his power was diminished when his regal title was taken from him and half his kingdom was divided up between his two brothers. Then, when this did not in fact curtail his tyranny, he was sent into exile by Tiberius Caesar to Lyons, a city in Gaul.

But if no human help at all can be gotten against a tyrant, we must turn to the king of all, God, who is an aid in times of trouble. For He has such power that He can turn the cruel heart of a tyrant to gentleness. As Solomon says, "The heart of a king is in the hand of God; . . . He will turn it wherever He wills." He even turned to gentleness the cruelty of the king of Assyria, who was preparing death for the Jews. He it was who so converted cruel King Nebuchadnezzar to such piety that he became a herald of divine power. "Now, therefore," he said, "I Nebuchadnezzar praise, exalt and glorify the king of heaven because all His works are true and His ways are judgments, and He is able to lay low those who walk arrogantly."

The tyrant whom He indeed judges unworthy of conversion He can remove from our midst or reduce them to a state of weakness, as we learn from the Sage, "God has destroyed the thrones of proud leaders, and made the gentle to sit there in their stead." He it is who, seeing the affliction of His people in Egypt and hearing their cry, cast down the tyrant Pharaoh with his army into the sea. He it is who not only cast out the aforementioned Nebuchadnezzar from his regal throne because of his former arrogance but even cast him out from human society and changed him into the likeness of a beast.

Nor is His hand weakened so that He cannot free His people from tyranny. He promised His people through Isaiah that He would give them rest from toil and lashings and hard servitude under which they had previously served. And, through Ezechiel, He says, "I will deliver My flock from their mouth," (that is, from the mouth of those who feed only themselves). But that the people should merit that such a benefit come from God, it must stop sinning, because it is by divine permission that the impious receive their rule, as a punishment for sin, as the Lord says through Hosea, "I will give you a king in my wrath," and in Job it is said, "He makes a man who is a hypocrite to reign because of the sins of the people." Fault must therefore be purged away that the scourge of tyrants may cease.

X

MACHIAVELLI

Machiavelli's *The Prince* is possibly the most famous work ever written about politics. It presents a powerful and original vision of the nature of government and rulership. The *Discourses* is a good deal less famous. But it too presents a striking view of political life, one that seems both to support and to undermine the claims of *The Prince*. Indeed, formulating a clear picture of the relationship between these two great works has long been a challenging task for scholars.

In 1498, the independent city-state of Florence acquired a republican form of government. At the age of twenty-nine, Niccolò Machiavelli was appointed head of the second chancery, a position of some importance. For the next fourteen years, he became ever more deeply involved in the government. He eventually became the chief aid to Piero Soderini, Florence's "gonfalonier," or head of state, and in this position he exerted great influence and was able to observe the intricacies and intrigues of political life at the highest levels. Among Machiavelli's more important duties were diplomatic missions, so that he traveled frequently, both to other Italian city-states and throughout Europe, dealing with popes, government heads, and other important leaders. He made several trips to France, as well as Switzerland and Germany, and wrote influential reports on his experiences.

The evidence suggests that he was a deeply loyal citizen of Florence and an ardent supporter of republican government. For this loyalty he paid a price. With the support of the pope's army, Florence's republican regime was overthrown in 1512 and replaced by an antirepublican government led by the city's most important aristocratic family, the Medici. Machiavelli lost his job. A short while later, he was implicated in a plot against the Medici and therefore was imprisoned. Had he confessed his complicity, he would have been executed. But even under torture, he refused to confess. Released from prison, he retired to a small farm on the outskirts of Florence and began his literary career in earnest.

In 1513, Machiavelli wrote both *The Prince* and the *Discourses*. The first of these was formally dedicated to Lorenzo de' Medici, Florence's ruler, evidently in an attempt to ingratiate himself with the new government and to obtain thereby an official appointment of some kind. This effort failed. But in the ensuing years, he continued to court the favor of the Medici, eventually with some success. In 1520, he became the official historiographer of the city of Florence and later performed other, relatively minor tasks for the regime. He also produced major literary works, including a magisterial history of Florence, an important treatise on the art of war, and comic plays, of which the most famous, *The Mandrake*, is often thought to be a masterpiece.

In 1527, the Medici were overthrown, and republican government was reinstated. This time, however, Machiavelli's involvement with the Medici caused the republicans to distrust him. He was denied his old job in the chancery of the republican regime, and he died shortly thereafter, evidently in deep disappointment.

The Prince presents itself, and has often been read, as embodying an entirely new approach to politics, something radically at odds with the Western tradition of political thought as developed from Plato to Thomas Aquinas. It does not aim to provide an analysis of ethical right and wrong from the standpoint of natural law, nor to describe the essence of the legitimate and just state. Rather, its goal is to enumerate a set of practical rules or principles that would be useful to any leader in effectively wielding and maintaining political power. The goal, in other words, is pragmatic, and the premises are the premises of hard-nosed realism. Given the facts of human nature and the realities of the world in which humans live, what kinds of policies can best achieve the ends of politics? When his project is understood along these lines, it hardly seems unusual that Machiavelli would conclude that sometimes the prince needs to act in ways that seem unethical, callous, even brutal and horrifying.

Many readers have believed that Machiavelli himself delights in such unethical, callous, and brutal behavior, that he celebrates it or, at the very least, accepts it with a shrug, indifferent to the harm it may cause. It is largely from such an interpretation that the word *machiavellian* derives. Other readers, however, have found a rather different resonance. For them, *The Prince* is a work of moral anguish. It never denies that goodness, traditionally conceived, really is good. It does not seek to undermine or to deny standard Christian ethics. But it sees with clear eyes that in the real world, good behavior can sometimes lead to disaster and that in order to get beneficial results—results that truly serve the interest of the people and that help make it possible for them to live good lives—bad behavior may be required.

Unlike *The Prince*, the *Discourses* is plainly a republican work. Formally, it is a commentary on the first ten books of Livy's great history of Rome. As such, it celebrates the Roman republic—much as Cicero did—and seeks to describe the essential spirit of republican government. Central to this spirit is the idea of civic virtue or civic republicanism. A republic depends on the patriotism of its citizens, on their allegiance to the regime, on their involvement in the public life of the city, and on their willingness to take up arms in its defense. When a city has such a citizenry, then it can enjoy the kind of freedom, cohesion, and security that makes for a flourishing civic community.

Both of Machiavelli's principal political writings rest on a common, if unstated, philosophical theory of the state. The purpose and goal of any state is to provide order and security. A state that succeeds in doing so is a healthy state, regardless of the means that it employs. But a state that fails to do so is sick. It provides its citizens not with peace and safety, but instead with chaos, confusion, anarchy, and violence, all the things that make living a good life impossible. Achieving a healthy state is the end of politics, but it is always a difficult end to achieve: human affairs operate under the unpredictable influence of *fortuna*, or chance; accident and contingency constantly contrive to confound our best-laid plans, hence to thrust us into anarchy and civil violence. To overcome *fortuna* requires *virtù*—an exceptional combination of insight, foresight, courage, and character that can be found sometimes in princes, sometimes in the citizens of a republic. Politically speaking, *virtù* is our only salvation. But even this is apt to be only temporary, for Machiavelli is, in the end, a pessimist. *Fortuna* is constant, *virtù* occasional, even rare. The best we can hope for are princely or republican regimes that can give us temporary relief, that can provide, for a time, the kind of orderliness and security that makes a city sound.

Further Reading: For the intellectual and historical background to Machiavelli's work, see the major, two-volume study by Quentin Skinner, *The Foundations of Modern Political Thought* (1978), especially Volume 1. Skinner's *Machiavelli* (1981) is also a fine introduction. An extremely influential essay is Isaiah Berlin's "The Originality of Machiavelli," in *Studies in Machiavelli* (1972), edited by Myron P. Gilmore. For important specialized studies, see Harvey C. Mansfield, *Machiavelli's New Modes and Orders: A Study of the Discourses on Livy* (1979); Hannah Pitkin, *Fortune Is a Woman: Gender and Politics in the Thought of Niccolò Machiavelli* (1984); and Anthony J. Parel, *The Machiavellian Cosmos* (1992). For Machiavelli's importance in the history of political thought, see the extremely influential work by J. G. A. Pocock, *The Machiavellian Moment: Florentine Political Thought and the Atlantic Republican Tradition* (1975).

Niccolò Machiavelli
(1469–1527)

Letter to Francesco Vettori

To His Excellency the Florentine Ambassador to his Holiness the Pope, and my benefactor, Francesco Vettori, in Rome.

Your Excellency. "Favors from on high are always timely, never late." I say this because I had begun to think I had, if not lost, then mislaid your goodwill, for you had allowed so long to go by without writing to me, and I was in some uncertainty as to what the reason could be. All the explanations I could think of seemed to me worthless, except for the possibility that occurred to me, that you might have stopped writing to me because someone had written to tell you I was not taking proper care of your letters to me; but I knew that I had not been responsible for their being shown to anyone else, with the exception of Filippo and Paolo.

Anyway, I have now received your most recent letter of the 23rd of last month. I was delighted to learn you are fulfilling your official responsibilities without fussing and flapping. I encourage you to carry on like this, for anyone who sacrifices his own convenience in order to make others happy is bound to inconvenience himself, but can't be sure of receiving any thanks for it. And since fortune wants to control everything, she evidently wants to be left a free hand; meanwhile we should keep our own counsel and not get in her way, and wait until she allows human beings to have a say in the course of events. That will be the time for you to work harder, and keep a closer eye on events, and for me to leave my country house and say: "Here I am!"

Since I want to repay your kind gesture, I have no alternative but to describe to you in this letter of mine how I live my life. If you decide you'd like to swap my life for yours, I'll be happy to make a deal.

I am still in my country house: Since my recent difficulties began I have not been, adding them all together, more than twenty days in Florence. Until recently I have been setting bird snares with my own hands. I've been getting up before dawn, making the bird-lime, and setting out with a bundle of cages on my back, so I look like Geta when he comes back from the harbor laden down with Amphitryo's books. I always caught at least two thrushes, but never more than six. This is how I spent September; since then I am sorry to say I have had to give up my rather nasty and peculiar hobby, so I will describe the life I lead now.

I get up in the morning at daybreak and go to a wood of mine where I am having some timber felled. I stay there two hours to check on the work done during the preceding day and to chat to the woodcutters, who are always involved in some conflict, either among themselves or with the neighbors. I could tell you a thousand fine stories about my dealings over this wood, both with Frosino da Panzano and with others who wanted some of the timber. Frosino in particular had them supply some cords without mentioning it to me, and when I asked for payment he wanted to knock off ten lire he said I had owed him for four years, ever since he beat me at cards at Antonio Guicciardini's. I began to cut up rough; I threatened to charge with theft the wagon driver who had fetched the wood. However, Giovanni Machiavelli intervened, and got us to settle our differences. Batista Guicciardini, Filippo Ginori, Tommaso del Bene, and a number of other citizens each bought a cord from me when the cold winds were blowing. I made promises to all of them, and supplied one to Tommaso. But in Florence it turned out to be only half

Reprinted from Machiavelli, *Selected Political Writings*, edited and translated by David Wootton (Indianapolis: Hackett Publishing Company, 1994) by permission of the publisher.

a cord, because there were he, his wife, his servants, and his sons to stack it: They looked like Gabburra on a Thursday when, assisted by his workmen, he slaughters an ox. Then, realizing I wasn't the one who was getting a good deal, I told the others I had run out of wood. They've all complained bitterly about it; especially Battista, who thinks this is as bad as anything else that has happened as a result of the battle of Prato.

When I leave the wood I go to a spring, and from there to check my bird-nets. I carry a book with me: Dante, or Petrarch, or one of the minor poets, perhaps Tibullus, Ovid, or someone like that. I read about their infatuations and their love affairs, reminisce about my own, and enjoy my reveries for a while. Then I set out on the road to the inn. I chat to those who pass by, asking them for news about the places they come from. I pick up bits and pieces of information, and study the differing tastes and various preoccupations of mankind. It's lunchtime before I know it. I sit down with my family to eat such food as I can grow on my wretched farm or pay for with the income from my tiny inheritance. Once I have eaten I go back to the inn. The landlord will be there, and, usually, the butcher, the miller, and a couple of kiln owners. With them I muck about all day, playing card games. We get into endless arguments and are constantly calling each other names. Usually we only wager a quarter, and yet you could hear us shouting if you were in San Casciano. So, in the company of these bumpkins, I keep my brain from turning moldy, and put up with the hostility fate has shown me. I am happy for fate to see to what depths I have sunk, for I want to know if she will be ashamed of herself for what she has done.

When evening comes, I go back home, and go to my study. On the threshold I take off my work clothes, covered in mud and filth, and put on the clothes an ambassador would wear. Decently dressed, I enter the ancient courts of rulers who have long since died. There I am warmly welcomed, and I feed on the only food I find nourishing, and was born to savor. I am not ashamed to talk to them, and to ask them to explain their actions. And they, out of kindness, answer me. Four hours go by without my feeling any anxiety. I forget every worry. I am no longer afraid of poverty, or frightened of death. I live entirely through them.

And because Dante says there is no point in studying unless you remember what you have learned, I have made notes of what seem to me the most important things I have learned in my dialogue with the dead, and written a little book *On princedoms* in which I go as deeply as I can into the questions relevant to my subject. I discuss what a principality is, how many types of principality there are, how one acquires them, how one holds onto them, why one loses them. And if any of my little productions have ever pleased you, then this one ought not to displease you; and a ruler, especially a new ruler, ought to be delighted by it. Consequently, I have addressed it to His Highness Giuliano. Filippo Casavecchia has seen it; he can give you a preliminary report, both on the text, and on the discussions I have had with him: though I am still adding to the text and polishing it.

You may well wish, Your Excellency, that I should give up this life, and come and enjoy yours with you. I will do so if I can; what holds me back at the moment is some business that won't take me more than six weeks to finish. Though I am a bit concerned the Soderini family is there, and I will be obliged, if I come, to visit them and socialize with them. My concern is that I might intend my return journey to end at my own house, but find myself instead dismounting at the prison gates. For although this government is well established and solidly based, still it is new, and consequently suspicious, nor is there a shortage of clever fellows who, in order to get a reputation like Pagolo Bertini's, would put me in prison, and leave me to worry about how to get out. I beg you to persuade me this fear is irrational, and then I will make every effort to come and visit you before six weeks are up.

I have discussed my little book with Filippo, asking him whether it was a good idea to present it or not; and if I ought to present it, then whether I should deliver it in person, or whether I should send it through you. My concern is that if I do not deliver it in person Giuliano may not read it; even worse, that chap Ardinghelli may claim the credit for my latest effort. In favor of presenting it is the fact that the wolf is at the door, for my funds are running down, and I cannot continue like this much longer without becoming so poor I lose face. In any case, I would like their lordships, the Medici, to start putting me to use, even if they only assign me some menial task, for if, once I was in their employment, I did not win their favor, I would have only myself to blame. As for my book, if they were to read it, they would see the fifteen years I have spent studying statecraft have not been wasted: I haven't been asleep at my desk or playing cards. Anyone should be keen to employ someone who has had plenty of experience and has learned from the mistakes he made at his previous employers' expense. As for my integrity, nobody should question it: For I have always kept my word, and I am not going to start breaking it now.

Someone who has been honest and true for forty-three years, as I have been, isn't going to be able to change character. And that I am honest and true is evident from my poverty.

So: I would like you to write to me again and let me have your opinion on this matter. I give you my regards. Best wishes.

Niccolò Machiavegli in Florence
10 December 1513.

The Prince

Niccolò Machiavelli to His Magnificence Lorenzo de' Medici

Those who wish to acquire favor with a ruler most often approach him with those among their possessions that are most valuable in their eyes, or that they are confident will give him pleasure. So rulers are often given horses, armor, cloth of gold, precious stones, and similar ornaments that are thought worthy of their social eminence. Since I want to offer myself to your Magnificence, along with something that will symbolize my desire to give you obedient service, I have found nothing among my possessions I value more, or would put a higher price upon, than an understanding of the deeds of great men, acquired through a lengthy experience of contemporary politics and through an uninterrupted study of the classics. Since I have long thought about and studied the question of what makes for greatness, and have now summarized my conclusions on the subject in a little book, it is this I send your Magnificence.

And although I recognize this book is unworthy to be given to Yourself, yet I trust that out of kindness you will accept it, taking account of the fact there is no greater gift I can present to you than the opportunity to understand, after a few hours of reading, everything I have learned over the course of so many years, and have undergone so many discomforts and dangers to discover. I have not ornamented this book with rhetorical turns of phrase, or stuffed it with pretentious and magnificent words, or made use of allurements and embellishments that are irrelevant to my purpose, as many authors do. For my intention has been that

my book should be without pretensions, and should rely entirely on the variety of the examples and the importance of the subject to win approval.

I hope it will not be thought presumptuous for someone of humble and lowly status to dare to discuss the behavior of rulers and to make recommendations regarding policy. Just as those who paint landscapes set up their easels down in the valley in order to portray the nature of the mountains and the peaks, and climb up into the mountains in order to draw the valleys, similarly in order to properly understand the behavior of the lower classes one needs to be a ruler, and in order to properly understand the behavior of rulers one needs to be a member of the lower classes.

I therefore beg your Magnificence to accept this little gift in the spirit in which it is sent. If you read it carefully and think over what it contains, you will recognize it is an expression of my dearest wish, which is that you achieve the greatness your good fortune and your other fine qualities seem to hold out to you. And if your Magnificence, high up at the summit as you are, should occasionally glance down into these deep valleys, you will see I have to put up with the unrelenting malevolence of undeserved ill fortune.

Chapter One: How many types of principality are there? And how are they acquired?

All states, all forms of government that have had and continue to have authority over men, have been and are either republics or principalities. And principalities are either hereditary, when their rulers' ancestors have long been their rulers, or they are new. And if they are new, they are either entirely new, as was Milan for Francesco Sforza, or they are like limbs added on to the hereditary state of the ruler who acquires them, as the kingdom of Naples has been added on to the kingdom of Spain. Those dominions that are acquired by a ruler are either used to living under the rule of one man, or accustomed to being free; and they are either acquired with soldiers belonging to others, or with one's own; either through fortune or through strength [*virtù*].

Chapter Two: On hereditary principalities.

I will leave behind me the discussion of republics, for I have discussed them at length elsewhere. I will concern myself only with principalities. The different types of principality I have mentioned will be the threads from which I will weave my account. I will debate how these different types of principality should be governed and defended.

I maintain, then, it is much easier to hold on to hereditary states, which are accustomed to being governed by the family that now rules them, than it is to hold on to new acquisitions. All one has to do is preserve the structures established by one's forebears, and play for time if things go badly. For, indeed, an hereditary ruler, if he is of no more than normal resourcefulness, will never lose his state unless some extraordinary and overwhelming force appears that can take it away from him; and even then, the occupier has only to have a minor setback, and the original ruler will get back to power.

Let us take a contemporary Italian example: The Duke of Ferrara was able to resist the assaults of the Venetians in '84, and of Pope Julius in 1510, only because his family was long established as rulers of that state. For a ruler who inherits power has few reasons and less cause to give offense; as a consequence he is more popular; and, as long as he does not have exceptional vices that make him hateful, it is to be expected he will naturally have the goodwill of his people. Because the state has belonged to his family from one generation to another, memories of how they came to power, and motives to overthrow them, have worn away. For every change in government creates grievances that those who wish to bring about further change can exploit.

Chapter Three: On mixed principalities.

New principalities are the ones that present problems. And first of all, if the whole of the principality is not new, but rather a new part has been added on to the old, creating a whole one may term "mixed," instability derives first of all from a natural difficulty that is to be found in all new principalities. The problem is that people willingly change their ruler, believing the change will be for the better; and this belief leads them to take up arms against him. But they are mistaken, and they soon find out in practice they have only made things worse. The reason for this, too, is natural and typical: You always have to give offense to those over whom you acquire power when you become a new ruler, both by imposing troops upon them, and by countless other injuries that follow as necessary consequences of the acquisition of power. Thus, you make enemies of all those to whom you have given offense in acquiring power, and in addition you cannot keep the goodwill of those who have put you in power, for you cannot satisfy their aspirations as they thought you would. At the same time you cannot use heavy-handed methods against them, for you are obliged to them. Even if you have an overwhelmingly powerful army, you will have needed the support of the locals to take control of the province. This is why Louis XII of France lost Milan as quickly as he gained it. All that was needed to take it from him the first time were Ludovico's own troops. For those who had opened the gates to him, finding themselves mistaken in their expectations and disappointed in their hopes of future benefit, could not put up with the burdensome rule of a new sovereign.

Of course it is true that, after a ruler has regained power in rebel territories, he is much more likely to hang on to it. For the rebellion gives him an excuse, and he is able to take firmer measures to secure his position, punishing delinquents, checking up on suspects, and taking precautions where needed. So, if the first time the King of France lost Milan all that was needed to throw him out was Duke Ludovico growling on his borders, to throw him out a second time it took the whole world united against him, and the destruction or expulsion from Italy of his armies. We have seen why this was so.

Nevertheless, he lost Milan both times. We have discussed why he was almost bound to lose it the first time; now we must discuss why he managed to lose it the second. What remedies should he have adopted? What can someone in the King of France's position do to hold on to an acquisition more effectively than he did?

Let me start by saying these territories that are newly added on to a state that is already securely in the possession of a ruler are either in the same geographical region as his existing possessions and speak the same language, or they are not. When they are, it is quite straightforward to hold on to them, especially if they are not used to governing themselves. In order to get a secure hold on them one need merely eliminate the surviving members of the family of their previous rulers. In other respects one should keep things as they were, respecting established traditions. If the old territories and the new have similar customs, the new subjects will live quietly. Thus, Burgundy, Brittany, Gascony, and Normandy have for long quietly submitted to France. Although they do not all speak exactly the same language, nevertheless their customs are similar, and they can easily put up with each other. He who acquires neighboring territories in this way, intending to hold on to them, needs to see to two things: First, he must ensure their previous ruler has no heirs; and second, he must not alter their old laws or impose new taxes. If he follows these principles they will quickly become inseparable from his hereditary domains.

But when you acquire territories in a region that has a different language, different customs, and different institutions, then you really have problems, and you need to have great good fortune and great resourcefulness if you are going to hold on to them. One of the best policies, and one of the most effective, is for the new ruler to go and live in his new territories. This will make his grasp on them more secure and more lasting. This is what the Sultan of Turkey has done in Greece. All the other measures he has taken to hold on to that territory would have been worthless if he had not settled there. For if you are on the spot, you can identify difficulties as they arise, and can quickly take appropriate action. If you are at a distance, you only learn of them when they have become serious, and when it is too late to put matters right. Moreover, if you are there in person, the territory will not be plundered by your officials. The subjects can

appeal against their exactions to you, their ruler. As a consequence they have more reason to love you, if they behave themselves, and, if they do not, more reason to fear you. Anyone who wants to attack the territory from without will have to think twice, so that, if you live there, you will be unlucky indeed to lose it.

The second excellent policy is to send colonies to settle in one or two places; they will serve to tie your new subjects down. For it is necessary either to do this, or to garrison your new territory with a substantial army. Colonies do not cost much to run. You will have to lay out little or nothing to establish and maintain them. You will only offend those from whom you seize fields and houses to give to your settlers, and they will be only a tiny minority within the territory. Those whom you offend will be scattered and become poor, so they will be unable to do you any harm. All the rest will remain uninjured, and so ought to remain quiet; at the same time they will be afraid to make a false move, for they will have before them the fate of their neighbors as an example of what may happen to them. I conclude such colonies are economical, reliable, and do not give excessive grounds for resistance; those who suffer by their establishment are in no position to resist, being poor and scattered, as I have said. There is a general rule to be noted here: People should either be caressed or crushed. If you do them minor damage they will get their revenge; but if you cripple them there is nothing they can do. If you need to injure someone, do it in such a way that you do not have to fear their vengeance.

But if, instead of establishing colonies, you rely on an occupying army, it costs a good deal more, for your army will eat up all your revenues from your new territory. As a result, your acquisition will be a loss, not a gain. Moreover, your army will make more enemies than colonies would, for the whole territory will suffer from it, the burden moving from one place to another as the troops are billeted first here, then there. Everybody suffers as a result, and everyone becomes your enemy. And these are enemies who can hurt you, for they remain, even if beaten, in their own homes. In every respect, then, an occupying army is a liability, while colonies are an asset.

In addition, anyone who finds himself with territory in a region with different customs from those of his hereditary possessions should make himself the leader and protector of neighboring powers who are weaker than he is, and should set out to weaken his powerful neighbors. He should also take care no outsider as powerful as himself has any occasion to intervene. Outside powers will always be urged to intervene by those in the region who are discontented, either because their ambitions are unsatisfied, or because they are afraid of the dominant powers. So, long ago, the Aetolians invited the Romans into Greece; and, indeed, in every other region the Romans occupied they were invited by local people. It is in the nature of things that, as soon as a foreign power enters into a region, all the local states that are weak rally to it, for they are driven by the envy they have felt for the state that has exercised predominance over them. As a result, the invader does not have to make any effort at all to win over these lesser states, because they all immediately ally themselves to the territory he has acquired there. He only has to take care they do not become too strong and exercise too much influence. He can easily, with his own troops and his new allies' support, strike down the powerful states, and make himself the arbiter of all the affairs of the region. Anyone who does not see how to play this role successfully will quickly lose what he has gained, and, while he holds it, will have innumerable difficulties and vexations.

The Romans, in the regions they seized, obeyed these principles admirably. They settled colonies; were friendly towards the weaker rulers, without building up their strength; broke the powerful; and did not allow foreign powers to build up support. Let me take just the region of Greece as an example. The Romans favored the Acheans and the Aetolians; they crushed the Kingdom of Macedon; they expelled Antiochus from the region. Despite the credit the Acheans and the Aetolians had earned with them, they never allowed them to build up any independent power; nor did the blandishments of Philip ever persuade them to treat him as a friend before they had destroyed his power; nor did Antiochus's strength intimidate them into permitting him to retain any territory in that region.

The Romans did in such matters what all wise rulers ought to do. It is necessary not only to pay attention to immediate crises, but to foresee those that will come, and to make every effort to prevent them. For if you see them coming well in advance, then you can easily take the appropriate action to remedy them, but if you wait until they are right on top of you, then the prescription will no longer take effect, because the disease is too far advanced. In this matter it is as doctors say of consumption: In the beginning the disease is easy to cure, difficult to diagnose; but, after a while, if it has not been diagnosed and treated early, it becomes easy to diagnose and hard to cure. So, too, in politics, for if you foresee problems while they are far off (which only a prudent man is able to do) they can easily be dealt with; but when, because you have failed to see them coming, you allow them to grow to the point that anyone can recognize them, then it is too late to do anything.

The Romans always looked ahead and took action to remedy problems before they developed. They never postponed action in order to avoid a war, for they understood you cannot escape wars, and when you put them off only your opponents benefit. Thus, they wanted to have a war with Philip and Antiochus in Greece, so as not to have one with them in Italy. At the time they could have avoided having a war at all, but this they did not want. They never approved the saying that nowadays is repeated *ad nauseam* by the wise: "Take advantage of the passage of time." Rather they relied on their strength [*virtù*] and prudence, for in time anything can happen, and the passage of time brings good mixed with evil, and evil mixed with good.

But let us return to the kings of France, and let us see whether they followed any of the principles I have outlined. I will discuss Louis, not Charles, for, since Louis held territory in Italy for a longer time, we can have a better understanding of the policies he was following. We will see he did the opposite of what one ought to do in order to hold on to territory in a region unlike one's hereditary lands.

King Louis was brought into Italy by the ambition of the Venetians, who hoped to gain half of the territory of Lombardy as a result of his invasion. I do not want to criticize the king's decision to ally with the Venetians. Since he wanted to get a foothold in Italy, and since he had no friends in that region (rather the opposite, for all the gateways to Italy were closed against him as a result of the actions of King Charles), he was obliged to take what allies he could get. His decision would have been a good one, if he had done everything else right. Now when the king had conquered Lombardy, he at once recovered the reputation Charles had lost for him. Genoa gave itself up and the Florentines became his friends. Everybody came forward to meet him as he advanced and sought his friendship: the Marquis of Mantua, the Duke of Ferrara, Bentivoglio, the Countess of Forlì, the rulers of Faenza, Pesaro, Rimini, Camerino, Piombino, the citizens of Lucca, Pisa, and Siena. Then the Venetians were able to see the risk they had chosen to run; in order to acquire a couple of fortresses in Lombardy, they had made the King of France master of two-thirds of Italy.

Now consider how easy it would have been for the king to preserve his authority in Italy if he had followed the principles I have laid out, and if he had protected and defended all his new friends. They were numerous, weak, and fearful, some afraid of the Church, some of the Venetians, and so had no choice but to remain loyal to him; and with their help he could easily have overwhelmed the surviving great powers. But he had no sooner got to Milan than he did the opposite, coming to the assistance of Pope Alexander so he could occupy the Romagna. He did not realize that by this decision he weakened himself, alienating his friends and those who had flung themselves into his arms; and at the same time strengthened the Church, adding to its already extensive spiritual authority an increased temporal power. And having made one error he was forced to make another, for, in order to put a stop to Alexander's ambitions, and to prevent his gaining control of Tuscany, he was obliged to march into Italy once more. Nor was he satisfied with having strengthened the Church and thrown away his alliances, but in addition, because he wanted the Kingdom of Naples, he agreed to divide it with the King of Spain. Where he had been all-powerful in Italy, he now shared his power with another, giving ambitious rulers in the region and those who were discontented with him someone to whom they could turn. Where he could have left in the Kingdom of Naples a king who was on his payroll, he threw him out, and replaced him with someone who might aspire to kick out the French.

It is perfectly natural and normal to want to acquire new territory; and whenever men do what will succeed towards this end, they will be praised, or at least not condemned. But when they are not in a position to make gains, and try nevertheless, then they are making a mistake, and deserve condemnation. If the King of France had the military capacity to attack Naples, he should have done so; if he did not have it, he should not have proposed to partition the territory. The division of Lombardy between France and Venice was justified because it gave the French a foothold in Italy; the division of Naples was blameworthy, for it was not justifiable on the same grounds.

Thus, Louis had made the following five mistakes: He wasted his alliance with the lesser states; he increased the strength of one of the more powerful Italian states; he invited an extremely powerful foreign state to intervene in Italy; he did not go and live in Italy; he did not establish settlements there. Even these mistakes might have had no evil consequences while he lived, had he not made a sixth, attacking the Venetians. Had he not strengthened the Church and brought the Spanish into Italy, then it would have been reasonable and appropriate to attack them; but having done what he had done, he should never have given his consent to a policy aimed at their destruction. For as long as they remained powerful, the others would never have been prepared to undertake an attack upon Lombardy. For the Venetians would not have consented to Lombardy's falling into the hands of others, and not themselves; while the others would not have wanted to take Lombardy from the King of France only to give it to the Venetians, and would not have had the courage to try to take it away from both of them.

And if someone were to reply that King Louis allowed Alexander to take the Romagna, and the King of Spain to have the Kingdom of Naples, in order to avoid a war, I would answer as I did above: One should never allow a problem to develop in order to avoid a war, for you end up not avoiding the war, but deferring it to a time that will be less favorable. And if others were to appeal to the promise the king had given to the pope, to help him seize the Romagna in return for the pope's giving him a divorce and making the Bishop of Rouen a cardinal, I would reply with what I will say later on the subject of whether and to what extent rulers should keep their word.

Thus, King Louis lost Lombardy because he did not follow any of the policies others have adopted when they have established predominance within a region and have wanted to hold on to it. There is nothing remarkable about what happened: It is entirely natural and predictable. I spoke about these matters with the Cardinal of Rouen in Nantes, when Valentino (as Cesare Borgia, son of Pope Alexander, was commonly called) was taking possession of the Romagna. The cardinal said to me that the Italians did not understand war; so I told him that the French did not understand politics, for if they did, they would not allow the church to acquire so much power. And in practice we have seen that the strength of the papacy and of the King of Spain within Italy has been brought about by the King of France, and they in turn have been the cause of his own ruin. From this one can draw a general conclusion that will never (or hardly ever) be proved wrong: He who is the cause of someone else's becoming powerful is the agent of his own destruction; for he makes his protegé powerful either through his own skill or through his own strength, and either of these must provoke his protegé's mistrust once he has become powerful.

Chapter Four: Why the kingdom of Darius, which Alexander occupied, did not rebel against his successors after Alexander's death.

When you think of the difficulties associated with trying to hold on to a newly acquired state, you might well be puzzled: Since Alexander the Great had conquered Asia in the space of a few years, and then died when he had scarcely had time to take possession of it, at that point you would expect the whole state to rebel. Nevertheless, Alexander's successors maintained possession of it and had no difficulty in keeping hold of it, beyond the conflicts that sprung up between themselves as a result of their own ambitions. My explanation is that the principalities recorded in history have been governed in two different ways: either by a single individual, and everyone else has been his servant, and they have helped to govern his kingdom as ministers, appointed by his grace and benevolence; or by a monarch together with barons, who, not by concession of the ruler, but by virtue of their noble lineage, hold that rank. Such barons have their own territories and their own subjects: subjects who recognize them as their lords and feel a natural affection for them. In those states that are governed by a single individual and his servants, the sovereign has

more authority in his own hands; for in all his territories there is no one recognized as having a right to rule except him alone; and if his subjects obey anyone else, they do so because he is the ruler's minister and representative, and they do not feel any particular loyalty to these subordinate authorities.

In our own day the obvious examples of these two types of ruler are the Sultan of Turkey and the King of France. All the kingdom of Turkey is ruled by a single monarch, and everyone else is his servant. He divides his kingdom into sanjaks, sending administrators, whom he replaces and transfers as he thinks best, to rule them. But the King of France is placed among a multitude of long-established nobles, whose rights are recognized by their subjects and who are loved by them. They have their own inherited privileges, and the king cannot take them away without endangering himself. If you compare these two states, you will realize it would be difficult to seize the sultan's kingdom, but, once you had got control of it, it would be very easy to hold on to it.

It would be difficult to occupy the lands of the sultan for two reasons: The local authorities of that kingdom will not invite you to invade, nor can you hope those around the ruler will rebel, making your task easier. And this for the reasons I have explained. For, since they are all his slaves, and indebted to him, it is harder to corrupt them; and even if you can corrupt them, they are not going to be much use to you, for they cannot command the obedience of the people, as I have explained. Consequently, anyone attacking the sultan must expect to find the Turks united in his defense and must rely more on his own strength than on the disorder of his opponents. But once he has defeated them and has destroyed their forces on the field of battle so completely they cannot muster an army, then he has no one to worry about except the sultan's close relatives. Once he has got rid of them, then there is no one left for him to fear, for there is no one else with influence over the people. Just as the invader, before his victory, had no reason to hope for support, so, after his victory, he has no reason to fear opposition.

The opposite is true in kingdoms governed like that of France. For it is easy to invade them, once one has gained the support of some local noble. For in such kingdoms one can always find malcontents who hope to benefit from innovation. These, as we have seen, can ease your entrance into the state and help you win victory. But then, when you try to hold on to power, you will find the nobility, both those who have been your allies and those you have defeated, present you with an infinity of problems. It simply is not sufficient to kill the ruler and his close relatives, for the rest of the nobility will survive to provide leadership for new insurrections. You cannot win their loyalty or wipe them out, so you will always be in danger of losing your kingdom should anything go wrong.

Now if you ask yourself what sort of state it was Darius ruled, you will see it was similar to that of the sultan. So it was necessary for Alexander, first to take on his forces and seize control of the territory. Once he was victorious, and Darius was dead, Alexander had a firm grip on his new lands, for the reasons I have given. And his successors, if they had stayed united, could have enjoyed them at their leisure; nor was there any resistance to them in that kingdom, apart from their own conflicts with one another. But states that are organized after the French model cannot be held onto, once seized, with such ease. This is why there were frequent rebellions in Spain, France, and Greece against the Romans. For there were many rulers in those territories, and as long as people remembered them, the Romans were always unsure of their grip. Once the memory of these rulers had faded completely away, thanks to the long duration of Roman rule, they became secure in their possession. Even after that, each faction among the Romans, when they fought among themselves, could call on the support of a section of those provinces, depending on the influence they had built up within them. The subjects of these territories, because their former rulers had no heirs, had no loyalties except to Roman leaders. Once you have considered all these matters, you will not be at all surprised at the ease with which Alexander held on to Asia or at the difficulties other conquerors (one might take Pyrrhus as one example among many) have had in keeping control of their acquisitions. The crucial factor in these differing outcomes is not the strength [*virtù*] or weakness of the conqueror but the contrasting character of the societies that have been conquered.

Chapter Five: How you should govern cities or kingdoms that, before you acquired them, lived under their own laws.

When the states one acquires by conquest are accustomed to living under their own laws and in freedom, there are three policies one can follow in order to hold on to them: The first is to lay them waste; the second is to go and live there in person; the third is to let them continue to live under their own laws, make them pay you, and create there an administrative and political elite who will remain loyal to you. For since the elite are the creation of the head of state, its members know they cannot survive without both his friendship and his power, and they know it is in their interest to do everything to sustain it. It is easier to rule a city that is used to being self-governing by employing its own citizens than by other means, assuming you do not wish to destroy it.

Examples are provided by the Spartans and the Romans. The Spartans took Athens and Thebes, establishing oligarchies there. However, they lost them again. The Romans, in order to hold on to Capua, Carthage, and Numantia razed them and never lost them. They sought to govern Greece according to more or less the same policies as those used by Sparta, letting the Greek cities rule themselves and enforce their own laws, but the policy failed, so in the end they were obliged to demolish many cities in that territory in order to hold on to them. The simple truth is there is no reliable way of holding on to a city and the territory around it, short of demolishing the city itself. He who becomes the ruler of a city that is used to living under its own laws and does not knock it down, must expect to be knocked down by it. Whenever it rebels, it will find strength in the language of liberty and will seek to restore its ancient constitution. Neither the passage of time nor good treatment will make its citizens forget their previous liberty. No matter what one does, and what precautions one takes, if one does not scatter and drive away the original inhabitants, one will not destroy the memory of liberty or the attraction of the old institutions. As soon as there is a crisis, they will seek to restore them. This is what happened in Pisa after it had been enslaved by the Florentines for a hundred years.

But when cities or provinces are used to being ruled by a monarch, and one has wiped out his relatives and descendants, then matters are very different. They are used to being obedient. Their old ruler is gone, and they cannot agree among themselves as to who should replace him. They do not know how to rule themselves. The result is that they are slower to take up arms, and it is easier for a new ruler to win them over and establish himself securely in power. But in former republics there is more vitality, more hatred, more desire for revenge. The memory of their former freedom gives them no rest, no peace. So the best thing to do is to demolish them or to go and live there oneself.

Chapter Six: About new kingdoms acquired with one's own armies and one's own skill [*virtù*].

No one should be surprised if, in talking about completely new kingdoms (that is, states that are governed by someone who was not a ruler before, and were themselves not previously principalities), I point to the greatest of men as examples to follow. For men almost always walk along the beaten path, and what they do is almost always an imitation of what others have done before. But you cannot walk exactly in the footsteps of those who have gone before, nor is it easy to match the skill [*virtù*] of those you have chosen to imitate. Consequently, a prudent man will always try to follow in the footsteps of great men and imitate those who have been truly outstanding, so that, if he is not quite as skillful [*virtù*] as they, at least some of their ability may rub off on him. One should be like an experienced archer, who, trying to hit someone at a distance and knowing the range [*virtù*] of his bow, aims at a point above his target, not so his arrow will strike the point he is aiming at, but so, by aiming high, he can reach his objective.

I maintain that, in completely new kingdoms, the new ruler has more or less difficulty in keeping hold of power depending on whether he is more or less skillful [*virtuoso*]. Now you only find yourself in this situation, a private individual only becomes a ruler, if you are either lucky, or skillful [*virtù*]. Both luck and skill enable you to overcome difficulties. Nevertheless, he who relies least on luck has the best prospect of success. One advantage is common to any completely new sovereign: Because he has no other

territories, he has no choice but to come in person and live in his new kingdom. Let us look at those who through their own skill [*virtù*], and not merely through chance, have become rulers. In my view, the greatest have been Moses, Cyrus, Romulus, Theseus, and others like them.

Obviously, we should not discuss Moses' skill, for he was a mere agent, following the instructions given him by God. So he should be admired, not for his own skill, but for that grace that made him worthy to talk with God. But let us discuss Cyrus and the others who have acquired existing kingdoms or founded new ones. You will find them all admirable. And if you look at the actions and strategies of each one of them, you will find they do not significantly differ from those of Moses, who could not have had a better teacher. If you look at their deeds and their lives, you will find they were dependent on chance only for their first opportunity. They seized their chance to make of it what they wanted. Without that first opportunity their strength [*virtù*] of purpose would never have been revealed. Without their strength [*virtù*] of purpose, the opportunity they were offered would not have amounted to anything.

Thus, it was necessary for Moses to find the people of Israel in Egypt, enslaved and oppressed by the Egyptians, so they, in order to escape from slavery, would be prepared to follow him. It was essential for Romulus to have no future in Alba, it was appropriate he should have been exposed at birth, otherwise he would not have formed the ambition of becoming King of Rome and succeeded in founding that nation. It was necessary that Cyrus should find the Persians hostile to the rule of the Medes, and the Medes weak and effeminate from too much peace. Theseus could not have demonstrated his strength of purpose [*virtù*] if he had not found the Athenians scattered. These opportunities made these men lucky; but it was their remarkable political skill [*virtù*] that enabled them to recognize these opportunities for what they were. Thanks to them their nations were ennobled and blessed with good fortune.

Those who become rulers through strength of purpose [*vie virtuose*], as they did, acquire their kingdoms with difficulty, but they hold on to them with ease. And much of the difficulty they have in getting to power derives from the new institutions and customs they are obliged to establish in order to found their governments and make them secure. One ought to pause and consider the fact that there is nothing harder to undertake, nothing more likely of failure, nothing more risky to pull off, than to set oneself up as a leader who plans to found a new system of government. For the founder makes enemies of all those who are doing well under the old system, and has only lukewarm support from those who hope to do well under the new one. The weakness of their support springs partly from their fear of their adversaries, who have the law on their side, partly from their own want of faith. For men do not truly believe in new things until they have had practical experience of them. So it is that, whenever those who are enemies of the new order have a chance to attack it, they do so ferociously, while the others defend it half-heartedly. So the new ruler is in danger, along with his supporters.

It is necessary, however, if we are going to make sense of his situation, to find out if our innovator stands on his own feet, or depends on others to prop him up. That is, we need to know if he is obliged to try to obtain his objectives by pleading, or whether he can resort to force. In the first case, he is bound to come to a bad end, and won't achieve anything. But when he can stand on his own feet, and can resort to force, then he can usually overcome the dangers he faces. Thus it is that all armed prophets are victorious, and disarmed ones are crushed. For there is another problem: People are by nature inconstant. It is easy to persuade them of something, but it is difficult to stop them from changing their minds. So you have to be prepared for the moment when they no longer believe: Then you have to force them to believe. Moses, Cyrus, Theseus, and Romulus would not have been able to make their peoples obey their new structures of authority for long if they had been unarmed. This is what happened, in our own day, to Friar Girolamo Savonarola. He and his new constitution were destroyed as soon as the multitude began to stop believing in him. He had no way of stiffening the resolution of those who had been believers or of forcing disbelievers to obey.

Thus the founders of new states have immense difficulties to overcome, and dangers beset their path, dangers they must overcome by skill and strength of purpose [*virtù*]. But, once they have overcome them, and they have begun to be idolized, having got rid of those who were jealous of their superior qualities, they are established, they are powerful, secure, honored, happy.

We have looked at some noble examples, and to them I want to add one less remarkable. Nevertheless, it has some points of similarity to them, and I want it to stand for all the other lesser examples I could have chosen. My example is Hiero of Syracuse. He was a private individual who became ruler of Syracuse. He, too, did not depend on luck once he had been given his opportunity. The people of Syracuse were oppressed and elected him as their military commander; so he deserved to be made their ruler. He was so remarkable [*di tanta virtù*], even before he became a ruler, history records "that he had everything one would look for in a king, except a kingdom." He disbanded the old militia and instituted a new one. Dropped his old friends and chose new ones. Since both his friends and his soldiers were his creatures, he had laid the foundations for constructing any political system he chose. He, too, had difficulties enough to overcome in acquiring power, and few in holding on to it.

Chapter Seven: About new principalities that are acquired with the forces of others and with good luck.

Those who, having started as private individuals, become rulers merely out of good luck, acquire power with little trouble but have a hard time holding on to it. They have no problems on the road to power, because they leap over all the obstacles; but dangers crowd around them once they are in power. I am talking about people who are given a state, either in return for money, or out of the goodwill of him who hands it over to them. This happened to many individuals in Greece, in the cities of Ionia and the Hellespont, who were made rulers by Darius, who wanted them to hold their cities for his own greater safety and glory. So, too, with those who, having been private citizens, were made emperors of Rome because they had corrupted the soldiers. Such rulers are entirely dependent on the goodwill and good fortune of whoever has given them power. Good will and good fortune are totally unreliable and capricious. Such rulers do not know how to hold on to their position and cannot do so. They do not know how, because they have always been private citizens, and only a brilliant and immensely skillful [*di grande virtù*] man is likely to know how to command without having had training and experience. They cannot because they have no troops of their own on whose loyalty and commitment they can count.

Moreover, states that spring up overnight, like all other things in nature that are born and grow in a hurry, cannot have their roots deep in the soil, so they shrivel up in the first drought, blow over in the first storm. Unless, as I have said, those who are suddenly made into rulers are of such extraordinary capacity [*virtù*] they can work out on the spot how to hold on to the gift fortune has unexpectedly handed them; and those preparations the others made before they became rulers, they must find a way of making after the event.

I want to add to the one and the other of these two ways of becoming a ruler, by skill [*virtù*] or by luck, two examples drawn from the events that have occurred in our own lifetimes: the examples of Francesco Sforza and Cesare Borgia. Francesco, by using the right methods and consummate skill [*virtù*], started out as a private citizen and ended up as Duke of Milan. And what he had acquired with painstaking effort, he held on to without trouble. On the other hand Cesare Borgia, who was called Duke Valentino by the common people, acquired his state thanks to the good fortune of his father, and when that came to an end he lost it. This despite the fact he used every technique and did all the things a prudent and skillful [*virtuoso*] man ought to do, to entrench himself in those territories that the arms and fortune of others had acquired for him. For, as I said above, he who does not prepare the foundations first can (in principle), if he is immensely skillful [*virtù*], make up for it later, although the architect will find catching up a painful process, and there is a real danger the building will collapse. So, if we look at all the things Borgia did, we will see he had laid solid foundations for future power. I do not think it irrelevant to discuss his policies, because I cannot think of any better example I could offer a new ruler than that of his actions. And if his strategy did not lead to success, this was not his fault; his failure was due to extraordinary and exceptional hostility on the part of fortune.

Pope Alexander VI, in setting out to make his son the duke into a ruler, was faced with considerable immediate and long-term difficulties. In the first place, he could find no way of making him the lord of any territory, except territory that belonged to the church. And he knew if he took land from the church to give to Cesare, he would have to overcome the opposition of the Duke of Milan, and also of the Venetians, for both Faenza and Rimini were already under Venetian protection. Secondly, he saw the armed forces of Italy, and particularly those he could hope to employ, were under the control of individuals who had reason to fear any increase in papal power. Consequently, he could not regard them as reliable. He could not trust the Orsini, the Colonna, or their associates, but there was no one else to whom he could turn. So it was necessary to break out of this framework, and to bring disorder to the territories of his opponents, so he could safely seize a part of them. This proved easy, for he found the Venetians, for reasons of their own, had decided to invite the French to invade Italy. He not only did not oppose this, but he facilitated it by dissolving the previous marriage of King Louis. So the king marched into Italy, with the help of the Venetians and the consent of Alexander. No sooner was he in Milan than the pope had borrowed forces from him for the attack on the Romagna, which was ceded to him out of fear of the King of France.

So, once Cesare had been made Duke of the Romagna, and the Colonnesi had been beaten, wanting to hang on to his new territories and make further conquests, he was faced with two obstacles. In the first place, his military forces did not appear reliable. In the second, the King of France might oppose him. He had made use of the troops of the Orsini, but they were likely to abandon him, and not only prevent him from making further acquisitions, but take from him what he had already acquired. And the same was true of the king. He had an indication of how far he could trust the Orsini when, after Faenza had been taken by storm, he attacked Bologna, for he discovered they had no appetite for that battle. And as for the king, he discovered his attitude when, having seized the Duchy of Urbino, he attacked Tuscany, for Louis made him abandon that enterprise. So the duke decided he must no longer depend on the troops and the good fortune of others.

The first thing he did was to weaken the factions of the Orsini and the Colonna in Rome. All the nobles who were allied to these families he won over to himself, making them members of his court, and giving them substantial pensions. He favored them with civil and military appointments appropriate to their standing. Thus, in the course of a few months, their attachment to their factions was dissolved, and they became committed to the duke. Next, he looked for a chance to crush the Orsini, having already defeated the forces of the Colonna family. He soon had his chance and he made the most of it. For the Orsini, having realized late in the day that the growing strength of the duke and the pope would be their ruin, called a meeting at Magione, near Perugia. From that meeting sprang the rebellion of Urbino and the uprisings in the Romagna that almost destroyed the duke; but he overcame all resistance with the help of the French. And, having got back his authority and realizing he could trust neither the French nor other external forces, he decided that, in order to prevent their allying against him, he must deceive them. He so successfully concealed his intentions that the Orsini, represented by Signor Paolo, made peace with him. The duke took every opportunity to ingratiate himself with Paolo, giving him money, clothes, and horses. So the leaders of the Orsini were brought, unsuspecting, to Sinigallia, where they were at his mercy. Having got rid of the leaders and won the allegiance of their followers, the duke could feel he had laid decent foundations for his future power. He had control of all the Romagna and the Duchy of Urbino, and it looked as though he had won over the Romagna and acquired the support of its population, who were beginning to enjoy a new prosperity.

Now, since it is worth paying attention to this question, and since it would be sensible to imitate Cesare's actions, I want to amplify what I have just said. Once the duke had subdued the Romagna, he found it had been under the control of weak nobles, who had rather exploited than governed their subjects and had rather been the source of conflict than of order, with the result the whole province was full of robbers, bandits, and every other type of criminal. So he decided it was necessary, if he was going to make the province peaceful and obedient to his commands, to give it good government. He put Mr. Remiro d'Orco, a man both cruel and efficient, in charge, and gave him absolute power. D'Orco in short order estab-lished peace and unity, and acquired immense authority. At that point, the duke decided such unchecked power was no longer necessary, for he feared people might come to hate it. So he established a civil court in the center of the province, placing an excellent judge in charge of it, and requiring every city to appoint a lawyer to represent it before the court. Since he knew the harsh measures of the past had given rise to some enmity towards him, in order to purge the ill-will of the people and win them completely over to him, he wanted to make clear that, if there had been any cruelty, he was not responsible for it, and that his hard-hearted minister should be blamed. He saw his opportunity and exploited it. One morning, in the town square of Cesena, he had Remiro d'Orco's corpse laid out in two pieces, with a chopping board and a bloody knife beside it. This ferocious sight made the people of the Romagna simultaneously happy and dumbfounded.

But let us get back to where we were. I was saying the duke found himself rather powerful and had taken precautions against immediate dangers, for he had built up a military force that he had planned himself and had in large part destroyed neighboring forces that could be a threat to him. So what remained, if he wanted to make further acquisitions, was the problem of the King of France; for he knew the king had, late in the day, realized his policy towards Borgia had been misconceived and would not allow him to make further conquests. So Borgia began to look for new alliances and to prevaricate with the French when they dispatched a force towards the Kingdom of Naples to attack the Spanish who were laying siege to Gaeta. His intention was to protect himself against them, which he would soon have succeeded in doing, if Alexander had gone on living.

These were the policies he pursued with regard to his immediate concerns. But there were future problems he also had to consider. In the first place, he had to worry that a new pope would be hostile to him and would try to take from him what Alexander had given him. He had four ways of trying to deal with this threat. In the first place, he set out to eliminate all the relatives of those rulers whose lands he had seized, to make it difficult for the pope to restore their previous rulers. Second, he sought to acquire the allegiance of the nobility of Rome, as I have explained, so he could use them to restrict the pope's freedom of action. Third, to make as many as possible of the members of the College of Cardinals his allies. Fourth, to acquire so much power, before the pope died, that he would be able on his own to resist a first attack. Of these four policies he had successfully carried out three by the time Alexander died; the fourth he had almost accomplished. Of the rulers he had dispossessed, he murdered as many as he could get his hands on, and only a very few survived. The Roman nobility were his supporters, and he had built up a very large faction in the College of Cardinals. As far as new acquisitions were concerned, he had plans for conquering Tuscany; he already held Perugia and Piombino; and he had taken Pisa under his protection. And, as soon as he would no longer have to worry about the King of France (which was already the case, for the French had already lost the Kingdom of Naples to the Spanish, with the result that both France and Spain were now obliged to try to buy his friendship), he would be free to seize Pisa. After which, Lucca and Siena would quickly give in, partly because they hated the Florentines, and partly because they would have been terrified. The Florentines could have done nothing.

If he had succeeded in all this (and he was on the point of succeeding in the very year Alexander died) he would have acquired so much strength and so much authority he would have become his own master. He would no longer have depended on events outside his control and on the policies of others, but would have been able to rely on his own power and strength [virtù]. But Alexander died only five years after Cesare Borgia had unsheathed his sword. He found himself with only his control over the Romagna firmly established, with everything else up in the air, caught between two powerful hostile armies, and dangerously ill. But the duke was so pugnacious and so strong [virtù], he so well understood what determines whether one wins or loses, and he had laid such sound foundations within such a short time, that, if he had not had these enemy armies breathing down his neck, or if he had been in good health, he could have overcome every difficulty.

I am justified in claiming he had laid sound foundations, for the Romagna remained loyal to him in his absence for more than a month; in Rome, although he was half dead, he was quite safe, and although the Ballioni, the Vitelli, and the Orsini congregated

in Rome, they could not muster a following to attack him; and, if he was not in a position to choose who should be pope, he could at least veto anyone he did not trust. So, if he had been well when Alexander died he would have been able to deal with his problems without difficulty. He told me himself, on the day Julius II was elected, that he had asked himself what he would do if his father died and had been confident he could handle the situation, but that it had never occurred to him that when his father died he himself would be at death's door.

So, now I have surveyed all the actions of the duke, I still cannot find anything to criticize. It seems to me I have been right to present him as an example to be imitated by all those who come to power through good luck and thanks to someone else's military might. For, since he was great-hearted and ambitious, he had no choice as to what to do; and he only failed to achieve his goals because Alexander died too soon, and he himself fell ill. So anyone who decides that the policy to follow when one has newly acquired power is to destroy one's enemies, to secure some allies, to win wars, whether by force or by fraud, to make oneself both loved and feared by one's subjects, to make one's soldiers loyal and respectful, to wipe out those who can or would want to hurt one, to innovate, replacing old institutions with new practices, to be both harsh and generous, magnanimous and open-handed, to disband disloyal troops and form new armies, to build alliances with other powers, so kings and princes either have to win your favor or else think twice before going against your wishes— anyone who thinks in these terms cannot hope to find, in the recent past, a better model to imitate than Cesare Borgia.

His only mistake was to allow Julius to be elected pope, for there he made a bad choice. The choice was his to make, for as I have said, if he could not choose who should be pope, he could veto anyone he did not like, and he should never have agreed to any cardinal's being elected with whom he had been in conflict in the past, or who, once he had been elected, would have been likely to be afraid of him. For men attack either out of fear or out of hatred. Those who had scores to settle with him included San Piero ad Vincula, Colonna, San Giorgio, Ascanio; all the others, if elected pope, would have had good reason to fear him, with the exception of Rouen and of the Spanish cardinals. The Spanish were his relatives and allies; Rouen was powerful, having the support of the King of France. So the duke's first objective should have been to ensure a Spaniard was elected pope; failing that, he should have agreed to the election of Rouen and vetoed that of San Piero ad Vincula. If he imagined recent gestures of goodwill make the powerful forget old injuries, he was much mistaken. So the duke made a mistake during the election of the pope, and this mistake was, in the end, the cause of his destruction.

Chapter Eight: Of those who come to power through wicked actions.

But since there are two other ways a private citizen can become a ruler, two ways that do not simply involve the acquisition of power either through fortune or strength [*virtù*], I feel I cannot omit discussion of them, although one of them can be more fully treated elsewhere, where I discuss republics. These are, first, when one acquires power through some wicked or nefarious action, and second when a private citizen becomes ruler of his own country because he has the support of his fellow citizens. Here I will talk about the first of these two routes to power, and will use two examples, one ancient, one modern, to show how it is done. These will be sufficient, I trust, to provide a model for anyone who has no alternative options. I do not intend to discuss in detail the rights and wrongs of such a policy.

Agathocles of Sicily became King of Syracuse, although he was not merely a private citizen, but of humble and poverty-stricken origins. He was the son of a potter, and from start to finish lived a wicked life; nevertheless, his wicked behavior testified to so much strength [*virtù*] of mind and of body that, when he joined the army, he was promoted through the ranks to the supreme command. Having risen so high, he decided to become the sole ruler and to hold on to power, which he had originally been granted by the consent of his fellow citizens, by violence and without being dependent on anyone else. Having entered into a conspiracy with a Carthaginian called Hamilcar, who was commander of a hostile army serving in Sicily, one morning he called together the people and the senate of Syracuse, as if he wanted to discuss matters of government policy, and, at a prearranged signal, had his soldiers kill all the senators and the richest citizens. With them out of the way, he made himself ruler of the city and held power without any resistance. Although the Carthaginians twice defeated his armies and even advanced to the walls of the city, he was not only able to defend his city, but, leaving part of his army behind to withstand the siege, he was able to attack the Carthaginians in Africa with the remainder of his forces. Within a short time he had forced them to lift the siege and was threatening to conquer Carthage. In the end they were obliged to come to terms with him, leaving Sicily to Agathocles in return for security in Africa.

If you consider Agathocles' bold achievements [*azioni e virtù*], you will not find much that can be attributed to luck; for, as I have said, he did not come to power because he had help from above, but because he worked his way up from below, climbing from rank to rank by undergoing infinite dangers and discomforts until in the end he obtained a monopoly of power, and then holding on to his position by bold and risky tactics.

One ought not, of course, to call it *virtù* [virtue or manliness] to massacre one's fellow citizens, to betray one's friends, to break one's word, to be without mercy and without religion. By such means one can acquire power but not glory. If one considers the manly qualities [*virtù*] Agathocles demonstrated in braving and facing down danger, and the strength of character he showed in surviving and overcoming adversity, then there seems to be no reason why he should be judged less admirable than any of the finest generals. But on the other hand, his inhuman cruelty and brutality, and his innumerable wicked actions, mean it would be wrong to praise him as one of the finest of men. It is clear, at any rate, that one can attribute neither to luck nor to virtue [*virtù*] his accomplishments, which owed nothing to either.

In our own day, when Alexander VI was pope, Oliverotto of Fermo, whose father had died a few years before, was raised by his maternal uncle, Giovanni Fogliani. As soon as he was old enough he joined the forces of Paolo Vitelli, so that, with a good military training, he could pursue a career in the army. When Paolo died, he signed up with his brother, Vitellozzo. In a very short time, because he was bright and had both a strong character and a lively spirit, he became Vitellozzo's second-in-command. Soon he thought it to be beneath his dignity to serve under another, and so he conspired to occupy Fermo, relying on the help of some citizens of that city who preferred to see their fatherland enslaved than free, and on the support of Vitellozzo. He wrote to his uncle, saying that, since he had been away from home for many years, he wanted to come to visit him and to see his city, and so, in a manner of speaking, reacquaint himself with his inheritance. He said he had only gone to war in order to acquire honor. So his fellow citizens would be able to see he had not been wasting his time, he wanted to arrive in state, accompanied by a hundred men on horseback, some of them his friends, and others his servants. He asked his uncle to ensure that the inhabitants of Fermo received him with respect: This would not only enhance his own reputation, but that of his uncle, who had raised him.

Giovanni did everything he could for his nephew. He ensured he was greeted by the people of Fermo with every honor, and he put him up in his own house. After a few days had gone by, and he had had time to make the arrangements necessary for the carrying out of his wicked plans, he held a lavish banquet at his uncle's, to which he invited his uncle and the most powerful citizens of Fermo. After the food had been eaten, and the guests had been entertained in all the ways that are customary upon such occasions, Oliverotto deliberately began discussing serious questions, talking about the greatness of Pope Alexander and his son Cesare, and about their undertakings. When his uncle Giovanni and the others picked up the subject, he sprang to his feet, saying such matters should be discussed in a more private place. He withdrew into another room, where Giovanni and all the other leading citizens followed. No sooner had they sat down than soldiers emerged from their hiding places and killed Giovanni along with all the rest. Once the killing was over, Oliverotto got on his horse and took possession of the city, laying siege to the government building. Those in authority were so terrified they agreed to obey him and to establish a new regime of which he was the head. With all those who had something to lose and would have been able to resist him dead, he was able to entrench himself by establishing new civilian and military institutions. Within a year of coming to power, he was not only securely in control of Fermo, but had become a threat to all the cities round about.

It would soon have been as difficult to get rid of him as to get rid of Agathocles, had he not allowed himself to be taken in by Cesare Borgia, when, as I have already explained, he got rid of the Orsini and the Vitelli at Sinigallia. Oliverotto was seized at the same time, and, a year after he had killed his uncle, he was strangled along with Vitellozzo from whom he had learned how to be bold [virtù] and how to be wicked.

Perhaps you are wondering how Agathocles and others like him, despite their habitual faithlessness and cruelty, have been able to live safely in their homelands year after year, and to defend themselves against their enemies abroad. Why did their fellow subjects not conspire against them? After all, mere cruelty has not been enough to enable many other rulers to hang on to power even in time of peace, let alone during the turmoil of war. I think here we have to distinguish between cruelty well used and cruelty abused. Well-used cruelty (if one can speak well of evil) one may call those atrocities that are committed at a stroke, in order to secure one's power, and are then not repeated, rather every effort is made to ensure one's subjects benefit in the long run. An abuse of cruelty one may call those policies that, even if in the beginning they involve little bloodshed, lead to more rather than less as time goes by. Those who use cruelty well may indeed find both God and their subjects are prepared to let bygones be bygones, as was the case with Agathocles. Those who abuse it cannot hope to retain power indefinitely.

So the conclusion is: If you take control of a state, you should make a list of all the crimes you have to commit and do them all at once. That way you will not have to commit new atrocities every day, and you will be able, by not repeating your evil deeds, to reassure your subjects and to win their support by treating them well. He who acts otherwise, either out of squeamishness or out of bad judgment, has to hold a bloody knife in his hand all the time. He can never rely on his subjects, for they can never trust him, for he is always making new attacks upon them. Do all the harm you must at one and the same time, that way the full extent of it will not be noticed, and it will give least offense. One should do good, on the other hand, little by little, so people can fully appreciate it.

A ruler should, above all, behave towards his subjects in such a way that, whatever happens, whether for good or ill, he has no need to change his policies. For if you fall on evil times and are obliged to change course, you will not have time to benefit from the harm you do, and the good you do will do you no good, because people will think you have been forced to do it, and they will not be in the slightest bit grateful to you.

Chapter Nine: Of the citizen-ruler.

But, coming to the alternative possibility, when a private citizen becomes the ruler of his homeland, not through wickedness or some act of atrocity, but through the support of his fellow citizens, so that we may call him a citizen-ruler (remember we are discussing power acquired neither by pure strength [*virtù*] nor mere luck—in this case one needs a lucky cunning), I would point out there are two ways to such power: the support of the populace or the favor of the elite. For in every city one finds these two opposed classes. They are at odds because the populace do not want to be ordered about or oppressed by the elite; and the elite want to order about and oppress the populace. The conflict between these two irreconcilable ambitions has in each city one of three possible consequences: rule by one man, liberty, or anarchy.

Rule by one man can be brought about either by the populace or the elite, depending on whether one or the other of these factions hopes to benefit from it. For if the elite fear they will be unable to control the populace, they begin to build up the reputation of one of their own, and they make him sole ruler in order to be able, under his protection, to achieve their objectives. The populace on the other hand, if they fear they are going to be crushed by the elite, build up the reputation of one of their number and make him sole ruler, in order that his authority may be employed in their defense. He who comes to power with the help of the elite has more difficulty in holding on to power than he who comes to power with the help of the populace, for in the former case he is surrounded by many who think of themselves as his equals, and whom he consequently cannot order about or manipulate as he might wish. He who comes to power with the support of the populace, on the other hand, has it all to himself: There is no one, or hardly anyone, around him who is not prepared to obey. In addition, one cannot honorably give the elite what they want, and one cannot do it without harming others; but this is not true with the populace, for the objectives of the populace are less immoral than those of the elite, for the latter want to oppress, and the former not to be oppressed. Thirdly, if the masses are opposed to you, you can never be secure, for there are too many of them; but the elite, since there are few of them, can be neutralized.

The worst a ruler who is opposed by the populace has to fear is that they will give him no support; but from the elite he has to fear not only lack of support, but worse, that they will attack him. For the elite have more foresight and more cunning; they act in time to protect themselves, and seek to ingratiate themselves with rivals for power. Finally, the ruler cannot get rid of the populace but must live with them; he can, however, get by perfectly well without the members of the elite, being able to make and unmake them each day, and being in a position to give them status or take it away, as he chooses.

In order to clarify the issues, let me point out there are two principal points of view from which one should consider the elite. Either they behave in a way that ties their fortunes to yours, or they do not. Those who tie themselves to you and are not rapacious, you should honor and love; those who do not tie themselves to you are to be divided into two categories. If they retain their independence through pusillanimity and because they are lacking in courage, then you should employ them, especially if they have good judgment, for you can be sure they will help you achieve success so long as things are going well for you, and you can also be confident you have nothing to fear from them if things go badly. But if they retain their independence from you out of calculation and ambition, then you can tell they are more interested in their own welfare than yours. A ruler must protect himself against such people and fear them as much as if they were publicly declared enemies, for you can be sure that, in adversity, they will help to overthrow you.

Anyone who becomes a ruler with the support of the populace ought to ensure he keeps their support; which will not be difficult, for all they ask is not to be oppressed. But anyone who becomes a ruler with the support of the elite and against the wishes of the populace must above all else seek to win the populace over to his side, which will be easy to do if he protects their interests. And since people, when they are well-treated by someone whom they expected to treat them badly, feel all the more obliged to their benefactor, he will find that the populace will quickly become better inclined towards him than if he had come to power with their support. There are numerous ways the ruler can win the support of the populace. They vary so much depending on the circumstances they cannot be reduced to a formula, and, consequently, I will not go into them here. I will simply conclude by saying a ruler needs to have the support of the populace, for otherwise he has nothing to fall back on in times of adversity.

Nabis, ruler of the Spartans, survived an attack by the confederate forces of all Greece, together with an almost invincible Roman army, and successfully defended both his homeland and his own hold on power. All he needed to do, when faced with danger, was neutralize a few; but if he had had the populace opposed to him, this would have been insufficient. Do not think you can rebut my argument by citing the well-worn proverb, "Relying on the people is like building on the sand." This is quite true when a private citizen depends upon them and gives the impression he expects the populace to free him if he is seized by his enemies or by the magistrates. In such a case one can easily find oneself disappointed, as happened to the Gracchi in Rome and to Mr. Giorgio Scali in Florence. But if you are a ruler and you put your trust in the populace, if you can give commands and are capable of bold action, if you are not non-plused by adversity, if you take other necessary precautions, and if through your own courage and your policies you keep up the morale of the populace, then you will never be let down by them, and you will discover you have built on a sound foundation.

The type of one-man rule we are discussing tends to be at risk at the moment of transition from constitutional to dictatorial government. Such rulers either give commands in their own name, or act through the officers of state. In the second case, their situation is more dangerous and less secure. For they are entirely dependent on the cooperation of those citizens who have been appointed to the offices of state, who can, particularly at times of crisis, easily deprive them of their power, either by directly opposing them or by simply failing to carry out their instructions. It is

too late for the ruler once a crisis is upon him to seize dictatorial authority, for the citizens and the subjects, who are used to obeying the constituted authorities, will not, in such circumstances, obey him, and he will always have, in difficult circumstances, a shortage of people on whom he can rely. For such a ruler cannot expect things to continue as they were when there were no difficulties, when all the citizens are conscious of what the government can do for them. Then everyone flocked round, everyone promised support, everyone was willing to die for him, when there was no prospect of having to do so. But when times are tough, when the government is dependent on its citizens, then there will be few who are prepared to stand by it. One does not learn the danger of such an erosion of support from experience, as the first experience proves fatal. So a wise ruler will seek to ensure that his citizens always, no matter what the circumstances, have an interest in preserving both him and his authority. If he can do this, they will always be faithful to him.

Chapter Ten: How one should measure the strength of a ruler.

There is another factor one should take into account when categorizing rulers: One should ask if a ruler has enough resources to be able, if necessary, to look after himself, or whether he will always be dependent on having alliances with other rulers. In order to clarify this question, I would maintain those rulers can look after themselves who have sufficient reserves, whether of troops or of money, to be able to put together a sound army and face battle against any opponent. On the other hand, I judge those rulers to be dependent on the support of others who could not take the field against any potential enemy, but would be obliged to take shelter behind the walls of their cities and castles, and stay there. We have talked already about those who can look after themselves, and we will have more to say in due course; to those who are in the second situation, all one can do is advise them to build defenseworks and stockpile arms, and to give up all thought of holding the open ground. He who has well fortified his city and who has followed the policies towards his own subjects that I have outlined above and will describe below, can be sure his enemies will think twice before they attack him, for people are always reluctant to undertake enterprises that look as if they will be difficult, and no one thinks it will be easy to attack someone who is well-fortified and has the support of the populace.

The cities of Germany are free to do as they please. They have little surrounding territory, and obey the emperor only when they want. They fear neither him nor any other ruler in their region, for they are so well-fortified everyone thinks it will be tedious and difficult to take them. They all have appropriate moats and ramparts, and more than enough artillery. They always keep in the public stores enough food and drink, and enough firewood, to be able to hold out for a year. Moreover, in order to be able to keep the populace quiet and to guarantee tax revenues, they always keep in stock enough supplies to keep their subjects occupied for a year in those crafts that are the basis of the city's prosperity and provide employment for the bulk of the people. They also emphasize military preparedness and have numerous ordinances designed to ensure this.

A ruler, therefore, who has a well-fortified city, and who does not set out to make enemies, is not going to be attacked; and, suppose someone does attack him, his adversary will have to give up in disgrace. For political circumstances change so fast it is impossible for anyone to keep an army in the field for a year doing nothing but maintaining a siege. And if you are tempted to reply that if the people have property outside the city walls and see it burning, then they will not be able patiently to withstand a siege, and that as time goes by, and their own interests are damaged, they will forget their loyalty to their ruler; then I reply that a ruler who is strong and bold will always be able to overcome such difficulties, sometimes encouraging his subjects to think relief is at hand, sometimes terrifying them with stories of what the enemy will do to them if they concede defeat, sometimes taking appropriate action to neutralize those who seem to him to be agitators. Moreover, it is in the nature of things that the enemy will burn and pillage the countryside when they first arrive, at which time the subjects will still be feeling brave and prepared to undertake their own defense. So the ruler has little to fear, for after a few days, when the subjects are feeling less courageous, the damage will already have been done, and it will be too late to prevent it. Then they will be all the more ready to rally to their ruler,

believing him to be in their debt, since they have had their houses burnt and their possessions looted for defending him. It is in men's nature to feel as obliged by the good they do to others, as by the good others do to them. So if you consider all the factors, you will see it is not difficult for a wise ruler to keep his subjects loyal during a siege, both at the beginning and as it continues, providing they are not short of food and of arms.

Chapter Eleven: About ecclesiastical states.

All that remains for us to discuss, at this point, is the ecclesiastical states. As far as they are concerned, all the problems are encountered before one gets possession of them. One acquires them either through strength [*virtù*] or through luck, but one can hold on to them without either. For they are maintained by their long-established institutions that are rooted in religion. These have developed to such a pitch of strength they can support their rulers in power no matter how they live and behave. Only ecclesiastical rulers have states, but no need to defend them; subjects, but no need to govern them. Their states, though they do not defend them, are not taken from them; their subjects, though they do not govern them, do not resent them, and they neither think of replacing their rulers nor are they in a position to do so. So these are the only rulers who are secure and happy. But because they are ruled by a higher power, which human intelligence cannot grasp, I will say no more about them; for, since they have been built up and maintained by God, only a presumptuous and rash person would debate about them. Nevertheless, if someone were to ask me how it comes about that the church has acquired so much temporal power, given that, until the papacy of Alexander [VI], the rulers of Italy, and indeed not only those who called themselves rulers, but every baron and lord, no matter how small, regarded the papacy's temporal power as of little significance, while now a King of France trembles at its power, for a pope has kicked him out of Italy and been the ruin of the Venetians: Though the answer to this question is well known, I think it will not be a waste of time to remind you of the main principles.

Before Charles, King of France, invaded Italy, control over this geographical region was divided between the pope, the Republic of Venice, the King of Naples, the Duke of Milan, and the Republic of Florence. These rulers were obliged to have two principal preoccupations: In the first place, they had to make sure no foreign power brought an army into Italy; in the second, they had to make sure none of the Italian powers increased its territory. The powers they were most concerned about were the pope and the Venetians. In order to prevent the Venetians from expanding all the rest had to cooperate, as happened when the Venetians tried to take Ferrara. In order to keep the pope in his place they relied on the nobles of Rome. These were divided into two factions, the Orsini and the Colonna, and so there was always occasion for friction between them. Because both factions were constantly in arms within sight of the pope, their strength kept the pope weak and sickly. Although there was occasionally a pope who had ambitions, Sixtus [IV] for example, yet neither luck nor skill enabled him to free himself of that handicap.

The real cause was the shortness of the popes' lives. On average, a pope lived ten years, which was scarcely enough time to crush one of the factions. Suppose a pope had almost destroyed the Colonna; his successor would prove to be an enemy of the Orsini, would rebuild the power of the Colonna, and would not have time to crush the Orsini. The result was the temporal power of the pope was not thought by the Italians to be of much importance. Then along came Alexander VI, who, more than all the other popes there have been, demonstrated how much a pope, using both money and arms, could get his own way. It was Alexander who, by making use of Duke Valentino and by taking advantage of the invasion of Italy by the French, brought about all those things I have mentioned above, when discussing the achievements of the duke. Although his objective was not to make the church, but rather the duke, powerful, nevertheless, he did make the church a power to be reckoned with. It was the church that, after he had died and the duke had been destroyed, inherited the results of his labors.

After him came Julius [II]. The church was already powerful, for it had control of the whole of the Romagna, and the barons of Rome had been crushed, and the two factions of Orsini and Colonna had, as a result of the hiding given them by Alexander, been eliminated. Moreover, Julius had opportunities to ac-

cumulate money of a sort that had not existed before Alexander. Julius not only took over where Alexander had left off, but made further advances. He planned to acquire Bologna, to destroy the power of the Venetians, and to throw the French out of Italy. He not only laid plans, but he succeeded in everything he undertook. His achievements were all the more admirable in that his goal was to build up the power of the Church, not of any private individual. He kept the factions of the Orsini and the Colonna in the feeble condition in which he had found them. Although they made some efforts to rise again, two things kept them down: in the first place, the new power of the church, which intimidated them; and in the second, the fact none of their number were cardinals, for it is the cardinals who have been at the origin of the conflicts between the factions. These two factions have never behaved themselves at times when they have had cardinals, for the cardinals, both in Rome and outside Rome, foster the factions, and the barons are obliged to come to their support. Thus the ambition of the prelates is the cause of the conflicts and tumults among the nobility.

Now His Holiness Pope Leo [X] has acquired the papacy, along with all its immense temporal power. We may hope, if his predecessors made it a military power to be reckoned with, he, who is so good and has so many virtues [virtù], will not only increase its power, but also make it worthy of respect.

Chapter Twelve: How many types of army are there, and what opinion should one have of mercenary soldiers?

So far I have discussed one by one the various types of one-man rule I listed at the beginning, and I have to some extent described the policies that make each type succeed or fail. I have shown the various techniques employed by numerous individuals who have sought to acquire and to hold on to power. Now my task is to outline the various strategies for offense and defense that are common to all these principalities. I said above it was necessary for a ruler to lay good foundations; otherwise, he is likely to be destroyed. The principal foundations on which the power of all governments is based (whether they be new, long-established, or mixed) are good laws and good armies. And, since there cannot be good laws where there are not good armies, and since where there are good armies, there must be good laws, I will omit any discussion of laws, and will talk about armies.

Let me begin by saying, then, that a ruler defends his state with armies that are made up of his own subjects, or of mercenaries, or of auxiliary forces, or of some combination of these three types. Mercenaries and auxiliaries are both useless and dangerous. Anyone who relies on mercenary troops to keep himself in power will never be safe or secure, for they are factious, ambitious, ill-disciplined, treacherous. They show off to your allies and run away from your enemies. They do not fear God and do not keep faith with mankind. A mercenary army puts off defeat for only so long as it postpones going into battle. In peacetime they pillage you, in wartime they let the enemy do it. This is why: They have no motive or principle for joining up beyond the desire to collect their pay. And what you pay them is not enough to make them want to die for you. They are delighted to be your soldiers when you are not at war; when you are at war, they walk away when they do not run. It should not be difficult to convince you of this, because the sole cause of the present ruin of Italy has been the fact that for many years now the Italians have been willing to rely on mercenaries. It is true that occasionally a ruler seems to benefit from their use, and they boast of their own prowess, but as soon as they face foreign troops their true worth becomes apparent. This is why Charles, King of France, was able to conquer Italy with a piece of chalk; and the person who said we were being punished for our sins spoke the truth. But our sins were not the ones of which he was thinking, but those I have been discussing. Because these were the sins of our rulers, our rulers as well as the common people had to pay the price for them.

I want now to make crystal clear the worthlessness of mercenary armies. Mercenary commanders are either excellent or not. If they are excellent, you cannot trust them, for they will always be looking for ways of increasing their own power, either by turning on you, their employer, or by turning on others whom you want them to leave alone. On the other hand, if they are not first rate [*virtuoso*], then they will be the ruin of you in the normal course of events. And if you want to reply the same problems will arise whoever makes up the army, whether they are mercenaries

or not, I will argue it depends on whether they take their orders from a sovereign or from a republic. A sovereign ought to go to war himself, and be his own general. A republic has to send one of its citizens. If it chooses someone who turns out not to be a successful soldier, it must replace him; if it chooses someone who is successful, it must tie his hands with laws, to ensure he keeps within the limits assigned to him. Experience shows individual sovereigns and republics that arm the masses are capable of making vast conquests; but mercenary troops are always a liability. Moreover, it is harder for a treacherous citizen to suborn an army consisting of his own fellow subjects than one made up of foreigners.

Rome and Sparta were armed and free for many centuries. The Swiss are armed to the teeth and do not have to take orders from anyone. In ancient history, we can take the Carthaginians as an example of the consequences of relying on mercenaries. They were in danger of being oppressed by their mercenary soldiers when the first war with Rome was over, despite the fact they employed their own citizens as commanders. Philip of Macedon was made general of the Theban armies after the death of Epaminondas; and, after he had won the war, he enslaved the Thebans. In modern times, Milan, after Duke Filippo died, employed Francesco Sforza to fight the Venetians. Once he had defeated the enemy at Caravaggio, he joined forces with them to attack the Milanese, his employers. Sforza his father, who was employed by Queen Giovanna of Naples, abandoned her without warning and without defenses. As a consequence, she was obliged to throw herself into the embrace of the King of Aragon in order to hold on to her kingdom. If the Venetians and the Florentines have in the past succeeded in acquiring new territory with mercenary armies, and if their commanders have not seized the conquests for themselves, but have held onto them for their employers, this, I would argue, is because the Florentines have had more than their share of luck. For of the first-rate [*virtuosi*] commanders, whom they would have had reason to fear, some have not been victorious, some have not been in sole command, and some have turned their ambitions elsewhere. It was John Hawkwood who did not win: We cannot know if he would have proved reliable had he been victorious, but no one can deny that if he had won Florence would have been his for the taking. Sforza always had to share command with the Braccheschi, and neither could act for fear of the other. Francesco turned his ambitions to Lombardy; Braccio turned his against the church and the Kingdom of Naples.

But let us look at what happened only a short time ago. The Florentines made Paolo Vitelli their commander. He was a very astute man, and, despite being of modest origin, he had acquired a tremendous reputation. If he had succeeded in taking Pisa, no one can deny the Florentines would have needed his goodwill, for, if he had transferred his support to their enemies, they would have been without defenses; and if they had managed to keep his support, they would have had no choice but to do as he told them.

Consider next the conquests made by the Venetians. You will see they ran no risks and won magnificent victories as long as they relied on their own troops, which was until they tried to conquer territory on the mainland. When they armed both the nobility and the populace they had a magnificent fighting force [*operorono virtuosissimamente*], but when they began to fight on the mainland they abandoned this sound policy [*questa virtù*], and began to copy the other Italian states. When they began their conquests on the mainland, because they had little territory there, and because their own reputation was fearsome, they had little to fear from their mercenary commanders. But as their conquests extended, as they did under Carmagnola, they began to discover their mistake. They recognized he was a first-rate [*virtuosissimo*] general, and that they had, under his command, defeated the Duke of Milan, but they realized he had lost his taste for war, and concluded they could no longer win with him, because he no longer wanted victory; but they could not dismiss him, or the land they had acquired would go with him. So, in order to neutralize him, they had to kill him. Since then they have employed as commanders of their forces Bartolemeo of Bergamo, Roberto of San Severino, the Count of Pitigliano, and others like them. With such commanders they had reason to fear defeat, not the consequences of victory. And indeed they were defeated at Vailà, where, in one day, they lost all they had acquired with so much effort in eight hundred years. For with mercenary troops one acquires new territory slowly, feebly, after many attempts; but one loses so much so quickly that it seems an act of God.

And, since these examples have been drawn from recent Italian experience, and since Italy has been entirely dependent on mercenary forces for many years, I want to trace the present state of affairs back to its source, so that, having seen the origin and development of the problem, it will be easier to see how to correct it. You need to understand, then, that in modern times, as soon as the authority of the Holy Roman Empire began to be rejected in Italy, and the pope began to acquire greater authority in temporal affairs, Italy began to be divided into a number of different states. Many of the larger cities went to war against the nobility of the surrounding countryside, who had been oppressing them, and who were, at first, supported by the emperor. The Church, on the other hand, favored the cities in order to build up its temporal authority. In many other cities individual citizens established princedoms. So Italy came to be more or less divided up between those who owed allegiance to the papacy and a number of independent republican city states. Since neither the priests nor the citizens of the republics were accustomed to fighting wars, they began to employ foreigners in their armies.

The first to win a reputation for these mercenary troops was Alberigo of Conio in the Romagna. Among those who were trained by him were Braccio and Sforza, who were, at the height of their powers, the arbiters of Italian affairs. After them came all the others who have commanded mercenary forces down to the present time. The outcome of all their prowess [*virtù*] has been that Italy has, in quick succession, been overrun by Charles, plundered by Louis, raped by Ferdinand, and humiliated by the Swiss.

The first objective these mercenary commanders have pursued has been to destroy the reputation of the infantry in order to build up that of their own forces. They did this because they have had no resources of their own, but have been dependent on their contracts. A few infantry would have done little for their reputation, while they could not afford to feed a large number. So they specialized in cavalry, for they could feed a reasonably large number, and with them win respect. It came to the point that in an army of twenty thousand soldiers there would not even be two thousand infantry. In addition, they have done everything they could to free themselves and their troops from trouble and from danger. During skirmishes between opposing forces they did not kill each other: Indeed, they not only took prisoners, but released them without demanding a ransom. They were in no hurry to assault fortifications under cover of darkness, while the defending troops were far from eager to mount sorties against their assailants. When they made camp they did not protect themselves with trenches or palisades. They passed the winters in barracks. And all these practices were permitted by their standing orders and were invented, as I said, so they could avoid effort and risk: so much so that they have reduced Italy to a despicable slavery.

Chapter Thirteen: About auxiliary troops, native troops, and composite armies.

Auxiliaries are the other sort of useless troops. You rely on auxiliaries when you appeal to another ruler to come with his own armies to assist or defend you. This is what Pope Julius did in recent times, when, having discovered the incompetence of his mercenary troops during the siege of Ferrara, he decided to rely on auxiliaries, and reached an agreement with King Ferdinand of Spain that he would come to his assistance with his men and arms. Auxiliary troops can be useful and good when fighting on their own behalf, but they are almost always a liability for anyone relying on their assistance. For if they lose, it is you who are defeated; if they win, you are their prisoner. There are plenty of examples of this in ancient history, but I do not want to stray from the contemporary case of Pope Julius II; he can have had no idea what he was doing when, in the hope of acquiring Ferrara, he placed himself entirely into the hands of a foreigner. But he was lucky: The outcome was neither defeat nor imprisonment, so he did not have to pay the price for his foolish decision. His auxiliaries were routed at Ravenna, but then the Swiss came along and drove out the victors, so that, contrary to everyone's expectation, including his own, he did not end up either a prisoner of his enemies, who had fled, or of his auxiliaries, for it was not they who had been victorious. Another example: The Florentines, having no troops of their own, brought ten thousand French soldiers to take Pisa. This decision placed them in more danger than at any other time during their troubles. Again, the Emperor of Constantinople, in order to attack his neighbors, brought ten thousand

Turks into Greece. They, when the war was over, had no intention of leaving: This was the beginning of Greece's enslavement to the infidels.

He, then, who has no desire to be the victor should use these troops, for they are much more dangerous than mercenaries. If your auxiliaries win you are ruined, for they are united in their obedience to someone else. If your mercenaries win it takes them more time and more favorable circumstances to turn against you, for they are not united among themselves, and it is you who recruited and paid them. If you appoint an outsider to command them, it takes him time to establish sufficient authority to be able to attack you. In short, where mercenaries are concerned the main risk is cowardice; with auxiliaries it is valor [*virtù*].

A wise ruler, therefore, will always avoid using mercenary and auxiliary troops, and will rely on his own forces. He would rather lose with his own troops than win with someone else's, for he will not regard it a true victory if it is won with troops that do not belong to him. I never hesitate to cite Cesare Borgia as a model to be imitated. This duke entered the Romagna with an auxiliary army, for his troops were all Frenchmen, and he used it to take Imola and Forlì. But since he did not feel such troops were reliable, he then switched over to mercenaries, believing that using them involved fewer risks, and so he hired the Orsini and the Vitelli. But in practice he found them unreliable, treacherous, and dangerous, and so he got rid of them and formed his own army. And it is easy to see the differences among these three types of army, for you only have to consider how the duke's reputation changed, depending on whether he was relying on the French alone, on the Orsini and the Vitelli, or on his own troops and his own resources. With each change of policy it increased, but he was only taken seriously when everyone could see he was in complete command of his own forces.

I wanted to stick to examples that are both recent and Italian, but I cannot resist mentioning Hiero of Syracuse, since I have already discussed him above. He, when he was made commander-in-chief by the Syracusans, as I have described, quickly realized their mercenary army was worthless, for it was made up of condottieri like our own Italian armies. He decided he could not risk either keeping them on, or letting them go, so he had them massacred. Thereafter, he went to war with troops of his own, not with other people's soldiers. I also want to remind you of an Old Testament story that is relevant. When David proposed to Saul that he should go and fight with Goliath, the Philistine champion, Saul, in order to give him confidence, dressed him in his own armor. David, having tried it on, rejected it, saying he could not give a good account of himself if he relied on Saul's weapons. He wanted to confront the enemy armed with his sling and his knife.

In short, someone else's armor either falls off, or it weighs you down, or it trips you up. Charles VII, father of King Louis XI, having through good luck and valor [virtù] driven the English out of France, recognized that it was essential to have one's own weapons and, so, issued instructions for the establishment of a standing army of cavalry and infantry. Later, his son King Louis abolished the infantry and began to recruit Swiss troops. It was this mistake, imitated by his successors, that was, as we can see from recent events, the cause of the dangers faced by that kingdom. For he built up the reputation of the Swiss while undermining his own military capacity, for he destroyed his own infantry and made his own cavalry dependent on the support of foreign troops, for they, having become accustomed to fighting alongside the Swiss, no longer think they can win without them. The result is the French dare not fight against the Swiss, and without the Swiss they are ineffective against anyone else. So the French armies have been mixed, partly mercenary and partly native. Such a mixed army is much preferable to one made up only of auxiliaries or only of mercenaries, but it is much inferior to one made up entirely of one's own troops. The French example is sufficient to make the point, for the Kingdom of France would be able to overcome any enemy if the foundations laid by Charles VII had been built upon, or even if his instructions had merely been kept in force. But men are foolish, and they embark on something that is attractive in its outward appearance, without recognizing the evil consequences that will follow from it: a point I have already made when talking about consumption.

A ruler who cannot foresee evil consequences before they have time to develop is not truly wise; but few have such wisdom. And if one studies the first destruction of the Roman Empire one discovers it came about as a result of the first recruitment of Gothic soldiers, for from that moment the armies of the Roman Empire began to grow feeble. And all the strength [virtù] that ebbed from the Romans accrued to the Goths. I conclude, therefore, that no ruler is secure unless he has his own troops. Without them he is entirely dependent on fortune, having no strength [virtù] with which to defend himself in adversity. Wise men have always believed and said that, "Nothing is so fragile as a reputation for strength that does not correspond to one's real capacities." Now one's own troops can be made up out of one's subjects, or one's citizens, or one's dependents: All others are either mercenaries or auxiliaries. And the correct way of organizing one's own troops is easy to find out by looking over the instructions given by the four rulers whose conduct I have approved, or by finding out how Philip, the father of Alexander the Great, and how many other republics and sovereigns levied and trained troops: I have complete confidence in their methods.

Chapter Fourteen: What a ruler should do as regards the militia.

A ruler, then, should have no other concern, no other thought, should pay attention to nothing aside from war, military institutions, and the training of his soldiers. For this is the only field in which a ruler has to excel. It is of such importance [virtù] that military prowess not only keeps those who have been born rulers in power, but also often enables men who have been born private citizens to come to power. On the other hand, one sees that when rulers think more about luxuries than about weapons, they fall from power. The prime reason for losing power is neglect of military matters; while being an expert soldier opens the way to the acquisition of power.

Francesco Sforza, because he had troops, became Duke of Milan, having begun life as a private citizen. His descendants, who had no taste for the sweat and dust of a soldier's life, started out as dukes and ended up as private citizens. For, among the other deleterious consequences of not having one's own troops, one comes to be regarded with contempt. There are several types of disgrace a ruler should avoid, as I will explain below. This is one of them. For there is no comparison between a ruler who has his own troops and one who has not. It is not to be expected that someone who is armed should cheerfully obey someone who is defenseless, or that someone who has no weapon should be safe when his employees are armed. For the armed man has contempt for the man without weapons; the defenseless man does not trust someone who can overpower him. The two cannot get on together. So, too, a ruler who does not know how to organize a militia, beyond the other dangers he faces, which I have already described, must recognize that he will not be respected by his troops, and that he cannot trust them.

So a ruler must think only of military matters, and in time of peace he should be even more occupied with them than in time of war. There are two ways he can prepare for war: by thinking and by doing. As far as actions are concerned, he should not only keep his troops in good order and see they are well-trained; he should be always out hunting, thereby accustoming his body to fatigue. He should take the opportunity to study the lie of the land, climbing the mountains, descending into the valleys, crossing the plains, fording rivers, and wading through marshes. He should spare no effort to become acquainted with his own land, and this for two reasons. First, the knowledge will stand him in good stead if he has to defend his state against invasion; second, his knowledge and experience on his own terrain will make it easy for him to understand any other landscape with which he has to become acquainted from scratch. The hills, the valleys, the plains, the rivers, the marshes of, for example, Tuscany have a good deal in common with those of the other regions of Italy. A knowledge of the terrain in one region will make it easy for him to learn about the others. A ruler who lacks this sort of skill does not satisfy the first requirement in a military commander, for it is knowledge of the terrain that enables you to locate the enemy and to get the edge over him when deciding where to camp, in what order to march, how to draw up the troops on the field of battle, and where to build fortifications.

Philopoemon, ruler of the Achaeans, is much praised by the historians, but in particular he is admired because during peacetime he thought about nothing but warfare. When he was out riding in the countryside with his friends, he would often halt and ask: "If the enemy were up on those hills, and we were down here with our army, who would have the better position? How should we advance, following the rule book, to attack him? If we wanted to retreat, how would we set about it? If they were retreating, how would we pursue them?" And so he would invite them to discuss, as they rode along, all the possible eventualities an army may have to face. He listened to their views, he explained his own and backed them up with arguments. Thanks to this continual theorizing he ensured that, if he was at the head of an army, he would be perfectly prepared for anything that might happen.

Such theorizing is not enough. Every ruler should read history books, and in them he should study the actions of admirable men. He should see how they conducted themselves when at war, study why they won some battles and lost others, so he will know what to imitate and what to avoid. Above all he should set himself to imitate the actions of some admirable historical character, as great men have always imitated their glorious predecessors, constantly bearing in mind their actions and their ways of behaving. So, it is said, Alexander the Great took Achilles as his model; Caesar took Alexander; Scipio took Cyrus. If you read the life of Cyrus that was written by Xenophon and then study the life of Scipio you will realize to what extent those qualities that are admired in Scipio derive from Cyrus: His chastity, his affability, his kindness, his generosity, all are modelled upon Cyrus as Xenophon portrays him. A wise ruler will follow these examples. He will never relax during peacetime, but will always be working to take advantage of the opportunities peace presents, so he will be fully prepared when adversity comes. When his luck changes, he must be ready to fight back.

Chapter Fifteen: About those factors that cause men, and especially rulers, to be praised or censured.

Our next task is to consider the policies and principles a ruler ought to follow in dealing with his subjects or with his friends. Since I know many people have written on this subject, I am concerned it may be thought presumptuous for me to write on it as well, especially since what I have to say, as regards this question in particular, will differ greatly from the recommendations of others. But my hope is to write a book that will be useful, at least to those who read it intelligently, and so I thought it sensible to go straight to a discussion of how things are in real life and not waste time with a discussion of an imaginary world. For many authors have constructed imaginary republics and principalities that have never existed in practice and never could; for the gap between how people actually behave and how they ought to behave is so great that anyone who ignores everyday reality in order to live up to an ideal will soon discover he has been taught how to destroy himself, not how to preserve himself. For anyone who wants to act the part of a good man in all circumstances will bring about his own ruin, for those he has to deal with will not all be good. So it is necessary for a ruler, if he wants to hold on to power, to learn how not to be good, and to know when it is and when it is not necessary to use this knowledge.

Let us leave to one side, then, all discussion of imaginary rulers and talk about practical realities. I maintain that all men, when people talk about them, and especially rulers, because they hold positions of authority, are described in terms of qualities that are inextricably linked to censure or to praise. So one man is described as generous, another as a miser [*misero*] (to use the Tuscan term; for "avaricious," in our language, is used of someone who has a rapacious desire to acquire wealth, while we call someone a "miser" when he is unduly reluctant to spend the money he has); one is called open-handed, another tight-fisted; one man is cruel, another gentle; one untrustworthy, another reliable; one effeminate and cowardly, another bold and violent; one sympathetic, another self-important; one promiscuous, another monogamous; one straightforward, another duplicitous; one tough, another easy-going; one serious, another cheerful; one religious, another atheistical; and so on. Now I know everyone will agree that if a ruler could have all the good qualities I have listed and none of the bad ones, then this would be an excellent state of affairs. But one cannot have all the good qualities, nor always act in a praiseworthy fashion, for we do not live in an ideal world. You have to be astute enough to avoid being thought to have those evil qualities that would make it impossible for you to retain power; as for those that are compatible with holding on to power, you should avoid them if you can; but if you cannot, then you should not worry too much if people say you have them. Above all, do not be upset if you are supposed to have those vices

a ruler needs if he is going to stay securely in power, for, if you think about it, you will realize there are some ways of behaving that are supposed to be virtuous [*che parrà virtù*], but would lead to your downfall, and others that are supposed to be wicked, but will lead to your welfare and peace of mind.

Chapter Sixteen: On generosity and parsimony.

Let me begin, then, with the qualities I mentioned first. I argue it would be good to be thought generous; nevertheless, if you act in the way that will get you a reputation for generosity, you will do yourself damage. For generosity used skillfully [*virtuosamente*] and practiced as it ought to be, is hidden from sight, and being truly generous will not protect you from acquiring a reputation for parsimony. So, if you want to have a reputation for generosity, you must throw yourself into lavish and ostentatious expenditure. Consequently, a ruler who pursues a reputation for generosity will always end up wasting all his resources; and he will be obliged in the end, if he wants to preserve his reputation, to impose crushing taxes upon the people, to pursue every possible source of income, and to be preoccupied with maximizing his revenues. This will begin to make him hateful to his subjects, and will ensure no one thinks well of him, for no one admires poverty. The result is his supposed generosity will have caused him to offend the vast majority and to have won favor with few. Anything that goes wrong will destabilize him, and the slightest danger will imperil him. Recognizing the problem, and trying to economize, he will quickly find he has acquired a reputation as a miser.

So we see a ruler cannot seek to benefit from a reputation as generous [*questa virtù del liberale*] without harming himself. Recognizing this, he ought, if he is wise, not to mind being called miserly. For, as time goes by, he will be thought of as growing ever more generous, for people will recognize that as a result of his parsimony he is able to live on his income, maintain an adequate army, and undertake new initiatives without imposing new taxes. The result is he will be thought to be generous towards all those whose income he does not tax, which is almost everybody, and stingy towards those who miss out on handouts, who are only a few. In modern times nobody has succeeded on a large scale except those who have been thought miserly; the others came to nothing. Pope Julius II took advantage of a reputation for generosity in order to win election, but once elected he made no effort to keep his reputation, for he wanted to go to war. The present King of France has fought many wars without having to impose additional taxes on his people, because his occasional additional expenditures are offset by his long-term parsimony. The present King of Spain could not have aspired to, or achieved, so many conquests if he had had a reputation for generosity.

So a ruler should not care about being thought miserly, for it means he will be able to avoid robbing his subjects; he will be able to defend himself; he will not become poor and despicable, and he will not be forced to become rapacious. This is one of those vices that make successful government possible. And if you say: But Caesar rose to power thanks to his generosity, and many others have made their way to the highest positions of authority because they have both been and have been thought to be generous. I reply, either you are already a ruler, or you are on your way to becoming one. If you are already a ruler, generosity is a mistake; if you are trying to become one then you do, indeed, need to be thought of as generous. Caesar was one of those competing to become the ruler of Rome; but if, having acquired power, he had lived longer and had not learned to reduce his expenditures, he would have destroyed his own position. You may be tempted to reply: Many established rulers who have been thought to be immensely generous have been successful in war. But my answer is: Rulers either spend their own wealth and that of their subjects, or that of other people. Those who spend their own and their subjects' wealth should be abstemious; those who spend the wealth of others should seize every opportunity to be generous. Rulers who march with their armies, living off plunder, pillage, and confiscations are spending other people's money, and it is essential they should seem generous, for otherwise their soldiers will not follow them. With goods that belong neither to you nor to your subjects, you can afford to be generous, as Cyrus, Caesar, and Alexander were. Squandering other people's money does not do your reputation any harm, quite the reverse. The problem is with squandering

your own. There is nothing so self-defeating as generosity, for the more generous you are, the less you are able to be generous. Generosity leads to poverty and disgrace, or, if you try to escape that, to rapacity and hostility. Among all the things a ruler should try to avoid, he must avoid above all being hated and despised. Generosity leads to your being both. So it is wiser to accept a reputation as miserly, which people despise but do not hate, than to aspire to a reputation as generous, and as a consequence, be obliged to face criticism for rapacity, which people both despise and hate.

Chapter Seventeen: About cruelty and compassion; and about whether it is better to be loved than feared, or the reverse.

Going further down our list of qualities, I recognize every ruler should want to be thought of as compassionate and not cruel. Nevertheless, I have to warn you to be careful about being compassionate. Cesare Borgia was thought of as cruel; but this supposed cruelty of his restored order to the Romagna, united it, rendered it peaceful and law-abiding. If you think about it, you will realize he was, in fact, much more compassionate than the people of Florence, who, in order to avoid being thought cruel, allowed Pistoia to tear itself apart. So a ruler ought not to mind the disgrace of being called cruel, if he keeps his subjects peaceful and law-abiding, for it is more compassionate to impose harsh punishments on a few than, out of excessive compassion, to allow disorder to spread, which leads to murders or looting. The whole community suffers if there are riots, while to maintain order the ruler only has to execute one or two individuals. Of all rulers, he who is new to power cannot escape a reputation for cruelty, for he is surrounded by dangers. Virgil has Dido say:

> Harsh necessity, and the fact my kingdom is new,
>   oblige me to do these things,
> And to mass my armies on the frontiers.

Nevertheless, you should be careful how you assess the situation and should think twice before you act. Do not be afraid of your own shadow. Employ policies that are moderated by prudence and sympathy. Avoid excessive self-confidence, which leads to carelessness, and avoid excessive timidity, which will make you insupportable.

This leads us to a question that is in dispute: Is it better to be loved than feared, or vice versa? My reply is one ought to be both loved and feared; but, since it is difficult to accomplish both at the same time, I maintain it is much safer to be feared than loved, if you have to do without one of the two. For of men one can, in general, say this: They are ungrateful, fickle, deceptive and deceiving, avoiders of danger, eager to gain. As long as you serve their interests, they are devoted to you. They promise you their blood, their possessions, their lives, and their children, as I said before, so long as you seem to have no need of them. But as soon as you need help, they turn against you. Any ruler who relies simply on their promises and makes no other preparations, will be destroyed. For you will find that those whose support you buy, who do not rally to you because they admire your strength of character and nobility of soul, these are people you pay for, but they are never yours, and in the end you cannot get the benefit of your investment. Men are less nervous of offending someone who makes himself lovable, than someone who makes himself frightening. For love attaches men by ties of obligation, which, since men are wicked, they break whenever their interests are at stake. But fear restrains men because they are afraid of punishment, and this fear never leaves them. Still, a ruler should make himself feared in such a way that, if he does not inspire love, at least he does not provoke hatred. For it is perfectly possible to be feared and not hated. You will only be hated if you seize the property or the women of your subjects and citizens. Whenever you have to kill someone, make sure you have a suitable excuse and an obvious reason; but, above all else, keep your hands off other people's property; for men are quicker to forget the death of their father than the loss of their inheritance. Moreover, there are always reasons why you might want to seize people's property; and he who begins to live by plundering others will always find an excuse for seizing other people's possessions; but there are fewer reasons for killing people, and one killing need not lead to another.

When a ruler is at the head of his army and has a vast number of soldiers under his command, then it is absolutely essential to be prepared to be thought cruel; for it is impossible to keep an army united and ready for action without acquiring a reputation for cruelty. Among the extraordinary accomplishments of Hannibal, we may note one in particular: He commanded a vast army, made up of men of many different nations, who were fighting far from home, yet they never mutinied and they never fell out with one another, either when things were going badly, or when things were going well. The only possible explanation for this is that he was known to be harsh and cruel. This, together with his numerous virtues [virtù], meant his soldiers always regarded him with admiration and fear. Without cruelty, his other virtues [virtù] would not have done the job. Those who write about Hannibal without thinking things through both admire the loyalty of his troops and criticize the cruelty that was its principal cause. If you doubt my claim that his other virtues [virtù] would have been insufficient, take the case of Scipio. He was not only unique in his own day, but history does not record anyone his equal. But his army rebelled against him in Spain. The sole cause of this was his excessive leniency, which meant his soldiers had more freedom than is compatible with good military discipline. Fabius Maximus criticized him for this in the senate and accused him of corrupting the Roman armies. When Locri was destroyed by one of his commanders, he did not avenge the deaths of the inhabitants, and he did not punish his officer's insubordination. He was too easygoing. This was so apparent that one of his supporters in the senate was obliged to excuse him by saying he was no different from many other men, who were better at doing their own jobs than at making other people do theirs. In course of time, had he remained in command without learning from his mistakes, this aspect of Scipio's character would have destroyed his glorious reputation. But, because his authority was subordinate to that of the senate, not only were the consequences of this defect mitigated, but it even enhanced his reputation.

I conclude, then, that, as far as being feared and loved is concerned, since men decide for themselves whom they love, and rulers decide whom they fear, a wise ruler should rely on the emotion he can control, not on the one he cannot. But he must take care to avoid being hated, as I have said.

Chapter Eighteen: How far rulers are to keep their word.

Everybody recognizes how praiseworthy it is for a ruler to keep his word and to live a life of integrity, without relying on craftiness. Nevertheless, we see that in practice, in these days, those rulers who have not thought it important to keep their word have achieved great things, and have known how to employ cunning to confuse and disorientate other men. In the end, they have been able to overcome those who have placed store in integrity.

You should therefore know there are two ways to fight: one while respecting the rules, the other with no holds barred. Men alone fight in the first fashion, and animals fight in the second. But because you cannot always win if you respect the rules, you must be prepared to break them. A ruler, in particular, needs to know how to be both an animal and a man. The classical writers, without saying it explicitly, taught rulers to behave like this. They described how Achilles, and many other rulers in ancient times, were given to Chiron the centaur to be raised, so he could bring them up as he thought best. What they intended to convey, with this story of rulers' being educated by someone who was half beast and half man, was that it is necessary for a ruler to know when to act like an animal and when like a man; and if he relies on just one or the other mode of behavior he cannot hope to survive.

Since a ruler, then, needs to know how to make good use of beastly qualities, he should take as his models among the animals both the fox and the lion, for the lion does not know how to avoid traps, and the fox is easily overpowered by wolves. So you must be a fox when it comes to suspecting a trap, and a lion when it comes to making the wolves turn tail. Those who simply act like a lion all the time do not understand their business. So you see a wise ruler cannot, and should not, keep his word when doing so is to his disadvantage, and when the reasons that led him to promise to do so no longer apply. Of course, if all men were good, this advice would be bad; but since men are wicked and will not keep faith with you, you need not keep faith with them. Nor is a ruler ever short of legitimate reasons to justify breaking his word. I could give an infinite number of

contemporary examples to support my argument and to show how treaties and promises have been rendered null and void by the dishonesty of rulers; and he who has known best how to act the fox has come out of it the best. But it is essential to know how to conceal how crafty one is, to know how to be a clever counterfeit and hypocrite. You will find people are so simpleminded and so preoccupied with their immediate concerns, that if you set out to deceive them, you will always find plenty of them who will let themselves be deceived.

Among the numerous recent cases one could mention, there is one of particular interest. Alexander VI had only one purpose, only one thought, which was to take people in, and he always found people who were willing victims. There never has been anyone who was more convincing when he swore an oath, nor has there been anybody who has ever formulated more eloquent oaths and has at the same time been quicker to break them. Nevertheless, he was able to find gulls one after another, whenever he wanted them, for he was a master of this particular skill.

So a ruler need not have all the positive qualities I listed earlier, but he must seem to have them. Indeed, I would go so far as to say that if you have them and never make any exceptions, then you will suffer for it; while if you merely appear to have them, they will benefit you. So you should seem to be compassionate, trustworthy, sympathetic, honest, religious, and, indeed, be all these things; but at the same time you should be constantly prepared, so that, if these become liabilities, you are trained and ready to become their opposites. You need to understand this: A ruler, and particularly a ruler who is new to power, cannot conform to all those rules that men who are thought good are expected to respect, for he is often obliged, in order to hold on to power, to break his word, to be uncharitable, inhumane, and irreligious. So he must be mentally prepared to act as circumstances and changes in fortune require. As I have said, he should do what is right if he can; but he must be prepared to do wrong if necessary.

A ruler must, therefore, take great care that he never carelessly says anything that is not imbued with the five qualities I listed above. He must seem, to those who listen to him and watch him, entirely pious, truthful, reliable, sympathetic, and religious. There is no quality that it is more important he should seem to have than this last one. In general, men judge more by sight than by touch. Everyone sees what is happening, but not everyone feels the consequences. Everyone sees what you seem to be; few have direct experience of who you really are. Those few will not dare speak out in the face of public opinion when that opinion is reinforced by the authority of the state. In the behavior of all men, and particularly of rulers, against whom there is no recourse at law, people judge by the outcome. So if a ruler wins wars and holds on to power, the means he has employed will always be judged honorable, and everyone will praise them. The common man accepts external appearances and judges by the outcome; and when it comes down to it only the masses count; for the elite are powerless if the masses have someone to provide them with leadership. One contemporary ruler, whom it would be unwise to name, is always preaching peace and good faith, and he has not a shred of respect for either; if he had respected either one or the other, he would have lost either his state or his reputation several times by now.

Chapter Nineteen: How one should avoid hatred and contempt.

Because I have spoken of the more important of the qualities I mentioned earlier, I want now to discuss the rest of them briefly under this general heading, that a ruler must take care (I have already referred to this in passing) to avoid those things that will make him an object of hatred or contempt. As long as he avoids these he will have done what is required of him, and he will find having a reputation for any of the other vices will do him no harm at all. You become hateful, above all, as I have said, if you prey on the possessions and the women of your subjects. You should leave both alone. The vast majority of men, so long as their goods and their honor are not taken from them, will live contentedly, so you will only have to contend with the small minority who are ambitious, and there are lots of straightforward ways of keeping them under control. You become contemptible if you are thought to be erratic, capricious, effeminate, pusillanimous, irresolute. You should avoid acquiring such a reputation as a pilot steers clear of the rocks. Make every effort to ensure

your actions suggest greatness and endurance, strength of character and of purpose. When it comes to the private business of your subjects, you should aim to ensure you never have to change your decisions once they have been taken, and that you acquire a reputation that will discourage people from even considering tricking or deceiving you.

A ruler who is thought of in these terms has the sort of reputation he needs; and it is difficult to conspire against someone who is respected in this way, difficult to attack him, because people realize he is on top of his job and has the loyalty of his employees. For rulers ought to be afraid of two things: Within the state, they should fear their subjects; abroad, they should fear other rulers. Against foreign powers, a good army and reliable allies are the only defense; and, if you have a good army, you will always find your allies reliable. And you will find it easy to maintain order at home if you are secure from external threats, provided, that is, conspiracies against you have not undermined your authority. Even if foreign powers do attack, if you have followed my advice and lived according to the principles I have outlined, then, as long as you keep a grip on yourself, you will be able to resist any attack, just as I said Nabis of Sparta was able to. But where your subjects are concerned, when you are not being attacked by foreign powers, you have to be wary of secret conspiracies. The best protection against these is to ensure you are not hated or despised, and the people are satisfied with your rule. It is essential to accomplish this, as I have already explained at length.

Indeed, one of the most effective defenses a ruler has against conspiracies is to make sure he is not generally hated. For conspirators always believe the assassination of the ruler will be approved by the people. If they believe the people will be angered, then they cannot screw up the courage to embark on such an enterprise, for conspirators have to overcome endless difficulties to achieve success. Experience shows the vast majority of conspiracies fail. For a conspirator cannot act alone, and he can only find associates among those whom he believes are discontented. As soon as you tell someone who is discontented what you are planning, you give him the means to satisfy his ambitions, because it is obvious he can expect to be richly rewarded if he betrays you. If he betrays you, his reward is certain; if he keeps faith with you, he faces danger, with little prospect of reward. So, you see, he needs either to be an exceptionally loyal friend or to be a completely intransigent enemy of the ruler, if he is to keep faith with you. So we can sum up as follows: The conspirators face nothing but fear, mutual distrust, and the prospect of punishment, so they lose heart; while the ruler is supported by the authority of his office and by the laws, and protected both by his supporters and by the forces of government. So, if you add to this inbuilt advantage the goodwill of the populace, then it is impossible to find anyone who is so foolhardy as to conspire against you. For in most situations a conspirator has to fear capture before he does the deed; but if the ruler has the goodwill of the people, he has to fear it afterwards as well, for the people will turn on him when the deed is done, and he will have nowhere to hide.

I could give an infinite number of examples to illustrate this, but I will confine myself to one only, a conspiracy that took place during the lifetime of our parents. Mr. Annibale Bentivoglio, grandfather of the present Mr. Annibale, was at the time ruler of Bologna. The Canneschi conspired against him and assassinated him. His only surviving relative was Mr. Giovanni, who was still in the cradle. But as soon as he was killed the people rose up and killed all the Canneschi. This happened because the family of Bentivoglio had, in those days, the goodwill of the people. Their loyalty was such that, there being no surviving member of the family in Bologna who could, now Annibale was dead, take over the government, and they having heard that in Florence there was a member of the family, someone who so far had been nothing more than the son of a blacksmith, the citizens of Bologna came to Florence to fetch him and made him the ruler of their city. He ruled it until Mr. Giovanni was old enough to take office.

I conclude, then, that a ruler need not worry much about conspiracies as long as the people wish him well; but if the people are hostile to him and hate him, then he should fear everything and everyone. States that are well-governed and rulers who are wise make every effort to ensure the elite are not driven to despair, and to satisfy the masses and keep them content; for this is one of the most important tasks a ruler must set himself.

Among the states that are well-ordered and well-ruled at the present time is France. There you will find innumerable good institutions that ensure the freedom of action and security of the king. First among them is the *parlement* and its authority. For whoever set up the government of that country understood the powerful are ambitious and insolent, and judged it necessary they should be bridled so they could be controlled, but on the other hand he recognized the hatred most people have for the powerful, whom they have reason to fear, and the consequent need to reassure and protect the great. So he did not want this to be the responsibility of the king, in order to avoid his alienating the powerful by favoring the people or alienating the people by favoring the powerful, and he established an independent tribunal, whose task it is, without incurring blame for the king, to crush the powerful and defend the weak. This arrangement is as intelligent and prudent as could be, and makes a substantial contribution to the security of the king and the stability of the kingdom. This institution enables us to recognize a significant general principle: Rulers should delegate responsibility for unpopular actions, while taking personal responsibility for those that will win favor. And once again I conclude a ruler should treat the powerful with respect, but at all costs he should avoid being hated by the people.

Many perhaps will think, if they consider the lives and deaths of some of the Roman emperors, that these provide examples contrary to the opinion I have expressed. For it would seem some of them lived exemplary lives and demonstrated great strength [*virtù*] of character, yet they fell from power, or rather they were killed by their retainers, who had conspired against them. Since I want to reply to this objection, I will discuss the characters of some of the emperors, explaining the reasons why they were destroyed, and show they do not tell against my argument. This will primarily involve pointing out factors that would seem significant to anyone who read the history of those times. I will confine myself to discussing all those emperors who came after Marcus Aurelius, up to and including Maximilian: that is, Marcus, his son Commodus, Pertinax, Julian, Severus, his son Antoninus Caracalla, Macrinus, Heliogabulus, Alexander, and Maximilian.

The first thing to be remarked is that, where in most states one only has to contend with the ambition of the great and the effrontery of the populace, the emperors of Rome had to face a third problem: They had to put up with the cruelty and greed of their soldiers. This was so difficult to do that it caused the downfall of many of the emperors, for it was almost impossible to satisfy both the soldiers and the populace. The people loved peace and quiet and, for this reason, liked their rulers to be unassuming; but the soldiers wanted the emperor to be a man of war and liked him to be arrogant, cruel, and rapacious. They wanted him to direct his aggression against the populace, so they could double their income and give free rein to their greed and cruelty. The result was those emperors who did not have a sufficiently intimidating reputation to keep both populace and soldiers in check (either because they did not think such a reputation desirable, or because they were incapable of acquiring it) were always destroyed. Most of them, especially those who acquired power without inheriting it, recognizing the difficulty of pleasing both soldiers and people, concentrated on pleasing the soldiers, thinking it could do little harm to alienate the populace. They had no choice, for, since rulers are bound to be hated by someone, their first concern must be to ensure they are not hated by any significant group; and, if they cannot achieve this, then they must make every possible effort to avoid the hatred of those groups that are most powerful. And so those emperors who had not inherited power and, thus, were in need of particularly strong support, attached themselves to the soldiers rather than to the people; a policy that proved successful or not, depending on whether the particular ruler in question knew how to establish his reputation with the army. For these reasons, then, Marcus, Pertinax, and Alexander, all of whom were unassuming, lovers of justice, haters of cruelty, sympathetic and kind, all came, apart from Marcus, to a tragic end. Marcus alone lived honorably and died peaceably, for he inherited power, and did not have to repay a debt to either the soldiers or the populace. Moreover, since he had many virtues [virtù] that made him widely respected, he was able, during his own lifetime, to keep both groups in their place, and he was never hated or despised. But Pertinax was made emperor against the wishes of the soldiers, who, being accustomed to an unbridled life under Commodus, were unable to tolerate the disciplined way of life Pertinax wanted to impose on them. So he

made himself hated, and to this hatred was added contempt, for he was an old man, and so his rule had scarcely begun before he fell from power.

Here we should note one can become hated for the good things one does, as much as for the bad. That is why, as I said above, a ruler who wants to hold on to power is often obliged not to be good, for when some powerful group—whether the populace, the soldiers, or the elite—whose support you feel it is essential to have if you are to survive, is corrupt, then you have to adapt to its tastes in order to satisfy it, in which case doing good will do you harm. But let us turn to Alexander. He was so good that among the other things for which he is praised is the fact that during the fourteen years he retained power, nobody was ever executed at his orders without due trial. Nevertheless, he was thought effeminate, and blamed for being under the influence of his mother, and so he came to be despised, the army conspired against him and killed him.

By contrast, let us consider the qualities of Commodus, of Severus, Antoninus Caracalla, and Maximinus. They were, you will find, in the highest degree bloodthirsty and rapacious. In order to satisfy the soldiery, they did not fail to commit every possible type of crime against the populace; and all of them, with the exception of Severus, came to a bad end. For Severus was such a strong ruler [in Severo fu tanta virtù] that, with the support of the army, even though the populace were oppressed by him, he could always rule successfully; for his strength [virtù] inspired awe in the minds of both soldiers and people: The people were always to a considerable degree stupefied and astonished by him, while the soldiers were admiring and satisfied. Because his deeds were commendable in a new ruler, I want to pause to point out how well he understood how to play the part both of the fox and of the lion: These are the two styles of action I have maintained a ruler must know how to imitate. Severus, because he knew what a coward Julian the new emperor was, persuaded the army he had under his command in Slavonia that it was a good idea to march on Rome to revenge the death of Pertinax, who had been killed by his praetorian guard. With this excuse, and without displaying any ambition to seize the throne, he set out for Rome; and his army was in Italy before anyone knew it had left its station.

When he reached Rome, the senate, out of fear, elected him emperor and had Julian put to death. Severus, having begun like this, faced two problems if he wanted to gain effective control of the whole empire: In Asia there was Niger, commander of the Asiatic armies, who had had himself proclaimed emperor; in the West there was Albinus, who also aspired to power. Because he thought it would be dangerous to take on both of them at once, he decided to attack Niger and deceive Albinus. So he wrote to Albinus saying now that he had been elected emperor by the senate, he wanted to share his authority with him. He offered him the title of Caesar and had the senate appoint him co-ruler. Albinus accepted these proposals at face value. But as soon as Severus had defeated and killed Niger and pacified the eastern empire, he returned to Rome and attacked Albinus in the senate, complaining that he, far from being grateful for the generosity he had been shown, had wickedly sought to assassinate him. Severus claimed to have no choice but to go and punish this ingrate. So he attacked him in France and deprived him of his offices and of his life.

Anyone who examines Severus's actions with care will find he was both a ferocious lion and a cunning fox. He will find he was feared and respected by all, and he was not hated by the armies. So it is no surprise Severus, who had not inherited power, was able to hold on to a vast empire, for his immense reputation was a constant defense against the hatred the populace might otherwise have felt for his exactions. Antoninus his son was also a man whose remarkable abilities inspired awe in the populace and gratitude in the soldiers. For he was a man of war, able to make light of the most arduous task and contemptuous of delicate food and all other luxuries. This made all his soldiers love him. Nevertheless, his ferocity and cruelty were without parallel. He did not only kill vast numbers of individuals, but, on one occasion, a large part of the population of Rome, and, on another, the whole of Alexandria. So he came to be loathed by everyone, and even his close associates began to fear him, with the result he was killed by a centurion while he was surrounded by his own troops. One should note rulers have no protection against an assassination like this, carried out by a truly determined individual, for anyone who is prepared to die can attack them. But,

nevertheless, rulers should not worry unduly about such assassins because they are extremely rare. You should try merely to avoid giving grave injury to anyone you employ who comes close to you in the course of business. Antoninus had done just this, for he had outrageously put to death a brother of the centurion who killed him, and had repeatedly threatened the centurion's own life; yet he employed him as a bodyguard. This was foolhardy, and the disastrous outcome could have been predicted.

Now we come to Commodus, who had no difficulty in holding on to power, because he had inherited it, being the son of Marcus. All he had to do was follow in his father's footsteps, and he would have been satisfactory to both soldiers and populace. But, because he was by nature cruel and brutal, he began to ingratiate himself with the soldiers and to encourage them to be undisciplined, so he would be able to give his own rapacity free rein against the people. On the other hand, he did not maintain his own dignity. Often, when he went to the amphitheater, he came down and fought with the gladiators, and he did other things that were despicable and incompatible with imperial majesty. So he became contemptible in the eyes of his soldiers. He was hated by the people and despised by the soldiers, so there was soon a conspiracy against him and he was killed.

There remains for us to discuss the character of Maximinus. He was a most warlike individual. The armies had been irritated by the feebleness of Alexander, whom I have already discussed, and so, with him out of the way, they elected Maximinus emperor. But he did not hold on to power for long, for there were two things that made him hateful and contemptible. In the first place, he was of the lowest social status, having once been a shepherd in Thrace (a fact known to everyone, and one that made them all regard him with disdain); in the second, when he was elected emperor he had delayed going to Rome and taking possession of the throne, but had acquired a reputation for terrible cruelty because his representatives, in Rome and throughout the empire, had acted with great ferocity. So everybody was worked up with disdain for his humble origins and agitated with hatred arising from their fear of his ferocity. First Africa rebelled, and then the senate and the whole population of Rome; soon all Italy was conspiring against him. His own army turned against him. They were laying siege to Aquileia, but were finding it hard to take the city, to which was added their distaste for his cruelty. Seeing so many united against him, they lost their fear of him and killed him.

I do not want to discuss Heliogabulus, Macrinus, and Julian, for they were entirely contemptible and fell from power quickly. We can now come to the end of this discussion. I would have you note the rulers of our own day do not face in such an acute form the problem of having to adopt policies that involve breaking the law in order to satisfy their soldiers' appetites; for, although you cannot afford entirely to ignore contemporary soldiers, you can handle them easily. Modern rulers do not face standing armies with long experience of ruling and administering provinces, such as the Roman armies had. But if in those days it was more important to give satisfaction to the soldiers than to the populace, that was because the soldiers were more to be feared than the populace. Now all rulers, with the exception of the sultans of Turkey and of Egypt, need to be more concerned to satisfy the populace than the soldiers, for the populace are the greater threat. I make an exception of the ruler of Turkey, for at all times he is surrounded by twelve thousand infantry and fifteen thousand cavalry, on whom depends the security and strength of his government. It is essential for him, more than anything else, to retain their loyalty. Similarly, the Sultan of Egypt is entirely at the mercy of his soldiers, so that he, too, must keep their loyalty, no matter what the consequences for the populace may be. And one should note the Sultan of Egypt is in a different position from all other rulers; for he is comparable to the Christian pope, who also cannot be described as either a hereditary or a new ruler. For the sons of the old ruler do not inherit his office and remain in power, but the new ruler is elected by a group who have the authority to appoint him. Since this arrangement has long been in existence, you cannot call the sultan a new ruler, for he faces none of the difficulties faced by those who are new to power. Even though he himself is new to power, the principle of succession is long-established, and ensures his authority is acknowledged as unquestioningly as would be the case if he were an hereditary ruler.

Let us return to our subject. I believe everyone should agree in the light of this discussion that hatred and contempt caused the fall of the emperors we have been considering, and will also understand how it comes about that, with one group of them following one line of policy and the other its opposite, in both groups one ruler was successful and the rest were killed. For it was pointless and dangerous for Pertinax and Alexander, who were new rulers, to try to imitate Marcus, who had inherited power; similarly it was a bad mistake for Caracalla, Commodus, and Maximinus to imitate Severus, for they lacked the strength [*virtù*] that would have been necessary for anyone following in his footsteps. Thus, a new ruler, who has not inherited power, should not follow the example of Marcus, but need not follow that of Severus. He ought to imitate in Severus those features that are essential for him to establish himself securely in power, and in Marcus those features that are effective and win glory for someone who is seeking to preserve a government that has already entrenched itself.

Chapter Twenty: Whether the building of fortresses (and many other things rulers regularly do) is useful or not.

Some rulers, in order to ensure they have a firm grip on power, have disarmed their subjects. Others have divided up the territories over which they rule. Some have positively encouraged opposition to their own authority. Others have set out to win over those who were hostile to them when they first came to power. Some have built fortresses. Others have destroyed them. It is impossible to pass definitive judgment on any of these policies until one considers the particular circumstances that existed in the state where the policy was adopted. Nevertheless, I will talk in general terms in so far as the subject itself permits.

No new ruler, let me point out, has ever disarmed his subjects; on the contrary, when he has found them disarmed, he has always armed them. For, when you arm them, their arms become yours, those who have been hostile to you become loyal, while those who have been loyal remain so, and progress from being your obedient subjects to being your active supporters. Because not every subject can be armed, provided you ensure those who receive arms stand to benefit, you will be more secure in your dealings with the others. When they recognize this diversity of treatment, it will make them all the more obliged to you;

while the unarmed will forgive you, for they will recognize it is necessary that those who face more dangers and have more onerous obligations should be better rewarded. But if you take their arms away from those who have been armed, you begin to alienate them. You make it clear you do not trust them, either because you think they are poor soldiers or disloyal. Whichever view they attribute to you, they will begin to hate you. And, since you cannot remain undefended, you will be obliged to rely on mercenary troops, with the consequences we have already discussed. No matter how good they are, they will be unable to defend you against a combination of powerful foreign powers and hostile subjects. So, as I have said, a new ruler who has not inherited power has always formed his own army. There are innumerable examples in history. But when a ruler acquires a new state, which is simply added on to his existing territories, then it is essential to disarm the people, with the sole exception of those who have actively supported you in taking power. And they too, over time, and as opportunity occurs, should be encouraged to become weak and effeminate. You should arrange things so that all the weapons in your new state are in the hands of those of your own troops who were closely associated with you in your old territories.

Our ancestors, particularly those who were thought wise, used to say it was necessary to hold Pistoia by encouraging factional divisions, and Pisa by building fortresses. So, in some of the territory they occupied, they encouraged divisions in order to have better control. This was a sound policy in the days when Italy experienced a balance of power; but I do not think it can be recommended now. For I do not believe any good ever comes of internal conflicts. It is certain that when enemy forces approach you run the risk that divided cities will go over to the other side, for the weaker of the two internal factions will attach itself to the invaders, and the stronger will not be able to retain power against enemies within and without the walls.

The Venetians, following, I believe, the same line of thought as our ancestors, encouraged the division of the cities under their control into the two factions of Guelfs and Ghibellines. Although they never allowed the conflicts between them to go so far as bloodshed, they encouraged these tensions so the inhabitants of these cities would be fully occupied with their own internal disagreements and would not unite against their masters. But history shows this policy did not pay off. For, when they were defeated at Vailà, one of the factions quickly plucked up courage and deprived them of all their territories. Such policies, indeed, imply the ruler is weak, for a robust government would never allow such divisions, since you only benefit from them in time of peace, when they enable you to manage your subjects more easily; when war comes, such a policy proves to be misconceived.

There is no doubt rulers become powerful as they overcome the difficulties they face and the opposition they encounter. So fortune, especially when she wants to make a new ruler powerful (for new rulers have more need of acquiring a reputation than ones who have inherited power), makes him start out surrounded by enemies and endangered by threats, so he can overcome these obstacles and can climb higher on a ladder supplied by his enemies. Therefore, many conclude a wise ruler will, when he has the opportunity, secretly foster opposition to his rule, so that, when he has put down his opponents, he will be in a more powerful position.

Rulers, and especially those who are new to power, have sometimes found there is more loyalty and support to be had from those who were initially believed to be opposed to their rule, than from those whom from the start they could count on. Pandolfo Petrucci, ruler of Siena, governed his state by relying more on those who were supposed to be hostile to him than on his supporters. But we cannot discuss this policy in general terms, because its success depends upon circumstances. I will only say those men who have been hostile when a ruler first acquires power, but who belong to those social groups that need to rely on government support in order to maintain their position, can always be won over by the new ruler with the greatest of ease. And they are all the more obliged to serve him faithfully because they know it is essential for them to undo by their actions the negative assessment that was initially made of them. Thus, the ruler can always get more out of them than out of those who, being all too confident of his goodwill, pay little attention to his interests.

And, since it is relevant to our subject, I do not want to fail to point out to rulers who have recently acquired a state through the support of people living within it, that they should give careful consideration to the motives of those who supported them. If they did not give their support out of natural affection for you, but gave it only because they were not happy with their previous government, you will find you can only retain their loyalty with much trouble and effort, for there is no way in which you will be able to keep them happy. If you think about it and consider the record of ancient and modern history, you will realize it will be much easier for you to win the loyalty of those men who were happy with the previous government and were therefore opposed to your seizure of power, than of those who, because they were unhappy with it, became your allies and encouraged you to take power from it.

Rulers have been accustomed, in order to have a more secure grip on their territories, to build fortresses. They are intended to be a bridle and bit for those who plan to rebel against you, and to provide you with a secure refuge in the event of an unexpected attack. I approve of this policy, for it was used by the Romans. Nevertheless, Mr. Niccolò Vitelli, in our own day, had two fortresses in Città di Castello destroyed so he could hold on to that state. Guido Ubaldo, the Duke of Urbino, when he returned to power, having previously been driven into exile by Cesare Borgia, completely destroyed all the fortresses in his territory. He believed that without them it would be harder to deprive him once again of power. The Bentivogli, when they recovered power in Bologna, adopted the same policy.

We must conclude that fortresses are useful or not, depending on circumstances, and that, if they are useful at one time, they may also do you harm at another. We can identify the relevant factors as follows: A ruler who is more afraid of his subjects than of foreign powers should build fortresses; but a ruler who is more afraid of foreign powers than of his subjects should do without them. The castle of Milan, which was built by Francesco Sforza, has done and will do more damage to the house of Sforza than any other defect in that state. For the best fortress one can have is not being hated by one's subjects; for if you have fortresses, but your subjects hate you, they will not save you, for your subjects, once they have risen in arms, will never be short of foreign allies who will come to their support.

In recent times, there is no evidence that fortresses have been useful to any ruler, except for the Contessa of Forlì, when her husband Count Girolamo died: Because she could take refuge in one she was able to escape the popular uprising, hold out until assistance came from Milan, and retake her state. Circumstances at the time were such that the populace could not get assistance from abroad; but later, even she gained little benefit from her fortresses when Cesare Borgia attacked her, and the populace, still hostile to her, joined forces with the invaders. So, both at first and later, it would have been safer for her not to have been hated by her people than to have fortresses. Consequently, having considered all these factors, I would praise both those who build fortresses and those who do not, but I would criticize anyone who, relying on his fortresses, thought it unimportant that his people hated him.

Chapter Twenty-One: What a ruler should do in order to acquire a reputation.

Nothing does more to give a ruler a reputation than embarking on great undertakings and doing remarkable things. In our own day, there is Ferdinand of Aragon, the present King of Spain. He may be called, more or less, a new ruler, because having started out as a weak ruler he has become the most famous and most glorious of all the kings of Christendom. If you think about his deeds, you will find them all noble, and some of them extraordinary. At the beginning of his reign he attacked Granada, and this undertaking was the basis of his increased power. In the first place, he undertook the reconquest when he had no other problems to face, so he could concentrate upon it. He used it to channel the ambitions of his Castilian barons, who, because they were thinking of the war, were no threat to him at home. Meanwhile, he acquired influence and authority over them without their even being aware of it. He was able to raise money from the church and from his subjects to build up his armies. Thus, this lengthy war enabled him to build up his military strength, which has paid off since. Next, in order to be able to engage in more ambitious undertakings, still exploiting religion, he practiced a pious cruelty, expropriating and expelling from his kingdom the Marranos: an act without parallel and truly despicable. He used religion once more as an excuse to justify an attack on Africa. He then attacked Italy and has recently invaded France. He is always plotting and carrying out great enterprises, which have always kept his subjects bewildered and astonished, waiting to see what their outcome would be. And his deeds have followed one another so closely that he has never left space between one and the next for people to plot uninterruptedly against him.

It is also of considerable help to a ruler if he does remarkable things when it comes to domestic policy, such as those that are reported of Mr. Bernabò of Milan. It is a good idea to be widely talked about, as he was, because, whenever anyone happened to do anything extraordinary, whether good or bad, in civil life, he found an imaginative way to reward or to punish them. Above all a ruler should make every effort to ensure that whatever he does it gains him a reputation as a great man, a person who excels.

Rulers are also admired when they know how to be true allies and genuine enemies: That is, when, without any reservations, they demonstrate themselves to be loyal supporters or opponents of others. Such a policy is always better than one of neutrality. For if two rulers who are your neighbors are at war with each other, they are either so powerful that, if one of them wins, you will have to fear the victor, or they are not. Either way, it will be better for you to take sides and fight a good fight; for, if they are powerful, and you do not take sides, you will still be preyed on by the victor, much to the pleasure and satisfaction of his defeated opponent. You will have no excuse, no defense, no refuge. For whoever wins will not want allies who are unreliable and who do not stand by him in adversity; while he who loses will not offer you refuge, since you were not willing, sword in hand, to share his fate.

The Aetolians invited Antiochus to Greece to drive out the Romans. Antiochus sent an ambassador to the Achaeans, who were allies of the Romans, to encourage them to remain neutral; while the Romans urged them to fight on their side. The ruling council of the Achaeans met to decide what to do, and Antiochus's ambassador spoke in favor of neutrality. The Roman ambassador replied: "As for what they say to you, that it would be sensible to keep out of the war, there is nothing further from your true interests. If you are without credit, without dignity, the victor will claim you as his prize."

It will always happen that he who is not your ally will urge neutrality upon you, while he who is your ally will urge you to take sides. Rulers who are unsure what to do, but want to avoid immediate dangers, generally end up staying neutral and usually destroy themselves by doing so. But when a ruler boldly takes sides, if your ally wins, even if he is powerful, and has the ability to overpower you, he is in your debt and fond of you. Nobody is so shameless as to turn on you in so ungrateful a fashion. Moreover, victories are never so overwhelming that the victor can act without any constraint: Above all, victors still need to appear just. But if, on the other hand, your ally is defeated, he will offer you refuge, will help you as long as he is able, and will share your ill-fortune, in the hope of one day sharing good fortune with you. In the second case, when those at war with each other are insufficiently powerful to give you grounds to fear the outcome, there is all the more reason to take sides, for you will be able to destroy one of them with the help of the other, when, if they were wise, they would be helping each other. The one who wins is at your mercy; and victory is certain for him whom you support.

Here it is worth noting a ruler should never take the side of someone who is more powerful than himself against other rulers, unless necessity compels him to, as I have already implied. For if you win, you are your ally's prisoner; and rulers should do everything they can to avoid being at the mercy of others. The Venetians allied with the King of France against the Duke of Milan, when they could have avoided taking sides; they brought about their own destruction. But when you cannot help but take sides (which is the situation the Florentines found themselves in when the pope and the King of Spain were advancing with their armies to attack Lombardy) then you should take sides decisively, as I have explained. Do not for a moment think any state can always take safe decisions, but rather think every decision you take involves risks, for it is in the nature of things that you cannot take precautions against one danger without opening yourself to another. Prudence consists in knowing how to assess risks and in accepting the lesser evil as a good.

A ruler should also show himself to be an admirer of skill [*virtù*] and should honor those who are excellent in any type of work. He should encourage his citizens by making it possible for them to pursue their occupations peacefully, whether they are businessmen, farmers, or are engaged in any other activity, making sure they do not hesitate to improve what they own for fear it may be confiscated from them, and they are not discouraged from investing in business for fear of losing their profits in taxes; instead, he should ensure that those who improve and invest are rewarded, as should be anyone whose actions will benefit his city or his government. He should, in addition, at appropriate times of the year, amuse the populace with festivals and public spectacles. Since every city is divided into guilds or neighborhoods, he ought to take account of these collectivities, meeting with them on occasion, showing himself to be generous and understanding in his dealings with them, but at the same time always retaining his authority and dignity, for this he should never let slip in any circumstances.

Chapter Twenty-Two: About those whom rulers employ as advisers.

A ruler's choice as to whom to employ as his advisers is of foremost importance. Rulers get the advisers they deserve, for good rulers choose good ones, bad rulers choose bad. The easiest way of assessing a ruler's ability is to look at those who are members of his inner circle. If they are competent and reliable, then you can be sure he is wise, for he has known both how to recognize their ability and to keep them faithful. But if they are not, you can always make a negative assessment of the ruler; for he has already proved his inadequacy by making a poor choice of adviser.

Nobody who knew Mr. Antonio of Venafro when he was adviser to Pandolfo Petrucci, ruler of Siena, could fail to conclude that Pandolfo was a brilliant man, for how else would he come by such an adviser? For there are three types of brains: One understands matters for itself, one follows the explanations of others, and one neither understands nor follows. The first is best, the second excellent, the third useless. It followed logically that if Pandolfo was not in the first rank, then he was at least in the second. For anyone who can judge the good or evil someone says and does, even if he does not have an original mind, will recognize what his adviser does well and what he does ill, and will encourage the first and correct the second. An adviser cannot hope to deceive such an employer, and will do his best.

But there is one infallible way for a ruler to judge his adviser. When you see your adviser give more thought to his own interests than yours, and recognize everything he does is aimed at his own benefit, then you can be sure such a person will never be a good adviser. You will never be able to trust him, for he who runs a government should never think of his own interests, but always of his ruler's, and should never suggest anything to his ruler that is not in the ruler's interests. On the other hand the ruler, in order to get the best out of his adviser, should consider his adviser's interests, heaping honors on him, enriching him, placing him in his debt, ensuring he receives public recognition, so that he sees that he cannot do better without him, that he has so many honors he desires no more, so much wealth he desires no more, so much status he fears the consequences of political upheaval. When a ruler has good advisers and knows how to treat them, then they can rely on each other; when it is otherwise, either ruler or adviser will suffer.

Chapter Twenty-Three: How sycophants are to be avoided.

I do not want to omit an important subject that concerns a mistake it is difficult for rulers to avoid making, unless they are very wise and good judges of men. My subject is sycophants, who pullulate at court. For men are so easily flattered and are so easily taken in by praise, that it is difficult for them to defend themselves against this plague, and in defending themselves they run the risk of making themselves despicable. For there is no way of protecting oneself against flattery other than by making it clear you do not mind being told the truth; but, when anyone can tell you the truth, then you are not treated with sufficient respect. So a wise ruler ought to find an alternative to flattery and excessive frankness. He ought to choose wise men from among his subjects, and give to them alone freedom to tell him the truth, but only in reply to specific questions he puts to them, not on any subject of their choice. But he ought to ask them about everything, and listen to their replies; then think matters over on his own, in his own way. His response to each of his advisers and their advice should make it apparent that the more freely they talk, the happier he will be. But he should listen to no one who has not been designated as an adviser, he should act resolutely once he has made up his mind, and he should cling stubbornly to his decisions once they have been taken. He who acts otherwise either is rushed into decisions by flatterers or changes his mind often in response to differing advice. Either way, people will form a poor opinion of him.

I want, on this subject, to refer to an example from recent history. The cleric Luca, an adviser to Maximilian, the present emperor, speaking of his sovereign, said that he did not ask for anyone's advice, and that he never did anything the way he wanted to: which was because he did not follow the principles I have just outlined. For the emperor is a secretive man, he keeps things to himself and never asks anyone's advice. But, when his decisions begin to be discovered, which is when they begin to be put into effect, he begins to be criticized by those who are close to him, and, as one might expect, he is persuaded to change his mind. The result is that he undoes each day what he did the day before; that nobody ever knows what he really wants or intends to do; and that one cannot rely upon his decisions.

A ruler, therefore, should always take advice, but only when he wants to, not when others want him to; he should discourage everybody from giving him advice without being asked; but he should be always asking, and, moreover, he should listen patiently to the answers, provided they are truthful. But if he becomes persuaded someone, for whatever reason, is not telling him the truth, he should lose his temper. There are many who think some rulers who have a reputation for being prudent do not really deserve to be thought so, claiming that the rulers themselves are not wise, but that they merely receive good advice. But without doubt they are mistaken. For this is a general rule without exceptions: A ruler who is not himself wise cannot be given good advice. Unless, I should say, he hands over all decisions to one other person and has the good luck to pick someone quite exceptionally prudent. But such an exceptional arrangement will not last long, for the man who takes all the decisions will soon take power. But a ruler who is not wise, if he takes advice from more than one person, will never get the same advice from everyone, nor will he be able to combine the different proposals into a coherent policy unless he has help. His advisers will each think about his own interests, and he will not be able to recognize their bias or

correct it. This is how it has to be, for you will find men are always wicked, unless you give them no alternative but to be good. So we may conclude that good advice, no matter who it comes from, really comes from the ruler's own good judgment, and that the ruler's good judgment never comes from good advice.

Chapter Twenty-Four: Why the rulers of Italy have lost their states.

The policies I have described, if prudently followed, will make a new ruler seem long-established and will rapidly make his power better entrenched than it would be if he had long held office. For the actions of a new ruler are much more closely scrutinized than those of an hereditary ruler; and new rulers, when they are seen to be strong [*virtuose*], attract much more support and make men more indebted to them than do hereditary rulers. For men are much more impressed by what goes on in the present than by what happened in the past; and when they are satisfied with what is happening now, they are delighted and ask for nothing more. So they will spring to a new ruler's defense, provided he plays his part properly. Thus, he will be doubly glorious: He will have begun a new tradition of government, underpinned and ornamented with good laws, good arms, good allies, and good examples; just as he is doubly shamed who, being born a ruler, has lost power through lack of skill in ruling.

And if you consider those Italian rulers who have lost power in recent years, such as the King of Naples, the Duke of Milan, and others, you will find: First, they all had in common an inadequate military preparation, for the reasons I have discussed above at length; second, you will see that some of them either were at odds with their own populace or, if they had the support of the populace, did not know how to protect themselves from the elite; for without these defects they would not have lost states that were strong enough to put an army in the field. Philip of Macedon (not the father of Alexander, but the Philip who was defeated by Titus Quintius) did not have a large state in comparison with the territory controlled by the Romans and the Greeks who attacked him; nevertheless, because he was a military man and a ruler who knew how to treat his populace and how to protect himself from the elite, he was able to sustain a war against superior forces for several years; and if, at the end, he lost control of several cities, he nevertheless retained his kingdom.

So our own rulers, each of whom had been in power for many years and then lost it, should not blame fortune but their own indolence. For when times were quiet they never once considered the possibility that they might change (it is a common human failing not to plan ahead for stormy weather while the sun shines). When difficult times did come, they thought of flight not of self-defense. They hoped the populace, irritated by the insolence of their conquerors, would recall them to power. This plan is a good one if there is no alternative policy available; but it is stupid to adopt it when there are alternatives. No one would be happy to trip and fall merely because he thought someone would help him back to his feet. Either no one comes to your assistance; or if someone does, you are the weaker for it, for your strategy for self-defense has been ignominious, and your fate has not been in your own hands. No method of defense is good, certain, and lasting that does not depend on your own decisions and your own strength [*virtù*].

Chapter Twenty-Five: How much fortune can achieve in human affairs, and how it is to be resisted.

I am not unaware of the fact that many have held and still hold the view that the affairs of this world are so completely governed by fortune and by God that human prudence is incapable of correcting them, with the consequence that there is no way in which what is wrong can be put right. So one may conclude that there is no point in trying too hard; one should simply let chance have its way. This view has come to be more widely accepted in our own day because of the extraordinary variation in circumstances that has been seen and is still seen every day. Nobody could predict such events. Sometimes, thinking this matter over, I have been inclined to adopt a version of this view myself. Nevertheless, since our free will must not be eliminated, I think it may be true that fortune determines one half of our actions, but that, even so, she leaves us to control the other half, or thereabouts. And I compare her to one of those torren-

tial rivers that, when they get angry, break their banks, knock down trees and buildings, strip the soil from one place and deposit it somewhere else. Everyone flees before them, everyone gives way in face of their onrush, nobody can resist them at any point. But although they are so powerful, this does not mean men, when the waters recede, cannot make repairs and build banks and barriers so that, if the waters rise again, either they will be safely kept within the sluices or at least their onrush will not be so unregulated and destructive. The same thing happens with fortune: She demonstrates her power where precautions have not been taken to resist her [*dove non è ordinata virtù a resisterle*]; she directs her attacks where she knows banks and barriers have not been built to hold her. If you think about Italy, which is the location of all these changes in circumstance, and the origin of the forces making for change, you will realize she is a landscape without banks and without any barriers. If proper precautions had been taken [*s'ella fussi reparata da conveniente virtù*], as they were in Germany, Spain, and France, either the flood would not have had the consequences it had, or the banks would not even have been overwhelmed. And what I have said is enough, I believe, to answer the general question of how far one can resist fortune.

But, turning rather to individuals, note we see rulers who flourish one day and are destroyed the next without our being able to see any respect in which they have changed their nature or their attributes. I think the cause of this is, in the first place, the one we have already discussed at length: A ruler who depends entirely on his good fortune will be destroyed when his luck changes. I also think a ruler will flourish if he adjusts his policies as the character of the times changes; and similarly, a ruler will fail if he follows policies that do not correspond to the needs of the times. For we see men, in those activities that carry them towards the goal they all share, which is the acquisition of glory and riches, proceed differently. One acts with caution, while another is headstrong; one is violent, while another relies on skill; one is patient, while another is the opposite: And any one of them, despite the differences in their methods, may achieve his objective. One also sees that of two cautious men, one will succeed, and the other not; and similarly we see that two men can be equally successful though quite different in their behavior, one of them being cautious and the other headstrong. This happens solely because of the character of the times, which either suits or is at odds with their way of proceeding. This is the cause of what I have described: that two men, behaving differently, achieve the same result, and of two other men, who behave in the same way, one will attain his objective and the other will not. This is also the cause of the fact that the sort of behavior that is successful changes from one time to another. Take someone who acts cautiously and patiently. If the times and circumstances develop in such a way that his behavior is appropriate, he will flourish; but if the times and circumstances change, he will be destroyed for he will continue to behave in the same way. One cannot find a man so prudent he knows how to adapt himself to changing circumstances, for he will either be unable to deviate from that style of behavior to which his character inclines him, or, alternatively, having always been successful by adopting one particular style, he will be unable to persuade himself that it is time to change. And so, the cautious man, when it is time to be headstrong, does not know how to act and is destroyed. But, if one knew how to change one's character as times and circumstances change, one's luck would never change.

Pope Julius II always acted impetuously; the style of action was so appropriate to the times and circumstances in which he found himself that the outcome was always successful. Consider his first attack on Bologna, when Mr. Giovanni Bentivoglio was still alive. The Venetians were not happy about it; nor was the King of Spain; he had discussed such an action with the French, who had reached no decision. Nevertheless, because he was ferocious and impetuous, he placed himself personally at the head of his troops. This gesture made the Spanish and the Venetians hesitate and do nothing: the Venetians out of fear, and the Spanish because they wanted to recover the territories they had lost from the Kingdom of Naples. On the other hand, he dragged the King of France along behind him. For the king saw it was too late to turn back, and he wanted an alliance with him in order to weaken the Venetians, so he concluded he could not deny him the support of French troops without giving him obvious grounds for resentment. So Julius, by acting impetuously, achieved something no other pope, no matter how

skillful and prudent, had been able to achieve. For, if he had delayed his departure from Rome until everything had been arranged and the necessary alliances had been cemented, as any other pope would have done, he would never have succeeded. The King of France would have found a thousand excuses, and his other allies would have pointed out a thousand dangers. I want to leave aside his other actions, for they were all similar, and they were all successful. He did not live long enough to experience failure. But, if the times had changed so that it was necessary to proceed with caution, he would have been destroyed. He would never have been able to change the style of behavior to which his character inclined him.

I conclude, then, that since fortune changes, and men stubbornly continue to behave in the same way, men flourish when their behavior suits the times and fail when they are out of step. I do think, however, that it is better to be headstrong than cautious, for fortune is a lady. It is necessary, if you want to master her, to beat and strike her. And one sees she more often submits to those who act boldly than to those who proceed in a calculating fashion. Moreover, since she is a lady, she smiles on the young, for they are less cautious, more ruthless, and overcome her with their boldness.

Chapter Twenty-Six: Exhortation to seize Italy and free her from the barbarians.

Having considered all the matters we have discussed, I ask myself whether, in Italy now, we are living through times suitable for the triumph of a new ruler, and if there is an opportunity for a prudent and bold [*virtuoso*] man to take control of events and win honor for himself while benefiting everyone who lives here. It seems to me so many factors come together at the moment to help out a new ruler that I am not sure if there has ever been a more propitious time for such a man. If, as I said, Moses could only demonstrate his greatness [*virtù*] because the people of Israel were slaves in Egypt; if we would never have known what a great man Cyrus was if the Persians had not been oppressed by the Medes; if the remarkable qualities of Theseus only became apparent because the Athenians were scattered abroad; so now, the opportunity is there for some bold Italian to demonstrate his greatness [*virtù*]. For see the conditions to which Italy has been reduced: She is more enslaved than the Jews, more oppressed than the Persians, more defenseless than the Athenians. She has no leader, no organization. She is beaten, robbed, wounded, put to flight: She has experienced every sort of injury. Although so far there has been the occasional hint of exceptional qualities in someone, so that one might think he had been ordained by God to redeem Italy, yet later events have shown, as his career progressed, that he was rejected by fortune. So Italy has remained at death's door, waiting for someone who could bind her wounds and put an end to the sack of Lombardy, to the extortion of Tuscany and of the Kingdom of Naples, someone who could heal her sores which long ago became infected. One can see how she prays to God that he will send her someone who will redeem her from this ill treatment and from the insults of the barbarians. One can see every Italian is ready, everyone is eager to rally to the colors, if only someone will raise them high.

At the moment, there is nowhere Italy can turn in her search for someone to redeem her with more chance of success than to your own illustrious family, which is fortunate and resourceful [virtù], is favored by God and by the church (indeed the church is now at its command). The undertaking is straightforward, if you keep in mind the lives and the deeds of the leaders I have mentioned. Of course those men were exceptional and marvelous; but, nevertheless, they were only men, and none of them had as good an opportunity as you have at the moment. For their undertakings were not more just than this one, or easier, nor was God more their ally than he is yours. This is truly just: "A war is just if there is no alternative, and the resort to arms is legitimate if they represent your only hope." These circumstances are ideal; and when circumstances are ideal there can be no great difficulty in achieving success, provided your family copies the policies of those I have recommended as your models. Beyond that, we have already seen extraordinary and unparalleled events. God has already shown his hand: The sea has been divided; a cloud has escorted you on your journey; water has flowed out of the rock; manna has fallen from on high. Everything has conspired to make you great. The rest you must do for yourselves. God does not want to have to do the whole thing, for he likes to

leave us our free will so we can lay claim to part of the glory by earning it.

There is no need to be surprised that none of the Italian rulers I have discussed has been able to accomplish what I believe your family can achieve, or to be disheartened if during all the wars that have been fought, all the political upheavals that have taken place, it has seemed as if the Italians have completely lost their capacity to fight and win [la virtù militare]. This is simply because the traditional way of doing things in Italy is mistaken, and no one has appeared who has known how to bring about change. Nothing does more to establish the reputation of someone who comes new to power than do the new laws and the new institutions he establishes. These, when they are well thought out and noble in spirit, make a ruler revered and admired. In Italy we have the raw materials: You can do anything you wish with them. Here we have people capable of anything [virtù grande], all they need are leaders who know what to do. When it comes to fighting one-on-one the Italians prove themselves to be stronger, quicker, cleverer. But when it comes to the clash of armies, the Italians are hopeless. The cause lies in the inadequacy of the leaders. Those who know what to do are not obeyed, and everyone thinks he knows what to do. So far there has been no one who has known how to establish an authority, based on fortune and ability [virtù], such that the others will obey him. This is the reason why, through the whole of the last twenty years, during all the wars that have taken place in that time, not a single army consisting solely of Italians has done well. Twenty years ago the Italians were defeated at Taro; since then at Alexandria, Capua, Genoa, Vailà, Bologna, Mestre.

So, if your illustrious family wants to follow in the footsteps of those excellent men who liberated the nations to which they belonged, you must, before you do anything else, do the one thing that is the precondition for success in any enterprise: Acquire your own troops. You cannot hope to have more faithful, more reliable, or more skillful soldiers. And if each soldier will be good, the army as a whole will be better still, once they see their ruler place himself at their head and discover he treats them with respect and sympathy. It is necessary, though, to get such an army ready, if we are to be able to defend Italy from the foreigners with Italian strength and skill [*con la virtù italica*].

It is true that the Swiss and Spanish infantries are thought to be intimidating; nevertheless, they both have their defects, so a third force could not only stand up to them, but could be confident of beating them. For the Spanish cannot withstand a cavalry charge; and the Swiss have reason to be afraid of infantry, should they come up against any as determined to win as they are. Thus, we have seen that the Spanish cannot withstand an attack by the French cavalry, and we will see in practice that the Swiss can be destroyed by the Spanish infantry. It is true that we have yet to see the Spanish properly defeat the Swiss, but we have seen an indication of what will happen at the Battle of Ravenna, when the Spanish infantry clashed against the German battalions, for the Germans rely on the same formation as the Swiss. There the Spanish, thanks to their agility and with the help of their bucklers, were able to get underneath the pikes of the Germans and were able to attack them in safety, without the Germans' having any defense. If the cavalry had not driven them off, they would have wiped them out. So, since we know the weakness of each of these infantries, we ought to be able to train a new force that will be able to withstand cavalry and will not be afraid of infantry. To accom-

plish this we need specially designed weapons and new battle formations. This is the sort of new undertaking that establishes the reputation and importance of a new ruler.

So you should not let this opportunity slip by. Italy, so long enslaved, awaits her redeemer. There are no words to describe with what devotion he would be received in all those regions that have suffered from foreign invasions which have flooded across the land. No words can describe the appetite for revenge, the resolute determination, the spirit of self-sacrifice, the tears of emotion that would greet him. What gates would be closed to him? What community would refuse to obey him? Who would dare be jealous of his success? What Italian would refuse to pledge him allegiance? Everyone is sick of being pushed around by the barbarians. Your family must commit itself to this enterprise. Do it with the confidence and hope with which people embark on a just cause so that, marching behind your banner, the whole nation is ennobled. Under your patronage, may we prove Petrarch right:

Virtue [*virtù*] will take up arms against savagery,
And the battle will be short.
For the courage of old is not yet dead
In Italian hearts.

Discourses

Book One

Preface

Men are by nature envious. It has always been as dangerous to propose new ways of thinking and new institutions as it is to seek unknown oceans and undiscovered continents. People are much quicker to criticize than to praise what others have done. Nevertheless, spurred on by an instinctive desire I have always had to do those things that I believe will further the common good and benefit everybody, I have refused to be intimidated. I have resolved to set out on a road no one has travelled before me. My journey may be tiresome and difficult, but I can hope it will prove rewarding, at least if people are willing to judge sym-

pathetically the purpose of my labors. If my limited intelligence, my lack of experience of contemporary politics, and my inadequate knowledge of classical history will make my efforts defective and of very limited use to others, I will at least be pointing out the way to someone with greater ability [*virtù*], more analytical skill, and better judgment, someone who will be capable of achieving what I have aimed at. Perhaps no one will praise my efforts; in any event, I do not deserve to be reproached.

Think of the respect in which we hold antiquity. Often, to take just one example, a single fragment of an antique statue will be purchased at enormous expense by someone who wants to look at it every day. He will give it a place of honor in his house and allow those who aspire to be sculptors to copy it. The sculptors then make every effort to do work comparable to it. Think, on the other hand, of the immensely skillful [*virtuosissime*] deeds the history books record for us, deeds done by ancient kingdoms and classical republics, by kings, generals, citizens, legislators, and others who have worn themselves out for their homelands. These deeds may be admired, but they are scarcely imitated. Indeed, everybody goes to great lengths to avoid copying them, even if it only concerns an insignificant detail. The result is not a trace of the classical military and political skills [*quella antiqua virtù*] survives. I cannot help but be both astonished and dismayed by this. Especially when I notice that when citizens find themselves caught up in legal disagreements, or when they fall ill, they always appeal to the legal decisions of the ancients, they always follow the medical remedies prescribed by them. For the civil laws are nothing other than decisions handed down by classical jurists, decisions that have been codified, and are now taught to lawyers by our own jurists. Similarly, medicine is simply the experience of classical doctors, on the basis of which contemporary doctors make their decisions. Nevertheless, in organizing republics, in administering states, in ruling kingdoms, in training armies and fighting wars, in passing judgment on subjects, and in planning new conquests, when it comes to all these activities, one does not find a single ruler or republic who tries to learn from the ancients.

I do not believe the cause of this is the feebleness contemporary religion has instilled in the world, nor the evil consequences that a supercilious indolence has had for many Christian countries and cities. The real problem is people do not properly understand the history books. When they read them they do not get out of them the meaning that is in them. They chew on them but do not taste them. The result is countless people read them and enjoy discovering in them the great variety of events they record, but never think of imitating them, presuming it would not be just difficult but would be simply impossible to do as the ancients did. As if the heavens, the sun, the elements, human beings had changed in their movement, organization, and capacities, and were quite different from what they were in days gone by. My intent has been to rescue men from this mistake, so I have decided I must write about all the books of Livy's history that have survived the ravages of time,

explaining whatever I think is important if one is to understand them. In doing so, I will draw on my knowledge of ancient and modern affairs. My hope is that those who read my comments will be able without difficulty to draw from them those practical benefits one ought to expect to gain from the study of history. Although my undertaking is a difficult one, nevertheless, helped by those who have encouraged me to embark on this enterprise, I believe I will have so much success that anyone coming after me will only have a little to do before he completes my task.

Chapter One: On the universal origins of any city whatever, and on how Rome began.

Those who read how the city of Rome began, who established its laws, and how it was organized will not marvel that so much excellence [*virtù*] was preserved in that city for so many centuries; and that later it gave birth to the vast empire the Roman republic eventually controlled. Since I want to talk first about its birth, I will start by saying all cities are constructed either by men born in the place where the city is built or by foreigners. In the first case, the inhabitants decide to build a city because they have been spread out in many tiny settlements in which they have not felt secure, for each settlement on its own, because of its location and because of the small number of its inhabitants, is incapable of resisting the assaults of an attacker. Nor are they in a position to assemble in joint defense when they see the enemy coming, either because it takes too long, or because, even if they could assemble in time, they would be obliged to abandon many of their settlements and would soon see them plundered by their enemies. So, to avoid these dangers, urged on either by their own individual judgments or by some one member of their group who has greater influence among them, they gather together to live in a single place they have chosen, one that will be more convenient to live in, and that will be easier to defend.

Athens and Venice are among the many cities that originated in this way. Athens, under the leadership of Theseus, was constructed by scattered inhabitants for the sort of reasons I have outlined. Venice was established by numerous little groups who had taken refuge on certain tiny islands at the end of the Adriatic sea. They were trying to escape the wars that continually broke out in Italy in the period following the collapse of the Roman empire as a result of the arrival of new groups of barbarians. They organized themselves, without there being any one individual in overall control, to live according to those laws that were, in their view, most conducive to their preservation. Their enterprise was a success because of the lengthy period of peace the site they had chosen ensured for them, for their lagoon was impenetrable, and the tribes who were invading Italy had no ships with which to attack them. So, from the most humble beginnings, they were able to rise to the eminent position they now occupy.

The second case, when foreigners come and build a city, takes two forms, depending on whether the immigrants are free men or men who owe allegiance to others. In the latter case a republic or a ruler may send out colonists in order to reduce the pressure of population in their existing settlements; or because they have recently conquered new territory and want to defend it effectively and inexpensively (the Romans built many such cities throughout their empire); or such a city may be built by a ruler who does not intend to live there, but to immortalize himself through it, as Alexander did by building Alexandria. Because such cities do not start out free, it rarely happens that they make great strides and come to be regarded as the capital cities of their own countries. It is in this category that we should place the construction of Florence, for (no matter whether it was built by Sulla's soldiers or by the inhabitants of the hilltops of Fiesole, who, given confidence by the long peace that the whole world benefited from under Augustus, came down to live in the plain of the Arno) it was built under Roman rule, nor could it, at the beginning, control any territory beyond what was assigned it at the pleasure of the emperor.

Cities are built by free men when a group of people, either under the command of a ruler or acting on their own, are forced to abandon the land of their birth and to seek new territory because of disease, or hunger, or war. They may occupy the cities that already exist in the territory they conquer, as Moses did, or they may build from scratch, as Aeneas did. It is in this latter case that one can fully appreciate the skill [*virtù*] of the architect as it is reflected in the fate of his city, for the history of the city will be more or less marvelous depending on whether its first founder is more or less skillful [*virtuoso*]. The skill [*virtù*] of the founder can be judged by two things: firstly, by his choice of a site for the construction of the new city; secondly, by the laws he draws up for it.

Men act either out of necessity or free choice. Since it seems that men are the most admirable [*maggior virtù*] where they have the least freedom of choice, one must consider whether it might not be better to choose an infertile region for the construction of a city so that its inhabitants will be forced to be industrious and prevented from being self-indulgent, and so that they will be more united, having less occasion for conflict because of the poverty of their land. We can see this happened at Ragusa, and in many other cities built in similar locations. Such a choice of location would be without doubt wiser and would lead to the best outcome, if men were content to live off their own possessions and did not want to try to get control of the property of others. But since men can only secure themselves by building up power, one must avoid building a city in a barren location, but rather settle the most fertile land, whose fecundity will make possible growth, so one will be able both to defend oneself against attackers and to defeat anyone who stands in the way of one's own power. In order to ensure the location does not lead to self-indulgence, one must design the laws to force people to do what the location does not force them to do. Thus, one should imitate those wise men who have lived in countries that have been delightful and fertile, countries apt to produce lazy men who are incapable of any manly [*virtuoso*] work. In order to avoid the disadvantages that would result from the delightfulness of the land if it caused self-indulgence, they required all those who were liable to military service to drill, so that by means of such regulations their inhabitants became better soldiers than those living in territory that is naturally harsh and infertile. The Kingdom of Egypt is an example of this: Despite the fact that the country is exceptionally fertile, the artificial necessity imposed by the laws was so effective that Egypt produced the finest men; and if their names had not been lost in antiquity, we would be able to see they deserved more praise than Alexander the Great and many others whose deeds remain fresh in our memory. And if you had examined the state of the sultan, with its regiments of Mamelukes and its Turkish militia, before they were abolished by the Sultan Selim, you would have seen there much drilling of soldiers and would have learned how much the Turks feared the self-indulgence the generosity of their country might induce in them, had they not introduced strict legal penalties to prevent it.

So I conclude it is wiser to choose to settle in a fertile place, provided the consequences of that fertility are kept within due limits by legislation. Deinocrates the architect came to Alexander the Great when Alexander wanted to build a city to magnify his own reputation. He showed him how he could build on Mount Athos: The site, apart from being easily defended, could be cut away so the new city would have the shape of a human body, which would be a remarkable and extraordinary thing and worthy of Alexander's greatness. But when Alexander asked him what the inhabitants of the city would live on he replied he had not given the matter any thought. Alexander laughed, and, leaving Mount Athos intact, built Alexandria in a place where people would want to settle because of the fecundity of the countryside and the ease of access to the sea and to the Nile.

Let us now consider the construction of Rome. If you take it that Aeneas was its first founder, you will think of it as one of the cities built by foreigners. If you believe it was founded by Romulus, you will think of it as founded by men born in the vicinity. Either way you will agree it was founded in freedom and was not under any outsider's authority. You will also recognize—we will return to this subject later—the extent to which the laws established by Romulus, Numa, and the other early legislators imposed an artificial necessity upon the inhabitants, so the fertility of the site, the ease of access to the sea, the frequent victories of their armies, and the extensive territory that fell under Roman control could not corrupt them even over the course of many centuries. Their laws ensured they had more admirable qualities [virtù] than any other city or republic has ever been able to boast of in its citizens.

The deeds of the Romans that are celebrated in Livy's history occurred either as a result of public or of private decisions and either inside or outside the city. I will begin by discussing those things that happened inside the city and as a result of public decision-making, that I take to be worthy of more detailed discussion, and we will need to explore all the conse-

quences that flowed from them. This first book, or at least this first part, will be taken up with a discussion of these matters.

Chapter Two: On the different types of republic that exist, and on how to categorize the Roman republic.

I want to leave aside any discussion of those cities that were under the authority of outsiders from the beginning, and to discuss only those that began completely free of external domination and were ruled by their own wills from the beginning, whether as republics or as princedoms. These cities, since they began in a variety of ways, have had a variety of constitutions and legal systems. In some, either at the very beginning or soon after their foundation, a single individual wrote all the laws at once—Lycurgus, for example, gave the Spartans their laws—while others acquired their laws by chance, little by little, according to the circumstances, as happened in Rome. We can call fortunate any republic in which there appears a leader so prudent he is able to give them a code of law they have no need to revise, but under which they can live securely. We know the Spartans obeyed the laws of Lycurgus for eight hundred years without corrupting them and without any serious internal conflict. On the other hand, we can call in some degree unfortunate any city that does not chance upon a prudent lawmaker, and is obliged to revise its laws for itself. And among these cities, moreover, those are most unfortunate that are furthest from having the right laws; and those are furthest astray whose constitution is quite unlike the one that would lead them to their true and ideal goal. For it is almost impossible for a city that finds itself in this situation to have enough good luck to be able to sort itself out. Those others that, if they do not have a perfect constitution, yet have started out in the right direction and are in a position to improve, can, as opportunity presents itself, become perfect. But this is certainly true: One never establishes a constitution without encountering danger. For enough men will never agree to a new law that changes the constitution of the city unless they are persuaded it is essential to pass it, and they will only be persuaded of this if they see themselves to be in danger, so it can easily happen that the republic is destroyed before she arrives at a perfect constitution. The republic of Florence is a good example of this: Defeat in the Battle of Arezzo led to her reorganization; defeat in the Battle of Prato in 1512 led to her dissolution.

I want now to discuss the constitution of Rome and the events that made it possible for her to achieve perfection. Some who have written about constitutions say they are of three types, which they call "monarchy," "aristocracy," and "democracy." They say anyone drawing up the constitution of a city must choose from these the one he thinks most appropriate. Others, who are widely thought to be wiser, say there are six types of constitution, of which three are inherently bad and three are inherently good, although even the good ones are so easily corrupted they, too, can quickly become pernicious. The good ones are the three I have already mentioned; the bad ones are three others that derive from these three, and each of which is so like the good constitution it most resembles that it is easy for one to turn into the other. Thus, monarchies easily become tyrannies, aristocracies become oligarchies, and democracies slide into anarchy. The result is that if a lawmaker establishes a constitution for a city that corresponds to one of the three good forms of government it will not last long, for no precaution is sufficient to ensure it will not slip into its opposite, for the good [*la virtute*] and the bad are, when it comes to constitutions, closely related.

These different types of government developed among men by accident. When the world began, it had few inhabitants, and they lived for a while apart from one another as the animals do. As their numbers multiplied they gathered together, and in order to be better able to defend themselves, they began to defer to one among their number who was stronger and braver than the rest. They made him, as it were, their leader and obeyed him. This was the origin of knowledge of those things that are good and honest as opposed to those that are pernicious and evil. For men saw that, if someone harmed his benefactor, his associates despised him and felt compassion for his victim. They learned to think ill of the ungrateful and to approve of those who were grateful. They came to realize the injuries that were done to someone else could equally be done to themselves. In order to avoid such evils, they gathered together to make laws and to lay down punishments for those who broke them: This was the invention of justice. Thereafter, when they had to choose a ruler, they no longer obeyed the strongest, but he who was most prudent and most just.

Later, however, they began to appoint their ruler by hereditary succession, not by election, with the immediate result that power was inherited by men who were inferior to their ancestors. They no longer acted virtuously [*lasciando l'opere virtuose*], but thought rulers were simply there to outdo other men in extravagance, lasciviousness, and in every other type of vice. The result was that rulers began to be hated, and, because they were hated, to be afraid. Because they were afraid, they went on the attack, and before long kings had become tyrants. These rulers faced the possibility of being destroyed. The conspiracies and plots hatched against them were not begun by those who were fearful or weak, but by those who surpassed their fellows in generosity, spiritedness, wealth, and nobility, for such men could no longer tolerate the dishonorable lives of their rulers. The masses then followed the lead provided by the elite and armed themselves against their ruler, and, when they had got rid of him, obeyed the elite as their liberators. The new rulers hated the idea of one-man rule and, so, established themselves collectively in power.

At first, remembering the evils of tyranny, they governed according to the laws they had established, putting their own interests second and the public good first. They directed and protected both public and private matters with great care. In due course, this government was inherited by their sons, who had never seen power change hands, had never suffered under evil government, and who were unwilling to continue treating their fellow subjects as their equals. They gave themselves over to avarice, to ambition, to chasing other men's wives. So aristocracy degenerated into an oligarchy in which the norms of civilized life were flouted. In a short time, the oligarchs suffered the same fate as the tyrants, for the masses became fed up with their government and gave their support to anyone who was planning any sort of resistance to their rule. Soon someone, with the assistance of the masses, was able to destroy them. Since they could still clearly remember one-man rule, and the harm it had done them, when they destroyed oligarchy they had no desire to restore monarchy, but instead established popular rule. This they organized in such a manner that neither the elite nor a powerful individual could have any influence whatsoever.

In the beginning, all states can command a certain amount of respect, so popular government survived for a while, but not for long, especially once the generation that had established it had passed away. It quickly degenerated into anarchy, in which neither private individuals nor public officials could command any respect. Each person did as he chose, with the result that every day innumerable crimes were committed. So, compelled by necessity, or advised by some good man, or desperate to escape from anarchy, they established once more the rule of one man. And from monarchy, step by step, they degenerated once again into anarchy, repeating the sequence I have already described.

This is the cycle through which all states revolve, and power is still passed, as it always has been, from hand to hand. But it rarely happens that the same people return to power, for scarcely a single state has survived long enough to travel several times through this cycle without being destroyed. Usually, while a state is torn apart by internal dissent, and as a result is weakened and deprived of good leadership, it is conquered by a neighboring state better organized than it is. But if this did not happen, then a state could repeat this cycle of constitutions over and over again.

I conclude all these forms of government are pestilential: The three good ones do not last long, and the three bad ones are evil. Those who know how to construct constitutions wisely have identified this problem and have avoided each one of these types of constitution in its pure form, constructing a constitution with elements of each. They have been convinced such a constitution would be more solid and stable, would be preserved by checks and balances, there being present in the one city a monarch, an aristocracy, and a democracy.

Lycurgus is the most admirable of those who have established constitutions of this sort. He constructed the constitution of Sparta so that it gave distinct roles to king, aristocracy, and people, with the result the state survived for eight hundred years, throughout which time his name was revered and the city lived in harmony. Matters turned out differently for Solon, who drew up the constitution of Athens. Because he

constructed a democracy, it survived such a short time that before Solon died he saw Athens under the tyranny of Pisistratus. Although forty years later Pisistratus's heirs were driven into exile and freedom was restored, because the Athenians re-established the democratic constitution drawn up by Solon, their freedom lasted no more than a century, despite the fact that in order to preserve it they introduced numerous reforms Solon had not considered. They did their best to control the insolence of the powerful and the license of the masses. Nevertheless, because they did not allow a proper role for one-man rule and for aristocracy, Athens survived, by comparison with Sparta, a very short time.

Let us turn to Rome. Even though Rome did not have a Lycurgus to establish from the beginning a constitution that would enable her to live free for centuries, nevertheless, she underwent so many political crises, because of the conflicts between the people and the senate, that chance eventually brought about something no legislator had been able to accomplish. For if Rome did not have the first type of good fortune, she had the second, and although her first constitution was defective, nevertheless, it did not cause her to turn off the right path that could lead her to perfection.

Romulus and all the other kings of Rome made many excellent laws, ones appropriate for a free state. But their goal was the establishment of a kingdom, not a republic, so when Rome became free she lacked many of the laws free government required, for these they had omitted to decree. And although the kings of Rome lost their power for the reasons and in the way I have outlined, nevertheless, those who threw them out quickly established two consuls who played the same role as the kings, so that they expelled from Rome the name of king but not the authority of kingship. The new republic was ruled by the consuls and the senate, so it was a mixture of only two of the three types of power I have described: of monarchy and aristocracy. It failed to give any authority to the populace.

When the Roman nobility became overbearing, for reasons I will explain later, the people rose up against them, with the result that, in order not to lose all power, the nobles were obliged to concede a share of power to the people. On the other hand, the consuls and the senate retained enough authority to be able to hold on to a share of power in the republic. So the tribunes of the people came to be established, after which the constitution of the republic became more stable, for now all three types of authority had a fair share in power. And fortune was so favorable to Rome that, although she passed from monarchy, to aristocracy, to democracy, going through each of the stages I have described for the reasons I have outlined, nevertheless, the aristocracy never seized all power from the monarchical element; nor did the people ever seize all power from the aristocracy; instead, power was added to power, and the mixture that resulted made for a perfect republic. Rome achieved this perfection because of the conflict between senate and people, as I will show at length in the next two chapters.

Chapter Three: On the circumstances under which the tribunes of the people came to be established in Rome, a development that made the constitution nearly perfect.

There is one thing that all those who discuss political life emphasize, and that is evident from the history of every state: It is essential that anyone setting up a republic and establishing a constitution for it should assume that all men are wicked and will always give vent to their evil impulses whenever they have the chance to do so. Even when some evil impulse is restrained and concealed for a time, there is always some hidden reason for this, one we do not recognize because we have not seen the vicious behavior the evil impulse would normally give rise to. But time will make clear what it is, for time, as they say, gives birth to truth.

When the Tarquins were expelled from Rome, there appeared to be a close collaboration between the populace and the senate. The nobles seemed to have given up their pride and to have become democratic in their outlook. One would have thought anyone would have been able to tolerate their rule, even someone from the lowest social class. The hypocrisy of the nobility continued to lie hidden as long as the Tarquins were alive, and during this period the reason for their behavior was invisible. For the nobles were afraid of the Tarquins and afraid, too, that if the populace were badly treated they would form an alliance with them; so they treated the populace well. But as soon as the Tarquins died and the

nobles felt they had nothing to fear, they began to treat the populace as outrageously as they had always wanted to, and they now harmed them in every way they could. This confirms what I just said: Men never do anything that is good except when forced to. Where there is a good deal of freedom of choice, and this freedom can be abused, then everything quickly becomes buried in confusion and disorder. Therefore, people say hunger and poverty make men industrious, while laws make them good. Where something works well on its own, without the support of the law, then there is no need for a law. But as soon as good habits break down, then laws at once become necessary. So with the Tarquins gone, fear of whom had kept the nobility in check, it was necessary to think of a new institution that would have the same effect as the Tarquins had had while they were alive. And so, after many conflicts, outcries, and crises had arisen between the populace and the nobility, it was decided to establish the tribunes in order to protect the populace. They were given so much authority and so high a status that thereafter they were always able to act as mediators between the populace and the senate and to control the arrogance of the nobility.

Chapter Four: On the tensions between the populace and the Roman senate, which made that republic free and powerful.

It would be wrong not to discuss those popular disorders that occurred in Rome between the death of the Tarquins and the creation of the tribunes. Afterwards, I will say a few things in reply to the many people who say Rome was a disorderly republic, one full of so much confusion that if good luck and military discipline [*virtù militare*] had not made up for its defects, it would have been inferior to every other republic. I cannot deny good luck and the army were causes of Rome's imperial greatness, though it seems to me these people do not realize that where there is a good army there must be a good constitution, and one will nearly always find a good army can make its own good luck.

But let us turn to the other particular characteristics of that city. I maintain those who criticize the clashes between the nobility and the populace attack what was, I would argue, the primary factor making for Rome's continuing freedom. They pay more attention to the shouts and cries that rise from such conflicts than to the good effects that derive from them. They do not take into account the fact that there are two distinct viewpoints in every republic: that of the populace and that of the elite. All the laws made in order to foster liberty result from the tensions between them, as one can easily see was the case in the history of Rome. For from Tarquin to the Gracchi, a period of more than three hundred years, the conflicts that broke out in Rome rarely resulted in men's being sent into exile, and even more rarely led to bloodshed. One cannot judge these conflicts as harmful, or the republic as divided, when over such a long period of time the differences between the parties led to no more than eight or ten citizens' being sent into exile, to a tiny number's being murdered, and indeed to only a few's being fined. Nor can there be any good grounds for calling a republic disorderly when it contains so many examples of individual excellence [*virtù*], for good individuals cannot exist without good education, and good education cannot exist without good laws, and good laws were the result of those very conflicts many people unthinkingly criticize. Anyone who scrutinizes the outcome of these conflicts will find they never led to exiles or murders that were contrary to the public good but always led to laws and institutions that favored public liberty.

And if someone were to argue the methods employed were extralegal and almost bestial—the people in a mob shouting abuse at the senate, the senate replying in kind, mobs running through the streets, shops boarded up, the entire populace of Rome leaving the city—I would reply such things only frighten those who read about them. Every city ought to have practices that enable the populace to give expression to its aspirations, especially those cities that want to be able to rely on the populace at times of crisis. The city of Rome had a number of practices of this kind. For example, when the populace wanted a law passed, either they demonstrated, as I have described, or they refused to enroll for military service, so that in order to pacify them it was necessary to give them at least part of what they wanted. The demands of a free people are rarely harmful to the cause of liberty, for they are a response either to oppression or to the prospect of oppression. When the populace is mistaken, then there is a remedy to hand in the open-air speech. Some sensible man has to get up and harangue them, showing them how they are wrong. The populace, as Cicero says, although they are ignorant, are capable of recognizing the truth, and it is easy for a man whom they have reason to respect to persuade them to change their mind by telling them the truth.

So people ought to be more sparing in their criticisms of the political system of Rome. If you consider all the good things the Romans achieved, you will have to admit the system that gave rise to such achievements must have been excellent. If popular demonstrations resulted in the creation of the tribunate, they should be praised without reserve, for, beyond giving the populace a role in government, the tribunes were set up to be the guardians of Roman liberty, as the next chapter will show.

Chapter Five: On whether the protection of liberty is best entrusted to the populace or to the elite, and on whether those who want to acquire power or those who want to maintain it are most likely to riot.

Those who have understood how to establish a republic have recognized one of the most urgent tasks is that of identifying a group with an interest in protecting liberty. Depending on whether this task is entrusted to the right group or not, political liberty will be preserved for a longer or a shorter time. Because in every state there is an elite and a populace, the question has been raised as to which group it is best to entrust with the task of protecting liberty. The Spartans and, in modern days, the Venetians have relied on the nobles; but the Romans relied on the populace. So we must ask ourselves which of these republics made the better choice. If we argue from first principles, we will find something to say on either side; but if we look at what happened in practice, we will conclude the nobility are more reliable, for liberty in Sparta and Venice has been longer-lived than in Rome. Let us look at the principles involved and first consider the arguments in favor of Rome's policy.

It would seem one ought to entrust something to people who have no desire to steal it. Now there is no question that if one considers the objectives of the nobles and the non-nobles, one must admit the former are very keen to dominate, and the latter want only not to be dominated. Consequently, the populace have a greater desire to live as free men, having less prospect of seizing power for themselves than the elite has. So if you put the populace in charge of protecting liberty, it is reasonable to believe that they will do a better job, and since they cannot hope to monopolize power themselves, they will ensure nobody else does. On the other hand, if you are defending the Spartan and Venetian policy you will say those who entrust the protection of liberty to the powerful accomplish two good things. In the first place, you satisfy some of the nobility's aspirations, and, because they have a greater role in the state as a result of having this power in their hands, they are more likely to be content. In the second, you take away a measure of authority from the populace, who are restless and insatiable. It is the populace who are responsible for innumerable conflicts and clashes in a republic. Their behavior is likely to make the nobility desperate, which in the long run will have evil consequences. You will cite Rome herself as an example. Because the tribunes of the people could claim to be the guardians of liberty, they were not satisfied with ensuring one consul was chosen from among the populace, but insisted both should be. Next they wanted the censor, the praetor, and all the other officials of the city government to be plebeians. Even this was not enough, for, driven on by the same madness, they began in time to worship those men whom they thought were capable of defeating the nobility. The result was the rise of Marius and the ruin of Rome. And indeed, anyone who balanced one set of arguments against the other would have difficulty making up his mind as to which group he should choose as the guardians of liberty, for he would be unable to decide which human aspiration was more dangerous for a republic: defending a status that has already been acquired, or acquiring a status one does not yet have.

In the end, anyone who examines the pros and cons with care will reach the conclusion that you are either thinking in terms of a republic whose goal is to conquer an empire, as Rome's was, or of one that merely wants to defend itself. If the first, then you must do everything as the Romans did; if the second, then you can copy Venice and Sparta, for the reasons I have already given and for others we will come to in the next chapter.

But let us turn to a discussion of which men are more dangerous to a republic, those who want to acquire new power, or those anxious not to lose the power they have. Marcus Menenius was appointed dictator, and Marcus Fulvius general of the horse. Both of them were plebeians. Their mission was to uncover certain conspiracies against Rome that had been hatched in Capua. The populace also gave them authority to enquire whether there were people in Rome who, out of ambition, were scheming to use extralegal means to be elected to the consulate or to other prestigious offices. The nobility thought the dictator had been given this mandate so he could attack them, and so they spread the word around Rome that it was not the nobles who were driven by ambition to use extralegal means to acquire honors, but the non-nobles. Unable to rely on their own abilities [*virtù*] or their inherited status, it was they who sought to acquire honors by corrupt means. In particular, they attacked Menenius, the dictator. This charge was so damaging that Menenius, having made a speech in which he protested against the calumnies directed at him by the nobles, resigned the dictatorship, and submitted himself to the judgment of the people. When his case had been considered, he was found to be innocent.

In such cases, it is easy to disagree as to who was the more ambitious, those who wanted to hold on to power or those who wanted to acquire it. For either aspiration can easily be the cause of tremendous conflict. Nevertheless, for the most part such conflicts are caused by those who already have power, for the fear of losing it gives them exactly the same ambitions as those who want to acquire power. Men do not feel they are secure in the possession of their property unless they are constantly acquiring more from someone else. Moreover, those who already have power are in a better position to use their influence and their resources to bring about change. In addition, their improper and self-interested behavior excites in the hearts of the powerless the desire to have power, either in order to take their revenge on their enemies by taking what they have from them, or in order to acquire for themselves that wealth and those honors they see their opponents abusing.

Chapter Nine: On how it is necessary to act alone if you want to draw up the constitution for a new republic from scratch, or reform an old one by completely changing its established laws.

Perhaps some people will think that I have jumped too far ahead in the history of ancient Rome, for I have not yet said anything about the men who drew up the Roman constitution, nor have I discussed those laws that dealt with religion or with military service. Since I do not want to keep those who want to read something about these matters waiting any longer, let me say that many will probably think the founding of Rome presents a bad example, for Romulus, in order to establish constitutional government, first killed his brother and then agreed to the killing of Titus Tatius, the Sabine, who had been elected to share office with him. You might think that the citizens of a state founded in this manner could claim that they were only following the example of their ruler if they attacked those who opposed their wishes while they sought to acquire power and authority. You would be right to think this, so long as you did not stop to consider the reasons that had led him to commit murder.

One ought to recognize this as a general principle: It rarely (if ever) happens that a republic or a kingdom has good institutions from the beginning, or is completely reformed along lines quite different from those on which it was previously organized, unless one person has sole responsibility. So one person alone must decide on the strategy, and he must make all the key decisions. A wise legislator when establishing a republic, if he wants to serve not his own interests but the public good, not to benefit his own heirs but the nation as a whole, should make every effort to ensure that all power lies in his own hands. A wise man will never criticize someone for an extralegal action undertaken to organize a kingdom or establish a republic. He will agree that if his deed accuses him, its consequences excuse him. When the consequences are good, as were the consequences of Romulus's act, then he will always be excused, for it is those who are violent in order to destroy who should be found guilty, not those who are violent in order to build anew.

A legislator should, however, use care and skill [*virtuoso*] to ensure that the power he has seized is not inherited by a successor; for, since men are more inclined to do evil than good, his successor is likely to use for selfish purposes the power he has been using for the public good. Moreover, one person alone may be best at drawing up plans, but the institutions he has designed will not survive long if they continue to depend on the decisions of one man. They will do better if many share the responsibilities, and if many are concerned to preserve them. For just as it is a bad idea to have many people plan something, for they will not agree about what is best, since there will be many differing opinions among them, so, too, when once they know what is right, they will not be able to agree to act contrary to it. Romulus deserved to be pardoned for the death of his brother and his colleague, for his actions were aimed at the public good and not at self-advancement. This is evident from the fact that he quickly established a senate to whose views he listened and whose advice he took. If you analyze the powers Romulus kept in his own hands, you will find that the only powers he kept were those of commanding the armies once war had been declared and of summoning the senate. This became apparent when Rome acquired freedom by driving out the Tarquins, for the Romans did not alter their established constitution at all, beyond replacing an hereditary monarch with two consuls elected annually. This shows that the original institutions of Rome were better adapted for a constitutional and participatory political system than for an absolute and tyrannical one.

There are an infinite number of examples that could be produced in support of what I have said in this chapter, such as Moses, Lycurgus, Solon, and other founders of monarchies and republics who could, because they had laid claim to a certain personal authority, establish laws aimed at the common good. But I want to leave these aside, as the point is obvious. Let me give only one additional example, not such a well-known one, but worth considering if one wants to establish a good constitution. Agis, King of Sparta, wanted to confine the Spartans within the limits that had been established for them by the laws of Lycurgus. He felt that his city, because it had in some measure deviated from its original constitution, had lost a good deal of its traditional excellence [*antica virtù*] and, with it, much of its strength and power. He had no sooner begun his reforms than he was assassinated by the Spartan ephors on the grounds that he was trying to establish a tyranny. But Cleomenes was appointed king to succeed him, and he developed the same aspirations, for he came across some memoranda and memoirs written by Agis. From them he learned the true opinions and intentions of his predecessor. He recognized that he could not do his country the service he intended if he did not concentrate all power in his own hands, for he thought that human beings were so self-interested that one could not do good to the majority if faced with the opposition of a powerful minority. So he seized on a suitable opportunity and had all the ephors and anyone else in a position to oppose him killed. Then he completely overhauled the laws of Lycurgus. This would probably have given Sparta a new lease on life and established for Cleomenes a reputation as great as that of Lycurgus, if the Macedonians had not been establishing their predominance, and if the other Greek cities had not been incapable of resisting them. For after Cleomenes' reforms, the Spartans were attacked by the Macedonians and discovered that, on their own, they were not strong enough to resist them. Their forces had nowhere to retreat and were defeated. So Cleomenes' plans, although wise and admirable, never came to fruition.

Having considered all these matters, I conclude that in order to establish the constitution of a republic one needs to have sole power; and that Romulus should be forgiven, not blamed, for the deaths of Remus and of Titus Tatius.

Chapter Twelve: On how important it is to give due weight to religion, and on how Italy, having been deprived of faith by the Church of Rome, has been ruined as a consequence.

Those rulers and those republics who want to keep their political systems free of corruption must above all else prevent the ceremonies of their religion from being corrupted and must keep them always in due veneration. For one can have no better indication of the prospective ruin of a society than to see that divine worship is held in contempt. It is easy to see why this is so, since we saw above that religions are established wherever men are born. Every religion grounds its spiritual life in one particular doctrine or practice. The religious life of the pagans was based on the

replies given them by their oracles and on the cult of divination and augury. All their other ceremonies, sacrifices, and rites depended on these, for it was easy for them to believe that a god who could foretell the good or evil that was going to happen to you could also determine your fate. It was this belief that gave rise to temples, to sacrifices, to prayers, and to all the other ceremonies with which the gods were venerated. They were authorized by the oracle of Delos, the temple of Jupiter Ammon, and by other celebrated oracles who were universally admired and worshipped. These oracles in time came to speak as they were instructed to by the powerful, and the deception involved was recognized by the populace. Thus, men came to be sceptics and became inclined to overthrow every good institution.

So the rulers of a republic or of a kingdom should uphold the basic principles of the religion to which they are committed. If they do this it will be easy for them to keep their state religious and, as a consequence, law-abiding and united. Everything that happens that fosters religious faith, even if they privately judge it to be false, they should support and encourage; the more prudent they are, the more scientific their outlook, the more they should do this. It is because sensible men have adopted this policy that belief in miracles has taken hold, even in religions that we know to be false. For wise men supported them without worrying about the truth of their claims, and their authority served to encourage belief in society as a whole.

There were many such miracles reported in Rome: for example, when the Roman soldiers were sacking the city of Veii some of them entered the temple of Juno. They went up to her statue and said, "Do you want to come to Rome?" Some thought she nodded in response; others heard her say yes. Since these men had a genuine religious faith (Livy's account makes this plain, for he reports that they entered the temple without being raucous, but acting devoutly and full of reverence) they thought they had heard the reply to their question that they had, perhaps, expected. This simple-minded belief was unhesitatingly encouraged and favored by Camillus and by the other rulers of the city.

If, when Christianity first became a state religion, such piety had been encouraged (as the founder of the religion instructed it should be), the Christian states and republics would now be more united and a good deal happier than they are. Nor is there any clearer indication of the decline of Christianity than the fact that those peoples who live closest to Rome, whose Church is the head of our religion, have the least faith. If you look back to the founding principles of Christianity, and contrast them with present practices, you will be bound to conclude that our religion will soon be destroyed or scourged.

Since many are of the view that the welfare of the cities of Italy depends on the Roman church, I want to argue the contrary case, employing those reasons that occur to me. I will appeal to two powerful arguments that, I believe, are compatible with each other. The first is that the wicked examples presented by the papal court have caused the whole of Italy to lose all piety and all religious devotion. This has innumerable unfortunate consequences and is the cause of numerous disorders. For just as respect for religion has a whole range of beneficial consequences, so contempt for religion has a whole range of evil consequences. Thus, we Italians owe this much to our Church and to our clergy: They have made us irreligious and wicked.

But this is not the half of what we owe them, for there is another reason why the Church is the cause of our ruin: the Church has been and still is responsible for keeping Italy divided. In truth, no geographical region has ever been unified or happy if it has not been brought under the political control of a single republic or ruler, as has happened in France and Spain. And the only reason why Italy has not been unified as they have been, the only reason why she does not have a republic or a prince who has been able to acquire control of the whole territory, is the existence of the church. The pope lives in Italy and has a temporal authority there, but he has not been powerful or skillful [virtù] enough to acquire absolute power throughout Italy and make himself her ruler; but on the other hand he has never been so weak that, faced with the prospect of losing his temporal possessions, he has been unable to call on some other state to defend him against whatever power has been on the rise in Italy. There is plenty of evidence for this in the past, for example when the papacy employed Charlemagne to kick out the Lombards, who had become rulers of almost the whole of Italy. In our own day the papacy destroyed the power of the Vene-

tians by obtaining the support of the French; and then got rid of the French with the help of the Swiss. So the church has not been powerful enough to conquer Italy, but has prevented anyone else from conquering her. This is the reason why Italy has never been united under one ruler, but has been divided among numerous princes and rulers, which has resulted in so much division and weakness that she has been reduced to being the victim, not only of powerful foreign states, but of anyone who cares to attack her. We Italians owe all this to our Italian church and to no one else.

If you wanted to have an incontrovertible test of the truth of my argument, you would need to be powerful enough to transport the court of Rome, with its temporal authority, from Italy to Switzerland. For the Swiss are the only people who still live as the ancients did, being uncorrupted in both their religion and their military service. You would see that in a short time the evil habits of the court of Rome would introduce more disorder into the territory of the Swiss than anything else that could ever happen there.

Chapter Thirteen: On how the Romans used religion to reorganize their city, to carry out their enterprises, and to put a stop to internal dissensions.

I think it might be helpful if I gave a few examples of occasions when the Romans used religion to reorganize their city and to carry out their enterprises. Although there are lots of examples to be found in Livy, nevertheless, I intend to confine myself to the few that follow. In the year after the Roman populace established tribunes with consular authority, all of whom, with one exception, were plebeians, there was plague and famine, and a number of prodigious events occurred. The nobles took advantage of this when it came to the election of new tribunes. They said the gods were angry because Rome had ill-treated its constituted authorities, and that there was no way of placating the gods except to elect the proper people as tribunes. The result was that the populace, unable to argue against these pious sentiments, elected tribunes who were all nobles.

Again, one can see how, when the city of Veii was under siege, the military commanders made use of religion to keep the soldiers ready for an attack. That same year the Alban lake had expanded remarkably. The Roman soldiers were weary with the lengthy siege and wanted to return home. Their commanders discovered that Apollo and some other oracles had declared that the year that Veii would be taken would be the year that the Alban lake overflowed its banks. This made the soldiers willing to put up with the frustrations of the siege, for they were seized with the hope that they would be able to take the town. They were willing to go on with the task, with the result that Camillus, once he was made dictator, took that city after it had been under siege for ten years. So religion, skillfully employed, helped the Romans seize Veii and helped, too, to restore the tribunate to the nobility. Without its help it would have been difficult to accomplish either objective.

I would not want to omit another example relevant to this subject. Terentillus, when he was tribune, provoked numerous conflicts in Rome. He wanted to propose some legislation for reasons I will outline below in the appropriate place. One of the first means employed by the nobility to resist him was religion, which they put to work in two different ways. In the first place, they had the Sibylline books consulted; they were interpreted as saying that the city was in danger of losing its liberty that year as a result of civil conflict. Although the tribunes exposed this as a stratagem, nevertheless, the prophecy so frightened the populace that they cooled in their support for Terentillus. The second was a response to the fact that a certain Appius Herdonius, with a throng of exiles and slaves, four thousand men in all, had occupied the Capitol by night, giving grounds to fear that if the Aequi and the Volsci, who were longstanding enemies of the Romans, took the opportunity to attack, they would be able to seize the city. Despite this, the tribunes did not let up in the determined insistence with which they advocated the adoption of Terentillus's law, dismissing Herdonius's attack as a fake. So a certain Publius Ruberius, a citizen whose manner was solemn and authoritative, came out of the senate and addressed the populace. Using words that were partly affectionate and partly threatening, he pointed out to them the danger in which the city stood and the untimely nature of their demands. He succeeded in compelling the populace to swear an oath that it would not go against the wishes of the consul. Restored to obedience, the populace retook the Capitol by force. But Publius Valerius, one of the consuls, died during the attack, and Titus Quintius was hurriedly appointed to replace him. He, in order to prevent the populace from catching its breath, and in order to ensure they did not have time to turn their thoughts to Terentillus's law, ordered them to march out of Rome against the Volsci, saying that the oath they had taken to stand by the consul obliged them to follow him. The tribunes argued against him, saying that the oath had been taken to the dead consul and not to him. Nevertheless, Livy describes how the populace, for fear of religion, preferred to obey the consul rather than believe the tribunes. He says this in praise of the old religion: "That negligence towards the gods that characterizes our own age had not yet developed. People did not yet feel free to reinterpret oaths and laws to suit themselves." Because of this, the tribunes were afraid that they would lose all their authority if they held out. They agreed with the consul that they would remain obedient to him, and that for one year there would be no more talk of the law of Terentillus, while the consuls agreed that for one year they would not lead the populace out to war. And so religion made it possible for the senate to overcome problems that, without its assistance, they would never have been able to overcome.

Chapter Seventeen: On how a corrupt people who come to be free can only hold on to their freedom with the greatest of difficulty.

In my view, if the kings of Rome had not been abolished, Rome would in a very short time have become weak and worthless. For if you consider the extent of the corruption that had set in among the kings, you will recognize that if there had been two or three generations of such rulers, then the corruption of the rulers would have infected the body of the nation. Once the society as a whole was corrupt, it would never again have been possible to reform it. But because the head was struck off before the body was infected, it was easy for them to accustom themselves to a free and well-organized political system. One should recognize as an indubitable truth that if a corrupt city, accustomed to one-man rule, acquires freedom and sees its ruler and all his relatives killed, it will never know what to do with its newfound liberty. It would be better for it to have a new ruler step into the shoes of the old. Without a new ruler it will never settle down, unless some individual who combines exceptional goodness with exceptional skill [*virtù*] keeps freedom alive in its midst; but this freedom will only survive as long as he does.

This is what happened at Syracuse with Dion and Timoleon. They both had the skill [*virtù*], under differing circumstances, to keep freedom alive in their city while they lived; but as soon as they died the old tyranny was restored. But the best example is that of Rome. When the Tarquins were thrown out the Romans were able to seize and maintain their freedom; but when Caesar was killed, when Gaius Caligula was killed, when Nero was killed, when the whole house of Caesar had been eliminated, at no point were they able so much as to lay claim to freedom, let alone maintain it. Events took a very different course, although all this happened in the same city, simply because, in the days of the Tarquins, the Roman people were not yet corrupt, while in later centuries they were rotten to the core. In the early days, in order to keep themselves firm of purpose and determined to prevent the restoration of the monarchy, all that was necessary was that they should swear that they would never agree to there being a king in Rome; in later centuries the authority and severity of Brutus, backed up by all the legions of the eastern empire, were insufficient to keep them committed to preserving the liberty that he, like the first Brutus, had restored to them. This was the result of the corruption that the faction of Marius had introduced into the populace; Caesar, having put himself at the head of this party, had been able to blind the populace to the fact that they were being enslaved, even as he himself placed the yoke upon their necks.

Although this example from the history of Rome is more important than any other, nevertheless, I would like to introduce some further examples of popular corruption drawn from contemporary history. I would say that nothing that could happen, no matter how destructive and violent, could accustom the peoples of Milan and of Naples to freedom, for those societies are completely corrupt. This was apparent after the death of Filippo Visconti, for although the Milanese sought to re-establish liberty, they could not do so, and had not the least idea of how to maintain it. Rome was therefore extremely lucky that her kings became corrupt quickly, so that they were soon kicked out, before their corruption had spread to the guts of the city. It is because the populace of Rome was not corrupt that the innumerable conflicts that broke out in Rome did not harm but actually helped the republic, for her citizens at least had the right objectives.

So we can draw this conclusion: Where the individuals are not corrupt, conflicts and other crises do no harm; where they are corrupt, the best-planned laws are useless, unless the laws are imposed by someone who uses ruthless methods to make people obey him, until the individuals themselves become good. I do not know if this has ever happened, or if it could ever happen. In practice one finds, as I said just before, that where a city has gone into decline because the individuals who make it up are corrupt, if it ever happens that it acquires freedom, it happens because of the skill [*virtù*] of one individual who is present by chance, not because of the strength [*virtù*] of the population as a whole, which is what is needed to maintain good institutions. As soon as the one leader dies, the city returns to its old habits. This is what happened in Thebes which, because of the skill [*virtù*] of Epaminondas, was able, so long as he was alive, to maintain a republican structure and to hold down an empire; but, as soon as he died, Thebes returned to its old internal conflicts. The problem is that an individual cannot live long enough to have time to discipline properly a city that has long been spoiled. One leader of exceptional longevity or two skilled [*virtuose*] leaders succeeding each other are not enough to establish order; but without one or the other, as I have said, there is no hope. By the time you discover this, however, you have undergone many dangers, and much blood has been spilled, and still liberty is not reborn. For this sort of corruption, this sort of incapacity for political freedom, is the result of the social inequality that has developed within the city. In order to restore equality, one would have to use quite exceptional measures. Few know how to use them, or, if they do know, are prepared to face what is involved, as I will explain in greater detail elsewhere.

Chapter Eighteen: On the way to preserve
political freedom in a corrupt but free city;
or to establish it in a corrupt and unfree city.

I think it is relevant to what we have been discussing,
and it would not be out of place, to consider whether
one can preserve political freedom in a corrupt but
free city, or whether one can establish it in a corrupt
and unfree city. On this subject, I say that it is very
difficult to do either one or the other; and although
it is almost impossible to formulate general rules, for
one would have to adjust one's policies in the light
of the extent of the corruption, nevertheless, since it
is good to think through every problem, I do not want
to omit a discussion of this one. Let us assume we
are dealing with an extremely corrupt city, so that we
can consider the most difficult case. Indeed, the case
would seem hopeless, for there are neither laws nor
institutions that will serve to restrain a universal corruption. For just as good habits need good laws if
they are to survive, so good laws will only be obeyed
if the subjects have good habits.

Moreover, the institutions and laws that have been
established in a republic at the time of its foundation,
when the individuals who made it up were good, are
no longer appropriate when they become bad. If the
laws of a city are relatively easily changed to take
account of changing circumstances, the institutions,
on the other hand, never change, or do so only at
long intervals. The result is that the new laws are
insufficient, because the institutions that remain unchanged distort their impact. In order to make clearer
what I mean, let me explain what the institutions of
the government, or rather of the state, were in Rome,
and then I will outline the laws with which the magistrates held the citizens in check. The fundamental
institutions of the state were embodied in the respective powers of the people, the senate, the tribunes,
and the consuls; in the ways in which magistrates
were chosen and appointed; and in the ways in which
legislation was passed. This fundamental constitution
changed little or not at all as circumstances changed.
What did change were the laws that restricted the
actions of citizens, such as the laws on adultery, the
laws controlling extravagance, those on political corruption, and many others, which were altered as the
citizens became progressively more corrupt. But since

the institutions of the state remained unchanged, although they were no longer appropriate once the
citizens had become corrupt, the revision of particular
laws was insufficient to prevent the progress of corruption; the outcome would have been different if not
only the laws had been changed, but the constitution
as well.

That I am justified in claiming that such institutions were not the right ones for a corrupt city is
particularly apparent if we look at two topics: the
election of magistrates and the passage of legislation.
The people of Rome did not give the consulate and
the rest of the highest offices in the city except to
those who sought them. This system was good at first,
for only those citizens who thought themselves worthy
of high office stood for election. Since defeat was
shameful, each candidate behaved well in the hope
of being judged worthy of election. However, this
system was disastrous when the city had become corrupt. For then it was not the most virtuous [*virtù*] but
the most powerful who stood for election, and the
weak, even if virtuous [*virtuosi*], were too frightened
to run for office. Things degenerated to this point
not all at once but bit by bit, as happens with all
cases of degeneration. Once the Romans had subdued
Africa and Asia, and had compelled almost the whole
of Greece to acknowledge their authority, they became confident that no one would conquer them,
and they no longer thought they had any enemies of
whom they ought to be afraid. This sense of security,
this absence of enemies who inspired respect, meant
that the people of Rome, in electing consuls, no
longer paid attention to competence [*virtù*], but
judged only on the basis of charm. They elected those
who were best at flattering Rome's citizens, not those
who were best at defeating Rome's enemies. Later,
even charm was not enough, and the people sank to
the point that they voted for those who had the most
patronage to distribute; so that good men, because
the system was faulty, never stood a chance.

Similarly, a tribune, or indeed any other citizen,
could propose a law to the people. Every citizen then
had the right to speak for or against the proposal
before a vote was taken. This was a good system, so
long as the citizens were good, for it is always a good
principle that anyone should be free to put forward
a proposal of benefit to the public; it is also a good

principle that everyone should be able to express his opinion on the subject, so that the people, when they have heard everyone's opinion, can then make the right decision. But once the citizens became corrupt this system became disastrous, for only the powerful proposed laws, and they did so not in order to further the liberty of all, but only in order to build up their own power. Everyone was too frightened to speak against their proposals, so that the people were either taken in, or else compelled to choose policies that would lead to their own destruction.

If one had wanted to preserve liberty in Rome despite the progress of corruption, it would have been necessary to go beyond passing new laws from time to time and to construct new political institutions. For the institutions and ways of life one needs to establish if men are corrupt are different from those that are appropriate if they are good; if one has different materials with which to work, one must build a quite different structure. But these institutions would either have had to be reformed all at once, as soon as it was realized that as a whole they were no longer appropriate, or else they would have had to be revised little by little, as each particular institution was seen to be in need of reform. Both of these procedures are, in my view, almost impossible to carry out. For if you want to revise institutions little by little and one by one, you need to have some wise man proposing change, someone who sees problems almost before they have developed and catches them at the moment of their birth. In the whole history of a city there might easily prove to be not a single person as wise as this. And even if there were such a person, he would never be able to persuade others to recognize the truth of his arguments, for men who have been used to living in a particular way have no desire to change it, especially when they do not find themselves standing toe-to-toe with a problem, but rather are asked to accept its existence on the basis of someone else's conjectures and hypotheses. On the other hand, if one hopes to change the institutions at a stroke, when everyone has come to recognize that they are defective, then I maintain defects that are easy to recognize are hard to correct. For such reforms, ordinary measures are insufficient, for we are dealing with a situation where the ordinary measures have proved defective. So one has to adopt extraordinary measures,

such as resorting to violence and civil war. One's primary goal must be to become sole ruler of the city, so that one can do with it as one pleases. In order to reconstruct the constitution of a city so that it fosters political liberty, one needs to be a man with good intentions; but people who resort to arms in order to seize power in a republic are people whose methods are bad. So you can see that there will hardly ever be an occasion when a good man, using wicked means, but using them in the service of good ends, will want to become sole ruler; or when a wicked man, having become sole ruler, wants to do good. It will not occur to him to use for good the power he has acquired by wicked means.

So I have now explained the difficulties that would have to be overcome if one were to try to preserve liberty in a corrupt city or to attempt to establish it from scratch. These difficulties are, in effect, insuperable. Even if one had the opportunity to carry out reform or revolution, one would have to introduce a constitution that was more monarchical than democratic. For men who were so ill-behaved that they could not be kept in order by the laws would need to be kept in check by a more or less arbitrary authority. If one sought to find some other way of making them good, one would either fail completely, or have to resort to extreme cruelty, as I explained above when discussing Cleomenes. He, in order to be sole ruler, had to kill the ephors, just as Romulus, for the same reason, had to kill both his brother and Titus Tatius the Sabine. They went on to use their power well. But you have to take into account the fact that neither of them was dealing with subjects who were as eaten away with corruption as those we have been discussing in this chapter. So it was not unreasonable for them to hope to build a free state; and they were able to turn their aspirations into reality.

Chapter Twenty-One: On how much those rulers and republics that do not have their own armies deserve to be criticized.

Those contemporary rulers and modern republics that do not have their own soldiers for defense and for offense ought to be ashamed of themselves. They should think of Tullus, and they will see that this shortcoming is not caused by a shortage of men fit for military duty, but by their own failure, for they should have known how to turn their subjects into soldiers. For Tullus became King of Rome when the city had been at peace for forty years. He could not find a single man who had ever been in battle. Nevertheless, when he decided he wanted to go to war, he did not think of hiring the Samnites, or the Tuscans, or of turning to others who were accustomed to military service. Instead, being a man of great wisdom, he decided to use his own troops. He was so skilled in his leadership [*fu tanta la sua virtù*] that it was possible for him to train the most excellent soldiers from scratch. This is truer than anything else: If a state has men but no soldiers, then the fault is the ruler's. There is no point in blaming the nature of the territory or the character of the inhabitants.

Here is a very recent example that confirms my claim. Everyone knows that only very recently the King of England attacked the King of France, and did so relying entirely on his own native troops. Now the English had been more than thirty years without fighting a war, so that their king could not recruit either soldiers or officers with experience of warfare; nevertheless, he did not hesitate to rely on untried troops to attack a kingdom full of experienced officers and disciplined soldiers, for the French army had for years past been continuously at war in Italy. The explanation for this is simply that the King of England was a prudent man, and his country was well administered, for during the years of peace they had continued to prepare for war.

Pelopidas and Epaminondas, the Thebans, when they had liberated Thebes and freed it from domination within the Spartan empire, found themselves ruling a city used to obeying, surrounded by a people who had become effeminate. But they did not hesitate, so well did they understand their business [*tanta era la virtù loro*], to call them to the colors and to march out with them against the Spartan armies whom they defeated. The historian of these events comments that these two very quickly showed not that men born in Lacedaemonia had the makings of good soldiers, but rather that wherever men are born, good soldiers are to be found, provided you can find someone who knows how to train them for military service, as we have seen Tullus knew how to train

the Romans. Virgil makes the point better than anyone else could, and in doing so shows that he agrees with it, when he says:

Tullus will herd the lazy men into the army.

Chapter Twenty-Seven: On how it is only on very rare occasions that men know how to be either completely bad or completely good.

Pope Julius II went to Bologna in 1505 to overthrow the Bentivogli, who had been rulers of the city for a hundred years. He also wanted to get rid of Giovampagolo Baglioni, who was tyrant of Perugia, because he had plotted against all the tyrants who controlled cities within the papal states. When he reached Perugia, realizing that everyone knew what his intention was, he had no expectation of being allowed to enter the city accompanied by his army, but he did get permission to enter without any troops, despite the fact that Giovampagolo was in the city with plenty of troops whom he had collected together to defend himself. So, swept along by the frenzy with which he undertook everything he did, Julius put himself into the hands of his enemy with only his personal guard to protect him.

Shortly afterwards, he left the city taking Giovampagolo with him, leaving a governor behind who would rule Perugia on behalf of the church. Astute men who were with the pope remarked on his rash boldness and on the cowardice of Giovampagolo. They could not understand how it came about that Giovampagolo had not made himself famous for evermore by getting rid of his enemy with a single blow. He would have been able to make himself wealthy from the plunder, for all the cardinals were travelling with the pope, and they had all their luxuries with them. They could not believe that he had held back out of goodness, nor that his conscience had restrained him. He was a violent man, who kept his sister as his mistress, and had killed cousins and nephews to take power. Compassion could not have made such a man hesitate. So they concluded the explanation was that men do not know how to be either admirably wicked or completely good. A truly wicked deed has its own grandeur or involves a certain nobility of conception: Most men are consequently not up to it.

So Giovampagolo, who thought nothing of committing incest and murdering his relatives in public, did not know how to carry out an enterprise that would have caused everyone to admire his spirit. He had a legitimate opportunity, but to tell the truth he did not dare, though he would have won eternal fame for being the first person to show the clergy just how little one should respect people who live and govern as they do. He could have done something whose grandeur would have more than compensated for any disgrace or any danger that might have resulted from it.

Chapter Forty-Two: On how easy it is for men to be corrupted.

One should also note, while we are discussing the Decemviri, how easy it is for men to be corrupted. Their characters are quickly transformed, no matter how good and well-trained they were. Think of how the young men that Appius had gathered around him began to be well-disposed towards tyranny because they stood to gain some small benefit by it, and of how Quintus Fabius, one of the second group of Decemviri, who was one of the best of men, was blinded by a little bit of ambition, and was persuaded by Appius's malice to change his good habits into evil ones, and become like his new mentor. If they consider such matters carefully, those who pass laws for republics or for kingdoms will be all the more eager to put a brake on human appetites, and deprive men of any hope that they can go wrong without being punished.

Chapter Forty-Six: On how men advance from one aspiration to another. At first they want only to defend themselves; later, they want to attack others.

When the Roman people had recovered their liberty, and returned to their original condition, except improved in so far as they had made many new laws that reinforced the authority of the populace, it seemed reasonable that Roman politics would quiet down for a while. In practice, however, the opposite proved to be the case, for every day new conflicts and discords broke out. Because Titus Livy very sensibly explains why this happened, it seems to me relevant at this point to report to you his precise words. He says

that it was always the case that if the populace were humiliated, the nobles grew haughty, and vice versa. Because the populace remained peaceably within their assigned limits, the young nobles began to insult them, and the tribunes were able to do little to defend them, for they, too, were under attack. The nobility, for its part, even though it thought that its younger members were overdoing it a bit, nevertheless was not distressed at the idea that if one group was going to make gains at the expense of the other, then it was they who stood to make gains at the expense of the populace. So the desire to defend their rights meant that each group advanced to the point where it oppressed the other.

The way these things work is this: When men are simply trying to avoid having reason to fear their opponents, they begin to give their opponents grounds to fear them. In defending themselves against attack, they attack others and put them on the defensive, as if there were no choice but to be either the attacker or the victim. So you can see one way in which republics fall apart; and also how men advance from one aspiration to another. There is nothing truer than the opinion Sallust attributes to Caesar: "All bad outcomes derive from good beginnings." As I have said, those citizens who live in a republic and are ambitious for themselves start out by trying to ensure that they cannot be attacked. They want not only to be safe from other private citizens, but even to be immune from prosecution. In order to accomplish this, they seek allies. These they acquire in ways that seem outwardly honest, either by lending private citizens money or by defending them against the powerful. Because this seems like a good way to behave [*pare virtuoso*], everyone is easily taken in by it, and so nothing is done to put a stop to it. So, an individual who carries on in this fashion, without being stopped, soon accumulates so much influence that other private citizens are afraid of him, and even government officials have to give him special treatment. Once he has got into this position, without anyone having taken the measures needed to put a stop to his accumulation of influence, it becomes very dangerous to do anything about it, for the reasons I explained above. It is dangerous to try to tackle a problem in a political system once it has become well-established.

In the end, it becomes straightforward: You must either eliminate him and run the risk of destroying yourself before you know it, or allow him to continue to accumulate power, in which case it will become obvious that he has mastered you, unless his death or some other lucky accident comes to your rescue. For once you have reached this point where both citizens and government officials are frightened of going against his wishes or even those of his allies, then it is relatively straightforward for him to ensure that everyone makes the decisions he wants made, and everyone turns against those he wants attacked. So a republic ought to have among its institutions one whose task it is to ensure citizens cannot do harm under the pretence of doing good, and that they can only establish reputations that help support, not undermine, political freedom. I will discuss how to accomplish this in another chapter.

Chapter Fifty-Five: On how easy it is to reach decisions in cities where the multitude is not corrupt; and on how it is impossible to establish one-man rule where there is social equality; and on how it is impossible to establish a republic where there is inequality.

Although we have already discussed at some length what one should expect, be it good or bad, in corrupt cities, nevertheless, I do not think it would be a digression if we considered a debate that took place in the senate over a motion introduced by Camillus. He proposed giving one-tenth of the plunder seized in Veii to the temple of Apollo. Since this plunder had fallen into the hands of the Roman populace, and since there was no other way of knowing what it was worth, the senate passed a decree that everyone should hand over to the treasury one-tenth of the loot that he had seized. This decree was never enforced, for the senate later adopted another proposal, and found a different way of compensating Apollo on behalf of the Roman people. Nevertheless, the very fact that it was passed is an indication of the extent to which the senate had confidence in the trustworthiness of the populace. In their opinion, everyone could be relied on to give an accurate account of all that he owed under the terms of the decree. As for the populace, they did not think for a moment of evading the decree by simply handing over less than they owed; they sought to have it repealed by openly protesting against it.

This example, along with many others that we have already discussed, shows the extent to which the Roman populace had a sense of public duty and of religious obligation, and how justified were those who had confidence in them. It is a simple fact that where such a sense of public duty is not to be found, one is entitled to be pessimistic. There is no point in being optimistic if you live in one of those regions that, in our own day, have become corrupt. Italy is the most far gone of them all; even France and Spain have been infected. If we do not see quite so many disorders in those countries as break out in Italy every day, the reason is not so much that the populace has a sense of public duty, for the truth is that their peoples are for the most part corrupted; rather it is because each has a king who keeps it united, not only because he is a strong leader [*non solamente per la virtù sua*], but because the institutions of those kingdoms are still intact. In the territory of Germany, it is evident that a sense of public duty and of religious obligation is still widespread among the populace; the result is that many self-governing republics survive there. They observe their own laws so well that nobody dares try to invade them from without or to subvert them from within.

In order to show that I am right to claim that the sense of public duty we associate with the ancients still predominates in them, I want to give one example comparable to the one I gave earlier concerning the senate and the Roman populace. In the German republics, it is customary, when they find they need to spend a considerable amount of money on public business, for the appropriate magistrates or councils to impose a tax on the inhabitants of the city of one or two percent of each person's assets. Once a decree has been passed according to whatever procedures are required by the local constitution, each person makes an appearance before the officials assigned to collect the tax, and, having taken an oath to pay what he owes, places in an official chest the sum of money that he, having consulted his conscience, thinks he ought to pay. He himself is the only witness to how much he pays. From this you can get some idea of how far a sense of public duty and of religious obligation is still to be found among these men. One is bound to think that each person pays what he really owes; for if he did not, the tax would not yield as much as they expected, judging by its yield on previous occasions over a long period of time; if it did not yield as much, the public would know they had been defrauded; and if they knew they were being defrauded they would change their method of collecting taxes. Such public spiritedness is all the more to be admired in our day and age because it is so rare.

Indeed, it survives only in Germany, and there are two reasons for this. The first is that the Germans do not have numerous contacts with their neighbors, for their neighbors rarely visit them, and they rarely visit their neighbors. They have been content with the products of the local economy, eating food grown and raised nearby, and dressing in wool from their own sheep. This removes the primary reason for contact with foreigners, and with it, the primary source of all corruption. They have avoided being infected with the customs of the French, the Spanish, or the Italians; and these three nations between them are the source of corruption throughout the world. The second reason is that those republics that have preserved popular sovereignty and resisted corruption do not tolerate any of their citizens to style himself a gentleman, or to live like one. So they maintain among themselves a genuine equality, and they are bitterly hostile to those lords and gentlemen who do exist in their region. If by chance some of them fall into their hands, they regard them as the germs of corruption and the causes of every possible immorality, and kill them.

In order to clarify the meaning of this term "gentleman," let me say that men are called "gentlemen" if they live in luxury without working. Their income arises from their estates, but they do not have to worry about cultivating them or going to any other trouble to make ends meet. Such people are pernicious influences in any republic and, indeed, in any part of the world. But even worse are those who, in addition to being wealthy, have a castle at their disposal and have subjects who obey them. Gentlemen of both types are to be found throughout the kingdom of Naples, in the papal states, in the Romagna, and in Lombardy. This is the reason why no republic has ever been established in those regions, nor any other form of popular sovereignty. For such types of men are totally hostile to a civilized way of life. To want to set up a republic in regions with this sort of social structure is to want the impossible; if one wanted to introduce a new political system in such regions,

supposing one had gained control of them, there would be no choice but to establish a monarchy. The reason is as follows: Where the individuals are so corrupt that the laws alone will not restrain them, then you need to establish alongside the laws a force greater than theirs, that is to say, the heavy hand of a king, who can use an absolute and unlimited power to put a halt to the unlimited ambition and corruption of the elite.

This argument is confirmed by the example of Tuscany. There you find that for a long time there have been three republics—Florence, Siena, and Lucca—crammed into a small geographical space. And the other cities of the region are either accustomed to subordination, as is apparent both from the character of their citizens and from their constitutions, or else defend, or at least would like to defend, their liberty. The reason is simple: In that region there are no lords of castles to be found and no (or at any rate very few) gentlemen. There is so much social equality that it would be easy for a wise man with some knowledge of ancient civilizations to establish some form of popular sovereignty. But it has been their great misfortune that, right down to the present, they have not chanced upon a leader who has been able to do it or has understood how to do it.

From this discussion I draw the following conclusion: Anyone who wants to set up a republic in a place where there is a fair number of gentlemen can only do it if he begins by killing them all. On the other hand, anyone who wants to set up a monarchy or a system of one-man rule in a place where there is a fair amount of social equality will never manage to do it unless he lifts out of that equality many individuals who are ambitious and restless, and makes them into gentlemen in fact if not in name, giving them castles and estates, and giving them control of men and property. Then he will be surrounded by an elite whom he can rely on to uphold his power, while they can rely on him to further their aspirations. As for the rest of the population, they will be obliged to submit to a yoke nothing but force could persuade them to tolerate. This way, those doing the forcing will be more than a match for those being forced, and so people will stay obediently in the ranks assigned to them. The task of making a region suited to monarchy into a republic, or one suited to republican government into a monarchy, is one for somebody of quite exceptional intelligence and force of personality. There have been many who have tried to do it, but very few have known how to carry it out in practice. For the scale of the enterprise is daunting in itself, and it means that often people fail when they have scarcely begun.

I believe that this opinion of mine—that where there are gentlemen one cannot establish a republic—may appear to be contradicted by the history of the Venetian republic, for there only those who are gentlemen are allowed to be elected to office. But my reply is that this example does not tell against me, for the gentlemen of Venice are rather gentlemen in name than in fact. For they do not have large incomes from country estates since their great wealth is founded on commerce and trade. Moreover, none of them has a castle or has any private jurisdiction over other men. In their case the name "gentleman" is a purely honorific title, one that has nothing to do with the factors that determine whether or not you are called a gentleman in any other city. Just as all republics have social distinctions that they refer to by one name or another, so Venice is divided into the gentlemen on the one hand and the populace on the other. They insist that the gentlemen have a monopoly, both in practice and in theory, of all the offices, while the rest are completely excluded from them. This does not lead to conflict in that territory, for the reasons I have explained. So we see that a republic can only be established where there is considerable social equality or where men are made to be equal; by contrast, the rule of one man requires considerable social inequality. If you ignore this principle you get a lopsided construction, and one that will not stand for long.

Chapter Fifty-Eight: On how the masses are wiser and more loyal than any monarch.

There is nothing more worthless and more unreliable than the masses. So says our Titus Livy, and all the other historians agree with him. For it often happens that, as one follows a political narrative, one sees the masses condemn someone to death, and then next moment lament his death, and long for his return. This is how the Roman populace behaved towards Manlius Capitolinus whom they first condemned to death and then longed for him to be alive. This is

what Livy says: "As soon as he was no longer a danger, the populace wanted him back." And elsewhere, when he describes the events that took place in Syracuse after the death of Hieronymus, nephew of Hiero, he says: "This is the nature of the masses: Either they obey humbly, or they domineer arrogantly."

I am not sure if I want to embark on an undertaking that is so hard and full of so many difficulties that I will either have to give up in disgrace or, if I carry on, be made to pay dearly for my persistence. I am not sure if I want to defend a view that, as I have said, is rejected by all the authorities. Nevertheless, I do not think, and never will think, that one should be blamed for putting forward an argument, so long as one relies on reason and has no intention of resorting to citing authorities or to force. In my view, then, the defect for which authors criticize the masses is a defect to be found in all men, considered as individuals, and, above all, in rulers. For anyone who is not constrained by the laws will make exactly the same errors as will the unbridled masses. One can easily recognize the truth of this, for there are and have been plenty of rulers but there are few who have been good and wise. I am speaking of rulers who have been able to break the bounds that ought to restrain them. I do not mean to include those kings who were to be found in Egypt when, at the beginning of recorded history, that territory was governed according to laws; or those who were to be found in Sparta; or those who in our own day have ruled in France. For government in France is more moderated by legal constraints than in any other presently-existing kingdom about which we are well-informed. The rulers who hold power under such constitutions are not to be included in the category I am discussing, for we want to consider the nature of individual men taken on their own and see if it is similar to that of the masses. Otherwise, we would have to consider the masses when they are similarly constrained by the laws so that we could compare them with constitutional monarchs. In such cases you would find the masses just as well-behaved as the monarchs, and you would find that they neither arrogantly domineer nor humbly obey.

Take for example the Roman populace who, for as long as the republic survived uncorrupted, never humbly obeyed and never arrogantly domineered; instead, they maintained their proper status honorably, respecting their institutions and obeying their governors. When it was necessary for them to join forces against an internal enemy, they did so, as they did against Manlius Capitolinus, against the Decemviri, and against others who tried to oppress them. But when it was necessary to obey dictators and consuls in order to preserve the republic, they did so. And if the Roman populace wished Manlius Capitolinus were alive once he was dead, it is not surprising; what it missed were his virtues [*virtù*], which were so great that remembering them made everyone regret his death. The same memories would have had the same consequences in a monarch, for all authors agree that virtue [*virtù*] is praised and admired even in one's enemies. If Manlius had been brought back to life while the populace mourned his death, it would have passed the same sentence on him as it did when it let him out of prison and shortly afterwards condemned him to death. So, too, we find examples of monarchs who are thought of as wise but have had someone put to death, and then bitterly regretted it. Alexander killed Cleitus and other friends of his; Herod killed Mariamne. But what our historian says about the nature of the masses is not intended to refer to those masses who are constrained by the laws, as the Roman populace was, but to those who are unbridled, as the populace of Syracuse was; they made the same errors as individuals who are enraged and unconstrained, the same errors as Alexander the Great and Herod made in the instances I have mentioned. Consequently, one should no more blame the masses in general than one does rulers in general, for both groups and individuals make mistakes when they have opportunities to go wrong and nothing prevents them. There are plenty of other examples of this beyond the ones I have mentioned, both among the Roman emperors and among other tyrants and monarchs. One finds far more examples of unreliable behavior and of shifts of policy and attitude among them than among any populace.

I conclude, therefore, that the common opinion, which holds that the populace, when they are in power, are unreliable, changeable, and disloyal is wrong. I maintain that they are no more guilty of these vices than are individual rulers. If someone were to criticize both multitudes and individuals who hold power, he might be right; but if he makes an

exception of the individuals, then he makes a mistake. For a populace in power, if it is well ordered, will be as reliable, prudent, and loyal as an individual, or rather it will be even better than an individual, even one who is thought wise. On the other hand, an individual who is not restrained by the laws will be even more disloyal, unreliable, and imprudent than a populace. The difference in their behavior would be a consequence, not of a difference in their natures, for all men are alike, and if any type of person is better than the rest, it is the common man who is; but would reflect whether they had more or less respect for the laws under which both prince and populace are supposed to live.

If you consider the Roman populace, you will see that for four hundred years they were hostile to the idea of monarchy, and were in love with the glory and the common good of their homeland; there are innumerable instances of their behavior that testify to both commitments. And if anyone cites against me the ingratitude that they showed towards Scipio, I would reply with what I said at length on this question above, when I showed that the populace was less ungrateful than an individual ruler.

But as far as prudence and predictability are concerned, I say that the populace is generally more prudent, more predictable, and has better judgment than a monarch. It is with good reason that people compare the voice of the populace to the voice of God, for one can see that there is a widespread belief that the predictions of a populace are uncannily accurate; indeed, it seems as if it has an inexplicable capacity [*occulta virtù*] to foresee what will bring it good fortune and what bad. As far as exercising their judgment is concerned, one sees that it is rare indeed that the people hear two speeches upholding different policies, and do not, if the speeches are equally effective [*virtù*], choose the better policy. They are almost always able to understand those truths that are explained to them. I have already admitted they sometimes make mistakes in matters involving their pride or what they take to be their interests. But monarchs often make mistakes when their passions are aroused, which happens much more often with a single ruler than it does with the populace. One also sees that, when it comes to making appointments to government offices, the populace makes much better choices than rulers do. You will never persuade the populace that it is a good idea to promote to an office a man who has a bad reputation and lives a decadent life. But rulers are easily persuaded to do this for all sorts of reasons. One sees a populace begin to be committed to opposing something, and then not change its mind for several centuries; the same cannot be said for rulers. For both the good judgment of the populace and its enduring commitments, I will rely simply on the example of the Roman people who, over a period of hundreds of years, during which they elected vast numbers of consuls and tribunes, did not make more than two or three appointments they afterwards had cause to regret. And they were, as I have said, so hostile to the idea of monarchy that no matter how much they were indebted to one of their citizens, if he aspired to be crowned king, then he could not hope to escape the lawful penalties.

One may also note, in addition, that cities where the populace is in power are capable of making immense territorial gains in very short periods of time, much greater than any that have been made by an individual ruler. This is what Rome did after it had expelled its kings, and Athens after it freed itself from Pisistratus. The only possible reason for this is that the populace is better at ruling than individuals are. Neither can I allow you to argue against my view by appealing to the things our historian says in the text I began by quoting and in other similar places. For if you go over all the cases of bad government by the populace, and all those by monarchs, all the achievements of the populace, and all those of monarchs, you will find the populace to be much superior in both goodness and glory. If individuals are superior to the populace in drawing up laws, establishing civic forms of life, creating constitutions and institutions, then the populace is equally superior to an individual when it comes to maintaining the institutions once they have been established. No doubt its achievements in this respect get credited to the original legislators.

So finally, to conclude my discussion, I say that just as some states based on one-man rule have endured over time, so have some republics. Both monarchies and republics need to be regulated by laws, for a king who can do whatever he wants is a madman on the loose, and a populace that can do what it wants is never wise. However, if we were to discuss the relative merits of a monarch who is obliged to obey the law and a populace restrained by legislation, you would find that the populace made a better ruler [*si vedra più virtù nel popolo*] than the monarch. If we were to discuss both types of government unconstrained by the law, you would find that the populace makes fewer mistakes than a monarch, and the ones it makes are less significant and easier to put right. For a populace that is licentious and disorderly needs only to be talked to by someone who is good, and he will find it easy to set it on the right path. A bad monarch will not listen to anyone, and the only way to correct him is to kill him. This enables one to judge the relative importance of the faults of the two types of government. To cure the faults of the people, you need only words; to cure those of a monarch, you need cold steel. Now it is obvious that a disease that is hard to cure is worse than one that is easy.

When a populace breaks free from restraint, there is no need to fear the foolish things it may do. It is not the present evil one has to worry about but the evil that may develop out of popular government, for a tyrant may seize power in the midst of the confusion. But the opposite is the case with bad monarchs. With them, one fears the present evil and hopes for some future improvement, for men persuade themselves that the evil deeds of their ruler may provoke people to lay claim to their freedom. So you can see that the difference between them is that under one type of government you fear what exists, under the other what might come to pass.

The cruel deeds of the multitude are directed at those whom it fears will endanger the common good; those of a monarch are directed at those whom he fears will endanger his own interests. Why then do people think ill of the populace? Because everyone freely speaks ill of them; they can do so without fear even when they are in power. But about monarchs one always speaks with great caution, and one is always fearful of the consequences. It does not seem to me irrelevant, since my present subject has led me towards it, to discuss in the next chapter which alliances one can most safely put one's trust in, those made with republics, or those made with monarchs.

Book Two

Chapter One: On whether skill [*virtù*] or good
fortune was a more significant factor in the
Romans' acquisition of an empire.

Many have been of the opinion—among them Plutarch who is an author whose judgment is always to
be respected—that the Roman people, in acquiring
an empire, benefited more from good fortune than
from skill [*virtù*]. One of the various reasons they put
forward to support this view is that it is evident, they
say, from the actions of the Romans themselves that
they attributed all their victories to good luck, for
they erected more temples to the goddess Fortune
than to any other god. It would seem Livy was more
or less of this opinion, for it is rare for him, whenever
he has a Roman speak about skill [*virtù*], not to couple
skill with luck.

But I do not want to admit the truth of this opinion
under any circumstances, and I do not believe there
are good arguments to support it. For if there has
never been a republic that has made as extensive
gains as Rome did, it is also evident there has never
been a republic better organized to make gains than
Rome was. It was the skill [*virtù*] of their armies that
enabled them to conquer an empire, and it was their
way of going about things, which dates back to their
first legislator, that enabled them to hold on to what
they had conquered, as I will explain at length below,
over the course of a number of chapters. Some people
say it was good fortune and not skill [*virtù*] that ensured the Roman people never had to face war against
two powerful enemies at the same time. Thus, they
only found themselves at war with the Latins, when,
if they had not really defeated the Samnites, they
were at least able to call on their support, for in
fighting the Latins they were helping the Samnites.
They did not campaign against the Tuscans until
they had first conquered the Latins and had almost
completely crippled the Samnites by defeating them
again and again. If two of these powers had allied
when they were fresh and undefeated, then without
doubt one could reasonably have predicted they
would destroy the Roman republic.

But, however it came about, it is true they never
had to fight two extremely powerful enemies at one
time. It seems the rise of one always caused the decline of another, or the decline of one made possible
the rise of another. This is apparent from the chronology of the wars they fought, for, leaving aside those
that took place before Rome was seized by the French,
one can see that while they were at war with the
Aequi and the Volsci, and so long as those tribes
remained powerful, nobody else attacked them. Only
after they had been subdued did the war with the
Samnites begin, and although the Latin tribes rebelled against the Romans before that war was over,
nevertheless, when that rebellion took place the Samnites entered into a league with the Romans and sent
their troops to help the Romans punish the Latins
for their insolence. Once they were subdued, the war
against the Samnites began again. When the Samnites
had been beaten in battle after battle, the war with
the Tuscans began; and when that had been settled,
the Samnites rebelled again as a result of the invasion
of Italy by Pyrrhus. When he had been forced to
retreat into Greece, they began the first war with the
Carthaginians; no sooner was this war over, but all
the French, on both sides of the Alps, allied against
the Romans, until they were defeated and butchered
in large numbers between Popolonia and Pisa, where
now stands the tower of St. Vincent.

After this war, there was a period of about twenty
years when they were not involved in any major conflicts, for they only fought against the Ligurians and
against those remnants of the French who held out
in Lombardy. This relative peace lasted until the
beginning of the Second Carthaginian War in which
Italy was embroiled for sixteen years. Having brought
this to a glorious conclusion, they found themselves
at war with Macedon, and, after that was over, with
Antiochus and with Asia. And after they had been
victorious in that war there was not a ruler or a republic in the whole world who, either alone or in alliance
with others, could hope to defy the Roman armies.

But anyone who considers the chronology of the
wars before this final victory and who studies the
policies of the Romans will realize they did not simply
rely on fortune. They also employed a quite remarkable prudence and skill [*virtù*]. For if you ask yourself
why they were so fortunate the answer will be obvious.
It is evident that when a ruler or a people acquire a
reputation such that every neighboring prince and
people is spontaneously afraid of attacking them and
fearful of being attacked by them, then it will always

be the case that no state will ever attack them unless it has no alternative.

The result is that the dominant state will have almost a free choice when it comes to deciding with which of its neighbors it wants to fight a war, and will be able, with a little effort, to pacify the others. They, partly out of fear of the dominant power and partly taken in by the techniques it will employ to give them a false sense of security, will be easy to pacify. The other powers who are not immediate neighbors and who do not have dealings with the victim, will regard the whole business as taking place a long way away and think it no concern of theirs. They will keep making this mistake until they are next in line. By which time they have no defense available except to rely on their own troops. But by then their own troops will be inadequate, for the dominant power will have become overwhelmingly strong.

I will not delay to discuss how the Samnites stood by and watched while the Romans defeated the Volsci and the Aequi, and, in order to be brief, I will confine myself to the case of the Carthaginians. They were very powerful and widely respected at the time the Romans were fighting against the Samnites and the Tuscans, for they already controlled the whole of Africa along with Sardinia, and Sicily, and part of Spain. Because they were so powerful, and because their territory was some distance from that of the Romans, it never occurred to them to attack them, or to come to the assistance of the Samnites and the Tuscans. Thus, they behaved as one does if one thinks time is on one's side, allying with the Romans, and trying to win their good will. They did not recognize their mistake until the Romans had conquered all the peoples between themselves and the Carthaginians, and had begun to challenge them for control of Sicily and Spain.

The same thing happened to the French as to the Carthaginians, and the same thing again to Philip, King of Macedon, and to Antiochus. Each one of them believed, while the people of Rome were occupied with one of the others, that Rome's enemies would win, and that there was plenty of time to defend themselves, either through diplomacy or war, against Rome's advancing power. So I am of the view that the good fortune the Romans had in never having to fight against two enemies at the same time is available to any ruler who acts as the Romans did and is as skillful [*virtù*] as they were.

Chapter Twenty-Nine: On how fortune blinds men's minds when she does not want them to thwart her plans.

If you will think sensibly about how people's lives are shaped, you will see that often events and accidents occur against which the heavens were determined we should have no protection. Seeing this sort of thing happened to the Romans, who were so skillful [*virtù*], pious, and well-organized, it is not surprising that it happens much more often to cities or regions who lack these advantages. Because this subject is a rather good one if one wants to show the influence of the heavens in human affairs, Livy discusses it at length and most eloquently.

He says that, because the heavens had some reason for wanting the Romans to recognize their power, they first made those Fabii who had been sent as ambassadors to the French make mistakes, with the result that their efforts served to incite the French to make war against the Romans, and then they ensured the Romans fell way below their normal standards when it came to making preparations for war. Fate had ensured that Camillus, who would have been able to handle such a difficult situation single-handedly, but for whose abilities there was no substitute, had been banished to Ardea. When the French began to march on Rome, the Romans, who had often appointed a dictator when faced with attacks by the Volsci and other hostile neighbors, failed to appoint one to deal with the French. Moreover, when it came to choosing soldiers, they chose poorly and without making any real effort. They were so slow to muster that they were only just in time to block the French advance where it had to cross the river Allia, a mere ten miles from Rome. There the tribunes pitched camp without taking any of the normal precautions. They did not reconnoiter the site, nor did they surround the camp with a ditch and palisade. In fact, they did not employ any precautions, either natural or supernatural. When it came to drawing up the battle lines they spread the ranks out so they were thin and weak. Neither soldiers nor officers lived up to the standards of the Roman army. The battle itself was bloodless, for the Romans fled before they were attacked, the bulk of the army making for Veii, while the rest withdrew to Rome. When they arrived in Rome they did not even stop by their houses but made straight for the Capitol, with the result the senate did not give any thought to defending the city, did not even bother to close the gates, but some of them fled, and others went with the rest into the Capitol. However, when it came to defending the Capitol, they finally began to get organized. They did not hamper the defense by admitting people who would be useless, while they stockpiled all the grain they could collect so they could withstand a siege. Of the vast numbers of those who were useless—the old, women, and children—the majority fled into the surrounding countryside, while the rest remained in Rome at the mercy of the French.

Anyone who read about all the Romans had achieved over the preceding years and then came to read about these events, would be quite incapable of believing these were the same people. When Livy has described this whole series of errors, he concludes with the remark: "So one can see the extent to which fortune will blind men's minds when she does not want them to deflect her onward momentum." This conclusion is as true as could be. It follows that men who regularly encounter extreme adversity or have the habit of success deserve less praise or less blame than one might think. For usually you will find they have been led to either tragedy or triumph because the heavens have pushed them decisively either one way or the other, either making it easy or virtually impossible for them to be able to act effectively [virtuosamente].

One thing fortune does is select someone, when she wants him to accomplish great things, who will be sufficiently bold and skillful [virtù] to recognize the opportunities she makes for him. In the same way, when she wants to bring about someone's destruction, she chooses a man who will help bring about his own undoing. If there is someone around who might get in her way, then she kills him, or deprives him of all the resources he would need to do any good. You can see this clearly in Livy's account. Fortune, in order to make Rome all the greater and build her up to the power she eventually attained, judged it necessary to give her a nasty shock (I will describe all that happened at length at the beginning of the next book), but did not want, at this point, to

destroy her completely. That is why she had Camillus banished, but not killed; had Rome seized by the enemy, but not the Capitol; determined that the Romans did nothing right when it came to defending Rome, but did everything right when it came to defending the Capitol. So that Rome would fall to the enemy, she ensured the bulk of the forces that had been defeated at the Allia would make for Veii, thus destroying any opportunity of defending the city. But in bringing this about she also laid the ground for Rome's liberation. A complete Roman army stood ready at Veii, and Camillus was nearby at Ardea. So they were able to make a determined effort to liberate their homeland under the command of a general whose reputation was not tarnished by defeat but was unblemished.

Perhaps I should add, in support of what I have said, an example from modern history; but I do not think it necessary, for this one example should be sufficient to satisfy anyone, and so I will move on. But I want to repeat that this is absolutely true, and all history testifies to it. Men can help fortune along, but they cannot resist it; they can swim with the tide, but they can never make headway against it. Of course, they should never give up, for they can never know what fortune has in mind. Her path is often crooked, her route obscure. So there is always reason to hope, and if one has hope one will never give up, no matter how hostile fortune may be, no matter how dreadful the situation in which one finds oneself.

Book Three

Chapter One: On how, if you want a [political or religious] movement or a state to survive for long you must repeatedly bring it back to its founding principles.

It is certainly true that everything in the world has a natural life expectancy. But usually creatures live out the full cycle the heavens have determined for them only if they do not abuse their bodies, but keep them in such good shape they either remain unchanged, or if they change it is to get healthier, not weaker. Now my subject is collective bodies, such as republics, political parties, and religious sects, and my claim is that those changes are healthy that bring them back to their founding principles. Consequently, the best constructed organizations, those that will live longest, are those that are organized in such a way they can be frequently reformed; it amounts to the same thing if, for some external reason independent of their structure, reform is thrust upon them. It is clearer than daylight that if organizations are not reformed they cannot survive.

The way to reform an organization is, as I just said, to bring it back to its founding principles. For all political and religious movements, all republics and monarchies must have some good in them at the start. Otherwise, they would not be able to start out with a favorable reputation, nor would they be able to make progress in the early days. But as time goes by, that original goodness becomes corrupted, and, unless something happens that brings them back to first principles, corruption inevitably destroys the organization. Medical doctors say, speaking of the human body, "Everyday it takes in something that, in the end, requires treatment."

This return to founding principles, in the case of states, occurs either through some external accident or through domestic wisdom. As for the first, you can see it was necessary for Rome to fall to the French if she was to have a hope of being reborn; being reborn, she acquired new strength and new skill [virtù], committing herself once again to respect for religion and justice, which, in the old Rome, had begun to be corrupted. This is very evident in Livy's history, when he points out that when they marched out with an army against the French and when they created tribunes with consular authority they did not perform any religious ceremonies. Even more strikingly, not only did they not punish the three Fabii who, contrary to the law of nations, had attacked the French, but they appointed them tribunes. One can reasonably presume the other sound laws that had been introduced by Romulus and by Rome's other wise rulers were increasingly treated with less respect than was reasonable and, indeed, necessary if Rome was to preserve political freedom.

Then this shock came from the outside so that all the institutions of the city could be renewed. It was made evident to the people that it was not only necessary to uphold religion and justice, but also to have respect for good citizens and to place more value on their judgment [virtù] than on the interests they felt

they would have to sacrifice if they adopted their policies. And this is, indeed, exactly what happened, for as soon as Rome recovered, they renewed all her old religious ordinances; punished the Fabii for beginning a conflict contrary to the law of nations; and moreover held the judgment [virtù] and goodness of Camillus in such esteem the senate and everyone else put their jealousy to one side and entrusted to him the leadership of the republic.

So it is necessary, as I have said, that men who live together in any sort of institution regularly take stock of themselves, either as a result of external shocks or of internal factors. As far as this second type of reform is concerned, it best arises either as a result of a legal requirement that the members of an institution frequently take stock, or because one good man appears among them and, by his own example and his skillful [virtuose] policies, has the same effect as such a law. So this improvement takes place in a state, either because of the skill [virtù] of a man, or because of the effect [virtù] of a law.

As far as legal authorities are concerned, the institutions that drew the Roman republic back to its first principles were the tribunes of the people, the censors, together with all those laws that were a barrier to the ambition and the insolence of men. Such laws and institutions have to be given life through the will power [virtù] of an individual citizen who determinedly sets out to enforce the laws despite the powerful opposition of those who seek to ignore them. Among such cases of the laws' being enforced, prior to the sack of Rome by the French, one may note the death of the sons of Brutus, the death of the ten citizens, and that of Maelius the corn dealer. After the sack of Rome, there is the death of Manlius Capitolinus, the death of the son of Manlius Torquatus, the prosecution brought by Papirius Cursor against Fabius, his commander of cavalry, and the charges brought against the Scipios. These cases involved going to extremes and caught people's attention. Whenever such a case occurred, it made men take stock; and as they became less common there was more opportunity for men to become corrupt, and reform became accompanied by ever greater danger and ever increasing conflict. For between two such dramatic legal decisions no more than ten years ought to go by. If the gap is longer men begin to develop bad habits and to break the laws; and if nothing happens to remind them of the penalties and to re-awaken their sense of fear, there are soon so many lawbreakers springing up all over the place that it is no longer possible to punish them without endangering stability.

Those who were in charge of the Florentine state from 1434 to 1494 used to say, when discussing this subject, that it was necessary to retake power every five years, otherwise power would slip away from them. What they meant by "retaking power" was inspiring the same fear and terror in their subjects they had inspired when they first came to power, when they had set out to crush those who had acted badly by the standards of the new system of government. But as the memory of that clampdown faded, people began to be emboldened to attempt innovations and to speak ill of their rulers. So it was necessary to provide a remedy by bringing matters back to first principles.

This reform of governments according to their first principles is sometimes the result of the simple virtue [virtù] of one man, without being based on any law that inspires him to act rigorously; such men are so respected and admired that good men want to imitate them, and bad men are ashamed to live according to principles at odds with theirs. The individuals in Roman history who are notable for having had such good effects are Horatius Cocles, Scaevola, Fabricius, the two Decii, Regulus Attilius, along with a few others. By their remarkable and virtuous [virtuosi] examples they had almost the same effects on their fellow citizens as good laws and good institutions had. If the individual instances of law enforcement I have mentioned, together with the examples provided by admirable individuals, had occurred at least every ten years in Rome, then it would certainly have been the case that Rome would never have become corrupt. But as both punishments and role models became less frequent, corruption began to spread. After Marcus Regulus there is not a single exemplary individual to be found. It is true the two Catos came along later, but there was such a long gap between Regulus and the first Cato, and then between the first and the second, and they were such isolated instances, that they could not by their own good example have any good effects. This is particularly true of the second Cato, who found the city very generally corrupted and could not by his own example improve the behavior of

his fellow citizens. This is all I need to say about republics.

But we should consider movements. We can see similar reforms are necessary if we take the example of our own religion. If this had not been brought back to first principles by St. Francis and St. Dominic it would have completely died away. They, by living lives of poverty and imitating the life of Christ, renewed religion in the minds of men at a time when they had lost all commitment to it. The new orders they founded were so effective that it is only because of them that the dishonesty of the prelates and of the hierarchy does not destroy the church, for the friars continue to live in poverty and have such influence with the people as a result of hearing confession and preaching that they persuade them it is wrong to criticize evil, and it is right quietly to obey the church authorities, and, if they make mistakes, to leave their punishment to God. And so the clergy do as much harm as they can, for they do not fear a punishment they do not see and in which they do not believe. Thus, this reform movement preserved, and continues to preserve, the Christian religion.

Kingdoms, too, need to renew themselves and to reform their laws so they accord with their original principles. One can see what a good effect this policy has in the Kingdom of France. That kingdom lives according to its laws and respects its institutions more than any other kingdom. These laws and institutions are upheld by the *parlements*, and especially the *Parlement* of Paris. They give them new life every time they enforce them against a prince of the kingdom or condemn the king in one of their judgments. So far, the *parlements* have maintained their role by being determined enforcers of the laws whenever the nobility break them; but should they ever leave first one and then more and more noblemen unpunished, the result would certainly be that they would either have to put things right by provoking a major crisis, or the whole system of government would break down.

One can therefore conclude that there is nothing more essential in any form of communal life, whether of a movement, a kingdom, or a republic, than to restore to it the reputation it had when it was first founded, and to strive to ensure there are either good institutions or good men who can bring this about, so that one is not dependent on having some external intervention before reform can occur. For although an external intervention is sometimes the best remedy, as it proved for Rome, it is so dangerous there are no circumstances in which one should hope for it.

In order to show you how the deeds of individuals made Rome great and had numerous good consequences for that city, I will turn to an account of individual leaders and a commentary on their actions. This third and final section of my commentary on the first ten books of Livy will deal with this subject. And although the kings of Rome did great and remarkable things, nevertheless, since history discusses them at length, I will leave them to one side and will say nothing more about them, except for mentioning one or two things they did in pursuit of their own private interests. I will begin, instead, by talking about Brutus, the father of Roman liberty.

Chapter Three: On how it is necessary, if one wants to preserve liberty when it has been newly won, to kill the sons of Brutus.

The harsh methods Brutus employed to preserve the liberty he had won for Rome were not merely useful, but necessary. His example is an exceptional one, with few parallels throughout history: a father sitting in judgment and not only condemning his sons to death, but supervising their execution. Those who study classical history will always learn from this that after a change in the system of government, whether it be from republic to tyranny, or from tyranny to republic, it is necessary to act decisively and in public against those who want to overthrow the new government. Anyone who sets up a tyranny and does not kill Brutus, anyone who introduces self-government and does not kill the sons of Brutus, cannot expect to survive long. Because I have already discussed this at length and in detail, I refer you to what I have already said on the subject.

I will simply add one memorable example that occurred in our own time and in our own country, that of Piero Soderini. He believed that he could overcome through patience and kindness the desire the sons of Brutus had to restore a different system of government. He was mistaken. Although he had wisdom enough to recognize the need to act, and although circumstances and the ambition of those who opposed him gave him the opportunity to eliminate them, nevertheless, he never resolved to do it. For not only did he believe he could overcome hostility through patience and kindness, and could buy off some of his enemies with rewards, he was of the view (and he often affirmed as much to his friends) that if he set out to attack his opponents boldly and to destroy his adversaries, he would have to claim extraordinary powers and set aside not only the laws but the principle of political equality. Even if he did not go on to make tyrannical use of his powers, he believed such an action would have so dismayed public opinion that after he died people would never agree again to appoint a gonfaloniere for life; and he believed this office was one that ought to be preserved and strengthened.

This was a genuine and significant consideration. But one should never put up with an evil consequence for the sake of some benefit if the evil consequence is more than likely to eliminate the benefit. He ought to have decided that since his deeds and his intentions would be judged by their outcome (assuming he lived long enough, and circumstances were not too unfavorable), he would be able, in due course, to demonstrate to everyone that he had acted in order to ensure the safety of the homeland and not out of private ambition. He ought to have been able to take steps to ensure no successor of his would be able to do for corrupt motives what he had done for patriotic ones. But he failed to see the mistake in his original view. He did not recognize that hostility is not overcome by time or bought off by gifts. So, because he did not know how to imitate Brutus, he fell from power, lost his reputation, and was forced into exile.

It is difficult to preserve a free state; but it is equally difficult to preserve a monarchy, as I will show in the next chapter.

Chapter Twenty-Nine: On how rulers are responsible for the failings of their subjects.

Princes should not complain of any failings to be found in the people over whom they rule. For such failings are likely to be caused either by their own negligence or because they themselves have the same faults. If you think of the peoples who in our own day have been thought of as being given over to robbery and such crimes, you will see their faults were entirely derived from those who ruled them and had the same failings. The Romagna, before Pope

Alexander VI eliminated the nobles who ruled over it, was well known for every type of crime. People knew that on the slightest excuse, murders and mayhem took place there. The cause of this was the wickedness of the rulers, not the incorrigible wickedness of their subjects, as the rulers claimed. For the rulers of the Romagna were poor but wanted to live as if they were rich. So they had to turn to plunder and invented various types of exaction. One of the dishonest methods they turned to was to pass laws prohibiting some activity or other. Then they encouraged people to ignore the laws and never punished those who broke them. Only when they were sure lots of people had put themselves in the wrong did they start enforcing the laws; not because they wanted people to be law-abiding, but because they wanted to collect the fines. Such policies had many evil consequences; above all, they impoverished the people without improving their behavior. Those who had been impoverished put their minds to ways of getting the better of those who were weaker than themselves. The result was all those evils I began by mentioning, all of which were caused by the rulers.

The truth of this is apparent from Livy's account of how, when the Roman legates were bringing the plunder they had taken from Veii as an offering to Apollo, they were seized by pirates from Lipari in Sicily and taken there as prisoners. When Timasitheus, their ruler, heard what sort of cargo this was, where it was going and who had sent it, he behaved as if he were a Roman though he had been born in Lipari, and explained to his people how wicked it would be to seize a religious offering. So, with popular approval, he let the legates continue on their journey with all their possessions. Our historian says: "Timasitheus inspired in the populace, who always copy their rulers, respect for religion." And Lorenzo de' Medici made the same point, remarking: "What the ruler does one day, many others do the next, for they all have their eyes on him."

Chapter Thirty-One: On how strong republics and fine men sustain the same outlook, no matter what happens, and never lose their dignity.

Our historian has Camillus do and say magnificent things in order to show us how a fine man ought to behave. One example is the following statement that he puts into his mouth: "Being dictator did not make me more self-confident, and being in exile will not make me doubt myself." From this you can see how great men are always themselves, no matter what happens to them. Their luck may change, and one moment they may be lifted up to the heights, the next crushed, but they themselves do not change, but always remain determined and seem so comfortable with their own style of behavior that everyone can easily see fortune has no power over them. Weak men behave very differently. For they become conceited and overexcited when they have good fortune, presuming that everything good that happens to them is a reward for excellent qualities [virtù] they do not, in fact, have. The result is they become intolerable and hateful to all those who have to deal with them. And this causes their luck to change quickly, and, as soon as they stare ill fortune in the face, they quickly develop the opposite vices, becoming inadequate and unselfconfident. Rulers who have weak characters like this are quicker to think of flight than of self-defense when times become tough, but then, since they have misused their period of good fortune, they have made no preparations against attack.

This virtue [virtù] of strength of character, and this vice of weakness of character, which I have been describing in individuals, can also be found in republics. One may take the Romans and the Venetians as examples. As for the first, no bad luck ever made them demoralized; and no good fortune ever made them overconfident, as is evident from their behavior after their army was routed at Cannae and after their victory fighting against Antiochus. After the rout, although it was extremely serious, for it was their third defeat, they never allowed themselves to feel inadequate. They sent armies into the field. They refused to ransom those of their soldiers who had been made prisoner, for this would have been a breach with tradition. They did not send emissaries to either Hannibal or Carthage to beg for peace. But, turning their backs on all such feeble policies, they thought only of carrying on the war, arming, since they were short of soldiers, old men and slaves. When Hanno the Carthaginian learned of this, he pointed out to the Carthaginian senate, as I have already mentioned, just how little they had gained by their victory at Cannae. So you can see how hard times did not dismay them or humiliate them.

On the other hand good fortune did not make them overconfident. Antiochus had sent ambassadors to Scipio to seek peace before the battle that he was to lose. Scipio had stated certain conditions for a settlement. They were that he must withdraw into Syria and that all other outstanding matters must be left to the decision of the Roman state. Antiochus rejected these terms. After he had fought the battle and lost he sent new ambassadors to Scipio with instructions to accept whatever conditions the victor chose to impose. The conditions Scipio offered them were exactly the same as those he had offered before the battle. He only added these words: "For the Romans, if they are beaten in battle, do not lose heart; and, if they win, they do not make a habit of being overconfident."

We have seen the Venetians exemplify the opposite characteristics. When things were going their way they thought they had made gains because of their own excellent qualities [*virtù*], which in fact they did not have. They became so full of themselves they called the King of France the son of St. Mark; they showed no respect towards the church; their aspirations extended far beyond Italy; and they had begun to dream of having an empire like that of the Romans. Then, when their luck turned, and they were half-defeated at Vailà by the King of France, they not only lost control of the whole of their territory because their subjects rebelled, but they ceded large parts of it to the pope and to the King of Spain out of feebleness and inadequacy. They sank so low they sent ambassadors to the emperor offering to be his vassals; they wrote letters to the pope full of cowardice and of submission in an attempt to persuade him to have pity on them. They were reduced to this miserable condition in four days after a semi-defeat, for after the battle their army, in retreat, was attacked, and about half of it destroyed.

Nevertheless, one of their generals who escaped reached Verona with more than twenty-five thousand soldiers, counting both infantry and cavalry. If the Venetians and their institutions had had any decent qualities [*virtù*], they could have regrouped and stood up to look fortune in the eye. There was still time for them either to win or lose more gloriously, or to obtain a more honorable settlement. But their feeble spirits, which had been shaped by the character of their institutions, which were unsatisfactory when it came to war, made them lose in one and the same moment both their territory and their self-confidence.

And this will always happen to anyone who behaves as they did. For this pattern of becoming overconfident at times of good fortune and inadequate at times of bad is a result of your habits of behavior and of your upbringing. If your education was foolish and weak, then you will be, too; if it was the opposite, then you will be the opposite. If you are brought up to have a decent understanding of the world, then you will be less inclined to get overexcited when things go well or to get dismayed when things go badly. If this is true of an individual it is also true of a group of people living together in the same state; they have the qualities that result from their society's habits of behavior.

Although earlier on I said that all states depend upon having a good army, and that if you do not have a good army you cannot hope to have either good laws or anything else worth having, I think it bears repeating. For at every point, as we read this history book, the importance of this fundamental requirement becomes apparent. And we see an army cannot be good if it is not kept in training, and you cannot keep it in training if it is not composed of your own subjects. States are not always at war, nor could they withstand it if they were. So you must be able to train your army during peacetime; but it is far too expensive to train an army in peacetime unless it consists of your own subjects.

Camillus, as I have said, had marched out with an army against the Tuscans. When his soldiers saw the size of the enemy army they were all dismayed, for it seemed to them they were so badly outnumbered that they would not be able to stand up to an enemy charge. When Camillus came to hear of the low morale among his soldiers, he went out and walked around the camp, chatting to a soldier here, another there, and got them to express their fears. In the end, without altering any of the dispositions he had made, he said, "Let each man do what he knows how to do, what he is used to doing." If you think about what he said and the way in which he set out to give his soldiers courage to face the enemy, you will realize you could not say this or pursue this sort of policy with an army that had not first been organized and trained, both in time of peace and in time of war. For a general who has soldiers who have never learned anything cannot trust them or expect them to do anything worthwhile; even if they had a second Hannibal in command, they would be defeated under him. For a commander cannot be everywhere while the battle takes place. So he is bound to be defeated unless he has first ensured there will be men throughout the army who share his outlook and have a good understanding of his routines and methods.

If a whole city is armed and organized as Rome was, so that every day its citizens, both in private and in public, have occasion to experience both the extent of their own strength [*virtù*] and the power of fortune, the result will always be that they will maintain the same attitude whatever happens to them and will always keep up their dignity without wavering. But if they are disarmed, and they put their trust in the tides of fortune and not in their own strength, then their temperament will change as their luck changes, and they will inevitably make a spectacle of themselves, just as the Venetians did.

WORKS CITED

Adcock, F. E., *Roman Political Ideas and Practice* (Ann Arbor: University of Michigan Press, 1964).

Annas, Julia, *An Introduction to Plato's Republic* (New York: Oxford University Press, 1981).

Berlin, Isaiah, "The Originality of Machiavelli," in *Studies in Machiavelli*, edited by Myron P. Gilmore (Florence, Italy: Sansoni, 1972).

Blundell, Mary Whitlock, *Helping Friends and Harming Enemies: A Study in Sophocles and Greek Ethics* (New York: Cambridge University Press, 1989).

Brickhouse, Thomas C., and Nicholas D. Smith, *Socrates on Trial* (Oxford: Oxford University Press, 1989).

————, and ————, *Plato's Socrates* (New York: Oxford University Press, 1994).

Brown, Peter, *The World of Late Antiquity* (New York: Harcourt Brace, 1989).

Chadwick, John, *The Decipherment of Linear B* (Cambridge: Cambridge University Press, 1958).

Connolly, William, *The Augustinian Imperative: A Reflection on the Politics of Morality* (Newbury Park, Calif.: Sage Publications, 1993).

Connor, W. R., *Thucydides* (Princeton, N.J.: Princeton University Press, 1984).

Cooper, John M., *Reason and the Human Good in Aristotle* (Cambridge: Harvard University Press, 1975).

Davis, Michael, *The Politics of Philosophy: A Commentary on Aristotle's Politics* (Lanham, Md.: Rowman and Littlefield, 1996).

de Romilly, Jacqueline, *The Great Sophists in Periclean Athens* (New York: Oxford University Press, 1992).

Engberg-Pedersen, Troels, *Aristotle's Theory of Moral Insight* (New York: Oxford University Press, 1983).

Euben, J. Peter, "Justice in the *Oresteia*," in *American Political Science Review* (1982).

————, *Greek Tragedy and Political Theory* (Berkeley: University of California Press, 1986).

Evans, J. A. S., *Herodotus, Explorer of the Past* (Princeton, N.J.: Princeton University Press, 1991).

Finley, M. I., *The World of Odysseus* (New York: Viking, 1954).

Gierke, Otto von, *Political Theories of the Middle Age* (Cambridge: Cambridge University Press, 1900).

Gould, John, *Herodotus* (New York: St. Martin's, 1989).

Hunter, Virginia, *Past and Process in Herodotus and Thucydides* (Princeton, N.J.: Princeton University Press, 1982).

Hussey, Edward, *The Presocratics* (London: Duckworth, 1972).

Inwood, Brad, *Ethics and Human Action in Early Stoicism* (New York: Oxford University Press, 1985).

Irwin, Terence, *Plato's Moral Theory* (New York: Clarendon Press, 1977).

Kagan, Donald, *The Outbreak of the Peloponnesian War* (Ithaca, N.Y.: Cornell University Press, 1969).

————, *The Fall of the Athenian Empire* (Ithaca, N.Y.: 1987).

Kahn, Charles H., *The Art and Thought of Heraclitus* (New York: Cambridge University Press, 1979).

Kraut, Richard, *Aristotle on the Human Good* (Princeton, N.J.: Princeton University Press, 1989).

Lateiner, Donald, *The Historical Method of Herodotus* (Toronto: University of Toronto Press, 1989).

Lord, Albert Bates, *The Singer of Tales* (Cambridge, Mass.: Harvard University Press, 1960).

Mansfield, Harvey C., *Machiavelli's New Modes and Orders: A Study of the Discourses on Livy* (Ithaca, N.Y.: Cornell University Press, 1979).

McKirahan, Richard D., Jr., *Philosophy before Socrates: An Introduction with Texts and Commentary* (Indianapolis: Hackett, 1994).

The Monist (1991).

Mulgan, R. G., *Aristotle's Political Theory: An Introduction* (New York: Clarendon Press, 1977).

Murphy, Mark C., "Consent, Custom and the Common Good in Aquinas's Account of Political Authority," in *Review of Politics* (1997).

Murray, Oswyn, *Early Greece* (Atlantic Highlands, N.J.: Humanities Press, 1980).

Parel, Anthony J., *The Machiavellian Cosmos* (New Haven, Conn.: Yale University Press, 1992).

Passerin D'Entreves, Alexander, *The Medieval Contribution to Political Thought* (Oxford: Oxford University Press, 1939).

———, *Natural Law* (London: Hutchinson's University Library, 1951).

Pitkin, Hannah, *Fortune Is a Woman: Gender and Politics in the Thought of Niccolò Machiavelli* (Berkeley: University of California Press, 1984).

Pocock, J. G. A., *The Machiavellian Moment: Florentine Political Thought and the Atlantic Republican Tradition* (Princeton, N.J.: Princeton University Press, 1975).

Rawson, Elizabeth, *Cicero: A Portrait* (Ithaca, N.Y.: Cornell University Press, 1983).

Redfield, J. M., *Nature and Culture in the Iliad: The Tragedy of Hector* (Chicago: University of Chicago Press, 1975).

Reeve, C. D. C., *Philosopher-Kings: The Argument of Plato's Republic* (Princeton: Princeton University Press, 1988).

———, *Socrates in the Apology* (Indianapolis: Hackett, 1989).

———, *Practices of Reason: Aristotle's Nicomachaean Ethics* (New York: Oxford University Press, 1992).

———, "Thucydides on Human Nature," in *Political Theory* (1999).

Romm, James, *Herodotus* (New Haven, Conn.: Yale University Press, 1998).

Salkever, Stephen, *Finding the Mean: Theory and Practice in Aristotle's Political Philosophy* (Princeton, N.J.: Princeton University Press, 1990).

Saxonhouse, Arlene, "Comedy in the Callipolis: Animal Imagery in the Republic," in *American Political Science Review* (1978).

Schein, Seth L., *The Mortal Hero: An Introduction to Homer's Iliad* (Berkeley: University of California Press, 1984).

Segal, Charles, *Sophocles' Tragic World: Divinity, Nature, Society* (Cambridge, Mass.: Harvard University Press, 1995).

Skinner, Quentin, *The Foundations of Modern Political Thought* (Cambridge: Cambridge University Press, 1978).

———, *Machiavelli* (Oxford: Oxford University Press, 1981).

Smith, R. E., *Cicero the Statesman* (Cambridge: Cambridge University Press, 1966).

Snodgrass, Anthony, *Archaic Greece* (Berkeley: University of California Press, 1981).

Steinberger, Peter J., "Ruling: Guardians and Philosopher/Kings," in *American Political Science Review* (1989).

———, *The Concept of Political Judgment* (Chicago: University of Chicago Press, 1993).

———, "Who Is Cephalus?" in *Political Theory* (1996).

———, "Was Socrates Guilty as Charged? Apology 24c–28a," in *Ancient Philosophy* (1997).

Steiner, George, *Antigones* (New York: Clarendon Press, 1984).

Strauss, Leo, *The City and Man* (Chicago: University of Chicago Press, 1978).

Syme, Ronald, *The Roman Revolution* (Oxford: Oxford University Press, 1960).

Tyrrell, William Blake, and Larry J. Bennett, *Recapturing Sophocles' Antigone* (Lanham, Md.: Rowman and Littlefield, 1998).

Vlastos, Gregory, *Socrates: Ironist and Moral Philosopher* (Ithaca, N.Y.: Cornell University Press, 1991).

Walker, Graham, *Moral Foundations of Constitutional Thought: Current Problems, Augustinian Prospects* (Princeton, N.J.: Princeton University Press, 1990).

Yack, Bernard, *The Problems of a Political Animal: Community, Justice and Conflict in Aristotelian Political Thought* (Berkeley: University of California Press, 1993).